marketing

marketing is the activity,
set of institutions, and processes
for creating, communicating,
delivering, and exchanging offerings
that have value for customers,
clients, partners, and society at large.

The definition of *marketing*, established by
the American Marketing Association, October 2007.

www.mhhe.com/grewal2e

Marketing

Marketing

Second Edition

Dhruv Grewal, PhD
Babson College
Michael Levy, PhD
Babson College

McGraw-Hill Irwin

Boston   Burr Ridge, IL   Dubuque, IA   New York   San Francisco   St. Louis
Bangkok   Bogotá   Caracas   Kuala Lumpur   Lisbon   London   Madrid   Mexico City
Milan   Montreal   New Delhi   Santiago   Seoul   Singapore   Sydney   Taipei   Toronto

McGraw-Hill
Irwin

MARKETING

Published by McGraw-Hill/Irwin, a business unit of The McGraw-Hill Companies, Inc., 1221 Avenue of the Americas, New York, NY, 10020. Copyright © 2010, 2008 by The McGraw-Hill Companies, Inc. All rights reserved. No part of this publication may be reproduced or distributed in any form or by any means, or stored in a database or retrieval system, without the prior written consent of The McGraw-Hill Companies, Inc., including, but not limited to, in any network or other electronic storage or transmission, or broadcast for distance learning.

Some ancillaries, including electronic and print components, may not be available to customers outside the United States.

This book is printed on acid-free paper.

3 4 5 6 7 8 9 0 WCK/WCK 0 9

ISBN   978-0-07-338095-7
MHID   0-07-338095-4

Vice president and editor-in-chief: *Brent Gordon*
Publisher: *Paul Ducham*
Executive editor: *Doug Hughes*
Editorial coordinator: *Devon Raemisch*
Marketing manager: *Katie Mergen*
Lead project manager: *Christine A. Vaughan*
Lead production supervisor: *Carol A. Bielski*
Designer: *Laurie J. Entringer*
Senior photo research coordinator: *Jeremy Cheshareck*
Photo researcher: *Mike Hruby*
Lead media project manager: *Brian Nacik*
Cover design: *Asylum Studios*
Typeface: *10/12 Palatino*
Compositor: *Aptara, Inc.*
Printer: *Quebecor World Versailles Inc.*

Library of Congress Cataloging-in-Publication Data

Grewal, Dhruv.
     Marketing / Dhruv Grewal, Michael Levy. -- 2nd ed.
       p. cm.
     Includes index.
     ISBN-13: 978-0-07-338095-7 (alk. paper)
     ISBN-10: 0-07-338095-4 (alk. paper)
     1. Marketing. I. Levy, Michael, 1950- II. Title.
   HF5415.G675 2010
   658.8--dc22
                            2008053218

www.mhhe.com

To our parents:

Saroj Grewal and the late Inder Grewal

and

Jacquie and Norman Levy

who instilled in us the value of perpetual learning.

about the authors

Authors Michael Levy (left) and Dhruv Grewal (right).

Dhruv Grewal

Dhruv Grewal, PhD (Virginia Tech), is the Toyota Chair in Commerce and Electronic Business and a professor of marketing at Babson College. His research and teaching interests focus on marketing foundations, marketing research, retailing, pricing, and value-based strategies. He was awarded the 2005 Lifetime Achievement in Behavioral Pricing Award by Fordham University. He is a "Distinguished Fellow" of the Academy of Marketing Science. He has also coauthored *Marketing Research* (2004, 2007).

Professor Grewal has published over 80 articles in journals such as the *Journal of Marketing, Journal of Consumer Research, Journal of Marketing Research, Journal of Retailing,* and *Journal of the Academy of Marketing Science.* He currently serves on numerous editorial review boards, including those of the *Journal of Retailing, Journal of the Academy of Marketing Science, Journal of Interactive Marketing,* and *Journal of Public Policy & Marketing.* He served as co-editor of the *Journal of Retailing* from 2001 to 2007.

Professor Grewal has won many awards for his teaching, including the 2005 Sherwin-Williams Distinguished Teaching Award, SMA; 2003 AMA Award for Innovative Excellence in Marketing Education; 1999 AMS Great Teachers in Marketing Award; Executive MBA Teaching Excellence Award (1998); School of Business Teaching Excellence Awards (1993, 1999); and Virginia Tech Certificate of Recognition for Outstanding Teaching (1989). He has co-chaired the 1993 AMS Conference, 1998 Winter AMA Conference, 1998 Marketing Science Institute Conference, 2001 AMA doctoral consortium, and 2006 Summer AMA Conference.

Professor Grewal has taught executive seminars and courses and/or worked on research projects with numerous firms, such as IRI, TJX, Radio Shack, Monsanto, McKinsey, Motorola, and numerous law firms. He has taught seminars in the United States, Europe, and Asia.

Michael Levy

Michael Levy, PhD (Ohio State University), is the Charles Clarke Reynolds Professor of Marketing and Director of the Retail Supply Chain Institute at Babson College. He received his PhD in business administration from The Ohio State University and his undergraduate and MS degrees in business administration from the University of Colorado at Boulder. He taught at Southern Methodist University before joining the faculty as professor and chair of the marketing department at the University of Miami.

Professor Levy has developed a strong stream of research in retailing, business logistics, financial retailing strategy, pricing, and sales management. He has published over 50 articles in leading marketing and logistics journals, including the *Journal of Retailing, Journal of Marketing, Journal of the Academy of Marketing Science,* and *Journal of Marketing Research.* He currently serves on the editorial review board of the *Journal of Retailing, Journal of the Academy of Marketing Science, International Journal of Logistics Management, International Journal of Logistics and Materials Management,* and *European Business Review.* He is coauthor of *Retailing Management,* seventh edition (2009), the best-selling college-level retailing text in the world. Professor Levy was co-editor of *Journal of Retailing* from 2001 to 2007. He co-chaired the 1993 Academy of Marketing Science conference and the 2006 Summer AMA conference.

Professor Levy has worked in retailing and related disciplines throughout his professional life. Prior to his academic career, he worked for several retailers and a housewares distributor in Colorado. He has performed research projects with many retailers and retail technology firms, including Accenture, Federated Department Stores, Khimetrics (SAP), Mervyn's, Neiman Marcus, ProfitLogic (Oracle), Zale Corporation, and numerous law firms.

Welcome to the second edition of
MARKETING!

Some exciting new additions in the 2nd edition include:

1. Incorporating the new 2007 American Marketing Association definition of marketing.

   The American Marketing Association states that "Marketing is the activity, set of institutions, and processes for creating, *capturing*,* communicating, delivering, and exchanging offerings that have value for customers, clients, partners, and society at large."

2. Given the spirit of the new definition, we have increased our focus on society at large by adding a new section on corporate social responsibility in Chapter 4.

3. The new definition continues to emphasize value. Our book, *Marketing,* second edition, emphasizes the value and the role of the customer in marketing organizations and activities.

4. Marketing practitioners and scholars have recognized the need to incorporate marketing metrics into their planning process. Metrics are used to explain why things happened and project the future. They make it possible to compare results across regions, strategic business units (SBUs), product lines, and time periods. There are state-of-the-art illustrations of marketing metrics throughout *Marketing,* second edition.

5. Chapter 2, "Developing Marketing Strategies and a Marketing Plan," has a new appendix that provides an illustrative marketing plan and tips for developing one.

*Word in italics was added by the authors.

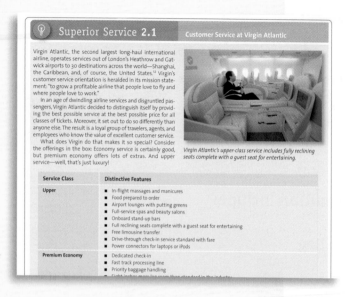

Superior Service 2.1 — Customer Service at Virgin Atlantic

Virgin Atlantic, the second largest long-haul international airline, operates services out of London's Heathrow and Gatwick airports to 30 destinations across the world—Shanghai, the Caribbean, and, of course, the United States.¹² Virgin's customer service orientation is heralded in its mission statement: "to grow a profitable airline that people love to fly and where people love to work."

In an age of dwindling airline services and disgruntled passengers, Virgin Atlantic decided to distinguish itself by providing the best possible service at the best possible price for all classes of tickets. Moreover, it set out to do so differently than anyone else. The result is a loyal group of travelers, agents, and employees who know the value of excellent customer service.

What does Virgin do that makes it so special? Consider the offerings in the box: Economy service is certainly good, but premium economy offers lots of extras. And upper service—well, that's just luxury!

Virgin Atlantic's upper-class service includes fully reclining seats complete with a guest seat for entertaining.

Service Class	Distinctive Features
Upper	■ In-flight massages and manicures ■ Food prepared to order ■ Airport lounges with putting greens ■ Full-service spas and beauty salons ■ Onboard stand-up bars ■ Full reclining seats complete with a guest seat for entertaining ■ Free limousine transfer ■ Drive-through check-in service standard with fare ■ Power connectors for laptops or iPods
Premium Economy	■ Dedicated check-in ■ Fast track processing line ■ Priority baggage handling

6. The United States has become increasingly dependent on services, and service industries account for 42 percent of the U.S. gross domestic product (GDP) and the lion's share of U.S. jobs. In this edition, we have developed a boxed insert highlighting "Superior Service" in the majority of the chapters in addition to the chapter on services (Chapter 12, "Services: The Intangible Product").

Power of the Internet 2.1 — Dove Evolutions

With the immense power of the Internet, Dove hopes to build "brand evangelists" for its beauty products and has therefore led the way in engaging its online customers. During the 2007 Academy Awards, for example, Dove ran two high-profile Internet marketing campaigns: "Evolution" and Dove Body Wash.

In 2006, Dove kicked off its online Real Beauty campaign by posting the "Evolution" video on YouTube. The first day saw 40,000 views; by the end of 2007, more than 5.5 million viewers had seen the spot.²⁷ The video is designed to demonstrate how perceptions of beauty get distorted by advertising. During the online video, a model transforms from a normal-looking woman to a billboard pin-up after undergoing hours of makeup. Even then, the image on the billboard gets altered by Photoshop. The video ends with a tagline: "No wonder our perception of beauty is distorted." At the bottom, it lists the address for the Dove Campaign for Real Beauty Web site (http:www.campaignforrealbeauty.com).

In 2007, "Evolution" won one of the most prestigious advertising awards, the Grand Prix for viral marketing at Cannes.²⁸ As the company explained, it chose the Internet as its release platform for "Evolution" because it freed the advertising team from time constraints. The marketers wanted to run a spot that was 74 seconds long, and U.S. television only sold advertising spots in 30 or 60 second increments. Furthermore, through the Internet, Dove could connect directly with its customers.

To get customers even more engaged with its brand, Dove also created a new campaign for the 2008 Oscar ceremony. Online, Dove invited consumers to create their own

Dove uses the Internet to promote the notion that beauty should not be defined by self-limiting stereotypes.

advertisements for Dove Body Cream Oil Body Wash, promising that the winning entry would be broadcast during the Oscar ceremony to a worldwide audience. On the Dove Cream Oil Web site on MSN.com (http:www.dovecreamoil.msn.com), users could upload their videos, use online editing tools, and vote on one another's submissions. Using the Internet to share videos encouraged these customers to think about the product, and interacting with other users got them emotionally engaged with the advertisements they viewed.²⁹

Thus, Dove has figured out several ways to use the power of the Internet to connect with its core customers and create high-impact marketing events—and at a reasonable price.

7. The Internet continues to provide marketers the opportunity to be creative, innovative, and entrepreneurial in their strategies and tactics. We have included a "Power of the Internet" boxed insert to highlight some of the most innovative strategies and tactics in every chapter.

When we, the authors, sat down to write this book, it seemed imperative that the evolution of the field and practice of marketing be at the forefront. We wanted to be sure that we were fully educating today's student about current marketing trends and practices, so we integrated newer concepts such as value creation, globalization, technology, ethics, and services marketing into the traditional marketing instruction. In this book, we examine how firms assess, analyze, create, deliver, communicate, and capture value. We explore both the fundamentals in marketing and new influencers, such as value-based pricing and the Internet, that are shaping the way businesses communicate with their customers in today's marketing environment.

Marketing, second edition, reflects not only the current trends in the marketplace, but also the needs of instructors and students. During the writing and revising of this book, we've sought the advice and expertise of hundreds of marketing and educational professionals, and we've taken all of their guidance to heart. We are grateful to the hundreds of individuals who participated in the focus groups, surveys, and personal conversations that helped mold this book, and we hope that you, the reader, will learn from and enjoy the results.

WHAT IS MARKETING?

Regardless of your age, your gender, or the city in which you live, you already know something about marketing.

You have been an involved consumer in the marketing process since childhood when, for example, you accompanied your mother or father to the supermarket and asked to buy a particular brand of cereal because you saw a friend eating it or heard about it on television. The prize inside the box of cereal was of value to you as a child; the nutritional information offered on the box panel was of value to your mother or father. Once you begin to explore the many ways in which companies and brands create value for their customers through marketing, you will also begin to appreciate the complex set of decisions and activities that are necessary to provide you with the products and services you use every day.

> **The function of marketing is multifaceted, but its fundamental purpose is to create value. Consider these examples:**

Why do people buy distressed jeans for well over a hundred dollars when they could buy Wrangler jeans at Wal-Mart for under twenty? The answer lies in marketing brand value: because brands like Diesel and Seven for All Mankind have created a cachet for their brands with edgy advertising and innovative washes and styles. When trendsetters start to wear these brands, others follow.

Do you want to sweetly say "I Love You" in 17 colors? Customized M&M's are the way to go. M&M's, the oval shaped chocolate candy with the hard shiny surface, have been providing customers value since their inception in 1941. They were initially sold to American GIs serving in World War II as a convenient snack that traveled well in any climate. Today, M&M's offer customers additional value by allowing them to order customized versions on the Internet (www. mymms.com).

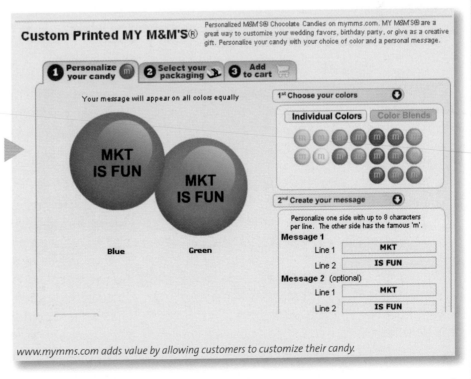

www.mymms.com adds value by allowing customers to customize their candy.

Those who teach the marketers of the future need to account for the consumer's ability to assess the marketplace at their fingertips and discern good value from poor value. This textbook, *Marketing*, second edition, is all about the core concepts and tools that help marketers create value for customers. Throughout this book you will find many other examples that define how companies create value for customers through branding, packaging, pricing, retailing, service, and advertising. We introduce the concept of value in Chapter 1 and carry it through the entire text:

- **The first section** of the text contains four chapters, and the central theme of the section is "Assessing the Marketplace." Following an introduction to marketing in Chapter 1, Chapter 2 then focuses on how a firm develops a marketing plan. A central theme of the chapter is how firms can effectively create, capture, deliver, and communicate value to their customers. Key elements of scenario planning are introduced and presented to demonstrate how to analyze and capitalize on opportunities presented. We provide an appendix after Chapter 2 that includes an illustrative marketing plan and points out tips for developing one. Chapter 3 focuses on "Marketing Ethics." An ethical decision framework is developed and presented. Important ethical concepts are linked back to the marketing plan introduced in Chapter 2. Finally, Chapter 4 ("Analyzing the Marketing Environment") focuses on how marketers can systematically uncover and evaluate opportunities. The role of corporate social responsibilities and their effects on various stakeholders are highlighted.

- **The second section** of the book deals with "Understanding the Marketplace" and is composed of three chapters. Chapter 5, "Consumer Behavior," focuses on understanding why consumers purchase products and services. The consumer decision-making process is highlighted. Chapter 6, "Business-to-Business Marketing," looks at why and how business-to-business buying takes place. Finally, Chapter 7 examines marketing from a global perspective.

- **The third section** of the book deals with "Targeting the Marketplace." Two chapters comprise this section. Chapter 8 focuses on "Segmentation, Targeting, and Positioning." In this chapter, we focus on how firms segment the marketplace, then pick a target market and finally position their good/service in line with their customers' needs and wants. Chapter 9, on marketing research, identifies the various tools and techniques that marketers use to uncover these needs and ensure that they create goods and services that provide value to their target markets.

- **The fourth section** of *Marketing*, second edition, devotes three chapters to "Value Creation." The first two, Chapter 10, "Product, Branding, and Packaging Decisions," and Chapter 11, "Developing New Products" cover the development and management of products and brands. While many of the concepts involved in developing and managing services are similar to those of physical brands, Chapter 12, "Services: The Intangible Product," addresses the unique challenges of the marketing of services.

- Pricing is the activity within a firm responsible for "Value Capture" (**Section 5**) by bringing in money and effecting revenues. *Marketing*, second edition, devotes two chapters to how firms price to capture value for the firm. Chapter 13 examines the importance of setting the right price, the relationship between price and quantity sold, break-even analysis, the impact of price wars, and how the Internet has changed the way people shop. Chapter 14 looks specifically at how to set prices.

- One important reason why Wal-Mart has become the world's largest retailer is their "Value Delivery" system (**Section 6**) They work with their vendors to make sure that merchandise is available when the customer wants it, at the right location, and in the right quantities. To achieve this, they have initiated many innovative programs and developed sophisticated transportation and warehousing systems. *Marketing*, second edition, devotes two chapters to value delivery. Chapter 15 takes a look at the entire supply chain, while Chapter 16 concentrates on retailing.

- Today's methods of "Value Communication" (**Section 7**) are more complex than in the past because new media and technologies, such as e-mail, blogs, the Internet, social marketing, m-commerce, and podcasts have been added to the advertising mix that previously utilized primarily radio and television to relay messages to consumers. *Marketing*, second edition, devotes three chapters to value communication. Chapter 17 introduces the breadth of integrated marketing communications. Chapter 18 is devoted specifically to advertising, while Chapter 19 covers personal selling.

In addition to our emphasis on value in *Marketing*, second edition, you will also find integrated and highlighted coverage of ethics, services, global marketing, and the power of the Internet:

- *Marketing*, second edition, contains an entire chapter on "Marketing Ethics." Placed early in the text (Chapter 3), it provides rich illustrations of corporate responsibility, and introduces an ethical decision-making framework that is useful for assessing potentially ethically troubling situations that are posed throughout the rest of the book. It therefore sets the tone for ethical material in each subsequent chapter. In addition, the vast majority of chapters contain an Ethical and Societal Dilemma box with a compelling ethical discussion and end-of-chapter discussion questions that force students to consider and evaluate ethical situations.

- The Internet has revolutionized the business world and is continually used by marketers to foster an entrepreneurial and innovative spirit. The majority of the chapters contain Power of the Internet boxes that depict recognizable and interesting applications of the Internet by firms.

- *Marketing*, second edition, defines services as an intangible product and devotes Chapter 12 to the topic. A balanced approach to presenting products and services is used throughout. Examples of great service businesses and how product-oriented businesses provide great service abound. In addition, the majority of the chapters contain a Superior Service box to highlight illustrations of companies satisfying their customers and differentiating themselves from competitors through their service strategies.

- Most firms are involved in global marketing. Giant firms such as Procter & Gamble, Starbucks, and United Airlines have global operations. But most firms, large and small, are involved because they get their materials, products, or services from firms located in other countries. Global examples are woven throughout each chapter of *Marketing*, second edition. In addition, Chapter 7 is devoted exclusively to the topic.

- Finally, you will also find the value theme integrated throughout the text in the Adding Value boxes in each chapter. This feature illustrates how firms find ultimate success by adding value to their products and services.

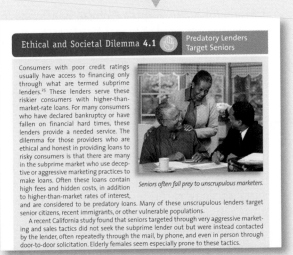

Ethical and Societal Dilemma 4.1 — Predatory Lenders Target Seniors

Consumers with poor credit ratings usually have access to financing only through what are termed subprime lenders.[25] These lenders serve these riskier consumers with higher-than-market-rate loans. For many consumers who have declared bankruptcy or have fallen on financial hard times, these lenders provide a needed service. The dilemma for those providers who are ethical and honest in providing loans to risky consumers is that there are many in the subprime market who use deceptive or aggressive marketing practices to make loans. Often these loans contain high fees and hidden costs, in addition to higher-than-market rates of interest, and are considered to be predatory loans. Many of these unscrupulous lenders target senior citizens, recent immigrants, or other vulnerable populations.

Seniors often fall prey to unscrupulous marketers.

A recent California study found that seniors targeted through very aggressive marketing and sales tactics did not seek the subprime lender out but were instead contacted by the lender, often repeatedly through the mail, by phone, and even in person through door-to-door solicitation. Elderly females seem especially prone to these tactics.

Adding Value 2.1 — FedEx Acquires Kinko's: Diversification or What?

When you've conquered express shipping and supply chain services, where do you look to increase earnings, cash flow, and returns?[27] For FedEx, the answer lay in diversification. In 1970, Paul Orfalea started the first Kinko's close to the University of California at Santa Barbara to provide appropriate products and services to college students at a reasonable price. From this single location in 1970, Kinko's had grown to more than 1,200 locations worldwide when FedEx acquired it.[48]

The benefits to both firms are significant. FedEx's global expertise and strong financial position can help Kinko's expand globally. Likewise, by using Kinko's as a storefront, FedEx can tap into a broader mix of small-, medium-, and large-scale businesses that use Kinko's printing and other services at its physical locations.

This acquisition looks at first like a simple case of diversification: new service/new market. But couldn't it also be perceived as market penetration: current service/current market? FedEx will earn more business among its current customers who like the lower cost and convenience of taking their packages to Kinko's. Likewise, current Kinko's customers might use Kinko's other services more often when they visit the store to send a FedEx package.

Furthermore, this growth strategy also could be interpreted as product development: new service/current market. After all, the current customers of both Kinko's and FedEx

WHY WILL INSTRUCTORS ENJOY USING THIS BOOK?

- **Tradition.** *Marketing*, second edition, draws from a history of outstanding marketing texts. Users of other books will feel confident and comfortable with the material in this second edition. We honor all the traditional marketing concepts, but make them current, relevant, and fun for your students to learn.

- **Assessment.** Business schools and accrediting organizations are demanding that students be accountable for specific material that is essential for any marketing practitioner. Of course, *Marketing*, second edition, provides students with knowledge of the language of marketing. In addition, students will come away with a set of tools that are essential to be successful in marketing careers. But the material goes beyond the printed page. The Online Learning Center contains an **Interactive Student Tool Kit**. The **Tool Kit** is a set of interactive exercises that are working models of the concepts presented in the text. Sophisticated, fun, and instructive, this Interactive Tool Kit contains up to three gradable assignments on each of the following concepts:

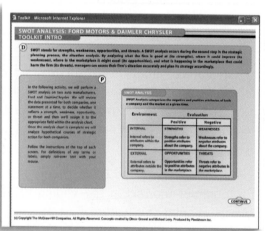

- SWOT Analysis (Chapter 2)
- Compensatory versus Noncompensatory Consumer Decision Making (Chapter 5)
- Vendor Evaluation Analysis (Chapter 6)
- Market Positioning Map (Chapter 8)
- Service Quality (Chapter 12)
- Break-even Analysis (Chapter 13)
- Developing an Advertisement (Chapter 18)

Marketing, second edition, has two new Tool Kits:
- Customer Lifetime Value (Chapter 9)
- Return on Marketing Investment (Chapter 17)

- **Outstanding Ancillary Materials.** In addition to the Tool Kit, *Marketing*, second edition, provides instructors with a broad spectrum of high-quality supplements:

- Two sets of state-of-the-art PowerPoint presentations for each chapter. One set contains pictures, screen grabs, key terms, interactive exhibits, and embedded videos. The other is a frills-free version, ideal for customizing.

- A user-friendly yet comprehensive Instructor's Manual (IM). In addition to the lecture notes and end-of-chapter solutions, you will also find additional cases, assignments, examples, and in-class activities that you can use to enhance your classroom lectures. This IM is available on the Instructor's side of the Online Learning Center.

- A video program on DVD, consisting of more than 15 segments in a variety of lengths to provide flexibility for your classroom. Some of the firms featured in these videos are Doritos, M&M's, Newman's Own Organics, Taco Bell, and Netflix.

- One of the most important aspects of the teaching package is the Test Bank. The Test Bank provides approximately 130 questions per chapter. Each question is keyed to chapter learning objectives and linked to the current AACSB standards. In the Test Bank you will find a balanced mixture of true/false, multiple-choice, short answer, and essay questions that are labeled as definition, conception, or application driven.

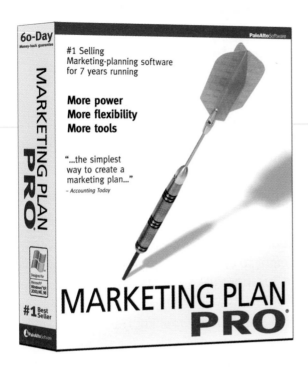

● **Marketing Plan Pro** is the most widely used marketing plan software program in the industry, and it includes everything students need to create professional, complete, and accurate marketing plans. Marketing Plan Pro can be packaged with *Marketing 2e* for a nominal fee.

● **McGraw-Hill Connect Marketing** is a web-based assignment and assessment platform that gives students the means to better connect with their coursework, with their instructors, and with the important concepts that they will need to know for success now and in the future. With Connect Marketing, instructors can deliver assignments, quizzes, and tests online. Nearly all the questions from the text are presented in an auto-gradable format and tied to the text's learning objectives. Instructors can edit existing questions and author entirely new problems. Track individual student performance – by question, assignment or in relation to the class overall – with detailed grade reports. Integrate grade reports easily with Learning Management Systems (LMS) such as WebCT and Blackboard. And much more.

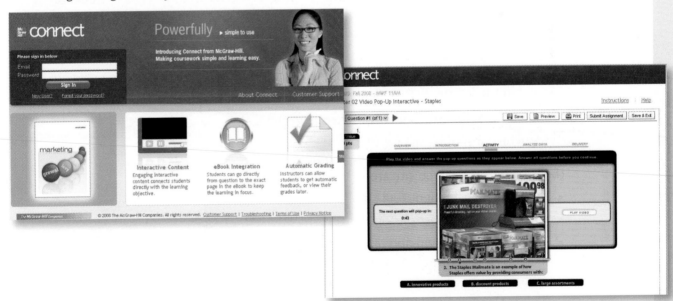

By choosing Connect Marketing, instructors are providing their students with a powerful tool for improving academic performance and truly mastering course material. Connect Marketing allows students to practice important skills at their own pace and on their own schedule. Importantly, students' assessment results and instructors' feedback are all saved online – so students can continually review their progress and plot their course to success.

WHY WILL STUDENTS ENJOY USING THIS BOOK?

- **A Compelling Read.** *Marketing*, second edition, was written with the student in mind. The examples are current and appealing, and feature a wide range of products and services that will be recognizable to a diverse group of readers.

- **Unique End-of-Chapter Applications and Exercises**

| Marketing Applications |

1. How has MTV created a sustainable competitive advantage?
2. Perform a SWOT analysis for your college or university.
3. Describe the primary target markets for McDonald's. How many target markets do you think this global giant pursues? How does it position its various products and services so that they appeal to its varied target markets?
4. Pick your favorite product, service provider, or retailer. How does it add value through the implementation of the four Ps?
5. Of the four growth strategies described in the chapter, which is the most risky? Which is the easiest to implement? Why?
6. Choose three companies. You believe the first builds customer value through product excellence, the second through operational excellence, and the third through customer excellence. Justify your answer.

- **Marketing Applications.** Each chapter concludes with eight to eleven Marketing Applications. These questions ask students to apply what they have learned to marketing scenarios that are relevant to their lives.

  - **Ethical Dilemma.** At least one of the Marketing Applications in each chapter poses an ethical dilemma based on material covered in the chapter. For instance, in Chapter 7 on global marketing, we pose the issue of a medical imaging service outsourcing its work to India, but not communicating the way this is done to patients. Students can apply the ethical decision-making framework introduced in Chapter 3 to these marketing situations.

  - **Net Savvy.** Each chapter contains two exercises that force students to the Internet to apply material covered in the text. For example, in Chapter 18, on advertising, we direct students to the Children's Advertising Review Unit, one of the major self-regulatory bodies for children's advertising, at www.caru.org. We ask students to choose a press release and discuss what action CARU took against the identified company or group and the legal and ethical issues addressed in the case.

  - **End-of-Chapter Cases.** Each chapter ends with a two- to three-page case covering a current marketing idea, concept, or company. Additional cases and case notes are found in the Instructor's Manual.

- **Web site for Students (www.mhhe.com/grewal2e)**
  The Online Learning Center will help students and instructors use *Marketing* effectively. Some of the features on the Web site are:

  - The Interactive Student Tool Kit

  - Multiple-choice questions on the student site

  - Marketer's Showdown and other selections from the book's video program, available as premium content

We've created this book and support package to give both instructors and students the best possible learning experience. We truly hope that you and your students fully enjoy this book and the tools that accompany it.

acknowledgments

We'd like acknowledge the considerable contributions of Britt Hackmann (Babson College), Elisabeth Nevins Caswell, and Colin Fox for their help throughout the development of this edition of *Marketing*.

We wish to express our sincere appreciation to Tracy Tuten Ryan for preparing the Instructor's Manual and the PowerPoint slides, Jeff Kulick for the Test Bank, Kelly Luchtman for the video production, and Elizabeth Gallagher for the new Tool Kits. The support, expertise, and occasional coercion from our publisher Doug Hughes and development editor Devon Raemisch are greatly appreciated. The book would also never have come together without the editorial and production staff at McGraw-Hill/Irwin: Katie Mergen, marketing manager; Christine Vaughan, lead project manager; Laurie Entringer, designer; Jeremy Cheshareck, senior photo research coordinator; Mike Hruby, photo researcher; Brian Nacik, lead media project manager; and Carol Bielski, lead production supervisor.

Our colleagues in the industry have been invaluable in providing us with case, video, advertising, and photo materials. They include: Jacquelyn A. Ottman (J. Ottman Consulting); Andrea Gallagher (IRI); Marty Ordman and Betta Gallego (Dole); Michael Buckley, Mark Bauer, and Max Ward (Staples); Peter Meehan and Nell Newman (Newman's Own Organics); Steve Swasey (NetFlix); Will Bortz (Taco Bell); Dan Sullivan (New Balance), Jenny Dervin (JetBlue); Susan Heaney (Avon Foundation); Nancy Hirshberg (Stonyfield Farms); Zoe Jackson (MOMA); Douglas Riggan (Burger King); Ryan Bowling (Mars North America); Ann Mukherjee (Frito-Lay), Molly Starmann (McDonald's) and Carol Sagers (McDonald's).

Over the years, we have had the opportunity to work with many talented and insightful colleagues. We have benefited from our research and discussions with them. Some of these colleagues are: Ross Petty, Danna Greenberg, Kate McKone-Sweet, Nancy Dlott and Anne Roggeveen (Babson College); Larry D. Compeau (Clarkson University); Rajesh Chandrashekaran (Fairleigh Dickinson University); Jeanne S. Munger (University of Southern Maine); Arun Sharma, A. Parasuraman, R. Krishnan, Howard Marmorstein, Anuj Mehrotra, Michael Tsiros, and Maria Giordano (all from University of Miami); Glenn Voss and Mitzi Montoya-Weiss (North Carolina State University); Kathleen Seiders (Boston College); Rob Palmatier (University of Cincinnati); Praveen Kopalle, Scott Neslin, and Kusum Ailawadi (Dartmouth); Robert Peterson and Andrea Godfrey (University of Texas at Austin); Don Lehmann (Columbia); Ruth Bolton, Steve Brown, and Terry Bristol (Arizona State University); Julie Baker and William Cron (Texas Christian University); Venkatesh Shankar, Len Berry, and Manjit Yadav (Texas A&M); Jerry Gotlieb (University of Western Kentucky); Hooman Estelami (Fordham University); Rajiv Dant and Ken Evans (University of Oklahoma); Monika Kukar Kinney (University of Richmond); Ronnie Goodstein (Georgetown); James Hess (University of Houston); Anthony Miyazaki and Walfried Lassar (Florida International University); Gopal Iyer and Tamara Mangleburg (Florida Atlantic University); David Hardesty (University of Kentucky); Greg Marshall (Rollins College); M. Joseph Sirgy, Julie Ozanne, and Ed Fern (Virginia Tech); Merrie Brucks and Ajith Kumar (University of Arizona); Valerie Folkes (University of Southern California); Carolyn Costley (University of Waikato); William Dodds (Ft. Lewis College); Ramon Avila (Ball State University); Douglas M. Lambert and Walter Zinn (The Ohio State University); Eugene Stone-Romeo (University of Central Florida); Joan Lindsey-Mullikin and Norm Borin (Cal Poly–San Luis Obispo); Abhijit

Biswas and Sujay Dutta (Wayne State University); Wagner Kamakura (Duke); Raj Srivastava (Emory); Cheryl Nikata (University of Illinois, Chicago); K. Sivakumar (Lehigh University); Namwoon Kim (Hong Kong Polytechnic University); Raj Suri (Drexel); Jean-Charles Chebat (HEC Montreal); Thomas Rudolph (St. Gallen University); Alan Dubinsky (Purdue University); Daniel J. Howard, Roger Kerin, Michael M. Van Breda, and Jack Webster; (Southern Methodist University); Charles A. Ingene (University of Mississippi); and Zhen Zhu (Suffolk University).

For their contributions to the first edition of *Marketing*, we gratefully acknowledge:

Dennis Arnett
Texas Tech University

Laurie Babin
University of Louisiana at Monroe

Ainsworth Bailey
University of Toledo

Joyce Banjac
Myers University

Harvey Bauman
Lees McRae College

Oleta Beard
University of Washington

Sandy Becker
Rutgers Business School

Ellen Benowitz
Mercer County Community College

Gary Benton
Western Kentucky University

Joseph Ben-Ur
University of Houston at Victoria

Patricia Bernson
County College of Morris

Harriette Bettis-Outland
University of West Florida

Parimal Bhagat
Indiana University of Pennsylvania

Jan Bingen
Little Priest Tribal College

John Bishop
University of South Alabama–Mobile

Nancy Bloom
Nassau Community College

Claire Bolfing
James Madison University

Karen Bowman
University of California

Tom Boyd
California State University–Fullerton

Nancy Boykin
Tarleton State University

Cathy Brenan
Northland Community and Technical College

Martin Bressler
Houston Baptist University

Claudia Bridges
California State University

Greg Broekemier
University of Nebraska–Kearney

Gary Brunswick
Northern Michigan University

John Buzza
Monmouth University

Rae Caloura
Johnson & Wales University

Michaelle Cameron
St. Edwards University

Lindell Chew
Linn University of Missouri

Dorene Ciletti
Duquesne University

Terry Clark
Southern Illinois University–Carbondale

Joyce Claterbos
University of Kansas

Gloria Cockerell
Collin County College

Paul Cohen
Florida Atlantic University

Mark E. Collins
University of Tennessee

Clare Comm
University of Massachusetts–Lowell

Sherry Cook
Southwest Missouri State University

Stan Cort
Case Western Reserve University

Keith Cox
University of Houston

Ian Cross
Bentley College

Geoffrey Crosslin
Kalamazoo Valley Community College

Joseph DeFilippe
Suffolk County Community College

George Deitz
University of Memphis

Kathleen DeNisco
Erie Community College

Tilokie Depoo
Monroe College

Monique Doll
Macomb Community College

Kimberly Donahue
Indiana University–Purdue University at Indianapolis

Jim D'Orazio
Cleveland State University

James Downing
University of Illinois–Chicago

Michael Drafke
College of DuPage

Leon Dube
Texas A&M University

Colleen Dunn
Bucks County Community College

John Eaton
Arizona State University–Tempe

Nancy Evans
New River Community College

Keith Fabes
Berkeley College

Tina Facca
John Carroll University

Joyce Fairchild
Northern Virginia Community College

David J. Faulds
University of Louisville

Larry Feick
University of Pittsburgh

Karen Flaherty
Oklahoma State University–Stillwater

Leisa Flynn
Florida State University

William Foxx
Auburn University

Douglas Friedman
Penn State University

Stanley Garfunkel
Queensborough Community College

S. J. Garner
Eastern Kentucky University

David Gerth
Nashville State Community College

Peggy Gilbert
Missouri State University

Kelly Gillerlain
Tidewater Community College

Jana Goodrich
Penn State–Behrend

Robin Grambling
University of Texas at El Paso

Kimberly D. Grantham
University of Georgia

James I. Gray
Florida Atlantic University

Kelly Gredone
Bucks County Community College

Michael Greenwood
Mount Wachusett Community College

Barbara Gross
California State University–Northridge

David Grossman
Florida Southern College

Hugh Guffey
Auburn University

Reetika Gupta
Lehigh University

John Hafer
University of Nebraska at Omaha

Allan Hall
Western Kentucky University

Joan Hall
Macomb Community College

Clark Hallpike
Elgin Community College

James E. Hansen
University of Akron

Dorothy Harpool
Wichita State University

Lynn Harris
Shippensburg University

Linda Hefferin
Elgin Community College

Lewis Hershey
Fayetteville State University

Tom Hickman
Loyola University

Robbie Hillsman
University of Tennessee at Martin

Nathan Himelstein
Essex County College

Adrienne Hinds
Northern Virginia Community College at Annandale

John Hobbs
University of Oklahoma

Don Hoffer
Miami University

Ronald Hoverstad
University of the Pacific

Kris Hovespian
Ashland University

James Hunt
University of North Carolina–Wilmington

Shane Hunt
Arkansas State University

Julie Huntley
Oral Roberts University

Sean Jasso
University of California–Riverside

Doug Johansen
University of North Florida

Candy Johnson
Holyoke Community College

Keith Jones
North Carolina A&T University

Janice Karlen
CUNY–LaGuardia Community College

Eric J. Karson
Villanova University

Imran Khan
University of South Alabama–Mobile

Todd Korol
Monroe Community College

Dennis Lee Kovach
Community College of Allegheny County

Dmitri Kuksov
Washington University in St. Louis

Jeff Kulick
George Mason University

Michelle Kunz
Morehead State University

John Kuzma
Minnesota State University at Mankato

Sandie Lakin
Hesser College

Timothy Landry
University of Oklahoma

Don Larson
Ohio State University

Felicia Lassk
Northeastern University

J. Ford Laumer
Auburn University

Kenneth Lawrence
New Jersey IT

Rebecca Legleiter
Tulsa CC Southeast Campus

Hillary Leonard
University of Rhode Island

Natasha Lindsey
University of North Alabama

Paul Londrigan
Mott Community College

Terry Lowe
Heartland Community College

Dolly Loyd
University of Southern Mississippi

Harold Lucius
Rowan University

Alicia Lupinacci
Tarrant Community College

Stanley Madden
Baylor University

Lynda Maddox
George Washington University

Cesar Maloles
California State University–East Bay

Karl Mann
Tennessee Tech University

Cathy Martin
University of Akron

Carolyn Massiah
University of Central Florida

Tamara Masters
Brigham Young University

Erika Matulich
University of Tampa

Bob Mayer
Mesa State College

Nancy McClure
University of Central Oklahoma

Mohan Menon
University of South Alabama

Michelle Meyer
Joliet Junior College

Ivor Mitchell
University of Nevada–Reno

Mark Mitchell
University of South Carolina

Steven Moff
Pennsylvania College of Technology

Rex Moody
University of Colorado

Farrokh Moshiri
University of California–Riverside

Dorothy Mulcahy
Bridgewater State College

James Munch
Wright State University–Dayton

Suzanne Murray
Piedmont Technical College

James E. Murrow
Drury University

Noreen Nackenson
Nassau Community College

Sandra Blake Neis
Borough of Manhattan Community College

John Newbold
Sam Houston State University

Keith Niedermeier
University of Pennsylvania

Martin Nunlee
Syracuse University

Hudson Nwakanma
Florida A&M University

Lois Olson
San Diego State University

Karen Overton
Houston Community College

Deborah L. Owens
University of Akron

Esther Page-Wood
Western Michigan University

Richard Pascarelli
Adelphi University

Michael Pearson
Loyola University

Jerry Peerbolte
University of Arkansas–Fort Smith

Glenn Perser
Houston Community College

Diane Persky
Yeshiva University

Susan Peters
California State Polytechnic University at Pomona

Renee Pfeifer-Luckett
University of Wisconsin–Whitewater

Gary Pieske
Minnesota State Community and Technical College

Jeff Podoshen
Temple University

Carmen Powers
Monroe Community College

Mike Preis
University of Illinois–Urbana-Champaign

Rosemary Ramsey
Wright State University

Srikumar Rao
Long Island University

Kristen Regine
Johnston & Wales University

Joseph Reihing
Nassau Community College

William Rice
California State University–Fresno

Patricia Richards
Westchester Community College

Eric Rios
Eastern University

Janet Robinson
Mount St. Mary's College

Heidi Rottier
Bradley University

Juanita Roxas
California State Polytechnic University

Donald Roy
Middle Tennessee State University

Shikhar Sarin
Boise State University

Carl Saxby
University of Southern Indiana

Diana Scales
Tennessee State University

James Schindler
Columbia Southern University

Jeffrey Schmidt
University of Oklahoma–Norman

Laura Shallow
St. Xavier University

Rob Simon
University of Nebraska–Lincoln

Erin Sims
DeVry University at Pomona

Lois J. Smith
University of Wisconsin

Brent Sorenson
University of Minnesota–Crookston

James Spiers
Arizona State University–Tempe

Geoffrey Stewart
University of Louisiana

John Striebich
Monroe Community College

Randy Stuart
Kennesaw State University

James Swanson
Kishwaukee College

James Swartz
California State Polytechnic University

Robert R. Tangsrud, Jr.
University of North Dakota

Steve Taylor
Illinois State University

Sharon Thach
Tennessee State University

Mary Tharp
University of Texas at San Antonio

Frank Tobolski
Lake in the Hills

Louis A. Tucci
College of New Jersey

Ven Venkatesan
University of Rhode Island at Kingston

Deirdre Verne
Westchester Community College

Steve Vitucci
Tarleton University Central Texas

Keith Wade
Webber International University

Wakiuru Wamwara-Mbugua
Wright State University–Dayton

Bryan Watkins
Dominican University, Priory Campus

Ron Weir
East Tennessee State University

Ludmilla Wells
Florida Gulf Coast University

Thomas Whipple
Cleveland State University

Tom Whitman
Mary Washington College

Kathleen Williamson
University of Houston–Clear Lake

Phillip Wilson
Midwestern State University

Doug Witt
Brigham Young University

Kim Wong
Albuquerque Technical Institute

Brent Wren
University of Alabama–Huntsville

Alex Wu
California State University–Long Beach

Poh-Lin Yeoh
Bentley College

Marketing 2e has benefited from the reviews, focus groups, and individual discussions with several leading scholars and teachers of marketing. Together, these reviewers spent hundreds of hours reading, discussing, and critiquing the manuscript.

We gratefully acknowledge:

Maria Aria
Camden County College

Dennis Arnett
Texas Tech University

Gerard Athaide
Loyola College of Maryland

Aysen Bakir
Illinois State University

Hannah Bell-Lombardo
Bryant University

Amit Bhatnagar
University of Wisconsin–Milwaukee

Linda Calderone
SUNY, Farmingdale

Nathaniel Calloway
University of Maryland, University College

Carlos Castillo
University of Minnesota–Duluth

Eve Caudill
Winona State University

Carmina Cavazos
University of Saint Thomas

Melissa Clark
University of North Alabama

Brent Cunningham
Jacksonville State University

Charlene Davis
Trinity University

Joseph Defilippe
Suffolk County Community College–Brentwood

Alan Friedenthal
Kingsborough Community College

George Goerner
Mohawk Valley Community College

Tom Greene
Eastern Washington University

Don Hanson
Bryant University

Jeffrey Harper
Texas Tech University

Charlane Held
Onondaga Community College

Jonathan Hibbard
Boston University

Craig Hollingshead
Texas A&M University–Kingsville

Donna Hope
Nassau Community College

Carol Johanek
Washington University, in St. Louis

Maria Johnson
Macomb Community College–Clinton Township

Rajiv Kashyap
William Paterson University

Josette Katz
Atlantic Cape Community College

Garland Keesling
Towson University

Marilyn Lavin
University of Wisconsin–Whitewater

Freddy Lee
California State University–Los Angeles

Guy Lochiatto
Massachusetts Bay Community College

Paul Londrigan
Mott Community College

Moutusi Maity
University of Wisconsin–Whitewater

Dennis Menezes
University of Louisville, Louisville

Linda Morable
Richland College

Brian Murray
Jefferson Community College

John Newbold
Sam Houston State University

Daniel Onyeagba
Argosy University–Atlanta

Terry Paul
Ohio State University–Columbus

Renee Pfeifer-Luckett
University of Wisconsin–Whitewater

Frank Alan Philpot
George Mason University

Susan Price
California Polytechnic State University

Lori Radulovich
Baldwin-Wallace College

Bruce Ramsey
Franklin University

Tom Rossi
Broome Community College

Linda Salisbury
Boston College

Nick Sarantakes
Austin Community College

Dwight Scherban
Central Connecticut State University

Dan Sherrell
University of Memphis

Karen Smith
Columbia Southern University

Randy Stuart
Kennesaw State University

Sue Taylor
Southwestern Illinois College

Sue Umashankar
University of Arizona

Deborah Utter
Boston University

Bronis Verhage
Georgia State University

Suzanne Walchli
University of the Pacific

Ludmilla Wells
Florida Gulf Coast University

Douglas Witt
Brigham Young University–Provo

Courtney Worsham
University of South Carolina

Joseph Yasaian
McIntosh College

Paschalina Ziamou
Bernard M. Baruch College

brief contents

table of contents

SECTION THREE   Targeting the Marketplace 241

SECTION FIVE   Value Capture 395

14 Strategic Pricing Methods 425

ASSESSING THE MARKETPLACE

Section One: Assessing the Marketplace contains four chapters. Following an introduction to marketing in Chapter 1, Chapter 2 focuses on how a firm develops a marketing plan. A central theme of the chapter is how firms can effectively create, capture, deliver, and communicate value to their customers. Chapter 3 focuses attention on Marketing Ethics. An ethical decision framework is developed and presented. The key ethical concepts are linked back to the marketing plan introduced in Chapter 2. Finally, Chapter 4, Analyzing the Marketing Environment, focuses on how marketers can systematically uncover and evaluate opportunities.

Assessing the Marketplace

Understanding the Marketplace

Targeting the Marketplace

Value Creation

Value Capture

Value Delivery: Designing the Channel and Supply Chain

Value Communication

1

CHAPTER

1

OVERVIEW OF MARKETING

- What is the role of marketing in organizations?
- How do marketers create value for a product or service?
- Why is marketing important both within and outside the firm?

Google. Facebook. YouTube. Three of the most common names in the latest Internet era, but what else do they have in common? Each firm, in its own way, has found a place in the lives of its customers by providing great value—that is, by giving more to customers than those customers spend in terms of their time and money.

Google: Remarkable for its rapid technology development, Google is the world's top Internet search engine, consistently outpacing competitors such as Yahoo!, MSN, AOL, Netscape, and Ask.com. But great technology means little unless customers believe that it gives them a more valuable experience than the competition can. Because its PageRank feature enables users to retrieve valuable search results without the clutter of irrelevant Web pages; because Google Docs let users create and share documents without an expensive productivity suite like Microsoft Office; and because Google Earth incorporates Google Search with satellite imagery, maps, and buildings, Google delivers on a specific promise.

It provides value to customers by allowing them to search the vast content of the Internet, as well as get driving directions so that they can make it to the restaurant on time. Google thus provides value to users and advertisers alike.

Facebook: To reconnect with a friend from high school or share photos with family, for millions of people, Facebook is the answer. Facebook's 90 million active users carry out millions of searches per month, making it the most popular people search engine in existence. Facebook also helps school communities, families, and coworkers keep in touch, share photos, and communicate.[1] In combination, these features offer great value for the Facebook community.

YouTube: Now owned by Google, YouTube represents part of the media revolution that is redefining how people view and share content. Since its founding in 2005, YouTube has grown steadily by offering valuable features to both users and advertisers. With YouTube, users may upload, view, and share video clips; through partnerships with the National Basketball Association (NBA), CBS, and the BBC, the site provides commercial content to its users. Advertisements from participating companies appear before videos, which increases the potential target markets for those advertising firms. In this arena, YouTube takes over where television left off. While the development of technologies such as DVRs and TiVo continues to hurt television's ability to deliver an effective medium for advertisers, YouTube has found a niche in which it can provide value for both advertisers and viewers.

They are all innovative, and they are all difficult to explain from a traditional business sense—what products or services do Google, Facebook, and YouTube really sell to earn their revenues? Yet the key commonality that marks all three examples of a new kind of firm is still a traditional approach to marketing: Each company succeeds because it provides good value to its customers.

● ● ●

WHAT IS MARKETING?

Unlike other subjects you may have studied, marketing already is very familiar to you. You start your day by agreeing to do the dishes in exchange for a freshly made cup of coffee. Then you fill up your car with gas. You attend a class that you have chosen and paid for. After class, you pick up lunch at the cafeteria, have your hair cut, buy a few songs or movies from Apple's iTunes, and take in a movie. In each case, you have acted as the buyer and made a decision about whether you should part with your time and/or money to receive a particular service or merchandise. If, after you return home from the movie, you decide to sell a CD on eBay, you have become a seller. And in each of these transactions, you were engaged in marketing.

The American Marketing Association states that "Marketing is the activity, set of institutions, and processes for creating, *capturing,* communicating, delivering, and exchanging offerings that have value for customers, clients, partners, and society at large."[2] What does this definition really mean? Good marketing is not a random activity; it requires thoughtful planning with an emphasis on the ethical implications of any of those decisions on society in general. Firms develop a marketing plan (Chapter 2) that specifies the marketing activities for a specific period of time. The marketing plan also is broken down into various components—how the product or service will be conceived or designed, how much it should cost, where and how it will be promoted, and how it will get to the consumer. In any exchange, the parties to the transaction should be satisfied. In our previous example, you should be satisfied or even delighted with the song you downloaded, and Apple should be satisfied with the amount of money it received from you. Thus, the core aspects of marketing are found in Exhibit 1.1. Let's see how these core aspects look in practice.

When you buy a song on iTunes, you are engaging in marketing.

Marketing Is about Satisfying Customer Needs and Wants

Understanding the marketplace, and especially consumer needs and wants, is fundamental to marketing success. In the broadest terms, the marketplace refers to the world of trade. More narrowly, however, the marketplace can be segmented or divided into groups of people who are pertinent to an organization for particular reasons. For example, even though the marketplace for toothpaste users may

EXHIBIT 1.1 Core Aspects of Marketing

- Marketing helps create value.
- Marketing is about satisfying customer needs and wants.
- Marketing occurs in many settings.
- Marketing
- Marketing can be performed by both individuals and organizations.
- Marketing entails an exchange.
- Marketing requires product, price, place, and promotion decisions.

include most of the people in the world, the makers of Crest could divide them into adolescent, adult, and senior users or perhaps into smokers, coffee drinkers, and wine drinkers. If you manufacture a toothpaste that removes coffee stains, you want to know for which marketplace segments your product is most relevant and then make sure that you build a marketing strategy that targets those groups.

Crest separates the toothpaste market into many segments.

Although marketers would prefer to sell their products and services to everyone, it is not practical to do so. Because marketing costs money, good marketers carefully seek out potential customers who have both an interest in the product and an ability to buy it. For example, most people need some form of transportation, and many people probably would like to own the new hybrid from Lexus. At $100,000, the Lexus LS 600h L is one of the most sophisticated hybrid cars on the market. But Lexus is not interested in everyone who wants an LS 600h L, because not everyone could manage to spend that much on a car. Instead, Lexus includes only those consumers who can afford such a product in its viable target market.[3] Although not all companies focus on such a specific, and wealthy, target, finding targeted potential buyers is the primary interest of marketers.

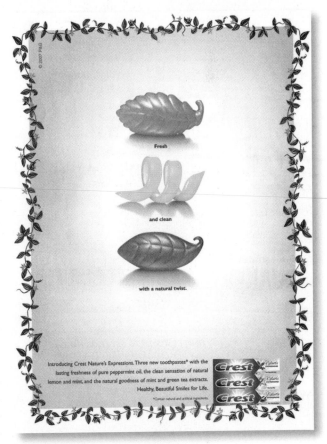

Marketing Entails an Exchange

Marketing is about an exchange—the trade of things of value between the buyer and the seller so that each is better off as a result. As depicted in Exhibit 1.2, sellers provide products or services, then communicate and facilitate the delivery of their offering to consumers. Buyers complete the exchange by giving money and information to the seller. Suppose you learn about a new Alicia

| EXHIBIT 1.2 | Exchange: Underpinning of Seller-Buyer Relationships |

Communications

Delivery

Information

Money

Goods/Services Producers
(Sellers)

Customers/Consumers
(Buyers)

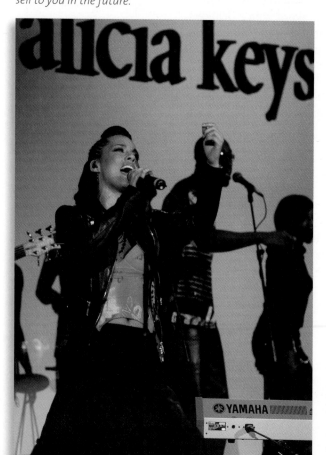

When you buy an Alicia Keys CD from BarnesNoble.com, you are involved in a marketing exchange. You get the CD and Barnes & Noble gets your money and important information that will help it sell to you in the future.

Keys CD by reading *Rolling Stone* magazine, which published a review of the CD and included an ad noting that the CD was available at Barnes & Noble and online (www.bn.com). You go online and purchase the CD. Along with gathering your necessary billing and shipping information, Barnes & Noble creates a record of your purchase, information that may be used in the coming months to inform you of the introduction of Alicia Keys' next CD and other related products. Thus, in addition to making money on this particular transaction, Barnes & Noble can use the valuable information it has obtained to facilitate an exchange in the future and solidify a relationship with you.

Marketing Requires Product, Price, Place, and Promotion Decisions

Marketing traditionally has been divided into a set of four interrelated decisions known as the marketing mix, or four Ps: product, price, place, and promotion as defined in Exhibit 1.3.[4] The four Ps, or marketing mix, are the controllable set of activities that the firm uses to respond to the wants of its target markets. But what does each of them mean?

Product: Creating Value Although marketing is a multifaceted function, its fundamental purpose is to create value by developing a variety of offerings, including goods, services, and ideas, to satisfy customer needs. Take, for example, water. Not too long ago, consumers perceived this basic commodity as simply water. It came out of a faucet and was consumed for drinking and washing. But taking a cue from European firms like Perrier (France) and San Pellegrino (Italy), several U.S.-based firms such as Poland Springs, Arrowhead, and Pepsi's Aquafina have created a product with benefits that consumers find valuable. In addition to easy access to water, an essential part of this created value is the products' brand image, which lets users say to the world, "I'm healthy," "I'm smart," and "I'm chic."[5]

EXHIBIT 1.3	The Marketing Mix	
Marketing Mix: 4 Ps	**Value**	
Product	Creating	
Price	Capturing	
Place	Delivering	
Promotion	Communicating	

Goods are items that you can physically touch. Reebok shoes, Coca-Cola, Budweiser, Kraft cheese, Tide, and countless other products are examples of goods. Reebok primarily makes shoes but also adds value to its products by, for example, designing them under its Rbk label to achieve fashionable appeal and enlisting popular celebrities like Scarlett Johansson to add their names to the designs. After taking on Nike in the athletic apparel and shoe markets, Reebok has now decided to go after the fashion market with its Rbk brand, especially its "Scarlett Hearts Rbk" line, a collection of workout-inspired gear designed by movie star Scarlett Johansson.

According to the company, Johansson's inspiration for the line came from her desire to "create a retro-inspired, sport lifestyle collection for the woman who is equal parts tomboy and glamour-girl."[6] Featuring photos of Johansson sprawled on couches wearing her hoodies, tanks, sneakers, and track pants, as well as videos in which she explains her choices for the logo (a heart), clothing, and the design process, the associated Web site provides an image of luxurious cool.

Unlike goods, **services** are intangible customer benefits that are produced by people or machines and cannot be separated from the producer. Travel-related industries like airlines and hotels, banking, insurance, spas, and entertainment all provide services. Getting money from your bank using an ATM or teller is another example of using a service. In this case, cash machines usually add value to your banking experience by being conveniently located, fast, and easy to use. The Ritz-Carlton Hotel Company adds value by providing over-the-top customer service. (See Superior Service 1.1 on page 9.)

Many offerings in the market represent a combination of goods and services. When you go to an optical center, you get your eyes examined (a service) and purchase new contact lenses (a good). If you enjoy Panic at the Disco you can attend a concert that, similar to other services like surgery or a football game, can be provided only at a particular time and place. At the concert, you can purchase a Panic at the Disco concert CD, a tangible good that caps and even extends a satisfying experience.

Ideas include thoughts, opinions, and philosophies, and intellectual concepts such as these also can be marketed. Groups promoting bicycle safety go to schools,

Firms like Pepsi have created value by bottling the simplest commodity, water, and calling it Aquafina.

How is a Panic at the Disco concert different from a Panic at the Disco CD?

give talks, and sponsor bike helmet poster contests for the members of their primary market—children. Then their secondary target market segment, parents and siblings, gets involved through their interactions with the young contest participants. The exchange of value occurs when the children listen to the sponsors' presentation and wear their helmets while bicycling, which means they have adopted, or become "purchasers," of the safety idea that the group marketed.

Price: Capturing Value   Everything has a price, though it doesn't always have to be monetary. Price, therefore, is everything the buyer gives up—money, time, energy—in exchange for the product. Marketers must determine the price of a product carefully on the basis of the potential buyer's belief about its value. For example, United Airlines can take you from New York to Denver. The price you pay for that service depends on how far in advance you book the ticket, the time of year, and whether you want to fly coach or business class. If you value the convenience of buying your ticket at the last minute for a ski trip between Christmas and New Year's Day and you want to fly business class, you can expect to pay four or five times as much as you would for the cheapest available ticket. That is, you have traded off a lower price for convenience. For marketers, the key to determining prices is figuring out how much customers are willing to pay so that they are satisfied with the purchase and the seller achieves a reasonable profit.

Place: Delivering the Value Proposition   The third P, place, represents all the activities (supply chain management) necessary to get the product to the right customer when that customer wants it. Specifically, *supply chain management* is the set of approaches and techniques that firms employ to efficiently and effectively integrate their suppliers, manufacturers, warehouses, stores, and other firms involved in the transaction, such as transportation companies, into a seamless value chain in which merchandise is produced and distributed in the right quantities, to the right locations, and at the right time, while minimizing systemwide costs and satisfying the service levels required by the customers.[7] Many marketing students initially overlook the importance of supply chain management because a lot of the activities are behind the scenes. But without a strong and efficient supply chain system, merchandise isn't available when customers want it. They are disappointed, and sales and profits suffer.

Superior Service 1.1 | Ritz-Carlton Hotel Makes Customer Service an Art[8]

The Ritz-Carlton Hotel Company, a winner of the Malcolm Baldrige National Quality Award, enjoys a great reputation as a top luxury hotel because it provides excellent customer service.

To do so, it trains its employees about the company's service values and how to execute them, which means Ritz-Carlton employees are prepared to go above and beyond expected service levels for each customer.

Employees attend daily, 15-minute "lineup" meetings to hear a "wow" story about exemplary service provided by an employee somewhere in the world. For example, when a guest at The Ritz-Carlton Resorts of Naples was about to miss an international flight because he had left some precious belongings in his hotel room, a hotel staff member personally collected and delivered the misplaced items to the airport. On another occasion, a Ritz-Carlton concierge booked a last-minute helicopter to whisk a frantic guest to his son's baseball game. The same story is told in hotels in 21 countries, so a waiter in Naples, Florida, will hear the same story as a concierge in Naples, Italy. These "wow" stories recognize an employee for his or her outstanding performance, motivate employees to embrace the 12 service values of the hotel, and reinforce each service value.

To help remind employees of these values, they all carry the chain's "Gold Standards," printed on a wallet-size card. The card contains the hotel's motto ("We Are Ladies and Gentlemen Serving Ladies and Gentlemen"), the three steps for high-quality service (warm and sincere greeting, anticipation and compliance with guests' needs, and fond farewell), and the 12 service values of the hotel, such as: I build strong relationships and create Ritz-Carlton guests for life (No. 1), or: I am proud of my professional appearance, language, and behavior (No. 10).

The result of such training and reinforcement is highly motivated employees who not only know the company's mission to deliver exceptional customer service but also understand how to apply its service values to everyday situations.

Ritz-Carlton understands the power of storytelling as a tactic to train employees. This training method might

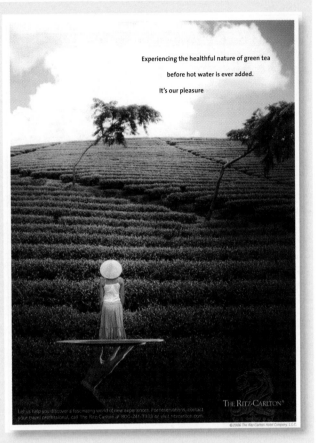

Experiencing the healthful nature of green tea before hot water is ever added. It's our pleasure

THE RITZ-CARLTON

The Ritz-Carlton Hotel Chain is an award-winning firm because it provides excellent customer service.

be productively applied to industries other than hotel chains.

Products can be duplicated, but customer service makes consumers emotionally attached and loyal to the experience and the associated brand.

But if the supply chain works, no one is disappointed. Imagine a seafood lover, landlocked in Idaho. She cannot manage to fly to Miami Beach regularly to visit Joe's Stone Crab; that just would not be practical. But Joe's wants to make sure it can provide her with the product she wants, so it has established a supply chain in which consumers can place orders through its Internet site (http://www.joesstonecrab.com). Joe's packages the orders and works with its supply chain partner, FedEx, to ensure the crabs get delivered to any location in the continental United States, including Idaho, by the end of the next business day. This service adds so much value that Joe's Stone Crabs can command a price premium—a medium-sized stone crab dinner for two is $123.95.[9] But for the seafood lover in Idaho, the ease with which she receives her seafood fix makes the price worthwhile. Power of the Internet 1.1 on the next page examines how Zappos' efficient supply chain made it a mega shoe, clothing, and accessories store that serves the world.

Promotion: Communicating the Value Proposition Even the best products and services will go unsold if marketers cannot communicate their value to customers. Countless Internet companies sank in the late 1990s, at least partly because

Power of the Internet 1.1

Zappos Delivers Shoes

Zappos.com, the online shoe, clothing, and accessories retailer, has grown from a shoe-only retailer with sales of $1.6 million in 2000 to a megastore with sales of over $1 billion annually. Prior to Zappos and a handful of other Internet shoe retailers, conventional wisdom was that personal service was necessary to sell shoes because customers needed to try them on and see how they looked on their feet. Also, if a retailer was out of stock of the desired shoes, a salesperson could switch customers to a satisfactory substitute. The advantage of an online shoe, clothing, and apparel retailer is the customer base is no longer limited by how far they will drive to a store. The market for an online retailer is limited only by the firm's ability to service customers' needs in a creative fashion.

Zappos has been successful in spite of these hurdles because it harnessed the power of the Internet to its advantage. Also, although Zappos. com began by advertising at expensive sports stadiums, it realized that it could not measure the return on this investment. So instead, it began decreasing advertising costs and spending more money on improving customer service through advanced supply chain management techniques such as free overnight shipping, free return shipping, and 24/7 fulfillment operations, making exchanging shoes almost as easy as in a store.

To make sure customers were getting what they wanted, when they wanted it, Zappos also strengthened its backend operations. The company previously used drop shipping, which means that an order taken by the retailer is shipped directly from the manufacturer to the customer. Although drop shipping eliminates the need to invest in and manage inventory, the retailer loses control. When Zappos could not guarantee when or if an item could be shipped, it upset customers. As a result, Zappos no longer uses drop shipping. It carries inventory in its warehouse instead. Zappos also

How does Zappos deliver value to its customers?

communicates with its thousands of manufacturers, which can log into an extranet that shows them how much of their product has been sold via Zappos.com. This real-time electronic relationship with its vendors keeps its shoe inventory at optimal levels—not more than it needs, but enough so it doesn't run out.

Zappos moved its fulfillment operations from a facility in California to one in Shepherdsville, Kentucky—conveniently, 20 miles from UPS's largest domestic shipping hub. This location also sits within 600 miles of two-thirds of the U.S. population. The location of the warehouse has helped the company expedite orders much more efficiently, from processing to shipment to delivery.

Zappos delivers value to its customers by offering them services they appreciate like free overnight and return shipping. To support this value proposition, Zappos has built strong relationships with its vendors.[10]

they did not communicate successfully with their customers. Some such firms had great products at very fair prices, but when customers could not find them on the Internet, the companies simply failed. Promotion thus is communication by a marketer that informs, persuades, and reminds potential buyers about a product or service to influence their opinions and elicit a response. Promotion generally can enhance a product or service's value, as happened for Calvin Klein fragrances. The company's provocative advertising has helped create an image that says more than "Use this product and you will smell good." Rather, the promotion sells youth, style, and sex appeal.

Calvin Klein is known for selling youth, fun, and sex appeal in its fragrance promotions. In this photo ck one models dance to the sounds of DJ Ruckus as they live in a billboard shaped like a giant ck one bottle overlooking the streets of Times Square in New York City.

Marketing Can Be Performed by Both Individuals and Organizations

Imagine how complicated the world would be if you had to buy everything you consumed directly from producers or manufacturers. You would have to go from farm to farm buying your food and then from manufacturer to manufacturer to purchase the table, plates, and utensils you need to eat that food. Fortunately, marketing intermediaries, such as retailers, accumulate merchandise from producers in large amounts and then sell it to you in smaller amounts. The process by which businesses sell to consumers is known as B2C (business-to-consumer) marketing, whereas the process of selling merchandise or services from one business to another is called B2B (business-to-business) marketing. With the advent of various Internet auction sites, such as eBay, consumers have started marketing their products and services to other consumers. This third category in which consumers sell to other consumers is C2C marketing. These marketing transactions are illustrated in Exhibit 1.4.

Individuals can also undertake activities to market themselves. When you apply for a job, for instance, the research you do about the firm, the resumé and cover letter you submit with your application, and the way you dress for

EXHIBIT 1.4 Marketing Can Be Performed by Both Individuals and Organizations

Manufacturer (makes computers)	Retailer (sells computers)	Consumer A	Consumer B
	B2B	B2C	C2C

an interview and conduct yourself during it are all forms of marketing activities. Accountants, lawyers, financial planners, physicians, and other professional service providers also constantly market their services one way or another.

Marketing Impacts Various Stakeholders

Most people think of marketing as a way to facilitate the sale of products or services to customers or clients. But marketing can also impact several other stakeholders, such as partners in the supply chain, employees, and society at large.

Supply chain partners, whether they are manufacturers, wholesalers, retailers, or other intermediaries like transportation or warehousing companies, are involved in marketing to each other. For instance, although manufacturers sell merchandise to retailers, the retailers often have to convince manufacturers to sell to them. After many years of not carrying Ralph Lauren products, JCPenney has co-introduced a line of clothing and home furnishings called American Living that is sold exclusively at JCPenney, but does not bear the Ralph Lauren name.[11]

Many firms develop marketing programs to attract the "best and brightest" employees. These programs, called employment marketing, involve undertaking marketing research to understand what potential employees are seeking, as well as what they think about the firm; developing a value proposition and an employment brand image; communicating that brand image to potential employees; and then fulfilling the brand promise by ensuring the employee experience matches that which was advertised. Firms often use advertising agencies that specialize in employment marketing to develop creative approaches to attract employees.[12] Starbucks' research, for example, revealed that existing employees liked their jobs. The rewards they receive from working at Starbucks go beyond pay and promotion opportunities. So Starbucks developed an employment marketing program based on the theme "Love

The dairy industry's "Got Milk" ad campaign has created high levels of awareness about the benefits of drinking milk and has increased milk consumption by using celebrities like David Beckham and Hilary Duff in its ads.

EXHIBIT 1.5 Marketing Evolution: Production, Sales, Marketing, and Value

Turn of the century | 1920 | 1950 | 1990

Production | Sales | Marketing | Value-based marketing

What You Do." Southwest uses a similar theme for its employment marketing program: "Feel Free to Actually Enjoy What You Are Doing."

Marketing often is designed to benefit an entire industry or society at large. The dairy industry has used a very successful, award-winning campaign with its slogan "Got Milk," aimed at different target segments. This campaign has not only created high levels of awareness about the benefits of drinking milk but also increased milk consumption in various target segments,[13] possibly through the use of a variety of celebrities from David Beckham, Hilary Duff, and Alex Rodriguez to Beyoncé and Carrie Underwood. Overall, this campaign benefits the entire dairy industry and promotes the health benefits of drinking milk to society at large.

Marketing Helps Create Value

Marketing didn't get to its current prominence among individuals, corporations, and society at large overnight. To understand how marketing has evolved into its present-day, integral business function of creating value, let's look for a moment at some of the milestones in marketing's short history (Exhibit 1.5).

Production-Oriented Era Around the turn of the 20th century, most firms were production oriented and believed that a good product would sell itself. Henry Ford, the founder of Ford Motor Co., once famously remarked, "Customers can have any color they want so long as it's black." Manufacturers were concerned with product innovation, not with satisfying the needs of individual consumers, and retail stores typically were considered places to hold the merchandise until a consumer wanted it.

Sales-Oriented Era Between 1920 and 1950, production and distribution techniques became more sophisticated, and the Great Depression and World War II conditioned customers to consume less or manufacture items themselves, so they planted Victory Gardens instead of buying produce. As a result, manufacturers had the capacity to produce more than customers really wanted or were able to buy. Firms found an answer to their overproduction in becoming sales oriented; they depended on heavy doses of personal selling and advertising.

Market-Oriented Era After World War II, soldiers returned home, got new jobs, and started families. At the same time, manufacturers turned from focusing on the war effort toward making consumer products. Suburban communities, featuring cars in every garage, sprouted up around the country, and the new suburban fixture, the shopping center, began to replace cities' central business districts as the hub of retail activity and a place to just hang out. Some products, once in limited supply because of World War II, became plentiful. And the United States entered a buyers' market—the customer became king! When consumers again had choices, they were able to make purchasing decisions on the basis of factors such as quality, convenience, and price. Manufacturers and retailers thus began to focus on what consumers wanted and needed before they designed, made, or attempted to sell their products and services. It was during this period that firms discovered marketing.

Value-Based Marketing Era   Most successful firms today are market oriented.[14] That means they generally have transcended a production or selling orientation and attempt to discover and satisfy their customers' needs and wants. Before the turn of the 21st century, better marketing firms recognized that there was more to good marketing than simply discovering and providing what consumers wanted and needed; to compete successfully, they would have to give their customers greater value than their competitors did.

Value reflects the relationship of benefits to costs, or what you *get* for what you *give*.[15] In a marketing context, customers seek a fair return in goods and/or services for their hard-earned money and scarce time. They want products or services that meet their specific needs or wants and that are offered at competitive prices. The challenge for firms is to find out what consumers are looking for and attempt to provide those very goods and services and still make a profit.

Every value-based marketing firm must implement its strategy according to what its customers value. Sometimes providing greater value means providing a lot of merchandise for relatively little money, such as a Whopper for 99¢ at Burger King or a diamond for 40 percent off the suggested retail price at Costco. But value is in the eye of the beholder and doesn't always come cheap. Satisfied BMW buyers believe their car is a good value because they have gotten a lot of benefits for a reasonable price. Similarly, people are willing to pay a premium for Apple's iPhone because of its extraordinary design and technology, even though cheaper substitutes are available.

A method of providing additional value to customers, known as value co-creation,[16] is to allow them the opportunity to act as collaborators in creating the product or service. For instance, when clients interact with their investment advisors to co-create their investment portfolios or when Nike allows customers to design their own sneakers, they are all involved in value co-creation. M&M's is involved in value co-creation by enabling customers to customize their orders on their Internet site. (See Adding Value 1.1.)

In the next section, we explore the notion of value-based marketing further. Specifically, we look at various options for attracting customers by providing them with better value than the competition does. Then we discuss how firms compete on the basis of value. Finally, we examine how firms transform the value concept into their value-driven activities.

CHECK YOURSELF

1. What is the definition of marketing?
2. Marketing is about satisfying _____ and _____ .
3. What are the four components of the marketing mix?
4. Who can perform marketing?
5. What are the various eras of marketing?

WHAT IS VALUE-BASED MARKETING?

Consumers make explicit and/or implicit trade-offs between the perceived benefits of a product or service and its cost. (See Exhibit 1.6.) Customers naturally seek options that provide the greatest benefits at the lowest costs. On the other side,

Adding Value 1.1 | My M&M's[17]

Creating value isn't just about the relationship between benefits and costs. In its traditional value proposition, Mars Inc., the maker of M&M's, offers its distinctive candy packaged in different sizes at many convenient locations, often for less than a dollar. But now Mars offers a unique choice to consumers. When consumers place orders for M&M's online, they may buy a set of eight 7-ounce bags for $47.92—enough to supply an entire crowd of chocolate lovers with their chocolate fix for weeks.[18] Now why would they do that?

When Mars initially introduced www.mymms.com during the 2006 holiday season, it promised visitors to its online shop that they could customize their own M&M's with personalized holiday greetings. Since then, the product has grown to fit a variety of occasions—from romance to business to birthdays. For example, to promote its new site, Mars hired a couple who communicated with each other only through custom M&M's for an entire month! You might not want to go to

such lengths, but on the My M&M's site, you can choose from a menu of different products that are not available in stores. Instead of the signature M, the personalized candy features the customer's own message, in 17 different color choices. And if the customized candy isn't enough, you can order embroidered bags for $85.

For those who are unsure quite what to say, Mars offers customizable messages for special events such as birthday parties, sporting events, graduations, and weddings—as well as wedding proposals! The updated candy classic goes beyond just personal relationships by offering options expressly for business customers that want to use custom M&M's as advertising or thank you gifts for special clients. Just imagine: You can communicate with clients, friends, family, or even spouses in a way that, well, melts in their mouths.

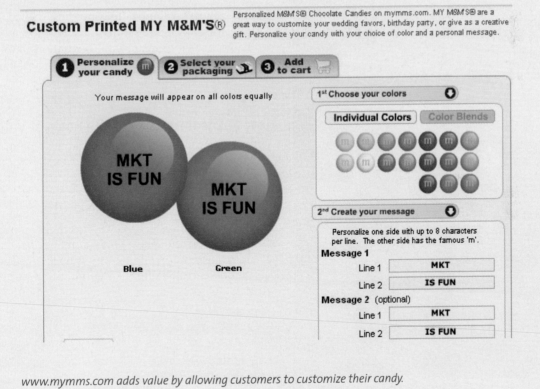

www.mymms.com adds value by allowing customers to customize their candy.

marketing firms attempt to find the most desirable balance between providing benefits to customers and keeping their own costs down.

To better understand value and to develop a value-based marketing orientation, a business must understand what customers view as the key benefits of a given product or service and how to improve on them. For example, some benefits of staying at a Sheraton hotel might include the high level of service quality provided by the personnel, the convenience of booking the room at Sheraton.com, and the overall quality of the rooms and meals offered. In broader terms, some critical benefits may be service quality, convenience, and merchandise quality. The customer's potential

| EXHIBIT 1.6 | Benefits and Costs Associated with Value |

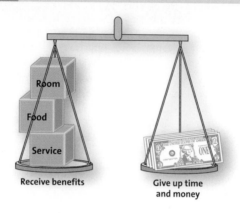

Receive benefits   Give up time
                                 and money

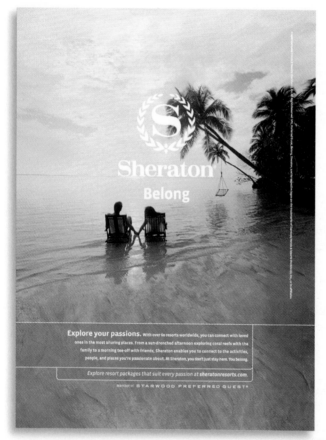

Sheraton provides value to its customers with a high level of service quality, the convenience of booking rooms online, and the overall quality of the rooms and meals offered.

cost elements, for the Sheraton hotel in our example, in terms of value-based marketing strategy, would include the price of the room and meals, the time it takes to book a room or check in at the hotel, and the risk of arriving at the hotel and finding it overbooked.

The other side of the value equation is the firm's ability to provide a better product/service mix or level of quality and convenience at the same cost or at a lower cost.

How Firms Compete on the Basis of Value

With such a simple formula, marketers should be able to deliver value consistently, right? Well, not exactly. In today's quickly changing world, consistently creating and delivering value is quite difficult. Consumer perceptions change quickly, competitors constantly enter markets, and global pressures continually reshape opportunities. Thus, marketers must keep a vigilant eye on the marketplace so they can adjust their offerings to meet customer needs and keep ahead of their competition.

Value-based marketing isn't just about creating strong products and services; it involves deciding which products/services to provide for whom. For example, Wal-Mart does not serve those customers who are looking to impress their friends with conspicuous consumption. Rather, Wal-Mart serves those who want convenient one-stop shopping and low prices—and on those values, it consistently delivers. But good value is not always limited just to low prices. Although Wal-Mart carries low-priced pots, pans, and coffee pots, cooking enthusiasts may prefer the product selection, quality, and expert sales assistance at Williams-Sonoma. The prices there aren't low like at Wal-Mart, but Williams-Sonoma customers believe they are receiving a good value too—because of the selection, quality, and service they receive—at Williams-Sonoma.

How Do Firms Become Value Driven?

Firms become value driven by focusing on three activities. First, they share information about their customers and competitors across their own organization and with other firms that help them in getting the product or service to the marketplace, such

Fashion designers for Zara, the Spain-based fashion retailer, collect purchase information and research customer trends to determine what their customers will want to wear in the next few weeks. They share this information with other departments to forecast sales and coordinate deliveries.

as manufacturers and transportation companies. Second, they strive to balance their customers' benefits and costs. Third, they concentrate on building relationships with customers.

Sharing Information   In a value-based, marketing-oriented firm, marketers share information about customers and competitors and integrate it across the firm's various departments. The fashion designers for Zara, the Spain-based fashion retailer, for instance, collect purchase information and research customer trends to determine what their customers will want to wear in the next few weeks; simultaneously, the logisticians—those persons in charge of getting the merchandise to the stores—use the same purchase history to forecast sales and allocate appropriate merchandise to individual stores. Sharing and coordinating such information represents a critical success factor for any firm. Imagine what might happen if Zara's advertising department were to plan a special promotion but not share its sales projections with those people in charge of creating the merchandise or getting it to stores.

Balancing Benefits with Costs   Value-oriented marketers constantly measure the benefits that customers perceive against the cost of their offerings. They use available customer data to find opportunities for better satisfying their customers' needs, keeping cost down, and in turn developing long-term loyalties. Such a value-based orientation has helped Target and Wal-Mart to outperform the Standard & Poor's retail index, Kohl's to outperform other department stores, and Ryanair and Southwest Airlines to outperform mainstream carriers.[19]

Until recently, it sometimes cost more to fly within Europe than to fly from the United States to Europe. But low-frills, low-cost carriers such as Ryanair and easyJet,[20] modeled on Southwest Airlines and JetBlue, now offer customers what they want: cheap intra-Europe airfares. Like their American counterparts, Ryanair and easyJet offer no food service and generally fly to and from out-of-the-way airports like Stansted, about 34 miles northeast of London. Many customers find value balanced against the minor inconveniences. Consider, for example, the London to Zurich, Switzerland, route for $50 or London to Athens, Greece, for $100. Values such as these are what have given low-cost carriers in the United States approximately 25 percent of the market share. Around the world, conventional airlines have started their own low-frills/low-cost airlines: Singapore Airlines provides Tiger, and Australia's Qantas offers Jetstar.

Building Relationships with Customers During the past decade or so, marketers have begun to realize that they need to think about their customer orientation in terms of relationships rather than transactions.[21] A *transactional orientation* regards the buyer–seller relationship as merely a series of individual transactions, so anything that happened before or after any transaction is of little importance. For example, used car sales typically are based on a transactional approach; the seller wants to get the highest price for the car, the buyer wants to get the lowest, and neither expects to do business with the other again.

A *relational orientation*, in contrast, is based on the philosophy that buyers and sellers should develop a long-term relationship. According to this idea, the lifetime profitability of the relationship is what matters, not how much money is made during each transaction. For example, UPS works with its shippers to develop efficient transportation solutions. Over time, UPS becomes part of the fabric of the shippers' organizations, and their operations become intertwined. In this scenario, they have developed a valuable long-term relationship.

Firms that practice value-based marketing use a process known as *customer relationship management (CRM)*, a business philosophy and set of strategies, programs, and systems that focus on identifying and building loyalty among the firm's most valued customers.[22] Firms that employ CRM systematically collect information about their customers' needs and then use that information to target their best customers with the products, services, and special promotions that appear most important to those customers.

Now that we've examined what marketing is and how it creates value, let's consider how it fits into the world of commerce, as well as into society in general.

To provide a great value, U.K.-based easyJet offers no food service and generally flies to and from out-of-the-way airports.

CHECK YOURSELF

1. What are two methods for increasing value?
2. How can a firm become value driven?

WHY IS MARKETING IMPORTANT?

Marketing once was only an afterthought to production. Early marketing philosophy went something like this: "We've made it; now how do we get rid of it?" However, marketing not only has shifted its focus dramatically, it also has evolved into a major business function that crosses all areas of a firm or organization, as illustrated in Exhibit 1.7. Marketing advises production about how much of the company's product to make and then tells logistics when to ship it. It creates long-lasting, mutually valuable relationships between the company and the firms from which it buys. It identifies those elements that local customers value and makes it possible for the firm to expand globally. Marketing has had a significant impact on consumers as well. Without marketing, it would be difficult for any of us to learn about new products and services. Understanding marketing can even help you find a job after you finish school.

EXHIBIT 1.7 Importance of Marketing

Expands global presence

Pervasive across organization

Can be entrepreneurial

Importance of marketing

Enriches society

Pervasive across supply chain

Makes life easier

Marketing Expands Firms' Global Presence

A generation ago, Coca-Cola was available in many nations, but Levi's and most other U.S. brands weren't. Blue jeans were primarily an American product—made in the United States for the U.S. market. But today most jeans, including those of Levi Strauss & Co., are made in places other than the United States and are available nearly everywhere. Thanks to MTV and other global entertainment venues, cheap foreign travel, and the Internet, you share many of your consumption behaviors with college students in countries all over the globe. The best fashions, music, and even food trends disseminate rapidly around the world.

Take a look at your next shopping bag. Whatever it contains, you will find goods from many countries—produce from Mexico, jeans from Italy, electronics from Korea. Global manufacturers and retailers continue to make inroads into the U.S. market. Companies such as Honda, Swatch, Sony, Heineken, and Nestlé sell as well in the United States as they do in their home countries. Sweden's fashion retailer H&M operates in 29 countries;[23] its upscale competitor, Spain's Zara, operates in over 70 countries.[24] The Dutch grocery store giant Ahold is among the top five grocery store chains in the United States, though you may never have heard of it because it operates under names such as Stop & Shop, GIANT, and Peapod in the United States.[25]

But how specifically does marketing contribute to a company's successful global expansion? Without the knowledge that firms gain by analyzing new customers' needs and wants on a segment-by-segment, region-by-region basis—one of marketing's main tasks—virtually no firm would succeed internationally or be able to expand globally. To appeal to its European customer base, McDonald's had to remodel its stores to the extent that most U.S. customers might not even recognize them as their familiar fast-food restaurant.[26] European consumers, who tend to view meals as occasions to be savored, have less interest in McDonald's American value offering—that is, consistent fast food at low prices. So the restaurant is redecorating in Europe, replacing bolted-down, plastic, yellow-and-white furniture with designer chairs and dark leather upholstery that create a more relaxed, sophisticated atmosphere. The chain is implementing nine different designs, depending on which one is most appropriate for the specific location and clientele. The designs range from "purely simple," with minimalist décor in neutral colors, to "Qualité," featuring large pictures of lettuces and tomatoes and gleaming stainless-steel kitchen utensils. The key to any successful makeover, whether it be global or local, is the same as the key to any strategy change: Make sure the change upgrade doesn't go so far that the firm loses its identity. McDonald's uniform quality control achieves this. Even if seated in upholstered leather chairs, customers have to know they're still in a McDonald's.

Marketing Is Pervasive across the Organization

In value-based marketing firms, the marketing department works seamlessly with other functional areas of the company to design, promote, price, and distribute products. Consider the Scion, designed for the less affluent youth market, which sometimes is referred to as "Generation Y" or "Millennials."[27] Scion's marketing department worked closely with engineers to ensure that the new car exceeded customers' expectations in terms of design but remained affordable. The company also coordinated the product offering with an innovative communications

Scion introduced a virtual road race in which participants received mileage points for sending Scion e-cards. At the end of the competition the driver with the most points won an onboard navigation system worth more than $2,000.

strategy. Because Generation Y is famous for its resistance to conventional advertising, Scion introduced a virtual road race in which participants received mileage points for sending Scion e-cards. The more "places" they visited, the more mileage points they received. At the end of the competition, each driver's points were totaled and compared with other racers' scores. The driver with the most points won an on-board navigation system worth more than $2,000. In addition, because Scion is a new car, the marketing department must work closely with the distribution department to ensure that advertising and promotions reach all distributors' territories and that distribution exists where those promotions occur. Marketing thus is responsible for coordinating all these aspects of supply and demand.

Marketing Is Pervasive across the Supply Chain

Firms do not work in isolation. Manufacturers buy raw materials and components from suppliers, which they sell to retailers or other businesses after they have turned the materials into products (see Exhibit 1.8). Every time materials or products are bought or sold, they are transported to a different location, which sometimes requires that they be stored in a warehouse operated by yet another organization. Such a group of firms that make and deliver a given set of goods and services is known as a supply chain.

As we discussed earlier, some supply chain participants have a transactional orientation in which the participating parties don't care much about their trading partners as the merchandise passes among them. Each link in the chain is out for its own best interest. Manufacturers, for example, want the highest price, whereas retailers want to buy the product at the lowest. As participants in transactions supply chain members do not enjoy any cooperation or coordination. But for the supply chain to provide significant value to the ultimate customer, the parties must establish long-term relationships with one another and cooperate to share data, make joint forecasts, and coordinate shipments. Effectively managing supply chain relationships often has a marked impact on a firm's ability to satisfy the consumer, which results in increased profitability for all parties.

Consider Levi Strauss & Co. and its close relationship with its major retailers. Not too many years ago, only about 40 percent of orders from the jeans manufacturer to its retailers arrived on time, which made it very difficult for retailers to keep all sizes in stock and therefore keep customers, who are generally not satisfied with anything less than the correct size, happy. Today, Levi's uses an automatic inventory replenishment system through which it manages the retailers' inventory itself. When a customer buys a pair of jeans, the information is transferred directly from the retailer to Levi's, which then determines which items the retailer needs to reorder and automatically ships the merchandise. The relationship benefits all parties: Retailers don't have to worry about keeping their stores stocked in jeans and save money because they don't have to invest as much money in inventory. Because

EXHIBIT 1.8 Supply Chain

Raw Material   Manufacturer   Retailer   Consumer

Levi Strauss & Co. works closely with its retailers to ensure its merchandise is available in the stores.

Levi's has control of the jeans inventory, it can be assured that it won't lose sales because its retailers have let their inventory run down. Finally, customers benefit by having the merchandise when they want it—a good value.

A supply chain comprises more than buyers and sellers, however. Firms build strategic alliances with consulting firms, marketing research firms, computer firms, and transportation firms, just to name a few. For example, UPS provides much more than a package delivery service; it also offers insurance services, supply chain management, and e-commerce support to small- and medium-sized customers. Through UPS Capital, firms can even obtain funds to finance their inventory or ease their cash flow.[28]

Marketing Makes Life Easier and Provides Employment Opportunities

Marketers provide you, as a consumer, with product and service choices, as well as information about those choices, to ensure that your needs are being met. They balance the product or service offering with a price that makes you comfortable with your purchase, and after the sale, they provide reasonable guarantees and return policies. Marketing's responsibility also includes offering pleasant and convenient places for you to shop. In essence, marketers make your life easier, and in that way, they add value.

Marketing also offers a host of employment opportunities that require a variety of skills. On the creative side, positions such as artists, graphic designers, voice talent, animators, music composers, and writers represent just a few of the opportunities available to talented individuals. On the analytical side, marketing requires database analysts, market researchers, and inventory managers who can quickly digest information, cross-reference data, and spot trends that might make or break a company. In the business arena, marketing requires strategists, project/product managers, sales associates, and analysts who are capable of designing and implementing complex marketing strategies that positively affect the bottom line.

Marketing Enriches Society

Should marketing focus on factors other than financial profitability, like good corporate citizenry? Many of America's best known corporations seem to think so, because they encourage their employees to participate in activities that benefit their communities and invest heavily in socially responsible activities and charities. For example, from the very start, when Kellogg functioned primarily as a purveyor of Corn Flakes, it maintained a strong commitment to enhancing the welfare of its many stakeholders—not just customers, but also employees and the community at large. As the company asserts:

- Our Values: At Kellogg Company, we act with integrity and show respect.
- Our Foods: We produce a range of foods to meet your tastes and health needs.
- Our Marketing Practices: Kellogg has a long-standing commitment to responsible marketing.
- In Our Communities: Great things can happen when a company is an active corporate citizen.
- Our Environment: We're helping to preserve and protect our natural resources.[29]

The firm's commitment to a broader civic responsibility, regardless of where it does business, stems from its corporate mission statement, which promises its "commitment to provide and maintain environmentally responsible practices for the communities in which we are located." Although initially a U.S. firm, Kellogg runs facilities in Australia, Germany, India, and Korea as well, and in all these communities, it engages in recycling campaigns and implements water management systems. Thus, the employees, its investors, and, perhaps most important, its customers are reassured, knowing that Kellogg aims to make all of its cartons out of 100 percent recycled fiber. When products suffer minor quality defects, such as too many yellow Froot Loops in a box, the company does not just waste them but instead donates them to charitable organizations and thus benefits the community as well.

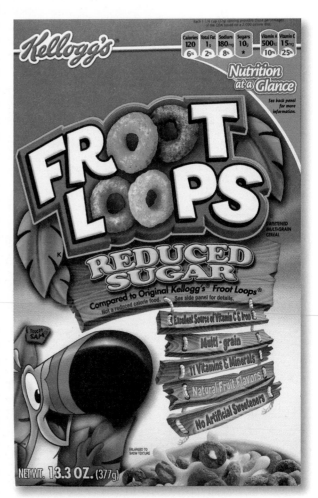

Similar sentiments are echoed by Colgate-Palmolive, which clearly states that "Our three fundamental values—Caring, Global Teamwork and Continuous Improvement—are part of everything we do."[30] Management at Ben & Jerry's, the Vermont-based ice cream producer, actively embrace social responsibility by focusing the company around three key types of missions: product, economic, and social (see Exhibit 1.9 on the next page).[31]

These firms, and hundreds more like them, recognize that including a strong social orientation in business is a sound strategy that is in both its own and its customers' best interest. It shows the consumer marketplace that the firm will be around for the long run and can be trusted with their business. In a volatile market, investors view firms that operate with high levels of corporate responsibility and ethics as safe investments. Similarly, firms have come to realize that good corporate citizenship through socially responsible actions should be a priority because it will help their bottom line in the long run.[32] Ethical & Societal Dilemma 1.1 examines how fast food companies are enriching society by becoming more socially responsible in their marketing to children.

Kellogg helps enrich society. If it puts too many yellow Froot Loops in a box, for instance, it donates it to charity instead of throwing the box away.

EXHIBIT 1.9	Ben & Jerry's Mission

■ **Product Mission**

To make, distribute and sell the finest quality all natural ice cream and euphoric concoctions with a continued commitment to incorporating wholesome, natural ingredients and promoting business practices that respect the Earth and the Environment.

■ **Economic Mission**

To operate the company on a sustainable financial basis of profitable growth, increasing value for our stockholders and expanding opportunities for development and career growth for our employees.

■ **Social Mission**

To operate the company in a way that actively recognizes the central role that business plays in society by initiating innovative ways to improve the quality of life locally, nationally and internationally.

Ethical and Societal Dilemma 1.1 Marketing Fast Food to Children

Recently, 11 major food manufacturers, responsible for two-thirds of all advertising directed at children,[33] agreed to limit their advertising to children. Foremost among those companies was McDonald's. In agreeing to restrict children's advertising to products that meet the requirements of the United States Department of Agriculture's (USDA) Dietary Guidelines for Americans, McDonald's took a decisive stand in the debate about developing culturally acceptable marketing strategies.

The increasing rates of childhood obesity, especially in the United States, have brought increased scrutiny to advertising that touts unhealthy food for children. Some parents' and health groups argue that when fast-food companies target children with their advertising, they are adding to the problem by making children believe fast food is always the way to go. Studies of children and advertising reveal that young consumers have trouble understanding the persuasive nature of advertising and simply accept at face value the things they see on television, on billboards, and in magazines.[34] On average, school-aged children watch 7,600 televised ads for food products every year.[35]

In response, McDonald's took a relatively bold step and committed to three principles that guide any of its marketing to children:

1. All national advertising primarily directed at children under 12 years of age may only feature meals that meet specific nutritional criteria consistent with healthy dietary choices. Specifically, the advertised meals must contain no more than 600 calories, no more than 35 percent of their calories from fat and 10 percent from saturated fat, and no more than 35 percent total sugar by weight.

2. Advertisements will prominently feature healthy lifestyle messages designed to appeal to children.

3. Third-party licensed characters (e.g., Donkey and Puss-in-Boots from *Shrek the Third*) in paid advertising directed toward children under the age of 12 years will promote healthy dietary choices. The use of such characters on the company's Web sites also is limited to the promotion of healthy dietary choices or healthy lifestyle messages.[36]

In commercials promoting a tie-in with *Shrek the Third*, Shrek, Donkey, Puss-in-Boots, and Gingy all share their apple slices and milk jugs, along with their Chicken McNuggets. Will such efforts affect perceptions of advertising aimed at children among parents and nutrition groups? Should they?

Marketing Can Be Entrepreneurial

Whereas marketing plays a major role in the success of large corporations, it also is at the center of the successes of numerous new ventures initiated by entrepreneurs, or people who organize, operate, and assume the risk of a business venture.[37] Key to the success of many such entrepreneurs is that they launch ventures that aim to satisfy unfilled needs. Some examples of successful ventures (and their founders) that understood their customers and added value include

- Ben & Jerry's (Ben Cohen and Jerry Greenfield).
- Bose Corporation (Ambar Bose).
- Kinko's (Paul Orfalea), now FedEx/Kinkos.
- Apple Inc. and Pixar Studios (Steve Jobs).
- *The Oprah Winfrey Show* and other ventures (Oprah Winfrey).

Steve Jobs is the cofounder, along with Ed Catmull, of Pixar Studios, a movie studio focused on cutting-edge, computer-animated films. The studio has been incredibly successful; its five top films (*Toy Story, Toy Story 2, A Bug's Life, Monsters, Inc.,* and *Finding Nemo*) earned more than $2 billion worldwide, along with 20 Academy Awards for the company in 20 years. But when a chasm opened between Pixar and its distributor, Disney, after a long and fruitful relationship, Disney executives learned just what value Pixar represented to their bottom line and acquired Pixar for $7.4 billion.[38]

Another extraordinary entrepreneur and marketer is Oprah Winfrey. A self-made billionaire before she turned 50, Oprah went from being the youngest person and first African-American woman to anchor news at WTVF-TV in Nashville, Tennessee, to being only the third woman in history to head her own production studio. Under the Oprah banner are a variety of successful endeavors including Harpo Films, Oprah's Book Club, Oprah.com, and the Oxygen television network. In addition to producing the two highest rated talk shows on TV, *The Oprah Winfrey Show* and *Dr. Phil*, Oprah's Harpo studio also has produced films such as *Beloved, The Women of Brewster Place,* and *The Great Debaters*. Oprah's philanthropic contributions are vast and varied. Through the Oprah Winfrey Foundation and Oprah's Angel Network, women around the world have raised over 50 million dollars for scholarships, schools, women's shelters, and building youth centers. Her efforts in the United States resulted in President Bill Clinton signing into law the national "Oprah Bill" to establish a national database of convicted child abusers.[39]

All of these distinguished entrepreneurs had a vision about how certain combinations of products and services could satisfy unfilled needs. All understood the marketing opportunity (i.e., the unfilled need), conducted a thorough examination of the marketplace, and developed and communicated the value of their product and services to potential consumers.

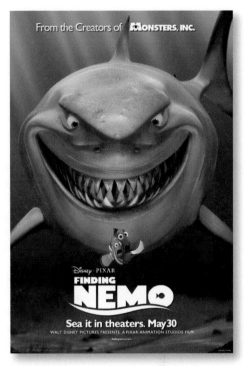

Entrepreneur Steve Jobs, founder of Apple Inc., also cofounded Pixar Studios along with Ed Catmull. Their computer-animated films, like Finding Nemo, *have won several Academy Awards.*

When you think of Oprah Winfrey, think big: Harpo Productions, Inc.; O, The Oprah Magazine; O at Home magazine; Harpo Films; the Oxygen television network; not to mention her philanthropic work with the Oprah Winfrey Foundation.

CHECK YOURSELF

1. List five functions that illustrate the importance of marketing.
2. A firm doing the right thing emphasizes the importance of marketing to _____ .

Summing Up

1. What is the role of marketing in organizations?

Marketing is the activity, set of institutions, and processes for creating, capturing, communicating, delivering, and exchanging offerings that have value for customers, clients, partners, and society at large. Marketing strives to *create value* in many ways. If marketers are to succeed, their customers must believe that the firm's products and services are valuable; that is, they are worth more to the customers than they cost. Another important and closely related marketing role is to capture value of a product or service based on potential buyers' beliefs about its value.

Marketers also enhance the value of products and services through various forms of *communication*, such as advertising and personal selling. Through communications, marketers educate and inform customers about the benefits of their products and services and thereby increase their perceived value.

Marketers facilitate the *delivery of value* by making sure the right products and services are available when, where, and in the quantities their customers want. Better marketers are not concerned about just one transaction with their customers. They recognize the value of loyal customers and strive to develop *long-term relationships* with them.

2. How do marketers create value for a product or service?

Value represents the relationship of benefits to costs. Firms can improve their value by increasing benefits, reducing costs, or both. The best firms integrate a value orientation into everything they do. If an activity doesn't increase benefits or reduce costs, it probably shouldn't occur. Marketers also have found that providing good value is one of the best ways to maintain a sustainable advantage over their competitors.

Firms become value driven by finding out as much as they can about their customers and those customers' needs and wants. They share this information with their partners, both up and down the supply chain, so the entire chain collectively can focus on the customer. The key to true value-based marketing is the ability to design products and services that achieve precisely the right balance between benefits and costs.

Value-based marketers aren't necessarily worried about how much money they will make on the next sale. Instead, they are concerned with developing a lasting relationship with their customers so those customers return again and again.

3. Why is marketing important both within and outside the firm?

Many brands and stores now appear in multiple countries, and marketing helps them expand globally. Successful firms integrate marketing throughout their organizations so that marketing activities coordinate with other functional areas such as product design, production, logistics, and human resources, enabling them to get the right product to the right customers at the right time.

Marketing helps facilitate the smooth flow of goods through the supply chain, all the way from raw materials to the consumer. From a personal perspective, the marketing function facilitates your buying process, and knowledge of marketing will help you in virtually any career you may decide to pursue.

Marketing also can be important for society through its embrace of solid, ethical business practices. Firms "do the right thing" when they sponsor charitable events and seek to reduce environmental impacts, and such efforts endear the firm to customers. Finally, marketing is a cornerstone of entrepreneurialism. Not only have many great companies been founded by outstanding marketers, but an entrepreneurial spirit pervades the marketing decisions of firms of all sizes.

Key Terms

- B2C (business-to-consumer) 11
- B2B (business-to-business) 11
- C2C (consumer-to-consumer) 11
- customer relationship management (CRM) 18
- employment marketing 12
- exchange 5
- goods 7
- ideas 7
- marketing 4
- marketing mix (four Ps) 6
- marketing plan 4
- relational orientation 18
- services 7
- supply chain 21
- transactional orientation 18
- value 14
- value co-creation 14

Marketing Applications

1. Do you know the difference between needs and wants? When water bottlers develop their marketing strategies, do they concentrate on satisfying their customers' needs or wants? What about a utilities company? A cellular phone provider? A humanitarian agency such as the Red Cross?

2. People can apply marketing principles to getting a job. If the person looking for a job is the product, describe the other three Ps.

3. One of your friends was recently watching TV and saw an advertisement that she liked. She said, "Wow, that was great marketing!" Was the ad in fact marketing?

4. Mercedes-Benz manufactures the Smart Car, which sells for around $15,000 and the SL 65 AMG 2-door Roadster for over $100,000. Is Mercedes providing the target markets for these cars with a good value? Explain why.

5. Assume you have been hired into the marketing department of a major consumer products manufacturer, such as Coca-Cola. You are having lunch with some new colleagues in other departments—finance, manufacturing, and logistics. They are arguing that the company could save millions of dollars if it just got rid of the marketing department. Develop an argument that would persuade them otherwise.

6. Why do marketers find it important to embrace societal needs and ethical business practices? Provide an example of a societal need or ethical business practice that a specific marketer is addressing.

Quiz Yourself

www.mhhe.com/ grewal2e

1. The "Got Milk" advertising campaign was designed to help market a(n):
   a. individual.
   b. firm.
   c. industry.
   d. organization.

2. The evolution of marketing progressed along the continuum:
   a. sales, marketing, value-based marketing, production.
   b. marketing, value-based marketing, production, sales.
   c. value-based marketing, production, sales, marketing.
   d. production, sales, marketing, value-based marketing.

(Answers to these two questions can be found on page 623.)

Go to www.mhhe.com/grewal2e to practice by answering an additional 11 questions.

Net Savvy

1. eBay (www.ebay.com) is the world's largest auction site. Visit its Web site and describe how it delivers value above and beyond that provided by conventional, in-person auctions, such as those you might find advertised in the weekend section of your local newspaper. Describe the ways in which the company communicates this value through its Web site.

2. Bluefly.com has successfully built its market by providing a great value to consumers. Visit its Web site and describe the ways in which it creates value for consumers and how it differs from a traditional apparel store. Under what circumstances would you shop at Bluefly.com versus a traditional apparel store?

Chapter Case Study

GOOGLE AND THE YOUTUBE ACQUISITION[40]

When in October 2006 Google paid $1.65 billion in stock to buy YouTube,[41] the match—Google's ad network combined with YouTube's growing Internet traffic—seemed heaven-sent. Yet Google continues to struggle to make a profit from its investment.

With over 80 million monthly users and the eighth largest audience on the Internet,[42] YouTube has become one of the Web's most popular sites. When it began in a garage in Menlo Park, California, in 2005, YouTube was a site for users to share, view, and comment on videos. But since then, the YouTube community has grown to include not just the amateurs who post feeds of their cat flushing the toilet or themselves singing oddly, but also mainstream media companies such as CBS and the BBC, as well as the National Basketball Association (NBA). As it has grown, YouTube has found new uses for its technology, from hosting branded "channels" and broadcasting commercial content from partner companies to trying to affect presidential elections by partnering with CNN to give "regular Joes" (and animated snowmen) the chance to ask the candidates questions.

YouTube users typically enter through the homepage or click a link directly to a particular video. After viewing videos, users can browse related items. Alternatively, viewers can perform keyword searches for specific items and receive results from the site's search engine listing relevant items and links to potentially interesting videos. Users can even search for videos by the individual poster's name to review all of that person's video uploads and comment history.

YouTube's business model relies on the site's ability to display ads to millions of YouTube users and on creating a compelling user experience that should encourage visitors to view more videos. Specifically, YouTube includes the following description of its business model on its Web site:

> YouTube is pursuing advertising as its business model, and is exploring a range of possibilities including PVAs (participatory video ads), promotions, sponsorships, contextual-based advertising, traditional banner advertising, etc. But more than anything else, we're committed to providing the best consumer experience to watch, upload, and share videos. When building a community, it is critical to get the model right.[43]

But building community does not always mean building profit, as Google is learning. YouTube inserts advertisements immediately before showing videos, but its ad profits are distinctly less than those that Google earns from its base navigation format. As more and more Google users spend their time accessing YouTube, the company's overall advertising profits may continue to dwindle, leaving Google little hope of recouping its investment.

Yet there are some indications that Google isn't that worried, because its acquisition of YouTube may have been driven more by its desire to expand its reach to more traditional media. If Google can offer television advertisers the ability to test market their ads on YouTube and return reports about which version of an ad is most successful among the YouTube community, it can provide companies a vital source of information.

In addition to questions regarding the profitability of YouTube, the site faces some serious legal challenges. Content owners are growing reluctant to license their media for use on YouTube; one company, Viacom, even sued YouTube for $1 billion in early 2007. In response, YouTube has introduced features such as the Video I.D. System that automatically removes copyrighted content, but these efforts have done little to allay the concerns of YouTube's traditional media partners.[44]

Questions

1. According to the breakdown in Exhibit 1.5, which of the four orientations best describes YouTube?

2. What was Google hoping to achieve by acquiring YouTube?

3. Which features create the most value for both users and advertisers?

4. In terms of creating value for its users and content providers, how does YouTube compare with traditional channels, such as television, movies, and DVDs? Explain your answer in terms of benefits, reduced costs, or a combination of these factors.

5. Visit the YouTube Web site and try some of its features. How can advertisers maximize the potential YouTube offers?

6. What risks do advertisers face if they choose to use YouTube?

DEVELOPING MARKETING STRATEGIES AND A MARKETING PLAN

Dunkin' Donuts versus Starbucks

People used to just make their coffee at home or maybe grab a cup of joe from the local diner. But in combination, Starbucks and Dunkin' Donuts have transformed and continue to lead the rapidly growing branded coffee market. Despite their radically different corporate histories, target markets, and positioning strategies, they manage to sell basically the same product. How can two companies both operate successfully in the same product market yet employ such divergent marketing strategies?

Starbucks: From its humble beginnings at the Pike Place Market in Seattle, Washington, Starbucks Coffee Company has grown from one store in 1971 to more than 8,200 company-owned stores across the world, as well as another 6,200-plus franchised stores. Although coffee remains its primary product, Starbucks also sells assorted coffee-related merchandise and accessories, ice cream, premade sandwiches, and branded beverages such as Tazo and Ethos Water.[1] It also has branched out into the music business, releasing compilations of the recordings that the stores play, and producing some CDs available only for purchase from the retail outlets—most famously, the recent release from music legend and former Beatle Sir Paul McCartney.

According to Starbucks' chair, Howard Shultz, "We're in the business of human connection and humanity, creating communities in a third place between home and work."[2] To achieve this "Third Place" strategy, Starbucks encourages customers to linger in the stores, rather than running in for coffee and then dashing back out. While they linger, the company hopes these consumers will purchase the occasional gourmet coffee beans or CD. The stores clearly personify this philosophy, from their comfortable, semiprivate seats to free outlets for laptops and available Wi-Fi. Some larger stores even go so far as to host miniconcerts to draw people in for longer periods of time. By focusing on creating a comfortable environment in which coffee and tea drinkers can meet friends or work alone, Starbucks has branded itself as a luxury provider of the coffee-drinking experience.

Dunkin' Donuts: Twenty years before Starbucks got its start, and on the opposite side of the country, William Rosenberg founded a chain of coffee shops around the Boston, Massachusetts, area. The chain quickly grew into a local New England institution,[3] then spread across the United States and overseas. Dunkin' Donuts today serves coffee, doughnuts, bagels, and breakfast sandwiches, in more than 6,000 restaurants.[4] Although the name still implies an emphasis on doughnuts—and customers can still enjoy the scent of baking pastries in stores—the company's true focus has shifted to coffee. Currently, 65 percent of Dunkin' Donuts' revenue comes from coffee.[5]

The marketing strategy Dunkin' Donuts has adopted of late represents a response to Starbucks' positioning as a luxury brand. Dunkin' prefers instead to reach out to the "average Joe." According to the chain's vice president of marketing, Dunkin' Donuts is focusing on "mainstream customers," who, as he noted in one interview, "have stuff they got to do, and most of what they want to do is not taking place in our stores."[6] In recent advertising campaigns, the firm relies on a celebrity, but not one associated with glamour or luxury. Instead, the ads show Rachael Ray, the proponent of simple, everyday tasks and host of *30 Minute Meals*, *Rachael Ray's Tasty Travels*, and the *Rachael Ray* show, rushing through her day, with only enough time to stop at Dunkin' for her coffee fix. Thus, to align with its perception of the market, Dunkin' Donuts' marketing strategy focuses on convenience and economy in an attempt to ensure that when practical, everyday people want a cup of coffee, they think first of their local, quick, easy-to-access, inexpensive Dunkin' Donuts.

● ● ●

In this chapter, we start by discussing a *marketing strategy*, which outlines the specific actions a firm intends to implement to appeal to potential customers. Then we discuss how to do a *marketing plan*, which provides a blueprint for implementing the marketing strategy. The chapter concludes with a tool called *scenario planning* that allows marketers to understand how forces in the environment will impact their marketing strategy in the future.

WHAT IS A MARKETING STRATEGY?

A **marketing strategy** identifies (1) a firm's target market(s), (2) a related marketing mix—their four Ps, and (3) the bases upon which the firm plans to build a sustainable competitive advantage. A **sustainable competitive advantage** is an advantage over the competition that is not easily copied, and thus can be maintained over a long period of time.

Starbucks and Dunkin' Donuts are appealing to different target markets, and they are implementing their marketing mixes—their four Ps—in very different ways. In essence, they have very different marketing strategies. Although both stores' customers seek a good cup of coffee and a pastry, Starbucks is also attempting to reach the customer who wants a coffee-drinking experience that includes a nice warm, social atmosphere and personal "baristas" to make their esoteric drinks. And people are willing to pay relatively high prices for all this. Dunkin' Donuts' customers, on the other hand, aren't particularly interested in the experience. They want a good tasting cup of coffee at a fair price, and they want to get in and out of the store quickly.

Building a Sustainable Competitive Advantage

What about their respective marketing mixes would provide a sustainable competitive advantage? After all, there are stores and restaurants that sell coffee and pastries in every neighborhood in which there is a Starbucks or a Dunkin' Donuts, and many of these have great coffee and pastries. If Starbucks or Dunkin' Donuts lowered their prices, their competition in the area would match the reduction. If they introduced a peppermint swirl cappuccino for the holiday season, other stores in the area could do the same. Thus, just because a firm implements an element of the marketing mix better than competition, it doesn't necessarily mean it is sustainable.

Establishing a competitive advantage means that the firm, in effect, builds a wall around its position in the market. When the wall is high, it will be hard for competitors outside the wall to enter the market and compete for the firm's target customers.

Over time, all advantages will be eroded by competitive forces, but by building high, thick walls, firms can sustain their advantage, minimize competitive pressure, and boost profits for a longer time. Thus, establishing a sustainable competitive advantage is the key to positive long-term financial performance.

There are four macro, or overarching, strategies that focus on aspects of the marketing mix to create and deliver value and to develop sustainable competitive advantages, as we depict in Exhibit 2.1:[7]

Recent Dunkin' Donuts advertising features Rachael Ray, host of 30 Minute Meals *the* Rachael Ray *show, and* Rachael Ray's Tasty Travels.

- **Customer excellence:** Focuses on retaining loyal customers and excellent customer service.
- **Operational excellence:** Achieved through efficient operations and excellent supply chain and human resource management.
- **Product excellence:** Having products with high perceived value and effective branding and positioning.
- **Locational excellence:** Having a good physical location and Internet presence.

Customer Excellence

Customer excellence is achieved when a firm develops value-based strategies for retaining loyal customers and provides outstanding customer service.

Retaining Loyal Customers Sometimes, the methods a firm uses to maintain a sustainable competitive advantage help attract and maintain loyal customers. For

EXHIBIT 2.1   Macro Strategies for Developing Customer Value

instance, having a strong brand, unique merchandise, and superior customer service all help solidify a loyal customer base. In addition, having loyal customers is, in and of itself, an important method of sustaining an advantage over competitors. Loyalty is more than simply preferring to purchase from one firm instead of another.[8] It means that customers are reluctant to patronize competitive firms. For example, loyal customers continue to shop at Dunkin' Donuts even if Starbucks opens more convenient locations or provides a slightly superior assortment or slightly lower prices.

More and more firms realize the value of achieving customer excellence through focusing their strategy on retaining their loyal customers. For instance, Starbucks doesn't think in terms of selling a single cup of coffee for $2. Instead, it is concerned with satisfying the customer who spends $25 per week, 50 weeks a year, for 10 years or more. This customer isn't a $2 customer; he's a $12,500 customer. Viewing customers with a lifetime value perspective, rather than on a transaction-by-transaction basis, is key to modern customer retention programs.[9] We will examine how the lifetime value of a customer is calculated in Chapter 9.

Marketers use several methods to build customer loyalty. One such way involves developing a clear and precise positioning strategy. For instance, loyal Dunkin' Donuts patrons have such a strong attachment to its products that they would rather go without than go to Starbucks.

Another method of achieving customer loyalty creates an emotional attachment through loyalty programs.[10] Loyalty programs, which constitute part of an overall customer relationship management (CRM) program, prevail in many industries from airlines to hotels to movies theaters to retail stores. With such programs, firms can identify members through the loyalty card or membership information the consumer provides when he or she makes a purchase. Using that purchase information, analysts determine which types of merchandise certain groups of customers are buying and thereby can tailor their offering to better meet the needs of their loyal customers. For instance, by analyzing their databases, financial institutions such as Bank of Montréal develop profiles of customers who have defected in the past and use that information to identify customers who may defect in the future. Once it identifies these customers, the firm can implement special retention programs to keep them.

Customer Service   Marketers also may build sustainable competitive advantage by offering excellent customer service,[11] though consistently offering excellent service can prove difficult. Customer service is provided by employees, and invariably, humans are less consistent than machines. On every visit, for example, Starbucks must attempt to ensure that every single barista greets customers in a friendly way and makes drinks consistently. But what happens when a barista comes to work in a bad mood or simply forgets to add nutmeg to a drink? Firms that offer good customer service must instill its importance in their employees over a long period of time so that it becomes part of the organizational culture.

Although it may take considerable time and effort to build a reputation for customer service, once a marketer has earned a good service reputation, it can sustain this advantage for a long time because a competitor is hard pressed to develop a comparable reputation. Superior Service 2.1 describes the superb customer service at Virgin Atlantic Airlines.

 ## Superior Service **2.1**   **Customer Service at Virgin Atlantic**

Virgin Atlantic, the second largest long-haul international airline, operates services out of London's Heathrow and Gatwick airports to 30 destinations across the world—Shanghai, the Caribbean, and, of course, the United States.[12] Virgin's customer service orientation is heralded in its mission statement: "to grow a profitable airline that people love to fly and where people love to work."

In an age of dwindling airline services and disgruntled passengers, Virgin Atlantic decided to distinguish itself by providing the best possible service at the best possible price for all classes of tickets. Moreover, it set out to do so differently than anyone else. The result is a loyal group of travelers, agents, and employees who know the value of excellent customer service.

What does Virgin do that makes it so special? Consider the offerings in the box: Economy service is certainly good, but premium economy offers lots of extras. And upper service—well, that's just luxury!

Virgin Atlantic's upper-class service includes fully reclining seats complete with a guest seat for entertaining.

Service Class	Distinctive Features
Upper	■ In-flight massages and manicures ■ Food prepared to order ■ Airport lounges with putting greens ■ Full-service spas and beauty salons ■ Onboard stand-up bars ■ Fully reclining seats complete with a guest seat for entertaining ■ Free limousine transfer ■ Drive-through check-in service standard with fare ■ Power connectors for laptops or iPods
Premium Economy	■ Dedicated check-in ■ Fast track processing line ■ Priority baggage handling ■ Eight inches more legroom than standard in the industry ■ China dinnerware and stainless steel cutlery ■ Free after-dinner liqueur
Economy	■ Full in-flight meals ■ Free individual entertainment for each seat (28 channels with movies, television shows, and games) ■ Free drinks ■ Amenity kits with stylishly fun socks, eye shades, toothbrushes, combs, rejuvenating toiletries, and seat-back stickers with slogans like "Do Not Disturb," "Wake Me For Meals," and "Wake Me For Duty Free."

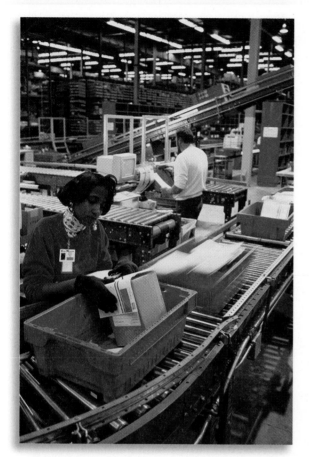

Some firms develop a sustainable competitive advantage through operational excellence with efficient operations and excellent supply chain management.

Operational Excellence

Firms achieve operational excellence, the second way to achieve a sustainable competitive advantage, through their efficient operations, excellent supply chain management, strong relationships with their suppliers, and excellent human resource management (which yields productive employees).

Efficient Operations All marketers strive for efficient operations to get their customers the merchandise they want, when they want it, in the required quantities, and at a lower delivered cost than that of their competitors. By so doing, they ensure good value to their customers, earn profitability for themselves, and satisfy their customers' needs. In addition, efficient operations enable firms either to provide their consumers with lower-priced merchandise or, even if their prices are not lower than those of the competition, to use the additional margin they earn to attract customers away from competitors by offering even better service, merchandise assortments, or visual presentations.

Excellent Supply Chain Management and Strong Supplier Relations Firms achieve efficiencies by developing sophisticated distribution and information systems as well as strong relationships with vendors. Like customer relationships, vendor relations must be developed over the long term and generally cannot be easily offset by a competitor.[13] Furthermore, firms with strong relationships may gain exclusive rights to (1) sell merchandise in a particular region, (2) obtain special terms of purchase that are not available to competitors, or (3) receive popular merchandise that may be in short supply.

In one such relationship, Levi Strauss & Co. has partnered with the world's largest retailer, Wal-Mart, even though for years it resisted selling to the retail giant because it believed such a partnership would tarnish its image and anger those of its customers willing to pay higher prices. But times have changed. Wal-Mart offers too much business to pass up, and Levi's market share has eroded. Its relationship with Wal-Mart even goes beyond an agreement to sell some jeans. Levi's has introduced a less expensive Signature line that is sold at Wal-Mart and other major retailers. To ensure the timely delivery of the line, Levi's has beefed up its distribution system accordingly.

Human Resource Management

Employees play a major role in the success of all firms. Those who interact with customers in providing services for customers are particularly important for building customer loyalty. Knowledgeable and skilled employees committed to the firm's objectives are critical assets that support the success of companies such as Southwest Airlines, Whole Foods, and The Container Store.[14]

J.C. Penney chairman and CEO Mike Ullman believes in the power of the employee for building a sustainable competitive advantage.[15] He said, "The associates are the first customers we sell. If it doesn't ring true to them, it's impossible to communicate and inspire the customer." To build involvement and commitment among its employees, Penney's has dropped many of the traditional pretenses that defined an old-style hierarchical organization. For instance, at the Plano, Texas, corporate headquarters, all employees are on a first-name basis, have a flexible workweek, and may attend leadership workshops intended to build an executive team for the future.

HEADLIGHTS THAT MOVE
IN THE DIRECTION
YOU ARE TURNING.
TECHNOLOGY CATCHES UP
TO COMMON SENSE.

AN ENTIRELY NEW ES. THE LEXUS ES 350.

THE PASSIONATE PURSUIT OF PERFECTION.

Lexus has developed a sustainable competitive advantage through product excellence. It utilizes headlights that move in the direction you are turning.

Product Excellence

Product excellence, the third way to achieve a sustainable competitive advantage, occurs by having products with high perceived value and effective branding and positioning. Some firms have difficulty developing a competitive advantage through their merchandise and service offerings, especially if competitors can deliver similar products or services easily. However, others have been able to maintain their sustainable competitive advantage by investing in their brand itself; positioning their product or service using a clear, distinctive brand image; and constantly reinforcing that image through their merchandise, service, and promotion. For instance, *BusinessWeek*'s top global brands—Coca-Cola, Microsoft, IBM, GE, Nokia, Toyota, Intel, McDonald's, Disney, and Mercedes—are all leaders in their respective industries, at least in part because they have strong brands and a clear position in the marketplace.[16]

One of the world's top brands, Lexus was conceived in 1983 when Toyota's Chairman Eiji Toyoda determined that the "time is right to create a luxury vehicle to challenge the best in the world." The Lexus LS 400 and ES250 were introduced in 1989; by 1990, the LS 400 was acclaimed by the trade press and industry experts as one of the best vehicles in the world. Today, the Lexus brand is synonymous with luxury and quality. How did Toyota take the Lexus concept from obscurity to a tangible vehicle that rivals such long-standing brands as Mercedes, BMW, and Porsche? Lexus developed its brand by focusing on the most important variables that predict whether a person will purchase a new luxury car: income, current car ownership, age of current vehicle, and distance from a dealership. Lexus has consistently reinforced its image by winning top awards from J.D. Power.[17]

Locational Excellence

Location is particularly important for retailers and service providers. Many say, "The three most important things in retailing are location, location, location." For

How has Southwest Airlines developed a sustainable competitive advantage?

example, most people will not walk or drive very far when looking to buy a cup of coffee. A competitive advantage based on location is sustainable because it is not easily duplicated.

Dunkin' Donuts and Starbucks have developed a strong competitive advantage with their location selection. They have such a high density of stores in some markets that it makes it very difficult for a competitor to enter a market and find good locations.

Multiple Sources of Advantage

In most cases, however, a single strategy, such as low prices or excellent service, is not sufficient to build a sustainable competitive advantage. Firms require multiple approaches to build a "wall" around their position that stands as high as possible. For example, Southwest Airlines has achieved success by providing customers with a good value that meets their expectations, offering good customer service, maintaining good customer relations, and offering great prices. By fulfilling all these strategies, Southwest Airlines has developed a huge cadre of loyal customers.

Southwest consistently has positioned itself as a carrier that provides good service at a good value—customers get to their destination on time for a reasonable price. At the same time, its customers know not to have extraordinary expectations. They don't expect food service, seat assignments, or flights out of the primary airports in a market area (e.g., flights are out of Midway as opposed to O'Hare in the Chicago area and out of Islip Long Island as opposed to LaGuardia or JFK in New York City). But they do expect—and even more important, get—on-time flights that are reasonably priced. By developing its unique capabilities in several areas, Southwest has built a very high wall around its position as the value player in the airline industry.

CHECK YOURSELF

1. What are the various components of a marketing strategy?
2. List the four macro strategies that can help a firm develop a sustainable competitive advantage.

THE MARKETING PLAN

Effective marketing doesn't just happen. Firms like Starbucks and Dunkin' Donuts carefully plan their marketing strategies to react to changes in the environment, the competition, and their customers by creating a marketing plan. A marketing plan is a written document composed of an analysis of the current marketing situation, opportunities and threats for the firm, marketing objectives and strategy specified in terms of the four Ps, action programs, and projected or pro-forma income (and other financial) statements.[18] The three major phases of the marketing plan are planning, implementation, and control.[19]

Although most people do not have a written plan that outlines what they are planning to accomplish in the next year, and how they expect to do it, firms do

EXHIBIT 2.2   The Marketing Plan

need such a document. It is important that everyone involved in implementing the plan knows what the overall objectives for the firm are and how they are going to be met. Other stakeholders, such as investors and potential investors, also want to know what the firm plans to do. A written marketing plan also provides a reference point for evaluating whether or not the firm met its objectives.

A marketing plan entails five steps, depicted in Exhibit 2.2. In Step 1 of the planning phase, marketing executives, in conjunction with other top managers, define the mission and/or vision of the business. For the second step, they evaluate the situation by assessing how various players, both in and outside the organization, affect the firm's potential for success (Step 2). In the implementation phase, marketing managers identify and evaluate different opportunities by engaging in a process known as segmentation, targeting, and positioning (STP) (Step 3). They then are responsible for implementing the marketing mix using the four Ps (Step 4). Finally, the control phase entails evaluating the performance of the marketing strategy using marketing metrics and taking any necessary corrective actions (Step 5).

As indicated in Exhibit 2.2, it is not always necessary to go through the entire process for every evaluation (Step 5). For instance, a firm could evaluate its performance in Step 5, then go directly to Step 2 to conduct a situation audit without redefining its overall mission.

We will first discuss each step involved in developing a marketing plan. Then we consider ways of analyzing a marketing situation, as well as identifying and evaluating marketing opportunities. We also examine some specific strategies marketers use to grow a business. Finally, we consider how the implementation of the marketing mix increases customer value. A sample marketing plan is provided in Appendix 2A, following this chapter.

EXHIBIT 2.3	Mission Statements

MADD's mission is to stop drunk driving, support the victims of this violent crime, and prevent underage drinking.

Starbucks' mission statement is to establish Starbucks as the premier purveyor of the finest coffee in the world while maintaining our uncompromising principles as we grow.

Disney, with its many business units, broadly describes its mission as its commitment to producing creative entertainment experience based on storytelling.

Sources: "About Us," www.MADD.org; www.starbucks.com/aboutus/environment.asp; and "Company Overview" www.corporate.disney.go.com.

Step 1: Define the Business Mission

The mission statement, a broad description of a firm's objectives and the scope of activities it plans to undertake,[20] attempts to answer two main questions: What type of business are we? What do we need to do to accomplish our goals and objectives? These fundamental business questions must be answered at the highest corporate levels before marketing executives can get involved. Most firms want to maximize stockholders' wealth by increasing the value of the firms' stock and paying dividends.[21] However, owners of small, privately held firms frequently have other objectives, such as achieving a specific level of income and avoiding risks. (See Exhibit 2.3 for several mission statement examples.) Nonprofit organizations, such as Mothers Against Drunk Driving (MADD), have nonmonetary objectives like eliminating drunk driving and underage drinking. In its mission statement, Starbucks explicitly recognizes that it must "establish [itself] as the premier purveyor of the finest coffee in the world while maintaining our uncompromising principles as we grow."[22] Disney's mission statement is sufficiently broad to encompass the many different types of businesses it operates. For all three firms, marketing holds the primary responsibility of enhancing the value of the company's products for its customers and other constituents.

Another key goal or objective often embedded in a mission statement is building a sustainable competitive advantage, namely, something the firm can persistently do better than its competitors. Although any business activity that a firm engages in can be the basis for a competitive advantage, some advantages are sustainable over a longer period of time, whereas others, like low prices, can be duplicated by competitors almost immediately.[23] For example, since the artificial sweetener Splenda entered the market in 2000, it has grown to $237 million in sales,[24] surpassing Equal and Sweet'N Low combined. Equal and Sweet'N Low could cut their prices to steal market share back from Splenda, but it would be hard for them to obtain a long-term advantage by doing so because Splenda could easily match any price reduction. Splenda has successfully attracted consumers because it has positioned itself as a healthy alternative to sugar that can be used for baking and not just a substitute for sugar. However, if it were easy for Sweet'N Low and Equal to copy Splenda's successful formula and marketing, they would do so. Attributes like formula and image thus can provide firms with a long-term (i.e., sustainable) competitive advantage. A competitive advantage acts like a wall that the firm has built around its position in a market. This wall makes it hard for outside competitors to contact customers inside—otherwise known as the marketer's target market. Of course, if the marketer has built a wall around an attractive market, competitors will attempt to break down the

What is the mission for a nonprofit organization like Mothers Against Drunk Driving (MADD)?

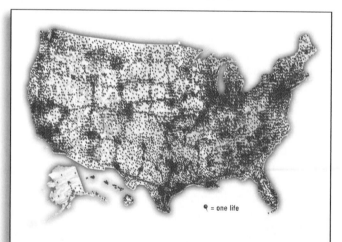

☞ = one life

If 17,000 people died tomorrow, would you notice?

Of course you would. There would be 24-hour news coverage. Dramatic headlines. And a devastating effect on our country forever. But last year, drinking and driving did kill about 17,000 people. It injured half a million more. But because it happened over a year rather than in a single day, most of us hardly noticed. It's a growing problem, with a simple answer. If you drink, find a safe way home. And help remove the marks that drunk driving leaves on our country.

wall. Over time, advantages will erode because of these competitive forces, but by building high, thick walls, marketers can sustain their advantage, minimize competitive pressure, and boost profits for a longer time. Thus, establishing a sustainable competitive advantage is key to long-term financial performance.

Step 2: Conduct a Situation Analysis Using SWOT

After developing its mission, a firm next must perform a situation analysis, using a SWOT analysis that assesses both the internal environment with regard to its **S**trengths and **W**eaknesses and the external environment in terms of its **O**pportunities and **T**hreats.

Consider how a corporation like Starbucks might conduct a SWOT analysis, as outlined in Exhibit 2.4. Because a company's strengths (Exhibit 2.4, upper left) refer to the positive internal attributes of the firm, in this example we might include Starbucks' international reputation as a quality coffee purveyor. Furthermore, to sell its varied products, Starbucks can rely on its massive retail store network of 14,000 locations worldwide.[25] Beyond the stores, Starbucks also licenses its brands to business partners that produce ready-to-drink products, such as Frappuccino® and Starbucks DoubleShot® drinks, and gourmet ice creams, which sell in grocery and convenience stores. These varied and plentiful retail locations represent a significant strength that the company can leverage to bring other products to market.

Opportunities (Exhibit 2.4, lower left) pertain to positive aspects of the external environment. Among Starbucks' many, many opportunities, the most significant may be its ability to build its current brand and businesses. In 2006, $108 million of Starbucks' $564 million in profits came from international business, and the huge, mostly untapped Chinese market offers a remarkable opportunity for enormous future growth. Operating stores in more than 37 countries while opening an average of 6 new stores every day outside of the United States,[26] Starbucks already has grown into an international brand but also has significant opportunities for much greater international expansion. In addition to such traditional growth, Starbucks continues to emphasize its social responsibility, including its support of fair-trade coffee and clean production conditions for coffee growers and beans. As the consumer environment appears poised to become even more "green," Starbucks' existing socially responsible practices may provide it an opportunity to appeal even more to green consumers.

Yet every firm has its weaknesses, and Starbucks is no exception. The weaknesses (Exhibit 2.4, upper right) are negative attributes of the firm, which in Starbucks'

Splenda has been successful because it is perceived as a healthy and sugar-free alternative to sugar and can be used for baking, unlike Equal and Sweet 'N Low.

EXHIBIT 2.4	SWOT Analysis for Starbucks	
Environment	**Evaluation**	
	Positive	**Negative**
Internal	**Strengths** ■ Strong brand identity ■ Retail store network ■ Grocery network	**Weaknesses** ■ Reliance on joint ventures and licensed outlets ■ Rapid growth erodes customer experience
External	**Opportunities** ■ Expansion outside of the U.S. market ■ Social and green marketing efforts	**Threats** ■ Potential saturation of the U.S. market ■ Intense competition in the specialty and overall coffee market ■ Potential declines in consumer demand for specialty coffee products, perhaps due to changing public opinions about caffeine or an economic downturn

Starbucks' strengths include a strong brand identity and a retail store and grocery network.

case might include its heavy reliance on its relationships with its joint venture and licensed outlet partners to open new stores. Without its joint ventures and licensed outlet partners, Starbucks' continued growth would be in serious jeopardy. Starbucks' precipitous growth has also called into question one of its original and primary benefits to consumers—the experience of watching their drinks being made by hand by a professional barista. This weakness was perceived to be large enough by management that Starbucks closed all of its stores for a few hours to provide an intense refresher course to its baristas.

Threats (Exhibit 2.4, lower right) represent the negative aspects of the company's external environment. For example, despite its expansion internationally, most Starbucks retail locations are in the United States, a market that some observers suggest may be close to saturation. If U.S. demand drops, whether because of economic conditions or shifts in the coffee market, Starbucks would be in real trouble. Additionally, Starbucks must keep abreast of any new research that suggests negative health effects from caffeine. Perhaps even more pressing, competitors such as Peet's Coffee and Caribou Coffee continue to pursue its position as the market leader, while other outlets like Dunkin' Donuts offer similar products at lower prices.

Step 3: Identifying and Evaluating Opportunities Using STP (Segmentation, Targeting, and Positioning)

After completing the situation audit, the next step is to identify and evaluate opportunities for increasing sales and profits using STP (segmentation, targeting, and positioning). With STP, the firm first divides the marketplace into subgroups or segments, determines which of those segments it should pursue or target, and finally decides how it should position its products and services to best meet the needs of those chosen targets.

Segmentation   Many types of customers appear in any market, and most firms cannot satisfy everyone's needs. For instance, among Internet users, some do research online, some shop, some look for entertainment, and many may do all three. Each of these groups might be a market segment consisting of consumers who respond similarly to a firm's marketing efforts. The process of dividing the market into groups of customers with different needs, wants, or characteristics—who therefore might appreciate products or services geared especially for them—is called market segmentation.

To segment the coffee drinker market, Starbucks uses a variety of methods, including geography (e.g., upscale locations, near college campuses) and people's

EXHIBIT 2.5   Market Segments for the Walt Disney Company

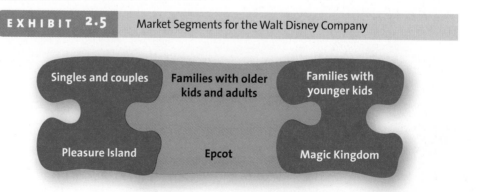

behavior (e.g., drinkers of caffeinated or decaffeinated products). After determining which of those segments represent effective targets, Starbucks develops a variety of products that match the wants and needs of the different market segments—caffeinated and decaffeinated coffees, teas, bottled water, and quick service food.

Let's also look at The Walt Disney Company. As an example, illustrated in Exhibit 2.5, Disney targets its Pleasure Island to singles and couples, Epcot to families with older children and adults, and the Magic Kingdom to families with younger children. Thus, Disney uses demographics like gender, age, and income to identify the young families it is pursuing for the Magic Kingdom but applies psychological or behavioral factors, like who prefers to party or go dancing, to identify the singles and couples it is pursuing for Pleasure Island.

Targeting   After a firm has identified the various market segments it might pursue, it evaluates each segment's attractiveness and decides which to pursue using a process known as target marketing or targeting. From our previous example, Disney realizes that its primary appeal for the Magic Kingdom is to young families, so the bulk of its marketing efforts for this business is directed toward that group, which includes, of course, both children and parents. In a recent ad campaign, Disney appealed to both groups, showing fantasy images of Cinderella's coach coming to the children's window as the parents sat downstairs and reviewed prices for a weeklong Disney vacation.

Coca-Cola targets many submarkets.

Soft drink manufacturers also have divided the market into many submarkets or segments. Coca-Cola, for instance, makes several different types of Coke, including regular, Coke II, Cherry Coke, Diet Coke, and caffeine-free—and then it adds in various combinations of these types. It also markets Sprite for those who don't like dark colas, Fruitopia and Minute Maid for more health-conscious consumers, and Dasani bottled water for purists.

Positioning   Finally, when the firm decides which segments to pursue, it must determine how it wants to be positioned within those segments.

Market positioning involves the process of defining the marketing mix variables so that target customers have a clear, distinctive, desirable understanding of what the product does or represents in comparison with competing products. Disney, for instance, defines itself as an entertainer. Its Florida Walt Disney World Resort owns and operates four theme parks, golf courses, 17 hotels and resorts, water parks, a sports complex, and a retail and dining complex.

After identifying its target segments, a firm must evaluate each of its strategic opportunities. A method of examining which segments to pursue is described in the Growth Strategies section later in the chapter. Firms typically are most successful when they focus on opportunities that build on their strengths relative

 ## Power of the Internet **2.1**   **Dove Evolutions**

With the immense power of the Internet, Dove hopes to build "brand evangelists" for its beauty products and has therefore led the way in engaging its online customers. During the 2007 Academy Awards, for example, Dove ran two high-profile Internet marketing campaigns: "Evolution" and Dove Body Wash.

In 2006, Dove kicked off its online Real Beauty campaign by posting the "Evolution" video on YouTube. The first day saw 40,000 views; by the end of 2007, more than 5.5 million viewers had seen the spot.[27] The video is designed to demonstrate how perceptions of beauty get distorted by advertising. During the online video, a model transforms from a normal-looking woman to a billboard pin-up after undergoing hours of makeup. Even then, the image on the billboard gets altered by Photoshop. The video ends with a tagline: "No wonder our perception of beauty is distorted." At the bottom, it lists the address for the Dove Campaign for Real Beauty Web site (http:www.campaignforrealbeauty.com).

In 2007, "Evolution" won one of the most prestigious advertising awards, the Grand Prix for viral marketing at Cannes.[28] As the company explained, it chose the Internet as its release platform for "Evolution" because it freed the advertising team from time constraints. The marketers wanted to run a spot that was 74 seconds long, and U.S. television only sold advertising spots in 30 or 60 second increments. Furthermore, through the Internet, Dove could connect directly with its customers.

To get customers even more engaged with its brand, Dove also created a new campaign for the 2008 Oscar ceremony. Online, Dove invited consumers to create their own

Dove uses the Internet to promote the notion that beauty should not be defined by self-limiting stereotypes.

advertisements for Dove Body Cream Oil Body Wash, promising that the winning entry would be broadcast during the Oscar ceremony to a worldwide audience. On the Dove Cream Oil Web site on MSN.com (http:www.dovecreamoil.msn.com), users could upload their videos, use online editing tools, and vote on one another's submissions. Using the Internet to share videos encouraged these customers to think about the product, and interacting with other users got them emotionally engaged with the advertisements they viewed.[29]

Thus, Dove has figured out several ways to use the power of the Internet to connect with its core customers and create high-impact marketing events—and at a reasonable price.

to those of their competition. In Step 4 of the marketing plan, the firm implements its marketing mix and allocates resources to different products and services.

With the growth of the Internet and the younger demographics of their core customer base, Unilever's Dove line of soaps and lotions has positioned itself to appeal to a younger, more Internet-savvy target market with innovative marketing campaigns. (See Power of the Internet 2.1.)

Step 4: Implement Marketing Mix and Allocate Resources

When the firm has identified and evaluated different growth opportunities by performing an STP analysis, the real action begins. It has decided what to do, how to do it, and how many resources should be allocated to it. In the fourth step of the planning process, marketers implement the actual marketing mix—product, price, promotion, and place—for each product and service on the basis of what they believe their target markets will value. At the same time, they make important decisions about how they will allocate their scarce resources to their various products and services.

Product and Value Creation   Products, which include services, constitute the first of the four Ps. Because the key to the success of any marketing program is the creation of value, firms attempt to develop products and services that customers perceive as valuable enough to buy. For many consumers, the product offered by Starbucks contains enough value that they will pay upwards of $4 for a single cup of coffee. But for other consumers, including 35–40 million Americans, existing coffee products have had absolutely no value, because drinking coffee caused them to suffer heartburn. Upon learning this information, Procter & Gamble (P&G), the consumer products giant, introduced Folgers' Simply Smooth, a coffee designed to be gentle on people's stomachs. Simply Smooth will not appeal to traditional

Folgers' Simply Smooth targets coffee lovers with sensitive stomachs.

coffee buyers, who value other elements of a coffee product, but it may create a new category of coffee drinkers, which would enable P&G to reach customers who typically would not have consumed any coffee products.[30]

Price and Value Capture Recall that the second element of the marketing mix is price. As part of the exchange process, a firm provides a product or a service, or some combination thereof, and in return, it gets money. Value-based marketing requires that firms charge a price that customers perceive as giving them a good value for the product they receive. Firms practice three types of pricing strategies. The first pricing strategy, cost-based pricing, is when a firm determines the costs of producing or providing its product and then adds a fixed amount above that total to arrive at the selling price. For example, a bookstore might purchase a book at the publisher's wholesale price and then mark it up a standard 35 percent. The second type, the competitor-based pricing strategy, is when a firm prices below, at, or above its competitors' offerings. For example, the same bookstore might decide to take the top 10 books on *The New York Times* bestseller list and price them $2 less than its primary competitors' prices.

Although relatively simple to implement, neither of these methods alone ensures that customers will perceive they are getting a good value for the products or services. That perception requires the third approach, termed value-based pricing, in which the firm first determines the perceived value of the product from the customer's point of view and then prices accordingly. For example, the bookstore might determine from its prior experience that students have various attitudes toward textbooks and their prices: Some students want a new book, whereas others accept a used one for a lesser price. Giving them a choice of both options provides value to both groups.

However, value-based pricing remains one of the least understood areas of business decision making, even though it is one of the few business activities with a direct impact on profits. Clearly, it is important for a firm to have a clear focus in terms of what products to sell, where to buy them, and what methods to use in selling them. But pricing is the only activity that actually brings in money by influencing revenues. If a price is set too high, it will not generate much volume. If a price is set too low, it may result in lower-than-necessary margins and profits. Therefore, price should be based on the value that the customer perceives.

Using a kiosk at a Staples store, customers connect and order from staples.com.

Place and Value Delivery For the third P, place, the firm must be able, after it has created value through a product and/or service, to make the product or service readily accessible when and where the customer wants it. Consider how Staples has integrated its stores with its Internet operations. Staples' overall goal has been to become the leading office product and service provider by combining its existing experience, extensive distribution infrastructure, and customer service expertise with Web-based information technology. In learning that its sales increased when customers used more than one channel of distribution (store and Internet), Staples turned the integration of its different channels into a seamless customer experience, a key value driver for the company. A consumer now can connect and order from www.staples.com, either from home or via a kiosk in the store. Therefore, even if a particular item is not readily available in the store, Staples is less likely to lose the customer's business. At the same time, the alternative channels have enabled Staples to discontinue slow-moving or expensive items from its in-store inventory, which reduces its costs. Instead, the company keeps some inventory of those slow-moving items at central warehouses and ships them directly to the customer. In this way, it has effectively integrated its stores with its Internet operation and used place to create value in its delivery process.

Promotion and Value Communication   The fourth and last P of the marketing mix is promotion. Marketers communicate the value of their offering, or the value proposition, to their customers through a variety of media including television, radio, magazines, sales forces, and the Internet—the last a real boon for specialty retailers across the globe.

Disney is one of the world's greatest promoters. For example, to market new reasons for consumers to visit its various properties, Disney teamed up with designer Kirstie Kelly to develop a "Princess Collection" of wedding dresses and accessories, which complement the *Disney Fairy Tale Weddings* program that allows couples to marry at a Disney theme park. For years, Disney has promoted the concept of princesses and fairy tales to young girls, but as those girls grew up, Disney needed a way to continue to promote its image to them. By aiming the wedding packages and gowns at engaged couples, Disney promises to create a magical experience for them. Kelly, a celebrity dress designer whose gowns typically retail around $20,000, has designed a line for Disney which it sells for between $1,000 and $3000. In addition to publicizing the dresses and wedding offers on travel and destination Web sites, Disney is hyping the collection through more traditional wedding outlets, such as international fashion shows. To make the process as simple as possible, brides can also view the featured dresses on www.DisneyBridal.com.[31]

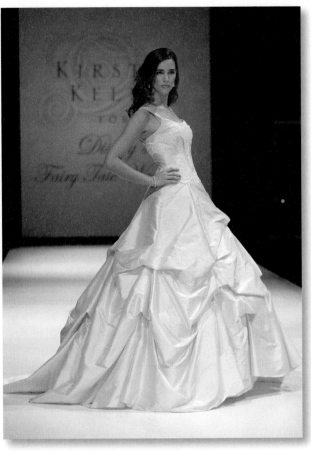

Disney has teamed up with designer Kirstie Kelly to develop a "Princess Collection" of wedding dresses and accessories.

Step 5: Evaluate Performance Using Marketing Metrics

The final step in the planning process includes evaluating the results of the strategy and implementation program using marketing metrics. A metric is a measuring system that quantifies a trend, dynamic, or characteristic.[32] Metrics are used to explain why things happened, and project the future. They make it possible to compare results across regions, SBUs, product lines, and time periods. The firm can determine why it achieved or did not achieve its performance goals with the help of these metrics. Understanding the causes of the performance, regardless of whether that performance exceeded, met, or fell below the firm's goals, enables firms to make appropriate adjustments.

Typically, managers begin by reviewing the implementation programs, and their analysis may indicate that the strategy (or even the mission statement) needs to be reconsidered. Problems can arise both when firms successfully implement poor strategies and when they poorly implement good strategies.

Who Is Accountable for Performance?   At each level of an organization, the business unit and its manager should be held accountable only for the revenues, expenses, and profits that they can control. Thus, expenses that affect several levels of the organization (such as the labor and capital expenses associated with operating a corporate headquarters) shouldn't be arbitrarily assigned to lower levels. In the case of a store, for example, it may be appropriate to evaluate performance objectives based on sales, sales associate productivity, and energy costs. If the corporate office lowers prices to get rid of merchandise and therefore profits suffer, then it's not fair to assess a store manager's performance based on the resulting decline in store profit.

Performance evaluations are used to pinpoint problem areas. Reasons performance may be above or below planned levels must be examined. Perhaps the managers involved in setting the objectives aren't very good at making estimates. If so, they may need to be trained in forecasting.

Actual performance may be different than the plan predicts because of circumstances beyond the manager's control. For example, there may have been a recession. Assuming the recession wasn't predicted, or was more severe or lasted longer than anticipated, there are several relevant questions: How quickly were plans adjusted? How rapidly and appropriately were pricing and promotional policies modified? In short, did the manager react to salvage an adverse situation, or did those reactions worsen the situation?

Performance Objectives and Metrics   Many factors contribute to a firm's overall performance, which make it hard to find a single metric to evaluate performance. One approach is to compare a firm's performance over time or to competing firms, using common financial metrics such as sales and profits. Another method of assessing performance is to view the firm's products or services as a portfolio. Depending on the firm's relative performance, the profits from some products or services are used to fuel growth for others.

Financial Performance Metrics   Some commonly used metrics to assess performance include revenues, or sales, and profits. For instance, sales are a global measure of a firm's activity level. However, a manager could easily increase sales by lowering prices, but the profit realized on that merchandise (gross margin) would suffer as a result. Clearly, an attempt to maximize one metric may lower another. Managers must therefore understand how their actions affect multiple performance metrics. It's usually unwise to use only one metric because it rarely tells the whole story.

In addition to assessing the absolute level of sales and profits, a firm may wish to measure the relative level of sales and profits. For example, a relative metric of sales or profits is its increase or decrease over the prior year. Additionally, a firm may compare its growth in sales or profits relative to other benchmark companies (e.g., Coke may compare itself to Pepsi).

The metrics used to evaluate a firm vary depending on (1) the level of the organization at which the decision is made and (2) the resources the manager controls. For example, while the top executives of a firm have control over all of the firm's resources and resulting expenses, a regional sales manager only has control over the sales and expenses generated by his or her salespeople.

Let's look at Starbucks' sales revenue and profits (after taxes) and compare them to those of another major food industry powerhouse, McDonald's (Exhibit 2.6). Clearly, on the revenues side Starbucks is growing at a faster pace (22 percent versus 9 percent for McDonald's). However, McDonald's profit as a percentage of sales is much higher (13% compared to 7%). Thus, it is important to simultaneously look at multiple performance metrics.

As the collective corporate consciousness of the importance of social responsibility grows, firms are starting to report corporate social responsibility metrics in major areas such as their impact on the environment, their ability to diversify their work-

EXHIBIT 2.6	Performance Metrics: Starbucks versus McDonald's			
		2005	**2006**	**% Change**
Starbucks[33]	Net Sales	$6.4B	$7.8B	22% growth
	Net Profit	$494M	$564M	14% growth
	Net Profit/Net Sales	7.7%	7.2%	
McDonald's[34]	Net Sales	$19.8B	$21.6B	9% growth
	Net Profit	$2.6B	$2.83B	8.8% growth
	Net Profit/Net Sales	13.1%	13.1%	

force, energy conservation initiatives, and their policies on protecting the human rights of their employees and the employees of their suppliers. The Ethical and Societal Dilemma 2.1 on page 50 examines how Starbucks is working to tackle important societal issues.

Portfolio Analysis   In portfolio analysis, management evaluates the firm's various products and businesses—its "portfolio"—and allocates resources according to which products are expected to be the most profitable for the firm in the future. Portfolio analysis is typically performed at the strategic business unit (SBU) or product line level of the firm, though managers also can use it to analyze brands or even individual items. An SBU is a division of the firm itself that can be managed and operated somewhat independently from other divisions and may have a different mission or objectives. For example, Goodyear is one of the largest tire firms in the world, selling its products on six continents in over 180 countries and with sales of over $20 billion. They have five SBUs that are organized by geography: North American Tire, European Union Tire, Eastern Europe, Middle East and Africa Tire, Latin America Tire, and Asia Pacific Tire.[35] A product line, in contrast, is a group of products that consumers may use together or perceive as similar in some way. One line of product for Goodyear could be car, van, SUV, and light truck while another line could be racing tires or aviation tires.

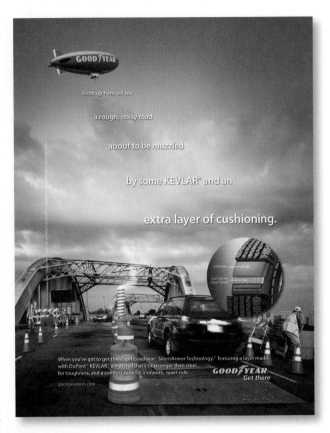

Goodyear, one of the largest tire firms in the world, organizes its strategic business units by geography.

One of the most popular portfolio analysis methods, developed by the Boston Consulting Group (BCG), requires that firms classify all their products or services into a two-by-two matrix, as depicted in Exhibit 2.7 on page 51.[36] The circles represent brands, and their sizes are in direct proportion to the brands' annual sales. The horizontal axis represents the relative market share. In general, market share is the percentage of a market accounted for by a specific entity,[37] and is used to establish the product's strength in a particular market. It is usually discussed in units, revenue, or sales. A special type of market share metric, relative market share, is used in this application because it provides managers with a product's relative strength, compared to that of the largest firm in the industry.[38] The vertical axis is the market growth rate, or the annual rate of growth of the specific market in which the product competes. Market growth rate thus measures how attractive a particular market is. Each quadrant has been named on the basis of the amount of resources it generates for and requires from the firm.

Stars   Stars (upper left quadrant) occur in high-growth markets and are high market share products. That is, stars often require a heavy resource investment in such things as promotions and new production facilities to fuel their rapid growth. As their market growth slows, stars will migrate from heavy users of resources to heavy generators of resources and become cash cows.

Cash cows   Cash cows (lower left quadrant) are in low-growth markets but are high market share products. Because these products have already received heavy investments to develop their high market share, they have excess resources that can be spun off to those products that need it. For example, in Exhibit 2.7, Brand C uses its excess resources to fund products in the question mark quadrant.

Question marks   Question marks (upper right quadrant) appear in high-growth markets but have relatively low market shares; thus, they are often the most

Ethical and Societal Dilemma 2.1 Starbucks Working to Make the Earth a Better Place

To ensure it adds value to the broader society that makes up its macroenvironment, Starbucks rates its own corporate social responsibility performance in five categories: its coffee, society, the environment, the workplace, and diversity. Brand equity is bolstered by being proactive along these socially responsible dimensions because customers feel good about their buying experience, and its relationships with suppliers, both locally and globally, are strengthened.

On World Water Day, Starbucks sponsored walks to symbolize and raise awareness about the average length that women and children walk to get drinking water each day.

With regard to its focus on sustainable coffee production, Starbucks introduced C.A.F.E. (Coffee and Farmer Equity) in 2004. The C.A.F.E. guidelines include a scorecard that rates coffee farmers according to their product quality, economic accountability, social responsibility, and environmental leadership. Third parties evaluate whether suppliers meet Starbucks' standards under the C.A.F.E. program. In just a few years, suppliers from 13 different countries had gained C.A.F.E. approval. To encourage further adoption of these standards by suppliers, Starbucks joined with the African Wildlife Foundation to enhance and improve sustainable farming practices in East Africa.

On a more local level, Starbucks sometimes experiences opposition from local communities that believe its stores will ruin the historical ambiance of an area. To take the needs of local communities into consideration, Starbucks attempts to address historic preservation, environmental, infrastructure, job, and urban revitalization concerns. For example, in La Mesa, California, Starbucks overcame opposition by supporting local events and businesses. In addition, it formed a joint venture with Johnson Development Corporation (JDC) to develop urban coffee opportunities. By opening in diverse urban areas, Starbucks helps stimulate economic growth in the areas by creating jobs, using local suppliers, and attracting other retailers to the area.

Starbucks has also launched a program that focuses on the needs of the more than 1 billion people globally who lack access to safe drinking water. On World Water Day, Starbucks sponsored three-mile walks in many cities, as well as a virtual online walk, to symbolize and raise awareness about the average length that women and children walk to get drinking water each day. To promote and inform the public about this serious health issue, Starbucks launched http://www.worldwaterday2006.org. Ethos Water, which Starbucks acquired in

(continued)

2005, contributes 5 cents for each bottle of water sold in Starbucks stores to humanitarian water programs around the world in countries such as Bangladesh, Ethiopia, and Kenya, with a goal of reaching $10 million by 2010, to help solve the world's water crisis.

Lack of water is not the only health worry facing people across the world. By partnering with nutrition experts to develop its menu, Starbucks attempts to follow the World Health Organization's plan to lessen diseases related to poor diet, lack of exercise, and obesity. The company's expanded menu offerings include nutritious options such as fresh fruit and yogurt parfaits. Simultaneously, it lowered the amount of trans fat in both its food and its drinks.

To address the health and welfare of its own employees (whom the company calls "partners"), Starbucks not only offers generous health benefits packages but also has undertaken a Thrive Wellness Initiative (TWI) for its 145,000 partners. The stated purpose of TWI is to care for well-being of employees. For example, the newest portion of the TWI is Kinetix, a program that offers classes on nutrition and exercise, as well as eight weeks of sessions with a personal trainer.

Finally, just as it expects its coffee producers to engage in environmentally friendly practices, Starbucks itself attempts to use renewable energy and reduce its negative impact on the environment. Furniture and fixtures in stores are made of sustainable building materials. As a member of the Sustainable Packaging Coalition, Starbucks also works to replace conventional packaging with green alternatives.

managerially intensive products in that they require significant resources to maintain and potentially increase their market share. Managers must decide whether to infuse question marks with resources generated by the cash cows, so that they can become stars, or withdraw resources and eventually phase out the products. Brand A, for instance, is currently a question mark, but by infusing it with resources, the firm hopes to turn it into a star.

EXHIBIT 2.7   Boston Consulting Group Product Portfolio Analysis

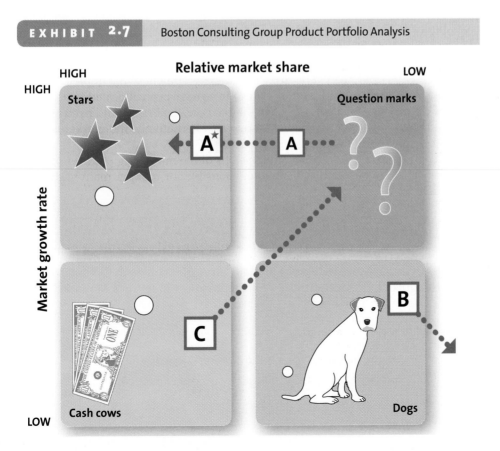

Dogs   Dogs (lower right quadrant) are in low-growth markets and have relatively low market shares. Although they may generate enough resources to sustain themselves, dogs are not destined for "stardom" and should be phased out unless they are needed to complement or boost the sales of another product or for competitive purposes. In the case depicted in Exhibit 2.7, the company has decided to stop making Brand B.

Although quite useful for conceptualizing the relative performance of products or services and using this information to allocate resources, the BCG approach, and others like it, is often difficult to implement in practice. In particular, it is difficult to measure both relative market share and industry growth. Furthermore, other measures easily could serve as substitutes to represent a product's competitive position and the market's relative attractiveness. Another issue for marketers is the potential self-fulfilling prophecy of placing a product or service into a quadrant. That is, suppose a product is classified as a dog though it has the potential of being a question mark. The firm might reduce support for the product and lose sales to the point that it abandons the product, which might have become profitable if provided with sufficient resources.

Because of these limitations, many firms have tempered their use of matrix approaches to achieve a more balanced approach to evaluating products and services and allocating their resources. Instead of assigning allocation decisions to the top levels of the organization, many firms start at lower management levels and employ checks and balances to force managers at each level of the organizational hierarchy to negotiate with those above and below them to reach their final decisions.

Strategic Planning Is Not Sequential

The planning process in Exhibit 2.2 suggests that managers follow a set sequence when they make strategic decisions. Namely, after they've defined the business mission, they perform the situation analysis, identify strategic opportunities, evaluate alternatives, set objectives, allocate resources, develop the implementation plan, and, finally, evaluate their performance and make adjustments. But actual planning processes can move back and forth among these steps. For example, a situation analysis may uncover a logical alternative, even though this alternative might not be included in the mission statement, which would mean that the mission statement would need to be revised. The development of the implementation plan also might reveal that insufficient resources have been allocated to a particular product for it to achieve its objective. In that case, the firm would need to either change the objective or increase the resources; alternatively, the marketer might consider not investing in the product at all.

Now that we have gone through the steps of the marketing plan, let's look at some growth strategies that have been responsible for making many marketing firms successful.

GROWTH STRATEGIES

Firms consider pursuing various market segments as part of their overall growth strategies, which may include the four major strategies shown in Exhibit 2.8.[39] The rows distinguish those opportunities a firm possesses in its current markets from

CHECK YOURSELF

1. What are the five steps in creating a marketing plan?
2. What tool helps a marketer conduct a situation analysis?
3. What is STP?

EXHIBIT 2.8	Market/Product and Services Strategies	
	Products and Services	
Markets	**Current**	**New**
Current	Market Penetration	Product Development
New	Market Development	Diversification

those it has in new markets, whereas the columns distinguish between the firm's current marketing offering and that of a new opportunity. Let's consider each of them in detail.

Market Penetration

A market penetration strategy employs the existing marketing mix and focuses the firm's efforts on existing customers. Such a growth strategy might be achieved by attracting new consumers to the firm's current target market or encouraging current customers to patronize the firm more often or buy more merchandise on each visit. A market penetration strategy generally requires greater marketing efforts, such as increased advertising and additional sales and promotions, or intensified distribution efforts in geographic areas in which the product or service already is sold.

To penetrate its target market, TV network MTV has found it needs new ways to engage its viewers. The young audience of text-messaging, video-gaming multitaskers to which MTV traditionally appeals will no longer accept plain video programming on their televisions. Thus, the network is working hard to develop additional strategies and outlets to retain viewers, as well as to encourage them to spend more time interacting with its content. For example, in addition to producing and airing reality shows such as "Newport Harbour," MTV creates virtual communities that fans of the show may join. By providing "NH" fans a forum to connect and debate about whether Chrissy will get back together with Clay, Allie's new crush, and their lives in college, MTV discovered that interactions with the audience through alternative channels increase ratings for the show.[40]

Natalie Martinez of the movie Death Race *visits MTV's* TRL *at MTV studios in New York City.*

Market Development and the Case for Global Expansion

A market development strategy employs the existing marketing offering to reach new market segments, whether domestic or international. International expansion generally is riskier than domestic expansion because firms must deal with differences in government regulations, cultural traditions, supply chains, and language. However, many U.S. firms, including MTV, enjoy a competitive advantage in global markets—such as Mexico, Latin America, Europe, China, and Japan—because, especially among young people, American culture is widely emulated for consumer products.

For example, because of rising prosperity worldwide and rapidly increasing access to cable television that offers U.S. programming, fashion trends from the

McDonald's is practicing a market development strategy by opening restaurants in China, like this one in Beijing.

United States have spread to young people in emerging countries. The global MTV generation prefers soft drinks to tea, athletic shoes to sandals, French fries to rice, and credit cards to cash. Since its founding in 1981, MTV has expanded well beyond the United States. MTV International (MTVI) is available in 440 million households in 167 countries and 28 languages.[41] To achieve this growth, MTV leveraged its existing media content but delivers culturally relevant content using local DJs and show formats.

Also in recent years, China's major cities have started to see more and more international products, but few foreign companies have targeted the rural Chinese consumer. However, Procter & Gamble (P&G), the consumer products manufacturer, is doing just that, and with remarkable results. Few companies have had as much success in the Chinese market as P&G, including more than $76 billion in annual global sales of products such as Tide, Gillette, Head & Shoulders, and Folgers Coffee.

For the past several years P&G has targeted the broader international market as a source of growth. North America accounts for 46 percent of its sales, and Northeast Asia and other developing markets constitute 31 percent.[42] To succeed in China, P&G engaged a network of 500,000 stores throughout cities and towns and deployed an army of customer research managers. These researchers move throughout China, often staying with families for several days, to identify important segments in the market. Some of their findings led P&G to focus on creating exotic flavors of Crest toothpaste for urban consumers, such as Morning Lotus Fragrance or Icy Mountain Spring. However, the researchers also warned that rural consumers prefer "Salt White," because they believe salt is a tooth whitener. P&G is applying similar segmentation approaches to its other products in China, including Olay moisturizing cream, Tide detergent, Rejoice shampoo, and Pampers diapers.[43]

Product Development

The third growth strategy option, a **product development strategy**, offers a new product or service to a firm's current target market. Consider MTV's show line-up: The network constantly develops new pilots and show concepts to increase the amount of time viewers can spend watching MTV. For example, each version of *The Real World* represents a new program designed to attract and retain both new and existing viewers.

Another example is International Flavors and Fragrances (IFF), the world leader in scent creation and food flavoring. IFF produces more than 31,000 compounds, 60 percent of which are flavors, whereas the other 40 percent are fragrances. Each new compound requires combining dozens of different aromas to create a unique scent or flavor. To stay in the forefront of this market, IFF must continually reevaluate its consumers and their needs; therefore, its market development strategy consists of carefully defining its target markets and expanding its offerings to meet their needs. For example, IFF invested $185 million dollars to develop new fragrances for deodorants, shampoos, and perfumes.[44] For its research, IFF draws on an electronic database of scents and the responses they evoke in consumers. Thousands of people in 30 countries have participated in IFF studies to understand what responses compounds provoke.

In turn, IFF's clients, which include Procter & Gamble, Unilever, Colgate, Estée Lauder, and Pepsi, use specific aromas to formulate new products each year, including Estée Lauder's perfume "Clinique Happy." Estée Lauder approached IFF to create a perfume that was the "essence of joy." After testing aromas with hundreds of test subjects, IFF created a citrus-heavy blend that consumers consistently associated with joy, well-being, and happiness. The product went on to be one of Estée Lauder's top perfume launches.[45] Other fragrances created by IFF for clients include "Cordovan" for the Banana Republic and "Beautiful Love" for Estée Lauder.[46]

Diversification

A **diversification strategy**, the last of the growth strategies from Exhibit 2.8, introduces a new product or service to a market segment that currently is not served. Diversification opportunities may be either related or unrelated. In a related diversification opportunity, the current target market and/or marketing mix shares something in common with the new opportunity. In other words, the firm might be able to purchase from existing vendors, use the same distribution and/or management information system, or advertise in the same newspapers to target markets that are similar to their current consumers. In contrast,

Adding Value 2.1 FedEx Acquires Kinko's: Diversification or What?

When you've conquered express shipping and supply chain services, where do you look to increase earnings, cash flow, and returns?[47] For FedEx, the answer lay in diversification. In 1970, Paul Orfalea started the first Kinko's close to the University of California at Santa Barbara to provide appropriate products and services to college students at a reasonable price. From this single location in 1970, Kinko's had grown to more than 1,200 locations worldwide when FedEx acquired it.[48]

The benefits to both firms are significant. FedEx's global expertise and strong financial position can help Kinko's expand globally. Likewise, by using Kinko's as a storefront, FedEx can tap into a broader mix of small-, medium-, and large-scale businesses that use Kinko's printing and other services at its physical locations.

This acquisition looks at first like a simple case of diversification: new service/new market. But couldn't it also be perceived as market penetration: current service/current market? FedEx will earn more business among its current customers who like the lower cost and convenience of taking their packages to Kinko's. Likewise, current Kinko's customers might use Kinko's other services more often when they visit the store to send a FedEx package.

Furthermore, this growth strategy also could be interpreted as product development: new service/current market. After all, the current customers of both Kinko's and FedEx will have greater exposure to some new service. But what about market penetration: current service/new market? By combining, both Kinko's and FedEx will reach new markets—namely, the other firm's current customer base. So, depending on how we define both the market and the service, FedEx's acquisition of Kinko's might be interpreted as any of the four growth strategies that have been described.

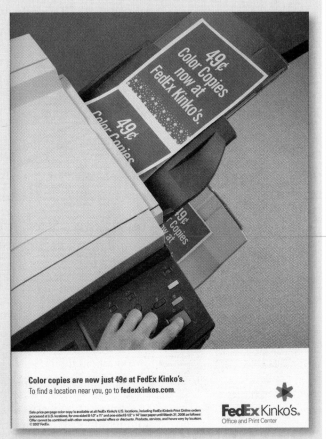

Color copies are now just 49¢ at FedEx Kinko's.
To find a location near you, go to **fedexkinkos.com**

What type of growth strategy did FedEx use when it acquired Kinko's?

in an unrelated diversification, the new business lacks any common elements with the present business. Unrelated diversifications do not capitalize on either core strengths associated with markets or with products. Thus, they would be viewed as being very risky. Adding Value 2.1 on the preceding page describes FedEx's acquisition of Kinko's, which may appear at first to be an unrelated diversification strategy. But is it?

SCENARIO PLANNING

Now that we have examined what is a marketing strategy, the process of developing a marketing plan, and alternative growth strategies, let's look at a process called scenario planning that integrates information obtained as part of the situation and opportunity analysis steps of the marketing plan to better understand the potential performance outcomes associated with different marketing mix applications.[49] By using the strategy elements that we discussed earlier, scenario planning enables a firm to predict, monitor, and adapt to the ever-changing future. All firms face strategic challenges in dealing with the opportunities and uncertainties of the marketplace due to the changes in cultural, demographic, social, technological, economic, and political forces. Thus, anticipating and interpreting change and leveraging resources to address those changes are key to developing winning value-based strategies.

As an outcome, a scenario planning exercise like the one outlined in Exhibit 2.9 develops a set of possible conclusions based on the plausible alternatives that a firm might pursue. By looking at alternative courses of action and imagining what might happen if they were taken, managers can better prepare for the future. To demonstrate how scenario planning works, we investigate a scenario plan for Wal-Mart to determine which strategic directions the giant retailer might pursue in coming years.

Step 1: Assess Strengths and Weaknesses

Step 1 includes the first half of a SWOT analysis: Assess the firm's strengths and weaknesses.

Strengths   Wal-Mart has many strengths, not the least of which is its sheer size—it is the largest company in the world. Just how big is it?[50]

- Wal-Mart is the world's largest retailer, with over $345 billion in sales.
- Its employs a workforce of 1.9 million people worldwide and 1.3 million people in the U.S.
- 180 million customers per week visit Wal-Mart worldwide.

However, being big isn't always a strength; a huge company sometimes suffers from its sluggish reactions to change and cumbersome hierarchical decision making. But size has generally been one of Wal-Mart's key strengths, perhaps because it has been able to develop inventory and information systems rapidly, expand into new retail businesses, and negotiate with vendors more effectively than most of its rivals. Wal-Mart's growth has been staggering.

EXHIBIT 2.9	Scenario Planning Process

Step 1: Assess the current situation by examining the firm's strengths and weaknesses. This helps us understand the company specific situation.

Step 2: Assess what could impact the firm by examining the firm's opportunities and threats.

Step 3: Identify different scenarios.

Step 4: Apply the marketing mix to the different scenarios.

Step 5: Assess the profitability of each scenario.

Another strength is Wal-Mart's unrelenting drive to provide the lowest price in every market in which it competes. On average, Wal-Mart saves the average household more than $2,500/year.[51] How does Wal-Mart do it? Its suppliers know they can only offer the retailer the lowest price, and forget about price increases. If they don't, they simply won't retain Wal-Mart as a customer, and for most suppliers, losing a customer of this size isn't an option. It also operates a bare-bones, no-frills operation.

Some experts believe that Wal-Mart's biggest strength rests in its supply chain. The originator of the hub-and-spoke distribution center system, Wal-Mart locates all its stores at the end of a "spoke" with a distribution center at the "hub." Using this system, each store easily can access distribution center deliveries. Furthermore, the distribution centers are among the most advanced in the world, with miles and miles of conveyor belts moving merchandise in and out at lightning speed.

Weaknesses Although Wal-Mart's weaknesses are few, they are potentially serious. No matter how hard it tries to be a good corporate citizen, it still manages to become the villain in many communities. Cities and towns of all sizes fear the demise of the small businesses that cannot compete with Wal-Mart's low prices. As a result of these demises, people lose their jobs and end up either unemployed or working for Wal-Mart at the substantially reduced wages that critics often deride Wal-Mart for imposing. Being the world's largest corporation also attracts substantial litigation, which leads to poor public relations.

How does Wal-Mart maintain its low prices?

Step 2: Assess Opportunities and Threats

In the second half of the SWOT analysis, we assess the firm's opportunities and threats. Consider some potential opportunities, many of which Wal-Mart already is investigating:[52]

- Expand aggressively into fashion apparel to compete more effectively with other lower-priced fashion retailers, like Target and H&M.
- Enter India.
- Expand offerings of health care, banking, and broadband access.[53]

Like any firm, Wal-Mart also faces several threats, but unlike many firms, these threats appear relatively mild in comparison with its opportunities. First, on a global scale, several retail powerhouses like Carrefour (France) and Metro (Germany) have impeded its global expansion. Second, small but nimble local retailers eat into its market in certain categories. Some such retailers can beat Wal-Mart on assortment and service but usually not on price. Third, given Wal-Mart's size, it exists under constant governmental surveillance for possible legal infringements as it expands into new categories, expands within a category, or enters new markets.

Step 3: Identify Different Scenarios

On the basis of the analysis performed in Steps 1 and 2, executives can identify some alternative scenarios that might happen in the next five years. Two of the scenarios could be as follows:

- Expand offering of health care, banking, and broadband access.
- Wal-Mart enters India.

Each of these alternative scenarios requires careful consideration and reflection to assess the risks, benefits, and costs of that move. To determine which are the best opportunities, it is useful to try to match the firm's competencies with the opportunity's attractiveness. Clearly, if the firm has a high competency to engage in an opportunity and the opportunity is attractive, it represents a likely opportunity to pursue.

Wal-Mart could examine the attractiveness of offering a broader array of health care, banking, and broadband services. This would allow them to move into more lucrative and potentially growing service opportunities. Alternatively, an expansion into India would allow it to go after a certain percentage of the over 1 billion consumers. Wal-Mart already buys over $1.6 billion worth of merchandise from India.[54] However, to attract the Indian consumer, Wal-Mart would need to carefully examine the Indian market.

Firms like Wal-Mart may have to adjust their communications mix to add more billboards as they expand in India.

Step 4: Apply the Marketing Mix to the Different Scenarios

In this step, the firm develops a potential strategy for each of the different scenarios created in Step 3. For simplicity, let's just consider the option of Wal-Mart entering India. It provides an intriguing yet straightforward option for several reasons. Because Wal-Mart is already buying over $1.6 billion worth of merchandise from India, the Indian government is not likely to throw roadblocks into its expansion efforts. The biggest potential problem is that, in India, Wal-Mart does not have the well-established supply chain it has in other markets. Wal-Mart is used to doing things in a big way. It will probably need different types of trucks, equipment, and warehouses to operate in the Indian environment. Another difficult challenge the company would face in India would be to find great urban locations that have the square footage that

Wal-Mart typically requires. Thus, Wal-Mart is opting to enter India with a joint venture with an Indian retailer that is looking at market expansion opportunities.

In addition to challenges on supply chain and location, Wal-Mart would also need to change the product assortment and store layouts to conform to the Indian consumers' tastes and preferences. For instance, most Indians buy fresh produce, meat, and other food items from street vendors or small stores, and the merchandise is often stored in bulk or in burlap sacks.[55] These stores can be messy, noisy, and cramped. As a result, the long wide aisles with neatly stacked packages, like one would find in a typical Wal-Mart store in the U.S., may not work well in India. Wal-Mart may also adjust its communication mix to take advantage of outdoor advertising opportunities (e.g., billboards, banners, buses) that are so popular in India. Finally, the prices of the merchandise would have to be in line with price expectation of the Indian middle class.

Step 5: Assess the Profitability of Each Scenario

After developing strategies for several options, as in Step 3, and applying the marketing mix as in Step 4, managers must finally assess the profitability of each option. In so doing, they weigh the expected revenues against the expected costs. The projects with the highest expected profit are the best to pursue. Therefore, it is likely that Wal-Mart forecasts indicated that the expected revenues from an expansion into India exceed its expected costs.

In this chapter we have considered how a firm develops its marketing strategy by completing a marketing plan. In particular, we have described how firms analyze their marketing situation, evaluate it, and then develop a segmentation, targeting, and positioning strategy in response. Then we studied how the marketing mix can be used to increase customer value. We detailed several generic strategies for growing a business and three overarching macro strategies that many firms have implemented successfully. Finally, we showed how scenario planning can be used to integrate information from external and internal corporate sources to assess the viability of various corporate strategies.

CHECK YOURSELF

1. Identify the steps of the scenario planning process.
2. How is scenario planning used in a firm?

Summing Up

1. **What is a marketing strategy?**

   A marketing strategy identifies (1) a firm's target markets(s), (2) a related marketing mix—their four Ps, and (3) the bases upon which the firm plans to build a sustainable competitive advantage. Firms use four macro strategies to build their sustainable competitive advantage. Customer excellence focuses on retaining loyal customers and excellent customer service. Operational excellence is achieved through efficient operations and excellent supply chain and human resource management. Product excellence entails having products with high perceived value and effective branding and positioning. Finally, locational excellence entails having a good physical location and Internet presence.

2. **How does a firm set up a marketing plan?**

   A marketing plan is composed of an analysis of the current marketing situation, its objectives, the strategy for the four Ps, and appropriate financial statements. A marketing plan represents the output of a three-phase process: planning, implementation, and control. The planning phase requires that managers define the firm's mission and vision and assess the firm's current situation. It helps answer the questions, "What business are we in now, and what do we intend to be in the future?" In the second phase, implementation, the firm specifies, in more operational terms, how it plans to implement its mission and vision. Specifically, to which customer groups does it wish to direct its marketing efforts, and how does it use its marketing mix to provide good value? Finally, in the control phase, the firm must evaluate its performance using appropriate metrics to determine what worked, what didn't, and how performance can be improved in the future.

3. **How are SWOT analyses used to analyze the marketing situation?**

Recall that SWOT stands for strengths, weaknesses, opportunities, and threats. A SWOT analysis occurs during the second step in the strategic planning process, the situation analysis. By analyzing what the firm is good at (its strengths), where it could improve (its weaknesses), where in the marketplace it might excel (its opportunities), and what is happening in the marketplace that could harm the firm (its threats), managers can assess their firm's situation accurately and plan its strategy accordingly.

4. **How does a firm choose what group(s) of people to pursue with its marketing efforts?**

Once a firm identifies different marketing opportunities, it must determine which are the best to pursue. To accomplish this task, marketers go through a segmentation, targeting, and positioning (STP) process. Firms segment various markets by dividing the total market into those groups of customers with different needs, wants, or characteristics who therefore might appreciate products or services geared especially toward them. After identifying the different segments, the firm goes after, or targets, certain groups on the basis of the firm's perceived ability to satisfy the needs of those groups better than competitors and profitably. To complete the STP process, firms position their products or services according to the marketing mix variables so that target customers have a clear, distinctive, and desirable understanding of what the product or service does or represents relative to competing products or services.

5. **How does the implementation of the marketing mix increase customer value?**

The marketing mix consists of the four Ps—product, price, promotion, and place—and each P contributes to customer value. To provide value, the firm must offer a mix of products and services at prices their target markets will view as indicating good value. Thus, firms make trade-offs between the first two Ps, product and price, to give custom-

ers the best value. The third P, promotion, informs customers and helps them form a positive image about the firm and its products and services. The last P, place, adds value by getting the appropriate products and services to customers when they want them and in the quantities they need.

6. **What is portfolio analysis and how is it used to evaluate marketing performance?**

Portfolio analysis is a management tool used to evaluate the firm's various products and businesses—its "portfolio"—and allocate resources according to which products are expected to be the most profitable for the firm in the future. A popular portfolio analysis tool developed by the Boston Consulting Group classifies all products into four categories. The first, stars, are in high growth markets and have high market shares. The second, cash cows, are in low-growth markets, but have high market share. These products generate excess resources that can be spun off to products that need them. The third category, question marks, are in high-growth markets, but have relatively low market shares. These products often utilize the excess resources generated by the cash cows. The final category, dogs, are in low-growth markets and have relatively low market shares. These products are often phased out.

7. **How can firms grow their businesses?**

Firms use four basic growth strategies: market penetration, market development, product development, and diversification. A market penetration strategy directs the firm's efforts toward existing customers and uses the present marketing mix. In other words, it attempts to get current customers to buy more. In a market development strategy, the firm uses its current marketing mix to appeal to new market segments, as might occur in international expansion. A product development growth strategy involves offering a new product or service to the firm's current target market. Finally, a diversification strategy takes place when a firm introduces a new product or service to a new customer segment. Sometimes a diversification strategy relates to the firm's current business, such as when a women's clothing manufacturer starts making and selling men's clothes, but a more risky strategy is when a firm diversifies into a completely unrelated business.

8. **How do marketers use scenario planning to determine which courses of action to take?**

Scenario planning integrates information on how the environment impacts a company's marketing strategy. Scenario planning is performed in five steps. In the first two steps, a company assesses its strengths, weaknesses, opportunities, and threats (SWOT). Third, it identifies different scenarios. Fourth, it applies the marketing mix to the different scenarios. Finally, it assesses the profitability of each scenario. The scenario(s) with the highest potential are considered for implementation.

Key Terms

- competitor-based pricing, 46
- control phase, 39
- cost-based pricing, 46
- customer excellence, 33
- diversification strategy, 55
- implementation phase, 39
- locational excellence, 37
- market development strategy, 53
- market growth rate, 49
- market penetration strategy, 53
- market positioning, 44
- market segment, 42
- market segmentation, 42
- market share, 49
- marketing plan, 38
- marketing strategy, 32
- mission statement, 40
- operational excellence, 36
- planning phase, 39
- product development strategy, 54
- product excellence, 37
- product line, 49
- products, 45
- relative market share, 49
- scenario planning, 56
- situation analysis, 41
- STP, 42
- strategic business unit (SBU), 49
- sustainable competitive advantage, 32, 40
- target marketing/targeting, 43
- value-based pricing, 46

Marketing Applications

1. How has MTV created a sustainable competitive advantage?

2. Perform a SWOT analysis for your college or university.

3. Describe the primary target markets for McDonald's. How many target markets do you think this global giant pursues? How does it position its various products and services so that they appeal to its varied target markets?

4. Pick your favorite product, service provider, or retailer. How does it add value through the implementation of the four Ps?

5. Of the four growth strategies described in the chapter, which is the most risky? Which is the easiest to implement? Why?

6. Choose three companies. You believe the first builds customer value through product excellence, the second through operational excellence, and the third through customer excellence. Justify your answer.

Quiz Yourself

www.mhhe.com/ grewal2e

1. In 2006, Ford Motor Company announced it would severely cut back automobile production. For parts companies supplying Ford Motor this represented a:
   a. weakness.
   b. opportunity.
   c. situational selling problem.
   d. threat.
   e. strategic business promotion efficiency.

2. Carla, a manager of a local coffee shop, in response to increased competition from Starbucks, has been directed by her regional marketing manager to cut prices on seasonal items, run an ad in the local paper, and tell distributors to reduce deliveries for the next month. Which stage of the strategic marketing planning process is Carla engaged in?
   a. Evaluate performance.
   b. Define the business mission.
   c. Situation analysis.
   d. Implement marketing mix and resources.
   e. Identify and evaluate opportunities.

(Answers to these two questions can be found on page 623.)

Go to www.mhhe.com/grewal2e to practice an additional 11 questions.

Toolkit

SWOT ANALYSIS

Assume you are a marketing analyst for a major company and are trying to conduct a situation analysis using SWOT analysis. Use the toolkit provided at www.mhhe.com/grewal2e, and complete the SWOT grids for each company using the appropriate items.

Net Savvy

1. The lines of food products produced under the Newman's Own and Newman's Own Organic labels align with the company's claims to engage in "Shameless Exploitation in Pursuit of the Common Good" (www.newmansown.com) and produce "Great Tasting Food That Happens to Be Organic" (www.newmansownorganics.com). Visit both sites and review the descriptions of the company, its mission, and its values. Discuss which aspects of its mission and values might be considered progressive. Does this progressive attitude create a special position for Newman's Own products in the market that contributes to a sustainable competitive advantage?

2. More and more firms seem to be entering the dating service industry. Visit www.eharmony.com and tour its Web site to find the types of activities and methods such companies use to help match compatible couples. Then visit www.match.com and do the same. Now, analyze the environment that might affect Internet dating services using a SWOT analysis.

Chapter Case Study

THE iPHONE: THE GREAT CONSUMER HOPE[56]

In 2004, when Apple announced it was developing an "iPod phone" in partnership with Motorola, consumers and Apple investors were filled with great anticipation. But the resulting ROKR phone prompted widespread disappointment, and less than a year later, Apple discontinued its iTunes support, making the handsets it had sold basically obsolete.

Despite the dismal failure of the first iPod phone, just three years later, Apple announced its iPhone. What could have made Apple decide to offer another cell phone, and what did it do differently when introducing the iPhone?[57]

APPLE INC.

Apple manufactures and sells computer, music, and phone hardware, along with related software. Since its incorporation in 1977[58] under the name Apple Computer Incorporated, Apple has introduced products that challenge the conventional approaches in the electronics industry. It pioneered modular design with the Apple II, engineered the initial graphical interfaces with the Macintosh, and offered the PowerBook as the first laptop to include a built-in track pad.[59]

In 2001, Apple changed how consumers listen to music when it entered the portable music player market. Since then, it has sold more than 100 million iPods, making it the market leader with a 74 percent market share in the MP3 arena.[60] According to most consumers and technology experts, the success of the iPod resulted from its incredible ease of use. By combining a music store, software, and portable player into one simple system, Apple eliminated the problems consumers faced with other music players and thus created value by simplifying the digital music experience.

THE ROKR

Three years after it introduced the iPod, Apple decided to partner with Motorola to produce a music phone. When Apple and Motorola came out with the ROKR in 2004, they had high hopes that they could capitalize on the popularity of portable electronics by combining two devices that members of the target market commonly carried: a cell phone and an MP3 player. It seemed like a perfect partnership, with Apple supplying access to affordable content and Motorola providing cell phone manufacturing and marketing experience. But the ROKR had a major flaw, according to cellular carriers such as Sprint and Cingular. These carriers earn revenue from the bandwidth used to download songs and the purchase price. But the ROKR could not purchase songs over the air and only played songs purchased through iTunes, so carriers made much less money from the ROKR phone and therefore did not push it.

Consumers also found the new cell phone disappointing, mainly because the phone was extremely slow to load music,[61] artificially capped capacity at 100 songs, and was sluggish when running iTunes.[62] Thus, half of its value proposition—that is, that it would replace MP3 players—failed to satisfy those who adopted the ROKR. After less than a year, Motorola discontinued its partnership with Apple and announced that the next-generation ROKR would not use iTunes.

Apple iPhone was named "Invention of the Year" by Time *magazine.*

THE HANDSET MARKET

When Apple decided to introduce its second version of a music cell phone, it faced significant barriers. As early as 2005, *Wired Magazine* pointed out that "music phones are the biggest threat Apple has faced since Windows."[63] Although Apple dominated the dedicated MP3 player market, more and more phone manufacturers were adding music playback to their handsets. Primary phone manufacturers, such as Nokia and Motorola, already had existing relationships with cellular carriers, so they achieved a distinct advantage in the U.S. market, where cellular carriers dominate the distribution market for handsets. (Only 0.05 percent of all cell phones are sold by noncarriers in the United States.)[64] To address this problem, Apple partnered with Cingular, now AT&T. But it could not negotiate price support, which meant that consumers would have to pay the entire $699 list price—a major issue indeed.

THE iPHONE

Despite these issues, Apple decided to develop the iPhone, but it made two important decisions about this release. First, it would redesign the buying process for cell phones. Second, Apple would introduce new iPod features unique to the iPhone.

To improve the cell phone purchasing process, Apple relied on simplification to make the ordeal as painless as possible. Customers who disliked shopping for phones could buy online and register through iTunes. Those who wanted to be among the first to get their hands on an iPhone could turn to AT&T sales locations and Apple stores, which provided no-risk trials. Apple even took control of the customer service and troubleshooting functions for the iPhone to ensure it determined all aspects of the user experience.

Then, to differentiate the iPhone from anything else available on the market, Apple developed unique features that were unavailable to iPod owners. In creating special value for technologically savvy, forward-thinking consumers, Apple designed the iPhone to feature a touchscreen, wireless capabilities, and a much larger viewing screen. By late 2007, Apple added these features to its iPod Touch.

THE LAUNCH

Despite the failure of the ROKR, the high purchase price of the iPhone, and the widespread tendency for consumers to get locked into long-term contracts with their existing cellular carriers, on the first day the iPhone was available, consumers lined up in the streets in hopes of having an opportunity to purchase it. In late 2007, *Time* named the iPhone the "Invention of the Year."[65]

Questions

1. How did Apple know that the cell phone market would be a good opportunity? What important differences led to the success of the iPhone and the failure of the ROKR?

2. Why did AT&T agree to partner with Apple? Could Apple have succeeded with another partner? Without a cellular partner?

3. What kind of industry analysis did Apple likely conduct before releasing the iPhone?

4. Do you think the iPhone will continue to be a success? What environmental factors support your position?

APPENDIX 2A

section 1

WRITING A MARKETING PLAN

> *Have a plan. Follow the plan, and you'll be surprised how successful you can be. Most people don't have a plan. That's why it's easy to beat most folks.*
>
> —Paul "Bear" Bryant, football coach, University of Alabama

WHY WRITE A MARKETING PLAN?[1]

As a student, you likely plan out much in your life—where to meet for dinner, how much time to spend studying for exams, which courses to take next semester, how to get home for winter break, and so on. Plans enable us to figure out where we want to go and how we might get there.

For a firm, the goal is not much different. Any company that wants to succeed (which means any firm whatsoever) needs to plan for a variety of contingencies, and marketing represents one of the most significant. A marketing plan—which we defined in Chapter 2 as a written document composed of an analysis of the current marketing situation, opportunities and threats for the firm, marketing objectives and strategy specified in terms of the 4Ps, action programs, and projected or pro-forma income (and other financial) statements—enables marketing personnel and the firm as a whole to understand their own actions, the market in which they operate, their future direction, and the means to obtain support for new initiatives.[2]

Because these elements—internal activities, external environments, goals, and forms of support—differ for every firm, the marketing plan is different for each firm as well. However, several guidelines apply to marketing plans in general; this Appendix summarizes those points and offers an annotated example.

MARKETING PLAN VERSUS BUSINESS PLAN

Of course, firms consider more than marketing when they make plans and therefore commonly develop business plans as well. Yet as this book highlights, marketing constitutes such an important element of business that business plans and marketing plans coincide in many ways.[3] Both marketing and business plans generally encompass

1. Executive summary.
2. Company overview.
3. Objectives or goals, usually according to strategic plan and focus.
4. Situation analysis.
5. Market/product/customer analysis.
6. Marketing strategy.
7. Financial projections.
8. Implementation plan.
9. Evaluation and control metrics.

However, a business plan also includes details about R&D and operations, and both may feature details about other key topics, depending on the focus of the company and the plan.

STRUCTURE OF A MARKETING PLAN

This section briefly describes each of the elements of a marketing plan.[4]

Executive Summary

The executive summary essentially tells the reader why he or she is reading this marketing plan—what changes require consideration, what new products need discussion, and so forth—and suggests possible actions to take in response to the information the plan contains.

Company Overview

In this section, the plan provides a brief description of the company, including perhaps its mission statement, background, and competitive advantages.

Objectives/Goals

This section offers more specifics about why readers are reading the marketing plan. What does the company want to achieve, both overall and with this particular marketing plan?

Situation Analysis

Recall from Chapter 2 that a situation analysis generally relies on SWOT considerations; therefore, this section describes the strengths, weaknesses, opportunities, and threats facing the company.

STP Analysis

The analysis proceeds by assessing the market in which the company functions, the products it currently offers or plans to offer in the future, and the characteristics of current or potential customers.

Marketing Strategy

The marketing strategy may be very specific, especially if the plan pertains to, for example, a stable product in a familiar market, or it may be somewhat open to varied possibilities, such as when the firm plans to enter a new market with an innovative product.

Financial Projections

On the basis of the knowledge already obtained, the marketing plan should provide possible developments and returns on the marketing investments outlined in the marketing strategy.

Implementation Plan

This portion of the marketing plan includes the timing of promotional activities, when monitoring will take place, and how expansions likely will proceed.

Evaluation Metrics and Control

The firm must have a means of assessing the marketing plan's recommendations; the marketing plan therefore must indicate the methods for undertaking this assessment, whether quantitatively or qualitatively.

Appendix

The final section(s) offers additional information that might be of benefit, such as a list of key personnel, data limitations that may influence the findings, and suggestions of the plan, relevant legislation, and so forth.

INFORMATION SOURCES[5]

When writing a marketing plan, you likely can turn to a variety of your firm's in-house information sources, including annual reports, previous marketing plans, published mission statements, and so on. In addition, various sources offer suggestions and examples that may provide you with direction and ideas. A reference librarian can help you find many of these sources, which likely are available through your university's library system.

- Knowthis.com—"a knowledge source for marketing" http://www.knowthis.com/tutorials/principles-of-marketing/ how-to-write-a-marketing-plan/21.htm.
- Encyclopedia of American Industries—introduces industry structure; arranged by SIC and NAICS codes.
- Standard & Poor's NetAdvantage—surveys of more than 50 different industries, with financial data about companies in each industry.
- Investext Plus—brokerage house reports.
- IBISWorld—market research on thousands of industries; classified by NAICS code.
- Statistical Abstract of the United States—a vast variety of statistics on a wealth of topics.
- U.S. Bureau of the Census—detailed statistical data gathered every 10 years on all aspects of the U.S. population.
- County Business Patterns: U.S. Bureau of the Census—payroll and employee numbers for most NAICS codes.
- Consumer Expenditure Study: U.S. Bureau of Labor Statistics—income and expenditures by household, classified by various demographics.

- LifeStyle Market Analyst—lifestyle information about geographic areas, lifestyle interest groups, and age and income groups.
- Mediamark Reporter—information about demographics, lifestyles, product and brand usage, and advertising media preferences.
- Scarborough Arbitron—local market consumer information for various media in 75 local markets for consumer retail shopping behavior, product consumption, media usage, lifestyle behavior, and demographics.
- Simmons Study of Media and Markets—products and consumer characteristics; various media audiences and their characteristics.
- Sourcebook America—demographic data, including population, spending potential index, income, race, and *Tapestry* data, presented by state, county, DMA, and zip code, as well as business data by county and zip code.
- Rand McNally Commercial Atlas and Marketing Guide—maps and tables showing demographic, industrial, transportation, railroad, airline, and hospital data.
- "Survey of Buying Power," Sales and Marketing Management—current state, county, city, and town estimates of population by age, retail sales by store group, effective buying income, and buying power index.
- Annual & 10-K reports from *Thomson One Banker, Edgar,* and *LexisNexis*—business descriptions, product listings, distribution channels, possible impact of regulations and lawsuits, and discussions of strategic issues.
- MarketResearch.com Academic—market research reports on a variety of consumer products.
- Mintel Reports Database—market research reports focusing on consumer products, lifestyles, retailing, and international travel industry.

LINGUISTIC AND VISUAL SUGGESTIONS

Again, recall that all marketing plans differ, because all firms differ. However, just as rules exist that dictate what makes for good writing, some rules or guidelines apply to all well-written marketing plans.

- Maintain a professional attitude in the writing and presentation.
- Keep descriptions and summaries concise. Get to the point.
- Use standard, edited English.
- Proofread the entire plan multiple times to catch grammatical, spelling, or other such errors that could dampen the professionalism of the writing.
- Adopt a businesslike tone; avoid flowery or jargon-filled writing.
- Employ direct, rather than passive, and present, rather than past, tense whenever possible (e.g., "We plan to achieve 30 percent growth in two years" rather than "The plan was that 30 percent growth would be achieved by the firm within two years").
- Be positive.
- Yet avoid meaningless superlatives (e.g., "Our goal is tremendous growth").
- Be specific; use quantitative information whenever possible.
- Insert graphics to convey important concepts succinctly, including photos, graphs, illustrations, and charts.
- However, avoid using so many visual elements that they clutter the plan.
- Lay out the plan clearly and logically.
- Organize sections logically, using multiple levels of headings, distinguished clearly by font differences (e.g., bold for first-level heads, italics for second-level heads).

- Consider the use of bullet points or numbered lists to emphasize important points.
- Exploit modern technology (e.g., graphics software, page layout software, laser printers) to ensure the plan looks professional.
- Adopt an appropriate font to make the text easy to read and visually appealing—avoid using anything smaller than 10-point font at a minimum.
- Avoid unusual or decorative fonts; stick with a common serif type to make the text easy to read.
- Consider binding the report with an attractive cover and clear title page.
- Generally aim for a plan that consists of 15–30 pages.

PEOPLEAHEAD MARKETING PLAN ILLUSTRATION[6]

PeopleAhead Marketing Plan: Condensed

> Instead of using separate "Executive Summary" and "Company Overview" sections, this marketing plan begins with a general overview that includes both aspects and answers the key questions: "What type of business are we?" and "What do we need to do to accomplish our objectives?" (see Chapter 2).

1. Executive Summary

PeopleAhead focuses on career advancement done right. Instead of making job search a one-time event, PeopleAhead provides a platform for people to find, advance, and develop their careers by sharing career goals, discussing professional development plans, and socializing with other professionals.

> As this plan does, a marketing plan should start with a positive, upbeat assessment of what the company does and what it hopes to continue doing.

PeopleAhead culminates the career advancement experience with its proprietary TrueMatch® technology, which identifies synergies between the companies hiring talent (employers) and PeopleAhead members (job candidates) who wish to be hired. By anonymously presenting only prequalified career opportunities to members, who confirm their interest and recommend others, PeopleAhead transforms the ineffective online hiring process into a highly efficient career-matching system. PeopleAhead was founded by Carlos Larracilla and Tom Chevalier to improve people's lives by helping them achieve their career aspirations. The vision for PeopleAhead was conceived of in January 2006, with a notion that personality alignment is critical to matching the right people with the right career opportunities. Since then, the idea has grown and morphed into a company that matches the right person with the right career opportunity by aligning personality, competencies, experience, and interests.

> Note the personalization of the company founders, which may help readers feel connected to the company.

Tom and Carlos combine human resources, system development, and sales experience to deliver a groundbreaking, TrueMatch®-branded talent matching network that makes it easier for people to achieve their career aspirations and improves the way companies identify individuals who will be able to contribute to their long-term success. The organizational chart of PeopleAhead is available in Appendix A.

2. Strategic Objectives

2.1. Mission

PeopleAhead's mission is to help individuals with career advancement and improve the human capital in companies. The site will act as a networking platform for professionals and career matching as opposed to job and resume-posting searches.

2.2. Goals:

- Use brand matching technology: TrueMatch®
- Build critical mass of users.
- Drive traffic to the Web site through marketing blitzes.
- Utilize word-of-mouth advertising from satisfied users.

2.3. Business Summary

- *Business Customers:* This group provides PeopleAhead's revenues. Customers purchase contact information about the Top Ten PROfiles gleaned from the individual member base that have been sorted and ranked by the TrueMatch® technology. PeopleAhead will focus on small and medium businesses (see Market Segmentation section), because these entities are underserved by large competitors in the online recruitment market, and because research shows that this demographic has a less efficient recruitment process that would benefit most readily from PeopleAhead's services. Within this segment, customers include HR managers who are responsible for the sourcing of candidates, functional area managers who require new talent for their team, and executives whose business objectives rely on human capital and efficiency of operations.
- *Individual Members:* This group does not pay for services but is the main source of data points for PeopleAhead's TrueMatch® system. PeopleAhead will focus on building a base of individual members who range from recent graduates to individuals with 5–7 years of continuous employment. Ideal members are those who are currently employed or will be graduating within nine months and are "poised" to make a career change. These individuals can utilize the services to the fullest extent and are valuable candidates for business customers.

2.4. Competitive Advantage

- *TrueMatch® offers a branded technology,* marketed to both business customers and individual candidates for its "black box" value proposition, which establishes PeopleAhead as the category leader for recruitment-matching software. This technology provides a point of differentiation from competitors, which may have technically similar matching software but constantly need to reinforce their marketing messages with explanations of their value proposition.
- *For individual candidates,* PeopleAhead will be the favored career advancement platform online, where individuals enthusiastically create a history and have connections (invited friends, coworkers, and mentors) in place that will make PeopleAhead a staple among their favorite Web sites. PeopleAhead delivers TrueMatch® career opportunities, professional development plans that let people establish a professional record, and valuable career advancement tools, including automatic position feedback, "recommend-a-friend," and team-based career networking.
- *For business customers,* PeopleAhead makes online sourcing and qualification of candidates quick and efficient by prequalifying potential candidates, seeking recommendations for hard-to-find individuals, and delivering only the Top 10 most

The paragraph provides a general outline of the firm's objectives; the bulleted list offers more specific goals, and the subsequent sections go into more detail about the various factors that may influence these objectives.

By referring to another section, the plan makes clear where it is heading and enables readers to cross-reference the information.

The plan acknowledges both a general, potential target market and the ideal targets.

As Chapter 2 suggests, the plan notes PeopleAhead's sustainable competitive advantage as part of its overall mission statement.

highly qualified candidates who have preconfirmed interest in the available position. PeopleAhead will be the most effective candidate-company matching platform available in the market, delivering prequalified, preconfirmed candidates.

In discussing both the external market and the internal advantages of PeopleAhead, the plan carefully distinguishes between individual job candidates and businesses, thus differentiating the focus and objectives according to this segmentation.

3. Situation Analysis—Online Recruitment

Online recruitment is the system whereby companies use the Web to locate and qualify prospective candidates for available positions. The methods employed by online recruitment service providers to serve this market range from resume aggregation to assessment test application to linking strategies. However, the common underlying objective is to locate candidates who would not be found by traditional recruitment methods and use computing power to qualify candidates quickly and with more accuracy than would be possible manually.

3.1. Industry Analysis

Large online recruitment Web sites make this a tedious process by requiring companies to search through many resumes manually to find the "right" candidate. Other sites solicit recommendations for positions. However, resumes are often "enhanced," such that almost all candidates appear qualified, and information found in the resume or provided through a recommendation is simply not sufficient to make an educated hiring decision. Companies need more information and intelligent tools that make this screening process more accurate.

3.1.1. Market Size:

The market size for both member segments in 2005 was as follows:

Figures provide a visually attractive break in the text and summarize a lot of information in an easy-to-read format.

Individual members segments

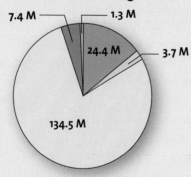

7.4 M — 1.3 M

24.4 M — 3.7 M

134.5 M

Senior college students	Current employees
Other college students	Unemployed
Graduate program students	

Company members segments

0.11 M — 0.10 M

1.33 M

5.27 M

- ☐ Very small enterprises   ☐ Medium enterprises
- ☐ Small enterprises   ☐ Large enterprises

The most critical issue in examining market size is the relationship between the number of companies and the number of workers employed, because sales are based on the number of positions (profiles purchased), not the number of companies that use the service.

The following figure shows the number of people employed by each enterprise market segment as of January 2006, according to the U.S. Department of Labor. This segment information will be useful in defining PeopleAhead's target market.

Employment by enterprise type

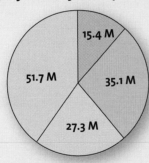

15.4 M

51.7 M

35.1 M

27.3 M

- ☐ Very small enterprises   ☐ Medium enterprises
- ☐ Small enterprises   ☐ Large enterprises

3.1.2. Market Growth

PeopleAhead will operate in the online recruitment market. The growth of this industry is subject to two primary constraints: U.S. economic health and online recruitment advertisement adoption rates. Understanding these constraints will help identify PeopleAhead's opportunity. General indicators suggest the U.S. economy (GDP) will grow at an average annual rate of 4% for the next decade.[7] Online recruitment advertising is expected to grow by 35% per year to reach $7.6 billion by 2010.[8] Not only is the market expanding, but it is exhibiting rapid adoption by new entities, as the following graph shows.[9]

Another visually attractive graph summarizes complicated information easily. The use of high-quality color can add a professional feel to a marketing plan.

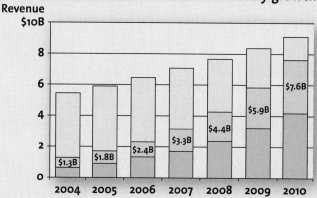

Recruitment advertisement industry growth

Legend:
- Total recruitment advertisement
- Total online recruitment market
- Main competitors: Monster, CareerBuilder, and Yahoo/HotJobs

3.1.3. Market Needs

- **The right person for the right position:** The right employee for one company or position is not the same for all others. Not only must companies locate intelligent individuals with relevant experience, but they also prefer people who are aligned with the position requirements in terms of personality, competencies, and fit with the company culture.

- **Prescreening qualification tools:** Increasing the number of candidates through online recruitment can be advantageous, but it can also be a hindrance. When sourcing candidates, recruiters need tools that help them qualify applicants.

- **Time savings:** Companies need to complete the online sourcing and qualification of candidates quickly. Leaving positions unfilled can cause critical performance gaps to emerge within the company.

3.1.4. Market Trends

The methods by which online recruitment service providers deliver candidates has been undergoing a migration from resume aggregation and search services like Monster and CareerBuilder to new Web 2.0 methodologies that include passive recruitment, "meta tagging," and social networking.

The underlying objective of these Web 2.0 services is to allow individuals to remain on a few, trusted Web sites while enabling companies to access those individuals for financial purposes. In parallel, the focus is moving from aggregation of unique visitors toward engaging existing users more intensively. Internet users are growing familiar with sites that encourage socializing, collaborating, and distributing private information online to help improve network benefits and need to be engaged to maintain contact.

> Before engaging in a firm-specific SWOT analysis (see Chapter 2), this marketing plan assesses the external market environment further and thus establishes a basis for the subsequent SWOT analysis.

3.2. SWOT Analysis

> Using a table and bullet points, the plan summarizes a lot of information succinctly and clearly.

	Positive	Negative
Internal	**STRENGTHS** • Industry best practices: The networking model used by PeopleAhead draws on the industry accepted "best practices" contact protocols drawn from multiple industries, including online feedback, recruitment, and social networking and offline professional networking. TrueMatch® software aligns business objectives with appropriate candidates. • Team expertise: The combined talents of the founders include human resources, system development, sales, and marketing. • Web development expertise: PeopleAhead has partnered with an award-winning European software development provider. This company provides quality usually reserved for high-budget projects, at terms that are favorable for a start-up company.	**WEAKNESSES** • Absence of industry "influentials": As a start-up, PeopleAhead does not currently have resources to attract influential industry managers. • Inability to guarantee critical mass: As is true of many Internet companies, the business must solve the "chicken and egg" puzzle to build critical mass. • Verifying efficiency of matching capabilities: In theory, the system has an absolute guarantee of effectivity; computations make decisions rather than humans. However, the matching capabilities must be verified as accurate to gain widespread acceptance. • Broad target market: Because PeopleAhead is targeting a wide range of businesses, the product being developed has not been "customized" ideally for each segment.
External	**OPPORTUNITIES** • Service gap: Recruiters are not pleased with current online recruitment vendors. • Industry gap: Job turnover is every 3.5 years per person. • Demand for productive candidates. • Online recruitment advertising: Growing by 35% per year, to reach $7.6 billion by 2010.[10]	**THREATS** • Convergence: existing competitors may form strategic alliances and establish powerful positions before PeopleAhead can establish itself. • Inability to protect model: Very little intellectual property created by online Web sites is protected by law. Although PeopleAhead will

> Note that the analysis uses outside sources to support its claims.

(continued)

External	OPPORTUNITIES	THREATS
	• Fragmented business models: Online recruitment is fragmented by recruitment methodology: active (people who need jobs), passive (people who are not looking but would move if enticed), poised (people unsatisfied with jobs they have), and network (finding people of interest based on who or what they know).	pursue aggressive IP protection strategies, the model could be copied or mimicked by competitors. • Inadequate differentiation: Inability to explain our differentiation would relegate PeopleAhead to (unfair) comparisons with competitors. Without differentiation, PeopleAhead will not be able to create scale through network effects.

3.3. Competition

Most online recruitment Web sites compete in the active recruitment market, including Monster, CareerBuilder, and Yahoo/HotJobs. The pervasive segment includes job seekers who actively look for jobs, post their resumes, and search for jobs on company Web sites. Most active recruiters offer free services to users and charge companies on a fee basis. Companies can post jobs and search for candidate resumes in the database (average fee for local searches is $500 and nationwide is $1,000). In this first-generation online recruitment business model, competitors face the challenge to make the process more user friendly and reduce the effort required to make these sites deliver results.

- **Monster:** Monster.com is the sixteenth most visited Web site in the United States, with more than 43 million professionals in its viewer base. It earned revenues of $275 million in the second quarter of 2006, up 39% from the previous year. Monster earns revenue from job postings, access to its resume database, and advertisements on Web sites of partner companies.

- **Careerbuilder:** Careerbuilder.com has experienced 75% growth for the past five years. In the second quarter of 2006, Careerbuilder became the top online recruitment seller in North America, surpassing Monster.com. This job post/resume search company uses its media ownership to attract "passive" candidates from partner Web sites. It achieves growth through affiliate partnerships that host job searches on affiliated Web pages, such as Google, MSN, AOL, USA Today, Earthlink, BellSouth, and CNN. Job posting is the primary activity, sold together with or separately from resume searches.

- **Passive Recruitment:** The second generation of online recruitment locates candidates who are not necessarily looking for jobs but who could be convinced to move to a new position if the right opportunity was presented. The most recognized competitors in this category include Jobster, LinkedIn, and H3 (Appendix B).

3.4. Company Analysis

PeopleAhead's mission is simple: improve people's lives through career advancement. PeopleAhead recognizes that career advancement means many things to many people and provides a fresh perspective on career networking that is flexible yet powerful.

- **Users are not alone:** Finding a job is not easy. Why search solo? PeopleAhead unites groups of friends, coworkers, and mentors to create natural, team-based career discovery.

- **Job posting is not natural:** People spend countless hours searching job listings and posting resumes, only to be overlooked because their writing style or resume format

---

If PeopleAhead chooses to adopt a competitor-based pricing strategy (see Chapter 13), detailed information about how other recruitment firms work will be mandatory.

Information about competitors' revenues, customers, growth, and so forth often is available publically through a variety of sources.

For information that may not belong in the main text, an appendix offers an effective means to provide detail without distracting readers.

This section offers the "product" component of the market/product/customer analysis. Because PeopleAhead's product is mostly a service (see Chapter 12), it focuses on some intangible features of its offering.

does not match an overburdened recruiter's preference. Good people make great companies, not resumes. PeopleAhead's TrueMatch® technology matches the right people with the right position. No posting, no applying—just good, quality matches.

- **Professionals being professionals:** There is a place online for social networking, pet networking, and music networking. So why is there no outlet for career networking online—the activity that consumes the majority of our professional lives? PeopleAhead is a place where professionals share their experiences, achievements and objectives with other professionals that care and can be found by employers who value their professionalism.

3.5. Customer Analysis

PeopleAhead's R&D efforts show that the impetus to improve recruitment effectivity is pervasive and that unmet needs revolve around a few core issues: the ability to find qualified talent, establishing a fit between the candidate and the company culture, verifying the candidate's career progression, and working quickly and cost effectively. The following customer characteristics represent ideal attributes that align with PeopleAhead's service offering. This information might be used in conjunction with the Marketing Strategy.

3.5.1. Business Customer

- **Industry:** Because companies that value human capital are more likely to take a chance on a start-up that promotes professional development, the broadly defined professional services industry, including insurance, banking, and consulting, is the primary focus.
- **Functional area:** PeopleAhead's system identifies "people" people, so positions that require human interaction are more aligned with system capabilities than those with stringent skill requirements, sets such as programming or accounting.
- **Size:** Large businesses (>1000 employees) have high volume requirements and demand vendors with proven track records; small businesses (<25 employees) hire fewer people and may not justify acquisition costs. PeopleAhead aligns best with medium-sized customers.
- **Hiring need:** PeopleAhead serves two types of searches very well: those with too many applicants and those with too few applicants. By drawing applicants that most systems overlook and delivering only the most qualified applicants, the system assures the right candidate is identified quickly.

3.5.2. Individual Member

- **Background:** People who value professional development and are familiar with computer networking technologies; most are likely college educated, motivated by career success, and aware of their professional competencies/deficiencies.
- **Situation:** Members should have a professional development plan to share with others who can help them achieve their objectives—likely people who are inquisitive about their professional future and not content with their current situation. The common industry terminology for this group of people is "poised candidates."

Outlook: Proactive people who research, plan, self-educate, and talk about their career. Probably the clearest example of proactivity is a student who devotes time, effort, and financial resources toward career advancement.

The last—and some would say most important—piece of the analysis puzzle: customers.

Although the introduction to this appendix and the plan's organization suggest that analyses of competitors, products, and customers are separate, as this plan shows, a firm usually cannot address one without considering the other. Here, in the "customer" section, the plan notes what its competitors fail to do and therefore why it offers a more valuable service.

Understanding a target customer is not just about numbers. PeopleAhead tries to consider what customers think and feel when searching for jobs too.

4. Marketing Strategy

4.1. Market Segmentation

4.1.1. Business Customers

- **Small enterprises.** Businesses with 10–99 employees. Companies with less than 10 employees are categorized as "Very Small Enterprises" and will not be a primary target market.
- **Medium enterprises.** Businesses with 100–1,000 employees.

4.1.2. Individual Members

- **Senior college students.** Students in the process of searching for a first career.
- **Graduate program students.** Mid-career candidates searching for new career opportunities, such as internships, part-time during enrollment, or full-time after graduation.
- **Current employees.** Persons who are currently employed but are poised to locate better career opportunities.
- **Unemployed.** Persons searching for job not included in previous segments.

4.2. Target Market

PeopleAhead plans to focus resources on small to medium enterprises (SMEs) in the New England Metro market, including Boston, Providence, Hartford, Stamford, Norwalk, Worcester, and Springfield. Online recruitment companies compete for national recruitment spending, but most job seekers are locally based, so market penetration is possible by covering a single geographical location. By maintaining this focus, PeopleAhead will be better equipped to build a critical mass of users that represent the job-seeking population and thus improve both users' and customers' experience, customer service, and the use of financial resources.

4.3. User Positioning

To the proactive professional, PeopleAhead is career advancement done right—providing a platform to discover, plan, and advance careers by uniting friends, coworkers, and mentors with companies searching for the right talent.

5. Marketing Mix

5.1. Products/Services Offered

The first planned offering is **group profiling:** users self-associate with groups to share development plans. Access to groupings is permission based and similar to social networking. Members will be able to share professional experiences with people they know. Group profiling may prompt "voyeur" networking, such that members join to view the profiles of the people they know.

PeopleAhead will then open **group profiling to business customers,** who will be granted access to groups of members to target people they want to hire.

The next added feature will be **user feedback** on professional development plans. PeopleAhead will track data from successful member profile matches to provide feedback for members who have not been matched successfully.

The plan continues with the same segmentation throughout. Here the plan discusses targeting and what makes each segment attractive.

By already identifying key markets in the previous section, the plan provides a foundation for a more specific targeting statement in this section.

The final step in the STP process: Positioning for the segmented, targeted market.

PeopleAhead's mission

Given its own section in this plan, a discussion of the marketing mix constitutes a key element of the strategic planning process (see Chapter 2).

According to well-known marketing concepts, the marketing mix consists of the 4Ps: product (service here), price, place (distribution here), and promotion.

The product (service) offering must establish the value for consumers: Why should they expend effort or resources to obtain the offering?

5.2. Price

In addition to a basic pricing schedule, PeopleAhead will offer bulk pricing and contract pricing to business customers to satisfy unique customer needs. The pricing model is expected to remain constant, but customer feedback will be analyzed to ensure alignment with their requirements.

Continuing the new customer acquisition plan, PeopleAhead will encourage new trials by offering promotional pricing to new customers.

5.3. Distribution

- **PeopleAhead Challenge:** The PeopleAhead Challenge will act as a primary user acquisition strategy. Selection will be focused on successful target segments demanded by customers.

- **Direct Sales:** Direct customer contact is the preferred method of communication during the first six months. Telesales is the anticipated eventual sales model, due to reduced costs and quicker customer sales cycle, but it limits intimacy between the customer and PeopleAhead. During the initial stages, intimacy and excellent customer service are more highly desired than reduced cost, and direct sales achieves that objective.

- **Industry Events:** Attendance at HR industry and recruitment events will supplement direct sales efforts.

- **Challenge Groups:** Word-of-mouth distribution by PeopleAhead members.

5.4. Promotion

- **Public Profiling:** When the product is ready, with proper precautions for protecting competitive advantages, PeopleAhead can increase its Web presence. Strategies include contributing articles to recruitment publishers, writing op/ed pieces, public profiling of the founders on Web sites like LinkedIn, Ziggs, and zoominfo, and blogging.

- **Blogger Community Testimonials:** Influential users of blogs will be invited to try the system and be granted "exclusive" access to the inner workings of the site. A subsequent linking blitz will put opinion pieces in front of recruiters, job seekers, and the investment community.

- **Strategic Alliances**: PeopleAhead offers a product that complements the services offered by many large organizations. Partner opportunities exist with

  a. Universities, colleges, academic institutions
  b. Professional associations, clubs, industry affiliation groups
  c. Online associations, groups, blogs
  d. Professional services firms, outplacement firms, and executive search firms

Strategic alliances serve multiple purposes: They can help PeopleAhead increase public exposure, increase the user base, expand product offerings, and increase revenue opportunities. These benefits will be considered and partnerships proposed prior to the official launch. For strategic purposes, PeopleAhead prefers to focus on product development in the near term (3 months) and then reassess potential alliances after system efficacy has been proven.

> Making the product (service) available where and when consumers want it may seem somewhat easier for PeopleAhead because of the vast development of the Internet; however, the firm still needs to consider how it can ensure people know where and how to access its offering.

> The plan offers a specific time frame, which recognizes the potential need to make changes in the future, as the market dictates.

Peopleahead.com

delivers:

» Target marketing for hard-to-fill positions

» Qualified & pre-confirmed candidates

» Intelligent candidate ranking tools

» Results

6. Financials

Start-up costs consist primarily of Web site design and development, legal representation (business formation, contract negotiation, and intellectual property protection), and general overhead. PeopleAhead projects start-up expenditures of $70,000 during inception, of which $30,000 has been funded by the founding team.

After the Web site launches, the cost structure will consist of sales agent salaries, general and administrative operating costs, and marketing. In the first year, marketing expenses are projected to be $6,250 per month. Monthly overhead likely will reach $24,750 and remain constant.

A.   Projected Income Statement

Pro Forma Income Statement

	Year 1	Year 2	Year 3	Year 4	Year 5
Sales	$56,453	$2,683,665	$8,170,655	$16,312,843	$30,921,013
Gross Margin	$54,194	$2,316,318	$7,383,829	$14,780,329	$28,244,172
Gross Margin %	96.00%	86.31%	90.37%	90.61%	91.34%
Net Profit	($156,906)	$717,403	$3,356,768	$7,035,155	$14,180,041

> The marketing plan needs to identify not only costs but also potential revenues to cover those costs.

> Certain assumptions or marketing research form the basis for its estimation of start-up costs.

> This section contains a lot of numbers in a small space; the graphs and tables help depict those numbers clearly and visually.

Revenue and net income projections

Revenue
$40M

($31M)

30

20

($16.3M)

($8.2M)   ($14.2M)

10   ($7M)

$56K   ($2.7M)($0.7M)   ($3.4M)

0

($157K)

−10

Year 1   Year 2   Year 3   Year 4   Year 5

▢ Revenues ▢ Net income (profit) ▮ Net income (loss)

7. Implementation Plan

The launch of PeopleAhead will use a phased approach, beginning with building brand awareness. Brand awareness should be developed through the founders' visible presence at professional events, online searches, membership in professional associations, networking, and strategic alliances. This visibility will help gain investment capital.

7.1. Objective—Growth

- During the first six months of commercial availability , the primary objective is to expand both the user and customer base to maintain a 100:1 user to customer ratio.
  - **Business Customers:** Sign 24 regular customers and 72 occasional customers. Execute 117 position matches.
  - **Individual Members:** Convert 10,000 people to PeopleAhead members.

7.2. Marketing Objectives—Growth

- **PeopleAhead Challenge:** Pursue groups that were effective during Beta trial and represent a cohesive set of profiles. Expand and refine the Challenge to reflect lessons learned.
- **Increase member networking activity:** Increase user numbers through networking initiated by existing members. Improve user experience to promote networking.
- **Increase profile completeness:** Increase user engagement with platform.
- **Generate traffic.**
- **Public relations campaign (PR):** Increase awareness of PeopleAhead brand through concentrated PR efforts directed at the target market of customers and users.

> This plan divides the objectives into three categories: overall objective, marketing, and financial. Although this is a marketing plan, it must also include other aspects that influence marketing, such as financial status.

7.3. Financial Objectives

- **Efficient marketing expenditures:** 9,000 target users (10,000 year-end total – 1,000 during beta) × $5.00 target acquisition cost = $45,000 budget.

- **Revenue:** $482.50 per position × 117 positions = $56,452.50 revenue.

7.4. Key Success Factors:

- **Economical marketing to relevant constituents:** PeopleAhead needs to establish communication (distribution) channels that pinpoint relevant constituents in a manner consistent with mission values. Limited by resources, chosen channels must aggregate many relevant eyes with free, minimal, or deferred costs involved.

- **Crafting of brand identity:** The contrast between PeopleAhead and competitors lies not only in product differentiation but also in the company's mission statement and delivery. One-time job search is available from thousands of online recruitment sources. Social networking has been covered from diverse angles, attracting many different audiences. The challenge is to associate www.PeopleAhead.com and True-Match® technology with "career advancement done right." The goal is to become the only company that a person thinks of for long-term career discovery, advancement, and development.

- **Efficient value delivery:** The base of customers (both individual and business) needs to receive the proposed value in a timely manner, with consideration given to quality versus quantity of results, alignment with existing objectives, and overall experience with the PeopleAhead brand.

- **Critical mass of business customers and individual users:** The matching process requires that both customers and users exist in the system from the outset of commercialization. This need brings to the forefront the "chicken and egg" scenario; establishing either customers or users requires the other constituent to exist already. The exact number that constitutes "critical mass" ranges from 100 users per position to 10 users per position, depending on compatibility between each constituency.

- **System effectivity:** The ability of PeopleAhead's TrueMatch® software to provide relevant candidate recommendations is critical. The effectiveness of the software depends on the algorithms that match users with positions and the networking protocol that initiates recommendations between users and the people they know. Proposing an inappropriate match could jeopardize the credibility of the system.

- **Intellectual property (IP) strategy:** PeopleAhead is engaged in two primary segments of online enterprise: online recruitment and social networking. Existing competitors have made many efforts to protect their methodologies through U.S. patents. However, precedent has not been established for the legal assertions made by these companies. As a result, PeopleAhead will assume an offensive IP strategy, consisting of diligent IP infringement review, patent application where appropriate, and aggressive trade secret protection of best practices.

- **Financial support:** The founders' investment is sufficient to form the business core and take delivery of PeopleAhead's Web site and software. Financial support will be required to fund operations, execute the IP strategy, and secure customers and users to meet financial targets. Without funding, PeopleAhead will not be able to proceed beyond the product development stage.

- **Sales process:** PeopleAhead's business model requires the acquisition of both business customers who have available positions and users who will be matched

> By offering quantitative, direct goals, PeopleAhead ensures that it can measure its progress toward those goals.

with those positions. These two constituents may be reached through different sales processes without overlap.

8. Evaluation & Control

PeopleAhead will evaluate user profiles to identify sets of profiles that are valuable to new business customers, which will aid in the selection of subsequent target market customers.

8.1. Business Customer

Face-to-face meetings, phone conversations, and e-mail survey contacts with people from a range of industries, company sizes, and functional areas provide a means to (1) build relationships with prospective customers, (2) understand customer needs, and (3) ensure alignment between PeopleAhead's product and customers' recruitment preferences. A summary of the key findings is listed here:

- **Employee fit:** Will the applicant fit our corporate culture? Will the applicant fit with the team we're considering? Will the applicants' competencies fit with the position requirements?
- **Pay for performance:** Objections to recruitment services focus not on price (though it is a consideration) but rather on lack of performance.
- **Unqualified applicants:** Many people who want a job apply, whether they are qualified or not. Recruiters then must scan resumes and weed out unqualified applicants instead of getting to know the qualified applicants.
- **Hard costs vs. soft costs:** Most companies track the recruitment costs of hiring providers, but few measure the time costs of hiring, opportunity costs of hiring the wrong employee, or productivity costs of leaving a position unfilled. Recruitment performance must be easy to measure. Value selling is difficult in the human resources departments.
- **Valuable recommendations:** Most recruiters use online recruitment as a necessary but ineffective means of candidate sourcing, secondary to recommendations. Recommendations include the recommender's judgment of the candidate's fit with the available position.

8.2. Individual Members

Periodic surveys of various prospective users of online recruitment services indicate (1) current services, (2) methods that work well, and (3) biggest problems with online recruitment providers. The following is a qualitative summary of the key findings:

- **Willingness to try:** Careers are important to people; they are averse to spending time uploading resume information to online recruitment Web sites only because of the lack of perceived value. They will spend time when the career opportunities are perceived as valuable.
- **Frustration:** Job seekers are frustrated with available online recruitment providers. Networking is the favored method for career advancement.
- **Lack of differentiation:** Regardless of the qualifications a job seeker possesses, it is difficult to make them evident in a traditional resume.
- **Motivation shift over time:** Early professionals are motivated by financial rewards. Mid-career professionals recommend people because it helps the people they know. Late career professionals hope to improve their own job search opportunities.

Appendix A. Organizational Chart of PeopleAhead

Appendix B. Competition: Passive Recruiters

> The evaluation section retains the segmentation scheme established previously between business customers and individual members.

> Additional useful information that might clutter the plan should appear in an appendix, but is not included in this illustration.

MARKETING ETHICS

- Why do marketers have to worry about ethics?
- What does it take for a firm to be considered socially responsible?
- How should a firm make ethically responsible decisions?
- How can ethics and social responsibility be integrated into a firm's marketing strategy?

R ecalls of high-profile products have screamed from recent headlines—pet food, toothpaste, and children's toys all seemed poised to harm American consumers. Product recalls represent a double-edged sword for marketers. They are costly to both the manufacturer and the retailer in negative short-term sales impacts, the cost of disposing of the recalled products, and the potential damage to the brand and store image. Manufacturers experience severe strains on their business relationships, both with retailers and customers. But despite these costs, recalls are absolutely necessary to protect consumers from dangerous or defective products. Companies face a challenge: lose millions of dollars and protect consumers, or avoid those high costs, and risk suffering even greater ones in the form of permanent damage to the corporate reputation.

Mattel, one of the largest toy companies in the world, produces Barbie dolls and accessories, Matchbox cars, and a variety of other well-known children's toys, including the extremely popular Laughing Elmo. Each year, Mattel manufactures

In one month, Mattel recalled more than 20 million potentially dangerous products.

more than 800 million toys, two-thirds of them in China.[1] In August 2007, Mattel learned that toys supposedly produced by one of its regular Chinese contractors had been subcontracted out to another factory that used lead paint. Realizing that lead is a dangerous neurotoxin that can

EXHIBIT 3.1	Mattel Recall Timeline[2]
Date	**Event**
August 2, 2007	Mattel recalls 1.5 million products because of dangerous levels of lead
August 14, 2007	Mattel recalls 17.4 million products that could be fatal if swallowed
September 4, 2007	Mattel recalls 850,000 products because of dangerous levels of lead

cause blood and brain disorders, especially in children, Mattel quickly decided to begin a recall (see the timeline in Exhibit 3.1). Between August 2 and September 4, 2007, Mattel recalled more than 20 million items[3] and sparked an international debate about children's toy safety and the responsibilities companies have to their customers. Although the Mattel case made headlines because it involved risks to children, it is hardly unique. During August 2007, six other firms also recalled their children's toys because of excessive levels of lead.[4]

● ● ●

Although Mattel acted fast to recall dangerous products, today's increasingly complex business environments make it hard to react quickly to every incident. Yet consumers hold the companies whose brand names they see on products, such as Mattel, responsible for the actions of their entire supply chain, forcing some companies to clamp down on their suppliers. Historically, companies have stressed price when they decided on their outsourcing contracts, but their responsibility today must be broadened to include labor, environmental, safety, and humanitarian concerns.

The ethical dilemma facing managers is how to balance shareholder interests and the needs of society. In the Mattel case, the balancing act meant that managers immediately chose to protect children at the expense of the company's short-term revenues.

Which is a more important corporate objective: making a profit or obtaining and keeping customers?[5] Although firms cannot stay in business without earning a profit, using profit as the sole guiding light for corporate action can lead to short-term decisions that may in fact cause the firm to lose customers in the long run. The balancing act may turn out to be the quest to place the company on the firmest footing possible. Mattel chose to maintain its strong relationships with its customers instead of looking solely to the short-term bottom line.

When customers believe they can no longer trust a company or that the company is not acting responsibly, they will no longer support that company by purchasing its products or services or investing in its stock. For marketers, the firm's ability to build and maintain consumer trust by conducting ethical transactions must be of paramount importance.

In this chapter, we start by examining what marketing ethics is and why behaving ethically is so important to successful marketing and to long-term profits. We then discuss how firms can create an ethical climate among employees and how their individual behavior can affect the ability of the firm to act ethically. To help you make ethical marketing decisions, we provide a framework for ethical decision making and then examine some ethical issues within the context of the marketing plan (from Chapter 2). Finally, we present some scenarios that highlight typical ethical challenges marketing managers often must face.

THE SCOPE OF MARKETING ETHICS

Business ethics refers to the moral or ethical dilemmas that might arise in a business setting. Marketing ethics, in contrast, examines those ethical problems that are specific to the domain of marketing. Firms' attempts to apply sound ethical principles must be a continuous and dynamic process.[6] The cartoon below illustrates the importance of making good ethical decisions. Because the marketing profession is often singled out among business disciplines as the root cause of a host of ethical lapses (e.g., unethical advertising, the promotion of shoddy products), anyone involved in marketing must recognize the ethical implications of their actions. These can involve societal issues, such as the sale of products or services that may damage the environment; global issues, such as the use of child labor; and individual consumer issues, such as deceptive advertising or the marketing of dangerous products.[7]

ETHICAL ISSUES ASSOCIATED WITH MARKETING DECISIONS

Unlike other business functions such as accounting or finance, people in marketing interact directly with the public. Because they are in the public eye, it should not be surprising that marketing and sales professionals sometimes rank poorly in ratings of the most trusted professions. In a recent Gallup survey, most professions were rated much higher than marketing—car salespeople came in last (tied with lobbyists) and advertising practitioners fared only slightly better.[8] (See Exhibit 3.2 on page 89.) For marketers, who depend on the long-term trust of their customers, this low ranking is very disappointing.

Yet there is some good news. In another survey, employees across the United States thought that the ethical climate in their firms had improved, with 83 percent of respondents stating that "top management keeps [its] promises and commitments."[9] Many consumers remain highly skeptical of business, however, and especially of marketing. But because the marketing function interacts with so many entities outside the firm on a regular basis, it has a tremendous opportunity to build the public's trust. Creating an ethical climate that establishes the health and well-being of consumers as the firm's number one priority just makes good business sense.

Creating an Ethical Climate in the Workplace

The process of creating a strong ethical climate within a marketing firm (or in the marketing division of any firm) includes having a set of values that guides decision making and behavior, like Johnson & Johnson's Credo. General Robert Wood Johnson wrote and published the first "Credo" for Johnson & Johnson (J&J)[10]—a one-page document outlining the firm's commitments and responsibilities to its various stakeholders. The J&J Credo can be summarized as follows:

Nurses and doctors are among the most trusted professionals.

We believe our first responsibility is to doctors, nurses, patients, mothers, fathers, and all others who use our products and services. We are responsible to our employees. We must respect their dignity and recognize their merit. Compensation must be fair and adequate and working conditions clean, orderly, and safe. We are responsible to the communities in which we live and work and to the world community as well. Our final responsibility is to our stockholders. When we operate according to these principles, the stockholders should realize a fair return.

Today, J&J continues to follow this credo in its daily business practices, as was evidenced by the infamous Tylenol recall. In the 1980s, seven people taking Tylenol died of cyanide poisoning. Without worrying initially about whether the poison got into the products during production or on the shelf, J&J immediately and voluntarily withdrew all Tylenol from the market until it could ensure its products' safety.

Not all firms operate according to the principles in J&J's Credo. For instance, Merck & Co. withdrew its highly successful drug Vioxx from the marketplace in 2004 because of evidence that it increased the chance of heart attacks and strokes in patients taking the drug.[11] But studies performed at least four years earlier had shown that patients taking Vioxx had an increased incidence of cardiovascular problems compared to an older drug. Although Merck continued to monitor these ongoing studies, it did not act nor did it initiate new studies. Would Merck have done better if it were working under J&J's Credo for ethical behavior?

Everyone within a firm must share the same understanding of its ethical values and how they translate into the business activities of the firm and must share a consistent language to discuss them. Once the values are understood, the firm must develop explicit rules and implicit understandings that govern all the firm's transactions. Top management must commit to establishing an ethical climate, and employees throughout the firm must be dedicated to this because the roots of ethical conflict often are the competing values of individuals. Each individual holds his or her own set of values, and sometimes those values result in inner turmoil and sometimes in conflicts between employees. For instance, a salesperson may believe that it is important to make a sale because her family depends on her for support, but at the same time, she may feel that the product she is selling is not appropriate for a particular customer. Once the rules are in place, there must be a system of controls that helps resolve such dilemmas and rewards appropriate behavior—that is, behavior consistent with the firm's values—and punishes inappropriate behavior.

Many professions, including marketing, have their own codes of ethics that firms and individuals in the profession agree to abide by. The generally accepted code in marketing, developed by the American Marketing Association (see Exhibit 3.3 on pages 90–91), flows from universal norms of conduct to the specific values to which marketers should aspire. Each subarea within marketing, such as marketing research, advertising, pricing, and so forth, has its own code of ethics that deals with the specific issues that arise when conducting business in those areas.

Now let's examine the ethical role of the individuals within the firm and how individuals contribute to the firm's ethical climate.

The Influence of Personal Ethics

Every firm is made up of individuals, each with his or her own needs and desires. Let's start by looking at why people may make *un*ethical decisions and how firms

EXHIBIT 3.2 Attitudes about the Ethical Standards of Various Professions

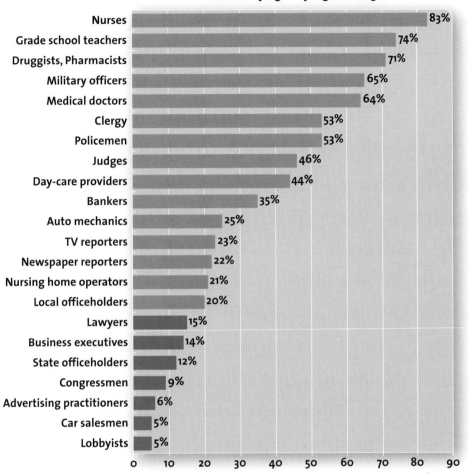

Percent saying "very high" or "high"

Profession	Percent
Nurses	83%
Grade school teachers	74%
Druggists, Pharmacists	71%
Military officers	65%
Medical doctors	64%
Clergy	53%
Policemen	53%
Judges	46%
Day-care providers	44%
Bankers	35%
Auto mechanics	25%
TV reporters	23%
Newspaper reporters	22%
Nursing home operators	21%
Local officeholders	20%
Lawyers	15%
Business executives	14%
State officeholders	12%
Congressmen	9%
Advertising practitioners	6%
Car salesmen	5%
Lobbyists	5%

0 10 20 30 40 50 60 70 80 90

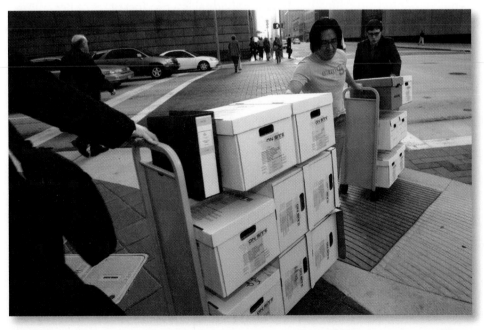

It is not always clear why people act unethically and sometimes illegally, but when they do, many people may be harmed. Here, file boxes are hauled to the federal courthouse for the fraud and conspiracy trial of former Enron executives.

EXHIBIT 3·3	American Marketing Association's Code of Ethics

ETHICAL NORMS AND VALUES FOR MARKETERS

Preamble

The American Marketing Association commits itself to promoting the highest standard of professional ethical norms and values for its members. Norms are established standards of conduct that are expected and maintained by society and/or professional organizations. Values represent the collective conception of what people find desirable, important and morally proper. Values serve as the criteria for evaluating the actions of others. Marketing practitioners must recognize that they not only serve their enterprises but also act as stewards of society in creating, facilitating and executing the efficient and effective transactions that are part of the greater economy. In this role, marketers should embrace the highest ethical norms of practicing professionals and the ethical values implied by their responsibility toward stakeholders (e.g., customers, employees, investors, channel members, regulators and the host community).

General Norms

1. Marketers must do no harm. This means doing work for which they are appropriately trained or experienced so that they can actively add value to their organizations and customers. It also means adhering to all applicable laws and regulations and embodying high ethical standards in the choices they make.
2. Marketers must foster trust in the marketing system. This means that products are appropriate for their intended and promoted uses. It requires that marketing communications about goods and services are not intentionally deceptive or misleading. It suggests building relationships that provide for the equitable adjustment and/or redress of customer grievances. It implies striving for good faith and fair dealing so as to contribute toward the efficacy of the exchange process.
3. Marketers must embrace, communicate and practice the fundamental ethical values that will improve consumer confidence in the integrity of the marketing exchange system. These basic values are intentionally aspirational and include honesty, responsibility, fairness, respect, openness and citizenship.

Ethical Values

Honesty—to be truthful and forthright in our dealings with customers and stakeholders.
- We will tell the truth in all situations and at all times.
- We will offer products of value that do what we claim in our communications.
- We will stand behind our products if they fail to deliver their claimed benefits.
- We will honor our explicit and implicit commitments and promises.

Responsibility—to accept the consequences of our marketing decisions and strategies.
- We will make strenuous efforts to serve the needs of our customers.
- We will avoid using coercion with all stakeholders.
- We will acknowledge the social obligations to stakeholders that come with increased marketing and economic power.
- We will recognize our special commitments to economically vulnerable segments of the market such as children, the elderly and others who may be substantially disadvantaged.

can establish a process for decision making that ensures they choose ethical alternatives instead.

Why People Act Unethically   Every individual is a product of his or her culture, upbringing, genes, and various other influences. In spite of these factors, however, people do continue to grow emotionally in their understanding of what is and is not ethical behavior. As a six-year-old child, you might have thought nothing of taking your brother's toy and bonking him on the head with it; as an adult, you probably have outgrown this behavior. But all of us vary in the way we view more complex situations, depending on our ethical understandings.

Think again of Mattel's and others' product recalls we discussed at the beginning of the chapter. How can certain manufacturers engage in such egregious behavior as using lead paint on toys marketed toward young children? What makes people take actions that create so much harm? Are all the individuals who contributed to that behavior just plain immoral? These simple questions have complex answers.

In many cases, people must choose between desirable outcomes. For example, a brand manager for a car company discovers from conversations with a member of the development team that the hot new energy-efficient hybrid model that is set to go into full production shortly has a potentially dangerous design flaw. There are two options for the brand manager: delay production and remedy the design flaw, which pushes production off schedule, delays revenue, and may result in layoffs and loss of the manager's bonus, or stay on schedule, put the flawed design

EXHIBIT 3·3	continued

Fairness—to try to balance justly the needs of the buyer with the interests of the seller.

- We will represent our products in a clear way in selling, advertising and other forms of communication; this includes the avoidance of false, misleading and deceptive promotion.
- We will reject manipulations and sales tactics that harm customer trust.
- We will not engage in price fixing, predatory pricing, price gouging or "bait-and-switch" tactics.
- We will not knowingly participate in material conflicts of interest.

Respect—to acknowledge the basic human dignity of all stakeholders.

- We will value individual differences even as we avoid stereotyping customers or depicting demographic groups (e.g., gender, race, sexual orientation) in a negative or dehumanizing way in our promotions.
- We will listen to the needs of our customers and make all reasonable efforts to monitor and improve their satisfaction on an ongoing basis.
- We will make a special effort to understand suppliers, intermediaries and distributors from other cultures.
- We will appropriately acknowledge the contributions of others, such as consultants, employees and coworkers, to our marketing endeavors.

Openness—to create transparency in our marketing operations.

- We will strive to communicate clearly with all our constituencies.
- We will accept constructive criticism from our customers and other stakeholders.
- We will explain significant product or service risks, component substitutions or other foreseeable eventualities that could affect customers or their perception of the purchase decision.
- We will fully disclose list prices and terms of financing as well as available price deals and adjustments.

Citizenship—to fulfill the economic, legal, philanthropic and societal responsibilities that serve stakeholders in a strategic manner.

- We will strive to protect the natural environment in the execution of marketing campaigns.
- We will give back to the community through volunteerism and charitable donations.
- We will work to contribute to the overall betterment of marketing and its reputation.
- We will encourage supply chain members to ensure that trade is fair for all participants, including producers in developing countries.

Implementation

Finally, we recognize that every industry sector and marketing subdiscipline (e.g., marketing research, e-commerce, direct selling, direct marketing, advertising) has its own specific ethical issues that require policies and commentary. An array of such codes can be accessed through links on the AMA Web site (marketingpower.com).

into production, achieve planned revenues and bonus, and hope it does not result in injuries to consumers and loss of revenue for the firm due to recalls later on. This type of dilemma occurs nearly every day in thousands of different business environments.

When asked in a survey whether they had seen any unethical behavior among their colleagues, chief marketing officers responded that they had observed employees participating in high pressure, misleading, or deceptive sales tactics (45 percent); misrepresenting company earnings, sales, and/or revenues (35 percent); withholding or destroying information that could hurt company sales or image (32 percent); and conducting false or misleading advertising (31 percent).[12] Did all the marketers in these situations view their actions as unethical? Probably not. There may have been extenuating circumstances. In marketing, managers often face the choice of doing what is beneficial for them and possibly the firm in the short run and doing what is right and beneficial for the firm and society in the long run.

For instance, a manager might feel confident that earnings will increase in the next few months and therefore believe it benefits himself, his branch, and his employees to exaggerate current earnings just a little. Another manager might feel considerable pressure to increase sales in a retail store, so she brings in some new merchandise, marks it at an artificially high price, and then immediately puts it on sale, deceiving consumers into thinking they are getting a good deal because they viewed the initial price as the "real" price. These decisions may have been justifiable at the time, but have serious consequences for the company.

Throughout *Marketing*, we provide illustrations of how the Internet has changed the way firms market their products and services for the better, but unfortunately, the Internet has become fertile ground for scam artists and thieves, as the nearby Power of the Internet 3.1 explains.

Power of the Internet 3.1   Unethical Internet Behavior

Internet crime is big business, estimated at $3.6 billion per year. And there are many ways to steal. One of the most popular methods of committing fraud on the Internet is phishing, or sending e-mails falsely claiming to be a legitimate business soliciting information to scam users into surrendering private information that will be used for identity theft.[13] The e-mails direct users to visit a bogus Web site that looks like a real one, where they are asked to update personal information, such as passwords and credit card, social security, and bank account numbers, that the legitimate organization already has. The Web site is set up to steal the user's information. The phishing e-mails come from a variety of phoney sources including banks; auction sites set up to look like eBay or PayPal; or charities, both "real" and invented. It is estimated that more than 3.6 million adults lose money every year as a result of phishing.[14]

Another scam entails the use of gift cards. A criminal uses cash earned by illegal activity to buy phone or gift cards. The criminal then sells the cards at a discounted value on auction sites. Thieves also rip off gift card numbers while cards are on a store display. Then when the proper owner of the card tries to use it, the funds are already spent. To counter this activity, major retailers do not display gift cards, or activate them only at the time of purchase.

A notorious but easy method of scamming both buyers and sellers has been on auction sites. Sellers post stolen or nonexistent merchandise on the sites, but never ship it to the winner. This now is relatively rare, since experienced buyers know that they should check out the seller, and in the case of eBay, buy only from those with numerous positive feedbacks. Fraudulent buyers can play havoc with Internet auctions. One popular tactic is to get the seller to use a fictitious escrow company. Once the sale is consummated, the buyer supposedly sends payment to the fictitious escrow company. But the money is never sent. The escrow company notifies the seller that the money has "safely" arrived. Then the seller sends the merchandise to the buyer, but never gets paid.

What is the "real" price? Did the manager bring the T-shirts in at an artificially high level and then immediately mark them down?

To avoid dire consequences, the short-term goals of each employee must be aligned with the long-term goals of the firm. In our hybrid car example, the brand manager's short-term drive to receive a bonus conflicted with the firm's long-term aim of providing consumers with safe, reliable cars. To align personal and corporate goals, firms need to have a strong ethical climate, explicit rules for governing transactions including a code of ethics, and a system for rewarding and punishing inappropriate behavior.

In the next section, we add the concept of corporate social responsibility to our discussion of ethics.

Ethics and Corporate Social Responsibility

Corporate social responsibility refers to the voluntary actions taken by a company to address the ethical, social, and environmental impacts of its business operations and the concerns of its stakeholders.[15] This goes beyond the individual ethics that we've discussed so far, but for a company to act in a socially responsible manner, the employees of the company must also first maintain high ethical standards and recognize how their individual decisions lead to optimal collective actions of the firm. Firms with strong ethical climates tend to be more socially responsible.

However, it is important to distinguish between ethical business practices and corporate social responsibility programs. Ideally, firms should implement programs that are socially responsible, AND its employees should act in an ethically responsible manner. (See Exhibit 3.4, upper left quadrant.) But being socially responsible is generally considered to be above and beyond the norms of corporate ethical behavior. For example, a firm's employees may conduct their activities in an ethically acceptable manner but the firm may still not be considered socially

EXHIBIT 3·4	Ethics versus Social Responsibility	
	Socially Responsible	**Socially Irresponsible**
Ethical	Both ethical and socially responsible	Ethical firm not involved with the larger community
Unethical	Questionable firm practices, yet donates a lot to the community	Neither ethical nor socially responsible

responsible because their activities have little or no impact on anyone other than their closest stakeholders: their customers, employees, and stockholders (Exhibit 3.4, upper right quadrant). In this case, employees would not, for instance, be involved in volunteer activities to clean up a local park or coach the community's youth baseball league—socially responsible activities that improve the communities in which the company operates.

Employees at some firms that are perceived as socially responsible can nevertheless take actions that are viewed as unethical (Exhibit 3.4, lower left quadrant). For instance, a firm might be considered socially responsible because it makes generous donations to charities but is simultaneously involved in questionable sales practices. Ethically, how do we characterize a firm that obtains its profits through illicit actions but then donates a large percentage of those profits to charity? The worst situation, of course, is when firms behave both unethically AND in a socially unacceptable manner (Exhibit 3.4, lower right quadrant).

Consumers and investors increasingly appear to want to purchase products and services from and invest in companies that act in socially responsible ways. Large global corporations, such as Coca-Cola, have recognized that they must be perceived as socially responsible by their stakeholders to earn their business. As a bonus, Coca-Cola earns both tangible and intangible benefits for acting in a socially desirable manner by helping to keep its employees healthy and disease free (see Superior Service 3.1 on the next page).

Wal-Mart, which has been the subject of many allegations of unethical business practices—such as purposefully driving smaller competitors out of business or requiring employees to work overtime without additional pay—topped the *BusinessWeek* survey of corporate givers by donating $250 million in 2006. (The second and third places went to Bank of America and Disney, which donated $200 and $170 million, respectively.)[16] Such corporations, when planning their strategic initiatives, increasingly include socially responsible programs. But being a socially responsible corporation does not ensure that all members of the firm or all subunits within it will act ethically; it means that the firm is committing time and resources to good projects in the world or community that may not directly relate to generating profit. At the same time, some of the firm's practices may remain questionable.

An employee is acting in a socially responsible manner if he coaches the community's youth baseball team.

We cannot expect every member of a firm to always act ethically. However, a framework for ethical decision making can help move people to work toward common ethical goals.

A Framework for Ethical Decision Making

Exhibit 3.5 outlines a simple framework for ethical decision making. Let's consider each of the steps.

Step 1: Identify Issues　　The first step is to identify the issue. For illustrative purposes, we'll investigate the use (or misuse) of data collected from consumers by a marketing research firm. One of the issues that might arise is the way the data are collected. For instance, are the respondents told about the real purpose of the study?

Superior Service 3.1   Coca-Cola Fights HIV/AIDS in Africa

The Coca-Cola Africa Foundation was formed to reduce the impact of HIV/AIDS on Coca-Cola's 60,000 employees and those of 40 independent bottlers in Africa. At present, 100 percent of Coca-Cola's independent bottling companies in 54 African countries are enrolled in the foundation's programs. All employees and their families are eligible to receive benefits, including access to antiretroviral drugs, testing, counseling, prevention, and treatment. The foundation's outreach also extends beyond employees into the community.[17]

The Coca-Cola Africa Foundation focuses its efforts on three key areas that affect the communities in which Coca-Cola operates: health care, education, and the environment. The many projects supported by the foundation cost millions of dollars each year, but Coca-Cola offers more than just funding. By using its distribution network, one of the most extensive in Africa, Coca-Cola can transport vital materials to rural communities across the continent. It also is able to reach areas of Africa to which AIDS/HIV workers have not previously had easy access and thereby ensure that people in

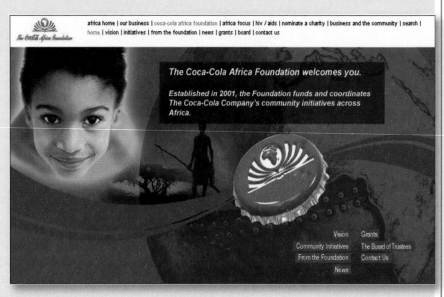

The Coca-Cola Africa Foundation provides millions of dollars each year to reduce the impact of HIV/AIDS on Coca-Cola's and independent bottlers' employees in Africa.

those areas can obtain information about the prevention and treatment of HIV/AIDS. Even Coca-Cola's marketing expertise is being used to raise awareness of key issues such as HIV prevention. By leveraging its corporate assets, Coca-Cola has made a positive contribution to African communities. They have expanded this program to India, China, and Russia.[18]

Another issue might be whether the results are going to be used in a way that might mislead or even harm the public, such as selling the information to a firm to use in soliciting the respondents.

Step 2: Gather Information and Identify Stakeholders In this step, the firm focuses on gathering facts that are important to the ethical issue, including all relevant legal information. To get a complete picture, the firm must identify all the individuals and groups that have a stake in how the issue is resolved.

Stakeholders typically include the firm's employees and retired employees, suppliers, the government, customer groups, stockholders, and members of the community in which the firm operates. Beyond these, many firms now also analyze the needs of the industry and the global community, as well as "one off" stakeholders, such as future generations, and the natural environment itself.

EXHIBIT 3.5   Ethical Decision-Making Framework

Step 1	Step 2	Step 3	Step 4
Identify issues	Gather information and identify stakeholders	Brainstorm and evaluate alternatives	Choose a course of action

EXHIBIT 3.6	Stakeholder Analysis Matrix for a Marketing Research Firm		
Stakeholder	**Stakeholders' Concerns**	**Result or Impact on the Stakeholder**	**Potential Strategies for Obtaining Support and Diminishing Impact**
The Public	■ Get inaccurate and biased results. ■ Publish false, misleading or out of context results.	■ Lose trust in marketing research professionals. ■ Lose trust in the marketing research process.	■ Report accurate results. ■ Report study context and methodology. ■ Comply with American Marketing Association's (AMA) Code of Ethics.
The Subjects/ Respondents	■ Invade privacy. Privacy will be compromised if they answer the survey. ■ Use marketing research as a guise to sell consumers goods or services.	■ Lose trust in the marketing research process. ■ Refuse to participate in future marketing research projects. ■ Provide incorrect information.	■ Comply with American Marketing Association's (AMA) Code of Ethics. ■ Protect respondents' confidential data. ■ Report aggregate rather than individuals' results.
The Client	■ Conduct research that was not needed. ■ Use an inadequate sample to generalize to their target market. ■ Disclose sensitive data to others.	■ Reduce their spending and reliance on marketing research. ■ Make marketing decisions without doing research or doing inadequate research.	■ Ensure that the marketing research vendor signs a confidentiality agreement. ■ Comply with American Marketing Association's (AMA) Code of Ethics.

Source: http://www.marketingpower.com (accessed September 1, 2008).

Exhibit 3.6 illustrates a stakeholder analysis matrix for our example.[19] Notice that each stakeholder has responsibilities to the others. In this case, the marketing researcher has ethical responsibilities to the public, the research subjects, and the client company, while the client has ethical responsibilities to the researcher, the subjects, and the public. Acknowledging the interdependence of responsibilities ensures that everyone's perspective is considered in the firm's decision making.

Step 3: Brainstorm Alternatives　After the marketing firm has identified the stakeholders and their issues and gathered the available data, all parties relevant to the decision should come together to brainstorm any alternative courses of action. In our example, these might include halting the market research project, making responses anonymous, instituting training on the AMA Code of Ethics for all researchers, and so forth. Management then reviews and refines these alternatives, leading to the final step.

Step 4: Choose a Course of Action　The objective of this last step is to weigh the various alternatives and choose a course of action that generates the best solution for the stakeholders using ethical practices. Management will rank the alternatives in order of preference, clearly establishing the advantages and disadvantages of each. It is also crucial to investigate any potential legal issues associated with each alternative. Of course, any illegal activity should immediately be rejected.

To choose the appropriate course of action, marketing managers will evaluate each alternative using a process something like the sample ethical decision-making metric in Exhibit 3.7 on the next page. The marketer's task here is to ensure that he or she has applied all relevant decision-making criteria and to assess his or her level of confidence that the decision being made meets those stated criteria. If the marketer isn't confident about the decision, he or she should reexamine the other alternatives.

EXHIBIT 3·7	Ethical Decision-Making Metric I							
				Confidence in Decision				
	Confident						Not Very Confident	
Criteria	1	2	3	4	5	6	7	
1. Have I/we thought broadly about any ethical issues associated with the decision that must be made?								
2. Have I/we involved as many people as possible who have a right to offer input or have actual involvement in making this decision and action plan?								
3. Does this decision respect the rights and dignity of the stakeholders?								
4. Does this decision produce the most good and the least harm to the relevant stakeholders?								
5. Does this decision uphold relevant conventional moral rules?								
6. Can I/we live with this decision alternative?								

Source: Adapted from Kate McKone-Sweet, Danna Greenberg, and Lydia Moland, "Approaches to Ethical Decision Making," Babson College Case Development Center, 2003.

By using such an ethical metric or framework, decision makers will include the relevant ethical issues, evaluate the alternatives, and choose a course of action that will help them avoid serious ethical lapses. Ethical & Societal Dilemma 3.1 illustrates how the ethical decision-making metric in Exhibit 3.7 can be used to make ethical business decisions.

CHECK YOURSELF

1. According to the American Marketing Association Code of Ethics, what are the six ethical values?
2. Identify the four stages in the ethical decision-making framework.

INTEGRATING ETHICS INTO MARKETING STRATEGY

Ethical decision making is not a simple process, though it can get easier as decision makers within the firm become accustomed to thinking about the ethical implications of their actions from a strategic perspective. In this section, we examine how ethical decision making can be integrated into the marketing plan introduced in Chapter 2. Exhibit 3.8 on page 99 summarizes the process, with an emphasis on identifying potential ethical pitfalls during each stage.

The questions vary at each stage of the strategic marketing planning process. For instance, in the planning stage, the firm will decide what level of commitment to its ethical policies and standards it is willing to declare publicly. In the implementation stage, the tone of the questions switches from "can we?" serve the market with the firm's products or services in an ethically responsible manner to "should we?" be engaging in particular marketing practices. The key task in the

Ethical and Societal Dilemma 3.1   A Questionable Promotion

Steve Jansen, the marketing manager for a retail store in a small town in the Midwest, received a notice about an upcoming promotion from the national chain to which his store belongs. The promotion is for a diet product called Lean-Blast, which targets women between the ages of 20 and 30. Jenna Jones, the celebrity who will be featured in the promotion, is a young actress who recently lost weight and transitioned from child star to adult actor. Jenna is very popular with younger girls, who still watch her early television series in reruns. The promotion is expected to generate a 30–40 percent increase in sales, and because LeanBlast has a high margin, the company looks for a sharp increase in revenue for this category. On the financial side, the promotion looks like a great opportunity for the store.

Recently, however, a local girl died from complications associated with an eating disorder. Her death at the age of 16 triggered a wide range of responses in the community to address eating disorders, as well as efforts to establish a healthier environment for young women.

Not only is Steve extremely nervous about the community's response to this campaign, he also is personally disturbed by the campaign because he knew the family of the girl who died. In addition, he has been thinking about his own adolescent daughters, who idolize Jenna, the celebrity endorsing the product. He wonders what his daughters' response will be to this campaign.

Using his training in ethical decision making, Steve sat down to evaluate his alternatives, beginning with identifying the various stakeholders that might be impacted by his decision. He came up with the following list: the employees, the shareholders, the customers, and the broader community. Each set of stakeholders has a different interest in the campaign and its outcome.

Steve then arrived at three possible alternatives:

1. Run the campaign as instructed.

2. Modify the campaign by stressing that products such as LeanBlast are to be used only by adult women who are overweight and only with the supervision of a medical professional.

3. Refuse to run this promotion in the local area.

Steve's next step was to evaluate each alternative through a series of questions similar to those in Exhibit 3.7:

Question 1: Have I thought about the ethical issues involved in my decision?

Steve feels confident that he has identified all the relevant ethical issues associated with this decision, so he gives this question a score of one.

Question 2: Do I need to include anyone else in the decision process?

Because this decision ultimately belongs to him, Steve feels the responsibility to make it, and he believes he has an adequate understanding of all affected parties' positions on the issue. He does not believe that additional input would assist his decision making. Again, he gives this question a score of one.

(Continued)

Ethical and Societal Dilemma 3.1

Question 3: Which of my alternatives respects the rights and dignity of the stakeholders and can be universally applied?[20]

In this case, Steve already has identified the relevant stakeholders as the local community, the customers, the employees, and the stockholders. The first alternative seems to violate the tenet of respect for persons, because many in the community will find the promotion offensive and contrary to the community's stated goals. The second alternative is an improvement over the first but still potentially offensive. Steve believes the third alternative—not running the promotion—is the right choice according to this criterion. Given this choice, he gives this question a score of one.

Question 4: Which alternative will produce the most good and the least harm?[21]

Using this criterion, the first alternative benefits those adult women who need and want LeanBlast. If the promotion achieves its projected revenues, it also benefits the employees and Steve, in that they will post above-average revenues in the category. The promotion also will draw traffic into the store and thereby increase storewide sales figures. However, the promotion harms those who have been affected by the recent tragedy, as well as those teenagers and young girls who would be drawn to the product in an attempt to emulate Jenna Jones's lean body image. Steve scores this alternative a six.

The second alternative requires that Steve supplement the promotion by spending extra funds to stress the proper use of products like LeanBlast, though it is not clear how effective the extra spending will be. Steve scores this alternative a four.

The third alternative costs the store the sales revenue it will lose by not participating in the promotion, and the national chain may assess Steve's store a penalty for failing to participate. The benefits of the third alternative are harder to quantify because most of them are social benefits. The costs, however, are very real in terms of lost revenue. Despite the potential loss, Steve scores this alternative a two.

Question 5: Do any of the alternatives violate a conventional moral rule?[22]

Here Steve has an even more difficult time. None of the alternatives violates a conventional moral rule; all fall within legitimate business practices. So, he gives this question a neutral four.

Question 6: Which alternatives can I personally live with?[23]

The first alternative is not one that Steve feels he can accept. He finds the choice of a young celebrity somewhat disturbing because her appeal is to a younger audience than the stated target market. Steve is forced to wonder whether the firm is trying to get younger women interested in its products. So, he gives this alternative a seven.

The second alternative is more acceptable to Steve, but he is still concerned about the impact of the promotion, regardless of any modifications he might make. He scores this alternative a neutral four.

Steve can most easily live with the third alternative of choosing not to run the promotion. This alternative is the one he can most easily justify and discuss with his family and friends. So, he gives this alternative a one.

On the basis of this exercise, Steve decides to call the national office to inform the parent company of his decision not to run the promotion in his store. Although Steve is extremely nervous while making this call, he is pleasantly surprised to hear that the national office also has been having some reservations about LeanBlast's choice of celebrity. Management clearly understands Steve's concerns about his community and in fact even offers to help Steve finance an educational session about eating disorders for his employees and the community. Steve decides that doing the right thing feels pretty good.

EXHIBIT 3.8   Ethical Issues and the Marketing Plan

Planning phase

•Does the firm want to include a commitment to ethics in its mission or vision statement?

•Is the firm prepared to support the development of an ethical climate that would maintain a strong ethical position?

Define the mission and/or vision

Perform a situation analysis

Implementation phase

•Should the firm be targeting this market with this product?

•Should the firm be relocating its production to another country?

•Should the firm be advertising its product in this market or in this manner?

•Should the firm be selling its product in this market or in this manner?

Identify and evaluate opportunities (segmentation, targeting & positioning)

Implement marketing mix and resources

Control phase

•Did any of the firm's actions have a negative impact on any stakeholder group?

•Are there any new circumstances that require a change in strategy to avoid an ethical issue?

•Is the firm prepared in the event of a potential ethical lapse?

Evaluate performance

control phase is to ensure that all potential ethical issues raised during the planning process have been addressed and that all employees of the firm have acted ethically. Let's take a closer look at how ethics can be integrated at each stage of the strategic marketing planning process.

Planning Phase

Marketers can introduce ethics at the beginning of the planning process simply by including ethical statements in the firm's mission or vision statements. Johnson & Johnson has its Credo; other firms use mission statements that include ethical precepts for shaping the organization. The mission statements from organizations such as The Body Shop and Ben & Jerry's Ice Cream are known for reflecting strong ethical perspectives. Even large firms such as General Mills provide a Code of Conduct Report that defines the priorities of the organization and its commitment to implanting those values in all that the firm does. Every year, General Mills issues a report discussing how the firm has performed against its own standards of ethical conduct. It also recently contributed $74 million in cash and products back to the communities in which it does business—more than 5 percent of its pretax profits.[24]

In addition, General Mills has announced it will be switching to whole grains in all its breakfast cereal lines, making it the first of the mass-marketed cereal manufacturers to do so. This switch has been applauded by nutritionists who claim it dramatically improves the dietary benefits of the cereals. General Mills made the switch not necessarily to increase consumer demand; rather, in keeping

General Mills is switching to whole grains in all of its breakfast cereal lines, which should improve the dietary benefits.

Adding Value 3.1   **Newman's Own: Making a Difference**[25]

Newman's Own began as a simple concept: The company would sell salad dressing in antique wine bottles with parchment labels and use the proceeds to benefit charities. In 1982, the founders of Newman's Own, actor Paul Newman and A. E. Hotchner, produced their first batch of salad dressing in Newman's basement to give as holiday gifts. When they also decided to check with a local grocer to see if it would be interested in the product, they found they could sell 10,000 bottles in two weeks. The rapid growth of Newman's Own surprised the founders, and the nonprofit organization quickly grew to include dozens of products, as well as a line of organic foods that Paul Newman's daughter, Nell Newman, would spin off on her own. Today, Newman's Own and Newman's Own Organic products are sold in 15 countries and include dozens of lines, from coffee to popcorn to dog food. Profits from Newman's Own—over $200 million since 1982—have been donated to thousands of charities, especially Newman's Hole in the Wall Gang camps for children with life-threatening diseases.

What about Newman's Own adding value? First, although not unique among food producers, Newman's Own is made of good, natural ingredients, and, of course, Newman's Own

Organics are organic. Unique to Newman's Own, however, are its association with the beloved actor, and that it gives all its profits to charity—the ultimate socially responsible act.

But not all of Newman's Own's success can be attributed to image or even to consumers who want something that reminds them of the man who played Butch Cassidy and Fast Eddie Felson. Some of Newman's Own's most popular items have resulted from partnerships with established companies, which allowed their well-known products to receive the "Newman's Own" touch. For example, Fig Newmans™ exists because a license from Kraft grants the company the right to use a name similar to Fig Newtons. In turn, Newman's Own licenses its brand for use on coffee and salad dressings at McDonald's. Associations with a firm with such a high profile mission as Newman's is beneficial to all.

The unique mission of the company and the entrepreneurial flair of the founders made this nonprofit a smashing, ongoing success. Employees of Newman's Own have the great satisfaction of giving back to society, various charities benefit from the donations, and customers enjoy good food with a clear conscience.

with its stated values, it improved its cereal products to improve the health of its consumers.[26]

During planning, ethical mission statements can take on another role as a means to guide a firm's SWOT analysis. Newman's Own (see Adding Value 3.1), for example, has what most of us would consider a simple but powerful mission statement.

Implementation Phase

An important element of continued commitment to a mission statement requires that the values stated in it remain consistent with the values of the company's primary target market. Sometimes, however, a firm's choice of target market for its products can lead to charges of unethical behavior. In segmenting a market, the marketer determines what aspects of the product, service, and overall marketing effort are important to particular groups of consumers. Groups may be responsive to the firm's efforts and still not represent an appropriate target market; thus, the firm can serve this market but should not.

When Turner Broadcasting, the parent company of the Cartoon Network, decided to advertise the *Aqua Teen Hunger Force* movie, it chose to use a nontraditional campaign to appeal to the rebellious instincts of its teenage target market. Instead of established media advertising, Turner Broadcasting hired a guerrilla marketing agency to put up LED light displays in 10 cities in the shape of a "Moonite," one of the characters featured in the television show and upcoming movie, with no other text or identification. The LED displays were placed near public transportation outlets and on several bridges to ensure they could be seen at night. In most cities, residents noted the displays and then gave them little further attention. But in Boston, worried residents mistook the cryptic devices for bombs and immediately notified the police, who responded by closing major roads and deploying canine and bomb squads. The police investigation cost the city of Boston $500,000, but it cost Turner Broadcasting far more. To settle any possible lawsuits, Turner paid the city of Boston $1 million and then sent another $1 million to the Department of Homeland Security as a show of goodwill. Turner Broadcasting wanted to market to its core audience—teenagers who would know exactly what the lighted character represented—but it failed to consider the ramifications of blinking lights and LED displays near public transportation venues in a city that had been touched deeply by the events of 9/11. If managers had thought through their strategy more fully, perhaps by using an ethical decision-making framework, they might have anticipated the potential for alarm in a post–9/11 world, or at least clearly communicated their ownership of the advertisement. Greater forethought could have helped Turner Broadcasting avoid an absurd problem that wound up costing it $2 million.[27]

When Procter & Gamble (P&G) teamed up with "tween" retailer Limited Too on a promotion featuring P&G's Secret Sparkle Body Spray, it promoted a contest open only to girls aged 7 to 14 years. But even as this group was being targeted, the Sparkle Body Spray product carried a warning label on its own packaging stating that it was to be kept out of children's reach. The spray also was being advertised in teen and tween magazines that attracted audiences under the age of 12 years.[28] Clearly, this promotion to young girls was inappropriate according to P&G's own labeling and was terminated when the Children's Advertising Review Unit of the Better Business Bureau stepped in and requested that P&G stop promoting the product to children. Had P&G considered all the potential ethical dilemmas at the implementation stage in its strategic marketing planning process, it might have avoided the issue of promoting spray to the same children it warned not to use the product.

The question of resource allocation in the implementation phase can also be an ethical minefield, and perhaps no business is more susceptible than the pharmaceutical industry.[29] For example, AIDS activists claim that pharmaceutical companies are not doing enough to develop affordable drugs for underdeveloped countries to treat AIDS among their poor citizens. Some public health officials also have sounded alarm bells about the lack of research into the next generation of antibiotics, at a time when bacteria continue to become increasingly resistant to existing drugs. Critics of the pharmaceutical industry can also point to the increasing number of "lifestyle" drugs, such as those for weight loss, wrinkles, male-pattern baldness, nail fungus, and such, as possible causes for the lack of new treatments for serious diseases, even though the pharmaceutical companies vehemently deny that they have been transferring assets from research on treatments for life-threatening illnesses to fund lifestyle drugs.

Turner Broadcasting advertised the movie Aqua Teen Hunger Force *using this LED light display. Mistaking the device as a bomb, Boston police closed roads and deployed canine and bomb squads. Had Turner used an ethical decision-making framework, it might have avoided a $2 million problem.*

During the last two decades, HIV/AIDS treatments and diagnostic testing kits have been developed in order to prevent the disease from getting worse. There are many implementation issues that arise with such advancements, such as how much the drugs should cost. If the drug is too expensive, then it is not accessible to those who can't afford it. Another issue that may arise is whether patients, rather than health-care providers, should be able to test whether they have a terminal disease. An HIV/ AIDS home-testing kit is very different from blood pressure kits, pregnancy tests, or cholesterol tests. Since HIV is a very serious illness, a positive test could cause a person to become severely depressed or even commit suicide. If counseling by a health-care professional is part of the process of telling a person that he or she is HIV/AIDS positive, then home-testing kits would not be marketable. [30]

Sourcing decisions are another problem area for some firms. Charges that they use sweatshop labor to produce their goods have been and continue to be made against many well-known companies. Locating production in an under-developed country can make economic sense, because it allows the company to take advantage of the lower production costs offered in poorer nations, but it also opens a Pandora's box of ethical issues, the most prominent of which deals with responsibility. Who is responsible for ensuring that the workers in the factories that produce the goods are treated fairly and paid a fair wage? Many firms, including Nike and Kmart, have had to face tough questioning from international labor rights organizations about the working conditions of employees making their products. Even the public faces of firms, such as Mary-Kate and Ashley Olsen and Kathy Lee Gifford, have been faulted for failing to take responsibility for the conditions in factories that produce products bearing their names. Environmental organizations have also joined the attack recently, noting that many overseas factories do not maintain the highest environmental standards.

Once the strategy is implemented, controls must be in place to be certain that the firm has actually done what it has set out to do. These activities take place in the next phase of the strategic marketing planning process.

Control Phase

During the control phase of the strategic marketing planning process, managers must be evaluated on their actions from an ethical perspective. Systems must be in place to check whether each potentially ethical issue raised in the planning process was actually successfully addressed. Systems used in the control phase must also react to change. The emergence of new technologies and new markets ensures that new ethical issues continually arise. Many firms have emergency response plans in place just in case they ever encounter a situation similar to the Tylenol tampering emergency or an industrial accident at a manufacturing plant. Ethics thus remains an ongoing crucial component of the strategic marketing planning process and should be incorporated into all the firm's decision making down the road.

CHECK YOURSELF

1. Should a marketing manager insist on assessing the ethics of a situation she or he is facing?
2. Identify one ethical issue that you might face in each of the three phases of a marketing plan.

UNDERSTANDING ETHICS USING SCENARIOS

In the final section of this chapter, we present a series of ethical scenarios designed to assist you in developing your skills at identifying ethical issues. There is no one right answer to the dilemmas below, just as there will be no correct answers to many of the ethical situations you will face throughout your career. Instead, these scenarios can help you develop your sensitivity toward ethical issues, as well as your ethical reasoning skills.

Exhibit 3.9 provides an alternative ethical decision-making metric to Exhibit 3.7 to assist you in evaluating these scenarios. By asking yourself these questions, you can gauge your own ethical response. If your scores there tend to be in the green area (1 and 2), then the situation *is not* an ethically troubling situation for you. If, on the other hand, your scores tend to be in the red area (6 and 7), it is ethically troubling and you know it. If your scores are scattered or in the yellow area, you need to step back and reflect on how you wish to proceed.

Scenario 1: R.J. Reynolds: Promotions to the Youth Market

Tobacco giant R.J. Reynolds sent a set of coasters featuring its cigarette brands and recipes for mixed drinks with high alcohol content to young adults, via direct mail, on their 21st birthdays (the legal age for alcohol consumption). The alcohol brands included in the recipes included Jack Daniels, Southern Comfort, and Finlandia Vodka. The reverse side of the coaster read, "Go 'til Daybreak, and Make Sure You're Sittin'." The campaign, called "Drinks on Us," clearly promoted abusive and excessive drinking. This campaign was eventually stopped because the cigarette company did not have permission to use the alcohol brands.

R.J. Reynolds is also producing candy- and fruit-flavored Camel cigarettes with names like Kauai Kolada, Twista Lime, Warm Winter Toffee, and Mocha Mint. These flavors were introduced in 1999, but have not been under strong enough fire from antismoking organizations for R.J Reynolds to stop marketing to young adults, the target market for these brands. A Harvard School of Public

EXHIBIT 3.9	Ethical Decision-Making Metric II							
		Decision						
		Yes		**Maybe**			**No**	
Test		1	2	3	4	5	6	7
The Publicity Test Would I want to see this action that I'm about to take described on the front page of the local paper or in a national magazine?								
The Moral Mentor Test Would the person I admire the most engage in this activity?								
The Admired Observer Test Would I want the person I admire most to see me doing this?								
The Transparency Test Could I give a clear explanation for the action I'm contemplating, including an honest and transparent account of all my motives, that would satisfy a fair and dispassionate moral judge?								
The Person in the Mirror Test Will I be able to look at myself in the mirror and respect the person I see there?								
The Golden Rule Test Would I like to be on the receiving end of this action and all its potential consequences?								

Source: Adapted from Tom Morris, *The Art of Achievement: Mastering the 7 Cs of Success in Business and in Life* (Kansas City, MO: Andrew McMeel Publishing, 2002); http://edbrenegar.typepad.com/leading_questions/2005/05/real_life_leade.html (accessed December 29, 2007).

Health study reported, "Flavored cigarettes can promote youth initiation and help young occasional smokers to become daily smokers by masking the natural harshness and taste of tobacco smoke and increasing the acceptability of a toxic product." Today tobacco companies spend $15.1 billion a year, or $41.5 million a day, on marketing. What should R.J. Reynolds do?[31]

Scenario 2: Victoria's Dirty Secret

Forest Ethics, a nonprofit environmental organization, launched a "Victoria's Dirty Secret" campaign against the lingerie store Victoria's Secret, protesting the enormous amount of paper used in its catalogs. The organization put full-page ads in magazines, chained themselves to stores, and faxed nasty letters to Victoria's Secret's corporate offices asking the company to use recycled paper or discontinue its catalog business. They became very "annoying," as the former COO of Limited Brands says, interrupting day-to-day operations. Forest Ethics even bought stock in the company so that its members could attend the shareholders' meeting to find out exactly what the company planned on doing in the future.

Victoria's Secret's catalog business generates more than $1 billion in sales, so eliminating the catalog business was not in the best interest of its shareholders. When the company tried to use recyclable paper, it found that it could not achieve the same quality glossy photos for the catalog. As a result, it did not change the paper that it used. The campaign lasted two years, yet its negative press did not have a negative effect on Victoria's Secrets' sales. If the company changes its mind and decides to stop printing catalogs, it would save the trees, but it might cause lost sales, and ultimately lost jobs. What should Victoria's Secret do?[32]

Scenario 3: Pregnant Teen TV Star

Jamie Lynn Spears, Britney Spears' younger sister, and the star of Nickelodeon's "Zoey 101," became pregnant at age 16, right before the fourth season. The story was front page news on every major tabloid, and the topic of water cooler gossip for quite some time.

The target audience for "Zoey 101" is 9–14-year-old children, especially girls. While there were rumors that the fourth season would be canceled, Nickelodeon decided to continue to air the show as planned. Should the show go on?[33]

Scenario 4: Who Is on the Line?

A California company, Star38, invented a computer program that allowed certain telephone users to avoid caller ID systems. For $19.99 per month and $0.07 per minute, a caller could log on to the company's Web site and type in the number he or she wanted to call, as well as the number he or she wanted to appear on the caller ID screen of the receiving phone. For an additional fee, the caller could create a name to appear along with the phony phone number. Star38 intended to sell its service to collection agencies, private detectives, and law enforcement agencies.

Is this an ethical business plan? Would your answer be the same if Star38 sold its services to any individual who signed up?

Marvin Smith, who runs a collection agency in Austin, Texas, is considering signing up for Star38. Should he?[34]

Scenario 5: West Virginia T-Shirts

A popular teen clothing retailer is selling a T-shirt for $22.50 picturing a map of West Virginia and the slogan: "It's All Relative in West Virginia." The governor of West Virginia has requested that the retailer remove the shirt from its stores and destroy all remaining inventory. In a letter to the president of the retail chain, the governor stated that this slogan is extremely offensive and perpetuates a negative stereotype of his state that undermines the state's efforts to portray the true spirit and values of its citizens.

The communications director for the retailer, in response to the governor's request, stated that the retailer had no plans to remove the shirt, a very popular item. He also stated that the retailer means no disrespect and in fact loves West Virginia. The retailer offers shirts depicting most of the 50 states, which it regards as a way of celebrating the states. By means of example, the communications director pointed to another T-shirt currently on sale: "New Hampshire: 40 Million Squirrels Can't Be Wrong."

Do you think the retailer's response to the governor was appropriate? Was the governor's request appropriate? What would you have done if you had been the retailer? Would your response be different if you knew that this retailer had previously been accused of using pornography in the marketing of its clothing?[35]

Scenario 6: Giving Credit Where Credit Isn't Due

A catalog retailer that carries home and children's items, such as children's furniture, clothing, and toys, was seeking a way to reach a new audience and stop the declining sales and revenue trends it was suffering. A market research firm hired by the cataloger identified a new but potentially risky market: lower-income single parents. The new market seemed attractive because of the large number of single parents, but most of these homes were severely constrained in terms of their monetary resources.

The research firm proposed that the cataloger offer a generous credit policy that would allow consumers to purchase up to $500 worth of merchandise on credit without a credit check, provided they signed up for direct payment of their credit account from a checking account. Because these were high-risk consumers, the credit accounts would carry extremely high interest rates. The research firm believed that even with losses, enough accounts would be paid off to make the venture extremely profitable for the catalog retailer.

Should the cataloger pursue this new strategy?

Scenario 7: The Jeweler's Tarnished Image

Sparkle Gem Jewelers, a family-owned and -operated costume jewelry manufacturing business, traditionally sold its products only to wholesalers. Recently however, Sparkle Gem was approached by the charismatic Barb Stephens, who convinced the owners to begin selling through a network of distributors she had organized. The distributors recruited individuals to host "jewelry parties" in their homes. Sparkle Gem's owners, the Billing family, has been thrilled with the revenue generated by these home parties and started making plans for the expansion of the distributor network.

However, Mrs. Billing just received a letter from a jewelry party customer, who expressed sympathy for her loss. Mrs. Billing was concerned and contacted the letter writer, who told her that Barb Stephens had come to the jewelry party at her church and told the story of Sparkle Gem. According to Stephens's story, Mrs. Billing was a young widow struggling to keep her business together after her husband had died on a missionary trip. The writer had purchased $200 worth of jewelry at the party and told Mrs. Billing that she hoped it helped. Mrs. Billing was stunned. She and her very much alive husband had just celebrated their 50th wedding anniversary.

What should Mrs. Billing do now?

Scenario 8: No Wonder It's So Good

Enjoy Cola is a new product produced by ABC Beverage and marketed with the slogan "Relax with Enjoy." Unlike other colas on the market, Enjoy does not contain caffeine and therefore is positioned as the perfect beverage to end the day or for a slow-paced weekend, and as a means to help consumers relax and unwind. The market response has been tremendous, and sales of Enjoy have been growing rapidly, especially among women.

ABC Beverage decided not to list on the ingredients label that Enjoy contains a small amount of alcohol because it is not required to do so by the government unless the alcohol content is more than 1 percent.

Mia Rodriguez, the marketing director for Enjoy, only recently learned that Enjoy contains small amounts of alcohol and is troubled about ABC's failure to disclose this information on the ingredients list. She worries about the impact of this omission on consumers who have alcohol sensitivities or those who shouldn't be consuming alcohol, such as pregnant women and recovering alcoholics.

What should Rodriguez do? What would you do in her position?

Scenario 9: Bright Baby's Bright Idea

Bartok Manufacturing produces a line of infant toys under the "Bright Baby" brand label. The Consumer Product Safety Commission (CPSC) recently issued a recall order for the Bright Baby car seat gym, a very popular product. According to the CPSC, the gym contains small parts that present a choking hazard. The CEO of Bartok Manufacturing, Bill Bartok, called an executive meeting to determine the firm's strategy in response to the recall.

Mike Henderson, Bartok's CFO, stated that the recall could cost as much as $1 million in lost revenue from the Bright Baby line. Noting that there had been no deaths or injuries from the product, just the *potential* for injury, Henderson proposed that the remaining inventory of car seat gyms be sold where there are no rules such as the CPSC's. Sue Tyler, the marketing director for Bartok, recommended that the product be repackaged and sold under a different brand name so that the Bright Baby name would not be associated with the product. Bartok, though a bit leery of the plan, agreed to go along with it to avoid the monetary losses.

What would you have recommended to the CEO?

Scenario 10: Money from Mailing Lists[36]

Sports Nostalgia Emporium sells autographed sports memorabilia online. Recently, the Director of Marketing, John Mangold, started using a mailing list he had purchased from Marketing Metrix, a marketing research firm that sells consumer information. Mangold relies on such purchased mailing lists to grow the company and sends printed catalogs to thousands of people each month. The mailing lists he gets from Marketing Metrix are much more effective than other mailing lists and generate almost twice as much revenue.

In a recent conversation with a sales representative from Marketing Metrix, Mangold discovered the reason its lists were so effective: Marketing Metrix tracks the online behavior of consumers and uses that information to create targeted lists. The mailing lists that Mangold has been using consist of consumers who visited the Web sites of Sports Nostalgia Emporium's competitors. Based on what he can discern, Mangold believes that these consumers are not aware that someone is collecting information about their online behavior, along with their names and addresses, and selling it to other firms.

Should Mangold continue to use the Marketing Metrix mailing list? If so, should he tell his new customers how he got their names and addresses? Do consumers need to give consent before firms can collect information about their behavior?

Scenario 11: The Blogging CEO[37]

David Burdick is the CEO of ACME Bubblegum, a successful public company. As one of the cofounders of the company, Burdick has enjoyed speaking and writing about the success of ACME Bubblegum for several years. Typically, he speaks at conferences or directly to the press, but recently, he has been blogging about his firm anonymously. Specifically, he defended a recent advertising campaign that was unpopular among consumers and pointedly attacked one of ACME Bubblegum's competitors. Burdick deeply enjoys his anonymous blogging and believes that none of his readers actually know that he works for ACME Bubblegum.

Should Burdick be allowed to praise his company's performance anonymously online? Should he be allowed to attack his competitors without disclosing his relationship with the company? How would you feel if the CEO of a company at which you shopped was secretly writing criticisms of his or her competition? How would you feel if you knew a writer for your favorite blog was actually closely involved in a company that the blog community discussed?

Summing Up

1. **Why do marketers have to worry about ethics?**

   The most important reason to worry about making ethically correct decisions is that it is simply the right thing to do! Being a part of an ethically responsible firm should be important to every employee, but it is particularly important to marketers because they interact most directly with customers and suppliers, which offers them a multitude of opportunities to be involved in ethical issues. It is often challenging to make ethically correct decisions because they can conflict with other personal or corporate objectives.

2. **What does it take for a firm to be considered socially responsible?**

   Individuals and firms can (and should) act ethically, but the outcome of their acts may not affect society in general. An ethical act may only affect the firm's immediate stakeholders, such as its employees, customers, and suppliers. To be socially responsible, a firm also must take actions that benefit the community in a larger sense, such as helping people who have been affected by a natural disaster like a hurricane.

3. **How should a firm make ethically responsible decisions?**

   First, firms can include ethics and social responsibility in their corporate mission. Second, they should institute policies and procedures to ensure that everyone working for the firm is acting in an ethically responsible manner. Third, firms can model their ethical policies after a well-established code of ethics like the one provided by the American Marketing Association. Fourth, when making ethically sensitive decisions, firms can utilize a metric such as Ethical Decision-Making Metric I, shown in Exhibit 3.7, or Ethical Decision-Making Metric II, shown in Exhibit 3.9.

4. **How can ethics and social responsibility be integrated into a firm's marketing strategy?**

   Firms should ensure that ethics and social responsibility issues are an integral part of their planning processes. Ethical and socially responsible considerations should be integrated into the firm's mission statement, as long as top management follows through and commits to supporting a strong ethical climate within the organization. When considering their marketing strategy, firms should ask not only "can we implement a certain policy?" but also "should we do it?" Finally, in the control phase, marketers must determine whether they truly have acted in an ethical and socially responsible manner. If not, they should make changes to the marketing strategy.

Key Terms

- business ethics, 87
- corporate social responsibility, 92
- ethical climate, 87
- marketing ethics, 87
- phishing, 92

Marketing Applications

1. Why are marketers likely to be faced with more ethical dilemmas than members of other functional areas, like finance, accounting, or real estate?

2. Develop an argument for why a children's toy manufacturer should build and maintain an ethical climate.

3. A pharmaceutical company gives generously to charities and sponsors cancer awareness programs. It also charges remarkably high prices and receives high margins for life-saving medications, mostly targeted toward elderly consumers. Evaluate this company from an ethical and social responsibility perspective.

4. A large U.S.-based dog food company is negotiating with a company in Korea to make a new line of organic dog food. The manufacturer wants a high-quality product at a reasonable cost but is concerned that the Korean workers will be underpaid and asked to work long hours in unpleasant conditions. Develop a stakeholder analysis matrix similar to that in Exhibit 3.6 to assess the impact of this decision on the relevant stakeholders.

5. Based on the dog food manufacturing scenario you developed for Question 4, provide responses to Ethical Decision-Making Metric I from Exhibit 3.7. Provide a rationale for your confidence score for each question.

6. A company that makes granola and other "healthy" snacks has the following mission statement: "Our goal is to profitably sell good-tasting, healthy products and to better society." Although its products are organic, they also are relatively high in calories. The company gives a small portion of its profits to the United Way. Evaluate the mission statement by using Ethical Decision-Making Metric II from Exhibit 3.9.

7. The granola company described in the previous question is thinking about starting an advertising campaign directed at children that would air on Saturday morning television. Explain why you think it should or should not do so by using the ethical decision-making metrics in both Exhibits 3.7 and 3.9. Which metric do you find more useful?

8. A health inspector found some rodent droppings in one batch of granola made by this same company. What should the company do? Base your decision on either of the ethical decision-making metrics in Exhibits 3.7 and 3.9, whichever you prefer.

Quiz Yourself

www.mhhe.com/
grewal2e

1. Johnson & Johnson's 1943 "Credo" was considered radical at the time because it:

   a. parodied the Communist Manifesto.
   b. proposed socialized medicine.
   c. put customers first.
   d. was issued by a general.
   e. sought to undermine American capitalism.

2. Recognizing that parents, children, teachers, staff, and taxpayers all have a vested interest in the problem of deteriorating school facilities, and then listening to each group's concerns, a school board would most likely next:

   a. identify issues of concern to lawmakers.
   b. assess the impact of their actions beyond the classroom.
   c. engage in brainstorming and evaluate alternatives.
   d. choose a course of action.
   e. all of the above

(Answers to these two questions are provided on page 623.)

Go to www.mhhe.com/grewal2e to practice an additional 11 questions.

Net Savvy

1. Perhaps no subdiscipline of marketing receives more scrutiny regarding ethical compliance than direct marketing, a form of nonstore retailing in which customers are exposed to and purchase merchandise or services through an impersonal medium such as telephone, mail, or the Internet.[38] Ethical

issues in direct marketing cover a broad spectrum because this means of selling is conducted through all forms of communication. The Direct Marketing Association (DMA) takes ethics very seriously and has numerous programs to ensure its member organizations comply with its Code of Ethics. Go to the Web site for the Direct Marketing Association (http://www. the-dma.org/). Click on "Advocacy Issues." How many different ways did you find that the DMA was involved in assisting consumers and the industry to create a more ethical marketplace?

2. An increasing number of firms are stating their strong commitment to corporate social responsibility initiatives. The Corporate Social Responsibility Newswire Service keeps track of these various initiatives and posts stories on its Web site about what various corporations are doing. Go to http://www.csrwire.com/ and choose one story. Write a description of the corporation and the initiative.

Chapter Case Study

WHOSE SIDE ARE YOU ON?[39]

Britt Smith was recently hired by a large architecture and engineering firm as an assistant account manager in the government contracts division. The firm specializes in building hospitals, schools, and other large-scale projects. Britt is excited to learn that she will be part of the marketing team that presents the firm's proposals to the clients. In this case the clients are primarily federal and state governmental agencies. The presentations are elaborate, often costing $50,000 or more to prepare. But the projects can be worth millions to the firm, so the investment is worth it. The firm has a solid record for building quality projects, on time, and the majority of the time within budget. The firm also has an impressive track record, being awarded government contracts an incredible 85 percent of the time. No other firm in the industry comes close to this record.

The first project Britt is assigned to is an enormous project to design a new military hospital complex. The team leader, Brian Jenkins, has stressed how crucial it is for the firm to land this contract. He hints that if the team is successful the members will be well compensated. In fact, Britt heard that the members of the winning team for the last contract this size each received a $10,000 bonus.

Not long after the project commences, Brian invites Britt to have lunch so they can get to know each other better. During lunch, a man approaches Brian and asks if he has received the information. The man says that he knows that with this information the firm is a sure winner. He also reminds Brian that he is due a bonus for getting such crucial information. After he leaves Brian explains that the man is George Miller, who was the former head of the division awarding the hospital contract. George has been helping Brian by talking to the decision team and getting information relevant to the bid. Brian explains that the information George has gathered about the internal discussions among the buying team will be what makes their proposal a clear winner, obviously good news for the team since a winning bid means bonuses are almost assured.

After lunch Britt looks at the firm's ethics manual that she was given just last week at a new employee orientation. Lobbying without disclosure and paying for insider information are clearly discussed as unethical practices in the manual. Yet Brian seemed perfectly comfortable discussing George's role with Britt.

Britt decides she should check with another team member about the use of insider information, so she asks Sue Garcia. Sue tells Britt that this kind of thing happens all the time. She jokes that most of the people in the division have at one time or another worked for the government. They all still know

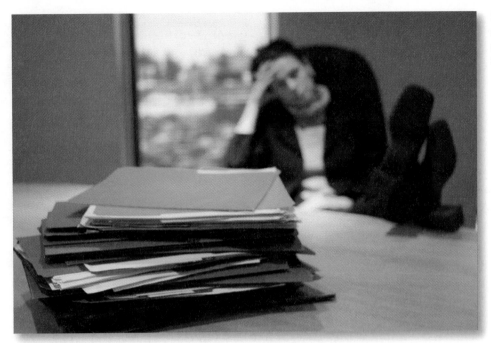

people in the various agencies. As far as Sue is concerned, friends will talk and that is not illegal, so there is no problem. It's a win–win situation: the government will get its building, the firm its funding, and the employees their bonuses.

Britt realizes that with her overdue credit card bill and her needed car repairs, the bonus money would really help out. Besides, she is the most junior member of the team. If all the others are comfortable with this practice, why should she be concerned? After all, it is just friends talking, isn't it?

Questions

1. Using the framework for ethical decision making presented in the chapter (Exhibit 3.5), analyze Britt's dilemma. Should she go to the company's ethics officer and report what she knows about the use of insider information?

2. Do you feel that Britt, as the most junior member of the team, has less of an ethical duty than more senior members of the team do? Why or why not?

3. If you were the ethics officer for this firm, would you address the belief among employees that it is acceptable to discuss a pending proposal with members of the decision team? If so, how? If you would not discuss this belief, why not?

4

section I

ANALYZING THE MARKETING ENVIRONMENT

LEARNING OBJECTIVES

- How do customers, the company, competitors, and corporate partners affect marketing strategy?

- Why do marketers have to think about their macroenvironment when they make decisions?

- How do corporate social responsibility programs help various stakeholders?

GE MONEY INTRODUCES EARTH REWARDS PLATINUM MASTERCARD CREDIT CARD

Companies such as GE are combining their mission and trends in the business environment to create new products that provide value for consumers and shareholders. In 2007, GE introduced the United States' first credit card designed to help consumers reduce pollution. In a crowded room at one of New York's most ecofriendly buildings, Seven World Trade Center, GE announced the latest addition to the ecomagination™ banner.[1] The "Earth Rewards" credit card is part of GE's plan to have $20 billion dollars in green sales by 2010.[2]

GE's commitment to helping the environment while improving its profitability is undeniable. In 2005, Jeffery Immelt, the CEO of GE, announced the "ecomagination" campaign to transform GE into a green company. In only one year, green projects contributed $12 billion to GE's sales. The new products range from aircraft engines that pollute less to energy-saving appliances and fluorescent lightbulbs. GE is also lobbying in Washington to create mandatory carbon regulations.

The new credit card reflects both GE's commitment to reducing consumer's carbon impact and the company's shrewd business acumen. GE hopes to combine U.S. consumers' escalating use of credit cards with their concern for the environment to create a product that provides new value for consumers. This initiative builds on GE's ecomagination™ initiative.[3]

When developing the "Earth Rewards" program, GE worked with the Pew Center on Global Change and World Resources Institute. The result was a comprehensive program that focuses on consumer education, improving socially responsible behavior at GE, and donations to high-impact environmental programs. To complement the card, GE created the My Earth Rewards Web site (http://www.myearthrewards.com) to support the new card. On the Web site consumers can calculate their carbon impact, read tips on reducing the amount of pollution they create, and learn about GE's efforts to reduce pollution. The "Earth Rewards" credit card lets consumers allocate up to 1 percent of their purchases toward initiatives that reduce carbon emissions, such as methane capture at landfills, renewable energy, and reforestation.[4] GE estimates that if an individual spends $750 dollars per month, the card will offset the average carbon impact of one U.S. consumer or about 10,000 pounds of carbon dioxide.[5]

Another way that GE is making the card more ecofriendly is by phasing out the use of paper. Instead of using paper applications, GE insists that consumers apply online or use the phone. Consumers are encouraged to receive electronic bill statements to reduce waste. And GE is committing to not using direct mail to connect with consumers. Instead it will advertise on ecofriendly Web sites, and use targeted Internet marketing such as advertisements on Google.[6]

GE is not alone in the field of carbon-friendly credit cards. Other financial institutions such as Bank of America, Barclay's Bank, and MBNA have also identified this trend and created cards to help consumers minimize their impact on the ecosystem or donate to wildlife preservation.

● ● ●

A MARKETING ENVIRONMENT ANALYSIS FRAMEWORK

As the opening vignette of this chapter suggests, marketers have become more aware of recent changes in what their customers want with regard to environmentally friendly products and have adapted their product and service offerings accordingly. By paying close attention to customer needs and continuously monitoring the business environment in which the company operates, a good marketer can identify potential opportunities.

Exhibit 4.1 illustrates the factors that affect the marketing environment, whose centerpiece, as always, is consumers. Consumers may be influenced directly by the immediate actions of the focal company, the company's competitors, and the corporate partners that work with the firm to make and supply products and services to consumers. The firm, and therefore consumers indirectly, is influenced by the macroenvironment, which includes various influences from culture and demographics, as well as social, technological, economic, and political/legal factors. We'll discuss each of these components in detail in this chapter and suggest how they might interrelate.

As illustrated in Exhibit 4.1, the consumer is the center of all marketing efforts. One of the goals of value-based marketing is to provide greater value to consumers than competitors offer. This provision requires that the marketing firm look at the entire business process from a consumer's point of view.[7] Consumers' needs and wants, as well as their ability to purchase, are affected by a host of factors that change and evolve over time. Firms use a variety of tools to keep track of their competitors' activities and communicate with their corporate partners.

EXHIBIT 4.1   Understanding the Marketing Environment

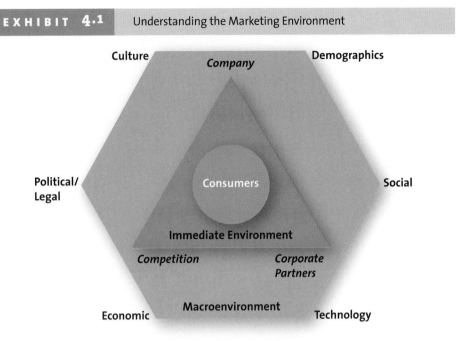

Furthermore, they monitor their macroenvironment to determine how such factors influence consumers and how they should respond to them. Sometimes, a firm can even anticipate trends.

For example, food products manufacturers have done an excellent job of monitoring consumers and responding to their needs and market trends. They have reacted to the desires of their customers to eat more healthy foods by providing new and improved products that are lower in calories, fat, and sodium, while at the same time higher in fiber.

THE IMMEDIATE ENVIRONMENT

Exhibit 4.2 on the next page illustrates the factors affecting consumers' immediate environment: the company's capabilities, competitors, and competitive intelligence, and the company's corporate partners.

Successfully Leveraging Company Capabilities

In the immediate environment, the first factor that affects the consumer is the firm itself. Successful marketing firms focus their efforts on satisfying customer needs that match their core competencies. The primary strength of Pepsi, for instance, rests in the manufacture, distribution, and promotion of carbonated beverages, but it has successfully leveraged its core competency in the bottled water arena with its Aquafina brand after recognizing the marketplace trend toward and consumer desire for bottled water. Marketers can use an analysis of the external environment, like the SWOT analysis described in Chapter 2, to categorize an opportunity as either attractive or unattractive and, if it appears attractive, to assess it relative to the firm's existing competencies.

Competitors and Competitive Intelligence

Competition also significantly affects consumers in the immediate environment. It is critical that marketers understand their firm's competitors, including their strengths, weaknesses, and likely reactions to marketing activities that their own firm undertakes. Firms use competitive intelligence (CI) to collect and synthesize information about their position with respect to their rivals. In this way, CI enables companies to anticipate changes in the marketplace rather than merely react to

EXHIBIT 4.2   Understanding the Immediate Environment

them.[8] It is estimated that the top 1,000 U.S. companies now spend about $1 billion a year on CI and will raise that to $10 billion over the next five years.[9]

The strategies for gathering CI can range from simply sending a retail employee to a competitor's store to check merchandise, prices, and foot traffic to more involved methods, such as

■ Reviewing public materials including Web sites, press releases, industry journals, annual reports, subscription databases, permit applications, patent applications, and trade shows.

■ Interviewing customers, suppliers, partners, or former employees.

■ Analyzing a rival's marketing tactics, distribution practices, pricing, and hiring needs.

These more sophisticated CI strategies are implicitly obvious in the modern razor market. Although men and women have been shaving for thousands of years, it wasn't until 1901 that anyone tried to sell a disposable, thin piece of metal sharp enough to shave hair. In its first year of production, the Gillette Safety Razor Company, as it was known then, sold 50 razor sets. The following year it sold 12 million—obviously, the company correctly anticipated a need and market trend. Today, American men spend almost $2 billion annually on razors and blades.

Gillette, the U.S. market leader, changed the landscape again by launching the enormously successful Mach3, a three-blade razor.[10] Not to be outdone, Schick, owned by Energizer Holdings introduced the Quattro razor, the world's first four-blade razor. The resulting battle for the title of "best razor" and for market share has resulted in a costly promotional and pricing battle. Razors that normally retail for up to $10 are being given away for free, and coupons for the corresponding razor blades appear everywhere.[11] In situations such as this, it becomes critical for firms like Gillette and Schick to keep close tabs on each other's activities using CI techniques. If Schick hadn't paid attention to the release of the Mach3, it might never have introduced the Quattro.

Although CI is widely regarded as a necessary function in today's world, certain methods of obtaining information have come under ethical and legal scrutiny. Take for example Gillette's case against Schick. Within hours of the press release introducing the Quattro, Gillette had filed a patent infringement lawsuit, claiming that the Quattro violates its Mach3 system's technology patent.[12] To have filed the suit so

Who copied whom? Gillette and Schick introduced similar razors almost simultaneously.

quickly, Gillette must have known about the impending launch well before Schick announced it, but how the company found out forms the core of the ethical question. According to the court papers that Gillette filed two weeks later, "a company engineer shared the results of scientific tests conducted on 10 Quattro cartridges obtained by the company." Schick quickly questioned how Gillette obtained the cartridges prior to their commercial release. Was it done in an ethically appropriate manner? But Schick's ethical argument apparently held little sway, as the U.S. Appeals Court ruled that Gillette's patent could extend to four or even five blades and was not limited to the number of blades currently installed in the Mach3.[13] Despite this ruling, Gillette and Schick continue to compete head-to-head. Gillette released the manual and battery-operated Fusion, one-upping the Quattro with five blades. Schick, in anticipation of the Fusion, created three stylized versions of the Quattro, the Schick Quattro Chrome, Midnight, and Power, to appeal to shavers on a more aesthetic level.[14]

Corporate Partners

The third factor that affects consumers in their immediate environment is the firm's corporate partners. Few firms operate in isolation. For example, automobile manufacturers collaborate with suppliers of sheet metal, tire manufacturers, component part makers, unions, transport companies, and dealerships to produce and market their automobiles successfully. Even firms like Dell, which makes its own computers and sells them directly to customers, must purchase components, consulting services, advertising, and transportation from others. Those parties that work with the focal firm are its corporate partners.

Let's consider an example that demonstrates the role these partners play and how they work together with the firm to create a single, efficient manufacturing system. Nau, which makes outdoor and ski clothing from renewable sources such as corn and recycled plastic bottles, is an example of a new type of ecofriendly company. Nau was founded by a team of entrepreneurs who left companies such as Nike and Patagonia. Most outdoor clothing manufacturing uses synthetic materials that are not renewable. Nau saw its challenge as how to develop clothing from sustainable materials that were rugged and beautiful, even though most sustainable materials are neither. The company's founders turned to its manufacturing partners around the world to develop new fabrics, such as PLA (polyactic acid), a fast-wicking biopolymer made from corn. To complement the new fabrics, the company ensures that it uses only organic cotton and wool from "happy sheep" provided by its partners in the ranching industry that embrace animal-friendly practices. Companies like Nau represent the cutting edge of sustainability and green business, and they also clearly show how "going green" prompts companies to work with their partners in innovative ways.[15]

Nau, a manufacturer of outdoor and ski clothing made from renewable sources, partners with its suppliers to develop new fabrics.

CHECK YOURSELF

1. What are the components of the immediate environment?

MACROENVIRONMENTAL FACTORS

In addition to understanding their customers, the company itself, their competition, and their corporate partners in the immediate environment, marketers must also understand the macroenvironmental factors that operate in the external environment, namely, the culture, demographics, social issues, technological advances, economic situation, and political/regulatory environment, or CDSTEP, as shown in Exhibit 4.3.

Culture

We broadly define culture as the shared meanings, beliefs, morals, values, and customs of a group of people.[16] Transmitted by words, literature, and institutions, culture gets passed down from generation to generation and learned over time. You participate in many cultures: Your family has a cultural heritage, so perhaps your mealtime traditions include eating rugelach, a traditional Jewish pastry, or sharing corned beef and cabbage to celebrate your Irish ancestry on St. Patrick's Day. Your school or workplace also shares its own common culture. In a broader sense, you also participate in the cultural aspects of the town and country in which you live. The challenge for marketers is to have products or services identifiable by and relevant to a particular group of people. Our various cultures influence what, why, how, where, and when we buy. Two dimensions of

EXHIBIT 4·3 The Macroenvironment

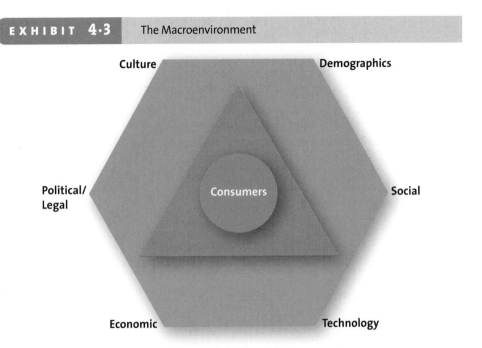

Culture

Demographics

Political/
Legal

Consumers

Social

Economic

Technology

culture that marketers must take into account as they develop their marketing strategies are the culture of the country and that of a region within a country.

Country Culture The visible nuances of a country's culture, such as artifacts, behavior, dress, symbols, physical settings, ceremonies, language differences, colors and tastes, and food preferences, are easy to spot. But the subtle aspects of culture generally are trickier to identify and navigate. BMW's Mini and other global automobile manufacturers have successfully bridged the cultural gap by

Some firms like BMW's Mini have successfully bridged the cultural gap by producing advertising that appeals to the same target market across countries.

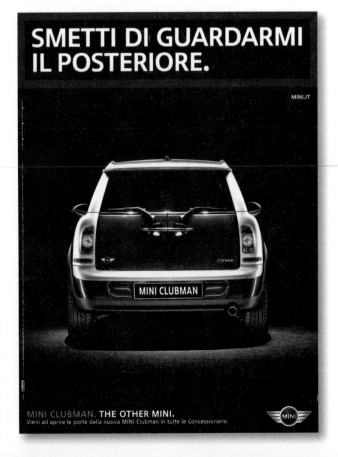

producing advertising that appeals to the same target market across countries. The pictures and copy are the same. The only thing that changes is the language.

Regional Culture   The region in which people live in a particular country affects the way they refer to a particular product category. For instance, 38 percent of Americans refer to carbonated beverages as "soda," whereas another 38 percent call it "pop," and an additional 19 percent call any such beverage a "Coke," even when it is Pepsi. Eat lunch in Indiana, and you'll have the best luck ordering a "pop" from the Midwesterner who owns the restaurant, but if you then head to Atlanta for dinner, you'd better order your "Coke," regardless of the brand you prefer. Head to Massachusetts, and the term is "soda," but if you move to Texas, you might be asked if you'd like a Dr Pepper—a generic term for carbonated beverages in the Lone Star state because it was first formulated there in 1885.[17] Imagine the difficulty these firms have in developing promotional materials that transcend these regional boundaries.[18]

Demographics

Demographics indicate the characteristics of human populations and segments, especially those used to identify consumer markets. Typical demographics such as age—which includes generational cohorts—gender, race, and income are readily available from market research firms like ACNielsen or the U.S. Census Bureau. For instance, Nielsen collects information about television viewership and sells it to TV networks and potential advertisers. The networks then use this information to set their advertising fees, whereas advertisers use it to choose the best shows on which to advertise. For a show popular among the desirable 18- to 35-year-old viewing segment, a network can charge the highest fees. But advertisers also might want to know whether a show is more popular with women than men or with urban or rural viewers. Armed with such information, advertisers ensure that viewers of Monday Night Football likely see more ads for beer and razors—products that speak largely to the game's mostly male demographic—whereas ads during daytime soap operas tend to feature cleaning products and diapers to appeal to the stay-at-home moms who often watch such shows. Demographics thus provide an easily understood "snapshot" of the typical consumer in a specific target market.

In the next few sections, we examine how firms use such demographics to assess their customers' needs and desires for merchandise and services and position themselves to deliver better value to those customers.

Marketers position their products and services differently, depending on which generational cohort they are targeting.

Generational Cohorts   Consumers in a *generational cohort*—a group of people of the same generation—have similar purchase behaviors because they have shared experiences and are in the same stage of life. For instance, Baby Boomers (people born after World War II, 1946–1964) and Generation Xers (people born between 1965 and 1976) both gravitate toward products and services that foster a casual lifestyle; however, they tend to do so for different reasons.[19] The aging Baby Boomers, who grew up with jeans and khakis and brought casual dressing into the business arena, are often trying to maintain their youth. Xers, in contrast, typically wear jeans and khakis because they are less impressed with the symbols of conspicuous consumption that their parents seem to have embraced. Although there are many ways to cut the generational pie, we discuss five major groups, as shown in Exhibit 4.4.

Seniors   Seniors make up America's fastest-growing group. But just because they are a large and growing segment, are they necessarily an important market segment

EXHIBIT **4·4**	Generational Cohorts				
Generational Cohort	**Tweens**	**Gen Y**	**Gen X**	**Baby Boomers**	**Seniors**
Range of Birth Years	1996–2000	1977–1995	1965–1976	1946–1964	Before 1946
Age in 2009	9–13	14–32	33–44	45–63	64 and older

for marketers to pursue? They're more likely to complain, need special attention, and take time browsing before making a purchase compared with younger groups. However, they generally have time to shop and money to spend.

Seniors also are the fastest-growing segment of Internet users;[20] 32 percent of people older than 65 years use the Internet.[21] When they are online, seniors are more likely to engage in activities that require capital, such as banking and investing, making hotel reservations, or purchasing products. Perhaps most surprisingly, 90 percent of all seniors with access to the Internet use e-mail and are just as likely as younger cohorts to gather their news, conduct product research, and use a photo service online.

However, seniors also tend to stick with older technologies and activities and are less likely to use the Internet for recreation. Rarely do seniors play online games, use instant messaging, or read blogs.[22] Similarly, few of them show up on such youth-oriented sites as Facebook or run up big cell phone bills texting their friends.

With their greater amounts of disposable income and time, what do seniors spend their money on? Travel, second homes, luxury cars, electronic equipment, investments, home furnishings, and clothing are frequent purchases.

Specifically, seniors like "made in the USA" items, natural fibers, recognizable brand names (but generally not designer labels), value, quality, and classic styles. They're typically loyal and willing to spend but also are extremely quality conscious and demand hassle-free shopping and convenient locations. Because most mature customers don't need the basics, they prefer to buy a few high-quality items rather than a large number of low-quality items.[23] Can you see how important it is for marketers to understand these facts about seniors?

Many seniors who live alone and on fixed incomes can fall prey to unscrupulous marketing practices. Marketers who offer promises of high-yield returns, "safe" investments, and even wonder cures find a vulnerable market in seniors. Some marketers prey on seniors' isolation and loneliness by "befriending" them and using that relationship to encourage the purchase of unnecessary products and services. A music store in Florida, for example, sold 11 different organs to an elderly woman suffering from Alzheimer's in the span of 18 months. According to another customer, a man whose fourth organ is worth more than his home, "What they do is, they get you involved, and they establish a sort of camaraderie . . . They have these socials and get-togethers, and they get real friendly," after which the sales staff engages in high-pressure tactics to get seniors to buy yet another organ, using financing provided by the music company.[24] Many states now have divisions within the state's attorney general's office to protect seniors from these abusive marketing practices. (See Ethical and Societal Dilemma 4.1 on the next page.)

Baby Boomers After World War II, the birth rate in the United States rose sharply, resulting in a group known as the Baby Boomers, the 78 million Americans born between 1946 and 1964. Although the Baby Boomer generation spans 18 years, experts agree that its members share several traits that set them apart from those born before World War II. First, they are individualistic. Second, leisure time represents a high priority for them. Third, they believe that they will always be able to

Ethical and Societal Dilemma 4.1 Predatory Lenders Target Seniors

Consumers with poor credit ratings usually have access to financing only through what are termed subprime lenders.[25] These lenders serve these riskier consumers with higher-than-market-rate loans. For many consumers who have declared bankruptcy or have fallen on financial hard times, these lenders provide a needed service. The dilemma for those providers who are ethical and honest in providing loans to risky consumers is that there are many in the subprime market who use deceptive or aggressive marketing practices to make loans. Often these loans contain high fees and hidden costs, in addition to higher-than-market rates of interest,

Seniors often fall prey to unscrupulous marketers.

and are considered to be predatory loans. Many of these unscrupulous lenders target senior citizens, recent immigrants, or other vulnerable populations.

A recent California study found that seniors targeted through very aggressive marketing and sales tactics did not seek the subprime lender out but were instead contacted by the lender, often repeatedly through the mail, by phone, and even in person through door-to-door solicitation. Elderly females seem especially prone to these tactics.

Two-thirds of the loans reviewed in the California study were found to be predatory: They contained onerous fees and penalties. Often the result of these loans is that the seniors lose the only large asset they have—their home. Attorneys general in California, Michigan, Rhode Island, and other states are now aggressively pursuing predatory lenders as well as educating seniors and other at-risk populations about these practices.

take care of themselves, partly evinced by their feeling of economic security, even though they are a little careless about the way they spend their money. Fourth, they have an obsession with maintaining their youth. Fifth and finally, they will always love rock 'n roll.

The Baby Boomers' quest for youth, in both attitude and appearance, provides a constantly growing market. Boomers spend $30 billion per year on antiaging products and have reenergized businesses ranging from food and cosmetics to pharmaceuticals and biotechnology.[26] Salon services used to be a purely feminine domain, but with Boomers turning 50 at the rate of seven per minute, salon services are recognizing the potential of positioning themselves as being in the rejuvenation business for both sexes.

The Baby Boomer cohort, which popularized personal fitness, also seeks to maintain their mental acuity as they age. To meet this demand, firms are introducing new products and services that help defy what are thought to be the mental effects of aging. A growing number of computer programs, including Nintendo's Brain Age, which has sold more than 10 million copies, promise to rejuvenate minds by exposing users to problem-solving exercises.[27] As Baby Boomers continue to age, the number and variety of age-defying products likely will continue to grow.

As they grow older, Baby Boomers shape the face of business, and their needs create new industries. As they move toward retirement, many Boomers are realizing that they have not saved enough for what may be a 30-year retirement. According to the Employee Benefit Research Group Institute, 32 percent

No matter how old they get, Baby Boomers will always love rock 'n roll.

of all employees aged 55 years or older have less than $25,000 in savings. To respond to this trend, lenders are creating new forms of loans, such as reverse mortgages that convert home equity into a steady stream of income. Typically these loans do not have to be repaid until the homeowner dies, moves permanently, or sells the home. In 2000, there were 6,000 reverse mortgages. By 2007, that number rose to 107,000 as Boomers began jumping at an opportunity to remain self-sufficient.[28]

Generation X   The next group, Generation X (Xers), includes those born between 1965 and 1976 and represents some 41 million Americans.[29] Vastly unlike their Baby Boomer parents, Xers are the first generation of latchkey children (those who grew up in homes in which both parents worked), and 50 percent of them have divorced parents.

Although fewer in number than Generation Y or Baby Boomers, Gen Xers possess considerable spending power because they tend to get married later and buy houses later in life. They're much less interested in shopping than their parents and far more cynical, which tends to make them astute consumers. They demand convenience and tend to be less likely to believe advertising claims or what salespeople tell them. Because of their experience as children of working parents, who had little time to shop, Xers developed shopping savvy at an early age and knew how to make shopping decisions by the time they were teenagers. As a result, they grew more knowledgeable about products and more risk averse than other generational cohorts. Finally, Xers are much less interested in status products than older generations, not because they can't afford luxury brands but because they just don't see the point. They ask, "Why shop at Neiman Marcus when Kohl's and Target are just as good, cheaper, and more convenient?"

Generation Y   With 60 million members in the United States alone, Generation Y is more than three times the size of Generation X and the biggest cohort since the original postwar baby boom. This group also varies the most in age, ranging from teenagers to young adults who have their own families.[30] Now that Gen Y is entering the workplace, it is becoming apparent that its members have different expectations and requirements than those of other cohorts. Gen Y puts a strong emphasis

Multitasking is no big deal for Gen Y.

on balancing work and life—these young adults want a good job, but they also want to live in a location that supports their lifestyle. According to one recent survey, 65 percent of 24- to 35-year-old respondents would choose a job according to its location rather than taking the best job they could find and being forced to live in a mediocre city.[31]

In another shift from previous generations, Gen Yers see no shame in moving back in with their parents after they graduate from college. Approximately 60 percent of college seniors cite their strong connection to their Baby Boomer parents and their warm feelings toward home as perfectly reasonable excuses to spend a few more years under their parents' roof. Their parents are finding this trend a bit shocking, especially because, when these children were younger, 40 percent claimed that they would be better off without parents. Exhibit 4.5 provides some interesting comparisons between Baby Boomers and their children in two different cohorts—Generation X and Generation Y.

Tweens Tweens—not quite teenagers, but not young children either—sit in beTWEEN. The importance of Tweens to marketers stems from their immense buying power, estimated to be $260 billion annually in the United States alone. Marketers feel the Tween effect in many areas, but particularly in the cell phone market. Tween users make great use of advanced features such as Web surfing, photo capabilities, and texting. Although smartphones such as the BlackBerry and the Treo historically targeted business users, companies today recognize the massive market for features these products possess among the Tween segment. Companies are also learning from their mistakes. When faced with the child-centric phone from AT&T that reduced features to basic calling, Tweens turned away in disgust. Tweens do not want to be treated like babies, and a phone that looked like it was made for a child was very unpopular, forcing AT&T to take it off the market.

Since Tweens are the first generation born after the emergence of the Internet, technology has no novelty for them. They communicate with friends via instant messaging while talking on a cell phone and flipping through television channels, all simultaneously. As a result, marketers are inventing increasingly innovative ways to reach them through the Internet. Marketers must be careful with this cohort though; once they get bored, Tweens are gone, off doing something else. So firms need to engage them quickly and with sincerity.

And what do Tweens like? In the food industry, they lean toward products like Heinz's green ketchup and Yoplait's GoGURT. For toys and clothing, they have made Club Libby Lu, Justice (owned by Tween brands), Hollister, and Claire's immensely popular.

EXHIBIT 4.5	Generational Cohort Comparisons	
Baby Boomers	**Generation X**	**Generation Y**
Diversity as a cause	Accept diversity	Celebrate diversity
Idealistic	Pragmatic/cynical	Optimistic/realistic
Mass movement	Self-reliant/individualistic	Self-inventive/individualistic
Conform to the rules	Reject rules	Rewrite the rules
Killer job	Killer life	Killer lifestyle
Became institutions	Mistrust institutions	Irrelevance of institutions
TV	PC	Internet
Have technology	Use technology	Assume technology
Task-technology	Multitask	Multitask fast
Ozzie and Harriet	Latchkey kids	Nurtured

Income   Income distribution in the United States has grown more polarized—the highest-income groups are growing, whereas many middle- and lower-income groups' real purchasing power keeps declining. Wealth among the top 1 percent of the American population is growing much faster than that of other groups. Income growth for the top 1 percent of the U.S. population is greater than the combined incomes of the bottom 20 percent of the population. The total income of the top 3 million Americans equals the income of the 166 million Americans at the bottom of the income pyramid.[32] The increase in wealthy families may be due to the maturing of the general population, the increase in dual-income households, and the higher overall level of education. It also may prompt some ethical concerns about the distribution of wealth. However, the broad range in incomes creates marketing opportunities at both the high and low ends of the market.

Although some marketers choose to target only affluent population segments, others have had great success delivering value to middle- and low-income earners. Consider, for example, the toys presented by the specialty retailer Hammacher Schlemmer versus the mass appeal of Wal-Mart's everyday low prices (EDLP), which has made it the world's largest toy retailer. Toy buyers at Wal-Mart are looking for inexpensive products; those at Hammacher Schlemmer go to great lengths to find exclusive, one-of-a-kind products, like the motorized water cannon pictured below right.[33]

Watch out for Tweens. They are fast, multitasking, technology savvy, and easily bored.

Another aspect of the income demographic relates to the concept of value. Why are customers searching for value more today than in recent decades? During the first three decades after World War II, most American families experienced real income growth, but in the late 1970s through early 2000s, that growth began to stagnate. Family incomes have stayed slightly ahead of inflation (the general rate of price increases), but their health care costs, property taxes, and tuition bills have risen much faster than inflation.

Education   Studies show that higher levels of education lead to better jobs and higher incomes.[34] (See Exhibit 4.6.) According the U.S. Bureau of Labor Statistics, employment that requires a college or secondary degree will account for 42 percent of projected job growth between 2000 and 2010. Moreover, average annual earnings are higher for those with degrees than for those without. Those who did not graduate from high school have an average annual salary of $18,083; high school grads earn $26,104; those with a bachelor's degree earn $42,087.[35]

This water cannon electric boat from Hammacher Schlemmer is a rechargeable electric watercraft powerful enough for riders to navigate lakes and ponds for up to six hours per charge, and it has a built-in motorized water cannon that can continuously spray a stream of water up to 35'. It can be yours for only $1995.95.

For some products, marketers can combine education level with other data like occupation and income and obtain pretty accurate predictions of purchase behavior. For instance, a full-time college student with a part-time job may have relatively little personal income but will spend his or her disposable dollars differently than would a high school graduate who works in a factory and earns a similar income. College students tend to play sports and go to nightclubs, whereas high school graduates are more likely watch sports and go to bars. Marketers need to be quite cognizant of the interaction among education, income, and occupation.

Gender   Years ago, gender roles appeared clear, but those male/female roles have been blurred. This shift in attitude

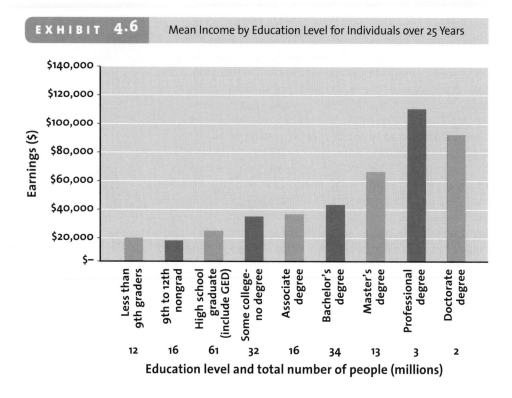

EXHIBIT 4.6   Mean Income by Education Level for Individuals over 25 Years

Education level	Total number of people (millions)
Less than 9th graders	12
9th to 12th nongrad	16
High school graduate (include GED)	61
Some college-no degree	32
Associate degree	16
Bachelor's degree	34
Master's degree	13
Professional degree	3
Doctorate degree	2

Education level and total number of people (millions)

and behavior affects the way many firms design and promote their products and services. For example, more firms are careful about gender neutrality in positioning their products and, furthermore, attempt to transcend gender boundaries whenever they can.

From cars to copiers, sweaters to sweeteners, women make the majority of purchasing decisions and then influence most of the remainder. One company that is making a concerted effort to specifically appeal to its female consumers is Nike. Rather than rely on stereotypical feminine appeals, Nike has recognized the increasing numbers of women who engage in physically challenging activities. In 2007, it held the fourth annual Women's Marathon in San Francisco. A 26.2-mile run is challenging in any situation, but the topography of San Francisco, with its hills and valleys, makes this marathon a particularly tough event. In addition to encouraging women to take the challenge through the name and advertising for the run, Nike also created special events for women along the course, such as a "chocolate mile," pedicure stations, and free massages. Every participant also received a "finisher's" necklace from Tiffany & Co. Nike is just one of many companies that recognize the potential of women consumers and market to them directly.[36]

Thousands of people line up for the start of the 2007 Nike Women's Marathon in San Francisco.

But that doesn't mean marketers have forgotten about men. Men are shopping more than they did a decade ago.[37] It is just that marketing to men is not easy. Manufacturers and retailers have tried to target the male consumer by appealing to the metrosexuals, or those having female habits like getting manicures and liking to shop. But they have been largely unsuccessful with this approach because "metrosexuals" consist only of a small portion of the population. Most men feel that they do not recognize themselves or relate well to the people shown in the advertisements using this approach.

There is a large portion of dads and men in their 20s and 30s who like "sports and beer." These men are concerned with the way they look, but do not spend extravagantly on things like $100 haircuts. There is also a large segment of dads who are shopping for their family for products for their household and children. Lastly, there are 70 million echo-boomers, those in their teens and early 20s who are avid shoppers for products that make them feel cool. This group has grown up with the Internet as a venue for shopping.

Marketers are learning that the best way to reach the male market is to interact with it. Men like to be involved and active in a purchase, rather than be persuaded by a sales campaign. For instance, on the basis of research with men, the children's stroller company Bugaboo International designed a high-tech black-and-chrome contraption with tires that could be on a dirt bike.

Ethnicity   Because of immigration and increasing birth rates among various ethnic and racial groups, the United States continues to grow more diverse.[38] Approximately 80 percent of all population growth in the next 20 years is expected to come from African American, Hispanic, and Asian communities. Minorities now represent approximately one-quarter of the population; by 2050, they will represent about 50 percent, and nearly a quarter of the population will be Hispanic.[39] Most of the foreign-born American population and recent immigrants tend to concentrate in a handful of metropolitan areas, such as New York, Los Angeles, San Francisco, and Chicago.[40]

Women are no longer the only family members doing the grocery shopping.

Spending by Hispanic consumers exceeds $863 billion per year; by 2011, predictions assert it will reach $1.2 trillion,[41] which would make Hispanic consumers the largest U.S. minority group in terms of disposable income. From 1990 to 2007, spending power among this group grew 300 percent, whereas non-Hispanic spending grew only 120 percent. Hispanic households tend to be larger than those of other groups, and 41 percent have annual incomes of at least $25,000, though Cubans tend to have much higher incomes than either Mexican or Puerto Rican consumers. In response to this growing purchasing power, some firms—both retailers and manufacturers—are focusing on the large and growing middle and affluent classes among minority groups. About 350,000 Hispanic immigrants come to the United States every year, and they and their U.S.-born children should increase the number of Hispanic Americans to more than 52.7 million in 2020.[42]

The Hispanic market is so large in some areas of the U.S. that marketers develop entire marketing programs just to meet Hispanics' needs.

Advertisers spent more than $3.3 billion in 2005 to market products to Hispanic consumers.[43] To attract and communicate with Hispanic consumers, marketers have invaded channels such as Telemundo, CNNenEspanol.com, and Vanidades with commercials for their products. The Hispanic market is particularly large in certain states and cities, such as California, Arizona, New Mexico, Texas, Miami, New York City, and Chicago.

Although African American households by and large remain less affluent than other groups, they also represent some retailers' best customers. For instance, African Americans spend proportionally more on women's dress shoes, clothing for teenagers, jewelry, women's athletic wear, and children's shoes than do other ethnic groups. Retailers that provide products and services that enhance personal appearance should take special note of this market. In general, African Americans spend more than their white counterparts on big-ticket items such as cars, clothing, and home furnishings. Many also have an affinity for brand name products because they equate them with quality.

The United States is like a salad bowl, made up of people from every corner of the world.

Although Asian Americans make up only about 3 percent of the U.S. population, they also represent the fastest-growing minority population. They tend to earn more, have more schooling, and be more likely to be professionally employed or own a business than whites. As is also true for Hispanic consumers, marketers should not assume that they can target all Asians with one strategy. The Chinese, Japanese, Indian, Korean, and Southeast Asian subgroups, such as the Vietnamese and Cambodian, all speak different languages and come from different regional and country cultures.

Social Trends

Various social trends appear to be shaping consumer values in the United States and around the world, including greener consumers, marketing to children, privacy concerns, and time-poor societies.

Greener Consumers[44]   Green marketing involves a strategic effort by firms to supply customers with environmentally friendly merchandise. Although this green trend is not new, it is growing. Many consumers, concerned about everything from the purity of air and water to the safety of beef and salmon, believe that each person can make a difference in the environment. For example, nearly half of U.S. adults now recycle their soda bottles and newspapers, and European consumers are even more green. Germans are required by law to recycle bottles, and the European Union does not allow beef raised on artificial growth hormones to be imported.

Demand for green-oriented products has been a boon to the firms that supply them. For instance, marketers encourage consumers to replace their older versions of washing machines and dishwashers with water- and energy-saving

Motivated by environmental concerns and rising gas prices, consumers are demanding more fuel-efficient hybrid cars.

models and to invest in phosphate-free laundry powder and mercury-free and rechargeable batteries. America's love affair with recycling also has created markets for recycled building products, packaging, paper goods, and even sweaters and sneakers. This raised energy consciousness similarly has spurred the growth of more efficient appliances, lighting, and heating and cooling systems in homes and offices. Health-conscious consumers continue to fuel the markets for organic foods, natural cleaning and personal care products, air- and water-filtration devices, bottled water, and organic fertilizers, as well as integrated pest management systems that do not rely on any manufactured chemicals. By offering environmental responsibility, these green products add an extra ounce of value that other products don't have.

Marketing to Children   In the past 20 years, child obesity has doubled and teenage obesity tripled in the United States, leading to skyrocketing rates of high blood pressure, high cholesterol, early signs of heart disease, and Type 2 diabetes among children. In response, the Center for Science and the Public Interest (CSPI) has proposed Guidelines for Responsible Food Marketing to Children, outlining a variety of changes to advertising directed at children. The CSPI notes that children are highly impressionable, and most food advertising to these young consumers touts high-calorie, low-nutrition products, associated in advertising with various

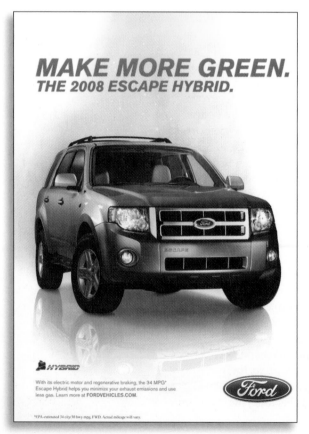

MAKE MORE GREEN.
THE 2008 ESCAPE HYBRID.

With its electric motor and regenerative braking, the 34 MPG* Escape Hybrid helps you minimize your exhaust emissions and use less gas. Learn more at FORDVEHICLES.COM.

*EPA-estimated 34 city/30 hwy mpg, FWD. Actual mileage will vary.

Adding Value 4.1 — Cereal Manufacturers Reformulating[45]

The trend toward healthier living and green business practices is spreading across industries. In the food industry, partly in response to consumer concerns and regulatory actions, marketers are focusing on the health benefits of foods and their impact on children's health. Many consumers also will pay more for such products. To respond to this trend, the Kellogg Company discontinued advertising sugary breakfast cereals to children and added recommended daily amounts of vitamins and minerals to all of its cereals.

After identifying the lack of whole-grain foods in the American diet as a significant opportunity for its breakfast cereal line, which includes Cheerios, Wheaties, Cinnamon Toast Crunch, and Kix, Kellogg began to reformulate all its products to focus on healthier food. However, its marketing research also revealed that consumers believed whole-grain flour would not taste as good as regular flour. Although 75 percent of the U.S. population thought they were eating enough whole grains, in reality, only about 10 percent of the population consumed enough.

Kellogg is not alone. To take advantage of the trend toward healthier eating seen in its market research findings, General Mills added whole grains to its already popular breakfast cereals, which amounts to an additional 1.5 billion servings of whole grain to the U.S. diet each year. To communicate the value of these whole-grain additions to consumers, General Mills uses online advertising and product promotions. It also features educational information on its breakfast cereal boxes so that consumers grow to understand the benefits of whole grain. To support its whole-grain initiative, General Mills created the Whole Grain Nation Web site (http://www.wholegrainlife.com), where consumers can find out about the health effects of whole grains on cholesterol, heart disease, and diabetes.

The trends in the food industry mirror the general trends toward consumer health and green consumption. As the various examples in this chapter show, companies that anticipate consumer needs and deliver superior products create value for themselves, their shareholders, and society.

toys, cartoons, and celebrities. The new guidelines require advertisers to market food in reasonably proportioned sizes. The advertised food items also must provide basic nutrients, have less than 30 percent of their total calories from fat, and include no added sweeteners. The advertising also cannot be aired during children's programming, and companies cannot link unhealthy foods with cartoon and celebrity figures. For example, Burger King no longer uses SpongeBob SquarePants to promote burgers and fries.[46] Adding Value 4.1 above describes how cereal manufacturers are responding to the need to create healthier products for children, as well as adults.

Privacy Concerns More and more consumers worldwide sense a loss of privacy. At the same time that the Internet has created an explosion of accessibility to consumer information, improvements in computer storage facilities and the manipulation of information have led to more and better security and credit check services. Yet, privacy breeches still occur. In January 2007, TJX Co., Inc., the owner of 2,500 discount stores, including the T.J. Maxx, Marshalls, Bob's Stores, and HomeGoods chains, announced that hackers had stolen the credit and debit card information of 45.7 million of its customers. In addition to their card numbers, another 455,000 customers suffered the exposure of their driver's license numbers as well.[47]

Have you ever felt that your privacy has been invaded by unsolicited telephone calls? The Federal Trade Commission (FTC), responding to consumer outcries regarding unwanted telephone solicitations, has registered the phone numbers of more than 145 million phone numbers in the Do Not Call Registry. This action was designed to protect consumers against intrusions that Congress determined to be particularly invasive.[48] Unfortunately, the Do Not Call Registry may have eliminated many honest telemarketers, leaving the wires open for the crooked groups who often use nontraceable recordings to reach potential customers at home. In the end, most companies are moving resources away from telephone campaigns and refocusing them elsewhere.

When "Leave It to Beaver" was on TV in the 1950s, viewers had only three or four channels from which to choose.

The Time-Poor Society   Reaching a target market has always been a major challenge, but it is made even more complicated by several trends that increase the difficulty of grabbing those markets' attention. First, in the majority of families, both parents work, and the kids are busier than ever. Since 1973, the median number of hours that people say they work has jumped from 41 to 49 a week. During that same period, reported leisure time has dropped from 26 to 19 hours a week.[49]

Second, consumers have many more choices about the ways they might spend their dwindling leisure hours. When *Leave It to Beaver* ruled television, most viewers could choose from only three or four channels, plus a handful of AM radio stations. Today, they have hundreds of each. Competing with television and radio are PDAs, DVDs, MP3 players, cell telephones, pagers, personal computers, and the Internet. In addition, as recording devices such as TiVo or DVR systems for cable television subscribers become more widespread, many time-strapped consumers simply record their favorite television shows to watch at their convenience. By fast-forwarding thorough the commercials, they can catch an entire one-hour show in approximately 47 minutes—which means they miss all the messages advertisers are attempting to send them.

Third, many consumers attempt to cope with their lack of leisure time by multitasking—watching television or listening to music while talking on the telephone or doing homework. Their divided attention simply cannot focus as well on advertisements that appear in those media.

Marketers must respond to the challenge of getting consumers' attention by adjusting, such as by moving their advertising expenditures from traditional venues like print media to instant messaging, Internet-based reviews and ads, movie screens, fortune cookies, baggage claim conveyor belts, billboards, airplane boarding passes, and ads in airports and on taxis, buses, and mass transport vehicles.[50]

Retailers are doing their part by making their products available to customers whenever and wherever they want. For instance, many retailers have become full-fledged multichannel retailers that offer stores, catalogs, and Internet shopping options. Others, like Office Depot and Walgreens, have extended their hours of operation so that their customers can shop during hours that they aren't working. In addition, automated processes like self-checkout lanes and electronic kiosks speed the shopping process and provide customers with product and ordering information. Grocery stores and home improvement centers have been particularly aggressive in developing strategies to help time-poor customers. See Superior Service 4.1.

Self-checkout lanes speed the shopping process, but do they improve customer service?

To find and develop such methods to make life easier for consumers in the time-poor society, marketers often rely on technology, another macroenvironmental factor and the topic of the next section.

Technological Advances

Technological advances have accelerated greatly during the past few decades, improving the value of both products and services. Since the birth of the first Generation Y baby in 1977, the world has realized the commercial successes of iPhones, cellular telephones, MP3 players, Internet access, personal digital assistants (PDAs), WiFi, and digital cameras. Flat-screen and high-definition televisions, as well as video on demand, have changed the way we view

Superior Service 4.1 — Grocery Retailers Help Time-Poor Customers

Traditional methods of shopping for and preparing food have always been time-consuming. Restaurants, and particularly fast-food restaurants, have helped lighten this burdensome task for decades. But as consumers become more time-pressed and as traditional grocery stores are feeling increased competition from superstores like Wal-Mart and Target and warehouse stores like Costco and Sam's Club, some grocery retailers are developing innovative methods of helping consumers put food on their families' tables.[51]

U.K.-based Tesco has recently opened its first stores in the U.S. under the Fresh & Easy Neighborhood Markets brand name.[52] How fresh and easy are they really? Tesco offers ready-to-heat meals, thus accentuating the "fresh" portion of its name. These new stores are relatively small and contain a tightly edited selection of merchandise, making it "easy" to shop.

Other grocery stores are taking a different stance on having fresh and easy products. Hannaford stores in the northeastern U.S. offer "Cooking School to Go" meals that have precut and premeasured ingredients for everything needed in a recipe.[53] The meals for two people cost $12, and the meals for 4 people cost $20. The packages are small and the containers are numbered so that cooking is very easy even for those who are "cooking challenged." There are no ingredients left out, not even the quarter teaspoon of cumin, or the teaspoon of canola oil. Hannaford also arranges their stores in a logical manner, facilitating a quick and easy shopping experience. For example, the cream and half-and-half are located next to the coffee, and the packaged granola is next to the bulk granola.

Hannaford has streamlined the checkout process by organizing checkout lines like a bank. One line is formed, and customers are helped at the next available register. Customers who have more than 25 items can choose "Go Cart Curb Service." The customer leaves the cart with a store employee, who scans all of the groceries and then meets the customer at the car in the covered bay. The customer can then use a wireless unit to pay for the groceries with a credit card.

television, and their impact is only expected to increase in the next few years. On the retail side, firms are able to track an item from the moment it was manufactured, through the distribution system, to the retail store, and into the hands of the final consumer using little radio-frequency identification device (RFID) chips that are affixed to the merchandise. Because they are able to determine exactly how much of each product is at a given point in the supply chain, retailers can also communicate with their suppliers—probably over the Internet—and collaboratively plan to meet their inventory needs. Exhibit 4.7 shows when some of these technological advances were introduced and their annual sales.

Many busy consumers never actually have the luxury of shopping in a mall. "Alpha moms"—tech-savvy, family-centric, working mothers—make most of

EXHIBIT 4·7   Advances in Technology

	Cell Phone	LCD Televisions	MP3 Player	Internet Access	Digital Camera	iPhone
Year Introduced	1984	1988	1991	1993	1998	2007
2006 Sales	$115.5 Million	$924 Million	$719 Million	$582 Million	$828 Million	$360 Million

Source: http://www.infotechtrends.com (accessed January 7, 2008).

Power of the Internet **4.1**   **Blogging: The Next Relationship Frontier**

No longer do we feel sorry for the lonely frequent Internet users, sitting alone in their homes, surfing the Web with no one to talk to. Many look for and find intimate relationships online. A Google search for "fan club" returns more than 70 million results, including sites for fans dedicated to Barry Manilow, the New York Rangers, and Moo-Cow. Web sites such as Bazaarvoice.com facilitate product reviews from customers. Perez Hilton, a celebrity blogger famous for his comments about celebrities, grew so popular that he earned his own television show on VH1. On sites that traditionally have been dominated by user-generated content (UGC), such as shared links, personal blogs, and varied message posts, marketers are adding their own commercial advertising, in the hope that it will appear more believ-able and authentic to the community-minded users of the sites.[54]

These Internet communities differ from a person's traditional social circle of friends and acquaintances in many ways, but one of the most significant is the absolute lack of secrets. Jeff Jarvis, the founder of *Entertainment Weekly* magazine, blogged about his bad experience with Dell. In turn, many other consumers found an outlet to complain about their similar experiences. Confronted with such widespread, and rapidly spreading, bad press, Dell took responsibility and admitted fault, then set up a "Dell Community" Web page on its site. Dell uses this page to gather customer feedback and improve its products and service, instead of ignoring or denying the frustrated sentiments its consumers are expressing.[55]

the purchasing decisions for their households, but with everything else they have to do, they simply cannot make time to visit store after store. Alpha moms average 87 minutes online every day. If marketers can figure out how to appeal to these busy women by monitoring their browsing or shopping behavior online, they can better target these customers with appropriate and timely promotions and discounts.[56]

Economic Situation

Marketers monitor the general economic situation, both in their home country and abroad, because it affects the way consumers buy merchandise and spend money. Some major factors that influence the state of an economy include the rate of inflation, foreign currency exchange rates, and interest rates.

Inflation refers to the persistent increase in the prices of goods and services.[57] Increasing prices cause the purchasing power of the dollar to decline; in other words, the dollar buys less than it used to.

In a similar fashion, foreign currency fluctuations can influence consumer spending. For instance, in the summer of 2002, the euro was valued at slightly less than U.S. $1. By the beginning of 2008, a euro was worth approximately $1.43. As the euro becomes more expensive compared with the dollar, merchandise made in Europe and other countries tied to the euro becomes more costly to Americans, whereas products made in the United States cost less for European consumers.

Tourists from other countries flock to the United States to shop because the value of the dollar is low compared to their own currency.

Finally, interest rates represent the cost of borrowing money. When customers borrow money from a bank, they agree to pay back the loan, plus the interest that accrues. The interest, in effect, is the cost to the customers or the fee the bank charges those customers for borrowing the money. Likewise, if a customer opens a savings account at a bank, he or she will earn interest on the amount saved, which means the interest becomes the fee the consumer gets for "loaning" the money to the bank. If the interest rate goes up, consumers have an incentive to save more, because they earn more for loaning the bank their money; when interest rates go down, however, consumers generally borrow more.

How do these three important economic factors—inflation, foreign currency fluctuations, and interest rates—affect firms' ability to market goods and services? Shifts in the three economic factors make marketing easier for some and harder for others. For instance, when inflation increases, consumers probably don't buy less food, but they may shift their expenditures from expensive steaks to less expensive hamburgers. Grocery stores and inexpensive restaurants win, but expensive restaurants lose. Consumers also buy less discretionary merchandise. Many retailers suffer seasonal losses when the economy is in trouble, because people spend less on their Christmas gifts. But off-price and discount retailers often gain ground at the expense of their full-price competitors. Similarly, the sale of expensive jewelry, fancy cars, and extravagant vacations will decrease, but curiously, the sale of low-cost luxuries, such as personal care products and home entertainment, tends to increase. It appears that, instead of rewarding themselves with a new Lexus or a health spa vacation, consumers buy a few cosmetics and rent a movie.

Another, perhaps unexpected, result of the devaluation of the U.S. dollar compared with other currencies might allow U.S. manufacturers to win and foreign makers to lose. During such inflationary times, "made in the U.S.A." claims become more important, which means that European or Asian manufacturers and U.S. retailers that buy from other countries must decide whether they should attempt to maintain their profit margins or accept a lower price to protect their U.S. customer base. Finally, when interest rates go up, consumers tend to save more, which makes it easier for financial institutions to sell products like mutual funds. But at the same time, people have less incentive to buy discretionary products and services because they are enticed by the higher interest rates to save. Therefore, though a financial institution's mutual fund division might benefit, its mortgage department might suffer because people don't buy houses when they feel they are not getting a good value for the money they must spend and borrow.

Political/Regulatory Environment

The political/regulatory environment comprises political parties, government organizations, and legislation and laws. Organizations must fully understand and comply with any legislation regarding fair competition, consumer protection, or industry-specific regulation. Since the turn of the century, the government has enacted laws that promote both fair trade and competition by prohibiting the formation of monopolies or alliances that would damage a competitive marketplace, fostering fair pricing practices for all suppliers and consumers, and promoting free trade agreements among foreign nations.

Legislation has also been enacted to protect consumers in a variety of ways. First, regulations require marketers to abstain from false or misleading advertising practices that might mislead consumers, such as claims that a medication can cure a disease when in fact it causes other health risks. Second, manufacturers are required to refrain from using any harmful or hazardous materials (e.g., lead in toys) that might place a consumer at risk. Third, organizations must adhere to fair and reasonable business practices when they communicate with consumers. For example, they must employ reasonable debt collection methods and disclose any finance charges and they also are limited with regard to their telemarketing and e-mail solicitation activities.

Last but not least, the government enacts laws focused on specific industries. These laws may be geared toward increasing competition, such as the deregulation of the telephone and energy industries, in which massive conglomerates like Ma Bell, the nickname for AT&T, were broken into smaller, competing companies. Or they may be in response to current events, such as the laws passed following the terrorist attacks of September 11, 2001, when the government ushered in

EXHIBIT 4.8	Competitive Practice and Trade Legislation

Year	Law	Description
1890	Sherman Antitrust Act	Prohibits monopolies and other activities that would restrain trade or competition. Makes fair trade within a free market a national goal.
1914	Clayton Act	Supports the Sherman Act by prohibiting the combination of two or more competing corporations through pooling ownership of stock and restricting pricing policies such as price discrimination, exclusive dealing, and tying clauses to different buyers.
1914	Federal Trade Commission	Established the Federal Trade Commission (FTC) to regulate unfair competitive practices and practices that deceive or are unfair to consumers.
1936	Robinson-Patman Act	Outlaws price discrimination toward wholesalers, retailers, or other producers. Requires sellers to make ancillary services or allowances available to all buyers on proportionately equal terms.
1938	Wheeler-Lea Act	Makes unfair and deceptive advertising practices illegal and gives FTC jurisdiction over food and drug promotion.
1993	North American Free Trade Agreement (NAFTA)	International trade agreement among Canada, Mexico, and the United States removing tariffs and trade barriers to facilitate trade among the three nations.

the Air Transportation Safety and System Stabilization Act to ensure that airlines could remain in business. A summary of the most significant legislation affecting marketing interests appears in Exhibits 4.8 and 4.9.

CHECK YOURSELF

1. What are the six key macroenvironmental factors?
2. Differentiate between country culture and regional culture.
3. Identify the different generational cohorts. What key dimension is used to classify an individual into a given cohort?
4. What are some important social trends shaping consumer values these days?

CORPORATE SOCIAL RESPONSIBILITY

In 1906, Upton Sinclair published *The Jungle*, his novel exposing the horrific conditions in meat-packing plants in American cities, that prompted President Theodore Roosevelt and Congress to force meat companies to take responsibility for the safety of their products. The notion of societal marketing and corporate social responsibility has changed significantly since then, and recent decades have seen its prevalence increase rapidly.[58] Corporate social responsibility (CSR), as defined in Chapter 3, refers to the voluntary actions taken by a company to address the ethical, social, and environmental impacts of its business operations and the concerns of its stakeholders.[59] Today, companies are undertaking a wide range of corporate social responsibility initiatives, such as establishing corporate charitable foundations, supporting and associating with existing nonprofit groups,

EXHIBIT 4.9	Consumer Protection Legislation

Year	Law	Description
1906	Federal Food and Drug Act	Created the Food and Drug Administration. Prohibited the manufacture or sale of adulterated or fraudulently labeled food and drug products.
1938	Food, Drug and Cosmetics Act	Strengthens the 1906 Federal Food and Drug Act by requiring that food be safe to eat and be produced under sanitary conditions; drugs and devices are safe and effective for their intended use; and cosmetics are safe and made from appropriate ingredients.
1966	Fair Packaging and Labeling Act	Regulates packaging and labeling of consumer goods; requires manufacturers to state the contents of the package, who made it, and the amounts contained within.
1966	Child Protection Act	Prohibits the sale of harmful toys and components to children. Sets the standard for child-resistant packaging.
1967	Federal Cigarette Labeling and Advertising Act	Requires cigarette packages to display this warning: "Warning: The Surgeon General Has Determined That Cigarette Smoking Is Dangerous To Your Health."
1972	Consumer Product Safety Act	Created the Consumer Product Safety Commission, which has the authority to regulate safety standards for consumer products.
1990	Children's Television Act	Limits the number of commercials shown during children's programming.
1990	Nutrition Labeling and Education Act	Requires food manufacturers to display nutritional contents on product labels.
1995	Telemarketing Sales Rule	Regulates fraudulent activities conducted over the telephone. Violators are subject to fines and actions enforced by the FTC.
2003	Controlling the Assault of Non-Solicited Pornography and Marketing Act of 2003 (CAN-SPAM Act)	Prohibits misleading commercial e-mail, particularly misleading subject and from lines.
2003	Amendment to the Telemarketing Sales Rule	Establishes a National Do Not Call Registry, requiring telemarketers to abstain from calling consumers who opt to be placed on the list.

supporting minority activities, and following responsible marketing, sales, and production practices. Social responsibility is even one of the eight key measures that *Fortune* magazine uses to create its list of the most admired companies (see Exhibit 4.10).

Some economists and social commentators suggest that CSR is unnecessary, that the goal of any corporation in a capitalist economy is single and simple: Make money. How does it benefit the company or its shareholders if a company worries about such unquantifiable issues as being a good citizen? Have companies decided that doing well for society is a better objective than profit maximization?

There is no easy answer to this question. When companies embrace CSR, they do so for a host of reasons. Many move beyond a shareholder perspective to recognize that they must appeal to a vast variety of *stake*holders, including their own employees, consumers and the marketplace, and society at large. In response, such companies undertake significant CSR efforts and then chronicle their CSR reports on the Web. Adding Value 4.2 on page 137 details GE's CSR report by highlighting the company's CSR activities as they pertain to different stakeholders, such as countries, suppliers, the environment, employees, and customers.

More and more firms are engaging in socially responsible activities in a systematic fashion, while still keeping in mind their own mission and strategy. In addition, the number of companies that report on their own CSR activities has steadily increased from just 267 in 1996 to 2,235 in 2006.[60] (See Exhibit 4.11 on page 138.)

EXHIBIT 4.10		Top 20 Admired Companies and Illustrative CSR Programs
Rank	**Company**	**Illustration of CSR Program**
1	Apple	Will eliminate the use of PVC, BFRs, and arsenic in its products by the end of 2008.
2	Berkshire Hathaway	Donates billions of dollars to the Bill and Melinda Gates Foundation.
3	General Electric	Ecomagination Campaign.
4	Google	Google.org funds for-profit entrepreneurship in Africa.
5	Toyota Motor	Over 100,000 Priuses sold (gas-electric hybrid engine).
6	Starbucks	Develops ecologically friendly growing practices.
7	FedEx	Delivered 440 tons of relief supplies at no charge to Hurricane Katrina victims.
8	Procter & Gamble	Live, Learn, and Thrive program improves the lives of children worldwide.
9	Johnson & Johnson	Funds nonprofits that fight HIV/AIDS around the world.
10	Goldman Sachs Group	Directs $1 billion into clean-energy investments.
11	Target	Donates 5% of its annual income to support local arts, education, and social services.
12	Southwest Airlines	Employees donate volunteer hours to Ronald McDonald Houses throughout the U.S.
13	American Express	Partners with National Trust for Historic Preservation through the WMF to preserve sites in the U.S and worldwide.
14	BMW	Member of the "Dow Jones Sustainability Group Index" since 1999.
14	Costco Wholesale	Pays better than normal wages and provides better benefits to its employees.
16	Microsoft	Developed a system with the American Red Cross for providing vital information on people's welfare in a disaster's aftermath.
17	United Parcel Service (UPS)	1,550 alternative-fuel delivery vehicles to cut fuel usage.
18	Cisco Systems	Established the Cisco Eco Board of leaders from 12 key areas of Cisco's businesses to drive environmental sustainability.
19	3M	Pollution Prevention Pays (3Ps) program focuses on conserving resources.
20	Nordstrom	Works with Strategic Paper Group to conserve resources used to produce catalogs.

Recently, more comprehensive research has attempted to understand and explain CSR.[61] Some of that research suggests the framework in Exhibit 4.12, which highlights the critical inputs and outputs involved with a corporate social responsibility program.

Inputs

The key inputs that a firm needs to understand and appreciate consist of three main categories: consumer, company, and cause. We look at each separately.

Consumer   As we have noted throughout this chapter, various demographic shifts and social trends affect consumers, and some of the more recent shifts have had

Adding Value 4.2 GE's Ecomagination

General Electric, a 128-year-old company that consists of various brands competing in industries such as consumer appliances; consumer electronics; network television, film, and media (NBC Universal); health care technology; aviation motors; lighting; and railway equipment, operates in many countries and emerging markets around the world.[62] As GE develops its operations in global arenas, the company must invest in a sustainable and responsible manner in not only local governments and its suppliers but also the environment and its people. To address issues such as global warming, water scarcity, and energy, GE uses a program it calls ecomagination™.[63] Much more than just a marketing campaign, ecomagination encompasses a valid business strategy that includes four commitments: to double investments in clean R&D, increase revenues from ecomagination products, reduce greenhouse gas emissions, and inform the public about these issues.

GE influences human rights throughout the world through its production practices. Banning the hiring of underage children and forced labor represents an obvious way to protect people in the world, but other company projects and products also focus on improving the lot of humanity worldwide. GE's commercial finance units actively invest in socially and environmentally beneficial projects, such as clean energy and water and energy capture from landfills. In Kuwait City, GE's Waste Water Reuse Facility recycles 65 percent of the sewage produced into water that may be used for irrigation and agriculture. Such projects improve the quality of life for people throughout

the community, and thus reach far beyond ensuring that factory facilities meet minimum human rights operations requirements.[64]

GE is committed to reducing greenhouse gas emissions (GHG) with its 1–30–30 plan. The "1" stands for the percentage that GE will reduce its GHG emissions worldwide by 2012; the first "30" indicates its commitment to reduce its GHG emissions by 30 percent by 2008; and the last "30" refers to the 30 percent improvement in its energy efficiency that it plans to achieve by the end of 2012. To meet these lofty goals, the company is integrating a "treasure hunt" process, developed by Toyota, to identify energy-saving and GHG-reduction opportunities. It has also launched an eCO2 Web site to recognize and reward the facilities and projects that make the greatest impact on GHG emissions reductions worldwide.

As part of its commitment to inform the public about environmental issues, GE has partnered with governments in various countries. In China, the firm partners with the Chinese National Development and Reform Commission (NDRC) to oversee and work with energy, aviation, rail, water, and consumer and industrial groups to initiate sustainable development and green products. In the United States, GE-owned NBC Universal is using its network to inform consumers about going green and the changes that each viewer, personally, can undertake to help in the larger effort. In addition, GE launched GreenIsUniversal.com, an informative site detailing various green issues and home to green-oriented blogs for discussion.[65]

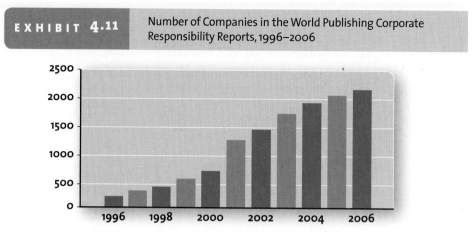

| EXHIBIT 4.11 | Number of Companies in the World Publishing Corporate Responsibility Reports, 1996–2006 |

Source: Richard Reeves, "Ethical Evangelists," *Management Today*, September 28, 2008.

tremendous impacts, such as the growing numbers of women in the workforce, senior citizens, and minorities. Corporate social responsibility programs must take these shifts and trends into account and react to them quickly. A few of the new trends include interest in the environment, respecting and protecting privacy in an electronic world, and ensuring healthiness of products, especially those aimed at children.

Company   In Chapter 2, we discussed the importance of the firm's strategy and the need to think ethically when developing that strategy. In a similar fashion, as a firm develops its CSR programs, it needs to think about its overall firm strategy. Programs and causes that fit well with their strategy and the industry in which they work likely will lead to better results for all stakeholders. For instance, Home Depot sells home improvement products, so when its 300,000 associates contribute more than 7 million hours of service annually through Team Depot to help rebuild communities (e.g., more than 160 homes for Habitat for Humanity; renovations of more than 20,000 homes for the elderly and disabled), its CSR activities seem to fit

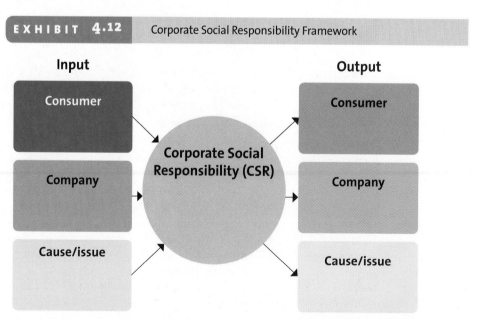

| EXHIBIT 4.12 | Corporate Social Responsibility Framework |

Source: Adapted from C. B. Bhattacharya and Sankar Sen, "Doing Better at Doing Good: When, Why and How Consumers Respond to Corporate Social Initiatives," *California Management Review*, 47 (Fall 2004), pp. 9–24.

America On the Move (AOM), is a nonprofit organization focused on making Americans healthier.

What's your goal?

America On the Move can help you get there! It's easy, fun and free!

America On the Move can help you reach your goal!

America On the Move Foundation is a national non-profit organization helping individuals, families and communities make positive small changes to improve health and quality of life. America On the Move (AOM) can also help YOU to achieve YOUR goal!

Getting Started:

No matter what your goal is, America On the Move is a good place to start. Try adding these two small changes to your day:

- Take 2000 more steps over your baseline (or the activity equivalent)
- Eat 100 fewer calories (by eating smarter)

It is simple to make small lifestyle changes that have big benefits on overall health. All it takes is walking an extra 2000 steps and eating smarter by consuming 100 fewer calories each day.

JAMES O HILL, PhD
Co-Founder
America On the Move

You can also register online at:
www.americaonthemove.org
or call **1-800-807-0077**

America on the move
Steps to a
Healthier Way of Life™

---

well with the firm's overall strategy. In addition, Home Depot donates more than $25 million in four target areas: affordable housing, at-risk youth, the environment, and disaster preparedness and relief. This sort of involvement further reinforces the fit between the firm's overall mission and the issues that it supports.

Cause/Issue The causes and societal issues currently represented by various nonprofit organizations seem almost innumerable; the actual number of nonprofit organizations in the United States exceeds 1.4 million.[66] Usually, each organization tackles a specific issue or cause, which enables firms to align their image with that of the cause. For example, Saks Fifth Avenue donated a percentage of its sales of a particular leather jacket to Help USA, a group that fights homelessness. Bloomingdale's gives annually to a wide variety of charities, including the National Colorectal Cancer Research Alliance, the Juvenile Diabetes Research Foundation, and Autism Speaks. Wal-Mart helps the Salvation Army raise money but also gave the charity $245 million. MAC Cosmetics' line of lipsticks and greeting cards raised $40 million for AIDS treatment.

Another nonprofit, America On the Move (AOM), is focused on making Americans healthier. A corporation considering whether it should support this organization must evaluate the salience of this issue, the reputation surrounding the cause, and again, the fit of the cause with the company. When PepsiCo decided to enhance its CSR efforts, it considered these three aspects. Improving the health of Americans is clearly a salient issue, whether through increasing breast cancer awareness or reducing levels of homelessness. In investigating the reputation of the cause, Pepsi found that since 2003, AOM had successfully helped launch a variety of initiatives, including the SmartChoices™ label on foods, and was run by a board staffed by reputable academics and professionals. A nonprofit dedicated to the cause of toenail fungus, staffed by a single sufferer, would not have the same level of salience or reputability.

Finally, with regard to the fit between AOM and Pepsi, the beverage company has announced its commitment to human sustainability and is adding fiber, vitamins, and nutrients while reducing fat, sugar, and sodium in its products. Because most recommendations on fighting obesity and living healthier suggest that people (and especially children) should consume 100 fewer calories per day and walk more, Pepsi agreed in 2006 to stop selling foods and drinks that did not meet the American Heart Association's nutritional guidelines in schools. Specifically, it pulled full-calorie soft drinks, juice drinks, and tea and reduced portion sizes. Furthermore, Pepsi had already pursued SmartChoices™ labels for many of its products, including Frito-Lay's Ruffles, which now contain less saturated fat. As AOM is dedicated to Americans' health and helped create the SmartChoices™ labels, Pepsi's sponsorship of this nonprofit organization appears to be an excellent fit that reinforces Pepsi's commitment to healthier products for the general public.

Output

The greater number of firms reporting on their CSR activities (Exhibit 4.11) suggests that more and more firms are realizing that doing good for society can also result in a better bottom line, because of happier employees, greater efficiency, and/or increased value for customers. Like the inputs, the outputs of these CSR activities found in Exhibit 4.12 are grouped into three main categories: consumer, company, and cause. We look at each separately.

Consumer   CSR often increases consumer awareness of the firm in the short run, which in turn leads to better brand equity and sales in the long run. The United Kingdom's grocery giant, Tesco, launched a massive advertising campaign to raise awareness of its program, offering one loyalty card point for each bag that a customer brings back, giving customers a way to feel good about and receive a reward for minimizing their amount of waste.

Company   At the same time as making the consumer aware and happy, the Tesco promotion also saved Tesco more than 10 million bags a week, which meant a significant cost savings. Other companies are working to reduce unnecessary packaging and print marketing materials, and still others are incorporating more recycled paper in their catalogs. Retailers like Target are embracing social responsibility in terms of how they build and operate their stores and therefore have turned to energy-efficient building construction. This initiative pays off not only in terms of being more socially responsible but also in terms of cost savings. Through its Zero Waste initiative, Wal-Mart has saved 478.1 million gallons of water, 20.7 million gallons of diesel fuel, and millions of pounds of solid waste. With its 100 percent renewable energy program, it expects to reduce yearly energy consumption by 30 percent in all of its new stores by 2014.[67]

In addition, such CSR activities can enhance the morale of employees. Happy employees have a sense of attachment to their employer. In service firms especially, employees represent the frontline when it comes to interacting with customers, so employees who are disappointed in or disgusted by their company cannot promote the company effectively. But if the company gives their employees a CSR message to deliver that they feel passionately about, they will deliver it with conviction, having an enormous impact on their customers.

Cause/Issue Finally, appropriate linkages between firms and their causes/issues benefit the cause and create better awareness of its objectives in the short run and more resources (workers and money) in the long run that it can devote toward its honorable mission.

CHECK YOURSELF

1. How has corporate social responsibility evolved since the turn of the 20th century?

2. Identify the inputs and outputs of the corporate social responsibility framework.

Summing Up

1. How do customers, the company, competitors, and corporate partners affect marketing strategy?

Everything a firm does should revolve around the customer; without the customer, nothing gets sold. Firms must discover their customers' wants and needs and then be able to provide a valuable product or service that will satisfy those wants or needs. If there were only one firm and many customers, a marketer's life would be a piece of cake. But because this situation rarely occurs, firms must monitor their competitors to discover how they might be appealing to their customers. Without competitive intelligence, a firm's customers might soon belong to its competitors. Though life certainly would be easier without competitors, it would be difficult, if not impossible, without corporate partners. Good marketing firms or departments work closely with suppliers, marketing research firms, consultants, and transportation firms to coordinate the extensive process of discovering what customers want and finally getting it to them when and where they want it. Each of these activities—discovering customer needs, studying competitors' actions, and working with corporate partners—helps add value to firms' products and services.

2. Why do marketers have to think about their macroenvironment when they make decisions?

To be successful, marketers must understand fully what is going on outside their firm. What are the chances that a fast-food hamburger restaurant would be successful in a predominantly Hindu neighborhood? Not good. Marketers must be sensitive to such cultural issues to be successful, and then they must also consider customer demographics—age, income, market size, education, gender, and ethnicity—to identify specific customer target groups. In any society, major social trends influence the way people live. Understanding these trends—such as green marketing, privacy issues, and the time-poor society—can help marketers serve their customers better. In no other time in history has technology moved so rapidly and had such a pervasive influence on the way we live. Not only do marketers help identify and develop technologies for practical, everyday uses, but technological advances help marketers provide consumers with more products and services more quickly and efficiently. The general state of the economy influences how people spend their discretionary income. When the economy is healthy, marketing success comes relatively easily. But when the economy gets bumpy, only well-honed marketing skills can yield long-term successes. Naturally, all firms must abide by the law, and many legal issues affect marketing directly. These laws pertain to competitive practices, such as antitrust legislation, and to protecting consumers from unfair or dangerous products through warning labels on cigarette packages and content labels on packaged food.

3. **How do corporate social responsibility programs help various stakeholders?**

To answer this question, we first have to identify the various stakeholders of a company, namely, customers, employees, stockholders, and the community. CSR benefits these stakeholders as follows:

- **Customers.** When companies adopt CSR, customers know that they can trust the firms to provide healthy, ethically acceptable products and services. Many customers also feel better about buying from a company that engages in responsible practices, which provides them with the additional value of feeling good about buying from that company.

- **Employees.** A firm committed to CSR likely treats its employees with decency and respect. For many employees (especially members of Generation Y), working for an irresponsible firm would be antithetical to their own morals and values.

- **Stockholders.** When a CSR initiative, such as using more efficient packaging, improves a company's profits by reducing costs, stockholders enjoy an immediate improvement in their investment. Some investors also choose which stocks to buy on the basis of the company's responsible stances.

- **Community.** This last stakeholder can be a local, national, or global community. The benefits of CSR in all cases are numerous—cleaner air and water, aid to the underprivileged, and healthier product options all can result from CSR by companies.

Key Terms

- Alpha moms 131
- Baby Boomers, 121
- competitive intelligence (CI), 115
- country culture, 119
- culture, 118
- demographics, 120
- echo-boomers, 127
- economic situation, 132

- foreign currency fluctuations, 132
- Generation X, 123
- Generation Y, 123
- generational cohort, 120
- green marketing, 128
- inflation, 132
- interest rates, 132
- macroenvironmental factors, 118

- metrosexuals, 126
- political/regulatory environment, 133
- regional culture, 120
- seniors, 120
- technological advances, 130
- Tweens, 124

Marketing Applications

1. Assume you are going to open a new store. Describe it. Who are your competitors? What would you do to monitor your competitors' actions? Who are your customers? What are you going to do to appeal to them? What are your social responsibilities, and how will you meet them?

2. In which generational cohort do you belong? What about your parents? How do you approach buying a computer differently than your parents would? What about buying an outfit to wear to a party? How can firms use their knowledge of generational cohorts to market their products and services better?

3. How can firms use customer demographics like income, market size, education, and ethnicity to market to their customers better?

4. Identify some of the ethnicity changes in the United States. Describe how they might affect the marketing practices of (a) a regional newspaper in Texas, (b) food retailers in cities, and (c) a home furnishing store in New York City.

5. Identify some recent technological innovations in the marketplace and describe how they have affected consumers' everyday activities.

6. Why should a T-shirt shop in the United States care about the value of the Hong Kong dollar?

7. Time-poor consumers have adopted various approaches to "buy" themselves more time, such as (a) voluntarily simplifying their complex lives, (b) using new technologies for greater empowerment and control, (c) using their time productively when traveling or commuting, and (d) multitasking. Identify and describe some products and services that consumers use to implement each of these strategies.

8. Identify a company that you believe does a particularly good job of marketing to different cultural groups. Justify your answer.

9. Choose a company that you believe is particularly socially responsible. Using the Corporate Social Responsibility Framework in Exhibit 4.12, justify your choice.

Quiz Yourself

www.mhhe.com/grewal2e

1. When marketers look at advertising media they often begin with viewer or listener profiles such as age, income, gender, and race. They then compare the media profile with their target audience. These marketers are using _____ to see if the media "fits" with their advertising agenda.
   a. country culture
   b. regional culture
   c. demographics
   d. macromarketing measures
   e. scenario planning

2. Many American consumers are purchasing hybrid automobiles even though they are more expensive and sometimes less fuel efficient when compared to compact conventional cars. Automobile marketers recognize that these consumers:
   a. value contributing to a greener environment.
   b. are economically irrational.
   c. are responding to global corporate pressure for social responsibility.
   d. would prefer an SUV.
   e. all of the above.

(Answers to these two questions are provided on page 623.)

Go to www.mhhe.com/grewal2e to practice an additional 11 questions.

Net Savvy

1. Seventh Generation is the leading brand of non-toxic, environmentally safe household products in the United States. Visit its Web site (http://www.seventhgeneration.com) and review the philosophy behind the business. Next, review the site to identify the products the company offers. Briefly summarize some of the consumer trends you think are reflected. Describe the ways in which Seventh Generation's products address the wants and needs of its customers.

2. The Internet has been a double-edged sword for consumers. On the one hand, it provides easy access to many businesses and sources for information. On the other hand, consumers must give up some of their privacy to access this information. The Electronic Privacy Information Center (http://www.epic.org), founded in 1994, attempts to focus public attention on privacy issues. Browse through its Web site. What steps does EPIC suggest consumers take to protect their privacy online? What policy recommendations does it make regarding legal restrictions on companies?

Chapter Case Study

STONYFIELD FARM: CHANGING THE ENVIRONMENT OF BUSINESS[68]

Overview

In 2001, Gary Hirshberg entered into a partnership with the multinational French corporation Groupe Danone after he had already built his organic Stonyfield Farm

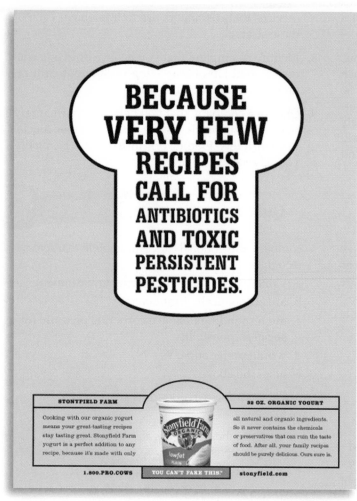

BECAUSE VERY FEW RECIPES CALL FOR ANTIBIOTICS AND TOXIC PERSISTENT PESTICIDES.

STONYFIELD FARM   32 OZ. ORGANIC YOGURT

Cooking with our organic yogurt means your great-tasting recipes stay tasting great. Stonyfield Farm yogurt is a perfect addition to any recipe, because it's made with only

all natural and organic ingredients. So it never contains the chemicals or preservatives that can ruin the taste of food. After all, your family recipes should be purely delicious. Ours sure is.

1.800.PRO.COWS   YOU CAN'T FAKE THIS.™   stonyfield.com

Stonyfield Farm's products are made with all natural and organic ingredients.

yogurt business from a small farm intended to fund his nonprofit ventures to a vast company with annual sales of $83 million. Three years later, with sales approaching $100 million, Groupe Danone increased its holding from 40 percent to 85 percent while maintaining Hirshberg as president and CEO.

A major reason for the company's rapid growth and popularity was its responsiveness to consumer demands for organic, natural food products. Stonyfield's popular yogurt and other products represented healthy alternatives to other brands, giving it a differential advantage in a marketplace in which more and more consumers had become choosier about the food products they bought. The company also supports various socially and environmentally beneficial causes. Because it provides superior value to consumers, Stonyfield Farm enjoys the number one market position for organic yogurt and is the number three branded yogurt in the industry.

Company History

In 1983, founders Gary Hirshberg and Samuel Kaymen started Stonyfield as an organic farming school to help revitalize New England agriculture and educate people about the environmental practices of local dairy farmers and the issues they face. Hirshberg and Kaymen began making high-quality yogurt as a way to raise money for their nonprofit school. Building on this tradition of environmental education, the company made pioneering social and environmental business practices central to their business, values, and growth. Essential to this goal is helping consumers realize the impact of their various purchases on the environment.

The Product

The company produces all natural and certified organic yogurts, smoothies, soy yogurt, frozen yogurt, ice cream, and milk. Their products contain no gelatins, artificial colors, artificial flavors, or other chemical additives used in many other brands. Stonyfield Farm yogurts contain inulin, a natural dietary fiber that helps boost calcium absorption, and six live active cultures that together enhance digestion, fortify the body's natural defenses, improve the absorption of nutrients and decrease the presence of harmful bacteria. The result: a healthier, better tasting product appreciated by health-conscious consumers.

Walking the Talk

Stonyfield's environmental initiatives center on two major themes: consumer education and modeling successful approaches of socially and environmentally responsible business practices. Ongoing consumer efforts include an educational campaign that presents the company's support for organic products, endorsement of humane animal treatment, and support of health and environmental initiatives. It models its principles of environmental sustainability through its efforts to use environmental packaging and extensive recycling practices and its award-winning efforts around climate change. Furthermore, it addresses both themes by donating 10 percent of its profits to organizations that protect and restore the planet.

In September 2000, the company launched its first national print advertising campaign, featuring celebrities perceived as positive role models. In the ads, these high-profile individuals spotlighted both environmental and social causes, in addition to endorsing Stonyfield Farm's products. Beginning in 2002, the company rolled out more traditional ads that featured its major selling point: organic products. The company launched its first national campaign in 2003, using a combination of television, radio, and print ads that communicate that the products are organic and good for the consumer and that the company has a sense of humor and a mission.[69]

Engaging Consumers

Stonyfield considers getting consumers involved a major key to its success. Although consumers appreciate the company's healthful approach to its products,

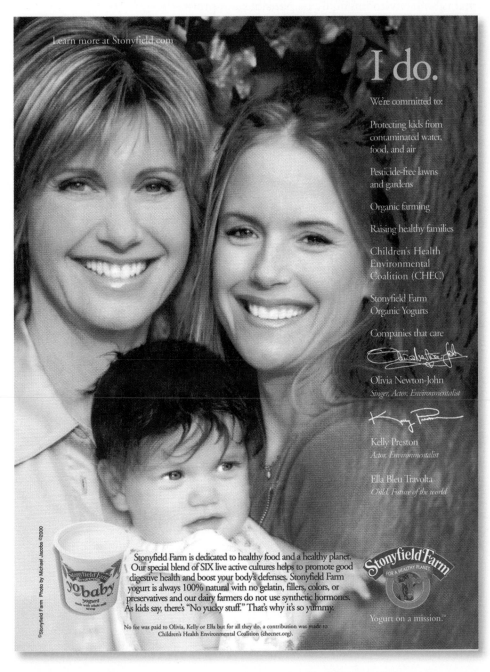

Stonyfield Farm's core values embody a high level of corporate social responsibility through consumer education and socially and environmentally responsible business practices.

they also like becoming empowered via the company's programs. One such program was "Vote for the Future," in which customers were asked to sign the back of a yogurt lid in support of sustainable energy policies. The lids were delivered to Washington, D.C., and customers who signed lids were entered into a "Flip Your Lid" contest that featured energy-efficient products and kits as prizes.

Stonyfield's social and environmental focus draws both positive recognition and the according financial benefits. Sales of Stonyfield products experienced double-digit, compound annual growth from $3 million in 1990 to $320 million in 2008. Recent trends reveal the continued success of Stonyfield. With its strategic partner, French food giant Groupe Danone, Stonyfield entered the European market, and the resulting growth in Stonyfield products achieved a rate of 18.9 percent in 2006—dwarfing the industry average growth rate of 6.8 percent.[70] With results like these, it is easy to see why Stonyfield is maintaining its focus on organic and sustainable business practices. These positive results, in combination with the fulfilment of its company objectives, enable Stonyfield to be a company that is both environmentally responsible and profitable.

Questions

1. Use the Corporate Social Responsibility Framework in Exhibit 4.12 to evaluate Stonyfield Farm's CSR program.
2. Many of Stonyfield Farm's green initiatives are costly and time consuming. Do you think they are worth it?

UNDERSTANDING THE MARKETPLACE

The three chapters in Section Two: Understanding the Marketplace focus on three levels of marketing: to individual consumers; from business to business; and on the global playing field. Chapter 5, Consumer Behavior, discusses why individual consumers purchase products and services. The consumer decision process is highlighted. Chapter 6, Business-to-Business Marketing, explores the whys and hows of business-to-business buying. Finally, Chapter 7 focuses on global markets. Thus, the three chapters in Section Two move from creating value for the individual consumer, to creating value for the firm or business, to creating value on the global level.

Assessing the Marketplace

Understanding the Marketplace

Targeting the Marketplace

Value Creation

Value Capture

Value Delivery: Designing the Channel and Supply Chain

Value Communication

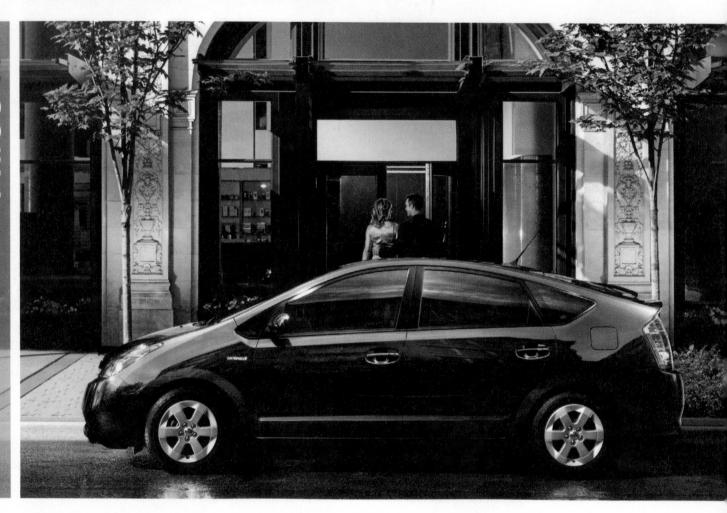

PRIUS 09

moving forw

CONSUMER BEHAVIOR

TOYOTA LEADS THE HYBRID CAR MARKET WITH ITS PRIUS

Good environmental practices historically have been bad for business, but in recent years, "going green" has started to make a lot of companies a lot of money. Now companies everywhere are adopting green business practices to appeal to new customers and improve their bottom lines. Unquestionably, the drive to go green has changed the marketplace, whether by reducing gasoline consumption, cutting carbon dioxide emissions, or creating the next eco-chic line of clothing. In the past few years, more consumers and governments have accepted the idea that carbon dioxide emissions are causing global warming. Combined with anxiety about rising oil prices, this has provided an opportunity for companies to create value by reducing their "carbon footprint" or helping consumers reduce their dependence on oil. Many of our day-to-day activities, from driving a car to turning on a light-bulb to enjoying a cup of coffee, have environ-mental impacts. And these little activities add up quickly. In the United States alone, the average consumer produces 10,000 pounds of carbon dioxide per year.[1]

As consumers become more sensitive about this, hybrid cars are becoming more popular. These vehicles are designed for a variety of different consumers from green advocates to those who simply want better mileage. In recognizing the opportunities associated with going green, Toyota led the charge among carmakers toward eco-friendly business. A decade before its competition, Toyota picked up on the trend and is reaping the benefits today. By using the past 10 years to develop a hybrid engine that can compete in a carbon-constrained economy, Toyota has earned superior profits for its shareholders and acceptance by a wide range of consumers. Today it may seem obvious that eco-chic products, such as the Toyota Prius, would be successful, but when Toyota began researching hybrid engines for the Prius, there was widespread doubt about its appeal. Clearly, the gamble has paid off. Toyota has sold its 1 millionth hybrid Prius, and demand for Toyota hybrids keeps growing.[2] In the coming years, Toyota plans to invest more in hybrid technology and introduce nine new hybrid cars in the United States by 2011.[3] The Prius thus provides an excellent example of a company identifying a consumer need and bringing a product to market to answer that need.

Consumers can choose among a wide array of hybrid cars, running the gamut from small, high-miles-per-gallon versions to large SUVs. The decision regarding which car to buy is a complex one that involves such variables as emotional response, personal style, and specific criteria including mileage, price, and safety. This plethora of considerations makes the car buyer's decision anything but simple. In turn, companies such as Toyota try to understand the consumer decision process and forecast what product attributes will sell the most cars. For the Prius, for example, developing a hybrid engine represented just one decision, but there were thousands of design details that were carefully determined, from the color palette to the amount of legroom.

● ● ●

All of us have often purchased services and products. We are all consumers, and we take this for granted. But we are also complex and irrational creatures who cannot always explain our own choices and actions, making the vitally important job of marketing managers even more difficult, as they are tasked with explaining consumers' behavior so that marketers have as good an understanding of their customers as possible.

To understand consumer behavior, we must ask *why* people buy products or services. Using principles and theories from sociology and psychology, marketers have been able to decipher many consumer choices and develop basic strategies for dealing with consumers' behavior. Generally, people buy one product or service instead of another because they perceive it to be the better value for them; that is, the ratio of benefits to costs is higher for the product or service than for any other.[4] However, "benefits" can be subtle and far from rationally conceived, as we shall see. Consider Katie Smith, who is considering a car purchase. She has just started college and misses her family's Ford Explorer. She lives on campus, near a bus stop that can take her downtown. She is considering whether to buy a monthly bus pass, a bike, or a car. In making the decision about how she will get around town, Katie asks herself:

- Which alternative gives me the best overall value—the best convenience at the lowest price?
- Which alternative is the best investment—the expenditure that will allow me the best resale value?

Because Katie might have several different reasons to choose a bus pass, a bike, or a car, it is critical for companies like Toyota (or Schwinn, Trek, and other bike makers, and even the city transit authority) to key in on the specific benefits that are most important to her. Only then can they create a marketing mix that will satisfy Katie.

In this chapter, we explore the process that consumers go through when they buy products and services. Then we discuss the psychological, social, and situational factors that influence this consumer decision process. Throughout the chapter, we emphasize what firms can do to influence consumers to purchase their products and services.

EXHIBIT 5.1 The Consumer Decision Process

Need Recognition → Information Search → Alternative Evaluation → Purchase → Post Purchase

THE CONSUMER DECISION PROCESS

The consumer decision process model represents the steps that consumers go through before, during, and after making purchases.[5] Because marketers often find it difficult to determine how consumers make their purchasing decisions, it is useful for us to break down the process into a series of steps and examine each individually, as in Exhibit 5.1.

Need Recognition

The consumer decision process begins when consumers recognize they have an unsatisfied need and want to go from their actual, needy state to a different, desired state. The greater the discrepancy between these two states, the greater the need recognition will be. For example, your stomach tells you that you are hungry, and you would rather not have that particular feeling. If you are only a little hungry, you may pass it off and decide to eat later. But if your stomach is growling and you cannot concentrate, the need—the difference between your actual (hungry) state and your desired (not hungry) state—is greater, and you'll want to eat immediately to get to your desired state. Consumer needs like these can be classified as functional, psychological, or both.[6]

Functional Needs Functional needs pertain to the performance of a product or service. For years, materials like GORE-TEX, Polartec, and Thinsulate have been viewed as functionally superior to others that might be used in rugged, high-performance outerwear. Knowing that consumers seek out these materials, high-end outdoor manufacturers such as The North Face prominently display the material content on each piece of clothing and equipment they offer.

Do Christian Louboutin's shoes satisfy functional or psychological needs?

Psychological Needs Psychological needs pertain to the personal gratification consumers associate with a product and/or service. Shoes, for instance, provide a functional need—to keep feet clean and protect them from the elements. So why would anyone pay $500 to $1,500 for shoes that may do neither? Because they seek to satisfy psychological needs. Christian Louboutin's shoes with their signature red sole may be the hottest shoe on the market.[7] Sarah Jessica Parker was spotted in a pair on the set of the *Sex and the City* movie, a pair showed up in an episode of *Dirty Sexy Money*, and BMW featured the shoe in a commercial. Nicole Kidman, Catherine Deneuve, Cameron Diaz, Ashley Olsen, Gwyneth Paltrow, and Angelina Jolie have also been photographed wearing Louboutin shoes. As a result of all this media attention, there is a strong demand for Louboutin shoes by women who just love exciting (and expensive) shoes.

Both these examples highlight that the vast majority of products and services are likely to satisfy both functional and psychological needs, albeit in different degrees. Whereas the functional characteristics of GORE-TEX are its main selling point, it also maintains a fashion appeal for mountain climber wannabes. In contrast, Christian Louboutin shoes satisfy psychological needs that overshadow the functional needs they serve. You can get a $15 haircut

Adding Value 5.1   H.O.G. Heaven[8]

It seems as though everybody wants a piece of H.O.G. Heaven these days. For years, Harley-Davidson motorcycles have been the premier form of two-wheeled transportation for motorcycle enthusiasts, and demand has exceeded supply. Even though other manufacturers, such as BMW, Yamaha, Suzuki, Honda, and Kawasaki, offer functional, dependable, fast motorcycles, they cannot compete with the Harley mystique.

A rich history, rider support, and its protected brand have contributed to Harley's cult-like following. Ten short years after William S. Harley and Arthur Davidson assembled their first motorcycles in a wooden shed in 1903, the company had opened a Milwaukee factory, won several racing awards, incorporated and introduced its first V-twin–powered motorcycle, and patented the classic "Bar and Shield" logo. It then went on to supply the U.S. military with motorcycles during World War I. Since 1916, Harley's magazine, *Enthusiast*, has featured such notables as Elvis Presley atop Harleys, during its run as the longest continually published motorcycle magazine.

Perhaps the single most important event in Harley-Davidson's history came in 1983 when the company formed the Harley Owner's Group (H.O.G.)—the largest factory-sponsored motorcycle club in the world, whose more than 1,000,000 members' sole mission is "to ride and have fun."[9] Not only do H.O.G. members receive copies of the *Enthusiast* and *Hog Tales*, H.O.G.'s official publication, but they also can take part in the Fly & Ride program, through which members get to fly to nearly 40 locations in the United States, Canada, Europe, and Australia, pick up a Harley at the local dealership, and tour the countryside. The best part about H.O.G. membership, though, is the camaraderie with like-minded devotees. In their 1,400 local chapters, supported by their local dealers, and during special events throughout the world, H.O.G. members have been able to share their love of Harleys as a community.

In addition to remarkable rider support, Harley-Davidson has taken great care to create and protect its global brand. Ranked among the top 50 most recognized global brands, Harley offers a full range of branded parts, accessories, and apparel through various outlets, including retail stores, dealerships, and online. The look, feel, and sound of a Harley are unmistakable—the company even tried to patent the "distinctive" exhaust sound made by its V-twin engines in 1994.

Although Harley-Davidson encourages the idea that its riders are "rugged individualists" who can customize their Hogs to reflect their individual tastes, the company actually has created a band of brand loyalists who believe function is more than two wheels and a motor. It's art, it's history, and it's community.

Everyone wants to own a Harley, even Jay Leno.

at SuperCuts or spend $50 or more to get basically the same thing at an upscale salon. Are the two haircuts objectively different? Yes, the answer might vary depending on which you believe represents a good haircut and a good value. Then, one person might value getting a really good deal; another might enjoy the extra attention and amenities associated with a fancy salon.

A key to successful marketing is determining the correct balance of functional and psychological needs that best appeals to the firm's target markets. Harley-Davidson, for instance, produces motorcycles that do much more than get their riders to the mall and back. Harleys are a way of life, as we discuss in Adding Value 5.1.

Search for Information

The second step, after a consumer recognizes a need, is to search for information about the various options that exist to satisfy that need. The length and intensity of the search are based on the degree of perceived risk associated with purchasing the product or service. If the way your hair is cut is important to your appearance and self-image, you may engage in an involved search for the right salon and stylist. Alternatively, an athlete looking for a short "buzz" cut might go to the closest, most convenient, and cheapest barber shop. Regardless of the required search level, there are two key types of information search: internal and external.

Internal Search for Information   In an internal search for information, the buyer examines his or her own memory and knowledge about the product or service, gathered through past experiences. For example, every time Katie, a cheeseburger junkie, wants lunch, she stops by In-N-Out Burger. She relies on her memory of past experiences when making this purchase decision.

External Search for Information   In an external search for information, the buyer seeks information outside his or her personal knowledge base to help make the buying decision. Consumers might fill in their personal knowledge gaps by talking with friends, family, or a salesperson. They can also scour commercial media for unsponsored and (it is hoped) unbiased information, such as that available through *Consumer Reports*, or peruse sponsored media such as magazines, television, or radio. Sometimes consumers get commercial exposures to products or services without really knowing it.

One source of information consumers turn to more and more frequently is the Internet.[10] For example, while leafing through a magazine at the grocery store, Katie saw a picture of Jessica Simpson wearing a pair of jeans she loved. When she got home, she turned on her computer and logged onto www.seenon.com and quickly discovered that the jeans were designed by William Rast.[11] Connecting to www.TrueJeans.com through the site, Katie entered her measurements and style preferences, and True Jeans returned recommendations of jeans that would be a good fit for her. Both types of search are examples of the external search for information. That is, Katie both looked up one of her favorite star's wardrobe and found jeans that will be a perfect fit for her, without having to go to the store or try on dozens of pairs of pants.

Another way that consumers can use the Internet is through a shopping bot such as Bizrate.com or a search engine like Google. The term *googol* was coined by Milton

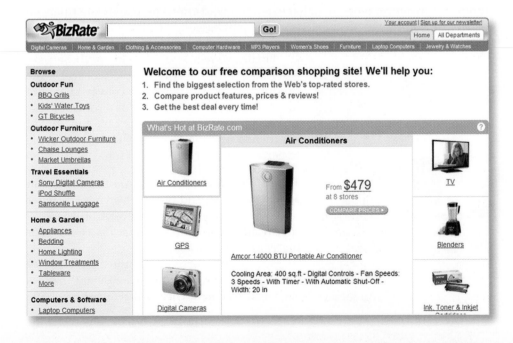

Sirotta, nephew of American mathematician Edward Kasner, to describe the number 1 followed by 100 zeros. There is not a googol of anything in the universe. And yet the founders of the Internet search engine Google adapted the term to reflect their mission of "organizing the immense, seemingly infinite amount of information available on the Web."[12] Today Google is the number one search engine, organizing more than 24 billion Web pages[13] and serving over 68 percent of all searches on the Internet.[14]

Factors Affecting Consumers' Search Processes   It is important for marketers to understand the many factors that affect consumers' search processes. Among them are the following four factors:

The Perceived Benefits versus Perceived Costs of Search   Is it worth the time and effort to search for information about a product or service? For instance, most families spend a lot of time researching the housing market in their preferred area before they make a purchase because homes are a very expensive and important purchase with significant safety and enjoyment implications, whereas they likely spend little time researching which inexpensive dollhouse to buy for the youngest member of the family.

The Locus of Control   People who have an internal locus of control believe they have some control over the outcomes of their actions, in which case they generally engage in more search activities. With an external locus of control, consumers believe that fate or other external factors control all outcomes. In that case, they believe it doesn't matter how much information they gather; if they make a wise decision, it isn't to their credit, and if they make a poor one, it isn't their fault. People who do a lot of research before purchasing individual stocks have an internal locus of control; those who purchase mutual funds are more likely to believe that they can't predict the market and probably have an external locus of control.

Actual or Perceived Risk   Three types of risk associated with purchase decisions can delay or discourage a purchase: performance, financial, and psychological. The higher the risk, the more likely the consumer is to engage in an extended search.

Performance risk involves the perceived danger inherent in a poorly performing product or service. An example of performance risk might be the possibility that your cell phone battery would go bad when you were waiting for a call to set up a job interview.

Financial risk is risk associated with a monetary outlay and includes the initial cost of the purchase, as well as the costs of using the item or service. Car manufacturers, for instance, recognize that extended warranties help alleviate financial risk for consumers who fear extensive postpurchase repair costs. Great warranties reduce the financial risk of buying a car.

Which of these products are convenience, shopping, and specialty goods?

Finally, psychological risks are those risks associated with the way people will feel if the product or service does not convey the right image. Katie Smith, thinking of a car purchase, looked up reviews of various cars and sought her friends' opinions because she wanted people to perceive her car as cool and fun.

Type of Product or Service   Another factor that affects the depth and type of search a consumer undertakes is the type of product or service—specifically, whether it is a *specialty, shopping,* or *convenience* product.

Specialty goods/services are products or services toward which the customer shows such a strong preference that he or she will expend considerable effort to search for the best suppliers. Environmentally minded consumers, who would only consider purchasing a Prius or other hybrid car, would devote lots of time and effort to selecting just the right one.

Shopping goods/services are products or services for which consumers will spend a fair amount of time comparing alternatives, such as apparel, fragrances, and appliances. When Katie decides to buy some new sneakers, she will go from store to store shopping—trying shoes on, comparing alternatives, and chatting with sales people.

Convenience goods/services are those products or services for which the consumer is not willing to spend any effort to evaluate prior to purchase. They are frequently purchased commodity items, usually purchased with very little thought, such as common beverages, bread, or soap.

When you get your hair cut, do you consider it to be a convenience, shopping, or specialty purchase?

Consumers can spend considerable time searching for both specialty and shopping goods or services; the difference lies in the kind of search. In some cases, the consumer's specific perceptions and needs help define the kind of search—and the type of product. For Katie, getting a haircut is a convenience purchase, so she visits the fastest, most convenient location. One of her friends is different and has tried various salons, each time comparing the haircut she received with her previous experiences. For her, a haircut is a shopping service. Katie has another friend who patronizes the hairstylist he perceives to be the best in town. He often waits weeks for an appointment and pays dearly for the experience. For him, getting a haircut is a specialty service.

Evaluation of Alternatives

Once a consumer has recognized a problem and explored the possible options, he or she must sift through the choices available and evaluate the alternatives. Alternative evaluation often occurs while the consumer is engaged in the process of information search. For example, a vegetarian consumer might learn about a new brand of yogurt that he or she can immediately rule out as a viable alternative because it contains some animal by-products. Consumers forgo alternative evaluations altogether when buying habitual (convenience) products; you'll rarely catch a loyal Pepsi drinker buying Coca-Cola.

Attribute Sets   Research has shown that a consumer's mind organizes and categorizes alternatives to aid his or her decision process. Universal sets include all possible choices for a product category, but because it would be unwieldy for a person to recall all possible alternatives for every purchase decision, marketers tend to focus on only a subset of choices. One important subset is retrieval sets, which are those brands or stores that can be readily brought forth from memory. Another is a consumer's evoked set, which comprises the alternative brands or stores that the consumer states he or she would consider when making a purchase decision. If a firm can get its brand or store into a consumer's evoked set, it has increased the likelihood of purchase and therefore reduced search time because the consumer will think specifically of that brand when considering choices. Katie Smith, for example, would like a hybrid car, if her parents will help her. She knows that not every carmaker (universal set) makes a hybrid car. She recalls that hybrid cars are available only on certain models such as the Toyota Prius and Camry, the Ford Escape, and the Honda Civic (retrieval set). But she wants a small car, so the Toyota Prius and the Honda Civic are the only models in her *evoked* set.

When consumers begin to evaluate different alternatives, they often base their evaluations on a set of important attributes or evaluative criteria. Evaluative criteria consist of a set of salient, or important, attributes about a particular product.

This Honda Civic hybrid, along with the Toyota Prius, are in Katie's evoked set of alternatives.

For example, a consumer looking to buy a new HDTV might take into consideration things like the selling price, brightness levels, picture quality, reputation of the brand, and the service support that the retailer offers. At times, however, it becomes difficult to evaluate different brands or stores because there are so many choices, especially when those choices involve technical criteria, as in the HDTV market.

Consumers utilize several shortcuts to simplify the potentially complicated decision process: determinant attributes and consumer decision rules. Determinant attributes are product or service features that are *important* to the buyer and on which competing brands or stores are perceived to *differ*.[15] Because many important and desirable criteria are equal among the various choices, consumers look for something special—a determinant attribute—to differentiate one brand or store from another. Determinant attributes may appear perfectly rational, such as a low price for milk, or they may be more subtle and psychologically based, such as the red soles on a pair of Christian Louboutin heels.

Consumer decision rules are the set of criteria that consumers use consciously or subconsciously to quickly and efficiently select from among several alternatives. These rules take several different forms: *compensatory, noncompensatory*, or *decision* heuristics.

Compensatory   A compensatory decision rule assumes that the consumer, when evaluating alternatives, trades off one characteristic against another, such that good characteristics compensate for bad characteristics.[16] For instance, Morgan Jackson is looking to buy a laptop and is considering several factors such as speed, weight, screen size, price, and accessories. But even if the laptop is priced a little higher than Morgan was planning to spend, a superb overall rating offsets, or compensates for, the higher price.

Although Morgan probably would not go through the formal process of making the purchasing decision based on the model described in Exhibit 5.2, this exhibit illustrates how a compensatory model would work.[17] Morgan assigns weights to the importance of each factor. These weights must add up to 1.0. So, for instance, processing speed is the most important, with a weight of .4, and screen size is least

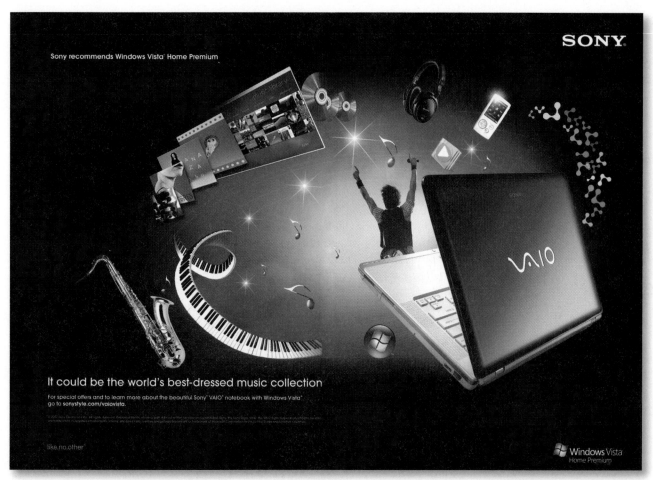

important with a weight of .1. She assigns weights to how well each of the laptops might perform, with 1 being very poor and 10 being very good. For instance, she thinks Sony has the best processing speed, so she assigns it a 10. Morgan multiplies each performance rating by its importance rating to get an overall score for each computer. The rating for Sony in this example is the highest of the three laptops $[(.4 \times 10) + (.1 \times 8) + (.3 \times 6) + (.2 \times 8) = 8.2)]$.

Noncompensatory Sometimes, however, consumers use a **noncompensatory decision rule**, in which they choose a product or service on the basis of one characteristic or one subset of a characteristic, regardless of the values of its other attributes.[18] Thus, although Sony received the highest overall score of 8.2, Morgan might still pick Lenovo because she is particularly price sensitive, and it had the highest score on price.

Although Morgan would buy a Sony if she used a compensatory decision rule, she would buy a Lenovo using a noncompensatory decision rule based on price alone.

EXHIBIT 5.2	Compensatory Purchasing Model for Buying a Car				
	Processing Speed	**Weight**	**Price**	**Screen Size**	**Overall Score**
Importance Weight	**0.4**	**0.1**	**0.3**	**0.2**	
Sony	10	8	6	8	8.2
Dell	8	9	8	3	7.1
Lenovo	6	8	10	5	7.2

Decision Heuristics   Not everyone uses compensatory or noncompensatory decision rules. Some use decision heuristics, which are mental shortcuts that help a consumer narrow down choices. Some examples of these heuristics include the following:

- *Price.* Consumers can choose the more expensive option, thinking they are getting better quality along with the higher price ("You get what you pay for"), or they might buy the one priced in the middle of the alternatives, neither the most expensive nor the cheapest, thinking that it is a good compromise between the two extremes.[19]

- *Brand.* Always buying brand name goods allows some consumers to feel safe with their choices. Purchasing a national brand, even if it is more expensive, gives many consumers the sense that they are buying a higher quality item.[20]

- *Product presentation.* Many times, the manner in which a product is presented can influence the decision process. For example, two comparable homes that are comparably priced will be perceived quite differently if one is presented in perfectly clean and uncluttered condition, with fresh flowers and the smell of chocolate chip cookies wafting about, whereas the other appears messy, has too much furniture for the rooms, and emits an unappealing smell. Consumers want to see that some effort has been put into the selling process, and just the way the product is presented can make or break a sale.[21]

Once a consumer has considered the possible alternatives and evaluated the pros and cons of each, he or she can move toward a purchase decision. Power of the Internet 5.1 illustrates how consumers evaluate different travel options and how Expedia has created value for consumers by making travel alternatives readily available.

Purchase and Consumption

Value is a strong driver of consumers' purchase decisions. Customers seek out and purchase the products and services that they believe provide them with the best value. Then, after consumers have access to the product or service, they usually consume it, or "put it to the test." A special type of consumption is called ritual consumption, which refers to a pattern of behaviors tied to life events that affect what and how we consume. These behaviors tend to have symbolic meanings and vary greatly by importance and by culture. They might take the form of everyday rituals such as going to Starbucks for a cappuccino or brushing your teeth with Crest, or they can be reserved for special occasions, such as holiday and birthday celebrations. Many firms try to tie their products and services to ritual consumption; just imagine, where would Hallmark be without holidays?

Postpurchase

The final step of the consumer decision process is *post*purchase behavior. Marketers are particularly interested in postpurchase behavior because it entails actual rather than potential customers. Satisfied customers, whom marketers hope to create, become loyal, purchase again, and spread positive word of mouth, so they are quite important. There are three possible positive postpurchase outcomes as illustrated in Exhibit 5.3 on page 160: customer satisfaction, postpurchase dissonance, and customer loyalty (or disloyalty).

Customer Satisfaction   Setting unrealistically high consumer expectations of the product through advertising, personal selling, or other types of promotion may lead to higher initial sales, but it eventually will result in dissatisfaction if the product fails to achieve high performance expectations. This failure can lead to dissatisfied customers and the potential for negative word of mouth.[22]

For example, Marriott recognized that it should worry when its market research suggested that it was serving large business groups well, but that small

Power of the Internet 5.1

Evaluating Travel Alternatives with Expedia[23]

To illustrate how the Internet is changing the way consumers make buying decisions, consider Expedia, the world's leading online travel service and the fourth-largest travel agency in the United States, a company that knows customers have high expectations in the competitive world of travel. Expedia's Web site (www.expedia.com) makes alternative evaluation easy through a variety of innovations. It allows customers to plan their travel by date, by price, by interest, or by activity. Travelers can book flights, hotel accommodations, car rentals, cruises, and vacation packages with the click of a mouse. The site also offers travel tools, such as travel alerts, flight status checks, seat selectors, airport information, currency converters, driving directions, weather reports, and passport information.

Before Web sites such as Expedia existed, consumers could purchase tickets only through travel agencies or directly from an airline. Travel agencies carefully guarded access to the reservation system, and there was no way to determine if there were less expensive flights available. Frequently consumers purchased tickets that were more expensive than other available options, but with the advent of Expedia and other travel Web sites consumers are now able to judge for themselves whether they are getting the best deal.

In addition to price, consumers can use Expedia to narrow their search from a universal set—all airlines—to their evoked set—say, only United, Delta, and American. They can also search according to determinant attributes, such as the lowest price or shortest flight. Some flyers use a noncompensatory decision rule; they will only fly United to Denver, no matter what the alternatives are, because they are members of the airline's frequent flyer program. Others will use a compensatory decision rule, so they will fly United or American to Denver, depending on which airline has the best combination of the lowest price, shortest flight, and minimum number of stops. Finally, some travelers choose an airline on the basis of key product signals, such as legroom, number of in-flight movie options, or quality of the food.

Companies such as Expedia are changing the way that consumers make decisions and helping to create consumers who are better informed about the costs and benefits of their purchasing options. As this trend continues, companies will have to focus on ways to demonstrate value to their customers to justify the price for their goods and services.

Expedia and other online travel services have changed the way consumers make their travel plans.

groups of business travelers were not enjoying their experience. Business travelers demand the best service and convenience from their hotels. To respond to the situation, Marriott conducted more market research to identify which services small groups of business travelers needed, and then made changes to its hotels to provide areas for conducting casual business and working in small groups, so that colleagues could collaborate outside of their rooms.[24]

EXHIBIT 5.3   Postpurchase Outcomes

Setting customer expectations too low is an equally dangerous strategy. Many retailers, for instance, don't "put their best foot forward." For instance, no matter how good the merchandise and service may be, if a store is not clean and appealing from the entrance, customers are not likely to enter.

Marketers can take several steps to ensure postpurchase satisfaction, such as:

- Build realistic expectations, not too high and not too low.
- Demonstrate correct product use—improper usage can cause dissatisfaction.
- Stand behind the product or service by providing money-back guarantees and warranties.
- Encourage customer feedback, which cuts down on negative word of mouth and helps marketers adjust their offerings.
- Periodically make contact with customers and thank them for their support. This contact reminds customers that the marketer cares about their business and wants them to be satisfied. It also provides an opportunity to correct any problems. Customers appreciate human contact, though it is more expensive for marketers than e-mail or postal mail contacts.

Postpurchase Dissonance   Sometimes, if expectation levels are not met and customers are in some way dissatisfied with the product or service, postpurchase dissonance results. Postpurchase dissonance, also known as buyers' remorse, is the psychologically uncomfortable state produced by an inconsistency between prior beliefs and actual behavior that evokes a motivation to reduce the dissonance. Postpurchase dissonance generally occurs when a consumer questions the appropriateness of a purchase after his or her decision has been made.

Postpurchase dissonance is especially likely for products that are expensive, are infrequently purchased, do not work as intended, and are associated with high levels of risk. Some dissonance is irrational; imagined benefits and reality entail an inevitable letdown. Marketers direct efforts at consumers after the purchase is made to address this issue. General Electric sends a letter to purchasers of its appliances, positively reinforcing the message that the customer made a wise decision by mentioning the high quality that went into the product's design and production. Some clothing manufacturers include a tag on their garments to offer the reassurance that because of their special manufacturing process, perhaps designed to provide a soft, vintage appearance, there may be variations in color that have no effect on the quality of the item. After a pang of dissonance, satisfaction may set in.

When Katie rented a movie classic, *Casablanca*, to watch in her dorm, she demonstrated a particular belief: "I love Ingrid Bergman and Humphrey Bogart." But her behavior was: "I cried all the way through it." Some dissonance resulted and manifested itself as an uncomfortable, unsettled feeling that she had made herself sad when she might have rented a comedy, or even done some homework. To reduce the dissonance, Katie could have taken several actions:

■ Canceled her Netflix subscription.

■ Paid attention to positive information, such as looking up old reviews of *Casablanca* or articles about Bogart and Bergman.

■ Sought positive feedback from friends, as when her friends who dropped by to watch it with her commented positively about the movie.

■ Sought negative information about products not selected, for example, read the reviews of all the mediocre new movies out this month.

After a while, satisfaction with her experience probably would have set in.

Customer Loyalty   In the postpurchase stage of the decision-making process, marketers attempt to solidify a loyal relationship with their customers. They want customers to be satisfied with their purchase and buy from the same company again. Loyal customers will buy only certain brands and shop at certain stores, and they include no other firms in their evoked set. As we explained in Chapter 2, such customers are therefore very valuable to firms, and marketers have designed customer relationship management (CRM) programs specifically to retain them.

Undesirable Consumer Behavior   Although firms want satisfied, loyal customers, sometimes they fail to attain them. Passive consumers are those that don't repeat-purchase or recommend the product to others. More serious and potentially damaging, however, is negative consumer behavior, such as negative word of mouth and rumors.

Negative word of mouth occurs when consumers spread negative information about a product, service, or store to others. When customers' expectations are met or even exceeded, they often don't tell anyone about it. But when consumers believe that they have been treated unfairly in some way, they usually want to complain, often to many people. To lessen the impact of negative word of mouth, firms provide customer service representatives—whether online, on the phone, or in stores—to handle and respond to complaints. If the customer believes that positive action will be taken as a result of the complaint, he or she is less likely to complain to family and friends or through the Internet and certain Web sites that are great purveyors of negative word of mouth.

Consumers often feel dissonance when purchasing products or services. It might be that uncomfortable feeling of mixed emotions—the movie makes me sad, but I love Bogart and Bergman.

CHECK YOURSELF

1. Name the five stages in the consumer decision process.

2. What differences mark the way a highly involved versus a less involved consumer looks at the information provided in an advertisement?

3. What is the difference between compensatory and noncompensatory decision rules?

FACTORS INFLUENCING THE CONSUMER DECISION PROCESS

The consumer decision process can be influenced by several factors, as illustrated in Exhibit 5.4. First are the elements of the marketing mix, which we discuss throughout this book. Second are psychological factors, which are influences internal to the customer, such as motives, attitudes, perception, and learning. Third, social factors, such as family, reference groups, and culture, also influence the decision process. Fourth, there are situational factors, such as the specific purchase situation, a particular shopping situation, or temporal state (the time of day), that affect the decision process.

Every decision people make as consumers will take them through some form of the consumer decision process. But, like life itself, this process does not exist in a vacuum.

Psychological Factors

Although marketers can influence purchase decisions, a host of psychological factors affect the way people receive marketers' messages. Among them are motives, attitudes, perception, learning, and lifestyle. In this section, we examine how such psychological factors can influence the consumer decision process.[25]

Motives   In Chapter 1, we argued that marketing is all about satisfying customer needs and wants. When a need, such as thirst, or a want, such as a Diet Coke, is not satisfied, it motivates us, or drives us, to get satisfaction. So, a motive is a need or want that is strong enough to cause the person to seek satisfaction.

People have several types of motives. One of the best known paradigms for explaining these motive types was developed by Abraham Maslow more than 30 years ago, called Maslow's Hierarchy of Needs.[26] Maslow categorized five groups of needs, namely, physiological (e.g., food, water, shelter), safety (e.g., secure employment, health), love (e.g., friendship, family), esteem (e.g., confidence, respect), and self-actualization (people engage in personal growth activities and attempt to meet their intellectual, aesthetic, creative, and other

EXHIBIT 5.4   Factors Affecting the Consumer Decision Process such needs). The pyramid in Exhibit 5.5 demonstrates the theoretical progression of those needs.

Physiological needs deal with the basic biological necessities of life—food, drink, rest, and shelter. Although for most people in developed countries these basic needs are generally met, there are those in both developed and less-developed countries who are less fortunate. However, everyone remains concerned with meeting these basic needs. Marketers seize every opportunity to convert these needs into wants by reminding us to eat at Taco Bell, drink milk, sleep on a Beautyrest mattress, and stay at a Marriott.

Safety needs pertain to protection and physical well-being. The marketplace is full of products and services that are designed to make you safer, such as airbags in cars and burglar alarms in homes, or healthier, such as vitamins and organic meats and vegetables.

Love needs relate to our interactions with others. Haircuts and makeup make you look more attractive, and deodorants prevent odor. Greeting cards help you express your feelings toward others.

Esteem needs allow people to satisfy their inner desires. Yoga, meditation, health clubs, and many books appeal to people's desires to grow or maintain a happy, satisfied outlook on life.

Finally, **self-actualization** occurs when you feel completely satisfied with your life and how you live. You don't care what others think. You drive a Prius because it suits the person you are, not because some celebrity endorses it or because you want others to think better of you.

Which of these needs applies when a consumer purchases a magazine? Magazines such as *Weight Watchers*, for instance, help satisfy *physiological* needs

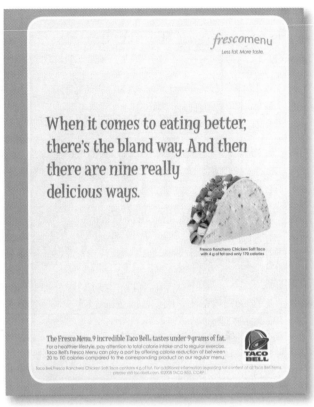

Taco Bell satisfies physiological needs.

EXHIBIT **5.5**	Maslow's Hierarchy of Needs

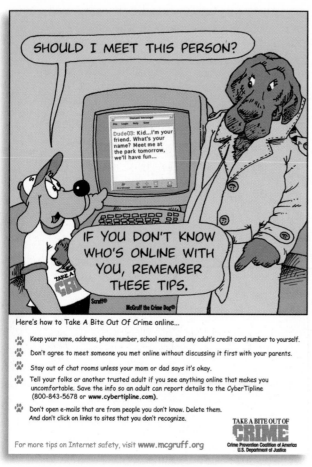

Ads for crime prevention satisfy safety needs.

Yoga satisfies esteem needs by helping people satisfy their inner desires.

like how to eat healthy but also *esteem* needs like how to be happy with one's life. Magazines like *Family Circle,* on the other hand, provide tips on how to make the home a *safer* place to live. Finally, magazines such as *Weddings* help satisfy *love and belonging* needs, because they provide instructions on topics such as how to prepare gracious invitations for friends and family. Many of these magazines fulfill several needs simultaneously, of course. Good marketers add value to their products or services by nudging people up the needs hierarchy and offering information on as many of the pyramid needs as they can.

Attitude

We have attitudes about almost everything. For instance, we like this class, but we don't like the instructor. We like where we live, but we don't like the weather. An **attitude** is a person's enduring evaluation of his or her feelings about and behavioral tendencies toward an object or idea. Attitudes are learned and long lasting, and they might develop over a long period of time, though they can also abruptly change. For instance, you might like your instructor for much of the semester—until she returns your first exam. The one thing attitudes have in common for everyone is their ability to influence our decisions and actions.

An attitude consists of three components. The **cognitive** component reflects what we believe to be true, the **affective** component involves what we feel about the issue at hand—our like or dislike of something, and the **behavioral component** is the actions we undertake with regard to that issue. For example,

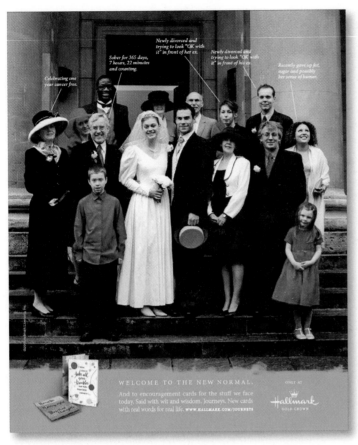

Greeting cards help you express your love needs.

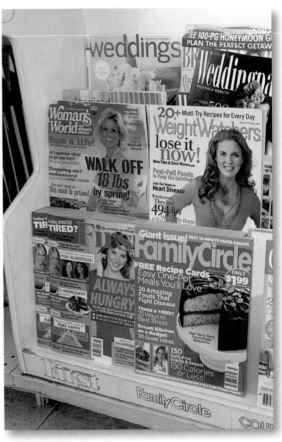

Which categories of Maslow's Hierarchy of Needs do these magazines fulfill?

Matt and Lisa Martinez see an advertisement for the movie *Pirates of the Caribbean* that shows Johnny Depp dueling with Geoffrey Rush. An announcer lists quotes from different respected movie critics indicating that the latest movie is great. On the basis of this advertisement, Matt and Lisa believe that the critics must be correct and that *Pirates of the Caribbean* is likely to be a good movie (cognitive component). Watching Johnny Depp talk about the movie in interviews prompts Matt and Lisa to think that the movie will be engaging because they like fantasy action adventures (affective component). After weighing their various movie options, Matt and Lisa go to see the movie (behavioral component).

Ideally, agreement exists among these components. When there is incongruence among the three, however—if Matt and Lisa found the reviews were mixed, but they went to see the movie anyway—cognitive dissonance might occur. Suppose, for instance, Matt and Lisa believe that another movie might be better, but they go to *Pirates of the Caribbean* instead. If the experience is not just great, their prior knowledge of mixed reviews could trigger buyers' remorse.

Although attitudes are pervasive and usually slow to change, the important fact from a marketer's point of view is that they can be influenced and perhaps changed through persuasive communications and personal experience. Marketing communication—through sales people, advertisements, free samples, or other such methods—can attempt to change what people believe to be true about a product or service (cognitive) or how they feel toward it (affective). If the marketer is successful, the cognitive and affective components work in concert to affect behavior. Continuing with our example, suppose that prior to viewing

Based on positive reviews (cognitive component) and positive feelings toward the actors (affective component), many people went to see Pirates of the Caribbean (behavior component) and came away with a positive attitude toward it.

the movie ad, Matt and Lisa thought that *Spider-Man* would be the next movie they would go see, but they had heard good things about *Pirates of the Caribbean*. The ad positively influenced the cognitive component of their attitude toward *Pirates of the Caribbean*, making it consistent with their affective component.

Perception Another psychological factor, perception, is the process by which we select, organize, and interpret information to form a meaningful picture of the world. Perception in marketing influences our acquisition and consumption of goods and services through our tendency to assign meaning to such things as color, symbols, taste, and packaging. Culture, tradition, and our overall upbringing determine our perception of the world. For instance, Lisa Martinez has always wanted an apartment in the Back Bay neighborhood of Boston because her favorite aunt had one, and they had a great time visiting for Thanksgiving one year. However, from his past experiences, Matt has a different perception. Matt thinks Back Bay apartments are small, expensive, and too small for a couple thinking about having children—though they would be convenient for single people who work in downtown Boston. The city of Boston has worked hard in recent years to overcome the long-standing negative perceptual bias that Matt and many others hold by working with developers to create larger, modern, and more affordable apartments and using promotion to reposition the perception of apartments in the Back Bay for young couples.

Learning Learning refers to a change in a person's thought process or behavior that arises from experience and takes place throughout the consumer decision process. For instance, after Katie recognized that she needed a car, she started looking for ads and searching for reviews and articles on the Internet. She learned from each new piece of information, so her thoughts about car features were different from those before she had read anything. She liked what she learned about the features of the Prius. She learned from her search, and it became part of her memory to be used in the future, possibly so she could recommend the car to her friends.

Learning affects both attitudes and perceptions. Throughout the buying process, Katie's attitudes shifted. The cognitive component came into play for her when she learned that no other car offered better mileage. Once she test-drove the Prius, she realized how much she liked the way it felt and looked, which involved the affective component. Then she purchased it—the behavioral component. Each time she was exposed to information about the car or to the car itself, she learned something different that affected her perception. Before she tried it, Katie hadn't realized how much fun it was to drive a small car; thus, her perception of the Prius changed through learning.

Lifestyle Lifestyle refers to the way consumers spend their time and money to live. For many consumers, the question of whether the product or service fits with their actual lifestyle, which may be fairly sedentary, or their perceived lifestyle, which might be outdoorsy, is an important one. Some of the many consumers sporting North Face jackets certainly need the high-tech, cold weather

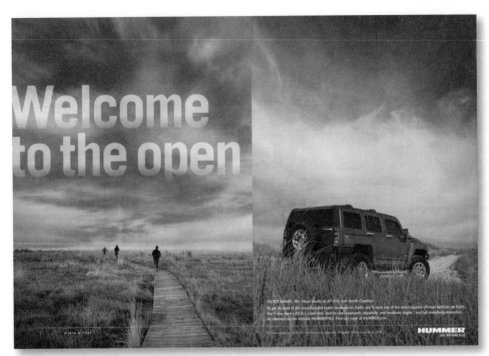

People buy a Hummer to emulate an outdoor lifestyle, even if it is only used to whiz over speed bumps in a parking lot.

gear because they are planning their next hike up Mount Rainier and want to be sure they have sufficient protection against the elements. Others, however, simply like the image that the jacket conveys—the image that they might be leaving for their own mountain-climbing expedition any day now—even if the closest they have come has been shoveling their driveway. Similarly, people buy the Hummer luxury four-wheel drive SUV so that they can get over almost any off-road obstacle, but they also like the leather seats with lumbar support, six-speaker audio system preloaded with XM satellite radio, remote keyless entry system, and the fact that they can whiz over speed bumps at the local grocery store.

A person's perceptions and ability to learn are affected by their social experiences, which we discuss next.

Social Factors

The consumer decision process is influenced from within by psychological factors, but also by the external, social environment, which consists of the customer's family, reference groups, and culture.[27] (See again Exhibit 5.4.)

Family   Many purchase decisions are made about products or services that the entire family will consume or use. Thus, firms must consider how families make purchase decisions and understand how various family members might influence these decisions.

When families make purchase decisions, they often consider the needs of all the family members. In choosing a restaurant, for example, all the family members may participate in the decision making. In other situations, however, different members of the family may take on the purchasing role. For example, the husband and teenage child may look through car magazines and *Consumer Reports* to search for information about a new car. But once they arrive at the dealership, the husband and wife, not the child, decide which model and color to buy, and the wife negotiates the final deal.

Children and adolescents play an increasingly important role in family buying decisions. Kids in the United States spend over $200 billion a year on personal items such as snacks, soft drinks, entertainment, and apparel. They directly influence the purchase of another $300 billion worth of items such as food, snacks, beverages, toys, health and beauty aids, clothing, accessories, gifts, and school supplies. Their indirect influence on family spending is even higher—$500 billion for items such as recreation, vacations, technology, and even the family car.[28] Even grandparents contribute to the economic impact of children in the United States. It is estimated that grandparents spend $27.5 billion dollars on purchases for grandchildren, and 72 percent of grandparents would spend more if the money were available to them.[29]

Influencing a group that holds this much spending power is vitally important. Traditional food retailers are already caught in a squeeze between Wal-Mart, which lures low-end customers, and specialty retailers like Whole Foods, which target the high end. Knowing how children influence food buying decisions is a strategic opportunity for traditional supermarkets and their suppliers to exploit. Getting this group to prefer one store, chain, or product over another can make a difference in the bottom line, as well as in the chances for survival in a difficult marketplace.[30]

Reference Groups   A reference group is one or more persons whom an individual uses as a basis for comparison regarding beliefs, feelings, and behaviors. A consumer might have various reference groups, including family, friends, coworkers, or famous people the consumer would like to emulate. These reference groups affect buying decisions by (1) offering information, (2) providing rewards for specific purchasing behaviors, and (3) enhancing a consumer's self-image.

Reference groups provide information to consumers directly through conversation or indirectly through observation. For example, Katie received valuable information from a friend about the Prius. On another occasion, she heard a favorite cousin who is an auto buff praising the virtues of the Prius's hybrid engine, which solidified her attitude about the car.

Some reference groups also influence behaviors by rewarding behavior that meets with their approval or chastising behavior that doesn't. For example, smokers are often criticized or even ostracized by their friends and made to smoke outside or in restricted areas.

Consumers can identify and affiliate with reference groups to create, enhance, or maintain their self-image. Customers who want to be seen as "earthy" might buy Birkenstock sandals, whereas those wanting to be seen as "high fashion" might buy Christian Louboutin shoes, as we discussed earlier in this chapter.

Some stores, like Abercrombie & Fitch, play on these forms of influence and hire sales associates they hope will serve as a reference group for customers who shop there. These "cool," attractive, and somewhat aloof employees are encouraged to wear the latest store apparel—thereby serving as living mannequins to emulate.

Family members often influence buying decisions.

Culture   We defined culture in Chapter 4 as the shared meanings, beliefs, morals, values, and customs of a group of people. As the basis of the social factors that impact your buying decisions, the culture or cultures in which you participate are not markedly different from your reference groups. That is, your cultural group might be as small as your reference group at school or as large as the country in which you live or the religion to which you belong. Like reference groups, cultures influence consumer behavior. For instance, the culture at Katie's college evokes an "environmentally friendly school." This influences, to some extent, the way she spends her leisure time and even what type of car she will buy. Adding Value 5.2 describes a cooking utensil company that adapts its products to the cooking cultures of local markets worldwide.

Adding Value 5.2 | OXO: Grating on Customers' Nerves—in a Good Way

OXO International provides innovative kitchenware that has been very successful in the United States. The OXO products, marketed under the Best Grips brand, are recognizable by their large black handles and distinctive design features. Recognized as one of the most innovative design companies in the United States, OXO creates value for its customers by using a concept called "Universal Design," which takes as its goal the design of products that are usable by the greatest number of people. Thus, OXO designs vegetable peelers that are safe for children to use and creates can openers that will function easily, even for seniors or people with arthritis. Initially, OXO imagined its core demographic would be Baby Boomers or those over the age of 60 years who require easy-to-use utensils. However, consumers of all ages currently use the products, which range from award-winning salad spinners to spatulas. Its success in the United States has enabled OXO to command a significant price premium for its utensils compared with generic products.

However, when OXO tried to expand outside of the United States market and into Japan, it found that Japanese consumers simply were not attracted to the OXO designs. Management had believed the Japanese market would be a good fit for OXO products, because the largest demographic segment in Japan is Baby Boomers, and the average age in

Japan is 10 years older than in the United States. Yet these consumers who presumably would appreciate the large, comfortable grips of the OXO utensils refused to purchase the products. Even the salad spinner, which had won awards in the United States and was the most popular OXO product, sold poorly.[31]

To understand why, OXO conducted several focus groups and quickly recognized several interesting characteristics of Japanese consumers. It turns out that Japanese cooks use kitchen utensils differently than do American cooks. For example, Americans hold spatulas like tennis rackets, whereas Japanese cooks hold them like pens. That slight difference meant that the grip that seemed large and comfortable to Americans was uncomfortable and unwieldy for the Japanese. To better serve Japanese consumers, OXO invested significant time to research how they cook at home.

The research resulted in an entirely new product line. Most notable was the creation of the Daikon radish grater. Radish graters are staples of Japanese kitchens, but no one had thought to improve on the design for decades. OXO took this opportunity to work with a Japanese design team and created a completely redesigned radish grater that earned the company a design award and rapid growth in the Japanese market.[32]

Situational Factors

Psychological and social factors typically influence the consumer decision process the same way each time. For example, your motivation to quench your thirst usually drives you to drink a Coke or a Pepsi, and your reference group at the workplace coerces you to wear appropriate attire. But sometimes, situational factors, or factors specific to the situation, override, or at least influence, psychological and social issues. These situational factors are related to the purchase and shopping situation, as well as to temporal states.[33]

Purchase Situation Customers may be predisposed to purchase certain products or services because of some underlying psychological trait or social factor, but these factors may change in certain purchase situations. For instance, Samantha Crumb considers herself a thrifty, cautious shopper—someone who likes to get a good deal. But her best friend is getting married, and she wants to buy the couple a silver tray. If the tray were for herself, she would probably go to Crate & Barrel or possibly even Wal-Mart. But since it is for her best friend, she went to Tiffany & Co. Why? To purchase something fitting for the special occasion of a wedding.

Shopping Situation Consumers might be ready to purchase a product or service but be completely derailed once they arrive in the store. Marketers use several techniques to influence consumers at this choice stage of the decision process. Consider the following techniques.

Store Atmosphere Some retailers and service providers have developed unique images that are based at least in part on their internal environment, also known as their atmospherics.[34] Research has shown that, if used in concert with other aspects of a retailer's strategy, music, scent, lighting, and even color can

Outback Steakhouse has developed internal environments that are not only pleasant but also consistent with their food and service.

positively influence the decision process.[35] Restaurants such as Outback Steakhouse and The Cheesecake Factory have developed internal environments that are not only pleasant but also consistent with their food and service.

Sales People   Well-trained sales personnel can influence the sale at the point of purchase by educating consumers about product attributes, pointing out the advantages of one item over another, and encouraging multiple purchases. The salesperson at Tiffany & Co., for instance, explained to Samantha why one platter was better than another, and suggested some serving pieces to go with it. Superior Service 5.1 examines how other retailers utilize sales people to positively influence the purchase situation.

Crowding   Customers can feel crowded because there are too many people, too much merchandise, or lines that are too long. If there are

---

 ## Superior Service **5.1**   Retailers Sell with Service

Some luxury retailers are changing their former strategy of having a snobby attitude toward customers.[36] To sustain customer loyalty, it is essential that retailers show every client that he or she is valuable. Henri Bendel of New York City and Colette in Paris sell designer clothing such as Missoni and Valentino, and are interested in helping all customers and educating them on the brands and merchandise. Henri Bendel offers free client services to help a customer find a new outfit, or even an anniversary gift. Small shoe boutiques such as Christian Louboutin and Salvatore Ferragamo that have only a few locations in the world are following suit in customer service. Even if a particular store does not have the shoe the customer is seeking, the staff will search all of the company's locations until they find it. At Ferragamo, all employees have to go through a mandatory customer service training program to empower them to function successfully in the luxury retail industry.

Research by appliance retailer Best Buy found that it was not doing a good job appealing to women because of the extremely loud audio department, the cluttered aisles, and the crowded lanes.[37] As a result, besides lowering its audio volume, making aisles wider, and adding play areas for children, Best Buy also trained its sales people to help female shoppers navigate the store. If they don't want to wander around, they can recline in a massage chair while a personal shopper gets the merchandise for them. Best Buy doesn't ignore the men, however. It just treats them slightly differently. For instance, women may want assistance on the phone to help them set up the electronic equipment. But men might be offended if a Best Buy salesperson called their house to help them with the installation.

Mitchells/Richards is a multimillion-dollar men's and women's clothing business with one store in Westport and a second store in Greenwich, Connecticut.[38] The company is focused on a philosophy of building relationships, always "hugging" the customer, and not just making transactions. Its employees treat all customers as celebrities or CEOs. In order for employees to be empowered to serve clients properly,

they have a sophisticated customer relationship management (CRM) program. The retailer's customer service goes far beyond just offering complimentary tailoring. The employees, including the sales associates, the tailors, the fitters, and the delivery people, know everything about their customers. They study their customers' profiles, which include the merchandise they have bought recently, merchandise they have *not* bought recently, and their upcoming events such as family birthdays, changes in spending habits, and even golf handicaps.

The Container Store sells products to help people organize their lives.[39] Multipurpose shelving and garment bags are available to organize closets. Portable file cabinets and magazine holders create order in home offices. Backpacks, modular shelving, and CD holders can make dorm rooms less cluttered. Recipe holders, bottles, jars, and recycling bins bring harmony to kitchens. Wherever you look in the store, there's always someone in a blue apron ready to help solve storage problems. Although storage items and many other similar products are available at other retailers, few competitors offer this high level of customer service. Considerable time is spent educating sales associates about the merchandise, who are then empowered to use their own intuition and creativity to solve customer problems. The company actively recruits its sales people, who are intrigued by helping people organize their lives.

Some retailers are bolstering their online sales service by providing an online chat capability that enables customers to click a button at any time and have an instant messaging e-mail or voice conversation with a customer service representative. This technology also enables electronic retailers to automatically send a proactive chat invitation to customers on the site. The timing of these invitations can be based on the time the visitor has spent on the site, the specific page the customer is viewing, or a product on which the customer has clicked. At Bluefly.com, for example, if a visitor searches for more than three items in five minutes, thereby demonstrating more than a passing interest, Bluefly will display a pop-up window with a friendly face offering help.[40]

too many people in a store, some people become distracted and may even leave.[41] Others have difficulty purchasing if the merchandise is packed too closely together. This issue is a particular problem for shoppers with mobility disabilities.

In-Store Demonstrations   The taste and smell of new food items may attract people to try something they normally wouldn't. Similarly, some fashion retailers offer "trunk shows," during which their vendors show their whole line of merchandise on a certain day. During these well-advertised events, customers are often enticed to purchase that day because they get special assistance from the sales people and can order merchandise that the retailer otherwise does not carry.

Promotions   Retailers employ various promotional vehicles to influence customers once they have arrived in the store. An unadvertised price promotion can alter a person's preconceived buying plan. Multi-item discounts, such as "buy 1, get 1 free" sales, are popular means to get people to buy more than they normally would. Because many people regard clipping coupons from the newspaper as too much trouble, some stores make coupons available in the store. Another form of promotion is offering a "free" gift with the purchase of a good or service. This type of promotion is particularly popular with cosmetics. Ethical and Societal Dilemma 5.1 details some of the concerns that go along with such promotions.

Packaging   It is difficult to make a product stand out in the crowd when it competes for shelf space with several other brands. This problem is particularly difficult

In-store demonstrations entice people to buy.

Ethical and Societal Dilemma 5.1 Is a "Free Gift" Really Free?

Some companies seek to short-circuit the consumer decision-making process by offering consumers a free gift as an additional incentive with their purchase. However, these gifts increase the cost of the product or service and therefore mislead consumers about the "real" cost. Are these giveaways a legitimate form of promotion, or do they unnecessarily increase the cost of products or services?

For instance, credit card companies frequently target college students with offers that include free gifts or donations to schools clubs or teams. According to the American Bankers Association, 25 percent of all student credit cards are received as part of an on-campus promotion, and there is a growing tendency toward signing up for credit cards on impulse. Although students are not typically seen as good credit risks, credit card companies target them for two reasons: Students represent potential lifetime customers who can develop brand loyalty and eventually use other financial products such as mutual funds, and secondly, credit card companies know that parents frequently help their children pay their debts, even if the parents are under no obligation to assist their children.[42]

One such credit card promotion by Citibank at The Ohio State University offered free sandwiches. The only catch was that a credit card application had to be submitted before any food was served. The Ohio state attorney general found out about the promotion and sued Citibank for violating the state's consumer protection laws. The attorney general accused Citibank of failing to clearly state the offer, and tempting students with a prize without disclosing the conditions. Even though Citibank claims that it did not condone the promotion, it is typical of credit card events around the country.

In response to the many credit card promotions targeting college-age students, some colleges and universities are moving to limit the number or type of promotions that can occur on campus. For example, in California, credit card companies cannot give away "free gifts," and in Oklahoma, colleges have been banned by the state legislature from selling student names and e-mail addresses to credit card companies.[43]

Does a free gift deceive a consumer, or is it simply a way to make an offer more attractive?

for consumer packaged goods, such as groceries and health and beauty products. Marketers therefore spend millions of dollars designing and updating their packages to be more appealing and eye catching.

Temporal State   Our state of mind at any particular time can alter our preconceived notions of what we are going to purchase. For instance, some people are "morning people," whereas others function better at night. A purchase situation may thus have different appeal levels depending on the time of day and the type of person the consumer is. Mood swings can alter consumer behavior. Suppose Samantha received a parking ticket just prior to shopping at Tiffany & Co. It is likely that she would be less receptive to the salesperson's influence than if she came into the store in a good mood. Her bad mood might even cause her to have a less positive postpurchase feeling about the store.

The factors that affect the consumer decision process—the marketing mix, psychological factors, social factors, and situational factors—are all impacted by the level of consumer involvement, the subject of the next section.

CHECK YOURSELF

1. Give some examples of needs suggested by Maslow's Hierarchy of Needs?
2. Which social factors likely have the most influence on
   a. The purchase of a new outfit for going out dancing?
   b. The choice of a college to attend?
3. List some of the tactics stores can use to influence consumers' decision processes.

INVOLVEMENT AND CONSUMER BUYING DECISIONS

Consumers make two types of buying decisions depending on their level of involvement: extended problem solving and limited problem solving, which includes impulse buying and habitual decision making. **Involvement** is the consumer's

EXHIBIT 5.6   Elaboration Likelihood Model

degree of interest in the product or service.[44] Consumers may have different levels of involvement for the same type of product. One consumer behavior theory, the elaboration likelihood model, illustrated in Exhibit 5.6, proposes that high- and low-involvement consumers process different aspects of a message or advertisement.

If both types of consumers viewed ads for hybrids produced by Toyota and Ford, the high-involvement consumer (e.g., Katie who is researching buying a hybrid) will scrutinize all the information provided (gas savings, eco-friendly) and process the key elements of the message more deeply. As a consequence, Katie, an involved consumer, is likely to either end up judging the ad to be truthful and form a favorable impression of the product or alternatively view the message as superficial and develop negative product impressions (i.e., her research suggests the product is not as good as it is being portrayed).

In contrast, a low-involvement consumer will likely process the same advertisement in a less thorough manner. Such a consumer might pay less attention to the key elements of the message (gas savings, eco-friendly) and focus on heuristic elements such as brand name (Toyota), price, and the presence of a celebrity endorser. The impressions of the low-involvement consumer are likely to be more superficial.

What type of buying decision does each of these products represent?

Extended Problem Solving

The buying process begins when consumers recognize that they have an unsatisfied need. Katie Smith recognized her need to have access to transportation when she went away to college. She sought information by asking for advice from her friends, reading consumer reports, and conducting research online. Once she decided that a car and not a bike or the bus was her best option, she visited several car dealerships to test-drive the models she was interested in and find out which dealer offered the best price. Finally, after considerable time and effort analyzing her alternatives, Katie purchased a Toyota Prius. This process is an example of extended problem solving, which is common when the customer perceives that the purchase decision entails a lot of risk. The potential risks associated with Katie's decision to buy her car include financial (did I pay too much?), physical (will it keep me safe in an accident?), and social (will my friends think I look cool?) risks. To reduce her perceived risk, Katie spent a lot of effort searching for information about cars before she actually made her purchase.

Limited Problem Solving

Limited problem solving occurs during a purchase decision that calls for, at most, a moderate amount of effort and time. Customers engage in this type of buying process when they have had some prior experience with the product or service and the perceived risk is moderate. Limited problem solving usually relies on past experience more than on external information. For some people even a car purchase could require limited effort.

A common type of limited problem solving is impulse buying, a buying decision made by customers on the spot when they see the merchandise.[45] When Katie went to the grocery store to do her weekly shopping, she saw a display case of popcorn and Dr Pepper near the checkout counter. Knowing that some of her friends were coming over to watch *Casablanca,* she stocked up. The popcorn and soda were an impulse purchase. Katie didn't go through the entire decision process; instead, she recognized her need and jumped directly to purchase without spending any time searching for additional information or evaluating alternatives. The grocery store facilitated this impulse purchase by providing easily accessible cues (i.e., by offering the popcorn and soda in a prominent display, at a great location in the store, and at a reasonable price).

Some purchases require even less thought. Habitual decision making describes a purchase decision process in which consumers engage in little conscious effort. On her way home from the grocery store, for example, Katie drove past an In-N-Out Burger and swung into the drive-through for a cheeseburger and Diet Coke. She did not ponder the potential benefits of going to Wendy's instead for lunch; rather, she simply reacted to the cue provided by the sign and engaged in habitual decision making. Marketers strive to attract and maintain habitual purchasers by creating strong brands and store loyalty (see Chapters 10 and 11) because these customers don't even consider alternative brands or stores.

CHECK YOURSELF

1. How do low- versus high-involvement consumers process information in an advertisement?
2. What is the difference between extended versus limited problem solving?

Summing Up

1. **What steps do you go through when you decide to buy a product or service?**

Consumers generally start their decision process by recognizing that they must buy something to satisfy a need or want. Sometimes the needs are simple: I need food because I am hungry. Often, however, they become more complex: I want to buy my girlfriend an engagement ring.

Once they recognize the need, consumers start searching for information. Generally, the more important the purchase, the more time and effort the consumer will spend on the search process. Firms facilitate this search by providing promotional materials and personal selling. Once they have enough information, consumers can evaluate their alternatives and make a choice.

In the next step of the decision process, consumers purchase and use the product or service. But the process doesn't simply stop there. After the sale, the consumer is either satisfied with the purchase or experiences postpurchase dissonance. All marketers want satisfied customers, but when instead they are confronted with dissatisfied customers who are in some way unsure about their purchase, they must proactively turn the situation around. If they don't, the customer may be gone for good.

2. How can understanding consumers' behavior help marketers sell products or services?

First and foremost, firms must design their products and services to meet their customers' wants and needs, but understanding certain aspects of consumer behavior can help as well. For instance, it is important to understand people's motives (i.e., what drives them to buy), their attitudes (i.e., how they feel about a product or service), and their perceptions (i.e., how information about that product or service fits into their world view). Knowledge about these psychological characteristics helps firms design and provide products and services that their customers want and need.

In addition, people don't live in a vacuum. Consumers are influenced by their family, their reference groups, and their culture. Understanding these social groups and people's roles within them provides important insights into consumers' buying behavior. Finally, though consumers already carry a host of psychological and social influences along with them on a shopping expedition, certain other factors can influence a purchase at the point of sale. Customers might change their buying behavior because a store layout is different from the one they are used to. Also, things can happen to customers, both positive and negative, once they are in a store that might alter their preconceived notion of what they plan to purchase. People can be just plain finicky, or can be in an unusually good or extremely bad mood, yet the more firms understand psychological, social, and situational factors, the more likely they will be to influence purchase decisions.

3. When purchasing a product or a service, do you spend a lot of time considering your decision?

The answer to how much time a consumer spends making a purchasing decision largely depends on the product or service being purchased. Some purchasing decisions require limited problem solving because the perceived risk of the purchase is low or the consumer has previous experience purchasing the product or service. Impulse and habitual purchases fall in this category. Sometimes, however, consumers enter into extended problem solving because the perceived risk of the purchase is great.

Key Terms

- affective component, 164
- attitude, 164
- behavioral component, 164
- cognitive component, 164
- compensatory decision rule, 156
- consumer decision rules, 156
- convenience goods/services, 155
- culture, 168
- decision heuristics, 158
- determinant attributes, 156
- esteem needs, 163
- evaluative criteria, 155
- evoked set, 155
- extended problem solving, 174
- external locus of control, 154
- external search for information, 153
- financial risk, 154

- functional needs, 151
- habitual decision making, 174
- impulse buying, 174
- internal locus of control, 154
- internal search for information, 153
- involvement, 172
- learning, 166
- lifestyle, 166
- limited problem solving, 174
- love needs, 163
- Maslow's Hierachy of Needs, 162
- motive, 162
- need recognition, 151
- negative word of mouth, 161
- noncompensatory decision rule, 157

- perception, 166
- performance risk, 154
- physiological needs, 163
- postpurchase dissonance, 160
- psychological needs, 151
- psychological risk, 154
- reference group, 168
- retrieval sets, 155
- ritual consumption, 158
- safety needs, 163
- self-actualization, 163
- shopping goods/services, 155
- situational factors, 169
- specialty goods/services, 154
- universal sets, 155

Marketing Applications

1. Describe two products: one you just went and purchased without much thought and one that took some deliberation on your part. Why did you spend a different amount of time and effort deciding on your purchases of the two products?

2. Assume you want to buy a new stereo system. What kinds of components would you consider? What types of needs would you be satisfying if you purchased that particular type of stereo?

3. Explain the factors that affect the amount of time and effort that a consumer might take when choosing a surgeon to perform a facelift. How would your answer change if the consumer were looking for moisturizing lotion?

4. When evaluating different alternatives for a Saturday night outing at a fine restaurant, explain the difference between the universal set, the retrieval set, and the evoked set. From which set of alternatives will the consumer most likely choose the restaurant?

5. What can retailers do to make sure they have satisfied customers after the sale is complete?

6. Tazo makes a blend of exotic green teas, spearmint, and rare herbs into a tea called Zen. Using Maslow's hierarchy of needs, explain which need(s) are being fulfilled by this tea.

7. Identify and describe the three social factors that influence the consumer decision process. Provide an example of how each of these might influence the purchase of the necessary products and services for a family vacation.

8. Trek has designed a new off-road bicycle designed to stand up to the rugged conditions of trail riding. Develop a theme for an advertising strategy that ensures all three components of attitude are positively covered.

9. What can a marketer do to positively influence a situation in which a consumer is ready to buy but has not yet done so?

10. You were recently hired by a retail and catalog company that promotes itself as an American firm selling only American-made goods. The products featured in advertising and in the catalogs tell the stories of the firms that produced the goods in the United States. The sales response to the firm's Made in America position has been incredible and growth has been impressive. One day while speaking to a vendor, you find out a shipment of merchandise will be delayed since the product is coming from overseas and is late. A few days later you hear a similar story. As it turns out, the firm just barely earns the Made in the USA label. Though technically the products meet a standard to be classified as American made, you worry that the firm is not being truthful to its customers. You decide to write a letter to the VP of Marketing detailing your concerns. What would you put in the letter?

 www.mhhe.com/ grewal2e

Quiz Yourself

1. Dawn flies regularly between Atlanta and Los Angeles. She almost always uses Delta and has accumulated a large number of Delta SkyMiles. However, Dawn uses an online fare comparison site each time she needs to book a ticket to see if competitors have a better price or a more convenient schedule. Dawn uses a _____ decision rule.
   a. compensatory
   b. noncompensatory
   c. ritual consumption
   d. social
   e. situational factor

2. Natalie and her fiancé Dow are planning their wedding. She knows her mother wants her to have a traditional church ceremony. She would like to have a ceremony on the beach like many of her friends had. Then there is the problem of who should officiate. Dow is from Thailand and would like to have a monk officiate. Natalie and Dow's wedding decisions are influenced by:
   a. impulse, habitual, and limited problem solving process.
   b. functional and psychological profit.
   c. universal, retrieval, and evoked sets.
   d. cognitive, affective, and behavioral environment.
   e. family, reference groups, and culture.

(Answers to these two questions are provided on page 623.)

Go to www.mhhe.com/grewal2e to practice an additional 11 questions.

Toolkit

CONSUMER BEHAVIOR

Jill is trying to decide, once and for all, which soft drink company is her favorite. She has created a chart to help her decide. She has rated Coca-Cola, Pepsi-Cola, and Jones Soda in terms of price, taste, variety, and packaging. She has also assessed how important each of these four attributes is in terms of her evaluations. Please use the toolkit provided at www.mhhe.com/grewal2e to determine which cola Jill will choose using a compensatory model. Which cola would she choose using a noncompensatory model? If you were Jill, which model would you use, the compensatory or the noncompensatory? Why?

Net Savvy

1. Visit the Harley-Davidson USA Web site (www.harley-davidson.com) and review the information provided about its Harley Owners Group (H.O.G.), by first going to the "Owners" tab at the top. Describe the efforts the company makes to maintain customer loyalty through its programs. What are the benefits to H.O.G. members? Discuss how these measures might be effective in creating value for members.

2. Customers use a variety of methods to provide feedback to companies about their experiences.

Planetfeedback.com was developed as one such venue. Visit its Web site (www.planetfeedback.com) and identify the types of feedback that customers can provide. Look over the feedback for Verizon by typing "Verizon" in the company search space. Summarize some of the most recent comments. What is the ratio of positive to negative comments about Verizon during the last year or so? Describe the effect these comments might have on customer perceptions of Verizon.

Chapter Case Study

THE SMART CAR PREPARES TO ENTER THE U.S. MARKET[46]

All the rage in crowded cities in Western Europe, the Smart car brand finally made its way across the Atlantic in January 2008. Although various models were available elsewhere, an entirely new model was introduced into the U.S. market: a two-person ultracompact called the "fortwo."[47] The year before the introduction of the Smart car, Daimler-Benz allowed consumers to reserve a Smart car by paying $99 dollars. Even though paying $99 dollars did not guarantee a place in line for a Smart car, but only an opportunity to purchase a Smart if there was one in a nearby dealership, over 30,000 consumers decided to pay the reservation fee in 2007. How does a reservation fee such as this one fit into the consumer decision process and why did Daimler-Benz decide to use this process in the United States?

The Smart car was conceived in 1994 through a joint venture between Mercedes-Benz and SMH, the Swiss manufacturer of Swatch watches, and named for "**S**watch, **M**ercedes, and **art**." Engineered with the environment in mind, the car originally was to use electric power or hybrid technology but ultimately was produced to consume either gasoline or diesel fuel, though it still achieves "green" status because of its anticorrosion undercoat and the powder coating on its steel body, which avoids polluting with wastewater and solvents. The body also features already colored, molded plastic panels to eliminate the need for paint booths and their resulting emissions.[48]

One of the hallmarks of the Smart car is its size. Its dimensions—eight feet long, five feet wide, and five feet tall—puts it five feet shorter and a foot narrower than the Volkswagen Beetle. The Smart car was designed as a part of an overall transportation strategy for Europe's bustling big cities. To support efforts to reduce congestion, the Smart car was to be used to reach local destinations, whereas longer trips would rely on rail and air transportation.

As the world's smallest car, Smart has earned affectionate nicknames: "the electric razor on wheels," "glorified go-cart," "high fashion by Hot Wheels," and "the rolling backpack," to cite just a few. Driving it has been likened to driving in a telephone booth, though some view it more as a high-tech toy whose cabin is part cockpit, part playpen. In exchange for the small size, the Smart car is an environmentalist's dream because of its ability to get 45 miles per gallon on the highway and 40 miles per gallon in the city,[49] its low emissions, and the recyclability of 85 percent of the materials used in its production. In markets in which gasoline costs upwards of $5 a gallon, the car has real appeal, especially among the eclectic crowd, with its hip, cool image.[50]

Although it sports only a three-cylinder, 50- to 60-horsepower engine, the Smart car is reported to purr like a kitten and offer some spunk. In addition to front and optional side airbags, air conditioning, remote control locking, and electric windows, Smart cars can change their colors if buyers purchase interchangeable snap-on body panels. When the mood hits, the owner pulls off the black panels, snaps on the red, and makes a whole new fashion statement.

The Market for Smart

Wholly owned by Daimler-Benz, Smart cars are currently sold in 37 countries, including Germany, Italy, Switzerland, Australia, Canada, Hong Kong, Israel, Japan, Lebanon, Mexico, South Africa, Taiwan, Turkey, and the United Kingdom.[51]

In the recent past, small cars have had a difficult time making big inroads into the U.S. automobile market. American consumers like the luxury and safety provided by their large, massive-horsepower cars, SUVs, and trucks—even when fuel prices skyrocket—partly because they are accustomed to a more sparsely populated geography, except for those U.S. consumers who live in sprawling metropolitan areas. Although uniquely styled cars like the PT Cruiser, Volkswagen Beetle, and

Smart cars are just plain cool!

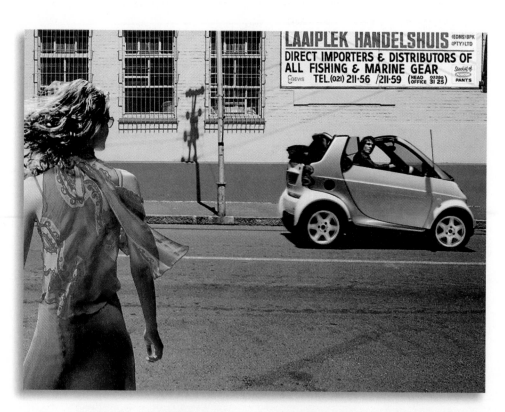

Mini Cooper have managed to get a piece of the limelight, they appeal only to small niches in the U.S. market.

For the past several years, the Smart has been available only through the gray market in the United States. On average, 1,000 Smart fortwos were imported each year into the United States and rebuilt to meet the more stringent American emission standards. Although the fortwo is an inexpensive car, the conversion and cost of importation could easily cost the owner two to three times the $11,000 price tag for the fortwo. Yet many consumers have been motivated to purchase this unique car in the gray market to make a fashion statement.[52]

In early 2007, when Daimler-Benz partnered with a U.S. dealer network to sell a new version of the fortwo in the United States, it decided to conduct an inexpensive word-of-mouth marketing campaign. The dealer network decided not to spend any money on media marketing and instead conducted a road show that brought the Smart fortwo to target cities all across the country. Over 50,000 people test-drove the fortwo, and 30,000 people decided to pay the $99 fee to add their name to the waiting list.[53] After signing up for the fortwo, customers on the waiting list received updates on the status of the fortwo, information about the benefits of driving a Smart, and additional options for purchase such as the opportunity to request colorful side panels and sunroofs. According to Daimler-Benz, 90 percent of consumers on the waiting list purchase a fortwo, but the waiting list exceeds the number of fortwos that are imported each year, so consumers have a long wait for their Smart.

Questions

1. Identify and discuss the type of decision process that consumers go through when purchasing this type of product. How have Smart cars created value?

2. Identify the determinant attributes that might set the Smart car apart from competing makes and models. What attributes might be of concern to consumers?

3. What are some differences between the U.S. market and other world markets that might make it tougher to sell the Smart car to U.S. consumers?

4. Explain whether you think the Smart car will be a success in the United States. Support and defend your position.

6

BUSINESS-TO-BUSINESS MARKETING

- How do B2B firms segment their markets?
- How does B2B buying differ from consumer buying behavior?
- What factors influence the B2B buying process?
- How has the Internet changed B2B marketing?

Think about the plastics in your life. Do you have a CamelBak water bottle or drink soda from a plastic bottle? Many of those products contain one or more of Eastman Chemical's products. Eastman is a Fortune 500 company with sales of $7.5 billion earned from more than 1,200 products. It employs 11,000 people to manufacture chemical products that go into everyday items such as Pepsi bottles, disposable diapers, golf clubs, and house paint. It is the world's largest producer of PET polymers for packaging, and in addition, it produces a wide range of inks, polymers, and plastics.[1]

Even though Eastman provides products that many might consider raw materials, the company is no stranger to marketing. During the Torino Olympic Games, Eastman Chemical manufactured 12,000 transparent seats for the ice hockey stadium to showcase a new material it had developed. Eastman Chemical also carefully introduced its new product Tritan, which is a copolyester that offers better impact and heat resistance than the copolymers that traditionally appear in plastic products. It brought an advertising agency into the process very early. The marketing plan took more than two years to create, because Eastman wanted to get the brand and messaging just right. The target market included product marketers, designers, and engineers who work in manufacturing industries, so Eastman created a message that would appeal to these scientists and innovators, prompting them to want to integrate Tritan into their inventions and thus make Eastman's innovation a success.

When the marketing campaign went live, it focused on how the product's key attributes—design freedom, flexibility, lower density, and greater resistance to heat—would help members of the target market do their jobs better. By using Tritan, they could design products that appealed more to consumers. For example, CamelBak, which manufactures rugged drink containers targeted at athletes, outdoor enthusiasts, and members of the military, adopted

Tritan for its latest incarnation, the CamelBak Better Bottle, with the promise that the new bottle would stand up better to the hazards of the dishwasher and resist cracking, even if dropped.[2]

The marketing activity, which included presentations at trade shows, print advertising in industry magazines, an online campaign, an e-mail blitz, and even direct mail,[3] was designed to get one product into more consumer products and took place entirely among companies. Such business-to-business (B2B) transactions occur every time one company sells to another; they represent an important part of the world economy.

● ● ●

Business-to-business (B2B) marketing refers to the process of buying and selling goods or services to be used in the production of other goods and services, for consumption by the buying organization, and/or for resale by wholesalers and retailers. Therefore, B2B marketing involves manufacturers, wholesalers, and service firms that market goods and services to other businesses but not to the ultimate consumer. The distinction between a B2B and a B2C transaction is not the product or service itself; rather, it is the ultimate *user of* that product or service. Had a CamelBak been sold to a wholesaler of landscaping supplies rather than a sporting goods retailer, which then sold it to a landscaping firm whose employees would use it on the job, the transaction would still be a B2B transaction because CamelBak is being used by a business rather than by an individual household consumer.

Wells Fargo Auto Finance works with automobile dealers (B2B) to coordinate loans to car buyers (B2C).

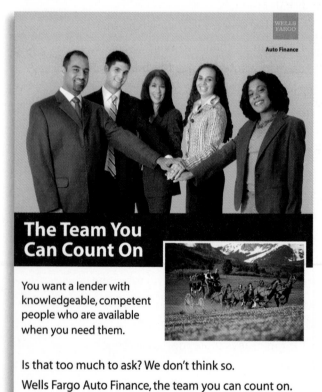

The Team You Can Count On

You want a lender with knowledgeable, competent people who are available when you need them.

Is that too much to ask? We don't think so.

Wells Fargo Auto Finance, the team you can count on.

Another major difference between the typical B2B and B2C transaction is the role of the salesperson. Sales people may be an important component of the communications mix for B2C transactions like real estate, insurance, jewelry, consumer electronics, and high-end apparel, because few consumers want to purchase an expensive piece of jewelry without some advice from a knowledgeable salesperson. But few consumers need help buying cereal and milk from the grocery store, so most fast moving consumer goods (FMCG) are sold without the aid of sales people. However, in most B2B sales, the salesperson becomes an integral component of the transaction.

The demand for B2B sales is often derived from B2C sales in the same supply chain. More specifically, **derived demand** is the linkage between consumers' demand for a company's output and its purchase of necessary inputs to manufacture or assemble that particular output. For instance, the demand for Eastman's Tritan copolyester, used to make CamelBak water bottles, derives from outdoor enthusiasts' demand for sturdy, flexible, portable water containers.

In this chapter, we will look at the different types of B2B markets and examine the B2B buying process with an eye toward how it differs from the B2C buying process, which we discussed in Chapter 5. Several factors influence the B2B buying process, and we discuss these as well. Finally, the chapter concludes with a discussion of the role of the Internet and its influence on the way B2B marketing is conducted.

B2B MARKETS

Just like organizations that sell directly to final consumers in B2C transactions, B2B firms focus their efforts on serving specific types of customer markets to create value for those customers.[4] For instance, Wells Fargo maintains a dedicated group to service its commercial banking clients. As the fifth largest U.S. bank, Wells Fargo manages assets of more than $492 billion, and its online capabilities generate a tremendous amount of traffic and span many different services. To create a better experience for its valuable commercial clients, it instituted a specialized group that would become a one-stop source for Internet banking services and products. The service provides commercial customers with a single portal that combines 50 products and services, spanning the areas of treasury, brokerage, and commercial paper, to ensure customers experience the same level of service. So far the initiative has been a success; more than 70 percent of the bank's commercial clients use the portal.[5]

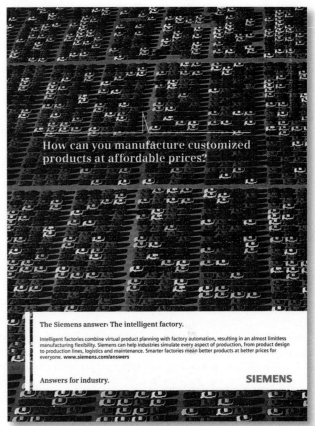

Siemens, Europe's largest conglomerate, works with businesses to help solve their problems.

As in this case, many firms find it more productive to focus their efforts on key industries or market segments rather than on ultimate consumers. Siemens and IBM both target industries: Siemens has identified core sectors, including health care, energy, and industry, that might benefit from its expertise, and IBM conducts thought leadership conferences to ensure its name stays in front of executives in its targeted industries.[6]

In our opening example of how Eastman Chemical markets its products, we described one type of B2B organization, that is, manufacturers or producers. However, resellers, institutions, and governments also may be involved in B2B transactions. Therefore, in the next sections, we describe each of these B2B organizations and how the government classifies them. (See Exhibit 6.1.)

EXHIBIT 6.1　　B2B Markets

Manufacturers or Producers

To make the products they sell to others, manufacturers and producers buy raw materials, components, and parts that allow them to manufacture their own goods. For example, Burt's Bees requires a vast variety of products to manufacture its more than 150 Earth-friendly, natural personal care products, including plastic for the product containers, perfumes, and beeswax. To match the rapidly growing demand for its moisturizers, hair products, and lip balms, Burt's Bees must manage its suppliers and transportation intermediaries closely to minimize any inventory shortages or overages, as well as to ensure on-time delivery to the more than 30,000 retail outlets in the United States, United Kingdom, Canada, Hong Kong, and Taiwan that carry its products.[7] Thus, not only does the manufacturer purchase products from other firms to make its products, but it also works with its corporate partners, like transportation companies, to facilitate the movement of the raw supplies to the factory and finished products to the stores.[8]

Burt's Bees purchases raw materials from around the world—B2B transactions.

Resellers

Resellers are marketing intermediaries that resell manufactured products without significantly altering their form. For instance, wholesalers and distributors buy CamelBaks and sell them to retailers—a B2B transaction; then retailers in turn resell those CamelBaks to the ultimate consumer—a B2C transaction. Thus, wholesalers, distributors, and retailers are all resellers. When you purchase an item for sports like a CamelBak, you likely consider the transaction a simple B2C sale, in which the reseller (retailer) sells you the item. But before you are able to use most sporting goods, they have passed through other transactions, some of which function to ensure you will like the items, as Adding Value 6.1 describes.

Institutions

Institutions, such as hospitals, educational organizations, and religious organizations, also purchase all kinds of goods and services. For instance, with an annual budget of $42 million for textbooks alone, the Chicago Public School system certainly qualifies as an institution with significant buying power. However, like most other not-for-profit institutions, the Chicago Public Schools face very tight budgets, and their textbook procurement method badly needed an overhaul. The school administrators realized that 30 percent of all book orders contained 10 or fewer books, which meant they missed any bulk discounts and suffered price discrepancies on 44 percent of their orders. They first revised their procurement strategy by centralizing control. They also set up an internal clearinghouse so that schools looking to buy certain textbooks and other schools looking to dispose of the same textbooks could complete the transaction seamlessly. These relatively simple changes are expected to save the schools approximately 33 percent of their annual book budget. With such success, the school system is applying these lessons to other purchasing activities, including capital construction, equipment and supplies, and food and janitorial services.[9]

Government

In most countries, the central government tends to be one of the largest purchasers of goods and services. For example the U.S. Federal Government spends about

Adding Value 6.1   **Paris Runways to Retail Stores**

Early each year, fashion designers display their new designs in runway shows in New York, London, Milan, and Paris. These fashion events are designed primarily to be media extravaganzas, but they also serve another purpose: Runway shows offer wholesale buyers an opportunity to inspect new lines of clothing and place orders. This dual purpose of a runway show creates value for buyers in two ways. First, they get a preview of fashion trends, which enables them to stay on top of market developments. Second, by throwing an extravagant party to accompany the runway shows, the designer is paying to create more buzz for the new line of clothing.

Attendees at fashion shows often consist of 10 times as many reporters as buyers, and those reporters generally publish their observations in some form, whether in a fashion magazine, a general readership newspaper, or even through television and magazine coverage—all of which means more publicity for the clothing line.[10] The widespread media attention that runway shows generate for designers' clothing thus makes it easier for retail stores to sell the new fashions. By promoting extravagant media events and helping cover the costs of advertising, the manufacturer or designer creates value for the retailer.

After ensuring that consumers will see, and ideally want, the featured fashions, the designers make their offerings available to the buyers. The buyers have seen the designs on models. Once those models leave the runway, the cloth-

ing moves into back room ateliers, where buyers from all over the world examine the clothing to determine how much to buy of each design.

Judging from the media coverage of runway events, the public might have the impression that such shows are the only way designers reveal their lines. In contrast, most designer sales occur during private meetings with buyers, both before and after the runway shows. Buyers meet with the designers and discuss the line. A model often will try on the size 2 clothing—the most common size for these sample designs—for the buyer to observe. The buyer's challenge then is to determine which items will sell best in the retail stores he or she represents while trying to imagine what the item will look like in larger sizes. Buyers must also negotiate purchases for orders that may not be delivered for as much as six months. Buyers also can suggest modifications to make the clothing more modest or more comfortable for their customers. The buyer's bonus is usually based on sales in the stores he or she represents, so the buyer must ensure that customers will be interested in the clothing he or she orders. Buyers and designers recognize the significant value of this relationship, which occasionally prompts buyers to purchase a few items from a designer, even if those items are not to their taste. Doing so ensures that the buyer will have access to the designer's collection for the next season.[11]

Fashion shows expose retail buyers to new fashions and create media buzz. But the buying takes place during private meetings between vendors and buyers.

The U.S. government spends over $5 billion a year on aerospace and defense for everything from nuts and bolts to this F-14 Tomcat jetfighter.

$2.8 trillion annually on procuring goods and services.[12] If you add in the amount state and local governments spend, these numbers reach staggering proportions. Specifically, with its estimated outlay of $504.8 billion dollars for fiscal year 2007, the Pentagon represents a spending force to be reckoned with,[13] especially when it comes to aerospace and defense (A&D) manufacturers, some of the Pentagon's greatest suppliers of products. Because the Pentagon represents such an important customer for most of these manufacturers, they have recognized the need to provide it with excellent value.[14]

B2B Classification System

The U.S. Bureau of the Census collects data about business activity in the United States through its classification scheme, which categorizes all firms into a hierarchical set of six-digit North American Industry Classification System (NAICS) codes.[15] Since the 1930s, the United States had used the Standard Industrial Classification (SIC) system, but the new NAICS, developed jointly with Canada and Mexico, provides comparable statistics about business activity in all of North America.

As the NAICS codes have evolved, more subcategories have been added to each sector. Consider, for example, the evolution of the telecommunications category shown in Exhibit 6.2. Under the 1987 SIC codes, broadcasting fell within the "Communications" sector, whose subcategories included telephones, telegraphs, and broadcasting. Today, though, with the rapid evolution of technology, broadcasting falls under a new sector known as "Information," which comprises publishing, motion pictures, broadcasting, Internet publishing, telecommunications, Internet service providers, and so on.[16] Older subcategories of Information, such as telegraphs, have been updated as "wired communication," and emerging technologies, such as cellular communications, have their own category as "wired telecommunications carriers."[17]

The NAICS classification system can be quite useful to B2B marketers for segmenting and targeting their markets. Suppose, for instance, that a high-tech telecommunications components manufacturer has developed a new product that will significantly speed data transmission. Which of the types of firms listed under NAICS classification 51511 (radio broadcasting) would be the most worthwhile to pursue as customers? To answer this question, the components manufac-

The NAICS classification system could help a high-tech telecommunications components manufacturer identify groups of customers to pursue.

EXHIBIT 6.2	Evolution of Telecommunications NAICS Codes	
1987 SIC	**2007 NAICS**	**2007 Subcategories**
48 Communication	51 Information	51511 Radio Broadcasting
483 Radio and Television Broadcasting	515 Broadcasting (except Internet)	515111 Radio Networks
483 Radio Broadcasting Stations	5151 Radio and Television Broadcasting	515112 Radio Stations

Source: http://www.census.gov/epcd/naics02/SICN02E.HTM#S48, accessed January 22, 2008; http://www.census.gov/epcd/naics07/, accessed January 22, 2008.

turer would first do research, probably using interviews conducted by company sales representatives, to determine which types of firms would find the new component most useful for their products. Then, using the NAICS data collected by the U.S. Census Bureau, the manufacturer could assess the number, size, and geographical dispersion of firms within each type, which might indicate both the product's potential and the types of firms that constitute the target market.

These different types of B2B markets and their distinct classifications lead to another way in which they differ from B2C markets, namely, how the B2B buying process differs from the process for B2C products and services.

CHECK YOURSELF

1. Identify the various types of B2B markets.
2. What are NAICS codes and how are they used?

THE BUSINESS-TO-BUSINESS BUYING PROCESS

The B2B buying process (Exhibit 6.3) parallels the B2C process, though it differs in many ways. Both start with need recognition, but the information search and alternative evaluation steps are more formal and structured in the B2B process. Typically, B2B buyers specify their needs in writing and ask potential suppliers to submit formal proposals, whereas B2C buying decisions are usually made by individuals or families and sometimes are unplanned or impulsive. Thus, for a family to buy a new hammer, all that is required is a trip to the hardware store and perhaps some brief discussion of which hammer will be best. For the Pentagon to buy 100,000 hammers, however, it must complete requisition forms, accept bids from manufacturers, and obtain approval for the expenditure. The final decision rests with a committee, as is the case for most B2B buying decisions, which often

EXHIBIT 6.3   Business-to-Business Buying Process

Need recognition → Product specification → RFP process → Proposal analysis and supplier selection → Order specification → Vendor/performance assessment using metrics

Toyota recognized the need to change its tire supplier when customers complained that their current supplier's tires did not perform adequately on snow-packed and off-the-road surfaces.

demand a great deal of consideration. Finally, in B2C buying situations, customers evaluate their purchase decision and sometimes experience postpurchase dissonance. However, formal performance evaluations of the vendor and the products sold generally do not occur, as they do in the B2B setting. Let's examine all six stages in the context of Toyota purchasing tires for its vehicles from Goodyear, Dunlop, and Firestone.[18]

Stage 1: Need Recognition

In the first stage of the B2B buying process, the buying organization recognizes, through either internal or external sources, that it has an unfilled need. For instance, Toyota's design teams might realize that their suppliers have increased the prices of the types of tires they use. At the same time, customers have complained that the tires they are currently using do not work very well on their all-wheel drive vehicles. Toyota's own driving tests on snow-packed and off-the-road surfaces also indicate the need for a change. Through suppliers' sales people, tradeshow demonstrations, ads in trade journals, Internet searches, and

In B2B transactions it is important to seek information to recognize a need.

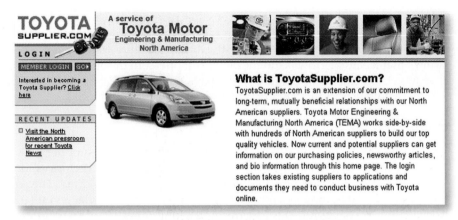

ToyotaSupplier.com is used to post RFPs so current and potential suppliers can get information on its purchasing policies and relevant news articles.

white papers, the company also has become aware of the benefits of different tire manufacturers.

Stage 2: Product Specification

After recognizing the need, the organization considers alternative solutions and comes up with potential specifications that suppliers might use to develop their proposals to supply the product. Because a significant share of Toyota vehicles are made and sold in North America, the company has made a strong commitment to engaging in long-term, mutually beneficial relationships with North American suppliers. In 2007, for instance, it spent nearly $29 billion for parts and materials from hundreds of North American suppliers and business partners.[19] Rather than working in a vacuum to determine its specifications for the new tires, Toyota's design teams and engineers actually go on site to vendors' plants to develop the specifications for prototypes with their experts.

Stage 3: RFP Process

The **request for proposals (RFP)** is a common process through which buying organizations invite alternative suppliers to bid on supplying their required components. The purchasing company may simply post its RFP needs on its Web site, work through various B2B linkages (which we discuss later in this chapter), or contact potential suppliers directly. Toyota, for example, has set up ToyotaSupplier.com so current and potential suppliers can get information on its purchasing policies and relevant news articles.[20]

In Step 4: Proposal Analysis, Vendor Negotiation, and Selection, Toyota decides to purchase from Goodyear because it has the best combination of strength of brand, ability to deliver, product quality, and ease of ordering.

Stage 4: Proposal Analysis, Vendor Negotiation, and Selection

The buying organization, in conjunction with its critical decision makers, evaluates all the proposals it receives in response to its RFP. Firms are likely to narrow the process to a few suppliers, often those with which they have existing relationships, and discuss key terms of the sale, such as price, quality, delivery, and financing. Some firms have a policy that requires them to negotiate with several suppliers, particularly if the product or service represents a critical component or aspect of the business. This policy keeps suppliers on their toes; they know that the buying firm can always shift a greater portion of its business to an alternative supplier if it offers better terms. For example, because Toyota negotiates with Dunlop and Firestone as well, Goodyear knows that it cannot grow lax in the benefits it offers. In the end, Toyota decides to purchase from Goodyear because it has the best combination of strength of brand, ability to deliver, product quality, and ease of ordering.

Stage 5: Order Specification

In the fifth stage, the firm places its order with its preferred supplier (or suppliers). The order will include a detailed description of the goods, prices, delivery dates, and in some cases, penalties if the order is not filled on time. The supplier then will send an acknowledgement that it has received the order and fill it by the specified date. For Toyota, this description includes the specific sizes and number of tires it wants, the price it will agree to pay for those tires, the date it expects to receive them, and the result if the wrong tires are delivered or delivered after the due date.

Stage 6: Vendor Performance Assessment Using Metrics

Just as in the consumer buying process, firms analyze their vendors' performance so they can make decisions about their future purchases. The difference is that, in a B2B setting, this analysis is typically more formal and objective. Let's consider how Toyota might evaluate Goodyear's performance, as in Exhibit 6.4, using the following metric:

1. The buying team develops a list of issues that it believes are important to consider in the evaluation of the vendor.
2. To determine how important each of these issues (in column 1) is, the buying team assigns an importance score to each (column 2). The more important the issue, the higher a score it will receive, but the importance scores must add up to 1. In this case, the buying team believes that product quality and strength of brand are most important, whereas meeting the delivery dates and the ease of ordering are less important.
3. In the third column, the buying team assigns numbers that reflect its judgments about how well the vendor performs. Using a five-point scale, where 1 equals "poor performance" and 5 equals "excellent performance," the buying team decides that Goodyear has fairly high performance on all issues except ease of ordering.
4. To get the overall performance of the vendor, in the fourth column, the team combines the importance of each issue and the vendor's performance scores by multiplying them together. Note that Goodyear performed particularly

EXHIBIT 6.4	Evaluating a Vendor's Performance		
(1) **Key Issues**	**(2)** **Importance Score**	**(3)** **Vendor's Performance**	**(4)** **Importance Performance**
Strength of brand	.30	5	1.5
Meets delivery dates	.20	4	.8
Product quality	.40	5	2.0
Ease of ordering	.10	3	.3
Total	1.0		4.6

well on the most important issues. As a result, when we add the importance/performance scores in column 4, we find that Goodyear's overall evaluation is quite high—4.6 on a 5-point scale!

CHECK YOURSELF

1. Identify the stages in the B2B buying process.
2. How do you do a vendor analysis?

FACTORS AFFECTING THE BUYING PROCESS

The six-stage B2B buying process may be influenced by three factors within the purchasing organization: the buying center, the buying organization's philosophy or corporate culture, and the buying situation.

The Buying Center

In most large organizations, several people typically are responsible for the buying decisions. These buying center participants can range from employees who have a formal role in purchasing decisions (i.e., the purchasing or procurement department) to members of the design team that is specifying the particular equipment or raw material needed to employees who will be using a new machine that is being ordered. All these employees are likely to play different roles in the buying process, which vendors must understand and adapt to in their marketing and sales efforts.

We can categorize six different buying roles within a typical buying center (Exhibit 6.5). One or more people may take on a certain role, or one person may take on more than one of the following roles: "(1) initiator, the person who first suggests buying the particular product or service; (2) influencer, the person whose views influence other members of the buying center in making the final decision; (3) decider, the person who ultimately determines any part of or the entire buying decision—whether to buy, what to buy, how to buy, or where to buy; (4) buyer, the person who handles the paperwork of the actual purchase; (5) user, the person who consumes or uses the product or service; and (6) gatekeeper, the person who controls information or access, or both, to decision makers and influencers."[21]

To illustrate how a buying center operates, consider purchases made by a hospital. Where do hospitals obtain their x-ray machines, syringes, and bedpans? Why

Many people are involved in making B2B purchasing decisions.

EXHIBIT 6.5   The Buying Center Roles

are some medical procedures covered in whole or in part by insurance, whereas others are not? Why might your doctor recommend one type of allergy medication instead of another?

The Initiator—Your Doctor   When you seek treatment from your physician, he or she *initiates* the buying process by determining the products and services that will best address and treat your illness or injury. For example, say that you fell backward off your snowboard and, in trying to catch yourself, shattered your elbow. You require surgery to mend the affected area, which includes the insertion of several screws to hold the bones in place. Your doctor promptly notifies the hospital to schedule a time for the procedure and specifies the brand of screws she wants on hand for your surgery.

The Influencer—The Medical Device Supplier, the Pharmacy   For years, your doctor has been using ElbowMed screws, a slightly higher-priced screw. Her first introduction to ElbowMed screws came from the company's sales representative, who visited her office to demonstrate how ElbowMed screws were far superior to those of its competition. Your doctor recognized ElbowMed as a good value. Armed with empirical data and case studies, ElbowMed's sales rep effectively *influenced* your doctor's decision to use that screw.

The Decider—The Hospital   Even though your doctor requested ElbowMed screws, the hospital ultimately is responsible for *deciding* whether to buy ElbowMed screws. The hospital supplies the operating room, instrumentation, and surgical supplies, and therefore, the hospital administrators must weigh a variety of factors to determine if the ElbowMed screw is not only best for the patients but also involves a cost that is reimbursable by various insurance providers.

The Buyer   The actual *buyer* of the screw will likely be the hospital's materials manager, who is charged with buying and maintaining inventory for the hospital in the most cost-effective manner. Whereas ElbowMed screws are specific to your type of procedure, other items, such as gauze and sutures, may be purchased through a group purchasing organization (GPO), which obtains better prices through volume buying.

The User—The Patient   Ultimately though, the buying process for this procedure will be greatly affected by the *user,* namely, you and your broken elbow. If you are uncomfortable with the procedure or have read about alternative procedures that you prefer, you may decide that ElbowMed screws are not the best treatment.

Ethical and Societal Dilemma 6.1 How Does the Doctor Know Best?

The pharmaceutical industry is constantly introducing new drugs and new uses for existing drugs. Thus doctors have to constantly update their knowledge of pharmaceuticals and what they are prescribed for, which is why pharmaceutical companies spend almost twice as much on promoting existing drugs than on new drug R&D.[22] One of the key information sources for doctors about changes in the pharmaceutical industry is the sales representatives who visit with the doctors. A recent study found that doctors want detailed information about drug safety, pricing, and prescribing in addition to information about new drugs. The doctors also want to understand the difference between the new drug and the old drug.

Unfortunately the study also found that the sales representatives do not provide all of these data to the doctors. The sales reps instead focus on the benefits of their new drugs and avoid volunteering pricing information, side effects data, or comparisons with existing products. Even safety data were skewed toward placing the new drugs in a favorable light. To make matters worse, the study found that when competitors' products were mentioned to doctors, they were generally discussed in unfavorable terms.

Perhaps the most troubling finding of the study was that doctors who were frequently visited by sales representatives often chose to treat patients with drug therapies and not alternative, nondrug therapies even if researchers consider the nondrug therapy superior. These doctors were also less likely to prescribe the generic equivalents to costly branded drugs. In other words, the sales representatives are having a dramatic impact on the doctors' choice in treatment of their patients.[23]

Because of the importance of the pharmaceutical industry and the life-saving, or -ending, capability of drugs, intense scrutiny focuses on pharmaceutical companies' marketing efforts. Most companies have stringent rules and regulations to ensure that their marketing remains ethical and respects patient privacy, but frequent allegations of misbehavior continue to emerge. Some commentators, such as former Pfizer vice president of marketing, Dr. Peter Rost, believe that most pharmaceutical marketing crosses the line of what is ethical. Although he used to design marketing campaigns for drugs, Rost now runs an online blog on *BrandWeek* that centers on pharmaceutical practices, with a special section allowing whistleblowers to share their experiences, such as one rep who claims his company pushed him to pay out more than $40,000 in "honorariums" to medical practitioners.[24]

What, if anything, should be done about the behavior of pharmaceutical sales representatives? What incentives could doctors or the medical community provide to encourage pharmaceutical companies to provide doctors with the desired information, while limiting their influence over patient care?

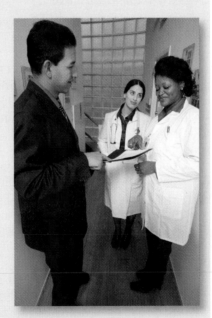

From an ethical perspective, what information should pharmaceutical sales representatives provide to doctors?

The Gatekeeper—The Insurance Company   Your insurer may believe that ElbowMed screws are too expensive and that other screws deliver equally effective results and therefore refuse to reimburse the hospital in full or in part for the use of the screws.

In the end, the final purchase decision must take into consideration every single buying center participant. Ethical and Societal Dilemma 6.1 examines how the

EXHIBIT 6.6   Organizational Buying Culture

"influencer" (the pharmaceutical sales representative and pharmaceutical companies) influences the "decider" (the physician) to suggest purchases ultimately made by the "user" (the patient).

Organizational Culture

A firm's organizational culture reflects the set of values, traditions, and customs that guide its employees' behavior. The firm's culture often comprises a set of unspoken guidelines that employees share with one another through various work situations. For example, in Wal-Mart's corporate headquarters, a cup is placed next to the coffee machine so the staff can pay for their drinks. Also, buyers are not allowed to accept even the smallest gift from a vendor, not even a cup of coffee. These small, seemingly insignificant gestures bolster the firm's overall corporate culture of being a low-cost operator whose buyers base decisions only on the products' and vendors' merits.

Organizational culture can have a profound influence on purchasing decisions, and corporate buying center cultures might be divided into four general types: autocratic, democratic, consultative, and consensus, as illustrated in Exhibit 6.6. Knowing which buying center culture is prevalent in a given organization helps the seller decide how to approach that particular client, how and to whom to deliver pertinent information, and to whom to make the sales presentations.

In an autocratic buying center, though there may be multiple participants, one person makes the decision alone, whereas the majority rules in a democratic buying center. Consultative buying centers use one person to make a decision but solicit input from others before doing so. Finally, in a consensus buying center, all members of the team must reach a collective agreement that they can support a particular purchase.[25]

Cultures act like living, breathing entities that change and grow, just as organizations do. Even within some companies, culture may vary by geography, by division, or by functional department. Whether you are a member of the buying center or a supplier trying to sell to it, it is extremely important to understand its culture and the roles of the key players in the buying process. Not knowing the roles of the key players could waste a lot of time—both yours and the buying center's—and could even alienate the real decision maker. However, a good understanding provides a means to establish effective working relationships, just as Volkswagen works with its suppliers to put a Volkswagen together, which we describe in Power of the Internet 6.1.

Power of the Internet 6.1   **Putting a Volkswagen Together[26]**

The German-based Volkswagen Group is the largest auto manufacturer in Europe with sales of over $153 billion dollars (£104 billion). It owns and distributes the Audi, Bentley, Bugatti, Lamborghini, Seat, Skoda, VW, and VW Financial Services brands.[27] It noted at one point that its purchasing agents spent 70 percent of their time searching for, analyzing, validating, and forwarding information about parts and components. That meant that they had only about 30 percent of their time to devote to activities that would add value to the firm, which was an unacceptable limitation. As Volkswagen grew, its suppliers were faced with increased complexity as well. Some suppliers had to log into as many as 20 different systems to manage their relationship with Volkswagen. To remain competitive VW needed to increase efficiency along every part of its value chain, including suppliers' efficiency. What could VW do? It recognized that its purchasing process needed to be made far more efficient. Volkswagen turned to IBM to help design a procurement system that would reduce the cost of parts so that that it could pass the savings on to customers and shareholders.

Volkswagen now manages its own Internet-based private network that links more than 7,619 suppliers of roughly $77 billion worth of components, automotive parts, and indirect raw materials. With its integrated software system iPAD, or Internal Purchasing Agent Desk, Volkswagen has cut processing time dramatically. With iPAD, purchasing agents receive product descriptions directly from suppliers online, so the search process, which used to take two hours, is now complete in nine minutes. Moreover, whereas agents used to spend, on average, 60 minutes per order, they now spend only 20. Using the Internet to integrate with its suppliers led to a 20 percent increase in staff productivity and paid for itself in one year by decreasing inventory costs and ordering time.[28]

Volkswagen also added capabilities that it lacked before changing its system. The online systems actively monitor part prices and competitive issues. The system alerts the procurement office of potential parts shortages before they occur and allows the procurement staff to focus on cost savings instead of unstructured paperwork.

In addition to improving its internal processes, Volkswagen has maintained strong relationships with its suppliers by setting up online tools to track invoices and payments and allowing suppliers to log on to its secure "Supplier Cockpit" Web site to find information pertinent to their products. Other online tools, including a catalog, auction, and request for proposals (RFP), are readily available. Perhaps most important though, Volkswagen focuses on continually promoting its close partnerships and collaboration with its vendors.

Systems such as this one demonstrate the significant value that can be created in the course of companies' external business-to-business relationships, as well as within the manufacturing process.

Volkswagen's software system, iPAD, has cut order processing time from two hours to nine minutes since VW's purchasing agents receive product descriptions directly from suppliers online.

Buying Situations

The type of buying situation also affects the B2B decision process. Most B2B buying situations can be categorized into three types: new buys, modified rebuys, and straight rebuys. (See Exhibit 6.7.) To illustrate the nuances between these three buying situations, we portray how colleges and universities develop relationships with some of their suppliers.

Most universities negotiate with sports apparel manufacturers such as Nike, Reebok, and New Balance to establish purchasing agreements for their sports teams. Schools, especially those with successful sports teams, have been very successful in managing these relationships with athletic equipment vendors. Large universities that win national championships, such as Louisiana State

EXHIBIT 6.7   Buying Situations

University or the University of Florida, can solicit sponsorships in exchange for free athletic equipment, whereas less popular teams or smaller schools, such as Appalachian State University, typically must accept an upfront sponsorship and then agree to buy from that vendor for a specified period of time. In exchange for this sponsorship, the vendors gain the right to sell apparel with the university logo and require the school's team to purchase only their equipment. Many apparel companies make a significant portion of their revenue through sponsorship deals that grant them the right to sell apparel with popular university logos.

Certain universities that attract significant media attention can negotiate very lucrative deals because they serve as a marketing outlet for the apparel company. For example, both the University of Michigan and The Ohio State University, despite widely publicized losses in the 2007 football season, signed contracts that

Schools like Louisiana State University negotiate with sports apparel manufacturers, such as Nike, to get free athletic equipment. The manufacturers, in turn, get to sell apparel with the university logo.

resulted in multimillion dollar sponsorships. Ohio State signed a nine-year, $26 million contract with Nike to provide athletic equipment and produce logo apparel, while Adidas signed an eight-year, $60 million deal with the University of Michigan.[29]

In a new buy situation, a customer purchases a good or service for the first time,[30] which means the buying decision is likely to be quite involved because the buyer or the buying organization does not have any experience with the item. In the B2B context, the buying center is likely to proceed through all six steps in the buying process and involve many people in the buying decision. Typical new buys might range from capital equipment to components that the firm previously made itself but now has decided to purchase instead.

For example, a small college might need to decide which apparel company to approach for a sponsorship. For smaller colleges, finding a company that will sponsor multiple sports teams—such as women's soccer as well as men's basketball—is the a priority, though it also must balance other considerations, such as the length of the contract. Some venders offer perks to attract new buyers; New Balance offers teams that sign up for long-term contracts custom fittings for their players' shoes. That is, each season, a sales team from New Balance visits the school and custom fits each player to achieve the best-fitting shoe possible.[31]

In a modified rebuy, the buyer has purchased a similar product in the past but has decided to change some specifications, such as the desired price, quality level, customer service level, options, or so forth. Current vendors are likely to have an advantage in acquiring the sale in a modified rebuy situation, as long as the reason for the modification is not dissatisfaction with the vendor or its products.

Thus, when The Ohio State University's sports department was negotiating whether to rebuy from Nike, one of the factors it considered was the size of the Adidas deal that the University of Michigan received. Even though Ohio State had just signed a seven-year contract with Nike for a $16.3 million sponsorship, the university grew dissatisfied with the arrangement and renegotiated a longer contract for an additional $10 million.[32] In this case, the established vendor acquired the sale, but at a significant cost.

Straight rebuys occur when the buyer or buying organization simply buys additional units of products that had previously been purchased. A tremendous amount of B2B purchases are likely to fall in the straight rebuy category.

For example, sports teams need to repurchase a tremendous amount of equipment that is not covered by apparel sponsorships, such as tape for athletes' ankles or weights for the weight room. The purchase of bottled water also typically involves a straight rebuy from an existing supplier.

These varied types of buying situations call for very different marketing and selling strategies. The most complex and difficult is the new buy, because it requires the buying organization to make changes in its current practices and purchases. As a result, several members of the buying center will likely become involved, and the level of their involvement will be more intense than in the case of modified and straight rebuys. In new buying situations, buying center members also typically spend more time at each stage of the B2B buying process, similar to the extended decision-making process that consumers use in the B2C process. In comparison, in modified rebuys, the buyers spend less time at each stage of the B2B buying process, similar to limited decision making in the B2C process (see Chapter 5).

In straight rebuys, however, the buyer is often the only member of the buying center involved in the process. Like a consumer's habitual purchase, straight rebuys often enable the buyer to recognize the firm's need and go directly to the fifth step in the B2B buying process, skipping the product specification, RFP process, and proposal analysis and supplier selection steps.

Regardless of the situation, more and more firms have begun to use the Internet to help facilitate buying for both buyers and sellers. Let's look at the various ways in which the Internet has transformed B2B marketing.

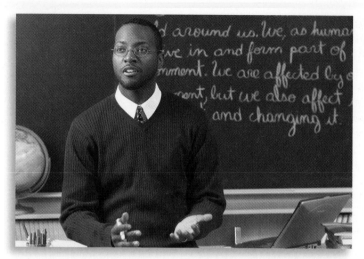

Dell sold 2,500 computers to the Douglas County School system. Is this a new buy, a modified new buy, or a straight rebuy?

Role of the Internet in Business-to-Business Marketing

As consumers, we often use the Internet to research products and buy them for ourselves, our family, and our friends. In a similar fashion, the B2B market has been radically altered in recent years through Internet technologies. For instance, the Internet has become the communication mode of choice, and sometimes of necessity, for connecting divisions and employees located in dispersed locations. Consider a salesperson on a sales call far from company headquarters. By logging in to the company's database, the salesperson can quickly find information about product availability and order status and even consult with supervisors about important negotiating points, such as price and discounts. Current trends suggest that B2B marketing will continue to rely increasingly on the Internet. Some companies, such as Intel, have even set ambitious goals, such as moving half of all advertising online.[33]

Another increasingly common use of the Internet involves virtual trade shows. Not unlike a traditional tradeshow—in which companies fly representatives to a convention site, set up complicated display booths, and attempt to convince potential buyers walking by the convention space to come to the booth to review their wares—today companies can set up "booths" inside a virtual space and engage in product demonstrations and conversations with potential clients. The virtual space can also host educational seminars and networking areas, just as a real-world trade show would do. Such virtual trade shows provide considerable savings, because the company has no need to fly a representative anywhere or purchase an expensive booth display. They also provide impressive ease of use for both the seller and the business customer. Members of the buying center can log onto the site whenever it is convenient for them, and the sellers can update their products, inventory levels, and pricing with the click of a button. Their widespread appeal has pushed virtual trade shows into consumer products, job fairs, and corporate training arenas—so far, at least.[34]

The Internet is equally useful for communications between businesses through private exchanges and auctions. A **private exchange** occurs when a specific firm (either buyer or seller) invites others to participate in online information exchanges and transactions. These exchanges help streamline procurement or distribution processes. Like Toyota with its ToyotaSource.com, as detailed in our discussion of the B2B buying process, IBM, General Motors, Ford, General Electric, Wal-Mart, and other large firms have formed private exchanges and included their key suppliers. Some, such as IBM and GE, even have mandated that their suppliers must deal with them primarily through such online exchanges, which provide the primary benefits of tremendous cost savings through the elimination of periodic negotiations and routine paperwork, as well as the ability to form a supply chain that can respond quickly to the buyer's needs.

For example, as we noted earlier in Power of the Internet 6.1, VW's suppliers derive their demand from the sales information VW provides to them. The suppliers in turn can provide needed component orders quickly and without requiring extensive inventory stockpiles. Because automotive parts can be very expensive and VW has factories all around the world, VW works with its suppliers to keep its inventory levels at a minimum. This effort leads to savings for VW, because it reduces the amount of money that VW has to invest in parts and storage space. These savings then can be passed on to consumers as lower prices, which provides VW with a very competitive position in the marketplace.

Superior Service **6.1** Virtual Hiring Saves Small Business Big Money

All businesses need IT assistance at some point to keep their computer systems up and running. Unfortunately, most small companies cannot afford a full-time IT staffer, so they have to turn to local help to solve their problems. In fact, only about 4 percent of small businesses keep a full-time IT employee on staff. As a result, it can be difficult and sometimes impossible for a small company to find the same level of service that large companies achieve through their talented, well-recruited IT staff. Fortunately, OnForce Inc. has created an alternative for small and medium businesses.

OnForce offers an online marketplace for computer repair and technology support that connects companies with independent IT consultants and technicians. The OnForce Web site actually uses auction technology to allow businesses to bid for IT support from more than 10,000 IT suppliers. By providing immediate access to a variety of suppliers, OnForce gives small businesses the power to negotiate for lower prices, as well as a choice of who will serve their company.

The OnForce Web site also enables small businesses to investigate the technicians who bid on their work orders. Before accepting the technician's offer, businesses can check the technician's customer service ratings from prior clients, compare qualifications, and determine if the technician has been convicted of a felony. OnForce also saves small businesses time. Compared with the length of time it takes to find, interview, and hire a local contractor, OnForce is amazingly fast: The median time from work order to the first offer from a technician is 15 minutes, and 95 percent of all postings find a match.[35]

The success of OnForce stems not only from the unique method it uses to bring businesses and technicians together but also because it delivers value in the form of excellent service to both parties. The business model is so successful that the U.S. company has expanded to Germany, Canada, and the United Kingdom.[36] Their secret to success seems so simple: It identified an area in which small businesses were not receiving the service they required and then designed a novel method to address the problem and give them the level of service they demanded.[37]

At another level, manufacturers and suppliers can work together to design better products, as Eastman Chemical and CamelBak did in the opening vignette to this chapter.[38] Manufacturers and retailers collect detailed information about their customers' preferences and other market trends, which they can share with those key suppliers involved in product design. This collaborative design process results in products that more closely match customer needs, thus creating and delivering higher customer value.

Private exchanges also have been formed on the manufacturer-to-retailer side of the supply chain and, in service industries, between skilled workers and small-to medium-sized companies. The Web site Guru.com, for example, was founded to help freelance professionals connect with companies that need their services, whether those services entail graphic design and cartooning or finance and accounting advice. Currently, 724,000 professionals list their offerings on this service-oriented professional exchange, and more than 30,000 companies regularly visit the site to post work orders.[39] Guru.com thus provides value to both companies and freelancers by offering not only a site for finding each other but also dispute resolution, escrow for payments, and a means to rate freelancer quality.[40] Superior Service 6.1 describes another highly focused service exchange site.

Furthermore, B2B transactions have increasingly turned to online auctions, whether English or reverse. In an English auction, goods and services are simply sold to the highest bidder. Thus, if a PC manufacturer has a number of unsold PCs, it can auction them through an exchange (perhaps even through eBay) and sell them to the buyer that bids the highest price for them. In the reverse auction, however, the buyer provides specifications to a group of sellers, which then bid down the price until the buyer accepts a specific bid. Firms like Dell, HP, Motorola, Palm, and Sun have lowered their procurement and component costs by using reverse auctions.[41]

Thus, in various ways, B2B marketing both differs from and mirrors the consumer behavior (B2C) process we detailed in Chapter 5. The differences, however, in the six stages of the buying process make sense in view of the many unique factors that come into play. The constitution of the buying center (initiator, influencer, decider, buyer, user, and gatekeeper), the culture of the purchasing firm (autocratic, democratic, consultative, or consensus), and the context of the buying situation (new buy, modified rebuy, straight rebuy) all influence the B2B buying process in various ways, which means that sellers must be constantly aware of these factors if they want to be successful in their sales attempts. Finally, just as it has done seemingly everywhere we look, the Internet has radically changed some elements of the B2B world, increasing the frequency of both private electronic exchanges and auctions.

CHECK YOURSELF

1. What factors affect the B2B buying process?
2. What are the six different buying roles?
3. What is the difference between new buy, rebuy, and modified rebuy?

Summing Up

1. How do B2B firms segment their markets?

The basic principles behind market segmentation remain the same for both B2B and consumer markets. Specifically, B2B firms want to divide the market into groups of customers with different needs, wants, or characteristics who therefore might appreciate products or services geared especially toward them. On a broad level, B2B firms divide the market into four types: manufacturers or producers, resellers, institutions, and government. Manufacturers purchase materials to make their products and components and expertise to help run their businesses, such as computer and telephone systems. Resellers are primarily wholesalers, distributors, or retailers that sell the unchanged products. Institutions include nonprofit organizations such as hospitals, schools, or churches. Finally, governments purchase all types of goods and services, but in the United States, defense is among the largest expenditures. To assist in their market segmentation, B2B businesses can use the NAICS, developed by the U.S. federal government in conjunction with Canada and Mexico, to identify potential customers by type and then develop marketing strategies to reach them.

2. How does B2B buying differ from consumer buying behavior?

At first glance, the B2B buying process looks similar to the consumer process described in Chapter 5. It starts with need recognition and ends with an evaluation of the product's or service's performance. But it is really quite different, primarily because of its formality. For instance, in the second stage, prod-

uct specification, the buying group spells out very specific requirements for the products or services it wants to purchase. Then, in the RFP process of the third stage, the buying firm announces its need for a product or service and solicits formal proposals. In the fourth stage, buyers analyze the various proposals and negotiate a deal. Unlike the consumer process, the fifth stage, in which the B2B firm places the order, is very formal and spells out every detail of the sales contract. Finally, in the sixth stage, buyers assess vendor performance.

3. What factors influence the B2B buying process?

In B2B situations, it is likely that several people, organized into a buying center, will be involved in making the purchase decision. The vendor must understand the relationships among the participants of the buying center to be effective. A firm's organizational culture can also influence the decision process. For instance, if a firm is trying to sell to a young, high-tech computer component manufacturer, it might be advised to send sales people who are fluent in technology-speak and can easily relate to the customer. Finally, the buying process depends to a great extent on the situation. If a firm is purchasing a product or service for the first time, the process is much more involved than if it is engaging in a straight rebuy.

4. How has the Internet changed B2B marketing?

The Internet has done more to change the way B2B marketing is conducted than any previous innovation has. Not only has the Internet made it easier for people to communicate within firms, it also facilitates the transfer of information among companies. Buyers can purchase products and services over the Internet through private exchanges, which are set up by one firm that invites other participants, and through B2B Internet auctions. These exchanges and auctions have created opportunities to streamline the procurement process, opened up markets to new buyers and sellers, and provided for more competitive market pricing.

Key Terms

- autocratic buying center, 194
- business-to-business (B2B) marketing, 182
- buyer, 191
- buying center, 191
- consensus buying center, 194
- consultative buying center, 194
- decider, 191
- democratic buying center, 194
- derived demand, 182
- English auction, 199
- gatekeeper, 191
- influencer, 191
- initiator, 191
- modified rebuy, 197
- new buy, 197
- North American Industry Classification System (NAICS) codes, 186
- organizational culture, 194
- private exchange, 198
- request for proposals (RFP), 189
- resellers, 184
- reverse auction, 199
- straight rebuy, 197
- user, 191

Marketing Applications

1. Provide an example of each of the four key types of B2B organizations.

2. What are the major differences between the consumer buying process discussed in Chapter 5 and the B2B buying process discussed in this chapter?

3. Assume you have written this textbook and are going to attempt to sell it to your school. Identify the six members of the buying center. What role would each play in the decision process? Rank them in terms of how much influence they would have on the decision, with 1 being most influential and 6 being least influential. Will this ranking be different in other situations?

4. Mazda is trying to assess the performance of two manufacturers that could supply music systems for its vehicles. Using the information in the table below, determine which manufacturer Mazda should use.

5. Provide an example of the three types of buying situations that the bookstore at your school might face when buying textbooks.

6. Describe the organizational culture at your school or job. How would knowledge of this particular organization's culture help a B2B salesperson sell products or services to the organization?

7. You have just started to work in the purchasing office of a major pharmaceutical firm. The purchasing manager has asked you to assist in writing an RFP for a major purchase. The manager gives you a sheet detailing the specifications for the RFP. While reading the specifications, you realize that they have been written to be extremely favorable to one bidder. How should you handle this situation?

Performance Evaluation of Brands			
Issues	**Importance Weights**	**Manufacturer A's Performance**	**Manufacturer B's Performance**
Sound	0.4	5	3
Cost	0.3	2	4
Delivery time	0.1	2	2
Brand cache	0.2	5	1
Total	1		

Quiz Yourself

1. After posting an RFP for telecommunication equipment, the University of Florida received six proposals from qualified vendors. Next, the University of Florida will:

   a. recognize proposal obstacles that the firm must comply with.

   b. revise need recognition through external sources.

   c. invite alternative suppliers to bid on supplying what is requested.

   d. proceed to proposal vendor analysis.

   e. evaluate the proposals and likely narrow the choice to a few suppliers.

2. Raycom Construction needs heavy duty equipment to install a new pipeline in northern Alaska. Raycom engineers will specify the type and capability requirements for the equipment to be purchased. The Raycom engineers will primarily play the _____ role in the company's buying center.

   a. buyer

   b. initiator

   c. influencer

   d. user

   e. gatekeeper

(Answers to these two questions are provided on page 623.)

Go to www.mhhe.com/grewal2e to practice an additional 11 questions.

Toolkit

B2B VENDOR ANALYSIS

Help David evaluate two software vendors. He has created a chart to help him decide which one to pick. He has rated the two vendors on brand strength, timeliness of deliveries, product quality, and ease of ordering. His firm is generally most interested in quality and then in timeliness. Reputation is somewhat important. The ease of ordering is least important. Please use the toolkit provided at http://www.mhhe.com/grewal2e to specify the importance weights and help David pick the best software vendor.

Net Savvy

1. Suppose you were working for Volkswagen. How would you use the North American Industry Classification System (NAICS) to assess the number of potential suppliers for tires? What is the NAICS classification code for tires? (You will have to do some research on the Internet to uncover this information.)

2. Levi Strauss & Co. maintains a Web site so that customers can shop online directly with the manufacturer. The Web site also refers consumers from its Web site directly to retailers. Go to http://www.levis.com, click on the link for the United States and then on "Store Locator." What do you find when you click this link? What happens when you click on the retailers' Web links? How is this type of linking beneficial to both Levis and to the various retailers? Now suppose you are seeking to purchase a specific product: women's, boot cut, or skinny jeans. What information does the Levi's Web site provide?

Chapter Case Study

WEYERHAEUSER: SERVING THE HOME BUILDING INDUSTRY[42]

Overview

With its annual sales of over $21.9 billion and 41,000 employees in 18 countries around the world, Weyerhaeuser has grown into one of the largest integrated

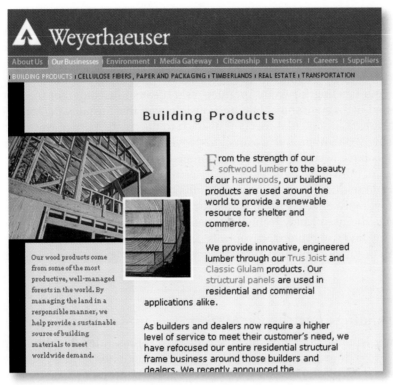

Weyerhaeuser, one of the largest integrated forest products companies in the world, is involved in growing and harvesting trees and manufacturing, distributing, and selling forest products.

forest products companies in the world.[43] Its principal operations involve growing and harvesting trees and manufacturing, distributing, and selling forest products. Weyerhaeuser is currently the world's largest producer of softwood lumber and pulp.

Weyerhaeuser's wood products businesses produce and sell softwood lumber, plywood, and veneer; oriented strand board and composite panels; hardwood lumber; and engineered lumber products. These products are sold primarily through the company's sales organizations and building materials distribution business, though Weyerhaeuser targets large builders in particular with its National Builder Program. As partners with a leader in the worldwide forest products industry, members are offered the convenience of a single reliable source for quality building supplies. Moreover, the program offers customized features and value-added services designed to meet each builder's unique needs, such as:[44]

- Access to Weyerhaeuser's in-depth product expertise and technical support.
- Input on product development to engineer greater value.
- Ongoing communication updates to enhance sales and profitability.
- Relationships at the executive level with key decision makers.
- Shared opportunities in e-commerce, environmental stewardship, joint marketing, and safety training.

Factors Affecting the Industry

In the wood products industry, changes in the political landscape in the past several years have affected environmental and land-use policies that regulate logging. In the late 1990s, logging on federal lands was cut back when the nesting areas of the spotted owl were made off-limits to loggers. Further restrictions were imposed due to additional concerns about other species. As a result, within the span of 10 years, the timber harvest on federal lands dropped by 75 percent.

Environmental concerns also fostered the growth of environmental certification and labeling for wood products as a means to ensure that the wood was harvested in an environmentally responsible way that sustains the forest ecosystem. These environmental concerns also led to the creative use of waste materials, like using wood byproducts as fuel to provide mills with electricity. Other scrap materials have been marketed to consumers as dyed mulch and shrink-wrapped bundles of firewood.

In addition to these environmental influences, some key technological advances have favorably affected the manufacturing of wood products for building. For example, the use of new technology and automation has greatly improved productivity, and computerized controls and laser scanners have maximized the amount of lumber obtained from a log, thus increasing output while consuming less wood.

The Building Construction Market

Housing is a major part of the U.S. economy, representing roughly 17 percent of the gross domestic product.[45] The largest volume items purchased by home builders are typically lumber and plywood, which represent roughly 20 percent of the total cost of the materials used to build a home.[46] The home construction industry also is highly cyclical, though repair and remodeling efforts are somewhat less so than new construction. The vibrancy of the industry varies along with several key factors, such as the overall health of the U.S. economy; demand levels for new home construction, improvements, and repairs; and the volume of home sales. During the first several years of the twenty-first century, the industry experienced strong growth after a pronounced lull, and residential construction permits and starts reached record highs, largely fueled by low interest rates. As the economy soured, the single residence home building construction market has become stagnant.

Although the industry is dominated by small firms, the largest builders represent a significant portion of new home sales. According to the most current government data, the top 1 percent of builders account for 40 percent of all new residential housing starts, and 1 percent of builders account for 34 percent of all new multifamily housing starts.[47] Industry concentration is likely to increase in the future through the increasing number of mergers and acquisitions.

For large wood products manufacturers like Weyerhaeuser, meeting the high expectations of large builders effectively is a business cornerstone. Because lumber represents a substantial portion of the total costs for builders, builders are careful to develop strong relationships with those manufacturers that can provide them with a good value for their money. Although the most important factor is obtaining competitively priced materials, builders also value product availability, speedy delivery, reliable products, and the ability to install quickly and efficiently.

Questions

1. Describe how you would expect large home building companies to purchase wood products from companies like Weyerhaeuser. Use the steps in the B2B buying process discussed in the chapter to facilitate your discussion.

2. Builders often consider wood products to be commodities, so companies like Weyerhaeuser work hard to provide additional value to gain a competitive

advantage in the marketplace. Describe some ways that Weyerhaeuser provides greater value to its customers than its competitors can. (It might help to review its Web site at http://www.weyerhaeuser.com.)

3. Identify the environmental factors discussed in the case that have influenced the industry during the past decade or so. What additional environmental factors might be important to the lumber industry, and how would they affect its B2B operations?

Marriott.
HOTELS & RESORTS

475 hotels · 69 countries

FLEXIBILITY

Business demands it. Which is why the social areas in our hotels are also functioning business areas. In both our group and private zones you can relax with a drink one minute, then have a meeting or go online the next. After all, the more we bend to help you, the more flexible you are for business.

THIS IS MARRIOTT

Marriott.com

CHAPTER

GLOBAL MARKETING

7

LEARNING OBJECTIVES

- What factors aid the growth of globalization?
- How does a firm decide to enter a global market?
- What ownership and partnership options do firms have for entering a new global market?
- What are the similarities and differences between a domestic marketing strategy and a global marketing strategy?
- How do ethical issues affect global marketing practices?

arriott International Inc., the operator of Marriott hotels worldwide for more than 80 years, generates revenues of $12 billion annually through its more than 3,000 hotels in 68 countries.[1] Its various brands range from the affordable Fairfield Inn to the luxurious Ritz-Carlton. Starting from a U.S. stronghold, Marriott has successfully expanded to earn a significant portion of its revenue from global properties. To use its full-service hotels as an example, only 34 percent of revenues come from U.S. operations; the remainder is derived from the Asia Pacific region (36 percent), the Middle East and Africa (11 percent), the Caribbean and Latin America (10 percent), and Europe (9 percent).[2]

With such global reach, Marriott knew when it decided to go after the international business traveler that its products and services could appeal to a global market segment, but it also needed to identify a way to reach this diverse group. Although the services that Marriott would

offer international travelers were very appealing, convincing experienced business travelers to change their hotel preferences would not be easy.

Marriott chose to run a massive advertising campaign targeting international travelers and invest in specific markets to build the various Marriott brands. For instance, after deciding on Beijing as the site for its 3,000th hotel,[3] Marriott thought to position that offering as the most luxurious hotel in the market that provided the largest standard-sized rooms anywhere in the city. According to the president of Marriott, the goal of developing a luxury reputation in China was not simply to encourage domestic travelers to stay in the new Marriott but rather to prompt Chinese businesspeople to recognize the brand and therefore choose to stay in Marriott's hotels when they traveled overseas.[4]

Marriott thus combined its positioning in international markets with a global marketing campaign that focused on what its marketing research had revealed international business travelers wanted: dependable luxury and absolute quality. The central concept behind the campaign focused on international forms of dance, because dance implies coordination, and the vast number of cultural dance variations would allow Marriott to express its worldwide commitment to specific local markets.[5]

Marriott marketers wanted to reach international travelers where they were most likely to be—hotel rooms, airplanes, and airports all over the world. Therefore, the company purchased media time on targeted global channels, such as CNN en Español, Al Jazeera, and France 24. It also approached airlines including Air China, Lufthansa, and Japan Air Lines to purchase in-flight television ads. Not limited to just televised promotions, the campaign also included traditional print placements in publications such as *The Economist* and online advertising. Marriott ads even showed up on YouTube (search for: Marriott Hotels: 30 International TV ad).[6]

So what do these decisions tell us about why Marriott has continued to succeed as a global hotel chain when others have failed? First, Marriott has been investing consistently in the global market for decades, not just a few years, and this consistent investment in foreign markets has built it brand equity around the world. Second, Marriott chooses specific and targetable market segments, even if they are global markets, so that it can craft a message that is just as relevant to travelers on Lufthansa as it is to travelers on Singapore Airlines. These steps, combined with its knowledge of brand building, learned from its experiences in countries all over the world, enable Marriott to compete remarkably well in the global market.

● ● ●

The increasing globalization of markets affects not only large U.S. corporations like Marriott, which actively go in search of new markets, but also small- and medium-sized businesses that increasingly depend on goods produced globally to deliver their products and services. Most people may not think about how globalization affects their daily lives, but just take a minute to read the labels on the clothing you are wearing right now. Chances are that most of the items, even if they carry U.S. brand names, were manufactured in another part of the world.

In the United States, the market has evolved from a system of regional marketplaces to national markets to geographically regional markets (e.g., Canada and the United States together) to international markets and finally to global markets. Globalization refers to the processes by which goods, services, capital, people, information, and ideas flow across national borders. Global markets are the result of several fundamental changes, such as reductions or eliminations of trade barriers by country governments, the decreasing concerns of distance and time with regard to moving products and ideas across countries, the standardization of laws across borders, and globally integrated production processes.[7]

Each of these fundamental changes has paved the way for marketing to flourish in other countries. The elimination of trade barriers and other governmental actions, for instance, allows goods and ideas to move quickly and efficiently around the world, which in turn facilitates the quick delivery of goods to better meet the needs of global consumers. When examining countries as potential markets for global products, companies must realize that these different countries exist at very different stages of globalization. The World Bank ranks countries according

Build it. *LEGO*

How do Legos get from its manufacturer in Denmark to a toy store near your home?

to their degrees of globalization on the basis of a composite metric that examines whether the factors necessary to participate in the global marketplace are present. Countries that score well on the scale represent the best markets for globalized products and services; those lowest on the scale represent the most troublesome markets.

Most Americans tend to take access to global products and services for granted. When we walk into a toy store, we expect to find Legos from Denmark; in the local sporting goods store, we anticipate finding Adidas shoes from Germany; and many consumers choose Nokia phones from Finland. But think about the process that enabled these products to arrive in your town. Or consider how a $12 digital camera for your keychain, made in Taiwan, which you purchased at Target, could be produced, transported halfway around the world, and sold for so little money. These are the questions we will be examining in this chapter.

We begin by looking at the growth of the global economy and the forces that led to it. We'll see how firms assess the potential of a given market, make decisions to go global, and—as Marriott did in the opening vignette—choose how they will sell globally. Then we explore how to build the marketing mix for global products and consider some of the ethical and legal issues of globalization.

GROWTH OF THE GLOBAL ECONOMY: GLOBALIZATION OF MARKETING AND PRODUCTION

Changes in technology, especially communications technology, have been the driving force for growth in global markets for decades. The telegraph, radio, television, computer, and, now, Internet increasingly connect distant parts of the world. Today, communication is instantaneous. Sounds and images from across the globe are delivered to TV sets, radios, and computers in real time, which enables receivers in all parts of the world to observe how others live, work, and play.

The globalization of production, also known as offshoring, refers to manufacturers' procurement of goods and services from around the globe to take advantage of national differences in the cost and quality of various factors of production

Many goods and services are provided from other countries, an activity known as offshoring. At this call center in Delhi, India, experts provide information to an Internet service provider in the U.K.

The key difference between the IMF and the World Bank is that the IMF focuses primarily on maintaining the international monetary system, whereas the World Bank concentrates on poverty reduction through low-interest loans and other programs. In this photo, outgoing World Bank President James D. Wolfensohn, right, Development Committee Chairman Trevor Manuel, the finance minister of South Africa, center, and International Monetary Fund Managing Director Rodrigo de Rato, far left, speak with reporters at the IMF headquarters in Washington.

(e.g., labor, energy, land, capital).[8] Although it originally focused on relocating manufacturing to lower cost production countries, the practice of offshoring has now grown to include products associated with a knowledge economy: medical services, financial advice, technological support, and consulting. The combined market for offshoring, including IT, call centers, and business process outsourcing, is expected to reach $450 billion by 2010.[9] Much of this demand comes from the banking sector; financial services are by far the largest private-sector market for offshoring, accounting for more than 35 percent of all offshoring.[10]

Many people believe that a majority of offshoring goes to India or China and the United States is a leader in offshoring. In fact, India represents only 11.5 percent of the offshoring market,[11] and European countries account for 54 percent of all offshoring contracts.[12] American firms historically have sent work to Canada, where they find a similar business environment but 20 percent lower labor costs and a historically advantageous exchange rate. With the relatively weak dollar, though, some of that business is coming back to the United States, because those cost savings no longer exist, and other jobs are going abroad to other key offshoring markets.[13]

Not all offshoring is about inexpensive labor. For some companies such as IBM, offshoring reflects its constant, global hunt for talent as it makes an effort to reduce costs. Krakow, Poland, which receives heavy investments from IBM, may be a low-cost location, especially in comparison with the United States, but it cannot compare to the cost savings available in China or India. However, Krakow also has invested heavily in technical education for its students, and the highly trained group of 150,000 engineers and technicians represents an attractive pool that IBM can tap to support its business.[14]

The growth of global markets also has been facilitated by organizations that are designed to oversee their functioning. Perhaps the most important of these organizations is represented by the General Agreement on Tariffs and Trade (GATT). The purpose of the GATT was to lower trade barriers, such as high tariffs on imported goods and restrictions on the number and types of imported products that inhibited the free flow of goods across borders. In 1948, 23 countries agreed to 45,000 tariff concessions that affected about one-fifth of world trade.[15] Over the years, successive rounds of trade negotiations have led to further reductions in trade barriers, as well as new rules designed to promote global trade further.

The original GATT also included the founding of the International Monetary Fund (IMF), but in 1994, the GATT was replaced by the World Trade Organization (WTO). The WTO differs from the GATT in that the WTO is an established institution based in Geneva, Switzerland, instead of simply an agreement. Furthermore, the WTO represents the only international organization that deals with the global rules of trade among nations. Its main function is to ensure that trade flows as smoothly, predictably, and freely as possible. The WTO also administers trade agreements, acts as a forum for trade negotiations, settles trade disputes, reviews national trade policies, and assists developing countries in their trade policy issues through technical assistance and training. Currently, the 148 members of the WTO account for 97 percent of global trade.[16]

As we noted, the original GATT established the IMF, whose primary purpose is to promote international monetary cooperation and facilitate the expansion and growth of international trade. Along with the IMF, the World Bank Group is dedicated to fighting

Ethical and Societal Dilemma 7.1 What's Wrong with Globalization?

One of the most persuasive arguments antiglobalization groups use is that many of the problems related to globalization can be attributed to the seemingly insatiable appetite of countries in North America and Europe, as well as Japan and other industrialized nations, for natural resources, oil, gasoline, timber, food, and so forth.[17] These nations consume 80 percent of the world's resources but are home to only 20 percent of the population. Should firms in industrialized nations be able to utilize these natural resources at a disproportionate rate, regardless of whether their shareholders demand profitable growth?

As the industrialized West has put into place laws that protect workers' rights, workers' safety, and the environment, U.S. firms also have outsourced production to less developed countries that either have no such laws or don't enforce them. Without laws to protect workers and the environment, the factories that produce these goods often exploit both the workers and the environment of these countries. Industrialized nations obtain the goods they crave at low costs, but at what price do these goods come to the country that provides them?

In many parts of the world, the changes wrought by globalization have moved so fast that cultures have not had time to adapt. Many countries fear that the price for economic success and participation in the global market may be the loss of their individual identities and cultures. The challenge thus becomes whether economic needs should be allowed to outweigh cultural preservation.

poverty and improving the living standards of people in the developing world. It is a development bank that provides loans, policy advice, technical assistance, and knowledge-sharing services to low- and middle-income countries in an attempt to reduce poverty.[18] Thus, the key difference between the IMF and the World Bank is that the IMF focuses primarily on maintaining the international monetary system, whereas the World Bank concentrates on poverty reduction through low-interest loans and other programs. For instance, the World Bank Group is the largest external funding source of education and HIV/AIDS programs.

Both these organizations affect the practice of global marketing in different ways, but together, they enable marketers to participate in the global marketplace by making it easier to buy and sell, financing deserving firms, opening markets to trade, and raising the global standard of living, which allows more people to buy goods and services.

However, these organizations have been criticized by a diverse group of nongovernmental organizations, religious groups, and advocates for workers and the poor. The primary criticism of the World Bank is that it is merely a puppet of Western industrialized nations that use World Bank loans to assist their globalization efforts. Others argue that the World Bank loans too much money to third-world countries, which makes it almost impossible for these often debt-ridden nations to repay the loans.[19] Ethical and Societal Dilemma 7.1 discusses some of the more general criticisms of globalization.

Globalization obviously has its critics, and those critics very well may have a point. But globalization also has been progressing at a steady and increasing pace. With that development in mind, let's look at how firms determine in which countries to expand their operations.

ASSESSING GLOBAL MARKETS

Because different countries, with their different stages of globalization, offer marketers a variety of opportunities, firms must assess the viability of various potential market entries. As illustrated in Exhibit 7.1, we examine four sets of criteria necessary

EXHIBIT 7.1 Components of a Country Market Assessment

to assess a country's market: economic analysis, infrastructure and technological analysis, government actions or inactions, and sociocultural analysis. Information about these four areas offers marketers a more complete picture of a country's potential as a market for products and services.

Economic Analysis Using Metrics

The greater the wealth of people in a country, generally, the better the opportunity a firm will have in that particular country. A firm conducting an economic analysis of a country market must look at three major economic factors using well-established metrics: the general economic environment, the market size and population growth rate, and real income.

Evaluating the General Economic Environment   Generally, healthy economies provide better opportunities for global marketing expansions, and there are several ways a firm can use metrics to measure the relative health of a particular country's economy. Each way offers a slightly different view, and some may be more useful for some products and services than for others.

To determine the market potential for its particular product or service, a firm should use as many metrics as it can obtain. One metric is the relative level of imports and exports. The United States, for example, suffers a trade deficit, which means that the country imports more goods than it exports. For U.S. marketers, this deficit can signal the potential for greater competition at home from foreign producers. Firms would prefer to manufacture in a country that has a trade surplus, or a higher level of exports than imports, because it signals a greater opportunity to export products to more markets.

The most common way to gauge the size and market potential of an economy, and therefore the potential the country has for global marketing, is to use standardized metrics of output. Gross domestic product (GDP), the most widely used of these metrics, is defined as the market value of the goods and services produced by a country in a year. Gross national income (GNI) consists of GDP plus the net income earned from investments abroad (minus any payments made to nonresidents who contribute to the domestic economy). In other words, U.S. firms that invest or maintain operations abroad count their income from those operations in the GNI but not the GDP.[20]

Another frequently used metric of an overall economy is the purchasing power parity (PPP), a theory that states that if the exchange rates of two countries are in equilibrium, a product purchased in one will cost the same in the other, if expressed in the same currency.[21] A novel metric that employs PPP to assess the relative economic buying power among nations is *The Economist*'s Big Mac Index, which suggests that exchange rates should adjust to equalize the cost of a basket of goods and services, wherever it is bought around the world. Using McDonald's Big Mac as the market basket, Exhibit 7.2 shows that the cheapest burger is in

EXHIBIT 7.2	Big Mac Index: Local Currency Under (−)/Over (+) Valuation against the Dollar		
	Big Mac Prices in Dollars*	**Implied PPP[†] of the Dollar**	**Under (−) /Over (+) Valuation against the Dollar, %**
United States[§]	3.41	−	−
Argentina	2.57	2.42	−22
Australia	2.95	1.01	−14
Brazil	3.61	2.02	+6
Britain	4.01	1.71[§§]	+18
Canada	3.68	1.14	+8
Chile	2.97	459	−13
China	1.45	3.23	−58
Czech Republic	2.51	15.5	−27
Denmark	5.08	8.14	+49
Egypt	1.68	2.80	−51
Euro area**	4.17	1.12[††]	+22
Hong Kong	1.54	3.52	−55
Hungary	3.33	176	−2
Indonesia	1.76	4,663	−48
Japan	2.29	82.1	−33
Malaysia	1.60	1.61	−53
Mexico	2.69	8.50	−21
New Zealand	3.59	1.35	+5
Peru	3.00	2.79	−12
Philippines	1.85	24.9	−46
Poland	2.51	2.02	−26
Russia	2.03	15.2	−41
Singapore	2.59	1.16	−24
South Africa	2.22	4.55	−35
South Korea	3.14	850	−8
Sweden	4.86	9.68	+42
Switzerland	5.20	1.85	+53
Taiwan	2.29	22.0	−33
Thailand	1.80	18.2	−47
Turkey	3.66	1.39	+7
Venezuela	3.45	2,170	−1

*At current exchange rates   [†]Purchasing power parity; local price divided by price in United States   [§]Average of New York, Chicago, Atlanta, and San Francisco   [§§]Dollars per pound   **Weighted average of prices in euro area   [††]Dollar per euro

Source: "Big Mac Index," *The Economist*, January 12, 2006, electronically accessed.

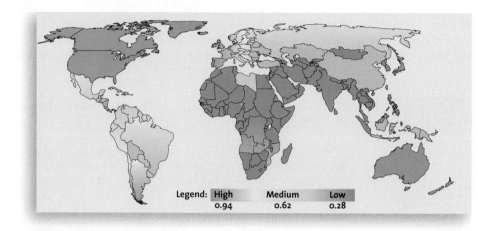

| EXHIBIT 7·3 | Global Human Development Index (HDI) Score |

Legend: High 0.94 Medium 0.62 Low 0.28

Source: http://www.nationmaster.com/red/graph/eco_hum_dev_ind-economy-human-development-index∫ =-1&b_map=1#.

China, where it costs $1.45, compared with an average American price of $3.41. In Switzerland, the same burger costs $5.20. This index thus implies that the Chinese yuan is 58 percent undervalued, whereas the Swiss franc is 53 percent overvalued in comparison with the U.S. dollar.

These various metrics help marketers understand the relative wealth of a particular country, though, as scholars have recently argued, they may not give a full picture of the economic health of a country because they are based solely on material output.[22] As a corollary metric to those described previously, the United Nations has developed the human development index (HDI), a composite metric of three indicators of the quality of life in different countries: life expectancy at birth, educational attainment, and whether the average incomes, according to PPP estimates, are sufficient to meet the basic needs of life in that country. For marketers, these metrics determine the lifestyle elements that ultimately drive consumption (recall that Chapter 5, on consumer behavior, discussed the influence of lifestyle on consumption). The HDI is scaled from 0 to 1; those countries that score lower than .5 are classified as nations with low human development, those that score .5–.8 have medium development, and those above .8 are classified as having high human development. Exhibit 7.3 shows a map of the world with the various HDI scores.

These macroeconomic metrics provide a snapshot of a particular country at any one point in time. Because they are standardized metrics, it is possible to compare countries across time and identify those that are experiencing economic growth and increased globalization.

Although an understanding of the macroeconomic environment is crucial for managers facing a market entry decision, of equal importance is the understanding of economic metrics of individual income and household size.

Evaluating Market Size and Population Growth Rate Global population has been growing dramatically since the turn of the 20th century (see Exhibit 7.4). The 2002 map (top) represents the world population as we know it today. The bottom map is a graphical depiction of what the population is expected to be in 2050. Note, for instance, how the populations of North and South America are expected to shrink relative to Africa. From a marketing perspective, however, growth has not been equally dispersed. Less-developed nations, by and large, are experiencing rapid population growth, while many developed countries are experiencing either zero or negative population growth. The countries with the highest purchasing power today may become less attractive in the future for many products and services because of stagnated growth.

EXHIBIT 7·4   Change in World Population

Population 2002

Population 2050

Source: www.worldmapper.org (accessed September 3, 2008).

Another aspect related to population and growth pertains to the distribution of the population within a particular region; namely, is the population located primarily in rural or urban areas? This distinction determines where and how products and services can be delivered. Long supply chains, in which goods pass through many hands, are necessary to reach rural populations and therefore add costs to products. India's 1.1 billion people live overwhelmingly in rural areas, though the population is moving toward urban areas to meet the demands of the growing industrial and service centers located in major cities such as Bangalore and New Delhi. This population shift, perhaps not surprisingly, is accompanied by rapid growth in the middle class.[23] Another major trend in India involves the age of the population; more than half of India's citizens are younger than 25 years;[24] in the United States, in contrast, the median age is 36.6 years.[25]

The business impacts of these combined trends of increasing urbanization, a growing middle class, and a youthful populace make India an absolutely enormous market for consumer goods. Take cell phones as an example. Fifteen years ago, the country hosted only 5 million total telecom connections, and that number included ground lines. Today, there are more than 200 million.[26] The rapid growth rates of industries create significant opportunities for global companies to sell

Ethical and Societal Dilemma 7.2   Is Global Retail Expansion Good for India?

Direct foreign investment, despite some recent relaxation of the laws, is still barred in India. But foreign firms are permitted to enter into joint ventures with Indian-owned firms. Although some retailers, notably GAP, Zara, and H&M have thus far stayed away from such arrangements because these firms don't want to give up complete operational control,[27] other retailers such as Wal-Mart, U.K.-based Tesco, and French-based Carrefour are looking at this rapidly growing, young, and increasingly prosperous country as a natural growth outlet.[28]

Ninety six percent of India's retailers are less than 500 square feet and are family owned.[29] Even in major cities like Delhi, some upscale shopping centers consist of clusters of tiny shops. In these small shops, clerks perch precariously on ladders to fetch items that are out of customers' reach, while other customers brush against each other as they wander crowded aisles. Some of the fanciest apparel stores are located up narrow, twisting staircases.

Customers are used to shopping in these small family-owned stores. They have been doing so their whole lives. It is therefore not clear whether or not they want to change their buying habits. For example, Kishore Biyani's supermarkets in Mumbai, India, were initially designed like most Western-style supermarkets.[30] But customers walked down the wide aisles, past neatly stocked shelves, and out the door without buying. Biyani soon recognized that part of his target market, lower middle–income customers, did not like the sterile environment. His other target market segment, wealthier families, generally employed servants to do the grocery shopping. These servants were accustomed to shopping in small, cramped stores filled with haggling customers. Most Indians buy fresh produce from street vendors or small stores, and the merchandise is kept under burlap sacks. Biyani therefore redesigned his stores to make them messier, noisier, and more cramped, much like a public market. Biyani's approach to retailing has worked. His company, Panaloon Retail (India), Ltd., is now the country's largest retailer with annual sales of approximately $900 million.

What will be the effect on the economy and culture of India if Wal-Mart and other large global retailers are successful in India? What will become of the small family-owned businesses? Will Indians continue the tradition of shopping in these stores, or will they switch to the bright lights and orderly, clean, and well-stocked atmosphere of the new competitors? What will happen to overall employment in the retail, transportation, and supply chain sectors? In the end, will small retailers in India go the way of similar retailers in the United States over the last 30 years in the wake of retail giants like Wal-Mart and others?

Retailing in India is evolving at a rapid pace.

products; in the telecommunications industry, for example, sellers of accessories such as ringtones and new batteries are enjoying a greatly expanded market. In general, India's economy is expected to continue to outpace world growth.[31]

Ethical and Societal Dilemma 7.2 raises the issue of whether it is in the best interest of a rapidly developing country to encourage foreign retailers to enter the country to stimulate the economy, but at the same time potentially harm family-owned businesses.

Evaluating Real Income A firm can make adjustments to an existing product to meet the unique needs of a particular country market. For instance, Procter & Gamble (P&G) is setting ambitious goals for its growth, including targeting one billion underserved consumers in developing countries. Creating products for the developing market takes more than just dropping prices, because for people who earn the equivalent of less than $1 a day, prices on P&G's existing products simply cannot go low enough. Therefore, P&G had to rethink its entire distribution network and all its product designs. To reach the rural Mexican market for example, P&G partnered with some of the 650,000 small stores and kiosks in rural Mexico instead of the supermarket chains that were predominately located in cities. These smaller stores needed a different kind of product than urban markets; rural Mexicans could not afford to purchase an entire bottle of Head & Shoulders but instead wanted to purchase single-use packets that cost about 19 cents each. The company also worked to identify ways that it could change products to better serve rural Mexico. For example, running water often is in short supply for low-income Mexicans, so P&G developed a single-use fabric softener, Downy Single Rinse, that consumers can add with detergent to eliminate the entire rinse cycle that most Americans use in their laundry. But why would P&G target rural Mexico? Because it knows that Mexicans spend about $16 billion annually in rural stores, and the only way to win the market is to offer consumers products that they can realistically afford.[32]

The Asian and European art market has strengthened as collectors take advantage of the weakened U.S. dollar.

On the other end of the spectrum are superwealthy consumers. As the U.S. dollar has fallen, the relative purchasing power of other regions has increased. The impact of this shift among the wealthy can best be depicted by the changes in the art world. Sotheby's and Christie's, two international auction houses, both sell major pieces of art. Most years, more than $11 billion worth of artwork passes through these two houses, though in recent years, the Asian art scene has been drawing the most attention. As Asian currencies appreciate, the number of collectors in the Asian art world has exploded. In 2007, Hong Kong art purchases were up 28 percent from the year before. At the same time, European art collectors also took advantage of the falling dollar to visit U.S. art shows, where they purchased nearly twice as much as they typically would. Thus, global trade creates opportunities for those who make expensive luxury goods as well as those companies that can find a way to produce low-cost, yet still profitable, products.[33]

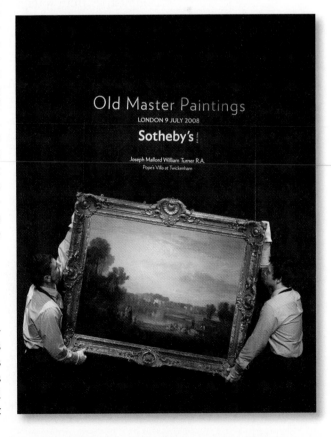

Analyzing Infrastructure and Technological Capabilities

The next component of any market assessment is an infrastructure and technological analysis. Infrastructure is defined as the basic facilities, services, and installations needed for a community or society to function, such as transportation and communications systems, water and power lines, and public institutions like schools, post

For a country to be a viable option for a new market entry, firms must assess its transportation, distribution channels, communications, and commercial infrastructure.

offices, and prisons. Marketers are especially concerned with four key elements of a country's infrastructure: transportation, distribution channels, communications, and commerce.

These four components are essential to the development of an efficient marketing system. First, there must be a system to transport goods throughout the various markets and to consumers in geographically dispersed marketplaces—trains, roads, refrigeration. Second, distribution channels must exist to deliver products in a timely manner and at a reasonable cost. Third, the communications system, particularly media access, must be sufficiently developed to allow consumers to find information about the products and services available in the marketplace. Fourth, the commercial infrastructure, which consists of the legal, banking, and regulatory systems, allows markets to function. In the next section, we focus on how issues pertaining to the political and legal structures of a country can affect the risk that marketers face in operating in a given country.

Analyzing Government Actions

Governmental actions, as well as the actions of nongovernmental political groups, can significantly influence firms' ability to sell goods and services, because they often result in laws or other regulations that either promote the growth of the global market or close off the country and inhibit growth. These issues include tariffs, quotas, boycotts, exchange controls, and trade agreements. (See Exhibit 7.5.)

Tariffs   A tariff (also called a duty) is a tax levied on a good imported into a country. In most cases, tariffs are intended to make imported goods more expensive and thus less competitive with domestic products,[34] which in turn protects domestic industries from foreign competition. In other cases, tariffs might be imposed to penalize another country for trade practices that the home country views as unfair. For example, the United States imposes a steep tariff on imported biofuel from Brazil, in response to the U.S. farming industry's claims that Brazil has an unfair advantage because sugar cane, native to Brazil, is a much more cost-efficient source of fuel ethanol than is American-produced corn.[35] The tax of 51 cents per gallon effectively prevents Brazilian sugar cane ethanol from reaching U.S. pumps.[36]

In lieu of tariffs, countries can utilize dumping laws to protect domestic companies against foreign competition. Dumping occurs when a foreign

EXHIBIT 7·5	Government Actions

Many U.S. quotas on foreign-made textiles have been eliminated. Some firms have chosen to redistribute the bulk of these savings to consumers—in Wal-Mart's case (left), 75 percent of the savings; whereas other firms, such as Bebe (right), are planning to redistribute only 25 percent of the savings and keep the rest as profit.

producer sells its offering in a foreign market at a price less than its production costs to gain market share.[37] When a foreign company is found to have engaged in dumping, U.S. law allows for fines, and those collected fines then get distributed to U.S. companies affected by the dumping practices. The Southern Shrimp Alliance, as one example, received more than $100 million in compensation from Asian shrimp fishers who were found guilty of dumping shrimp in the U.S. market.[38]

Quotas   A quota designates the maximum quantity of a product that may be brought into a country during a specified time period. Many U.S. quotas on foreign-made textiles were eliminated in 2005, which increased the amount of imported apparel products sold in the United States. Some firms have chosen to redistribute the bulk of these savings to consumers—in Wal-Mart's case, 75 percent of them—whereas others, such as Bebe, are planning to distribute only 25 percent and keep the rest as profit.[39]

However, tariffs and quotas also can impose a fundamental and potentially devastating blow to a firm's ability to sell products in another country. Tariffs artificially raise prices and therefore lower demand, and quotas reduce the availability of imported merchandise. Conversely, tariffs and quotas benefit domestically made products because they reduce foreign competition.

Boycott   A boycott pertains to a group's refusal to deal commercially with some organization to protest against its policies. Boycotts might be called by governments or nongovernmental organizations, such as trade unions or environmental groups. Although most are called by nongovernmental organizations, they still can be very political. The modern war in Iraq initially prompted some American boycotts, such as the memorable refusals by some consumers to purchase French products—and the renaming in the Congressional lunchroom of French toast to "Liberty toast"— in response to France's refusal to join the U.S. war effort. More recently, however, various other countries have issued their own calls for boycotts of U.S. products and services. A recent survey indicates that 20 percent of respondents from Europe and Canada claim that they consciously avoid purchases of U.S. products as a form of protest against U.S. foreign policy, especially its actions in Iraq. The survey also asked the respondents if they were intentionally avoiding purchasing the products offered by 40 well-known U.S. corporations. Corporations viewed as being "more American" fared the worst. For example, 60 percent of respondents said that they would not buy Marlboro products, and 48 percent claimed they would "definitely avoid" using American Express. The other brands that respondents stated they were "most avoiding" included ExxonMobil, AOL, Chevron, Texaco, United Airlines, Budweiser, Chrysler, Barbie dolls, Starbucks, and General Motors. Adding to the bad news for U.S. corporations, 50 percent of the survey respondents stated that

The decline of the value of the U.S. dollar against the euro and other important world currencies has made imports to the U.S. more expensive, and exports from the U.S. less expensive.

they distrusted U.S. firms because of their perceived involvement in foreign policy.[40] The long-term impact of such boycotts on the ability of U.S. firms to market in other countries, as a result of global antiwar sentiment, remains as yet unknown.

Exchange Control Exchange control refers to the regulation of a country's currency exchange rate, the measure of how much one currency is worth in relation to another.[41] A designated agency in each country, often the Central Bank, sets the rules for currency exchange, though in the United States, the Federal Reserve sets the currency exchange rates. In recent years, the value of the U.S. dollar has decreased significantly compared with other important world currencies such as the euro and the pound sterling (U.K.). The fall of the dollar has had a twofold effect on U.S. firms' ability to conduct global business. For firms that depend on imports of finished products, raw materials that they fabricate into other products, or services from other countries, the cost of doing business has gone up dramatically. At the same time, buyers in other countries find the costs of U.S. goods and services much lower than they were before.

A method of avoiding an unfavorable exchange rate is to engage in countertrade. Countertrade is trade between two countries where goods are traded for other goods and not for hard currency. For instance, the Philippine government has entered into a countertrade agreement with Vietnam. The Philippine International Trading Corp is importing rice and paying for half of it with fertilizer, coconuts, and coconut by-products.[42]

Trade Agreements Marketers must consider the trade agreements to which a particular country is a signatory or the trading bloc to which it belongs. A trade agreement is an intergovernmental agreement designed to manage and promote trade activities for a specific region, and a trading bloc consists of those countries that have signed the particular trade agreement.[43]

Some major trade agreements cover two-thirds of the world's international trade: the European Union (EU), the North American Free Trade Agreement (NAFTA), Central America Free Trade Agreement (CAFTA), Mercosur, and the Association of Southeast Asian Nations (ASEAN).[44] These trade agreements are summarized in Exhibit 7.6. The EU represents the highest level of integration

EXHIBIT 7.6	Trade Agreements
Name	**Countries**
European Union	There are 27 member countries of the EU: Austria, Belgium, Bulgaria, Cyprus, Czech Republic, Denmark, Estonia, Finland, France, Germany, Greece, Hungary, Ireland, Italy, Latvia, Lithuania, Luxembourg, Malta, Netherlands, Poland, Portugal, Romania, Slovakia, Slovenia, Spain, Sweden, and the United Kingdom.[45] There are three official candidate countries to join the EU: Croatia, Macedonia, and Turkey.
NAFTA	United States, Canada, and Mexico.
CAFTA	United States, Costa Rica, the Dominican Republic, El Salvador, Guatemala, Honduras, and Nicaragua.
Mercosur	Full members: Argentina, Brazil, Paraguay, Uruguay, and Venezuela.
ASEAN	Brunei Darussalam, Cambodia, Indonesia, Laos, Malaysia, Myanmar, Philippines, Singapore, Thailand, and Vietnam.

| EXHIBIT 7·7 | Map of the European Union |

Source: http://en.wikipedia.org/wiki/European_Union.

across individual nations, whereas the other agreements vary in their integration levels.

European Union   The EU is an economic and monetary union that currently contains 27 countries, as illustrated in Exhibit 7.7. Croatia, Macedonia, and Turkey head a list of additional petitioners for membership, but they have not yet been granted full membership.[46] The European Union represents a significant restructuring of the global marketplace. By dramatically lowering trade barriers between member nations, the union has changed the complexion of the global marketplace.

Having one currency, the euro, across Europe has simplified the way many multinational companies market their products. For instance, prior to the conversion to the euro on January 1, 1999, firms were unable to predict exchange rates. This barrier made it difficult to set consistent prices across countries. After the euro replaced the traditional European currencies, stable prices resulted. Products could be preticketed for distribution across Europe. In addition, patent requirements were simplified because one patent application could cover multiple countries. Similarly, the rules governing data privacy and transmission, advertising, direct selling, and other marketing issues have been streamlined and simplified, allowing more seamless trade.

The European Union has resulted in lowering trade barriers and strengthening global relationships among member nations.

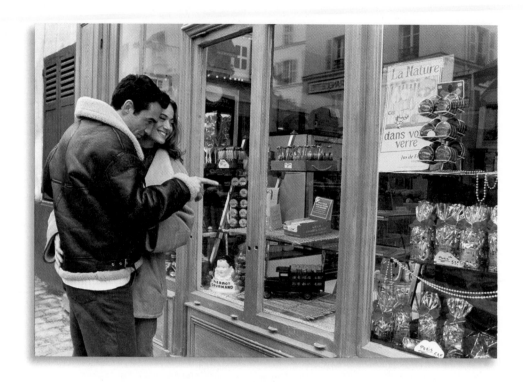

North American Free Trade Agreement (NAFTA)   NAFTA is limited to trade-related issues, such as tariffs and quotas, among the United States, Canada, and Mexico.

Central American Free Trade Agreement (CAFTA)   CAFTA is a trade agreement among the United States, Costa Rica, the Dominican Republic, El Salvador, Guatemala, Honduras, and Nicaragua.[47]

Mercosur   Translated from the Spanish, Mercosur means the Southern Common Market. This group covers most of South America. In 1995, Mercosur member nations created the Free Trade Area of the Americas (FTAA), primarily in response to NAFTA.

Association of Southeast Asian Nations (ASEAN)   Originally formed to promote security in Southeast Asia during the Vietnam War, ASEAN changed its mission to building economic stability and lowering trade restrictions among the six member nations in the 1980s.

These trading blocs affect how U.S. firms can conduct business in the member countries. Some critics contend that such blocs confer an unfair advantage on their member nations because they offer favorable terms for trade, whereas others believe they stimulate economies by lowering trade barriers and allowing higher levels of foreign investment.

Analyzing Sociocultural Factors

Understanding another country's *culture* is crucial to the success of any global marketing initiative. Culture, or the shared meanings, beliefs, morals, values, and customs of a group of people, exists on two levels: visible artifacts (e.g., behavior, dress, symbols, physical settings, ceremonies) and underlying values (thought processes, beliefs, and assumptions). Visible artifacts are easy to recognize, but businesses often find it more difficult to understand the underlying values of a culture and appropriately adapt their marketing strategies to them.[48]

One important cultural classification scheme that firms can use is Geert Hofstede's cultural dimensions concept, which sheds more light on these underlying values. Hofstede believes cultures differ on five dimensions:[49]

1. **Power distance:** Willingness to accept social inequality as natural.
2. **Uncertainty avoidance:** The extent to which the society relies on orderliness, consistency, structure, and formalized procedures to address situations that arise in daily life.
3. **Individualism:** Perceived obligation to and dependence on groups.
4. **Masculinity:** The extent to which dominant values are male oriented. A lower masculinity ranking indicates that men and women are treated equally in all aspects of society; a higher masculinity ranking suggests that men dominate in positions of power.[50]
5. **Time orientation:** Short- versus long-term orientation. A country that tends to have a long-term orientation values long-term commitments and is willing to accept a longer time horizon for, say, the success of a new product introduction.

To illustrate two of the five dimensions, consider the data and graph in Exhibit 7.8. Power distance is on the vertical axis and individualism is on the horizontal axis. Several Latin American countries cluster high on power distance but low on individualism; the United States, Australia, Canada, and the United Kingdom, in contrast, cluster high on individualism but low on power distance. Using this information, firms should expect that if they design a marketing campaign that stresses equality and individualism, it will be well accepted in English-speaking countries, all other factors being equal. The same campaign, however, might not be as well received in Latin American countries.

Another means of classifying cultures distinguishes them according to the importance of verbal communication.[51] In the United States and most European countries, business relationships are governed by what is said and written down, often through formal contracts. In countries such as China and South Korea, however, most relationships rely on nonverbal cues, so that the situation or context means much more than mere words. For instance, business relationships in China

---

EXHIBIT 7.8   Country Clusters

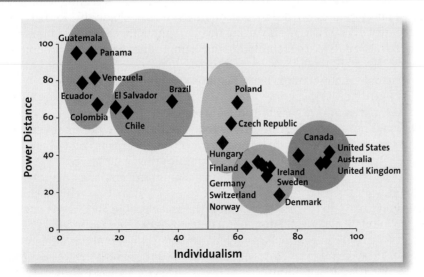

Source: Based on data available at http://www.geert-hofstede.com. Data from: Geert Hofstede, *Culture's Consequences,* 2nd ed. (Thousand Oaks, CA: Sage, 2001). Copyright © Geert Hofstede, reproduced with permission.

often are formalized by just a handshake, and trust and honor are often more important than legal arrangements.

Overall, culture affects every aspect of consumer behavior: why people buy, who is in charge of buying decisions, and how, when, and where people shop. After marketing managers have completed the four parts of the market assessment, they are better able to make informed decisions about whether a particular country possesses the necessary characteristics to be considered a potential market for the firm's products and services. In the next section, we detail the market entry decision process, beginning with a discussion of the various ways firms might enter a new global market.

CHECK YOURSELF

1. What are key metrics that can help analyze the economic environment of a country?
2. What types of government actions should we be concerned about as we evaluate a country?
3. What are five important cultural dimensions?

CHOOSING A GLOBAL ENTRY STRATEGY

When a firm has concluded its assessment analysis of the most viable markets for its products and services, it must then conduct an internal assessment of its capabilities. As we discussed in Chapter 2, this analysis includes an assessment of the firm's access to capital, the current markets it serves, its manufacturing capacity, its proprietary assets, and the commitment of its management to the proposed strategy. These factors ultimately contribute to the success or failure of a market expansion strategy, whether at home or in a foreign market. After these internal market assessments, it is time for the firm to choose its entry strategy.

A firm can choose from many approaches when it decides to enter a new market, which vary according to the level of risk the firm is willing to take. Many firms actually follow a progression in which they begin with less risky strategies to enter their first foreign markets and move to increasingly risky strategies as they gain confidence in their abilities and more control over their operations, as illustrated in Exhibit 7.9. We examine these different approaches that marketers take when entering global markets, beginning with the least risky.

Exporting Exporting means producing goods in one country and selling them in another. This entry strategy requires the least financial risk but also allows for only a limited return to the exporting firm. Global expansion often begins when a firm receives an order for its product or service from another country, in which case it faces little risk because it has no investment in people, capital equipment, buildings, or infrastructure. By the same token, it is difficult to achieve economies of scale when everything has to be shipped internationally. The Swiss watchmaker Rolex sells relatively small numbers of expensive watches all over the world. Because its transportation costs are relatively small compared with the cost of the watches, the best way for it to service any market is to export from Switzerland.

Franchising Franchising is a contractual agreement between a firm, the fran-chisor, and another firm or individual, the franchisee. A franchising contract

EXHIBIT 7·9   Global Entry Strategies

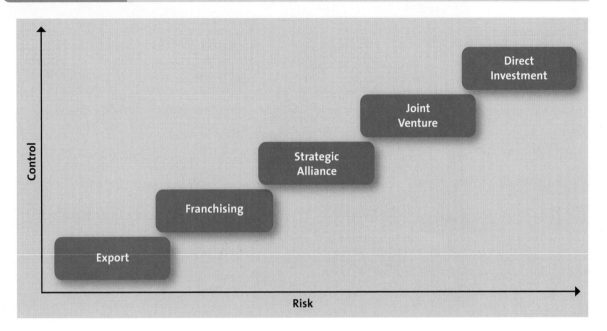

allows the franchisee to operate a business—a retail product or service firm or a B2B provider—using the name and business format developed and supported by the franchisor. Many of the best-known retailers in the United States are also successful global franchisers, including McDonald's, Pizza Hut, Starbucks, Domino's Pizza, KFC, and Holiday Inn, all of which have found that global franchising entails lower risks and requires less investment than does opening units owned wholly by the firm. However, when it engages in franchising, the firm has limited control over the market operations in the foreign country, its potential profit is reduced because it must be split with the franchisee, and, once the franchise is established, there is always the threat that the franchisee will break away and operate as a competitor under a different name.

Strategic Alliance   Strategic alliances refer to collaborative relationships between independent firms, though the partnering firms do not create an equity partnership; that is, they do not invest in one another. For example, you might not know its name yet, but Chery Automobile Company, China's fourth largest automotive firm, hopes that you will soon and therefore is betting its future on a series of high-profile strategic alliances. Foremost among the alliances is its agreement to work with Chrysler to sell Chery-made A1 sedans in Mexico under the Dodge brand. Both sides have high hopes for the deal: Chery anticipates rapid growth in its foreign sales, and Chrysler hopes to gain access to the prototypes of well-designed compact cars, which it has had trouble developing. The strategic alliance agreement indicates the companies will use the Chery platform to create a variety of styles for both Chrysler and Chery. With increased access to the international market, its collaboration with Chrysler should help Chery become a major player in the world automotive market.[52]

Joint Venture   A joint venture is formed when a firm entering a new market pools its resources with those of a local firm to form a new company in which ownership, control, and profits are shared. In addition to sharing the financial burden, the local partner offers the foreign entrant greater understanding of the market and access to resources such as vendors and real estate. Also in the car market, the largest joint venture consists of a collaboration between Volkswagen and First

Volkswagen's Audi division has a joint venture with Chinese manufacturer First Automotive Works (FAW).

Automotive Works (FAW), another Chinese carmaker.[53] The joint venture focuses on VW's Audi brand but also produces additional cars for the Chinese market. Through its joint venture, VW gained a real head start in China. As the first premium international car brand to manufacture in China, Audi was chosen as the premium car for the 2008 Olympics. By combining VW's experience with the FAW sales network, Audi has been able to establish a strong position in the Chinese market. According to a recent J.D. Power sales satisfaction survey of 31 luxury cars, Audi ranked first in China.[54]

China, like many other countries, usually requires joint ownership of firms entering its domestic markets, though these restrictions are loosening as a result of WTO negotiations. Furthermore, problems with this entry approach can arise when the partners disagree or if the government places restrictions on the firm's ability to move its profits out of the foreign country and back to its home country.

Direct Investment   **Direct investment** requires a firm to maintain 100 percent ownership of its plants, operation facilities, and offices in a foreign country, often through the formation of wholly owned subsidiaries. This entry strategy requires the highest level of investment and exposes the firm to significant risks, including the loss of its operating and/or initial investments. For example, a dramatic economic downturn caused by a natural disaster, war, political instability, or changes in the country's laws can increase a foreign entrant's risk considerably. Many firms believe that in certain markets, these potential risks are outweighed by the high potential returns; with this strategy, none of the potential profits must be shared with other firms. In addition to the high potential returns, direct investment offers the firm complete control over its operations in the foreign country.

ING Group, a financial services firm based in The Netherlands, decided to enter the U.S. market through a wholly owned subsidiary. Attracted by the United States' position as the world's largest financial services market, as well as regulations friendly to ING's desire to provide banking services, insurance, and asset management products (e.g., mortgages, investment accounts), ING began an aggressive entry into the U.S. market and has not looked back since. Forgoing traditional bank branches, ING established ING Direct and operates purely online. Currently ING employs over 10,000 people in the United States.[55] Although it began with online savings accounts, ING has expanded into investment accounts and online mortgage services and now has 6 million customers and more than $77 billion in assets in the United States[56]—as well as an advertising campaign that gently pokes fun at people's lack of awareness about what the company does.[57]

As we noted, each of these entry strategies entails different levels of risk and rewards for the foreign entrant. But even after a firm has determined how much risk it is willing to take, and therefore how it will enter a new global market, it still must establish its marketing strategy, as we discuss in the next section.

CHECK YOURSELF

1. Which entry strategy has the least risk and why?
2. Which entry strategy has the most risk and why?

CHOOSING A GLOBAL MARKETING STRATEGY

Just like any other marketing strategy, a global marketing strategy includes two components: determining the target markets to pursue and developing a marketing mix that will sustain a competitive advantage over time. In this section, we examine marketing strategy as it relates specifically to global markets.

Target Market: Segmentation, Targeting, and Positioning

Global segmentation, targeting, and positioning (STP) is more complicated than domestic STP for several reasons. First, firms considering a global expansion have much more difficulty understanding the cultural nuances of other countries. Second, subcultures within each country also must be considered. Third, consumers often view products and their role as consumers differently in different countries.[58] A product or service often must be positioned differently in different markets. For example, MySpace, the social networking community created by News Corp., enjoys a position as a multimedia-heavy social networking site, and favorite of college students, in the United States, but that strategy does not work as well in other parts of the world. To cope with these local differences, News Corp. has redesigned MySpace to fit the local conditions in more than 22 countries. In India and Latin America, News Corp. released a low-bandwidth version that does not automatically stream videos, because the typical Internet connection in those areas is not very rapid. On the other end of the spectrum, markets such as Taiwan have Internet connections that are far more rapid than those in the United States, as well as an even more Internet-savvy culture. Therefore, in those markets, MySpace has been redesigned to act as a blogging service and offers additional tools to help users promote their own blogs and profiles.[59]

The most efficient route is to develop and maintain a global positioning strategy; one position means only one message to get out. For instance, Tropicana is the best-selling orange juice brand in the United States and owns 6 percent of the global juice market. Tropicana's parent company, PepsiCo, therefore takes a global positioning strategy that stresses around the world that Tropicana is "fresh-squeezed Florida orange juice."[60] However, another well-known American brand, Heinz ketchup, is moving away from a single, global strategy. Consumers in the United States appreciate their ketchup, just as it stands, but to expand globally, Heinz recognizes that it must "tweak" its position, and even its ketchup recipe, to align with local tastes.[61]

When it identifies its positioning within the market, the firm then must decide how to implement its marketing strategies using the marketing mix. Just as firms adjust their products and services to meet the needs of national target markets, they must alter their marketing mix to serve the needs of global markets.

The Global Marketing Mix

During the early stages of globalization, in the 1950s and 1960s, large U.S. firms were uniquely positioned in the global marketplace because they had the unique skills necessary to develop, promote, and market brand name consumer products. In the 1970s and 1980s, however, Japanese firms dominated the global marketplace because they could exploit their skills in production, materials management, and new product development. Today, retailers such as Wal-Mart, financial services firms such as Citicorp, and software firms such as Microsoft are dominating the newest stage of globalization by exploiting their technological skills.[62] In the following section, we explore the four Ps (product, price, promotion, place) from a global perspective.

Global Product or Service Strategies   There are three potential global product strategies:

- Sell the same product or service in both the home country market and the host country.
- Sell a product or service similar to that sold in home country but include minor adaptations.
- Sell totally new products or services.

The strategy a firm chooses depends on the needs of the target market. The level of economic development, as well as differences in product and technical standards, helps determine the need for and level of product adaptation. Cultural differences such as food preferences, language, and religion also play a role in product strategy planning. For example, Campbell discovered that though Russia and China are two of the largest markets for soup in the world, cooks in those countries have unique demands. Chinese consumers drink 320 billion bowls of soup each year, and Russian buyers consume 32 billion servings, compared with only 14 billion bowls of soup served in the United States. However, Chinese cooks generally refuse to resort to canned soup; though the average Chinese consumer eats soup five times each week, he or she also takes great pride in preparing it personally with fresh ingredients. In contrast, Campbell found that Russian consumers, though they demand very high quality in their soups, had grown tired of spending hours preparing their homemade broths. To identify opportunities in these markets, Campbell sent teams of social anthropologists to study how Chinese and Russian cooks prepare and consume soup. Primarily, the soup company found that it would need to change its products to focus more on broths and bases, which would enable local cooks to save preparation time but also add their own flair to the meals and make them seem homemade. Campbell also changed its recipes slightly to reflect local tastes.[63]

The level of economic development also affects the global product strategy because it relates directly to consumer behavior. For instance, consumers in devel-

The level of economic development affects the global product strategy. Consumers in the United States prefer larger motorcycles with more amenities, like the Honda Goldwing on the left with the air bag deploying. Motorcycles in India are generally smaller, like the Pleasure scooter on the right, which is a joint venture between Honda Motor Company of Japan and Hero Group, the world's largest manufacturer.

oped countries tend to demand more attributes in their products than do consumers in less developed countries. In the United States, Honda does not offer its line of "urban" motorcycles, available in Mexico and China, because the product line resembles a motor scooter more than a motorcycle, which does not tend to appeal to American consumers. Motorcycles sold in the United States have more horsepower and bigger frames and come with an array of options that are not offered in other countries.

Some firms also might standardize their products globally but use different promotional campaigns to sell them. The original Pringles potato chip product remains the same globally, as do the images and themes of the promotional campaign, with limited language adaptations for the local markets, though English is used whenever possible. However, the company does change Pringles' flavors in different countries, including paprika-flavored chips sold in Italy and Germany.[64]

Not just manufacturers must adapt their offering. On the retail side, for example, Whole Foods is making shopping an experience in the United Kingdom to compete with the local organic supermarket chains (see Adding Value 7.1).

Despite the persistent differences across borders, marketers have found a growing convergence in food consumption in many product categories. Nestlé is a good example of a company that has both influenced and exploited this global convergence in tastes:[65] It is the world's largest producer of baby foods, with brands such as Gerber and several brands of infant formula, and since it began selling infant formula in 1867, it has expanded to nearly every country in the world.[66]

Global Pricing Strategies   Determining the selling price in the global marketplace is an extremely difficult task.[67] Many countries still have rules governing the competitive marketplace, including those that affect pricing. For example, in parts of Europe including Belgium, Italy, Spain, Greece, and France, sales are allowed only twice a year, in January and June or July. In most European countries, retailers can't sell below cost, and in others they can't advertise reduced prices in advance of sales or discount items until they have been on the shelves more than a month. For firms such as Wal-Mart and other discounters, these restrictions threaten their core competitive positioning as the lowest-cost provider in the market. Other issues, such as tariffs, quotas, antidumping laws, and currency exchange policies, can also affect pricing decisions.[68]

Competitive factors influence global pricing in the same way they do home country pricing, but because a firm's products or services may not have the same positioning in the global marketplace as they do in their home country, market prices must be adjusted to reflect the local pricing structure. Spain's fashion retailer Zara, for instance, is relatively inexpensive in the EU but is priced about 65 percent higher in the United States, putting them right in the middle of their moderately priced competition.[69] Since it is important for Zara to get its fashions to the United States in a timely manner, it incurs additional transportation expenses, which it passes onto its North American customers. Finally, as we discussed earlier in this chapter, currency fluctuations impact global pricing strategies.

Global Distribution Strategies   Global distribution networks form complex value chains that involve middlemen, exporters, importers, and different transportation systems. These additional middlemen typically add cost and ultimately increase the final selling price of a product. As a result of these cost factors, constant pressure exists to shorten distribution channels wherever possible.

The number of firms with which the seller needs to deal to get its merchandise to the consumer determines the complexity of a channel. In most developing

Adding Value 7.1   Whole Foods Woos London

Whole Foods made its first entry into the European market by opening a flagship store in London. The three-story supermarket in the United Kingdom features 80,000 square feet of organic shopping supported by 28 checkout lanes and 500 employees.[70]

Thus far, Whole Foods is receiving a warm reception in London, because it is adding its own particular organic flair to the organic grocery market. Londoners are accustomed to a wide variety of high-quality foods that range from feathered pheasant from Borough Market to curry at Marks & Spencer and even to gourmet offerings at the famous Harrods. The U.K. organics market is extremely competitive and includes all the major chains, such as Tesco, Sainsbury, and Marks & Spencer, which all offer organic lines of products that are less expensive than those provided by Whole Foods. However, Whole Foods has found ways to create value for London shoppers other than price.[71]

In particular, Whole Foods is focusing on the shopping experience and playing up its mystique as the U.S. organic supermarket. Each market will highlight food counters to increase interactions with the staff, as well as to help consumers pick out the right meats, cheeses, and produce. In terms of products, Whole Foods also has increased the breadth and depth of its organic line to far exceed those of its competitors. In addition to products, the chain will offer a variety of experiential services, such as facials and chair massages.

But the real value additions for London shoppers arrive in the form of locally grown organic foods that they cannot buy anywhere else. Building on its experience in the United States, Whole Foods has established relationships with local farmers in the United Kingdom and is bringing their foods to London shelves. The ability to buy locally grown organic food is seducing English shoppers. They're literally eating it up![72]

Whole Foods' first European store in London.

countries, manufacturers must go through many different types of distribution channels to get their products to end users, who often lack adequate transportation to shop at central shopping areas or large malls. Therefore, these consumers shop near their homes at small, family-owned retail outlets. To reach these small retail outlets, most of which are located far from major rail stations or roads, marketers have devised a variety of creative solutions. Unilever's strategy in India is a prime example of how a global company can adopt its distribution network to fit local conditions. Unilever trained 25,000 Indian women to serve as distributors, who in turn extended Unilever's reach to 80,000 villages

Superior Service 7.1 **Buy Your Ticket for China Online**

Purchasing tickets for events in China can be a risky experience. Not only is the demand for events high, which makes it hard to get tickets, but the tickets many consumers are able to buy actually might be fake. Online ticket companies, like Ticketmaster, finally are rushing to fill this gap.

Historically, venues in China have been reluctant to create online purchasing options, which meant that it was difficult or impossible for consumers who lived far away from the site of the event to ever buy tickets. The paper tickets and high demand combined to create enormous lines and confusion. Furthermore, counterfeiting and fraud ran rampant because the paper tickets were easy to copy. But all that is changing as new online ticket vendors begin to sprout in China.

More and more entertainment options in this rapidly modernizing country have created the pressing need for a convenient means to purchase tickets. From the Summer Olympics to Faye Wong concerts and Broadway musicals, there have never been more opportunities for fans to attend live events in China. Ticketmaster is hoping to cash in on this demand by using modern ticketing technology to equalize access to tickets, cut out shady ticket dealers, and make the industry more profitable.

Ticketmaster brought its expertise in dealing with high-volume ticketing events to the Beijing Olympics and is easing the ticket sales process for domestic and international Olympic fans alike. In a country that could generate 200,000 visitors every second as soon as the Olympic ticketing Web site opened, Ticketmaster had to be well prepared for the volume of requests it would receive. Because of its long experience with selling tickets, both over the phone and online, Ticketmaster also is well positioned to create value by serving its customers efficiently and effectively. Thus, in the constantly changing environment that marks China, companies such as Ticketmaster are responding to customer needs, seizing the opportunity to make money by providing superior service to brand new customers.[73]

across India. The program generates $250 million each year just in villages that otherwise would be too costly to serve.[74] For an example of a firm that is using a new distribution strategy to deliver superior service in China, see Superior Service 7.1.

Global Communication Strategies The major challenge in developing a global communication strategy is identifying the elements that need to be adapted to be effective in the global marketplace. For instance, literacy levels vary dramatically across the globe. In Argentina, 3.8 percent of the adult population is illiterate, compared with 6 percent in the Philippines and a whopping 61 percent in Liberia.[75] Media availability also varies widely; some countries offer only state-controlled media. Advertising regulations differ too. In an attempt at standardization, the EU recently recommended common guidelines for its member countries regarding advertising to children and is currently reviewing a possible ban on "junk food" advertising.[76]

Differences in language, customs, and culture also complicate marketers' ability to communicate with customers in various countries. Language can be particularly vexing for advertisers. For example, in the United Kingdom, a thong is only a sandal, whereas in the United States, it can also be an undergarment. To avoid the potential embarrassment that language confusion can cause, firms spend millions of dollars to develop brand names that have no preexisting meaning in any known language, such as Accenture (a management consulting firm) or Avaya (a subsidiary of Lucent Technologies, formerly Bell Labs).

Within many countries there are multiple variants on a language. For example, China hosts three main languages, and firms such as Mercedes-Benz have adapted their names for each language. Thus, Mercedes-Benz is known by three Chinese names in Asia: *peng zee* in Cantonese for Hong Kong, *peng chi* in Mandarin for Taiwan, and *ben chi* in Mandarin for mainland China. Nokia, in contrast, chose to use only one name throughout China and thus is known as *nuo jee ya* in Mandarin.[77] As China continues to develop, having more than one name to represent a product or service likely will become increasingly inefficient.

Even with all these differences, many products and services serve the same needs and wants globally with little or no adaptation in their form or message. Firms with global appeal can run global advertising campaigns and simply translate the wording in the advertisements and product labeling. Other companies use the Internet to customize their global marketing campaigns for certain markets. For an example of how Pepsi uses the Internet to reach the Chinese market, see Power of the Internet 7.1.

 Power of the Internet 7.1   **Pepsi Engages the Chinese over the Web**

Pepsi has red aspirations: It wants to be the cola of choice for China, but it currently has gained only a 30 percent market share and continues to trail the most popular "red" cola, Coke, which enjoys 50 percent of the market. But things, as they often do, are changing. Pepsi has begun using the Internet to engage Chinese consumers—and in so doing, it is earning a great response.

In the past few years, use of the Internet among Chinese consumers has increased dramatically. Although there are only 137 million Chinese consumers online, which places the Internet penetration rate at approximately 10 percent of the country, these users tend to be affluent urban consumers—exactly those consumers that most foreign brands want to target.[78]

Pepsi is using two approaches to reach Chinese consumers over the Internet. First, it posts online videos in an attempt to find popular and inexpensive brand promoters within the Chinese market. The "Back Dorm Boys" gained international net prominence with their lip-synched YouTube videos (http://www.youtube.com/watch?v=nlmuCbLMC9g) and appealed to a particularly enormous following in China. Pepsi teamed with this comic group to create additional Web videos for its Chinese Web site (www.pepsi.cn) and then featured their talents on a Pepsi Max television spot. By using the Internet to find spokespeople, Pepsi not only saved itself money but also extended its appeal to a young, cola-drinking audience.[79]

Second, Pepsi offers online competitions to Chinese consumers. In one of its most successful competitions, Pepsi solicited online photos people took of themselves rooting for Team China in the Olympics. The competition, by far the largest online event that Pepsi has ever created, prompted 2.46 million photo submissions and tallied more than 140 million votes. The prize? To have one's photo placed on Pepsi cans all over China.[80]

To combat Coke's dominant market share in China, Pepsi uses the Internet to promote its products with celebrities like soccer star David Beckham.

However, other products require a more localized approach because of cultural and religious differences. In a classic advertisement for Longines watches, a woman's bare arm and hand appear, with a watch on her wrist. The advertisement was considered too risqué for Muslim countries, where women's bare arms are never displayed in public, but the company simply changed the advertisement to show a gloved arm and hand wearing the same watch.

Even among English speakers there can be significant differences in the effectiveness of advertising campaigns. Take the popular "What Happens in Vegas Stays in Vegas" advertising campaign, which has been very successful and spawned numerous copycat slogans in the United States. Essentially, the U.S. mass market thought the provocative campaign pushed the envelope, but just far enough to be entertaining. However, when the Las Vegas tourism group extended its advertising to the United Kingdom, it found that the ad campaign was not nearly as effective. After conducting focus groups, the group found that British consumers did not find the advertisements edgy *enough* for their more irreverent British tastes. In response, the advertising agency began studying British slang and phrases to find ways to make the campaign even sexier and more provocative.[81]

Regulatory actions in the host country can also affect communication strategies. For example, the WTO has become involved in several cases pertaining to firms' rights to use certain names and affiliations for their products and promotions. Several products in the EU have established worldwide brand recognition on the basis of where they are made. For instance, the EU currently allows only ham made in Parma, Italy, to be called Parma ham and sparkling wine made in the Champagne region of France to be called Champagne. However, the EU has also refused to grant requests from non-EU countries for similar protection, notably Florida orange juice.[82] The WTO is expected to ask the EU to either remove all such protections or grant them to non-EU countries as well.

In one case, similar arguments have even led to a global beer brawl, in which the American beer giant Budweiser must contend with claims by the tiny, 700-year-old Czech brewery Budvar that the American company stole its name. The two companies could coexist in an uneasy truce before the fall of the Berlin Wall, because Budweiser could not access Budvar's Eastern European market, and Budvar could not easily get its products out of that area. But since then, the competition between them has heated up, leading some countries to provide

When you say, "I'll have a Bud," do you mean a Budweiser or a Budvar from the Czech Republic?

exclusive registrations to one of the two and other countries to place them both on shelves. Most indications suggest the WTO will deny both companies' claims to the exclusive use of the Budweiser/Budvar names, meaning that someday soon, American consumers may have to clarify what they mean when they say, "I'll have a Bud."[83]

CHECK YOURSELF

1. What are the components of a global marketing strategy?
2. What are the three global product strategies?

ETHICAL ISSUES IN GLOBAL MARKETING

Although ethical issues abound domestically, an extra layer of complexity arises for global marketing. Firms that market globally must recognize that they are, in essence, visitors in another country and, as such, must be aware of the ethical concerns of their potential customers, both at home and abroad. In this section, we examine three areas of particular concern: environmental challenges, labor issues, and impact on host country culture.

Environmental Concerns

Among the various environmental concerns that exist, people throughout the world are worried about the amount of waste being generated, especially in developed countries. Waste can include, but is not limited to, the excessive use of natural resources and energy, refuse from manufacturing processes, excess trash created by consumer goods packages, and hard-to-dispose-of products like tires, cell phones, and computer monitors.

Many developed countries produce almost two tons of household and industrial waste per person per year![84] Although developing countries do not produce nearly the same level of waste, much of the waste in these areas is not properly disposed of.

Global Labor Issues

Global labor issues, especially concerns about working conditions and wages paid to factory workers in developing countries, have become increasingly prominent.[85] Many large U.S. firms have been questioned by various groups, including nongovernmental organizations and human rights activists, about the degree to which workers employed by the companies are paid less than a living wage or are forced to work long hours in poor working conditions.[86]

In this context, high prices offer no guarantee of a supply chain free of sweatshops. Apple Inc. has been repeatedly questioned about the working conditions in the manufacturing plants that produce iPods and iPhones. Even though iPod boxes proudly state that the music player was designed in California, the entire manufacturing process has been subcontracted to Taiwanese and Chinese manufacturers.[87] Because Apple does not own the plants in which its goods are produced, it must negotiate with factory owners to improve or ensure adequate working conditions and wages, while at the same time attempting to get the cheapest prices. Because Apple negotiates very hard on price, suppliers sometimes try to make money by paying laborers less, making them work long hours, or providing them only with unsafe working conditions. Labor conditions for Chinese workers in "iPod city" recently became more well known among U.S. consumers, and Apple responded quickly with an investigation and clarifying statements to the media.[88] Issues such as fair wages and labor conditions must be especially important to Apple, because the core demographic for the iPod and its other innovative products consists of creative people who are willing to tailor their purchasing to a political viewpoint.[89] Apple simply cannot afford to have its affluent customers wondering if it is profiting from human suffering.

Thus, in response to pressure from consumers, Apple has begun investing in social responsibility and has joined an industry group that supports the Electronic Industry Code of Conduct (EICC). The EICC, signed by a group of companies, including the founding firms Hewlett-Packard, Dell, and IBM, exacts a promise to ensure safe labor conditions, workers' rights, and environmental responsibility in the global electronics supply chain.[90] Apple acknowledges that social responsibility is an ongoing process and now conducts audits and monitors suppliers to ensure safer working conditions.[91]

Impact on Host Country Culture

The final ethical issue involves cultural imperialism, or the belief that one's own culture is superior to that of other nations. Cultural imperialism can take the form of an active, formal policy or a more subtle general attitude.[92] Critics of U.S. firms entering foreign markets claim that U.S. products and services overwhelm the local culture, often replacing its foods, music, movies, and traditions with those of the West.

In Iran, for example, the ruling clerics have forbidden the celebration of Valentine's Day. Despite strict Iranian laws regarding the interactions of men and women, especially unmarried men and women, Valentine's Day has become the second largest holiday in Iran after the Persian New Year. These Iranians were exposed to Valentine's Day through the Internet and satellite television, two information sources the government cannot control. In recent years, stores have begun displaying the holiday-themed products that arrive through underground distribution channels months in advance. Risking legal action, florists, gift shops, and restaurants make special accommodations for the holiday. Many parents sponsor Valentine's Day parties with both men and women in attendance. Apparently, there is no stopping love. The holiday is so popular that politicians even use Valentine's Day imagery to woo young voters in Iranian elections.[93]

For other Iranians, though, this type of celebration represents a threat to Iran's culture. Many U.S. firms find themselves squarely in the middle of this cultural conflict. Various countries around the world encompass competing desires: the desire to modernize and participate in the global marketplace versus the desire to hold on to traditional cultural values and ways of life. There is no simple way to resolve these dilemmas. Firms that enter new markets simply must tread lightly to ensure that their business practices, products, and services do not create any unnecessary friction or offense in the host country.

Summing Up

1. What factors aid the growth of globalization?

Technology, particularly in communications, has facilitated the growth of global markets. Firms can communicate with their suppliers and customers instantaneously, easily take advantage of production efficiencies in other countries, and bring together parts and finished goods from all over the globe. International organizations such as the World Trade Organization, the International Monetary Fund, and the World Bank Group also have reduced or eliminated tariffs and quotas, worked to help people in less-developed countries, and facilitated trade in many areas.

2. **How does a firm decide to enter a global market?**

First, firms must assess the general economic environment. For instance, countries with a trade surplus, strong domestic and national products, growing populations, and income growth generally are relatively more favorable prospects. Second, firms should assess a country's infrastructure. To be successful in a particular country, the firm must have access to adequate transportation, distribution channels, and communications. Third, firms must determine whether the proposed country has a political and legal environment that favors business. Fourth, firms should be cognizant of the cultural and sociological differences between their home and host countries and adapt to those differences to ensure successful business relationships.

3. **What ownership and partnership options do firms have for entering a new global market?**

Firms have several options for entering a new country, each with a different level of risk and involvement. Direct investment is the most risky but potentially the most lucrative. Firms that engage in a joint venture with other firms already operating in the host country share the risk and obtain knowledge about the market and how to do business there. A strategic alliance is similar to a joint venture, but the relationship is not as formal. A less risky method of entering a new market is franchising, in which, as in domestic franchise agreements, the franchisor allows the franchisee to operate a business using its name and strategy in return for a fee. The least risky method of entering another country is exporting.

4. **What are the similarities and differences between a domestic marketing strategy and a global marketing strategy?**

The essence of a global marketing strategy is no different from that of a domestic strategy. The firm starts by identifying its target markets, chooses specific markets to pursue, and crafts a strategy to meet the needs of those markets. However, additional issues make global expansion more difficult. For instance, should the product or service be altered to fit the new market better? Does the firm need to change the way it prices its products in different countries? What is the best way to get the product or service to the new customers? How should the firm communicate its product or service offering in other countries?

5. **How do ethical issues affect global marketing practices?**

In particular, firms must be cognizant of the impact their businesses have on the environment. When producing merchandise or employing service personnel in another country, they must be certain that the working conditions and wages are fair and adequate, even if the workers are employed by a third party. Finally, marketers must be sensitive to the impact their business has on the culture of the host country.

Key Terms

- boycott, 219
- countertrade, 220
- cultural imperialism, 235
- direct investment, 226
- dumping, 218
- duty, 218
- environmental concerns, 234
- exchange control, 220
- exchange rate, 220
- exporting, 224
- franchisee, 224
- franchising, 224
- franchisor, 224
- General Agreement on Tariffs and Trade (GATT), 210
- global labor issues, 234
- globalization, 208
- globalization of production, 209
- gross domestic product (GDP), 212
- gross national income (GNI), 212
- human development index (HDI), 214
- infrastructure, 217
- International Monetary Fund (IMF), 210
- joint venture, 225
- offshoring, 209
- purchasing power parity (PPP), 212
- quota, 219
- strategic alliance, 225
- tariff, 218
- trade agreements, 220
- trade deficit, 212
- trade surplus, 212
- trading bloc, 220
- World Bank Group, 210
- World Trade Organization (WTO), 210

Marketing Applications

1. What is globalization? Why is it important for marketers to understand what globalization entails?

2. The World Trade Organization, World Bank, and International Monetary Fund all work in different ways to facilitate globalization. What role (or roles) does each organization play in the global marketplace?

3. Moots is a high-end bicycle manufacturer located in Steamboat Springs, Colorado. Assume the company is considering entering the U.K., Chinese, and Indian markets. When conducting its market assessment, what economic factors should Moots consider to make its decision? Which market do you expect will be more lucrative for Moots? Why?

4. Now consider the political, economic, and legal systems of China, India, and the United Kingdom. Explain why you think one country might be more hospitable to Moots than the others.

5. Volkswagen sells cars in many countries throughout the world, including Mexico and Latin America. How would you expect its market position to differ in those countries compared with that in the United States?

6. CITGO, the petroleum company owned by the Venezuelan government, sells its products throughout the world. Do you anticipate that its market positioning and advertising differ in different countries? Why or why not?

7. What are the benefits of being able to offer a globally standardized product? What types of products easily lend themselves to global standardization?

8. What is cultural imperialism? Why would a recording company like Def Jam Records need to be aware of and sensitive to this issue?

9. Provide an example of a potentially ethically troubling practice by a non-U.S. firm doing business in the United States.

10. Assume you work for a U.S.-based medical imaging services firm that positions itself as having experts that personally review and diagnose clients' films and tests. Clients are unaware that most of the diagnosis and review work, bookkeeping, and other record keeping are done by a company in India. The local doctor's office simply reviews the recommendations and signs off on the diagnosis. Yet as your manager points out, the American medical practice still supervises each patient's account. After recent news stories about the practice of offshoring sensitive transactions, clients have been commenting about how grateful they are to have a local firm. What, if anything, should you tell your clients about the firm's practice of offshoring?

Quiz Yourself

www.mhhe.com/grewal2e

1. The Big Mac Index is a novel metric of:
   a. GDP
   b. purchasing power parity
   c. per capita GNI
   d. economic appetite
   e. international trade calories

2. Many of the best-known American retailers, like KFC and McDonald's, have expanded globally using:
   a. franchising.
   b. exporting.
   c. joint venture.
   d. direct investment.
   e. strategic alliance.

(Answers to these two questions are provided on page 623.)

Go to www.mhhe.com/grewal2e to practice an additional 11 questions.

Net Savvy

1. For many small businesses, the idea of entering a foreign market is frightening. The U.S. national government, as well as most state governments, now offers assistance designed specifically for small-business owners. One such organization is the Massachusetts Export Center. Visit its Web site

at http://www.mass.gov/export/ and examine the types of services it provides for businesses. Now click on the Export Statistics link. To what five countries did Massachusetts export the most? Do any of these countries surprise you?

2. Boeing is a global brand, yet in each country, it alters its promotions to meet local tastes. Go to www.boeing.com/worldwide.html and visit the U.K. site. Now click through to three non-Western countries. How are these Web sites different?

Chapter Case Study

P&G TAKES ON THE WORLD, ONE SMILE AT A TIME[94]

The People's Republic of China was founded October 1, 1949, with Beijing as its capital. During the remainder of the 20th century, China, which is roughly the size of the continental United States, has experienced civil unrest, major famine, foreign occupation, and a strict one-party Communist regime under Mao Zedong. However, since 1978, China's leadership, while maintaining communist political ideals, also has embraced market-oriented economic development, which has led to startlingly rapid gains. For many Chinese, recent developments have dramatically improved their living standards and their levels of personal freedom.

The shift from a centrally planned system to increasing liberalization in the economy since that 1978 change prompted a tenfold increase in China's gross domestic product (GDP). Measured in terms of purchasing power parity (PPP), China is the second largest economy in the world, after only the United States. With regard to general economic growth, the country suffers from a drastically unequal distribution, in which the coastal areas have developed the most and the most rapidly. Such uneven economic development creates a significant migrant workforce, estimated to number around 150 million people, who subsist on part-time, low paying jobs in villages and cities.[95]

Despite such inequality in development, the economic outlook for China appears good—GDP growth rates are forecast to reach 10.1 percent for 2008. The economic

Since 1988, when P&G entered the Chinese market, it has developed and distributed many new products to meet the unique needs of this very diverse market.

policy hinges on creating more jobs, and mounting external pressure suggests revaluing the Chinese currency, the Renminbi.[96]

However, actual growth of the 1.3 billion strong Chinese population slowed as a result of government population controls, which limited each family to only one child. Although China's median age is slightly younger than that of the United States currently, at 33.2 years old, the one-child policy means that China is one of the most rapidly aging countries in the world. Today, approximately 70 percent of the population falls between the ages of 15 and 65 years.

These market conditions make China an excellent target for consumer goods, assuming they can be produced at the right price. With only 10 percent of the population below the poverty line[97] and a market of nearly 1.3 billion consumers, it should be obvious why a wide variety of companies, including the consumer goods giant Procter & Gamble (P&G), are targeting the Chinese market with some of their most popular brands.

For its investments in China, P&G has decided on a slow-growth strategy, which enables it to study the market and adapt popular American products to Chinese tastes. For instance, P&G is positioning its Crest toothpaste as a major consumer brand, which demands that the company employ some of its most sophisticated product development and consumer targeting techniques.

In 1988, P&G first brought Head & Shoulders to mainland China; since then, it has slowly introduced dozens of other popular American brands, including Oil of Olay, Pampers, and Whisper. These brands now account for $2.5 billion in annual income for the consumer products goliath. To support these sales, it employs 6,300 workers in China and has built a sophisticated distribution network.

However, the well-developed Chinese coastal cities, where P&G currently sells most of its products, are becoming increasingly competitive as more and more global companies join in the hunt for the massive Chinese market. To continue growing and reaching China's untapped rural market, P&G is targeting rural Chinese with what it considers household staples, such as Crest toothpaste.

The first step P&G took before entering the rural market was to examine the distribution network. Most rural Chinese consumers shop in small stores and lack access to the supermarkets that can be found in the cities. To adapt to this distribution challenge, P&G has created an army of sales representatives who visit and service these stores. It even agreed to work with the China's Commerce Ministry to train locals in 10,000 villages in the ways and methods of running retail stores.

After building its distribution system, P&G conducted extensive, and expensive, market research to identify toothpaste product attributes that were most important to Chinese consumers. It turns out that their tastes are remarkably heterogeneous. Therefore, P&G created several flavors targeted at different, specific demographics within China—Crest Salt White for certain rural areas, and Morning Lotus Fragrance, reserved for city dwellers.

So far, this two-pronged approach—that is, building a hard-to-mimic distribution network and adapting global products to local tastes—has made Crest a success in China. But competitors, such as Dutch Unilever and the local Chinese company Nice Group, are doing their best to imitate P&G. At the moment, P&G has the advantage, and it hopes to hold on to it by helping Chinese consumers develop strong brand preferences.

Questions

1. Consumers' tastes for toothpaste in China typically vary from region to region, as well as across various demographic dimensions, such as age, income, and education. In contrast, tastes for toothpaste are fairly narrow in the United States. Why is there such a pronounced difference between these two markets?

2. Instead of partnering with a local company in a joint venture, P&G is building its own distribution network. What type of entry strategy is this, and are there any other entry strategies that would be appropriate for P&G to use in this situation? Why or why not? If so, which ones?

3. Describe how P&G's distribution and product variation gives it an advantage over its competitors. Is there anything you would have done differently to enter this market?

TARGETING THE MARKETPLACE

Section Three: Targeting the Marketplace has two chapters. Chapter 8 focuses on segmentation, targeting, and positioning. In this chapter, we examine how firms segment the marketplace, then pick a target market, and finally position their goods/services in line with their customers' needs and wants. Chapter 9 on marketing research identifies the various tools, techniques, and metrics that marketers use to uncover customers' needs and wants and to ensure that they create goods and services that provide value to their target markets.

Assessing the Marketplace

Understanding the Marketplace

Targeting the Marketplace

Value Creation

Value Capture

Value Delivery: Designing the Channel and Supply Chain

Value Communication

SEGMENTATION, TARGETING, AND POSITIONING

LEARNING OBJECTIVES

- How does a firm decide what type of segmentation strategy to use—undifferentiated, differentiated, concentrated, or micromarketing?

- What is the best method of segmenting a market?

- How do firms determine whether a segment is attractive and therefore worth pursuing?

- What is positioning, and how do firms do it?

Today, the Coca-Cola Company is one of the largest consumer packaged goods companies in the world, but when it first introduced Coca-Cola in 1886, sales averaged a modest nine drinks per day.[1] Its growth, driven largely by a remarkably disciplined approach to marketing, has led to Coke products being sold in more than 200 countries at an astounding rate of 1 billion servings per day.[2] Yet Coca-Cola continually faces the unique challenge of a mature cola market, which means growth rates overall are low, and to increase sales, it must either take customers away from other beverage companies or encourage existing customers to drink more cola—neither of which is an easy task. Part of the company's solution pertains to its approach to new product development.[3]

For example, Coke creates unique products for various specific market segments. Because those unique products appeal to specific groups, Coke can increase its sales without cannibalizing the sales of its other products. Stopped drinking soda in an attempt to limit the amount of caffeine you drink? Coke wants you to know that it feels your pain and therefore offers Caffeine-Free Coca-Cola and Diet Coke. Still like your caffeine during the day but want to minimize the amount you drink right before bedtime? Why not purchase a case of each, saving your regular Coke for when you need a midday pick-me-up and your Caffeine-Free Coke for your after-dinner soda needs? By introducing decaffeinated versions of its traditional sodas, Coca-Cola could increase the number of sodas it sells each day without cannibalizing sales, because the consumers targeted by these products already had been avoiding drinking Coca-Cola to reduce their caffeine intake.

Through its efforts to identify and target such specific market segments, Coca-Cola has grown its stable of consumer brands to more than 400 products.[4] Consider the plight of Diet Coke. "Real men" didn't want to drink a diet soda, which they stigmatized as a "girly" drink that only women would consume. But Coca-Cola had a response for them too: the high-profile launch of Coke Zero, which avoided the dreaded word "diet"[5] and specifically targeted men through its packaging, promotions, and image. By targeting men between the ages of 18 to 34 years who wanted to drink a low-calorie cola but would not purchase Diet Coke, Coca-Cola increased its sales of Coke-branded products by one-third.[6]

A successful new product introduction needs to combine an innovative product with a marketing campaign that communicates the value of that new product to the targeted segment. Thus, for the Coke Zero launch, Coca-Cola designed a campaign supported by advertisements on television and radio, in print, on outdoor billboards, and online, as well as widespread sampling programs and opportunities.[7] Little mention was made of the lack of calories or dietetic element of the new offering; instead, the advertising focused on the similarity of the taste between Coke and Coke Zero and used dark, bold colors. To appeal to those young men who proclaimed, "I'm not drinking any diet junk," the media strategy also tried to expose as many of them as possible to the new product, spending a significant bulk of the media budget on outdoor advertising.[8] The marketing campaign even included a fantasy football game, "Fantasy Football Fever," available on the Coke Zero Web site (www.cocacolazero.com), that was regularly featured in ESPN fantasy sports podcasts.

By using gender to segment the diet cola market, Coca-Cola was able to customize the advertising for Coca-Cola Zero to appeal to men, whereas Diet Coke ads could concentrate on women. In turn, Coke gained closer connections for its different products with each product's targeted market segment, and Coke Zero became one of the most successful launches in the company's long history.[9] The company plans to continue to focus all of its flagship brands more tightly in the future by adapting the company's products and marketing mix to the changing market climate. Market segmentation, done properly, pays, enabling this company to have a Coke (or Diet Coke or Coke Zero or . . .) and a smile!

Some people like fruit-based drinks, while others like highly caffeinated energy drinks. Some people want a diet product; others care primarily about how well the product hydrates after a workout. Still other people demand affordable beverages, whereas some prefer it to be organic. More likely though, a group of people desires a drink that is dark in color, cola flavored, and contains caffeine; whereas another group demands drink that is low calorie, citrus flavored, and light in color. Each of these product attributes potentially appeals to a different group of people.

In Chapter 1, we learned that marketing is about satisfying consumers' wants and needs. A company could make one type of beverage and hope that every consumer would buy it, but that's the kind of mistake that causes a company to go out of business. Or, as we described in Chapter 2, beverage manufacturers could analyze the market to determine the different types of drinks people want and then make several varieties that cater to the wants of specific groups. It is not enough just to make the product, however. Drink manufacturers such as Coca-Cola must position their drinks in the minds of their target market so those consumers understand why a particular drink meets their needs better than competitive products do.

In Chapter 2, we described the steps involved in a marketing plan: The manager first defines the firm's mission and objectives and then performs a situation analysis. The third step of the marketing plan is to identify and evaluate opportunities by performing an STP (segmentation, targeting, and positioning) analysis—which makes up the topic of this chapter.

In the opening vignette, Coca-Cola identified the various groups of cola drinkers that would respond similarly to the firm's marketing efforts. These are also known as market segments. Those who like caffeine-free regular cola are one market segment; people who prefer diet cola with caffeine are a different segment. After evaluating each market segment's attractiveness, Coca-Cola decided to concentrate its new product on one group of consumers—its target market—because it believed it could satisfy their needs better than its competitors could. As we noted in Chapter 2, the process of dividing the market into groups of customers who have different needs, wants, or characteristics and who therefore might appreciate products or services geared especially for them is called market segmentation.

Once the target market was identified, Coca-Cola had to convince the targeted group that, when it comes to soft drinks, their choice should be Coca-Cola Zero. It is achieving this task by defining the marketing mix variables so that the target customers have a clear, distinctive, desirable understanding of what the product or services do or represent, relative to competing products—a process we described in Chapter 2 as market positioning. In particular, Coca-Cola has designed a gender-based advertising campaign that has positioned Coca-Cola Zero as the only diet drink with the taste of a regular Coca-Cola. It has also made sure that the drink is available almost anywhere its customers would want to buy it.

THE SEGMENTATION, TARGETING, POSITIONING PROCESS

In this chapter, we discuss how a firm conducts a market segmentation or STP analysis (see Exhibit 8.1). We'll first discuss market segmentation, or how a segmentation strategy fits into a firm's overall strategy and objectives and which segments are worth pursuing. Then we discuss how to choose a target market or markets by evaluating each segment's attractiveness and, on the basis of this evaluation, choosing which segment or segments to pursue. Finally, we describe how a firm develops its positioning strategy.

Although the STP process in Exhibit 8.1 makes it appear that the decision making is linear, this need not be the case. For instance, although a firm starts with a strategy, it may be modified as information about the segments' attractiveness is determined.

EXHIBIT 8.1   The Segmentation, Targeting, and Positioning Process

Step 1: Establish Overall Strategy or Objectives

The first step in the segmentation process is to articulate the vision or the objectives of the company's marketing strategy clearly. The segmentation strategy must be consistent with and derived from the firm's mission and objectives, as well as its current situation—its strengths, weaknesses, opportunities, and threats (SWOT). Coca-Cola's objective, for instance, is to increase sales in a mature industry. The company recognized its strengths were its brand name and its ability to place new products on retailers' shelves, but its primary weakness was that it didn't currently have a product line for the emerging market segments. Identifying this potentially large and profitable market segment before many of its mainstream competitors offered a great opportunity, though following through on that opportunity could lead to a significant threat: competitive retaliation. Coca-Cola's choice to pursue health-conscious men thus is clearly consistent with its overall strategy and objectives.

Establishing a basic segmentation strategy is not always as straightforward as it was for Coca-Cola, however. Exhibit 8.2 illustrates several segmentation strategies. Sometimes it makes sense to not segment at all. In other situations, a firm should concentrate on one segment or go after multiple segments at once. Finally, some firms choose to specialize in their product or service line to meet the needs of very small groups—perhaps even one person at a time. We discuss each of these basic segmentation types next.

Undifferentiated Segmentation Strategy, or Mass Marketing   When everyone might be considered a potential user of its product, a firm uses an undifferentiated segmentation strategy. (See Exhibit 8.2.) If the product or service is perceived to provide the same benefits to everyone, there simply is no need to develop separate strategies for different groups. Although not a common strategy in today's complex marketplace, an undifferentiated strategy can be effective for very basic commodities, such as salt or sugar. However, even those firms that offer salt and sugar now are trying to differentiate their products.

An undifferentiated strategy also is common among smaller firms that offer products or services that consumers perceive to be indistinguishable, such as a neighborhood bakery. But again, more marketing-savvy entrepreneurs typically try to differentiate themselves in the marketplace. The corner bakery thus becomes "Le Croissant" or "Bagel Delight." By making their commodity-like products appear special, they

EXHIBIT 8.2   Segmentation Strategies

add value for the customer and differentiate themselves from their competition.

What about gasoline? Everyone with a car needs it. Yet gasoline companies have vigorously moved from an undifferentiated strategy to a differentiated one by segmenting their market into low-, medium-, and high-octane gasoline users.

Differentiated Segmentation Strategy

Firms using a differentiated segmentation strategy target several market segments with a different offering for each (see Exhibit 8.2, top). The Gap, for instance, employs four store formats—Banana Republic, The Gap, and Old Navy—to appeal to fashion-forward, traditional, and more price-sensitive segments, respectively—and Piperlime (www.piperlime.com), The Gap's online-only shoe store. Beyond these four segments, The Gap has further differentiated the market into GapKids, babyGap, GapMaternity, and GapBody. In a similar fashion, adidas Group appeals to various segments through its various companies, including adidas, Reebok, Reebok-CCM Hockey, Rockport, and the TaylorMade-adidas Golf lines of clothing and footwear.

Au Bon Pain ("the place of good bread" in French) is a national chain of bakeries found in urban and suburban crossroads, and even airports. The company makes its commodity-like products appear special by associating them with a French image.

Firms embrace differentiated segmentation because it helps them obtain a bigger share of the market and increase the market for their products overall. The more retail formats The Gap develops to reach different market segments, the more apparel and accessories it can and will sell. Offering several different shoe lines enables adidas to appeal to more potential customers than if it had just one line. Furthermore, providing products or services that appeal to multiple segments helps diversify the business and therefore lowers the company's overall risk. For example, if a line directed toward one segment is performing poorly, the impact on the firm's profitability can be offset by revenue from another line that continues to do well.

But a differentiated strategy can be expensive. Consider The Gap's investment in chinos alone. The firm must develop, manufacture, transport, store, and promote chinos separately for each of its store concepts.

Concentrated Segmentation Strategy

When an organization selects a single, primary target market and focuses all its energies on providing a product to fit that market's needs, it is using a concentrated segmentation strategy (see Exhibit 8.2, right). Entrepreneurial start-up ventures often benefit from using a concentrated strategy, which allows them to employ their limited resources more efficiently.

For example, if you've never shopped at Abercrombie & Fitch (A&F), the chances are that you're older than 30 years of age. If you have, we bet you're younger than 30, right? Since its inception, A&F has pursued a calculated concentrated segmentation strategy by deliberately targeting the young and good looking with a hip, edgy image. Thus, if older or "unhip" consumers don't find it appealing, that doesn't bother A&F one bit. Its whole brand experience is designed to create an impression of exclusivity for its 18- to 22-year-old customers.[10] For instance, rather than display items in brightly lit windows, as most clothing retailers do, it carefully shutters off the outside of its stores so that customers have to enter to see the merchandise. Once inside, they confront not a brightly lit interior that helps customers find what they're looking for but rather a dark, loud environment with an almost overwhelming scent of heavy cologne. The stores

Abercrombie & Fitch targets the college-age market with a hip, edgy image.

are carefully designed to make shopping an emotional experience for core customers, but for the parents of these customers, that experience is just plain too unpleasant. Of course, if you don't like it, that's fine— because you're not part of the target market anyway.[11]

Micromarketing[12]   Take a look at your collection of belts. Have you ever had one made to match your exact specifications? (If you're interested, try www.leathergoods-connection.com.) When a firm tailors a product or service to suit an individual customer's wants or needs, it is undertaking an extreme form of segmentation called **micromarketing** or **one-to-one marketing** (see Exhibit 8.2, bottom). Small producers and service providers generally can tailor their offering to individual customers more easily, whereas it is far more difficult for larger companies to achieve this degree of segmentation. Nonetheless, companies like Dell and Lands' End have capitalized on Internet technologies to offer "custom-made" computers, dress shirts, chinos, and jeans. Firms that interact on a one-to-one basis with many people to create custom-made products or services are engaged in **mass customization**, providing one-to-one marketing to a large group of people.

　　Some consumers appreciate custom-made goods and services because they are made especially for them, which means they'll meet the person's needs exactly. If a tailor measures you first and then sews a suit that fits your shoulders, hips, and leg length exactly, it probably will fit better than an off-the-rack suit that you pick up at a department store. But such products and services are typically more expensive than ready-made offerings and often take longer to obtain. You can purchase

Using mass customization, at Build-A-Bear Workshop stores, kids can custom make teddy bears and other stuffed animals.

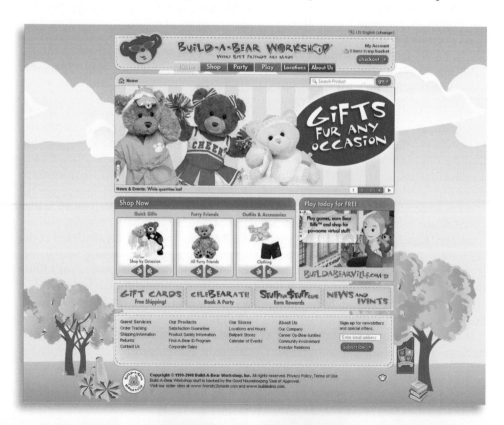

a pair of Lands' End chinos at Sears and wear them out of the store. The firm's custom chinos, in contrast, take three to four weeks to make and deliver. And if you visited an old-fashioned tailor, the processes of measuring you, ordering the material, and sewing the pants might take several months.

The degree to which firms should segment their markets—from no segmentation to one segment to multiple segments to one-to-one segments—depends on the balance the firm wants to achieve between the added perceived customer value that segmentation can offer and its cost. Now let's take a look at how firms describe their segments.

Step 2: Describe Segments

The second step in the segmentation process is to describe the different segments, which helps firms better understand the profile of the customers in each segment, as well as the customer similarities within a segment and dissimilarities across segments. Soft-drink marketers, for instance, have broken up the carbonated beverage landscape into caffeinated or decaffeinated, regular (with sugar) or diet, and cola versus something else. This segmentation method is based on the benefits that consumers derive from the products.

As we see next, marketers also use geographic, demographic, psychographic, benefit, geodemographic, loyalty, and composite segmentation approaches. Examples of these are found in Exhibit 8.3.

Geographic Segmentation Geographic segmentation organizes customers into groups on the basis of where they live. Thus, a market could be grouped by country (Germany, China), region (northeast, southeast), or areas within a region (state, city, neighborhoods, zip codes). Not surprisingly, geographic segmentation is most useful for companies whose products satisfy needs that vary by region.

Firms can provide the same basic goods or services to all segments even if they market globally or nationally, but better marketers make adjustments to meet the needs of smaller geographic groups. For instance, a national grocery store chain like Safeway or Albertson's runs similar stores with similar assortments in various locations across the United States. Within those similar stores though, a significant percentage of the assortment of goods will vary by region, city, or even neighborhood, depending on the different needs of the customers who surround each location.

Consider a new Saks Fifth Avenue department store. The chain has chosen the location for its new store carefully, knowing that each store needs to reflect and support the purchasing needs of the community that it serves. After determining that a new location can, in general, support its overall product mix, the Saks organization closely considers the characteristics of the location and builds a store-specific product

EXHIBIT **8.3**	Methods for Describing Market Segments
Segmentation Method	**Sample Segments**
Geographic	Continent: North America, Asia, Europe, Africa Within U.S.: Pacific, mountain, central, south, mid-Atlantic, northeast
Demographic	Age, gender, income
Psychographic	Innovators, thinkers, achievers, experiencers, believers, strivers, makers, survivors
Benefits	Convenience, economy, prestige
Geodemographic	Urban, exurban, established, sophisticated townhouses, bohemians, affluent retirees
Loyalty	Not loyal, somewhat loyal, completely loyal

Saks Fifth Avenue has nine market segments to describe the sites where it has stores and adapts the merchandise accordingly.

mix that reflects the geography it serves. The New York flagship store, for example, accounts for one-fifth of the company's annual revenue, and the target market at this location tends to include 46–57-year-old women who prefer classic styles for work and slightly more modern looks for the weekend. But such a selection does not resonate with Birmingham, Alabama. Through market research, Saks found that its merchandise was too conservative for the slightly younger customer base there, who would travel as far as Atlanta, Georgia, to shop. To adapt its merchandise to each geographic area, Saks has come up with nine segments to describe the sites where it has stores, classified according to the degree of fashion—"Park Avenue" classic, "uptown" modern, "Soho" trendy, or contemporary—as well as the preferred pricing levels—"good," "better," and "best," ranging from moderately priced to expensive—that characterize customers of that particular store. With this combination of spending levels and styles, Saks can deliver the appropriate merchandise to each of its stores.[13]

Demographic Segmentation   Demographic segmentation groups consumers according to easily measured, objective characteristics such as age, gender, income, and education. These variables represent the most common means to define segments because they are easy to identify and because demographically segmented markets are easy to reach. For instance, if Kellogg's wants to advertise its Froot Loops cereal to kids, it easily determines that the best time for television ads would be during cartoons shown on Saturday morning (though proposed restrictions on advertising foods to children may force Kellogg's to find another time slot). By considering the viewer profiles of various TV shows, Kellogg's can find the ones that fit its target market's demographic profile.

One important demographic, gender, plays a very important role in how firms market products and services to men versus women.[14] For instance, TV viewing habits vary significantly between men and women. Men tend to channel surf—switching quickly from channel to channel—and watch prime time shows more often if they are action oriented and have physically attractive cast members. Women, in contrast, tend to view shows to which they can personally relate through the situational plot or characters and those recommended by friends. Thus, a company like Gillette, which sells razors for both men and women, will consider the gender appeal of various shows when it buys advertising time on television.

However, demographics may not be useful for defining the target segments for other companies. For example, demographics are poor predictors of the users of activewear, such as jogging suits and athletic shoes. At one time, firms like Nike assumed that activewear would be purchased exclusively by young, active people, but the health and fitness trend has led people of all ages to buy such merchandise. Furthermore, relatively inactive consumers of all ages, incomes, and education find activewear more comfortable than traditional street clothes.

Psychographic Segmentation   Of the various methods for segmenting, or breaking down the market, psychographics is the one that delves into how

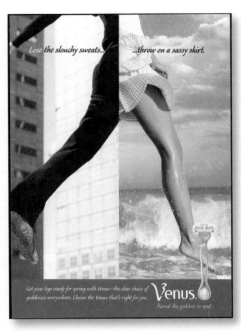

consumers actually describe themselves. Usually marketers determine (through demographics, buying patterns, or usage) into which segment an individual consumer falls. Psychographics studies how people self-select, as it were, on the characteristics of how they choose to occupy their time (behavior) and what underlying psychological reasons determine those choices.[15] For example, a person might have a strong need for inclusion or belonging, which motivates him or her to seek out activities that involve others, which in turn influences the products he or she buys to fit in with the group. If a consumer becomes attached to a group that enjoys literary discussions, he or she is motivated to buy the latest books and spend time in stores such as Barnes & Noble. Such self-selection by the consumer could be very valuable knowledge for bookstore managers trying to find new ways of attracting customers. Determining psychographics involves knowing and understanding three components: self-values, self-concept, and lifestyles.

Self-values are goals for life, not just the goals one wants to accomplish in a day. They are the overriding desires that drive how a person lives his or her life. Examples might be the need for self-respect, self-fulfillment, or a specific sense of belonging. This motivation causes people to develop self-images of how they want to be and then images of a way of life that will help them arrive at these ultimate goals. From a marketing point of view, self-values help determine the benefits the target market may be looking for from a product. The underlying, fundamental, personal need that pushes a person to seek out certain products or brands stems from his or her desire to fulfill a self-value.

People's self-image, or self-concept, is the image people ideally have of themselves.[16] For instance, a person who has a goal to belong may see, or want to see, himself as a fun-loving, gregarious type whom people wish to be around. Marketers often make use of this particular self-concept through communications that show their products being used by groups of laughing people who are having a good time. The connection emerges between the group fun and the product being shown and connotes a lifestyle that many consumers seek, in fact.

Lifestyles, the third component of people's psychographic makeup, are the way we live.[17] If values provide an end goal and self-concept is the way one sees oneself in the context of that goal, lifestyles are how we live our lives to achieve goals. For instance, someone with a strong sense of community and doing good for others will probably be attracted to MTV's Think community described in Adding Value 8.1.

Marketers like Benetton want their ads to appeal to people's self-concepts: "I'm like them (or I want to be like them), so I should buy their products."

 Adding Value 8.1   **MTV Uses Lifestyle Segmentation to Target the Think Community**

Many people think of MTV as just a broadcaster, but the music channel is adding value by providing many other services to its viewing community. One such initiative, the Think community (think.mtv.com), uses lifestyle segmentation to target a group of individuals interested in doing good deeds.[18] This site is therefore different from other social networks, like Facebook or MySpace, because it is designed to appeal only to those looking for a resource and reference group interested in social issues, whether they are casual volunteers or lifelong activists.

The Think community offers members the chance to be rewarded for their volunteer work. Those who earn such recognition also get self-fulfilling forms of rewards, including the opportunity to hang out with socially conscious celebrities, gain access to MTV media events, and even win scholarships and grants to support the good deeds.[19] As part of an effort to help prepare young people for college and a career, the Think community tries to provide a means for people to connect to an inspiring world that extends beyond their hometown.

But why did MTV feel the need to target this group? According to one MTV study, 80 percent of young people said that taking action to help their community seemed important, but only 19 percent of them described themselves as very involved. Thus, MTV recognized an opportunity to use its global broadcast platform to add value for its viewers by giving them an easy way to get involved. Whether young people choose to work for a better environment, fight discrimination, or help educate the world, the Think community provides them with direction and thus is creating new ways to mobilize youth with tools such as cell phones, forums, and digital cameras. MTV also hopes that by making engagement easy, the Think community will ensure that youth get and then stay involved.[20]

In addition to Think, MTV appeals to this "get involved" lifestyle segment by having memberships in several corporate social responsibility (CSR) groups in the United States and abroad.[21] It also partners with established nonprofits such as the United Way. The motives for these actions may be completely noble, but they also benefit the music-oriented network. In one high-profile case in which creating value for the community also created high ratings for the network, MTV partnered with the United Way to create an alternative spring break for students who wanted to go to New Orleans to help repair the damage after Hurricane Katrina. Not only was MTV swamped with applications from those who wanted to go help the people of New Orleans, but the show also earned remarkably high ratings![22]

From big initiatives like creating the Think community to small things like "greening" the set of *The Real World*, MTV keeps trying to engage the "get involved" segment of its viewers.[23] In so doing, it is adding value for viewers without sacrificing financial success.

EXHIBIT **8.4** VALS™ Framework

The most widely used psychographic tool is VALS™, owned and operated by SRI Consulting Business Intelligence (SRIC-BI).[24] Consumers are classified into the eight segments shown in Exhibit 8.4 based on their answers to the questionnaire (http://www.sric-bi.com/VALS/presurvey.shtml). The vertical dimension of the VALS framework indicates level of resources, including income, education, health, energy level, and degree of innovativeness. The upper segments have more resources and are more innovative than those on the bottom.

The horizontal dimension shows the segments' primary psychological motivation for buying. Consumers buy products and services because of their primary motivations— that is, how they see themselves in the world and how that self-image governs their activities. The three primary motivations of U. S. consumers are ideals, achievement, and self-expression. People who are primarily motivated by ideals are guided by knowledge and principles. Those who are motivated by achievement look for products and services that demonstrate success to their peers. Consumers who are primarily motivated by self-expression desire social or physical activity, variety, and risk.

VALS™ enables firms to identify target segments and their underlying motivations. It shows correlations between psychology and lifestyle choices. For instance, a European luxury automobile manufacturer used VALS™ to identify online, mobile applications that would appeal to affluent, early-adopter consumers within the next five years.[25] The VALS™ analysis enabled the company to prioritize the most promising applications to develop. In another case, VALS™ was used to help a medical center identify customers most interested and able to afford cosmetic surgery. Based on the underlying motivations of its target customers, the center and its ad agency developed an ad campaign so successful that it had to be pulled early to avoid overbooking at the surgi-center.

Firms are finding that psychographic segmentation schemes like VALS™ are often more useful for predicting consumer behavior than are demographics. This is because people who share demographics often have very different psychological traits. Take, for example, Jack and John, both are 30-year-old, married, college graduates. Demographically, they are the same, but Jack is risk-averse and John is a risk taker. Jack is socially conscious and John is focused on himself. Lumping Jack and John together as a target does not make sense because the ways they think and act are totally different from each other.

There are limitations to using psychographic segmentation, however. Psychographics are more expensive to identify in potential customers. With demographics, for example, a firm like Nike can easily identify its customers as, say, men or women and then direct its marketing strategies to each group differently. The problem is that not all men are alike, as we saw with Jack and John. Women are not all alike either! To identify VALS Thinkers or Makers, companies use the VALS questionnaire in surveys or focus groups. VALS provides segment descriptions linkages with consumer product and media data, communication styles, and zip code locations.[26]

Benefit Segmentation   Benefit segmentation groups consumers on the basis of the benefits they derive from products or services. Because marketing is all about satisfying consumers' needs and wants, dividing the market into segments whose needs and wants are best satisfied by the product benefits can be a very powerful tool. It is effective and also relatively easy to portray a product's or service's benefits in the firm's communication strategies.

An excellent illustration of benefit segmentation is the Royal Bank of Canada's approach to customer segmentation. It considers that its customers may fall into as many as 80 market segments, but its primary categorization centers around the benefits that customers are seeking from a bank. It divides personal (i.e., nonbusiness) customers into five primary benefit groups: Youth, Nexus, Borrowers/Builders, Wealth Accumulators, and Wealth Preservers.[27] As the names of these segments suggest, Royal Bank approaches them according to the benefits they want their bank to provide, such as the accumulation or the preservation of their wealth.

The flyPhone, a multimedia cell phone manufactured by Firefly Mobile, offers another good illustration of benefit segmentation. The flyPhone combines an MP3 player, video player, camera, and games, but because the flyPhone is a phone particularly targeted at Tweens, it also includes sophisticated parental controls. Parents can limit incoming or outgoing calls and prevent new addresses or numbers from being added to the phone.[28] Using a benefit segmentation approach, Firefly Mobile designed a phone that appeals to both parents and their children according to the benefits the product offers: the Tweens get a cool phone, and their parents can enjoy the benefit of providing such a cool product while still limiting the cost and protecting their children.[29]

It is just as easy to identify Thinkers (left) as it is Makers (right). A person is given the VALS questionnaire and the VALS program at SRIC-BI runs the answers through the computer for scoring to determine the VALS type.

Geodemographic Segmentation   Because "birds of a feather flock together," geodemographic segmentation uses a combination of geographic, demographic, and lifestyle characteristics to classify consumers. Consumers in the same neighborhoods tend to buy the same types of cars, appliances, and apparel and shop at the same types of retailers. Two of the most widely used tools for geodemographic segmentation are PRIZM (Potential Rating Index by Zip Market), developed by Claritas (www.claritas.com), and ESRI's (www.esri.com) Tapestry. Using detailed demographic data and information about the consumption and media habits of people who live in each U.S. block tract (zip code + 4), PRIZM can identify more than 60 geodemographic segments or neighborhoods, and Tapestry offers 65. Each block group then can be analyzed and sorted by more than 60 characteristics, including income, home value, occupation, education, household type, age, and several key lifestyle variables. The information in Exhibit 8.5 describes three PRIZM clusters.

Geodemographic segmentation can be particularly useful for retailers because customers typically patronize stores close to their neighborhood. Thus, retailers can use geodemographic segmentation to tailor each store's assortment to the preferences of the local community. This kind of segmentation is also useful for finding new locations; retailers identify their "best" locations and determine what types of people live in the area surrounding those stores, according to the geodemographic clusters. They can then find other potential locations where similar segments reside.

EXHIBIT 8.5   PRIZM Clusters

Cluster Name	Boomtown Singles: Middle Income Young Singles	Hispanic Mix: Urban Hispanic Singles and Families	Gray Power: Affluent Retirees in Sunbelt Cities
Description	This Cluster plays host to the youth of 100 fast-growing second cities in the south, midwest, and west. They are young professionals and "techies" in public and private service industries who live in multiunit rentals, enjoy music, and vacation in the Caribbean.	This Cluster collects the nation's bilingual, Hispanic barrios, which are chiefly concentrated in the Atlantic metro corridor, Chicago, Miami, Texas, Los Angeles, and the southwest. These neighborhoods are populated by large families with many small children. They rank second in percentage of foreign-born members and are first in transient immigration.	This Cluster represents over 2 million senior citizens who have pulled up stakes and moved to the country or the Sunbelt to retire among their peers. Although these neighborhoods are found nationwide, almost half are concentrated in 13 retirement areas. They are health and golf fanatics with fat investment portfolios.
Age Groups	Under 24, 25–34	Under 24, 25–34	55–64, 65+

Loyalty Segmentation   Firms have long known that it pays to retain loyal customers. Loyal customers are those who feel so strongly that the firm can meet their relevant needs best that any competitors are virtually excluded from their consideration; that is, these customers buy almost exclusively from the firm.[30] These loyal customers are the most profitable in the long term.[31] In light of the high cost of finding new customers and the profitability of loyal customers, today's companies are using loyalty segmentation and investing in retention and loyalty initiatives to retain their most profitable customers.

Airlines, for instance, definitely believe that all customers aren't created equal. At United Airlines, the customers who have flown the most miles with the company, the "Premier Executive 1K," receive guaranteed reservations even on sold-out flights, priority check-in, special seating priorities, and priority waitlist status.[32] None of these special services are available to the occasional flyer.

Using Multiple Segmentation Methods   Although all segmentation methods are useful, each has its unique advantages and disadvantages. For example, segmenting by demographics and geography is easy because information about who the customers are and where they are located is readily available, but these characteristics don't help marketers determine their customers' needs. Knowing what benefits customers are seeking or how the product or service fits a particular lifestyle is important for designing an overall marketing strategy, but such segmentation schemes present a problem for marketers attempting to identify specifically which customers are seeking these benefits. Thus, firms often employ a combination of segmentation methods, using demographics and geography to identify and target marketing communications to their customers, then using benefits or lifestyles to design the product or service and the substance of the marketing message.

Step 3: Evaluate Segment Attractiveness

The third step in the segmentation process involves evaluating the attractiveness of the various segments. To undertake this evaluation, marketers first must determine whether the segment is worth pursuing, using several descriptive criteria: Is the segment identifiable, substantial, reachable, responsive, and profitable (see Exhibit 8.6)?

Identifiable   Firms must be able to identify who is within their market to be able to design products or services to meet their needs. It is equally important to ensure that the segments are distinct from one another because too much overlap between segments means that distinct marketing strategies aren't necessary to meet segment members' needs.

EXHIBIT 8.6   Evaluation of Segment Attractiveness

Adding Value 8.2   CVS Identifies Its Target Market by Lifestyle and Demographics

Every day, roughly 4 million women, approximately 85 percent of all customers, walk through the doors of one of CVS's approximately 6,200 stores to purchase something from the largest pharmacy chain in the United States.[33] The issue facing CVS is which is the best segment of these customers to target? According to CVS's research, women control the majority of health care spending, including the one in four women who provides care to someone in her own home. Yet the vast majority of these caregivers (93 percent) felt that no company offered them help with this challenging task.

CVS recognized an unmet need: supporting female caregivers who make the health care decisions in their households. To meet their needs and thus succeed in the pharmacy market, CVS turned to a sophisticated lifestyle/demographics-based segmentation strategy. On the basis of its own segmentation of shoppers in its stores, CVS identified three female shopper segments, each with its own name and lifestyle:

■ Caroline, who is 25 to 34 years of age and single or newly married

■ Vanessa, a 35- to 54-year-old who typically is involved in caring for her children and possibly her parents

■ Sophie, a 55-year-plus consumer of prescription medications[34]

Of these segments, "Vanessa" makes up the majority of female CVS shoppers. As their families' caregivers, Vanessas take responsibility for stocking the family first-aid kit with Band-Aids, taking children to the doctor, picking up shaving cream for their husbands, ensuring their aging parents have the prescriptions they need, and grabbing a gift card for the coworker whose birthday they forgot until the last minute.[35] Because these women make most of the household purchasing decisions for their families, CVS chose to target them with services that attempt explicitly to support their roles as family caregivers.

For example, CVS's new advertising campaign is trying to win over this influential group with targeted advertising and added services, such as in-store clinics.[36] To communicate its in-store changes and services to the target segment, one advertisement portrays an animated woman performing symbolic acts of caring, such as giving a bird a ribbon from her hair. Before their eyes, viewers then see this giving woman transform into a CVS pharmacist. The $25 million media campaign targets both the Vanessa and Sophie lifestyle segments, so the pharmacy purchased television spots during shows that appeal to this fairly broad group, such as *Dancing with the Stars*, *Extreme Makeover Home Edition*, *Brothers and Sisters*, *Oprah*, and *The Ellen DeGeneres Show*.[37]

As this example shows, research used to identify viable market segments using multiple methods enables companies to deliver maximum value to their customers. In this case CVS is customizing its product and service mix to best serve its largest target market segment: Vanessas, the 35- to 54-year-old female caregivers.

As noted earlier in this chapter, The Gap has identified several distinct segments to pursue. Recognizing that many of its core customers have families, The Gap opened GapKids and babyGap. Its research also indicated an opportunity to compete with The Limited Brands' Victoria's Secret in the women's intimate apparel market, so it opened GapBody. Finally, though The Gap is largely successful with middle-of-the-road customers, it was too expensive for some customers and not fashion-forward enough for others. Its Old Navy and Banana Republic stores appeal better to these markets. The segment of people interested in purchasing shoes at Piperlime, Gap's online shoe store, is more difficult to accurately identify since everyone needs shoes. Adding Value 8.2 provides an example of how CVS identifies its target market and defines it by both lifestyle and demographics.

Substantial   Once the firm has identified its potential target markets, it needs to measure their size. If a market is too small or its buying power insignificant, it won't generate sufficient profits or be able to support the marketing mix activities. Although The Gap had identified potential new target markets to pursue, it was imperative for the company to determine whether the market for women's intimate apparel was relatively small, in which case the company would fit the products into its regular stores. If the market was large, the products would require their own space. The Gap experimented cautiously with the new concept by first placing a section of intimate apparel in some of its stores. Over time, Gap managers realized the potential of the concept and began to roll out GapBody stores.

The Gap has identified several distinct segments to pursue. Two of its brands—GapKids (left) and The Gap (right)— appeal to different target markets.

Reachable The best product or service cannot have any impact, no matter how identifiable or substantial the target market is, if that market cannot be reached (or accessed) through persuasive communications and product distribution. The consumer must know the product or service exists, understand what it can do for him or her, and recognize how to buy it.

Talbots, a chain of traditional apparel stores that also sells on the Internet and through catalogs, has a straightforward plan for reaching its target customers: college-educated women between 35 and 55 years of age with an average household income of $75,000 or more.[38] The company simply locates its new stores in places where it has gotten a lot of Internet and catalog business. Advertisements appear in media that are consistent with the lifestyle Talbots is trying to portray— traditional, conservative, and with good taste. However, when Talbots determined that its ability to reach men and children through its brand extensions, Talbots Men and Talbots Kids, was poor enough that those lines had become unprofitable, it decided to shut them down to refocus on its primary target market of women.[39]

Firms trying to reach college students have a much more difficult time because students' media habits are quite diverse, and they generally are cynical about firms that try too hard to sell to them. High-end fashionable jeans companies, for instance, often underpromote their lines or promote them very subtly through traditional media because, if their customers start to believe the brand is too mainstream, they won't buy it. Another hard-to-reach segment is composed of people with disabilities. For how one company is trying to make this segment easier to reach, see Superior Service 8.1.

Superior Service 8.1   Serving the Underserved

Some segments are almost always overlooked and find it hard to get the services and products they need. The disabled population certainly faces this situation in the United States. More than 54 million Americans live with some form of disability, but they remain a very difficult segment to reach because disabilities cut across age, economic situation, and geography.[40] Such cross-segment identities create significant challenges for marketers who want to reach out to the disabled community. At the same time, people with disabilities represent an extremely large market. The U.S. market for goods and services specific to disabilities is greater than $300 billion, and the discretionary income of people with disabilities exceeds $135 billion.[41]

Disaboom Inc., a recent start-up, is working to solve some of the problems that the disabled face. Founded by Dr. Glen House, a physician who is also a quadriplegic, Disaboom is based on his firsthand knowledge of the challenges faced by the disabled community, which inspired him to provide a comprehensive, evolving source of information for disabled communities.[42] A free community, Disaboom combines a social environment, providing features such as an online dating community, forums, and blogs, with practical resources pertaining to living with disabilities, including medical information, classifieds, and job postings. To round out the community, Disaboom has not been afraid to buy other companies. For example, it recently acquired the largest dating Web site for people with disabilities, www.LoveByrd.com. Through a combination of creating its own content and partnering with other groups that help people with disabilities, such as the American Association of People with Disabilities, Disaboom has reached a critical mass that has enabled it to start an online community.

Like many online communities, such as Facebook and MySpace, Disaboom is a for-profit company, though the Disaboom users do not contribute directly to profits, because the revenue comes from advertisers.[43] It has already partnered with companies such as Johnson & Johnson, Ford, General Motors, and Netflix.[44] These advertisers jumped at the chance to support the site, because doing so grants them access to the large disability market. For instance, Ford used the site to spread the word about the $1,000 credit that it gives to consumers who need to add wheelchair lifts or other accessibility options to their automobiles. The mobility motoring manager at Ford noted that the partnership with Disaboom has been a resounding success that far exceeded the carmaker's expectations.[45]

Responsive   For a segmentation strategy to be successful, the customers in the segment must react similarly and positively to the firm's offering. If, through the firm's distinctive competencies, it cannot provide products or services to that segment, it should not target it. For instance, General Motors (GM) has introduced a line of cars to the large and very lucrative luxury car segment. People in this market typically purchase Porsches, BMWs, Audis, and top-of-the-line Lexuses. In contrast, GM has been somewhat successful competing for the middle-priced family-oriented car and light truck segments. Thus, though the luxury car segment meets all the other criteria for a successful segment, GM took a big risk in attempting to pursue this market.

Is GM successful competing against Porsche, BMW, Audi, and Lexus with vehicles like this Cadillac Escalade?

Developing a market segmentation strategy over the Internet usually is somewhat easier than developing it for traditional channels. Power of the Internet 8.1 on page 262 explains why.

Profitable   Marketers must also focus their assessments on the potential profitability of each segment, both current and future. Some key factors to keep in mind in this analysis include market growth (current size and expected growth rate), market competitiveness (number of competitors, entry barriers, product substitutes), and market access (ease of developing or accessing distribution channels and brand familiarity). Some straightforward calculations can help illustrate the profitability of a segment:[46]

$$\text{Segment profitability} = (\text{Segment size}$$
$$\times \text{Segment adoption percentage}$$
$$\times \text{Purchase behavior}$$
$$\times \text{Profit margin percentage})$$
$$- \text{Fixed costs}$$

where

Segment size = Number of people in the segment

Segment adoption percentage = Percentage of customers in the segment who are likely to adopt the product/service

Purchase behavior = Purchase price × number of times the customer would buy the product/service in a year

Profit margin percentage = (Selling price − variable costs) ÷ selling price

Fixed costs = Advertising expenditure, rent, utilities, insurance, and administrative salaries for managers

To illustrate how a business might determine a segment's profitability, consider Camillo's start-up lawn service. He is trying to determine whether to target homeowners or businesses in a small Midwestern town. Exhibit 8.7 estimates the profitability of the two segments. The homeowner segment is much larger than the business segment, but there are already several lawn services with established customers. There is much less competition in the business segment. So, the segment adoption rate for the homeowner segment is only 1 percent, compared to 20 percent for the business segment. Camillo can charge a much higher price to businesses and they utilize lawn services more frequently. The profit margin for the business segment is higher as well because Camillo can utilize large equipment to cut the grass and therefore save on variable labor costs. However, the fixed costs for purchasing and maintaining the large equipment are much higher for the business segment. Further, he needs to spend more money obtaining and maintaining the business customers. He would use less expensive door-to-door flyers to reach the household customers. Finally, on the basis of these assumptions, Camillo decides the business segment is more profitable for his lawn service.

This analysis provides an estimate of the profitability of two segments at one point in time. It is also useful to evaluate the profitability of a segment over the lifetime of one of its typical customers. To address this issue, marketers consider factors such as how long the customer will remain loyal to the firm, the defection

EXHIBIT 8.7	Profitability of Two Market Segments for Camillo's Lawn Service	
	Homeowners	**Businesses**
Segment size	75,000	1,000
Segment adoption percentage	1%	20%

Purchase behavior
  Purchase price
  Frequency of purchase
	
	$100
	12 times
		
		$500
		20 times

Profit margin percentage	60%	80%
Fixed costs	$400,000	$1,000,000
Segment profit	$140,000	$600,000

Which segment will be more profitable to Carhartt in the long run: a more fashion-forward segment inspired by movie stars like Tom Cruise in War of the Worlds (left), or its traditional market for rugged work clothes (right)?

rate (percentage of customers who switch on a yearly basis), the costs of replacing lost customers (advertising, promotion), whether customers will buy more or more expensive merchandise in the future, and other such factors. We explicitly address the lifetime value of customers in the next chapter.

For instance, Carhartt has been making rugged work clothes in the United States since 1889. Recently, a more affluent, urban, fashion-oriented customer has been attracted to the brand. Which of these two very different segments—buyers of traditional work clothes or fashion-forward consumers—will be more profitable to Carhartt in the long term? Even if the fashion-forward segment buys several of the more expensive items, Carhartt's appeal to that segment probably will be fleeting because these customers view their clothes as fashion rather than everyday work clothes.

Now that we've evaluated each segment's attractiveness (Step 3), we can select the target markets to pursue (Step 4).

Step 4: Select Target Market

The fourth step in the STP process is to select a target market. The key factor likely to affect this decision is the marketer's ability to pursue such an opportunity or target segment. Thus, as we mentioned in Chapter 2, a firm assesses both the attractiveness of the target market (opportunities and threats based on the SWOT analysis and the profitability of the segment) and its own competencies (strengths and weaknesses based on SWOT analysis) very carefully.

To illustrate how one firm selects target markets, consider Hallmark, the U.S.'s largest greeting card company with more than $4.1 billion in annual sales and a brand recognized around the globe.[47] Hallmark cards are available in grocery stores, discount stores, drug stores, and specialty card stores. Ninety percent of U.S. households purchase at least one greeting card per year. Everyone needs greeting cards from time to time, right?

First, using a geographic segmentation strategy, Hallmark is continuing its global expansion, particularly to India and China. Also, it is using a benefit segmentation strategy by targeting those seeking the convenience of sending a card over the Internet. The industry was worried that these e-cards, which are generally free, would negatively affect traditional card sales, but in fact

How has Hallmark selected its target markets?

Power of the Internet 8.1

Easy Does It with Internet-Based Segmentation[48]

Internet-based segmentation facilitates the implementation of segmentation strategies in several ways. First, it offers the possibility to cater to very small segments, sometimes as small as one customer at a time, very efficiently and inexpensively (e.g., mortgage and insurance sites that provide personalized quotes). A personalized Web site experience can be executed at a significantly lower cost than would be possible in other venues, such as in a retail store or over the phone, and sometimes even at negligible costs. For example, frequent fliers of American Airlines are able to check prices and choose special services online at a fraction of the cost that the company would incur for a phone or ticket counter interaction with an agent.[49]

Second, segmentation over the Internet simplifies the identification of customers and provides a great deal of information about them. Cookies, small text files a Web site stores in a visitor's browser, provide a unique identification of each potential customer who visits a Web site and detail how the customer has searched through the site. Marketers also can ask visitors to fill out an online registration form.

Third, through the Internet the company can make a variety of recommendations to customers on the basis of their site visit patterns and how they search the site. For example, Amazon.com and other e-tailers provide recommendations for related products to customers browsing and/or searching their site, which are based on matching their profiles to those of other customers. This tactic helps to boost sales of similar and complementary products.

Fourth, the marketing strategy can be customized in real time according to known data about the customer. For example, Staples can offer merchandise at different prices in different parts of the country by simply asking customers to enter their zip code.

However, the growth of Internet-based segmentation also has prompted increased consumer concerns and public policy mandates. Consumers are often worried about their privacy, especially when asked to identify themselves through site registrations or even by accepting cookies when visiting a site. Responding to both privacy concerns and industry self-regulations, most Internet sites now include privacy policies that clearly state what types of consumer information are collected and how that information is used. Consumers also are given a choice to "opt out" if they do not

want their information shared with third parties or to be part of the firm's future marketing campaigns.

Although cookies themselves do not contain consumer-specific information, the use of consumer site visit information, along with data gathered from other sources, has potential legal consequences and may affect customer relationships. For example, when Amazon.com tried to offer different prices on the same day for certain DVDs, many observers criticized the practice as discrimination among consumer segments. Amazon argued that the price differences were the result of a pricing test being conducted; however, consumers and participants in chat forums like DVD Talk Forum disagreed. Many observers now contend that charging different prices to different customers is not bad as long as it is used to discount, rather than charge premium, prices.

Another concern surrounding Internet-based segmentation emerges when it gets combined with e-mail marketing campaigns. Even legitimately collected e-mail lists can cause trouble for companies that seek to contact customers. When Right Start, a baby and infant product retailer, sent out its first newsletter to test an e-mail list that it had purchased, it was immediately contacted and notified that it would be put on a spammer list if it did not desist.[50] In response to Internet-based marketing, consumers are taking steps to prevent their information from being shared with others, which makes it even harder for companies to reach and identify them. In the past, consumers might have simply ignored poorly targeted e-mails or direct mail, but now they actively use spam filters and add their names to do-not-contact lists. Thus, though the Internet can be a powerful tool to reach consumers, a growing segment of savvy users is refusing to be reached in this way.

The final consideration that a marketer must address before building the Internet into its market segmentation approach is the level of access to the Internet. Although broadband penetration certainly is increasing rapidly, some segments remain well behind the national average and can be difficult to reach without using direct mail. For instance, only 54 percent of Hispanics in the United States have access to the Internet.[51] Companies that want to reach this segment therefore should conduct careful market research before beginning their marketing campaign to verify that they are using the right means to contact and segment their target market.

the availability of e-cards has helped to boost sales. Hallmark.com has a link on its home page for Free-Cards to promote its brand name via the Internet. Internet users are exposed to traditional advertising, and Hallmark can sell and promote its movies made for the Hallmark Channel and sell gifts ornaments and other popular personal expression items. Exhibit 8.8 on p. 264 provides an illustration of how a firm like Hallmark might match its competencies with the attractiveness of various alternative segments and use this process to pick the best fit.

Sometimes firms' target market selection also can raise serious ethical concerns. Ethical and Societal Dilemma 8.1 examines the issue of marketing certain products to teens.

Ethical and Societal Dilemma 8.1   Designer Labels Target Teens

What happens when marketing to a segment works too well? Take, for example, designer labels targeting teens 13 to 17 years of age. In 2007, designer labels accounted for 15.4 percent of teen clothing purchases; just three years earlier, these labels earned only 9.6 percent. Yet among adults older than 18 years old, the 7 percent market share designer labels maintain has remained constant for around seven years.[52] So what can explain these trends?

High-end designers are taking advantage of teens' desire for fashion and bragging rights to sell apparel to younger consumers by targeting them intensively with advertising and product placements. Luxury brands targeting kids include Dolce & Gabbana and Armani, which have created their own separate teen lines, as well as Michael Kors, Coach, Dooney & Bourke, and Dior, which target these young consumers with accessories. Even retailers are cashing in on the trend; department stores such as Nordstrom have added Burberry and Prada products to their children's departments. As a result, Tweens are showing up for their middle school classes with their $225 Dooney & Bourke gym bags in tow.[53]

The effects of intense advertising to kids also appear in the form of more sophisticated brand opinions among younger and younger consumers. Four years ago, 15 percent of teens claimed to love Armani; today, that level has reached 27 percent. In schools across the country, the effects of increased advertising to kids also results in massive increases in "fashion bullying"—when students are targeted because they do not wear the "right" clothing or designers. More than one-third of all middle school students say that they have been bullied because of what they wear. Although this form of bullying certainly is not new, guidance counsellors say that fashion bullying has reached a new level of intensity as more designers launch collections targeted at kids.

In response to these concerns, some companies, including Coach and Tiffany & Co., have taken steps to reduce their exposure to the teen market. Tiffany's increased silver prices because too many teenagers were visiting their stores, which created the risk of alienating its traditional core consumers—those who purchase the high-end retailer's most expensive items. Even though 5 percent of Coach sales are to teenagers, the company has chosen not to market to them directly and limits exposure among the 13- to 18-year-old segment to publicity through secondary sources such as fashion and gossip magazines.[54]

Fashion companies thus face an ethical dilemma: How much should they target teens? Clearly, these companies hope to gain lifetime aficionados by reaching out to consumers at a young age, with the goal of turning them into loyal return customers. However, some advertising appears to be encouraging fashion bullying. Furthermore, luxury purchases such as designer handbags and totes are specifically designed to be artificially exclusive. When teens buy luxury goods at more than twice the rate of the general population, it suggests that parents are funding a fashion habit that they may not engage in themselves and that may not be sustainable for those children when they grow up and have to pay their own way. Should the designers care?

Step 5: Identify and Develop Positioning Strategy

The last step in developing a market segmentation strategy is positioning. Market positioning involves a process of defining the marketing mix variables so that target customers have a clear, distinctive, desirable understanding of what the product does or represents in comparison with competing products. This strategy can be realized by communicating particular messages in persuasive communications and through different media.

Positioning strategies generally focus on either how the product or service affects the consumer or how it is better than competitors' products and services. When positioning against competitors, the objective is to play up how the brand being marketed provides the desired benefits better than do those of competitors. Firms thus position their products and services according to value, salient attributes, and symbols, and against competition.

EXHIBIT 8.8 Hallmark's Assessment of Potential Target Markets

SEGMENT ATTRACTIVENESS

	High	Medium	Low
High			
Medium	India & China	Internet	
Low			

FIRM COMPETENCY

Value   Value is a popular positioning method because the relationship of price to quality is among the most important considerations for consumers when they make a purchase decision. Value positioning may open up avenues to attract new customer segments that the company previously had neglected. For example, while Procter & Gamble's (P&G's) competitors, such as Unilever and Colgate, found success with lower-priced "value" products like Suave shampoo and Alberto VO5, P&G seemed to ignore the 80 percent of the world that could not afford its products. In an attempt to correct this oversight, P&G company managers are now working globally to understand "price-sensitive customers" in various regions and sharing strategies to promote P&G products. For example, they've taken flagship products like Ivory soap and dropped the price 10–15 percent below that of rivals such as Dial.[55]

Salient Attributes   One of the most common positioning strategies focuses on the product attributes that are most important to the target market. Volvo, the car company traditionally positioned for the safety-conscious driver, wants to stretch its safety image to one focused on driving performance and excitement. The company expects the positioning adjustment to be a long and concentrated effort, because so many of Volvo's boxier vehicles remain on the road today, which reinforces its more conservative image. Volvo's goal is not to abandon the safety notions associated with the brand but rather to expand its image to compete with other top luxury brands.[56]

Can Volvo position its cars to be more exciting with higher performance without losing its traditional position that appeals to safety-conscious drivers?

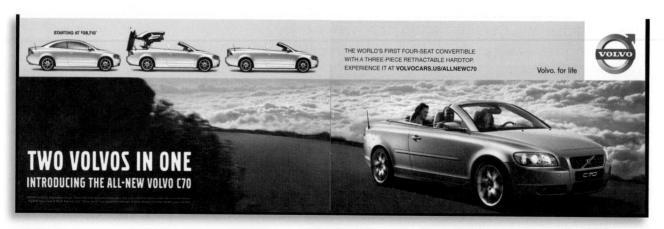

STARTING AT $38,710

TWO VOLVOS IN ONE
INTRODUCING THE ALL-NEW VOLVO C70

THE WORLD'S FIRST FOUR-SEAT CONVERTIBLE WITH A THREE-PIECE RETRACTABLE HARDTOP. EXPERIENCE IT AT **VOLVOCARS.US/ALLNEWC70**

Volvo. for life

Symbol   A well-known symbol can also be used as a positioning tool. What comes to mind when you think of Colonel Sanders, the Jolly Green Giant, the Gerber Baby, or Tony the Tiger? Or consider the Texaco star, the Nike swoosh, or the Ralph Lauren polo player. These symbols are so strong and well known that they create a position for the brand that distinguishes it from its competition. Many such symbols are registered trademarks that are legally protected by the companies that developed them.

Competition   Firms can choose to position their products or services against a specific competitor or an entire product/service classification. For instance, 7-Up positioned its product as "the Uncola" to differentiate it from caramel-colored cola beverages like Pepsi and Coke. Goodrich tires were promoted as "the other guys," or the ones without the blimp, to set them apart from Goodyear tires. Marketers must be careful, however, that they don't position their product too closely to their competition. If, for instance, their package or logo looks too much like a competitor's, they might be opening themselves up to a trademark infringement lawsuit. For example, numerous store brands have been challenged for having packaging confusingly similar to that of national brands. Similarly, McDonald's sues anyone who uses the "Mc" prefix including McSleep Inns and McDental Services, even though in the latter case there was little possibility that consumers would believe the fast-food restaurant company would branch out into dental services. However, courts have allowed parody jeans for full-figured women to be sold under the Lardasche label, despite the objections of Jordache jeans.

What if you ate vegetables just because you liked them?

The Jolly Green Giant is such a well-known symbol that it can be used as a positioning tool.

Now that we have identified the various methods by which firms position their products and services, we discuss the actual steps they go through in establishing that position.

CHECK YOURSELF

1. Identify the steps in the segmentation process
2. What are the four segmentation strategies?
3. What are the various segmentation methods?
4. Identify four positioning strategies.

POSITIONING STEPS

When developing a positioning strategy, firms go through five important steps. Before you read about these steps, though, examine Exhibit 8.9, a hypothetical perceptual map of the soft drink industry in the United States. A perceptual map displays, in two or more dimensions, the position of products or brands in the consumer's mind. We have chosen two dimensions for illustrative purposes: strong versus light taste (vertical) and fun versus healthy (horizontal). Also, though this industry is quite complex, we have simplified the diagram to include only a few players in the market. The position of each brand is denoted by a small circle,

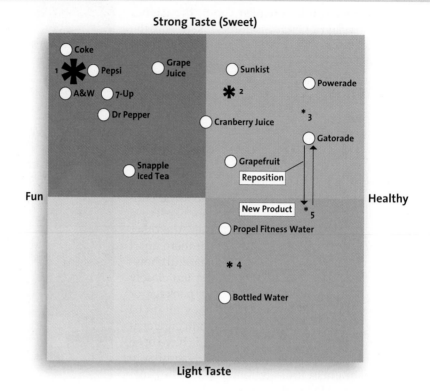

EXHIBIT 8.9   Perceptual Map for U.S. Soft Drink Industry

and the numbered asterisks denote consumers' ideal points—where a particular market segment's ideal product would lie on the map. The larger the asterisk, the larger the market.

To derive a perceptual map such as this, marketers follow five steps.

1. **Determine consumers' perceptions and evaluations of the product or service in relation to competitors'.** Marketers determine their brand's position by asking consumers a series of questions about their and competitors' products. For instance, they might ask how the consumer uses the existing product or services, what items the consumer regards as alternative sources to satisfy his or her needs, what the person likes or dislikes about the brand in relation to competitors, and what might make that person choose one brand over another.

2. **Identify competitors' positions.** When the firm understands how its customers view its brand relative to competitors', it must study how those

Gatorade with football player Jason Taylor (left) and POWERade with soccer player David Beckham (right) are positioned to compete for target market 3 in Exhibit 8.9.

same competitors position themselves. For instance, POWERade ("Liquid Hydration + Energy Drink") positions itself closely to Gatorade ("Is It In You?"), which means they appear next to each other on the perceptual map and appeal to target market 3. They are also often found next to each other on store shelves, are similarly priced, and are viewed by customers as sports drinks. Gatorade also knows that its sports drink is perceived to be more like POWERade than like its own Propel Fitness Water (located near target market 4), Coke (target market 1), or Sunkist orange soda (target market 2).

3. **Determine consumer preferences.** The firm knows what the consumer thinks of the products or services in the marketplace and their positions relative to one another. Now it must find out what the consumer really wants, that is, determine the "ideal" product or service that appeals to each market. For example, a huge market exists for traditional Gatorade, and that market is shared by POWERade. Gatorade also recognizes a market, depicted as the ideal product for segment 5 on the perceptual map, of consumers who would prefer a less sweet, less calorie-laden drink that offers the same rejuvenating properties as Gatorade. Currently, no product is adequately serving market 5.

4. **Select the position.** Continuing with the Gatorade example, the company has three choices to appeal to the "less sweet sports drink" target market 5. It could develop a new product to meet the needs of market 5. Alternatively, it could adjust or reposition its marketing approach—its product and promotion—to sell original Gatorade to market 5 (arrow pointing down from Gatorade to the ideal point for segment 5). Finally, it could ignore what target market 5 really wants and hope that consumers will be attracted to the original Gatorade because it is closer to their ideal product than anything else on the market (arrow pointing up from the ideal point for segment 5 to Gatorade).

5. **Monitor the positioning strategy.** Markets are not stagnant. Consumers' tastes shift, and competitors react to those shifts. Attempting to maintain the same position year after year can spell disaster for any company. Thus, firms must always view the first three steps of the positioning process as ongoing, with adjustments made in step four as necessary.

CHECK YOURSELF

1. What is a perceptual map?
2. Identify the five positioning steps.

REPOSITIONING

Sometimes firms try to change their positioning. Tiffany & Co. has long been known for luxury jewelry, which it markets to wealthy segments of the population and delivers in its signature blue boxes.[57] However, in the 1990s, the company decided to reposition its image by expanding its product assortment to appeal more to the middle class, following the widespread trend of "affordable luxury."

Tiffany introduced a silver charm bracelet, priced at $110, and a "Return to Tiffany" line that became very popular among teenagers and resulted in explosive sales growth for the company. The company hoped it would gain lifetime customers from this strategy—adults who had bought the jewelry when they were teenagers would continue to buy the brand throughout their lives.

Instead, the short-term success of the less expensive silver jewelry alienated older, more affluent clientele who now viewed Tiffany as an inexpensive, common brand. In response, the company has again attempted to reposition its image by increasing prices on its silver products by 30 percent. Its continued attempts to reclaim its position as a luxury jeweler include store renovations, with chilled water and champagne available to shoppers, private viewing rooms to create an intimate feel, and featured high-end products like $2.5 million pink diamond rings.

Repositioning is difficult, and in the case of Tiffany, a particularly challenging undertaking. Despite its efforts to regain its original image, many consumers in this target segment remain convinced that pretty much anyone can wear Tiffany jewelry.

Summing Up

1. How does a firm decide what type of segmentation strategy to use—undifferentiated, differentiated, concentrated, or micromarketing?

Most firms use some form of segmentation strategy. An undifferentiated strategy is really no segmentation at all and works only for products or services that most consumers consider to be commodities. The difference between a differentiated and a concentrated strategy is that the differentiated approach targets multiple segments, whereas the concentrated targets only one. Larger firms with multiple product/service offerings generally use a differentiated strategy; smaller firms or those with a limited product/service offering often use a concentrated strategy. Firms that employ a micromarketing or one-to-one marketing strategy tailor their product/service offering to each customer—that is, it is custom made. In the past, micromarketing was reserved primarily for artisans, tailors, or other craftspeople who would make items exactly as the customer wanted. Recently, however, larger manufacturers and retailers have begun experimenting with custom-made merchandise as well. Service providers, in contrast, are largely accustomed to customizing their offering. Hair salons could not flourish if every customer got the same cut.

2. What is the best method of segmenting a market?

There is really no one "best" method to segment a market. Firms choose from various methods on the basis of the type of product/service they offer and their goals for the segmentation strategy. For instance, if the firm wants to identify its customers easily, geographic or demographic segmentation likely will work best. But if it is trying to dig deeper into why customers might buy its offering, then lifestyle, benefits, or loyalty segmentation work best. Geodemographic segmentation provides a nice blend of geographic, demographic, and psychographic approaches. Typically, a combination of several segmentation methods is most effective.

3. How do firms determine whether a segment is attractive and therefore worth pursuing?

Marketers use several criteria to assess a segment's attractiveness. First, the customer should be *identifiable*—companies must know what types of people are in the market so they can direct their efforts appropriately. Second, the market must be *substantial* enough to be worth pursuing. If relatively few people appear in a segment, it is probably not cost-effective to direct special marketing mix efforts toward them. Third, the market must be *reachable*—the firm must be able to reach the segment through effective communications and distribution. Fourth, the firm must be *responsive* to the needs of customers in a segment. It must be able to deliver a product or service that the segment will embrace. Finally, the segment must be *profitable*, both in the near term and over the lifetime of the customer.

4. What is positioning, and how do firms do it?

Positioning is the "P" in the STP (segmentation, targeting, and positioning) process. It refers to how customers think about a product, service, or brand in the market relative to competitors' offerings. Firms position their products and services according to several criteria. Some focus on their offering's *value*—customers get a lot for what the product or service costs. Others determine the most *important attributes* for customers and position their offering on the basis of those attributes. The product's *use* can offer another positioning method. Cars, for example, can be positioned all the way from basic transportation (Toyota Corolla) to pure luxury (Bentley Continental). Symbols can also be used for positioning, though few products or services are associated with symbols that are compelling enough to drive people to buy. Finally, one of the most common positioning

methods relies on the favorable comparison of the firm's offering with the products or services marketed by competitors. When developing a positioning strategy and a perceptual map, firms go through five steps. First they determine consumers' perceptions and evaluations of the product or service in relation to competitors. Second, they identify competitors' positions. Third, they determine consumer preferences. Fourth, they select the position. Finally, they monitor the positioning strategy.

Key Terms

- benefit segmentation, 254
- concentrated segmentation strategy, 247
- demographic segmentation, 250
- differentiated segmentation strategy, 247
- geodemographic segmentation, 255

- geographic segmentation, 249
- ideal point, 266
- lifestyles, 251
- loyalty segmentation, 256
- mass customization, 248
- micromarketing, 248
- one-to-one marketing, 248
- perceptual map, 265

- psychographics, 250
- self-concept, 251
- self-values, 251
- undifferentiated segmentation strategy (mass marketing), 246
- Value and Lifestyle Survey (VALS), 253

Marketing Applications

1. You have been asked to identify various strategies for segmenting a market, which then will be used to choose one strategy for your pet supply store. List and discuss each of the overall strategies that can be used to develop a segmentation approach. Provide an example of each of the four strategies the pet store might use.

2. What overall segmentation strategy would you suggest for a small entrepreneur starting his own business? Justify why you would recommend that particular approach.

3. The concept of "mass customization" seems like a contradiction in terms. How and why would a retailer use mass customization?

4. A number of methods are used to segment markets. Identify the typical customer for each of the six methods discussed in the text.

5. You have been asked to evaluate the attractiveness of a group of identified potential market segments. What criteria will you use to evaluate those segments? Why are these appropriate criteria?

6. A small-business owner is trying to evaluate the profitability of different segments. What are the key factors you would recommend she consider? Over what period of time would you recommend she evaluate?

7. Think about the various nationwide restaurant chain brands that you know (e.g., Burger King, Applebee's, Ruth's Chris Steakhouse). How do those various brands position themselves in the market?

8. Put yourself in the position of an entrepreneur who is developing a new product to introduce into the market. Briefly describe the product. Then, develop the segmentation, targeting, and positioning strategy for marketing the new product. Be sure to discuss (a) the overall strategy, (b) characteristics of the target market, (c) why that target market is attractive, and (d) the positioning strategy. Provide justifications for your decisions.

9. Think of a specific company or organization that uses various types of promotional material

to market its offerings. The Web, magazine ads, newspaper ads, catalogs, newspaper inserts, direct mail pieces, and flyers might all be sources for a variety of promotional materials. Locate two or three promotional pieces for the company and use them as a basis to analyze the segments being targeted. Describe the basic segmentation strategy reflected in these materials, and describe characteristics of the target market according to the materials. Be sure to include a copy of all the materials used in the analysis.

10. You have been hired recently by a large bank in its credit card marketing division. The bank has relationships with a large number of colleges and prints a wide variety of credit cards featuring college logos, images, and the like. You have been asked to oversee the implementation of a new program targeting the freshman class at the schools with which the bank has a relationship. The bank has already purchased the names and home addresses of the incoming freshman class. You have been told that no credit checks will be required for these cards as long as the student is over 18 years of age. The bank plans a first day of school marketing blitz that includes free hats, T-shirts, and book promotions, as well as free pizza, if the students simply fill out an application. Do you think it is a good idea to offer this program to these new students?

www.mhhe.com/grewal2e

Quiz Yourself

1. Adidas Group owns Reebok, adidas, and Taylor-Made brands. Adidas uses the different brands to pursue a(n) _____ strategy.
   a. concentrated segmentation
   b. micromarketing segmentation
   c. benefit segmentation
   d. differentiated segmentation
   e. undifferentiated segmentation

2. Talbots' target customers are college-educated women between 35 and 55 years old with average household income of $75,000 or more. Talbots is describing its market using a _____ segmentation approach.
   a. self-actualization
   b. geodemographic
   c. psychographic
   d. demographic
   e. geographic

(Answers to these two questions are provided on page 623.)

Go to www.mhhe.com/grewal2e to practice an additional 11 questions.

Toolkit

MARKET POSITION MAP ANALYSIS

Assume you are a brand manager for a major manufacturer. You have identified a number of market segments and are trying to understand how its products are positioned relative to other manufacturers'. Use the toolkit provided at www.mhhe.com/grewal2e to conduct a market position analysis.

Net Savvy

1. Go to the "My Best Segments" portion of the Claritas Web site, www.mybestsegments.com. Click on the tab that says "ZIP Code Look-Up," then enter your zip code to learn which segments are the top five in your zip code. Follow the links for each of the five most common PRIZM segments to obtain a segment description. Write up a summary of your results. Discuss the extent to which you believe these are accurate descriptions of the main segments of people who reside in your zip code.

2. Go to the SRI Consulting Business Intelligence Web site (http://www.sric-bi.com/VALS/presur-

vey.shtml), and click on the link to complete the VALS survey. After you submit your responses, a screen will display your primary and secondary VALS types. Click on the colored names of each segment to get additional information about them, and print out your results. Assess the extent to which these results reflect your lifestyle, and identify which characteristics accurately reflect your interests and activities and which do not.

Chapter Case Study

CHINA MOBILE GROWS THROUGH SEGMENTATION[58]

A few years ago, farmers in the town of Dagoucun in Tibet had to travel 20 kilometers to make a phone call, and they would truck their produce to distant cities in hopes of finding a buyer. But last year, the village received cell phone service through China Mobile, and today, farmers receive crop prices on their phones and are discovering which more marketable crops they should plant for ready sale, such as herbs for traditional medicine. Instead of farmers going to the city, the buyers contact them to pick up produce. In towns all over this area, similar changes are causing the Chinese cellular market to keep exploding, and one of the driving forces behind this change is China Mobile.[59]

Where is the world's largest cellular phone company? You might have guessed Finland, the home base of Nokia, or the United States, but you'd be wrong. China Mobile is the world's largest provider of cell phone service with more than 332 million subscribers—more than the entire population of the United States—and it continues to grow at the astounding rate of 5 million customers per month.[60] Each year it transmits over 353.38 billion text messages and 1.2 trillion minutes of voice traffic.[61] Because of its immense size, it has been rewarded with a market capitalization of $220 billion, making it the most valuable cellular carrier on Earth and the largest company on the Hong Kong Stock Exchange.[62]

Company

China Mobile spun off from China's state telecommunication company in 2000 and built its success by marketing in urban China. As cell phone penetration in Chinese cities rose to nearly 100 percent, China Mobile realized that China's interior, home to more than 700 million people, experienced cell phone penetration of only 12 percent.[63] To reach this enormous rural market, China Mobile invested in 230,000 cellular towers, a number that dwarfs the investment of Cingular, the largest U.S. carrier, with its 47,000 towers. With nearly a quarter billion towers throughout China, 97 percent of the Chinese population have access to China Mobile's signal. Thus, whether they're riding inside subway cars in Beijing or climbing to the top of Mount Everest, customers can still use their China Mobile phones.[64]

The company operates across all 31 of China's provinces,[65] offering traditional telecommunication services as well as a variety of multimedia offerings through its partnerships with News Corp, MTV, Warner Music, the NBA, and local cable companies. Part of its success stems from its strong focus on value-added services, such as ringtones, and its dedication to working with partners to make the cell phone the primary medium for communication. In a country where computer penetration remains low, cell phones provide the main means of access to the Internet for consumers.

Marketing Strategy

Beyond these strategic decisions, China Mobile's tremendous success also results from the company's careful and targeted segmentation of the Chinese cellular market. Segments of Chinese mobile phone users, according to the company, include wealthy businessmen, college students, and rural farmers. To serve these groups, various service plans aim to maximize handset penetration, then increase the use of value-added services that appeal to certain groups, such as ringtones.

To target the rural customer segment, China Mobile has a special low cost program with several value-added services.

Rural Segment   In the rural segment, China Mobile faces the challenge of winning customers without sacrificing its profit margins. The average income in rural China is only $400 per year, which leaves little discretionary spending room for expensive cell phones.[66] However, by carefully targeting rural populations with the right mix of services, the company has been able to maintain its profit margins. Furthermore, to keep costs low, China Mobile buys little in the way of advertising and instead relies on influential locals to persuade others to purchase handsets and prepaid cards.

The China Mobile service plan for farmers costs $0.25 per month, though placing or receiving individual calls and text messages entails an extra cost. What makes China Mobile's rural plans more attractive than those of its competitors remains the vast array of available value-added products. For example, the basic service plan includes free access to China Mobile's Agricultural Information Service, which delivers information about the production, supply, and sale of agricultural products; tips on managing rural administrative affairs; and details that affect rural residents' livelihood, such as crop prices or tips on duck farming, all delivered via text message.[67]

Wealthy Businessmen Segment   In a completely different market, China Mobile still must compete in the saturated urban segment; it does so by targeting wealthy businessmen who demand services that will make their lives more enjoyable. To attract this segment, China Mobile offers Go-Tone, which is relatively expensive at $6.40 per month, to provide mobile access to exclusive golf clubs and special VIP waiting rooms in Chinese airports.

China Mobile targets the college segment with a relatively low cost program and special services like exclusive concerts featuring popular performers.

College Segment   Not unlike farmers, college students worry about costs, but their wishes and demands are markedly different. To attract budget-conscious students, China Mobile offers the M-Zone plan for $2 a month. Targeted at customers who are avid music lovers in their 20s, M-Zone keeps them informed and grants them access to recent hits and releases by well-known artists. These consumers are predominately interested in short text messages and music downloads. Therefore, in addition to phone-related features, China Mobile offers this segment exclusive concerts featuring popular performers.[68]

Creating Value through Additional Services   Across all three of these segments, China Mobile offers services that are available only to its subscribers, whether those services pertain to weather, campus information, banking services, police information, or city services. It also enables subscribers to access the Internet.

Results of China Mobile's Segmentation Efforts

China Mobile's success, largely due to its well-thought-out segmentation program, seems in no real danger of stopping. The growth it has gained across its segments has garnered global attention for the relatively new firm. For example, Millward Brown, a global marketing research firm, ranks China Mobile fourth among the top 100 most powerful brands, and *BusinessWeek* calls it the top among its "20 Best Chinese Brands."[69]

Questions

1. Which types of segmentation strategies does China Mobile use to categorize the Chinese market? Are these types effective in this market? Provide support for your answer.

2. In many areas of rural China, China Mobile is the only cell phone carrier. So why would it go to the trouble of creating value-added services to serve a captive segment like farmers?

3. What methods do you think China Mobile uses to prevent customers from choosing a less expensive plan? For example, why do college students choose the $2 M-Zone plan instead of the $0.25 rural plan? How do you think that China Mobile identified the services for which college students would be willing to pay more?

The problem is that not all men are alike, as we saw with Jack and John. Women are not all alike either! To identify VALS Thinkers or Makers, companies use the VALS questionnaire in surveys or focus groups. VALS provides segment descriptions linkages with consumer product and media data, communication styles, and zip code locations.

It is just as easy identify Thinkers (left) as it as it is Makers (right). A person is given the VALS questionnaire and the Vals program at SRIC-BI runs the answers through the computer or coring to determine the VALS type.

CHAPTER

MARKETING RESEARCH AND INFORMATION SYSTEMS

LEARNING OBJECTIVES

- How do marketers use information systems to create greater value for customers?

- Can certain marketing research practices cause a firm to encounter ethical problems?

- What are the necessary steps to conduct marketing research?

- What are primary and secondary data, and when should each be used?

As one of the largest restaurant chains in the world, McDonald's runs more than 30,000 stores in 100 countries.[1] Each day, 52 million people eat food from a McDonald's restaurant, making it one of the most well-known and valuable brands in the world. One of the keys to McDonald's success has been creating a consistent look and feel throughout all of its stores for the past 30 years, yet changing tastes and demographics, and intense competition in the quick service restaurant industry like Panera Bread, have made the colorful plastic interiors look dated. To fix that problem, McDonald's has turned to a key tool in the marketing toolkit, marketing research, to redesign its stores from the bottom up.[2] McDonald's management had two primary goals for the redesign: to refresh and update the McDonald's restaurant experience and to improve the overall customer experience.

To reach these goals, McDonald's turned to an outside marketing research firm that specializes in design. They videotaped and analyzed how customers ate in quick service restaurants. They also collected and analyzed information about their customers.[3] On the basis of these analyses, McDonald's identified three actionable segments of customers. To accommodate all three of these different segments, the fast-food chain decided to develop a store layout that incorporates different seating areas: a linger section, a grab-and-go section, and a family section, each with a distinct personality. The linger section focuses on young adults who want to hang out and be social by providing armchairs, sofas, and Wi-Fi. The grab-and-go section appeals to customers who eat alone, giving them plasma televisions that stream news and local weather and that they can watch from their bar stools, set before tall counters. Finally, the family section features comfortable seating for groups. Each section also plays different music inside the store.[4]

The new store design, which McDonald's is rolling out worldwide through a series of store remodeling efforts, does not mean that the company is abandoning its iconic yellow and red colors, but the red is now muted, and sage green joins the mix. New restaurants feature less plastic and more brick and wood, and the lighting includes hanging lights that create a more intimate environment and highlight the framed artwork and photos hanging on the walls.[5] By using marketing research, McDonald's learned how to serve its customers better. And better service means better profits.

● ● ●

As the McDonald's example shows, marketing research is a key prerequisite to successful decision making. It consists of a set of techniques and principles for systematically collecting, recording, analyzing, and interpreting data that can aid decision makers involved in marketing goods, services, or ideas.[6] When marketing managers attempt to develop their strategies, marketing research can provide valuable information that will help them make segmentation, positioning, product, place, price, and promotion decisions.

Firms invest billions of dollars in marketing research every year. For instance, as the largest U.S.-based marketing research firm, The Nielsen Company earns annual worldwide revenues of almost $3.7 billion.[7] Why do marketers find this research valuable? First, it helps reduce some of the uncertainty under which they currently operate. Successful managers know when research might help their decision making and then take appropriate steps to acquire the information they need. Second, marketing research provides a crucial link between firms and their environments, which enables them to be customer oriented because they build their strategies by using customer input and continual feedback. Third, by constantly monitoring their competitors, firms can anticipate and respond quickly to competitive moves.

If you think market research is applicable only to corporate or retailing ventures, think again. Not-for-profit organizations and governments also use research to serve their constituencies better. The political sector has been slicing and dicing the voting public for decades to determine relevant messages for different demographics. Politicians desperately want to understand who makes up the voting public to determine how to reach them. But not only do they want to know your political views; they also want to understand your media habits, such as what magazines you subscribe to, so they can target you more effectively.

In this chapter, we examine how marketing information systems create value for firms and their customers. We also discuss some of the ethical implications of using the information marketing information systems collect, followed by a discussion of the overall marketing research process. The chapter concludes with an examination of customer lifetime value, a popular marketing metric that uses secondary data to determine a customer's value to a firm.

Politicians and not-for-profit organizations do research to understand their constituencies.

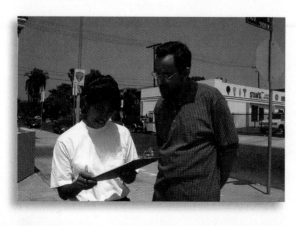

USING MARKETING INFORMATION SYSTEMS TO CREATE BETTER VALUE

In today's networked business world, marketers use increasingly sophisticated methods of gathering and employing marketing information to help them provide greater value to customers. A marketing information system (MkIS) is a set of procedures and methods that apply to the regular, planned collection, analysis, and presentation of information that then may be used in marketing decisions. An MkIS provides a means to accumulate information from sources both internal and external to the organization for the purpose of making it routinely available to managers for making more informed decisions. For example, Overstock.com, one of the largest online shopping Web sites,[8] developed a system to track the search habits of its shoppers. Overstock.com uses more than 40 attributes, which it collects during shopping sessions, to determine which incentives to offer each customer at checkout time. For example, it tracks variables such as geographic origin, keywords, time of day, and gender. By combining this information with the enormous amount of historic transaction data that it has collected, Overstock.com can offer the right incentives that help it close the sale. Using this system, Overstock.com also divides its customers into more than 300 segments and employs its marketing research to customize their direct mail and online shopping experiences.[9] Customers that enter "discount" into a Google search to find Overstock.com get flagged as price sensitive, so the company offers them a larger discount than it does customers who access the Web site directly.[10] This system also enables the company to better meet the needs of its best customers, thus improving the overall value of its offering.

Although an MkIS can be expensive, if used properly, it can be a valuable investment. Nowadays, companies usually find it necessary to go beyond using routine reports and must generate customized analyses. For example, Burger King might be interested in comparing two different promotions for a new menu item targeted to the same geographic region of the country. By initiating a query of the number of menu items sold in the zip codes that constitute the targeted area, an analyst could compare the effectiveness of each marketing program or take the analysis one step further and determine the total revenue generated from those customers, broken down into the amount they spent on the meal, number of items sold, and sales of other items such as soft drinks, fries, and desserts. In this way, the MkIS helps the company determine which promotion generated the most interest in the new menu item and whether the promotion increased or decreased average store sales.

Since the use of MkIS has become more widespread, organizations of all types have vast amounts of data available to them. One of the most valuable resources such firms have at their disposal is their rich cache of customer information and purchase history. However, it can be difficult to make sense of the millions and even billions of pieces of individual data, which are stored in large computer files called data warehouses. For this reason, firms find it necessary to use data mining techniques to extract valuable information from their databases. Data mining uses a variety of statistical analysis tools to uncover previously unknown patterns in the data or relationships among variables. Through data mining, for example, McDonald's discovered three types of quick service restaurant customers and recognized that the best way to serve them was by changing the seating options. A gardening retailer might learn through its data mining that 25 percent of the time its customers buy a garden hose, they also purchase a sprinkler. Or an investment firm might use statistical techniques to group clients according to income, age, type of securities purchased, and prior investment

Marketers use data mining techniques to determine what items people buy at the same time so they can be promoted and displayed together.

experience. This categorization identifies different segments, to which the firm can offer valuable packages that meet their specific needs. The firm can tailor separate marketing programs to each of these segments. Data mining thus can be useful for a broad range of organizations.

THE ETHICS OF USING CUSTOMER INFORMATION

As we noted in Chapter 3, upholding strong business ethics requires more than a token nod to ethics in the mission statement. A strong ethical orientation must be an integral part of a firm's marketing strategy and decision making. In Chapter 3, we discussed how marketers have a duty to understand and address the concerns of the various stakeholders in the firm.

As technology continues to advance rapidly, especially in terms of a firm's ability to link data sets and build enormous databases that contain information on millions of customers, marketing researchers must be careful to not abuse their ability to access these data, which can be very sensitive. Recent security breaches at some of the United States' largest retailers, banks, and credit-reporting services have shown just how easily this stored data can be abused.

Many consumers may be surprised to know just who has their personal information. For example, when 650,000 JCPenney credit card holders suffered information theft, it was not JCPenney's fault. Rather, GE Money, which managed the credit cards, had contracted data storage responsibility to a specialist in data security, Iron Mountain.[11] Iron Mountain then lost the data. But regardless of who did what, for consumers, the effect is the same. In this case, GE Money paid to offer credit monitoring to those consumers whose information had been stolen to ensure that thieves could not also steal their identities. The risk of data theft also is very real for both consumers and companies. The average cost of data theft to companies is about $200 per account.[12] That means that a loss of 650,000 customer records could potentially cost GE Money $128 million! The lesson for marketing researchers is to respect and protect the privacy of individual customers absolutely and without question. From charitable giving to medical records to Internet tracking, consumers are more anxious than ever about preserving their fundamental right to privacy.

More and more, consumers want to be assured that they have control over the information that has been collected about them through various means, such as a Web site or product registration or rebate form. Consumers' anxiety has become so intense that the U.S. government has promulgated various regulations, such as the "junk fax prevention act" and "Do Not Call" and "Do Not Email" lists, to give citizens control over who contacts them.[13] When conducting marketing research, researchers must assure respondents that the information they provide will be treated as confidential and used solely for the purpose of research. Without such assurances, consumers will be reluctant to either provide honest responses to marketing research inquiries or even agree to participate in the first place.

Many firms voluntarily notify their customers that any information provided to them will be kept confidential and not given or sold to any other firm. Several organizations, including the Center for Democracy and Technology and the Electronic Privacy Information Center, have emerged as watchdogs over data mining of consumer information. In addition, national and state governments in the United States play a big part in protecting privacy. In addition to the "Do Not Call" and "Do Not Email" initiatives, companies now are required to disclose their privacy practices to customers on an annual basis. Therefore, marketers must adhere to legislative and company policies, as well as respect consumers' desires for privacy.[14]

Finally, it is extremely important to adhere to ethical practices when conducting marketing research. The American Marketing Association, for example, provides three guidelines for conducting marketing research: (1) It prohibits selling or fundraising under the guise of conducting research, (2) it supports maintaining research integrity by avoiding misrepresentation or the omission of pertinent research data, and (3) it encourages the fair treatment of clients and suppliers. Numerous codes of conduct written by various marketing research societies all reinforce the duty of researchers to respect the rights of the subjects in the course of their research. The bottom line: Marketing research should be used only to produce unbiased, factual information.

THE MARKETING RESEARCH PROCESS

Managers consider several factors before embarking on a marketing research project. First, will the research be useful; will it provide insights beyond what the managers already know and reduce uncertainty associated with the project? Second, is top management committed to the project and willing to abide by the results of the research? Related to both of these questions is the value of the research. Marketing research can be very expensive, and if the results won't be useful or management does not abide by the findings, it represents a waste of money.

Whirlpool Corporation
Building unmatched loyalty
one customer at a time.

While Whirlpool chose to pursue a "World Washer" strategy in Europe that was contrary to its own research findings, its European competitors continued to innovate by responding to preferences in different regions by offering products to meet their special needs.

Consider Whirlpool's approach to the European market for washing machines.[15] Although the findings of a major marketing research program indicated that there were significant regional differences in consumer preferences, managers stayed committed to their strategy of introducing the "World Washer," which could be sold in all EU markets. Although Whirlpool considered its research to be a worthwhile project, it was not particularly valuable to the firm because it continued to pursue a strategy that was contrary to its own research findings. Research showed that offering the same machine to different regions failed to address those different preferences in the marketplace, like Britons' preference to wash laundry more frequently using quieter machines than their neighbors in the rest of Europe. Yet instead of a localization strategy, Whirlpool relies on innovation to design its new products. One of its new washing machines in Europe, the Aqua Steam, can inject steam into the washing machine to remove stains at high temperatures or even sterilize baby clothing.[16] While the company has maintained its World Washer strategy, its European competitors have continued to innovate by responding to preferences in different regions by offering products to meet their special needs.

The marketing research process itself can be divided into five steps (see Exhibit 9.1). Although the stages of the marketing research process are presented in a step-by-step progression, of course research does not always happen that way. Sometimes, researchers go back and forth from one step to another as the need arises. For example, marketers may establish a specific research objective, which they follow with data collection and preliminary analysis. If they uncover new information during the collection step or if the findings of the analysis spotlight new research needs, they might redefine their objectives and begin again

EXHIBIT 9.1   The Marketing Research Process

Step 1:	Step 2:	Step 3:	Step 4:	Step 5:
Defining Objectives	Designing the Research Project	Data Collection	Analyzing Data	Presenting Results

from a new starting point. A major automobile manufacturer once set out to identify consumer responses to its new company logo, only to discover in preliminary focus groups that some of the respondents thought the company had gone out of business! Clearly, those researchers had to regroup and set out in a different direction with an entirely different objective.

Another important step in embarking on a research project is to plan the entire project in advance. For example, when setting up a questionnaire, marketers should consider the data collection process and anticipate the types of analyses that might produce meaningful results for decision makers. Open-ended questions on a questionnaire can slow down the coding process and make it difficult to run some sophisticated statistical analyses. If the decision makers want a sophisticated analysis fast, a questionnaire filled with open-ended questions may not be the best choice. But if they really need insightful, exploratory answers, they should turn to such open-ended questions to ensure they get respondents' own ideas. By planning the entire research process well in advance of starting the project, researchers can avoid unnecessary alterations to the research plan as they move through the process.

Step 1: Defining the Objectives and Research Needs

Because research is both expensive and time-consuming, it is important to establish in advance exactly what information is required to answer specific research questions and how that information should be obtained. Researchers assess the value of a project through a careful comparison of the benefits of answering some of their questions and the costs associated with conducting the research. For instance, going back to Whirlpool's European washing machine study, suppose the company had a choice of conducting in-depth interviews with several hundred washing machine owners at a cost of $200 per interview or doing an online survey with the same number of respondents but at a cost of only $2 per questionnaire. Which data collection method should Whirlpool use? Clearly the questionnaires are much less expensive, but the in-depth interviews provide richer information that would be virtually impossible to access through questionnaires.

When designing a marketing research project, a firm like Smellswell Cologne must first specify its objectives—what it really needs to know!

As this simple example shows, there are always value trade-offs in marketing research. Researchers can always design a more expensive study and eke out more and better information, but in the end, they should choose the method that will provide them with the information they need at the lowest cost.

Marketing research efforts and resources can be wasted if research objectives are poorly defined. Poor design arises from three major sources: basing research on irrelevant research questions, focusing on research questions that marketing research cannot answer, and addressing research questions to which the answers are already known. For companies with track records of anticipating new technologies, fashions, or gadgets that consumers will demand, as well as the core competencies to deliver them in a timely manner, lengthy marketing research studies likely will not add significantly to the benefits of their own intuition. However, timely and focused marketing research could help them refine their ideas and prototypes. When researchers have determined what information they need to address a particular problem or issue, the next step is to design a research project to meet those objectives.

Step 2: Designing the Research Project

The second step in the marketing research project involves design. In this step, researchers identify the type of data needed and determine the type of research necessary to collect it. Recall that the objectives of the project drive the type of data needed, as outlined in Step 1. Let's look at how this second step works, using a hypothetical example about marketing men's cologne.

Smellswell Cologne, a marketer of a national brand of men's cologne, sets out to evaluate its position in the marketplace relative to its competitors. The specific purpose of the marketing research is twofold: to determine current relative market share (as defined in Chapter 2) and to assess how that position will change in the next few years.

Identifying the marketing metric needed for the first purpose—determining relative market share—is fairly straightforward. It requires finding the company's sales during a particular time frame relative to that of the largest firm in the industry.[17]

Identifying the marketing metric needed for the second purpose—assessing the extent to which the firm's market position will improve, stay the same, or deteriorate—is not as easy to obtain. For instance, the company's marketers might want to assess customers' brand loyalty, because if the company enjoys high levels of loyalty, the future looks rosier than if loyalty is low. Smellswell Cologne's relative market share in relation to that of its competitors over time can also shed light on the future of its market position. The firm will want to know which firms have been gaining relative market share and which are losing.

Thus, after the firm has identified its specific objectives and needs, it must consider whether the data required are secondary or primary in nature.

Secondary Data   Secondary data are pieces of information that have already been collected from other sources and usually are readily available. Census data, the company's sales invoices, and information from trade associations, the Internet, books, and journal articles are all readily available, free (or inexpensive) sources of secondary data.

In addition, marketers can purchase syndicated data, which are data available for a fee from commercial research firms such as Information Resources Inc. (IRI), National Purchase Diary Panel, and ACNielsen. Exhibit 9.2 contains information about various firms that provide syndicated data. This type of information, in our hypothetical cologne example, might include the prices of different colognes, sales figures, growth or decline in the category, and advertising and promotional spending. Consumer packaged goods firms that sell to wholesalers may not have the means to gather pertinent data directly from the retailers

EXHIBIT 9.2	Syndicated Data Providers and Their Services
ACNielsen (www.acnielsen.com)	With its *Market Measurement Services,* the company tracks the sales of consumer packaged goods, gathered at the point of sale in retail stores of all types and sizes.
Information Resources Inc. (www.infores.com)	*InfoScan* store tracking provides detailed information about sales, share, distribution, pricing, and promotion across a wide variety of retail channels and accounts.
J.D. Power and Associates (www.jdpower.com)	Widely known for its automotive ratings, it produces quality and customer satisfaction research for a variety of industries.
Mediamark Research Inc. (www.mediamark.com)	Supplies multimedia audience research pertaining to media and marketing planning for advertised brands.
National Purchase Diary Panel (www.npd.com)	Tracking services provide information about product movement and consumer behavior in a variety of industries.
NOP World (www.nopworld.com)	The *mKids US* research study tracks mobile telephone ownership and usage, brand affinities, and entertainment habits of American youth between 12 and 19 years of age.
Research and Markets (www.researchandmarkets.com)	Promotes itself as a "one-stop shop" for market research and data from most leading publishers, consultants, and analysts.
Roper Center for Public Opinion Research (www.ropercenter.uconn.edu)	The *General Social Survey* is one of the nation's longest running surveys of social, cultural, and political indicators.
Simmons Market Research Bureau (www.smrb.com)	Reports on the products American consumers buy, the brands they prefer, and their lifestyles, attitudes, and media preferences.
Yankelovich (www.yankelovich.com)	The *MONITOR* tracks consumer attitudes, values, and lifestyles shaping the American marketplace.

that sell their products to the consumer, which makes syndicated data a valuable resource for them. Some syndicated data providers also offer information about shifting brand preferences and product usage in households, which they gather from consumer panels. Adding Value 9.1 describes the valuable information that IRI provides to its customers.

A marketing research project often begins with a review of the relevant secondary data, which provides both advantages and disadvantages. The data can be quickly accessed at a relatively low cost; the Census of Retail Trade and County Business Patterns, for example, provides data about sales of different types of retail establishments. These patterns may be the only accurate sources available to a small new business that wants to determine the size of its potential market. For such a firm, gathering accurate and comprehensive data on its own would be quite difficult.

Internally, companies also generate a tremendous amount of secondary data from their day-to-day operations. For example, companies such as CVS use sales data to study how customers shop. At CVS, customers scan their loyalty cards at the checkout counter in exchange for discounts. By scanning their cards, customers also give CVS an extensive library of information about their purchasing habits. The combination of sales data and loyalty card information lets retailers identify high-value customers, as well as the specific kinds of products that the most unprofitable customers purchase. Since CVS first created its ExtraCare loyalty card, more than 50 million customers have signed up for the program.[18] With 50 million informants who generate data each time they shop at CVS, the drugstore chain can determine which discounts to offer, where to send direct mail, and how it should alter the product mix that each store carries. It has learned, for instance, that the average cardholder shops at CVS 11 times per year, but the top 30 percent of its shoppers visit a store 27 times per year.[19] By identifying common characteristics of frequent shoppers, CVS can ensure that it meets their needs effectively and target similar consumers with its advertising. Secondary data can also be used by firms to assess the profitability of their customers by determining the customer lifetime value (CLV). More details about calculating CLV are found in Appendix 9A.

Adding Value 9.1   IRI and the Value of Information[20]

Information Resources Inc. (IRI), one of the top U.S. research organizations, provides market research and analytical services to the consumer packaged goods, health care, and retail industries. Ninety-five percent of the *Fortune* Global 500 in the consumer packaged goods and retail industries use IRI market research to make their business decisions.[21] For its clients—which include Anheuser-Busch, ConAgra, CVS, Johnson & Johnson, and PepsiCo—IRI collects, monitors, and manages a variety of data in some of the most active research markets in the world, including the United States and Europe.

From appropriate channel usage to desired packaging, IRI tracks a host of data to deliver detailed findings that are designed to grow and enhance clients' operations. Recently, IRI published a report tracking the increase in private-label brands (i.e., a brand owned by the store that sells it) in the consumer packaged goods industry. If a grocery store chooses to offer its own brand of detergent, it must engage in competition with various branded detergents, such as Tide, Cheer, and All. In the past, private-label products often were positioned as more affordable versions of popular brands and tended to target and attract price-conscious consumers. However, according to IRI's findings, recent trends indicate private-label sales are growing across consumer segments. To identify these trends in private-label sales, IRI collects point-of-sale data from almost 40,000 retail outlets throughout the country, then cross-references these data with data collected from the 70,000 households that make up the Consumer Network Household Panel that IRI had armed with personal scanners to track their household purchases.

The findings from this research then can be used to identify effective promotional activities, fine-tune category

IRI research on private-label bottled water provides information to bottling companies that enables them to adjust their marketing strategies to react to competitive action.

offerings, and predict shopping patterns. In this case, IRI notes that in 15 percent of product categories, private labels have gained an above-average market share, but they are losing share to national brands. Furthermore, IRI found that the national brands that gained market share from a private label and encouraged consumers who had bought private labels in the past to switch over to their branded products are investing heavily in marketing their brands. In the bottled water segment, for example, SoBe Life Water is promoting its offering as a viable alternative to private-label waters.

Some interesting patterns with regard to consumer reactions to price changes have also emerged from IRI's analysis. As prices for certain staples such as chicken, peanut butter, milk, and pasta increase, consumers opt to switch to less expensive private-label offerings. This trend is especially strong for chicken, for which producers have reduced the number of coupons they offered while simultaneously increasing their prices. On the basis of these findings, the IRI data suggest that producers should identify how brand loyal and price sensitive their customers really are before they make decisions about whether to stop offering coupons or raise prices.[22] As these two examples show, IRI's research delivers actionable insights that businesses throughout the world value.

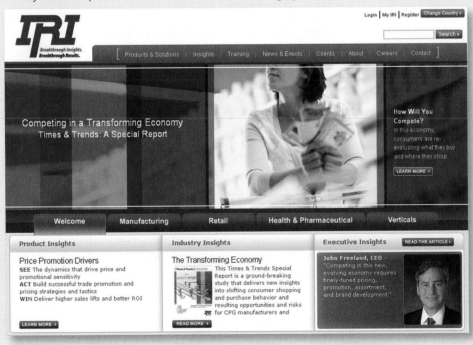

The homepage for IRI explains some of its many market research products.

Sometimes, however, secondary data are not adequate to meet researchers' needs. Because the data initially were acquired for some purpose other than the research question at hand, they may not be completely relevant. For instance, the U.S. Census is a great source for demographic data about a particular market area, and it can be easily accessed at a low cost. However, the data are collected only at the beginning of every decade, so they quickly become outdated. For example, if a firm were interested in opening a retail flooring store in the next year, it would have to rely on U.S. Census data collected in 2000, when housing starts were at much higher levels than they were just a few years later. If it hoped to locate in an area in which housing starts are projected to decline even further in the next several years, these data would be too old to provide much in the way of insights. Researchers must also pay careful attention to how the secondary data were collected. Despite the great deal of data available on the Internet, easy access does not ensure that the data are trustworthy.

Primary Data   In many cases, the information researchers need is available only through primary data, or data collected to address specific research needs. Marketers collect primary data using a variety of means, such as observing consumer behavior, conducting focus group interviews, or surveying customers using the mail, telephone, in-person interviews, or the Internet. Primary data collection can help eliminate some of the problems inherent to secondary data.

A major advantage of primary research is that it can be tailored to fit the pertinent research questions, though it also has its own set of disadvantages. For one thing, it is usually more costly to collect primary than secondary data, and the collection typically takes longer. Furthermore, marketers often require sophisticated training and experience to design and collect primary data that are unbiased, valid, and reliable. (For a summary of the advantages and disadvantages of each type of research, see Exhibit 9.3.)

Step 3: Data Collection Process

Data collection begins only after the research design process. Depending on the nature of the research problem, the collection can employ either exploratory or conclusive research.

As its name implies, exploratory research attempts to begin to understand the phenomenon of interest; it also provides initial information when the problem lacks any clear definition. Exploration can include informal methods, like reviewing available secondary data, or more formal methods that encompass qualitative research, such as observation techniques, in-depth interviews, focus groups, and projective techniques (see Exhibit 9.4, left side).

If the firm is ready to move beyond preliminary insights, it likely is ready to engage in conclusive research, which provides the information needed to confirm those insights and which managers can use to pursue appropriate courses of action. For marketing researchers, because it is often quantitative in nature, conclusive research offers a means to confirm implicit hunches through surveys, formal studies such as specific experiments, scanner and panel data, or some combination of these. (See Exhibit 9.4, right side.) In the case of formal research, it also enables the researcher to test his or her predictions.

The major advantage of using primary data like focus groups for market research is that it can be tailored to fit the pertinent research questions. But it usually is more expensive and takes longer to collect than secondary data.

EXHIBIT 9.3	Advantages and Disadvantages of Secondary and Primary Data		
Type	**Examples**	**Advantages**	**Disadvantages**
Secondary Research	■ Census data ■ Sales invoices ■ Internet information ■ Books ■ Journal articles ■ Syndicated data	■ Saves time in collecting data because they are readily available ■ Reduces data collection costs	■ May not be precisely relevant to information needs ■ Information may not be as timely as needed ■ Sources may not be original, and therefore usefulness is an issue ■ Methodologies for collecting data may not be relevant or may contain bias in the subject matter
Primary Research	■ Observed consumer behavior ■ Focus group interviews ■ Surveys	■ Specific to the immediate data needs and topic at hand ■ Offers behavioral insights generally not available from secondary research	■ Usually more costly to collect ■ Typically takes longer to collect ■ Often requires more sophisticated training and experience to design and collect unbiased, valid, reliable data

Many research projects use exploratory research as the first phase of the research process and follow it up with conclusive research. Let's attempt to understand this progression by studying both methods in detail.

Exploratory Research Methods   Managers commonly use several exploratory research methods: observation, in-depth interviewing, focus group interviews, and projective techniques (Exhibit 9.4, left side).

Observation   An exploratory research method, observation entails examining purchase and consumption behaviors through personal or video camera scrutiny. For example, researchers might observe customers while they shop or when they go about their daily lives, during which processes they use a variety of products. Observation can last for a very brief period of time (e.g., two hours watching teenagers shop for clothing in the mall), or it may take days or weeks (e.g., researchers live with families to observe their use of products). When consumers are unable to articulate their experiences, observation research becomes particularly useful; how else could researchers determine which educational toys babies choose to play with or confirm details of the buying process that consumers might not be able to recall accurately? Ethical & Societal Dilemma 9.1 describes observational research and raises the question, Should people be informed that they are being watched?

In-Depth Interview   An in-depth interview is an exploratory research technique in which trained researchers ask questions, listen to and record the answers, and then pose additional questions to clarify or expand on a particular issue. For instance, in addition to simply watching teenagers shop for apparel, interviewers

EXHIBIT 9.4	Exploratory versus Conclusive Data Collection

Ethical and Societal Dilemma 9.1   Watching Consumers[23]

How does sitting in a mall or standing in a store checking out the people in the corner add up to bona fide market research? Well, for corporate ethnographers Emma Gilding and Paco Underhill, it's just another day on the job. Gilding helped found Ogilvy & Mather's (O&M) Discovery Group; Underhill created Envirosell.

Gilding's projects range from American Express to Huggies diapers and a number of pharmaceutical products. In general, ethnographers only follow people who apply for a study. These applicants go through a screening process that is based on a predetermined set of qualifications, such as age, gender, and brand familiarity. Those who qualify are paid to allow a camera crew, which documents their every move, to follow them during their daily routines for a day or more.[24] Gilding is quick to point out that any unnatural behaviors the cameras may bring about soon subside as subjects fall into their normal routines. Furthermore, and importantly, study participants are fully informed and have given their consent to being the subjects of a marketing research study. One company that recently engaged Gilding's services is Diebold, an ATM and voting machine manufacturer. Diebold wanted to design a new ATM and hired Gilding to run a two-part study to gather information about the exact elements that the new machines needed to feature. Gilding first filmed bank customers conducting automatic transactions to see how these customers interacted with ATMs. After studying the information, Diebold created a working prototype of the new version, and Gilding filmed customer interactions with the new product to ensure that the product changes helped consumers conduct their banking more easily.[25]

Envirosell has performed projects for firms ranging from Staples to Wells Fargo. For Staples, it observed consumers in 12 stores, videotaping their movements through the stores for eight hours each research day, as a means to better understand how consumers actually shopped around the various departments to gather products, view signs, and interact with sales associates. Envirosell researchers also conduct interviews with shoppers. On the basis of the results of these studies, Staples has rolled out a new store format that focuses on solving customer problems by combining service with self-service rather than just selling individual items. Staples associates can now provide a higher level

might stop them one at a time in the mall to ask them a few questions, such as: "We noticed that you went into and came out of Abercrombie & Fitch very quickly without buying anything. Why was that?" If the subject responds that no one had bothered to wait on her, the interviewer might ask a follow-up question like, "Oh? Has that happened to you before?" or "Do you expect sales assistance there?" The results often provide insights that help managers better understand the nature of their industry, as well as important trends and consumer preferences, which can be invaluable for developing marketing strategies.

An in-depth interview is an exploratory research technique in which trained researchers ask questions, listen to and record answers, and then pose additional questions to clarify or expand on a particular issue.

In-depth interviews provide quite a few benefits. They can provide a historical context for the phenomenon of interest, particularly when they include industry experts or experienced consumers. They also can communicate how people really feel about a product or service at the individual level, a level that rarely emerges from other methods that use group discussions. Finally, marketers can use the results of in-depth interviews to develop surveys.

Focus Group Interviews In focus group interviews, a small group of persons (usually 8 to 12) comes together for an intensive discussion about a particular topic. Using an unstructured method of inquiry, a trained moderator guides the conversation on the basis of a predetermined general outline of the topics of interest. Researchers usually of service in those areas that demand it, and the new store format gives customers the tools to be self-sufficient if they choose to browse on their own.

Using ethnographic approaches, research teams also can identify information that would not be accessible to them through more traditional marketing research means—a respondent to a simple questionnaire or people involved in an interview probably would not be able to provide insightful information about the patterns they follow when walking through a store or a mall.

Do you believe it is ethical for a firm to record the movements and activities of customers as they shop in a store? Would your opinion be different if the customers were informed that they were being watched?

In some cases, researchers obtain consent from the consumers they are watching and videotaping; in other cases, they do not. The ethical dilemma for marketing researchers centers around whether using observational techniques in which the subjects are not informed that they are being studied, like viewing customers in a mall or a retail store, violates the rule of fair treatment. Observing uninformed consumers very well may lead to important insights that would not otherwise be discovered. But do the results justify the methodology?

record the interactions by video- or audiotape so they can carefully comb through the interviews later to catch any patterns of verbal or nonverbal responses.

In particular, focus groups gather qualitative data about initial reactions to a new or existing product or service, opinions about different competitive offerings, or reactions to marketing stimuli, like a new ad campaign or point-of-purchase display materials.

The Jones Apparel Group, for example, used focus groups to develop new products and an advertising campaign for its L.E.I. brand. A *Fortune* 500 company that produces apparel and accessories under the brand names Nine West, Jones New York, and AK Anne Klein,[26] Jones Apparel Group believed the L.E.I. brand was not connecting with its target market—juniors 13 to 17 years of age—and wanted to give the brand a facelift. To identify why consumers were not buying the brand, it conducted extensive focus groups, which revealed that juniors wanted the brand to be more inspirational and patriotic. Jones Apparel Group also discovered, because the focus groups told it, that juniors were spending a lot of time online. Therefore, it has increased its use of the Internet, including sponsoring a contest on MySpace that involved consumers uploading photos of themselves waving the American flag. So far, the response to the brand update has been "outstanding."[27]

The widespread use of the Internet has prompted several other changes in marketing research practices, as Power of the Internet 9.1 details. In particular, virtual focus groups have started to make inroads into the market researchers'

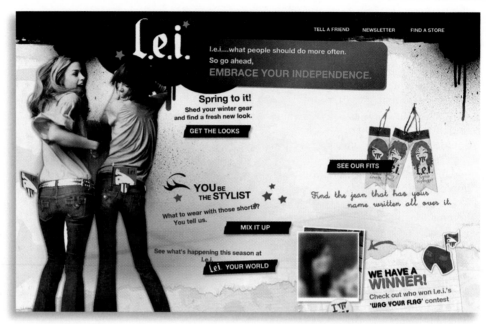

Jones Apparel Group learned a lot about its target market—13-to 17-year-olds—by doing focus groups.

Lego's Star Wars Imperial Destroyer, with 3,100 parts and a $300 price tag, was designed with the help of virtual focus groups.

toolkit. Lego, for instance, invited more than 10,000 kids to participate in a virtual focus group that it hoped would give the company ideas for new products.[28] The participants saw short lists of proposed toys and clicked on the ones they liked. They ranked their choices and even suggested new ideas. These ideas were fed, in turn, to other potential customers and were rated against the ideas from Lego's own toy creators. The new suggestions, in turn, got creative juices flowing among still other potential customers. The resulting product, the Star Wars Imperial Destroyer, was different from anything else in Lego's 73-year history— it was Lego's largest and most expensive set ever, with 3,100 parts and a $300 price tag. Its first production run, planned to last a year, sold in less than five weeks.

Projective Technique   A projective technique is a type of qualitative research in which subjects are provided a scenario and asked to express their thoughts and feelings about it. For example, consumers may be shown a cartoon that has a consumer looking at a shelf display in a supermarket with a text box above the consumer. The respondent would write in thoughts about the issue in the text box. Thus, the cartoon allows the respondent to visualize the situation and project his or her thoughts or feelings by filling out the text box.

Conclusive Research Methods   Conclusive research can be descriptive in nature—such as when it profiles a typical user or nonuser of a particular brand according to a survey. It can also be experimental—such as when a soft-drink producer conducts a taste test to determine which formulation of a green, high caffeine drink is preferred by customers. Conclusive research can also be collected from the merchandise that is scanned at a store or from a group of customers, known as a panel, who record all of their purchases. In this section, we will discuss each of these conclusive research techniques—survey, experiment, scanner, and panel.

Survey Research   A survey is a systematic means of collecting information from people that generally uses a questionnaire. A questionnaire is a form that features

Power of the Internet **9.1**   **Virtual Worlds Yield Real Marketing Research**

Makena Technologies has a rather unusual product to sell: It makes virtual worlds for companies. For Coca-Cola, it designed and developed a bottle-shaped island that online consumers could visit to purchase Coca-Cola–branded merchandise. Yet beyond the virtual world, customized to appeal to brand consumers, the Makena software platform also provides an advertising and marketing research platform. To understand just what companies can do when they can watch your every online move, take a close look at the virtual worlds that MTV created with Makena technology.

Virtual MTV (http://www.vmtv.com/) involves a collection of virtual worlds that allow users to interact with characters from their favorite shows or perform a heelflip bumpside in a virtual skate park.[29] In this online space, users socialize with other avatars or with staff members while they move about, perhaps finding a spot to watch some music videos, buy clothing, or just chat with other users.[30]

But MTV has bigger plans than just a game and social Web site. Immediately after creating its virtual worlds, MTV hired a marketing research firm, MauroNewMedia, a specialist in marketing research in "new media," such as virtual reality and online gaming, to study the behavior of 500,000 users over a six-month period. Even though MauroNewMedia did not link users' real identities to their avatars, it could conduct research that seems almost impossible in real life. In particular, it combines its exper-

tise with eye-tracking technology, online testing, and data mining to study how users interact with virtual worlds.[31] MTV's goal was to evaluate the possibilities and promise of targeted marketing and marketing research in virtual worlds; the results from the study likely come as no surprise. That is, it is extremely easy to conduct research in virtual worlds. On the Makena platform, the hosts of virtual worlds can pinpoint exactly when individual avatars take a look at specific ads and products.[32] In turn, marketing researchers can identify which kinds of ads appeal most to which kinds of users and then create custom messages designed just for them.

Second Life, the largest online virtual world, also has attracted a group of marketing research firms interested in understanding the behavior of its virtual denizens. Firms such as The Market Truth pay Second Life residents a small fee to participate in surveys that ask about their brand preferences and other market information, then try to relate their visible avatar choices, such as their apparent sex or age, with psychographic characteristics that would let companies divide Second Life users into useful segments.[33]

As virtual worlds mature, even more marketers likely will start to use them not just to advertise but also to collect information about user preferences. Researchers, however, are aware that since Second Life users may take on different identities than in real life, they may react differently to marketing stimuli in the virtual world.

In the virtual world at www.there.com firms like Coca-Cola and MTV can pinpoint when individual avatars take a look at specific ads and products.

EXHIBIT 9.5   Structured versus Unstructured Response

a set of questions designed to gather information from respondents and thereby accomplish the researchers' objectives. Individual questions on a questionnaire can be either unstructured or structured. Unstructured questions are open ended and allow respondents to answer in their own words. An unstructured question like "What are the most important characteristics for choosing a brand of shampoo?" yields an unstructured response. However, the same question could be posed to respondents in a structured format by providing a fixed set of response categories, like price, fragrance, ability to clean, and dandruff control, and then asking respondents to rate the importance of each. Structured questions thus are closed-ended questions for which a discrete set of response alternatives, or specific answers, is provided for respondents to evaluate (see Exhibit 9.5).

Developing a questionnaire is part art and part science. The questions must be carefully designed to address the specific set of research questions. Moreover, for a questionnaire to produce meaningful results, its questions cannot be misleading in any fashion (e.g., open to multiple interpretations), and they must address only one issue at a time. Furthermore, they must be worded in vocabulary that will be familiar and comfortable to those being surveyed. More specifically, the questions should be sequenced appropriately: general questions first, more specific questions next, and demographic questions at the end. Finally, the layout and appearance of the questionnaire must be professional and easy to follow, with appropriate instructions in suitable places. For some tips on what *not* to do when designing a questionnaire, see Exhibit 9.6.

Marketing surveys can be conducted either online or offline, but online marketing surveys offer researchers the chance to develop a database quickly with many responses, whereas offline marketing surveys provide a more direct approach that includes interactions with the target market.

Web surveys have steadily grown as a percentage of all quantitative surveys. Online surveys have a lot to offer managers with tight deadlines and smaller budgets,[34] including the following benefits:

- **Response rates are relatively high.** Typical response rates run from 1 to 2 percent for mail and 10 to 15 percent for phone surveys. For online surveys, in contrast, the response rate can reach 30 to 35 percent, or even higher in business-to-business research.

- **Respondents may lie less.** Respondents lie in any medium. Have you ever wondered, for example, how many administrative assistants fill out mail

EXHIBIT 9.6	What Not to Do When Designing a Questionnaire	
Issue	**Good Question**	**Bad Question**
Avoid questions the respondent cannot easily or accurately answer.	When was the last time you went to the grocery store?	How much money did you spend on groceries last month?
Avoid sensitive questions unless they are absolutely necessary.	Do you take vitamins?	Do you dye your hair?
Avoid double-barreled questions, which refer to more than one issue with only one set of responses.	1. Do you like to shop for clothing? 2. Do you like to shop for food?	Do you like to shop for clothing and food?
Avoid leading questions, which steer respondents to a particular response, irrespective of their true beliefs.	Please rate how safe you believe a BMW is on a scale of 1 to 10, with 1 being not safe and 10 being very safe.	BMW is the safest car on the road, right?
Avoid one-sided questions that present only one side of the issue.	To what extent do you believe fast food contributes to adult obesity using a five-point scale? 1: Does not contribute, 5: Main cause	Fast food is responsible for adult obesity: Agree/Disagree
Avoid questions with implicit assumptions, which presume the same point of reference for all respondents.	Should children be allowed to drink Coca-Cola in school?	Since caffeine is a stimulant, should children be allowed to drink Coca-Cola in school?
Avoid complex questions and those that may seem unfamiliar to respondents.	What brand of wristwatch do you typically wear?	Do you believe that mechanical watches are better than quartz watches?

Source: Adapted from A. Parasuraman, Dhruv Grewal, and R. Krishnan, *Marketing Research,* 2nd ed. (Boston: Houghton Mifflin, 2007), Ch. 10.

surveys for their bosses? And what sort of answers they might give? Because the Internet has a higher perception of anonymity than telephone or mail contacts, respondents are more likely to be more truthful.

- **It is inexpensive.** An average 20-minute phone interview can cost $30 to $40, compared with $7 to $10 for an online interview. Costs likely will continue to fall more as users become more familiar with the online survey process.

- **Results are processed and received quickly.** Reports and summaries can be developed in real time and delivered directly to managers in simple, easy-to-digest reports, complete with color, graphics, and charts. Traditional phone or mail surveys require laborious data collection, tabulation, summary, and distribution before anyone can grasp their results.

The Internet can also be used to collect data other than that available from quantitative surveys. If consumers give a firm permission to market to them, the firm can collect data about their usage of its Web site and other Internet applications. In addition, open-ended questionnaires can be used to collect more in-depth qualitative data.

Online marketing surveys enable researchers to develop a database quickly with many responses at a relatively low cost.

Commonly Used Survey-Based Metrics Marketing researchers use scales to measure certain concepts such as attitudes, perceived quality, value, and willingness to buy, perceptions (e.g., quality, value), and loyalty (e.g., purchase intentions). The concepts were discussed in Chapter 5. These constructs are measured using multiple questions that ask respondents to provide their response to a 5-point or 7-point scale. Some illustrative scales are provided in the survey found in Exhibit 9.7: Section A measures attitudes, B measures perceived quality, C measures value, D measures purchase intentions, and E collects some shopping behavior and demographics.[35]

EXHIBIT 9·7   Sample Metrics

Please take a few minutes to tell us about your experience at McDonald's. The information you provide will be maintained in a confidential manner. For each question, please respond by checking the box that applies or writing your response in the space provided.

Please Evaluate Your Experience at McDonald's

A. Attitude	Strongly Disagree	Disagree	Neither Agree or Disagree	Agree	Strongly Agree
I was very happy with McDonald's	①	②	③	④	⑤
Eating at McDonald's made me feel good	①	②	③	④	⑤
I am excited to have McDonald's products	①	②	③	④	⑤

B. (Measure of Perceived Quality)	Strongly Disagree	Disagree	Neither Agree or Disagree	Agree	Strongly Agree
The food appears to be good quality	①	②	③	④	⑤
The food appears to be well prepared	①	②	③	④	⑤
The food was tasty	①	②	③	④	⑤

C. (Measure of Value)	Strongly Disagree	Disagree	Neither Agree or Disagree	Agree	Strongly Agree
Taking advantage of the price deal would make me feel good	①	②	③	④	⑤
I would get a lot of pleasure knowing that I would save money at a reduced price	①	②	③	④	⑤
McDonald's food prices are low	①	②	③	④	⑤

D. (Willingness to Buy Measure)	Strongly Disagree	Disagree	Neither Agree or Disagree	Agree	Strongly Agree
If I was hungry, I would eat McDonald's	①	②	③	④	⑤
There is a high likelihood that McDonald's would be a strong option for a meal	①	②	③	④	⑤
There is a high likelihood I would eat at McDonald's for a meal	①	②	③	④	⑤

E. Please Tell Us About Yourself

In the last month, how many times have you been to McDonald's?   # _____

On average, how much do you spend each visit at McDonald's? $ _____

Please record your age   _____

Please record your gender

Male ○   Female ○

THANK YOU!

Assume you were working at McDonald's and wanted to see how your customers evaluated the food and offers. A survey like the one in Exhibit 9.7 could be administered to customers. Suppose 100 customers filled out the survey and the results of the first question, "I was very happy with McDonald's," were:

1	2	3	4	5
Strongly Disagree	Disagree	Neither Agree nor Disagree	Agree	Strongly Agree
N = 5	N = 5	N = 10	N = 30	N = 50

Their responses are indicated by "N = ." Marketers could report several metrics. But two common metrics would be that 80 percent of respondents had high satisfaction since they responded to "agree" or "strongly agree." It could also be reported that satisfaction was high because the mean was 4.15 on the 5-point scale.

Experimental Research　Experimental research is a type of quantitative research that systematically manipulates one or more variables to determine which variables have a causal effect on another variable. For example, suppose McDonald's is trying to determine the most profitable price for a new menu bundled item (hamburger, fries, and drink). Assume that the fixed cost of developing the item is $300,000 and the variable cost, which is primarily composed of the cost of the food itself, is $2.00. McDonald's puts the item on the menu at four different prices in four different markets. (See Exhibit 9.8.) In general, the more expensive the item, the less it will sell. But by running this experiment, the restaurant chain determines that the most profitable item is the second least expensive item. These findings suggest some people may have believed the least expensive item was too expensive, so they refused to buy it. The least expensive item sold fairly well, but McDonald's did not make as much money on each item sold. In this experiment, the changes in price likely caused the changes in quantities sold and therefore affected the restaurant's profitability.

Scanner Research　Scanner research is a type of quantitative research that uses data obtained from scanner readings of UPC codes at check-out counters. Whenever you go into your local grocery store, your purchases are rung up using scanner systems. The data from these purchases are likely to be acquired by leading marketing research firms, such as Information Resources Inc. or AC Nielsen, which use this information to help leading consumer packaged good firms (e.g., Kellogg's, Pepsi, Sara Lee) assess what is happening in the marketplace. For example, a firm can determine what would happen to sales if it reduced the price of its least popular

EXHIBIT **9.8**	Hypothetical Pricing Experiment for McDonald's

	1	2	3	4	5
Market	Unit Price	Market Demand at Price (in Units)	Total Revenue (Col. 1 × Col. 2)	Total Cost of Units Sold ($300,000 Fixed Cost + $2.00 Variable Cost)	Total Profits (Col. 3 − Col. 4)
1	$4	200,000	$800,000	700,000	$100,000
2	5	150,000	$750,000	600,000	$150,000
3	6	100,000	$600,000	500,000	$100,000
4	7	50,000	$350,000	400,000	($50,000)

Using an experiment, McDonald's would "test" the price of a new menu item to determine which is the most profitable.

product by 10 percent in a given month by lowering the price in some markets and leaving it the same in others. Do sales increase, decrease, or stay the same?

Panel Research   Panel research is a type of quantitative research that involves collecting information from a group of consumers (the panel) over time. The data collected from the panelists may be from a survey or a record of purchases. These data provide consumer packaged good firms with a comprehensive picture of what individual consumers are buying or not buying. Thus, one key difference between scanner research and panel research is the nature of aggregation. Scanner research typically focuses on weekly consumption of a particular product at a given unit of analysis (e.g., individual store, chain, region), whereas panel research focuses on the total weekly consumption by a particular person or group of people.

Regardless of how it gets done, though, collecting data can be an expensive process for entrepreneurs working on a shoestring budget. Tips for conducting marketing research on a shoestring budget are provided in Adding Value 9.2.

Step 4: Analyzing Data

The next step in the marketing research process—analyzing and interpreting the data—should be both thorough and methodical. To generate meaningful information, researchers analyze and make use of the collected data. In this context, data can be defined as raw numbers or other factual information that, on their own, have limited value to marketers. However, when the data are interpreted, they become information, which results from organizing, analyzing, and interpreting data and putting the data into a form that is useful to marketing decision makers. For example, a checkout scanner in the grocery store collects sales data about individual consumer purchases. Not until those data are categorized and examined do they provide information about which products and services were purchased together or how an in-store promotional activity translated into sales.

The purpose of converting data to information is to describe, explain, predict, and/or evaluate a particular situation, as Harrah's does in Superior Service 9.1. For example, an entrepreneur might learn that her core customers live in various

Adding Value **9.2**   **Marketing Research on a Shoestring Budget**

Imagine your company needs some research conducted but has a relatively small budget. Fortunately, marketing research does not have to have a high price tag, though it always takes drive and knowledge. Here are some ways to uncover the information you and your company might need without breaking the bank.

Objective: What is it that you need to know?

- **Network.** Use your phone directory on your cell phone and call friends and professional colleagues. In most cases, researchers probably already know people in the industry who will be able to share their knowledge. They can help marketers determine what their objectives should be in upcoming research projects.

Customer Analysis: Who are your customers, and what do they want?

- **Customers.** Talk with current and prospective customers. Ask them the right questions, and they will provide the necessary answers. This approach is remarkably cheap because it entails only the researcher's labor, though it will require a large time commitment. Marketers need to take care how they ask the questions though; people tend to provide answers that they think the questioner wants or that seem socially acceptable.

- **Online.** Use a search engine like Google by simply typing in some appropriate keywords.

- **U.S. Census Bureau.** The U.S. Census Bureau is an important source of information. At www.census.gov, industry, demographic, and economic reports are all accessible for free. Although not known for its ease of use, the Web site offers a wealth of information.

Competitive Analysis: What are your competitors doing?

- **Web sites.** Visit competitors' Web sites, if they have them. Learn about their products and services, pricing, management team, and philosophies. Read their press releases. You can even infer what part of the business is thriving through reading their career pages.

- **SEC Filings.** If competitors are public, they are required to file 10K forms annually with the Securities Exchange Commission (SEC). Search for SEC filings using www.finance.yahoo.com or www.moneycentral.msn.com/home.asp, both of which provide sales and expense numbers, in addition to other important information in the footnotes.

- **Go There.** If competitors are smaller mom-and-pop stores, visit them. Hang out in front of the store armed with a pad and paper and count the number of people who walk in, then the percentage of people that walk out having purchased something. Use logic and judgment. Have the customers purchased items that appear to have higher profit margins? Find out where and what competitors are advertising.

- **NAICS Codes.** For a wider view of the competitive industry, review the North American Industry Classification System (NAICS) codes. The NAICS identifies companies operating in an industry sector with a six digit code. The government's Web site at www.census.gov/epcd/www/naics.html helps pinpoint the correct NAICS code and can generate an industry-specific report. For example, if you want to identify women's clothing stores, you would go to number 44812. The first two digits, 44, identify merchandise retailers (as would 45). The third digit breaks down the merchandise retailers further. For example, retailers selling clothing and clothing accessories are in classification 448, while general merchandise retailers are in classification 452. The fourth digit subdivides clothing and accessory retailers (448) into clothing stores (4481), shoe stores (4482), and jewelry and luggage stores (4483). The fifth digit provides a further breakdown into men's clothing stores (44811) and women's clothing stores (44812). The sixth digit (not shown here) is used to capture differences in the three North American countries that use the classification scheme, the United States, Mexico, and Canada.

Focus Groups, Surveys, and Analyst Reports: What detailed information can you gather?

- **Be Specific.** Determine precisely what information is required; it is very costly to pay for research that does not assist in a decision or provide strategic direction.

- **Surveys.** Determine what form will provide the most value. Phone surveys cost about $40 per interview, mailings average from $5,000 to $15,000 for 200 responses, and e-mail surveys usually are much cheaper.

- **Focus Groups.** Although focus groups can be more expensive, there are ways to cut corners. Develop the questions in-house, and don't outsource the moderator or facility. It is important, however, to find the right participants.

- **Analyst Reports.** Prewritten reports, covering a broad price range and a wide variety of questions, are available for purchase from the hundreds of companies that write and sell reports. Two of the best known are found at www.forrester.com and www.hoovers.com.

Superior Service **9.1**

Harrah's Knows Its Customers Appreciate Superior Service[36]

As one of the largest casino operators in the world, Harrah's Entertainment runs more than 50 casinos in 13 states and five countries under a variety of brand names, including Caesar's Palace, Horseshoe, and Harrah's. Its facilities typically include hotel and convention space, restaurants, and entertainment facilities.[37] But the company runs another type of facility as well, one that few gamers likely would find as entertaining: It collects a vast amount of information about its millions of customers' preferences and gaming activities. Specifically, Harrah's tracks thousands of details about each visitor, from how much they gamble on each visit to whether they like NASCAR racing.

When Harrah's assigned managers to study the collected information, it found what it considered a surprising result. Conventional wisdom in the gambling industry states that "high rollers" are the most important customers, whereas Harrah's found that the most profitable customers were average, middle-aged working people who gambled only $100–$500 per trip but also visited several times per year.[38]

Next, Harrah's studied these most profitable visitors and found that they were not interested in typical casino incentives, such as free rooms or meals. Instead, what these loyal customers wanted was better service. From this research, Harrah's decided to create their Total Rewards loyalty card program, which classifies four tiers of players—Gold, Platinum, Diamond, and Seven Stars—according to their playing level. Each segment also consists of approximately 90 different groups, based on geodemographics, psychographics, and playing patterns.

In the Total Rewards program, customers can earn reward credits toward future vacations, sporting events, and merchandise. They also get more of what they want,

namely, better service through shorter waits in line. While competing casino operators are trying to lure customers by adding amenities like luxury spas, upscale shopping centers, and fabulous shows, Harrah's is garnering a very loyal following by catering to those who prefer to drop by for an hour after work to play the slots. Total Gold customers must stand in regular lines at the reception desk and restaurants, whereas Total Platinum customers are directed to shorter lines, and the ultra-privileged Total Diamond customers bypass most lines altogether. The company has also made sure that its entire four-tier promotion remained very conspicuous, which makes customers more interested in rising to the higher tiers. Harrah's use of marketing research thus, in an unavoidable pun, has really paid off big![39]

Harrah's uses marketing research to provide its distinct customer segments with the services they want.

suburbs around the outskirts of town. This piece of data takes on new meaning when she learns that none of these customers came to her store in response to the clever and expensive recent direct mail campaign she conducted. By analyzing data she collected through a survey, she discovers that her core customers are working professionals who are drawn to the store when they walk by it on their way to and from work, not people from the upscale apartments in the downtown region that she had targeted with her direct mail advertisements.

Data analysis might be as simple as calculating the average purchases of different customer segments or as complex as forecasting sales by market segment using elaborate statistical techniques. Cablecom, Switzerland's largest cable operator, has begun increasing the sophistication of its marketing research analyses. Since its founding in 1994, the cable company has grown to serve more than 16 million customers in 17 countries, offering cable television, broadband Internet, mobile phone services, and fixed-network telephony.[40] Much of its growth stems from its efforts to satisfy current customers and attract new ones. As the company continued to grow, it quickly learned that it was much easier to retain customers than to try to win them back. Thus, Cablecom turned to rigorous marketing research to understand why and when customers cancel their service. By analyzing the enormous amount of information that it possesses about its customers, Cablecom has developed statistical models that identify, at up to 78 percent accuracy, when a customer is dissatisfied with his or her service. Once the company identifies an unhappy customer, it can follow up and proactively address that customer's issues. By mining customer data and information, the company also reduced its churn levels from 19 percent to 2 percent. Churn is the number of participants who discontinue their use of a service divided by the average number of total participants. With these changes, the company can focus on what it does best, namely, delivering telecommunication service to homes.[41]

Step 5: Presenting Results

In the final phase in the marketing research process, the analyst prepares the results and presents them to the appropriate decision makers. A typical marketing research report includes an executive summary, the body of the report (which discusses the research objectives, methodology used, and detailed findings), the conclusions, the limitations, and appropriate supplemental tables, figures, and appendixes. To be effective, a written report must be short, interesting, methodical, precise, lucid, and free of errors.[42] Furthermore, the reports should use a style appropriate to the audience, devoid of technical jargon, and include recommendations that managers can actually implement.

CHECK YOURSELF

1. What are the steps in the marketing research process?
2. What is the difference between primary and secondary research?
3. What is the difference between exploratory and conclusive research?
4. What are some commonly used survey based metrics?

Summing Up

1. **How do marketers use information systems to create greater value for customers?**

   A marketing information system (MkIS) is a set of procedures and methods for the regular, planned collection, analysis, and presentation of information that marketers can use to make marketing decisions. An MkIS provides a means to accumulate information from sources both internal and external to the organization, which then makes that information routinely available to managers for their informed decision making. In turn, an MkIS enables firms to understand better what customers want through analyses of their purchases. This specialized knowledge can translate into purchasing and promotion programs that are tailor-made for customers.

2. **Can certain marketing research practices cause a firm to encounter ethical problems?**

   Marketing researchers have obligations to their subjects and to society to behave in an ethical manner. This responsibility means that marketing researchers must take every precaution to ensure the confidentiality of the data they collect from consumers and the privacy of study participants. Researchers should never misrepresent the purpose of a study; for example, a sales pitch should never be cast as a marketing research study. Finally, the results of research studies should be reported fully. If data or parts of the study are ignored, the results might be misinterpreted.

3. **What are the necessary steps to conduct marketing research?**

There are five steps in the marketing research process. The first step is to define objectives and research needs, which sounds so simple that managers often gloss over it. But this step is crucial to the success of any research project because, quite basically, the research must answer those questions that are important for making decisions. In the second step, designing the research project, researchers identify the type of data that is needed, whether primary or secondary, on the basis of the objectives of the project from Step 1, and then determine the type of research that enables them to collect those data. The third step involves deciding on the data collection process and collecting the data. Depending on the research objectives and the findings from the secondary data search, researchers will choose either exploratory or conclusive research. Exploratory research usually involves observation, in-depth interviews, or projective techniques, whereas if the project calls for conclusive research, the researchers may perform a survey or an experiment, or use scanner and panel data. The fourth step is to analyze and interpret the data, and the fifth and final step is to prepare the findings for presentation. Although these steps appear to progress linearly, researchers often work backward through the process as they learn at each step.

4. **What are primary and secondary data, and when should each type be used?**

Secondary data are pieces of information that have been collected from other sources, such as the U.S. Census, internal company sources, the Internet, books, articles, trade associations, or syndicated data services. Primary data are data collected to address specific research needs, usually through observation, focus groups, interviews, surveys, or experiments. Research projects typically start with secondary research, which provides a background for what information is already known and what research has been done previously. Also, compared with primary research, secondary research is quicker, easier, and less expensive, and it requires less methodological expertise. However, secondary research likely was collected for reasons other than those pertaining to the specific problem at hand, which means the information may be dated, biased, or simply not specific enough to answer the research questions. Primary research, in contrast, can be designed to answer very specific questions, but it also can be expensive and time-consuming.

Key Terms

- churn, 297
- conclusive research, 284
- data, 294
- data mining, 277
- data warehouses, 277
- experimental research, 293
- exploratory research, 284
- focus group interview, 286

- in-depth interview, 285
- information, 294
- marketing information system (MkIS), 277
- marketing research, 276
- observation, 285
- panel research, 294
- primary data, 284

- projective technique, 288
- questionnaire, 288
- scanner research, 293
- secondary data, 281
- structured questions, 290
- survey, 288
- syndicated data, 281
- unstructured questions, 290

Marketing Applications

1. A large department store collects data about what its customers buy and stores these data in a data warehouse. If you were the store's buyer for men's shoes, what would you want to know from the data warehouse that would help you be a more successful buyer?

2. Identify a not-for-profit organization that might use marketing research, and describe one example of a meaningful research project that it might conduct. Discuss how this project would be useful to the organization.

3. Marketing researchers do not always go through the steps in the marketing research process in sequential order. Provide an example of a research project that might not follow this sequence.

4. A bathroom fixture supply store is trying to determine if there is a significant market for its type of merchandise in a specific location where it is considering putting a store. Would it be most likely to use primary or secondary data, or a combination of the two, to answer this question?

5. A high-tech firm has just developed a new technology to correct bad vision without surgery or contact lenses. The company needs to estimate the demand for such a service. Would it use primary or secondary data, or a combination of the two?

6. A bank manager notices that by the time customers get to the teller, they seem irritated and impatient. She wants to investigate the problem further, so she hires you to design a research project to figure out what is bothering the customers. What type of research method would you recommend? Is it an exploratory or conclusive method?

7. PomWonderful has developed a coffee-flavored pomegranate beverage, and it wants to determine if it should begin to market it throughout the United States. The company used two separate studies for the advertising campaign:

   ■ A focus group to identify the appropriate advertising message for the new beverage.

   ■ A survey to assess the effectiveness of the advertising campaign for the new PomWonderful beverage.

   Which study was exploratory and which was conclusive? What other studies would you recommend PomWonderful undertake?

8. Suppose your university wants to modify its course scheduling procedures to better serve students. What are some secondary sources of information that might be used to conduct research into this topic? Describe how these sources might be used. Describe a method you could use to gather primary research data about the topic. Would you recommend a specific order in obtaining each of theses types of data? Explain your answer.

9. Marshall is planning to launch a new sandwich shop and is trying to decide what features and price would interest consumers. He sends a request for a proposal to four marketing research vendors, and three respond, as described in the table below.

   Which vendor should Marshall use? Explain your rationale for picking this vendor over the others.

Vendor A	Vendor B	Vendor C
The vendor that Marshall has used in the past estimates it can get the job done for $200,000 and in two months. The vendor plans to do a telephone-based survey analysis and use secondary data from the U.S. Census.	Marshall's key competitor has used this vendor, which claims that it can get the job done for $150,000 and in one month. This vendor plans to do a telephone-based survey analysis and use secondary data. During a discussion pertaining to its price and time estimates, the vendor indicates it will draw on insights it has learned from a recent report prepared for one of Marshall's competitors.	This well-known vendor has recently started to focus on the restaurant industry. It quotes a price of $180,000 and a time of one month. The vendor plans to conduct a Web-based survey analysis and use secondary data.

Quiz Yourself

www.mhhe.com/ grewal2e

1. Company sales invoices, Census data, and trade association statistics are examples of:
   a. primary data.
   b. data mines.
   c. secondary data.
   d. simplistic data.
   e. exploratory data.

2. Bianca's discount home furnishings store is in a strip mall. She wants to know what other businesses in the strip mall her customers visit when they come to her store. To collect information for this objective, Bianca will most likely use:
   a. door-to-door surveys.
   b. focus group interviews.
   c. observation.
   d. sales invoices.
   e. Census data.

(Answers to these two questions are provided on page 623.)

Go to www.mhhe.com/grewal2e to practice an additional 11 questions.

Net Savvy

1. Go to the Web site for the Gallup Organization (www.gallup.com), which administers public opinion polls. Choose two different topics from the site with recent survey results and identify at least two that focus on different topics. Print out the results to both, and identify the objectives of the surveys. How are they similar, and how do they differ? Discuss one of the major findings from each survey, and provide an interpretation of the data.

2. Visit the Epinions.com Web site (www.epinions.com), a clearinghouse for consumer reviews about different products and services. Think of a particular business with which you are familiar, and review the ratings and comments for that business. Discuss the extent to which this site might be useful to a marketer for that company who needs to gather market research about the company and its competitors. Identify the type of research this process involves—secondary or primary? Exploratory or conclusive?

Chapter Case Study

HOLLYWOOD: RESEARCHING A BLOCKBUSTER[43]

If you made a $150 million investment in a movie, you likely would do everything you could to make it a success, right? So would movie studios, and that's why they invest in rigorous marketing research before they ever release a new movie. The entire movie-making process—which spans optioning, actor selection, script acceptance, advertising, theatrical releases, home media, television rights, and library sales—can take up to three years or more. Thus, even though the process of making a movie—or at least most movies—is more art than science, some very scientific research techniques have become best practices in the movie industry.[44]

Among the most well-known uses of marketing research in Hollywood is prerelease test screenings. During these early, invitation-only viewings of a movie, audiences react to, comment on, and provide feedback about the initial cuts of a film. In most cases today, the movie studio contracts this process out to one of the firms that specialize in audience feedback, such as Nielsen NRG, a division of the Nielsen Company, which itself focuses on serving the entertainment industry.[45] The marketing research company carefully selects several audiences to reflect diverse demographic segments; that way, the movie studio has sufficient information to estimate both the earning potential of the movie among different target markets and the changes it might make to improve that potential.

Let's use a fictional example to examine the test screening process: Paramount is making a blockbuster movie about an archeologist who successfully fights off an alien invasion of Earth but dies in the end, heroically saving the love of his life. Depending on its research budget, the marketing research company that Paramount hires might start by surveying potential viewers about their interest in action films, aliens, and the actors who play the main characters.

Imagine that this research suggests that two market segments likely will enjoy the film and therefore that these filmgoers should be represented at test screenings—namely, men under 25 years and women under 25 years of age. The research firm then must determine the level of detail it should measure, depending on its mandate from the studio. Some movie studios just want a general sense of the film's popularity so that they can allocate their advertising budgets effectively. But Paramount is betting a lot on this summer blockbuster, so it wants scene-by-scene feedback from the prescreening audiences.

At this point, the research firm has several additional choices about how to collect information during the movie. During the screening, it might engage in human observation and carefully record which scenes make the audience laugh or applaud. Alternatively, with mechanical observation, the research firm plants microphones throughout the theater to record the decibel levels of the laughter the movie provokes.[46] In our hypothetical case, let's assume the research firm opts to hand out keypads to the audience members, on which they record whether they like or dislike each scene in the movie as it appears on the screen. At the end of the screening, the research firm conducts in-depth interviews with all audience members to get a better sense of their overall impressions of the film.

How well do you know movie audiences? What do you think they said in response to our alien movie? Those familiar with the industry would likely predict, as we do in our fictional example, that the research firm will find that approximately 90 percent of the audience, and nearly 100 percent of the women, disliked the ending, in which the main character dies. After the research firm takes these results to Paramount, the movie studio likely will choose to change the ending of the film and ensure a happy ending for both the hero and his true love.

Test screenings are just one of the many methods that movie studios employ to increase the chances that they will make a blockbuster. Two other areas that receive a lot of attention are actor selection and advertising budget allocation.

To continue the alien movie example, let's go back in time a bit and suppose that the director has yet to start filming but is trying to choose between Leonardo DiCaprio and Harrison Ford for the lead male role and Kate Winslet and Cameron Diaz for the lead female role. Some directors simply choose the actors that make them feel most comfortable, but another option is to use research from the Hollywood Stock Exchange (http://www.hsx.com). This "exchange" actually is a prediction market that HSX Research runs. Prediction markets try to harness the wisdom of crowds to predict future outcomes; in this case, HSX has created a game that enables consumers to buy and sell shares of movies and actors in a simulated stock market. According to HSX Research, the 1.6 million traders on the HSX Web site predict the popularity of a movie or actor months in advance with remarkable accuracy.[47] In turn, publications like *Forbes* and *The New York Times* cite the Hollywood Stock Exchange as a key example of how firms can efficiently collect information by making market research participants think they are participating in a game. Some industry experts claim that a movie's HSX stock price is the most accurate predictor of actual box office receipts.[48]

The movie-making process is long and involves large amounts of money. Test screenings and prediction markets are just two of the most common methods to evaluate a movie, but as the value and cost of movies continue to increase, so will the use of marketing research.

Questions

1. Do you think that marketing research improves movies' quality, improves the chance of making a blockbuster, or both?

2. Does it matter whether you do the research in-house or hire a marketing research firm?

3. Visit the top 15 movie stocks according to HSX (http://www.movies.hsx. com/moviestockindex.htm). Do you agree with the predictions of the Hollywood Stock Exchange? How would you use a tool like this if you were a movie producer?

4. Other than prediction markets, which marketing research techniques would you plan to use if you were investing millions of dollars in a movie?

5. What are some ways that a movie studio can test advertisements for a movie, both before the launch and after the movie appears in theaters?

USING SECONDARY DATA TO ASSESS CUSTOMER LIFETIME VALUE (CLV)

This appendix examines how secondary data from customer transactions can help determine the value of a customer over time. Specifically, **customer lifetime value (CLV)** refers to the expected financial contribution from a particular customer to the firm's profits over the course of their entire relationship.[1]

To estimate CLV, firms use past behaviors to forecast future purchases, the gross margin from these purchases, and the costs associated with servicing the customers. Some costs associated with maintaining customer relationships include communicating with customers through advertising, personal selling, or other promotional vehicles to acquire their business initially and then retain them over time.

Measures of customer lifetime value typically apply to a group or segment of customers and use available secondary data. A basic formula for CLV,[2] with the assumption that revenues and profits arrive at the start of the year, is as follows:

$$CLV = \sum_{t=1}^{T} \frac{[\text{profit at t} \times \text{retention rate}^{t-1}]}{(1 + i)^{t-1}} - \text{acquisition costs}$$

To implement this CLV formula, we must answer the following questions:

1. How many years (t) can we expect to do business with a customer? The total number of years is denoted by T.

2. What can we expect the annual profits to be from an individual customer or an average customer? These profits are based on sales minus the costs of merchandise and the costs of serving and retaining the customer.

3. What is the retention rate, that is, the average percentage of customers who continue to purchase from the firm from one time period to another? A 90 percent retention rate means that if we have 100 customers in the first year, we will have 90 at the beginning of the second year.

4. What is the discount rate (i)? The discount rate is based on the idea that a dollar is worth less in the future than it is today, so the company can use it to adjust future profits and determine a customer's value today for the customer's purchases in the future. For example, if the discount rate is 10 percent, $100 in profits at the beginning of year 2 are worth only $90.91 (100/(1 + .1)) at the beginning of year 1.

Consider Gregory Missoni, a fairly new client of Very Clean Cleaners who switched from his other dry cleaner because Very Clean sent him $100 worth of coupons in a direct mailing.

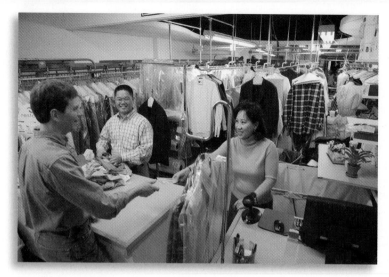

Very Clean Cleaners should consider a Customer's Lifetime Value to determine its service levels.

Greg just picked up his $200 shirt from Very Clean and found that the dry cleaner had broken a brown button and replaced it with a white button. When he complained, the clerk acted as if it were no big deal. Greg explained to the clerk that it was a very expensive shirt that deserved more careful handling, then asked to speak with the manager. At this point, how important is it that the manager makes sure Greg is satisfied, so that he will continue to bring his dry cleaning to Very Clean Cleaners? To answer this question, the manager uses the following information:

- It cost Very Clean $100 to acquire Greg as a customer. Thus, the acquisition cost is $100.

- Very Clean expects Greg to remain a client for 5 years (time horizon T = 5 years).

- Very Clean expects to make a $1,000 profit each year from Greg's dry cleaning.

- On average, 10 percent of customers defect to another cleaner each year. Therefore, the expected retention rate is 90 percent.

- The discount rate is 10 percent per year (i in this illustration). For simplicity, Very Clean assumes all profits are accrued at the beginning of the year.

Applying the formula, such that CLV equals the profits from years 1–5, less the acquisition costs, we obtain:

$$CLV = \underbrace{\frac{\$1,000 \times (.90)^0}{(1+.1)^0}}_{\text{Year 1}} + \underbrace{\frac{\$1,000 \times (.90)^1}{(1+.1)^1}}_{\text{Year 2}} + \underbrace{\frac{\$1,000 \times (.90)^2}{(1+.1)^2}}_{\text{Year 3}}$$
$$+ \underbrace{\frac{\$1,000 \times (.90)^3}{(1+.1)^3}}_{\text{Year 4}} + \underbrace{\frac{\$1,000 \times (.90)^4}{(1+.1)^4}}_{\text{Year 5}} - \$100$$

Or

CLV = $1,000 + $818.2 + $669.4 + $547.7 + $ 448.1 − $100 = $3,383.40

Let's see how the formula works. The expected profit from Greg is $1,000 per year. Very Clean assumes profits accrue at the beginning of the year, so the profits for the first year equal $1,000; they are not affected by the retention rate or the discount rate.

However, the retention and discount rates have effects on the profits for the subsequent time periods. In the second year, the retention rate, which Very Clean determined was 90 percent (i.e., 90 percent of customers continue to do business with it) modifies profits, such that expected profits in the second year equal $1,000 × 90% = $900. Moreover, the discount rate is applied such that the profits received in the second year are worth less than if they had been received in the first year. Therefore, the $900 received at the beginning of the second year must be divided by 1.1, which is equivalent to $818.20.

Using similar calculations for the third year, the expected profits adjusted for retention are $1,000 × .9 × .9 = $810. The discount rate then reduces the profit to $810 ÷ 1.1^2 = $669.40 in today's dollars. (Note that the discount rate is squared because it refers to two years in the future.) After calculating the adjusted and discounted profits for the fourth and fifth years in similar fashion, we realize the sum

VALUE CREATION

Section Four devotes three chapters to how marketing contributes to value creation. Chapter 10 and Chapter 11 explore strategies and tactics in the development and management of successful products and their brands. While many of the concepts involved in developing and managing services are similar to those of physical brands, Chapter 12 addresses the unique challenges of the marketing of services.

Assessing the Marketplace

Understanding the Marketplace

Targeting the Marketplace

Value Creation

Value Capture

Value Delivery: Designing the Channel and Supply Chain

Value Communication

of estimated discounted profits for five years is $3,483.40. However, we still must subtract the $100 spent to acquire Greg, which provides a CLV of $3,383.40.

According to this analysis, it would be a good idea for the manager to take a long-term perspective when evaluating how to respond to Greg's complaint about his button. Greg cannot be viewed as a $2.50 customer, as he would be if Very Clean determined his value based on the cost of laundering his shirt, nor should he be viewed as a $200 customer, based on the cost of the shirt. He actually is worth a lot more than that.

For illustrative purposes, we have simplified the CLV calculations in this example. We assumed that the average profits remain constant at $1,000. But firms usually expect profits to grow over time, or else grow, level off, and then perhaps decline. Retention costs, such as special promotions used to keep Greg coming back, also do not appear in our illustration, though such additional costs would reduce annual profits and CLV. Finally, we assume a five-year time horizon; the CLV obviously would differ for longer or shorter periods. For an infinite time horizon, with first period payments upfront, the formula becomes fairly simple:[3]

$$CLV = profits \times \left[1 + \frac{\text{retention rate}}{(1 + \text{discount rate} + \text{retention rate})} \right]$$
$$- \text{acquisition costs}$$

$$= \$1,000 \times \left[1 + \frac{.9}{(1 + .1 - .9)} \right] - \$100$$
$$= \$1,000 \times (1 + 4.5) - \$100$$
$$= \$5,500 - \$100 = \$5,400$$

This illustration thus explains how firms can use secondary data to calculate CLV; it further demonstrates the importance of knowing a customer's lifetime value when executing marketing tactics and strategies. Several Customer Lifetime Value problems can be accessed at www.mhhe.com/grewal2e.

PRODUCT, BRANDING, AND PACKAGING DECISIONS

- How do firms adjust their product lines to changing market conditions?
- Why are brands valuable to firms?
- How do firms implement different branding strategies?
- How do a product's packaging and label contribute to a firm's overall strategy?

In 1984, Michael Jordan was a top-three draft pick, chosen by the Chicago Bulls after Hakeem Olajuwon and Sam Bowie had gone to other teams. He was predicted to be good, but few likely could have predicted he would change the face of basketball and become what many sports fans consider the best player that will ever be.

Around the same time, the athletic shoe company Nike was in a tough spot, facing diminishing sales as the running shoe mania that had swept the United States in the early 1980s appeared to be coming to an end, taking Nike's profits with it. Intrigued by Jordan's charisma and friendly appeal, demonstrated in a couple of previous endorsement deals, the company approached the young star.[1]

At the time, endorsement deals for athletic shoes centered primarily on getting the athlete to wear the products on the field or court. For example, Converse kept basketball great Larry Bird supplied in sneakers, but he never appeared in specific advertising for the company. The shoe companies tended to avoid investing too much in a single athlete. Yet Nike went a different route with Jordan, proposing that it would create an entire line named after him and would run advertising featuring him, in addition to asking him to wear the shoes.

The first Air Jordans were notably different from the conventional basketball shoe. Primarily, they were bright red and black, not white, which meant that every time Jordan wore them on the court, the NBA fined him $5,000 for being out of uniform. It was a marketing bonanza. Nike happily paid each fine, thrilled with the press that the controversy stirred. And people bought the shoes in droves, even despite the then-astronomical price of $125 per pair.

Within a couple of years, Jordan was gaining more and more recognition, especially after he won the 1986 Slam Dunk contest with a high-flying leap from the top of the arc, his legs splayed, and his arm, ball in palm, seeming to touch the sky. So when Nike got around to designing the Air Jordan III, it again did something few other endorsement advertisers had ever done: It asked Jordan to help it design the new shoe, then replaced Nike's well-known, valuable "swoosh" logo with a silhouette of Jordan dunking the ball.

The strategy represented a huge risk, because the swoosh logo was widely recognized as a branding tool. But by betting on Jordan's popularity, as well as the popularity of the shoes bearing his name, Nike created yet another logo that provided it widespread recognition and great value. Eventually, Nike spun Air Jordans off into its own subbrand, with the now world-famous Jordan silhouette as the only logo on the shoe.

The Air Jordan XXIII, released in January 2008, promises to be another big seller, especially considering the metaphoric connection it has to Jordan's playing number (23) during his championship years with the Bulls. But Nike isn't relying solely on Jordan's appeal anymore to ensure sufficient sales of its $185 sneaker. It also promises a shoe made of sustainable materials, made through a manufacturing process that creates minimal waste.[2]

The unsurpassed success of the collaboration between a beloved national athlete and the shoe company prompted the latter to continue down the same path with others. Some deals succeeded as well as Jordan's; Tiger Woods has extended the company's reach into the world of golf, and his deal requires that he wears all Nike gear, not just a pair of shoes. With the famous swoosh appearing on his shirts and hats every time Woods wins yet another tournament, Tiger is closely associated with Nike.[3]

But deals with other athletes have been less successful; Nike signed Michelle Wie to a deal when she was 15 years old, and the teen phenom has yet to win a major tournament on the LPGA golf circuit. Even more worrisome for Nike is the potential backlash against its brand when its endorsees run into legal trouble, as when Kobe Bryant was accused of rape. He continued to be retained by Nike, and ultimately was exonerated. However, when Michael Vick was convicted of dogfighting, he was dropped as an endorser by the company.

● ● ●

As a key element of a firm's marketing mix (the four Ps), product strategies are central to the creation of value for the consumer. A **product** is anything that is of value to a consumer and can be offered through a voluntary marketing exchange. In addition to *goods,* such as soft drinks, or *services,* such as a stay in a hotel, products might also be *places* (e.g., Universal Studio theme park), *ideas* (e.g., "stop smoking"), *organizations* (e.g., The American Red Cross), *people* (e.g., Arnold Schwarzenegger), or *communities* (e.g., MotleyFool.com) that create value for consumers in their respective competitive marketing arenas.

This chapter begins with a discussion of how firms adjust their product lines to meet and respond to changing market conditions. Then we turn our attention to branding—why are brands valuable to the firm, and what are the different branding strategies firms use? We also never want to underestimate the value of a product's packaging and label. These elements must send out a strong message from the shelf: Buy me! The final section of this chapter examines packaging and labeling issues.

PRODUCT ASSORTMENT AND PRODUCT LINE DECISIONS

The complete set of all products offered by a firm is called its product assortment or product mix. An abbreviated version of Colgate-Palmolive's product assortment is shown in Exhibit 10.1. The product assortment typically consists of various product lines, which are groups of associated items, such as items that consumers use together or think of as part of a group of similar products. Colgate-Palmolive's product lines include oral care, personal care, home care, and pet nutrition.

Within each product line, there are often multiple product categories. A product category is an assortment of items that the customer sees as reasonable substitutes for one another or are used under similar circumstances. For example, in the oral care product line, Colgate-Palmolive offers several categories: toothpaste, toothbrushes, kids' oral care products, whitening products, floss, and oral first aid. Each category within a product line may use the same or different brands, which are the names, terms, designs, symbols, or any other features that identify one seller's good or service as distinct from those of other sellers.[4] For instance, Colgate-Palmolive offers several brands of toothbrushes (e.g., Plus, Whitening, Massager, Navigator).

Product assortments can also be described in terms of their breadth and depth. A firm's product line breadth (sometimes also referred to as variety) represents the number of product lines offered by the firm; Colgate-Palmolive has four. Product line depth, in contrast, is the number of categories within a product line. Within Colgate-Palmolive's oral care line, for example, there are several categories—toothpaste, toothbrushes, kids' products, and so forth. Its pet nutrition product line, however, comprises fewer categories and therefore has less depth.

EXHIBIT 10.1	Colgate-Palmolive Product Assortment			
	Product Lines			
	Oral Care	**Personal Care**	**Home Care**	**Pet Nutrition**
Product Categories	*Toothpaste* (Colgate Total) *Toothbrush* (Colgate Plus) *Kids' products* (Colgate Barbie Bubble Fruit toothpaste) *Whitening products* (Colgate Simply White) *Floss* (Colgate Total Dental Floss) *Oral first aid* (Colgate Orabase)	*Deodorants* (Speed Stick) *Bar soap* (Irish Spring) *Body wash* (Soft Soap) *Hand wash* (Soft Soap) *Men's toiletries* (Skin Bracer Aftershave)	*Dishwashing liquid* (Palmolive) *Automatic dishwashing liquid* (Palmolive) *Household cleaners* (Ajax) *Dish wipes* (Palmolive) *Fabric conditioners* (Ultra, Suavitel)	Hill's Pet Nutrition, Inc.—subsidiary *Dog food* (Science Diet) *Cat food* (Science Diet)

Source: www.colgate.com, accessed September 9, 2008.

Pepsi has realized significant growth of sales and profits by its introduction of the Diet Pepsi Max line.

Within each product category are a number of individual items called stock keeping units (SKUs), which are the smallest unit available for inventory control. Within the toothpaste category, for instance, Colgate-Palmolive offers 39 Colgate SKUs that represent various sizes, flavors, and configurations of Colgate Luminous, Colgate Max, Colgate Total, and Colgate Fresh Confidence.[5] The category depth is the number of SKUs within a category.

The decision to expand or contract product lines and categories depends on several industry-, consumer-, and firm-level factors. Among the industry factors, firms expand their product lines when it is relatively easy to enter a specific market (entry barriers are low) and/or when there is a substantial market opportunity.[6] When firms add new product categories and brands to their product assortments, they often earn significant sales and profits, as was the case with Doritos' Cool Ranch product line, Oil of Olay's Definity antiaging products, Chrysler's minivans, and Pepsi's Diet Max line.[7]

However, unchecked and unlimited product line extensions may have adverse consequences. Too much variety in the product assortment is often too costly to maintain, and too many brands may weaken the firm's brand reputation.[8] In the past several years, for example, Revlon undertook a significant restructuring. It introduced a new line, Vital Radiance, aimed at women over the age of 45 years. But when it realized this line was cutting into the sales of its other brands, Revlon eliminated the Vital Radiance line, forced out its CEO, and cut jobs in an attempt to refocus on those products and markets that were doing well.[9]

Now let's look at why firms change their product mix's breadth or depth, as well as product line decisions for services.

Change Product Mix Breadth

Firms may change their product mix breadth by either adding to or deleting categories.

Increase Breadth   Firms often add new product categories to capture new or evolving markets, increase sales, and compete in new venues. Since the growth of "designer" jeans has slowed, several designers have branched out. True Religion Brand Jeans are increasing its merchandise categories to become more of an all-encompassing lifestyle brand rather than just a denim company. It now makes apparel, belts, swimwear, a fragrance, and handbags. Similarly, Seven For All Mankind, Antik, and other premium denim companies are branching out into other categories.[10]

Decrease Breadth   Sometimes it is necessary to delete entire product lines to address changing market conditions or meet internal strategic priorities. Shortly after expanding its offerings to include a line of heated breakfast sandwiches,

Starbucks began phasing out the offerings. According to Starbucks' CEO Howard Schultz, the decision marks the company's effort to "build for the long-term and get back to the roots and the core of our heritage, which is the leading roaster of specialty coffee in the world."[11] Without having to worry about sandwiches, the coffee chain can focus instead on competing effectively with competitors such as Dunkin' Donuts and increase its flexibility to invest in new product lines in the future.

In the 1980s frozen yogurt became a low-fat, healthy substitute for ice cream. In the 1990s, the government allowed ice-cream companies to advertise "reduced fat" on their labels. This caused a sharp decline in the sales of frozen yogurt. TCBY, which began as a frozen yogurt shop, sold ice cream from 1996 to 2004, but recently reduced its breadth by eliminating ice cream so that it can concentrate on its original product category, frozen yogurt. The chain is renovating its stores, and touting the immune system and weight control benefits of eating frozen yogurt in its promotions.[12]

Change Product Assortment Depth

As with product line breadth, firms occasionally either add to or delete from their product line depth.

Increase Depth Firms may add items or SKUS to address changing consumer preferences or preempt competitors while boosting sales. Johnson & Johnson's Band-Aid was introduced in 1920 with a one-size-fits-all product. Today it has more than 40 products that help to heal cuts and scrapes. Band-Aid is constantly increasing its depth by introducing new products that solve every possible wound or blister problem. One of its most recent products, called Blister Block, prevents the formation of blisters.[13]

Decrease Depth From time to time it is also necessary to delete SKUs to realign resources. The decision to delete SKUs is never taken lightly. Generally, substantial investments have been made to develop and manufacture the products. Consumer goods firms make pruning decisions regularly to eliminate unprofitable items and refocus their marketing efforts on more profitable items. The spice company McCormick eliminates dozens of products each year including sauces, Golden Dipt products, and Grill Mates seasonings. The company's growth strategy focuses on introducing new products, increasing overall profit margins, and reducing the complexity of its product lines. Increased commodity costs have also forced lower margin products to be eliminated. McCormick's B2B sales to food manufacturers have increased 51 percent because these firms switched to the new, more desirable products.[14]

Product Line Decisions for Services

Many of the strategies used to make product line decisions for physical products can also be applied to services. For instance, a service provider like a bank typically offers different product lines for its business and retail (consumer) accounts; those product lines are further divided into categories based on the needs of different target markets.

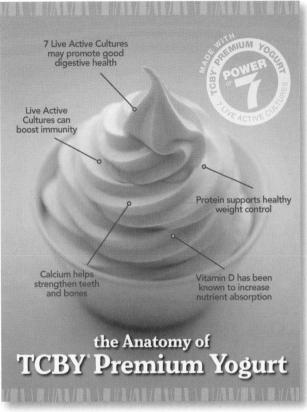

the Anatomy of
TCBY® Premium Yogurt

7 Live Active Cultures may promote good digestive health

Live Active Cultures can boost immunity

Protein supports healthy weight control

Calcium helps strengthen teeth and bones

Vitamin D has been known to increase nutrient absorption

TCBY has decreased its breadth by eliminating ice cream so it can concentrate on the health benefits of yogurt.

Johnson & Johnson's Band-Aid Brand has more than 40 SKUs.

On the retail side, banks offer savings and checking accounts to individual consumers. The different types of accounts thus are equivalent to SKUs. Bank of America (BofA), one of the world's largest financial institutions, which serves more than 59 million customers in the United States and additional customers in 175 other countries,[15] offers a variety of checking account products to meet the needs of its different target markets. For example, with Bank of America Advantage Checking®, customers who maintain higher balances are rewarded with preferred interest and free banking services. For customers older than 55 years of age, BofA offers Bank of America Advantage for Seniors®, which allows customers to invest in CDs and use up to $2,500 of their value, without early withdrawal penalties, for expenditures or emergencies. BofA even offers college accounts, like CampusEdge® Checking, with low opening deposits and low fees.[16]

CHECK YOURSELF

1. What is the difference between product line breadth versus depth?
2. Why change product line breadth?
3. Why change product line depth?

BRANDING

Branding provides a way for a firm to differentiate its product offerings from those of its competitors and can be used to represent the name of a firm and its entire product assortment (General Motors), one product line (Chevrolet), or a single item (Corvette). Brand names, logos, symbols, characters, slogans, jingles, and even distinctive packages constitute the various brand elements firms use,[17] which they usually choose to be easy for consumers to recognize and remember. For example, most consumers are aware of the Mercedes-Benz star and would recognize it even if the word Mercedes-Benz did not appear on the product or in an advertisement. Exhibit 10.2 summarizes these brand elements.

Most consumers are aware of the Mercedes-Benz star and would recognize it even if the word "Mercedes-Benz" did not appear on the product or in an advertisement.

300 horsepower is fast.
400 will take your breath away.
That's why we gave it 451.

Mercedes-Benz

EXHIBIT 10.2	What Makes a Brand?
Brand Element	**Description**
Brand name	The spoken component of branding, it can describe the product or service/product characteristics and/or be composed of words invented or derived from colloquial or contemporary language. Examples include Comfort Inn (suggests product characteristics), Saturn (no association with the product), or Avanade (invented term).
URLs (uniform resource locators) or domain names	The location of pages on the Internet, which often substitutes for the firm's name, such as Yahoo! and Amazon.
Logos and symbols	Logos are visual branding elements that stand for corporate names or trademarks. Symbols are logos without words. Examples include the Nike swoosh and the Mercedes star.
Characters	Brand symbols that could be human, animal, or animated. Examples include the Pillsbury Doughboy and the Keebler Elves.
Slogans	Short phrases used to describe the brand or persuade consumers about some characteristics of the brand. Examples include State Farm's "Like A Good Neighbor" and Dunkin Donuts' "America Runs On Dunkin."
Jingles	Audio messages about the brand that are composed of words or distinctive music. Examples are Intel's four-note sound signature that accompanies the "Intel Inside" slogan.

Source: Kevin Lane Keller, *Strategic Brand Management*, 2nd ed. (Upper Saddle River, NJ: Prentice Hall, 2003).

Value of Branding for the Customer and the Marketer

Brands add value to merchandise and services beyond physical and functional characteristics or the pure act of performing the service.[18] Let's examine some ways in which brands add value for both customers and the firm.

Brand makes a difference: Could you tell the difference between these brands by tasting them?

Brands Facilitate Purchasing   Brands are often easily recognized by consumers and, because they signify a certain quality level and contain familiar attributes, brands help consumers make quick decisions.[19] Consumers recognize orange juice brands like Sunny Delight, Tropicana, Florida's Natural, Simply Orange, Minute Maid, and Odwalla. From promotions, past purchases, or information from friends and family, they have a perception of a brand's level of quality, how it tastes, how healthy it is, whether it is a good value, and most important, whether they like it and want to buy it. Brands enable customers to differentiate one firm or product from another. Without branding, how could we easily tell the difference between Minute Maid and Tropicana without a taste?

Brands Establish Loyalty   Over time and with continued use, consumers learn to trust certain brands. They know, for instance, that Band-Aid bandages always perform in the exact same way. Many customers become loyal to certain brands in much the same way that you or your friends likely have become loyal to your college. They wouldn't consider switching brands and, in some cases, feel a strong affinity to certain brands. For instance, Coca-Cola drinkers don't drink Pepsi, and wouldn't dare touch a Dr Pepper. Companies are applying innovative techniques to strengthen brand loyalty on their Internet sites, as Power of the Internet 10.1 describes.

Brands Protect from Competition and Price Competition   Strong brands are somewhat protected from competition and price competition. Because such brands are more established in the market and have a more loyal customer base, neither competitive pressures on price nor retail-level competition is as threatening to the firm. For instance, Chemise Lacoste is known for its polo shirts. Although many

Power of the Internet 10.1

Luxury Designers Build Loyalty through Web Site Branding[20]

Because 99 percent of people who earn a minimum household income of $150,000 have Internet access at home, luxury brands are starting to find ways to benefit from the online video and interactive Web features available on the Internet. Luxury brands used to depend on print ads and retailers for advertising, but reaching out to customers on Web sites, especially those with cutting-edge features, is proving valuable.

Older Web technology could make products look too much the same; what is the visual difference between a $499 Marc Jacobs shoe and $14 Target shoe? But modern Internet technology evokes a stronger connection with the brand and the products than do print ads. Leading this revolution is Createthe Group, which has created Web site designs for high-fashion sites such as Miu Miu, Balenciaga, and Marc Jacobs. Through these designers' Web sites designers can offer more content to consumers than they could through retailers.

For example, the Christian Dior Fall/Winter Haute Couture extravaganza was available online the morning after the show. Balenciaga.com (www.balenciaga.com) focuses on its fashion heritage by featuring archival footage from the 1960 spring/summer runway show. Prada.com (www.prada.com) features 20 short films about its production process, including shots showing artists sketching handbags, the making of a Prada ballerina slipper, and more. The featured craftsmanship reminds consumers why they pay premiums for these products. And then there's the Marc Jacobs site, which posts insider gossip and news from the employees—content that luxury consumers live for.

Consumers spend more time on these Web sites than ever before, probably because the video, three-dimensional branding, and luxury appeals help create emotional connections with customers. Luxury retailers can distinguish themselves from other producers by allowing customers to feel as though they really know what goes on behind the scenes.

---

similar brands are available and some retailers offer their own brands, Lacoste is perceived to be of superior quality, garners a certain status among its users, and can therefore command a premium price.

Brands Reduce Marketing Costs   Firms with well-known brands can spend relatively less on marketing costs than firms with little-known brands because the brand sells itself. People have become familiar with Target's red-and-white bull's-eye logo, so its advertisements don't need to explain who the company is or what it does. People just know.

Brands Are Assets   Brands are also assets that can be legally protected through trademarks and copyrights and thus constitute a unique ownership for the firm. Firms sometimes have to fight to keep their brands "pure." Rolex and other Swiss watch companies are ever watchful to ensure that the value of their brands is not diluted with counterfeit merchandise or sales through nonauthorized dealers. Louis Vuitton fights an ongoing battle to keep handbags with slightly altered versions of its logos from sidewalks and shops. In the Internet age, the fight has extended to keyword branding; American Airlines has brought suit against Google, asserting that the search engine infringes on its trademark by using "American Airlines" as a keyword that triggers paid advertisements posted by other companies.[21]

Brands Impact Market Value   Having well-known brands can have a direct impact on the company's bottom line. The value of a brand can be calculated by

The Rolex brand is such a valuable asset that to protect it, the firm must continually watch for counterfeit merchandise and sales through nonauthorized dealers.

EXHIBIT 10.3	The World's Ten Most Valuable Brands		
Rank	**Brand**	**Country of Ownership**	**Brand Value in 2007 ($ Billions)**
1	Coca-Cola	U.S.	65.3
2	Microsoft	U.S.	58.7
3	IBM	U.S.	57.1
4	GE	U.S.	51.6
5	Nokia	Finland	33.7
6	Toyota	Japan	32.1
7	Intel	U.S.	30.9
8	McDonald's	U.S.	29.4
9	Disney	U.S.	29.2
10	Mercedes	Germany	23.6

Source: http://www.ourfishbowl.com/images/surveys/Interbrand_BGB_2007.pdf (accessed March 15, 2008).

assessing the earning potential of the brand over the next 12 months.[22] The world's 10 most valuable brands appear in Exhibit 10.3.

Brand Equity

The value of a brand translates into brand equity, or the set of assets and liabilities linked to a brand that add to or subtract from the value provided by the product or service.[23] Like the physical possessions of a firm, brands are assets the firm can build, manage, and harness over time to increase its revenue, profitability, and overall value. Firms spend millions of dollars on promotion, advertising, and other marketing efforts throughout a brand's life cycle. These marketing expenditures, if done carefully, result in greater brand recognition, awareness, and consumer loyalty for the brand.

Ralph Lauren has mastered the art of building brand equity by defining its own version of value. The name Ralph Lauren, the ubiquitous polo player, and associated brands like Ralph Lauren, Purple Label, RLX, and Pink Pony have engendered a loyal following throughout North America and the rest of the world. Ralph Lauren merchandise can command prices 50 to 100 percent higher than similar-quality merchandise from lesser known and appreciated designers and manufacturers. The brand, under the tight control of its parent company, has been licensed for tabletop, bed and bath, furniture, paints, broadloom, and gift items.[24] A licensed brand is one in which there is a contractual arrangement between firms, whereby one firm allows another to use its brand name, logo, symbols, and/or characters in exchange for a negotiated fee.[25] These licensed products are manufactured and distributed by firms other than Ralph Lauren, but the brand association earns them greater value.

How do we know how "good" a brand is, or how much equity it has? Experts look at four aspects of a brand to determine its equity: brand awareness, perceived value, brand associations, and brand loyalty.

Brand Awareness　Brand awareness measures how many consumers in a market are familiar with the brand and what it stands for and have an opinion about that brand. The more aware or familiar customers are with a brand, the easier their decision-making process will be. Familiarity matters most for products that are bought without much thought, such as soap or chewing gum. However, brand awareness is also important for infrequently purchased items or items the consumer has never purchased before. If the consumer recognizes the brand, it probably has attributes that make it valuable.[26] For those who have never purchased a Toyota, for instance, just being aware of the brand can help facilitate a purchase.

These brands are so strong that they have become synonymous with the product itself.

Certain brands gain such predominance in a particular product market over time that they become synonymous with the product itself; that is, the brand name starts being used as the generic product category. Examples include Kleenex tissue, Clorox bleach, Xerox copiers, Band-Aid adhesive bandages, and Rollerblade skates. Companies must be vigilant in protecting their brand names, because if they are used so generically, over time, the brand itself can lose its trademark status.

Marketers create brand awareness through repeated exposures of the various brand elements (brand name, logo, symbol, character, packaging, or slogan) in the firm's communications to consumers. Such communication media include advertising and promotions, personal selling, sponsorship and event marketing, publicity, and public relations[27] (see Chapters 17–19). Because consumer awareness is one of the most important steps in creating a strong brand, firms are willing to spend tremendous amounts of money advertising the brand, especially when they think they can reach a lot of potential consumers. Therefore, 30-second spots on television during the Super Bowl sell for an average of $2.7 million, and the last few spots in the game go for as much as $3.3 million.[28]

Perceived Value   Perceived value of a brand is the relationship between a product or service's benefits and its cost. Customers usually determine the offering's value in relationship to that of its close competitors. If they feel a less expensive brand is about the same quality as a premium brand, the perceived value of the cheaper choice is high. For instance, private-label brands, which are brands developed by retailers rather than manufacturers, are generally less expensive than brands developed by manufacturers. These brands, commonly found in supermarkets, drug stores, and in apparel stores, have seen such a rise in popularity in recent years because of their high perceived value.

Brand awareness alone does not ensure a strong brand. Consumers could be aware of a brand but have a negative opinion of its value or of the firm's reputation. Philip Morris is well known as a tobacco company, especially for its Marlboro brands. The Philip Morris holding company, which still owns Philip Morris and at one time owned Kraft Foods, was forced to change its name to Altria Group to shield Kraft Foods against the negative publicity associated with tobacco.[29]

Sarah Jessica Parker designed a sportswear and shoe line for Steve & Barry's with all items priced under $20.

Good marketing raises customers' quality perceptions relative to price; thus, it increases perceived value. Many customers tend to associate higher prices with higher quality, but they also have become more informed and perceptive in recent years. Retailers like Target and Kohl's specialize in providing great value. Certainly, merchandise at these stores is not always of the highest possible quality, and the apparel is not the most fashion-forward. But customers don't necessarily want to buy a paring knife that will last for 50 years or a wastebasket that is suitable for display in a living room, nor do they need to show up at school looking like they came from a fashion show runway. At the same time, these retailers are finding ways to make their offerings even more valuable, such as by hiring high-fashion designers to create reasonably priced lines to feature in their stores. Target pioneered this affordable, well-designed trend with Isaac Mizrahi. H&M has been very successful in hiring Stella McCartney, Karl Lagerfeld, and most recently Roberto Cavalli. Customers are able to snatch up well-designed pieces for H&M prices. Sarah Jessica Parker designed a sportswear and shoe line for Steve & Barry's with all items priced under $20. Although Sarah Jessica Parker is more of a celebrity than a designer, her fashion image is still bringing a special touch to the line. The "Armani Lounge" in the Chelsea Football Club Director's Suite at Stamford Bridge, U.K., is designed by Giorgio Armani.[30]

Brand Associations   **Brand associations** reflect the mental links that consumers make between a brand and its key product attributes, such as a logo, slogan, or famous personality. These brand associations often result from a firm's advertising and promotional efforts. For instance, Toyota's hybrid car, the Prius, is known for being economical, a good value, and stylishly good for the environment. BMW and Audi are associated with performance. Firms also attempt to create specific associations for their brands with positive consumer emotions, such as fun, friendship, good feelings, family gatherings, and parties. State Farm Insurance advertises that "like a good neighbor, State Farm is there." Hallmark Cards associates its brand with helping people show they care with quality: "When you care enough to send the very best." The company's crown logo and its slogan are recognized by over 90 percent of American consumers. The programs on Hallmark television channel are consistent with the brand's wholesome family image.[31]

Firms sometimes even develop a personality for their brands, as if the brand were human. **Brand personality** refers to such a set of human characteristics associated with a brand,[32] which has symbolic or self-expressive meanings for consumers.[33] Brand personality elements could include personal issues such as gender, age, or personality, and/or physical traits such as fresh, smooth, round, clean, or floral.[34] McDonald's has created a fun-loving, youth-oriented brand personality with its golden arches, brightly lit and colored restaurants, exciting and youthful packaging and advertising, and spokesperson and mascot Ronald McDonald, the clown. But in Europe, where consumers embrace a more "sit-down-to-eat" lifestyle than in the United States, McDonald's restaurants are starting to feature cafe lattes, lime-green designer chairs, and dark leather upholstery. To create a brand personality that appeals more to young adults and professionals and combat its image of unappealing décor, the restaurant chain is spending more than $828 million to remodel 1,280 European outlets.[35]

Brand Loyalty   **Brand loyalty** occurs when a consumer buys the same brand's product or service repeatedly over time rather than buy from multiple suppliers within the same category.[36] Therefore, brand-loyal customers are an important source of value for firms. First, such consumers are often less sensitive to price. In return, firms sometimes reward loyal consumers with loyalty or customer relationship management (CRM) programs, such as points customers can redeem for extra discounts or free services, advance notice of sale items, and invitations to special events sponsored by the company. Second, the marketing costs of reaching loyal consumers are much lower because the firm does not have to spend money on advertising and promotion campaigns to attract these customers. Loyal consumers simply do not need persuasion or an extra push to buy the firm's brands. Third, loyal customers tend to praise the virtues of their favorite products, retailers, or services to others. This positive word-of-mouth reaches potential customers and reinforces the perceived value of current customers, all at no cost to the firm. Finally, a high level of brand loyalty insulates the firm from competition because, as we noted in Chapter 2, brand-loyal customers do not switch to competitors' brands, even when provided with a variety of incentives.

Firms can manage brand loyalty through a variety of CRM programs. They create associations and clubs to provide a community feeling among loyal customers. Perhaps the firms best able to create such a sense of community are sports teams, which enjoy existing customer loyalty and then can improve it through their CRM efforts. For example, the United Kingdom–based soccer club Manchester United may not have won a championship title since 2004, but the term "ManU" means something to soccer fans all over the world.[37] These fans can join the club's "One United" community. Their membership card arrives with a personalized letter from the club's coach, Sir Alex Ferguson, which allows them online access to purchase ManU-related products, read topical articles, participate in discussion forums, and even download ManU screensavers. Dedicated fans do their banking with ManU Finance, obtain their mobile phones through ManU Mobile (available with, of course, ManU ringtones), and join one of the more than 200 local fan clubs located in 24 countries.[38]

A multitude of other firms, like airlines, hotels, long-distance telephone providers, credit card companies, and retailers, also have developed frequent buyer/user programs to reward their loyal customers. The better CRM programs attempt to maintain continuous contact with loyal customers by sending them birthday cards or having a personal sales associate contact them to inform them of special events and sales. Adding Value 10.1 illustrates just how close a brand can come to a consumer's life—if consumers will let it.

Adding Value 10.1   The Brands Singles Choose to Find Them a Friend

In Seattle, natural grocery store chain Whole Foods holds a "singles" night every month, during which it offers wine tastings and snacks, as well as an opportunity for people to mingle and interact.[39] Singles wear red or blue ribbons, depending on whether they are looking for a male or female partner. Is Whole Foods trying to turn into Match.com in the produce aisle? In reality, Whole Foods is simply expanding the brand experience for its customers, meaning that the retailer not only sells commodities but also creates communities. Human interactions within the store environment ideally turn into increased sales.

Similarly, REI, the leading outdoor equipment company, offers kayak training; PetSmart and Petco offer dog training and classes for pet owners; and Cabela's offers classes on trout fishing and gun cleaning in stores that include stuffed game, artificial trout streams, and restaurants.

The Nike store in Portland, Oregon, hosts running groups that meet two times per week, after which the runners meet at the Niketown store for refreshments. Members who have logged more than 100 miles earn special recognition, and the Nike Plus Web site communicates with runners' Apple iPods to track their running metrics. More than half of the 200,000 runners involved in Nike's program use this system, visiting the Web site more than four times per week. In comparison, even Starbucks' core customers frequent its stores only about 15 times per month.

By extending their brands to match customers' lifestyles and creating and showing support for their communities, companies earn more loyal customers, which turns into higher profits. For customers, in the end, the brand

REI offers kayak training to help build a community and its brand.

experience is what resonates. If they can find a friend, training partner, or even spouse who shares similar interests, whether that be natural foods, well-trained dogs, or grueling marathons, they're likely to develop a strong affection for the company. That affection could even get passed down for generations, as couples tell their "how we met" stories to their children and grandchildren: "Well, I was in the cracker aisle, and there was your mother in the cookie aisle...."

CHECK YOURSELF

1. How do brands create value for the customer and the firm?
2. What are the components of brand equity?

BRANDING STRATEGIES

Firms institute a variety of brand-related strategies to create and manage key brand assets, such as the decision to own the brands, establishing a branding policy, extending the brand name to other products and markets, cooperatively using the brand name with that of another firm, and licensing the brand to other firms.

Brand Ownership

Brands can be owned by any firm in the supply chain, whether manufacturers, wholesalers, or retailers. There are two basic brand ownership strategies: manufacturer brands and private-label brands.

Manufacturer Brands   **Manufacturer brands**, also known as **national brands**, are owned and managed by the manufacturer. Some famous manufacturer brands are Nike, Coca-Cola, KitchenAid, and Marriott. With these brands, the manufacturer develops the merchandise, produces it to ensure consistent quality, and invests in a marketing program to establish an appealing brand image. The majority of the brands marketed in the United States are manufacturer brands, and manufacturing firms spend millions of dollars each year to promote their brands. For example, for the Simple Pleasures product line of its Tide brand, Procter & Gamble spends $32 million annually on media—and that is only one of approximately 35 Tide product lines that P&G owns.[40] By owning their brands, manufacturers retain more control over their marketing strategy, are able to choose the appropriate market segments and positioning for the brand, and can build the brand and thereby create their own brand equity.

Private-Label Brands[41]   Private-label brands, also called store brands, house brands, or own brands, are products developed by retailers. Some manufacturers prefer to make only private-label merchandise because the costs of developing and marketing a manufacturer's brand are prohibitive. Other firms manufacture both their own brand and merchandise for other brands or retailers. In many cases, retailers develop the design and specifications for their private-label products and then contract with manufacturers to produce those products. In other cases, national brand vendors work with a retailer to develop a special version of its standard merchandise offering to be sold exclusively by the retailer. In these cases, the national brand manufacturer is responsible for the design and specification as well as the production of the merchandise.

In the past, sales of private-label brands were limited. National brands had the resources to develop loyalty toward their brands through aggressive marketing. It was difficult for smaller local and regional retailers to gain the economies of scale in design, production, and promotion needed to develop well-known brands.

In recent years, as the size of retail firms has increased through growth and consolidation, more retailers have the scale economies to develop private-label merchandise and use this merchandise to establish a distinctive identity. In addition, manufacturers are more willing to accommodate the needs of retailers and develop exclusive cobrands for them. Private-label products now account for an average of 16 percent of the purchases in North America and roughly 22 percent in Europe.[42]

There are four categories of private brands: premium, generic, copycat, and exclusive cobrands.

Premium brands   Premium brands offer the consumer a private label that is comparable to, or even superior to, a manufacturer's brand quality, sometimes with modest price savings. Examples of premium private labels include Wal-Mart's Sam's Choice (U.S.), Loblaw's President's Choice (Canada), Tesco Finest (U.K.), Marks & Spencer's St. Michael (U.K.), Woolworth Select (Australia), Pick and Pay's Choice (South Africa), and Albert Heijn's AH Select (Netherlands).[43]

President's Choice is Canadian retailer Loblaw's premium private label. It competes on quality, not price. Kellogg has two scoops of raisins in its cereal, but President's Choice cereal has four and is still cheaper. The Decadent chocolate chip cookie under the President's Choice label has 39 percent chocolate chips by weight, compared with 19 percent in Chips Ahoy! In addition, it uses real butter instead of hydrogenated coconut oil and quality chocolate instead of artificial chips. The resulting product is Canada's market leader in chocolate chip cookies, despite being sold only in 20 percent of the market held by Loblaw.[44]

Generic brands   Generic brands target a price-sensitive segment by offering a no-frills product at a discount price. These products are used for commodities like milk and eggs in grocery stores and underwear in discount stores. However, even in these markets, the popularity and acceptance of generic products has declined. Consumers question the quality and origin of the products, and retailers have found

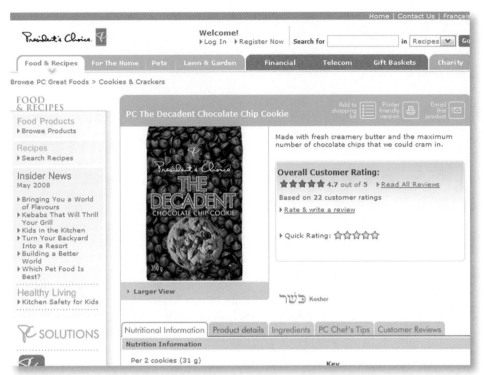

President's Choice Decadent chocolate chip cookie is a premium private label that is Canada's market leader because of its high-quality ingredients.

better profit potential and the ability to build brand equity with manufacturer and store brands. For example, many fruits and vegetables sold through supermarket chains now carry either the manufacturer's brand name (Dole bananas) or the store's.

Copycat brands   Copycat brands imitate the manufacturer's brand in appearance and packaging, generally are perceived as lower quality, and are offered at lower prices. Copycat brands abound in drugstores. Many retailers track manufacturer's brands as they introduce new products and then modify them to meet the needs of their target customers. For instance, CVS and Walgreen's brands are placed next to the manufacturer's brands and often look like them. Both the Pepto-Bismol and CVS's generic equivalent are similarly packaged and contain pink liquid.

Exclusive cobrands   An exclusive cobrand is a brand that is developed by a national brand vendor, often in conjunction with a retailer, and is sold exclusively by the retailer. The simplest form of an exclusive cobrand is when a national brand manufacturer assigns different model numbers and has different exterior features for the same basic product sold by different retailers. For example, a Sony TV sold at Best Buy might have a different model number than a Sony TV with similar features available at Circuit City. These exclusive models make it difficult for consumers to compare prices for virtually the same television sold by different retailers. Thus, the retailers are less likely to compete on price when selling these exclusive cobrands, their margins for the products are higher, and they are motivated to devote more resources toward selling the exclusive cobrands than they would for similar manufacturer's brands.[45]

A more sophisticated form of exclusive cobranding is when a manufacturer develops an exclusive product or group of related products for a retailer. For example, cosmetics powerhouse Estée Lauder sells three brands of cosmetics and skin care products—American Beauty, Flirt!, and Good Skin—exclusively at Kohl's. The products are priced between mass-market brands such as Cover Girl or Maybelline (sold mainly in drugstores, discount stores, and supermarkets) and

EXHIBIT 10.4		**Exclusive Cobrands**	
Retailer	**Manufacturer/ Designer**	**Product Category**	**Product Name**
Kohl's	Estée Lauder	Cosmetics	American Beauty, Flirt!, and Good Skin
Whole Foods	Whole Foods	Food	365 Organic
Sharper Image[46]	ARG Manufacturing	Kitchen tools	Sharper Image
Macy's[47]	Martha Stewart	Soft home (sheets, towels)	Martha Stewart Collection
JCPenney[48]	Ralph Lauren	Home goods, apparel, and accessories	American Living
Furniture First[49]	Serta	Bedding	Mattress First

Lauder's higher-end brands, sold primarily in more fashion-forward department stores such as Macy's. Whole Foods' very successful 365 Organic brand gives customers an opportunity to buy high-quality products that are less expensive compared to other brands in the store. Examples of these and several other exclusive cobrands you might recognize are found in Exhibit 10.4.

Naming Brands and Product Lines

Firms use several very different strategies to name their brands and product lines: corporate or family brands, corporate and product line brands, and individual brands.

Corporate or Family Brands   A firm can use its own corporate name to brand all its product lines and products, such as the General Electric Company (GE), which brands its appliances prominently with the GE brand name. Similarly, all products sold through The Gap stores bear only The Gap brand name. When all products are sold under one corporate or family brand, the individual brands benefit from the overall brand awareness associated with the family name.

Corporate and Product Line Brands   A firm also could use combinations of the corporate and product line brands to distinguish its products. For example, Kellogg's uses its family brand name prominently on its cereal brands (e.g., Special K, Froot Loops, Rice Krispies). In other cases, the individual brand's name is more prominently displayed on the package than the Kellogg's name, as in the case of Pop-Tarts, Eggo, Cheez-Its, and Nutri-Grain. In addition, Kellogg's owns other brands, such as Keebler, that are not overtly associated with the family brand.

Individual Brands   A firm can use individual brand names for each of its products. For example, in its house and home products line, Procter & Gamble markets various detergent products (Tide, Gain, Cheer, Downy, Febreze), paper products (Bounty, Charmin), household cleaners (Mr. Clean, Swiffer), and dishwashing products (Cascade, Dawn, Joy). Furthermore, it markets brands in various other product lines, such as personal and beauty products (Olay, Old Spice, Secret, Cover Girl), health and wellness products (Prilosec OTC, Glide, Puffs), baby products (Pampers, Luvs), and pet nutrition and care products (Iams).[50]

Choosing a Name   Although there is no simple way to decide how to name a brand or a product line, the more the products vary in their usage or performance, the more likely it is that the firm should use individual brands, just as the examples of consumer packaged goods manufacturers (e.g., P&G, Colgate-Palmolive) demonstrate. Choosing a name also can be an exercise in creativity, as the alco-

Sometimes Frito-Lay uses its family brand name on its products, while other times the individual brand's name is more prominently displayed.

holic beverage market shows. Wines named "Cardinal Zin" and "Dirty Laundry" enable these wineries to distinguish themselves from more traditionally named products, especially in a market as diverse and full of offerings as the wine market. The name can also indicate a strong brand image: By renaming its craft beer "Dead Frog," the previously titled Backwoods Brewing Company prompted laughs, some shock, and a sense that the company was cutting-edge and entertaining among its consumers—as well as a virtual guarantee that they would remember the name.[51]

Brand Extension

A **brand extension** refers to the use of the same brand name for new products being introduced to the same or new markets.[52] The dental hygiene market, for instance, is full of brand extensions; Colgate and Crest sell toothpaste, toothbrushes, and other dental hygiene products, even though their original product line was just toothpaste.

There are several advantages to using the same brand name for new products. First, because the brand name is already well established, the firm can spend less in developing consumer brand awareness and brand associations for the new product.[53] Gillette's Braun brand started selling kitchen appliances (coffeemakers, toasters, food processors, blenders, juicers) in the United States, then extended into various other product categories, including shaving (dry razors, beard care), beauty care products (cordless hair stylers), oral care products (power toothbrushes), and steam irons.[54]

Second, if either the original brand or the brand extension has stong consumer acceptance, that perception will carry over to the other product. Following its success in the PC market, Dell extended its brand name to monitors, printers, handheld computers, digital juke boxes, LCD televisions, servers, and network switches, among other products.[55] Similarly, consumers who had not used the Neutrogena brand before trying the brand extension, Neutrogena On-the-Spot Acne Patch, might be encouraged to try Neutrogena's core product line of moisturizing lotions, especially if their experience with the acne patch has been positive.[56]

Crest uses a brand extension strategy, since they use the same brand name for many related products.

Finally, when brand extensions are used for complementary products, a synergy exists between the two products that can increase overall sales. For example, Frito-Lay markets both chips and dips under its Frito-Lay and Doritos brand names.[57] When people buy the chips, they tend to buy the dips as well.

The Walt Disney Company began as an animation and movie studio and has expanded its brand to include television networks (Disney, ABC, ESPN)[58] and theme parks around the world. Disney's more recent brand extensions have been spurred by market expansion into sophisticated demographic segments. Disney's new line of wedding gowns, created in partnership with designer Kirstie Kelly, is inspired by the Disney characters that brides-to-be grew up with: Snow White, Belle, Sleeping Beauty, Jasmine, and Ariel.[59] Other brand Disney extensions include Chardonnay with Costco, lighting products with the Minka Group, Fashion bath and bedding collection with Dan River, outdoor tabletops and entertaining products with Zak Designs, Furniture with Drexel Heritage, Disney Jeans, and a sporting line.[60]

Not all brand extensions are successful, however. Some can dilute brand equity.[61] **Brand dilution** occurs when the brand extension adversely affects consumer perceptions about the attributes the core brand is believed to hold.[62] Sir Richard Branson's Virgin conglomerate has successfully branched out from record stores to health clubs to book publishing to tourism to cosmetics, but it also has experienced some serious failures, especially in the alcoholic and cola beverages markets.[63] Its brand of vodka was a failure, and Virgin Cola failed in the United States and achieved only a 3 percent market share in the United Kingdom. The primary risk that Virgin runs from extending its brand too far is not being able to satisfy all its customers of all its brands. As long as the customer has a nice flight on Virgin Atlantic, he or she may try Virgin Mobile. But if that same person has a bad experience with his or her cell phone contract, Virgin Atlantic—and the other Virgin brands—may lose a customer forever. Finally, if the brand extension is very similar to the core brand, it even could cause cannibalization of sales from the core brand.

To prevent the potentially negative consequences of brand extensions, firms consider the following:

- Marketers should evaluate the fit between the product class of the core brand and that of the extension.[64] If the fit between the product categories is high, consumers will consider the extension credible, and the brand association will be stronger for the extension. Thus, when the pastry maker Entenmann's introduced a line of coffee, it made sense to consumers and improved the brand's image.[65]

- Firms should evaluate consumer perceptions of the attributes of the core brand and seek out similar attributes for the extension because brand-specific associations are very important for extensions.[66] For example, if HP printers were associated with reliability, performance, and value, consumers would expect the same brand-specific attributes in other products that carried the HP brand name.

- Firms should refrain from extending the brand name to too many products and product categories to avoid diluting the brand and damaging brand equity. Donald Trump has been quite successful lending his name to various property, business, and television lines, but when he tried to extend himself to branding steaks and a home rug line, he prompted mostly derision; as one observer jokingly asked, "the Trump rug collection? For the head or the floor?"[67]

- Firms should consider whether the brand extension will be distanced from the core brand, especially if the

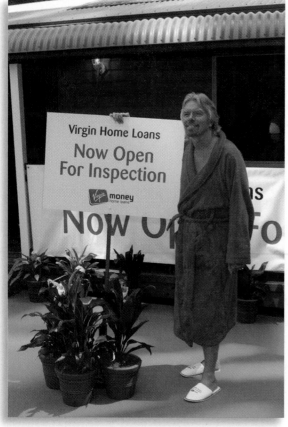

Sir Richard Branson has successfully extended the Virgin brand beyond its core businesses of air travel and music stores. One of his latest ventures is Virgin Home Loans.

firm wants to use some but not all of the existing brand associations. When Marriott introduced its budget line of hotels, it downplayed the Marriott name, calling the new chain Fairfield Inn. And did you even know that Marriott International owns 99 percent of the Ritz-Carlton chain of luxury hotels? Not many people do, and that ignorance is by the company's design. The information is buried on Ritz-Carlton's Web site.[68]

Cobranding

Cobranding is the practice of marketing two or more brands together, on the same package or promotion. Primarily due to credit card companies, such as Visa and MasterCard, the practice has greatly increased in the past decade. Airlines were among the first to cobrand with credit card companies (such as the United Airlines Visa Card), but recently, firms in other industries, such as banking, retail, and restaurants, have begun forming similar alliances. Starbucks was the first in the quick-service restaurant industry to offer its own Starbucks credit card in alliance with Visa.[69]

Cobranding can enhance consumers' perceptions of product quality[70] by signaling "unobservable" product quality through links between the firm's brand and a well-known quality brand. For example, NutraSweet's claim to be a sugar substitute that was safe and left no aftertaste got a boost after both Coca-Cola and Pepsi started offering products that contained NutraSweet and included a reference to it on its labels and in its promotions. Microsoft has joined with Ford Motors to offer its Sync brand of "in-car communication and entertainment systems" in certain models under the Ford, Lincoln, and Mercury brand names (e.g., Ford Explorer, Lincoln MKZ, Mercury Sable). Commercials name all these brands in touting the new technology, and the Sync Web site features logos from Microsoft, Mercury, Lincoln, and Ford on the introductory page.[71]

Cobranding can also be a prelude to an acquisition strategy. FedEx entered into a cobranding arrangement with Kinko's, whereby it provided FedEx delivery services at Kinko's retail outlets.[72] Then in early 2004, FedEx acquired Kinko's for an estimated $2.4 billion and began rebranding Kinko's as FedEx Kinko's.[73] The combined company has entered into another cobranding agreement with Adobe, in which the latest version of Acrobat would feature an icon users could click to forward their Acrobat document directly to any FedEx Kinko's for printing.[74] But this strategy has been less successful. Faced with complaints from printing companies that compete with FedEx Kinkos, Adobe agreed to remove the button in another update just two months after announcing its cobranding attempt.[75]

This example suggests just one of the risks to cobranding; another risk becomes apparent when the customers of each of the brands turn out to be vastly different. For example, the Burger King and Häagen-Dazs cobranding strategy failed because the customer profiles for each brand were too different.[76] Cobranding may also fail if the brands' owners cannot resolve financial disputes about revenue or royalty sharing.[77] Finally, the firms that own the brands may change their priorities, as a result of which the cobranded product may no longer be available. In this scenario, the customer relationships and loyalty created with the cobranded product would be lost.[78]

Brand Licensing

Brand licensing is a contractual arrangement between firms, whereby one firm allows another to use its brand name, logo, symbols, and/or characters in exchange for a negotiated fee.[79] Brand licensing is common for toys, apparel, accessories, and entertainment products, such as video games; in the United States alone, it generates more than $100 billion in retail sales per year.[80] The firm that provides the right to use its brand (licensor) obtains revenues through royalty payments from the firm that has obtained the right to use the brand (licensee). These royalty payments sometimes take the form of an up-front, lump-sum licensing fee or may be based on the dollar value of sales of the licensed merchandise.

Giorgio Armani, the well-known fashion designer, not only produces apparel collections, but also has developed a line of high-end electronics in conjunction with Samsung Electronics. As Armani says, "We make as much of a personal statement with mobile phones or the televisions in our living rooms as we do with the shoes and bags we wear." The electronics line will join the other products bearing the Armani name, like chocolates, housewares, flowers, and even a hotel in Dubai.[81] Other electronics companies have partnered with designers as well, including Dolce & Gabbana's design of a Razr for Motorola and a Prada-designed cell phone for LG Electronics. The Porsche name appears on Grundig radios, watches, luggage sets, and tennis rackets. The computer world has even capitalized on the Porsche brand name with the game *Need for Speed: Porsche Unleashed*. If Porsche isn't luxurious enough, racing game fans can drive a virtual Maserati in *Gran Turismo 5* for the PlayStation.

One very popular form of licensing is the use of characters created in books and other media. Such entertainment licensing has generated tremendous revenues for movie studios. Disney, for instance, flooded retail stores with Jack Sparrow after the release of each of the three *Pirates of the Caribbean* films. *Star Wars* memorabilia has continued to be successful since the first film was released in the 1970s. A long-standing staple of licensing has been major league sports teams that play in the NBA, NFL, or NHL, as well as various collegiate sports teams.

Licensing is an effective form of attracting visibility for the brand and thereby building brand equity while also generating additional revenue. There are, however, some risks associated with it. For the licensor, the major risk is the dilution of its brand equity through overexposure of the brand, especially if the brand name and characters are used inappropriately.[82]

Consider, for instance, the famous—or possibly infamous—alligator shirt. In 1933, the company founded by Frenchman René Lacoste (the licensor), famous as a tennis player and for his nickname "the alligator," entered into a licensing agreement with André Gillier (the first licensee) to produce a high-quality white knit shirt with a ribbed collar, short sleeves, and a crocodile emblazoned on the right

The famous tennis player René "the alligator" Lacoste (left in 1927 photo) cofounded a firm that made a white knit shirt with an alligator emblazoned on the right breast. The brand is still sold today (right) at Lacoste boutiques and stores like Neiman Marcus.

breast. The line expanded to include other casual apparel items, and in 1966, the Lacoste name was licensed to American manufacturer Izod (the second licensee). Alligator-emblazoned apparel could be found in better department stores and country club golf and tennis shops into the late 1980s. But Izod also began to sell the alligator apparel in discount stores, and quality and sales suffered. The alliance continued until 1992, when Lacoste severed its ties with Izod. Lacoste has since regained its prestige image and can be found in boutiques and exclusive specialty department stores around the world.[83]

Licensors also run the risk of improperly valuing their brand for licensing purposes or entering into the wrong type of licensing arrangement. For example, Marvel Entertainment Inc.'s previous deals with movie studios for the use of its comic book characters were "undervalued," because the firm took lump-sum licensing fees up front rather than pegging its royalty fees to sales. As a result, the firm probably left money on the table for deals on the first *X-Men* and *Blade* films.[84] In entertainment licensing, both licensors and licensees run the risk that characters based on books and movies will be only a fad. Moreover, the success or failure of merchandise based on movies is directly affected by the success or failure of the movie itself.

Brand Repositioning

Brand repositioning or rebranding refers to a strategy in which marketers change a brand's focus to target new markets or realign the brand's core emphasis with changing market preferences.[85] Although repositioning can improve the brand's fit with its target segment or boost the vitality of old brands, it is not without costs and risks. Firms often need to spend tremendous amounts of money to make tangible changes to the product and packages, as well as intangible changes to the brand's image through advertising. These costs may not be recovered if the repositioned brand and messages are not credible to the consumer or if the firm has mistaken a fad for a long-term market trend.

Abercrombie & Fitch (A&F), founded in 1892, was the largest high-quality sporting goods and outfitting store for camping, fishing, and hunting gear. Its customers were mainly professional hunters, explorers, trappers, and outdoorsmen, and included Theodore Roosevelt, Amelia Earhart, Katharine Hepburn, and Howard Hughes. In fact, their 12-story building on Madison Avenue and 45th Street in Manhattan had a log cabin on the roof, a casting pool for fishermen to sample rods and flies, an armored rifle range in the basement, a golf school, and a dog and cat kennel. Although these special features may seem commonplace today at stores like REI and Bass Pro Shops that have equally enticing attractions, it was innovative during A&F's sporting goods heyday from 1907 through the early 1960s. The store carried unique exotic items such as hot air balloons, yachting pennants, portable trampolines, treadmills for exercising dogs, and other high-end toys for grownups. In 1988, Abercrombie & Fitch was acquired by Limited Brands after years of struggling and bankruptcy. Limited Brands repositioned it into a casual luxury lifestyle brand for college students age 18–22.[86] Limited Brands spun off Abercrombie & Fitch in 1988 as an independent company and began to open new concepts to extend its market reach.

Procter & Gamble's Head & Shoulders is repositioning its popular antidandruff shampoo and conditioners. The company's repositioning strategy broadens its appeal to those looking for a glamorous health-oriented product from its roots as a clinically proven antidandruff aid. The key to this successful repositioning is gaining new customers without losing its appeal to its loyal customer base. The repositioning strategy includes a more glamorous youth-oriented promotional theme, new packaging, and the addition of Kristin Davis from Sex & the City as the global face for the brand.[87]

CHECK YOURSELF

1. What is the difference between manufacturer, private-label, and generic brands?
2. What is cobranding?
3. What are some advantages and disadvantages of brand extensions?

PACKAGING

Packaging is an important brand element with more tangible or physical benefits than the other brand elements. Packages come in different types and offer a variety of benefits to consumers, manufacturers, and retailers. The primary package is the one the consumer uses, such as the toothpaste tube. From the primary package, consumers typically seek convenience in terms of storage, use, and consumption.

The secondary package is the wrapper or exterior carton that contains the primary package and provides the UPC label used by retail scanners. Consumers can use the secondary package to find additional product information that may not be available on the primary package. Like primary packages, secondary packages add consumer value by facilitating the convenience of carrying, using, and storing the product.

Labatt Blue is reinforcing its brand throughout the product's journey to the point of consumption at a tailgate party, picnic, or barbeque. The two-layer plastic package holds 28 cans and actually chills the beer without a cooler. There is a tear-away section to access the beer and pack ice around the cans. The inner bag prevents the melting ice from dripping. The perforated divider inserts become paperboard coasters to be used at the outdoor event.[88]

The secondary package can also be an important marketing tool for the manufacturer if it is used to convey the brand's positioning. Cosmetics companies, for instance, consider the secondary package to be primarily about brand image, so their secondary packages are designed to match the image they want to portray and are immediately recognizable.[89]

Retailers' priorities for secondary packaging, however, differ. They want convenience in terms of displaying and selling the product. In addition, secondary packages often may be packed into larger cartons, pallets, or containers to facilitate shipment and storage from the manufacturer to the retailer. These shipping packages benefit the manufacturer and the retailer in that they protect the shipment during transit; aid in loading, unloading, and storage; and allow cost efficiencies due to the larger order and shipment sizes.

Because packages are critical to the firm's brand positioning and shelf appeal, many innovations in design and materials have occurred in the past few decades. Some examples include:[90]

- **FlexCan, stand-up, reclosable zipper pouches:** Capri Sun's stand-up pouch juice drink took the lead. Now a variety of products and pouch types are available, including pouches with reclosable zippers to maintain product freshness.

- **DailyGloss:** This type of packaging has many individually sealed pouches, and is normally used for pills or chewing gum. Adapted for lip gloss, individual doses can be easily accessed without affecting the rest of the package.

The secondary package is especially important to cosmetics companies. It is used to reinforce the image and be immediately recognizable.

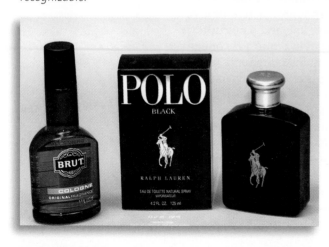

- **Smart lids:** The plastic cap on a portable paper cup changes color depending on temperature of the contents. When cold, the lid is brown, when hot, the lid turns red.

- **Labatt Blue:** The aluminum beer can is wrapped in an insulated layer which protects the contents from heat transferred from warm hands and the outside temperature. The can is also more comfortable to hold because of the thermal barrier.

- **Aseptic drink bottles:** TetraPak and IP provided designs and machinery that increased the shelf life of beverages without refrigeration. They are used primarily by juice marketers.

- **Child-resistant/senior-friendly packages:** Products that are harmful to children under the age of five years, such as drugs and medicines, solvents, chemicals, and pesticides, now are packaged with child-resistant tops. In 1995, the Consumer Products Safety Council amended the child-resistant packaging protocol so that older adults could easily open such packaging.

- **Snack 'n' seal:** These packages are used to increase the product's freshness, resealability, and ease of opening. Originally used for baby wipes and now for baked goods like Chips Ahoy! and Oreo cookies, these packages have individually sealed subpackages with a reclosable feature.

This Chips Ahoy! package has individually sealed subpackages with a reclosable feature to keep the product fresh.

Product Labeling

Labels on products and packages provide information the consumer needs for his or her purchase decision and consumption of the product. In that they identify the product and brand, labels are also an important element of branding and can be used for promotion. The information required on them must comply with general and industry-specific laws and regulations, including the constituents or ingredients contained in the product, where the product was made, directions for use, and/or safety precautions.

Many labeling requirements stem from various laws, including the Federal Trade Commission Act of 1914, the Fair Packaging and Labeling Act of 1967, and the Nutrition Labeling Act of 1990. Several federal agencies, industry groups, and consumer watchdogs carefully monitor product labels. The Food and Drug Administration is the primary federal agency that reviews food and package labels and ensures that the claims made by the manufacturer are true.

Ethical and Societal Dilemma 10.1 illustrates the problems food manufacturers face with regard to the types of ingredients they use in their products, as well as the associated labeling concerns. These concerns are further compounded when the products are sold across international borders.

A product label is much more than just a sticker on the package; it is a communication tool. Many of the elements on the label are required by laws and regulations (i.e., ingredients, fat content, sodium content, serving size, calories), but other elements of the label remain within the control of the manufacturer. How manufacturers use labels to communicate the benefits of their products to consumers varies by the product. Many products highlight specific ingredients, vitamin content, or nutrient content (e.g., iron). This focus signals to consumers that the product offers these benefits. Although often overlooked, the importance of the label as a communication tool should not be underestimated.

Ethical and Societal Dilemma 10.1   What's in the Food? Is It on the Label?

How is it that an American jar of mayonnaise has double the saturated fat of a jar sold in London?[91] The culprit is soy oil, a genetically altered ingredient used to make mayonnaise in the United States. In the United Kingdom, however, putting soy oil into a product poses a problem: Genetically modified food has become a serious issue for consumers there. Consumer protests have led to the adoption of new labeling requirements that are designed to alert consumers to the presence of genetically modified ingredients. Companies like Hellmann's thus avoid mentioning the difference in ingredients, and substitute vegetable oil for soy oil in the United Kingdom. Vegetable oil is lower in saturated fats, which leads to the difference between a jar of mayonnaise in the two countries.

For food manufacturers, it is not just consumer protests that are causing product changes; there are also increasing concerns about the global rise in obesity. Many countries are investigating whether to regulate the marketing of food products or require products deemed "unhealthy" or "junk food" to carry warning labels. In response, manufacturers are scrambling to reformulate certain products to be lower in fat, salt, sugar, and calories. Some products are promoting these new changes, such as calcium-enriched Kraft Macaroni & Cheese and General Mills' whole grain cereals.

To address consumers' heightened sensitivity to health concerns, some firms, in a questionable attempt to make products appear healthier, have played games with the serving sizes listed on the label. Thus, one label for a candy bar might list information as it pertains to one serving, considered to be the entire bar, whereas the label for another candy bar also lists the information for one serving, but defines a serving as half the bar. Although not inaccurate, this type of labeling has the potential to mislead consumers into thinking a product is healthier than it truly is. Companies also might tout the health benefits of their products while downplaying less attractive product attributes. For example, some consumer packaged goods manufacturers advertise that their products are low fat, but in order to make them still taste good, they add sugar and/or salt.

Even restaurants are getting in on this practice. Subway touts itself as a healthy fast-food alternative, but in actuality, a regular 12-inch roast beef sandwich with cheese and mayonnaise has more calories and fat than a Big Mac from McDonald's. Consumers who believe they are eating healthier by stopping at Subway also tend to indulge themselves in treat items, like chips and a soda to go with their "healthier" sandwich. In response, some states are considering legislation that would require chain restaurants to post all nutrition information on prominent placards in their stores.[92]

Should firms provide full disclosure on labels and try to make products healthier, or should they make products that they think consumers want and let them make their own health decisions?

Summing Up

1. **How do firms adjust their product lines to changing market conditions?**

Market conditions change. New opportunities arise, firms or even industries mature and die. Competition may become more intense or competitors may move on to pursue other opportunities. As firms grow they change their product lines by adding either new product categories or new SKUs within a product category. The decision to add products should be made carefully. Excessive product line expansions can confuse consumers and dilute the appeal of the brand's core products. Sometimes, products or product lines become unprofitable, the firm's priorities change, or consumer preferences shift. When this happens, firms must prune their product lines by deleting items or possibly even entire product categories.

2. **Why are brands valuable to firms?**

Brands facilitate the consumer search process. Some customers are loyal to certain brands, which essentially protects those brands from competition.

In addition, brands are valuable in a legal sense, in that trademarks and copyrights protect firms from counterfeiters and knockoff artists. Firms with well-known brands can spend relatively less on marketing because the brand and its associations help sell the product. Finally, brands have real market value as a company asset.

3. How do firms implement different branding strategies?

Firms use a variety of strategies to manage their brands. First, they must decide whether to offer manufacturer, private-label, or generic brands. Second, they have a choice of using an overall corporate brand or a collection of product line or individual brands. Third, to reach new markets or extend their current market, they can extend their current brands to new products. Fourth, firms can cobrand with another brand to create sales and profit synergies for both. Fifth, firms with strong brands have the opportunity to license their brands to other firms. Sixth and finally, as the marketplace changes, it is often necessary to reposition a brand.

4. How do a product's packaging and label contribute to a firm's overall strategy?

Like brands, packaging and labels help sell the product and facilitate its use. The primary package holds the product, and its label provides product information. The secondary package provides additional consumer information on its label and facilitates transportation and storage for both retailers and their customers. Labels have become increasingly important to consumers because they supply important safety, nutritional, and product usage information.

Key Terms

- brand, 311
- brand association, 319
- brand awareness, 317
- brand dilution, 326
- brand equity, 317
- brand extension, 325
- brand licensing, 327
- brand loyalty, 320
- brand personality, 320
- brand repositioning (rebranding), 329
- breadth, 311
- category depth, 312
- cobranding, 327

- copycat brands, 323
- corporate and product line brands, 324
- corporate brand (family brand), 324
- depth, 311
- exclusive cobrand, 323
- generic brands, 322
- house brands, 322
- individual brands, 324
- licensed brand, 317
- manufacturer brands (national brands), 321
- own brands, 322

- perceived value, 318
- premium brands, 322
- primary package, 330
- private-label brands, 322
- product, 310
- product assortment, 311
- product category, 311
- product lines, 311
- product mix, 311
- secondary package, 330
- stock keeping units (SKUs), 312
- store brands, 322

Marketing Applications

1. Prepared foods at Whole Foods Market, the world's largest retailer of organic foods, are very profitable. To make them even more profitable, suggest two strategies that would alter the product mix breadth and depth.

2. Suppose you have just been hired by a pillow manufacturer as a marketing consultant. The manufacturer has been making private-label pillows for other companies for 75 years but is thinking about developing its own pillow brand for sale.

Discuss the advantages and disadvantages of such a strategy.

3. Identify a specific brand that has developed a high level of brand equity. What specific aspects of that brand establish its brand equity?

4. Are you loyal to any brands? If so, pick one and explain why you believe you are loyal, beyond that you simply like the brand. If not, pick a brand that you like and explain how you would feel and

act differently toward the brand if you were loyal to it.

5. Nike owns several brands: Converse, Chuck Taylor, Cole-Haan, Jumpman, and Air Jordans, among others. Each brand features many models, each of which has a unique identifying name. Wouldn't it be easier to just identify them all as Nikes? Justify your answer.

6. Identify a specific company that has recently introduced a new brand extension to the marketplace. Discuss whether you believe the brand extension example you provided will benefit or harm the firm.

7. The Chicago Marathon cobranded with LaSalle Bank, a Chicago-based institution. But when Bank of America purchased LaSalle in 2007, the marathon became cobranded with the new owner as the Bank of America Chicago Marathon (see www.chicagomarathon.com). What are the benefits and potential liabilities of each partnership from all three groups' points of view?

8. Do you think all food sold in a grocery store should have an ingredient and nutrition label? Consider the perspectives of consumers, the manufacturer, and the store.

9. You are the brand manager for a firm that makes herbs, spices, and other food additives. You have had complaints from some of your retail outlets that they are finding empty bottles of pure vanilla

Bank of America is cobranded with the Chicago Marathon.

extract stashed around the store. Apparently, due to the high (35 percent) alcohol content of pure vanilla extract, people are grabbing the cute little bottles, having a drink, and getting rid of the evidence. Anecdotal evidence from store employees indicates that the majority of the imbibers are teenagers. The cost of placing a tamper proof cap on the extract is a relatively insignificant percentage of the purchase price, but will make it more difficult to open, particularly for older customers. Also, there has been a significant rise in sales to retailers as a result of the vanilla bean "addicts." What should you do?

www.mhhe.com/ grewal2e

Quiz Yourself

1. Toothpaste, toothbrush, whitening products, kids' oral products, and floss are all _____ within Colgate-Palmolive's Oral Care product line.
   a. product categories
   b. primary packaging parts
   c. product breadth
   d. product assortments
   e. private label brands

2. It is almost impossible to watch a sporting event on television without seeing Nike's "swoosh" check mark, which is Nike's:

   a. name.
   b. symbol.
   c. design.
   d. term.
   e. all of the above.

(Answers to these two questions are provided on page 623).

Go to www.mhhe.com/grewal2e to practice an additional 11 questions.

Net Savvy

1. Visit the Sara Lee Web site (www.saralee.com). Identify and briefly describe its different *product lines*. Now identify one of its *product categories*, and discuss the *product line depth* of that particular category. Be sure to justify your answers.

2. Interbrand Corporation is a leading brand consultancy firm headquartered in New York that conducts research on the monetary value of different brands. Visit the company's Web site (www.interbrand.com) and access the most recent "Best Global Brands" survey. Identify the top five brands, their brand values, and their countries of origin. Describe changes in the rankings of these firms from the previous year. Identify the brands with the greatest increase and the greatest decrease in terms of percentage change in brand value from the previous year.

Chapter Case Study

BAND-AID® BRAND PRODUCTS:[93] BUILDING ON THE VALUE OF THE BRAND[94]

Part of global giant Johnson & Johnson's Consumer Products Company, Band-Aid® is widely known as a leader in the wound care market. With its dominant share of the market, the brand is widely recognized and respected by consumers and health care professionals alike. Known as an innovator of wound care products, the company continues to introduce new products that exploit creative technologies, one of which led *Good Housekeeping* magazine to name Band-Aid® Brand Liquid Bandage a "Good Buy" award winner. From its early beginnings to today, the company has excelled at providing value to its customers and demonstrated that people across the world can trust the brand.

The Brand Begins

Necessity is the mother of invention, and in the case of Band-Aid® the saying applies. Back in 1920, when Earl Dickson came home from his cotton-buying job at Johnson & Johnson, he would always find a hot meal that his wife Josephine had prepared for him. He also found visible burns and cuts on Josephine from her kitchen labors, which prompted Earl to piece together gauze squares and adhesive tape to cover her wounds. Soon, Earl decided to prepare ready-made bandages in this fashion, with pieces of gauze at intervals along the tape so that Josephine could cut the premade strip and tend to her wounds throughout the day. When the product was first launched in the market, the bandages were made by hand, were not sterile, and had annual sales of just $3,000.

The Company Today

Today, Band-Aid® products are machine-made and completely sterile. A visit to the company's Web site (www.bandaid.com) reveals the distance Band-Aid® has come from the early tape and gauze product, as well as the modern demand for over-the-counter first-aid products in a variety of categories.[95]

In keeping with its long history of product innovations, the company continues to invest in new product development and marketing (see Exhibit 10.5). Band-Aids® come in a host of styles, including those with popular characters for kids; uniquely shaped bandages for various parts of the body; antibiotic Band-Aids® to help fight germs; waterproof

Band-Aids® come in a host of styles, including those with popular characters for kids.

EXHIBIT 10.5	Examples of Band-Aid® Product Innovations
Year	**Product Innovation**
1920	Band-Aid® brand adhesive bandages—3" wide and 18" long—introduced to the market
1924	First machine-made, sterile bandages
1940	Packaging adds red strings to open bandage packages
1951	Plastic strips
1956	Decorated bandages
1958	Sheer vinyl bandages
1994	Sport-strip bandages
1997	Antibiotic adhesive bandages with ointment on the pad
2000	Advanced healing strips for wound care
2001	Liquid bandage that promotes fast healing
2003	Scar-healing technology that fades red and raised scars
2005	Celebrates 85th anniversary with limited edition tins
2006	Relaunch of *plus* Antibiotic
2007	"I am stuck on BAND-AID Brand" jingle with new commercial

products with aloe to treat burns; scar-healing strips; bandages in clear plastic, stretchy cloth, and round and square shapes; and treated and untreated pads. Moreover, the Band-Aid® franchise has expanded to include various ointments, gauze, tapes, and kits for a plethora of first-aid needs. For example, One-Step Cleansing + Infection Protection Foam antiseptic cleans and heals wounds without the need for antibiotic ointment; Calamine Spray dries rashes from poison ivy; Bug-Bite Relief Patches relieve itching and prevent scratching; and FIRST AID TO GO!® Mini First-Aid Kits include essential travel-sized products.

Band-Aid also knows the benefits of good packaging. To celebrate its 85th anniversary, the company made retro tins available in limited quantities. Consumers may appreciate the convenience of modern cardboard boxes, but they also appreciate the nostalgia associated with flipping up the lid on a tin canister. Moreover, to promote its product lines targeted at children, Band-Aid features large, cartoon versions of its licensed characters, including Barbie, Dora the Explorer, and Spider-Man on the boxes as well as the bandages.

But new product introductions by Band-Aid® don't come cheap. For instance almost half of a yearly marketing budget was used to introduce three new product extensions. Advanced Healing Blister Block, a round, waterproof cushioning strip to heal and prevent foot blisters, received $7 million in marketing support to tout its ability to promote fast, natural healing. Finger Care Tough Strips obtained a marketing budget of $5 million and was rolled out as an extension of regular finger care products. Finally, Extra Large Tough Strips were also supported with $5 million for marketing.[96]

The company is in an enviable position. People around the world see the value of Band-Aid® products to heal, prevent, and repair minor nicks, cuts, scrapes, wounds, and bruises. Ongoing product innovations and line expansions likely will help the company continue to be the most recognized name in tape, bandages, and gauze.

Questions

1. Visit the company's Web site (www.bandaid.com) and identify and describe the different product lines that it markets.

2. How would you describe its product line breadth?

3. Review the different product categories in each of the company's product lines. Which has the greatest depth? Which has the least?

4. Review the company's products designed for children. To what extent do these use manufacturer (national) branding? Private-label (store) branding? Licensed branding? Justify your answers. What added value do these products offer compared with regular Band-Aid® protection products?

ALL POINTS
INTERNATIONAL
MUSIC
FESTIVAL

FOSSIL
ALL POINTS
INTERNATIONAL
MUSIC FESTIVAL

WARRANTY BOOKLET

INSTRUCTION MANUAL

CHAPTER

11

DEVELOPING NEW PRODUCTS

- How can firms create value through innovation?
- What is the diffusion of innovation theory, and how can managers use it to make product line decisions?
- How do firms create new products and services?
- What is a product life cycle, and how can the concept be applied to product line decisions?

When stellar new products enter the market, many people's first response goes something like this: "What a great idea! Why didn't somebody think of this before?" For the team at Inventables, a Chicago-based innovation company—whose mission statement claims its dedication to "build a living showcase of what's possible to deliver inspiration and innovation to the dreamers of the world"—the answer would be because no one had used its program to spark their creativity before.[1]

Inventables hires "Technology Hunters," people with some experience in materials science, to go out into the world and find what is new and interesting. By interviewing designers, scouring trade shows, reviewing trade journals and magazines, conducting research in foreign markets, and talking with the network of informants the company has developed, it ensures it has access to the most recent breakthroughs in

science, technology, and material innovation. For example, Inventables noted recent developments in nanoscience and now lists luminescent nanocrystals within its research portfolio.

Not sure what luminescent nanocrystals can do for you? That's okay—you aren't Inventables' main customer. Instead, Inventables offers its research and innovation expertise to product companies looking for new applications. It's those applications that one day will be in your hand. For example, imagine a paint that contains luminescent nanocrystals; the walls of your dorm room could glow like the light sticks that children carry on Halloween and concert fans love to wave to prompt an encore from their favorite band.

Inventing is hard work, and Inventables tries to take some of the legwork out of it for consumer goods (e.g., Avon, Kraft, Tupperware), consumer electronics (e.g., Bissell, Samsung, Whirlpool), toys (e.g., Disney, Fisher-Price, Mattel), and other (e.g., BMW, Hallmark, the U.S. Army) organizations that it counts as its clients. After determining, researching, and summarizing what is new and exciting, Inventables gathers together various concepts, ideas, and materials into its Innovation Center, a display that contains actual samples that product developers may explore. Each sample is tagged with a brief description and several suggestions about how the related technology might be applied. The Center gets delivered to each company that orders it and can be updated regularly with new findings. Each company deals with the Center in its own way, whether by encouraging product developers to interact with it daily or by hosting innovation sessions during which everyone comes together to play and experiment with the sample materials.

The items that Inventables provides to its customers come from five categories: materials, mechanisms, electronics, processes, and "wow" products. Included items must demonstrate something new, solve a problem in an unconventional way, or be found only in a niche market but remain largely unknown elsewhere.

Thus, when the watchmaker Fossil signed up to receive Inventables' services, it received exposure to a combination push-button/LCD switch. Previously, the switch had been used primarily as a cheaper alternative to a digital touch screen or as an interface element in automation equipment. These applications certainly did not fit the watch industry, but by playing with the item in their own hands, developers at Fossil realized that the technology could change the way people use stopwatches. Instead of having to find and press a tiny button on the side—which, as almost any runner will tell you, becomes an especially challenging task after a strenuous run—people instead could just slap at the face of the watch to turn off the counter.

In addition to its sample suggestions, Inventables maintains a portfolio of ideas that are not quite ready for production yet, but sure would be great if someone figured out how to make them work. Imagine, for example, a clear toaster that enables you to watch your bread cook, ensuring no more burnt toast ever. Why didn't someone think of that before?

● ● ●

Now imagine living 200 years ago. You cook your meals on a stove fueled by coal or wood. As a student, you do your homework by hand, illuminated only by candlelight. You get to school on foot, by horseback, or in a horse-drawn carriage, if you're really fortunate. Your classroom is small and basic, and you have very few classmates. The professor simply lectures and writes on a chalkboard.

Fast forward to today. You finish your homework on a laptop computer with word-processing software that appears to have a mind of its own and can correct your spelling automatically. Your climate-controlled room has ample electric light. While you work on your laptop, you can also be talking with a friend using the hands-free headset of your wireless phone. On your way to school, in your car, you pick up fast food from a convenient drive-through window while listening to your personal selection of songs on your iPod. Your friend calls you on the way to school about a slight change to the homework, so you go on your BlackBerry, make the change to your assignment, and e-mail it from your phone to the professor. When you arrive at college, you sit in a 200-person classroom in which you can plug in your laptop, take notes on your computer, and digitally record the lecture while the professor uses PowerPoint presentations to aid in his discussions. These PowerPoint presen-

tations are enlarged at the front
of the room and you are also following along on your own laptop
because they were downloadable. In class, you are planning a last-minute party,
so you send out a Facebook invitation to the friends that you want to invite to get
a headcount. You then instant-message your roommate, notifying her that she can
order food and drinks for X amount of people. If you oversleep, no matter, you can
watch a podcast of your professor's lecture any time you want.

Our lives are defined by the many new products and services developed through
scientific and technological advances and refined either with the help of companies
like Inventables or by firms' internal product development teams. Whereas scientific
research opens up the world of ideas, technological research transforms these ideas
into interesting and useful services, tangible products, and effective processes.

This is the second chapter that deals with the first P in the marketing mix:
product. Continuing our discussion from the preceding chapter, we explore how
companies such as Inventables add value to firms' product and service offerings
through innovation. We also look at how firms develop new products and services
on their own. We conclude the chapter with an examination of how new products
and services are adopted by the market and how firms change their marketing mix
as the product or service moves through its life cycle.

None of these products were available a few years ago.

INNOVATION AND VALUE

Innovation is the process by which ideas are transformed into new products and
services that will help firms grow. Without innovation and its resulting new products and services, firms would have only two choices: continue to market current
products to current customers or take the same product to another market with similar customers.

Although innovation strategies may not work in the short run, overriding long-
term reasons compel firms to introduce new products and services. First, as they
add new products to their offerings, firms
can create and deliver value more effectively by satisfying the changing needs of
their current and new customers or simply
by keeping customers from getting bored
with the current product or service offering.
For example, Unilever's Dove Beauty Bar
line initially focused just on items people
could use to wash their faces, but the product line has since successfully extended into
hair, face, and skin care lines, all under the
Dove umbrella. Today, Dove loyalists can
enjoy not only bar soap for their face but
also hand soap, antiperspirants and deodorants, moisturizing lotions, cleansers, toners,
shampoo, conditioner, styling products, and
much more.[2]

By adding new products, Unilever's Dove brand creates and delivers value more effectively by satisfying the changing needs of its current and new customers or simply by keeping customers from getting bored with its current product offerings.

Second, the longer a product exists in the marketplace, the more likely it is that the market will become saturated. Without new products or services, the value of the firm will ultimately decline.[3] Imagine, for example, if car companies simply assumed and expected that people would keep their cars until they stopped running. If that were the case, there would be no need to continually come up with new and innovative models. The companies could just stick with the models that sell well. But few consumers actually keep the same car until it stops running. Even those who want to stay with the same make and model often want something new, just to add some variety to their lives. Therefore, car companies revamp their models at least every year, whether with new features like GPS or a more powerful engine, or by redesigning the entire look of the vehicle. By doing so, firms sustain their growth by getting consumers excited by the new looks and new features, prompting many car buyers to exchange their old vehicle years before its functional life is over.[4]

Third, the portfolio of products that innovation can create helps the firm diversify its risk and therefore enhances firm value better than a single product can.[5] If some products in a portfolio are doing poorly, others may be doing well. Firms with multiple products are better able to withstand external shocks, including changes in consumer preferences or intensive competitive activity. For this reason, firms like 3M demand that a specific percentage of their sales each year must come from new products introduced within the previous few years.

Fourth, in some industries, such as the arts, books, and software, most sales come from new products. For example, a motion picture generates most of its theater, DVD, and cable TV revenues within a year of its release. Consumers of computer software and video games demand new products in much the same way that fashion mavens demand new apparel styles.

The degree to which a new product or service adds value to the firm and for customers also depends on how new it really is. When we say a "new product," we don't necessarily mean that the product has never existed before; completely new-to-the-market products represent fewer than 10 percent of all new product introductions each year. It is more useful to think of the degree of newness of a product on a continuum from truly "new-to-the-world"—as WiFi was a few years ago—to "slightly repositioned," such as the repositioning of Kraft's Capri Sun brand of ready-to-drink beverages, repackaged in a bigger pouch to appeal more to teens.

Truly new product introductions, truly new-to-the-world products that create new markets, can add tremendous value to firms. These new products, also called **pioneers** or **breakthroughs**, establish a completely new market or radically change both the rules of competition and consumer preferences in a market.[6] The Apple iPod is a pioneer product. Not only did it change the way people listen to music, but it also created an entirely new industry devoted to accessories, such as

Have you ever heard of any of these products? No wonder. They all failed. Orajel (left) was a "fluoride-free" toothpaste targeted toward young children. Dunk-A-Balls cereal (center) was shaped like basketballs so children could play with them before eating them. The Garlic Cake (right) was supposed to be served as an hors d'oeuvre, but the company forgot to mention potential usage occasions to consumers, so people wondered why they would want to eat one.

Apple has introduced several pioneer products in recent years, including the iPhone.

cases, earbuds, docking stations, and speakers. Although Apple offers many of these accessories itself, other companies have jumped on the bandwagon, ensuring that you can strap your iPod to your arm while on the move or insert it into the base of a desk lamp equipped with speakers to get music and light from your desk. And don't forget: The iPod also launched perhaps the most notable other recent pioneer, the iPhone.[7]

Pioneers have the advantage of being first movers; as the first to create the market or product category, they become readily recognizable to consumers and thus establish a commanding and early market share lead. Studies also have found that market pioneers can command a greater market share over a longer time period than later entrants can.[8]

This finding does not imply, however, that all pioneers succeed.[9] In many cases, imitators capitalize on the weaknesses of pioneers and subsequently gain advantage in the market. Because pioneering products and brands face the uphill task of establishing the market alone, they pave the way for followers, who can spend less marketing effort creating demand for the product category and instead focus directly on creating demand for their specific brand. Also, because the pioneer is the first product in the market, it often has a less sophisticated design and may be priced relatively higher, leaving room for better and lower-priced competitive products. A majority of new products are failures: As many as 95 percent of all new consumer goods fail, and products across all markets and industries suffer failure rates of 50 to 80 percent.[10]

Even if they succeed, new-to-the-world products are not adopted by everyone at the same time. Rather, they diffuse or spread through a population in a process known as *diffusion of innovation.*

DIFFUSION OF INNOVATION

The process by which the use of an innovation—whether a product or a service—spreads throughout a market group, over time and over various categories of adopters, is referred to as diffusion of innovation.[11] The theory surrounding diffusion of innovation helps marketers understand the rate at which consumers are likely to adopt a new product or service. It also gives them a means to identify

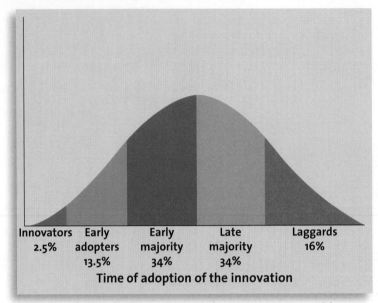

Source: Adapted from Everett M. Rodgers, *Diffusion of Innovation* (New York: The Free Press, 1983).

potential markets for their new products or services and predict their potential sales, even before they introduce the innovations.

As the diffusion of innovation curve in Exhibit 11.1 shows, the number of users of an innovative product or service spreads through the population over a period of time and generally follows a bell-shaped curve. A few people buy the product or service at first, then increasingly more buy, and finally fewer people buy as the degree of the diffusion slows. These purchasers can be divided into five groups according to how soon they buy the product after it has been introduced.

Innovators

Innovators are those buyers who want to be the first on the block to have the new product or service. These buyers enjoy taking risks and are regarded as highly knowledgeable. You probably know someone who is an innovator—or perhaps you are one for a particular product or service category. For example, the person who stood in line overnight to be sure to get a ticket for the very first showing of the latest Batman movie is an innovator in that context. Firms that invest in the latest technology, either to use in their products or services or to make the firm more efficient, also are considered innovators. Typically, innovators keep themselves very well informed about the product category by subscribing to trade and specialty magazines, talking to other "experts," searching the Internet, and attending product-related forums, seminars, and special events. Typically, innovators represent only about 2.5 percent of the total market for any new product or service.

However, these innovators are crucial to the success of any new product or service because they help the product gain market acceptance. Through talking about and spreading positive word of mouth about the new product, they prove instrumental in bringing in the next adopter category, known as early adopters.

Early Adopters

The second subgroup that begins to use a product or service innovation is the early adopters. They generally don't like to take as much risk as innovators do but instead wait and purchase the product after careful review. Thus, this market waits for the first reviews of the Batman movie, *The Dark Knight,* before purchasing a ticket, though they likely still go a week or two after it opens. Early adopters tend to enjoy novelty and often are regarded as the opinion leaders for particular product categories.

This group, which represents about 13.5 percent of all buyers in the market, acts as opinion leaders who spread the word. As a result, early adopters are crucial for bringing the other three buyer categories to the market. If the early adopter group is relatively small, the number of people who ultimately adopt the innovation likely will also be small.

Early Majority

The **early majority**, which represents approximately 34 percent of the population, is crucial because few new products and services can be profitable until this large group buys them. If the group never becomes large enough, the product or service typically fails.

The early majority group differs in many ways from buyers in the first two stages. Its members don't like to take as much risk and therefore tend to wait until "the bugs" are worked out of a particular product or service. If we continue our application to movies, this group probably rents *The Dark Knight* from a video store when it first comes out on video. Thus, they experience little risk, because all the reviews are in, and their costs are lower because they're renting the movie instead of going to the theater. When early majority customers enter the market, the number of competitors in the marketplace usually also has reached its peak, so these buyers have many different price and quality choices.

An innovator is, for example, the person who stood in line all night just to see the opening of the latest Batman movie, The Dark Knight.

Late Majority

At 34 percent of the market, the **late majority** is the last group of buyers to enter a new product market; when they do, the product has achieved its full market potential. Perhaps these movie watchers wait until the latest Batman movie is always in stock or just put it low on their Netflix queue, to be delivered after the other consumers interested in watching it have already seen it. By the time the late majority enters the market, sales tend to level off or may be in decline.

Laggards

Laggards make up roughly 16 percent of the market. These consumers like to avoid change and rely on traditional products until they are no longer available.[12] In some cases, laggards may never adopt a certain product or service. When *The Dark Knight* eventually releases on regular television networks, they are likely to go ahead and watch it.

Using the Diffusion of Innovation Theory

Using the diffusion of innovation theory, firms can predict which types of customers will buy their new product or service immediately after its introduction, as well as later as the product gets more and more accepted by the market. With this

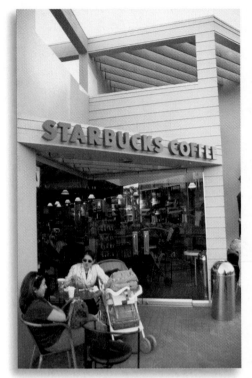

What has made Starbucks so successful? It has a strong relative advantage *over other coffee venues. It is* compatible *with people's current behavior. Products and locations are easily* observable *by others. It is* not complex *and is easy* to try.

knowledge, the firm can develop effective promotion, pricing, and other marketing strategies to push acceptance among each customer group. However, because different products diffuse at different rates, marketers must understand what the diffusion curve for the new product looks like, as well as the characteristics of the target customers in each stage of the diffusion. The speed with which products diffuse depends on several product characteristics.

Relative Advantage   If a product is perceived to be better than substitutes, then the diffusion will be relatively quick. Many believe, for example, that Starbucks' meteoric rise to success is because it is a superior substitute to doughnut or traditional coffee shops.

Compatibility   Similarly, the ritual of "having a coffee" is well ingrained in many cultures, including American culture. "Having coffee" is consistent with people's past behavior, their needs, and their values. Since people are accustomed to drinking coffee, it has been relatively easy for Starbucks to acquire customers in the United States. The diffusion has been much slower in countries like China and Japan, where tea has been the traditional drink.

Observability   The ubiquitous Starbucks logo can be easily seen on cups in and around Starbucks stores. When products are easily observed, their benefits or uses are easily communicated to others, thus enhancing the diffusion process. A Botox treatment to reduce wrinkles, on the other hand, is not easily observed by others and therefore has diffused more slowly.

Complexity and Trialability   Products that are relatively less complex are also relatively easy to try. These products will generally diffuse more quickly than those that are not so easy to try. Purchasing a tall nonfat latte, for instance, is a lot easier than purchasing a new car with a GPS system.

The diffusion of innovation theory thus comes into play in the immediate and long-term aftermath of a new product or service introduction. But before the introduction, firms must actually develop those new offerings. In the next section, we detail the process by which most firms develop new products and services and how they initially introduce them into the market.

CHECK YOURSELF

1. What are the five groups on the diffusion of innovation curve?
2. What factors enhance the diffusion of a good or service?

HOW FIRMS DEVELOP NEW PRODUCTS

The new product development process begins with the generation of new product ideas and culminates in the launch of a new product and the evaluation of its success. The stages of the new product development process, along with the important objectives of each stage, are summarized in Exhibit 11.2.

Idea Generation

To generate ideas for new products, a firm can use its own internal research and development (R&D) efforts, collaborate with other firms and institutions, license technology from research-intensive firms, brainstorm, research competitors' products and services, and/or conduct consumer research; see Exhibit 11.3. Firms that

EXHIBIT 11.2   The Product Development Process

IDEA GENERATION	CONCEPT TESTING	PRODUCT DEVELOPMENT	MARKET TESTING	PRODUCT LAUNCH	EVALUATION OF RESULTS
Development of viable new product ideas.	Testing the new product idea among a set of potential customers.	Development of prototypes and/or the product.	Testing the actual products in a few test markets.	Full-scale commercialization of the product.	Analysis of the performance of the new product and making appropriate modifications.

want to be pioneers rely more extensively on R&D efforts, whereas those that tend to adopt a follower strategy are more likely to scan the market for ideas. Let's look at each of these idea sources.

Internal Research and Development   Many firms have their own R&D departments, in which scientists work to solve complex problems and develop new ideas.[13] Historically, firms such as IBM in the computer industry, Black and Decker in the consumer goods industry, 3M in the industrial goods industry, and Merck and Pfizer in the pharmaceuticals industry have relied on R&D development efforts for their new products. In other industries, such as software, music, and motion pictures, product development efforts also tend to come from internal ideas and R&D financial investments.

The product development costs for these firms are quite high, and the resulting new product or service has a good chance of being a technological or market breakthrough. Firms expect such products to generate enough revenue and profits to make the costs of R&D worthwhile; however, R&D investments generally are considered continuous investments, so firms may lose money on a few new products. In the long run, though, these firms are betting that a few extremely successful new products, often known as blockbusters, can generate enough revenues and profits to cover the losses from other introductions that might not fare so well.

R&D Consortia   In recent years, more and more firms have been joining consortia, or groups of other firms and institutions, possibly including government and educational

EXHIBIT 11.3   Sources of New Product Ideas

Black & Decker relies on internal research and development efforts for new product ideas.

institutions, to explore new ideas or obtain solutions for developing new products. Here, the R&D investments come from the group as a whole, and the participating firms and institutions share the results.

The National Institutes of Health (NIH) is supporting a five-year, $71 million project to conduct clinical trials of treatments for rare diseases and disorders. A clinical trial is a medical study that tests the safety and effectiveness of a drug or treatment in people.[14] To be classified as rare, a disease must affect less than 200,000 people. Pharmaceutical companies are often reluctant to do research and develop products to treat these diseases because the market is too small to make a profit. There are about 6,000 rare diseases that impact 25 million Americans. The NIH sponsors medical foundations to do research to treat rare diseases. This research is disseminated to the medical community, thus encouraging drugs and therapies to be developed more quickly and at a lower cost than would be possible if the research were privately funded. The NIH currently is working with 10 research consortia and 30 patient advocacy groups in 50 sites in the United States, the United Kingdom, Japan, and Brazil.[15]

Licensing For many new scientific and technological products, firms buy the rights to use the technology or ideas from other research-intensive firms through a licensing agreement. This approach saves the high costs of in-house R&D, but it means that the firm is banking on a solution that already exists but has not been marketed. For example, many pharmaceutical firms license products developed by biotechnology firms such as Amgen, Biogen, and Genentech. Because most biotechnology firms are smaller, tend to be very research focused, and lack the resources and expertise to market their own innovations, they are content to obtain some development financing and royalties on sales of their product from the pharmaceutical firms.[16]

Brainstorming Firms often engage in brainstorming sessions during which a group works together to generate ideas. One of the key characteristics of a brainstorming session is that no idea can be immediately accepted or rejected. The moderator of the session may channel participants' attention to specific product features and attributes, performance expectations, or packaging, but only at the end of the session do the members vote on the best ideas or combinations of ideas. Those ideas that receive the most votes are carried forward to the next stage of the product development process.

In some cases, companies have trouble moving through these steps alone, which prompts them to turn to outside firms like Inventables, which we discussed in the chapter opener, and IDEO. IDEO is a design firm based in Palo Alto, California, that offers not new products themselves but rather a stellar service that helps clients generate new product and service ideas in industries such as health care, toys, and computers. IDEO employs anthropologists, graphic designers, engineers, and psychologists whose special skills help foster creativity and innovation. The firm has worked with Procter & Gamble, HMO Kaiser Permanente, Nestlé, Hewlett-Packard, Vodafone, Samsung, AT&T Wireless, NASA, and the BBC, to name a few.

Competitors' Products   A new product entry by a competitor may trigger a market opportunity for a firm, which can use reverse engineering to understand the competitor's product and then bring an improved version to market. Reverse engineering involves taking apart a product, analyzing it, and creating an improved product that does not infringe on the competitor's patents, if any exist. This copycat approach to new product development is widespread and practiced by even the most research-intensive firms. Copycat consumer goods show up in grocery and drugstore products, as well as in technologically more complex products like automobiles and computers.

Customer Input   Listening to the customer is essential for successful idea generation.[17] Studies have found that as many as 85 percent of all new business-to-business (B2B) product ideas come from customers.[18] Because customers for B2B products are relatively few, firms can follow their use of products closely and solicit suggestions and ideas to improve those products either by using a formal approach, such as focus groups, interviews, or surveys, or through more informal discussions. The firm's design and development team then works on these suggestions, sometimes in consultation with the customer. This joint effort between the selling firm and the customer significantly increases the probability that the customer eventually will buy the new product.

Such collaboration is not necessarily limited just to new products, but can also help a company innovate in areas such as packaging. Many consumers experience "wrap rage"—a great frustration with packaging that makes it seemingly impossible to get at the actual products. So many companies are moving away from the traditional clamshells, which are the curved plastic package around many electronics goods, because they are so difficult to open. For instance, Costco has replaced the clamshells with packaging made of coated paperboard that still requires scissors to open, but is flat and therefore can be opened easily. This innovation benefits the seller because it prevents easy theft of expensive electronics products. Consumers benefit as well because it is easier to open.[19]

One successful customer input approach is to analyze lead users, those innovative product users who modify existing products according to their own ideas to suit their specific needs.[20] If lead users customize a firm's products, other customers might wish to do so as well. Thus, studying lead users helps the firm understand general market trends that might be just on the horizon. Manufacturers and retailers of fashion products often spot new trends by noticing how trendsetters have altered their clothing and shoes. For instance, designers of high-fashion jeans distress their products in different ways depending on signals they pick up "on the street." One season, jeans appear with whiskers, the next season they have holes, the next, paint spots.

Another way to garner input from customers is to sponsor contests. Staples, for instance, is concentrating on the development of new private-label products. They sponsor InventionQuest to encourage the public to create office supply inventions. Winners receive up to $25,000 and 8 percent royalty on sales. Products like Rubber Bandits (extra long rubber bands with a write-on label) or TackDots (small rubber disks with adhesive on the back, used to hang notes or pictures in small spaces like a computer monitor) are new private-label products that have been introduced as a result of the InventionQuest contest. Staples has received over 22,000 ideas from the public.[21]

These innovative consumers are called lead users *because they modify existing products according to their own ideas to suit their specific needs.*

At the end of the idea-generation stage, the firm should have several ideas that it can take forward to the next stage: concept testing.

Concept Testing

Ideas with potential are developed further into concepts, which in this context refer to brief written descriptions of the product; its technology, working principles, and forms; and what customer needs it would satisfy.[22] A concept might also include visual images of what the product would look like.

Concept testing refers to the process in which a concept statement is presented to potential buyers or users to obtain their reactions. These reactions enable the developer to estimate the sales value of the product or service concept, possibly make changes to enhance its sales value, and determine whether the idea is worth further development.[23] If the concept fails to meet customers' expectations, it is doubtful it would succeed if it were to be produced and marketed. Because concept testing occurs very early in the new product introduction process, even before a real product has been made, it helps the firm avoid the costs of unnecessary product development.

The concept for an electric scooter might be written as follows:

> The product is a lightweight electric scooter that can be easily folded and taken with you inside a building or on public transportation. The scooter weighs 25 pounds. It travels at speeds of up to 15 miles per hour and can go about 12 miles on a single charge. The scooter can be recharged in about two hours from a standard electric outlet. The scooter is easy to ride and has simple controls—just an accelerator button and a brake. It sells for $299.[24]

Concept testing progresses along the research techniques described in Chapter 9. The firm likely starts with exploratory research, such as in-depth interviews or focus groups, to test the concept, after which it can undertake conclusive research through Internet or mall-intercept surveys. Video clips on the Internet might show a virtual prototype and the way it works so that potential customers can evaluate the product or service. In a mall-intercept survey, an interviewer would provide a description of the concept to the respondent and then ask several questions to obtain his or her feedback.

The most important question pertains to the respondent's purchase intentions if the product or service were made available. Marketers also should ask whether the product would satisfy a need that other products currently are not meeting. Depending on the type of product or service, researchers might also ask about the expected frequency of purchase, how much customers would buy, whether they would buy it for themselves or as a gift, when they would buy, and whether the price information (if provided) indicates a good value. In addition, marketers usually collect some information about the customers so they can analyze which consumer segments are likely to be most interested in the product. The airline industry is testing a technology that is expected to significantly alleviate the lost baggage problem. (See Superior Service 11.1.)

Some concepts never make it past concept testing stage, particularly if respondents seem uninterested. Those that do receive high evaluations from potential consumers, however, move on to the next step, product development.

Product Development

Product development or product design entails a process of balancing various engineering, manufacturing, marketing, and economic considerations to develop a product's form and features or a service's features. An engineering team develops a product prototype that is based on research findings from the previous concept testing step, as well as their own knowledge about materials and technology. A prototype is the first physical form or service description of a new product, still in rough or tentative form, that has the same properties as a new product but is produced through different manufacturing processes—sometimes even crafted individually.[25]

Superior Service 11.1   Airlines Can Improve Luggage Efficiency through RFID[26]

Many problems arise during commercial flights, but the problem of lost luggage might be reduced significantly through the use of radio frequency identification (RFID) tags. These tags replace luggage tags, so that airlines can track each bag as it moves from point A to point B. The RFID system at the Las Vegas airport, for instance, has resulted in less lost baggage, less sorting, and more knowledge about the specific location of bags.

The International Air Transport Association (IATA) may decide to require all airlines to use RFID luggage tags, but airlines have been reluctant to adopt the bagging system because of its additional price. Each tag costs about 15 cents per tag, compared with 4 cents per tag for the existing paper tags that airlines use.

The RFID luggage tags reduce the hassle and money required of airlines and their passengers. U.S. airlines spend about $400 million annually on lost luggage, including reimbursing customers and delivering misplaced bags. With RFID, predictions suggest lost luggage may be reduced by 20 percent, and only 1 percent of bags will have to be manually sorted, compared with the 10–20 percent manually sorted with existing luggage tags. The RFID system is 99 percent accurate in reading tags, a significant improvement over current systems.

The potential mandate from the IATA that all airlines use an RFID tagging system could make flying more enjoyable for customers. The technology offers a huge advantage to customers and could even influence which airlines they choose. Lost or delayed luggage can ruin a traveling experience, so those airlines with a virtually guaranteed luggage arrival system should achieve a strong competitive advantage.

Product prototypes are usually tested through alpha and beta testing. In alpha testing, the firm attempts to determine whether the product will perform according to its design and whether it satisfies the need for which it was intended.[27] Rather than use potential consumers, alpha tests occur in the firm's R&D department. For instance, Ben & Jerry's Ice Cream alpha tests all its proposed new flavors on its own employees at its corporate headquarters in Vermont. It may be a great job, but it can also be fattening!

Many people, consumer groups, and governmental agencies are concerned when alpha testing involves tests on animals, particularly when it comes to pharmaceuticals and cosmetics. Ethical and Societal Dilemma 11.1 on the next page discusses these concerns in the United States and the European Union.

In contrast, beta testing uses potential consumers, who examine the product prototype in a "real use" setting to determine its functionality, performance, potential problems, and other issues specific to its use. The firm might develop several prototype products that it gives to users, then survey those users to determine whether the product worked as intended and identify any issues that need resolution.

Household products manufacturer Kimberly-Clark uses virtual testing in the beta-testing phase of its product development process. The consumer goods company uses a virtual store aisle that mimics a real-life shopping experience by creating a realistic picture of the interior of the store. A retina-tracking device records the movement of a test customer who "shops" the virtual aisle of a store and chooses certain products to investigate further in the virtual simulation. Thus, consumer companies can demonstrate the likely success, or failure, of a product without actually having to produce it for a market and, potentially, expose its secrets to competitors.[28]

Market Testing

The firm has developed its new product or service and tested the prototypes. Now it must test the market for the new product with a trial batch of products. These tests can take two forms: premarket testing or test marketing.

Premarket Tests Firms conduct premarket tests before they actually bring a product or service to market to determine how many customers will try and then continue to use the product or service according to a small group of potential

Ethical and Societal Dilemma 11.1 Should Firms Test on Animals?

Product testing on animals has been a primary issue for animal rights activists for years.[29] As public opposition to animal testing increases, so do many companies' declarations that they "do not test products on animals." However, such statements can be misleading because even though the whole product may not have been tested on animals, the individual ingredients may have been. To help clarify any confusion, companies can apply to the Coalition for Consumer Information on Cosmetics (CCIC), a national group formed by eight animal welfare group members such as the United States Humane Association and the Doris Day

The Leaping Bunny Logo can be purchased from the Coalition for Consumer Information on Cosmetics (CCIC) if a company's products are certified to be free from cruelty to animals.

consumers. One popular proprietary premarket test version is called BASES II, conducted by the research firm ACNielsen. During the test, potential customers are exposed to the marketing mix variables, such as the advertising, then surveyed and given a sample of the product to try.[31] After some period of time, during which the potential customers try the product, they are surveyed about whether they would buy/use the product again. This second survey indicates an estimation of the probability of a consumer's repeat purchase. From these data, the firm generates a sales estimate for the new product that enables it to decide whether to introduce the product, abandon it, redesign it before introduction, or revise the marketing plan. An early evaluation of this sort—that is, before the product is introduced to the whole market—saves marketers the costs of a nationwide launch if the product fails.

Sometimes firms simulate a product or service introduction, in which case potential customers view the advertising of various currently available products or services along with advertising for the new product or service. They receive money to buy the product or service from a simulated environment, such as a mock Web page or store, and respond to a survey after they make their purchases. This test thus can determine the effectiveness of a firm's advertising as well as the expected trial rates for the new product.

Test Marketing   A method of determining the success potential of a new product, **test marketing** introduces the offering to a limited geographical area (usually a few cities) prior to a national launch. A test marketing effort uses all the elements

Animal League, and be certified as "cruelty free." They then can purchase the trademarked Leaping Bunny Logo from CCIC for use on their labels.

One of the founding principles of The Body Shop, and one that has resonated well with its customers, is that its products are free of animal testing. Another major cosmetics manufacturer, Procter & Gamble, has eliminated animal testing on more than 80 percent of its products. It uses a combination of in vitro testing, computer modeling, and historical data to determine the safety of new products and ingredients. These methods are more expensive than more traditional methods, but P&G claims that the results are better. If performed correctly, new chemicals can either be dropped from consideration or pushed forward in as little as three days compared to the six months previously required for animal testing.

In other fields, animal welfare groups continue to push to stop the use of animal testing altogether. The People for the Ethical Treatment of Animals (PETA) publicly cites companies it accuses of engaging in animal testing and praises those that do not. Its Web site links to another site encouraging consumers to be "sweethearts" by buying Valentine's candy from Hershey's instead of Mars (maker of M&M's candy) because Mars tests the effects of cocoa on rats, whereas Hershey's does not.[30]

The European Union has passed a ban on animal testing altogether. Beginning in 2009, any cosmetic tested on animals, even in other parts of the world, cannot be sold in the European Union. However, the cosmetics industry is worried that this ban will not only affect their companies' sales, but also their customers' ability to find the products they want. The EU cosmetics industry successfully lobbied for an extension on certain areas of toxicity testing to provide more time to find alternatives. The cosmetics industry believes it will be difficult to find alternative testing methods in time, and if they cannot, then they will have fewer ingredients to make the products consumers want.

The issues involved in animal testing are complex. At the broadest level, should firms be allowed to develop products that customers want, even if there is some potential harm to the environment or to those animals that share the environment with humans? More specifically, should firms be allowed to test products on animals, even when those products are not specifically designed to improve the health and well-being of their human users? Does the testing that is performed endanger the lives or health of the animals?

of the marketing mix: It includes promotions like advertising and coupons, just as if the product were being introduced nationally, and the product appears in targeted retail outlets, with appropriate pricing. On the basis of the results of the test marketing, the firm can estimate demand for the entire market.

Test marketing costs more and takes longer than premarket tests, which may provide an advantage to competitors that could get a similar or better product to market first without test marketing. For this reason, some firms, such as Newman's Own Organic, launch new products (e.g., its Fig Newmans™) without extensive consumer testing and rely instead on intuition, instincts, and guts.[32]

Test marketing, however, is a strong predictor of product success because the firm can study actual purchase behavior, which is more reliable than a simulated test. For instance, Folgers realized that 35–40 million Americans had eliminated or reduced their coffee intake because of their concerns about its effects on their stomachs. So it began to test market a new product called Simply Smooth, a low-acid version of its well-known coffee brand. Folgers first considered how the product would sell with a small test market. After positive results, it began a rollout nationwide.[33]

Many firms use BehaviorScan to improve the probability of success during the test marketing phase of a new product introduction. BehaviorScan utilizes consumer panel data collected passively at the point of sale in stores and through home scanning to measure individual household first-time trial and repeat purchases. New products are placed in stores within 1 week of introduction, rather than the typical 8- to 12-week period. Since more sales data are collected in a shorter period of time than with conventional test marketing methods, first-year sales can be estimated after just 16 to 24 weeks in the test market.[34] Once the market demand is estimated, the firm can determine how aggressively the product should be introduced nationally.

Product Launch

If the market testing returns with positive results, the firm is ready to introduce the product to the entire market. This most critical step in the new product introduction requires tremendous financial resources and extensive coordination of all aspects of the marketing mix. If the new product launch is a failure, it may be difficult for the product—and perhaps the firm—to recover. Some new products show great promise, though, as Exhibit 11.4 describes.

EXHIBIT 11.4   Innovative New Products

	Product	Description
	Wheat Thins Chips—Veggie	Crackers that have the consistency of a chip and are flavored like vegetables.
	Jimmy Dean Pancakes & Sausage on a Stick	Chocolate chip pancake batter wrapped around a sausage on a stick.
	DanActive Immunity boosting beverages	Probiotic drink that strengthens the body's defenses against cold weather and stress.
	Annie's Organic Cheddar Bunnies	An organic version of Goldfish in the shape of a rabbit for kids.
	Wind-defying umbrella from Hammacher Schlemmer	Resists gusts of wind up to 35 mph that turn umbrellas inside out.

So what does a product launch involve? First, on the basis of the research it has gathered on consumer perceptions, the tests it has conducted, and competitive considerations, the firm confirms its target market (or markets) and decides how the product will be positioned. Then the firm finalizes the remaining marketing mix variables for the new product, including the marketing budget for the first year.[35]

Promotion　The test results help the firm determine an appropriate integrated marketing communications strategy.[36] Promotion for new products is required at each link in the supply chain. If the products are not sold and stocked by retailers, no amount of promotion to consumers will sell the products. Promotions to retailers to get them to purchase the new products are often a combination of introductory price promotions, special events, and personal selling. Introductory price promotions are limited-duration lower-than-normal prices designed to provide retailers with an incentive to try the products. Manufacturers may run a special event in the form of an introductory celebration or a party in conjunction with an interesting event like a sporting event or the Academy Awards. Fashion retailers have elaborate runway shows to introduce their new products. Finally, as in many B2B sales situations, personal selling may be the most efficient way to get retailers to purchase their products.

Manufacturers also use promotion to generate demand for new products with consumers. If manufacturers can create demand for the products with consumers, they will go to retailers asking for it, thus further inducing retailers to carry the products. These promotions are often coupled with short-term price reductions, coupons, or rebates. Sometimes manufacturers promote new products in advance of the product launch just to create excitement with potential customers. Automobile and motorcycle manufacturers, for instance, advertise their new products months before they are available on the dealers' floors.

For products that are somewhat complex or conceptually new, marketers may need to provide for more consumer education about the product's benefits than they would for simpler and more familiar products. For technical products, technical support staff must be trained to answer customer questions that may arise immediately after the launch. And for other new ideas, the promotion may simply represent an effort to add value to a relatively well-known product, as Adding Value 11.1 describes.

Place　The manufacturer coordinates the delivery and storage of the new products with its retailers to assure that it is available for sale when the customer wants it, at the stores the customer is expecting to find it, and in sufficient quantities to meet demand. Manufacturers work with their retailers on decisions such as:

- Should the merchandise be stored at retailers' distribution centers or distributed directly to stores?
- What initial and fill-in quantities should be shipped?
- Should the manufacturer be involved in reordering decisions?
- Should the merchandise be individually packaged so it is easy to display in the stores?
- Should price stickers be affixed on the merchandise at the factory or at the store?
- Should the manufacturer be involved in the maintenance of the merchandise once in the store?

Coupons or rebates are often used when a new product is introduced.

Adding Value 11.1   Marilyn Monroe Would Love It: Diamonds for Hair Care[37]

In the drive to create the next big thing in hair care products, consumer goods companies search for innovations in a variety of areas—packaging, brand image, and performance benefits, to name a few. But little changes occur in the basics of hair care, which still relies on product lines like shampoo, conditioner, and styling products. To make its latest lines stand out, Nivea has added something new, something that intrinsically has value in financial markets but is being integrated more for its image appeal in this case: diamonds.

With the new Diamond Gloss line, Nivea promises that consumers get actual diamonds ground up into their beauty products. But the value doesn't come from inclusion of the dust of the most expensive gemstones in the world. Instead, the company promises added value in the form of a shine like diamonds.

Women who wash and condition their hair with Diamond Gloss products will get "added brilliance" and "light reflection," making their hair seem shinier and healthier. Note that

Does adding crushed diamonds to hair products enhance their value?

the crushed up diamonds do nothing to improve hair health, and the company is careful to avoid making that claim. Rather, it promotes the idea that the diamonds themselves, when applied to hair, will make it shine like a diamond would.

Under a different brand name, Nivea's parent company, Beiersdorf AG, offers Cellular Radiance Concentrate Pure Gold by la prairie, a liquid skin serum in which 24-carat gold is dissolved. According to the company's promotions, "the tiny particles melt into the skin to produce an incomparable radiance and a look that speaks of vitality." Again, gold's value in the serum has nothing to do with its trading price or any actual, proven effect on skin. Rather, the value comes from the idea that a consumer can glitter like gold.

The value to the consumer comes from the idea of luxury these products promise. Diamonds in our hair and gold on our faces—the ultimate in precious value.

Price   Like the promotion of new products, setting prices is a supply chain–wide decision. Manufacturers must decide at what price they would like products to sell to consumers on the basis of the factors to be discussed in Chapters 13 and 14. They often encourage retailers to sell at a specified price known as the manufacturer's suggested retail price (MSRP). Although retailers often don't abide by the MSRP, manufacturers can withhold benefits such as cooperative advertising or even refuse to deliver merchandise to noncomplying retailers. It is sometimes easier to start with a higher MSRP and then over time lower it than it is to introduce the new product at a low price and then try to raise it.

When setting the MSRP, manufacturers also consider the price at which the new products are sold to the retailers. The retailers not only need to make a profit on each sale, but they may also receive a slotting allowance from the manufacturer, which is a fee paid simply to get new products into stores or to gain more or better shelf space for their products.

Timing   The timing of the launch may be important, depending on the product.[38] Hollywood studios typically release movies targeted toward general audiences (i.e., those rated G or PG) during the summer when children are out of school. New automobile models traditionally are released for sale during September, and fashion products are launched just before the season of the year for which they are intended.

Evaluation of Results

After the product has been launched, marketers must undertake a critical postlaunch review to determine whether the product and its launch were a success or failure and what additional resources or changes to the marketing mix are needed, if any. Firms measure the success of a new product by three interrelated factors: (1) its satisfaction of technical requirements, such as performance; (2) customer acceptance; and (3) its satisfaction of the firm's financial requirements, such as sales and profits.[39] If the product is not performing sufficiently well, poor customer acceptance will result, which in turn leads to poor financial performance.

The new product development process, as we have seen, when followed rationally and sequentially, helps avoid such domino-type failures. The *product life cycle*, discussed in the next section, helps marketers manage their products' marketing mix during and after its introduction.

CHECK YOURSELF

1. What are the steps in the new product development process?
2. Identify different sources of new product ideas.

THE PRODUCT LIFE CYCLE

The product life cycle defines the stages that new products move through as they enter, get established in, and ultimately leave the marketplace and thereby offers marketers a starting point for their strategy planning. Exhibit 11.5 illustrates a typical product life cycle, including the industry sales and profits over time. In their life cycles, products pass through four stages: introduction, growth, maturity, and decline. When innovators start buying the product, the product enters the introduction stage of its life cycle. In the growth stage, the product gains acceptance, demand and sales increase, and competitors emerge in the product category. In the maturity stage, industry sales reach their peak, so firms try to rejuvenate their products by adding new features or repositioning them. If these efforts succeed, the product achieves new life.[40] If not, it goes into decline and eventually exits the market.

EXHIBIT 11.5   Product Life Cycle

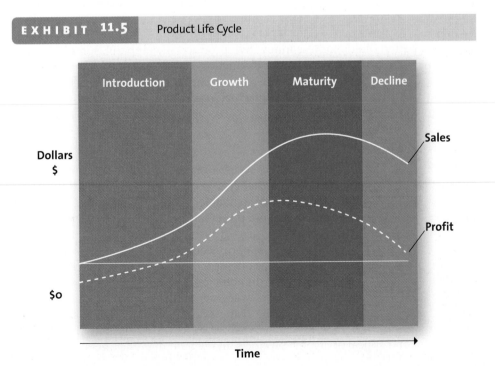

EXHIBIT 11.6	Characteristics of Different Stages of the Product Life			
	Introduction	**Growth**	**Maturity**	**Decline**
Sales	Low	Rising	Peak	Declining
Profits	Negative or low	Rapidly rising	Peak to declining	Declining
Typical consumers	Innovators	Early adopters and early majority	Late majority	Laggards
Competitors (number of firms and products)	One or few	Few but increasing	High number of competitors and competitive products	Low number of competitors and products

Not every product follows the same life cycle curve; many products stay in the maturity stage for a very long time. For example, "white good" categories, such as clothes washers, dryers, and refrigerators, have been in the maturity stage for a very long time and will remain there indefinitely until a superior product comes along to replace them.

The product life cycle offers a useful tool for managers to analyze the types of strategies that may be required over the life of their products. Even the strategic emphasis of a firm and its marketing mix (four Ps) strategies can be adapted from insights about the characteristics of each stage of the cycle, as we summarize in Exhibit 11.6.

Let's look at each of these stages in depth.

Introduction Stage

The introduction stage for a new, innovative product or service usually starts with a single firm, and innovators are the ones to try the new offering. Some new-to-the-world products and services that defined their own product category and industry include the telephone (invented by Alexander Graham Bell in 1876), the transistor semiconductor (Bell Laboratories in 1947), the Walkman portable cassette player (Sony in 1979), the Internet browser (Netscape in 1994), personal digital assistant (Palm in 1996), iTunes (Apple in 2001), and Blu-Ray (Sony in 2006). Sensing the viability and commercialization possibilities of this market-creating new product, other firms soon enter the market with similar or improved products at lower prices. The same pattern holds for less innovative products like apparel, some CDs, and even a new soft drink flavor. The introduction stage is characterized by initial losses to the firm due to its high start-up costs and low levels of sales revenue as the product begins to take off. If the product is successful, firms may start seeing profits toward the end of this stage.

Growth Stage

The growth stage of the product life cycle is marked by a growing number of product adopters, rapid growth in industry sales, and increases in both the number of competitors and the number of available product versions.[41] The market becomes more segmented and consumer preferences more varied, which increases the potential for new markets or new uses of the product or service.[42] Innovators start rebuying the product, and early majority consumers enter.

Also during the growth stage, firms attempt to reach new consumers by studying their preferences and producing different product variations—varied colors, styles, or features—which enable them to segment the market more precisely. The goal of this segmentation is to ride the rising sales trend and firmly establish the firm's brand, so as not to be outdone by competitors. In recognizing the growing demand for and appeal of organic products, many food manufacturers are working hard to become the first brand that consumers think of when they consider organic products. Del Monte was the first of the major canned vegetable sellers to go organic, releasing organic versions of its tomatoes, green beans, corn, and sweet peas, along with an organic chicken broth product under its College Inn line. The cans feature bold "organic" banners across the front and promise that no pesticides were used to produce the food items. Even though Del Monte products have been around for over 100 years, in this growth category, the company must work to establish its distinctive appeal in the organic market in particular.[43]

As firms ride the crest of increasing industry sales, profits in the growth stage also rise because of the economies of scale associated with manufacturing and marketing costs, especially promotion and advertising. At the same time, firms that have not yet established a stronghold in the market, even in narrow segments, may decide to exit in what is referred to as an "industry shakeout." Adding Value 11.2 describes TiVo's move from the introduction to growth stage of the product life cycle.

These new-to-the-world products defined their own product category and industry. The telephone (left) was invented in 1876 and the Walkman (right) came out in 1979.

Adding Value 11.2   The TiVo® Experience and the Consumer[44]

The digital video recorder (DVR) enables consumers to choose what television shows to watch and when, to pause and rewind whenever they want, and even to get an instant replay of their favorite TV shows. Silicon Valley–based TiVo Inc. was the pioneer and dominant brand in this market for several years after the introduction of DVRs in 1999. TiVo's unit is a box that sits atop consumers' television sets that, depending on the model, allows a consumer to record and play back 150 hours or more of standard definition or high definition TV programming on its hard drive using standard video compression formats. Each night, the unit dials into a server and downloads weeks' worth of program information from the consumer's cable or satellite provider. Consumers pay for the initial unit as well as a monthly subscription fee.

However, TiVo's primary competitors, including satellite providers such as Dish Network and cable providers such as Time Warner and Comcast, are making great inroads on its market share. Currently, approximately 19 percent of U.S. households have DVR capabilities, and according to The Carmel Research Group, the DVR market will grow rapidly. By 2010, it expects penetration rates to increase to 46 percent, or around 52.5 million households. Of these adoptees, approximately 4.3 million consumers currently use the TiVo® DVR and service. In the future, cable providers are anticipated to take the lead in the market, grabbing 61 percent of the DVR market, followed by satellite providers with 32 percent, and, at the back of the pack, TiVo with just 2 percent.*

To avoid this market share erosion, TiVo's challenge is to get consumers not only to adopt the technology but also to prefer its brand of DVRs. The company plans to woo customers by providing better consumer information; selectively distributing through electronics retailers that can better promote the product, such as Best Buy; keeping the technology and installation process as simple as possible; and entering into partnerships with cable and satellite providers, such as Comcast, Cox, and DIRECTV, that agree to use the TiVo software in their devices. In addition, to compete better against cable providers, the company embraced a three-pronged strategy: lower costs on some models, offer greater support service, and establish agreements with cable companies, by which they provide TiVo branded boxes to their customers. Yet the name once synonymous with DVR is facing a tough road ahead in its efforts to remain consumers' first choice.

It's Easy to Set Up!

▸ Get TiVo® HD DVR + TiVo service
▸ Replace your cable box with TiVo HD
▸ Get the best of broadcast + broadband when you connect to your wired or wireless home network

Comparison Chart

	TiV HD DVR	Other DVRs**
Recording Capacity	20 hours HD	Typically 20 HD hours or less
Record and Watch in HDTV	●	●
Record 2 Shows at Once†	●	●
Search Broadband & Broadcast TV*	●	
Online Scheduling	●	
Download Movies Directly to Your DVR*	●	
Watch YouTube videos*	●	
Stream Music with Rhapsody	●	
Transfer shows to your iPod	●	
Expandable Storage‡	●	
TiVoToGo*	●	
Over-the-air recording	●	
Kidzone	●	
Compatible Broadcast Sources	Cable, Antenna	Cable, Satellite

TiVo Service Pricing
Pay as you go: $12.95/month with a 1-year subscription
OR
Get 2 months free: prepay $129 for 1-year of service
Get one year free: prepay $299 for 3 years of service
Get a product lifetime service subscription for only $399
See www.tivo.com for pricing and service details

† CableCARD™ decoder may be required for dual tuner functionality and to resolve dual digital cable channels.
* Broadband Internet connection required.
‡ Compatible e-SATA hard drive is required. Visit www.tivo.com/expand. Sold separately.
** Explore® 8300™ HD DVR.

TiVo offers many benefits not available with a simple DVR.

* This figure reflects TiVo's anticipated market share for its standalone DVRs and does not cover TiVo's deployment of DVRs with service providers.

Maturity Stage

The maturity stage of the product life cycle is characterized by the adoption of the product by the late majority and intense competition for market share among firms. Marketing costs (e.g., promotion, distribution) increase as these firms vigorously defend their market share against competitors. At the same time, they face intense competition on price as the average price of the product falls substantially compared with the shifts during the previous two stages of the life cycle. Lower prices and increased marketing costs begin to erode the profit margins for many firms. In the later phases of the maturity stage, the market has become quite saturated, and practically all potential customers for the product have already adopted the product. Such saturated markets are prevalent in developed countries. In the United States, most consumer packaged goods found in grocery and discount stores are already in the maturity stage.

Firms may pursue several strategies during this stage to increase their customer base and/or defend their market share, such as entry into new markets and market segments and developing new products.

Entry into New Markets or Market Segments   Because the market is saturated at this point, firms may attempt to enter new geographical markets, including international markets (as we discussed in Chapter 7), that may be less saturated. For example, Whirlpool has started manufacturing washing machines for Brazil, China, and India that it prices lower than those it sells in the United States to attract the large consumer base of lower-income consumers in these countries.[45] In many developing economies, the large and growing proportion of middle-class households is just beginning to buy the home, kitchen, and entertainment appliances that have been fairly standard in U.S. households for several decades. In India alone, the roughly 487 million middle-class consumers will spend $420 billion on a variety of consumer products in the next four years.[46]

However, even in mature markets, firms may be able to find new market segments. Emerging new trends or changes in consumer tastes may fragment mature markets, which would open new market opportunities. As the popularity of the Internet increased, for example, firms such as Expedia, Orbitz, Priceline, and Travelocity found that they could provide the easy access and convenience of online bookings for air travel, hotel stays, and car rentals. Consumers who prefer such access and convenience, as well as the ability to compare prices across different service providers, increasingly are using the Internet to make their travel plans.

New market opportunities also may emerge through simple product design changes, such as in the market for "wipes." Just a few years ago, baby wipes accounted for most of the sales of personal wipes, but Procter & Gamble's Oil of Olay Facial Cleansing Cloths and Unilever's Ponds Age-Defying wipes have gained significant market share.[47] In the household sector, products such as P&G's Swiffer duster, the electrostatic wipe for mopping floors, and Swiffer WetJet (its detergent) have expanded the market greatly. Clorox has added premoistened Armor All wipes to its do-it-yourself car cleaning line[48] and the Clorox® ToiletWand™ for consumers who don't enjoy unsightly and unsanitary toilet brushes hanging around in their bathrooms.[49] Although the household cleaning and cosmetic markets are both well established and mature, marketers working in these product categories saw trends early and moved to create new products that offer value for consumers.

Just a few years ago, baby wipes accounted for most of the sales of personal wipes. Firms have seen the opportunity to enter new markets, so products have proliferated.

Development of New Products Despite market saturation, firms continually introduce new products with improved features or find new uses for existing products because they need constant innovation and product proliferation to defend market share during intense competition. Firms such as 3M, P&G, and Hewlett-Packard, for instance, continuously introduce new products. Innovations by such firms ensure that they are able to retain or grow their respective market shares.

Sometimes new products are introduced by less-than-famous companies. Consider, for instance, the NanoCar, which is one-billionth the size of a regular automobile. Although not appropriate for a Sunday drive, it is fully functioning with parts such as axles, a laser-based security system to prevent theft or tampering, and an electrostatic motor to get it around. It is used to conduct research on a molecular scale to help unravel the mysteries of atomic science.[50]

The NanoCar is one-billionth the size of a regular car and is used to conduct research on a molecular scale.

Decline Stage

Firms with products in the decline stage either position themselves for a niche segment of diehard consumers or those with special needs or they completely exit the market. The few laggards that have not yet tried the product or service enter the market at this stage. Take vinyl long-playing records (LPs) for example. In an age of CDs and Internet-downloaded music in MP3 and other formats, it may seem surprising that vinyl records are still made and sold. But though the sales of vinyl LPs have been declining in the past 15 years, about 2 million still are sold in the United States each year. Granted, this is a minuscule number compared with the 800 million CDs sold each year, but diehard music lovers prefer the unique sound of a vinyl record to the digital sound of CDs and music in other formats. Because the grooves in vinyl records create sound waves that are similar to those of a live performance, and therefore provide a more authentic sound, nightclub DJs, discerning music listeners, and collectors prefer them. Even some younger listeners have been buying vinyl records, influenced perhaps by their parents' collections, the sound, or simply the uniqueness of an LP.

Aiding this continued demand is the fact that there are simply too many albums of music from the predigital era that are available only on vinyl. It may take many years, maybe even decades, for all the music from earlier generations to be digitized. Until that time, turntable equipment manufacturers, small record-pressing companies such as Music Connection in Manhattan, and new and emerging record companies, such as Premier Crue Music, continue to have a market that demands their LPs.[51]

The Shape of the Product Life Cycle Curve

In theory, the product life cycle curve is assumed to be bell shaped with regard to sales and profits. In reality, however, each product or service has its own individual shape; some move more rapidly through their product life cycles than others, depending on how different the product or service is from products currently in the market and how valuable it is to the consumer. New products and services that consumers accept very quickly have higher consumer adoption rates very early in their product life cycles and move faster across the various stages.

For example, DVD players and DVDs moved much faster than VCRs across the life cycle curve and have already reached the maturity stage, likely because consumers who already owned VCRs were accustomed to recording TV shows and playing prerecorded movies and programs. It also was easy to switch VCR customers to DVD technology because DVDs were more durable and had better resolution than videotapes. Finally, prices for DVDs and DVD players dropped more quickly and drastically than did VCR prices, which made the new technology a better value.

Strategies Based on Product Life Cycle: Some Caveats

Although the product life cycle concept provides a starting point for managers to think about the strategy they want to implement during each stage of the life cycle of a product, this tool must be used with care. The most challenging part of applying the product life cycle concept is that managers do not know exactly what shape each product's life cycle will take, so there is no way to know precisely what stage a product is in. If, for example, a product experiences several seasons of declining sales, a manager may decide that it has moved from the growth stage to decline and stop promoting the product. As a result, of course, sales decline further. The manager then believes he or she made the right decision because the product continues to follow a predetermined life cycle. But what if the original sales decline was due to a poor strategy or increased competition—issues that could have been addressed with positive marketing support? In this case, the product life cycle decision became a self-fulfilling prophecy, and a growth product was doomed to an unnecessary decline.[52]

Fortunately, new research, based on the history of dozens of consumer products, suggests that the product life cycle concept is indeed a valid idea, and new analytical tools now provide "rules" for detecting the key turning points in the cycle.[53] In the pharmaceutical industry, where breakthrough innovations are few and far between, firms use the product life cycle to identify the consumer promotions needed at each stage to get the most out of their existing brands.[54]

CHECK YOURSELF

1. What are the stages in the product life cycle?
2. How do sales and profits change during the various stages?

Summing Up

1. How can firms create value through innovation?

New products and services keep current customers coming back for more and induce new customers into the market. Multiple products and services also help diversify the firm's portfolio, thus lowering its overall risk and enhancing its value. Although risky, new-to-the-world products have tremendous potential because they are the first in the market to offer something that has never before been available.

2. What is the diffusion of innovation theory, and how can managers use it to make product line decisions?

The diffusion of innovation theory can help firms predict which types of customers will buy their products or services immediately upon introduction, as well as later as they gain more acceptance in the market. The firm can then develop marketing strategies to encourage acceptance among each customer group. Diffusion of innovation also can help predict sales.

3. How do firms create new products and services?

When firms develop new products, they go through several steps. First, they generate ideas for the product or service using several alternative techniques, such as internal research and development, R&D consortia, licensing, brainstorming, tracking competitors' products or services, or working with customers. Second, firms test their concepts by either describing the idea of the new product or service to potential customers or showing them images of what the product would look like. Third, the design process entails determining what the product or service will actually include and provide. Fourth, firms test market their designs. Fifth, if everything goes well in the test market, the product is launched. Sixth, firms must evaluate the new product or service to determine its success.

4. What is a product life cycle, and how can the concept be applied to product line decisions?

The product life cycle helps firms make marketing mix decisions on the basis of the product's stage in its life cycle. In the introduction stage, companies attempt to gain a strong foothold in the market quickly by appealing to innovators. During the growth stage, the objective is to establish the brand firmly. When the product reaches the maturity stage, firms compete intensely for market share, and many potential customers already own the product or use the service. Eventually, most products enter the decline phase, during which firms withdraw marketing support and eventually phase out the product. Knowing where a product or service is in its life cycle helps managers determine its specific strategy at any given point in time.

Key Terms

- alpha testing, 351
- beta testing, 351
- breakthrough, 342
- clinical trial, 348
- concept, 350
- concept testing, 350
- decline stage, 357
- diffusion of innovation, 343
- early adopter, 344
- early majority, 345

- first movers, 343
- growth stage, 357
- innovation, 341
- innovator, 344
- introduction stage, 357
- introductory price promotion, 355
- laggard, 345
- late majority, 345
- lead user, 349

- maturity stage, 357
- pioneer, 342
- premarket test, 351
- product design, 350
- product development, 350
- product life cycle, 357
- prototype, 350
- reverse engineering, 349
- slotting allowance, 356
- test marketing, 352

Marketing Applications

1. Some people think that a product should be considered "new" only if it is completely new to the market and has never existed before. Describe or give examples of other types of new products.

2. Apple has introduced a new three-quarter-inch-thick laptop. How quickly do you think this product will diffuse among the U.S. population? Describe the types of people that you expect will be in each of the diffusion of innovation categories.

3. Are there any advantages for companies that are the first to introduce products that create new markets? Justify your answer. If you see advantages, explain why some new products still fail.

4. Identify and describe the ways that companies generate new product ideas. Which of these ways involve the customer? How can firms assess the value of the ideas that customers generate?

5. Describe an example of a new product or service that is targeted at the college student market. Using the concept testing discussion in the chapter, describe how you would conduct a concept test for this product or service.

6. The New York Knicks' point guard Stephon Marbury has introduced a new line of basketball shoes, the "Starbury" line, that retails for around $15. What might make the shoes and other athletic wear in this line more or less valuable to consumers, compared with, say, a pair of $130 Zoom I Kobe sneakers?

7. Hummer is about to introduce a new model SUV and is currently in the market testing phase of the new product development process. Describe two ways that Hummer might conduct initial market testing prior to launching this new model.

8. Kellogg has just introduced several new organic versions of its classic breakfast cereals. As the manager responsible for these products, how would you assess their success? Why do you believe these issues are important?

9. What type of deodorant do you use? What stage of the product life cycle is it in? Is the deodorant manufacturer's marketing strategy—its four Ps—consistent with the product's stage in its life cycle? Explain.

10. In what stage of the product life cycle is a new model of a PlayStation video game console? Is Sony's marketing strategy—its four Ps—consistent with the product's stage in its life cycle? How is it different from that of the deodorant in the previous question? Explain.

11. You have recently been hired by a cosmetics company in the product development group. The firm's brand is a top-selling, high-end line of cosmetics. The head of the development team has just presented research that shows that "tween"

girls, aged 11 to 15, are very interested in cosmetics and have the money to spend. The decision is made to create a line of tween cosmetics based on the existing adult line. As the product moves through development you begin to notice that the team seems to lean toward a very edgy and sexual theme for the line, including naming the various lines "envy," "desire," "prowess," and "fatal attraction." You begin to wonder, is this concept too much for girls in the targeted age group?

www.mhhe.com/grewal2e

Quiz Yourself

1. Whenever Donald considers upgrading his personal computer system, he consults with Jeremy, a knowledgeable friend who always has the latest technology. For Donald, Jeremy is a(n) _____ in the diffusion of innovation curve.

    a. innovator
    b. laggard
    c. late majority
    d. early majority
    e. early adopter

2. Zappos.com, an online shoe store, worked to overcome the problem of new product

_____ with its easy, no-hassle return procedure.

    a. relative advantage
    b. compatibility
    c. observability
    d. complexity
    e. trialability

(Answers to these two questions are provided on pages 623–624.)

Go to www.mhhe.com/grewal2e to practice an additional 11 questions.

Net Savvy

1. Go to www.inventables.com and click on the Product tab. Review the Example Research. Then peruse the Concept Studio. What type of innovations appear on each of these pages? Choose one selection from each and try to imagine potential applications of these ideas. Do you believe the new products will be successful? Why or why not? For which selection, Research or Concept, is it more challenging to come up with an application? Why?

2. The automotive industry is constantly adding new and different products and technologies to cars and trucks. Conduct an Internet or library database search for innovative new automotive technologies. Choose products that fit each stage of the product life cycle, and justify your choices.

Chapter Case Study[55]

A QUICK BITE, A QUICK SNOOZE: THE LAUNCH OF METRONAPS[56]

The founders of MetroNaps claim their idea came to them in a real-life moment to which many officer workers probably can relate: Observing his coworkers at a New York investment bank, Arshad Chowdhury realized many of them were sneaking off to the bathroom to "rest their eyes" for 15 minutes or simply falling asleep at their desks. The problem seemed clear to him. People simply were not getting enough sleep. But the solution seemed less obvious, especially in the 24/7 modern environment, in which people are bombarded with information, entertainment, and deadlines, making it difficult for them to unwind and get to sleep at night.

When Chowdhury started researching a bit further, he noted that for more than two decades, studies had suggested that naps improve job performance. But most companies tend to discourage napping. They believe that it can cut productivity when workers stop their tasks to sprawl out on top of their desks.

What these sleep-deprived people really needed was a way to get away for a little shut-eye, a difficult undertaking, especially in urban environments. So MetroNaps

MetroNaps offers a sleeping pod to rent in convenient locations.

instead offers a sleeping pod, rented in 20-minute increments, in convenient locations, including its first location in the Empire State Building, which opened in 2004. The first 20 minutes of nap time costs customers $14; for an additional 20 minutes, they pay $9.50 more.

Workers, often on their lunch hour, rent an EnergyPod, which looks something like an ergonomically designed lawn chair from a futuristic space movie. The shield provides some privacy, headphone jacks allow music listeners to plug in, and the timer in the armrest starts the pod shaking gently and increases lighting levels when time is up so customers can't oversleep.

The company has ventured into the B2B market by selling EnergyPods to companies that believe that a little nap can actually improve their workers' health and overall productivity. MetroNaps lists, among others, Procter & Gamble, Cisco, and the Savannah College of Art and Design as clients. It also promotes the benefits of EnergyPods to spas and fitness centers that want to give clients a place to nap after a relaxing massage or workout. Its related products include T-shirts proclaiming the wearer a "napaholic," headphones, and "Nap Passes" that offer gift certificates for nap times.

Yet not everyone is completely convinced of the viability of MetroNaps product/service combination. Chowdhury admits that his most difficult obstacle remains the attempt to overcome the stigma associated with napping, especially in the hypermanic modern business world.

Questions

1. How easily do you believe MetroNaps will be accepted in the United States? What might accelerate or impede the diffusion of this innovation? Describe the type of client that will be their early adopters and early majority. What about the late majority and laggards?

2. How could the founders of MetroNaps have utilized the New Product Development Process shown in Exhibit 11.2?

SERVICES: THE INTANGIBLE PRODUCT

The rental car industry is plagued by low customer satisfaction ratings.[1] Customers, often tired from long plane flights, must wait in line, toting heavy bags, only to find out that the car model they requested is unavailable. But one car rental agency stands out by creating a different scenario. For the eighth time in nine years, J.D. Power & Associates ranked Enterprise Rent-A-Car highest in terms of customer service. Yet Enterprise still refuses to rest on its laurels. By focusing on customer service, Enterprise is earning loyal customers and high profits in a tough industry.

Since its founding in 1957, Enterprise Rent-A-Car has grown into a rental company that offers a fleet of more than 700,000 cars. It also has grown in its scope; 90 percent of the U.S. population lives within 15 miles of one of the 7,000 Enterprise Rent-A-Car locations. With sales of more than $9 billion, Enterprise represents one of the largest private companies in the United States.[2] The key to its success has been a simple guideline, set out by founder Jack Taylor: "Take care of your customers and employees, and the profits will follow."

Enterprise believes that meeting customer expectations simply is not sufficient; you need to exceed them, or 70 percent of customers will not buy from you again.[3] In turn, the key to Enterprise's success is making sure that each and every customer is "Completely Satisfied." Every month, Enterprise measures customer satisfaction scores for each location, using hundreds of thousands of telephone surveys. Only customers who rank their experience as "Completely Satisfied" count toward the positive customer service ranking for each branch. Enterprise measures complete satisfaction because its goal is never just a single car rental. It wants to build a lifelong relationship with each customer it attracts.[4]

To create an environment in which employees can deliver superb customer service, Enterprise invests in those same employees. Because its customer service relies heavily on frontline employees, Enterprise works hard to build a strong team. Its successful efforts rely extensively on encouraging its existing employees to recruit others they know who would make suitable employees. If an existing Enterprise employee recommends someone who gets hired, he or she receives a financial reward, and the new employee enjoys a built-in mentor, enabling that person to feel like part of the team from the very start. This commitment to employees has won Enterprise a spot on *BusinessWeek's* "50 Best Places to Launch a Career" and helped establish one of the best on-campus recruiting programs in the country.

In addition to focusing on employees, Enterprise carefully considers the potential impacts on customers before it makes any decisions. For example, the rental company, known for its neighborhood locations, has expanded into airport locations, because Enterprise believes its employees, with their strong customer service drive, can do a better job helping customers flying in from out of town as they attempt to find their way to their destination and grapple with their luggage. These dedicated customer service specialists not only provide clear directions and perhaps something to drink but also make the rental process easier overall.

As noted, despite its strong showing and positive reviews, Enterprise continues to push the envelope to find new ways to exceed customer expectations. Although J.D. Power rates customer satisfaction with rental services on the basis of the pickup process, rental car quality, shuttle bus/van service, return process, and costs/fees, Enterprise is moving beyond these criteria to establish its latest effort to improve customer service. For example, Enterprise found that customers were increasingly concerned with the environment, so it began to offer the opportunity for customers to opt-in and pay an extra $1.25 per rental to purchase a carbon offset. These funds then get contributed to efforts to remove CO_2 from the atmosphere. The company promises to match each customer's contribution (up to $1 million). Therefore, if 100,000 customers participate, more than 30 million pounds of CO_2 will get removed from the atmosphere. Many customers have chosen to participate, apparently because they recognize the extra value Enterprise is offering; that is, customers like to do business with companies that are concerned about the environment.

Enterprise Rent-A-Car thus provides a great example of how a company, even one in an industry known for poor customer satisfaction, can differentiate itself, not necessarily through better products (e.g., cars), but by offering superior service.

The opening vignette focuses our attention on Enterprise, a firm that provides excellent service as well as products. Whereas a **service** is any intangible offering that involves a deed, performance, or effort that cannot be physically possessed,[5] **customer service** specifically refers to human or mechanical activities firms undertake to help satisfy their customers' needs and wants. By providing good customer service, firms add value to their products or services.

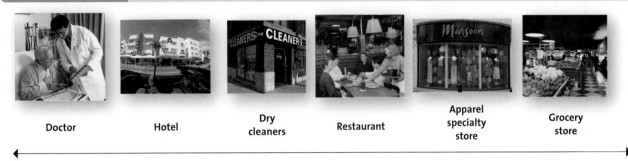

EXHIBIT 12.1   The Service–Product Continuum

| Doctor | Hotel | Dry cleaners | Restaurant | Apparel specialty store | Grocery store |

Service dominant   **Product dominant**

Exhibit 12.1 illustrates the continuum from a pure service to a pure product. Most offerings, like Enterprise Rent-A-Car's, lie somewhere in the middle and include some service and some product. As we noted in Chapter 2, even those firms that are engaged primarily in selling a product, like an apparel store, typically view service as a method to maintain a sustainable competitive advantage. This chapter moves on to take an inclusive view of services as anything from pure service businesses to a business that uses service as a differentiating tool to help it sell physical products.

Economies of developed countries like the United States have become increasingly dependent on services. For example, service industries like retail and information services account for 42 percent[6] of the U.S. gross domestic product (GDP), the lion's share of U.S. jobs, and almost 100 percent of U.S. job growth.[7] This dependence and the growth of service-oriented economies in developed countries have emerged for several reasons.

First, it is generally less expensive for firms to manufacture their products in less-developed countries. Even if the goods are finished in the United States, some of their components likely were produced elsewhere. In turn, the proportion of service production to goods production in the United States, and other similar economies, has steadily increased over time. Second, household maintenance activities, which many people performed by themselves in the past, have become quite specialized. Food preparation, lawn maintenance, house cleaning, laundry and dry cleaning, hair care, and automobile maintenance all are often performed by specialists in the modern economy.

Third, people place a high value on convenience and leisure. Most households have little time for the household maintenance tasks mentioned in the previous point, and many are willing to pay others to do their chores. Fourth, as the U.S. population ages, the need for health care professionals—not only doctors and nurses but also caregivers in assisted living facilities and nursing homes—also increases. Along the same lines, an ever greater number of retired Americans are traveling more and utilizing various forms of leisure services.

As the population ages, the need for health care professionals increases.

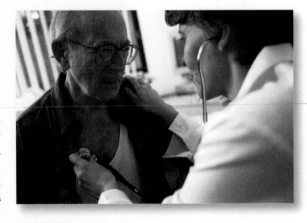

SERVICES MARKETING DIFFERS FROM PRODUCT MARKETING

The marketing of services differs from product marketing because of the four fundamental differences involved in services: Services are intangible, inseparable, variable, and perishable.[8] (See Exhibit 12.2.) This section examines these differences and discusses how they affect marketing strategies.

EXHIBIT 12.2	Core Differences between Services and Goods

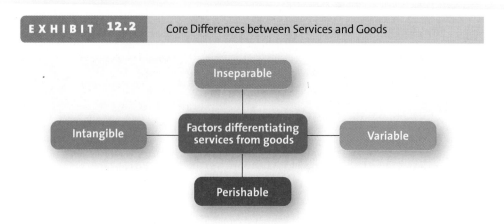

Intangible

As the title of this chapter implies, the most fundamental difference between a product and a service is that services are intangible—they cannot be touched, tasted, or seen like a pure product can. When you get a physical examination, you see and hear the doctor, but the service itself is intangible. This intangibility

IPic offers much more than just a movie.

can prove highly challenging to marketers. For instance, it makes it difficult to convey the benefits of services—try describing whether the experience of visiting your dentist was good or bad and why. Health care service providers (e.g., physicians, dentists) offer cues to help their customers experience and perceive their service more positively, such as a waiting room stocked with television sets, beverages, and comfortable chairs to create an atmosphere that appeals to the target market.

Similarly, IPic Theaters enhances its service offering by providing a new twist on the movie experience. The luxury experience in an IPic theater works to create an "evening out" environment for couples over the age of 21 years. Instead of selling single seats, IPic fills its theaters with six-foot wide seats for two. The movies it shows are the same; it is just the service that has changed. And the theater chain has seen its sales explode.[9] By focusing on making the theater experience about an enjoyable luxury event for a couple instead of an individual, IPic Theaters has differentiated itself from its competitors. Each ticket includes complimentary popcorn, a plush, oversized "loveseat for two," and restaurant-prepared food during movies shown after 6:00 p.m., accompanied by beer, wine, or martinis.[10]

Furthermore, a service cannot be shown directly to potential customers—how do you depict a sense of luxury in a movie theater?—which also makes it difficult to promote. Marketers must therefore creatively employ symbols and images to promote and sell services, like Six Flags does in using its advertising to evoke images of happy families and friends enjoying a roller coaster ride. Professional medical services provide appropriate images of personnel doing their jobs in white coats surrounded by high-tech equipment. Educational institutions promote the quality of their services by touting their famous faculty and alumni, as well as their accreditations. They also often use images of happy students sitting spellbound in front of a fascinating professor or going on to lucrative careers of their own.

Because of the intangibility of services, the images marketers use reinforce the benefit or value that a service provides. Professional service providers, such as doctors, lawyers, accountants, and consultants, depend heavily on consumers' perceptions of their integrity and trustworthiness. Yet the promotional campaigns some of these professionals use have been criticized by their peers and consumer welfare groups. Ethical and Societal Dilemma 12.1 discusses the tension created when service providers use marketing tactics to attract clients to their service but still attempt to maintain a perception of integrity and trustworthiness.

Inseparable Production and Consumption

Another difference between services and products is that services are produced and consumed at the same time; that is, service and consumption are inseparable. Because service production can't be separated from consumption, astute service marketers provide opportunities for their customers to get directly involved in the service. Health care providers have found, for instance, that the more control they allow their patients in determining their course of treatment, the more satisfied those patients are.[11]

Because the service is inseparable from its consumption, customers rarely have the opportunity to try the service before they purchase it. And after the service has been performed, it can't be returned. Imagine telling your dentist that you want a "test" cavity filled before he or she starts drilling a real one. Because the purchase risk in these scenarios can be relatively high, service firms sometimes provide extended warranties and 100 percent satisfaction guarantees. The Choice Hotels chain, for instance, states: "We guarantee total guest satisfaction at Comfort

The Choice Hotels chain guarantees total guest satisfaction.

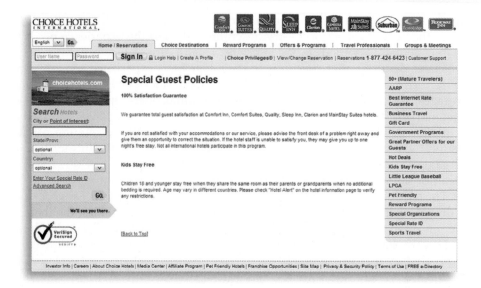

Inn, Comfort Suites, Quality, Sleep Inn, Clarion and MainStay Suites hotels. If you are not satisfied with your accommodations or our service, please advise the front desk of a problem right away and give them an opportunity to correct the situation. If the hotel staff is unable to satisfy you, they may give you up to one night's free stay."[12]

Ethical and Societal Dilemma 12.1   Who Are You Going to Call?

At one time, lawyers in many states were prohibited from advertising their services because many believed that marketing by lawyers would undermine the integrity of the profession. Over time, the laws were repealed. But in the face of the advertising that has ensued, many are questioning whether the marketing tactics of some lawyers have gone too far.

The term "ambulance chaser" usually is used derogatorily to refer to lawyers who solicit clients when they are stressed or their ability to make rational decisions is limited, such as just after a car accident. The term was coined when some personal injury lawyers literally followed ambulances and offered legal services to the injured parties. Critics of lawyers who market their services point to the aggressive advertising and promotional programs these attorneys use, which often prey on potential clients' vulnerabilities after they have been injured or in some way been negatively impacted by the actions of others. The lawyers who market themselves this way claim they are providing a valuable service to society.

To respond to the need for ethical guidance, many professional associations offer guidelines and example cases to help members determine which types of advertisements might be considered unethical by peers and other interested parties. For example, the American Bar Association (ABA) has drafted a set of rules that its members must abide by when creating their advertising. It also offers a variety of resources to help lawyers determine what kinds of advertising are appropriate. Among those resources, the ABA offers a Web site dedicated to "Information on Professionalism and Ethics in Lawyer Advertising," court rulings about advertising, and links to state-specific lawyer association advertising rules.[13] For example, one of the rules that ABA-certified lawyers are expected to follow bans any usage of pop-up ads or the use of actors when advertising law services.[14]

For practicing lawyers and other professionals, the ethical dilemma remains: How to balance their need to gain clients through marketing with their need to retain an image of professionalism and integrity. Can marketing be used to communicate the benefits of legal services without preying on the vulnerabilities of consumers?

Variable

The more humans are needed to provide a service, the more likely there is to be variability in the service's quality. A hair stylist may give bad haircuts in the morning because he or she went out the night before. Yet that stylist still may offer a better service than the undertrained stylist working in the next station over. A restaurant, which offers a mixture of services and products, generally can control its food quality but not the variability in food preparation or delivery. If a consumer has a problem with a product, it can be replaced, redone, destroyed, or, if it is already in the supply chain, recalled. In many cases, the problem can even be fixed before the product gets into consumers' hands. But an inferior service can't be recalled; by the time the firm recognizes a problem, the damage has been done.

As we noted in the opening vignette, Enterprise Rent-A-Car has worked to standardize its service delivery across the United States and, to that end, provides extensive training to its associates. Go to any Enterprise outlet at any airport, and chances are you will be greeted in the same personalized way. The airport shuttle drivers will load and unload your bags. When you get off the shuttle, you will be greeted by name, and your car will be ready to go in minutes. This smooth and pleasant service transaction is the result of the company's very specific service standards and excellent training program.

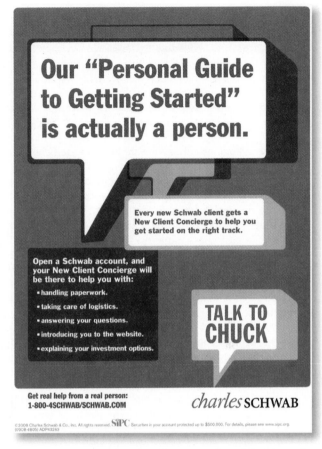

Because each customer's needs differ, investment firm Charles Schwab personalizes each service offering.

Marketers also can use the variable nature of services to their advantage. A micromarketing segmentation strategy can customize a service to meet customers' needs exactly (see Chapter 8). Geek Housecalls has a micromarketing segmentation strategy and will come to your home or office to repair or service your PC—setting up a network, cleaning your hard drive, or even tutoring you on the operation of a particular program. Clients are matched with their very own "personal geek" on the basis of their needs, which allows for a fully personalized service offering. Another firm that has built much of its success on a micromarketing perspective is The Charles Schwab Corporation. Founded in 1973, The Charles Schwab Corporation earned its success by working closely with customers to create custom investing and savings plans that would be sure to prepare them for their retirement. Schwab currently manages more than $1.4 trillion in client savings for 8.4 million clients.[15] Because each customer's needs differ, Schwab fully personalizes each service offering. When creating a portfolio for customers, Schwab brokers attempt to design a careful mix of brokerage, banking, bond trading, annuities, savings accounts, and mortgages that will best suit each client.[16]

In an alternative approach, some service providers tackle the variability issue by replacing people with machines. For simple transactions like getting cash, using an ATM is usually quicker and more convenient—and less variable—than waiting in line for a bank teller. Many retailers are installing kiosks with broadband Internet access in their stores. In addition to offering customers the opportunity to order merchandise not available in the store, kiosks can provide routine customer service, freeing employees to deal with more demanding customer requests and problems and reducing service variability. For example, customers can use kiosks to locate merchandise in the store and determine whether

Computer crashing? Network down? Call Geek Housecalls.

Adding Value **12.1**   Adding Convenience through Self-Checkout Machines[17]

Thought of as a gimmick when they were first introduced in 1995, self-checkout machines have gained converts and are heading into more arenas. The machines are multiplying in grocery and discount stores at blistering speed. Wal-Mart, Kroger, Home Depot, Best Buy, Costco, and IKEA already use them. Even libraries nationwide are installing self-checkout machines for books.

Self-checkouts are successful and increase customer loyalty because they appeal to those shoppers who want to move on quickly and believe they can zip through their checkouts faster by using the machines. Some experts say the reason customers think self-checkout is faster is that they are active when using it, unlike waiting for a cashier, which leaves customers with nothing to do and may make it seem as though time is dragging. Others contend that self-checkout actually does save between 15 seconds and 15 minutes, depending on the size of an order.

Widespread ATM machine usage has paved the way for self-checkout machines and other self-service kiosks. Many customers now perceive self-service as a normal and quick way to check out with their purchases.

If customers like the machines, retailers love them. Kiosks replace employees at the point of sale and thus decrease labor costs. In airports, passengers now commonly check in using kiosks. Compared with the $3 per customer it costs airlines to pay an agent to help check passengers in, the cost of a kiosk is as low as $0.14. Among best-in-class companies, 47 percent had achieved a return on their kiosk investments within three years of installation. Expect to find kiosks in even more industries, such as fast food chains, not just airports and checkout lines. Customers gain satisfaction and express greater brand loyalty as a result of

increasing self-service options for payment, ordering, and assistance. According to IBM's director of marketing and strategy for retail stores, every time you see a door, there's an opportunity for a kiosk to be deployed.[18]

Do self-checkout machines increase or reduce consumers' perception of service?

specific products, brands, and sizes are available. Kiosks can also be used to automate existing store services, such as gift registry management, rain checks, film drop-off, credit applications, and preordering service for bakeries and delicatessens. Adding Value 12.1 describes how some retailers and other service providers are reducing service variability with self-service checkout machines.

The technological delivery of services can cause additional problems. Some customers either do not embrace the idea of replacing a human with a machine for business interactions or have problems using the technology. In other cases, the technology may not perform adequately, such as self-checkout scanners that fail to scan all merchandise or ATMs that run out of money or are out of order.

The Internet has reduced service variability in several areas. Prior to the mid-1990s, customers engaged in one-on-one interactions when they purchased travel items (e.g., airlines, hotel, rental car), concert and movie tickets, insurance, mortgages, and merchandise. Today, these purchases can be made directly via the Internet, and if the customer wants more information than is available online, most Web sites provide ways to contact customer service personnel by e-mail or telephone.

Beyond online benefits, the Internet has also reduced in-store service variability. At Staples, for instance, in-store kiosks provide information, prices, avail-

Since services are perishable, service providers like ski areas offer less expensive tickets at night to stimulate demand.

ability, and product information to customers. They represent a useful supplement for sales people, who can't possibly be knowledgeable about every aspect of the many high-tech products the company carries.

Perishable

Services are perishable in that they cannot be stored for use in the future. You can't stockpile your membership at Gold's Gym like you could a six-pack of V-8 juice, for instance. The perishability of services provides both challenges and opportunities to marketers in terms of the critical task of matching demand and supply. As long as the demand for and the supply of the service match closely, there is no problem, but unfortunately, this perfect matching rarely occurs. A ski area, for instance, can be open as long as there is snow, even at night, but demand peaks on weekends and holidays, so ski areas often offer less expensive tickets during off-peak periods to stimulate demand. Airlines, cruise ships, movie theaters, and restaurants confront similar challenges and attack them in similar ways.

As we have seen, providing great service is not easy, and it requires a diligent effort to analyze the service process piece by piece. In the next section, we examine what is known as the Gaps Model, which is designed to highlight those areas where customers believe they are getting less or poorer service than they should (the gaps) and how these gaps can be closed.

CHECK YOURSELF

1. What are the four marketing elements that distinguish services from products?
2. Why can't we separate firms into just service or just product sellers?
3. What are some of the ethical issues associated with marketing professional services?

PROVIDING GREAT SERVICE: THE GAPS MODEL

Customers have certain expectations about how a service should be delivered. When the delivery of that service fails to meet those expectations, a **service gap** results. The Gaps Model (Exhibit 12.3) is designed to encourage the systematic examination of all aspects of the service delivery process and prescribe the steps needed to develop an optimal service strategy.[19]

As Exhibit 12.3 shows, there are four service gaps:

1. The **knowledge gap** reflects the difference between customers' expectations and the firm's perception of those customer expectations. Firms can close this gap by matching customer expectations with actual service through research.

2. The **standards gap** pertains to the difference between the firm's perceptions of customers' expectations and the service standards it sets. By setting appropriate service standards and measuring service performance, firms can attempt to close this gap.

3. The **delivery gap** is the difference between the firm's service standards and the actual service it provides to customers. This gap can be closed by getting employees to meet or exceed service standards.[20]

4. The **communication gap** refers to the difference between the actual service provided to customers and the service that the firm's promotion program promises. If firms are more realistic about the services they can provide and at the same time manage customer expectations effectively, they generally can close this gap.

As we discuss the four gaps subsequently, we will apply them to the experience that Marcia Kessler had with a motel in Maine. She saw an ad for a package weekend that quoted a very reasonable daily rate and listed the free amenities available at Paradise Motel: free babysitting services, a piano bar with a nightly

EXHIBIT 12.3   Gaps Model for Improving Service

Sources: Michael Levy and Barton Weitz, *Retailing Management,* 7th ed. (Burr Ridge, IL: McGraw-Hill, 2009). Adapted from Valarie Zeithaml, A. Parasuraman, and Leonard Berry, *Delivering Quality Customer Service* (New York: The Free Press, 1990) and Valarie Zeithaml, Leonard Berry, and A. Parasuraman, "Communication and Control Processes in the Delivery of Service Quality," *Journal of Marketing,* 52, no. 2 (April 1988), pp. 35–48.

singer, a free Continental breakfast, a heated swimming pool, and newly decorated rooms. When she booked the room, Marcia discovered that the price advertised was not available during the weekend, and a three-day minimum stay was required. After checking in with a very unpleasant person at the front desk, Marcia and her husband found that their room appeared circa 1950 and had not been cleaned. When she complained, all she got was "attitude" from the assistant manager. Resigned to the fact that they were slated to spend the weekend, she decided to go for a swim. Unfortunately, the water was "heated" by Booth Bay and stood at around 50 degrees. No one was using the babysitting services because there were few young children at the resort. It turns out the piano bar singer was the second cousin of the owner, and he couldn't carry a tune, let alone play the piano very well. The Continental breakfast must have come all the way from the Continent, because everything was stale and tasteless. Marcia couldn't wait to get home.

What service gaps did Marcia experience while on vacation at the Paradise Motel in Maine?

The Knowledge Gap: Knowing What Customers Want

An important early step in providing good service is knowing what the customer wants. For example, the motel offered babysitting services, but most of its customers did not have kids, had not brought them on their trip, or simply did not want to use the service. Had the motel known that no one would take advantage of this service, it might have trained the babysitters to get the rooms cleaned in time for the guests' arrival.

To reduce the knowledge gap, firms must understand the customers' expectations. To understand those expectations, firms undertake customer research and increase the interaction and communication between managers and employees.

Understanding Customer Expectations   Customers' expectations are based on their knowledge and experiences.[21] Marcia's expectations were that her room at the motel in Maine would be ready when she got there, the swimming pool would be heated, the singer would be able to sing, and the breakfast would be fresh. If the resort never understood her expectations, it is unlikely it would ever be able to meet them.

Expectations vary according to the type of service. Marcia's expectations might have been higher, for instance, if she were staying at a Ritz-Carlton rather than the Paradise Motel. At the Ritz, she might expect employees to know her by name, be aware of her dietary preferences, and have placed fresh fruit of her choice and fresh-cut flowers in her room before she arrived. At the Paradise Motel, she expected easy check-in/checkout, easy access to a major highway, a clean room with a comfortable bed, and a TV, at a bare, minimum.

People's expectations also vary depending on the situation. As long as they delivered expected services, Marcia might be satisfied with both the preceding hotel properties, depending on the circumstances. If she had been traveling on business, the Paradise Motel might have been fine (had the room at least been clean and modern), but if she were celebrating her 10th wedding anniversary, she probably would prefer the Ritz. Thus, the service provider needs to not only know and understand the expectations of the customers in its target market, but also have some idea of the occasions of service usage.

To help ensure that JetBlue understands customers' expectations, it surveys at least six customers from every flight it operates.[22] The airline brings together top executives to discuss what customers are saying and how it should respond. It learned, for instance, that when its pilots stand in the aisle in the cabin to talk to passengers over the plane's public-address system, the response is extremely favorable—especially when the pilot appears at the beginning of the flight or when there is some kind of delay. As a result, new pilots are now taught how to address passengers, including practicing announcements as part of their training using flight simulators. And every JetBlue pilot is given a printed guide to making announcements.

Evaluating Service Quality Using Well-Established Marketing Metrics   To meet or exceed customers' expectations, marketers must determine what those expectations are. Yet because of their intangibility, the service quality, or customers' perceptions of how well a service meets or exceeds their expectations, often is difficult for customers to evaluate.[23] Customers generally use five distinct service dimensions to determine overall service quality: reliability, responsiveness, assurance, empathy, and tangibles (Exhibit 12.4).

If you were to apply the five service dimensions to your own decision-making process when you select a college—which provides the service of education—you might find results like those in Exhibit 12.5.

If your expectations include an individualized experience at a state-of-the-art institution, perhaps University B is a better alternative for you. But if you are relying heavily on academic performance and career placement from your university experience, then University A might be a better choice in terms of the five service dimensions. If a strong culture and tradition are important to you, University A offers this type of environment. What your expectations are has a lot to do with your perception of how your university falls within these service dimensions.

Marketing research (see Chapter 9) provides a means to better understand consumers' service expectations and their perceptions of service quality. This research can be extensive and expensive, or it can be integrated into a firm's everyday interactions with customers. Today, most service firms have developed voice-of-customer programs and employ ongoing marketing research to assess how well they are meeting their customers' expectations. A systematic voice-of-customer (VOC) program collects customer inputs and integrates them into managerial decisions.

EXHIBIT 12.4   Building Blocks of Service Quality

RELIABILITY:
The ability to perform the service dependably and accurately.

RESPONSIVENESS:
The willingness to help customers and provide prompt service.

ASSURANCE:
The knowledge of and courtesy by employees and their ability to convey trust and confidence.

EMPATHY:
The caring, individualized attention provided to customers.

TANGIBLES:
The appearance of physical facilities, equipment, personnel, and communication materials.

EXHIBIT 12.5	Collegiate Service Dimensions	
	University A	**University B**
Reliability	Offers sound curriculum with extensive placement services and internships.	Curriculum covers all the basics but important courses are not always available. Career placement is haphazard at best.
Responsiveness	Slow to respond to application. Very structured visitation policy. Rather inflexible with regard to personal inquiries or additional meetings.	Quick response during application process. Open visitation policy. Offers variety of campus resources to help with decision making.
Assurance	Staff seems very confident in reputation and services.	Informal staff who convey enthusiasm for institution.
Empathy	Seems to process student body as a whole rather than according to individual needs or concerns.	Very interested in providing a unique experience for each student.
Tangibles	Very traditional campus with old-world look and feel. Facilities are manicured. Dorm rooms are large, but bathrooms are a little old.	New campus with modern architecture. Campus is less manicured. Dorm rooms are spacious with newer bathrooms.

An important marketing metric to evaluate how well firms perform on the five service quality dimensions (Exhibit 12.4) is the zone of tolerance, which refers to the area between customers' expectations regarding their desired service and the minimum level of acceptable service—that is, the difference between what the customer really wants and what he or she will accept before going elsewhere.[24] To define the zone of tolerance, firms ask a series of questions about each service quality dimension that relates to:

- The desired and expected level of service for each dimension, from low to high.
- Customers' perceptions of how well the focal service performs and how well a competitive service performs, from low to high.
- The importance of each service quality dimension.

Exhibit 12.6 illustrates the results of such an analysis for Lou's Local Diner, a family-owned restaurant. The rankings on the left are based on a 9-point scale, on which 1 is low and 9 is high. The length of each box illustrates the zone of tolerance for each service quality dimension. For instance, according to the length of the reliability box, customers expect a fairly high level of reliability (top of the box) and will also accept only a fairly high level of reliability (bottom of the box). On the other end of the scale, customers expect a high level of assurance (top of the box) but will accept a fairly low level (bottom of the box). This difference is to be expected, because the customers also were asked to assign an important score to the five service quality dimensions so that the total equals 100 percent. Looking at the average importance score, we conclude that reliability is relatively important to these customers, but assurance is not. So customers have a fairly narrow zone of tolerance for service dimensions that are fairly important to them, and a wider range of tolerance for those service dimensions that are less important. Also, note that Lou's Local Diner always rates higher than its primary competitor, Well-Known National Chain, on each dimension.

Further note that Well-Known National Chain scores below the zone of tolerance on the tangibles dimension, meaning that customers are not willing to accept the way the restaurant looks and smells. Lou's Local Diner, in contrast, performs above the zone of tolerance on the responsiveness dimension—maybe even too well. The local restaurant may wish to conduct further research to verify which responsiveness aspects it is performing so well, and then consider toning those aspects down. For example, being responsive to customers' desires to have a

Lou's Local Diner always rates higher than its primary competitor, Well-Known National Chain, on each service quality dimension.

diner that serves breakfast 24 hours a day can be expensive and may not add any further value to Lou's Diner because customers would accept more limited times.

A very straightforward and inexpensive method of collecting consumers' perceptions of service quality is to gather them at the time of the sale. Service providers can ask customers how they liked the service—though customers often are reticent to provide negative feedback directly to the person who provided the service—or distribute a simple questionnaire. Starbucks randomly selects customers to rate their experience by printing out a Web address at the bottom of its receipts. Using this method, a complaining customer does not have to make the complaint directly to the barista who may have caused the problem, but Starbucks still gets almost instantaneous feedback. Regardless of how information is collected, companies must take care not to lose it, which can happen if there is no effective mechanism for filtering it up to the key decision makers. Furthermore, in some cases, customers cannot effectively evaluate the service until several days or weeks later. Automobile dealers, for instance, often call their customers a week after they perform a service like an oil change to assess their service quality.

Another excellent method for assessing customers' expectations is making effective use of customer complaint behavior. Even if complaints are handled effectively to solve customers' problems, the essence of the complaint is too often lost on managers. For instance, a large PC retailer responded to complaints about the lack of service from sales people and issues with products by providing an e-mail address for people to contact the service department. This contact proved to be a bit difficult when the problem was that the computer wasn't working.[25]

Even firms with the best formal research mechanisms in place must put managers on the front lines occasionally to interact directly with the customers. Unless the managers who make the service quality decisions know what their service providers are facing on a day-to-day basis, and unless they can talk directly to the cus-

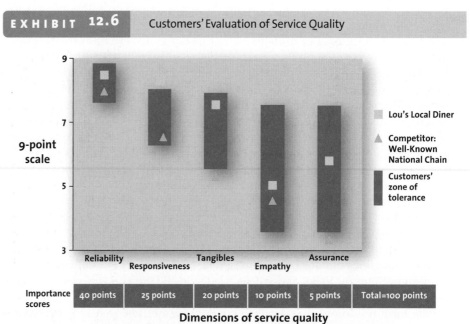

EXHIBIT 12.6   Customers' Evaluation of Service Quality

9-point scale

■ Lou's Local Diner

▲ Competitor: Well-Known National Chain

Customers' zone of tolerance

Dimensions of service quality

| Importance scores | 40 points | 25 points | 20 points | 10 points | 5 points | Total=100 points |

Reliability   Responsiveness   Tangibles   Empathy   Assurance

Note: The scale ranges from a 9 indicating very high service quality on a given service quality dimension to a 1 indicating very low service quality.

tomers with whom those service providers interact, any customer service program they create will not be as good as it could be.

The Standards Gap: Setting Service Standards

Getting back to our Paradise Motel in Maine, suppose it set out to determine its customers' service expectations and gained a pretty good idea of them. Its work is still far from over; the next step is to set its service standards and develop systems to ensure high-quality service. How can it make sure that every room is cleaned by 2:00 p.m.? That the breakfast is checked for freshness and quality every day? The manager needs to set an example of high service standards, which will permeate throughout the organization, and the employees must be thoroughly trained not only to complete their specific tasks but also how to treat guests.

Achieving Service Goals through Training   To deliver consistently high-quality service, firms must set specific, measurable goals based on customers' expectations; to help ensure that quality, the employees should be involved in the goal setting. For instance, for the Paradise Motel, the most efficient process would be to start cleaning rooms at 8:00 a.m. and finish by 5:00 p.m. But many guests want to sleep late, and new arrivals want to get into their room as soon as they arrive, often before 5:00. So a customer-oriented standard would mandate that the rooms get cleaned between 10:00 a.m. and 2:00 p.m.

Service providers, like this housekeeper at a hotel, generally want to do a good job, but they need to be trained to know exactly what a good job entails.

Service providers generally want to do a good job, as long as they know what is expected of them.[26] Motel employees should be shown, for instance, exactly how managers expect them to clean a room and what specific tasks they are responsible for performing. In general, more employees will buy into a quality-oriented process if they are involved in setting the goals. For instance, suppose an employee of the motel refuses to clean the glass cups in the rooms because she believes that disposable plastic cups are more ecological and hygienic. If management listens to her and makes the change, it should make the employee all the more committed to the other tasks involved in cleaning rooms.

For frontline service employees, pleasant interactions with customers do not always come naturally. Although people can be taught specific tasks related to their jobs, it is simply not enough to tell employees to "be nice" or "do what customers want." A quality goal should be specific: Greet every customer/guest you encounter with "Good morning/afternoon/evening, Sir or Miss." Try to greet customers by name.

In extreme cases, such training becomes even more crucial. From long ticket lines to cancelled flights to lost baggage to safety concerns, customer service incidents are on the rise in the airline industry. Faced with these mounting complaints, some airlines are attempting to implement better employee training geared toward identifying and defusing potentially explosive situations. In another travel-related industry, Homewood Suites, a division of Hilton Hotels, relies on a program that uses video iPods for training the 6,000 people who work in the chain's 204 hotels. Training content is organized into categories so that employees can choose the video that is most appropriate for them. By using this iPod system, the company can continuously update its training program.[27]

Commitment to Service Quality   Service providers take their cues from management. If managers strive for excellent service, treat their customers well, and demand the same attitudes from everyone in the organization, it is likely employees will do the same. Take, for example, Whole Foods Market, the Texas-based organic food grocer. Whole Foods is legendary for its focus on customer service—a focus that has made it one of the most successful grocery chains in the world. Whole Foods bases its philosophy on three things: "Whole Foods, Whole People,

Whole Planet."[28] By rewarding excellent employees and promoting from within, Whole Foods has fostered an environment in which stores compete to take care of customers the best. For example, in one incident in the Northeast United States during a snowstorm, the new register IT system crashed. Instead of refusing to sell food to the Hartford, Connecticut, customers who had braved the snowstorm to get to the store, the store manager allowed these tired, cold, and wet customers to take the food home without paying. Cashiers simply bagged the customers' groceries and wished them happy holidays. In the manager's mind, it was not right to "punish" the customers for a mistake that Whole Foods' IT department had made. Talk about customer service![29]

Pulte Homes Inc., which in recent years has won more awards in J.D. Power's annual survey of customers than any other new-home builder, has a strong commitment to customer service.[30] It surveys customers immediately after they buy a house and then several years later to make sure they are still happy. When Pulte wasn't satisfied with the marks it was getting from customers for overall satisfaction, it created a customer-relations department of 1,200 people and established a program to ensure that it paid closer attention to its customers' desires throughout the sales and building process.

The Delivery Gap: Delivering Service Quality

The delivery gap is where "the rubber meets the road," where the customer directly interacts with the service provider. Even if there are no other gaps, a delivery gap always results in a service failure. Marcia experienced several delivery gaps at the Paradise Motel: the unclean room, the assistant manager's attitude, the unheated swimming pool, the poor piano bar singer, and the stale food.

Delivery gaps can be reduced when employees are empowered to act in the customers' and the firm's best interests and supported in their efforts so they can do their jobs effectively.[31] Technology can also be employed to reduce delivery gaps. (See Exhibit 12.7.)

Empowering Service Providers   In this context, empowerment means allowing employees to make decisions about how service gets provided to customers. When frontline employees are authorized to make decisions to help their customers, service quality generally improves. Nordstrom provides an overall objective—satisfy customer needs—and then encourages employees to do whatever is necessary to achieve the objective. For example, a Nordstrom shoe sales associate decided to break up two pairs of shoes, one a size 10 and the other a size 10½, to sell a hard-to-fit customer. Although the other two shoes were unsalable, the customer purchased 5 other pairs that day and became a loyal Nordstrom customer as a result. Empowering service providers with only a rule like "Use your best judgment" (as Nordstrom does) might cause chaos. At Nordstrom, department managers avoid abuses by coaching and training sales people to understand what "Use your best judgment" means.

EXHIBIT 12.7   Methods to Reduce Delivery Gaps

However, empowering service providers also can be difficult and costly. In cases in which the service is very repetitive and routine, such as at a fast-food restaurant, it might be more efficient and easier for service providers to follow a few simple rules. For instance, if a customer doesn't like his hamburger, ask him what he would like instead or offer him a refund. If an exceptional circumstance that does not fit the rules arises, then a manager should handle the issue.

Empowerment becomes more important when the service is more individualized. Suppose a man purchased an expensive wristwatch and accidentally dropped and broke it before he even left the store. The sales associate who waited on him should be empowered to do whatever it takes to satisfy him and to take responsibility for the problem rather than to turn it over to someone else.

Quicken Loans, an online loan provider, cannot rely on a sales clerk to resolve a problem in person, but it has found a way to enable customers to find the best rates on loans and mortgages, which saves those customers valuable time. If it only offered a simple listing of loan rates, Quicken Loans would be no different than its competitors and could not have achieved its successful reputation. Instead, it empowers its employees to solve customers' problems and gives them the authority to follow through with its customer service policy: "Every Client. Every Time. No Exceptions. No Excuses."[32] New mortgage bankers and loan officers receive more than 200 hours of training their first year, as well as additional training throughout the year for them—and their spouses! The training excites the associates and sparks their desire to find better solutions for customers, many of whom are unaware of the complicated processes involved in making mortgages and complicated loans. The approach seems to be working; Quicken Loans earned a 94 percent customer satisfaction rate,[33] enjoys financial success, remains involved in an ongoing multiple-store expansion, and has been on the top of *Fortune* magazine's "100 Best Companies to Work For" in America for several years running.[34] Power of the Internet 12.1 (on the next page) examines a T-shirt manufacturer that empowers its customers to enhance its customer service.

Providing Support and Incentives A service provider's job can often be difficult, especially when customers are unpleasant or less than reasonable. But the service provider cannot be rude or offensive just because the customer is. The old cliché, "Service with a smile," remains the best approach. To ensure that service is delivered properly, management needs to support the service provider in several ways.

First, managers and coworkers should provide emotional support to service providers by demonstrating a concern for their well-being and standing behind their decisions. Because it can be very disconcerting when a waiter is abused by a customer who believes her food was improperly prepared, for instance, restaurant managers must be supportive and help the employee get through his emotional reaction to the berating experienced.[35] Such support can extend to empowering the waiter to rectify the situation by giving the customer new food and a free dessert, in which case the manager must understand the waiter's decision, not punish him for giving away too much.

Fast-food chain Wing Zone understands the stress that angry customers can cause order takers, and has devised a method of providing emotional support. Its entry-level employees, who are mostly college students, don't have the experience needed to handle these customers. Therefore, they've been trained to hand off overly demanding customers to the nearest manager right away. Wing Zone's managers then put the complaints back on the customers, asking them how they'd like the company to handle the problem. When both parties can't find some middle ground, managers refer the customer to the corporate office's toll-free number and Web site to file a formal complaint.[36]

Second, service providers require instrumental support—the systems and equipment—to deliver the service properly. Many retailers provide state-of-the-art instrumental support for their service providers. In-store kiosks help sales

Power of the Internet 12.1

Employees and Customers: Service on All Sides

Based in Chicago, the T-shirt manufacturer Threadless exemplifies employee/customer empowerment and service. Not "employee empowerment <u>and</u> customer service"; on Threadless's Web site and in its company philosophy, there is no separating the two.[37] The clothing company takes a different route than most manufacturers throughout the production process for its offerings. First, design comes from consumers. A fervent online community, dedicated to the idea of underground T-shirt design, submits ideas and mock-ups of their perfect T. To encourage more ideas, winning designers receive a $2,000 cash payment, along with a $500 merchandise credit on the site. The site provides a simple means to submit ideas, including a downloadable submission kit that offers would-be designers a simple template, straightforward printing instructions, and a list of reasons for which designs might be rejected.

Second, product decisions also come from the community. Threadless's 500,000 registered members (up from 35,000 in 2005)[38] vote on the designs posted, enabling members to voice their preferences in an *American Idol*–style vote count. Using vote totals and their own impressions, the company's executives select a few carefully chosen designs to produce, such as "Attack of the Mole People," "Ziggy Stardog," and "Tyger Tyger."

Third, the online retailer provides the means for members to purchase new shirts in those very designs that they had a hand in designing and selecting. The site organizes its multitude of offerings into various categories so that customers can search by availability, size, style, or line (e.g., TypeTees, Select, or Kids). True T-afficionados can register for the 12 Club, which ensures they get an exclusive, limited edition T-shirt once a month.

During the seven years the company has been in business, it has received 200,000 design submissions, but only 1,000 have been chosen as winners. Threadless also has added a critique section to its site, with the hope that it can provide a service that keeps repeat losers from growing discouraged and taking their T-shirt business—whether that means design or purchase—elsewhere. The critique section gives the erstwhile designers and ongoing customers a means to submit a work in progress and get feedback from the wider community. Thus, members can participate in the Threadless community, if they so choose, without having to enter the bruising competition.

Threadless empowers its customers to design T-shirts.

Finally, to ensure designers and wearers know who joins them in their interests, Threadless invites submissions of photos of members wearing their instantly recognizable shirts. Its "Threadspotting" section also features public displays, usually identified by excited members.

associates provide more detailed and complete product information and enable them to make sales of merchandise that is either not carried in the store or is temporarily out of stock.

Third, the support that managers provide must be consistent and coherent throughout the organization. Patients expect physicians to provide great patient care using state-of-the-art procedures and medications, but because they are tied to managed-care systems (health maintenance organizations or HMOs), many doctors must squeeze more people into their office hours and prescribe less optimal, less expensive, courses of treatment. These conflicting goals can be so frustrating and emotionally draining on physicians and other health care providers that some have found work outside of medicine.

Conflicting service goals also can occur within an organization.[39] For instance, inventory managers might restrict purchasing levels to lower the company's inventory investment, but that attempt at greater efficiency causes sales people stress because they are out of stock of merchandise their customers want. Managers therefore must balance the sometimes conflicting needs of inventory managers and sales people by providing clear guidance and oversight in attending to the expectations of customers.

Fourth, a key part of any customer service program is providing rewards to employees for excellent service. Numerous firms have developed a service reputation by ensuring that their employees recognize the value the firm places on customer service. Travelocity, for example, features employees who champion the customer service experience in a weekly e-mail. It believes that engaged employees are the key to customer satisfaction. Travelocity therefore works to create an atmosphere that reinforces the commitment to customers by encouraging employees to nominate colleagues who exemplify its commitment to customers. Through constant feedback about who is serving the customer best, as well as smaller events such as monthly lunches with the CEO for selected employees, Travelocity creates a business environment that recognizes and rewards customer service.[40] The results for Travelocity include a wealth of awards, such as a top ranking on the Customer Online Respect Survey and a designation as the "World's Leading Travel Internet Site" for eight consecutive years.[41]

Home Depot has a customer service initiative that includes an "Orange Juiced" program, named after employees' signature orange aprons, that earmarks as much as $25,000 per quarter to stores that provide the best customer service.[42] Individual employees can receive bonuses of as much as $2,000 per month or $10,000 per quarter. Home Depot determines which store is rewarded by looking at several factors: reviews by peers and managers, focus groups, and "voice of the customer" surveys. Between 150,000 and 250,000 customers call the company's 800 number each week or visit its Internet site—printed at the bottom of their receipt—to rate their customer service experience.

Home Depot earmarks as much as $25,000 per quarter to stores that provide the best customer service.

Use of Technology   Technology has become an increasingly important facilitator of the delivery of services. Since the mid-1990s, with the widespread usage of the Internet, firms have invested heavily in technologies that have enabled customers to buy more quickly, more easily, and with more information than in the past. As noted earlier, electronic kiosks have found their way into the services of many retailers. Ticketing kiosks at airports allow customers to get boarding passes and seat assignments, often in less than a minute. Many hotels, including Marriott, have installed self–check-in kiosks that enable customers to charge their rooms, encode and dispense key cards, and secure identification.[43]

Some firms are using technology to help personalize their service. Electronics superstore Best Buy is using RFID to personalize and enhance the customer experience.[44] **RFIDs (radio frequency identification devices)** are tiny computer chips that automatically transmit to a special scanner all the information about a container's contents or individual products. Customers receive a card with an embedded RFID transmitter. Then, from home, customers can browse the Best Buy Web site for information on the products in which they are interested. This information is entered onto the transmitter so store management knows exactly who a customer is and what he or she is interested in the moment the customer enters the store. Customers can add information on whether they want help from a personal shopping assistant when they enter the store, whether they want to be left to shop on their own, or whether they want the customer service representative to give them some time to browse before offering to help. This allows customers to tailor the shopping experience to exactly their likes and dislikes. The information on the chip also allows Best Buy to offer instant rebates and validate warranty information

A retail store assistant (RSA) facilitates the shopping experience.

on the spot without the customer having to fill out reams of paperwork.

Another use of technology in the service delivery process is a retail store assistant (RSA).[45] An RSA can be a kiosk or a device attached to the customer's shopping cart. Instead of bringing a shopping list to the store, a customer can swipe a loyalty card or enter a phone number at an RSA.[46] Any information the customer has entered online from home will show up on the customer's profile. Depending on the customer's shopping habits that are stored in the retailer's database, he or she will be offered special offers. The RSA matches the customer's purchase record with the appropriate coupons being offered. On the back of the coupons is a map of the store and the location of all items, eliminating the need to explore every aisle. If a printed piece of paper is too cumbersome, the list and information could also be transferred via Bluetooth technology to a mobile device, such as a phone.

Even car companies are developing new technologies to improve the service experience associated with driving a car. BMW, Maybach, Rolls-Royce, and Mercedes-Benz use telematics, which is the long-range communication of computer-based information,[47] to create a unique driving experience for their customers. The most common form of telematics is a GPS navigation system, but some companies go even further than telling drivers how to get to the nearest drugstore or movie theater. Instead, these innovative companies monitor everything on the car, from its oil pressure to its engine status, and then provide a means for the car to telephone its owner and identify any problems or service events needed, such as a tune-up or an oil change. This revolutionary combination of information and the driving experience helps car makers improve their services.[48] Other applications of such service offerings may sound straight out of the future, but they also might not be too far away. Imagine a refrigerator that could tell you when you're getting low on milk. Isn't that a service many time-pressured consumers would pay to add to the functions of their existing refrigerator?

Using technology to facilitate service delivery can provide many benefits, such as access to a wider variety of services, a greater degree of control by the customer over the services, and the ability to obtain information. Management also benefits from the increased efficiency in service processes through reduced servicing costs, and, in some cases, can develop a competitive advantage over less service-oriented competitors.[49]

The advent of Web-enabled service thus is changing customers' perceptions about the availability and types of services offered, though those perceptions vary. Some customers embrace technology, while others resent it. Many multichannel retailers have experienced a new Web-related service challenge: abandoned shopping carts on Internet sites. This technology-related issue signals that customers may have become disappointed, frustrated, or angry while shopping and have decided to take their money elsewhere.[50]

The Communications Gap: Communicating the Service Promise

Poor communication between marketers and their customers can result in a mismatch between an ad campaign's or a salesperson's promises and the service the firm can actually offer. Paradise Motel's ad promised reasonable rates and many free amenities. Yet Marcia Kessler found the advertised rate was available only on weekdays, and the amenities underwhelming. The ad raised customer expectations to an unrealistic level, setting the Paradise up for service failures.

Although firms have difficulty controlling service quality because it can vary from day to day and provider to provider, they do have control over how they communicate their service package to their customers. If a firm promises more than it can deliver, customers' expectations won't be met. An advertisement may lure a customer into a service situation once, but if the service doesn't deliver on the promise, the customer will never return. Dissatisfied customers also are likely to tell others about the underperforming service, using word of mouth or, increasingly, the Internet, which has become an important channel for dissatisfied customers to vent their frustrations.

The communications gap can be reduced by managing customer expectations. Suppose you need an operation, and the surgeon explains, "You'll be out of the hospital in five days and back to your normal routine in a month." You have the surgery and feel well enough to leave the hospital three days later. Two weeks after that, you're playing tennis again. Clearly, you will tend to think your surgeon is a genius. However, regardless of the operation's success, if you had to stay in the hospital for 10 days and it took you two months to recover, you would undoubtedly be upset.

Promising only what you can deliver, or possibly even a little less, is an important way to control the communications gap.[51] For instance, when Federal Express first issued its next-day delivery guarantee—"absolutely, positively there by 10:30 a.m."— it achieved a competitive advantage until others matched its promise. Now Federal Express often gives next-day service when the customer has paid only for second-day service. If the package arrives on the second day, it meets expectations. If it arrives a day early, it exceeds them.

A relatively easy way to manage customer expectations is to coordinate the mechanism through which the expectation is created and the means by which the service is provided. Expectations typically are created through promotions, advertising, or personal selling. Delivery is another function altogether. If a salesperson promises a client that an order can be delivered in one day, and that delivery actually takes a week, the client will be disappointed. However, if the salesperson coordinates the order with those responsible for the service delivery, the client's expectations likely will be met.

Customer expectations can be managed when the service is delivered. Recorded messages tell customers who have phoned a company with a query how many minutes they will have to wait before the next operator is available. Business-to-business sellers automatically inform online customers of any items that are out of stock. Whether online or in a store, retailers can warn their customers to shop early during a sale because supplies of the sale item are limited. People are generally reasonable when they are warned that some aspect of the service may be below standard. They just don't like surprises!

CHECK YOURSELF

1. Explain the four service gaps identified by the Gaps Model.
2. List at least two ways to overcome each of the four service gaps.

SERVICE RECOVERY

Despite a firm's best efforts, sometimes service providers fail to meet customer expectations. When this happens, the best course of action is to attempt to make amends with the customer and learn from the experience. Of course, it is best to avoid a service failure altogether, but when it does occur, the firm has a unique opportunity to demonstrate its customer commitment.[52] Effective service recovery

When a service failure occurs, like receiving a poor meal at a restaurant, a firm's goodwill can be recovered by giving the customer a free dessert.

efforts can significantly increase customer satisfaction, purchase intentions, and positive word of mouth, though customers' postrecovery satisfaction levels usually fall lower than their satisfaction level prior to the service failure.[53]

The Paradise Motel in Maine could have made amends with Marcia Kessler after its service failures if it had taken some relatively simple, immediate steps: The assistant manager could have apologized for his bad behavior and quickly upgraded her to a suite and/or given her a free night's lodging for a future stay. The motel could also have given her a free lunch or dinner to make up for the bad breakfast. None of these actions would have cost the motel much money. Yet by using the customer lifetime value approach described in Chapter 9, the motel would have realized that by not taking action, it lost Marcia, who over the next few years could have been responsible for several thousand dollars in sales, as a customer forever. Furthermore, Marcia is likely to spread negative word of mouth about the motel to her friends and family because of its failure to recover. Quite simply, effective service recovery entails (1) listening to the customer, (2) providing a fair solution, and (3) resolving the problem quickly.[54]

Listening to the Customer

Firms often don't find out about service failures until a customer complains. Whether the firm has a formal complaint department or the complaint is offered directly to the service provider, the customer must have the opportunity to air the complaint completely, and the firm must listen carefully to what he or she is saying.

Customers can become very emotional about a service failure, whether the failure is serious (a botched surgical operation) or minor (the wrong change at a restaurant). In many cases, the customer may just want to be heard, and the service provider should give the customer all the time he or she needs to "get it out." The very process of describing a perceived wrong to a sympathetic listener is therapeutic in and of itself. Service providers therefore should welcome the opportunity to be that sympathetic ear, listen carefully, and appear (and actually be) anxious to rectify the situation to ensure it doesn't happen again.[55]

Finding a Fair Solution

Most people realize that mistakes happen. But when they happen, customers want to be treated fairly, whether that means distributive or procedural fairness.[56] Their perception of what "fair" means is based on their previous experience with other firms, how they have seen other customers treated, material they have read, and stories recounted by their friends.

Distributive Fairness   **Distributive fairness** pertains to a customer's perception of the benefits he or she received compared with the costs (inconvenience or loss). Customers want to be compensated a fair amount for a perceived loss that resulted from a service failure. If, for instance, a person arrives at the airport gate and finds her flight is overbooked, she may believe that taking the next flight that day and receiving a travel voucher is adequate compensation for the inconvenience. But if no flights are available until the next day, the traveler may require additional compensation, such as overnight accommodations, meals, and a round-trip ticket to be used at a later date.[57]

The key to distributive fairness, of course, is listening carefully to the customer. One customer, traveling on vacation, may be satisfied with a travel voucher, whereas another may need to get to the destination on time because of a business appointment. Regardless of how the problem is solved, customers typically want tangible restitution—in this case, to get to their destination—not just an apology. If providing tangible restitution isn't possible, the next best thing is to assure the customer that steps are being taken to prevent the failure from recurring.

A mother approached Buck Rogers, who was the general manager of the Daytona Cubs minor league baseball team, to inform him that a rowdy patron near her and her young child had been swearing constantly during the game. Rogers immediately offered to change her seat, but the mother did not find this offer sufficient because she believed she could probably hear the swearing fan from anywhere in the ballpark. The woman indicated she would never come back. Trying to find an acceptable solution and not lose the fan, Rogers offered her a free admission to another game and told her that when she returned, her son could throw out the first pitch. The end result of this quick thinking: The woman and her son returned many times.[58]

Procedural Fairness With regard to complaints, procedural fairness refers to the perceived fairness of the process used to resolve them. Customers want efficient complaint procedures over whose outcomes they have some influence. Customers tend to believe they have been treated fairly if the service providers follow specific company guidelines. Nevertheless, rigid adherence to rules can have deleterious effects. CVS, the largest drugstore chain in the United States, requires a manager's approval for every return, no matter how small. This process can take several minutes and irritate everyone in the checkout line. In this case, the procedure the company uses to handle a return may overshadow potential positive outcomes. Therefore, as we noted previously, service providers should be empowered with some procedural flexibility to solve customer complaints.

Flexibility entails discretion. Consider the local convenience store that sells both cigarettes and alcohol. The storeowner has implemented a policy that everyone who appears to be under 30 years of age who attempts to purchase these items must show valid identification. If the store clerks comply, the customers accept it as part of the purchasing protocol and perceive it as fair for everyone. If a customer looks over 30 years of age, however, but the store clerk asks for identification, this can create a service failure.

A "no questions asked" return policy has been offered as a customer service by many retailers for years. But because of its high cost as a result of customers abusing the policy, many retailers have modified their return policy. Some large retailers, for instance, now limit their returns to 90 days, since this is considered a reasonable amount of time for customers to return an item. Home Depot's return policy was originally to take back all merchandise, but now, if customers don't have a receipt, they can only get store credit based upon the lowest selling price of the item. If they have a receipt, they can get cash back. Target requires that customers have a receipt and return the merchandise in 90 days to get a refund. In addition, for some consumer electronics products that have been opened, customers must pay a 15 percent restocking fee.

Resolving Problems Quickly

The longer it takes to resolve a service failure, the more irritated the customer will become and the more people he or she is likely to tell about the problem. To resolve service failures quickly, firms need clear policies, adequate training for their employees, and empowered employees. Health insurance companies, for instance, have made a concerted effort in recent years to avoid service failures that occur because customers' insurance claims have not been handled quickly or to the customers' satisfaction. USAA, a member-owned financial services organization that caters to members of the military and their families, employs telephone representatives who work directly with "action agents" within the organization to resolve customer complaints and identify service failures quickly. Its efforts have paid off; USAA has a high annual customer renewal rate and owns and manages more than $96 billion in assets for 6 million members.[59]

Retailers' return policies have become more restrictive because of customer abuse.

The CREST Method of Resolving Service Failures

The CREST method, when carefully and sincerely implemented, can help resolve many service failures.

- **C:** "Calm the customer" by actively listening and empathizing.

- **R:** "Repeat the problem" so that the customer knows he or she was heard and understood. For example, respond, "Now, Mrs. Jones, you paid your mortgage on time, but still were assessed the penalty fee, is that correct?"

- **E:** Use "empathy statements," such as, "Yes, Mrs. Jones, I can see your point. I would feel the same way."

- **S:** "Solve the problem" by indicating what action will be taken to resolve the issue. Say, for example, "I will contact Dave in our mortgage area, and call you this afternoon."

- **T:** Make a "timely response" to ensure that the problem is resolved in a defined span of time that is acceptable to both parties.[60]

Simple as it may sound, to recover effectively from service failures, firms must not only listen to the customers' complaints but act on them expeditiously.

CHECK YOURSELF

1. Why must companies worry about service recovery?
2. Name the two types of fairness that consumers might demand from a service recovery.
3. What does CREST stand for?

Summing Up

1. How does the marketing of services differ from the marketing of products?

First and foremost, services are intangible—they can't be seen or touched—which makes it difficult to describe a service's benefits or promote it to others. Service providers attempt to reduce the service's intangibility by enhancing its delivery with more tangible attributes, like a nice atmosphere or price benefits. Second, services are produced and consumed at the same time. Third, services are more variable than products, though service providers attempt to reduce this variability through standardization, training, service bundling, and technology. Fourth, because consumers can't stockpile perishable services, marketers provide incentives to stagger demand over time.

2. Why is it important that service marketers know what customers expect?

A knowledge gap occurs when marketers don't understand what their customers want. They may not be providing customers enough or the right service, in which case customers will be disappointed. To understand customer expectations, marketers analyze service quality through comprehensive studies and by interacting with customers.

3. What can firms do to help employees provide better service?

First, firms should provide training to employees regarding how to do their job and interact with customers. Second, they need to demonstrate a strong commitment to service and lead through example. Third, they can empower service providers to solve service issues and problems. Fourth, they should provide employees with both emotional support and the tools they need to do a good job. Fifth, the service program should be consistent throughout the organization. Sixth, service providers need incentives that encourage them to do a good job.

4. **What should firms do when a service fails?**

In the best-case scenario, the service does not fail in the first place. But failures are inevitable, and when they do happen, the firm must make amends to the customer. Listen carefully to the customer.

Let the customer air his or her complaint. Find a fair solution to the problem that not only compensates the customer for the failure but also follows procedures that the customer believes are fair. Resolve the problem quickly.

Key Terms

- communication gap, 376
- customer service, 368
- delivery gap, 376
- distributive fairness, 388
- emotional support, 383
- empowerment, 382
- inseparable, 371
- instrumental support, 383

- intangible, 370
- knowledge gap, 376
- perishable, 375
- procedural fairness, 389
- RFID (radio frequency identification device), 385
- service, 368
- service gap, 376

- service quality, 378
- standards gap, 376
- variability, 373
- voice-of-customer (VOC) program, 378
- zone of tolerance, 379

Marketing Applications

1. Those companies from which you purchase products and services are not pure sellers of services, nor are they pure sellers of products. What services does a bagel shop provide? What goods does the post office provide?

2. You have been sitting in the waiting room of your mechanic's shop for more than an hour. With the knowledge that products are different from services, develop a list of the things the shop manager could do to improve the overall service delivery. Consider how the shop might overcome problems associated with the tangibility, separability, variability, and perishability of services.

3. You have conducted a zone of tolerance analysis for a local car wash. You find that the length of the reliability and responsiveness boxes are much greater than those of the other three service quality dimensions. You also find that the car wash is positioned above the zone box on reliability but below the box on responsiveness. What should you tell the manager of the car wash to do?

4. Design a simple system for collecting customer information about the services of your car wash client.

5. Think back to your last job. What training did your employer provide regarding how to interact with customers and provide good customer service? What could your employer have done to prepare you better to interact with customers?

6. Provide an example of a specific situation in which a service provider could have avoided a service failure if he or she had been empowered to do so. What should that person have done?

7. What types of support and incentives could your university provide advisors to help make them more attentive to students' needs?

8. What technologies do you use that help facilitate your transactions with a specific retailer or service provider? Would you rather use the technology or engage in a face-to-face relationship with a person? How, if at all, would your parents' answer to these two questions be different?

9. A local health club is running a promotional campaign that promises you can lose an inch a month off your waist if you join the club and follow its program. How might this claim cause a communications gap? What should the club do to avoid a service failure?

10. Suppose the health club didn't listen to your advice and ran the promotional campaign as is. A new member has come in to complain that not only did he not lose inches off his waist, he actually gained weight. How should the health club manager proceed?

11. You are hired by a career consulting firm that promises to market new graduates to high-paying employers. The firm provides potential clients

with an impressive list of employers. It charges the clients a fee, and then a separate finder's fee if the client gets a position. The firm aggressively markets its services and has a large client base. You learn that the firm simply takes submitted résumés and posts them to a variety of online job search engines. The firm never actually contacts any firms on its clients' behalf. The CEO, himself a recent college grad, tells you that the firm never promises to actually contact potential employers, only that they have access to employers and will distribute clients' résumés. What do you think of the career consulting firm's practices?

www.mhhe.com/grewal2e

Quiz Yourself

1. A _____ gap reflects the difference between customers' expectations and the firm's perception of those customer expectations.
   a. seniority
   b. knowledge
   c. standards
   d. delivery
   e. communication

2. When approached by a customer, Nordstrom's employees have been trained to drop whatever they are doing, listen carefully, and provide caring, individualized attention to that customer. Nord-strom employees have been trained to emphasize _____ in the five service quality dimensions.
   a. assurance
   b. reliability
   c. tangibles
   d. responsiveness
   e. empathy

(Answers to these two questions are provided on page 624.)

Go to www.mhhe.com/grewal2e to practice an additional 11 questions.

Toolkit

SERVICES ZONE OF TOLERANCE

Use the Toolkit provided at www.mhhe.com/grewal2e to assess the zone of tolerance for several service providers.

Net Savvy

1. What services does JetBlue (www.jetblue.com) offer? Go to JetBlue's Web site, click on "About JetBlue," then "Why You'll Like Us." Compare the services of JetBlue, American Airlines (www.aa.com) and Virgin America (www.virginamerica.com) to each other using the five service quality dimensions (tangibility, responsiveness, reliability, assurance, and empathy). For www.aa.com, go to "Travel Information," then "During Your Flight," for its services. For www.virginamerica.com, go to "Our Difference," and then "See Our Difference."

2. Evaluate the ease with which you can make hotel reservations using Marriott's (www.marriott.com) Internet reservation system. Marriott subscribes to the BBBOnline Privacy Program. What is this program? Why do you believe that Marriott includes its seal on its Web site?

Chapter Case Study

PUTTIN' ON THE RITZ[61]

Luxury hotels are booming, and hotels are adding more and more expensive rooms to compete for the highest-end customers.[62] Despite that vast number of hotels in the luxury hotel market, though, the undisputed leaders remain Ritz-Carlton hotels. Ritz-Carlton competes by simply offering the best service. So what exactly does this hotel chain do differently than its competitors, and how does it maintain its advantage based on superior service?

Ritz-Carlton, owned by the hotel group Marriott International, consists of 70 hotels in 23 countries around the world. Ritz hotels employ 32,000 people worldwide and train their employees in the efforts necessary to create the perfect service experience.[63] The history of Ritz-Carlton began in 1927 with the opening of the Ritz-Carlton Boston, a hotel renowned for the lengths it would go to for its guests, such as reupholstering the chairs in Winston Churchill's room in red fabric to match his favorite color or redecorating the décor of Joan Crawford's room with a theme of peppermint Lifesavers, her favorite candies.[64]

Ritz-Carlton's superior customer service also is based on highly trained employees who care for their guests, as well as a sophisticated customer relationship management (CRM) system that ensures that Ritz guests receive consistent and superlative service.

Attention to Employees

Ritz-Carlton combines extensive employee training and careful hiring practices to create an environment that embraces the customer. For example, employees are instructed to never say the word "No" to a guest, and each concierge receives a $2,000 daily fund for each guest that the concierge can use to solve problems for hotel customers. Ritz guests are often surprised by the little things that hotel employees do, but this high-quality service gets eternally reinforced by constant training. For instance, on every shift, on every Ritz property, a 15-minute meeting acts as a refresher to remind employees to act on one of the 12 "Service Values" that constitute the company's "Gold Standard."

The Ritz-Carlton's motto is: We are Ladies and Gentlemen serving Ladies and Gentlemen.

Training is only one part of the excellent customer service; before it even gets to that point, the Ritz-Carlton starts by hiring the right kind of employees. It looks for people who are "warm" and "caring" and works to instill the Ritz-Carlton motto: "We are Ladies and Gentlemen serving Ladies and Gentlemen."[65] Before the opening of the Ritz-Carlton Dallas, each employee had undergone more than 80 hours of training. Of the 400 employees who would run the hotel, half transferred in from other Ritz hotels to ensure that the new opening would maintain the customer service and attention to every detail for which the company continues to be so well known.

Sophisticated IT Systems

To support its performance, the Ritz uses a CRM system called Mystique that collects information about guests, from their special requests, to informal observations by employees. This system is relatively difficult to implement because observations need to be "actionable" and confirmed by various aspects of the customer's stay. For example, if a customer orders a martini with pearl onions three times, the bartender should enter it into the system as the customer's favorite drink, but if that same customer orders a similar martini only once, it likely is not something worth noting. Yet employees are constantly trying to "wow" their customers, so any knowledge that helps them do so in the future provides value to both employees and customers.

Ritz-Carlton's goal is to encourage guests to engage actively with the Ritz-Carlton brand. Its research shows that customers who connect with the brand spend 23 percent more than other customers. That makes customer service an important driver of company value. After all, a mere 4 percent increase in customer engagement would be worth approximately $40 million in sales to the company! Employees are trained how to engage their customers, realizing, for example, that a rock star and a retired corporate executive probably should be treated differently. Employees are taught to alter their style depending on the situation, because their interactions should differ when greeted by a guest who says, "Good evening, young man; how are you?" versus another who nods, "Hey dude, how's it going?"

Recognition of the Best

Finally, beyond the impressive loyalty that Ritz-Carlton enjoys from its customers, it has earned some of the most prestigious awards in quality, including the Malcolm Baldrige Award. To share what it has learned with other companies, Ritz-Carlton recently created a customer service training program that costs $1,700 per person. Now banks, hospitals, law firms, and car dealerships—industries often criticized for providing poor service—send their employees to training programs to improve their own level of service. Even employees of Lexus dealerships, Macy's, and Starbucks have been attendees at Ritz training programs.

Students in Ritz's training program learn about how the hotel chain provides the best service to its customers and how they might borrow some of its techniques in their own industry. The people who do the laundry, maintain the landscaping, park guests' cars, and open the doors at the Ritz are all involved in training employees from other companies that turn to the Ritz for help. They offer advice on how to help guests or customers in their own areas of expertise and also how to perform outside of their job description, when called on, even during busy periods, to ensure superb customer service all the time.

Questions

1. Using the building blocks (five dimensions) of service quality (see again Exhibit 12.4), evaluate the Ritz-Carlton hotel chain.
2. Compare the Ritz-Carlton's service quality performance with that of the most recent hotel in which you stayed.
3. Using the Gaps Model, identify the service gaps you might have noticed during your most recent hotel stay. How might those gaps be closed?

VALUE CAPTURE

Section Five has two chapters on pricing dedicated to value capture. Chapter 13 examines the importance of setting the right price, the relationship between price and quantity sold, break-even analysis, the impact of price wars, and how the Internet has changed the way people shop. Chapter 14 looks specifically at how to set prices.

Assessing the Marketplace

Understanding the Marketplace

Targeting the Marketplace

Value Creation

Value Capture

Value Delivery: Designing the Channel and Supply Chain

Value Communication

PRICING CONCEPTS FOR ESTABLISHING VALUE

LEARNING OBJECTIVES

- Why should firms pay more attention to setting prices?
- What is the relationship between price and quantity sold?
- Why is it important to know a product's break-even point?
- Who wins in a price war?
- How has the Internet changed the way some people use price to make purchasing decisions?

The story of how, when, and where jeans got their start is part of American folk history and an ideal example of someone finding a market niche and filling it: When he moved to San Francisco to open a store during the California Gold Rush, Levi Strauss found his customers kept asking for work pants that could stand up to rough wear and tear. After discovering a little-used fabric, denim, and working with an inventor who had figured out how to put rivets in clothing, Strauss had a product that seemed incomparable. With its broad appeal and myriad uses, the blue jean appeared to be a "can't miss," which allowed Strauss to charge the then-steep price of $1 per pair.

We might laugh today at the idea of jeans for a dollar, especially when we consider that in 2005, an anonymous eBay bidder paid $60,000 for an original pair of 1850 Levi's 501s. For most consumers, the reasonable price to pay for jeans falls somewhere in between these extremes. But what is the reasonable price? When it comes to jeans, do we get what we pay for, or does price not matter, because they're all the same?

These different ideas about price reflect the concept of value. Today, Levi's 501 jeans retail for around $45, but 7 for All Mankind sells plenty of its popular styles for $200, and some consumers will spend ten times that much for a pair of bejeweled, Roberto Cavalli premium denim jeans. These various prices for what is essentially the same item—a pair of jeans—reflect the value that each offering provides. A consumer interested in a simple, basic closet staple probably sees little reason to spend thousands of dollars and therefore finds value in the known quality, fit, and accessibility of Levi's. Another consumer, who wants great fashion and a hip image,

How much are you willing to pay for a pair of 7 for All Mankind jeans?

prefers the edgy feel of 7 for All Mankind. And for those consumers who can afford them, like Aerosmith's Steven Tyler (pictured on p. 396), Cavalli provides unique styling, distinctive accents, and perhaps even platinum rivets.

In essence, if consumers value the brand and the potential benefits a higher price might signify, they likely will buy the higher-end jeans. However, a consumer who values lower prices will likely purchase Levi's. Thus, knowing how consumers arrive at their perceptions of value is critical to developing successful pricing strategies. Nonetheless, a good pricing strategy must consider other factors as well, which is why developing one is a formidable challenge to all firms. Do it right, and the rewards to the firm will be substantial. Do it wrong, and failure will be swift and severe. But even if a pricing strategy is implemented well, consumers, economic conditions, markets, competitors, government regulations, and even a firm's own products change constantly—and that means that a good pricing strategy today may not remain an effective pricing strategy tomorrow.

● ● ●

A lot rides on marketers setting the right price, so we take two chapters to explain the role of price in the marketing mix. First, in this chapter, we explain what "price" is as a marketing concept, why it is important, how marketers set pricing objectives, and how various factors influence price setting. In the next chapter, we extend this foundation by focusing on specific pricing strategies that capitalize on capturing value.

Imagine that a consumer realizes that to save money on a particular item, she will have to drive an additional 20 miles. She may judge that her time and travel costs are not worth the savings, so even though the price tag is higher at a nearby store, she judges the overall cost of buying the product there to be lower. To include aspects of price such as this, we may define price as the overall sacrifice a consumer is willing to make to acquire a specific product or service. This sacrifice necessarily includes the money that must be paid to the seller to acquire the item, but it also may involve other sacrifices, whether nonmonetary, like the value of the time necessary to acquire the product or service, or monetary, like travel costs, taxes, shipping costs, and so forth, all of which the buyer must give up to take possession of the product.[1] It's useful to think of overall price like this to see how the narrower sense of purchase price fits in.

Previously, we have defined *value* as the relationship between the product's benefits and the consumer's costs, which is another way of looking at the same thing. Consumers judge the benefits the product delivers against the sacrifice necessary to obtain it, then make a purchase decision based on this overall judgment of value. Thus, a great but overpriced product can be judged as low in value and may not sell as well as an inferior but well-priced item. In turn, we cannot define price without referring specifically to the product or service associated with it. The key to successful pricing is to match the product or service with the consumer's value perceptions.

In this equation, price also provides information about the quality of products and services. If firms can price their products or services too high, can they price them too low as well? Quite simply, yes. Although price represents the sacrifice consumers make to acquire the product or service, looked at the other way around it also provides helpful signals to consumers. A price set too low may signal low quality, poor performance, or other negative attributes about the product or service. Would you trust your looks to a plastic surgeon advertising rhinoplasty surgery (commonly referred to as a nose job) for only $299.99? We discuss this aspect of price in further detail when we talk about specific pricing strategies in the next chapter, but for now, note that consumers don't necessarily want a low price all the time or for all products. Rather, what they want is high value, which may come with a relatively high or low price, depending on the bundle of benefits the product or service delivers. If the firm wants to deliver value and value is judged by the benefits relative to the cost, then pricing decisions are absolutely critical to the effort to deliver value.

Because price is the only element of the marketing mix that does not generate costs, but instead generates revenue, it is important in its own right. Every other element in the marketing mix may be perfect, but with the wrong price, sales and thus revenue will not accrue. Research has consistently shown that consumers usually rank price as one of the most important factors in their purchase decisions.[2]

Knowing that price is so critical to success, why don't managers put greater emphasis on it as a strategic decision variable? Price is the most challenging of the four Ps to manage, partly because it is often the least understood. Historically, managers have treated price as an afterthought to their marketing strategy, setting prices according to what competitors were charging or, worse yet, adding up their costs and tacking a desired profit on to set the sales price. Prices were rarely changed except in response to radical shifts in market conditions. Even today pricing decisions are often relegated to standard rules of thumb that fail to reflect our current understanding of the role of price in the marketing mix.

For example, retailers sometimes use a 100 percent markup rule, otherwise known as "keystoning." That is, they simply double what they paid for the item when they price it for resale. Yet what happens if the store receives a particularly good deal from the manufacturer on an item? If consumers are not sensitive to price changes for the product, should marketers blindly pass this lower price on to consumers? Why lower the price if it will not stimulate more sales? In this case, it might be better for the store not to follow its standard markup practice and instead take the additional profit. Similarly, if the store's cost for an item goes up and consumers are particularly sensitive to price increases for that product, the store might want to take less than 100 percent markup.

As we said, all this is crucial because consumers may use the price of a product or service to judge its quality.[3] Price is a particularly powerful indicator of quality when consumers are less knowledgeable about the product category. For example, most college students know little about upholstered furniture, so if a student found himself in an IKEA store and had to make a decision about which sofa to purchase, he might judge the quality of the various sofas according to their prices and assume that a higher price means higher quality, and he would probably be right.

In summary, marketers should view pricing decisions as a strategic opportunity to create value rather than as an afterthought to the rest of the marketing mix. Let us now turn to the five basic components of pricing strategies.

THE FIVE Cs OF PRICING

Successful pricing strategies are built around the five critical components (the five Cs) of pricing found in Exhibit 13.1.

We examine these components in some detail because each makes a significant contribution to formulating good pricing policies.[4] To start, the first step is to develop the company's pricing objectives.

Company Objectives

By now, you know that different firms embrace very different goals. These goals should spill down to the pricing strategy, such that the pricing of a company's products and services should support and allow the firm to reach its overall goals. For example, a firm with a primary goal of very high sales growth will likely have a different pricing strategy than a firm with the goal of being a quality leader.

Each firm, then, embraces objectives that seem to fit with where management thinks the firm needs to go to be successful, in whatever way they define success.

EXHIBIT 13.1	Five Cs of Pricing

EXHIBIT 13.2	Company Objectives and Pricing Strategy Implications
Company Objective	**Examples of Pricing Strategy Implications**
Profit-oriented	Institute a companywide policy that all products must provide for at least an 18 percent profit margin to reach a particular profit goal for the firm.
Sales-oriented	Set prices very low to generate new sales and take sales away from competitors, even if profits suffer.
Competitor-oriented	To discourage more competitors from entering the market, set prices very low.
Customer-oriented	Target a market segment of consumers who highly value a particular product benefit and set prices relatively high (referred to as premium pricing).

These specific objectives usually reflect how the firm intends to grow. Do managers want it to grow by increasing profits, increasing sales, decreasing competition, or building customer satisfaction?

Company objectives are not as simple as they might first appear; they often can be expressed in slightly different forms that mean very different things. Exhibit 13.2 introduces some common company objectives and corresponding examples of their implications for pricing strategies. These objectives are not always mutually exclusive, because a firm may embrace two or more noncompeting objectives.

Profit Orientation Even though all company methods and objectives may ultimately be oriented toward making a profit, firms implement a profit orientation specifically by focusing on target profit pricing, maximizing profits, or target return pricing.

- Firms usually implement target profit pricing when they have a particular profit goal as their overriding concern. To meet this targeted profit objective, firms use price to stimulate a certain level of sales at a certain profit per unit.

- The maximizing profits strategy relies primarily on economic theory. If a firm can accurately specify a mathematical model that captures all the factors required to explain and predict sales and profits, it should be able to identify the price at which its profits are maximized. Of course, the problem with this approach is that actually gathering the data on all these relevant factors and somehow coming up with an accurate mathematical model is an extremely difficult undertaking.

- Other firms are less concerned with the absolute level of profits and more interested in the rate at which their profits are generated relative to their investments. These firms typically turn to target return pricing and employ pricing strategies designed to produce a specific return on their investment, usually expressed as a percentage of sales.

Sales Orientation Firms using a sales orientation to set prices believe that increasing sales will help the firm more than will increasing profits. For example, a new health club might focus on unit sales, dollar sales, or market share and therefore be willing to set a lower membership fee and accept less profit at first to focus on and generate more unit sales. In contrast, a high-end jewelry store might focus on dollar sales and maintain higher prices. The jewelry store relies on its prestige image, as well as the image of its suppliers, to provoke sales. Even though it sells fewer units, it can still generate high dollar sales levels.

Finally, some firms may be more concerned about their overall market share than about dollar sales per se (though these often go hand in hand) because

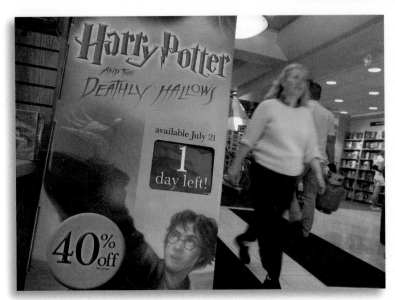

Large retailers discounted the price of the new Harry Potter book to increase market share.

they believe that market share better reflects their success relative to the market conditions than do sales alone. A firm may set low prices to discourage new firms from entering the market, encourage current firms to leave the market, take market share away from competitors—all to gain overall market share. For example, the release of the last installment of J. K. Rowling's popular series prompted some of the largest booksellers, including Wal-Mart and Amazon.com, to offer *Harry Potter and the Deathly Hallows* for less than half its list price. In so doing, these retail giants ensured that Potter fans would preorder, order, or buy just from them, pushing up their market share and outcompeting smaller booksellers that could not afford to take similar price cuts.[5] In addition, by offering a discount coupon for a future purchase with every preorder of *Deathly Hallows*, Amazon attempted to increase its future sales as well. In this case, profits on the book itself are of little concern; the focus is on increasing sales.

Adopting a market share objective does not always imply setting low prices. Rarely is the lowest-price offering the dominant brand in a given market. Heinz Ketchup, Philadelphia Brand Cream Cheese, Crest toothpaste, and Nike athletic shoes have all dominated their markets, yet all are premium-priced brands. **Premium pricing** means the firm deliberately prices a product above the prices set for competing products to capture those customers who always shop for the best or for whom price does not matter. Thus, companies can gain market share simply by offering a high-quality product at a fair price as long as they use effective communication and distribution methods to generate high value perceptions among consumers. Although the concept of value is not overtly expressed in sales-oriented strategies, it is at least implicit because, for sales to increase, consumers must see greater value.

Competitor Orientation   When firms take a **competitor orientation**, they strategize according to the premise that they should measure themselves primarily against their competition. Some firms focus on **competitive parity**, which means they set prices that are similar to those of their major competitors. Another competitor-oriented strategy, **status quo pricing**, changes prices only to meet those of the competition. For example, when Delta increases its average fares, American Airlines and United often follow with similar increases; if Delta rescinds that increase, its competitors tend to drop their fares too.[6] Value is only implicitly considered in competitor-oriented strategies, but in the sense that competitors may be using value as part of their pricing strategies, copying their strategy might provide value.

Customer Orientation   A **customer orientation** explicitly invokes the concept of value. Sometimes a firm may attempt to increase value by focusing on customer satisfaction and setting prices to match consumer expectations. Or a firm can use a "no-haggle" price structure to make the purchase process simpler and easier for consumers, thereby lowering the overall price and ultimately increasing value. For example, the car company Saturn has relied on a "no-haggle" price policy.

Firms may offer very high-priced, "state-of-the-art" products or services in full anticipation of limited sales. These offerings are designed to enhance the company's reputation and image and thereby increase the company's value in the minds of consumers. Paradigm, a Canadian speaker manufacturer, produces what many audiophiles consider a high-value product, yet offers speakers priced

SATURN SKY RED LINE TURBO

Saturn has a "no-haggle" price policy to make the purchase process easier for customers, thereby lowering the overall price and increasing value.

as low as $189 per pair. However, Paradigm also offers a very high-end pair of speakers for $6,000. Although few people will spend $6,000 on a pair of speakers, this "statement" speaker communicates what the company is capable of and can increase the image of the firm and the rest of its products—even that $189 pair of speakers. Setting prices with a close eye to how consumers develop their perceptions of value can often be the most effective pricing strategy, especially if it is supported by consistent advertising and distribution strategies.

After a company has a good grasp on its overall objectives, it must implement pricing strategies that enable it to achieve those objectives. As the second step in this process, the firm should look toward consumer demand to lay the foundation for its pricing strategy.

Customers

When firms have developed their company objectives, they turn to understanding consumers' reactions to different prices. The second C of the five Cs of pricing focuses on the customers. Customers want value, and as you likely recall, price is half of the value equation.

To determine how firms account for consumers' preferences when they develop pricing strategies, we must first lay a foundation of traditional economic theory that helps explain how prices are related to demand (consumers' desire for products) and how managers can incorporate this knowledge into their pricing strategies.[7] But first read through Adding Value 13.1 on the next page, which considers how some companies achieve success by allowing customers to decide how much value their products offer.

Demand Curves and Pricing
A **demand curve** shows how many units of a product or service consumers will demand during a specific period of time at different prices. Although we call them "curves," demand curves can be either straight or curved, as Exhibit 13.3 shows. Of course, any demand curve relating demand to price assumes that everything else remains unchanged. For the sake of experiment, marketers creating a demand curve assume that the firm will not increase its expenditures on advertising and that the economy will not change in any significant way.

Can you tell the difference between the $6,000 and the $189 speaker?

Adding Value 13.1   Pay What You Want—Really

At the Terra Bite Lounge in Kirkland, Washington, coffee shop customers pay what they want to pay, and then leave the money in a lockbox. And yet, the coffee shop is profitable—maybe even because it does not set prices. The 200 customers per day that the shop hosts spend an average of $2–3 per person. Terra Bite Lounge is not the first to come up with this concept; the One World Café in Salt Lake City has been profitable for two years and brought in $350,000 in revenue, with a 5 percent profit margin in 2007.[8]

For this concept to work, employees and customers must be comfortable with the payment method. Customers who feel that they may be paying too much or too little can tarnish the atmosphere. In the same way, employees who do not leave the pricing solely up to the customer can make customers uncomfortable.

Such restaurants embrace a charitable concept, arguing that by offering patrons food and drink for the price they can afford, they ensure everyone has a chance to eat. For those who can afford to purchase items, the associated image of charity may be valuable in itself.

The idea is not limited to food providers either; the band Radiohead caused quite a stir in the music industry when it released its 2007 album, *In Rainbows*, solely online, not in stores, and asked its fans to pay as much as they wanted

to download it. Even when given the chance to download the album for free, approximately 40 percent of visitors voluntarily paid for it.[9] When the band released *In Rainbows* more conventionally through traditional retail channels, it encouraged buyers to participate in "do it yourself" packaging by recycling their old CD cases instead of paying for a new one to come with their new CD.

At the Terra Bite Lounge, customers pay what they want.

Exhibit 13.3 illustrates the classic downward-sloping demand curve in which, as price increases, demand for the product or service decreases. In this case, consumers will buy more CDs as the price decreases. In Adding Value 13.1, the demand for Radiohead's *In Rainbows* likely increased when the band reduced the cost down to essentially nothing. We can expect to uncover a demand curve similar to this one for many, if not most, products and services.

The horizontal axis in Exhibit 13.3 measures the quantity demanded for the CDs in units and plots it against the various price possibilities indicated on the

EXHIBIT 13.3   Demand Curve for Compact Discs

vertical axis. Each point on the demand curve then represents the quantity demanded at a specific price. So, in this instance, if the price of a CD is $10 per unit ($P_1$), the demand is 1,000,000 units (Q_1), but if the price were set at $15 ($P_2$), the demand would only be 500,000 units (Q_2). The firm will sell far more CDs at $10 each than at $15 each. Why? Because of the greater value this price point offers.

Knowing the demand curve for a product or service enables a firm to examine different prices in terms of the resulting demand and relative to its overall objective. In our preceding example, the music retailer will generate a total of $10,000,000 in sales at the $10 price ($10 × 1,000,000 units) and $7,500,000 in sales at the $15 price ($15 × 500,000 units). In this case, given only the two choices of $10 or $15, the $10 price is preferable as long as the firm wants to maximize its sales in terms of dollars and units. But what about a firm that is more interested in profit? To calculate profit, it must consider its costs, which we cover in the next section.

Interestingly enough, not all products or services follow the downward-sloping demand curve for all levels of price depicted in Exhibit 13.3. Consider prestige products or services, which consumers purchase for their status rather than their functionality. The higher the price, the greater the status associated with it and the greater the exclusivity, because fewer people can afford to purchase it. Loro Piana, a high-end fashion designer, purposefully set out to control the vicuña market so that it could produce exclusive sweaters made from the fleece of these rare animals that can be sheared only every two years. Vicuña fleece, though remarkably soft and warm, is also incredibly hard to procure and rare to find, which means Loro Piana can charge $5,900 for a sweater. Consumers know they are among the few people in the world who can say that they cuddled up in vicuña during the last winter storm.[10] In this case, a higher price also leads to a greater quantity sold—up to a certain point. The price demonstrates just how rare, exclusive, and prestigious the product is. When customers value the increase in prestige more than the price differential between the prestige product and other products, the prestige product attains the greater value overall.

However, prestige products can also run into pricing difficulties. The Fender Telecaster and Stratocaster guitars are absolute necessities for any self-respecting guitar hero, but for students just learning or hobbyists, the price of owning a Fender "axe" was simply too much. In response, Fender introduced a separate, budget-priced line of similar guitars under a different brand name, so as not to dilute the prestige of the Fender name. The Squier line, made in Japan with automated manufacturing and less expensive parts, offers a look similar to the famous Fender guitars and performance just a notch below the originals. Today, an American-made "Eric Clapton" Fender Stratocaster lists for $2,142.84, whereas a Squier Stratocaster model retails for around $350.[11]

Exhibit 13.4 illustrates a demand curve for another hypothetical prestige service, a Caribbean cruise. As the graph indicates, when the price increases from $1,000 ($P_1$) to $5,000 ($P_2$), the quantity demanded actually increases from 200,000 (Q_1) to 500,000 (Q_2) units. However, when the price increases to $8,000 ($P_3$), the demand then decreases to 300,000 (Q_3) units.

Although the firm likely will earn more profit selling 300,000 cruises at $8,000 each than 500,000 cruises at $5,000 each, we do not know for sure until we bring costs into the picture. However, we do know that more consumers are willing to book the cruise as the price increases initially from $1,000 to $5,000 and that most consumers will choose an alternative vacation as the price increases further from $5,000 to $8,000.

We must consider this notion of consumers' sensitivity to price changes in greater depth.

Price Elasticity of Demand
Although we now know something about how consumers react to different price levels, we still need to determine how consumers respond to actual changes in price. These responses vary depending

John Frusicante of the Red Hot Chili Peppers uses a Fender Stratocaster.

EXHIBIT 13.4   Demand Curve for Caribbean Cruise (a prestige product)

on the product or service. For example, consumers are generally less sensitive to price increases for necessary items, like milk, because they have to purchase the items even if the price climbs. When the price of milk goes up, demand does not fall significantly because people still need to buy milk. However, if the price of steak rises beyond a certain point, people will buy less because they can turn to the many substitutes for this cut of meat. Marketers need to know how consumers will respond to a price increase (or decrease) for a specific product or brand so they can determine whether it makes sense for them to raise or lower prices.

Price elasticity of demand measures how changes in a price affect the quantity of the product demanded. Specifically, it is the ratio of the percentage change in quantity demanded to the percentage change in price.

We can calculate it with the following formula:

$$\text{Price elasticity of demand} = \frac{\%\text{ change in quantity demanded}}{\%\text{ change in price}}$$

The demand curve provides the information we need to calculate the price elasticity of demand. For instance, what is the price elasticity of demand if we increase the price of our CD from $10 to $15?

Consumers are less sensitive to the price of milk than to steak. When the price of milk goes up, demand does not fall significantly because people still need to buy milk. However, if the price of steak rises beyond a certain point, people will buy less because they can turn to many substitutes for steak.

$$\% \text{ change in quantity demanded } = \frac{(1,000,000 - 500,000)}{1,000,000} = 50\%, \text{ and}$$

$$\% \text{ change in price } = \frac{(\$10 - \$15)}{10} = -50\%, \text{ so}$$

$$\text{Price elasticity of demand } = \frac{50\%}{-50\%} = -1.$$

Thus, the price elasticity of demand for our CD is − 1.

In general, the market for a product or service is price sensitive (or **elastic**) when the price elasticity is less than –1, that is, when a 1 percent decrease in price produces more than a 1 percent increase in the quantity sold. In an elastic scenario, relatively small changes in price will generate fairly large changes in the quantity demanded, so if a firm is trying to increase its sales, it can do so by lowering prices. However, raising prices can be problematic in this context, because doing so will lower sales. To refer back to our grocery examples, a retailer can significantly increase its sales of filet mignon by lowering its price because filets are elastic.

The market for a product is generally viewed as price insensitive (or **inelastic**) when its price elasticity is greater than –1, that is, when a 1 percent decrease in price results in less than a 1 percent increase in quantity sold. Generally, if a firm must raise prices, it is helpful to do so with inelastic products or services because in such a market, fewer customers will stop buying or reduce their purchases. However, if the products are inelastic, lowering prices will not appreciably increase demand; customers just don't notice or care about the lower price.

Consumers are generally more sensitive to price increases than to price decreases.[12] That is, it is easier to lose current customers with a price increase than it is to gain new customers with a price decrease. Also, the price elasticity of demand usually changes at different points in the demand curve unless the curve is actually a straight line, as in Exhibit 13.3. For instance, a prestige product or service, like our Caribbean cruise example in Exhibit 13.4, enjoys a highly inelastic demand curve up to a certain point so that price increases do not affect sales significantly. But when the price reaches that certain point, consumers start turning to other alternatives because the value of the cruise has finally been reduced by the extremely high price.

American consumers have experienced the full force of this elasticity phenomenon during the past few years as the U.S. dollar has lost ground to other major world currencies, particularly the euro. In 2000, the exchange rate was $0.90 for a euro; in 2007, the currencies had traded places, and the exchange rate was over $1.46.[13] Therefore, a German-made Mercedes-Benz that may have cost $39,000 in 2005 would have cost over $63,000 in 2007 if Mercedes hadn't absorbed any of the cost of the currency devaluation. While American consumers have seen the value of products made in other countries, particularly the higher-priced Western European countries, erode with the dollar, Europeans have begun to perceive shopping in the United States to be like one big bargain basement.

A Mercedes-Benz that cost $39,000 in 2005 would now cost over $63,000 due to the devaluation of the dollar against the euro.

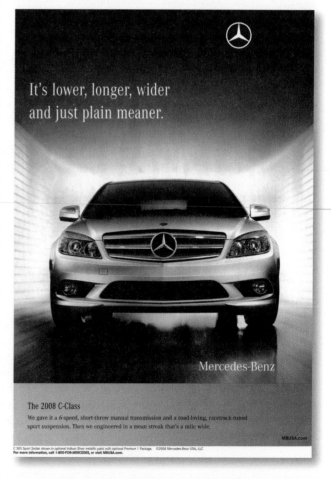

It's lower, longer, wider and just plain meaner.

Mercedes-Benz

The 2008 C-Class

We gave it a 6-speed, short-throw manual transmission and a road-loving, racetrack-tuned sport suspension. Then we engineered in a mean streak that's a mile wide.

MBUSA.com

Factors Influencing Price Elasticity of Demand   We have illustrated how price elasticity of demand varies across different products and at different points along a demand curve, as well as how it can change over time. What causes these differences in the price elasticity of demand? We discuss a few of the more important factors next.

Income Effect   Generally, as people's income increases, their spending behavior changes: They tend to shift their demand from lower-priced products to higher-priced alternatives. That is, consumers buy hamburger when they're stretching their money but steak when they're flush. Similarly, they may increase the quantity they purchase and splurge on a movie a week instead of one per month. In turn, when the economy is good and consumers' incomes are rising overall, the price elasticity of steak or movies may actually drop, even though the price remains constant. Conversely, when incomes drop, consumers turn to less expensive alternatives or purchase less. This income effect refers to the change in the quantity of a product demanded by consumers due to a change in their income.

If there are many close substitutes for a product, customers will be sensitive to small price changes, and the product will be highly elastic. If, for instance, Skippy raises its price, many customers will switch to another brand.

Substitution Effect   The substitution effect refers to consumers' ability to substitute other products for the focal brand. The greater the availability of substitute products, the higher the price elasticity of demand for any given product will be. For example, there are many close substitutes for the various brands of peanut butter. If Skippy raises its prices, many consumers will turn to Jif, Peter Pan, or another brand because they are more sensitive to price increases when they can easily find lower-priced substitutes. Extremely brand-loyal consumers, however, are willing to pay a higher price, up to a point, because in their minds, Skippy still offers a better value than the competing brands, and they believe the other brands are not adequate substitutes.

Keep in mind that marketing plays a critical role in making consumers brand loyal. And because of this brand loyalty and the lack of what consumers judge to be adequate substitutes, the price elasticity of demand for some brands is very low. For example, Polo/Ralph Lauren sells millions of its classic polo shirts at $75 while shirts of equal quality but without the polo player logo sell for much less. Getting consumers to believe that a particular brand is unique, different, or extraordinary in some way makes other brands seem less substitutable, which in turn increases brand loyalty and decreases the price elasticity of demand.

Cross-Price Elasticity   Cross-price elasticity is the percentage change in the quantity of Product A demanded compared with the percentage change in price in Product B. For example, when the price of DVD players dropped rapidly in the years 2000–2004, the demand for DVDs also increased rapidly. We refer to products like DVDs and DVD players as complementary products, which are products whose demands are positively related, such that they rise or fall together. In other words, a percentage increase in the quantity demanded for Product A results in a percentage increase in the quantity demanded for Product B.[14] However, when the price for DVD players dropped, the demand for VCRs went down, so DVD players and VCRs are substitute products because changes in their demand are negatively related. That is, a percentage increase in the quantity demanded for Product A results in a percentage decrease in the quantity demanded for Product B.[15] In addition, on the Internet, shopping bots like www.MySimon.com and www.Bizrate.com have made it much easier for people to shop for substitutable products like consumer electronics, which likely has affected the price elasticity of demand for such products.[16]

Superior Service 13.1   Great Service Lowers Price Elasticity

Why can some hotels, doctors, and retailers get away with charging more than their competitors and keep customers coming back for more? In some cases, it is the service. Consider the Ritz-Carlton chain of hotels. When it opens a new hotel, each employee undergoes more than 80 hours of training. About half the staff are transferred from other Ritz hotels to ensure that the new opening maintains the customer service and attention to every detail for which the company is well known.[17]

Every shift, every day, on every Ritz property, a 15-minute meeting acts as a refresher to remind employees to act on one of the 12 "Service Values" that constitute the company's "Gold Standard." Employees are empowered to do whatever it takes to solve guest problems. For example, employees are allotted $2,000 per day per guest to solve any problems that a guest may have—without supervisor approval.[18]

To support its performance, the Ritz collects information about guests, from special requests to informal observations. This system is relatively difficult to implement, because observations need to be "actionable" and confirmed by various aspects of the customer's stay. For example, if a customer orders a martini with pearl onions three times, the bartender should enter it into the system as the customer's favorite drink, but if that same customer orders a similar martini only once, it likely is not something worth noting. Yet employees are constantly trying to "wow" their customers, so any knowledge that helps them to do so in the future provides value to both employees and customers.[19]

Are you tired of waiting an hour or more to see your primary care doctor, only to get a hurried five minute audience? Some patients are signing up for concierge doctor services that promise to keep on-time appointments, be available 24/7, and give medical tests that the physician, not the insurance company, deems necessary.[20] Doctors promise to limit their patient load to 600 instead of the usual 2,500 to 3,000. Sound interesting? It should. It can cost as much as $15,000 per year. Clearly those who utilize this service are not price sensitive.

What makes the best customers of specialty department stores like Neiman Marcus, Nordstrom, and Saks Fifth Avenue continue to buy as if the merchandise were free? Part of the answer, of course, is that these stores have great merchandise, some of which is unavailable at other stores in the area. But also, these stores provide outstanding service—service so good that many people don't mind paying a relatively high price for the merchandise. Salespeople get to know their good customers as well as they know their merchandise. They will do whatever it takes to exceed their customers' expectations. For instance, if a store is out of an item that a good customer is requesting, it is not unreasonable to expect a salesperson not only to try to get it from other affiliated stores, but if all else fails, to go to a competitor's store to find the item.

Not everyone who walks in the door gets this level of service, however. These stores give premier services to premier customers, those who spend a lot of money in their stores. For instance, Neiman Marcus's top 100,000 customers spend more than $12,000 per year at the store, whereas the rest of its customers spend more like $600 per year.[21] Its loyalty program for its best customers offers a luxury vehicle like the Lexus ISF for customers who earn 5 million points or spend $5 million. Nordstrom and Saks offer their best customers perks like free shipping, vacations, and invitations to special events.

The way a product or service is marketed to customers can have a profound effect on its price elasticity. Specifically, Superior Service 13.1 describes how good marketing in the form of great customer service can make customers less sensitive to price. Prior to this point, we have focused on how changes in prices affect how much customers buy. Clearly, knowing how prices affect sales is important, but it cannot give us the whole picture. To know how profitable a pricing strategy will be, we must also consider the third C, costs.

Costs

To make effective pricing decisions, firms must understand their cost structures so they can determine the degree to which their products or services will be profitable at different prices. In general, prices should *not* be based on costs because consumers make purchase decisions based on their perceived value; they care little about the firm's costs to produce and sell a product or deliver a service. For example, a variety of factors—a larger middle class in many developing Asian and South American countries, increased fuel costs, demand for grain-based ethanol—have driven the price of soybeans, grain, and corn through the roof. Yet when Sara Lee

Sara Lee tried to pass cost increases along to its customers, but sales dropped as a result.

tried to cover some of these cost increases by hiking prices on its breads by 6.5 percent, consumers would have none of it, and sales dropped 7.4 percent.[22] Consumers use just the price they must pay and the benefits they may receive to judge value; they will not pay a higher price for an inferior product simply because the firm cannot be as cost efficient as its competitors or because events out of their control drive the cost of raw materials or labor higher.

Though Sara Lee may have trouble passing its costs on to consumers, other companies can do so with few negative repercussions. The same factors that drove grain and ethanol prices higher for the bread company affect popcorn producers, and yet Jolly Time, the company that supplies popcorn to most movie theaters in the United States, estimates that 4 billion Americans continue to consume the salty snack at the movies despite a 40 percent price increase.[23]

Although companies incur many different types of costs as a natural part of doing business, there are two primary cost categories: variable and fixed.

Variable Costs   Variable costs are those costs, primarily labor and materials, that vary with production volume. As a firm produces more or less of a good or service, the total variable costs increase or decrease at the same time. Because each unit of the product produced incurs the same cost, marketers generally express variable costs on a per-unit basis. Continuing with our Sara Lee example, the majority of the variable costs are the cost of the ingredients, primarily flour. Each time Sara Lee makes a loaf of bread, it incurs the cost of the ingredients.

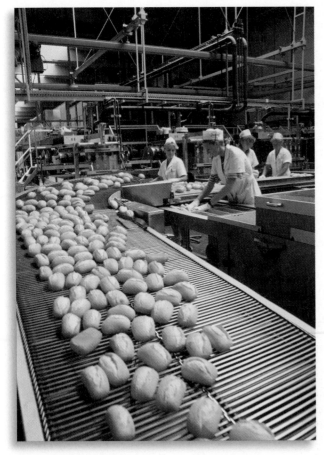

In the service industry, variable costs are far more complex. A hotel, for instance, incurs certain variable costs each time it rents a room, including the costs associated with the labor and supplies necessary to clean and restock the room. Note that the hotel does not incur these costs if the room is not booked. Suppose that a particular hotel calculates its total variable costs to be $10 per room; each time it rents a room, it incurs another $10 in variable costs. If the hotel rents out 100 rooms on a given night, the total variable cost is $1,000 ($10/room × 100 rooms).

In either case, however, variable costs tend to change depending on the quantity produced. If Sara Lee makes 100,000 loaves of bread in a month, it would have to pay a higher price for ingredients on a per pound basis than if it were producing a million loaves. Similarly, a very large hotel will be able to get a lower per unit price on most, if not all, the supplies it needs to service the room because it purchases such a large volume. However, as the hotel company continues to grow, it may be forced to add more benefits for its employees or increase wages to attract and keep long-term employees. Such changes will increase its overall variable labor costs and affect the total variable cost of cleaning a room. Thus, though not always the case, variable costs per unit may go up or down (for all units) with significant changes in volume.

The unit variable costs of producing bread go down as quantity goes up. But fixed costs stay the same.

Fixed Costs   Fixed costs are those costs that remain essentially at the same level, regardless of any changes in the volume of production. Typically, these costs include items such as rent, utilities, insurance, administrative salaries (for executives and higher-level managers), and the depreciation of the physical plant and equipment. Across reasonable fluctuations in production volume, these costs remain stable; whether Sara Lee makes 100,000 loaves or a million, the rent it pays for the bakery remains unchanged.

Total Cost   Finally, the total cost is simply the sum of the variable and fixed costs. For example, in one year, our hypothetical hotel incurred $100,000 in fixed costs. We also know that because the hotel booked 10,000 room nights, its total variable cost is $100,000 (10,000 room nights × $10/room). Thus, its total cost is $200,000.

Next, we illustrate how to use these costs in simple analyses that can inform managerial decision making about setting prices.

Break-Even Analysis and Decision Making

A useful technique that enables managers to examine the relationships among cost, price, revenue, and profit over different levels of production and sales is called break-even analysis. Central to this analysis is the determination of the break-even point, or the point at which the number of units sold generates just enough revenue to equal the total costs. At this point, profits are zero.

How do we determine the break-even point? Although profit, which represents the difference between the total cost and the total revenue (total revenue or sales = selling price of each unit sold × number of units sold), can indicate how much money the firm is making or losing at a single period of time, it cannot tell managers how many units a firm must produce and sell before it stops losing money and at least breaks even.

Exhibit 13.5 presents the various cost and revenue information we have discussed in a graphic format. The graph contains three curves (recall that even though they are straight, we still call them curves): fixed costs, total costs, and total revenue. The vertical axis measures the revenue or costs in dollars, and the horizontal axis measures the quantity of units sold. The fixed cost curve will always appear as a horizontal line straight across the graph because fixed costs do not change over different levels of volume.

The total cost curve starts where the fixed cost curve intersects the vertical axis at $100,000. When volume is equal to zero (no units are produced or sold), the fixed costs of operating the business remain and cannot be avoided. Thus, the lowest point the total costs can ever reach is equal to the total fixed costs. Beyond

EXHIBIT 13.5   Break-Even Analysis

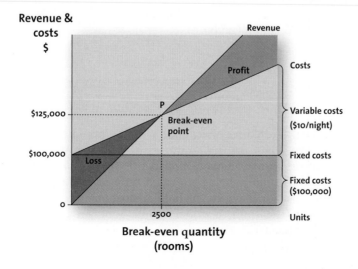

that point, the total cost curve increases by the amount of variable costs for each additional unit, which we calculate by multiplying the variable cost per unit by the number of units, or quantity.

Finally, the total revenue curve increases by the price of each additional unit sold. To calculate it, we multiply the price per unit by the number of units sold. The formulas for these calculations are as follows:

$$\text{Total variable cost} = \text{variable cost per unit} \times \text{quantity}$$

$$\text{Total cost} = \text{fixed cost} + \text{total variable cost}$$

$$\text{Total revenue} = \text{price} \times \text{quantity}$$

We again use the hotel example to illustrate these relationships. Recall that the fixed costs are \$100,000 and the variable costs are \$10/room rented. If the rooms rent for \$50 per night, how many rooms must the hotel rent over the course of a year to break even? If we study the graph carefully, we find the break-even point at 2,500, which means that the hotel must rent 2,500 rooms before its revenues equal its costs. If it rents fewer rooms, it loses money (the red area); if it rents more, it makes a profit (the green area). To determine the break-even point in units mathematically, we must introduce one more variable, the **contribution per unit**, which is the price less the variable cost per unit.

In this case,

$$\text{Contribution per unit} = \$50 - \$10 = \$40$$

Therefore, the break-even point becomes

$$\text{Break-even point (units)} = \frac{\text{fixed costs}}{\text{contribution per unit}}$$

In this case,

$$\text{Break-even point (units)} = \frac{\$100,000}{\$40} = 2,500 \text{ room nights}$$

When the hotel has crossed that break-even point of 2,500 rooms, it will then start earning profit at the same rate of the contribution per unit. So if the hotel rents 4,000 rooms—1,500 rooms more than the break-even point—its profit will be \$60,000 (1,500 rooms × \$40 contribution per unit).

Let's extend this simple break-even analysis to show how many units a firm must produce and sell to achieve a target profit. Say the hotel wanted to make \$200,000 in profit each year. How many rooms would it have to rent at the current price? In this instance, we need only add the targeted profit to the fixed costs to determine that number:

$$\text{Break-even point (units)} = \frac{(\text{fixed costs} + \text{target profit})}{\text{contribution per unit}}$$

or

$$7,500 \text{ rooms} = \frac{(\$100,000 + \$200,000)}{\$40}$$

Although a break-even analysis cannot actually help managers set prices, it does help them assess their pricing strategies because it clarifies the conditions in which different prices may make a product or service profitable. It becomes an even more powerful tool when performed on a range of possible prices for comparative purposes. For example, the hotel management could analyze various prices, not just \$50, to determine how many hotel rooms it would have to rent at what price to make a \$200,000 profit.

In a hotel, the cost of the physical structure, including the lobby, is fixed—it is incurred even if no rooms are rented. The costs of washing the towels and sheets are variable—the more rooms that are rented, the more the costs.

Naturally, however, there are limitations to a break-even analysis. First, it is unlikely that a hotel has one specific price that it charges for each and every room, so the price it would use in its break-even analysis probably represents an "average" price that attempts to account for these variances. Second, prices often get reduced as quantity increases because the costs decrease, so firms must perform several break-even analyses at different quantities.

Third, a break-even analysis cannot indicate for sure how many rooms will be rented or, in the case of products, how many units will sell at a given price. It only tells the firm what its costs, revenues, and profitability will be given a set price and an assumed quantity. To determine how many units the firm actually will sell, it must bring in the demand estimates we discussed previously.

Competition

Because the fourth C, competition, has a profound impact on pricing strategies,[24] we use this section to focus on its effect, as well as on how competitors react to certain pricing strategies. There are three levels of competition—oligopolistic, monopolistic, and pure—and each has its own set of pricing challenges and opportunities (see Exhibit 13.6).

When a market is characterized by oligopolistic competition, only a few firms dominate. Firms typically change their prices in reaction to competition to avoid upsetting an otherwise stable competitive environment. Often cited examples of oligopolistic markets include the soft drink market and the market for education at elite universities (where tuition represents the price).

Sometimes reactions to prices in oligopolistic markets can result in a price war, which occurs when two or more firms compete primarily by lowering their prices. Firm A lowers its prices; Firm B responds by meeting or beating Firm A's new price. Firm A then responds with another new price, and so on. Price wars often appear in the airline industry when a low-cost provider like JetBlue enters a market in which established carriers already exist. But what motivates firms to enter price wars?[25] In the airline example, the new entrants might want to gain market share, whereas the established airlines drop their prices to preserve their market share. Other reasons include avoiding the appearance of being insensitive to consumers and simply overreacting to a price decrease offered by competitors. In many cases, companies do not need to respond to price cuts with price cuts

EXHIBIT 13.6 Competition

of their own because consumers do not buy solely on the basis of price. Better service, higher quality, and brand loyalty might be used as competitive strategies instead.[26]

Monopolistic competition occurs when there are many firms competing for customers in a given market but their products are differentiated. When so many firms compete, product differentiation rather than a strict pricing competition tends to appeal to consumers. Thus, when Apple entered the cellular phone market with its greatly anticipated iPhone, it priced the iPhone at a premium level. Even though some consumers complained the price was too high and Apple was forced to drop the cost in the months immediately after the introduction, the innovation's positioning, which focused on the iPhone's smart design, multiple functions, and convenience, was sufficiently attractive that the phones sold out in most retail outlets within hours.

With **pure competition**, different companies that consumers perceive as substitutable sell commodity products. In such markets, price usually is set according to the laws of supply and demand. For example, wheat is wheat, so it does not matter to a commercial bakery whose wheat it buys. However, the secret to pricing success in a pure competition market is not necessarily to offer the lowest price, because doing so might create a price war and erode profits. Instead, some firms have brilliantly decommoditized their products. For example, coffee beans used to be regarded as all the same, and then Starbucks, Peet's, Seattle's Best, and others distinguished their brands by promoting their beans as a gourmet alternative to other types of beans. Recently, these coffee retailers further distinguished their brands by promoting **fair trade** coffee, which is a socially

Does this fair trade coffee compete in a pure competitive market, or has it sufficiently differentiated itself?

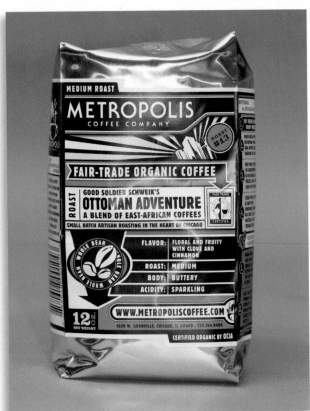

Ethical and Societal Dilemma **13.1**

The Battle: Retailers versus Manufacturers. The Winner: Consumers?

When the Supreme Court broke with precedent and ruled that manufacturers could set minimum retail prices, interested parties on all sides—manufacturers, retailers, and consumers—took notice. Essentially, the Court found that the long-standing prohibition on price fixing, which occurs, for example, when retailers and manufacturers collude to charge higher prices, did not apply when it comes to **retail price maintenance (RPM)** policies. Retail price maintenance is an attempt by a vendor to dictate or control the retail price.

Therefore, a manufacturer may now tell the retailers that stock its products the minimum amount they may charge for those products. In theory, it might seem preposterous that a manufacturer would establish a minimum price; wouldn't it want to sell as many of its products as it can? But as we have seen in this chapter, some manufacturers want their products to sell for high prices as part of their image. Retailers willing to discount merchandise to get customers into the store or to clear out obsolete products at the end of the season could easily undermine such a strategy.

Some, including Justice Stephen Breyer, who dissented from the majority opinion, suggest the Supreme Court's decision will cost the typical American consumer up to $1,000 in additional costs each year. If a manufacturer of, say, high-tech electronics refuses to allow a low-price retailer like Costco to sell its products at low retail prices, consumers will be forced to pay more for such items.

Others argue the decision will actually be good for consumers. Without RPM policies, consumers often free-ride, meaning that they gather information from high-service, high-price retailers and then go buy the item for a lower price at a discount retailer. Thus, retailers in some markets have little incentive to offer effective service levels when they will lose the sale to a lower-priced competitor. If they cannot compete on price, though, because the manufacturer will not allow sharp price reductions, more retailers may have to compete on service, which should mean better quality for consumers.

In addition, the battle is not quite over. Although it may seem that manufacturers are in control, it also may be difficult for those without a strong brand to stand up to retailers. For example, retailers that do not want to agree to RPM may simply stop doing business with that manufacturer. However, manufacturers of luxury brands, such as Sony or Liz Claiborne, likely possess enough strength to enforce pricing agreements, because retailers really need and want them.[27] So in the end, who will win, the retailers or the manufacturers? Regardless of who wins that battle, will consumers be able to achieve victory in the war?

responsible movement that ensures that producers receive fair prices for their products.

When a commodity can be differentiated somehow, even if simply by a sticker or logo, there is an opportunity for consumers to identify it as distinct from the rest, and in this case, firms can at least partially extricate their product from a pure competitive market.

Channel Members

Channel members—manufacturers, wholesalers, and retailers—can have different perspectives when it comes to pricing strategies. Consider a manufacturer that is focused on increasing the image and reputation of its brand but working with a retailer that is primarily concerned with increasing its sales. The manufacturer may desire to keep prices higher to convey a better image, whereas the retailer wants lower prices and will accept lower profits to move the product, regardless

To discourage the gray market, Fujitsu warns consumers that the manufacturer's product warranty becomes null and void unless the item has been purchased from an authorized dealer.

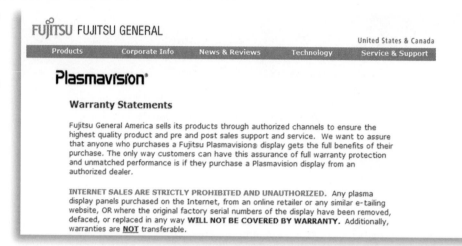

of consumers' impressions of the brand. Unless channel members carefully communicate their pricing goals and select channel partners that agree with them, conflict will surely arise. Ethical and Societal Dilemma 13.1 on the previous page illustrates the conflict that can arise between channel members when setting retail prices.

Channels can be very difficult to manage, and distribution outside normal channels does occur. A gray market, for example, employs irregular but not necessarily illegal methods; generally, it legally circumvents authorized channels of distribution to sell goods at prices lower than those intended by the manufacturer.[28] Many manufacturers of consumer electronics therefore require retailers to sign an agreement that demands certain activities (and prohibits others) before they may become authorized dealers. But if a retailer has too many high-definition TVs in stock, it may sell them at just above its own cost to an unauthorized discount dealer. This move places the merchandise on the street at prices far below what authorized dealers can charge, and in the long term, it may tarnish the image of the manufacturer if the discount dealer fails to provide sufficient return policies, support, service, and so forth.

To discourage this type of gray market distribution, some manufacturers, such as Fujitsu, have resorted to large disclaimers on their Web sites, packaging, and other communications to warn consumers that the manufacturer's product warranty becomes null and void unless the item has been purchased from an authorized dealer.[29]

CHECK YOURSELF

1. What are the five Cs of pricing?
2. Identify the four types of company objectives.
3. What is the difference between elastic versus inelastic demand?
4. How does one calculate the break-even point in units?

MACRO INFLUENCES ON PRICING

Thus far, we have focused mainly on product- and firm-specific factors—the five Cs—that influence pricing. Now we turn to the broader factors that have a more sweeping effect on pricing in general. In this section, we consider the Internet and various economic factors.

The Internet

The shift among consumers to acquiring more and more products, services, and information online has made them more price sensitive and opened new categories of products to those who could not access them previously. Gourmet foods, books, music, movies, and electronics are just a few of the product categories that present a significant online presence. Because they have gained access to rare cheeses, breads, meats, spices, and confections, consumers are demanding more from their local grocery stores in terms of selection and variety and have become more sensitive about prices. Furthermore, consumers' ability to buy electronics at highly discounted prices online has pushed bricks-and-mortar stores to attempt to focus consumers' attention on prepurchase advice and expertise, consulting services, and after-sales service—and away from price.

The Internet also has introduced search engines that enable consumers to find the best prices for any product quickly, which again increases their price sensitivity and reduces the costs associated with finding lower-price alternatives.[30] Not only do consumers know more about prices, they know more about the firms, their products, their competitors, and the markets in which they compete.

Another implication of the Internet for prices has been the growth of online auction sites such as eBay. Gone are the days when sellers had to offer their unwanted items to local buyers at "fire sale" prices. Although there certainly are good deals to be had on eBay, many items can fetch a premium price because bidders tend to get caught up in the bidding process. Also, unique and special-interest items, which previously required professional appraisals before their value could be established, now have millions of potential bidders clearly articulating a value for everything from a seven-carat canary diamond engagement ring selling for $189,000 to a 1960 Porsche 356 Roadster selling for $86,500. Today, many consumers use eBay's prior auction section to determine the prices at which products have sold in the past and establish a value for new offerings.

Power of the Internet 13.1 describes eBay pricing strategies for sellers and buyers.

Economic Factors

Two interrelated trends that have merged to impact pricing decisions are the increase in consumers' disposable income and status consciousness. Some consumers appear willing to spend money for products that can convey status in some way. Products once considered only for the very rich, such as Rolex watches and Mercedes-Benz cars, are now owned by more working professionals. Although such prestige products are still aimed at the elite, more and more consumers are making the financial leap to attain them.

At the same time, however, a countervailing trend finds customers attempting to shop cheap. The popularity of everyday low-price retailers like Wal-Mart and Target, extreme value stores such as Dollar General, and wholesale clubs like Costco among customers who can afford to shop at

Stores like H&M have introduced disposable chic to America.

Power of the Internet 13.1   **Pricing on eBay**

Researchers have published dozens of papers using eBay as their data source.[31] One research question often investigated is, "What can sellers do to get the highest price?" Here are a few tips:

1. **Set the starting price relatively low.** It is important to start prices relatively low to stimulate interest among potential bidders. For instance, starting a Nikon camera auction at $0.01 resulted in significantly higher final prices than the average price for all camera auctions. In another case, when the seller started an auction for a kitchen sink at $225, it ended without a single bidder. When reauctioned with a starting price of $75, the sink sold for $275. There is one exception to the start-low rule: If the item is somewhat idiosyncratic and therefore might not have many bids, it is best to set the price closer to the item's actual value.[32]

2. **Use reserve prices with caution, especially for low-priced items.** A reserve price in an auction is secret to potential bidders, and is the minimum amount at which a seller will sell an item. Sellers use reserve prices as protection against selling an item too low. Using a reserve price reduces the probability that the auction will end in a sale. In an experiment using relatively low-value Pokémon trading cards, researchers found that auctions utilizing reserves on average resulted in fewer serious bidders per auction and lower final sale prices. However, other research suggests that for items over $25.00, the reserve might push revenues higher when the auctions end in a successful sale.[33]

3. **Use photos to generate bids.** Listings with photos receive much more traffic than listings without photos. More traffic to the listing results in bids, and the more bids, the higher the sale price.[34]

4. **Don't flood the market.** To sell multiples of an item, don't sell them all at the same time. The market appreciates the illusion of scarcity. Items that are scarce or even unique are perceived to be more valuable. Also, spacing out the listings increases the size of the potential market because people float in and out of the market.

5. **Spell-check.** Misspellings decrease the amount of traffic an auction receives. People search for specific words. If those words are spelled wrong, the item won't pop up. One study found that Michael Jordan shirts listed "Micheal" went unsold almost twice as often as those that were spelled correctly. When sold, the misspelled brand names resulted in lower final sale prices.[35]

6. **Hype it up.** It is good to exaggerate a little. For instance, in selling a handbag, say, "Runway special! A must-have for fall!" Also, if the suggested retail price is relatively high, mention it. One study found that auctions that mention the high retail price in an item description sell for 7 percent more on average.[36]

7. **Hold longer auctions.** Longer auctions tend to fetch higher prices. Research shows that three-day and five-day auctions yield approximately the same prices, seven-day auctions are about 24 percent higher, and 10-day auctions 42 percent higher on average.[37]

8. **Don't end auctions when everyone else does.** A study found that auctions ending during peak hours on eBay are actually 9.6 percent less likely to result in a sale. About 35 percent of auctions end between 5 p.m. and 8:59 p.m., when only 25 percent of bids are placed.[38]

9. **Charge for shipping—but not too much.** Bidders don't pay much attention to shipping costs when placing bids. In one study, CDs listed with a starting price of one cent with $3.99 shipping averaged 21 percent higher final sale prices than CDs set with an opening price of $4 and no shipping charge. When the CDs were listed with a $2 starting price and a $6 shipping cost, five of the 20 CDs went unsold.[39]

10. **Avoid negative feedback.** Sellers who have even a few positive feedback reports are more likely than sellers who have no history to receive bids and to have their auctions result in a sale. Positively rated sellers also receive higher bids.[40]

By implementing these sellers' strategies from a buyers' perspective, one might be able to get some good deals. For instance, if an item has lots of bids, it may sell for an artificially high price. It pays to check out items without pictures or with misspelled words since they get fewer bids and therefore usually end up selling for less. Finally, look for short-duration auctions with items at high starting or reserve prices.

department and specialty stores illustrates that it is cool to save a buck. Retailers like Old Navy and H&M also have introduced disposable chic and cross-shopping into middle America's shopping habits. In this context, **cross-shopping** is the pattern of buying both premium and low-priced merchandise or patronizing both expensive, status-oriented retailers and price-oriented retailers. These stores offer fashionable merchandise at great values—values so good that if items last for only a few wearings, it doesn't matter to the customers. The net impact of these contradictory trends on prices has been that some prestige items have become more expensive, whereas many other items have become cheaper.

Finally, the economic environment at local, regional, national, and global levels influences pricing. Starting at the top, the growth of the global economy has changed the nature of competition around the world. Many firms maintain a presence in multiple countries—products get designed in one country, the parts are manufactured in another, the final product assembled in a third, and after-sales service is handled by a call center in a fourth. By thinking globally, firms can seek out the most cost-efficient methods of providing goods and services to their customers.

By thinking globally, firms can seek out the most cost-efficient methods of providing goods and services to their customers.

On a more local level, the economy still can influence pricing. Competition, disposable income, and unemployment all may signal the need for different pricing strategies. For instance, rural areas are often subjected to higher prices because it costs more to get products there and because competition is lower. Similarly, retailers often charge higher prices in areas populated by people who have more disposable income and enjoy low unemployment rates.

CHECK YOURSELF

1. How have the Internet and economic factors affected the way people react to prices?

Summing Up

1. **Why should firms pay more attention to setting prices?**

   Price is the only element of the marketing mix that generates revenues. It is also half the value equation. Although costs and other factors should be taken into consideration in setting prices, the most important factor is how the customer views the price in relationship to what he or she receives.

2. **What is the relationship between price and quantity sold?**

   Generally, when prices go up, the quantity sold goes down. Sometimes, however—particularly with prestige products and services—demand actually increases with price. Furthermore, some products and services are more elastic, or sensitive, to price than others. This degree of elasticity

also changes at various price levels. Consumers' sensitivity to price is influenced by how expensive a product or service is and whether substitute or complementary products or services are available.

3. **Why is it important to know a product's break-even point?**

   Break-even analysis offers a flexible tool that provides managers with an understanding of the relationships among prices, costs, revenues, and profits at different demand levels. It also indicates the conditions in which different prices can make a product or service profitable. However, a break-even analysis cannot provide managers with "the best" price because it does not include demand estimates at different price points.

4. Who wins in a price war?

A price war occurs when two or more firms compete by sequentially lowering their prices. The question of who wins depends on what the firms are trying to accomplish. If a firm wants to gain market share and is strong enough to sustain price cuts, it has a good chance of victory. But competing firms may risk financial peril if they lower their prices or lose significant market share if they don't. Often, however, it is the consumer who wins. If competitors match each other's price cuts, there are no market share gains, and the consumer just gets a lower price.

5. How has the Internet changed the way some people use price to make purchasing decisions?

Because it is so easy to get information on the Internet, people generally have become more aware of and sensitive to price. This trend has forced both manufacturers and retailers to become more price competitive. Some consumers even know more about the relative value of different products than the firms from which they are buying. Online auctions like eBay not only provide consumers with the relative value of millions of products but also enhance their value by establishing a global market for products that would have been geographically limited in the past.

Key Terms

- break-even analysis, 411
- break-even point, 411
- competitive parity, 402
- competitor orientation, 402
- complementary products, 408
- contribution per unit, 412
- cross-price elasticity, 408
- cross-shopping, 418
- customer orientation, 402
- demand curve, 403
- elastic, 407
- fair trade, 414

- fixed costs, 410
- gray market, 416
- income effect, 408
- inelastic, 407
- maximizing profits, 401
- monopolistic competition, 414
- oligopolistic competition, 413
- premium pricing, 402
- prestige products or services, 405
- price, 398
- price elasticity of demand, 406
- price war, 413

- profit orientation, 401
- pure competition, 414
- reserve price, 418
- retail price maintenance, 415
- sales orientation, 401
- status quo pricing, 402
- substitute products, 408
- substitution effect, 408
- target profit pricing, 401
- target return pricing, 401
- total cost, 411
- variable costs, 410

Marketing Applications

1. You and your two roommates are starting a pet grooming service to help put yourselves through college. There are two other well-established pet services in your area. Should you set your price higher or lower than that of the competition? Justify your answer.

2. One roommate believes the most important objective in setting prices for the new pet grooming business is to generate a large profit, while keeping an eye on your competitors' prices; the other roommate believes it is important to maximize sales and set prices according to what your customers expect to pay. Who is right and why?

3. Assume you have decided to buy an advertisement in the local newspaper to publicize your new pet grooming service. The cost of the ad is $1,000. You have decided to charge $40 for a dog grooming, and you want to make $20 for each dog. How many dogs do you have to groom to break even on the cost of the ad? What is your break-even point if you charge $50 per dog?

4. Is there a difference between a $5,900 Loro Piana vicuña sweater and a $100 cashmere sweater? Have you ever purchased a higher-priced product or service because you thought the quality was better than that of a similar, lower-priced product or service? What was the product or service? Do you believe you made a rational choice?

5. How does the fluctuating value of the euro affect the price of German cars sold in the United States?

6. On your weekly grocery shopping trip, you notice that the price of spaghetti has gone up 50 cents a pound. How will this price increase affect the demand for spaghetti sauce, rice, and Parmesan cheese? Explain your answer in terms of the price elasticity of demand.

7. Zinc Energy Resources Co., a new division of a major battery manufacturing company, recently patented a new battery that uses zinc-air technology. The unit costs for the zinc-air battery are: The battery housing is $8, materials are $6, and direct labor is $6 per unit. Retooling the existing factory facilities to manufacture the zinc-air batteries amounts to an additional $1 million in equipment costs. Annual fixed costs include sales, marketing, and advertising expenses of $1 million; general and administrative expenses of $1 million; and other fixed costs totaling $2 million. Please answer the following questions.

   a. What is the total per-unit variable cost associated with the new battery?

   b. What are the total fixed costs for the new battery?

   c. If the price for the new battery was set at $35, what would the break-even point be?

8. How do pricing strategies vary across markets that are characterized by monopolistic, oligopolistic, and pure competition?

9. Suppose you are in the market for a new Sharp LCD television. You see one advertised at a locally owned store for $300 less than it costs at Circuit City. The salesperson at the local store tells you that the television came from another retailer in the next state that had too many units of that model. Explain who benefits and who is harmed from such a gray market transaction: you, Sharp, Circuit City, the local store?

10. Has the Internet helped lower the price of some types of merchandise? Justify your answer.

Quiz Yourself

www.mhhe.com/ grewal2e

1. If a shoe company has $1 million in fixed costs, its average shoe sells for $50 a pair, and variable costs are $30 per unit, how many units does the company need to sell to break even?
   a. 5,000
   b. 10,000
   c. 50,000
   d. 100,000
   e. 500,000

2. Ferrari and Lamborghini are manufacturers of very expensive automobiles. Their limited edition cars often sell for $300,000 or more. The cars are considered by most consumers a prestige product, for which demand is likely to be:
   a. cross-price elastic.
   b. price inelastic.
   c. price elastic.
   d. status quo elastic.
   e. derived demand inelastic.

(Answers to these two questions are provided on page 624.)

Go to www.mhhe.com/grewal2e to practice an additional 11 questions.

Toolkit

BREAK-EVEN ANALYSIS

A shoe manufacturer has recently opened a new manufacturing plant in Asia. The total fixed costs are $50 million. They plan to sell the shoes to retailers for $50, and their variable costs (material and labor) are $25 per pair. Calculate the break-even volume. Now see what would happen to the break-even point if the fixed costs were increased to $60 million due to the purchase of new equipment, or the variable costs were decreased to $20 due to a new quantity discount provided by the supplier. Please use the toolkit provided at www.mhhe.com/grewal2e to experiment with changes in fixed cost, variable cost, and selling price to see what happens to break-even volume.

Net Savvy

1. Several different pricing models can be found on the Internet. Each model appeals to different customer groups. Go to www.eBay.com and try to buy this book. What pricing options and prices are available? Do you believe that everyone will choose the least expensive option? Why or why not? Now go to www.Amazon.com. Is there more than one price available for this book? If so, what are those prices? If you had to buy another copy of this book, where would you buy it, and why would you buy it there?

2. Prices can vary, depending on the market being served. Because Dell sells its computers directly to consumers all around the world, the Dell Web site makes it easy to compare prices for various markets. Go to www.dell.com. Begin on the Dell USA site and determine the price of a Dimension 3000 desktop computer. Next go to the Dell United Kingdom Web site and another country of your choice to find the price of the same computer. (If you need to convert currency to U.S. dollars, go to www.xe.com.) How does the price of the desktop computer vary? What would account for these differences in price?

Chapter Case Study

FINDING THE BEST PRICE: BIZRATE VERSUS EBAY[41]

Economists point to auction Web sites such as eBay as the best means to represent the value of any given product, because the price is determined solely by the value that the consumer attaches to it. That is, the value of the item is accurately reflected in the price paid. Thus, the prices paid for items on eBay must be some of the lowest prices available, right?

Recently, various Internet search engines, such as www.shopzilla.com, www.pricegrabber.com, and www.pricescan.com, have gained popularity. Perhaps one of the most popular is www.bizrate.com.

Do auction Web sites or price search engines really give consumers the lowest price? To address this question, we performed searches using both Bizrate and eBay for two specific products: a Sony model DSC-H9 Cyber-shot digital camera and a Yamaha home theater receiver, model RX-V861. At bizrate.com, we found nine stores that sold the Yamaha home theater receiver at prices ranging from a low of $400 to a high of $678. For the Sony camera, we found three stores offering it at prices from $326 to $629.

At eBay, the prices for the Yamaha home theater receiver started at $419 and moved up to $599; the Sony digital camera prices ranged from $305 to $430.

Thus, it appears from analyzing these two products alone that the lowest prices are available through both channels, but the high-end prices are lower at eBay. eBay displays similar products together on the same page, which may explain why the range of prices found on eBay is narrower than that on Bizrate.

Product	Bizrate		eBay	
	Low	High	Low	High
Sony digital camera	$326	$629	$305	$430
Yamaha home theater receiver	$400	$678	$419	$599

Questions

1. How has the Internet changed price competition for well-known, branded products?

2. Would the nature of price competition on the Internet be different if we had looked for commodities or esoteric luxury products?

3. Do you think this accessibility to detailed price comparisons has reduced price competition, such that all sellers price at the same level?

4. What assumptions do you tend to make about a product that seems priced very low? Very high?

STRATEGIC PRICING METHODS

- How should firms set their prices?
- What psychological factors affect the way consumers make pricing decisions?
- In what conditions should a price skimming or a market penetration strategy be used?
- What tactics do sellers use to reduce prices to retailers? To consumers?
- How can firms avoid legal and ethical problems when setting or changing their prices?

If you start with a name and strategy that inherently promises low prices, how do you change your image so that you can start offering higher quality and charging more for those better quality items? For Payless Shoe, this question is more than just an academic exercise. In 2005, Payless undertook a complete overhaul of its entire marketing mix, including its self-identifying pricing strategy.

Pressure from large discount retailers such as Wal-Mart meant Payless was struggling to compete on its long-standing value standard: price. It had always promised every customer who ever thought of its name that they would, indeed, pay less. But competing with the everyday low pricing (EDLP) master Wal-Mart simply was not feasible anymore.

So Payless made a move into the fashion-forward segment in an effort to deliver more trendy merchandise and compete with mass market retailers such as H&M and Target. For example, it hired the developer of Cole Haan footwear and handbag collections to update every element of the company's marketing mix. Then it partnered with designers such as Laura Poretzky and Lela Rose to design fun and fashionable shoes for its target market: young women.

Armed with these better looking shoes, Payless started moving away from a traditional EDLP strategy and is experimenting with prices as high as $60—significantly higher than Wal-Mart and other low-price competitors. Payless based this decision in part on the changing demographics of its target market. The average household incomes of Payless customers in 2005 reached $50,000, and this segment values great style, as well as low prices.

To get consumers to accept the change from EDLP to higher pricing tactics, Payless also had to alter other aspects of its marketing mix. In particular, to support its efforts to gain a reputation for fashion-forward shoes, Payless currently is in the process of renovating its stores so that when customers enter, they recognize a difference. Once they perceive the retailer a bit differently, they may begin to believe that it really does have something new, different, and valuable to offer. Payless has added new carpeting, better lighting, and better fixtures; the new store designs are similar to an upscale specialty store.

The shoe retailer thus offers one example of how a company, known primarily for its offer that customers will pay less, might move into a different strategic pricing approach. Only time will tell if it will be successful.[1]

● ● ●

Coming up with the "right" price is never easy, as the Payless example shows. How will Payless's decision to undertake a radical change in its pricing strategy affect future sales—both of its own products and those of potential competitors, such as Wal-Mart, H&M, and Target? To answer such questions, we examine various pricing strategies in this chapter.

The previous chapter was devoted to examining what "price" is, why it is important, how marketers set pricing objectives, and the factors that influence prices. In this chapter, we extend that foundation by focusing on specific pricing strategies that capitalize on capturing value, as well as the psychological aspects of pricing that convey value. We also examine the implications of various pricing strategies and some of the more important legal and ethical issues associated with pricing.

PRICING STRATEGIES

Firms embrace different objectives, face different market conditions, and operate in different manners; thus, they employ unique pricing strategies that seem best for the particular set of circumstances in which they find themselves. Even a single firm needs different strategies across its products and services and over time as market conditions change. The choice of a pricing strategy thus is specific to the product/ service and target market. Although firms tend to rely on similar strategies when they can, each product or service requires its own specific strategy because no two are ever exactly the same in terms of the marketing mix. Cost-based, competitor-based, and value-based strategies are discussed in this section (see Exhibit 14.1).

EXHIBIT 14.1   Pricing Strategies

Cost-Based Methods

As their name implies, cost-based pricing methods determine the final price to charge by starting with the cost. Cost-based methods do not recognize the role that consumers or competitors' prices play in the marketplace. Although relatively simple, compared with other methods used to set prices, cost-based pricing requires that all costs can be identified and calculated on a per-unit basis. Moreover, the process assumes that these costs will not vary much for different levels of production. If they do, the price might need to be raised or lowered according to the production level. Thus, with cost-based pricing, prices are usually set on the basis of estimates of average costs.

Competitor-Based Methods

Most firms know that consumers compare the prices of their products with the different product/price combinations competitors' offer. Thus, using a competitor-based pricing method, they may set their prices to reflect the way they want consumers to interpret their own prices relative to the competitors' offerings. For example, setting a price very close to a competitor's price signals to consumers that the product is similar, whereas setting the price much higher signals greater features, better quality, or some other valued benefit.

Other companies use this method to gain market share or to exploit a cost advantage they have achieved. For example, when Intel slashed its prices to compete against AMD, a rival computer chipmaker, AMD suffered significant losses in its earnings, revenues, and stock prices. When two companies such as these compete by setting prices according to what the competitor charges, the result is

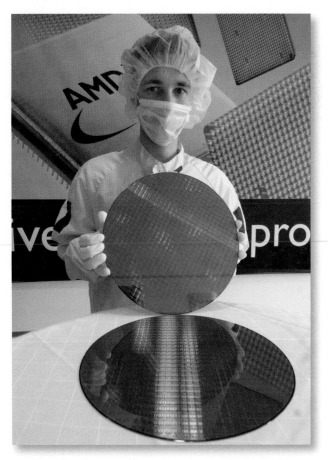

When computer chipmaker Intel (left) slashed its prices, competitor AMD (right) suffered significant losses in earnings, revenues, and stock prices.

Ferrari uses premium pricing.

often a price war, and in this case, Intel seems to be the victor.[2]

Price wars also can be damaging to companies. Unless it has a real cost advantage and therefore can lower prices without harming profits, a company may find that a price war leads only to an empty victory. That is, it may have earned greater market share at the expense of its competitor, but it may have lost most of its profits by doing so.[3]

According to some research, the effectiveness of such competitor-based pricing may depend on culture. In Western markets, most of which are quite mature, marketing means more than price, and marketing strategies rely more on "finesse" to attract customers. In developing nations, such as China, though, price remains the primary consideration, and a price drop among price-sensitive Chinese consumers prompts quick responses and a lot more sales.[4] Thus, competitor-based pricing offers the possibility of both significant benefits and significant risk, depending on the context.

Another competitor-based method is premium pricing, which means the firm deliberately prices a product above the prices set for competing products to capture those consumers who always shop for the best or for whom price does not matter. For example, can a $250,000 Ferrari be that much better than a $230,000 Ferrari? Regardless, some consumers will want to pay the additional $20,000 to get what they perceive as the very best.

The idea of premium pricing is not limited to truly luxury products like Ferraris, for which even the "inexpensive" version remains out of reach for most consumers. For example, in modern markets, the idea of "going green" appeals to many consumers, who appear willing to pay more for organic, healthy products. Clothing providers from Target to Nike to the designer Stella McCartney produce higher-priced organic and green products that promise no pesticides were used in the cotton and that the fuel that powers production facilities runs on corn husks.[5] "Green" Red Tab Levi's 501 jeans cost $68, compared with $40 for nonorganic jeans, but consumers who prefer to be environmentally responsible seem more than willing to pay the cost premium, especially if doing so does not require them to give up all sense of fashion. As more celebrities and high-end designers endorse healthy products for a healthy environment, more consumers follow their lead and embrace organic fashion as the "cool" thing to do. In turn, more companies follow a premium pricing strategy to communicate to consumers that their products cost more, but only because they're better in some way.

Value-Based Methods

Value-based pricing methods include approaches to setting prices that focus on the overall value of the product offering as perceived by the consumer. Consumers determine value by comparing the benefits they expect the product to deliver with the sacrifice they will need to make to acquire the product. Of course, different consumers perceive value differently. So how does a manager use value-based pricing methods? We consider two key approaches.

Improvement Value Method   With the first method, the manager must estimate the improvement value of a new product or service. This **improvement value** represents an estimate of how much more (or less) consumers are willing to pay for a product relative to other comparable products. For example, suppose a major telecommunications company has developed a new cell phone. Using any of a host of research methods—such as consumer surveys—the manager could get customers to assess the new product relative to an existing product and provide an estimate of how much better it is, or its improvement value.

EXHIBIT 14.2	Improvement Value		
Incremental Benefits	**Improved Value**	**Benefit Weight**	**Weighted Factor**
Clarity	20%	0.40	8%
Range	40%	0.20	8%
Security	10%	0.10	1%
Battery life	5%	0.20	1%
Ease of use	30%	0.10	3%
Overall		1.00	21%

Exhibit 14.2 illustrates how to calculate the improvement value. Consumers evaluate how much better (or worse) the new cell phone is than an existing product on five dimensions: clarity, range, security, battery life, and ease of use. According to the respondents to the survey, the new cell phone has 20 percent more clarity than the comparison phone. These consumers also weight the importance of the five attributes by allocating 100 points among them to indicate their relative importance; for the clarity dimension, this weighting is .40. When the manager multiplies the improvement weight by the relative importance percentage, clarity (20% × 0.40) emerges with a weighted factor of 8 percent. The marketer repeats the process for each benefit and sums the weighted factors to arrive at an approximation of the improvement value of the new product from customers' point of view. In this illustration, the improvement value is equal to 21 percent, so if the other cell phone costs $100, the firm should be able to charge customers a value-based price as high as $121 ($100 × 1.21).

Is the improvement value on this new cell phone sufficiently greater than competitive products that Motorola can charge a higher price for it?

Cost of Ownership Method   Another value-based method for setting prices determines the total cost of owning the product over its useful life. Using the cost of ownership method, consumers may be willing to pay more for a particular product because, over its entire lifetime, it will eventually cost less to own than a cheaper alternative.[6]

Consider, for example, that an energy efficient fluorescent lightbulb costs $3.00 and is expected to last 6,000 hours. Alternatively, a conventional lightbulb costs $1.00 but its average life is only 1,500 hours. Even though the fluorescent bulb is expected to last 4 times longer than a conventional bulb, it only costs 3 times as much. Using the cost of ownership method, and considering the cost per hour, the fluorescent bulb manufacturer could charge $4.00 for each bulb to be equivalent to the cost of the conventional bulb. But since research indicated that many consumers are reluctant to spend $4.00 for a bulb when they are used to getting them for $1.00, the manufacturer chose to charge only $3.00.

Although value-based pricing strategies can be quite effective, they also necessitate a great deal of consumer research to be implemented successfully. Sellers must know how consumers in different market segments will attach value to the benefits delivered by their products. They also must account for changes in consumer attitudes because the way customers perceive value today may not be the way they perceive it tomorrow. For instance, must-have holiday toys like Tickle Me Elmo dolls once went for hundreds of dollars when they were first introduced. They are now available for less than $35 at stores like Wal-Mart. If they

Power of the Internet 14.1

Do We Have to Pay Twice as Much to See Miley or Hannah?

When Hannah Montana tickets went on sale for her 2007, 54-date tour, online ticket brokers snapped up the entire supply within minutes. Parents faced the awful task of telling their heartbroken Tweens, the primary market for Miley Cyrus's alter ego character, that they would not be going. Rather than confront that task, some turned to the online brokers, which offered the tickets, with a face value of $63, for $237 on StubHub and as much as $2,000 on other online sites.

Ticketmaster, the initial source for most concert tickets, tries to block resellers from buying up blocks of tickets using software with a Captcha feature that displays squiggly letters only legible to humans. But brokers such as RMG Technologies own software that can encode Captcha and thus enable IP addresses to purchase tickets in huge quantities.[7] With virtual monopoly control over tickets, BMG can post the tickets on eBay's StubHub or Craigslist and charge almost as much as it wants. In response, Ticketmaster has announced that it has no choice but to sue RMG, its best single customer.

At the same time, at least two states, Arkansas and Missouri, filed suit against the brokers, alleging fraud and violations of consumer protection laws. According to Arkansas Attorney General Dustin McDaniel, brokers advertised tickets for sale before they even existed to determine buyer interest in buying those tickets at inflated prices.[8]

As a result of the technological capabilities of RMG and other online ticket brokers, concert ticket prices have skyrocketed overall. Hannah Montana prompted the biggest price race to date, but other popular shows, such as Bruce Springsteen, Van Halen, The Police, Beyoncé, and Justin Timberlake, come close. The drive to find tickets even prompts consumer fraud; one mother submitted an essay her daughter wrote about her father, killed in duty in Iraq, to win a contest for Hannah Montana tickets, then was forced to return them when contest officials discovered that the entire story was fabricated.[9]

If parents will tell falsehoods about dead fathers to win tickets for their children, what won't they pay in monetary costs? Ticketmaster faces a difficult choice: It might eliminate all Internet ticket purchases and force consumers to go back to standing in line, which seems unfeasible. It can simply accept the power of online ticket brokers, which seems unlikely. Or it can keep trying to improve its software technology, though that too may be a losing battle. Regardless of Ticketmaster's choice, it appears fans will have to accept a new pricing model based on who holds the power of the ticket.

Online ticket brokers have turned the industry's pricing model on its ear $2,000 for a $63 ticket to see Hannah Montana, give me a break!

eventually become collectables, they might again sell for far more than that in online auction sites. Therefore, firms must be actively and constantly engaged in consumer research. Furthermore, the emergence of the Internet may have altered the methods consumers use to determine value, as Power of the Internet 14.1 recognizes.

CHECK YOURSELF

1. What are the three different strategies for setting prices?
2. How can you use value-based strategies for setting prices?

What is a Tickle Me Elmo doll worth? It depends on customers' perception of value. When first introduced, they went for hundreds of dollars. Now they are available for less than $35 at stores like Wal-Mart.

PSYCHOLOGICAL FACTORS AFFECTING VALUE-BASED PRICING STRATEGIES

Understanding the psychology underlying the way consumers arrive at their perceptions, make judgments, and finally invoke a choice is critical to effective pricing strategies, so marketers must examine some of the more important psychological processes that influence consumers' reactions to and use of price. When consumers are exposed to a price, they assign meaning to it by placing it into a category, like "expensive," "a deal," "cheap," "overpriced," or even "fair."

In this section, we examine some of the factors that influence this psychological process of adding meaning to, or evaluating, price.[10]

Consumers' Use of Reference Prices

A reference price is the price against which buyers compare the actual selling price of the product and that facilitates their evaluation process. In some cases, the seller itself provides an external reference price, a higher price to which the consumer can compare the selling price to evaluate the deal.[11] Typically, the seller labels the external reference price as the "regular price" or an "original price." When consumers view the "sale price" and compare it with the provided external reference price, their perceptions of the value of the deal will likely increase.[12] In the advertisement in Exhibit 14.3, Sears has provided an external reference price, in smaller print and labeled "Reg.," to indicate that $24.99 is the regular price of Lee jeans. In addition, the advertisement highlights the current "sale" price of $21.99. Thus, the external reference price suggests to consumers that they are getting a good deal and will save money.

Consumers may also rely on an internal reference price to judge a price offering by accessing price information stored in their memory—perhaps the last price they paid or what they expect to pay.[13] For instance, when a consumer has been seated in a restaurant and first views the price of a large pepperoni pizza, she only has her internal reference price for comparison. If the price of the pizza on the menu is $12 and the consumer's internal reference price is $10 because she recalls that as the price she usually pays for a large pepperoni pizza at another restaurant, she may judge the menu price as high.

A more complex element of reference prices is the relationship among them. That is, external reference prices influence internal reference prices.[14] When consumers are repeatedly exposed to higher reference prices, their internal reference prices shift toward the higher external reference prices, assuming their initial internal reference price was not too far away from it. The net effect is that consumers will perceive the product or service in question to have a relatively lower selling price, and it therefore becomes a better deal in their perceptions.

Everyday Low Pricing (EDLP) versus High/Low Pricing

With an everyday low pricing (EDLP) strategy, companies stress the continuity of their retail prices at a level somewhere between the regular, nonsale price and the deep-discount sale prices their competitors may offer.[15] By reducing consumers' search costs, EDLP adds value; consumers can spend less of their valuable time comparing prices, including sale prices, at different stores. For example, Wal-Mart relies on EDLP to communicate to consumers that, for any given group of often-purchased items, its prices are lower than those of any other company in that market. This claim does not necessarily mean that every item that consumers may purchase will be priced lower at Wal-Mart than anywhere else—in fact, some competitive retailers will offer lower prices on some items. However, for an average purchase, Wal-Mart's prices tend to be lower overall.

Alternatively, some retailers prefer a high/low pricing strategy, which relies on the promotion of sales, during which prices are temporarily reduced to encourage purchases. In the end, which consumers prefer which strategy depends on how those consumers evaluate prices and quality. Some prefer not to expend the time to find the lowest price and favor EDLP as an efficient way to get low, even if not the very lowest, prices. Alternatively, other consumers may relish the challenge of getting the lowest price or be so price sensitive that they are willing to expend the time and effort to seek out the lowest price every time.

But even this categorization gets more complicated, in that it needs to include quality perceptions as well. Some consumers perceive that stores that use EDLP carry lower-quality goods, whereas high/low pricing stores tend to carry better-quality

Wal-Mart relies on an everyday low price (EDLP) pricing strategy.

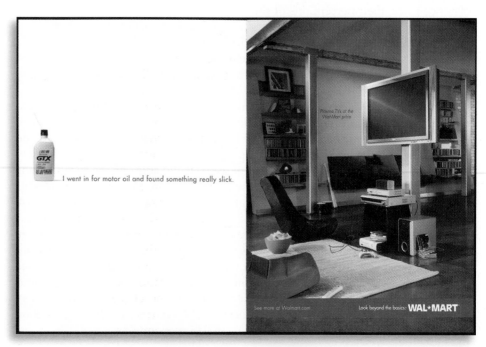

items. As the opening vignette showed, when Payless wanted to move away from the lower-quality, EDLP positioning, it had to change both its pricing and its quality. In part, this perception forms because consumers view the initial price at a high/low store as the reference price. In the end, however, the consumer's decision, once again and as always, comes down to value.

Odd Prices

Have you ever wondered why prices rarely end in round amounts, like $3.00 or $23.00? In various product categories, odd prices, or those that end in odd numbers, usually 9, are very common, such as $11.99, $3.98, $7.77, and $3.99. Although not documented, most marketers believe that odd pricing got its start as a way to prevent sales clerks from just pocketing money. Because the price was odd, the clerk would have to open the cash register for change, which required that the sale be rung up on the register.

Odd prices signal to consumers that the price is low.

Today, it seems that odd pricing simply may be so traditional that sellers are afraid to round off their prices for fear that consumers will respond negatively. Also, some sellers may believe that consumers mentally truncate the actual price, making the perceived price appear lower than it really is. For example, if the price is $21.99, consumers may focus more on the $21 than on the 99 cents, which may cause them to perceive the price as significantly lower than $22.00, even though that difference is only a penny. Another explanation is that consumers infer that an odd price must have been precisely calculated to wind up with such an odd result. Thus, the price must be fair, because the seller obviously could have rounded it up and taken in a little more money for each item. The main finding from research on the odd pricing approach is that odd prices signal to consumers that the price is low.[16]

The bottom line is that if sellers want to suggest a deal to be had, odd prices may be appropriate. However, odd prices also can suggest low quality.[17] Some consumers may perceive higher value because of the low price (especially if quality is less important to them than price), whereas others may infer lower value on the basis of the low-quality image the odd price suggests (especially if price is less important to them than quality).

The Price–Quality Relationship

Imagine that you have an important date tonight, and you are cooking a special, romantic, Italian dinner. You go to the grocery store to buy the food and realize that your recipe for the antipasto appetizer calls for lupini beans (a large bean usually imported from Italy). You've never even heard of lupini beans, much less purchased or used them in a recipe. Luckily, the store has three different brands of lupini beans. But how do you choose which brand to buy? The three choices are priced at $3.99, $3.79, and $3.49. Are you going to risk the success of this dinner to save a mere $0.50 on a can of beans? Probably not. Without other information to help you make a choice, you will likely go for the $3.99 can of beans because, like most consumers, you believe that they must be of higher quality because they cost more.

But not all consumers rely on price to judge quality. When consumers know the brands, have had experience with the products, or have considerable knowledge about how to judge the quality of products objectively, price becomes less important.[18] The store, brand name, product warranties/guarantees, and where the product was produced also represent information consumers use to judge quality. Nonetheless, price generally plays a critical role in consumers' judgments of quality.[19]

Given these various psychological pricing factors that come into play for consumers, marketers must consider how they function when they set prices. In the next section, we discuss how to apply psychological factors in the pricing decisions for new products.

NEW PRODUCT PRICING

Developing pricing strategies for new products is one of the most challenging tasks a manager can undertake. When the new product is similar to what already appears on the market, this job is somewhat easier because the product's approximate value has already been established. But when the new product is truly innovative, or what we call "new to the world," determining consumers' perceptions of its value and pricing it accordingly becomes far more difficult.

Consider, for example, the value to consumers of innovations like the polio vaccine, cell phones, the Internet, satellite radio, or air bags. When the pharmaceutical firm Merck received approval of Gardasil, a cervical cancer vaccine, it faced difficult decisions on a variety of fronts, including pricing. No other vaccines currently available offer the promise of protecting women against cervical cancer, so how could Merck determine the value of the benefit its new product offers? Complicating the issue are the ethical and legal considerations associated with this product. Because cervical cancer primarily results from a sexually transmitted virus, some parents and organizations argue that giving the vaccine to the recommended patients—girls and young women between the ages of 11 and 26 years—implicitly undermines abstinence messages. Thus, some consumers will refuse Gardasil at any price, whereas others may believe that a vaccine that can prevent a disease that affects approximately 10,000 women annually and is responsible for the death of approximately 4,000 is worth almost any amount of money.[20] These difficult assessments require good marketing research that can uncover the value of an innovation in the eyes of consumers. Therefore, we turn our attention to two distinct pricing strategies for new products: skimming and penetration.

Price Skimming

In many markets, and particularly for new and innovative products or services, innovators and early adopters (see Chapter 11) are willing to pay a higher price to obtain the new product or service. This strategy, known as price skimming, appeals to these segments of consumers who are willing to pay the premium price to have the innovation first. Did any of your friends wait in line for hours, desperate to be the first to own a new iPhone? If so, those people likely reside in the innovator segment of the cell phone market, which made them willing to pay the very highest prices to obtain this brand-new phone with its exciting product enhancements. When Apple first introduced the new technology, these consumers willingly paid the $599 retail price. However, after this high-price market segment becomes saturated and sales begin to slow down, companies generally lower the price to capture (or skim) the next most price sensitive market segment, which is willing to pay a somewhat lower price. For most companies, the price dropping process can continue until the demand for the product has been satisfied, even at the lowest price points.

For price skimming to work, the product or service must be perceived as breaking new ground in some way, offering consumers new benefits currently unavailable in alternative products. When they believe it will work, though, firms use skimming strategies for a variety of reasons. Some may start by pricing relatively high to signal high quality to the market. Others may decide to price high at first to limit demand, which gives them time to build their production capacities. Similarly, some firms employ a skimming strategy to try to quickly earn back some of the high research and development investments they made for the new product. Finally, firms employ skimming strategies to test consumers' price sensitivity. A firm that prices too high can always lower the price, but if the price is initially set too low, it is almost impossible to raise it without significant consumer resistance.

For a skimming pricing strategy to be successful, competitors cannot be able to enter the market easily; otherwise, price competition will likely force lower prices and undermine the whole strategy. Competitors might be prevented from entering the market through patent protections, their inability to copy the innovation (because it is complex to manufacture, its raw materials are hard to get, or the product relies on proprietary technology), or the high costs of entry.

Skimming strategies also face a significant potential drawback in the relatively high unit costs often associated with producing small volumes of products. Therefore, firms must consider the trade-off between earning a higher price and suffering higher production costs.

Finally, firms using a skimming strategy for new products must face the consequences of ultimately having to lower the price as demand wanes. Margins suffer, and customers who purchased the product or service at the higher initial price may become irritated when the price falls. For example, only two months after its release, Apple dropped the price of the iPhone $200, to $399, to attract more customers, especially in the midst of the 2007 holiday season. In Apple's case, the decision prompted complaints from among the high-price market segment that had paid more, but as Steve Jobs, Apple's CEO, noted in an open letter to customers, "There is always change and improvement, and there is always someone who bought a product before a particular cutoff date and misses the new price or the new operating system or the new whatever. This is life in the technology lane. If you always wait for the next price cut or to buy the new improved model, you'll never buy any technology product because there is always something better and less expensive on the horizon."[21] Despite this claim that early adopters simply

Apple used a price skimming strategy when it introduced the iPhone, but quickly lowered the price to attract more customers.

should expect to pay more, Apple also offered a $100 rebate to those who had paid $599 in an attempt to mitigate the frustration its customers felt when they confronted an obvious instance of price skimming.

Market Penetration Pricing

Instead of setting the price high, firms using a market penetration strategy set the initial price low for the introduction of the new product or service. Their objective is to build sales, market share, and profits quickly. In direct opposition to a skimming strategy, the low market penetration price encourages consumers to purchase the product immediately rather than wait for the price to drop. Although it is not always the case, many firms expect the unit cost to drop significantly as the accumulated volume sold increases, an effect known as the experience curve effect. With this effect, as sales continue to grow, the costs continue to drop, allowing even further reductions in the price.

In addition to offering the potential to build sales, market share, and profits, penetration pricing discourages competitors from entering the market because the profit margin is relatively low. Furthermore, if the costs to produce the product drop because of the accumulated volume, competitors that enter the market later will face higher unit costs, at least until their volume catches up with the early entrant.

Like a skimming strategy, a penetration strategy has its drawbacks. First, the firm must have the capacity to satisfy a rapid rise in demand—or at least be able to add that capacity quickly. Second, low price does not signal high quality. Of course, a price below their expectations decreases the risk for consumers to purchase the product and test its quality for themselves. Third, firms should avoid a penetration pricing strategy if some segments of the market are willing to pay more for the product; otherwise, the firm is just "leaving money on the table." Adding Value 14.1 illustrates how the skimming and penetration pricing strategies are used in the world of high fashion.

 Adding Value 14.1   **Price Skimming versus Market Penetration in the World of High Fashion[22]**

To obtain a custom-made suit from Brioni, a luxury clothing company based in Italy and the provider of all the suits Pierce Brosnan wore when he played James Bond, a man would need to wait approximately two months as tailors painstakingly hand-cut and -sewed the jacket and pants to match the specific measurements the customer provided. In approximately the same amount of time, the fast-fashion Spain-based retailer Zara can identify a new trend, such as the propensity of their customers to wear trench coats, communicate the trend to its designers, have the coats manufactured, and send them to stores around the globe. In today's fashion industry, the same man might buy both the Brioni suit and the Zara trench coat to wear together. Style is no longer dictated by price, and both price skimming luxury designers and penetration pricing retailers can be successful.

Because of the very efficient supply chains employed by fast-fashion chains such as Zara or its Sweden-based competitor H&M, they often can copy a designer's fashion and get it to the stores at much lower prices. To combat the stores offering lower-priced, but still well-designed, clothing, high-end designers rely on prices that communicate their dedication to their artisan heritage, the special quality of the detail in their clothing, and the inability to obtain such luxuries at low cost.

Both Zara's trench coats and Brioni's suits continue to sell well, sometimes even to the same people. This concept, known as cross-shopping, is exemplified in Adena Halpern's 2006 memoir, *Target Underwear and a Vera Wang Gown*.[23] For the most part though, the masses enjoy the fashionable access that H&M and Zara offer at an affordable price, and the luxury market embraces the detail and cutting-edge design of designers like Brioni or Chanel and willingly pays the price.

Several luxury fashion designers have decided to get a piece of the mass market. For example, Vera Wang is designing an apparel line that is sold at Kohl's; and Karl Lagerfeld is providing a ready-to-wear line for H&M, while remaining in charge of Chanel couture. Middle-of-the-road stores with average-design clothes and average prices are the ones that are struggling. They are neither hip and inexpensive nor expensive and elaborate.

CHECK YOURSELF

1. What are alternative pricing strategies to consider in introducing a new product?

PRICING TACTICS

It is important to distinguish clearly between pricing strategies and pricing tactics. A *pricing strategy* is a long-term approach to setting prices broadly in an integrative effort (across all the firm's products) based on the five Cs (company objectives, costs, customers, competition, and channel members) of pricing discussed in Chapter 13. Pricing tactics, in contrast, offer short-term methods to focus on select components of the five Cs. Generally, a pricing tactic represents either a short-term response to a competitive threat (e.g., lowering price temporarily to meet a competitor's price reduction) or a broadly accepted method of calculating a final price for the customer that is short term in nature. We separate our discussion of pricing tactics into those aimed at intermediaries in a business-to-business (B2B) setting and those directed at end consumers.

Business-to-Business Pricing Tactics and Discounts

The pricing tactics employed in B2B settings differ significantly from those used in consumer markets. Among the most prominent are seasonal and cash discounts, allowances, quantity discounts, and uniform delivered versus zone pricing. (See Exhibit 14.4.)

Seasonal Discounts   A seasonal discount is an additional reduction offered as an incentive to retailers to order merchandise in advance of the normal buying season. For instance, Lennox may offer its air conditioner dealers an additional seasonal discount if they place their orders and receive delivery before April 1, prior to the warm months when air conditioner sales are highest. If it can ship earlier in the season, Lennox can plan its production schedules more easily and lessen its finished goods inventory. Its dealers, however, must weigh the benefits of a larger profit because of the discount versus the extra cost of carrying the inventory for a longer period of time.

EXHIBIT 14.4	Business-to-Business Pricing Tactics
Tactic	**Description**
Seasonal discounts	An additional reduction offered as an incentive to retailers to order merchandise in advance of the normal buying season.
Cash discounts	An additional reduction that reduces the invoice cost if the buyer pays the invoice prior to the end of the discount period.
Allowances	Advertising or slotting allowances (additional price reductions) offered in return for specific behaviors. Advertising allowances are offered to retailers if they agree to feature the manufacturer's product in their advertising and promotional efforts. Slotting allowances are offered to get new products into stores or to gain more or better shelf space.
Quantity discounts	Providing a reduced price according to the amount purchased.
Uniform delivered versus zone pricing	Uniform delivered price: shipper charges one rate, no matter where the buyer is located. Zone price: different prices depending on the geographical delivery area.

Cash Discounts   A cash discount reduces the invoice cost if the buyer pays the invoice prior to the end of the discount period. Typically, it is expressed in the form of a percentage, such as "3/10, n/30," or "3%, 10 days, net 30," means the buyer can take a 3 percent discount on the total amount of the invoice if the bill is paid within 10 days of the invoice date; otherwise the full, or net, amount is due within 30 days. Why do B2B sellers offer cash discounts to customers? By encouraging early payment, they benefit from the time value of money. Getting money earlier rather than later enables the firm to either invest the money to earn a return on it or avoid borrowing money and paying interest on it. In both instances, the firm is better off financially.

Allowances   Another pricing tactic that lowers the final cost to channel members is allowances, such as advertising or slotting allowances, offered in return for specific behaviors. An advertising allowance offers a price reduction to channel members if they agree to feature the manufacturer's product in their advertising and promotional efforts. Slotting allowances are fees paid to retailers simply to get new products into stores or to gain more or better shelf space for their products. Some argue that slotting allowances are unethical because they put small manufacturers that cannot readily afford allowances at a competitive disadvantage. Demanding large slotting allowances could be considered a form of bribery—"paying off" the retailer to get preferential treatment.

Quantity Discounts   A quantity discount provides a reduced price according to the amount purchased. The more the buyer purchases, the higher the discount and, of course, the greater the value.

A cumulative quantity discount uses the amount purchased over a specified time period and usually involves several transactions. This type of discount particularly encourages resellers to maintain their current supplier because the cost to switch must include the loss of the discount. For example, automobile dealers often attempt to meet a quota or a sales goal for a specific time period, such as a quarter or a year. If they meet their quotas, they earn discounts on all the cars they purchased from the manufacturer during that time period in the form of a rebate check. For this very reason, you will often find good deals on cars at the end of a quarter or fiscal year. If the dealership can just sell a few more cars to meet its quota, the rebate earned can be substantial, so taking a few hundred dollars less on those last few cars is well worth the opportunity to receive a rebate check worth many times the amount of the losses.

A noncumulative quantity discount, though still a quantity discount, is based only on the amount purchased in a single order. It therefore provides the buyer with an incentive to purchase more merchandise immediately. Such larger, less frequent orders can save manufacturers order processing, sales, and transportation expenses. For example, a jeans store might get a 40 percent discount off the manufacturer's suggested retail price for placing a $500 order; a 50 percent discount for an order of $501–$4,999, and a 60 percent discount for an order of greater than $5,000.

Uniform Delivered versus Zone Pricing   These pricing tactics are specific to shipping, which represents a major cost for many manufacturers. With a uniform delivered pricing tactic, the shipper charges one rate, no matter where the buyer is located, which makes things very simple for both the seller and the buyer. Zone pricing, however, sets different prices depending on a geographical division of the delivery areas. For example, a manufacturer based in New York City might divide the United States into seven different zones and use different shipping rates for each zone to reflect the average shipping cost for customers located therein. This way, each customer in a zone is charged the same cost for shipping. Zone pricing can be advantageous to the shipper because it reflects the actual shipping charges more closely than uniform delivered pricing can.

Women's
Non-Iron
Classic Fit
Shirts
2 for $149
Reg. $89.50 each

FROM THE ARCHIVES

Country Club Collection
Our line of lifestyle clothing, introduced in April of 2003, met standards of quality, comfort and class. Not strictly for golf or tennis, this tightly focused line of clothing is designed for

Golden Fleece® Logo Mini Umbrella
$50.00

Tattersall Umbrella
$60.00
See Product in Outfit

Brooks Brothers Plaid Mini Umbrella
$50.00

Royal Stewart Umbrella
$298.00

Sterling Handle Stick Umbrella
$1,198.00

Brooks Brothers uses price lining for its umbrellas: $50 or $60, $298, and $1198—or good, better, best.

Pricing Tactics Aimed at Consumers

When firms sell their products and services directly to consumers, rather than to other businesses, the pricing tactics they use naturally differ. In this section, we analyze some tactics for products and services aimed directly at consumers: price lining, price bundling, and leader pricing (Exhibit 14.5).

Price Lining When marketers establish a price floor and a price ceiling for an entire line of similar products and then set a few other price points in between to represent distinct differences in quality, the tactic is called price lining.

Consider the specific price lines used by Brooks Brothers. The firm prices its umbrellas at three price points: $50 or $60, $298, and $1,198—or good, better, and best. The lowest-priced version, a "Classic stick umbrella in Brooks Brothers signature tattersall," at $60, still communicates a high level of quality compared with umbrellas offered by competitors, such as department stores or drugstores, that are priced much lower. The two higher-priced lines then communicate even higher levels of quality—a consumer spending almost $1,200 on an umbrella expects it to provide a remarkable level of quality. Yet the descriptions of the two higher-priced versions are not notably different. Brooks

Jewel grocery stores practice price lining. Jewel's private label (left) has the lowest price; Smuckers (right) has a higher price; and the St. Dalfour brand from France (middle) has the highest price.

EXHIBIT 14.5	Pricing Tactics Aimed at Consumers
Tactic	**Description**
Price lining	Establishing a price floor and a price ceiling for an entire line of similar products and then setting price points in between to represent distinct differences in quality.
Price bundling	Pricing of more than one product for a single, lower price.
Leader pricing	Building store traffic by aggressively pricing and advertising a regularly purchased item, often priced at or just above the store's cost.

EXHIBIT 14.6	An Illustration of Price Bundling					
Customer	Willing to Pay for Product A	Buy Product A at $7	Willing to Pay for Product B	Buy Product B at $4	Revenue for Products A & B	Buy Bundle at $9
A	8	Yes	1	No	9	Yes
B	3	No	6	Yes	9	Yes
C	8	Yes	7	Yes	15	Yes
D	5	No	2	No	7	No
Sell at	7		4		9	

Brothers describes the $1,198 as a "Stick umbrella with handmade silver handle. Made in Italy." For the $298 version, still rather expensive by many people's standard, Brooks Brothers provides this description: "Royal Stewart printed folding umbrella. Handmade leather handle. Made in Italy."[24] Clearly, the handle is different on the two offerings, but is that sufficient to communicate such vastly different perceived quality levels? Instead, Brooks Brothers relies on price to convey its different quality offering. A price of $1,198 leaves little room for ambiguity!

Price Bundling   When firms are stuck with a slow-moving item, to encourage sales, they sometimes will "bundle" it with a faster-moving item and price the bundle below what the two items would cost separately. Sometimes, however, firms bundle products together just to encourage customers to stock up so they won't purchase competing brands, to encourage trial of a new product, or to provide an incentive to purchase a less desirable product or service to obtain a more desirable one in the same bundle. This practice of selling more than one product for a single, lower price is called price bundling.

We present a price bundling example in Exhibit 14.6. Imagine we have two products to offer for sale, A and B. The first column designates four different customers, A–D. Each subsequent column indicates the average price that each of these customers is willing to pay for Product A alone, Product B alone, and finally the total revenue if they purchase both A and B. If we price Product A at $7 and Product B at $4, the total revenue would be $22, because only customers A and C would buy Product A (revenue = $14) and only customers B and C would buy Product B (revenue = $8). However, if we bundled both products at a price of $9, our total revenue would be $27, because customers A, B, and C would all pay $9 for both items.

Leader Pricing   Leader pricing is a tactic that attempts to build store traffic by aggressively pricing and advertising a regularly purchased item, often priced at or just above the store's cost. The rationale behind this tactic argues that, while in the store to get the great deal on, say, milk, the consumer will also probably pick up other items he or she needs. The store has priced these items at higher profit margins, so their purchase will more than cover the lower markup on the milk. Imagine the marketing potential of various combinations of products; the store uses leader pricing on cocktail sauce, which gives employees the perfect opportunity to ask, "How about a pound of fresh shrimp to go with the cocktail sauce you're purchasing?" Leader pricing can be illegal under circumstances that are discussed later in the chapter.

Consumer Price Reductions

The final price a customer pays for a product or service often has been adjusted from the original price because marketers have used various techniques designed

| EXHIBIT 14.7 | Consumer Price Reductions |

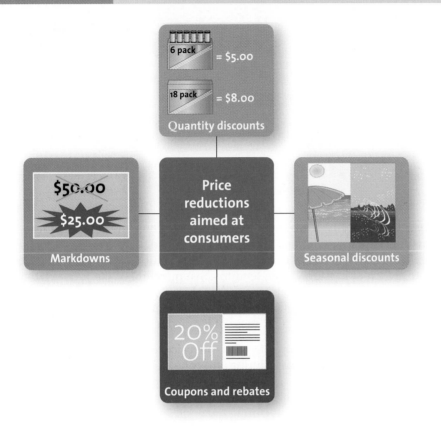

to enhance value. Some of these techniques include markdowns, quantity discounts, coupons, and rebates (Exhibit 14.7).

Markdowns Markdowns are the reductions retailers take on the initial selling price of the product or service.[25] An integral component of the high/low pricing strategy we described previously, markdowns enable retailers to get rid of slow-moving or obsolete merchandise, sell seasonal items after the appropriate season, and match competitors' prices on specific merchandise. For example, after the holidays, manufacturers of popular gift items, such as gaming systems, often reduce prices to attract consumers who were unwilling to brave long lines or pay higher prices to get the latest version of the Microsoft Xbox or Sony Playstation system.[26] Retailers must get rid of merchandise that isn't selling because holding on to such items hurts the retailer's image and ties up money in inventory that could be used more productively elsewhere.

Retailers also use markdowns to promote merchandise and increase sales. Particularly when used in conjunction with promotions, markdowns can increase traffic into the store, which many retailers view as half the battle. Once customers are in the store, retailers always hope they will purchase other products at regular prices.

Quantity Discounts for Consumers We have already discussed how firms use quantity discounts in the B2B marketplace, but the most common implementation of a quantity discount at the consumer level is the size discount. For example, there are three sizes of General Mills' popular cereal Cheerios—10-, 15-, and 20-ounce boxes priced at approximately $3.89, $4.49, and $5.99, respectively.

Stores like Aldi use a pricing tactic called leader pricing to build store traffic by aggressively pricing and advertising regularly purchased items, often at or just above the store's cost.

Customers get a size discount for buying larger sizes. With Cheerios, the larger the box, the less it costs per ounce.

The larger the quantity, the less the cost per ounce, which means the manufacturer is providing a quantity discount. The goal of this tactic is to encourage consumers to purchase larger quantities each time they buy. In turn, these consumers are less likely to switch brands and often tend to consume more of the product, depending on the product usage characteristics. Typically, buying a larger package of toilet tissue does not mean consumers will use it faster, but buying a larger box of cereal may encourage them to eat more of it or eat it more often.[27]

Seasonal Discounts   Seasonal discounts are price reductions offered on products and services to stimulate demand during off-peak seasons. You can find hotel rooms, ski lift tickets, snowmobiles, lawn mowers, barbeque grills, vacation packages, flights to certain destinations, and Christmas cards at discounts during their "off" seasons. Some consumers even plan their buying around these discounts, determined to spend the day after Christmas stocking up on discounted wrapping paper and bows for the following year.

Shoppers at Ukrop's use their loyalty card at a kiosk and receive unadvertised personalized coupons.

Coupons   Coupons offer a discount on the price of specific items when they're purchased. Coupons are issued by manufacturers and retailers in newspapers, on products, on the shelf, at the cash register, over the Internet, and through the mail.[28] Retailers use coupons because they are thought to induce customers to try products for the first time, convert those first-time users to regular users, encourage large purchases, increase usage, and protect market share against competition. However, the impact of coupons on profitability is questionable.

Coupon promotions, like all temporary promotions, may be stealing sales from a future period without any net increase in sales. For instance, if a supermarket runs a coupon promotion on sugar, households may buy a large quantity of sugar and stockpile it for future use. Thus, unless the coupon is used mostly by new buyers, the net impact on sales is negligible, and there will be a negative impact on profits due to the amount of the redeemed coupons and cost of the coupon redemption procedures. Coupons may annoy, alienate, and confuse consumers and therefore do little to increase store loyalty. Customers see an ad for a supermarket with a headline reading "Double Coupons" but don't realize there might be conditions, such as a minimum purchase required, or that it may only apply to certain manufacturers.

Recognizing these problems, some retailers like Macy's have reduced coupon usage and cut the number of days on which customers can redeem coupons. Although minimizing coupon usage could hurt the department store chain, Macy's hopes to offer more everyday value and will continue to offer coupons to its credit card holders, its most valuable customers.[29]

Grocery stores like Ukrop's are using coupons more strategically by tying them to their customer relationship management (CRM) systems.[30] Shoppers scan their loyalty cards at a kiosk located near the store entrance and receive up to eight coupons and messages selected just for them, based on their shopping history. This program allows Ukrop's and its vendors to give unadvertised personalized offers to the chain's most valuable customers.

Rebates Rebates provide another form of discounts for consumers off the final selling price. In this case, however, the manufacturer, instead of the retailer, issues the refund as a portion of the purchase price returned to the buyer in the form of cash. Rebates can be even more frustrating than coupons for consumers, but the idea is similar. Whereas a coupon provides instant savings when presented, a rebate promises savings, usually mailed to the consumer at some later date, only if the consumer carefully follows the rules. The "hassle factor" for rebates thus is higher than for coupons. The consumer must first buy the item during a specified time period, then mail in the required documentation—which usually includes the original sales receipt—and finally wait four to six weeks (or more!) for a check to arrive.

Manufacturers generally like rebates because as much as 90 percent of consumers never bother to redeem them. Manufacturers also embrace this form of price reduction because it lets them offer price cuts to consumers directly. With a traditional wholesale price cut from its vendors, retailers can keep the price on the shelf the same and pocket the difference. Rebates can also be rolled out and shut off quickly. That allows manufacturers to fine-tune inventories or respond quickly to competitors without actually cutting prices. Finally, because buyers are required to fill out forms with names, addresses, and other data, rebates become a great way for vendors to build a customer data warehouse. From the retailer's perspective, rebates are more advantageous than coupons since they increase demand in the same way coupons may, but the retailer has no handling costs.

Leasing For some products, discounts, coupons, and rebates may not be sufficient to bring the price to within consumers' reach. With a lease, consumers pay a fee to purchase the right to use a product for a specific amount of time. They never own the product, they are just renting it. Leasing products opens up new, less price sensitive, target markets. Some consumers also like leases because they get tired of the product before its useful life is over, and they don't have to worry about selling it, trading it, or throwing it away. Car companies have used leasing options for years to appeal to consumers who plan to keep their cars only for a few years and will want to trade in for a new model sooner rather than later. Other industries are recognizing that what works for Toyotas and Chevy trucks also works for gowns, handbags, art, and luxury cars. As Superior Service 14.1 notes, though consumers lease products, it is the ancillary service that makes it so valuable.

With so many different pricing strategies and tactics, it is no wonder that unscrupulous firms find ample opportunity to engage in pricing practices that can hurt consumers. We now take a look at some of the legal and ethical implications of pricing.

CHECK YOURSELF

1. What are some consumer-oriented pricing tactics?
2. What are some retailer-oriented pricing tactics?

Superior Service 14.1   Oh, This Old Porsche? I'm Just Leasing It This Month . . .

A red Ferrari or a turbo Porsche—or how about a Bentley GTC convertible? Members of the Classic Car Club can drive one each week by paying initiation fees and annual dues of $7,000 to $23,000, plus a daily rental. Customers can drive around in an Audi R8 sports car during a vacation and then show up at a business meeting in a Bentley sedan. It is like Zip Car for the well-to-do. It is not just luxury cars, however. Consumers are leasing everything from fashion to art, putting hard-to-own luxury items within reach of more people.[31] The focus on owning luxury products has become less important than having multiple options, limiting financial exposure, and experiencing products that most people cannot afford to own.

Leasing luxury products involves more than just the product. Those firms that do it well also provide excellent service. For example, the Classic Car Club invites members to weekly happy hour events, offers special activities such as driving a race car around a track, and provides reciprocal privileges for renting in locations where the Club does not exist.

The Wardrobe Company leases designer gowns from Dolce & Gabbana, Carolina Herrera, and Behnaz Sarafpour for 15 percent of the retail price. For frequent event attendees, these prices provide quite a deal! Bag, Borrow, or Steal allows its members to rent premium handbags and jewelry. There are also firms that rent art for a house to make it more appealing to potential buyers.

The flexibility and convenience of leasing ensures customers do not have to make big decisions about big products and yet still get to enjoy the experience. In this sense, the service of providing the lease goods is just as important as the products themselves. Many customers avoid serious investments and their attendant risk, but they still appreciate the experience of carrying a Louis Vuitton bag for a week or driving a different Ferrari each month. Leasing allows these customers to fulfill their psychological needs and gain the extra perks that go along with the products.

Want to impress a date? Lease a car from Classic Car Club.

LEGAL AND ETHICAL ASPECTS OF PRICING

Prices tend to fluctuate naturally and respond to varying market conditions. Thus, though we rarely see firms attempting to control the market in terms of product quality or advertising, they often engage in pricing practices that can unfairly reduce competition or harm consumers directly through fraud and deception. A host of laws and regulations at both the federal and state levels attempt to prevent unfair pricing practices, but some are poorly enforced, and others are difficult to prove.

Deceptive or Illegal Price Advertising

Although it is always illegal and unethical to lie in advertising, a certain amount of "puffery" is typically allowed (see Chapter 18). But price advertisements should never deceive consumers to the point of causing harm. For example, a local car dealer's advertising that it had the "best deals in town" would likely be considered puffery. In contrast, advertising "the lowest prices, guaranteed" makes a very specific claim and, if not true, can be considered deceptive.

Deceptive Reference Prices   Previously, we introduced external reference prices, which create reference points for the buyer against which to compare the selling price. If the reference price is bona fide, the advertisement is informative. If the reference price has been inflated or is just plain fictitious, however, the advertisement is deceptive and may cause harm to consumers. But it is not easy to determine whether a reference price is bona fide. What standard should be used? If an advertisement specifies a "regular price," just what qualifies as regular? How many units must the store sell at this price for it to be a bona fide regular price—half the stock? A few? Just one? Finally, what if the store offers the item for sale at the regular price but customers do not buy any? Can it still be considered a regular price? In general, if a seller is going to label a price as a regular price, the Better Business Bureau suggests that at least 50 percent of the sales have occurred at that price.[32]

Loss Leader Pricing   As we discussed previously, leader pricing is a legitimate attempt to build store traffic by pricing a regularly purchased item aggressively but still above the store's cost. Loss leader pricing takes this tactic one step further by lowering the price *below* the store's cost. Some states prohibit loss leader pricing by requiring some minimum markup, but such laws are difficult to enforce. No doubt you have seen "buy one, get one free" offers at grocery and discount stores. Unless the markup for the item is 100 percent of the cost, these sales obviously do not generate enough revenue from the sale of one unit to cover the store's cost for both units, which means it has essentially priced the total for both items below cost, unless the manufacturer is absorbing the cost of the promotion to generate volume. Costco uses American consumers' ongoing efforts to find the lowest prices on gasoline to attract them to its stores. Accused of illegal loss leader pricing by rivals in 11 states, Costco swears it does no such thing; it simply prices gasoline to earn the barest of margins. As long as the price is not below cost, the practice is legal, and Costco has used its pricing of this commodity successfully to drive significant business into its stores. However, other gasoline purveyors argue that Costco's tactics injure competition in a way that runs counter to the laws of various states.[33]

Similarly, offering selected prescription drugs at $4 per refill might not earn Wal-Mart significant profits. However, by drawing customers into the stores to pick up their inexpensive prescriptions, the retail giant imagines they will be tempted to pick up some other items as well, thus increasing its overall share of their wallets. Wal-Mart's $4 prescription drug offer has prompted responses across the ethical spectrum; whereas some commentators view it as a benefit for lower-income consumers who previously could not afford their medications, others argue that Wal-Mart may be taking a loss on these prescriptions, which is an unfair and sometimes illegal competitive practice.[34]

Is this a legitimate sale, or is the retailer using deceptive reference prices?

Bait and Switch   Another form of deceptive price advertising occurs when sellers advertise items for a very low price without the intent to really sell any. This bait-and-switch tactic is a deceptive practice because the store lures customers in with a very low price on an item (the bait), only to aggressively pressure these customers into purchasing a higher-priced model (the switch) by disparaging the low-priced item, comparing it unfavorably with the higher-priced model, or professing an inadequate supply of the lower-priced item. Again, the laws against bait-and-switch practices are difficult to enforce because sales people, simply as a function of their jobs, are always trying to get customers to trade up to a higher-priced model without necessarily deliberately baiting them. The key to proving deception centers on the intent of the seller, which is also difficult to prove.

Predatory Pricing

When a firm sets a very low price for one or more of its products with the intent to drive its competition out of business, it is using predatory pricing. Predatory pricing is illegal under both the Sherman Act and the Federal Trade Commission Act because it constrains free trade and represents a form of unfair competition. It also tends to promote a concentrated market with a few dominant firms (an oligopoly).

But again, predation is difficult to prove. First, one must demonstrate intent, that is, that the firm intended to drive out its competition or prevent competitors from entering the market. Second, the complainant must prove that the firm charged prices lower than its average cost, an equally difficult task. Despite numerous charges and the bankruptcies of many of its competitors, for example, no one has been able to prove that Wal-Mart engages in predation. Rather, it just competes extremely effectively when it comes to price.

Price Discrimination

There are many forms of price discrimination, but only some of them are considered illegal under the Clayton Act and the Robinson-Patman Act. When firms sell the same product to different resellers (wholesalers, distributors, or retailers) at different prices, it can be considered price discrimination; usually, larger firms receive lower prices.

We have already discussed the use of quantity discounts, which is a legitimate method of charging different prices to different customers on the basis of the quantity they purchase. The legality of this tactic stems from the assumption that it costs less to sell and service 1,000 units to one customer than 100 units to 10 customers. But quantity discounts must be available to all customers and not be structured in such a way that they consistently and obviously favor one or a few buyers over others. Subtle forms of price discrimination, such as rebates, free delivery, advertising allowances, and other methods used to lower the price without actually changing the invoice, are specifically prohibited by the Robinson-Patman Act. It is, however, perfectly legitimate to charge a different price to a reseller if the firm is attempting to meet a specific competitor's price. In addition, a barter agreement, in which buyers and sellers negotiate a mutually agreed upon price, is commonplace and absolutely legal in retail settings such as car sales and collectibles markets.

Furthermore, the Robinson-Patman Act does not apply to sales to end consumers, at which point many forms of price discrimination occur. For example, students and seniors often receive discounts on food and movie tickets, which is perfectly acceptable under federal law.

However, a series of recent court decisions in 10 states has caused some sellers to rethink the meaning of price discrimination. These 10 states have now banned "ladies' nights" in bars because the practice violates the rights of men and compromises various state antidiscrimination statutes (see Ethical and Societal Dilemma 14.1).

Is this price discrimination illegal?

ADMISSION PRICES
General Admission $9.25
Bargain Matinee $7.00
Friday-Sunday and Holiday periods before 4:00 PM
Monday-Thursday during Non-Holiday periods before 6:00 PM
Children (2-12) $6.50
Seniors (60 & Over)

Ethical and Societal Dilemma 14.1 Oh Yes, It's Ladies Night … No More

Despite the enduring popularity of Kool and the Gang's 1979 hit, it may not be ladies' night anymore in several states. Traditionally, bars have chosen one night per week and designated it "ladies' night," the night when women are admitted either for free or at a reduced rate and, once inside, served drinks at reduced prices. A New Jersey man named David Gillespie went to the Coastline bar on one ladies' night and was charged a $5 admission and full price for drinks; when he requested the discounted ladies' night prices, he was refused.[35]

Gillespie sued under New Jersey's Law Against Discrimination and won. Essentially, the courts found that because the bar offered public accommodation, it could not discriminate in either entry or service on the basis of gender. Coastline did not argue that higher prices were being charged to men but instead offered in its defense that the difference in prices had a legitimate business purpose and no intent of hostility toward men. In fact, it argued, 80 percent of the patrons in the bar on ladies' night were men.

The decision has met with mixed reviews. The former Governor of New Jersey, James McGreevey, issued a written statement denouncing it as "bureaucratic nonsense," and an "overreaction that reflects a complete lack of common sense and good judgment." One TV commentator cried "Is there nothing sacred?" For now, however, the law stands, and it is ladies' night no more. Other states, including California, Colorado, Iowa, and Pennsylvania, maintain similar laws on their books, whereas some state supreme courts, such as those in Illinois and Washington, find the offers permissible means to attract target customers.[36]

A similar case in Las Vegas centers on health clubs. Todd Phillips is suing under Nevada's 2005 ban on gender discrimination, alleging that gyms' offers of lower fees and special workout areas for women make them illegal. The case is of particular interest to the gym's casino neighbors, many of which continue to offer ladies' nights promotions.[37]

Putting aside your own potential gender biases for a moment, do you believe that women should get lower prices in bars and health clubs? Is this a real case of discrimination that should be protected under the law or an effective pricing strategy?

Should bars be allowed to have "ladies' night," when women are admitted either for free or at a reduced rate and, once inside, served drinks at reduced prices? Is this illegal price discrimination?

Price Fixing

Price fixing is the practice of colluding with other firms to control prices. Recently, the five largest music companies—Universal Music, Sony Music, Warner Music, BMG Music, and EMI—and three of the largest music retailers—Musicland Stores, Trans World Entertainment, and Tower Records—agreed to pay $67.4 million and distribute $75.7 million in CDs to public and nonprofit groups to settle a lawsuit for alleged price fixing during the late 1990s.[38]

This particular case of price fixing is especially interesting because it includes both horizontal and vertical price fixing. Horizontal price fixing occurs when competitors that produce and sell competing products collude, or work together, to control prices, effectively taking price out of the decision process for consumers. In this particular case, prosecutors alleged that horizontal price fixing had occurred among the record companies, which specified pricing terms associated with the sale and distribution of CDs. Vertical price fixing occurs when parties at different levels of the same marketing channel (e.g., manufacturers and retailers) collude to control the prices passed on to consumers. In the music industry case, prosecutors alleged that the music companies colluded with music retailers to maintain retail prices for CDs.

Whereas horizontal price fixing is clearly illegal under the Sherman Antitrust Act, vertical price fixing falls into a gray area. In 1997, Supreme Court Justice Sandra Day O'Connor rendered a decision that vertical price fixing does not always violate antitrust laws.[39] Thus, the practice of vertical price fixing is not always illegal but rather must be reviewed on a case-by-case basis to determine its legality.

As these legal issues clearly demonstrate, pricing decisions involve many ethical considerations. In determining both their pricing strategies and their pricing tactics, marketers must always balance their goal of inducing customers, through price, to find value and the need to deal honestly and fairly with those same customers. Whether another business or an individual consumer, buyers can be influenced by a variety of pricing methods; it is up to marketers to determine which of these methods works best for the seller, the buyer, and the community.

CHECK YOURSELF

1. What common pricing practices are considered to be illegal or unethical?

Summing Up

1. How should firms set their prices?

The various methods of setting prices each have their own set of advantages and disadvantages. The fixed percentage and mark-up approaches are quick and easy but fail to reflect the competitive environment or consumer demand. Although it is always advisable to be aware of what competitors are doing, using competitor-based pricing should not occur in isolation without considering consumers' reactions. Taking a value-based approach to pricing, whether the improvement value or the total cost of ownership, in conjunction with these

other methods provides a nicely balanced method of setting prices.

2. What psychological factors affect the way consumers make pricing decisions?

Customers take different perspectives and use different sources to set a particular value for a product or service. For instance, some use the manufacturer's suggested retail price as a reference point, whereas others prefer to consider the total prices of all their purchases at a particular store. These latter customers tend to prefer stores that use an everyday low pricing strategy because the average prices of their purchases likely will be low. For those customers who equate price with quality—the higher the price, the higher the quality—a high/low strategy is appealing because they not only can gauge quality by the initial higher price but also can use it as their reference price. For almost all customers though, odd prices, like those that end in 9, tend to signal a good deal.

3. In what conditions should a price skimming or a market penetration strategy be used?

When firms use a price skimming strategy, the product or service must be perceived as breaking new ground or customers will not pay more than what they pay for other products. Firms use price skimming to signal high quality, limit demand, recoup their investment quickly, and/or test people's price sensitivity. Moreover, it is easier to price high initially and then lower the price than vice versa. Market penetration, in contrast, helps firms build sales and market share quickly, which may discourage other firms from entering the market. Building demand quickly also typically results in lowered costs as the firm gains experience making the product or delivering the service.

4. What tactics do sellers use to reduce prices to retailers? To consumers?

Pricing tactics can be divided into those that affect resellers such as retailers and those that affect consumers. On the B2B side, seasonal discounts give retailers an incentive to buy prior to the normal selling season, cash discounts prompt them to pay their invoices early, and allowances attempt to get retailers to advertise the manufacturer's product or stock a new product. In addition, quantity discounts can cause retailers to purchase a larger quantity over a specific period of time or with a particular order. Finally, zone pricing bases the cost of shipping the merchandise on the distance between the retailer and the manufacturer—the farther away, the more it costs. On the consumer side, marketers can use price lining to indicate different quality levels to consumers or bundle products to offer lower prices than those charged if the products were purchased separately. To get customers into their stores, retailers also price certain products or services at very low prices, with the hope that these same customers will also buy other, more profitable items. In some methods similar to those used in B2B contexts, sellers offer seasonal and quantity discounts to individual buyers as well. Finally, coupons and rebates offer consumers additional price reductions.

5. How can firms avoid legal and ethical problems when setting or changing their prices?

There are almost as many ways to get into trouble by setting or changing a price as there are pricing strategies and tactics. Three of the most common legal issues pertain to advertising deceptive prices. Specifically, if a firm compares a reduced price with a "regular" or reference price, it must actually have sold that product or service at the regular price. In many states, advertising the sale of products priced below the retailer's cost constitutes an unfair competitive practice, as does bait-and-switch advertising. Charging different prices to different customers is sometimes, but not always, illegal, whereas any collusion among firms to fix prices is always illegal.

Key Terms

Marketing Applications

1. Suppose you have been hired as the pricing manager for a drugstore chain that typically adds a fixed percentage onto the cost of each product to arrive at the retail price. Evaluate this technique. What would you do differently?

2. Some high fashion retailers, notably H&M and Zara, sell what some call "disposable fashion"—apparel priced so reasonably low that it can be disposed of after just a few wearings. Here is your dilemma: You have an important job interview and need a new suit. You can buy the suit at one of these stores for $199 or at Brooks Brothers for $500. Of course, the Brooks Brothers suit is of higher quality and will therefore last longer. How would you use the two value-based approaches described in this chapter to determine which suit to buy?

3. Consider the last purchase you made on sale. How did you use external and internal reference prices to determine the product's value? Do you believe the external reference price was deceptive? Why or why not?

4. Identify two stores at which you shop, one of which uses everyday low pricing and another that uses a high/low pricing strategy. Do you believe that each store's chosen strategy is appropriate for the type of merchandise it sells and the market of customers to whom it is appealing? Justify your answer.

5. As the product manager for Whirlpool's line of washing machines, you are in charge of pricing new products. Your product team has developed a revolutionary new washing machine that relies on radically new technology and requires very little water to get clothes clean. This technology will likely be difficult for your competition to copy. Should you adopt a skimming or a penetration pricing strategy? Justify your answer.

6. What is the difference between a cumulative and a noncumulative quantity discount?

7. If you worked for a manufacturing firm located in Oregon and shipped merchandise all over the United States, which would be more advantageous, a zone or a uniform delivered pricing policy? Why? What if your firm were located in Kansas—would it make a difference?

8. Coupons and rebates benefit different channel members. Which would you prefer if you were a manufacturer, a retailer, and a consumer? Why?

9. Suppose the president of your university got together with the presidents of all the universities in your athletic conference for lunch. They discussed what each university was going to charge for tuition the following year. Are they in violation of federal laws? Explain your answer.

10. Imagine that you are the newly hired brand manager for a restaurant that is about to open. Both the local newspaper and a gourmet food magazine recently ran articles about your new head chef, calling her one of the best young chefs in the country. In response to these positive reviews, the company wants to position its brand as a premium, gourmet restaurant. Your boss asks what price you should charge for the chef's signature filet mignon dish. Other restaurants in the area charge around $25 for their own filet offerings. What steps might you undertake to determine what the new price should be?

11. You have been hired by a regional supermarket chain as the candy and snack buyer. Your shelves are dominated by national firms, like Wrigley's and Nabisco. The chain imposes a substantial slotting fee to allow new items to be added to their stock selection. Management reasons that it costs a lot to add and delete items, and besides, these fees are a good source of revenue. A small, minority-operated, local firm produces several potentially interesting snack crackers and a line of gummy candy, all with natural ingredients, added vitamins, reduced sugar, and a competitive price—and they also happen to taste great. You'd love to give the firm a chance, but its managers claim the slotting fee is too high. Should your firm charge slotting fees? Are slotting fees fair to the relevant shareholders—customers, stockholders, vendors?

12. Though not illegal, many firms operating over the Internet have been experimenting with charging different consumers different prices for the same product or service. Since stores in different parts of the country might have different prices, some Web sites require zip code information before providing prices. Why would retailers charge different prices in different markets or zip codes? Is it ethical for retailers to do so? Is it a good business practice?

Quiz Yourself

www.mhhe.com/grewal2e

1. In determining the price for his company's new pocket digital camera, Matt is assessing what consumers consider the regular or original price for similar cameras available in the market. Matt is assessing the _____ influence on pricing strategy.
   a. improvement value
   b. odd-even
   c. everyday low pricing
   d. reference-based
   e. cost of ownership

2. When Apple Computer Company introduced their iPhone in 2007, they priced the new combination iPod, Internet, and cellular telephone at

$599, considerably higher than either their iPod or competing cellular phones. Apple Computer was probably pursuing a _____ pricing strategy.
   a. market penetration
   b. slotting allowance
   c. price fixing
   d. reference
   e. skimming

(Answers to these two questions are provided on page 624.)

Go to www.mhhe.com/grewal2e to practice an additional 11 questions.

Net Savvy

1. Go to www.coupons.com. In which product categories does this Web site offer coupons? Choose a product from each category.

   - How effective are coupons for selling these types of products? Why?

   - Find a product marked by a pencil icon, with the notice "Sign Up and Save." Why is the manufacturer asking for this information?

   - Do any sellers offer rebates through this Web site? Why or why not?

   - What are the benefits to the seller of using coupons.com over other integrated marketing communication options? Click on the "Who

   We Are" tab at the top of the site for some hints.

   - How do you think coupons.com makes money? For example, consider what companies are advertising on the site. Do the same companies offer coupons?

2. Visit the Web site for Bag, Borrow, or Steal (www.bagborroworsteal.com) and select handbags. Click on the "organize by price" link, then choose two different offerings on extreme ends of the pricing spectrum. How much do they cost to "borrow" for a week? What distinguishes these two bags and justifies the price difference, according to the Web site? Which would you borrow?

Chapter Case Study

BATTLE ROYAL: APPLE VERSUS AMAZON[40]

As commentators far and wide have acknowledged, Apple radically changed the music industry when it introduced the iPod and its affiliated iTunes site. The very way musicians and media companies marketed music had to change in response, and one of the most significant changes occurred with regard to pricing.

Apple set the pricing model: Most songs on iTunes sell for around $0.99, and album costs usually equal the single-song price multiplied by the number of songs on that album. In creating this pricing model, Apple also instituted a technology unique to digital music, namely, digital rights management (DRM). This technology ensures that songs will expire or prevents them from being shared multiple times or on multiple devices. Thus, one consumer cannot download a song, copy it innumerable times, and share it with all of her friends. Although DRM technology therefore protects copyright holders, it also seems to frustrate consumers.

Apple also dictated that its iPods, iPhones, and related devices would only play songs equipped with its own proprietary FairPlay DRM solution or those without any DRM protection at all. Producers were faced with an either-or choice: Use iTunes or go DRM free. And many music companies, including Warner Music Group, swore they would never allow their songs to be sold without DRM protection.

Apple has thus far refused to license FairPlay to any other music players. Therefore, the company has almost a "stranglehold" on the digital music market and limits the markets for media companies to iPod or iPhone owners who use the FairPlay DRM.

Everything changed when Amazon.com started selling music downloads of Universal and EMI songs without any DRM protection at all. The days in which music companies could tell listeners when and how they might listen to their songs essentially were over. The online retailer's offering contains about 2 million songs that sell, on average, for 40 percent less than they would cost through iTunes.

The likely result seems to be an all-out price war. In just a few years, Apple and iTunes could be forced to engage in the kind of deep discounting that Tower Records and CD Wherehouse undertook in the years before digital downloads swept both aside. Such a price war could help rejuvenate the sales of songs and albums, and perhaps lower prices for consumers.

The price war also could quickly decrease the margins of music stores like Amazon and Apple. In announcing its new music store, Amazon didn't say how the discounts would affect its margins, but the implications cannot be minor.

Yet according to one music industry insider, the industry "needs to have a lot of successful retailers or they won't have a growing market. You can't satisfy consumers if there is only one place to buy music. In every industry, you see market growth when there are lots of different places to buy the product."

The music companies that have signed up with Amazon currently are making less on each copy sold, and the copies include no protections against copying or expiration dates. The situation appears likely headed into a price war, which will mean smaller margins for all the players.

Questions

1. Who are the key players in this industry?

2. Why do you think different music companies, such as Warner and Universal, have taken such different stances on DRM protection?

3. What would represent an effective response by Apple to Amazon's lower prices? Should it lower download prices to match the offer? Why or why not?

4. If a price war will reduce margins, as the case suggests, why would any company embrace this strategy?

VALUE DELIVERY: DESIGNING THE CHANNEL AND SUPPLY CHAIN

CHAPTER 15

Supply Chain Management

CHAPTER 16

Retailing and Multichannel Marketing

Section Six deals with the value delivery system. It is critical that merchandise is delivered in time to stores to meet customer demand. To achieve this, retailers have initiated many innovative programs with their vendors and developed sophisticated transportation and warehousing systems. We devote two chapters to value delivery. Chapter 15 takes a look at the entire supply chain, while Chapter 16 concentrates on retailing and multichannel marketing.

Assessing the Marketplace

Understanding the Marketplace

Targeting the Marketplace

Value Creation

Value Capture

Value Delivery: Designing the Channel and Supply Chain

Value Communication

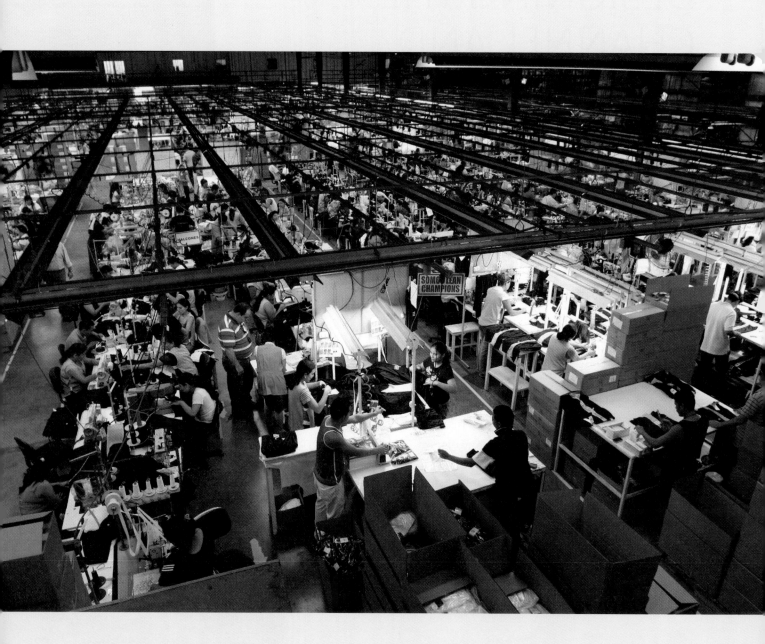

SUPPLY CHAIN MANAGEMENT

LEARNING OBJECTIVES

■ What is supply chain management?

■ How do supply chains add value?

■ How does a supply chain work?

■ How is a supply chain managed?

Nicole Miller, the New York dress designer and manufacturer, sells to many boutiques and large retailers. In the 1980s, Nicole Miller sent its typical daily orders of three dresses from its small Madison Avenue location to 1,200 specialty stores, with handwritten invoices enclosed in the packages. All processes—allocating, preparing, and shipping orders—involved manual labor. If one customer ordered 200 units to be sent to 25 different stores, Nicole Miller employees would have to spend hours packaging and invoicing all of the various shipments.

Today, the company has expanded to include 20 of its own freestanding retail stores, though a majority of its products are sold through specialty and department stores.[1] Nicole Miller has radically upgraded its ability to get its merchandise to the selling floor quickly with much less human effort.

Before it updated its systems, store employees had to add Universal Product Codes (UPC, the black-and-white bar codes found on most merchandise) and price tags to each item by hand. The items were recorded into inventory twice, once while at the production facility and once at the store, because the stores had separate computer systems from those of the corporate offices. When the retail system converted to the use of the UPC, though, the retail stores and corporate offices became more coordinated.

In the past, apparel manufacturers, including Nicole Miller, typically delivered orders to the retailers' distribution centers in whatever way they chose. It was then up to the distribution centers to allocate the merchandise according to the stores' needs. Today, many large retailers have transferred much of this allocation function to manufacturers like Nicole Miller, forcing them to upgrade their systems. Nicole Miller's retail customers prefer to receive a box at their distribution centers and be able to ship it directly to their stores, without having to open the carton to re-sort, put tags on the merchandise, and place it on hangers. Since Nicole Miller sends merchandise to retailers' distribution centers ready to go on the retail floor, employees don't have to spend many hours of nonproductive (nonselling) time getting the merchandise ready to go on sale.

For Nicole Miller to work seamlessly with its retailers, it decided to set up an electronic data interchange (EDI) with the department and specialty stores that sell its clothing and accessories, which allowed both parties to talk to each other, computer to computer. Both entities in this supply chain know what merchandise to send and receive, and both can easily track where it is in the supply chain from the time the retailer places the order, through the transportation process, to when it is placed on the retail floor, and is finally sold. Nicole Miller also can let the retailer know exactly when the distribution center can expect the order by sending it an electronic advance shipping notice (ASN). This notice allows the distribution center to get ready to receive the merchandise by having space and people available. Rather than create an invoice with each shipment, it uses specially generated carton labels, which provide detail about each item in every box, including the vendor's name, the carton's contents, and the store's destination. The moment the labels are attached to the carton, Nicole Miller transmits the appropriate ASN, via EDI, to its retail trading partner, ensuring quicker payments. The store manager electronically acknowledges receipt of the merchandise without anyone having to type in or write down any information.

This supply chain information system has been symbiotic for Nicole Miller and its retailers. By having access to retail sales data, Nicole Miller has improved its ability to forecast, create new designs, and develop new strategies. Analysis of these data also enables Nicole Miller to see the entire market picture, so it can work with its retailers to provide them with the merchandise they need when they need it.

Overall, integrated systems have helped move merchandise into stores faster; eliminated repetitive data entries; sped up invoicing, distribution, and shipments; and enabled companies—both manufacturers and retailers—to provide a closer match with what customers demand.

In this chapter, we discuss the third P, place, which includes all activities required to get the right product to the right customer when that customer wants it.[2] Students of marketing often overlook or underestimate the importance of place in the marketing mix simply because it happens behind the scenes. Yet place, or supply chain management as it is commonly called, adds value for customers because it gets products to customers efficiently—quickly and at low cost.

As we noted in Chapter 1, **supply chain management** refers to a set of approaches and techniques firms employ to efficiently and effectively integrate their suppliers, manufacturers, warehouses, stores, and transportation intermediaries into a seamless operation in which merchandise is produced and distributed in the

EXHIBIT 15.1   Simplified Supply Chain

right quantities, to the right locations, and at the right time, as well as to minimize systemwide costs while satisfying the service levels their customers require.[3] As we learned in the opening vignette, Nicole Miller employs a greatly improved supply chain compared with the one it relied on in the past, because the company owns or at least has considerable control over the various phases within that chain. As a result, it is able to conceive, design, manufacture, transport, and, ultimately sell high-fashion apparel much more quickly and efficiently than many of its major competitors.

Exhibit 15.1 shows a simplified supply chain, in which manufacturers make products and sell them to retailers or wholesalers. The exhibit would be much more complicated if we had included suppliers of materials to manufacturers and all of the manufacturers, wholesalers, and stores in a typical supply chain. Wholesalers are firms that buy products from manufacturers and resell them to retailers, and retailers sell products directly to consumers. Manufacturers ship to a wholesaler, or, in the case of many multistore retailers, to the retailer's distribution center (as is the case for Manufacturer 1 and Manufacturer 3) or directly to stores (Manufacturer 2).

Although Exhibit 15.1 shows the typical flow of manufactured goods, many variations to this supply chain exist. Some retail chains, like Home Depot and Costco, function as both retailers and wholesalers; they act as retailers when they sell to consumers directly and as wholesalers when they sell to other businesses, like building contractors or restaurant owners. When manufacturers such as Dell or Avon sell directly to consumers, they are performing both production and re-tailing activities. When Dell sells directly to a university or business, it becomes a business-to-business (B2B) transaction, but when it sells to students or employees individually, it is a B2C (business-to-consumer) operation.

SUPPLY CHAIN, MARKETING CHANNELS, AND LOGISTICS ARE RELATED

People often talk about supply chain management, marketing channel management, and logistics management as if they were the same thing. A marketing channel is the set of institutions that transfer the ownership of and move goods from the point of production to the point of consumption; as such, it consists of all the institutions and marketing activities in the marketing process.[4] Thus, a marketing channel and a supply chain are virtually the same and the terms could be used interchangeably.

Logistics management describes the integration of two or more activities for the purpose of planning, implementing, and controlling the efficient flow of raw materials, in-process inventory, and finished goods from the point of origin to the point of consumption. These activities may include, but are not limited to, customer service, demand forecasting, distribution communications, inventory control, materials handling, order processing, parts and service support, plant and warehouse site selection, procurement, packaging, return goods handling, salvage and scrap disposal, traffic and transportation, and warehousing and storage.[5] Therefore, logistics management is that element of supply chain management that concentrates on the movement and control of physical products; supply chain management as a whole also includes an awareness of the relationships among members of the supply chain or channel and the need to coordinate efforts to provide customers with the best value.

So, are marketing channel management, supply chain management, and logistics management the same or different? To answer this question, we must look at how firms have handled these activities in the past. Marketing channel management traditionally has been the responsibility of marketing departments, under the direction of a marketing vice president. Logistics was traditionally the responsibility of operations, under a vice president of operations. Although their goals were similar, they often saw solutions differently, and sometimes they worked in conflict. For instance, the marketing department's goal might have been to make sales, whereas logistics wanted to keep costs low. Firms have come to realize there is tremendous opportunity in coordinating marketing and logistics activities not only within a firm but also throughout the supply chain. Thus, because supply chain management takes a systemwide approach to coordinating the flow of merchandise, it includes both channel management and logistics and is therefore the term that we use in this chapter.

SUPPLY CHAINS ADD VALUE

Why would a manufacturer want to use a wholesaler or a retailer? Don't these supply chain members just cut into their profits? Wouldn't it be cheaper for consumers to buy directly from manufacturers? In a simple agrarian economy, the best supply chain may in fact follow a direct route from manufacturer to consumer: The consumer goes to the farm and buys food directly from the farmer. Modern "eat local" environmental campaigns suggest just such a process. But before the consumer can eat a fresh steak procured from a local farm, she needs to cook it first. Assuming the consumer doesn't know how to make a stove and lacks the materials to do so, she must rely on a stove maker. The stove maker, who has the necessary knowledge, in turn must buy raw materials and components from various suppliers, make the stove, and then make it available to the consumer. If the stove maker isn't located near the consumer, the stove must be transported to where the consumer has

| **EXHIBIT 15.2A** | Direct Supply Chain without a Retailer |

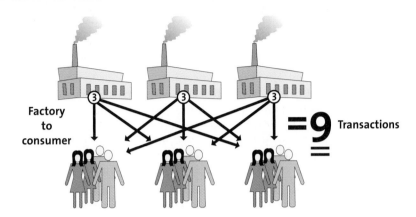

Factory to consumer

=9 Transactions

access to it. To make matters even more complicated, the consumer may want to view a choice of stoves, hear about all their features, and have the stove delivered and installed.

Each participant in the supply chain thus adds value. The components manufacturer helps the stove manufacturer by supplying parts and materials. The stove maker then turns the components into the stove. The transportation company gets the stove to the retailer. The retailer stores the stove until the customer wants it, educates the customer about product features, and delivers and installs the stove. At each step, the stove becomes more costly but also more valuable to the consumer.

Even more simple supply chains add value at each step: The farmer who sold the steak to the consumer had to raise and then slaughter the animal, which means that the steak had more value to the consumer than an entire cow would.

Exhibits 15.2A and 15.2B show how using supply chain partners can provide value overall. Exhibit 15.2A shows three manufacturers, each of which sells directly to three consumers in a system that requires nine transactions. Each transaction costs money—for example, the manufacturer must fill the order, package it, write up the paperwork, and ship it—and each cost is passed on to the customer. Exhibit 15.2B shows the same three manufacturers and consumers, but

How many companies are involved in making and getting a stove to your kitchen?

| **EXHIBIT 15.2B** | Indirect Supply Chain with a Retailer |

Factory to store to consumer

=3

+3

6 Transactions

this time they go through a retailer. The number of transactions falls to six, and as transactions are eliminated, the supply chain becomes more efficient, which adds value for customers by making it more convenient and less expensive to purchase merchandise.

Supply Chain Management Streamlines Distribution

Supply chain management offers the 21st century's answer to a host of distribution problems faced by firms. As recently as the early 1990s, even the most innovative firms needed 15 to 30 days—or even more—to fulfill an order from the warehouse to the customer. The typical order-to-delivery process had several steps: order creation, usually using a telephone, fax, or mail; order processing, using a manual system for credit authorization and assignment to a warehouse; and physical delivery. Things could, and often did, go wrong. Ordered goods were not available. Orders were lost or misplaced. Shipments were misdirected. These mistakes lengthened the time it took to get merchandise to customers and potentially made the entire process more expensive.

Faced with these predicaments, firms began stockpiling inventory at each level of the supply chain (retailers, wholesalers, and manufacturers), but keeping inventory where it is not needed becomes a huge and wasteful expense. If a manufacturer has a huge stock of items stuck in a warehouse, it not only is not earning profits by selling those items but also must pay to maintain and guard that warehouse.

Therefore, more recently firms have swung in the other direction, as Adding Value 15.1 points out. Zara gains its competitive advantage by bringing fashions to the store and the customers much faster than other apparel retailers. It holds minimal inventory, produces new fashion quickly, and rarely gets stuck with old inventory. Deliveries show up at stores twice a week; the newly delivered items rarely remain on retail shelves for more than a week. But this speedy system is not limited to the retail side; Zara also takes only four to five weeks to design a new collection and then about a week to manufacture it, so it continually cycles though its inventory of fabric and materials necessary to make its clothing. Its competitors, in comparison, need an average of six months to design a new collection and another three weeks to manufacture it.

Supply Chain Management Affects Marketing

Every marketing decision is affected by and has an effect on the supply chain. When products are designed and manufactured, how and when the critical components reach the factory must be coordinated with production. The sales department must coordinate its delivery promises with the factory or distribution centers. A distribution center, a facility for the receipt, storage, and redistribution of goods to company stores or customers, may be operated by retailers, manufacturers, or distribution specialists.[6] Furthermore, advertising and promotion must be coordinated with those departments that control inventory and transportation. There is no faster way to lose credibility with customers than to promise deliveries or run a promotion and then not have the merchandise when the customer expects it.

Five interrelated activities emerge in supply chain management: making information flow, making merchandise flow, managing inventory, designing the supply chain, and managing the relationships among supply chain partners. In the next few sections, we examine each of these activities.

CHECK YOURSELF

1. How does supply chain management add value?

Adding Value 15.1   Move It Fast

The second largest clothing retailer in the world,[7] Zara International competes with local retailers in most of its markets, but also chains like The Gap (largest), Sweden's Hennes & Mauritz (H&M), and Italy's Benetton. Although its competition has strived to beat Zara at its own game, it is still arguably the leader in "fast fashion"—it conceives of, manufactures, and delivers fashionable merchandise rapidly and responds to customer demand for the merchandise quickly.

Important differences mark the ways the four close competitors operate. The Gap and H&M own most of their stores but outsource all their manufacturing. In contrast, Benetton has invested relatively heavily in manufacturing, but licensees run its stores. Zara not only owns a majority of its stores but also produces a majority of its own clothes, mostly at its ultramodern manufacturing complex in northwestern Spain. In another departure from the pack, Zara makes over 40 percent of its own fabric—far more than most of its rivals.

From its base in Spain, Zara also operates its own flexible worldwide distribution network. The company derives its competitive advantage from an astute use of information and technology. All its stores are electronically linked to the headquarters in Spain. Store managers, together with a fleet of sharp-eyed, design-savvy trend spotters on Zara's staff, routinely prowl fashion hot spots such as university campuses and happening nightclubs. Their job is to function as the company's eyes and ears, to spot the next wave. Using wireless handheld devices, they send images back to corporate headquarters so that designers can produce blueprints for close-at-hand manufacturers to start stitching, resulting in garments that will be hanging in Zara stores within weeks.

Zara's efficient supply chain system is based on providing customers with what is fashionable at a very good value.[8] The factories are all located in Spain, Portugal, Morocco, and Turkey, which are close to its European stores, making it possible to ship the clothes directly from the factory to the stores. Although the company incurs higher labor costs than in other parts of the world, it also incurs smaller transportation costs as a result of the shortened transportation distances. Whereas previously the company assigned sales people to attach security alarm tags to clothing, requiring the work of 10 people for 12 hours per week, it now attaches the tags at the factories, thereby reducing labor costs. Shipments are rushed onto the selling floor as soon as they arrive. Apparel is even delivered on plastic shipping hangers, so no time is wasted getting merchandise ready for sale. Sales people then switch the garments to wood hangers when they have some downtime.

The handheld computers on each store manager's belt show which garments are the best sellers. When they notice an item selling really quickly, the managers can instantly order more, and if available, it will arrive a couple of days later. Another key to Zara's strategy involves the size of the clothing collections—always small. With fewer items, the company ensures that its merchandise will sell out, so it avoids the problem of stale merchandise on the shelf and rarely has to resort to expensive markdowns.

However, The Gap, H&M, and Benetton recognize that Zara might not be able to maintain its supply chain competitive advantage forever, because Zara's factories all cluster close to its European stores instead of spanning the globe. It plans to build a logistics center in Asia, but not until 2013. To make up for the higher costs in other countries, caused by the shipping challenges, it has increased its prices, and its competitors see a chink in the armor. In the United States, Zara's prices are 40 percent more than they are in Spain. Don't think for a second that The Gap, based in the United States, does not recognize where its prices need to be to successfully compete with Zara.

Zara's advanced supply chain and information systems enable it to get its relatively inexpensive high fashion apparel to stores in New York (left) and Paris (right) in a matter of a few weeks.

MAKING INFORMATION FLOW

Information flows from the customer to stores, to and from distribution centers, possibly to and from wholesalers, to and from product manufacturers, and then on to the producers of any components and the suppliers of raw materials. To simplify our discussion and because information flows are similar in other supply chain links and B2B channels, we shorten the supply chain in this section to exclude wholesalers, as well as the link from suppliers to manufacturers. Exhibit 15.3 illustrates the flow of information that starts when a customer buys a Sony DVD player at Best Buy. The flow follows these steps:

Flow 1 (Customer to Store): The sales associate at Best Buy scans the Universal Product Code (UPC) tag on the DVD player packaging, and the customer receives a receipt. The UPC tag is the black-and-white bar code found on most merchandise. It contains a 13-digit code that indicates the manufacturer of the item, a description of the item, information about special packaging, and special promotions.[9] In the future, RFID tags, discussed at the end of this chapter, may replace UPC tags.

Flow 2 (Store to Buyer): The point-of-sale (POS) terminal records the purchase information and electronically sends it to the buyer at Best Buy's corporate office. The sales information is incorporated into an inventory management system and used to monitor and analyze sales and to decide to reorder more DVDs, change a price, or plan a promotion. Buyers also send information to stores on overall sales for the chain, how to display the merchandise, upcoming promotions, etc.

Flow 3 (Buyer to Manufacturer): The purchase information from each Best Buy store is typically aggregated by the retailer as a whole, which creates an order for new merchandise and sends it to Sony. The buyer at Best Buy may also communicate directly with Sony to get information and negotiate prices, shipping dates, promotional events, or other merchandise-related issues.

EXHIBIT 15.3   Information Flows

Power of the Internet 15.1 | Neiman Marcus Expedites Shipments through Customs

Neiman Marcus receives most of its apparel, accessories, jewelry, and home products from other countries. Because it deals with fashions that have short product life cycles, good communication with its suppliers is essential.[10]

A major impediment to getting its deliveries in a timely manner involved the delays caused by the U.S. Customs and Border Protection. These agencies demand comprehensive and complicated paperwork before they will allow shipments into the United States, and with so much paperwork, incomplete information and errors are common, which kept Neiman Marcus' shipments from arriving in time. The company therefore instituted an Internet-based system that remains in contact with every business partner that touches a shipment to ensure that the documents get prepared properly for U.S. Customs. Trust is one thing; this system guarantees that the work gets done correctly. Any missing paperwork prompts an automatic alert to the appropriate business partner, which can then send the missing paperwork to U.S. Customs while the shipment is still en route, rather than wait to be notified by Customs after it has arrived. Missing or incorrect documents found by Customs once the shipment has arrived can delay the process even more. This initiative eliminated a full two days from the shipping cycle.

As an added bonus, Neiman Marcus uses the system to comply more closely with import regulations. The duty/tariff laws of different countries vary and can change quickly. To keep up to date with these changes in the more than 60 countries with which it does business, Neiman Marcus requires vendors to guarantee that they will update any tariff changes on the Internet-based system within 24 hours of the country's rule change. Shipments then receive a HTSUS (harmonized tariff schedule of the United States), which makes it easier for U.S. Customs to identify the import shipments and move them through the clearance process. As a result, Neiman Marcus shipments have a low risk rating and move through Customs much faster than those of many of its competitors.

Power of the Internet 15.1 examines how Neiman Marcus works with its suppliers to expedite a key issue in this flow: U.S. Customs import processes.

Flow 4 (Store to Manufacturer): In some situations, the sales transaction data are sent directly from the store to the manufacturer, and the manufacturer decides when to ship more merchandise to the distribution centers and the stores. In other situations, especially when merchandise is reordered frequently, the ordering process is done automatically, bypassing the buyers.

Flow 5 (Store to Distribution Center): Stores also communicate with the Best Buy distribution center to coordinate deliveries and check inventory status. When the store inventory drops to a specified level, more DVDs are shipped to the store, and the shipment information is sent to the Best Buy computer system.

Flow 6 (Manufacturer to Distribution Center and Buyer): When the manufacturer ships the DVDs to the Best Buy distribution center, it sends an advanced shipping notice to the distribution centers. An advanced shipping notice (ASN) is an electronic document that the supplier sends the retailer in advance of a shipment to tell the retailer exactly what to expect in the shipment. The center then makes appointments for trucks to make the delivery at a specific time, date, and loading dock. When the shipment is received at the distribution center, the buyer is notified and authorizes payment to the vendor.

Data Warehouse

Purchase data collected at the point of sale (information flow 2 in Exhibit 15.3) goes into a huge database known as a data warehouse. The information stored in the data warehouse is accessible on various dimensions and levels, as depicted in the data cube in Exhibit 15.4.

As shown on the horizontal axis, data can be accessed according to the level of merchandise aggregation—SKU (item), vendor, category (e.g., dresses), or all merchandise. Along the vertical axis, data can be accessed by level of the

EXHIBIT 15.4   Retail Data Warehouse

company—store, divisions or the total company. Finally, along the third dimension, data can be accessed by point in time—day, season, or year.

The CEO might be interested in how the corporation is generally doing and could look at the data aggregated by quarter for a merchandise division, a region of the country, or the total corporation. A buyer may be more interested in a particular manufacturer in a certain store on a particular day. Analysts from various levels of the retail operation extract information from the data warehouse to make a plethora of marketing decisions about developing and replenishing merchandise assortments.

In some cases, manufacturers also have access to this data warehouse. They communicate with retailers using electronic data interchange (EDI) and use supply chain systems known as vendor-managed inventory and collaborative planning, forecasting, and replenishment (CPFR), which are all discussed next.

Electronic Data Interchange

In information flows 3, 4, and 6 in Exhibit 15.3, the retailer and manufacturer exchange business documents through EDI. Electronic data interchange (EDI) is the computer-to-computer exchange of business documents from a retailer to a vendor and back. In addition to sales data, purchase orders, invoices, and data about returned merchandise can be transmitted back and forth.

Many retailers now require vendors to provide them with notification of deliveries before they take place using an advanced shipping notice. If the ASN is accurate, the retailer can dispense with opening all the received cartons and checking in merchandise. In addition, EDI enables vendors to transmit information about on-hand inventory status, vendor promotions, and cost changes to the retailer, as well as information about purchase order changes, order status, retail prices, and transportation routings.

Typically, EDI is transmitted over the Internet through either intranets or extranets. Intranets are secure communication systems contained within one company, such as between buyers and distribution centers. In contrast, an extranet is a collaborative network that uses Internet technology to link businesses with their suppliers, customers, or other businesses. These extranets are typically private and secure, in that they can be accessed only by certain parties. Thus, some but not all manufacturers would have access to a retailer's extranet.

Especially through extranets, EDIs have gone beyond merely communicating order and shipping information. Suppliers, through their extranet, can describe and show pictures of their products, and buyers can issue requests for proposals. The two parties then can electronically negotiate prices and specify how the product will be made and how it should look.

For example, Cabela's, which has long worked to outfit outdoor enthusiasts and hunters through its catalogs, realized that when it expanded into brick-and-mortar stores as well, it had to update its order management system. If, for instance, a customer in Colorado placed a catalog order, it would be processed in Wheeling, West Virginia. If the item was not in stock there, the old system would show "out of stock" to the customer, even though it was available at a different distribution center.[11] To address this problem, Cabela's integrated all its distribution channels into its retail order and fulfillment system, which links together all members of the company's supply chain—manufacturers (up to 2,000 of them), distribution centers, stores, individual customers, and the retailer as a whole. With greater knowledge of exactly where products are in the supply chain, Cabela's not only enhances customer service and supplies consumers more efficiently but also achieves much greater inventory visibility and minimizes its supply chain costs.

The use of EDI provides three main benefits to supply chain members. First, EDI reduces the cycle time, or the time between the decision to place an order and the receipt of merchandise. Information flows quicker using EDI, which means that inventory turnover is higher. Second, EDI improves the overall quality of communications through better recordkeeping; fewer errors in inputting and receiving an order; and less human error in the interpretation of data. Third, the data transmitted by EDI are in a computer-readable format that can be easily analyzed and used for a variety of tasks ranging from evaluating vendor delivery performance to automating reorder processes.

Because of these benefits, many retailers are asking their suppliers to interface with them using EDI. However, small- to medium-sized suppliers and retailers face significant barriers, specifically, cost and the lack of information technology

Cabela's order and fulfillment system links all members of its supply chain to enhance customer service.

(IT) expertise, to become EDI enabled. However, EDI remains an important component of any vendor-managed inventory system.

Vendor-Managed Inventory

Vendor-managed inventory (VMI) is an approach for improving supply chain efficiency in which the manufacturer is responsible for maintaining the retailer's inventory levels in each of its stores.[12] By sharing the data in the retailer's data warehouse and communicating that information via EDI, the manufacturer determines a **reorder point**—a level of inventory at which more merchandise is required. When inventory drops to the order point, the manufacturer generates the order and delivers the merchandise. Although VMI can be used to replenish inventory at retail stores, the approach is usually applied to replenish inventories at the retailer's distribution center.[13]

In ideal conditions, the manufacturer replenishes inventories in quantities that meet the retailer's immediate demand, reducing stockouts with minimal inventory. In addition to better matching retail demand to supply, VMI can reduce the vendor's and the retailer's costs. Manufacturer sales people no longer need to spend time generating orders on items that are already in the stores, and their role shifts to selling new items and maintaining relationships. Retail buyers and planners no longer need to monitor inventory levels and place orders.

Frito-Lay and other snack food, candy, and beverage vendors have been involved with VMI in supermarkets for a long time. However, technological advances have increased the sophistication of VMI. The sharing of POS transaction data, for instance, allows manufacturers to sell merchandise on **consignment**; the manufacturer owns the merchandise until it is sold by the retailer, at which time the retailer pays for the merchandise. Consignment selling provides an incentive for the manufacturer to pick SKUs and inventory levels that will minimize inventory and generate sales. Because the manufacturer is bearing the financial cost of owning the inventory, retailers are more willing to allow the manufacturer to be responsible for determining the inventory plan and appropriate assortment for each store.

Although it is a more advanced level of collaboration than simply using EDI and sharing information, VMI has its limitations. Whereas the manufacturer coordinates the supply chain for its specific products, it does not know what other actions the retailer is taking that might affect the sales of its products in the future. For example, Pepsi might not know that a supermarket will be having a big promotion in three weeks for a new beverage introduced by Coca-Cola. Without this knowledge, Pepsi would ship too much merchandise to the supermarket.

Collaborative Planning, Forecasting, and Replenishment

Collaborative planning, forecasting, and replenishment (CPFR) is the sharing of forecast and related business information and collaborative planning between retailers and vendors to improve supply chain efficiency and product replenishment.[14] Although retailers share sales and inventory data when using a VMI approach, the manufacturer remains responsible for managing the inventory. In contrast, CPFR is a more advanced form of retailer–manufacturer collaboration that involves sharing proprietary information, such as business strategies, promotion plans, new product developments and introductions, production schedules, and lead time information. Superior Service 15.1 describes how manufacturers and retailers work together to provide better merchandise selection for their customers.

Pull and Push Supply Chains

Information flows such as that described previously illustrate a **pull supply chain**—a supply chain in which orders for merchandise are generated at the store

Superior Service 15.1   The CPFR Promise: Make Everybody Happy

Motorola, manufacturer of mobile phone handsets, decided to develop a CPFR program when it realized that if a retailer that carried its merchandise was out of stock on a certain phone, more than half of all customers would just purchase a competitor's phone. This would result in not only a lost service contract but possibly a lost customer for life. However, because a particular phone model might comprise multiple SKUs—multiple colors, available modes, memory capabilities, production dates, and so forth—accurate demand forecasting is extremely complex.

To improve the situation, Motorola had to change the way information flowed from manufacturer to retailer and back. Formerly, the manufacturer's sales representative communicated with the retailer's purchasing department to make ordering, forecasting, and delivery decisions. With the new CPFR system, Motorola combined category management, supply chain planning, and execution processes to increase product availability and reduce transportation, logistics, and inventory costs. This was no small task! Today, both retailers and Motorola review cross-linked metrics, including retailer forecasts; Motorola measures delivery, the retailer measures inventory, and Motorola looks at order changes.[15] Together, they forecast with great accuracy, which benefits the manufacturer, because Motorola retains a customer; the retailer, who can satisfy customers; and customers, who can get the phone they want when they want it.

Another CPFR system connects the warehouse retailer BJ's Wholesale Club with its supply chain partner, Pharmavite, a manufacturer of high-quality vitamins and dietary supplements that sells under the brand names NatureMade, OLAY, and Nature's Resource. This CPFR system not only improves the level of in-stock merchandise and sales but also uncovers gaps in the distribution process and decreases forecasting errors. The CPFR software helped refine forecasts, plan promotions, execute orders, and manage exceptions. As a result, in quantifiable terms, the supply chain reduced on-hand inventory by 30 percent, increased BJ's comparable-store sales by 24 percent, improved inventory turns by 42 percent, attained a 98 percent average forecast accuracy, and maintained more than 99 percent in-stock levels.[16]

Supply chain systems like Motorola's CPFR improve the customer experience.

level on the basis of sales data captured by POS terminals. Basically, in this type of supply chain, the demand for an item pulls it through the supply chain. An alternative and less sophisticated approach is a **push supply chain**, in which merchandise is allocated to stores on the basis of forecasted demand. Once a forecast is developed, specified quantities of merchandise are shipped (pushed) to distribution centers and stores at predetermined time intervals.

In a pull supply chain, there is less likelihood of being overstocked or out of stock because the store orders merchandise as needed on the basis of consumer demand. A pull approach increases inventory turnover and is more responsive to changes in customer demand. A pull approach becomes even more efficient than a push approach when demand is uncertain and difficult to forecast because the forecast is based on consumer demand.[17]

Although generally more desirable, a pull approach is not the most effective in all situations. First, a pull approach requires a more costly and sophisticated information system to support it. Second, for some merchandise, retailers do not have the flexibility to adjust inventory levels on the basis of demand. For example, commitments must be made months in advance for fashion and private-label apparel. Because these commitments cannot be easily changed, the merchandise has to be preallocated to the stores at the time the orders are formulated. Third, push supply chains are efficient for merchandise that has steady, predictable demand, such as milk and eggs, basic men's underwear, and bath towels. Because both pull and push supply chains have their advantages, most retailers use a combination of these approaches.

MAKING MERCHANDISE FLOW

Exhibit 15.5 illustrates different types of merchandise flows:

1. Sony to Best Buy's distribution centers, or
2. Sony directly to stores.
3. If the merchandise goes through distribution centers, it is then shipped to stores,
4. and then to the customer.

Making merchandise flow involves first deciding if the merchandise is going to go from the manufacturer to a retailer's distribution center or directly on to stores. Once in a distribution center, multiple activities take place before it is shipped on to a store.

Distribution Centers versus Direct Store Delivery

As indicated in Exhibit 15.5, manufacturers can ship merchandise directly to a retailer's stores—direct store delivery (flow 2)—or to their distribution centers (flow 1). Although manufacturers and retailers may collaborate, the ultimate

EXHIBIT 15.5   Merchandise Flows

decision is usually up to the retailer and depends on the characteristics of the merchandise and the nature of demand. To determine which distribution system—distribution centers or direct store delivery—is better, retailers consider the total cost associated with each alternative and the customer service criterion of having the right merchandise at the store when the customer wants to buy it.

There are several advantages to using a distribution center:

- More accurate sales forecasts are possible when retailers combine forecasts for many stores serviced by one distribution center rather than doing a forecast for each store. Consider a set of 50 Target stores, serviced by a single distribution center, that each carries Michael Graves toasters. Each store normally stocks 5 units for a total of 250 units in the system. By carrying the item at each store, the retailer must develop individual forecasts, each with the possibility of errors that could result in either too much or too little merchandise. Alternatively, by delivering most of the inventory to a distribution center and feeding the stores merchandise as they need it, the effects of forecast errors for the individual stores are minimized, and less backup inventory is needed to prevent stockouts.

The use of distribution centers helps reduce stockouts.

- Distribution centers enable the retailer to carry less merchandise in the individual stores, which results in lower inventory investments systemwide. If the stores get frequent deliveries from the distribution center, they need to carry relatively less extra merchandise as backup stock.

- It is easier to avoid running out of stock or having too much stock in any particular store because merchandise is ordered from the distribution center as needed.

- Retail store space is typically much more expensive than space at a distribution center, and distribution centers are better equipped than stores to prepare merchandise for sale. As a result, many retailers find it cost-effective to store merchandise and get it ready for sale at a distribution center rather than in individual stores.

But distribution centers aren't appropriate for all retailers. If a retailer has only a few outlets, the expense of a distribution center is probably unwarranted. Also, if many outlets are concentrated in metropolitan areas, merchandise can be consolidated and delivered by the vendor directly to all the stores in one area economically. Direct store delivery gets merchandise to the stores faster and thus is used for perishable goods (meat and produce), items that help create the retailer's image of being the first to sell the latest product (e.g., video games), or fads. Finally, some manufacturers provide direct store delivery for retailers to ensure that their products are on the store's shelves, properly displayed, and fresh. For example, employees delivering Frito-Lay snacks directly to supermarkets replace products that have been on the shelf too long and are stale, replenish products that have been sold, and arrange products so they are neatly displayed.

The Distribution Center

The distribution center performs the following activities: coordinating inbound transportation; receiving, checking, storing, and cross-docking; getting merchandise "floor ready"; and coordinating outbound transportation. To illustrate these activities being undertaken in a distribution center, we'll continue our example of Sony DVDs being shipped to a Best Buy distribution center.

Management of Inbound Transportation   Traditionally, buyers focused their efforts, when working with vendors, on developing merchandise assortments, negotiating prices, and arranging joint promotions. Now, buyers and planners are much more involved in coordinating the physical flow of merchandise to the stores. The DVD buyer has arranged for a truckload of DVDs to be delivered to its Houston, Texas, distribution center on Monday between 1:00 and 3:00 P.M. The buyer also specifies how the merchandise should be placed on pallets for easy unloading.

The truck must arrive within the specified time because the distribution center has all of its 100 receiving docks allocated throughout the day, and much of the merchandise on this particular truck is going to be shipped to stores that evening. Unfortunately, the truck was delayed in a snowstorm. The dispatcher—the person who coordinates deliveries to the distribution center—reassigns the truck delivering the DVDs to a Wednesday morning delivery slot and charges the firm several hundred dollars for missing its delivery time. Although many manufacturers pay transportation expenses, some retailers negotiate with their vendors to absorb this expense. These retailers believe they can lower their net merchandise cost and better control merchandise flow if they negotiate directly with trucking companies and consolidate shipments from many vendors.

Receiving and Checking Using UPC and Radio Frequency Identification (RFID) Device   Receiving is the process of recording the receipt of merchandise as it arrives at a distribution center. Checking is the process of going through the goods upon receipt to make sure they arrived undamaged and that the merchandise ordered was the merchandise received.

In the past, checking merchandise was a very labor-intensive and time-consuming process. Today, however, many distribution systems using EDI are designed to minimize, if not eliminate, these processes. The advance shipping notice (ASN) tells the distribution center what should be in each carton. A UPC label or radio frequency identification (RFID) tag on the shipping carton that identifies the carton's contents is scanned and automatically counted as it is being received and checked. Radio frequency identification (RFID) tags are tiny computer chips that automatically transmit to a special scanner all the information about a container's contents or individual products. Adding Value 15.2 explains how American Apparel is using RFID tags.

RFID tags make receiving and checking merchandise accurate, quick, and easy.

Approximately as large as a pinhead, RFID tags consist of an antenna and a chip that contains an electronic product code that stores far more information about a product than bar (UPC) codes can. The tags also act as passive tracking devices, signalling their presence over a radio frequency when they pass within a few yards of a special scanner. The tags have long been used in high-cost applications, such as automated highway toll systems and security identification badges.

The prospect of affordable tags is exciting supply chains everywhere. If every item in a store were tagged as described in Adding Value 15.2, RFID technology could be used to locate mislaid products, deter theft, and even offer customers personalized sales pitches through displays mounted in dressing rooms. Ultimately, tags and readers could replace bar codes and checkout labor altogether. Customers could just walk through a door equipped with a sensor, which would read all the tags electronically and charge the purchases directly to the customer's credit card.

Adding Value **15.2**   American Apparel: Now with RFID Chips

American Apparel operates 180 stores in 13 countries. It also manufactures its own clothes in Los Angeles. At the manufacturing facility, RFID tags get attached to each item that will be for sale in stores. Because the store merchandising calls for having only one color, style, and size on the retail floor at one time, every single time an item gets purchased, it must be replaced from the stockroom.

Prior to the use of RFID tags, only about 90 percent of its items were on the sales floor at any given time. Once it started putting RFID tags on the individual items, this percentage rose to 99 percent, which resulted in a sales increase of approximately 15 to 25 percent.[18] As soon as an item gets misplaced—because it is sold, mistakenly returned to the stockroom, or stolen—the stockroom workstation receives a notice to replace that item. Whereas restocking the store used to take six employees to complete the task, it now requires only two.

Each case of merchandise has an RFID shipping label that contains the information about every item inside the case. When the case reaches the store, the RFID shipping label gets scanned again, and the inventory is added to the store's inventory.[19]

American Apparel has improved its inventory accuracy and attained better-stocked sales floors by using RFID tags.

The weekly inventory of all items in the store now takes just two people two hours, for a total of four worker-hours, compared with the 24 worker-hours it previously required. Sales people thus have more time to help customers and perform other value-adding tasks pertinent to their position.

American Apparel attaches RFID tags to its merchandise to improve product availability and sales.

The main value of RFID is that it eliminates the need to handle items individually by enabling distribution centers and stores to receive whole truckloads of merchandise without having to check in each carton. Still, the watchword, for both retailers and manufacturers of consumer products, is caution. For most supply chain members, long-term investments in RFID technology are still too risky and expensive. Experts believe it will be 5 to 10 years before RFID tags are prevalent on most consumer products.

Yet several of the most prominent retailers already are taking advantage of this new technology. Wal-Mart, Metro (Germany's largest retailer), Target, Best Buy, and Albertson's are all experimenting with RFID programs.[20] To meet these demands, vendors have been forced to make significant investments to acquire the necessary technology and equipment.

In a cross-docking distribution center, merchandise moves from vendors' trucks to the retailer's delivery trucks in a matter of hours.

Storing and Cross-Docking After the merchandise is received and checked, it is either stored or cross-docked. When merchandise is stored, the cartons are transported by a conveyor system and forklift trucks to racks that go from the distribution center's floor to its ceiling. Then, when the merchandise is needed in the stores, a forklift driver goes to the rack, picks up the carton, and places it on a conveyor system that routes the carton to the loading dock of a truck going to the store.

Merchandise cartons that are cross-docked are prepackaged by the vendor for a specific store. The UPC labels on the carton indicate the store to which it is to be sent. The vendor also may affix price tags to each item in the carton. Because the merchandise is ready for sale, it is placed on a conveyor system that routes it from the unloading dock at which it was received to the loading dock for the truck going to the specific store—thus, the name cross-docked. The cartons are routed on the conveyor system automatically by sensors that read the UPC label on the cartons.

Cross-docked merchandise is in the distribution center only for a few hours before it is shipped to the stores.

Merchandise sales rate and degree of perishability or fashionability typically determine whether cartons are cross-docked or stored. For instance, because Sony's DVDs sell so quickly, it is in Best Buy's interest not to store them in a distribution center. Similarly, cross-docking is preferable for fashion apparel or perishable meat or produce.

Getting Merchandise Floor Ready   For some merchandise, additional tasks are undertaken in the distribution center to make the merchandise floor ready. Floor-ready merchandise is merchandise that is ready to be placed on the selling floor. Getting merchandise floor ready entails ticketing, marking, and, in the case of some apparel, placing garments on hangers. At Tesco's Fresh & Easy Neighborhood Markets in California, it is essential that products ship in ready-to-sell units so that it has little manipulation or sorting to do at the distribution center or in the stores. To move the store-ready merchandise it receives from suppliers quickly into the store, Tesco demands that products sit on roll cages rather than pallets. Then, store employees can easily wheel them onto the retail floor. The stores' backrooms only have two or three days' worth of backup inventory, and since the stores are relatively small, about 10,000 square feet, it is important to keep inventory levels low and receive lots of small, accurate deliveries from its suppliers.[21]

Ticketing and marking refers to affixing price and identification labels to the merchandise. It is more efficient for a retailer to perform these activities at a distribution center than in its stores. In a distribution center, an area can be set aside and a process implemented to efficiently add labels and put apparel on hangers. Conversely, getting merchandise floor ready in stores can block aisles and divert sales people's attention from their customers. An even better approach from the retailer's perspective is to get vendors to ship floor-ready merchandise, thus totally eliminating the expensive, time-consuming ticketing and marking process.

Preparing to Ship Merchandise to a Store   At the beginning of the day, the computer system in the distribution center generates a list of items to be shipped to each store on that day. For each item, a pick ticket and shipping label is generated. The pick ticket is a document or display on a screen in a forklift truck indicating how much of each item to get from specific storage areas. The forklift driver goes to the storage area, picks up the number of cartons indicated on the pick ticket, places UPC shipping labels on the cartons that indicate the stores to which the items are to be shipped, and puts the cartons on the conveyor system, where they are automatically routed to the loading dock for the truck going to the stores.

Shipping Merchandise to Stores   Shipping merchandise to stores from a distribution center has become increasingly complex. Most distribution centers run 50–100 outbound truck routes in one day. To handle this complex transportation problem, the centers use sophisticated routing and scheduling computer systems that consider the locations of the stores, road conditions, and transportation operating constraints to develop the most efficient routes possible. As a result, stores are provided with an accurate estimated time of arrival, and vehicle utilization is maximized.

Inventory Management through Just-In-Time Systems

Customers demand specific SKUs, and they want to be able to buy them when needed. If, for instance, you want to buy a pair of size 10 Nike Shox NZ iD, you probably aren't going to purchase a size 9 Nike Apres 18 Women's Slide sandals just because the retailer is out of the shoes you want. At the same time, firms can't afford to carry more than they really need of an SKU, because to do so is very expensive. Suppose, for instance, a shoe store carries $1 million worth of inventory at its own expense. Experts estimate that it would cost between 20 and 40 percent of the value of the inventory, or $20,000 to $40,000 per year, to hold that inventory! So firms must balance having enough inventory to satisfy customer demands with not having more than they need.

To help reconcile these seemingly conflicting goals, many firms have adopted just-in-time (JIT) inventory systems. Just-in-time inventory systems, also known as quick response (QR) systems in retailing, are inventory management systems designed to deliver less merchandise on a more frequent basis than traditional inventory systems. The firm gets the merchandise "just-in-time" for it to be used in the manufacture of another product, in the case of parts or components, or for sale when the customer wants it, in the case of consumer goods. The JIT systems lower inventory investments, but product availability actually increases.[22]

Toyota largely initiated the concept of JIT systems for its car manufacturing plants, but other manufacturers have adopted the concept avidly. Consider, for example, the supply chain for Tubular Steel, a national distributor of carbon, alloy, and stainless steel pipe, tubing, and bar products. The company proffers itself as a service and solutions firm, promising that it can save its customers significant costs by enabling them to adopt its JIT system. Even for new orders, Tubular Steel promises a quote within 24 hours and delivery soon thereafter from its more than 60,000 tons of stock, held in eight regional distribution centers. For example, Tubular Steel worked with Sunshine, a packaging provider, to list the parts needed for each of Sunshine's products, along with the part number and its usage sequence. When Sunshine placed orders with Tubular Steel, based on product numbers, the company produced each individual part, cut to length, and labeled each part with Sunshine's part number, then packed the parts in the order in which they were used and labeled each box to match to the product in production. Therefore, Sunshine received only the parts it needed at the moment it needed them to assemble a particular piece of equipment. The JIT process has been very successful in streamlining Sunshine Packaging's preproduction process.[23]

The benefits of a JIT system include reduced lead time, increased product availability, and lower inventory investment.

Reduced Lead Time   By eliminating the need for paper transactions by mail, overnight deliveries, or even faxes, the EDI in the JIT system reduces lead time, or the

Zappos distribution center is conveniently located 20 miles from UPS's largest domestic shipping hub and within 600 miles of two-thirds of the U.S. population.

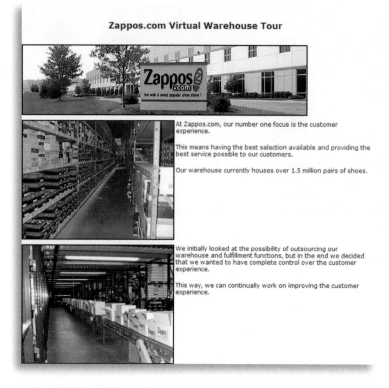

amount of time between the recognition that an order needs to be placed and the arrival of the needed merchandise at the seller's store, ready for sale. Because the vendor's computer acquires the data automatically, no manual data entry is required on the recipient's end, which reduces lead time even more and eliminates vendor recording errors. Even better, the shorter lead times further reduce the need for inventory because the shorter the lead time, the easier it is for the retailer to forecast its demand.

For example, Zappos, an online shoe retailer, moved its distribution center from California to Shepherdsville, Kentucky—conveniently, 20 miles from UPS's largest domestic shipping hub. This location also sits within 600 miles of two-thirds of the U.S. population. The location of the warehouse helped the company expedite orders much more efficiently, from processing to shipment to delivery.[24]

Adidas manufactures sporting goods and distributes them throughout the world to different retailers and wholesalers. Adidas introduces 10,000 new apparel items and 4,000 new footwear items every three months. A high percentage of orders are for priority requests, which must get delivered within one or two days, a very short lead time. Therefore, in addition to providing transportation services, UPS works with Adidas by providing it with special labeling, garments on hanger, and advanced shipping notices, services that further reduce the time it takes to get merchandise on the shelves and ready for sale.[25]

Increased Product Availability and Lower Inventory Investment   In general, as a firm's ability to satisfy customer demand by having stock on hand increases, so does its inventory investment; that is, it needs to keep more backup inventory in stock. But with JIT, the ability to satisfy demand can actually increase while inventory decreases. Because the firm can make purchase commitments or produce merchandise closer to the time of sale, its own inventory investment is reduced. Firms also need less inventory because they're getting less merchandise in each order, but they receive shipments more often. Inventory is even further reduced because the firms aren't forecasting sales quite as far into the future. For instance, fashion retailers that don't use QR must make purchase commitments as much as six months in advance and receive merchandise well ahead of actual sales, whereas QR systems align deliveries more closely with sales.

The ability to satisfy customer demand by keeping merchandise in stock also increases in JIT systems as a result of the more frequent shipments. For instance, if a Zara store runs low on a medium-sized Kelly green sweater, its QR system ensures a shorter lead time than those of more traditional retailers. As a result, it is less likely that the Zara store will be out of stock for its customers before the next sweater shipment arrives.

Costs of a JIT System   Although firms achieve great benefits from a JIT system, it is not without its costs. The logistics function becomes much more complicated with more frequent deliveries. With greater order frequency also come smaller orders, which are more expensive to transport and more difficult to coordinate.

Therefore, JIT systems require a strong commitment by the firm and its vendors to cooperate, share data, and develop systems like EDI and CPFR. Successful JIT systems require not only financial support from top management but also a psychological commitment to partnering with vendors. In some cases, larger firms even pressure their less powerful supply chain partners to absorb many of these expensive logistics costs.

CHECK YOURSELF

1. What happens at each step of the merchandise flow in a typical supply chain?

2. Why are just-in-time supply chain systems becoming so popular?

MANAGING THE SUPPLY CHAIN

Supply chains are composed of various entities that are buying, such as retailers or wholesalers; selling, such as manufacturers or wholesalers; or helping facilitate the exchange, such as transportation companies. Like interactions between people, these relationships can range from close working partnerships to one-time arrangements. In almost all cases, though, they occur because the parties want something from one another. For instance, Home Depot wants hammers from Stanley Tool Company, Stanley wants an opportunity to sell its tools to the public, and both companies want UPS to deliver the merchandise.

The Home Depot and Stanley Tool Company have a mutually beneficial partnership. The Home Depot buys tools from Stanley because their customers find value in Stanley products. Stanley sells tools to Home Depot because they have established an excellent market for its products.

Each member of the supply chain performs a specialized role. If one member believes that another isn't doing its job correctly or efficiently, it usually can replace that member. So, if Stanley isn't getting good service from UPS, it can switch to FedEx. Likewise, if Home Depot believes its customers don't perceive Stanley tools to be a good value, it may buy from another tool company. Home Depot could even decide to make its own tools or use its own trucks to pick up tools from Stanley. However, even if a supply chain member is replaced, the function it performed remains, so someone needs to complete it.

If a supply chain is to run efficiently, the participating members must cooperate. Often, however, supply chain members have conflicting goals. For instance, Stanley wants Home Depot to carry all its tools but not those of its competitors so that Stanley can maximize its sales. But Home Depot carries a mix of tool brands so it can maximize the sales in its tool category. When supply chain members are not in agreement about their goals, roles, or rewards, supply chain or channel conflict results.

Open, honest communication is a key to supply chain relationships. Buyers and vendors, such as retailers and manufacturers, must understand what drives the other's business, their roles in the relationship, each firm's strategies, and any problems that might arise over the course of the relationship.

For example, Wal-Mart and Procter & Gamble (P&G) recognize that it is in their common interest to remain profitable business partners. Wal-Mart's customers demand and expect to find P&G products in their stores, and P&G needs the sales generated by being in the world's largest retailer. Wal-Mart cannot demand prices so low that P&G cannot make money, and P&G must be flexible enough to accommodate the needs of its biggest customer. With a common goal, both firms have an incentive to cooperate because they know that by doing so, each can boost sales. Common goals also help sustain the relationship when expected benefit flows aren't realized. If one P&G shipment fails to reach a Wal-Mart store on time due to an uncontrollable event like misrouting by a trucking firm, Wal-Mart will not suddenly call off the whole arrangement. Instead, Wal-Mart is likely to view the incident as a simple mistake and remain in the relationship, because Wal-Mart knows that both it and P&G are committed to the same goals in the long run.

There are two non–mutually exclusive ways to manage a supply chain: coordinate the channel using a vertical marketing system or develop strong relationships with supply chain partners.

Managing Supply Chains through Vertical Marketing Systems

Although conflict is likely to occur in any supply chain, it is generally more pronounced when the supply chain members are independent entities. Supply chains that are more closely aligned, whether by contract or ownership, share common goals and therefore are less prone to conflict.

In an independent or conventional supply chain, the several independent members—a manufacturer, a wholesaler, and a retailer—each attempt to satisfy their own objectives and maximize their own profits, often at the expense of the other members, as we portray in Exhibit 15.6 (left).

None of the participants has any control over the others. For instance, the first time Zara purchases cotton fabric from Tessuto e Colore in Northern Italy, both parties try to extract as much profit from the deal as possible, and after the deal has been consummated, neither party feels any responsibility to the other. Over time, Zara and Tessuto might develop a relationship in which their transactions become more routinized and automatic, such that Zara depends on Tessuto for fabric, and Tessuto depends on Zara to buy a good portion of its output. This scenario represents the first phase of a vertical marketing system, which is a supply chain in which the members act as a unified system, as in Exhibit 15.6 (right). There are three types, or phases, of vertical marketing systems, each with increasing levels of formalization and control. The more formal the vertical marketing system, the less likely conflict will ensue.

| EXHIBIT 15.6 | Independent versus Vertical Marketing Channels |

Independent marketing channel

Manufacturer
Wholesaler
Retailer
Consumer

Vertical marketing channel

Manufacturer
Wholesaler
Retailer
Consumer

Administered Vertical Marketing System   The Zara/Tessuto supply chain relationship offers an example of an administered vertical marketing system. In an administered vertical marketing system, there is no common ownership and no contractual relationships, but the dominant channel member controls the channel relationship. In our example, because of its size and relative power, Zara imposes some control over Tessuto; it dictates, for instance, what Tessuto should make and when it should be delivered. Zara also has a strong influence over the price. If either party doesn't like the way the relationship is going, however, it can simply walk away.

Contractual Vertical Marketing System   Over time, Zara and Tessuto may formalize their relationship by entering into contracts that dictate various terms, such as how much Zara will buy each month, at what price, and the penalties for late deliveries. In contractual vertical marketing systems like this, independent firms at different levels of the supply chain join together through contracts to obtain economies of scale and coordination and to reduce conflict.[26]

Franchising is the most common type of contractual vertical marketing system; franchising companies and their franchisees account for $1.53 trillion in economic activity—an astonishing 35 percent of all retail sales in this country—and employ more than 18 million people.[27] Franchising is a contractual agreement between a franchisor and a franchisee that allows the franchisee to operate a retail outlet using a name and format developed and supported by the franchisor. Exhibit 15.7 lists the United States' top franchise opportunities. These rankings, determined by *Entrepreneur* magazine, are created using a number of objective measures, such as financial strength, stability, growth rate, and size of the franchise system.[28]

In a franchise contract, the franchisee pays a lump sum plus a royalty on all sales in return for the right to operate a business in a specific location. The franchisee also agrees to operate the outlet in accordance with the procedures prescribed by the franchisor. The franchisor typically provides assistance in locating and building the business, developing the products or services sold, management training, and advertising. To maintain the franchisee's reputation, the franchisor also makes sure that all outlets provide the same quality of services and products.

A franchise system combines the entrepreneurial advantages of owning a business with the efficiencies of vertical marketing systems that function under single ownership (a corporate system, as we discuss next). Franchisees are

Zara and Tessuto e Colore in Northern Italy might develop a vertical marketing system in which transactions have become routinized and automatic, such that Zara depends on Tessuto for fabric, and Tessuto depends on Zara to buy a good portion of its output.

EXHIBIT 15.7	Top Franchise Opportunities		
Rank	**Franchise Name/Description**	**Number of U.S. Outlets**	**Start-up Cost**
1	7-Eleven Convenience store	5,580	$65–227K
2	Subway Submarine sandwiches and salads	21,344	$76.1–227.8K
3	Dunkin' Donuts Coffee, doughnuts, baked goods	5,451	$255.7K–1.1M
4	Pizza Hut Pizza	4,757	$1.1–1.7M
5	McDonald's Hamburgers, chicken, salads	11,674	$506K–1.6M
6	Sonic Drive In Restaurants Drive-in restaurant	2,655	$820K–2.3M
7	KFC Corp. Chicken	4,371	$1.1–1.7M
8	InterContinental Hotels Group Hotels	2,541	Varies
9	Domino's Pizza Pizza, breadsticks, buffalo wings	4,581	$118.5–460.3K
10	RE/MAX Int'l. Real estate	4,344	$35.5–197K

Source: Entrepreneur's Top 10 Franchise 500, http://www.entrepreneur.com/franchises/rankings/franchise500-115608/2008 .html (accessed May 28, 2008).

motivated to make their stores successful because they receive the profits, after they pay the royalty to the franchisor. The franchisor is motivated to develop new products, services, and systems and to promote the franchise because it receives royalties on all sales. Advertising, product development, and system development are all done efficiently by the franchisor, with costs shared by all franchisees.

Corporate Vertical Marketing System Because Zara deals with "fast fashion," it is imperative that it have complete control over the most fashion-sensitive items. So Zara manufactures these items itself and contracts out its less fashionable items to other manufacturers.[29] The portion of its supply chain that Zara owns and controls is called a corporate vertical marketing system. Because Zara's parent company, Inditex, owns the manufacturing plants, warehouse facilities, retail outlets, and design studios, it can dictate the priorities and objectives of that supply chain, and thus conflict is lessened.

Managing Supply Chains through Strategic Relationships

There is more to managing supply chains than simply exercising power over other members in an administered system or establishing a contractual or corporate vertical marketing system. There is also a human side.

In a conventional supply chain, relationships between members often are based on the argument over the split of the profit pie—if one party gets ahead, the other party falls behind. Sometimes this type of transaction is acceptable if the parties have no interest in a long-term relationship. For instance, if Nicole Miller sees a fad for a particular fabric, it may only be interested in purchasing from a particular vendor once. In that case, it might seek to get the best one-time price, even if it means the supplier will make very little money and therefore might not want to sell to Nicole Miller again.

More often than not, however, firms seek a strategic relationship, also called a partnering relationship, in which the supply chain members are committed to maintaining the relationship over the long term and investing in opportunities that are mutually beneficial. In a conventional or administered supply chain, there are significant incentives to establishing a strategic relationship, even without contracts or ownership relationships. Both parties benefit because the size of the profit pie has increased, so both the buyer and the seller increase their sales and profits. These strategic relationships are created explicitly to uncover and exploit joint opportunities, so members depend on and trust each other heavily; share goals and agree on how to accomplish those goals; and are willing to take risks, share confidential information, and make significant investments for the sake of the relationship. Successful strategic relationships require mutual trust, open communication, common goals, and credible commitments.

Mutual Trust   Mutual trust holds a strategic relationship together. Trust is the belief that a partner is honest (i.e., reliable, stands by its word, sincere, fulfills obligations) and benevolent (i.e., concerned about the other party's welfare). When vendors and buyers trust each other, they are more willing to share relevant ideas, clarify goals and problems, and communicate efficiently. Information shared between the parties thus becomes increasingly comprehensive, accurate, and timely. For instance, a CPFR system for mutual inventory forecasting would not be possible without mutual trust.

With trust, there's also less need for the supply chain members to constantly monitor and check up on each other's actions because each believes the other won't take advantage, even given the opportunity. The RFID systems that enable sealed cartons to be checked into a distribution center without being opened also would be impossible without mutual trust. However, though RFID tags can greatly enhance efficiency in a supply chain and though they rely on trust in that supply chain, they pose serious privacy concerns for consumers, as we discuss in Ethical and Societal Dilemma 15.1.

Ethical and Societal Dilemma 15.1 What Does Your Tag Know about You?

Although RFIDs (radio frequency identification devices) can provide a lot of value for a company by streamlining the supply chain, they also strike fear in the hearts of some consumers when they are used on individual items.[30] Retailers of higher-priced or theft-prone items particularly like RFID tags, which enable them to easily track the merchandise's whereabouts. They also facilitate warranty services and recalls because the tag has information about when the item was purchased, where, and by whom.

So, suppose you buy a notebook computer with an affixed RFID tag. As the item is scanned at the point of sale, the retailer adds personal information to the database, such as your name, when the item was purchased, the selling price, and your purchase history with the retailer. This information then might be read by an unauthorized reader, such as another retailer in the mall. Also, in the same way that RFID tags track the whereabouts of a carton of merchandise, the tag can pinpoint your location after the sale as you carry your new computer around campus.

Some people thus are concerned that RFID tags will encroach on their personal privacy. They believe that once the product is purchased, it belongs to them, and information regarding its use is no one's business except their own. Companies manufacturing RFID tags therefore are developing countermeasures to these potential concerns, such as a kill function that disables the tag at the checkout point, or removing the tag when the product is purchased.

Nicole Miller has a strategic partnership with retailers like JCPenney.

Open Communication   To share information, develop sales forecasts together, and coordinate deliveries, Nicole Miller (the clothing manufacturer from the opening vignette) and its suppliers maintain open and honest communication. This maintenance may sound easy in principle, but most businesses don't tend to share information with their business partners. But open, honest communication is a key to developing successful relationships, because supply chain members need to understand what is driving each other's business, their roles in the relationship, each firm's strategies, and any problems that arise over the course of the relationship.

Common Goals   Supply chain members must have common goals for a successful relationship to develop. Shared goals give both members of the relationship an incentive to pool their strengths and abilities and exploit potential opportunities together. Such commonality also offers an assurance that the other partner won't do anything to hinder the achievement of those goals within the relationship.

Nicole Miller works with its retailers by providing pre-ticketed merchandise on hangers. It also exchanges information using an advanced EDI system.

For example, Nicole Miller and its local suppliers recognize that it is in their common interest to be strategic partners. Nicole Miller needs the quick response local manufacturers afford, and those manufacturers recognize that if they can keep Nicole Miller happy, they will have more than enough business for years to come. With common goals, both firms have an incentive to cooperate because they know that by doing so, both can boost sales. For instance, if Nicole Miller needs a special production run to make an emergency shipment to New York, the suppliers will work to meet the challenge. If one of Nicole Miller's suppliers has difficulty getting a particular fabric or financing its inventory, it is in Nicole Miller's best interest to help it because they are committed to the same goals in the long run.

Credible Commitments   Successful relationships develop because both parties make credible commitments to, or tangible investments in, the relationship. These commitments go beyond just making the hollow statement, "I want to be your partner"; they involve spending money to improve the products or services provided to the customer.[31] For example, if Nicole Miller makes a financial commitment to its suppliers to help them develop state-of-the-art manufacturing facilities and computer systems for improved communication, it is making a credible commitment—putting its money where its mouth is.

Just like many other elements of marketing, managing the supply chain can seem like an easy task at first glance: Put the merchandise in the right place at the right time. But the various elements and actors involved in a supply chain create its unique and compelling complexities and require that firms work carefully to ensure they are achieving the most efficient and effective chain possible.

CHECK YOURSELF

1. What are the different types of vertical marketing systems?
2. How do firms develop strong strategic partnerships with their supply chain partners?

Summing Up

1. **What is supply chain management?**

    Supply chain management refers to the effort to coordinate suppliers, manufacturers, warehouses, stores, and transportation intermediaries so that the merchandise the customer wants is produced in the right quantities and sent to the right locations at the time the customer wants it. Logistics concentrates on the movement and control of the products, whereas supply chain management includes the managerial aspects of the process as well.

2. **How do supply chains add value?**

    Without a supply chain, consumers would be forced to find raw materials, manufacture products, and somehow get them to where they could be used, all on their own. Each supply chain member adds value to the product by performing one of these functions. Supply chain man-

    agement also creates value for each firm in the chain and helps bind together many company functions, including manufacturing, inventory management, transportation, advertising, and marketing.

3. **How does a supply chain work?**

    For a supply chain to operate properly, the flow of information and merchandise must be coordinated, and supply chain members must work together to their mutual benefit. In more sophisticated supply chains, information flows seamlessly between supply chain members through EDI. Many of the best supply chains use a JIT or QR inventory management system, which provides the right amount of inventory just when it is needed. The JIT systems thus improve product availability and reduce inventory investments.

4. **How is a supply chain managed?**

The more closely aligned the supply chain members are with each other, the less likely there will be significant conflict. An administered supply chain occurs when a dominant and powerful supply chain member has control over the other members. In a contractual supply chain (e.g., franchising), coordination and control are dictated by contractual relationships between members. Corporate supply chains can operate relatively smoothly because one firm owns the various levels of the chains. Supply chains also can be effectively managed through strong relationships developed with supply chain partners. To create such relationships, the partners must trust each other, communicate openly, have compatible goals, and be willing to invest in each other's success.

Key Terms

- administered vertical marketing system, 477
- advanced shipping notice (ASN), 463
- checking, 470
- collaborative, planning, forecasting, and replenishment (CPFR), 466
- consignment, 466
- contractual vertical marketing system, 477
- corporate vertical marketing system, 478
- cross-dock, 471
- cycle time, 465
- dispatcher, 470
- distribution center, 460

- electronic data interchange (EDI), 464
- extranet, 464
- floor-ready merchandise, 472
- franchising, 477
- independent (conventional) supply chain, 476
- intranet, 464
- just-in-time inventory systems, 473
- lead time, 473
- logistics management, 458
- marketing channel, 458
- pick ticket, 472
- pull supply chain, 466
- push supply chain, 467
- quick response, 473

- radio frequency identification (RFID) tag, 470
- receiving, 470
- reorder point, 466
- strategic relationship (partnering relationship), 479
- supply chain conflict (channel conflict), 476
- supply chain management, 456
- ticketing and marketing, 472
- Universal Product Code (UPC), 462
- vendor-managed inventory, 466
- vertical marketing system, 476
- wholesaler, 457

Marketing Applications

1. Describe supply chain management by identifying the major activities that it involves. Identify several ways that supply chain management adds value to a company's offerings, with regard to both consumers and business partners.

2. Discuss the similarities and differences among the concepts of supply chains, marketing channels, and logistics.

3. In what ways can the flow of information be managed in the supply chain? How can the ready flow of information increase a firm's operating efficiencies?

4. Describe how B2B transactions might employ EDI to process purchase information. Considering the information discussed in Chapter 6 about B2B buying situations, determine which buying situation (new task, modified rebuy, or straight rebuy) would most likely align with the use of EDI technology. Justify your answer.

5. What are the differences between the use of a traditional distribution center and one that relies on cross-docking? Discuss the extent to which one is more efficient than the other, being sure to detail your reasoning.

6. Discuss the advantages to a retailer like Victoria's Secret of expending the time and effort to get merchandise floor ready at either the point of manufacture or in the distribution center rather than having retail store staff members do it in the stores. Provide the logic behind your answer.

7. A JIT inventory system appears to be an important success factor for Zara. Choose a local retailer and examine the advantages and disadvantages of its use of a JIT system. Do you believe it should use JIT? Why?

8. Give an example of a retailer that participates in an independent (conventional) supply chain and one involved in a vertical marketing system. Discuss the advantages and disadvantages of each.

9. For each of the following consumer products, identify the type of vertical marketing system used, and justify your answer: (a) Bertolli pasta sold through grocery stores, (b) Krispy Kreme donuts sold through franchises, and (c) www. polo. com by Ralph Lauren.

10. Why might a big company like Dell want to develop strategic partnerships with locally owned computer stores? Describe what Dell would have to do to maintain such relationships.

11. You are hired as an assistant brand manager for a popular consumer product. One day in an emergency meeting, the brand manager informs the group that there is a problem with one of the suppliers and that he has decided to send you over to the manufacturing facilities to investigate the problem. When you arrive at the plant, you learn that a key supplier has become increasingly unreliable in terms of quality and delivery. You ask the plant manager why the plant doesn't switch suppliers, because it is becoming a major problem for your brand. He informs you that the troubled supplier is his cousin, whose wife has been very ill, and he just can't switch right now. What course of action should you take?

Quiz Yourself

www.mhhe.com/ grewal2e

1. Franchising involves a(n) _____ supply chain.
   a. cooperative
   b. corporate
   c. contractual
   d. administered
   e. conventional

2. Flora is frustrated with her company's supply chain management information system. She wants to be able to receive sales data, initiate purchase orders, send and receive invoices, and receive returned merchandise documentation. Flora needs a(n):
   a. cross-docking extranet.
   b. electronic data interchange.
   c. floor-ready intranet.
   d. vertical conflict reduction.
   e. radio frequency identification system.

(Answers to these two questions are provided on page 624)

Go to www.mhhe.com/grewal2e to practice an additional 11 questions.

Net Savvy

1. Zappos.com, an online shoe seller, has received praise for its stellar supply chain management. Go to www.zappos.com/warehouse_tour.html, look through the warehouse tour, and see how a shoe ultimately reaches the customer. How does its distribution center enable Zappos to adhere to its marketing communications message and provide excellent customer service?

2. Several examples in this chapter highlight ways that Zara International, a division of Inditex, successfully manages its supply chain. Visit Inditex's Web site (www.inditex.com) and review the company's commitment to corporate social responsibility, particularly the section that pertains to its Code of Conduct. Considering the discussion in this chapter about strategic relationships, how does Inditex address the factors necessary for mutually beneficial partnerships, according to its code of conduct?

Chapter Case Study

WAL-MART: PIONEER IN SUPPLY CHAIN MANAGEMENT[32]

Wal-Mart dominates the retailing industry in terms of its sales revenue, its customer base, and its ability to drive down costs and deliver good value to its customers.

After all, the world's largest corporation takes pride in having received numerous accolades for its ability to continuously improve efficiency in the supply chain while meeting its corporate mandate of offering customers Everyday Low Prices.

Tight inventory management is legendary at Wal-Mart through its just-in-time techniques, some of which are homegrown, that allow the firm to boast one of the best supply chains in the world. Wal-Mart has not only transformed its own supply chain but influenced how vendors throughout the world operate. For example, retailers everywhere are now placing much more emphasis on vendors' on-time and accurate deliveries. To meet these requirements, vendors have had to upgrade their inventory management and delivery systems to ensure they are doing business the way their large retailer customers prefer.[33] Recognized for its ability to obtain merchandise from global sources, Wal-Mart also pioneered the strategy of achieving high levels of growth and profitability through its precision control of manufacturing, inventory, and distribution. Although the company is not unique in this regard, it is by far the most successful and most influential corporation of its kind and has put into practice various innovative techniques.

And when Wal-Mart does something, it does it on a massive scale. Wal-Mart's computer system, for example, is second only to that of the Pentagon in storage capacity. Its information systems analyze more than 10 million daily transactions from point-of-sale data and distribute their analysis in real time both internally to its managers and externally via a satellite network to Wal-Mart's many suppliers, who use the information for their production planning and order shipment.

Much of the popularity of supply chain management has been attributed to the success of Wal-Mart's partnership with Procter & Gamble. During the 1980s, the two collaborated in building a software system that linked P&G to Wal-Mart's

Wal-Mart has developed a sustainable competitive advantage through efficient supply chain management.

distribution centers, taking advantage of advances in the world's telecommunications infrastructure. When a Wal-Mart store sold a particular P&G item, the information flowed directly to P&G's planning and control systems. When the inventory level of P&G's products at Wal-Mart's distribution center got to the "reorder point," the system automatically alerted P&G to ship more products. This information helped P&G plan its production. Wal-Mart was also able to track when a P&G shipment arrived at one of its distribution warehouses, which enabled it to coordinate its own outbound shipments to stores. Both Wal-Mart and P&G realized savings from the better inventory management and order processing, savings that in turn were passed on to Wal-Mart's consumers through its low everyday prices.

Wal-Mart's Innovations

Wal-Mart has pioneered many innovations in the purchase and distribution processes of the products it sells. As many as 20 years ago, Wal-Mart drove the adoption of UPC bar codes throughout the retail industry; it also pioneered the use of electronic data interchange (EDI) for computerized ordering from vendors. Its hub-and-spoke distribution network ensures goods are brought to distribution centers around the country and then directed outward to thousands of stores, each of which is within a day's travel. Through the use of cross-docking, one of its best-known innovations, goods get trucked to a distribution center from suppliers and then are immediately transferred to trucks bound for stores,

Wal-Mart speeds merchandise from its distribution centers to stores.

without ever being placed into storage.[34] In addition, Wal-Mart uses a dedicated fleet of trucks to ship goods from warehouses to stores in less than 48 hours, as well as to replenish store inventories about twice a week. Thus, with flow-through logistics, the company speeds the movement of goods from its distribution centers to its retail stores around the world.

Today the retail giant continues to push the supply chain toward greater and greater efficiency. It has well-established systems for the continuous replenishment of merchandise, vendor-managed inventory, cross-docking, strategic collaborations with producers in the manufacturing planning cycle, order and delivery, and direct shipments from manufacturers. It also strives to apply new technologies. For example, it has gotten some of its suppliers to adopt RFID technology and is using RFID in some of its own distribution centers.[35] Its continuous use of innovations thus leads to lower inventory and operating costs, which enables Wal-Mart to keep its costs in check.

Wal-Mart furthermore has made an art of managing the flow of products and information among its suppliers, distribution centers, and individual stores through technology, the application of which allows for precision control of logistics and inventory. It is this type of innovation that has put Wal-Mart at the top of the retailing game. Not all organizations can pull this approach off so well. Wal-Mart is a unique case in which a single, very powerful firm took primary responsibility for improving performance across its own supply chain. By developing a superior supply chain management system, it has reaped the rewards of higher levels of customer service and satisfaction, lower production and transportation costs, and more productive use of its retail store space. Fundamentally, it boils down to Wal-Mart's ability to link together suppliers, distribution centers, retail outlets, and, ultimately, customers, regardless of their location. Although operational innovation isn't the only ingredient in Wal-Mart's success, it has been a crucial building block for its strong competitive position.

Questions

1. How does an individual firm like Wal-Mart manage a supply chain, particularly considering that supply chains include multiple firms with potentially conflicting objectives? Describe some of the conflicts that could arise in such a circumstance.

2. What are some of the ways that Wal-Mart's supply chain management system has provided it the benefits of higher levels of product availability and lower merchandise acquisition and transportation costs? Provide specific examples of each benefit.

RETAILING AND MULTICHANNEL MARKETING

LEARNING OBJECTIVES

- What are the issues manufacturers consider when choosing retail partners?
- What types of retailers are available for distributing products?
- How do manufacturers and retailers work together to develop a strategy?
- Why is multichannel marketing becoming such a prevalent channel strategy?

As fast as the dry cleaners, as friendly as the concierge at a hotel—can Apple stores leap tall buildings too?[1] Apple retail stores, crucial for the company's success and accounting for 20 percent of the company's revenue, have led to its recognition as one of *Fortune*'s Most Admired Companies. Before it opened its own retail stores, Apple allowed product sales through large retailers, which meant the company depended on these large electronics retailers. The retailers had no special incentive to market Apple products, nor did they have the training necessary to sell the technologically advanced items. Apple therefore realized that the only way it could ensure its unique products really stood out was by taking the responsibility for selling into its own hands.

In the course of this decision, Apple spent significant time and effort designing its stores. The company leased warehouse space to create a prototype store that it could then replicate all over the country. After a few iterations, the ultimate Apple Store emerged, based on a design that considered how customers shop for products, not on just the product categories themselves.

Its largest store in the United States, located in Boston, appears like a glass cube with a glowing Apple logo surrounded by traditional Boston buildings. Its New York City location was the first to utilize this avant garde glass cube design. In this location, the cube houses a spiral staircase that leads to the underground store. Even some of the smaller stores carry this theme, with ceilings that make the stores appear as if they are lit by the sun. The computers are connected to the Internet, and customers are free to surf the Internet and chat online. If you are in need of an Internet Café, Apple stores even provide the service free!

The Apple Store has become more than just a retailer to sell its iMacs, iPods, AppleTVs, and so forth. The store offers an array of free services and is designed to allow customers to try out the different products before buying them. This benefit is especially important for early adopters who want to try new technologies as soon as they are available. For customers who need more assistance with products, the store offers Personal Shopping. A customer can make an appointment with a "Specialist" at a store to learn about the products of interest, without being obligated to make a purchase. For free technical services, the store offers a Genius Bar, with "Geniuses" who have been trained at the corporate headquarters on Apple products.

The stores also offer free workshops, focusing on everything from the basics of using Apple products to using Adobe Photoshop to create business presentations. For professional photographers, musicians, and filmmakers, workshops teach the detailed applications that they can use to optimize their finished products. The Apple stores also offer camps for children, workshops for families, and more.

When customers enter the store, a person wearing an orange shirt, the "Concierge," directs them where they need to go. The store avoids checkout counters; instead, using EasyPay, sales people use wireless credit-card readers to check out customers.

Apple also can brag about achieving the best-per-square-foot sales in the country—$4,500 per square foot, far more than Saks Fifth Avenue at $363, Best Buy at $930, and even Tiffany & Co. at $2,746.[2] If companies had middle names, "innovative" would be Apple's. The company continues to demonstrate its willingness to do what it takes to be unique, while still producing the best technology and the best customer service in the retail industry.

● ● ●

Retailing sits at the end of the supply chain, where marketing meets the consumer. As Apple realized before it started to open its retail stores, regardless of how good a firm's strategy is or how great the product or service is, if it isn't available when the customer wants it, where he or she wants it, at the right price, and in the right size, color, and style, it simply won't sell. It is primarily the retailer's responsibility to make sure that these customers' expectations are fulfilled.

Retailing is defined as the set of business activities that add value to products and services sold to consumers for their personal or family use. Our definition includes products bought at stores, through catalogs, and over the Internet, as well as services like fast-food restaurants, airlines, and hotels. Some retailers claim they sell at "wholesale" prices, but if they sell to customers for their personal use, they are still retailers, regardless of how low their prices may be. Wholesalers (see Chapter 15) buy products from manufacturers and resell them to retailers or industrial or business users.

Cosmetic designer Traver Rains (left) celebrates the introduction of the MAC Heatherette collection (right) at an event at a MAC store in South Beach, Florida.

Retailing today is changing, both in the United States and around the world. No longer do manufacturers rule many supply chains, as they once did. Retailers like Wal-Mart, Carrefour (a French hypermarket), Home Depot, Tesco, Metro (a German retail conglomerate), and Kroger[3]—the largest retailers in the world—dictate to their suppliers what should be made, how it should be configured, when it should be delivered, and, to some extent, what it should cost. These retailers are clearly in the driver's seat.

This chapter extends Chapter 15's discussion of supply chain management by examining why and how manufacturers utilize retailers. The manufacturer's strategy depends on its overall market power and how consistent a new product or product line is with its current offering. Consider the following scenarios:

■ **Scenario 1:** Cosmetics conglomerate Estée Lauder's subsidiary brand M-A-C is introducing a new line of mascara.

■ **Scenario 2:** Estée Lauder is introducing a line of scarves, leather goods, and other accessories—products not currently in its assortment.

■ **Scenario 3:** Britt, a young entrepreneur, is launching a new line of environmentally friendly (green) cosmetics.

Each of these scenarios is different and requires the manufacturer to consider different alternatives for reaching its target markets through retailers.

Exhibit 16.1 illustrates four factors manufacturers consider to establish their strategy for working with retailers.[4] In choosing retail partners, the first factor, manufacturers assess how likely it is for certain retailers to carry their products.

EXHIBIT 16.1   Factors for Establishing a Relationship with Retailers

| Choosing retail partners | Identifying types of retailers | Facilitating retail strategy | Managing a multichannel strategy |

Manufacturers also consider where their target customers expect to find the products, because those are exactly the stores in which they want to place their products. The overall size and level of sophistication of the manufacturer will determine how many of the supply chain functions it performs and how many it will hand off to other channel members. Finally, the type and availability of the product and the image the manufacturer wishes to portray will determine how many retailers within a geographic region will carry the products.

In the second factor, manufacturers identify the types of retailers that would be appropriate to carry its products. Although the choice is often obvious—such as a supermarket for fresh produce—manufacturers may have a choice of retailer types for some products.

As we discussed in Chapter 15, a hallmark of a strong marketing channel is that manufacturers and retailers coordinate their efforts in it. In the third factor, manufacturers and retailers therefore develop their strategy by implementing the four Ps.

Finally, many retailers and some manufacturers are exploring a **multichannel strategy** in which they sell in more than one channel (e.g., store, catalog, and Internet). The fourth factor therefore consists of examining the circumstances in which sellers may prefer to adopt a particular strategy. Although these factors are listed consecutively, manufacturers may consider them all simultaneously or in a different order.

CHOOSING RETAILING PARTNERS

Imagine, as a consumer, trying to buy a new leather jacket without being able to visit a retailer or buy it online. You would have to figure out exactly what size, color, and style of jacket you wanted. Then you would need to contact various manufacturers, whether in person, by phone, or over the Internet, and order the jacket. Assuming it fit you reasonably well, you still might need to take it to a tailor to have the sleeves shortened. It would not be very convenient.

Manufacturers like Estée Lauder use retailers such as Macy's because doing so creates value by pulling all these actions together. The store offers a broad selection of leather jackets, scarves, and other accessories that it has carefully chosen in advance. Customers can see, touch, feel, and try on each item while in the store. They can buy one scarf or leather jacket at a time or buy an outfit that works together. Finally, the store provides a salesperson to help customers coordinate their outfit and a tailor to make the whole thing fit perfectly.

When choosing retail partners, manufacturers must look at the basic channel structure, where their target customers expect to find the products, channel member characteristics, and distribution intensity.

Revlon might have a difficult time getting CVS to buy a new mascara because its supply chain is not vertically integrated.

Channel Structure

The level of difficulty a manufacturer has in getting retailers to purchase its products is determined by the degree to which the channel is vertically integrated, as described in Chapter 15; the degree to which the manufacturer has a strong brand or is otherwise desirable in the market; and the relative power of the manufacturer and retailer.

Scenario 1 represents a corporate vertical marketing system. Because M-A-C is made by Estée Lauder and operates its own stores, when the new mascara line gets introduced, the stores simply receive the new line automatically. They have no choice. In contrast, Revlon would have a much more difficult time getting CVS to buy a new mascara line, because these supply chain partners are not vertically integrated.

When an established firm like Estée Lauder enters a new market with scarves, leather, and accessories, as is the case in Scenario 2, it cannot just place the products with any retailer. It must determine where its customers would expect to find higher-end scarves, leather goods, and accessories, and then use its established relationships with cosmetics buyers, the power of its brand, and its overall reputation to leverage its position in this new product area.

Britt (Scenario 3) would have an even more difficult time getting a retailer to buy and sell her green cosmetics line, because she lacks power in the marketplace—she is small, and her brand is unknown. It would be difficult to get buyers to see her, let alone consider her line. She might face relatively high slotting allowances (Chapter 14) just to get space on retailers' shelves. But like Estée Lauder in Scenario 2, when choosing retailers to which to sell, Britt should consider where the end customer expects to find her products, as well as some important retailer characteristics.

Customer Expectations

From a retailer's perspective, it is important to know from which manufacturers its customers want to buy. Manufacturers, in contrast, need to know where their target market customers expect to find their products and those of their competitors. As we see in the hypothetical example in Exhibit 16.2, Estée Lauder currently sells cosmetics at Dillard's Department Stores, Macy's, and Sears (orange arrows). Its competitor Nars sells at Dillard's and Macy's but also to JCPenney (green arrows). A survey of Estée Lauder customers shows that they would expect to find its clothes at Kohl's, Dillard's, Macy's, and JCPenney (blue box). On the basis of this information, Estée Lauder decides to try to start selling at Kohl's and JCPenney but stop selling at Sears to provide greater convenience to customers.

Customers generally expect to find certain products at some stores but not at others. For example, Estée Lauder would not choose to sell to CVS or Dollar General because its customers would not expect to shop at those stores for high-end cosmetics or clothing like Estée Lauder's. Instead, CVS might carry less expensive cosmetic brands, like Revlon and Maybelline, and bargain closeouts probably appear at Dollar General. But Estée Lauder's customers definitely expect to find its clothing offerings at major department stores.

EXHIBIT 16.2 Estée Lauder and Nars Distribution

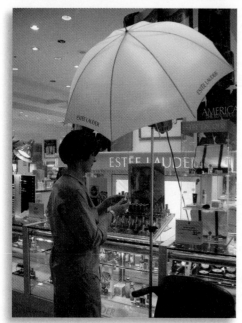

Most consumer packaged goods companies, such as Pepsi (top), strive for intensive distribution—they want to be everywhere. But cosmetics firms like Estée Lauder (bottom) use an exclusive distribution strategy by limiting their distribution to a few select, higher-end retailers in each region.

Channel Member Characteristics

Several factors pertaining to the channel members themselves will help determine the channel structure. Generally, the larger and more sophisticated the channel member, the less likely that it will use supply chain intermediaries. Britt will probably use a group of independent sales people to help sell her line of green cosmetics, whereas a large manufacturer like Estée Lauder will use its own sales force that already has existing relationships in the industry. In the same way, an independent grocery store might buy merchandise from a wholesaler, but Wal-Mart, the world's largest grocer, only buys directly from the manufacturer. Larger firms often find that by performing the channel functions themselves, they can gain more control, be more efficient, and save money.

Distribution Intensity

When setting up distribution for the first time, as is the case with Britt's green cosmetics (Scenario 3), or introducing a new product line, as is the case with Estée Lauder's new line of scarves, leather, and accessories (Scenario 2), firms decide the appropriate level of distribution intensity—the number of channel members to use at each level of the marketing channel. Distribution intensity commonly is divided into three levels: intensive, exclusive, and selective.

Intensive Distribution   An intensive distribution strategy is designed to get products into as many outlets as possible. Most consumer packaged goods companies, such as Pepsi, Procter & Gamble, Kraft, and other nationally branded products found in grocery and discount stores strive for and often achieve intensive distribution. Pepsi, for instance, wants its product available everywhere—grocery stores, convenience stores, restaurants, and vending machines. The more exposure it gets, the more it sells.

Exclusive Distribution   Manufacturers also might use an exclusive distribution policy by granting exclusive geographic territories to one or very few retail customers so no other customers in the territory can sell a particular brand. Exclusive distribution can benefit manufacturers by assuring them that the most appropriate retailers represent their products. Cosmetics firms like Estée Lauder, for instance, limit their distribution to a few select, higher-end retailers in each region. They believe that if they sell their products to drugstores, full-line discount stores, and grocery stores, this distribution would weaken their image.

In cases of limited supply or when a firm is just starting out, providing an exclusive territory to one customer helps ensure enough inventory to offer the customer an adequate selection. By granting exclusive territories, Britt's green cosmetics line guarantees its retailers adequate supply, which gives them a strong incentive to market her products. The retailers that Britt uses know there will be no competing retailers to cut prices, so their profit margins are protected, which also gives them an incentive to carry more inventory and use extra advertising, personal selling, and sales promotions.

Selective Distribution   Between the intensive and exclusive distribution strategies lies selective distribution, which uses a few selected customers in a territory. Like exclusive distribution, selective distribution helps a seller maintain a particular image and control the flow of merchandise into an area, so many shopping goods manufacturers use it. Recall that shopping goods are those products for which consumers are willing to spend time comparing alternatives, such as most apparel items, home items like branded pots and pans or sheets and towels, branded hardware and tools, and consumer electronics. Retailers still have a strong incentive to sell the products but not to the same extent as if they had an exclusive territory.

As we noted in Chapter 15, like any large complicated system, a marketing channel is difficult to manage. Whether the balance of power rests with large retailers like Wal-Mart or with large manufacturers like Procter & Gamble, it behooves channel members to work together to develop and implement their channel strategy. In the next section, we explore the different types of retailers with an eye toward which would be most appropriate for M-A-C Cosmetics, Estée Lauder's new line of scarves, leather, and accessories, and Britt's new line of environmentally friendly cosmetics.

CHECK YOURSELF

1. What issues should manufacturers consider when choosing retail partners?
2. What is the difference between intensive, exclusive, and selective levels of distribution intensity?

IDENTIFY TYPES OF RETAILER

Although it may seem clear which type of retailer Estée Lauder and Britt may wish to pursue when attempting to place their new lines, the choice is not always easy. Manufacturers need to understand the general characteristics of different types of retailers so they can determine the best channels for their product. For instance, the characteristics of a retailer that are important to a food manufacturer may be quite different than those of a cosmetics manufacturer. In the next few sections, we examine the various types of retailers, identify some major players, and discuss some of the issues facing each type (Exhibit 16.3).

Food Retailers

The food retailing landscape is changing dramatically. Twenty years ago, consumers purchased food primarily at conventional supermarkets. Now

EXHIBIT 16.3 Types of Retailers

Kroger is the world's second largest food retailer. Wal-Mart is the largest.

ALDI is a limited assortment supermarket chain that carries only 2,000 SKUs.

conventional supermarkets account for only 56 percent of food sales (not including restaurants). The fastest-growing segment of the food retail market is the remaining 44 percent of food sales made by supercenters, warehouse clubs, convenience stores, and new concepts such as extreme value food retailers.[5] While Wal-Mart and other general merchandise retailers are offering more food items, traditional supermarkets are carrying more nonfood items, and many offer pharmacies, health care clinics, photo processing centers, banks, and cafés.

The world's largest food retailer, Wal-Mart, has more than $134 billion in sales of supermarket-type merchandise, followed by Kroger (U.S. corporate headquarters), Carrefour (France), Ahold (Netherlands), and Albertson's (U.S.).[6] The largest supermarket chains in the United States are Kroger, Safeway, Supervalu, Ahold USA, and Publix.[7]

Supermarkets   A conventional supermarket is a self-service food store offering groceries, meat, and produce with limited sales of nonfood items, such as health and beauty aids and general merchandise.[8] Perishables like meat and produce account for 50 percent of supermarket sales and typically have higher margins than packaged goods.[9]

Whereas conventional supermarkets carry about 30,000 stockkeeping units (SKUs), limited assortment supermarkets or extreme value food retailers stock only 2,000 SKUs.[10] The two largest limited assortment supermarket chains in the United States are Save-A-Lot and ALDI. Rather than carry 20 brands of laundry detergent, limited assortment stores offer one or two brands and sizes, one of which is a store brand. Stores are designed to maximize efficiency and reduce costs. For example, merchandise is shipped in cartons or crates that can serve as displays so that no unloading is needed. Some costly services that consumers take for granted, such as free bags and paying with credit cards, are not provided. Stores are typically located in shopping centers with low rents. By trimming costs, limited assortment supermarkets can offer merchandise at 40 to 60 percent lower prices than conventional supermarkets.[11]

Although conventional supermarkets still sell a majority of food merchandise, they are under substantial competitive pressure from other types of food retailers, full-line discount chains, supercenters, warehouse clubs, extreme value retailers, convenience stores, and restaurants. To compete successfully against intrusions by other food retailing formats, conventional supermarkets are differentiating their offerings by (1) emphasizing fresh perishables, (2) targeting health-conscious and ethnic consumers with new lines of natural and organic items, (3) providing a better in-store experience with a better overall atmosphere and demonstrations, and (4) offering more private-label brands. Superior Service 16.1 notes how Wegmans employs such tactics to ensure its customers are satisfied and keep coming back to shop at its stores.

Superior Service 16.1

Wegmans Services Its Employees—and Its Customers Too

For many grocery stores, meeting customers' needs is what they do.[12] For Wegmans, exceeding customers' needs and expectations is what it does and how it operates. In an industry in which 84 percent of consumers don't believe that traditional supermarkets can provide anything different from nontraditional grocers such as Wal-Mart, Wegmans has developed a strong and loyal customer base.

From its start in Rochester, New York, privately owned Wegmans has expanded in the past 90 years to reach customers in New York, New Jersey, Pennsylvania, Virginia, and, most recently, Maryland. By any count, Wegmans is successful. Its sales per square foot are $9.29, approximately 50 percent higher than the industry average. Considering that its new stores are 130,000 square feet each—three times the size of a typical supermarket—Wegmans must be doing something right. In 2004, Wegmans received 7,000 letters, half of which were requests for a store to be built in a new community. When the Dulles store in Virginia opened, more than 15,500 customers, typical traffic for a week in a typical supermarket, came through on opening day.

Wegmans respects and services both its customers and its employees. When it earned *Fortune*'s coveted "Best Company to Work For" Award, Wegmans noted that part of its success as a retailer stems from its success as an employer. In the past 20 years, Wegmans has paid more than $54 million in college scholarships to both full-time and part-time employees. On a different educational front, employees who work in the meat and fish departments must graduate from a "university" program that takes between 30 and 55 hours and gives employees knowledge that assists them in furthering their careers.

Furthermore, because Wegmans prides itself on its customer service and satisfaction, it gives its employees power to assist customers in any way they see fit, without the approval of a supervisor. For example, one customer purchased the largest turkey Wegmans had for Thanksgiving and then discovered it was too large to cook at home. A Wegmans' employee cooked the turkey for the customer without charge.

In another case, a woman was looking for a particular item. When the employee couldn't find the location of the item immediately, the customer said, "Go on back to whatever you were doing." A few minutes later, the employee found the customer in another section of the store and exclaimed, "There you are! I finally found it!" The employee took the time away from her current task to help a customer, even after she was no longer expected to be of assistance.

Wegmans offers far more than you would find in a traditional supermarket—a real service bonanza. Drop off your child at the in-store day care center. Saunter through the bookstore for Oprah's newest book club recommendation. Drop off your dry cleaning and overdue video rental. Pick up your dry cleaning. When you tire of browsing the flower and international newspaper sections, you can finally start on your grocery list. But before you run through the checkout, don't forget to pick up that bottle of champagne the cheese shop attendant told you would complement the white Castello cheese he handpicked for you.

Wegmans may sell many of the same products as other grocery retailers, but it's not the same. Employees at every level work to service the customer and exceed their needs and expectations. As a result, Wegmans' store count is growing at a steady pace, and so is its loyal customer base.

Wegmans invests in its employees. This strategy pays off by providing customers with great service.

Supercenters Supercenters, the fastest growing retail category, are large stores (150,000–220,000 square feet) that combine a supermarket with a full-line discount store. Wal-Mart operates 2,300 supercenters in the United States—four times more than its leading competitors Meijer, Kmart, Fred Meyer (a division of Kroger), and Target combined. By offering broad assortments of grocery and general merchandise products under one roof, supercenters provide a one-stop shopping experience.

Warehouse Clubs Warehouse clubs are large retailers (at least 100,000–150,000 square feet) that offer a limited and irregular assortment of food and general merchandise with little service at low prices for ultimate consumers and small businesses. The largest warehouse club chains are Costco, Sam's Club (a division of Wal-Mart), and BJ's Wholesale Club, a distant third. Costco differentiates itself

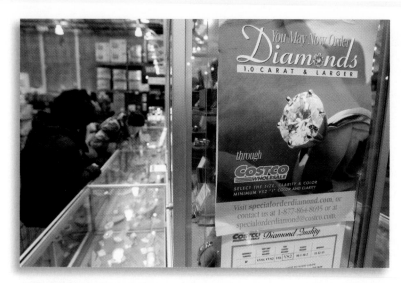

At Costco, customers can buy 1.0 carat and larger diamonds as well as huge bags of carrots.

by offering unique upscale merchandise not available elsewhere at low prices. For example, you can buy a 5-carat diamond ring for $127,999.99. Sam's Club focuses more on small businesses, providing services such as group health insurance as well as products.

Both Estée Lauder's and Britt's products could be sold in warehouse clubs, but they are probably not the best choices. Both product lines will have an upscale image, which is inconsistent with any warehouse club. If, however, either firm has an overstocked situation caused by overestimating demand or returned merchandise from retailers, warehouse clubs are a potential outlet.

Convenience Stores   Convenience stores provide a limited variety and assortment of merchandise at a convenient location in 2,000–3,000 square foot stores with speedy checkout. They are the modern version of the neighborhood mom-and-pop grocery/general store. Convenience stores enable consumers to make purchases quickly, without having to search through a large store and wait in a long checkout line. Milk, eggs, and bread once represented the majority of their sales, but now the majority of sales come from gasoline and cigarettes.

Convenience stores also face increased competition from other formats. Supercenter and supermarket chains are attempting to increase customer store visits by offering gasoline and tying gasoline sales to their frequent shopper programs. Drugstores and full-line discount stores also are setting up easily accessed areas of their stores with convenience store merchandise.

In response to these competitive pressures, convenience stores are taking steps to decrease their dependency on gasoline sales by offering fresh food and healthy fast food, tailoring assortments to local markets, and making their stores even more convenient to shop by opening smaller stores closer to where consumers shop and work. Finally, convenience stores are adding new services, such as financial service kiosks that give customers the opportunity to cash checks, pay bills, and buy prepaid telephone minutes, theater tickets, and gift cards.

Trader Joe's has evolved from a convenience store into a unique grocery store that offers unique items at low prices. Adding Value 16.1 provides insight into what has made it so successful.

General Merchandise Retailers

The major types of general merchandise retailers are department stores, full-line discount stores, specialty stores, category specialists, home improvement centers, off-price retailers, and extreme value retailers.

Department Stores   Department stores are retailers that carry a broad variety and deep assortment, offer customer services, and organize their stores into distinct departments for displaying merchandise. The largest department store chains in the United States are Macy's, Sears, JCPenney, Kohl's, Nordstrom, Dillards, and Saks.[13] Department stores would be an excellent retail channel for Estée Lauder's and Britt's new lines.

Traditionally, department stores attracted customers by offering a pleasing ambience, attentive service, and a wide variety of merchandise under one roof. They sold both soft goods (apparel and bedding) and hard goods (appliances, furniture, and consumer electronics). But now most department stores focus almost

Adding Value 16.1 Trader Joe's Offers the Unexpected[14]

Trader Joe's is a grocery store that offers unique items at low prices. The store originally evolved into what it is today because of strong competition from the fast-growing convenience store 7-Eleven. Today, though, Trader Joe's is not viewed in the same light as a convenience store, especially a 7-Eleven. It caters to an earthy, crunchy person, as well as to upscale shoppers looking for exceptional products.

Its limited assortment of products appeals to both gourmands and gourmets. It carries only 2,000 products, compared with 30,000 at a regular grocery store, and focuses on special items, such as prepared or organic foods, rather than mass-market products. It does not sell brands like Coke or Budweiser, nor will it sell every type of laundry detergent. There is one kind of laundry detergent, but 10 kinds of hummus. Trader Joe's offers Joe-Joe's cookies at Christmas, which look like Oreos but taste like Girl Scout's Thin Mints.

Unlike regular grocery stores, which carry 16 percent private-label products, 80 percent of Trader Joe's products are private labels. The company develops small businesses to become its vendors, making the products it sells exclusive to its stores. Between its limited assortment and products available only at Trader Joe's, the product selection is very special and hand picked. Many grocery stores, like Kroger and Safeway, are catching on to the success of private-label brands and increasing their private-label offerings.

Trader Joe's also focuses on the customer experience by mimicking a vacation during the shopping trip. All employees wear Hawaiian shirts, give out food and drink samples from huts, and use nautical terminology. The employees, as a result, feel relaxed and can have fun at work. Full-time employees earn $48,000 per year on average and have the opportunity to make six figures annually, much more than the typical grocery store employee. The company also provides health-care benefits for even part-time employees, an extremely unusual benefit in any retail sector.

Trader Joe's employees help enhance the shopping experience by wearing Hawaiian shirts and giving out food and drink samples.

exclusively on soft goods. Each department within the store has a specific selling space allocated to it, as well as sales people to assist customers. The department store often resembles a collection of specialty shops.

Department store chains can be categorized into three tiers. The first tier includes upscale, high-fashion chains with exclusive designer merchandise and excellent customer service, such as Neiman Marcus, Bloomingdale's (part of Macy's Inc.), Nordstrom, and Saks Fifth Avenue (part of Saks Inc.). Macy's and Dillards are in the second tier of upscale traditional department stores, in which retailers sell more modestly priced merchandise with less customer service. The value-oriented third tier—Sears, JCPenney, and Kohl's—caters to more price-conscious consumers. To better compete, department stores are (1) attempting to increase the amount of exclusive and private-label merchandise they sell, (2) strengthening their customer loyalty programs, and (3) expanding their online presence.

Full-Line Discount Stores **Full-line discount stores** are retailers that offer a broad variety of merchandise, limited service, and low prices. Discount stores offer both private labels and manufacturer brands, but except for Target, these brands are typically less fashion oriented than the brands in department and specialty stores. The largest full-line discount store chains are Wal-Mart, Kmart (part of Sears Holding), and Target.

Although full-line discount stores typically carry scarves, leather goods, accessories, and cosmetics, they are not good options for Estée Lauder's or

Britt's new lines. Customers do not expect higher-end products in full-line discount stores.

Wal-Mart accounts for almost 66 percent of full-line discount store retail sales in the United States, so the most significant trend in this sector is Wal-Mart's conversion of full-line discount stores into supercenters. Wal-Mart is expected to reach 3,300 supercenters by 2010, while its conventional stores should decrease to approximately half their current level.[15] This change in emphasis is the result of the increased competition faced by full-line discount stores and the operating efficiencies of supercenters. Full-line discount stores confront intense competition from category specialists that focus on a single category of merchandise, such as Dick's Sporting Goods, Office Depot, Circuit City, Bed Bath & Beyond, Sports Authority, and Lowe's.

As Wal-Mart closes its full-line discount stores and opens supercenters, Target is becoming one of the most successful retailers in terms of sales growth and profitability. Target succeeds because its stores offer fashionable merchandise at low prices in a pleasant shopping environment. It has developed an image of "cheap chic" by teaming with designers such as Behnaz Sarafpour, Isaac Mizrahi, Proenza Schouler, and Patrick Robinson to produce inexpensive, exclusive merchandise.

Specialty Stores   Specialty stores concentrate on a limited number of complementary merchandise categories and provide a high level of service in relatively small stores. Specialty stores tailor their retail strategy toward very specific market segments by offering deep but narrow assortments and sales associate expertise. Estée Lauder's M-A-C line of cosmetics sells in the company's own retail specialty stores, as well as in some department stores. Certain specialty stores would be excellent outlets for the new lines by Estée Lauder and Britt. Customers likely expect to find Estée Lauder lines of scarves, leather, and accessories in women's apparel, gift, or leather stores. Britt's line of green cosmetics would fit nicely in a cosmetics specialty store like Sephora.

Sephora, France's leading perfume and cosmetic chain—a division of the luxury goods conglomerate LVMH (Louis Vuitton–Moët Hennessy)—is an example of an innovative specialty store concept. In the United States, prestigious cosmetics are typically sold in department stores. Each brand has a separate counter with a commissioned salesperson stationed behind the counter to help customers. Sephora

Sephora is an innovative specialty store that sells cosmetics.

is a cosmetic and perfume specialty store offering a deep assortment in a self-service, 6,000–9,000-square-foot format. Its stores provide more than 15,000 SKUs and more than 200 brands, including its own, private-label brand. Merchandise is grouped by product category, with the brands displayed alphabetically so customers can locate them easily. Customers are free to shop and experiment on their own. Product testing is encouraged. The knowledgeable sales people, always available to assist customers, are paid a salary by Sephora, unlike department store cosmetic sales people, who are compensated in part by incentives provided by the vendors. The low-key, open-sell environment results in customers spending more time shopping.

Drugstores Drugstores are specialty stores that concentrate on pharmaceuticals and health and personal grooming merchandise. Pharmaceuticals often represent more than 50 percent of drugstore sales and an even greater percentage of their profits. The largest drugstore chains in the United States are Walgreens, CVS, and Rite Aid—three chains that account for about 66 percent of U.S. drugstore sales, up from 43 percent in 2000.[16]

Although Estée Lauder's new line would not be consistent with the merchandise found in drugstores, Britt's green cosmetics may be a welcome addition. Some drugstores have recognized consumer demand for green products, even though Britt's cosmetics may be priced higher than its competitors. Britt must decide whether her high-end products will suffer a tarnished image if she sells them in drugstores or if drugstores are a good channel for increasing brand awareness.

Drugstores, particularly the national chains, are experiencing sustained sales growth because the aging population requires more prescription drugs. Although the profit margins for prescription pharmaceuticals are higher than those for other drugstore merchandise, these margins are shrinking as a result of government health care policies, HMOs, and public outcry over lower prices in other countries, especially Canada.

Drugstores are also being squeezed by considerable competition from pharmacies in discount stores and supermarkets, as well as prescription mail-order retailers. In response, the major drugstore chains are building larger stand-alone stores to offer a wider assortment of merchandise, more frequently purchased food items, the convenience of easy ordering and drive-through windows for picking up prescriptions, and in-store medical clinics. Walgreens is even adding women's apparel, most of which is priced below $15.[17] To build customer loyalty, the chains are changing the role of their pharmacists from simply dispensing pills to providing health care assistance, such as explaining how to use a nebulizer.

Category Specialists Category specialists, also known as big box retailers or category killers, are discount stores that offer a narrow but deep assortment of merchandise. Most category specialists predominantly use a self-service approach, but they offer assistance to customers in some areas of the stores. For example, the office supply store Staples has a warehouse atmosphere, with cartons of copy paper stacked on pallets, plus equipment in boxes on shelves. But in some departments, such as computers or electronics and other high-tech products, it provides sales people who staff the display area to answer questions and make suggestions.

By offering a complete assortment in a category at somewhat lower prices than their competition, category specialists can "kill" a category of merchandise for other retailers, which is why they are frequently called category killers. Using their category dominance, they exploit their buying power to negotiate low prices and are assured of supply when items are scarce. Department stores and full-line discount stores located near category specialists often have to reduce their offerings in the category because consumers are drawn to the deep assortment and low prices at the category killer.

Lowe's is one of the U.S.'s largest home improvement center chains. This category specialist offers equipment and material used by do-it-yourselfers and contractors to make home improvements.

One of the largest and most successful types of category specialists is the home improvement center. A home improvement center is a category specialist offering equipment and material used by do-it-yourselfers and contractors to make home improvements. The largest U.S. home improvement chains are Home Depot and Lowe's. Like warehouse clubs and office supply category specialists, home improvement centers operate as retailers when they sell merchandise to consumers and as wholesalers when they sell to contractors and other businesses. Although merchandise in home improvement centers is displayed in a warehouse atmosphere, sales people are available to assist customers in selecting merchandise and to tell them how to use it.

Extreme Value Retailers   Extreme value retailers are small, full-line discount stores that offer a limited merchandise assortment at very low prices. The largest extreme value retailers are Family Dollar Stores and Dollar General.[18]

Like limited assortment food retailers, extreme value retailers reduce costs and maintain low prices by buying opportunistically from manufacturers that have excess merchandise, offering a limited assortment, and operating in low-rent locations. They offer a broad but shallow assortment of household goods, health and beauty aids, and groceries. Many value retailers, particularly Family Dollar and Dollar General, target low-income consumers, whose shopping behavior differs from typical discount store or warehouse club customers. For instance, though these consumers demand well-known national brands, they often cannot afford to buy large-sized packages.

Despite some of these chains' names, few sell merchandise for a just dollar. In fact, the two largest—Family Dollar and Dollar General—do not employ a strict dollar limit and sell merchandise for up to $20. The names imply a good value but do not limit customers to the arbitrary dollar price point. Because this segment of the retail industry is growing rapidly, vendors often create special, smaller packages just for them.

Extreme value retailers would not be an obvious choice of consumers for Estée Lauder's and Britt's new lines, because they are not consistent with the brands' image. But if these manufacturers find themselves in an overstock situation, they could utilize these retailers to get rid of the merchandise. For the same reason, they might use off-price retailers.

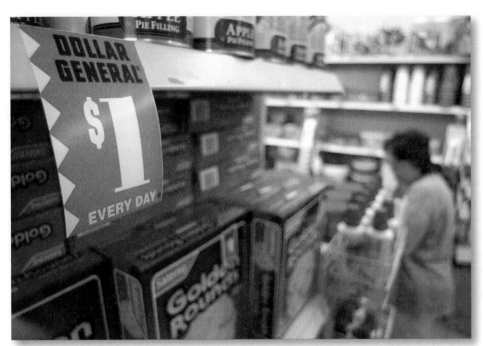

Dollar General is one of the U.S.'s largest extreme value retailers. It has small, full-line discount stores that offer a limited assortment at very low prices.

Off-Price Retailers Off-price retailers, also known as close-out retailers, offer an inconsistent assortment of brand name merchandise at low prices. America's largest off-price retail chains are TJX Companies (which operates Marshalls, Winners, HomeGoods, TJMaxx, AJWright, and HomeSense), Ross Stores, Burlington Coat Factory, Big Lots Inc., and Tuesday Morning. Off-price retailers sell brand name and even designer-label merchandise at 20–60 percent less than department store prices through their unique buying and merchandising practices.[19] Most merchandise is bought opportunistically from manufacturers or other retailers with excess inventory at the end of the season. The merchandise might be in odd sizes or unpopular colors and styles, or it may be irregulars (merchandise that has minor mistakes in construction). Typically, merchandise is purchased at one-fifth to one-fourth of the original wholesale price. Off-price retailers can buy at low prices because they do not ask suppliers for advertising allowances, return privileges, markdown adjustments, or delayed payments.

This outlet mall in San Marco, Texas, has tenants such as Neiman Marcus Last Call, Zegna, Escada, and Salvatore Ferragamo.

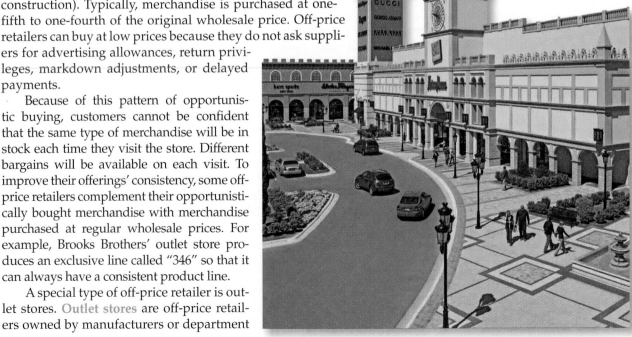

Because of this pattern of opportunistic buying, customers cannot be confident that the same type of merchandise will be in stock each time they visit the store. Different bargains will be available on each visit. To improve their offerings' consistency, some off-price retailers complement their opportunistically bought merchandise with merchandise purchased at regular wholesale prices. For example, Brooks Brothers' outlet store produces an exclusive line called "346" so that it can always have a consistent product line.

A special type of off-price retailer is outlet stores. Outlet stores are off-price retailers owned by manufacturers or department or specialty store chains. Those owned by manufacturers are also referred to as **factory outlets**. Manufacturers view outlet stores as an opportunity to improve their revenues from irregulars, production overruns, and merchandise returned by retailers. Outlet stores also allow manufacturers some control over where their branded merchandise may be sold at discount prices. Retailers with strong brand names such as Saks (Saks OFF 5th) and Brooks Brothers operate outlet stores too. By selling excess merchandise in outlet stores rather than at markdown prices in their primary stores, these department and specialty store chains can maintain an image of offering desirable merchandise at full price.

Now that we've explored the types of stores we can examine how manufacturers and retailers coordinate their retail strategy using the four Ps.

CHECK YOURSELF

1. What are the different types of food retailers? What differences mark their strategies?
2. What are the different types of general merchandise retailers? What differences mark their strategies?

FACILITATING RETAIL STRATEGY USING THE FOUR Ps

Like other marketers, retailers perform important functions that increase the value of the products and services they sell to consumers. We now examine these functions, classified into the four Ps.

Product

To distinguish itself from the competition, Macy's has an exclusive relationship with Tommy Hilfiger in which it is the only department store to offer the popular brand.

A typical grocery store carries 20,000 to 30,000 different items; a regional department store might carry as many as 200,000. Providing the right mix of merchandise and services that satisfies the needs of the target market is one of retailers' most fundamental activities. Offering assortments gives customers a choice. But to reduce transportation costs and handling, manufacturers typically ship cases of merchandise to retailers, such as cartons of mascara or boxes of leather jackets. Because customers generally don't want or need to buy more than one of the same item, retailers break the cases and sell customers the smaller quantities they desire.

Manufacturers don't like to store inventory because their factories and warehouses are typically not available to customers. Consumers don't want to store more than they need because it takes up too much space. Neither group likes to store inventory that isn't being used because doing so ties up money that could be used for something else. Retailers thus provide value to both manufacturers and customers by performing the storage function, though many retailers are beginning to push their suppliers to hold the inventory until they need it. (Recall our discussion of JIT inventory systems in Chapter 15.)

It is difficult for retailers to distinguish themselves from their competitors through the merchandise they carry because competitors can purchase and sell many of the same popular brands. So many retailers have developed private-label brands (also called store brands), which are products developed and marketed by a retailer and available only from that retailer. For example, if you want an I.N.C. dress, you have to go to Macy's.

Retailers often work together with their suppliers to develop an exclusive cobrand, which we described in Chapter 10 as a brand that is developed by a national brand vendor, often in conjunction with a retailer, and is sold exclusively by the retailer. So, for instance, since Estée Lauder has such a strong brand name and already has a strong retail network, it might want to develop an exclusive cobrand with Kohl's. This brand would have a name like Lauder, so that customers would know it was made by Estée Lauder, but it would be available only at Kohl's. Exclusive cobrands have a double benefit—they are exclusively available at only one retailer, and they offer name recognition similar to that of a national brand. The disadvantages of exclusive cobrands include that they can be sold by only one retailer, and the retailer has to share its profits with the national brand manufacturer.

Price

Price helps define the value of both the merchandise and the service, and the general price range of a particular store helps define its image. Although both Saks Fifth Avenue and JCPenney are department stores, their images could not be more different. Thus, when Estée Lauder considers which of these firms is most appropriate for its new line of scarves, leather, and accessories, it must keep customers' perceived images of these retailers' price–quality relationship in mind. It does not, for instance, want to attempt to sell its new line at JCPenney if it is positioning the line with a relatively high price. Price must always be aligned with the other elements of retailing strategy: product, promotion, place, personnel, and presentation. A customer would not expect to pay $20 for a lipstick sold in her local grocery store, but she might question a lipstick's quality if its price is significantly less than $20 at Neiman Marcus. As we discovered in Chapters 13 and 14, there is much more to pricing than simply adding a markup onto a product's cost. Manufacturers must consider at what price they will sell the product to retailers so that both the manufacturer and the retailer can make a reasonable profit. At the same time, both the manufacturer and the retailer are concerned about what the customer is willing and expecting to pay.

Bass Pro Shops Outdoor World in Lawrenceville, Georgia, uses its 43-foot climbing wall as a way to promote its store.

Promotion

Retailers and manufacturers know that good promotion, both within the retail environments and in the media, can mean the difference between flat sales and a growing consumer base. Advertising in traditional media such as newspapers, magazines, and television continues to be important to get customers into the stores. But new avenues to communicate with customers electronically are becoming increasingly important. Once in the store, however, retailers use displays and signs, placed at the point of purchase or in strategic areas such as the end of aisles, to inform customers and stimulate purchases of the featured products.

A coordinated effort between the manufacturer and retailer helps guarantee that the customer receives a cohesive message. The extent to which manufacturers work with their retailers to coordinate promotional activities can ensure that both the manufacturer and the retailer can maintain their consistent images. For example, Estée Lauder might work with its most important retailers to develop advertising and point-of-sale signs.

It may even help defray the costs of advertising by paying all or a portion of the advertising's production and media costs, an agreement called cooperative (co-op) advertising.

Store credit cards and gift cards are more subtle forms of promotion that also facilitate shopping. Retailers also might offer pricing promotions—such as coupons, rebates, in-store or online discounts, or perhaps buy-one-get-one-free offers—to attract consumers and stimulate sales. These promotions play a very important role in driving traffic to retail locations, increasing the average purchase size, and creating opportunities for repeat purchases. But retail promotions also are valuable to customers; they inform customers about what is new and available and how much it costs.

In addition to more traditional forms of promotion, many retailers are devoting more resources to their overall retail environment as a means to promote and showcase what the store has to offer. Their displays of merchandise, both in the store and in windows, have become an important form of promotion. Since many shopping activities can be rather mundane, those retailers that can distinguish themselves with unusual and exciting store atmospherics add value to the shopping experience. Bass Pro Shops Outdoor World in Lawrenceville, Georgia, for instance, offers a 30,000-gallon aquarium stocked with fish for casting demonstrations, an indoor archery range, and a 43-foot climbing wall. These features enhance customers' visual experiences, provide them with educational information, and enhance the store's sales potential by enabling customers to "try before they buy."

A variety of factors influence whether customers will actually buy once they are in the store, some of which are quite subtle. Consumers' perceptions of value and their subsequent patronage are heavily influenced by their perceptions of the store's "look and feel." Music, color, scent, and crowding can also significantly affect the overall shopping experience.[20] Therefore, the extent to which stores offer a more pleasant shopping experience fosters a better mood, resulting in greater spending.

Personal selling and customer service representatives are also part of the overall promotional package. Retailers must provide services that make it easier to buy and use products, and retail associates, whether in the store, on the

As a special promotion, Dillard's Department Store customers in Scottsdale, Arizona, received a passport containing in-store savings for its Lifestyle Squad event.

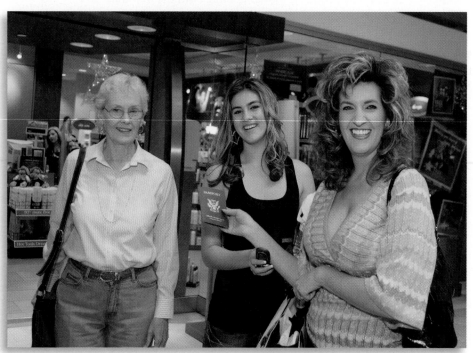

phone, or over the Internet, provide customers with information about product characteristics and availability. They can also facilitate the sale of products or services that consumers perceive as complicated, risky, or expensive, such as an air conditioning unit or a diamond ring. Manufacturers can play an important role in getting retail sales and service associates prepared to sell their products. Britt, for example, could conduct seminars about how to use and sell her new line of green cosmetics. In some retail firms, these salesperson and customer service functions are being augmented, or even replaced, by technology in the form of in-store kiosks, the Internet, or self-checkout lanes.

To make their locations more convenient, Walgreens has some free-standing stores, unconnected to other retailers, so the stores can offer a drive-up window for customers to pick up their prescriptions.

The knowledge retailers can gain from their store personnel and customer relationship management (CRM) databases is key for developing loyal customers and operating loyalty programs. Traditionally, retailers treated all their customers the same way, but today, the most successful retailers concentrate on providing more value to their best customers. Using direct salesperson contact, targeted promotions, and services, they attempt to increase their share of wallet—the percentage of the customer's purchases made from that particular retailer—with their best customers. For instance, Internet retailers can use consumer information to provide a level of personal service that previously was available only through expensive sales people in the best specialty stores.

Place

Retailers already have realized that convenience is a key ingredient to success, and an important aspect of this success is convenient locations.[21] As the old cliché claims, the three most important things in retailing are "location, location, location." Many customers choose stores on the basis of where they are located, which makes great locations a competitive advantage that few rivals can duplicate. For instance, once Starbucks saturates a market by opening in the best locations, it will be difficult for Peet's to break into that same market—where would it put its stores?

In pursuit of better and better locations, retailers are experimenting with different options to reach their target markets. The United States' largest drugstore retailer, Walgreens, has free-standing stores, unconnected to other retailers, so the stores can offer a drive-up window for customers to pick up their prescriptions. Other stores, like Brookstone, have opened stores where they have a captive market—airports.

EXPLORING MULTIPLE CHANNEL OPTIONS

Thus far in this chapter we have explored the most traditional method for a manufacturer to get merchandise to the ultimate consumer, namely, through retailers. There are, however, other options: For instance, a manufacturer can sell directly to consumers using its own stores, catalogs, or the Internet. In this section, we explore the relative advantages of each of these options from both a manufacturer's and a retailer's perspective. We also consider the synergies inherent to providing products through multiple channels.

Channels for Selling to Consumers

Each channel—stores, catalogs, and the Internet—offers its own unique benefits for selling to consumers. See Exhibit 16.4.

EXHIBIT 16.4	Benefits Provided by Different Channels	
Stores	**Catalogs**	**Internet**
Browsing	Convenience	Broader selection
Touching and feeling merchandise	Information	More information
Personal service	Safety	Personalization
Cash and credit payment		Touch and feel attributes
Entertainment and social interaction		
Instant gratification		
Risk reduction		

Store Channel

Stores offer several benefits to customers that they cannot get when they shop through catalogs or on the Internet.

Browsing Shoppers often have only a general sense of what they want (e.g., a sweater, something for dinner, a gift) but don't know the specific item they want. They go to a store to see what is available before they decide what to buy. Although some consumers surf the Web and look through catalogs for ideas, many still prefer browsing in stores.

At LegoLand in Minneapolis's Mall of America, customers can browse, touch, and feel the product, enjoy personal service, be entertained, and interact with others.

Touching and Feeling Products Perhaps the greatest benefit offered by stores is the opportunity for customers to use all five of their senses—touching, smelling, tasting, seeing, and hearing—when examining products.

Personal Service Sales associates have the capability to provide meaningful, personalized information. Sales people can be particularly helpful when purchasing a complicated product, like consumer electronics, or something the customer doesn't know much about, like a diamond ring.

Cash and Credit Payment Stores are the only channel that accepts cash payments. Some customers prefer to pay with cash because it is easy, resolves the transaction immediately, and does not result in potential interest payments. Some customers also prefer to use their credit card or debit card in person rather than to electronically send the payment information via the Internet.

Entertainment and Social Experience In-store shopping can be a stimulating experience for some people, providing a break in their daily routine and enabling them to interact with friends.

Immediate Gratification Stores have the advantage of allowing customers to get the merchandise immediately after they buy it.

Risk Reduction When customers purchase merchandise in stores, the physical presence of the store reduces

Stores provide entertainment or a social experience to customers. They can also touch before purchase and get instant gratification by buying after a demonstration like at this Williams-Sonoma House demonstration by interior designer Charlotte Moss in Beverly Hills, California.

their perceived risk of buying and increases their confidence that any problems with the merchandise will be corrected.

Catalog Channel

The catalog channel provides some benefits to customers that are not available from the store or Internet channels. Catalogs, like all nonstore formats, offer the convenience of looking at merchandise and placing an order from almost anywhere 24/7. However, catalogs also have some advantages over other nonstore formats.

Convenience   The information in a catalog is easily accessible for a long period of time. Consumers can refer to the information in a catalog anytime by simply picking it up from the coffee table. The development of magalogs—catalogs with magazine-type editorial content—enhances consumers' desire to keep catalogs readily available. Williams-Sonoma produces a magalog featuring its gourmet cooking tools and foods for sale, along with kitchen tips and recipes.

Information   Catalogs have information about the products and how they can be used. For example, Pottery Barn (PB) Kids' catalog shows how its products can be put together in a child's room.

Safety   Security in malls and shopping areas is becoming an important concern for many shoppers, particularly the elderly. Nonstore retail formats have an advantage over store-based retailers in that they enable customers to review merchandise and place orders from a safe environment—their homes.

Internet Channel

Shopping over the Internet provides the convenience offered by catalogs and other nonstore formats. However, the Internet, compared with store and catalog channels, also has the potential to offer a greater selection of products and more personalized information about products and services in a relatively short amount of time. It also offers sellers the unique opportunity to collect information about how

People living in London, Ontario, can shop electronically at Harrod's in London, England, in less time than it take, them to visit their local supermarket.

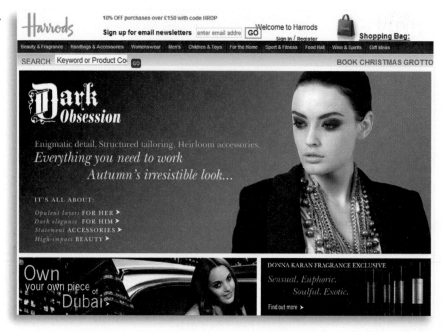

consumers shop—information that they can use to improve the shopping experience across all channels.

Broader Selection   One benefit of the Internet channel, compared with the other two channels, is the vast number of alternatives available to consumers. By shopping on the Internet, consumers can easily "visit" and select merchandise from a broader array of retailers. People living in London, Ontario, can shop electronically at Harrod's in London, England, in less time than it takes them to visit their local supermarket. Web sites typically offer deeper assortments of merchandise (more colors, brands, and sizes) than are available in stores. This offering enables them to satisfy consumer demand for less popular styles, colors, or sizes and still keep their overall inventory costs low.[22]

More Information to Evaluate Merchandise   Using an Internet channel, firms can provide as much information as each customer wants and more information than he or she could get through store or catalog channels. Customers shopping electronically can drill down through Web pages until they have enough information to make a purchase decision. Unlike in catalogs, the information on an electronic channel database can be frequently updated and will always be available—24/7, 365 days per year. Furthermore, retaining knowledgeable sales associates is difficult and, in many cases, not cost-effective. The cost of adding information to an Internet channel is likely to be far less than the cost of continually training thousands of sales associates.

The depth of information available on a Web site even can provide solutions to customer problems. Home Depot walks customers on its Web site through the steps of installation and repair projects, thereby giving do-it-yourselfers confidence prior to tackling home improvement tasks. The directions include the level of difficulty and a list of the tools and materials needed to complete the project successfully.

Virtual communities, networks of people who seek information, products, and services and communicate with one another about specific issues, also help customers solve problems by providing information not readily available through other channels. People who participate in these networks, known as **social shoppers**, seek not just information for future use but also an enhanced emotional connection with other participants during the shopping experience.[23] Some of these social shoppers may spend two or three times the amount of time traditional shoppers spend shopping, and then not make a purchase. It is the experience of shopping they enjoy more than the product or service. Social shopping is explored further in Chapter 17.

Pricegrabber.com and Epinions.com are long-established sites for buyers to compare products and write reviews about more technical products.[24] Other sites, like ThisNext.com, Kaboodle.com, Wists.com, and StyleHive.com, are spearheading a new type of community dedicated to social shopping, which combines shopping and social networking.[25] For instance, if a person is interested in Kona coffee, she would go to www.ThisNext.com and register to create her own pages to collect information about the items she finds. In addition to describing the items and posting Web addresses, she can post images and rate the products. Other people interested in Kona coffee then could find this and similar information easily.[26]

Sears and Macy's have added the ability for customers to post apparel reviews to their Web sites. Other retailers that have added customer comments to their sites include Home Depot, Petco, Cabela's, and Bass Pro Shops. These reviews are not only helpful to their customers but also provide valuable feedback to buyers about what customers like and don't like. Retailers are ideally suited to offer these problem-solving sites for customers because they have the skills to put together merchandise assortments, services, and information to attract members.

Personalization The most significant potential benefit of the Internet channel is its ability to personalize the information for each customer economically, whether in terms of personalized customer service or personalized offerings.

Personalized Customer Service Traditional Internet channel approaches for responding to customer questions—such as FAQ (frequently asked questions) pages and offering an 800 number or e-mail address to ask questions—often do not provide the timely information customers are seeking. To improve customer service from an electronic channel, many firms offer live, online chats. An *online chat*

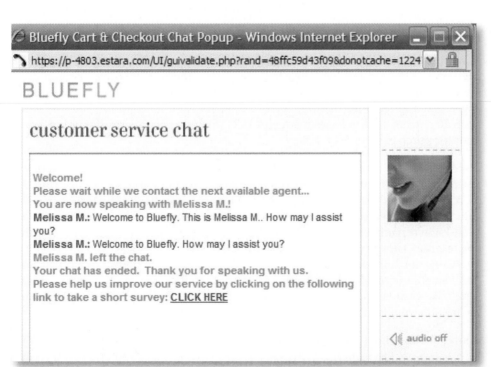

At Bluefly.com, if a visitor lingers on certain items, a window will pop up, offering help.

provides customers with the opportunity to click a button at any time and have an instant messaging e-mail or voice conversation with a customer service representative. This technology also enables firms to send a proactive chat invitation automatically to customers on the site. The timing of these invitations can be based on the time the visitor has spent on the site, the specific page the customer is viewing, or a product on which the customer has clicked. At Bluefly.com, for example, if a visitor searches for more than three items in five minutes, thereby demonstrating more than a passing interest, Bluefly will display a pop-up window with a friendly face offering help.[27]

Personalized Offering   The interactive nature of the Internet also provides an opportunity for retailers to personalize their offerings for each of their customers. For example, at many Web sites, you can create a personal homepage, like My Yahoo, that is tailored to your individual needs. Using a cookie, a small computer program that provides identifying information installed on your hard drive, Amazon serves up personalized homepages with information about books and other products of interest based on visitors' past purchases. Amazon.com will also send interested customers customized e-mail messages that notify them that their favorite author or recording artist has published a new book or released a new CD. Another personalized offering that online retailers are able to present to customers is recommendations of complementary merchandise. Just as a well-trained salesperson would make recommendations to customers prior to checkout, an interactive Web page can make suggestions to the shopper about items that he or she might like to see, such as what other customers who bought the same item also purchased.

Some Internet retailers, like Overstock.com, are able to personalize promotions and homepages on the basis of several attributes tied to the shopper's current or previous Web sessions, such as the time of day, time zone as determined by a computer's Internet address, and assumed gender.[28] Using this information, a retailer can target promotions for collectables to those who have previously searched for similar merchandise or deals on down parkas to those living in colder climates. It can also test the effectiveness of different promotions in real time. For instance, if a 5 percent discount works better than $5 off, it will stick with the more successful promotion.

Selling Merchandise with "Touch-and-Feel" Attributes   When you buy products, some critical information might include "look-and-see" attributes, like color, style, and grams of carbohydrates, or "touch-and-feel" attributes, like how the shirt fits, the ice cream flavor tastes, or the perfume smells. Fit can be predicted well only if the apparel has consistent sizing and the consumer has learned over time which size to buy from a particular brand. Because of the problems of providing touch-and-feel information, apparel retailers experience return rates of more than 20 percent on purchases made through an electronic channel but only 10 percent for purchases made in stores.

Role of Brands   Brands provide a consistent experience for customers that helps overcome the difficulty of not being able to touch and feel merchandise prior to purchase online. Because consumers trust familiar brands, products with important touch-and-feel attributes, such as clothing, perfume, flowers, and food, with well-known name brands sell successfully through nonstore channels including the Internet, catalogs, and TV home shopping.

Consider branded merchandise like Tommy Hilfiger perfume. Even if you can't smell a sample of the perfume before buying it online, you know that it will smell like your last bottle because the manufacturer of Tommy Hilfiger makes sure each bottle smells the same.

Using Technology   Firms with electronic channels are using technology to convert touch-and-feel information into look-and-see information that can be com-

To overcome the limitations associated with trying on clothing, H&M uses virtual models that are constructed on the basis of the shopper's response to questions about his or her body dimensions.

municated through the Internet. Web sites are going beyond offering the basic image to giving customers the opportunity to view merchandise from different angles and perspectives using 3D imaging and/or zoom technology. JCPenney.com has a new interactive shopping tool, for instance, that lets shoppers mix and match 142,000 combinations of window treatments in visual room settings to preview how a particular choice might look at home.[29] The use of these image-enhancing technologies has increased conversion rates (the percentage of consumers who buy the product after viewing it) and reduced returns.

To overcome the limitations associated with trying on clothing, apparel retailers have started to use virtual models on their Web sites. These virtual models enable consumers to see how selected merchandise looks on an image with similar proportions to their own and then rotate the model so the "fit" can be evaluated from all angles. The virtual models are either selected from a set of "prebuilt" models or, as H&M (www.hm.com) does, constructed on the basis of the shopper's response to questions about his or her height, weight, facial, leg, and other body dimensions. At MyShape.com and Zafu.com, consumers respond to a series of questions about their bodies' shape.[30] On the basis of the answers, the site recommends the best-fitting clothing. Landsend.com was among the first to offer custom clothing, such as jeans and khakis featuring selected details like type of wash, rise, and leg shape. At Timberland.com, customers can design custom boots in a variety of colors, monograms, sole colors, and stitching.

Gifts In some situations, touch-and-feel information might be important, but the information in a store is not much better than the information provided electronically. For example, suppose you're buying a bottle of perfume for your mother. Even if you go to the store and smell the samples of all the new scents, you might not get much information to help you determine which one your mother would like. In this situation, stores offer little benefit over an electronic channel in terms of useful information provided about the merchandise. But buying gifts electronically offers the benefit of saving you the time and effort of packing and sending the gift to your mother. For this reason, gifts represent a substantial portion of sales made through the Internet channel.

Power of the Internet 16.1   How Much Is an Amazon.com Customer Worth?[31]

You may be surprised how much an Amazon.com customer is really worth to the company. Apart from having a well-run Internet business, Amazon.com has always focused its strategy around its customers. The Internet retailer began as a book e-tailer and now sells almost everything under the sun, including an array of Web services. It also allows other merchants to sell goods on its Internet site. So, Amazon sells everything. What else?

Jeff Bezos, the company's founder and CEO, has a well-known "obsession" with customers. The customer experience is an important competitive advantage at Amazon.com, and the online retailer uses its technology capabilities to enhance that experience for each and every customer. In addition to its proprietary recommendation system, Amazon.com figures out what its customers want and how to get it to them quickly. In one instance, a customer ordered a $500 Playstation3, intending it to be a Christmas present. When the package did not arrive, the customer visited Amazon's site, which provided a link for him to track the package. The tracking software indicated the game already had been delivered and signed for, but it was nowhere to be found. The logical conclusion was that it had been stolen. The customer contacted Amazon.com through the site, and with few questions asked, Amazon sent the customer another Playstation3, without charging additional shipping charges.

In this case, Amazon.com lost $500, plus shipping, on a mistake that was not even its fault. But because it provided the technical means for the customer to find out what happened and then solved the issue, it not only saved a kid's Christmas but also probably turned the relieved parent into a loyal Amazon.com customer for life. In the end, this customer also likely will communicate his extraordinary experience to many other potential Amazon customers.

Furthermore, because, as one of its limitations, Internet shopping does not give customers the items they buy immediately, as store shopping would, Amazon decided to launch a program that allows customers to pay an annual fee of $79 for unlimited two-day free shipping. In one year, it has foregone more than $600 million in shipping revenue. Although some Wall Street analysts may frown on "unnecessary costs" like these, Amazon maintains 72 million active customers, defined as those that spent at least $184 per year on the site. The average spending per customer the previous year was $150.

For Amazon, maintaining a customer-centric company means exploiting the technology it has developed and knowing that money it spends on customer service does not benefit the bottom line in the short term. The customer service failure recovery undertaken for the missing Playstation3 cost the company a considerable amount of money, but in the long term, the company likely has gained a lifetime customer.

Services Some service providers have been very successful over the Internet, because the look-and-see attributes of their offering can be presented very effectively online. For example, REI Adventures (www.rei.com/adventures) is a subsidiary of REI, the multichannel outdoor sporting goods retailer. You can shop for trips by location, activity, or specialty, such as family, private departures, women, and youth. The site provides biographies of the tour guides in each region and vivid descriptions that make you want to pack your bags and go.

Although Amazon.com began as a bookseller, you can now buy just about anything on its site. But the availability of merchandise alone didn't make Amazon the largest Internet-only retailer. Its commitment to customer service garners loyal and profitable customers, as Power of the Internet 16.1 explains.

Using the Internet to Improve Multichannel Shopping Experience[32]

An electronic channel can provide firms with valuable insights into how and why customers shop and are dissatisfied or satisfied with their experiences. For example, information about how customers shop a merchandise category would be useful for designing a store or a Web site.

The store and Web site layouts need to reflect whether customers shop by brands, size, color, or price point. Customer willingness to substitute one brand for another, for example, is valuable information for assortment planning. To collect this information from a store or catalog would be quite difficult; someone would have to follow shoppers around the store or observe them going through catalog pages. However, collecting data as customers navigate through a Web site is quite easy.

Perceived Risks in Electronic Shopping

Although most consumers have had the opportunity to try out electronic shopping, they also have some concerns about buying products through an electronic channel. The two critical perceived risks are (1) the security of credit card transactions on the Internet and (2) potential privacy violations. Although many consumers remain concerned about credit card security, extensive security problems have been rare. Almost all Internet sellers use sophisticated technologies to encrypt communications.[33] In 2006 however, the security encryption systems for TJX companies (owners of Marshall's and TJ Maxx) were hacked, exposing 45.7 million credit and debit cards to theft. As a result, customers are leery, and banks are suing the retailer for neglecting to encrypt this secure information properly.[34]

Consumers also are concerned about the ability of Internet sellers to collect information about their purchase history, personal information, and search behavior on the Internet. Consumers may be worried about how this information will be used in the future. Will it be sold to other firms, or will the consumer receive unwanted promotional materials online or in the mail? To answer these questions, consider Ethical and Societal Dilemma 16.1 on the next page.

EVOLUTION TOWARD MULTICHANNEL MARKETING

Traditional store-based and catalog retailers and some manufacturers are placing more emphasis on their electronic channels and evolving into multichannel retailers—that is, retailers that use some combination of stores, catalogs, and the Internet to sell merchandise—for four reasons. First, the electronic channel gives them an opportunity to overcome the limitations of their primary existing format, as we described in the previous sections. Second, by using an electronic channel, they can expand their market reach. Third, providing a multichannel offering builds share of wallet, or the percentage of total purchases made by a customer from a particular seller. Fourth, an electronic channel enables firms to gain valuable insights into their customers' shopping behavior.

Overcoming the Limitations of an Existing Format

One of the greatest constraints facing store-based retailers is the size of their stores. The amount of merchandise that can be displayed and offered for sale in stores is limited. By blending stores with Internet-enabled kiosks, retailers can dramatically expand the assortment offered to their customers. For example, Wal-Mart and Home Depot have a limited number of major appliance floor models in their stores, but customers can use a Web-enabled kiosk to look at an expanded selection of appliances, get more detailed information, and place orders.

Another limitation that store-based retailers face is inconsistent execution. The availability and knowledge of sales associates can vary considerably across stores or even within a store at different times during the day. This inconsistency is most problematic for retailers selling new, complex merchandise. For example, consumer electronic retailers such as Best Buy find it difficult to communicate the features and benefits of the newest products to all of their sales associates. To address this problem, Best Buy installed kiosks designed to be used by sales associates and customers to obtain product information.

A catalog retailer also can use its electronic channel to overcome the limitations of its catalog. Once a catalog is printed, it cannot be updated with price changes and new merchandise. Therefore, retailers like Lands' End use Internet sites to

The definition of personal privacy depends on whom you are talking to and in which country. Some people define personal information as all information that is not publicly available; others include both public (e.g., driver's license, mortgage data) and private (hobbies, income) information. Internet retailers need to take the necessary precautions to protect consumer privacy by incorporating privacy safety software such as firewalls and encrypting data every time it is transferred to prevent it being intercepted.[35]

Who is responsible for ensuring consumer privacy? In the United States, Americans rely on retailers to protect consumer privacy. Existing legislation for consumer privacy is restricted to the protection of information in government functions and practices in credit reporting, video rentals, banking, and health care. However, the European Union (EU), Australia, New Zealand, and Canada have different and more stringent consumer privacy laws. Some of the provisions of the EU directive on consumer privacy include the following:

- Businesses can collect consumer information only if they have clearly defined the purpose, such as completing the transaction.

- The purpose must be disclosed to the consumer from whom the information is being collected.

- The information can be used only for that specific purpose.

- The business can keep the information only for the stated purpose. If the business wants to use the information for another purpose, it must initiate a new collection process.

- Businesses operating in Europe can export information from EU countries only to importing countries with similar privacy policies. Thus, U.S. retailers, hotel chains, airlines, and banks cannot transfer information from Europe to the United States because the United States does not have similar privacy policies.

Basically, the EU perspective is that consumers own their personal information, so retailers must get consumers to agree explicitly to share this personal information. This agreement is referred to as an **opt in**. In contrast, personal information in the United States is generally viewed as being in the public domain, and retailers can use it in any way they desire. American consumers must explicitly tell retailers not to use their personal information—they must **opt out**.[36]

The EU has delayed enforcement of its directive. The United States is currently negotiating a safe harbor program that would enable U.S. companies abiding by the EU directives to export information. However, because of increasing concerns about consumer privacy, Congress is considering new legislation on consumer privacy. The Federal Trade Commission has developed the following set of principles for fair information practices:

- *Notice and awareness.* Covers the disclosure of information practices, including a comprehensive statement of information use, such as information storage, manipulation, and dissemination.

- *Choice/consent.* Includes both opt-out and opt-in options and allows consumers the opportunity to trade information for benefits.

- *Access/participation.* Allows for the confirmation of information accuracy by consumers.

- *Integrity/security.* Provides controls for the theft of and tampering with personal information.

- *Enforcement/redress.* Provides a mechanism to ensure compliance by participating companies.[37]

In summary, there is growing consensus that personal information must be fairly collected, that the collection must be purposeful, and that the data should be relevant, maintained as accurate, essential to the business, subject to the rights of the owning individual, kept reasonably secure, and transferred only with the permission of the consumer. To address these concerns, many Internet sellers that collect customer information have privacy policies. The Electronic Privacy Information Center (www.epic.org) recommends that privacy policies clearly state what information is collected from each visitor and how it will be used, give consumers a choice as to whether they give information, and allow them to view and correct any personal information held by an online retail site. Internet sellers need to assure their customers that information about them is held securely and not passed on to other companies without the customer's permission.

provide customers with real-time information about stock availability and price reductions on clearance merchandise.

Expanding Market Presence

Adding an electronic channel is particularly attractive to firms with strong brand names but limited locations and distribution. For example, retailers such as Harrod's, IKEA, and Neiman Marcus are widely known for offering unique, high-quality merchandise, but they require customers to travel to England or major U.S. cities to buy many of the items they carry. Interestingly, most of these store-based retailers currently are multichannel retailers through their successful catalog and Internet offerings.

Increasing Share of Wallet[38]

Although offering an electronic channel may draw some sales from other channels, using it with other channels can result in consumers making more total purchases from the seller. Traditional single-channel retailers can use one channel to promote the services offered by other channels. For example, the URL of a store's Web site can be advertised on in-store signs, shopping bags, credit card billing statements, POS receipts, and the print or broadcast advertising used to promote the stores. The retailer's electronic channel can be used to stimulate store visits by announcing special store events and promotions. Store-based retailers can leverage their stores to lower the cost of fulfilling orders and processing returned merchandise if they use the stores as "warehouses" for gathering merchandise for delivery to customers. Customers also can be offered the opportunity to pick up and return merchandise at the retailer's stores rather than pay shipping charges. Many retailers will waive shipping charges when orders are placed online or through the catalog if the customer physically comes in the store.

The URL of Levi's Web site can be used on its shopping bags to promote both its stores and Web site.

Gaining Insights into Customers' Shopping Behaviors

As we mentioned previously, it is difficult to observe customers' behavior in stores or when they shop catalogs, because most people prefer not to have sales clerks constantly tailing them in stores or visiting their homes, pestering them with questions about why they have taken each action they take. Therefore, online retailing provides key insights into the choices consumers make. However, people often shop differently in the different channels; for example they might browse extensively online but dash into and out of stores to get what they need. If a retailer gathers data about a customer's actions in all of its channels, it should be able to put together a clearer, more detailed picture of how and why customers patronize—or don't patronize—its channels and offerings.

Will Manufacturers Bypass Retailers and Sell Directly to Consumers?

Disintermediation occurs when a manufacturer sells directly to consumers, bypassing retailers. Retailers are concerned about disintermediation because manufacturers can get direct access to their consumers by establishing a retail site on the Internet. Naturalizer brand shoes and accessories are sold through its Web site (www.naturalizer.com) and at the same time directly to retailers such as Zappos.com or Macy's. However, Exhibit 16.5 illustrates why most manufacturers are reluctant to engage in retailing.

Manufacturers lack many of the critical skills necessary to sell merchandise electronically, and retailers are typically more efficient in dealing with customers directly than are manufacturers. They have considerably more experience than manufacturers in distributing merchandise directly to customers, providing

EXHIBIT 16.5	Capabilities Needed for Multichannel Retailing		
Capabilities	**Store-Based Retailers**	**Catalog Retailers**	**Merchandise Manufacturers**
Develop assortments and manage inventory	High	High	Low
Manage people in remote locations	High	Low	Low
Efficiently distribute merchandise to stores	High	Low	High
Present merchandise effectively in a printed format and distribute catalogs	Medium	High	Low
Present merchandise effectively on a Web site	Medium	High	Low
Process orders from individual customers electronically	Medium	High	Low
Efficiently distribute merchandise to homes and accept returns	Medium	High	Low
Integrate information systems to provide a seamless customer experience across channels	Low	Medium	Low

complementary assortments, and collecting and using information about customers. Retailers also have an advantage because they can provide a broader array of products and services, such as various brands or special offerings, to solve customer problems. For example, if consumers want to buy the components for a home entertainment center from a variety of manufacturers, they must go to several different Internet sites and still cannot be sure that the components will work together or arrive at the same time.

Manufacturers that sell directly to consumers risk losing the support of the retailers they bypass. Therefore, many manufacturers, such as Energizer (www.energizer.com), the world's largest producer of batteries and flashlights, use their Web sites only as a marketing tool to show customers which products are available and then direct them to nearby stores where they can purchase the products.

Summing Up

1. What are the issues manufacturers consider when choosing retail partners?

Because manufacturers want their offerings available where, when, and in the form that customers prefer, they must consider whether customers expect to find their products at specific retailers. For example, customers probably do not expect, or want, to find a value-priced product at a luxury retailer. The manufacturer also must consider the basic channel structure in which it functions, along with the characteristics of the members of that

channel. Finally, manufacturers need to determine the distribution intensity they prefer: exclusive, intensive, or selective.

2. What types of retailers are available for distributing products?

Retailers generally fall into one of two categories: food retailers and general merchandise retailers. Each of the categories consists of various formats, including supermarkets, supercenters, warehouse clubs, convenience stores, department stores, discount stores, specialty retailers, drugstores, category specialists, extreme value retailers, and off-price stores.

3. **How do manufacturers and retailers work together to develop a strategy?**

To develop a coordinated strategy—which represents a key goal for an effective channel partnership between retailers and manufacturers—these functions need to consider all of the four Ps in conjunction: product, place, promotion, and price.

4. **Why is multichannel marketing becoming such a prevalent channel strategy?**

The various types of retail channels—stores, catalogs, and the Internet—each offer their own benefits and limitations, including those related to availability, convenience, and safety, among others. If a retailer adopts a multichannel strategy, it can exploit the benefits and mitigate the limitations of each channel and help expand its overall market presence. Furthermore, a multichannel strategy offers it the chance to gain a greater share of customers' wallets and more insight into their buying behaviors.

Key Terms

- big box retailers, 499
- category killers, 499
- category specialists, 499
- close-out retailers, 501
- convenience stores, 496
- conventional supermarket, 494
- conversion rates, 511
- cookie, 510
- cooperative (co-op) advertising, 504
- department stores, 496
- disintermediation, 515
- distribution intensity, 492

- drugstores, 499
- exclusive distribution, 492
- extreme value food retailers, 494
- extreme value retailers, 500
- factory outlets, 502
- full-line discount stores, 497
- home improvement center, 500
- intensive distribution, 492
- irregulars, 501
- limited assortment supermarkets, 494
- multichannel retailers, 513
- multichannel strategy, 490

- off-price retailers, 501
- online chat, 509
- opt in, 514
- opt out, 514
- outlet stores, 501
- retailing, 488
- selective distribution, 492
- share of wallet, 505
- social shoppers, 508
- specialty stores, 498
- supercenters, 495
- virtual communities, 508
- warehouse clubs, 495

Marketing Applications

1. Nike and Puma both make sneakers. Do they pursue an intensive, an exclusive, or a selective distribution intensity strategy? Would you suggest any changes to this strategy?

2. Why don't traditional department stores have the same strong appeal to American consumers that they once enjoyed during their heyday in the last half of the twentieth century? Discuss which types of retailers are now competing with department stores.

3. Assume that adidas, the shoe manufacturer, has decided to sell expensive wristwatches for men and women. What factors should it consider when developing its strategy for choosing retail partners?

4. Some argue that retailers can be eliminated from the distribution channel because they only add costs to the final product without creating any value-added services in the process. Do you agree with this perspective? Is it likely that consumers will make most purchases directly from manufacturers in the near future? Provide justification for your answers.

5. Many years ago, the corporations that sold gasoline made the strategic move to include a substantial offering of food items. Today, it is rare to find a gas station that does not sell food items. Into which category of food retailer did these service stations fall? Do you think this was a prudent strategic direction for these corporations? Explain your logic.

6. Assume you have been given some money but told that it must be invested in a retailer's stock. In which type of retailer would you choose to

invest? Which specific retailer? Provide a rationale for your answers.

7. Provide examples of how manufacturers work with retailers to jointly plan and implement the four Ps.

8. Why are so many bricks-and-mortar retailers adopting a multichannel strategy?

9. You can purchase apparel at a discount store, specialty store, category specialist, off-price retailer, department store, or Internet-only store. From which of these types of stores do you shop? Explain why you prefer one type over another.

10. Suppose you are the confectionary buyer for a regional chain of grocery stores. The store policy is to charge a "substantial" slotting fee for the placement of new items. Slotting fees were originally designed to cover the costs of placing new products on the shelves, such as adjustments to computer systems and realignment of warehouse and store space. Over the years, these fees have become larger, and they are now a significant source of revenue for the chain. A local minority-owned manufacturer of a popular brand of specialty candy would like to sell to your chain, but claims that the slotting fee is too high and does not reflect the real cost of adding their candy. Discuss the ethical implications of such a policy. What should the chain do?

---

www.mhhe.com/
grewal2e

Quiz Yourself

1. The Gap, Lenscrafters, and Foot Locker are all examples of:
   a. department stores.
   b. off-price retailers.
   c. discount stores.
   d. specialty stores.
   e. extreme value retailers.

2. Wal-Mart and Target dominate the _____ industry in the United States.

   a. department store
   b. off-price retailer
   c. discount store
   d. specialty store
   e. csategory specialist

(Answers to these two questions are provided on page 624)

Go to www.mhhe.com/grewal2e to practice an additional 11 questions.

Net Savvy

1. How do Jcrew.com and Gap.com provide value to their customers beyond the physical products that they sell? Why would a customer purchase online instead of going to the store? Under what circumstances would the customer prefer a store-based experience?

2. Using either your own experience or that of a friend, select a familiar multichannel retailer. Evaluate its Web site in terms of how well it provides value to its customers. Do you believe that offering multiple selling channels to customers enhances their shopping experience? How does it help the retailer? Explain your answer.

Chapter Case Study

STAPLES, INC.[39]

Staples operates in the highly competitive, $240 billion office products market, which historically has been served by traditional office products retailers. These traditional retailers purchase a significant portion of their merchandise from wholesalers that purchase merchandise from manufacturers. Traditional office supply retailers often employ commissioned sales people who use the wholesaler's catalog to present their business customers with products to select.

But due to their ability to sell at lower prices, mass merchandisers, warehouse clubs, and discount retailers have taken market share away from these traditional retailers, and the industry has grown substantially in the past two decades with the emergence of office supply superstores like Staples, Office Depot, and Office Max. In addition, mail order firms, contract stationery businesses, electronic commerce wholesalers, and manufacturers that sell directly to the consumer all compete for sales. However, though the office products business has changed in recent years, a significant portion of the market is still served by small retailers.

Regardless, the superstores have dramatically changed the landscape of the office supply industry. First, they greatly expanded the use of the retail store format to distribute office supply products, capitalizing in part on the significant increase in the number of home offices. Prior to the mid-1980s, office supply customers primarily placed their orders through commissioned sales people. Second, an even more recent change in this industry has been the greater use of the Internet for ordering office supply products. These changes have resulted in a very price-competitive market for office supplies, dominated by a small number of providers.

COMPANY BACKGROUND

Originally opened in 1986 by executive-turned-entrepreneur Tom Stemberg, Staples' sales exceeded $19 billion in 2007.[40] Staples has been credited with pioneering the high-volume office products superstore concept. By evolving its original mission of slashing the costs and eliminating the hassles of running an office, to making it easy to buy office products, Staples has become the world's largest office products company.

To distinguish itself in this competitive industry, Staples strives to provide a unique shopping experience to customers in all its market segments. Central to maintaining customer satisfaction is developing strong customer relationship skills and broad knowledge about office products in all associates hired by the company. Therefore, Staples includes formal training as an integral part of the development of its associates. Another truly important aspect of customer service is the availability of merchandise. In the office supply industry, customers have very specific needs, such as finding an ink cartridge for a particular printer, and if the store is out of stock of a needed item, the customer may never come back.

Staples uses various channels of distribution to address the needs of its different segments. Smaller businesses are generally served by a combination of retail stores, catalog, and the Internet. Retail operations focus on serving the needs of consumers and small businesses, whereas the catalog and Internet operations focus on customers who need delivery of their office products and other specialized services. The typical Staples retail store has approximately 7,000 stockkeeping units (SKUs), but Staples.com offers about 45,000 SKUs.

Staples believes that the Internet channel has helped it increase its sales while reducing its overhead costs. It has developed three standalone Web sites: Staples.com, a public Web site; Quill.com, an e-commerce site for medium-sized businesses; and StaplesLink.com, a secure, customized, e-commerce procurement Web site for large customers with contracts with Staples. In addition, the company has placed Staples.com kiosks in its stores so that customers can make purchases of any product, even if they are not stocked in the store. Customers can pay for these purchases at the register or through Staples.com and have the product delivered to their home or business.[41] This multichannel approach allows Staples to increase its productivity by stocking only fast-moving items in stores but not sacrificing product availability.

MULTICHANNEL INTEGRATION

Staples' overall goal has been to become the leading office products and service provider by combining its existing experience, extensive distribution infrastructure, and customer service expertise with Web-based information technology. As a result, the integration of different channels of distribution into one seamless customer experience has been of particular interest to the company. Staples, like many other multichannel retailers, has found that many customers use multiple channels to make their Staples purchases and that sales increase when customers use more than one channel (customers that shop two channels spend twice as much as a single-channel shopper; a tri-channel shopper spends about three times as much as a single-channel shopper). Therefore, the greater the number of channels a particular customer shops, the greater the overall expenditure he or she is likely to make.

Staples faces several challenges in integrating its channels of distribution, most of which are related to its Internet channel. First, it must consider the extent to which the Internet may cannibalize its retail store sales. The most attractive aspect of the Internet is its potential to attract new customers and sell more to existing customers. But if overall sales are flat, that is, if online retailing only converts retail store sales to Internet sales, Staples suffers increased overhead costs and poorer overall productivity. Second, Staples must be concerned about the stock position of its retail stores compared with that of alternative channels. Since a retail store cannot carry as much merchandise as the Internet channel, the challenge is keeping an appropriate balance between minimizing stockouts and avoiding the proliferation of too many SKUs in the retail stores. Finally, Staples has to contend with price competition, both within its own multichannel organization and from competitors.

Questions

1. Assess the extent to which Staples has developed a successful multichannel strategy. What factors have contributed to its success?

2. What are the advantages and disadvantages of using kiosks as a part of its approach?

3. How should Staples assess which SKUs to keep in its stores versus on the Internet?

4. How can they respond to lower prices on the Internet than in stores, both between their own channels and competitive retailers?

VALUE
COMMUNICATION

CHAPTER 17
Integrated Marketing Communications

CHAPTER 18
Advertising, Public Relations, and Sales Promotions

CHAPTER 19
Personal Selling and Sales Management

In Section Seven we explore value communication. Today, value communication methods are more complex because of new technologies that have added e-mail, blogs, Internet, and podcasts to the advertising mix that once utilized only radio, television, newspapers, and magazines to relay messages to consumers. Chapter 17 introduces the breadth of integrated marketing communications. Chapter 18 discusses advertising, public relations, and sales promotions. Chapter 19 covers personal selling.

Assessing the Marketplace

Understanding the Marketplace

Targeting the Marketplace

Value Creation

Value Capture

Value Delivery: Designing the Channel and Supply Chain

Value Communication

INTEGRATED MARKETING COMMUNICATIONS

LEARNING OBJECTIVES

- How do customers perceive marketing communications?
- Why are some media channels growing while others are shrinking?
- How should firms use marketing metrics to plan for and measure integrated marketing communications (IMC) success?
- Why are some governmental agencies and consumer groups concerned about certain innovative IMC strategies?

The carbonated beverage market is a relatively saturated one in which mostly brand-loyal consumers stick with their favorites and their consistent drink patterns. So for a company that wants to increase its market share, where should it turn?

The answer to this question relies a little bit on some topics already covered—effective branding, going global, retailing effectively. But it also requires an approach that ensures companies can communicate the value of their offerings in diverse, well-rounded ways. Consider, for example, the latest trend in soda marketing: diet colas that avoid the label "diet."

When Diet Pepsi Max and Coke Zero began to enter the marketplace, the two cola giants worked hard to deliver a consistent message that indicated to consumers that this was not their mothers' diet drink. Facing a generally feminine reputation—"only women drink diet soda"—the cola makers recognized an untapped market consisting largely of younger men who were way too tough (or too worried about appearing tough) to drink diet colas.

After developing products to fill this untapped niche (see Chapter 11), PepsiCo and Coca-Cola needed to tell consumers that these drinks could offer value to male consumers. To avoid any confusion, the entire package of marketing communications had to send this message consistently. Therefore, the colas come in dark, masculine colors like black and red for Coke Zero and dark blue and steel grey for Diet Pepsi Max. The names themselves avoid overly explicit references to dieting; Coca-Cola calls its offering a "calorie-free cola" instead of ever using the term "diet." And though

Diet Pepsi Max uses the word, it is the smallest of the title terms on the bottles and cans; MAX is what appears largest, boldest, and capitalized.

To go along with its innovative product and market-specific packaging, Pepsi launched an advertising campaign entitled, "Wake up, people!" Commercials promote Diet Pepsi Max as a solution to yawning, which becomes contagious and interrupts vital moments in life, such as a wedding or a job interview. During the 2008 Super Bowl, the brand reached millions of viewers with an ad full of drowsy people who popped awake and began bobbing their heads to the dancehall favorite, "What Is Love?" after they drank the ginseng-infused, higher caffeine beverage. The ad also appeals to pop culture by acknowledging the cultural phenomenon created around the tune by the *Saturday Night Live* skit featuring two brothers whose heads never stopped bouncing.[1]

If the Super Bowl seems not specific enough to male consumers, perhaps NASCAR may be more so. Therefore, Coke is focusing more on the Daytona 500, releasing advertising in which two actors, claiming to be employees of regular Coca-Cola, extend a running joke about suing Coke Zero for "taste infringement" by trying to solicit NASCAR drivers to do whatever it takes to ensure no Coke Zero appears in the winner's circle. In one exchange with Jeff Burton, after referring to the Coke Zero brand as "soda pirates," the fake brand managers corner Jamie McMurray outside the Sprint Cup garage and ask, "Would you be willing to throw a race?" A stunned McMurray replies, "I don't think so, no. . . ."[2]

On the Internet, Pepsi offers ads on Facebook, Yahoo, pepsimax.com, and wake-uppeople.com. In addition, it is attempting to use the still untraditional mode of viral marketing through its Web site, which features a yawn-a-thon, a page on which people can donate their yawns by uploading photos, as well as a means for consumers to send wake-up calls to their friends narrated by Ben Stein, the comedian best known for his snore-inducing turn as a teacher in *Ferris Bueller's Day Off*.[3]

Coke also plays on its ongoing theme online, allowing visitors to cocacolazero.com to send an e-mail to a friend they believe may be copying them (as Coke Zero is reputed to be copying Coca-Cola) and "sue" them for such violations as "Joke Theft," "Biting on Style," or "Getting the Same Tattoo."[4]

As these popular campaigns attest, each element of an integrated marketing communication (IMC) strategy must have a well-defined purpose and support and extend the message delivered by all the other elements.

● ● ●

Throughout this book, we have focused our attention on how firms create value by developing products and services. In Chapters 10, 11, and 12, we also focused on how they deliver value to customers. However, consumers are not likely to come flocking to new products and services unless they are aware of them. Therefore, marketers must consider how to communicate the value of a new product and/or service—or more specifically, the value proposition—to the target market. The "calorie-free" cola examples illustrate how a firm can develop a communication strategy to demonstrate the value of its product, but let's begin our subsequent consideration by examining what IMC is, how it has developed, and how it contributes to value creation.

Integrated marketing communications (IMC) represents the Promotion P of the four Ps. It encompasses a variety of communication disciplines—general advertising, personal selling, sales promotion, public relations, direct marketing, public relations, electronic media and community building—in combination to provide clarity, consistency, and maximum communicative impact.[5] Instead of consisting of separated marketing communication elements with no unified control, IMC programs regard each of the firm's marketing communications elements as part of a whole, each of which offers a different means to connect with the target audience. This integration of elements provides the firm with the best means to reach the target audience with the desired message, and it enhances the value story by offering a clear and consistent message.

There are three elements in any IMC strategy: the consumer, the channels through which the message is communicated, and the evaluation of the results of the communication, as we depict in Exhibit 17.1. This chapter is organized around these three elements. In the first section, the focus is on *consumers*, so we examine how consumers receive communications, whether via media or other methods, as well as how the delivery of that communication affects a message's form and contents. The second section examines the various *communication channels* that make up the components of IMC and how each is used in an overall IMC strategy. The third section considers how the level of complexity in IMC strategies leads marketers to design new ways to measure the *results* of IMC campaigns. The chapter concludes with a discussion of some legal and ethical issues arising from the use of these new forms of marketing communications.

EXHIBIT 17.1   Integrated Marketing Communications

COMMUNICATING WITH CONSUMERS

As the number of communication media has increased, the task of understanding how best to reach target consumers has become far more complex. In this section, we examine a model that describes how communications go from the firm to the consumer and the factors that affect the way the consumer perceives the message. Then we look at how marketing communications influence consumers—from making them aware that a product or service exists to moving them to buy.

The Communication Process

Exhibit 17.2 illustrates the communication process. Let's first define each component and then discuss how they interact.

The Sender   The message originates from the sender, who must be clearly identified to the intended audience. For instance, an organization such as Home Depot working with one of their vendors, Stanley Tools, can send a message that it is having a special Father's Day sale.

The Transmitter   The sender works with the creative department, whether in-house or from a marketing (or advertising) agency, to develop marketing communications. Stanley Tools likely develops ad material with its advertising agency and provides the material to Home Depot. Such an agency or intermediary is the transmitter.

Encoding   Encoding means converting the sender's ideas into a message, which could be verbal, visual, or both. Home Depot may take out full-page ads in every major newspaper proclaiming: "Amazing Father's Day Deals at 25 Percent Off!" A television commercial showing men examining and testing tools at Home Depot is another way to encode the message that "there are great deals to be had." As the old saying goes, a picture can be worth a thousand words. But the most important facet of encoding is not what is sent but rather what is

EXHIBIT 17.2	The Communication Process

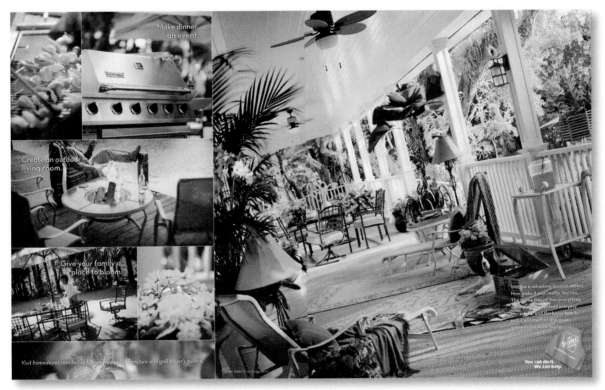

Which component of the communication process does this Home Depot ad exemplify?

received. Home Depot shoppers must believe that the sale is substantial enough to warrant a trip to a store.

The Communication Channel   The communication channel is the medium—print, broadcast, the Internet—that carries the message. Home Depot could transmit through television, radio, and various print advertisements, and it realizes that the media chosen must be appropriate to connect itself (the sender) with its desired recipient. So Home Depot might advertise on HGTV and in *Better Homes and Gardens*.

The Receiver   The receiver is the person who reads, hears, or sees and processes the information contained in the message and/or advertisement. The sender, of course, hopes that the person receiving it will be the one for whom it was originally intended. For example, Home Depot wants its message received and decoded properly by the families of fathers who are likely to shop in its stores. Decoding refers to the process by which the receiver interprets the sender's message.

Noise   Noise is any interference that stems from competing messages, a lack of clarity in the message, or a flaw in the medium, and it poses a problem for all communication channels. Home Depot may choose to advertise in newspapers that its target market doesn't read, which means the rate at which the message is received by those to whom it has relevance has been slowed considerably. As we have already defined, encoding is what the sender intends to say, and decoding is what the receiver hears. If there is a difference between them, it is probably due to noise.

Feedback Loop   The feedback loop allows the receiver to communicate with the sender and thereby informs the sender whether the message was received and decoded properly. Feedback can take many forms: a customer's purchase of the item, a complaint or compliment, the redemption of a coupon or rebate, and so forth. If Home Depot observes an increase in store traffic and sales, its managers know

Receivers decode messages differently. What does the Taco Bell sign mean to you?

that their intended audience received the message and understood that there were great Father's Day bargains to be found in the store.

How Consumers Perceive Communication

The actual communication process is not as simple as the model in Exhibit 17.2 implies. Each receiver may interpret the sender's message differently, and senders often adjust their message according to the medium used and the receivers' level of knowledge about the product or service.

Receivers Decode Messages Differently   Each receiver decodes a message in his or her own way, which is not necessarily the way the sender intended. Different people shown the same message will often take radically different meanings from it. For example, what does the image on the left convey to you?

If you are a user of this brand, it may convey satisfaction. If you recently went on a diet and gave up your favorite Mexican food, it may convey dismay or a sense of loss. If you have chosen to be a nonuser, it may convey some disgust. If you are a recently terminated employee, it may convey anger. The sender has little, if any, control over what meaning any individual receiver will take from the message.[6]

Senders Adjust Messages According to the Medium and Receivers' Traits   Different media communicate in very different ways, so marketers make adjustments to their messages and media depending on whether they want to communicate with suppliers, shareholders, customers, or the general public, as well as the specific segments of those groups.[7] For example, Peapod is a Chicago-based company that takes grocery orders online and then delivers the orders to customers' doors. It found that its business dropped dramatically in the late spring, as winter-weary Chicagoans finally ventured out to get some sun and perhaps hit the grocery store on their own. Therefore, Peapod refocused its advertising efforts. Instead of using direct mail or traditional advertising, it contracted with companies that would insert coupons for Peapod's services into employees' pay envelopes. By adjusting its communication medium and message, Peapod could attract customers, tired after a long day of work, who wanted their groceries waiting for them at home—regardless of whether the sun was shining.[8]

Online grocery retailer, Peapod, adjusted its communication medium and message to attract more customers.

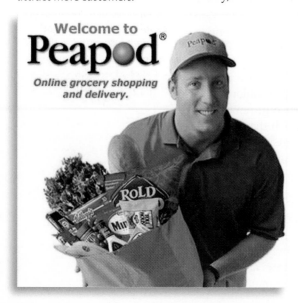

The AIDA Model

Clearly, IMC is not a straightforward process. After being exposed to a marketing communication, consumers go through several steps before actually buying or taking some other action. There is not always a direct link between a particular marketing communication and a consumer's purchase.

To create effective IMC programs, marketers must understand how marketing communications work. Generally, marketing communications move consumers stepwise through a series of mental stages, for which there are several models. The most common is the AIDA model (Exhibit 17.3),[9] which suggests that Awareness leads to Interest, which leads to Desire, which leads to Action. At each stage, the consumer makes judgments about whether to take the next step in the process. Customers actually have three types of responses, so the AIDA model is also known as the "think, feel, do" model. In making a purchase decision, consumers go through each of the AIDA steps to some degree, but the steps may not always follow the AIDA order. For instance, during an impulse purchase, a consumer may "feel" and "do" before he or she "thinks."

EXHIBIT 17.3	The AIDA Model

Action

Desire

Interest

Awareness

Think   Feel   Do

Awareness Even the best marketing communication can be wasted if the sender doesn't gain the attention of the consumer first. Brand awareness refers to a potential customer's ability to recognize or recall that the brand name is a particular type of retailer or product/service. Thus, brand awareness is the strength of the link between the brand name and the type of merchandise or service in the minds of customers.

There are a number of awareness metrics, from aided recall to top-of-mind awareness. Aided recall is when consumers indicate they know the brand when the name is presented to them. Top-of-mind awareness, the highest level of awareness,

Senders must adjust messages according to the receivers' traits. LG, for instance, uses the ad on the left to target consumers for its Super Blu dual format high-definition player. The LG ad on the right is targeted to the B2B audience. A B2B customer can interact directly with a firm's products using its digital display.

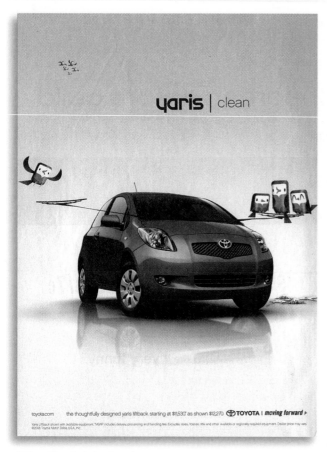

When Toyota introduced the Yaris, it used multiple communication channels to catch the attention of its younger target market.

occurs when consumers mention a specific brand name first when they are asked about a product or service. For example, Harley Davidson has top-of-mind awareness if a consumer responds "Harley" when asked about American-made motorcycles. High top-of-mind awareness means that a product or service probably will be carefully considered when customers decide to shop for it. Manufacturers, retailers, and service providers build top-of-mind awareness by having memorable names; repeatedly exposing their name to customers through advertising, locations, and sponsorships; and using memorable symbols.

When Toyota introduced the Yaris, a smaller, well-designed car that tried to appeal to younger customers, the carmaker swarmed consumers with notifications. In addition to traditional print and television advertising, the Yaris appears on its own MySpace page, the Yaris Web site, and direct messages sent to mobile phones. Then, playing on the popularity of the Fox network's show *Prison Break*, Yaris sponsored a special insert in *TV Guide* devoted to the show, in which pictures of the Yaris models appear to be tattooed on a man's chest—just as a crucial plot point hinges on a tattoo in *Prison Break*.[10] With this multichannel approach, Toyota ensured that not just those looking for a new car but also anyone interested in television would get to know its new product line. Even if someone passed over or ignored one of the communication channels, odds remained good that another would catch the potential customer's attention.

Interest   Once the consumer is aware that the company or product exists, communication must work to increase his or her interest level. It isn't enough to let people know that the product exists; consumers must be persuaded that it is a product worth investigating. Marketers do so by ensuring that the ad's message includes attributes that are of interest to the target audience. To appeal to younger consumers hoping to find a car with good fuel efficiency, Toyota's ads for the Yaris show it plucking a single coin from a piggy bank or smashing a "spider" with gas pumps for legs.[11] Through these communications, Toyota hopes to pique consumers' interest so much that they do something about it.

Desire   After the firm has piqued the interest of its target market, the goal of subsequent IMC messages should move the consumer from "I like it" to "I want it." For instance, in addition to emphasizing its fuel efficiency and affordability, Toyota tries to make the Yaris appear rather tough to differentiate it from "softer" fuel-efficient cars and thus make the car seem unique.[12]

Action   The ultimate goal of any marketing communication is to drive the receiver to action. If the message has caught consumers' attention and made them interested enough to consider the product as a means to satisfy a specific desire of theirs, they likely will act on that interest by making a purchase.

This step-by-step model applies particularly well to expensive, high-involvement products, like a new car. However, for other types of products, the IMC process appears more circular, such that marketers and consumers engage in ongoing dialog in which marketers provide messages either to induce or respond to consumers' initial comments or feedback.[13]

The Lagged Effect   Sometimes consumers don't act immediately after receiving a marketing communication because of the lagged effect—a delayed response to a marketing communication campaign. It generally takes several exposures to an ad before a consumer fully processes its message.[14] In turn, measuring the effect of a current campaign becomes more difficult because of the possible lagged response to a previous one.[15] Suppose you purchased a Yaris right after reading through the advertising booklet contained in *TV Guide*. The advertising insert may have pushed you to buy, but other communications from Toyota, such as television ads and articles in automotive magazines that you saw weeks earlier, probably also influenced your purchase.

Now that we've examined various aspects of the communication process, let's look at how specific media are used in an IMC program.

CHECK YOURSELF

1. What are the different steps in the communication process?

2. What is the AIDA model?

ELEMENTS OF AN INTEGRATED MARKETING COMMUNICATION STRATEGY

For any communications campaign to succeed, the firm must deliver the right message to the right audience through the right media. Reaching the right audience is becoming more difficult, however, as the media environment grows more complicated.

Advances in technology have led to satellite radio, wireless technology, pop-up and banner ads on Web sites, brand-sponsored Web sites, viral advertisements, PDA messaging, and text messaging, all of which vie for consumers' attention. Print media have also grown and become more specialized. In 1970, 6,690 magazines were published in the United States; today, there are almost 16,000 magazines, more than 12,000 journals, almost 10,000 newspapers, more than 14,000 newsletters, and approximately 12,000 catalogs.[16] Approximately 75 new publications also get launched every month.[17]

This proliferation of media has led many firms to shift their promotional dollars from advertising to direct marketing, Web site development, product placements, and other forms of promotion in search of the best way to deliver

As print media has grown and become more specialized, advertisers are better able to target their audience.

messages to their target audiences. Exhibit 17.4 illustrates just how profound the changes in media expenditures can be in just one year. Note that newspaper advertising decreased 4.7 percent, while Internet display advertising and Internet–paid searches (which is when the advertiser pays to increase its ranking in search engines) increased 16.7 and 18.5 percent, respectively. Media fragmentation has also occurred on television. Networks are dedicated to certain types of sports (Outdoor Life Network, Golf Channel), children (Nickelodeon), ethnic minorities (Black Family Channel, Univision), and classic movies (AMC, Turner Classic Movies). Each of these channels allows IMC planners to target their desired audience narrowly.

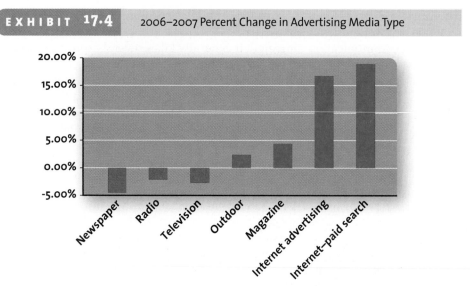

Source: TNS Media Intelligence, http://www.tns-mi.com/news/09112007.htm (accessed May 13, 2008); *eMarketer.com*, April 2007.

We now examine the individual elements of IMC and the way each contributes to a successful IMC campaign (see Exhibit 17.5). Some elements—advertising, sales promotion, public relations, and personal selling—appear in detail in subsequent chapters; we discuss them only briefly here.

Advertising

Perhaps the most visible of the IMC components, advertising, according to the American Marketing Association, entails "the placement of announcements and persuasive messages in time or space purchased in any of the mass media by business firms, nonprofit organizations, government agencies, and individuals who seek to inform and/or persuade members of a particular target market or audience about their products, services, organizations, or ideas."[18] In Chapter 18, we discuss the purpose of advertising and its various types, but for now, we note that advertising is extremely effective for creating awareness of a product or service and generating interest. Mass advertising can entice consumers into a conversation with marketers. However, advertising must break through the clutter of other messages to reach its intended audience. And as marketers attempt to find ways to reach their target audiences, advertising has become increasingly pervasive. Not so long ago, most of many firms' promotional budgets was spent on advertising. Since the 1990s, however, advertising's share of total promotional dollars has fallen as the budgets for other forms of sales promotion, especially direct marketing, have increased, resulting in a more balanced approach to the use of marketing communications elements.

Personal Selling

Personal selling is the two-way flow of communication between a buyer and a seller that is designed to influence the buyer's purchase decision. Personal selling can take place in various settings: face-to-face, video teleconferencing, on the telephone, or over the Internet. Although consumers don't often interact with professional sales people, personal selling represents an important component of many IMC programs, especially in business-to-business (B2B) settings.

The cost of communicating directly with a potential customer is quite high compared with other forms of promotion, but it is simply the best and most efficient way to sell certain products and services. Customers can buy many products and services without the help of a salesperson, but sales people simplify the buying process by providing information and services that save customers time and effort. In many cases, sales representatives add significant value, which makes the added expense of employing them worthwhile. We devote Chapter 19 to personal selling and sales management.

Sales Promotions

Sales promotions are special incentives or excitement-building programs that encourage the purchase of a product or service, such as coupons, rebates, contests, free samples, and point-of-purchase displays. Marketers typically design these incentives for use in conjunction with other advertising or personal selling programs. Many sales promotions, like free samples or point-of-purchase displays, are designed to build short-term sales, though others, like contests and sweepstakes, have become integral components of firms' CRM programs as means to build customer loyalty. We discuss such sales promotions in Chapter 18.

Direct Marketing

The component of IMC that has received the greatest increase in aggregate spending recently is direct marketing, or marketing that communicates directly with target customers to generate a response or transaction.[19] The direct marketing toolkit contains a variety of marketing communication initiatives, including telephone, mail, program-length television commercials (infomercials), catalogs, and Internet-based initiatives such as e-mail and m-commerce.

Internet-based technologies have had a profound effect on direct marketing initiatives. E-mail, for instance, can be directed to a specific consumer. However, when the same message is delivered electronically to all recipients, electronic communications more closely resemble advertising. Firms use e-mail to inform customers of new merchandise and special promotions, confirm the receipt of an order, and indicate when an order has been shipped.

As technology and customers together become more sophisticated, more firms are augmenting their e-mail communications with m-commerce (mobile commerce), which involves communicating with and even selling to customers through wireless handheld devices, such as cellular telephones and personal

Retailers like Borders Books send personalized e-mails to their customers with messages based on past purchases.

digital assistants (PDAs).[20] Tech-savvy customers use their cell phones and PDAs to obtain sports scores, weather, music videos, and text messages in real time. It thus is a natural evolution for firms to tap into this trend. Consider some of these innovative m-commerce applications:

- Grand Rapids, Michigan–based hypermarket Meijer offers consumers the opportunity to learn in advance when the retailer's gasoline prices are going to go up, before the hikes actually hit the pump.[21]

- GPShopper is an Internet-style search engine that lets shoppers search a chain's entire inventory to see if an item is in stock at a nearby store.[22] This service is available for stores such as Best Buy, Toys "R" Us, and Sports Authority.

- Retailers can send coupons directly to shoppers' cell phones.[23] Redemption rates have been as high as 40 percent, compared with less than 2 percent for many print and online campaigns. Shoppers text a code found on store signs to get the coupon, then display it on their phone at checkout.

- Customers can buy products instantly using text messages, a process that eliminates the need to go to a store or even visit a Web site.[24] If a customer sees an ad for a coat in a magazine, he or she can order it by sending the text code that appears next to the item through a cell phone or PDA. Not limited to merchandise, some concert halls are using this technology to sell tickets, and some charities are taking donations by text message.

Personalized direct mail remains especially effective for targeting multicultural consumer groups. Media companies cannot help but notice the nuances of large target markets, such as Hispanic consumers. Their country of origin, generation, degree of English fluency, and language they speak in their homes play huge roles in determining how Hispanic consumers respond to media appeals. A Puerto Rican consumer is very different from one from Spain.

Furthermore, among Hispanic people who only speak Spanish, 54 percent lack access to the Internet in their homes. By targeting these consumers through direct mail, marketers make sure they appeal to this important market segment.[25] Unlike mass media, which communicate to a wide audience, direct marketing allows for personalization of the message, a key advantage.

The increased use of customer databases has enabled marketers to identify and track consumers over time and across purchase situations, which has contributed to the rapid growth of direct marketing. Marketers have been able to build these databases, thanks to consumers' increased use of credit and debit cards, store-specific credit and loyalty cards, and online shopping, all of which require the buyer to give the seller personal information that becomes part of its database. Because firms understand customers' purchases better when they possess such information, they can more easily focus their direct marketing efforts appropriately. Ethical and Societal Dilemma 17.1 details both the benefits and the concerns associated with how firms use such information to market to customers one at a time.

Direct marketing, or one-to-one programs, create a win–win situation for customers and the firm. Customers get their needs addressed efficiently; firms are able to gather large amounts of data about customers, including their needs and wants, purchase intentions, and levels of satisfaction. This information enables the firm to develop products and services that offer higher value to customers, which in turn gives those customers an incentive to remain loyal to the firm.

Ethical and Societal Dilemma 17.1   Identifying Web Users

Whereas previously companies bought ads on Web sites related to the product being promoted (e.g., a healthy drink on the GNC Web site), more targeted advertising now pursues a particular customer rather than all visitors to a particular Web site.[26] For instance, a behavioral advertising firm like Tacoda can track how a person moves through a Web browser, so that it knows when the user frequents certain sites and thus determines the particular interests of that consumer. On the basis of the consumer's interests, firms like Tacoda then strategically place advertising on specific sites—but only on that person's browser. Another person who goes to the same Web site at the same time will receive a different ad, more in line with his or her own interests.

In a nod to privacy concerns, this method of targeting advertising does not provide personal profiles of consumers, but rather information about their search activity on the browser. Even when multiple users employ the same computer, advertising firms can distinguish patterns and identify which user is at the computer at certain times. So, for instance, if you share your computer with your roommate, advertisers know which of you is using the computer at a particular time, given your browsing habits. Those consumers who do not want their preferences passed on can opt out by changing their browser settings.

As beneficial as this tracking technology may seem for advertisers, it also might enable clever hackers to target computer browsers more easily. If it falls into the wrong hands, information about consumers' browsing and purchasing habits might allow others to impose on users' privacy and security. Furthermore, the technology currently requires consumers to opt out, rather than asking them to opt in, which may leave some consumers unaware of all to which they are agreeing when they employ these sites.

Do you believe that your personal privacy is being unjustly invaded by firms that provide you with targeted advertising based on your browsing habits? Or do you think advertising firms engaged in these activities are providing you with information that may make your buying decisions more pleasant and efficient?

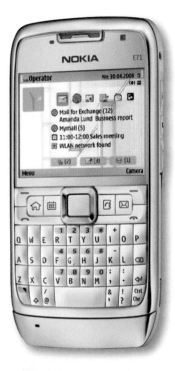

Public Relations (PR)

Public relations is the organizational function that manages the firm's communications to achieve a variety of objectives, including building and maintaining a positive image, handling or heading off unfavorable stories or events, and maintaining positive relationships with the media. Public relations activities support the other promotional efforts by the firm by generating "free" media attention, as we discuss further in Chapter 18.

Electronic Media

Although we have discussed several electronic media promotional vehicles previously in this chapter, we will now examine Web sites, corporate blogs, social marketing, and online games.

Web Site Firms are increasing their emphasis on communicating with customers through their Web sites. They use their Web sites to build their brand image and educate customers about their products or services and where they can be purchased. Retailers and some manufacturers sell merchandise directly to consumers over the Internet. For example, in addition to selling merchandise, Office Depot's Web site has a Business Resource Center that provides advice and product knowledge, as well as a source of networks to other businesses. There are forms that businesses use to comply with Occupational Safety and Health Act (OSHA) requirements, check job applicant records, estimate cash flow, and develop a sexual harassment policy; workshops for running a business; and local and national business news. By providing this information on its Web site, Office Depot reinforces

Direct marketers use PDAs and cell phones to reach potential customers.

its image as the essential source of products, services, and information for small businesses.

Corporate Blogs   Corporate blogging has risen from obscure, random company postings to a valuable Web addition in virtually no time. A blog (Weblog) contains periodic posts on a common Web page. As a new form of marketing communication, a well-received blog can create positive word of mouth, connect customers by forming a community, increase sales because the company can respond directly to customers' comments, and develop a long-term relationship with the company.[27]

Insincere postings or fake blogs that are actually disguised advertising campaigns are problematic. By its very nature, a blog is transparent and contains authors' honest observations, which can help customers determine their trust and loyalty levels. Anything less than total honesty will break that bond and damage the relationship. When handled appropriately, though, blogs can serve as trusted platforms for damage control.

At about the same time that the natural and organic grocery store chain Whole Foods Markets attempted to purchase its competitor Wild Oats, it was publicly disclosed that its CEO, John Mackey, had been actively blogging on the Yahoo Finance Web site for eight years. Using the alias, "Rahodeb" (an anagram of his wife Deborah's name), he wrote poorly of Wild Oats, saying that it would probably go into bankruptcy. At the same time he praised Whole Foods (and himself, noting in one posting that Rahodeb thought Mackey's new haircut was "cute"). The FTC, angered by his false identification, has used this information in its case against the Whole Foods takeover of Wild Oats arguing that Mackey's opinions and statements are strong evidence of his intent to make Whole Foods a monopoly.[28]

Since corporate blogging is still in its infancy, there is no standard format or purpose. Consider the following corporate blogs for illustrative purposes:

- Southwest Airlines' blog, "Nuts about Southwest," is used primarily to connect customers with the company's employees, letting them in on the culture and operations. The corporate contributors include everyone from mechanics, to executives, to pilots. The blog is also used for new product launches, and as a method of collecting information upon which to base corporate decisions. The blog has reached more than one million customers.[29]

- Whole Foods Market's blog tackles a broad range of issues, all under the rubric "Whole Foods Lifestyle." It includes topics like recycling and cooking. The comments are posted under general posting so that users can more easily navigate the site.[30]

- Overstock.com's blog is fairly unstructured, allowing customers to communicate about anything that they want. The site has a separate blog, called "Deep Capture," in which the CEO, Patrick Byrne, comments on issues in the world that bother him and responds to comments that users may have for him.[31]

Social Shopping   Firms communicate with their customers through word of mouth (WOM), or communication between people about a firm.[32] A relatively new pathway for WOM communication is through social shopping. Social shopping is a communication channel in which consumers use the Internet to engage in the shopping process by exchanging preferences, thoughts, and opinions among friends, family, and others.[33] Customers or users review, communicate about, and aggregate information about products, prices, and deals.

Many firms, especially retailers, encourage customers to post reviews of products they have bought or used and even have visitors to their Web sites rate the quality of the reviews. Research has shown that these online product reviews in-

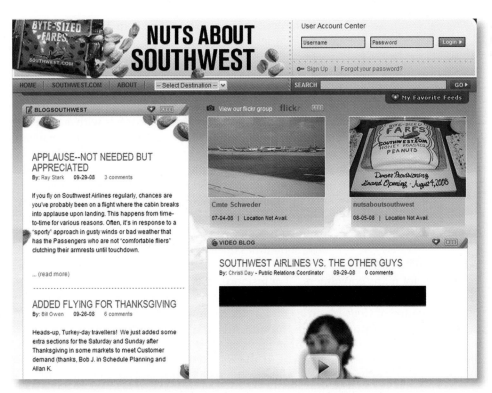

Southwest Airlines' blog "Nuts about Southwest" connects customers with employees.

crease customer loyalty and provide a competitive advantage for sites that offer them.[34] One survey reveals that, of the shoppers who bought from sites with reviews, 40 percent said the review was the main reason they made the purchase. That group of product review users was also 21 percent more satisfied with its purchases than other buyers and 18 percent more likely than other buyers to buy from that site the next time it needed similar products.

ShopStyle.com is a social shopping site that enables shoppers to put together outfits from different retailers and discuss them with friends.

Visitors to the Tag Body Spray Web site can view this game in which visitors take on the role of a male character who must get past various virtual roadblocks—the family dog, parents, a younger brother—to gain access to the female "honey" who will find his Tag-enhanced scent appealing.

The Internet site www.ShopStyle.com features clothing and accessories from hundreds of other Internet stores. Shoppers can browse different looks that feature items across several retailers, put together outfits on their own, and then share and discuss them with friends. Some retailers are actively influencing the social shopping process. For example, ShopStyle.com featured a contest with a prize donated by Shopbop (www.shopbop.com), an online retailer.[35] Customers exposed to the contest on ShopStyle may have been lured to Shopbop's site to buy. Nordstrom and Bluefly. com also host pages on ShopStyle.com that feature outfits they sell. The Gap maintains interactive pages on www. Stylehive.com, a MySpace-like site on which shoppers exchange tips and post pictures of their favorite sites.

It is sometimes unclear whether the outfits posted or the advice given on a Web site is paid for by the retailer, which creates an ethically troubling issue for many consumers.[36] For instance, a Stylehive user named "Nataliezee" posts her favorite picks for outfits. Although her biography notes that she's an associate editor of *Craft Magazine*, it doesn't mention that the magazine has a deal with Stylehive to feature its wares prominently and use the advice of "Nataliezee."

Many firms feature customer reviews on their own Web sites.[37] In some cases, these reviews pose a potential risk if the review is negative. A dissatisfied customer's online comments could criticize the firm or the products it offers. Even a negative online review can have a silver lining for firms, though. Negative reviews can help customers affirm that they've vetted all their concerns before making a decision, as long as the reviews aren't overwhelmingly negative. Some negative reviews also add a sense of legitimacy to the information offered.

Online Games   One particularly successful way to reach younger consumers is through short online games that allow consumers to interact with the site and possibly other players. In line with its hipster image, young male target market, and claim that it is "uniquely designed to attract the ladies," Tag Body Spray includes on its Web site a game in which visitors take on the role of a male character who must get past various virtual roadblocks—the family dog, parents, a younger brother—to gain access to the female "honey" who will find his Tag-enhanced scent appealing.

Community Building   Many firms operate Web sites devoted to community building. These sites offer an opportunity for customers with similar interests to learn about products and services that support their hobbies and share information with others. Visitors to these Web sites can also post questions seeking information and/or comments about issues, products, and services. For example, at www.theknot.com, a community site targeting couples planning their weddings, a bride-to-be might ask how to handle an overly zealous bachelor party being planned by the best man. Others who have experienced this problem then post their advice.

Community building need not always be an electronic initiative, however. REI, an outdoor apparel and equipment retailer, offers adventure travel planning resources for hiking trips, bike tours, paddling, adventure cruises, whitewater rafting, climbing, wildlife viewing, and snowshoeing. Customers can select from more than 90 trips worldwide, including weekend getaways, and experience travel REI-style, with small groups and experienced local guides. By offering these trips, REI creates a community of customers who engage in activities using the merchandise that REI sells. The community thus reinforces REI's brand image.

Over time, technology will continue to improve, and other new means of communicating with consumers will be added to the IMC channel mix. For now, let's look at how the components of IMC fit together with marketing metrics to achieve the organization's strategic objectives.

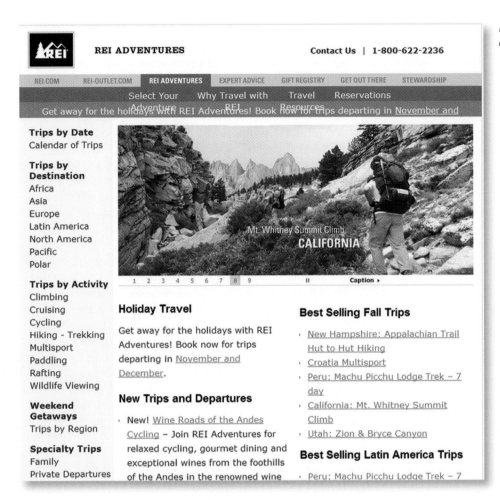

REI builds communities by offering adventure travel tours.

CHECK YOURSELF

1. What are the different elements of an IMC program?

PLANNING FOR AND MEASURING IMC SUCCESS

We begin by examining how marketers set strategic goals before implementing any IMC campaign. After they have established those goals, marketers can set the budget for the campaign and choose marketing metrics they will use to evaluate whether it has achieved its strategic objectives.

Goals

As with any strategic undertaking, firms need to understand the outcome they hope to achieve before they begin. These goals can be short-term, such as generating inquiries, increasing awareness, and prompting trial. Or they can be long-term in nature, such as increasing sales, market share, and customer loyalty. Selling beverages was the primary and long-term goal of the Coke and Pepsi campaigns described in the opening vignette, but in the short term, these companies also wanted to establish brand awareness and purchase intentions. Thus, their campaigns were designed to get consumers' attention first through television ads, then encourage them to log on to their Web sites to access additional promotional material.

These goals, both short- and long-term, should be explicitly defined and measured. They constitute part of the overall promotional plan, which is usually a subsection of the firm's marketing plan. Another part of the promotional plan is the budget.

Setting and Allocating the IMC Budget

Firms use a variety of methods to plan their marketing communications budgets. Because all the methods of setting a promotional budget have both advantages and disadvantages, no one method should be used in isolation.[38]

The objective-and-task method determines the budget required to undertake specific tasks to accomplish communication objectives. To use this method, marketers first establish a set of communication objectives, then determine which media best reach the target market and how much it will cost to run the number and types of communications necessary to achieve the objectives. This process—set objectives, choose media, and determine costs—must be repeated for each product or service. The sum of all the individual communication plan budgets becomes the firm's total marketing communications budget. In addition to the objective-and-task method, various rule-of-thumb methods can be used to set budgets (see Exhibit 17.6).

These rule-of-thumb methods use prior sales and communication activities to determine the present communication budget. Although they are easy to implement, they obviously have various limitations, as noted in the exhibit. Clearly, budgeting is not a simple process. It may take several rounds of negotiations among the various managers, who are each competing for resources for their own areas of responsibility.

Once the IMC budget is set, firms decide how much of the budget to allocate to specific communication elements, types of merchandise, geographic regions, or long and short-term objectives. For example, an apparel manufacturer must decide how much of its IMC budget to spend in each area of the United States and on men's versus women's apparel.

Research indicates that allocation decisions are more important than the decision about the amount to spend on communications.[39] In other words, firms often

EXHIBIT 17.6		Rule-of-Thumb Methods
Method	**Definition**	**Limitations**
Competitive parity	The communication budget is set so that the firm's share of communication expenses equals its share of the market.	Does not allow firms to exploit the unique opportunities or problems they confront in a market. If all competitors use this method to set communication budgets, their market shares will stay approximately the same over time.
Percentage-of-sales	The communication budget is a fixed percentage of forecasted sales.	Assumes the same percentage used in the past, or by competitors, is still appropriate for the firm. Does not take into account new plans (e.g., to introduce a new line of products in the current year).
Affordable budgeting	Marketers forecast their sales and expenses, excluding communication, during the budgeting period. The difference between the forecast sales and expenses plus desired profit is reserved for the communication budget. That is, the communication budget is the money available after operating costs and profits have been budgeted.	Assumes communication expenses do not stimulate sales and profit.

can realize the same objectives by reducing the size of the communication budget but allocating it more effectively.

An easy way to make such allocation decisions is to use a percentage of sales or match competitive spending. But rules of thumb probably won't maximize profits because they ignore the possibility that IMC programs might be more effective for some merchandise categories or for some regions than for others.

Instead, firms should attempt to allocate their IMC budget to those regions or categories where they can get "the most bang for their buck." For instance, an apparel manufacturer may find that its customers have a high awareness and very favorable attitude toward its women's clothing but not know much about its men's clothing. In this situation, a dollar spent on advertising men's clothing might generate more sales than a dollar spent on women's clothing, even though the sales of women's clothing are greater than the sales of men's clothing.

Measuring Success Using Marketing Metrics

Once a firm has decided how to set its budget for marketing communications and its campaigns have been developed and implemented, it reaches the point that it must measure the success of the campaigns, using various marketing metrics. Each step in the IMC process can be measured to determine how effective it has been in motivating consumers to move to the next step in the buying process. However, recall that the lagged effect influences and complicates marketers' evaluations of a promotion's effectiveness, as well as the best way to allocate marketing communications budgets. Because of the cumulative effect of marketing communications, it may take several exposures before consumers are moved to buy, so firms cannot expect too much too soon. They must invest in the marketing communications campaign with the idea that it may not reach its full potential for some time. In the same way, if firms cut marketing communications expenditures, it may take time before they experience a decrease in sales.

When measuring IMC success, the firm should examine when and how often consumers have been exposed to various marketing communications. Specifically, they use measures of *frequency* and *reach* to gauge consumers' *exposure* to marketing communications. For most products and situations, a single exposure to a communication is hardly enough to generate the desired response. Therefore, marketers measure the frequency of exposure—how often the audience is exposed to a communication within a specified period of time. The other measure used to measure consumers' exposure to marketing communications is reach, which describes the percentage of the target population exposed to a specific marketing communication, such as an advertisement, at least once.[40] Marketing communications managers usually state their media objectives in terms of gross rating points (GRP), which represents reach multiplied by frequency (GRP = reach × frequency).

GRP can be measured for print, radio, or television, but when they are compared, they must refer to the same medium. Suppose that Kenneth Cole places seven advertisements in *Vogue* magazine, which reaches 50 percent of the "fashion forward" target segment. The total GRP generated by these seven magazine advertisements is 50 reach × 7 advertisements = 350 GRP. Now suppose Kenneth Cole includes 15 television ads as part of the same campaign, run during the program *America's Next Top Model*, which has a rating (reach) of 9.2. The total GRP generated by these 15 advertisements is 138 (9.2 × 15 = 138). However, advertisements typically appear during more than one television program, so the total GRP actually equals the sum of the GRP generated during *America's Next Top Model* and that which Kenneth Cole gains by advertising during 12 showings of *Project Runway*, which earns a rating of 1.8. The total reach then is 138 + (1.8 × 12 = 21.6) = 159.6.

Although GRP is an adequate measure for television and radio advertisements, assessing the effectiveness of any Web-based communications efforts in an IMC campaign generally requires Web tracking software to indicate how much

How does a firm like Kenneth Cole measure the effectiveness of its Web-based communications efforts compared to more traditional IMC media like print, radio, or television?

time viewers spend on particular Web pages and the number of pages they view. Click-through tracking measures how many times users click on banner advertising on Web sites. Online couponing is a promotional Web technique in which consumers print a coupon directly from a site and then redeem the coupon in a store. Another promotional Web technique is online referring, in which consumers fill out an interest or order form and are referred to an offline dealer or firm that offers the product or service of interest. All these methods can be easily measured and assessed.

Planning, Implementing, and Evaluating IMC Programs— An Illustration of Google Advertising

Hypothetically, imagine Transit, an upscale sneaker store in New York City modeled after vintage New York City subway trains. Transit's target market is young, well-educated, hip men and women aged 17–34. The owner's experience indicates the importance of personal selling for this market because they (1) make large purchases and (2) seek considerable information before making a decision.

Transit is an upscale sneaker store in New York City modeled after vintage New York City subway trains.

Thus, Jay Oliver, the owner, spends part of his communication budget on training his sales associates.

Oliver has realized his communication budget is considerably less than that of other sneaker stores in the area. He has therefore decided to concentrate his limited budget on a specific segment and use electronic media exclusively in his IMC program.

The IMC program Oliver has developed emphasizes his store's distinctive image and uses his Web site, social shopping, and some interesting community building techniques. For instance, he has an extensive customer database (CRM) from which he draws information for matching new merchandise with his customers' past purchase behaviors and little personal nuggets of information that he or other sales associates have collected on the customers. He then e-mails specific customers information about new products that he believes they will be interested in. He also encourages customers to use blogs hosted on his Web site. Customers chat about the "hot" new sneakers, club events, and races. He does everything with a strong sense of style.

In order to reach out to new customers, he is using search engine marketing (SEM) to market Transit. In particular, he is using Google AdWords, a search engine marketing tool offered by Google that allows firms to show up in searches based on the keywords potential customers use. (A banner ad is not produced, just the search result.) For example, Oliver must assess what are the best keywords to use. Someone may be looking for sneakers, sneakers in New York City, athletic shoes, etc. Using Google AdWords, Oliver can assess the effectiveness of his advertising expenditures by measuring the reach, relevance, and return on investment for each of the keywords that were used. To estimate reach, Oliver can ascertain the number of clicks, the number of impressions (times the ad appears in front of the user), and the click-through rate (CTR) (number of clicks/number of impressions).[41]

The relevance of the ad describes how useful an ad message was to the customer doing the search. For Google AdWords, AdRank is used to rank the ads in a Google search. AdRank is calculated on the basis of the quality score determined through click-through rate and the price that the company pays for the advertising. For instance, in a search for "sneaker store," the Transit ad showed up fourth, suggesting high relevance.[42]

Using the following formula, Oliver can determine an ad's return on investment (ROI):

$$ROI = \frac{(Sales \times Gross\ margin\% - Marketing\ expenditure)}{Marketing\ expenditure}$$

For instance, by using the two keyword searches on page 544, Oliver can see how much the advertising cost him (Column 3), the gross margin (sales × gross margin%) that were produced as a result (Column 4), and the ROI (Column 6). For "sneaker store," the Transit Web site had a lot more clicks than the clicks that were received from "New York City sneakers," 110 versus 40, respectively (Column 2).

How does Transit use Google AdWords to determine the effectiveness of its advertising expenditures on Google?

Even though the gross margin was lower for the keywords "sneaker store" at \$35/day versus \$40/day for the keywords "New York City sneakers," the ROI was much greater for the "sneaker store" keyword combination. In the future, Oliver should continue this keyword combination in addition to producing others that are similar to it, in the hope that he will attain an even greater return on investment.

(1) Keyword	(2) Clicks	(3) Marketing Expenditure	(4) Gross Margin	(5) (Col. 4 − Col. 3)	(6) ROI (Col. 5 ÷ Col. 3 × 100)
Sneaker store	110	\$10/day	\$35/day	\$25	250%
New York City sneakers	40	\$25/day	\$40/day	\$15	60%

To evaluate his IMC program, Oliver compares the results of the program with his objectives. To measure his program's effectiveness, he conducted an inexpensive online survey using the following questions:

Communication Objectives	Questions
Awareness	What stores sell sneakers?
Knowledge	Which stores would you rate outstanding on the following characteristics?
Attitude	On your next shopping trip for sneakers, which store would you visit first?
Visit	Which of the following stores have you been to?

Here are the survey results for one year:

Communication Objective	Before Campaign	6 Months After	One Year After
Awareness (% mentioning store)	38%	46%	52%
Knowledge (% giving outstanding rating for sales assistance)	9	17	24
Attitude (% first choice)	13	15	19
Visit (% visited store)	8	15	19

The results show a steady increase in awareness, knowledge of the store, and choice of the store as a primary source of sneakers. This research provides evidence that the IMC program was conveying the intended message to the target audience.

As IMC programs become more sophisticated, measurement is not the only concern. There are a host of legal and ethical issues that marketers need to worry about, so in the last section, we examine some current legal and ethical IMC issues.

CHECK YOURSELF
1. What are three rule-of-thumb methods used for setting IMC budgets?
2. How would a firm evaluate the effectiveness of its Google advertising?

LEGAL AND ETHICAL ISSUES IN IMC

Integrated marketing communications brings together many diverse forms of communication under one umbrella. But in the United States, each form of communication media traditionally has been regulated separately. For example, cigarette advertising was banned from television and radio in 1969 under the Public Health Smoking Act but could still appear in print and on billboards, and cigarette companies still sponsored various entertainment and sporting events. However, after 1997, cigarette companies voluntarily agreed to remove cigarette advertising from billboards and end all sponsorship of sports and entertainment events in the United States.[43] For now, cigarette advertising is permitted only in print media and online. In Chapter 18, we detail the various agencies that regulate the different forms and media for advertising in the United States. In this section, we discuss some controversies surrounding commercial speech and new forms of potential deception.

What Is Commercial Speech?

When IMC brings all these different media together, it often employs a mix of commercial and noncommercial speech, which the United States legally distinguishes. However, the courts are starting to have a difficult time determining which is which. Commercial speech[44] is defined as a message with an economic motivation, that is, to promote a product or service, to persuade someone to purchase, and so on. Marketers can only make commercial claims that are fact based, not mere opinions. A statement such as "our product X is superior to our competitor's product Y" must be substantiated. Thus, when Powerade, a Coca-Cola product, ran advertisements in which a horse and buggy shot ahead of competitive racers after drinking Powerade, with the tagline, "10 is better than 50," Pepsi brought suit, claiming the ads were deceptive by offering a comparison with Gatorade. That is, Powerade was claiming it had 10 calories instead of Gatorade's 50; that claim was not contested. But by making the horse and buggy go faster, Coke was also implying that Powerade improved performance—a claim it could not substantiate.[45]

Noncommercial speech, in contrast, is a message that does not have an economic motivation and therefore is fully protected under the First Amendment. Firms can express matters of opinion, such as when the president of the firm tells an audience, "Our company makes the best products," without needing to offer substantiation for the claim as long as those claims are not designed with an economic motivation.

Advertising and direct marketing are forms of commercial speech, whereas PR is not. For instance, in *Kasky v. Nike*, Nike claimed that a letter to the editor written by its CEO was part of a PR campaign and thus not an advertising message.[46] Unfortunately for Nike, the California courts felt otherwise and found that Nike's letter was an advertisement and qualified as commercial speech, which meant that the claims made in the letter had to be substantiated.

Summing Up

1. **How do customers perceive marketing communications?**

   On the surface, marketing communications look simple: People become aware of a product or service, then grow interested, then desire it, and finally take an action such as purchasing it. But it isn't quite that simple. First, there is the cumulative effect of marketing communications. Ads from the past, for instance, help influence consumers' actions in the future. Second, everyone interprets commercial messages differently, thus making it difficult for a marketer to be assured that a particular, clear signal is getting through. Third, to be effective, marketers must adjust their messages to fit the media and the receiver's knowledge level.

2. **Why are some media channels growing while others are shrinking?**

   In the past, most of a firm's promotional budget was spent on advertising. Although advertising still demands a sizable portion, other media channels have taken up a substantial chunk of the total budget. Direct marketing expenditures are growing because the number of direct marketing media options, particularly online options, has increased in recent years. While outbound telephone calls have declined, Internet-based technologies like e-mail and m-commerce have increased. Public relations also has become increasingly important as other media forms become more expensive and as consumers grow more skeptical of commercial messages. Finally, the Internet has spawned some innovative new ways to promote products and services.

3. How should firms use marketing metrics to plan for and measure IMC success?

Planning and allocating an IMC budget should encompass a combination of factors. The process could start by setting the overall IMC budget as a percentage of sales. Then, the firm might examine what other firms are spending on similar product categories. When it gets down to planning the budget for individual product categories or items, the firm should set its objectives for the campaign and allocate enough money to meet those objectives.

Marketers rely on a mix of traditional and nontraditional measures to determine IMC success. Because potential customers generally need to be exposed to IMC messages several times before they will buy, firms estimate the degree to which customers are exposed to a message by multiplying frequency (the number of times an audience is exposed to a message) by reach (the percentage of the target population exposed to a specific marketing communication). Measuring Internet IMC effectiveness requires different measures, such as click-through tracking that measures how many times users click on banner advertising on Web sites.

4. Why are some governmental agencies and consumer groups concerned about certain innovative IMC strategies?

If a message is designed to promote or sell a product or service, it is generally considered commercial speech, but if the message has no promotional or selling intent, it is fully protected by the First Amendment. The line becomes blurred, however, when normally noncommercial venues are used to sell something. Another practice that is causing a stir emerges when the sender of a commercial message is not clearly identified. Activities such as bogus Web sites or online reviews, in which the identity of the sponsor of an activity or event is intentionally kept from prospective customers, can be considered deceptive promotional practices.

Key Terms

- advertising, 532
- affordable budgeting, 540
- AIDA model, 528
- aided recall, 529
- blog (Weblog), 536
- brand awareness, 529
- clicks, 543
- click-through rate (CTR), 543
- click-through tracking, 542
- commercial speech, 545
- communication channel, 527
- competitive parity, 540
- decoding, 527
- direct marketing, 533
- encoding, 526

- feedback loop, 527
- frequency, 541
- gross rating points (GRP), 541
- impressions, 543
- integrated marketing communications (IMC), 525
- lagged effect, 531
- m-commerce (mobile commerce), 533
- noise, 527
- noncommercial speech, 545
- objective-and-task method, 540
- online couponing, 542
- online referring, 542
- percentages of sales, 540

- personal selling, 533
- public relations, 535
- reach, 541
- receiver, 527
- relevance, 543
- return on investment (ROI), 543
- rule-of-thumb methods, 540
- sales promotions, 533
- search engine marketing (SEM), 543
- sender, 526
- social shopping, 536
- top-of-mind awareness, 529
- transmitter, 526
- Web tracking software, 541

Marketing Applications

1. Assume that the contemporary apparel company Juicy Couture has embarked on a new IMC strategy. It has chosen to advertise on TV during the NBC *Nightly News* and in print in *Time* magazine. The message is designed to announce new styles for the season and uses a 17-year-old woman as the model. Evaluate this strategy.

2. Using the steps in the AIDA model, explain why a potential consumer in question 1 who views Juicy

Couture's advertising may not be ready to go out and purchase a new pair of jeans.

3. Suppose a snack company introduces a new product called SumSeeds—sunflower seeds with energy boosters like caffeine, taurine, lysine, and ginseng. How would you expect this product's IMC program to differ from that for regular sunflower seeds sold as snacks?

4. It's holiday time, and you've decided to purchase a jewelry item for the person of your choice at Tiffany & Co. Evaluate how Tiffany's advertising, personal selling, public relations, and electronic media might influence your purchase decision. How might the relative importance of each of these IMC elements be different if your parents were making the purchase?

5. Suppose you saw your instructor for this course being interviewed on TV about the impact of a big storm on an upcoming holiday's sales. Is this interview part of your college's IMC program? If so, do you believe it benefits the college? How?

6. A retail store places an ad in the local newspaper for yoga wear. The sales of the featured items increase significantly for the next two weeks; sales in the rest of the sportswear department go up as well. What do you think are the short- and long-term objectives of the ad? Justify your answer.

7. As an intern for Michelin tires, you have been asked to develop an IMC budget. The objective of the IMC strategy is to raise Michelin's market share by 5 percent in the United States in the next 18 months. Your manager explains, "It's real simple; just increase the budget 5 percent over last year's." Evaluate your manager's strategy.

8. You were sitting in the school cafeteria yesterday, and a young man from your marketing class, whom you don't know well, asked if he could sit down. He then started telling you about this very cool new Apple product that allows you to record class lectures and play them back on an MP3 player. Although you recognize the merit in the product, you later find out that he works for Apple. Do you believe his action constitutes an ethical IMC strategy? How will it affect your attitude toward Apple and the potential that you will purchase the product?

Quiz Yourself

www.mhhe.com/
grewal2e

1. Often a(n) _____ accomplishes the task of encoding IMC messages.
   a. advertising agency
   b. consumer interest group
   c. media channel
   d. noise reduction specialist
   e. viral public relations expert

2. Ingrid wants her company to expand its use of public relations. She argues that, as other IMC alternatives become more expensive and _____, public relations should be a larger part of her company's IMC efforts.

   a. online couponing has declined
   b. consumers have become more skeptical of marketing claims
   c. Web tracking software has become more sophisticated
   d. gross rating points have become marginalized
   e. commercial speech has become more effective

(Answers to these two questions are provided on page 624.)

Go to www.mhhe.com/grewal2e to practice an additional 11 questions.

Toolkit

RETURN ON MARKETING EXPENDITURES

Suppose Jay Oliver (marketing manager of Transit sneaker store) is considering two search engine marketing (SEM) options to reach out to new customers to market Transit. In particular, he is using Google AdWords, a search engine marketing tool offered by Google that allows firms to show up in searches based on the keywords potential customers use. Transit is targeting young adults age 17–28. The sneaker market is about $500,000,000 sales annually, and the target market is about 35% of that. Their gross margins are 20%. Oliver estimates that Transit will capture a 2% market share of the target market with a $500,000 advertising and keyword budget (option 1) and a 3% market share with a $1,000,000 advertising and keyword budget (option 2). Which marketing plan produces the higher ROI for the year? Please use the toolkit provided at www.mhhe.com/grewal2e to assess the ROI of the two options.

Net Savvy

1. Visit http://www.thephelpsgroup.com and click on the "Our Work" tab at the top. In the Work Portfolio, compare the IMC for the different companies. What were the goals of the integrated marketing campaign? Which IMC components were used in that particular campaign? How do those components contribute to the success of the IMC campaign in achieving its stated goals?

2. The Direct Marketing Association is the primary source of information about direct marketing activities for both academics and practitioners. The Web site for the DMA, at http://www.the-dma.org/, contains a wealth of information about direct marketing practices and self-regulation. How many different target markets does the DMA address on its home page? Click on the "Information for Consumers" button located on the left side of the home page. What services does the DMA provide for consumers? Why do you think it offers those services?

Chapter Case Study

JIGSAW: A MENACE TO YOUR PHONE[47]

The televised advertisements for Lion's Gate Entertainment's *Saw* films seem scary enough, with their images of toes being cut off and screaming actors, along with flashes of the films' frightening trap-maker Jigsaw. Yet to maintain the buzz surrounding the film series through four (and likely more) installations, the movie studio goes much farther.

Lion's Gate wanted to push the DVD release of *Saw III* and therefore engaged in an elaborate plan, fitting for the detailed games and traps that frequent the movies themselves, that would send images of the blood-soaked torture flick to millions of fans' cell phones. The market for slasher movies tends to include younger men, most of whom likely viewed the film during its theatrical release. But to induce them to think about the movie again for the DVD release, Lion's Gate and its advertising agency, Initiative, created ads that could double as entertainment. As the executive vice president of Initiative noted, "Advertising and content are really not that different, especially in the entertainment space."[48]

Working with MobiTV, a company that offers subscribers live television on their cell phones, the company created a 24/7 *Saw III* channel that provided never-before-seen outtakes, behind-the-scenes footage, and cast interviews. To tout the channel, MobiTV also ran interactive ads on its own service. If users were watching, say, the Discovery Channel on their phones, they might see an ad for the *Saw* channel. Thus, the IMC campaign increased awareness of not only the DVD release but the advertising for the DVD release in a virtual cycle of attention building.

Not content to rely just on consumers who subscribe to MobiTV, the campaign also reached out to another form of entertainment widely accessed by the target market: comedians. It may seem that comedy and movies focusing on dismemberments and violence have little in common, but by prompting comedy acts like Richard Villa to mention the movie in their stand-up routines and sketches, an entirely different group of viewers were in turn prompted to remember their affection for the films.

Comedy not an odd enough partner for horror? What about a musical? Lion's Gate also teamed with Warcon Records to produce a *Saw III*–themed live music show in support of both the film and its soundtrack. "A Musical Evening Inspired by the Soundtrack of SAW III" took over New York's Webster Hall, featuring

Lion's Gate uses multiple media channels to introduce its Saw *films.*

appearances by bands from the film's soundtrack, with headlining acts such as Helmet, The Smashup, and Hydrovibe. Shawnee Smith, the actress who plays Amanda in the *Saw* movies, served as the emcee.

For the performance, the hall installed a special museum, displaying film props, torture devices, and the creepy Billie puppet. And of course, attendees could join the "Circle of Blood" fan club.[49]

Fans of this caliber certainly are not willing to let the producers of the film have all the fun. Inspired by these creative efforts, various fans push the product themselves, in a form of advertising specially enabled by modern technology. MySpace even hosts a *Saw* music video, posted by a member who calls himself "Saw III."[50]

The result of these varied and innovative marketing communications? The *Saw* franchise continues to rake in movie dollars. In particular, for its DVD release, *Saw III* became the top-selling and top-rented release of the week, and the halo effect of its success pushed the DVDs of the first two films into the top 20, according to ACNielsen.

Questions

1. How effective do you think Lion's Gate's advertising through untraditional media channels has been for its films?

2. The *Saw* movies tend to appeal mostly to younger, male viewers. Therefore, is Lion's Gate's strategy a long- or a short-term strategy? Why?

3. How do the film's producers create value for their target market?

CHAPTER

18

ADVERTISING, PUBLIC RELATIONS, AND SALES PROMOTIONS

The story of the founding of The Gap has reached almost mythic proportions—how Doris and Don Fisher, frustrated with a lack of customer service in other stores and mindful of the generation gap (hence the store's name) between younger and adult consumers, especially in the "hippie" mecca of San Francisco in 1969, opened a store to sell jeans and music and eventually turned it into a giant clothing retailer that owns multiple successful brands (e.g., Old Navy, Banana Republic). The story itself has been part of much of The Gap's advertising through the years.

Its first major ad campaign in 1974 played on the theme, encouraging consumers to "Fall into the Gap." Other popular campaigns followed, such as the award-winning "Individuals of Style" ads that featured hip celebrities sporting Gap clothing in a way that marked them as individuals—and promised consumers that buying Gap items could help them do the same, even as the company continued to expand its presence into virtually every mall in America. By 1997, *Advertising Age* magazine had named The Gap its advertiser of the year.[1]

But just a decade later, the company seemed to have lost its advertising way. Its 2006 "Peace Love Gap" holiday campaign, designed to "promote the importance of spreading peace and love," did little to spread the retailer's profits. Sagging sales continued; December 2006 sales dipped by 8 percent.[2] Its ads simply failed to connect with customers, resulting in confusion about both the brand and its target customer—in addition to that significant sales decline.

Following its "Peace" advertisements, The Gap promoted its participation in a widely reported cause-related marketing campaign, in which it joined with U2's lead singer Bono to launch the product (RED) line of clothing that would benefit AIDS relief organizations. The product (RED)-themed ads featured glamorous celebrities such as Penelope Cruz and Christy Turlington clad in red Gap clothing and suggesting consumers could change the world if they would just buy a Gap T-shirt.

But few consumers really identify with an international film star or a supermodel. Nor, apparently, do most women appreciate the skinny jean look. Television commercials in 2006 featured skinny jeans, a style few women saw as appropriate for their body types, especially when the ads featured emaciated-looking models. The mass market appeal the company had hoped to achieve never materialized.

In August 2007, the company tried again with an entirely new campaign in which it chose to move away from its recent efforts and perhaps closer to its storied past. In its more recent attempts, The Gap has focused on print ads, forgoing television advertising altogether (when is the last time you saw a Gap ad on TV?). In a bit of a nod to its advertising heyday, the campaign featured famous and semifamous comedians, film stars, and musicians, photographed in black and white, wearing basic Gap clothing.[3]

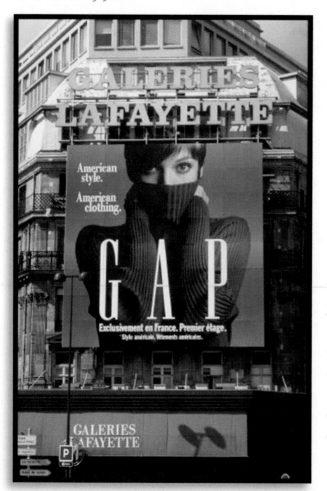

Gap's American style in France: This billboard is in front of the famous Parisian department store, Galeries Lafayette.

Thus, the campaign aimed to reestablish the brand image in customers' minds, especially with the tagline, "Classics Redefined." The celebrities chosen promote an idea of integrity to the public, including John Mayer, Lucy Liu, Selma Blair, Sarah Silverman, Regina King, Aaron Eckhart, and Ami Yumi. The campaign avoided stars that the public likely sees and hears about on a daily basis, like Jessica Simpson, or those who seem far out of reach, like Turlington or Cruz.

The simplicity of the ads also tried to remind consumers of what The Gap initially was designed to evoke: the primary place for basic T-shirts and khaki pants. Although some of the spokespeople are older than the targeted market of consumers in their late 20s to early 30s, the retailer hopes this market might view even these relatively young celebrities as classics who transcend age.

Maybe this time The Gap will achieve a successful ad campaign. In the past, it has often used celebrities for its advertising, but those campaigns usually made the spokespeople appear trendy and cool. This new campaign is taking a different approach—using black-and-white photos of minor celebrities to evoke simplicity and relate better to customers.

Advertising is a paid form of communication, delivered through media from an identifiable source, about an organization, product, service, or idea, designed to persuade the receiver to take some action, now or in the future.[4] This definition provides some important distinctions between advertising and other forms of promotion, which we have discussed in the previous chapter. First, advertising is not free; someone has paid, with money, trade, or other means, to get the message shown. Second, advertising must be carried by some medium—television, radio, print, the Web, T-shirts, sidewalks, and so on. Third, legally, the source of the message must be known or knowable. Fourth, advertising represents a persuasive form of communication, designed to get the consumer to take some action. That desired action can range from "Don't drink and drive" to "Buy a new Mercedes."

Some activities that are called advertising really are not, such as word-of-mouth advertising. Even political advertising technically is not advertising because it is not for commercial purposes and thus is not regulated in the same manner as true advertising.

Advertising encompasses an enormous industry and clearly is the most visible form of marketing communications—so much so that many people think of marketing and advertising as synonymous. Global advertising expenditures are projected to increase by 6.8 percent between 2007 and 2008, reaching $500 billion in total, with almost half that amount being spent in the United States alone. It is not just a perception that advertising is everywhere; it *is* everywhere.[5]

Yet how many of the advertisements you were exposed to yesterday do you remember today? Probably not more than three or four. As you learned in Chapter 5, perception is a highly selective process. Consumers simply screen out messages that are not relevant to them. When you notice an advertisement, you may not react to it. Even if you react to it, you may not remember it later. Even if you do, you still may not remember the brand or sponsor, or, worse yet (from the advertiser's point of view), you may remember it as an advertisement for another product.[6]

To get you to remember their ad and the brand, advertisers must first get your attention. As we discussed in Chapter 17, the increasing number of communication channels and changes in consumers' media usage have made the job of advertisers far more difficult.[7] As our opening example about The Gap demonstrated, advertisers continually struggle in their efforts to use creativity and a mix of media that offer better opportunities to reach their target markets.

As a consumer, you are exposed only to the end product—the finished advertisement. But many actions must take place before you actually get to see an ad, as the Toolkit available for this chapter will show you (see page 581). In this chapter, we examine what it takes to undertake a successful advertising campaign, from identifying a target audience to creating the actual ad and assessing performance. Although our discussion is generally confined to advertising, much of the process for developing an advertising campaign is applicable to many of the IMC media vehicles discussed in Chapter 17. We conclude our discussion of advertising with the regulatory and ethical issues in advertising, then move on to examine public relations, and then sales promotions and their use.

Designing and carrying out a successful advertising program requires much planning and effort. Exhibit 18.1 shows the key steps in the process, each of which helps ensure that the intended message reaches the right audience and has the desired effect. Now let's examine each of these steps.

EXHIBIT 18.1   Steps in Planning and Executing an Ad Campaign

Step 1	Step 2	Step 3	Step 4	Step 5	Step 6	Step 7
Identify target audience	Set advertising objectives	Determine the advertising budget	Convey the message	Evaluate and select media	Create advertisements	Assess impact

1. IDENTIFY TARGET AUDIENCE

SLIP INTO SOMETHING
TIMELESS THIS SEASON

Who is the target audience for this ad, men or women?

The success of an advertising program depends on how well the advertiser can identify its target audience. Firms conduct research to identify their target audience, then use the information they gain to set the tone for the advertising program and help them select the media they will use to deliver the message to that audience.

During this research, firms must keep in mind that their target audience may or may not be the same as current users of the product. Think about jewelry. Research shows that in a typical year, some 43 percent of the U.S. adult population—more than 85 million people—purchase jewelry. Although women have a significantly higher purchase incidence (48 percent) than men (36 percent), men spend approximately twice as much on their jewelry purchases than do women. Perhaps it is no surprise that the majority of men's jewelry purchases are gifts for women.[8] So what do these pieces of information tell advertisers? Essentially, if they want to sell jewelry, they need to appeal to either women who will purchase for themselves or men who will purchase for the women in their lives.

Some advertising messages also may be directed at portions of audiences who are not part of the marketer's target market but who participate in the purchase process. Chrysler, for instance, runs ads for its minivans during Saturday morning children's viewing hours. These ads are designed to build brand awareness on the part of the children, who, Chrysler hopes, will influence their parents' minivan choices.[9] It also lined up an endorsement by Jimmy Neutron, the cartoon boy genius, for ads running on the Nickelodeon network and during family-friendly shows, such as *Dancing with the Stars*.[10] As Adding Value 18.1 reveals, though, children are not the only ones Chrysler hopes to attract with its specifically targeted advertising.

2. SET ADVERTISING OBJECTIVES

Advertising campaign objectives are derived from the overall objectives of the marketing program and clarify the specific goals that the ads are designed to accomplish. Generally, these objectives appear in the **advertising plan**, a subsection of the firm's overall marketing plan that explicitly analyzes the marketing and advertising situation, identifies the objectives of the advertising campaign, clarifies a specific strategy for accomplishing those objectives, and indicates how the firm can determine whether the campaign was successful.[11] An advertising plan is crucial because it will later serve as the yardstick against which advertising success or failure is measured.

Generally, in advertising to consumers, the objective is a **pull strategy** in which the goal is to get consumers to *pull* the product into the supply chain by demanding it. **Push strategies** also exist and are designed to increase demand by focusing on wholesalers, distributors, or sales people, as we describe Chrysler doing with its dealers in Adding Value 18.1. These campaigns attempt to motivate the seller to highlight the product, rather than the products of competitors, and thereby push the product to consumers. In this chapter, we will focus on pull strategies. Push strategies are examined in Chapters 15, 16, and 19.

All advertising campaigns aim to achieve certain objectives: to inform, persuade, and remind customers. Another way of looking at advertising objectives is to examine an ad's focus. Is the ad designed to stimulate demand for a particular product or service, or more broadly for the institution in general? Also, ads can

Adding Value 18.1 A New Image to Appeal to the Wealthy

Chrysler, the American car company best known for its tough, adventurous Dodge and Jeep brands, recently hired the head of Toyota's luxury Lexus marketing division to help the company refurbish its brand. Clearly, Chrysler is reaching out to a new market.[12]

Many car buyers today prefer imports over domestic cars, and Chrysler is trying to appeal to them in its new advertising campaign. Rather than rely on the rugged image of its famous divisions, the company wants to gain an upscale image. To do so, it has begun to study premium car customers and what features they want.

Lexus offers a potentially effective model, using marketing events that tie its luxury sedan to the Neiman Marcus brand and the sponsorship of a *Vogue* magazine fashion show at the Pebble Beach classic car show. By hiring an executive from Lexus to head its marketing efforts, Chrysler hopes to gain similar experience and ideas.

As Chrysler changes its image, it also plans to improve its relationships with its business customers—dealerships. Dealers complained that the company's ad campaigns failed to add any value, because they did not showcase new models or highlight product features. Today, Chrysler is determined to listen to the dealerships and work with them to drive sales. In a sense, then, Chrysler must appeal to two separate audiences: end users and retailers.

Its newest tagline seems to indicate that Chrysler's efforts are paying off. The description "Engineered Beautifully" gives a luxury feel that also communicates the quality of the design—not quite the same feel as the Dodge line's "Grab Life by the Horns." If Chrysler products can live up to their advertising campaign, the company may yet be successful in picking up a whole new set of upscale customers.

Will ads like this appeal to the luxury car market?

be used to stimulate demand for a product category or an entire industry, or for a specific brand, firm, or item. First we look at the broad overall objectives of inform, persuade, and remind. Then we examine advertising objectives based on the focus of the ad: product versus institutional and primary versus selective.

Informative Advertising

Informative advertising communicates to create and build brand awareness, with the ultimate goal of moving the consumer through the buying cycle to a purchase. Such advertising helps determine some important early stages of a product's life cycle (see Chapter 11), particularly when consumers have little information about the specific product or type of product. Retailers often use informative advertising

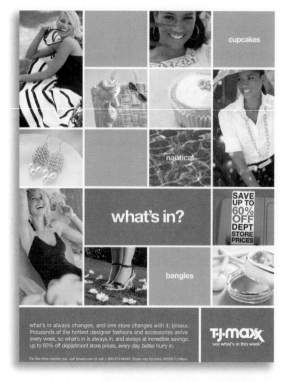

This ad informs consumers about "what's in" at T.J. Maxx.

to tell their customers about an upcoming sales event or the arrival of new merchandise, as in the advertisement on the left, designed to inform consumers that T.J. Maxx has new merchandise available.

Persuasive Advertising

When a product has gained a certain level of brand awareness, firms use **persuasive advertising** to motivate consumers to take action. Persuasive advertising generally occurs in the growth and early maturity stages of the product life cycle, when competition is most intense, and attempts to accelerate the market's acceptance of the product. In later stages of the product life cycle, persuasive advertising may be used to reposition an established brand by persuading consumers to change their existing perceptions of the advertised product. Firms, like Cover Girl in the ad below, often use persuasive advertising to convince consumers to take action—switch brands,[13] try a new product, or even continue to buy the advertised product.

Reminder Advertising

Finally, **reminder advertising** is communication used to remind or prompt repurchases, especially for products that have gained market acceptance and are in the maturity stage of their life cycle. Such advertising certainly appears in traditional media, such as television or print commercials, but it also encompasses other forms of advertising. For example, if you decide to buy cat food, do you carefully consider all the options, or do you just grab the first thing you see on the shelf? When your grocery store places a display of Purina Whisker Lickin's Deli Slices chicken and tuna flavor treats for cats on the end of the cereal aisle, it relies on the top-of-the-mind awareness that Purina has achieved with this product. That is, Deli Slices maintains a prominent place in cat owners' memories that triggers their response without them having to put any thought into it. The end cap display thus prompts you, and many other consumers, to respond by buying a package, just the response Purina hoped to attain.

Cover Girl's persuasive ads attempt to motivate consumers to take action: try the product, switch brands, or continue to buy the product.

EXHIBIT 18.2 — Types of Advertising

	Product Focused	**Institutional**
Primary Demand	Diet Coke generates demand for all diet sodas.	Got Milk? generates demand for the entire fluid milk category.
Selective Demand	Diet Coke generates demand for Coca-Cola's diet soda.	McDonald's demonstrates its commitment to the community through its support of Ronald McDonald House Charities.

End-of-aisle displays like this one for Purina Whisker Lickin's Deli Slices treats for cats reminds customers and prompts purchases.

Focus of Advertisements

The ad campaign's objectives determine the specific ad's focus. To illustrate, consider the two dichotomies depicted in Exhibit 18.2. The first dichotomy is between product-focused advertisements, which focus on informing, persuading, or reminding consumers about a specific product or service, and institutional advertisements, which inform, persuade, and remind consumers about issues related to places, politics, an industry, or a particular corporation. The second dichotomy distinguishes those ads designed to generate demand for the product category or an entire industry (primary demand) from those designed to generate demand for a specific brand, firm, or item (selective demand).

Perhaps the best-known primary demand advertising campaign is the long-running institutional campaign "Got Milk?" to encourage milk consumption by appealing to consumers' needs to affiliate with the milk-moustached celebrities shown in the ads.[14] A recent incarnation of the Got Milk? campaign, titled "Bones," also focuses on the beneficial properties of milk for building strong bones. This

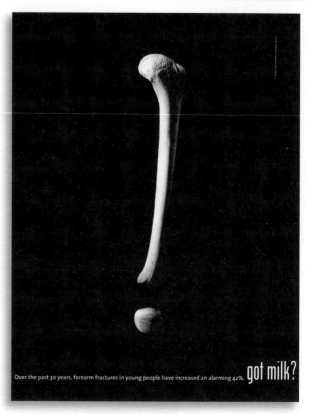

One of the best-known campaigns for generating primary demand is the "Got Milk?" campaign (left). The latest incarnation of the campaign, titled "Bones" (right) has a more informative appeal, combined with a mild emotional fear appeal.

Public service advertising, like McGruff the Crime Dog, focuses on public welfare and generally is sponsored by nonprofit institutions, civic groups, religious organizations, trade associations, or political groups.

new focus represents a switch to a more informative appeal, combined with a mild emotional fear appeal in its assertion that failing to drink milk can lead to medical problems. Its Spanish-language ad campaign, "Toma Leche," similarly touts milk as a "wonder tonic" that fights cavities, sleeplessness, and bone loss.

A special class of primary demand advertising is public service advertising (PSA), which focuses on public welfare and generally is sponsored by nonprofit institutions, civic groups, religious organizations, trade associations, or political groups.[15] PSAs represent a form of social marketing, which is the application of marketing principles to a social issue to bring about attitudinal and behavioral change among the general public or a specific population segment.[16] Because PSAs are a special class of advertising, under Federal Communications Commission (FCC) rules, broadcasters must devote a specific amount of free airtime to them. Some recent successful PSA campaigns include a campaign to preserve the oceans, featuring scenes from Disney's *The Little Mermaid*; a reminder about the foreclosure crisis faced by many American consumers, in which a family sitting down to dinner avoids answering a persistently ringing phone; and a fictional talent show citing the dangers of cyberbullying.[17] Other PSAs have been running for years and have created their own pop culture standards, like Smokey the Bear (wildfire prevention), McGruff the Crime Dog (crime prevention), and Rosie the Riveter (women going to work during World War II).[18]

Because they often are designed by top advertising agencies for nonprofit clients, PSAs usually are quite creative and stylistically appealing. For example, what is your reaction to the truth® public service antismoking campaign summarized in Ethical and Societal Dilemma 18.1?

Ethical and Societal Dilemma 18.1 Getting to the truth®

Just as is the case for other social marketing issues, getting young people to either stop smoking or never start offers a difficult challenge. Accomplishing attitudinal and/or behavioral changes with regard to an addictive product may be the toughest challenge of all for advertisers. Yet such changes were exactly the goal the American Legacy Foundation had in mind when it set out to "de-market" cigarettes to teenagers and children in 1999.

The foundation came into being as part of the historic tobacco settlement between various states' attorneys general and the tobacco industry. One clause of the settlement demanded that $300 million per year be set aside for a Public Education Fund. And part of this Public Education Fund was devoted to "raising generations that would be smoke free."

The first step was to get young people's attention—never an easy task. The American Legacy Foundation decided to use fear appeals and shock ads to deliver the message. The truth® campaign, the largest national youth-focused antitobacco education campaign ever, is designed to engage teens by exposing tobacco companies' marketing and manufacturing practices, as well as to highlight the toll of tobacco in relevant and innovative ways.[19] Specifically, the truth® provides "a hard-hitting media campaign that uses edgy television, radio and print ads," as well as a quirky, humor-filled Web site, "confronting the tobacco industry with smoking-related death statistics or exposing the companies' marketing tactics."[20] Among the most vivid ads are those that depict body bags piled up in front of Philip Morris headquarters, gasping rats to dramatize that cigarettes include an ingredient in rat poison, and a dog walker offering to sell dog urine to tobacco companies because cigarettes contain urea.[21] The Web site also pokes sarcastic fun at some of the companies' marketing tactics, including an animated feature called "The Useful Cigarette" that facetiously mentions how cigarettes could help people stay warm because they contain antifreeze and could be great for Goths who want to take off their black nail polish because they contain acetone, the main ingredient in nail polish remover.[22]

But how far is too far? Is this "in-your-face" style effective? Do advertisers need to go to these extremes to deliver their messages? According to the truth's own site, it does, and it has been successful, reducing smoking among youth by 300,000 by 2002.[23] In addition, according to an organization dedicated to helping the truth persevere, 75 percent of teens can identify truth ads.[24] However, for youths who already smoke, other research has shown that the campaign has had the opposite effect: Instead of convincing them to quit smoking, the campaign has reinforced their commitment to the addictive act. Should the truth continue to receive funding from the Big Tobacco settlement? Is it an effective means to provide a public service?

If you smoke, would this ad make you stop? If you don't smoke, would this ad influence you to refrain from starting?

To illustrate how a brand moves from generating primary demand in the introductory stage of its product life cycle to generating selective demand during the growth and maturity stages, consider Pfizer's brand Rogaine. When it first appeared on the market, Rogaine was considered quite innovative and required a doctor's prescription. No other products at the time existed to tackle the problem of "male pattern baldness." Pfizer's early ad campaigns were designed to inform consumers and generate demand for the product category. But as the category began to grow and mature, competitive treatments entered the market, especially once the product no longer required a prescription. As the market grew, Pfizer realized that both men and women experienced thinning hair; to market effectively to both groups, it had to design different campaigns. The appeal used for men is much more emotional, that for women much more informational. Even the color schemes and graphics on the packages are vastly different. The advertiser's ability to understand the needs of the target market thus is crucial, because it helps the firm determine which type of advertising and appeal to use.

Regardless of whether the advertising campaign's objective is to inform, persuade, or remind; to focus on a particular product or the institution in general; or to stimulate primary versus selective demand, each campaign's objectives must be specific and measurable. For a brand awareness campaign, for example, the objective might be to increase brand awareness among the target market by 50 percent within six months. Another campaign's goal may be to persuade 10 percent of a competitor's customers to switch to the advertised brand. Once the advertising campaign's objectives are set, the firm sets the advertising budget.

3. DETERMINE THE ADVERTISING BUDGET

The various budgeting methods for marketing communication (Chapter 17) also apply to budgeting for advertising. First, firms must consider the role that advertising plays in their attempt to meet their overall promotional objectives. Second, advertising expenditures vary over the course of the product life cycle. Third, the nature of the market and the product influence the size of advertising budgets. The nature of the market also determines the amount of money spent on advertising. For instance, less money is spent on advertising in B2B (business-to-business) marketing contexts than in B2C (business-to-consumer) markets. Personal selling, as we discuss in Chapter 19, likely is more important in B2B markets.

4. CONVEY THE MESSAGE

In this step, marketers determine what they want to convey about the product or service. First, the firm determines the key message it wants to communicate to the target audience. Second, the firm decides what appeal would most effectively convey the message. We present these decisions sequentially, but in reality, they must be considered simultaneously.

The Message

The message provides the target audience with reasons to respond in the desired way. A logical starting point for deciding on the advertising message is to tout the key benefits of the product or service. The message should communicate its problem-solving ability clearly and in a compelling fashion. In this context, advertisers must remember that products and services solve problems, whether real or perceived. That is, people are not looking for 1/4-inch drill bits; they are looking for 1/4-inch holes.[25] Because there are many ways to make a 1/4-inch hole, a firm like Black & Decker must convey to consumers that its drill bit is the best way to get that hole.

Another common strategy differentiates a product by establishing its unique benefits. This distinction forms the basis for the unique selling proposition (USP), which is often the common theme or slogan in an advertising campaign. Briefly, a good USP communicates the unique attributes of the product and thereby becomes a snapshot of the entire campaign. Some of the most famous USPs include the following:

Red Bull . . . Gives You Wings

Capital One . . . What's in your wallet?

Kellogg's Raisin Bran . . . Two scoops in every box of Kellogg's Raisin Bran

State Farm Insurance . . . Like a good neighbor, State Farm is there

TNT . . . We know drama

Is Black & Decker doing a good job of selling a solution?

The selling proposition communicated by the advertising must be not only *unique* to the brand but also *meaningful* to the consumer; it furthermore must be *sustainable* over time, even with repetition.

The Appeal

According to early theories of rhetoric (the study of the principles and rules of composition), there are three main types of appeals that an argument may use: logos (logical), ethos (ethical), and pathos (emotional). Advertisers similarly use different appeals to portray their product or service and persuade consumers to purchase them, though advertising tends to combine the types of appeals into two categories: informational and emotional.

Informational Appeals Informational appeals help consumers make purchase decisions by offering factual information and strong arguments (i.e., logos) built around relevant issues that encourage consumers to evaluate the brand favorably on the basis of the key benefits it provides.[26] Kimberly-Clark, for example, relies

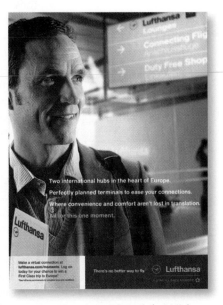

USPs are a common theme or slogan in an advertising campaign. Chevrolet (left) uses, "An American Revolution." IBM's (middle) USP is, "Stop Talking. Start Doing." Lufthansa's (right) slogan is, "There's no better way to fly."

heavily on informational appeals to sell Kleenex Anti-Viral tissues. Note the copy used on the company's Web site:

> Only KLEENEX® Anti-Viral Tissue has a moisture-activated middle layer that is scientifically proven to kill cold and flu viruses. When moisture from a runny nose, cough or sneeze comes in contact with KLEENEX® Anti-Viral Tissue's special middle layer, cold and flu viruses are trapped and killed.[27]

This appeal is perfectly suited to this type of product. The source of its competitive advantage is a tangible feature of the product. And by stressing the superior benefits of this product over regular facial tissue, the advertising copy directly delivers an informational persuasive message.[28]

Emotional Appeals   An **emotional appeal** aims to satisfy consumers' emotional desires rather than their utilitarian needs. These appeals therefore focus on feelings about the self. The key to a successful emotional appeal is the use of emotion to create a bond between the consumer and the brand. The emotions most often invoked in advertising include fear, safety, humor, happiness, love (or sex), comfort, and nostalgia.

Let's look again at Kimberly-Clark's Kleenex line; it uses a completely different and emotional appeal for its regular facial tissue. Facial tissues can be closely tied to emotional moments that create the need to wipe away tears of joy or sorrow, and Kleenex attempts to reinforce this emotional trigger by sponsoring the TNT TearJerker Movies. It also has a separate interactive Web site called Letitout. com, where users can post videos and pictures about emotional experiences on the blog and send virtual Kleenexes to their friends. Kleenex was the official supplier of the 2008 Olympics and produced *Let It Out®: The Movie*, a documentary on Olympians' experiences that evoke pride, joy, pain, and defeat.

Its "Let It Out" ads also chronicle the attempts of a therapist-like spokesman to get people in the street to stop on his couch and tell him about something—their love for their mother, how much they miss someone they've lost—that prompts them to reach for the Kleenex conveniently placed on a table in front of the couch. Unlike the Anti-Viral campaign, this campaign relies on the implied need for Kleenex during dramatic films and tough moments in life. Tangible product features, no longer the persuasive mechanism used to deliver the selling message as they are in informational appeals, do not even appear in the emotional appeal.

Although the term "emotion" often conveys the image of tears, many other effective appeals are used in advertising. People need a sense of self-esteem, so Jenny Craig advertisements tend to feature celebrities and regular people talking about how much better they feel about themselves after they've joined the program and lost weight. Weight loss ads also tend to play a bit on consumers' fears, showing "before and after" pictures as if the heavier version were a horror to behold. Fear appeals in politics are as old as the origin of paper. The Nazis used fear appeals to promulgate hate toward Jews during the Holocaust. Lyndon Johnson's infamous "Daisy" ad showed a nuclear explosion in a child's eye. Today candidates use fear appeals for issues as mundane as garbage removal to as serious as sexual predators. Clearly, fear appeals often work best when the threat appears to be directed toward children or some other innocent victim.

Another common appeal, sex and love, turns products that may or may not be sexy into sex-based products. Nivea promises that its moisturizing lotion makes the difference "between staying in and going out," suggesting a direct relation between its smoothing lotion and users' sex appeal. Levi's features a man in his apartment struggling to get his jeans on, and with each tug, a street scene enters further into his room. In a relatively new twist on the sex appeal, though, Levi's filmed two versions of the ad: one in which the street scene

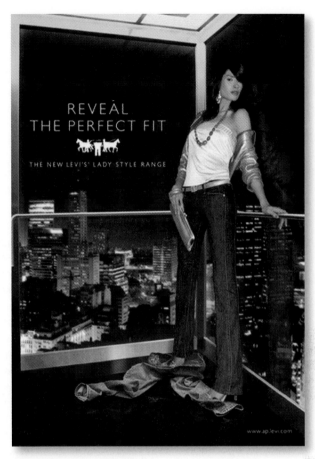

Firms use emotional appeals to satisfy consumers' emotional desires rather than their utilitarian needs. The ad on the left appeals to people's fear of environmental crisis, while the ad on the right has sex appeal.

contains a woman in a phone booth, who eventually walks off, arm-in-arm, with the Levi's-wearing main character, and another in which the object of his affection is a man.[29]

5. EVALUATE AND SELECT MEDIA

The content of an advertisement is tied closely to the characteristics of the media that firms select to carry the message, and vice versa. Media planning refers to the process of evaluating and selecting the media mix—the combination of the media used and the frequency of advertising in each medium—that will deliver a clear, consistent, compelling message to the intended audience.[30] For example, Target may determine that a heavy dose of television, radio, print, and billboards is appropriate for the holiday selling season between Thanksgiving and the end of the year.

Because the media buy, the actual purchase of airtime or print pages, is generally the largest expense in the advertising budget, marketers must make their decisions carefully. Television advertising is by far the most expensive. Total U.S. advertising expenditures per medium have remained roughly constant for some time, though some shifts are currently taking place. For example, whereas television advertising is consistent at approximately 44 percent, Internet advertising is jumping from about 7 to 8 percent. Spanish-language media also are growing by more than 14 percent, whereas newspaper advertising is losing almost an entire percentage point.[31] To characterize these various types of media, we again use a dichotomy: mass and niche media.

Mass and Niche Media

Mass media channels include national newspapers, magazines, radio, and television and are ideal for reaching large numbers of anonymous audience members. **Niche media** channels are more focused and generally used to reach narrower segments, often with unique demographic characteristics or interests. Cable television and specialty magazines such as *Skateboarder* or *Cosmo Girl* all provide examples of niche media. In some cases, niche media offer advertisers the opportunity to change and even personalize their messages, which is generally not an option with mass media. For example, magazine advertisers can print response cards with the name of the subscriber already on the card or change advertisements to reflect local differences, such as climate or preferences.

Choosing the Right Medium

For each class of media, each alternative has specific characteristics that make it suitable for meeting specific objectives (see Exhibit 18.3). For example, consumers use different media for different purposes, to which advertisers should match their messages. Television is used primarily for escapism and entertainment, so most television advertising relies on a mix of visual and auditory techniques.

How, then, could the third largest office supply dealer, OfficeMax, differentiate itself from its dominant rivals, Office Depot and Staples? It approached the holiday season with a **viral marketing campaign**—a campaign that facilitates and encourages people to pass along a marketing message. It is nicknamed viral because the number of people exposed to a message mimics the process of passing a virus or disease from one person to another.[32] The company set up a toll-free

EXHIBIT 18.3	Types of Media Available for Advertising	
Medium	**Advantages**	**Disadvantages**
Television	■ Has wide reach. ■ Incorporates sound and video.	■ Has high cost. ■ Has cluttered airways. ■ Has more potential spillover.
Radio	■ Is relatively inexpensive. ■ Can be selectively targeted. ■ Has wide reach.	■ No video limits presentation. ■ Consumers give less focused attention than TV. ■ Exposure periods are short.
Magazines	■ Are very targeted. ■ Subscribers pass along to others.	■ Are relatively inflexible. ■ Have long lead times.
Newspapers	■ Are flexible. ■ Are timely. ■ Can localize.	■ Can be expensive in some markets. ■ Involve potential loss of control over placement. ■ Advertisements have short life span.
Internet	■ Can be linked to detailed content. ■ Is highly flexible and interactive. ■ Allows for specific targeting.	■ Costs not easily comparable to other media. ■ Is becoming cluttered. ■ Blocking software prohibits delivery.
Outdoors	■ Is relatively inexpensive. ■ Offers opportunities for repeat exposure. ■ Is flexible.	■ Is not easily targeted. ■ Has placement problems in some markets. ■ Exposure time is very short.
Direct Mail	■ Is highly targeted. ■ Is flexible. ■ Allows for personalization.	■ Is relatively expensive. ■ Is a cluttered environment. ■ Is often considered "junk mail."

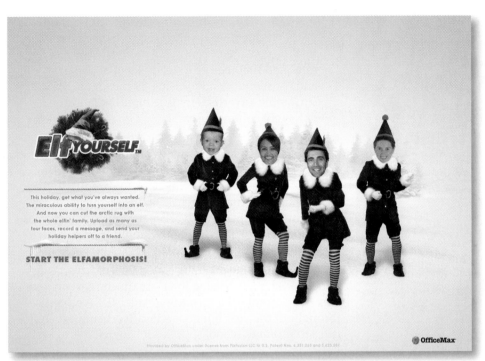

OfficeMax uses a successful viral marketing campaign in which people can send customized "elf" messages to their friends during the holidays.

phone number that visitors could use to record a message that got transformed to sound like an elf's voice, then visitors could upload their own faces and paste them onto the dancing elf. A link to the Web site was e-mailed to friends and families and OfficeMax's thousands of employees. The site received more than 36 million visitors and more than 11 million elves were created. *Good Morning America* and other programs even used the program to "elf" their on-air personalities. The following year, OfficeMax expanded the elf campaign into four dancing elves, prompting 193 million visits and the creation of 123 million new elves. The site ranked among the 1,000 most popular in 50 countries. OfficeMax even took out an ad in *The Wall Street Journal* to apologize to corporate America for the loss of productivity caused by the dancing elves.

The results of the campaign showed that more than one-third of those who visited the site were influenced to shop at OfficeMax. Another one-third said the campaign improved their perceptions of the retailer. Ninety-five percent said that they would visit the ElfYourself.com Web site again the next year. The viral campaign thus was able to connect people and customers online to create dialogue rather than monologue, in OfficeMax's terminology. In the process, the company built its brand and created a piggyback campaign that customers will await each year.[33]

Communication media also vary in their ability to reach the desired audience. For instance, radio is a good medium for products such as grocery purchases or fast food because many consumers decide what to purchase either on the way to the store or while in the store. Because many people listen to the radio in their cars, it becomes a highly effective means to reach consumers at a crucial point in their decision process. As we discussed in Chapter 17, each medium also varies in its reach and frequency. Advertisers can determine how effective their media mix has been in reaching their target audience by calculating the total GRP (reach × frequency) of the advertising schedule, which we discuss next.

Determining the Advertising Schedule

Another important decision for the media planner is the advertising schedule, which specifies the timing and duration of advertising. There are three types of schedules:[34]

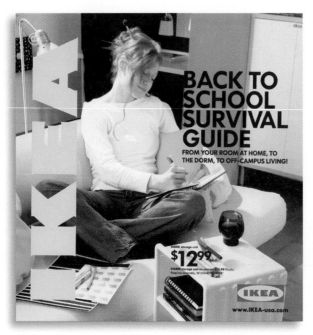

IKEA uses a pulsing strategy when they set their advertising schedule. They advertise throughout the year, but have more advertising directed at the back-to-school market in August.

- A **continuous** schedule runs steadily throughout the year and therefore is suited to products and services that are consumed continually at relatively steady rates and that require a steady level of persuasive and/or reminder advertising. For example, Procter & Gamble advertises its Tide brand of laundry detergent continuously.

- **Flighting** refers to an advertising schedule implemented in spurts, with periods of heavy advertising followed by periods of no advertising. This pattern generally functions for products whose demand fluctuates, such as tennis racquets, which manufacturers may advertise heavily in the months leading up to and during the summer.

- **Pulsing** combines the continuous and flighting schedules by maintaining a base level of advertising but increasing advertising intensity during certain periods. For example, the furniture retailer IKEA advertises throughout the year but boosts its advertising expenditures to promote school supplies in August.

6. CREATE ADVERTISEMENTS

After the advertiser has decided on the message, type of ad, and appeal, its attention must shift to the actual creation of the advertisement. During this step, the message and appeal are translated creatively into words, pictures, colors, and/or music. Often, the execution style for the ad will dictate the type of medium used to deliver the message. For example, although automobile manufacturers and their dealers advertise in many media, the media must fit the message.[35] To demonstrate an image, they can use television and magazines. To promote price, they can use newspapers and radio. To appeal to specific target markets, they can use some of the electronic media vehicles described in Chapter 17. When using multiple media to deliver the same message, however, they must maintain consistency across the execution styles—that is, integrated marketing—so that the different executions deliver a consistent and compelling message to the target audience.

MINI Cooper has developed an innovative method of advertising to its current customers with this interactive billboard. Owners receive an RFID chip–embedded key fob (upper right corner). Every time a customer passes the billboard, he or she receives a customized message.

Why is this gorilla smiling? Because the kangaroos have arrived at the Buenos Aires Zoo. This Clio-winning ad delivers a compelling visual, a call to action (visit the zoo), and the advertiser's identification.

Although creativity plays a major role in the execution stage, advertisers must remain careful not to let their creativity overshadow the message. Whatever the execution style, the advertisement must be able to attract the audience's attention, provide a reason for the audience to spend its time viewing the advertisement, and accomplish what it set out to do. In the end, the execution style must match the medium and objectives.

Print advertising can be especially difficult because it is a static medium: no sound, no motion, only one dimension. Instead, print relies on several key components that appear in most ads: the headline, or large type designed to draw attention and be read first; the body copy, which represents the main text portion of the ad; the background or backdrop for the ad, usually a single color; the foreground, which refers to everything that appears on top of the background, and the branding that identifies the sponsor of the ad. The advertiser must convey its message using these compelling visuals, background colors or images, a logo, and limited text.

The ad above is an example of a very effective print ad, so effective that it won a Clio, the top advertising award.[36] From the start, this compelling ad makes viewers wonder why the gorilla is smiling, and the answer, that "The kangaroos have arrived," is likely to prompt amused awareness that a new exhibit has opened. The background and foreground match in their coloring, because this advertisement really wants to emphasize the foreground image instead of relying on bright colors to attract readers' attention. Once it has grabbed them with the funky image, the ad ensures that viewers know who is advertising and how to answer the ad's call to action (i.e., visit the zoo) by including the zoo name and logo, even larger than the tagline. In other ads, the advertiser might include a Web address or telephone number to enable the target audience to answer different calls to action. For the Buenos Aires Zoo though, this ad delivers all the necessary elements: a compelling visual, a call to action, and the advertiser's identification.

For radio and television, some important execution elements include identifying the appropriate talent (actors or singers) to deliver the message and choosing the correct music and visuals. As we noted in this chapter's opener, The Gap has flirted with different types of celebrities to represent its image in advertising. Attempting to be more accessible to its target market, it has shied away from supermodels in favor of celebrities that it believes its customers can better relate to.

7. ASSESS IMPACT USING MARKETING METRICS

The effectiveness of an advertising campaign must be assessed before, during, and after the campaign has run. **Pretesting** refers to assessments performed before an ad campaign is implemented to ensure that the various elements are working in an integrated fashion and doing what they are intended to do.[37] **Tracking** includes monitoring key indicators, such as daily or weekly sales volume, while the advertisement is running to shed light on any problems with the message or the medium. **Posttesting** is the evaluation of the campaign's impact after it is has been implemented. At this last stage, advertisers assess the sales and/or communication impact of the advertisement or campaign.

Measuring sales impact can be especially challenging because of the many influences other than advertising on consumers' choices, purchase behavior, and attitudes. These influences include the level of competitors' advertising, economic conditions in the target market, sociocultural changes, and even the weather, all of which can influence consumer purchasing behavior. Advertisers must try to identify these influences and isolate those of the particular advertising campaign.

For frequently purchased consumer goods in the maturity stage of the product life cycle such as soda, sales volume offers a good indicator of advertising effectiveness. Because their sales are relatively stable, and if we assume that the other elements of the marketing mix and the environment have not changed, we can attribute changes in sales volume to changes in advertising. Exhibit 18.4 illustrates a hypothetical sales history for Red Bull soda in a grocery store chain. Using a statistical technique called time-series analysis, sales data from the past is used to forecast the future. The data in Exhibit 18.4 can be decomposed into its basic trend (green), the seasonal influences (red), and the **lift** or additional sales caused by the advertising (orange). In this case, the lift caused by the advertising campaign is substantial.

For other types of goods in other stages of the product life cycle, sales data offer but one of the many indicators that marketers need to examine to determine advertising effectiveness. For instance, in high-growth markets, sales growth alone can be misleading because the market as a whole is growing. In such a situation, marketers measure sales relative to those of competitors to determine their relative market share. Firms find creative ways to identify advertising effectiveness. For

EXHIBIT 18.4 Sales History for Red Bull in a Grocery Store Chain

example, digital cable allows them to present a specific advertisement to certain neighborhoods and then track sales by local or regional retailers.

Some product categories experience so many influences that it is almost impossible to identify advertising's contribution to any individual consumer's choice to purchase a particular product, especially for addictive products such as cigarettes and alcohol or those with potentially negative health consequences, such as fast food or high-sugar breakfast cereals. Although many people firmly believe that advertising for these products contributes significantly to obesity in children, academic research has not been able to show a causal relationship. Other factors, such as parental and peer influence, tend to reflect a stronger causal relationship than does advertising.[38]

CHECK YOURSELF

1. What are the steps involved in planning an ad campaign?
2. What is the difference between informational, persuasive, and reminder advertising?
3. What are the pros and cons of the different media types?

REGULATORY AND ETHICAL ISSUES IN ADVERTISING

In the United States, the regulation of advertising involves a complex mix of formal laws and informal restrictions designed to protect consumers from deceptive practices. Many federal and state laws, as well as a wide range of self-regulatory agencies and agreements, affect advertising (Exhibit 18.5). The primary federal agencies that regulate advertising activities are the Federal Trade Commission (FTC), Federal Communications Commission (FCC), and Food and Drug Administration (FDA). In addition to these agencies, others, such as the Bureau of Alcohol, Tobacco and Firearms and the U.S. Postal Service, regulate advertising to some degree.

The FTC is the primary enforcement agency for most mass media advertising. Occasionally, the FTC and FCC join together to investigate and enforce regulations on particular advertising practices. One special class of products is dietary supplements, many of which are classified as food products and therefore do not

EXHIBIT 18.5	Federal Agencies That Regulate Advertising	
Federal Agency	**General Purpose**	**Specific Jurisdiction**
Federal Trade Commission (FTC) (established 1914)	Enforces federal consumer protection laws.	Enforces truth in advertising laws; defines deceptive and unfair advertising practices.
Federal Communications Commission (FCC) (1934)	Regulates interstate and international communications by radio, television, wire, satellite, and cable.	Enforces restrictions on broadcasting material that promotes lotteries (with some exceptions); cigarettes, little cigars, or smokeless tobacco products; or that perpetuates a fraud. Also enforces laws that prohibit or limit obscene, indecent, or profane language.
Food and Drug Administration (1930)	Regulates food, dietary supplements, drugs, cosmetics, medical devices (including radiation-emitting devices such as cell phones), biologics (biological issues), and blood products.	Regulates package labeling and inserts, definition of terms such as "light" and "organic," and required disclosure statements (warning labels, dosage requirements, etc.).

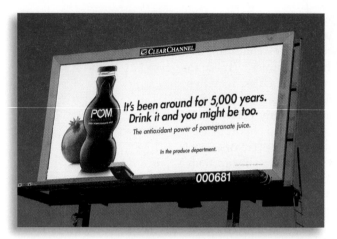

Is this ad an example of puffery or deception?

fall under the FDA's strict standards for drug advertising. Thus, companies can make unsubstantiated claims about them if they offer an accompanying disclosure statement, such as "This statement has not been evaluated by the FDA" or "This product is not intended to diagnose, treat, cure, or prevent any disease."[39]

This does not mean, however, that firms are free to say whatever they want in their promotions. Airborne, for instance, is a dietary supplement and health formula that is claimed to help ward off harmful bacteria and germs, and help prevent the flu and the common cold. It contains herbal extracts, amino acids, antioxidants, electrolytes, synthetic vitamins, and other ingredients, and can be purchased in many U.S. retail stores without a prescription. To settle a class-action lawsuit claiming that there is no evidence that the supplement wards off harmful bacteria and germs, the manufacturer agreed to pay former customers $23.3 million.[40] Another class-action lawsuit against dairy company Dannon alleges that claims on advertisements and labeling for its Activia brand of yogurt that the product is "proven" to improve one's "intestinal rhythm" and "regulate your digestive system" are all unsubstantiated. It further claims that deceptive advertising has enabled Dannon to sell hundreds of millions of dollars worth of ordinary yogurt at a 30 percent price premium over regular yogurt to consumers.[41]

Many product categories fall under self-regulatory restrictions or guidelines. For example, advertising to children is regulated primarily through self-regulatory mechanisms designed by the National Association of Broadcasters and the Better Business Bureau's Children's Advertising Review Unit. The only formal regulation of children's advertising appears in the Children's Television Act of 1990, which limits the amount of advertising broadcast during children's viewing hours.[42]

Recently, to make matters even more complicated for advertisers, state attorneys general's offices have begun to inquire into various advertising practices and assert their authority to regulate advertising in their states. The EU also has increased its regulation of advertising for EU member nations. Many of these state and European regulations are more restrictive than existing federal or self-regulatory requirements.

The line between what is legal and illegal is more difficult to discern when it comes to **puffery**, which is the legal exaggeration of praise, stopping just short of deception, lavished on a product.[43] Take, for instance, the following claims found in a classified real estate section: "Lovely Townhome, Feels Like Single Family," "Stunningly Beautiful," "Best Price in Town," "Bargain of the Year." Since all of these claims are highly subjective, and none could be proven true or false, they are considered to be puffery and therefore allowed under the law.

How do the courts determine what makes an ad deceptive, rather than simply puffery? The FTC's position is that it "will not pursue cases involving obviously exaggerated or puffing representations, i.e., those that ordinary consumers do not take seriously."[44] In general, the less specific the claim, the less likely it is considered to be deceptive. For instance, if Burger King claimed it had the best hamburgers in the world, it would probably be considered puffery. But if it claimed to make the top 1 percent of all hamburgers, it would be deceptive, unless, of course it could prove that claim.

In an actual case, the American Italian Pasta Company was found not to be in violation of the truth-in-advertising law (Lanham Act) for using its slogan, "America's Favorite Pasta." The court reasoned, "it fell into the category of (1) exaggerated statements of bluster or boast upon which no reasonable consumer would rely; and (2) vague or highly subjective claims of product superiority. . . ."[45] In the end, puffery is OK as long as consumers know that the firm is stretching the truth through exaggeration. But if the consumer knows it's puffery, then why bother?[46]

PUBLIC RELATIONS

As you may recall from Chapter 17, public relations (PR) involves managing communications and relationships to achieve various objectives, such as building and maintaining a positive image of the firm, handling or heading off unfavorable stories or events, and maintaining positive relationships with the media. In many cases, public relations activities support other promotional efforts by generating "free" media attention and general goodwill.

Designers, for example, vie to have celebrities, especially those nominated for awards, wear their fashions on the red carpet. These sightings can create both positive and negative publicity. When Reese Witherspoon wore a Nina Ricci yellow cocktail dress to the Golden Globes, the dress got so much press that the designer's cachet increased significantly. Chanel, Valentino, Zac Posen, and Christian Dior are all red carpet veterans that commonly provide dresses or tuxedos to celebrities, whose images will be broadcast around the world.[47] The controversy surrounding Diablo Cody's refusal to wear Stuart Weitzman–designed diamond-encrusted shoes to the Oscars seems to have created negative publicity for both the screenwriter and the designer, yet both names remained in the news for far longer than those of most participants in the awards ceremony.[48] The placement of designer apparel at media events benefits both the designer and the celebrity. And neither happens by accident. Public relations people on both sides help orchestrate the events to get the maximum benefit for both parties.

Good PR has always been an important success factor. Yet in recent years, the importance of PR has grown as the cost of other forms of marketing communications has increased. At the same time, the influence of PR has become more powerful as consumers have become increasingly skeptical of marketing claims made in other media.[49] In many instances, consumers view media coverage generated through PR as more credible and objective than any other aspects of an IMC program, because the firm does not "buy" the space in print media or time on radio or television.

For example, TOMS Shoes, a company founded by Blake Mycoskie, illustrates how a well-orchestrated IMC effort, using a combination of promotional and PR campaigns, can enhance a firm's image while supporting a worthwhile cause.[50] Mycoskie took a traditional Argentinean shoe, known as *alpargatas*, and began selling and marketing them to consumers outside the generally impoverished nation in which they originated. The company's Web site proclaims that Mycoskie's inspiration was simple. He noted the comfort of the shoes and the extreme poverty of Argentina, so he promises, again with great simplicity: "You buy a pair of TOMS, and I give a pair to a child on your behalf." This message is found on his Web site, and other press vehicles, including a mention as the "Good Guy of the Month" in Oprah Winfrey's *O, The Oprah Winfrey Magazine*. TOMS shoes embraces cause-related marketing, which refers to commercial activity in which businesses and charities form a partnership to market an image, product, or service for their mutual benefit.[51] That is, the company is not just about making and selling shoes but also partners with groups such as Insight Argentina, an organization offering volunteer activities in Argentina to help that area address its most pressing social issues.[52]

Another very popular PR tool is event sponsorship. Event sponsorship occurs when corporations support various activities (financially or otherwise), usually in the cultural or sports and entertainment sectors. Some of them are big name events; the titles of most college football playoff games now include the

EXHIBIT 18.6   Elements of a Public Relations Toolkit

PR Element	Function
Publications: Brochures, special-purpose single-issue publications such as books	Inform various constituencies about the activities of the organization and highlight specific areas of expertise.
Video and audio: Programs, public service announcements	Highlight the organization or support cause-related marketing efforts.
Annual reports	Give required financial performance data and inform investors and others about the unique activities of the organization.
Media relations: Press kits, news releases, speeches, event sponsorships	Generate news coverage of the organization's activities or products/services.
Electronic media: Web sites, e-mail campaigns	Web sites can contain all the previously mentioned toolbox elements, while e-mail directs PR efforts to specific target groups.

name of their sponsors (e.g., the Allstate Sugar Bowl). Others are slightly less famous; for example, Rollerblade USA, the maker of Rollerblade in-line skates, sponsors Skate-In-School, a program it developed with the National Association for Sport and Physical Education (NAPSE) to promote the inclusion of rollerblading in physical education curricula. Firms often distribute a PR toolkit to communicate with various audiences. Some toolkit elements are designed to inform specific groups directly, whereas others are created to generate media attention and disseminate information. We depict the various elements of a PR toolkit in Exhibit 18.6.

CHECK YOURSELF

1. Why do companies utilize public relations as part of their IMC strategy?
2. What are the elements of a public relations toolkit?

SALES PROMOTION

Advertising rarely provides the only means to communicate with target customers. As we discussed in Chapter 17, a natural link appears between advertising and sales promotion. Sales promotions are special incentives or excitement-building programs that encourage consumers to purchase a particular product or service, typically used in conjunction with other advertising or personal selling programs. Many sales promotions, like free samples or point-of-purchase (POP) displays, attempt to build short-term sales, whereas others, like loyalty programs, contests, and sweepstakes, have become integral components of firms' long-term customer relationship management (CRM) programs, which they use to build customer loyalty. In this section, we examine the various tools firms use for their sales promotions and how those tools complement the advertiser's efforts to achieve its strategic objectives.

We present the tools used in sales promotions, along with their advantages and disadvantages, in Exhibit 18.7 and discuss them next. Then, we examine some ways in which integrated marketing communication (IMC) programs make use of sales promotions.

The tools of any sales promotion can be focused on either channel members, such as wholesalers or retailers, or end-user consumers. Just as we delineated for advertising, when sales promotions are targeted at channel members, the marketer is employing a push strategy; when it targets consumers themselves, it is using a pull strategy. Some sales promotion tools can be used with either a push or pull strategy. We now consider each of the tools and how they are used.

Types of Sales Promotion

Coupons   A coupon is a certificate with a stated price reduction for a specific item or percentage of a purchase. Coupons are commonly used in supermarkets, but other retailers such as department stores and restaurants also use coupons to lure customers away from the competition. Manufacturers also distribute coupons for their products that can be used at retailers that stock their products. To attract customers, some supermarkets even accept coupons distributed by competing retailers.

Some retailers have linked coupons directly to their loyalty programs. Drugstore giant CVS, for instance, tracks its customers' purchases from its Extra Care loyalty card and gives

This sales promotion deal for Payless ShoeSource is a short-term price promotion that encourages consumers to buy a second pair of shoes at one-half off.

EXHIBIT 18.7	Kinds of Sales Promotion	
Promotion	**Advantages**	**Disadvantages**
Coupons	■ Stimulates demand. ■ Allows for direct tracing of sales.	■ Has low redemption rates. ■ Has high cost.
Deals	■ Encourages trial. ■ Reduces consumer risk.	■ May reduce perception of value.
Premiums	■ Builds goodwill. ■ Increases perception of value.	■ Consumers buy for premium not product. ■ Has to be carefully managed.
Contests	■ Increases consumer involvement. ■ Generates excitement.	■ Requires creativity. ■ Must be monitored.
Sweepstakes	■ Encourages present consumers to consume more.	■ Sales often decline after.
Samples	■ Encourages trial. ■ Offers direct involvement.	■ Has high cost to the firm.
Loyalty Programs	■ Creates loyalty. ■ Encourages repurchase.	■ Has high cost to the firm.
POP Displays	■ Provides high visibility. ■ Encourages brand trial.	■ Is difficult to get a good location in the store. ■ Can be costly to the firm.
Rebates	■ Stimulates demand. ■ Increases value perception.	■ Is easily copied by competitors. ■ May just advance future sales.
Product Placement	■ Displays products nontraditionally. ■ Demonstrates product uses.	■ Firm often has little control over display. ■ Product can be overshadowed.

MediaCart delivers point-of-decision promotions from a shopping cart.

them coupons that are tailored just for them.[53] Kroger Co. registered its loyalty card members with Shortcuts.com, allowing customers to go online and choose which coupons they want to redeem. The coupon offerings that the customer chooses are automatically deducted when the loyalty card is scanned at the register.[54]

Coupons received by mobile phones are starting to be offered by some firms. Although almost a third of consumers would like to receive mobile coupons, only about 1 percent of advertisers currently offer them.[55]

A new product, the MediaCart, delivers point-of-decision advertising from a shopping cart. Although it doesn't provide paper coupons in a traditional way, it does inform customers about special deals as they pass them in the aisle. Each video screen is embedded with a radio frequency identification (RFID) chip that interacts with chips installed on store shelves. In addition to providing advertising and special offers, it can record shopping habits, shopper dwelling times, and how shoppers travel through the store—all critical information that the retailer can use to provide a better shopping experience for customers and thus increase sales.

Traditional coupons carried in newspapers, magazines, in-store displays, and direct mail have very low redemption rates of less than 1 percent; on the other hand, redemption rates from these newer forms of coupons are much higher and are gaining in popularity.[56] The reason why traditional coupons are waning in favor of electronically generated coupons is that consumers can seek out these coupons or marketers can individually target customers, whereas many people have no interest in purchasing products or services offered by traditional coupons.

Deals   A **deal** refers generally to a type of short-term price reduction that can take several forms, such as a "featured price," a price lower than the regular price; a "buy one, get one free" offer; or a certain percentage "more free" offer contained in larger packaging. Another form of a deal involves a special financing arrangement, such as reduced percentage interest rates or extended repayment terms. Deals encourage customers to try a product because they lower the risk for consumers by reducing the cost of the good. Deals can also alter perceptions of value—a short-term price reduction may signal a different price/quality relationship than would be ideal from the manufacturer's perspective.

Premiums   A **premium** offers an item for free or at a bargain price to reward some type of behavior, such as buying, sampling, or testing. These rewards build goodwill among consumers, who often perceive high value in them. Premiums can be distributed in a variety of ways: They can be included in the product packaging, such as the toys inside cereal boxes; placed visibly on the package, such as a coupon for free milk on a box of Cheerios; handed out in the store; or delivered in the mail, such as the free perfume offers Victoria's Secret mails to customers.

Furthermore, premiums can be very effective if they are consistent with the brand's message and image and highly desirable to the target market. However, finding a premium that meets these criteria at a reasonable cost can be a serious challenge. At Burger King, the average order cost is $5, while the average premium the fast-food giant distributes costs the company less than 50 cents. Is a 50 cent premium enough to stimulate sufficient demand? Or is it too expensive for Burger King to offer?

Contests A contest refers to a brand-sponsored competition that requires some form of skill or effort. 3M, makers of Post-it Notes, is hosting a "One Million Uses and Counting" global consumer contest on YouTube.[57] Each contestant is required to create and upload a short video to the official Post-it YouTube channel demonstrating a unique use of Post-it Notes. All submissions receive a free trial of Post-it Digital Notes. The winner receives a cash award and the winning video may be featured as "America's No. 1 Choice" on Post-it.com and on the Post-it Notes YouTube channel for three consecutive months.

If you won the Delta Grammy Sweepstakes, you could hear John Legend sing on an in-flight concert.

Sweepstakes A form of sales promotion that offers prizes based on a chance drawing of entrants' names, sweepstakes do not require the entrant to complete a task other than buying a ticket or filling out a form. Often the key benefit of sweepstakes is that they encourage current consumers to consume more if the sweepstakes form appears inside the packaging or with the product. Many states, however, specify that no purchase can be required to enter sweepstakes.

Samples Sampling offers potential customers the opportunity to try a product or service before they make a buying decision. Distributing samples is one of the most costly sales promotion tools but also one of the most effective. Quick service restaurants and grocery stores frequently utilize sampling. For instance, Starbucks provides samples of new products to customers. Costco uses so many samples that customers can have an entire meal. Sometimes trial-size samples come in the mail or are distributed in stores.

Hotels utilize a variation on the sampling theme. Guests "sample" the hotel and its amenities, and can then purchase everything from the pillow they sleep on to the shampoo they use. The Westin was the first hotel to sell parts of the hotel room, starting with its Heavenly Bed. When it first offered the bed for individual sale, the hotel's satisfaction ratings shot up 5 percent, and room occupancy rates increased.[58] Hotels at Home (www.hotelsathome.com), a catalog and e-commerce business, offers products from more than 2,400 hotel chains worldwide, including Westin, Hilton, and Sheraton. Their customers are less likely to return products than typical online shoppers, because they already have had a "test drive" during their hotel stay. Hotels at Home allows customers to cherry pick—buy a Marriot bed and a Westin pillow.

At Hotels at Home (www.hotelsathome.com) you can buy the same products you find at hotels like Westin, Hilton, and Sheraton.

Loyalty Programs   As part of a sales promotion program, loyalty programs are specifically designed to retain customers by offering premiums or other incentives to customers who make multiple purchases over time. Such sales promotions are growing increasingly popular and are often tied to long-term CRM systems. (Loyalty programs are examined in Chapters 2 and 16.)

Point-of-Purchase Displays   Point-of-purchase (POP) displays are merchandise displays located at the point of purchase, such as at the checkout counter in a supermarket. Retailers have long recognized that the most valuable real estate in the store is at the POP (point of purchase). Customers see products like a magazine or a candy bar while they are waiting to pay for their purchases, and impulsively purchase them. In the Internet version of a point-of-purchase display, shoppers are stimulated by special merchandise, price reductions, or complementary products that Internet retailers feature on the checkout screen.

Rebates   Rebates are a particular type of price reduction in which a portion of the purchase price is returned by the seller to the buyer in the form of cash. Many products, such as consumer electronics, offer significant mail-in rebates that may lower the price of the item significantly. Some companies enjoy the added bonus of good PR when they appear on consumer Web sites like fatwallet.com or slickdeals.net—sites that post rebate offers and the rules for getting them in one easily accessed place.[59] Firms offer such generous rebates because the likelihood that consumers will actually apply for the rebate is low. The firms garner considerable value from rebates because they attract consumers but they may not have to pay off all the rebates offered.

Some companies may have taken the idea of minimal risk too much to heart, prompting complaints from some consumers that the rebates are too difficult to redeem. In some cases, the complaints have led to lawsuits in which consumers claimed the rebate offers were misleading. Such consumer backlash has prompted Best Buy and Office Max to abandon the entire concept, while others like Staples have begun advertising a separate "Easy Rebates" program.[60]

Product Placement   When marketers use product placement, they include their product in nontraditional situations, such as in a scene in a movie or television program.[61] Perhaps the most famous visible movie product placement was Hershey's Reese's Pieces in the film *ET*. The product actually became part of the storyline, offered the candy high levels of visibility, and resulted in a large increase in sales.[62] The placement also became the stuff of movie legend; Steven Spielberg, the director, had wanted to use M&M's candy but could not get permission from Mars to do so.

Although Hershey's did not pay to place Reese's Pieces in *ET*, other firms have been more than willing to shell out for product placements. Various companies spend approximately $4.38 billion on product placements in movies annually (e.g., Sony laptops in the James Bond feature *Casino Royale*) and television (e.g., Applebee's restaurant in *Friday Night Lights*). For their deals with *American Idol*, Ford, Coca-Cola, and AT&T pay approximately $30 million each to gain product placements and advertising space.[63]

MTV's reality TV show, *The Hills*, is the highest rated show on the network, and features multiple product placements. Heidi Montag, one of the main stars of *The Hills*, works for SBE Entertainment Group, which manages hotels, restaurants, and nightclubs. *The Hills* regularly gives viewers updates on SBE's newest projects. For example, SBE just bought the Sahara Hotel

Point-of-purchase (POP) displays are located at the point of purchase such as a checkout counter in a supermarket. They are very effective for stimulating impulse purchases.

in Las Vegas. The four protagonist California girls on *The Hills* party at SBE-owned nightclubs such as S-Bar and Hyde, and then frequent Pinkberry, a frozen yogurt chain. Two of the characters on the show, Lauren Conrad and Whitney Port, interned at *Teen Vogue*, and now work for the PR firm People's Revolution, owned by Kelly Cutrone. Designer Marc Jacobs, a Michael Kors boutique storefront, BMWs, Mercedes, Audis, Bentleys, Christian Louboutin shoes, Chanel, and Balenciaga bags all make not-so-subtle appearances on the show. Of course, every member of the cast has an iPhone.

The most recent trend sees product placements in other forms of media, including books, video games, and music. The authors of *Cathy's Book*, a 2006 publication, agreed to change all makeup references in the text to Cover Girl products, so, whereas initially the main character just wore lip gloss, in the revised edition she wears "a killer coat of Lipslicks in 'Daring.'"[64] Complaints from some observers led the authors to remove the mentions for the paperback release, but by then, the novel had already sold approximately 48,000 copies. Furor similarly erupted over Russell Simmon's admission that he had entered into negotiations with McDonald's to get some of the rappers he represents to include mentions of Big Macs in their rhymes.[65] Research continues to suggest that consumers recall product placements relatively well.[66]

Hummer successfully placed its product on CSI: Miami.

MTV's "The Hills" cast, Lauren 'Lo' Bosworth, Lauren Conrad, and Whitney Port, host the VIP grand opening of Bowlmor Lanes West Coast Outpost STRIKE in Orange County, California.

Using Sales Promotion Tools

Marketers must be careful in their use of promotions, especially those that focus on lowering prices. Depending on the item, consumers may stock up when items are offered at a lower price, which simply shifts sales from the future to now and thereby leads to short-run benefits at the expense of long-term sales stability. For instance, using sales promotions like coupons to stimulate sales of household cleaning supplies may cause consumers to stockpile the products and decrease demand for those products in the future. But a similar promotion used with a perishable product like Dannon yogurt should increase its demand at the expense of competitors like Yoplait.

Many firms are also realizing the value of **cross-promoting**, when two or more firms join together to reach a specific target market. To achieve a successful cross-promotion, the two products must appeal to the same target market and together create value for consumers. Burger King, for instance recently ran a three-firm cross promotion: Motts Strawberry-Flavored Applesauce, designed to attract health-conscious parents; *Star Wars* memorabilia, designed to attract collectors and fans of the movie; and BK King of the Courts 3-on-3 College Basketball Tournament, designed to attract college students and fans of college basketball. Each of these cross-promotions targets a different market and attempts to create value in a slightly different way for Burger King consumers. However, the ultimate, overall goal for Burger King is to generate increased sales and greater brand loyalty.

The goal of any sales promotion is to create value for both the consumers and the firm. By understanding the needs of its customers, as well as how best to entice them to purchase or consume a particular product or service, a firm can develop promotional messages and events that are of interest to and achieve the desired response from those customers. Traditionally, the role of sales promotion has been to generate short-term results, whereas the goal of advertising was to generate long-term results. As this chapter demonstrates, though, both sales promotion and advertising can generate both long- and short-term effects. The effective combination of both types of activities leads to impressive results for the firm and the consumers.

Evaluating Sales Promotions Using Marketing Metrics

Many sales promotion opportunities undertaken by retailers are initiated by manufacturers. For example, Sharp might offer the following special promotion to Costco: During a one-week period, Costco can order 37-inch Sharp Aquos LCD HDTVs at $300 below the standard wholesale price. However, if Costco elects to buy these HDTVs at the discounted price, then it must feature them prominently on its Web page for $1099.00 ($325 below the suggested retail price). In addition, Costco must agree to purchase enough of this particular model to have front-of-store displays in each of its stores.

Before Costco decides whether to accept such a trade promotion and then promote the Sharp HDTV to its customers, it needs to assess the promotion's impact on its own profitability. Such a promotion may be effective for Sharp but not for Costco.

To evaluate a trade promotion, the retailer considers:

- The realized margin from the promotion.
- The cost of the additional inventory carried due to buying more than the normal amount.
- The potential increase in sales from the promoted merchandise.
- The long-term impact on sales of the promotion.
- The potential loss suffered when customers switch to the promoted merchandise from more profitable TVs.
- The additional sales made to customers attracted to the store by the promotion.[67]

When the HDTV's price is reduced to $1099.00, Costco will sell more Sharp HDTVs than it normally does. But Costco's margin on the HDTVs will be less because the required retail discount of $325 isn't offset by the normal wholesale discount of $300. In addition, Costco might suffer losses because the promotion encourages customers to buy these special HDTVs, which have a lower margin than Costco makes on its other HDTVs. In contrast, the promotion may attract customers who don't normally shop at Costco but who will visit to buy the Sharp HDTV at the discounted price. These customers might buy additional merchandise, providing a sales gain to the store that it wouldn't have realized if it hadn't promoted this item.

CHECK YOURSELF

1. What are various forms of sales promotions?
2. What factors should a firm consider when evaluating a sales promotion?

Summing Up

1. How do firms plan and execute advertising campaigns?

Firms (1) identify their target market, (2) set advertising objectives, (3) set the advertising budget, (4) depict their product or service, (5) evaluate and select the media, (6) create the ad, and (7) assess the impact of the ad.

2. **Why do firms advertise, and why do they engage in public relations?**

When firms are advertising to consumers, they are using a pull strategy; when advertising to supply chain members to induce them to carry and sell products, they are using a push strategy. All advertising campaigns are designed to either inform, persuade, or remind customers. Ads can also be used to stimulate demand for a particular category or industry, or for a specific brand, firm, or item. Finally, ad campaigns are used to stimulate either primary or selective demand. Ultimately, public relations has the same aim.

3. **What appeals do advertisers use to get customers' attention?**

Advertising appeals are either informational or emotional. Informational appeals influence purchase decisions with factual information and strong arguments built around relevant key benefits that encourage consumers to evaluate the brand favorably. Emotional appeals indicate how the product satisfies emotional desires rather than utilitarian needs.

4. **How do firms determine which media to use?**

Firms can use mass media channels like newspapers or television to reach large numbers of anonymous audience members. Niche media, such as cable television and specialty magazines, are generally used to reach narrower segments with unique demographic characteristics or interests. When choosing the media, firms must match their objectives to the media. Also, certain media are better at reaching a particular target audience than others.

5. **What legal and ethical issues are of concern to advertisers?**

Advertising is regulated by a plethora of federal and state agencies. The most important federal agencies are the FTC, which protects consumers against general deceptive advertising; the FCC, which has jurisdiction over radio, television, wire, satellite, and cable and covers issues regarding the use of tobacco products and objectionable language; and the FDA, which regulates food, dietary supplements, drugs, cosmetics, and medical devices.

6. **Why do firms integrate public relations programs into their IMC strategies?**

Public relations programs are used to build and maintain a positive image of the firm, head off unfavorable stories or events, and maintain positive relationships with the media. Firms can accomplish these public relations objectives by working with or providing the media with products or favorable information to be used in articles, television appearances, etc. They can also work with charities or co-sponsor events.

7. **How do sales promotions supplement a firm's IMC strategy?**

Sales promotions are special incentives or excitement-building programs that encourage purchase and include coupons, deals, premiums, contests, sweepstakes, samples, POP displays, rebates, and product placement. They either push sales through the channel, as is the case with contests directed toward retail sales people, or pull sales through the channel, as coupons and rebates do. Sales promotions usually occur in conjunction with other elements of a firm's IMC strategy, such as price promotions.

Key Terms

- advertising, 553
- advertising plan, 554
- advertising schedule, 565
- background, 567
- body copy, 567
- branding, 567
- cause-related marketing, 571
- contest, 575
- continuous advertising schedule, 566
- coupon, 573
- cross-promoting, 577
- deal, 574
- emotional appeal, 562
- event sponsorship, 571
- flighting advertising schedule, 566

- foreground, 567
- headline, 567
- informational appeal, 561
- informative advertising, 555
- institutional advertisements, 557
- lift, 568
- loyalty program, 576
- mass media, 564
- media buy, 563
- media mix, 563
- media planning, 563
- niche media, 564
- persuasive advertising, 556
- point-of-purchase (POP) display, 576
- posttesting, 568
- premium, 574

- pretesting, 568
- primary demand advertising, 557
- product placement, 576
- product-focused advertisements, 557
- public relations (PR), 571
- public service advertising (PSA), 558
- puffery, 570
- pull strategy, 554
- pulsing advertising schedule, 566
- push strategy, 554
- rebate, 576
- reminder advertising, 556
- sales promotion, 572

Marketing Applications

1. Choose one of the ads featured in this book and identify its page number. What are the objectives of this ad? Does the ad have more than one objective? Explain your answer.

2. Using the same ad, explain what kind of appeal it uses. How do you know?

3. Microsoft spends millions of dollars each year on advertising for many different purposes. Using the 2 × 2 matrix in Exhibit 18.2, provide an example of how it might design a campaign for each type of ad.

4. Name a current advertising slogan you believe is particularly effective for developing a unique selling proposition.

5. Bernard's, a local furniture company, target markets to college students with apartments and households of young people purchasing their first furniture items. If you worked for Bernard's, what type of media would you use for your advertising campaign? Justify your answer.

6. Should Bernard's use continuous, pulsing, or flighting for its advertising schedule? Why?

7. Suppose Porsche is introducing a new line of light trucks and has already created the advertising campaign. How would you assess the effectiveness of the campaign?

8. Suppose now that Porsche is planning a sales promotion campaign to augment its advertising campaign for the new line of light trucks. Which push and pull sales promotion tools do you believe would be most effective? Why?

9. Choose an ad that you believe unreasonably overstates what the product or service can do. (If you can't think of a real ad, make one up.) Explain whether the ad is actually deceptive or just puffery. How would your answer change if you lived in France?

10. You are invited to your six-year-old niece's birthday party and bring her the new superhero doll being advertised on television. She's thrilled when she unwraps the gift but is in tears a short time later because her new doll is broken. She explains that on TV, the doll flies and does karate kicks, but when she tried to play with the doll this way, it broke. You decide to call the manufacturer, and a representative tells you he is sorry your niece is so upset but that the ad clearly states the doll does not fly. The next time you see the televised ad, you notice very small print at the bottom that states the doll does not fly. You decide to write a letter to the FTC about this practice. What information should you include in your letter?

www.mhhe.com/ grewal2e

Quiz Yourself

1. Smokey the Bear, Mothers Against Drunk Driving (MADD), and crash test dummies Vince and Larry are examples of successful _____.
   a. selective demand strategies
   b. public puffery campaigns
   c. pretracking publicity
   d. product-focused advertisements
   e. public service announcements

2. Campbell Soup Company ran a series of radio ads tied to local weather forecasts. Before an impending storm, the ads said, "Time to stock up on Campbell Soup." During the storm, the ads said, "Stay home and stay warm with Campbell Soup."

The first ad was _____ advertising, while the second ad was _____ advertising.
   a. informative; persuasive
   b. persuasive; reminder
   c. reminder; persuasive
   d. discussive; informative
   e. institutional; persuasive

(Answers to these two questions are provided on page 624.)

Go to www.mhhe.com/grewal2e to practice an additional 11 questions.

Toolkit

MAKE AN ADVERTISEMENT

Suppose you have been hired to develop a new ad for a product or service to target the college student market. The ad will appear in college student newspapers around the world. Please use the toolkit provided at www.mhhe.com/grewal2e to develop the ad.

Net Savvy

1. Go to the Web site for the Children's Advertising Review Unit (CARU), one of the major self-regulatory bodies for children's advertising, at www.caru.org. Click on the About CARU link and examine the history and activities of CARU. How does this form of regulation complement the more formal regulation of federal and state agencies? Now look under the News and Publications link. Choose one of the press releases and discuss what action CARU took against the identified company or group. What was the main issue in the case?

2. PR Newswire attempts to provide information for "professional communicators." Visit its Web site at www.prnewswire.com and explore the services and products it has to offer. What would you consider this organization's primary purpose? To whom does PR Newswire address the advertising appeals on its Web site?

Chapter Case Study

WHAT IS POPULARITY ANYWAY?[68]

When it comes to social networking sites—those Web forums that enable friends to stay in contact, describe themselves and their interests, and measure their popularity by the number of registered friends they maintain, the rules of advertising change radically. Who is advertising to whom, and how can companies—both the networking sites and others that want in on the game—make the best use of appealing to consumers?

Consider your own Facebook or MySpace site, assuming you have one. Are all your real-life friends your online friends too? Do you actually know all the friends registered on your online site? In all likelihood, you host online friends you've never met, meaning that your circle of virtual friends is pretty huge compared with the number of people whom you see in person or talk to face to face on a regular basis. That means the audience on social sites also potentially is much bigger than that for other forms of media.

Such huge audiences mean huge interest by advertisers. Advertising on social networking sites actually consists of at least three areas, though: Members advertise themselves to gain more friends, the sites advertise to get more members, and outside companies hope to advertise their products to appeal to the vast networks of consumers active on the sites. Let's look at examples of each of these realms in turn.

Members Advertising Themselves

Regardless of whether online popularity translated into primary votes, the 2008 presidential candidates took care to make their Facebook and MySpace pages appealing, especially to the younger voters who would tend to use social networking sites. Their Web sites included links to their pages, and in some news releases, they touted the number of friends they had attracted.

Tila Tequila, the model, singer, blogger, and actress, began her career modeling and, although featured on the 2006 covers of *Maxim* and *Stuff* magazines, was relatively unknown.[69] She did not become a celebrity until she joined MySpace in 2003, and became famous because of fans of her site. Tila mass–e-mailed 30,000 to 50,000 people to look at her MySpace page, and they all joined. This was in the early stages of MySpace, when people were only friends with people they were actually friends with, and did not venture out into the online community to make friendships. She appeared on NBC's *Identity* as 1 of 12 strangers, with her claim to fame being that she had over 1 million MySpace friends. Shortly thereafter, she became the star of *A Shot at Love with Tila Tequila,* which became the MTV network's top show for people aged 18–34.

Most Facebook users aren't trying to be celebrities or running to become the president of the United States, yet the competition for more and more friends can be fierce, even if the only one who seems to care about it is the member.

Sites Advertising Their Services

In this area, the advertising tends to be rather untraditional; social networking sites appear to have little use for print, television, or radio and instead rely on advertising within their own Web sites to spark interest.

Facebook not only assures its individual users that it provides a way for them to "connect . . . with the people around you" but also promises advertisers that they can "reach the exact audience [they] want."[70] Thus, Facebook tries to appeal to two different audiences: the users and the advertisers who remain so interested in those users.

Similarly, MySpace prompts users to invite their friends to join, appealing to their need for social acceptance by vowing that the more friends who join (and in turn encourage their own friends to join, and so on), the larger the user's network will grow.[71]

Outside Companies Advertising on Sites

Social networks are so popular that marketers yearn for more ways to capitalize quickly on the markets associated with them. Newspapers, television spots, and other traditional advertising media continue to lose ground as consumers spend more time on blogs and online.

For example, with Facebook's advertising programs, companies can target specific groups of people. If a group of online friends reveal an interest in ski equipment, or another group really wants to know about Burton snowboards, marketers can target both groups on the basis of these interests. Alternatively, customers may get alerts when their friends have made a purchase that matches their interests. As a result, consumers can attract other friends who might be interested in the same offer, spurring purchases along the way. This viral marketing aspect is a dream for companies.[72]

From a market research point of view, companies can learn much more about their customers from their interests, their past purchases, and their movement through the social network. Customers appear keen to submit their opinions about their friends' purchases, interests, polls, and blogs. Reviews or votes about BOTOX® treatments, ASICS running sneakers, or the play of the Chargers in the AFC playoffs all constitute new ways that customers communicate with one another—and with marketers who are paying attention.

Because modern customers spend a significant amount of time reading reviews and looking at alternative products before actually making a purchase, reviews by other customers have significant impact. People also are likely to trust other users more than an advertising message.

Marketers thus are learning a lot about their customers—everything from how to communicate with them to their likes, dislikes, and preferences. The social atmosphere on the Web should continue to grow, providing an ever-increasing pool of information and marketing opportunities.

Questions

1. Should social networking sites start branching out beyond their own sites to advertise, such as by running television ads? Why or why not?

2. What type of appeal usually gets people to join a social networking site? What type of appeals do members use to get others to become their online friends? What type of appeals do companies advertising on social networking sites use? Explain the differences in your answers.

3. How might you measure the value of the advertising by each of the three groups discussed in this case study? Which would be easier or more difficult to measure? What types of analyses might you use?

PERSONAL SELLING AND SALES MANAGEMENT

CRUISIN' IN A PINK CADILLAC

As a direct sales company, Mary Kay Inc. products are sold by individual self-employed sellers known as Independent Beauty Consultants, who grow their own businesses by selling Mary Kay® skin care, fragrance, and cosmetic products to customers—or by sharing the business opportunity with other potential Independent Beauty Consultants.[1] When a Beauty Consultant shares the Mary Kay opportunity with others, she has the opportunity to earn commissions based upon the retail sales of other individuals who choose to become Independent Beauty Consultants as well.

For example, Gloria Mayfield Banks, an Independent Elite Executive National Sales Director, has earned more than $5 million in commissions since starting her Mary Kay business. After completing her MBA degree from Harvard University School of Business, she began a sales career at IBM and focused on the computer industry. But after a divorce, Banks became a single par-

ent of two children and began struggling financially. She thus turned to searching for part-time work that would provide her with flexibility but also offer her sufficient payback for her hard work.

Just two months after becoming a Mary Kay Independent Beauty Consultant in 1988, Banks decided to pursue it on a full-time basis. Within a year, she set a sales record, all the while sharing the Mary Kay opportunity with others who, over time, have accomplished millions of dollars in retail sales. And as a perk unique to Mary Kay, Banks has earned the use of nine pink Cadillacs, all symbols of her incredible success.

The unmistakable pink cars may be the most obvious but they are not the only perk that Mary Kay offers to successful Independent Beauty Consultants. The financial rewards are open-ended and generous: Beauty Consultants retain the gross profits on each product they sell, which are often as high as 50 percent of the suggested retail price, as well as the opportunity to earn commissions based on the retail sales of team members. In terms of nonfinancial rewards, Mary Kay adopts a specific and determined philosophy: faith first, family second, career third. Such a corporate attitude promotes a different environment than that usually found in the corporate world where often career is the only priority. From the moment a Beauty Consultant signs her Independent Beauty Consultant agreement, she is eligible for various small gifts and symbolic rewards that mark even seemingly small successes. During team sales meetings, Beauty Consultants receive recognition from their peers and Independent Sales Directors for their accomplishments and therefore become ever more motivated to continue on their successful paths. The meetings serve as motivating events, cheering each member on to bigger and better successes.

● ● ●

Just like advertising, which we discussed in the last chapter, personal selling is so important in integrated marketing communications that it deserves its own chapter. Almost everyone is engaged in some form of selling. On a personal level, you sell your ideas or opinions to your friends, family, employers, and professors. Even if you have no interest in personal selling as a career, a strong grounding in the topic will help you in numerous career choices. Consider, for instance, Harry Turk, a very successful labor attorney. He worked his way through college selling sweaters to fraternities across the country. Although he loved his part-time job, Harry decided to become an attorney. When asked whether he misses selling, he said, "I use my selling skills every day. I have to sell new clients on the idea that I'm the best attorney for the job. I have to sell my partners on my legal point of view. I even use selling skills when I'm talking to a judge or jury." In this chapter, we take a straightforward business perspective on selling.

THE SCOPE AND NATURE OF PERSONAL SELLING

Many sales people now can rely on virtual offices, which enable them to communicate via the Internet with colleagues and customers.

Personal selling is the two-way flow of communication between a buyer or buyers and a seller that is designed to influence the buyer's purchase decision. Personal selling can take place in various situations: face-to-face, via video teleconferencing, on the telephone, or over the Internet. Over 14 million people are employed in sales positions in the United States,[2] including those involved in business-to-business (B2B) transactions—like manufacturers' representatives selling to retailers or other businesses—and those completing business-to-consumer (B2C) transactions, such as retail sales people, real estate agents, and insurance agents. Sales people are referred to in many ways: sales representatives or reps, account executives, agents. And as Harry Turk found, most professions rely on personal selling to some degree.

Sales people don't always get the best coverage in popular media. In Arthur Miller's play and the subsequent movie *Death of a Salesman*, the main character, Willie Loman, leads a pathetic existence and suffers from the loneliness inherent in being a traveling salesman.[3] The characters in David Mamet's play *Glengarry Glen Ross* (which was also made into a movie) portray sales people as crude, ruthless, and of questionable character. Unfortunately, these powerful Pulitzer Prize–winning pieces of literature weigh heavily on our collective

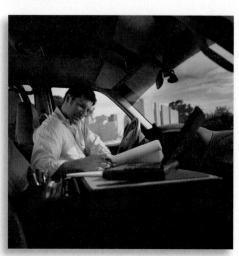

consciousness and often overshadow the millions of hardworking professional sales people who have fulfilling and rewarding careers and who add value to their firm and provide value for their customers.

Professional selling can be a satisfying career for several reasons. First, many people love the lifestyle. Sales people are typically out on their own. Although they occasionally work with their managers and other colleagues, sales people are usually responsible for planning their own day. This flexibility translates into an easier balance between work and family than many office-bound jobs can offer. Many sales people now can rely on virtual offices, which enable them to communicate via the Internet with colleagues and customers. Because sales people are evaluated primarily on the results they produce, as long as they meet and exceed their goals, they experience little day-to-day supervision.

Professional selling can be a very lucrative career and is very visible to management.

Second, the variety of the job often attracts people to sales. Every day is different, bringing different clients and customers, often in a variety of places. Their issues and problems and the solutions to those problems all differ and require creativity.

Third, professional selling and sales management can be a very lucrative career. Sales is among the highest-paying careers for college graduates, and compensation often includes perks, such as the use of a company car and bonuses for high performance. A top performer can have a total compensation package of over $150,000; even lower-level sales people can make well over $50,000. Although the monetary compensation can be significant, the satisfaction of being involved in interesting, challenging, and creative work is rewarding in and of itself.

Fourth, because sales people are the frontline emissaries for their firm, they are very visible to management. Furthermore, it is fairly straightforward for management to identify top performers, which means that those high-performing sales people who aspire to management positions are in a good position to get promoted.

Personal Selling and Marketing Strategy

Although personal selling is an essential part of many firms' integrated marketing communications strategy, it offers its own unique contribution to the four Ps. Because of the one-to-one nature of sales, a salesperson is in a unique position to customize a message for a specific buyer. As a result, a preplanned sales presentation or demonstration can be altered at any time as the need arises. For instance, in a personal selling situation, the salesperson can probe the buyer for his or her potential reservations about a product or service, educate the buyer when appropriate, and ask for the order at the appropriate time. Also, unlike other types of promotion, the sales presentation can be directed toward those customers with the highest potential. This highly directed approach to promotion is important because experts estimate that the average cost of a single B2B sales call is about $392.[4]

Sales people input customer information into their PDAs to develop a customer database for CRM systems.

As we discussed in Chapter 15, building strong supply chain relationships is a critical success factor. Who in the organization is better equipped to manage this relationship than the salesperson, the frontline emissary for the firm? The most successful sales people are those who build strong relationships with their customers. They don't view themselves as being successful if they make a particular sale or one transaction at a time. Instead, they take a long-term perspective. Thus, building on the strategic relationship concept introduced in Chapter 15, relationship selling is a sales philosophy and process that

A good CRM system provides sales people with the information they need to suggest specific items and services to individual customers.

emphasizes a commitment to maintaining the relationship over the long term and investing in opportunities that are mutually beneficial to all parties. Relationship sales people work with their customers to find mutually beneficial solutions to their wants and needs. A Lenovo sales team, for instance, may be working with your university to provide you with the computer support and security you need for all four years you spend working with the school's network or computer labs.

Research has shown that a positive customer–salesperson relationship contributes to trust, increased customer loyalty, and the intent to continue the relationship with the salesperson.[5] To help build strong relationships, many firms undertake active customer relationship management (CRM) programs that identify and focus on building loyalty with the firm's most valued customers. Because the sales force interacts directly with customers, its members are in the best position to help a firm accomplish its CRM objectives.

Such CRM programs have several components. There is a customer database or data warehouse. Whether the salesperson is working for a retail store or manages a selling team for an aerospace contractor, he or she can record transaction information, customer contact information, customer preferences, and market segment information about the customer. Once the data have been analyzed and CRM programs developed, sales people can help implement the programs. For instance, bankers and brokers use a "high-touch approach" in which they frequently call on their best customers or contact them by phone. A salesperson can contact customers when there are new products or changes to existing product lines. He or she can probe customers about what they liked or disliked about their recent transactions with the firm. Or the purpose of the call can be purely social. If done properly, customers will feel special and important when a salesperson calls just to see how things are going.

Mitchells/Richards, upscale apparel boutiques in Westport and Greenwich, Connecticut, prides itself on the service that its sales people are able to provide. Its CRM system is specifically designed to keep track of what the customers have purchased in the past; sizes, color and style preferences; and little personal tidbits about the customers and their families. This information enables the sales people to suggest specific items and services to individual customers. Even if a customer's favorite salesperson isn't available, by accessing the CRM system another salesperson can step in and provide knowledgeable and attentive service.

Yet as they work to develop these relationships with their customers, all companies must be sure to maintain customer trust. Relationships are based on give-and-take. For example, especially online, companies prefer to gather a lot of information about their customers, usually to ensure that they provide the best offers to these relationship partners. But when customers must provide more information to a company—perhaps more than they wanted to or more than they think is necessary for the company to determine the best offers for them—the relationship likely starts to seem unbalanced, which upsets customers' sense of justice or fairness. Southwest Airlines sends birthday cards to its most valuable customers—seemingly a nice gesture. But some customers receive the cards and start to wonder whether Southwest has too much information about them. How did the airline obtain their birth dates in the first place?[6]

The Value Added by Personal Selling

Why have sales people in the supply chain? They are expensive, and as we discuss later in this chapter, they can be a challenge to manage. Some firms, especially certain retailers, have made the decision not to use a sales force and become, for the most part, almost completely self-service. But those that use personal selling as part of their integrated marketing communications program do so because it adds value to their product or service mix—that is, personal selling is worth more than it costs. Personal selling adds value by educating and providing advice, saving the customer time, and making things easier for the customer.[7]

Sales People Provide Information and Advice   Imagine how difficult it would be to buy a custom suit, a house, or a car without the help of a salesperson. Similarly, UPS wouldn't dream of investing in a new fleet of airplanes without the benefit of Boeing's selling team. Sure, it could be done, but customers see the value in and are willing to pay indirectly for the education and advice sales people provide. On the consumer side of this example, you might pick up an envelope from a stand-alone UPS box, fill out the form yourself, and ship a letter overnight, but when you have to ship holiday gifts to friends and relatives around the world, you might turn to a UPS Store to get assistance from the staff in packaging everything carefully and ensuring that the gifts arrive in time. Retail sales people similarly can provide valuable information about how a garment fits, new fashions, or directions for operating products. Boeing's sales team can provide UPS with the technical aspects of the aircraft, as well as the economic justification for the purchase.

The Internet has certainly changed the way many consumers make travel decisions. Thousands use sites like Expedia.com and Travelocity.com or visit airlines, Amtrak, hotels, and car rental firms online to make reservations directly. But when booking a complicated trip or planning to visit an exotic locale, or for those who don't feel comfortable buying online, the personal travel agents add significant value. They can help with itineraries, give helpful insights, and even save the customer money.

Sales People Save Time and Simplify Buying   Time is money! Customers perceive value in time and labor savings. In many grocery and drugstore chains, sales people employed by the vendor supplying merchandise straighten stock, set up displays, assess inventory levels, and write orders. In some cases, such as bakeries or soft drink sales, sales people and truck drivers even bring in the merchandise and stock the shelves. These are all tasks that retail employees would otherwise have to do.

Sometimes, however, turning over too many tasks to suppliers' sales people can cause problems. Imagine a grocery store that has turned its inventory management function over to a supplier, like the consumer packaged goods firm Kraft. The supplier might place competitors' products in disadvantageous shelf positions. Unless the relationship involves significant trust or the grocery has precautionary measures in place, the Kraft sales representative might place plenty of Kraft Thousand Island dressing on the shelf but leave little room for its competitors' products, designating a suboptimal amount of shelf space to Wishbone's Thousand Island offering. Although this relationship benefits Kraft, it may not help the grocer, especially if that retailer earns better margins on the competitors' products. Sales people certainly can help facilitate a buying situation, but they should never be allowed to take it over.

The same might be said of your own personal shopping. When you go to buy a new car, the salesperson likely will work hard to convince you that you should purchase a specific make or model. Although a car salesperson has a significant amount of knowledge about the products and therefore can simplify the car buying process, the final decision must remain up to you, the consumer.

THE PERSONAL SELLING PROCESS

Although selling may appear a rather straightforward process, successful sales people follow several steps. Depending on the sales situation and the buyer's readiness to purchase, the salesperson may not use every step, and the time

EXHIBIT 19.1   The Personal Selling Process

required for each step will vary depending on the situation. For instance, if a customer goes into The Gap already prepared to purchase some chinos, the selling process will be fairly quick. But if IBM is attempting to sell personal computers for the first time to a university, the process may take several months. With this in mind, let's examine each step of the selling process (Exhibit 19.1).

Step 1: Generate and Qualify Leads

The first step in the selling process is to generate a list of potential customers (leads) and assess their potential (qualify). Sales people who already have an established relationship with a customer will skip this step, and it is not used extensively in retail settings. In B2B situations, however, it is important to work continually to find new and potentially profitable customers.

The real estate market offers a prime example. In particular, wealthy customers looking to buy a home likely consider real estate agents an absolute necessity. Some people may be able to find a house and close the deal on their own or with limited assistance, but many well-known celebrities want someone else to handle the process, not just for their ease, but also to conceal their identity. When a famous actor or award-winning singer puts a $100 million home up for sale, password-protected Web sites can feature floor plans and inside views for the shopping convenience of interested buyers. But to obtain the password to get into the site, the customer must be prequalified as a billionaire.[8] The agent thus provides an additional service to these shy sellers and buyers—a go-between who protects everyone's privacy.

Such high-powered real estate agents often rely on their reputations to attract customers, though sales people can generate leads in a variety of ways.[9] They can discover potential leads by talking to their current customers and networking at events such as industry conferences or chamber of commerce meetings. The Internet has been a boon for generating leads. For instance, sales people can gather information collected on the firm's Web site or Google a few key words and instantly generate enough potential leads to keep them busy for weeks. For example www.itsmyporsche.com is an online community of Porsche owners. By browsing the site, sales people can find people in their area looking for a particular car. In the case of hard-to-find or vintage Porsches, the site could help sales people locate buyers worldwide.

Trade shows also offer an excellent forum for finding leads. These major events are attended by buyers who choose to be exposed to products and services offered by potential suppliers in an industry. Thus, consumer electronics buyers make sure that they attend the annual International Consumer Electronics Show (CES) in Las Vegas, the world's largest trade show for consumer technology (www.cesweb. org). The show is attended by 140,000 people from over 110 countries including vendors; developers; and suppliers of consumer technology hardware, content, technology delivery systems, and related products and services. Nearly 2,700 vendor exhibits take up 1.8 million net square feet of exhibit space, showcasing the very latest products and services. Vendors often use the CES to introduce new products, including the first camcorder (1981), high-definition television (HDTV) (1998), and Internet protocol television (IP TV) (2005). In addition to providing an opportunity for retail buyers to see the latest products, the CES conference program features prominent speakers from the technology sector—perhaps most famously, Microsoft's Bill Gates.[10]

A great place to generate leads is at a trade show.

Cold calls are a method of prospecting in which sales people telephone or go to see potential customers without appointments.[11] Telemarketing is similar to a cold call, but it always occurs over the telephone. Sometimes professional telemarketing firms, rather than the firm's sales people, make such calls. However, cold calls and telemarketing have become less popular than they were in the past. First, the success rate is fairly low because the potential customer's need has not been established ahead of time. As a result, these methods can be very expensive. Second, both federal and state governments have begun to regulate the activities of telemarketers. Federal rules prohibit telemarketing to consumers whose names appear on the national Do-Not-Call list, which is maintained by the Federal Trade Commission. Even for those consumers whose names are not on the list, the rules prohibit calling before 8:00 a.m. or after 9:00 p.m. (in the consumer's time zone) or after the consumer has told the telemarketer not to call. Federal rules also prohibit unsolicited fax messages and unsolicited telephone calls, as well as e-mail messages to cell phones.

After sales people generate leads, they must qualify those leads by determining whether it is worthwhile to pursue them and attempt to turn them into customers. In a retail setting, qualifying potential can be a very dangerous and potentially illegal practice. Retail sales people should never "judge a book by its cover" and assume that a person in the store doesn't fit the store's image or cannot afford to purchase there. Imagine going to an upscale jewelry store to purchase an engagement ring, only to be snubbed because you are dressed in your everyday, casual school clothes. But in B2B settings, where the costs of preparing and making a presentation can be substantial, the seller must assess a lead's potential. Sales people should consider, for instance, whether the potential customer's needs pertain to a product or a service. They should also assess whether the lead has the financial resources to pay for the product or service.[12]

Retail sales people should never "judge a book by its cover" and assume that a person in the store doesn't fit the store's image or cannot afford to purchase there.

Step 2: Preapproach

The preapproach occurs prior to meeting the customer for the first time and extends the qualification of leads procedure described in Step 1. Although the salesperson has learned about the customer during the qualification stage, in this step, he or she must conduct additional

These sales people are role playing. The woman standing at the easel is acting out a simulated buying situation while her colleagues act as the buying group. Afterward they will critique her presentation.

research and develop plans for meeting with the customer. Suppose, for example, a management consulting firm wants to sell a bank a new system for finding checking account errors. The consulting firm's salesperson should first find out everything possible about the bank: How many checks does it process? What system is the bank using now? What are the benefits of the consultant's proposed system compared with the competition? The answers to these questions provide the basis for establishing value for the customer.

Having done the additional research, the salesperson establishes goals for meeting with the customer; it is important that he or she know ahead of time exactly what should be accomplished. For instance, the consulting firm's salesperson can't expect to get a commitment from the bank that it will buy on the first visit. But a demonstration of the system and a short presentation about how the system would benefit the customer would be appropriate. It is often a good idea to practice the presentation prior to the meeting using a technique known as **role playing**, in which the salesperson acts out a simulated buying situation while a colleague or manager acts as the buyer. Afterward, the practice sales presentation can be critiqued and adjustments can be made.

Step 3: Sales Presentation and Overcoming Reservations

The Presentation   Once all the background information has been obtained and the objectives for the meeting are set, the salesperson is ready for a person-to-person meeting. Let's continue with our bank example. During the first part of the meeting, the salesperson needs to get to know the customer, get his or her attention, and create interest in the presentation to follow. The beginning of the presentation may be the most important part of the entire selling process, because this is where the salesperson establishes exactly where the customer is in his or her buying process (Exhibit 19.2). (For a refresher on the B2B buying process, see Chapter 6.)

Suppose, for instance, the bank is in the first stage of the buying process, need recognition. It would not be prudent for the salesperson to discuss the pros and cons of different potential suppliers because doing so would assume that the customer already had reached Stage 4, proposal analysis and customer selection. By asking a series of questions, however, the salesperson can assess the bank's need for the product or service and adapt or customize the presentation to match the customer's need and stage in the decision process.[13]

Asking questions is only half the battle; carefully listening to the answers is equally important. Some sales people, particularly inexperienced ones, believe that to be in control, they must do all the talking. Yet it is impossible to really understand where the customer stands without listening carefully. What if the COO says, "It seems kind of expensive"? If the salesperson isn't listening carefully, he or she won't pick up on the subtle nuances of what the customer is really thinking. In this case, it probably means the COO doesn't see the value in the offering.

When the salesperson has gotten a good feel for where the customer stands, he or she can apply that knowledge to help the customer solve its problem or satisfy its need. The salesperson might begin by explaining the features or characteristics of the system that will reduce checking account errors. It may not be obvious, solely on the basis of these features, however, that the system adds value beyond the bank's current practices. Using the answers to some of the questions the salesperson posed earlier in the meeting, he or she can clarify the product's advantages over current or past practices, as well as the overall benefits of adopting the new system. The salesperson might explain, for instance, that the bank can expect a

EXHIBIT 19.2   Aligning the Personal Selling Process with the B2B Buying Process

20 percent improvement in checking account errors and that, because of the size of the bank and number of checks it processes per year, this improvement would represent $2 million in annual savings. Because the system costs $150,000 per year and will take only three weeks to integrate into the current system, it will add significant and almost immediate value.

Handling Reservations An integral part of the sales presentation is handling reservations or objections that the buyer might have about the product or service. Although reservations can arise during each stage of the selling process, they are very likely to occur during the sales presentation. Customers may raise reservations pertaining to a variety of issues, but they usually relate in some way to value, such as that the price is too high for the level of quality or service.

Good sales people know the types of reservations buyers are likely to raise. They may know, for instance, that their service is slower than competitors' or that their selection is limited. Although not all reservations can be forestalled, effective sales people can anticipate and handle some. For example, when the bank COO said the check service seemed expensive, the salesperson was ready with information about how quickly the investment would be recouped.

As in other aspects of the selling process, the best way to handle reservations is to relax and listen, then ask questions to clarify any reservations. For example, the salesperson could respond to the COO's reservation by asking, "How much do you think the bank is losing through checking account errors?" Her answer might open up a conversation about the positive trends in a cost/benefit analysis. Such questions are usually more effective than trying to prove the customer's reservation is not valid, because the latter approach implies the salesperson isn't really listening and could lead to an argument. In an attempt to handle reservations and start the process of closing the sale, a salesperson may offer creative deals or incentives that may be unethical.

Step 4: Closing the Sale

Closing the sale means obtaining a commitment from the customer to make a purchase. Without a successful close, the salesperson goes away empty handed, so many sales people find this part of the sales process very stressful. Although losing a sale is never pleasant, sales people who are involved in a relationship with their customers must view any particular sales presentation as part of the progression toward ultimately making the sale. An unsuccessful close on one day may just be a means of laying the groundwork for a successful close the next meeting.

Although we have presented the selling process in a series of steps, closing the sale rarely follows the other steps so neatly. However, good sales people listen carefully to what potential customers say and pay attention to their body language. Reading these signals carefully can help sales people achieve an early close. Suppose that our hypothetical bank, instead of being in the first step of the buying process, is in the final step of negotiation and selection. An astute salesperson will pick up on these signals and ask for the sale.

Step 5: Follow-Up

> "It ain't over till it's over."
> —Yogi Berra[14]

With relationship selling, it is never really over, even after the sale has been made. The attitudes customers develop after the sale become the basis for how they will purchase in the future. The follow-up therefore offers a prime opportunity for a salesperson to solidify the customer relationship through great service quality. Let's apply the five service quality dimensions we discussed in Chapter 12 to the follow-up:[15]

- **Reliability.** The salesperson and the supporting organization must deliver the right product or service on time.

- **Responsiveness.** The salesperson and support group must be ready to deal quickly with any issue, question, or problem that may arise.

- **Assurance.** Customers must be assured through adequate guarantees that their purchase will perform as expected.

- **Empathy.** The salesperson and support group must have a good understanding of the problems and issues faced by their customers. Otherwise, they cannot give them what they want.

  - **Tangibles.** Because tangibles reflect the physical characteristics of the seller's business, such as its Web site, marketing communications, and delivery materials, their influence is more subtle than that of the other four service quality dimensions. That doesn't mean it is any less important. For instance, retail customers are generally more pleased with a purchase if it is carefully wrapped in nice paper instead of being haphazardly thrown into a crumpled plastic bag. The tangibles offer a signal that the product is of high quality, even though the packaging has nothing to do with the product's performance.

A postsale follow-up letter, call, or e-mail is the first step in initiating a new order and sustaining the relationship.

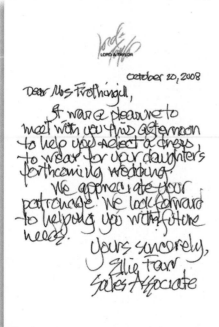

When customers' expectations are not met, they often complain—about deliveries, the billing amount or process, the product's performance, or after-sale services such as installation or training. Effectively handling complaints is critical to the future of the relationship. As we noted in Chapter 12, the best way to handle complaints is to listen to the customer, provide a fair solution to the problem, and resolve the problem quickly.

The best way to nip a postsale problem in the bud is to check with the customer right after he or she takes possession of the product or immediately after the service has been completed. This speed demonstrates responsiveness and empathy. It also shows the customer that the salesperson and the firm care about customer satisfaction. Finally, a postsale follow-up call, e-mail, or letter takes the salesperson back to the first step in the sales process for initiating a new order and sustaining the relationship.

Many technological advances help facilitate the selling process, as we find in the next section. Superior Service 19.1 examines how Toyota Camrys are sold in China.

 ## Superior Service **19.1**   The Fancy Chinese Camry

Good sales people know how to service their customers. In China, Toyota sold 500,000 cars last year; and one salesperson alone sells about 60 Camry sedans per month. That's approximately 2 cars a day! In China, the Camry embodies a high-end vehicle. Although the car body is cosmetically similar to the Camry sold in the United States, and is only slightly different, it sells for $27,000–$37,000 in China, compared to around $4,000 for the average car in China.

Toyota's strategy to build a status-conscious brand starts the moment customers enter the dealership. Those interested in a Camry are checked in and ushered to a graceful showroom by employees who greet them by name. Another employee immediately enters all contact details into a database so that the sales staff can conduct follow-up communication after their initial visit. The plush service area contains a white baby grand player piano, playing soothing melodies, along with leather couches, Internet access, free coffee, and snacks. If they tire of listening to music, potential buyers can sneak a peek at the service bay, which the showroom overlooks, and appreciate the transparency of the operation—a rare décor choice in China.

When the salesperson arrives, he or she never appears desperate to sell a car, because such an attitude implies there is something wrong with the product. Instead, the company fixes the prices for its vehicles and prohibits any haggling with customers. At the point of the sale, most customers simply pay cash for their new car, which gets wrapped in a giant red ribbon and delivered so that the buyer can celebrate his or her purchase with friends and family.

That celebration might even include the employee who sold the car. Toyota sales people in China consider customers friends and therefore remain willing to do virtually anything to keep them happy—even after the sale has been completed. One customer phoned the dealership to say that his car would not start late on a rainy night. The salesperson immediately arranged for the car to be towed and fixed, then sent the owner two cases of mandarin oranges as a token gesture. In another case, a driver who had had too much to drink turned not to a taxi company but to his Toyota salesperson, who immediately went to pick up the inebriated customer.

For such acts, the salesperson will gain referrals, because these customers will certainly tell others to buy a car from that employee in the future (unless the drunk driver is too embarrassed to admit his folly, that is). From a single car sale, a salesperson earns just $7–14, depending on how many extra features the customer selects, which gets added to a base salary of $140 per month. Thus, a Toyota Camry salesperson cannot afford to buy the cars he or she sells.[16]

Toyota salespeople in China consider customers friends and therefore remain willing to do anything to keep them happy.

CHECK YOURSELF

1. What are the steps in the personal selling process?
2. How does the selling process impact the business to business buying process?

THE IMPACT OF TECHNOLOGY AND THE INTERNET ON PERSONAL SELLING

Technology and the Internet have had significant impacts on the role of personal selling in recent years. Sales people have instant access to their customers and their firm through cell phones, PDAs (personal digital assistants), and the Internet. They can make appointments, take orders, solve problems, and get information at any time and from almost any place.

Prior to the Internet's explosion, it was cumbersome to perform research on products, customers, or competitors. Sales people would rely on a research staff for this information, and it could take weeks for the research to be completed and sent through the mail. Customer information, if it was available at all, was typically a manual system that individual sales people kept in a notebook or on a series of cards. There were no customer data warehouses and no formal CRM systems. Today, sales people have all this information at their fingertips, as long as they are connected to the Internet and are willing to exploit its capabilities.[17] They can easily access their company's customer database and surf the Web for product and competitive information at any time and virtually anywhere.

Technology has also made sales training programs more effective, easier, and, often, less expensive than in the past. Rather than incur the time and expense of flying a group of sales people to one location, companies can conduct distance learning and training through videoconferencing. Some firms also offer online training courses. Sales people can view the material, which contains product information or selling techniques, and take tests on the information at a time convenient to them. Instead of the traditional, bulky, and sometimes overlooked bulletins and product catalogs, companies can distribute material effectively via e-mail.

Because customers also have better access to information through these technological innovations, sales people have gained time to participate in the more creative and technical aspects of selling. Customers can check their order status and pricing or get product information from the selling firm's extranet. They can even place their own order electronically, if they so choose, without the aid of a salesperson. In some cases, because the selling job has become more streamlined as a result of such technological advances, firms have been able to trim back their sales force expenses without any simultaneous loss in productivity. To learn how technology has changed the way college textbooks are sold, for example, consider Power of the Internet 19.1.

Online technology also has changed the very definition of who sellers are. With eBay, anyone can sell a product personally, because

Technology has changed the lives of sales people and sales training. Companies can conduct distance learning and training through videoconferencing.

Power of the Internet 19.1

Technology-Facilitated Textbook Selling

Have you ever considered how the textbook you are reading right now might have been sold with the aid of technology? Sam Hussey is a senior account manager for McGraw-Hill/Irwin, the publisher of this text, in Massachusetts. In his early years with the firm, he would go on campus with a briefcase full of books. He'd stop by various professors' offices, talk to them about possible book adoptions, and show them the various features of the books in his bag. He would communicate with the home office and his customers by phone, fax, or mail. If a professor needed a book in a hurry, Hussey would call the distribution center, and a person would take down all the information by hand—a time-consuming and potentially error-prone system. Although Hussey maintained all his customer information in a "little black book," McGraw-Hill/Irwin had no comprehensive customer database. The company did not know, for instance, which instructors were using which books. Without that information, it was impossible to implement an adequate CRM system.

Things are different for Hussey today. Because McGraw-Hill/Irwin now has an integrated CRM system, he knows exactly who is using which specific texts. He can plan his sales calls so that he knows whom he plans to see, what books they are currently using, and which books he plans to sell. Once in a professor's office, he can demonstrate—on his computer or the professor's—special features of the text, accompanying PowerPoint slides, or the

book-related Internet content. If the professor needs a book, Hussey places the order over the Internet. Because McGraw-Hill/Irwin keeps most of its book contents in a digital database, Hussey can create custom course material for professors, including text, cases, and articles. He uses an electronic ordering system, linked to the publisher's custom publishing operation, to create a sample book that will be delivered to the professor in about a week. Once approved, the book can be printed and delivered to the local bookstore for purchase by students, just like you.

Sam Hussey, senior account manager at McGraw-Hill/Irwin, has a very different job today than he did just a few years ago—all because of advances in technology.

the online auction service gives each person who accesses the site access to a worldwide market of customers. The best individual merchants even can become PowerSellers if their sales totals or volume hits a certain level. Some enterprising personal sellers also maintain their own virtual store within the site that offers the security and reputation of eBay, combined with the personal attention and care the sellers provide on a one-to-one basis.

To increase their sales, many online retailers now offer more support for online consumers, such as online chats, to help consumers understand the merchandise better. The additional features and information help keep shoppers on the site for longer periods of time, which often means more sales.

However, sales people who do not add value or an online assistant who does not provide real assistance to satisfy the customer may be more disappointing than no online support at all. For example, a customer on the Dell Web site orders a computer but does not receive a confirmation e-mail. The customer uses the online help service to confirm that the order had been placed, but the sales assistant cannot track the order; instead, she simply repeats phrases such as, "I understand how frustrated you must feel." The customer's frustration only grows as a result of the service interaction.

Overall, the communication between a retailer and a customer must be effective and add value to the shopping experience. Customers expect answers to their questions when they communicate with online personnel. When customers feel let down because of poor performance by a salesperson or Web site, they often become lost forever to the disappointing online retailer.[18]

ETHICAL AND LEGAL ISSUES IN PERSONAL SELLING

Although ethical and legal issues permeate all aspects of marketing, they are particularly important for personal selling. Unlike advertising and other communications with customers, which are planned and executed on a corporate level, personal selling involves a one-to-one, and often face-to-face, encounter with the customer. Thus, sellers' actions are not only highly visible to customers but also to other stakeholders, such as the communities in which they work.

Ethical and legal issues arise in three areas in personal selling. First, there is the relationship between the sales manager and the sales force. Second, in some situations, an inconsistency might exist between corporate policy and the salesperson's ethical comfort zone. Third, both ethical and legal issues can arise when the salesperson interacts with the customer, especially if that salesperson or the selling firm collects significant information about the customer. To maintain trustworthy customer relationships, companies must take care that they respect customer privacy and respect the information comfort zone—that is, the amount of information a customer feels comfortable providing.[19]

The Sales Manager and the Sales Force

Like any manager, a sales manager must treat people fairly and equally in everything he or she does. With regard to the sales force, this fairness must include hiring, promotion, supervision, training, assigning duties and quotas, compensation and incentives, and firing.[20] Federal laws cover many of these issues. For instance, equal employment opportunity laws make it unlawful to discriminate against a person in hiring, promotion, or firing because of race, religion, nationality, sex, or age.

Sales people must live within their own ethical comfort zone. Should insurance sales people disclose inadequate hurricane coverage and risk not making the sale?

The Sales Force and Corporate Policy

Sometimes sales people face a conflict between what they believe represents ethical selling and what their company asks them to do to make a sale. Suppose an insurance agent, whose compensation is based on commission, which is a percentage of the agent's sales, sells a homeowner's policy to a family that has just moved to New Orleans, an area prone to flooding as a result of hurricanes. Even though the policy covers hurricane damage, it does not cover water damage from hurricanes. If the salesperson discloses the inadequate coverage, the sale might be lost because additional flood insurance is very expensive. What should the salesperson do? Sales people must live within their own ethical comfort zone. If this, or any other situation, is morally repugnant to the salesperson, he or she must question whether they want to be associated with the company.[21]

Sales people also can be held accountable for illegal actions sanctioned by the employer. If the homeowner asks if the home is above the floodplain or whether water damage from flooding is covered by the policy, and it is company policy to intentionally mislead potential customers, both the salesperson and the insurance dealership could be susceptible to legal action.

Perhaps nowhere is ethical selling more hotly debated than in the pharmaceutical industry. Physicians have become accustomed to the perks offered by the pharmaceutical representatives who visit their office and restock their shelves with product samples, extras such as free tickets to Broadway musicals and pens—tons and tons of pens. It's a fine line between buying a prospect's time to demonstrate your wares and bribing him or her to prescribe your firm's drugs.

According to Pennsylvania-based Scott-Levin Consulting, promotional budgets for pharmaceuticals have reached nearly $14 billion, with roughly 56,000 people in the sales force. Incidentally, that's about one sales rep and $100,000 dollars for every 11 practicing physicians.

Pharmaceutical companies hand out samples liberally as a central part of their marketing program. The National Institute for Healthcare Management suggests the cost figure reaches about $7.2 billion in samples each year. Many patients benefit from these samples; however, most companies only give out samples of their high-priced products. The net result, according to a study by Washington University, becomes that many doctors dispense and prescribe drugs that are not their primary drug of choice.

At the end of the day, many ethical decisions rest on the shoulders of the independent sales representatives. Are they using tactics that promote the best health care options for the patients, or are they simply pushing their product? On a broader scale, are they inflating medication costs as a result of these selling methods so that, ultimately, the customer cannot afford the prescription anyway?

Are pharmaceutical sales people promoting the best health care option for the patients, or are they simply pushing their product?

The Salesperson and the Customer

As the frontline emissaries for a firm, sales people have a duty to be ethically and legally correct in all their dealings with their customers. Not only is it the right thing to do, it simply means good business. Long-term relationships can deteriorate quickly if customers believe that they have not been treated in an ethically proper manner. Unfortunately, sales people sometimes get mixed signals from their managers or simply do not know when their behaviors might be considered unethical or illegal. Formal guidelines can help, but it is also important to integrate these guidelines into training programs in which sales people can discuss various issues that arise in the field with their peers and managers. Most important, however, is for sales managers to lead by example. If managers are known to cut ethical corners, it shouldn't surprise them when their sales people do the same. Ethical and Societal Dilemma 19.1 considers the ethical issues that pharmaceutical sales people face.

MANAGING THE SALES FORCE

Like any business activity involving people, the sales force requires management. Sales management involves the planning, direction, and control of personal selling activities, including recruiting, selecting, training, motivating, compensating, and evaluating, as they apply to the sales force.[23]

Large companies with established brands like Pepsi often use a company sales force instead of independent agents. Because the sales people are company employees, the manufacturer has more control over what they do. Pepsi's sales people, like this one in Mexico, deliver products, stock the shelves, and keep track of inventory.

Managing a sales force is a rewarding yet complicated undertaking. In this section, we examine how sales forces can be structured, some of the most important issues in recruiting and selecting sales people, sales training issues, ways to compensate sales people, and finally, how to supervise and evaluate sales people.

Sales Force Structure

Imagine the daunting task of putting together a sales force from scratch. Will you hire your own sales people, or should they be manufacturer's representatives? What will be each salesperson's primary duties: order takers, order getters, sales support? Finally, will they work together in teams? In this section, we examine each of these issues.

Company Sales Force or Manufacturer's Representative A company sales force comprises people who are employees of the selling company. Independent agents, also known as manufacturer's representatives, or "reps," are sales people who sell a manufacturer's products on an extended contract basis but are not employees of the manufacturer. They are compensated by commissions and do not take ownership or physical possession of the merchandise.

Manufacturer's representatives are useful for smaller firms or firms expanding into new markets because such companies can achieve instant and extensive sales coverage without having to pay full-time personnel. Good sales representatives have many established contacts and can sell multiple products from noncompeting manufacturers during the same sales call. Also, the use of manufacturer's representatives facilitates flexibility; it is much easier to replace a rep than an employee and much easier to expand or contract coverage in a market with a sales rep than with a company sales force.

Company sales forces are more typically used for established product lines. Because the sales people are company employees, the manufacturer has more control over what they do. If, for example, the manufacturer's strategy is to provide extensive customer service, the sales manager can specify exactly what actions a company sales force must take. In contrast, because manufacturer's representatives are paid on a commission basis, it is difficult to persuade them to take any action that doesn't directly lead to sales.

Order takers process routine orders or reorders or rebuys for products.

Salesperson Duties Although the life of a professional salesperson is highly varied, sales people generally play three important roles: order getting, order taking, and sales support.

Order Getting An order getter is a salesperson whose primary responsibilities are identifying potential customers and engaging those customers in discussions to attempt to make a sale. An order getter is also responsible for following up with the customer to ensure that the customer is satisfied and to build the relationship. In B2B settings, order getters are primarily involved in new buy and modified new buy situations (see Chapter 6). As a result, they require extensive sales and product knowledge training. The Coca-Cola salesperson who goes to Safeway's headquarters to sell a special promotion of Vanilla Coke is an order getter.

Order Taking An order taker is a salesperson whose primary responsibility is to process routine orders or reorders or rebuys for products. Colgate employs order takers around the globe who go into stores and distribution centers that already carry Colgate products to check inventory, set up displays, write new orders, and make sure everything is going smoothly.

Sales Support Sales support personnel enhance and help with the overall selling effort. For example, if a Best Buy customer begins to experience computer problems, the company has a Geek Squad door-to-door service as well as support in the store. Those employees who respond to the customer's technical questions and repair the computer serve to support the overall sales process.

Combination Duties Although some sales people's primary function may be order getting, order taking, or sales support, others fill a combination of roles. For instance, a computer salesperson at Staples may spend an hour with a customer educating him or her about the pros and cons of various systems and then make the sale. The next customer might simply need a specific printer cartridge. A third customer might bring in a computer and seek advice about an operating system problem. The salesperson was first an order getter, next an order taker, and finally a sales support person.

Some firms use selling teams that combine sales specialists whose primary duties are order getting, order taking, or sales support but who work together to service important accounts. As companies become larger and products more complicated, it is nearly impossible for one person to perform all the necessary sales functions.

Recruiting and Selecting Sales People

When the firm has determined how the sales force will be structured, it must find and hire sales people. Although superficially this task may sound as easy as posting the job opening on the Internet or running an ad in a newspaper, it must be performed carefully because firms don't want to hire the wrong person—sales people are very expensive to train.

The most important activity in the recruiting process is to determine exactly what the salesperson will be doing and what personal traits and abilities a person should have to do the job well. For instance, the Coca-Cola order getter who goes to Safeway to pitch a new product will typically need significant sales experience, coupled with great communication and analytical skills. Coke's order takers need to be reliable and able to get along with lots of different types of people in the stores, from managers to customers.

When recruiting sales people, is it better to look for candidates with innate sales ability, or can a good training program make anyone a successful salesperson? In other words, are good sales people born or are they made?[24] By a margin of seven to one in a survey of sales and marketing executives, respondents believed that training and supervision are more critical determinants of selling success than the salesperson's inherent personal characteristics.[25] Yet some of those same respondents noted that they knew "born sales people" and that personal traits are important for successful sales careers. So, it appears that to be a successful salesperson, while it helps to have good training, the first requirement is to possess certain personal traits.

What are those personal traits? Managers and sales experts have identified the following:[26]

■ **Personality.** Good sales people are friendly, sociable, and, in general, like being around people. Customers won't buy from someone they don't like.

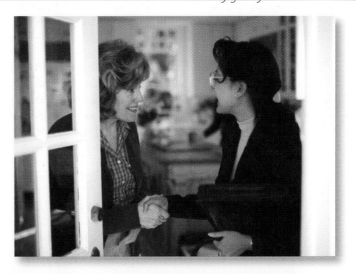

Good sales people, particularly in difficult selling situations such as door-to-door sales, don't easily take no for an answer. They keep coming back until they get a yes.

- **Optimism.** Good sales people tend to look at the bright side of things. Optimism also may help them be resilient—the third trait.

- **Resilience.** Good sales people don't easily take no for an answer. They keep coming back until they get a yes.

- **Self-motivation.** As we have already mentioned, sales people have lots of freedom to spend their days the way they believe will be most productive. But if the sales people are not self-motivated to get the job done, it probably won't get done.

- **Empathy.** Empathy is one of the five dimensions of service quality discussed previously in this chapter and in Chapter 12. Good sales people must care about their customers, their issues, and their problems.

Sales Training

Even people who possess all these personal traits need training. All sales people benefit from training about selling and negotiation techniques, product and service knowledge, technologies used in the selling process, time and territory management, and company policies and procedures.

Firms use varied delivery methods to train their sales people, depending on the topic of the training, what type of salesperson is being trained, and the cost versus the value of the training. For instance, an on-the-job training program is excellent for communicating selling and negotiation skills because managers can observe the sales trainees in real selling situations and provide instant feedback. They can also engage in role-playing exercises in which the salesperson acts out a simulated buying situation and the manager critiques the salesperson's performance.

A much less expensive, but for some purposes equally valuable, training method is the Internet. Online training programs have revolutionized the way training happens in many firms. Firms can provide new product and service knowledge, spread the word about changes in company policies and procedures, and share selling tips in a user-friendly environment that sales people can access anytime and anywhere. Distance learning sales training programs through teleconferencing enable a group of sales people to participate with their instructor or manager in a virtual classroom. And testing can occur online as well. Online sales training may never replace the one-on-one interaction of on-the-job training for advanced selling skills, but it is quite effective and efficient for many other aspects of the sales training task.

Motivating and Compensating Sales People

An important goal for any effective sales manager is to get to know his or her sales people and determine what motivates them to be effective. Some sales people prize their freedom and like to be left alone, whereas others want attention and are more productive when they receive accolades for a job well done. Still others are motivated primarily by monetary compensation. Great sales managers determine how best to motivate each of their sales people according to what is most important to each individual. Although sales managers can emphasize different motivating factors, except in the smallest companies, the methods used to compensate sales people must be fairly standardized and can be divided into two categories: financial and nonfinancial.

Financial Rewards   Sales people's compensation usually has several components. Most sales people receive at least part of their compensation as a salary, a fixed sum of money paid at regular intervals. Another common financial incentive is a commission, which, as we've already mentioned, is money paid as a percentage of the sales volume or profitability. A bonus is a payment made at management's discretion when the salesperson attains certain goals; bonuses usually are given only periodically, such as at the end of the year. A sales contest is a short-term incentive designed to elicit a specific response from the sales force. Prizes might be cash or other types of financial incentives. For instance, Volkswagen may give a free trip to Germany for the salesperson who sells the most high-end Phaetons.

The bulk of any compensation package is made up of salary, commission, or a combination of the two. The advantage of a salary plan is that sales people know exactly what they will be paid, and sales managers therefore have more control over their sales people. For instance, salaried sales people can be directed to spend a certain percentage of their time handling customer service issues. Under a commission system, however, sales people have only one objective—make the sale! Thus, a commission system provides the most incentive for the sales force to sell.

With more than 14 percent of the market, the electronics giant Best Buy has overcome many obstacles to beat its competition. Much of Best Buy's success follows the company's customer-focused strategy that employs a noncommissioned sales force. The move, which prompted industry scorn and alienated several vendors, turned out to serve the company well in the long run and has revolutionized an industry once characterized by the "hard sell."[27]

Nonfinancial Rewards   As we have noted, good sales people are self-motivated. They want to do a good job and make the sale because it makes them feel good. But this good feeling also can be accentuated by recognition from peers and management. For instance, the internal monthly magazine at the cosmetics firm Mary Kay provides an outlet for not only selling advice but also companywide recognition of individual sales people's accomplishments.[28]

Nonfinancial rewards should have high symbolic value, as plaques, pens, or rings do. Free trips or days off are also effective rewards. More important than what the reward is, however, is the way it is operationalized. For instance, an award should be given at a sales meeting and publicized in the company newsletter. It should also be done in good taste, because if the award is perceived as tacky, no one will take it seriously.[29] Mary Kay recognizes sales people's success with unusually large rewards that have both high symbolic and high material value. About 94,000 Independent Beauty Consultants and sales directors have earned the use of one of the famous pink Cadillacs, but it is also possible to gain rewards and recognition such as a set of faux pearl earrings within the first week of becoming a consultant.

Evaluating Sales People by Using Marketing Metrics   Sales people's evaluation process must be tied to their reward structure. If sales people do well, they should receive their just rewards, in the same way that if you do well on your exams and assignments in a class, you should earn a good grade. However, sales people should be evaluated and rewarded for only those activities and outcomes that fall under their control. For instance, if Macy's makes a unilateral decision to put Diesel jeans in all its stores after a negotiation with Diesel's corporate headquarters in Italy, the Diesel sales representatives responsible for individual Macy's stores should not receive credit for making the sale, nor should they get all the windfall commission that will ensue from the added sales.

Considering this guiding principle—evaluate and reward sales people for what they do and not for what they don't do—how should sales managers evaluate their sales people? The answer is never easy because measures must be tied to performance, and there are many ways to measure performance in a complex job like selling. For example, evaluating performance on the basis of monthly sales alone fails to consider how profitable the sales were, whether any progress was made to build new business that will be realized sometime in the future, or the level of customer service the salesperson provided. Because the sales job is multifaceted with many contributing success factors, sales managers should use multiple measures.[30]

Evaluation measures are either *objective* or *subjective*. Sales, profits, and the number of orders represent examples of objective measures. Although each is somewhat useful to managers, such measures do not provide an adequate perspective for a thorough evaluation because there is no means of comparison with other sales people. For instance, suppose salesperson A generated $1 million last year, but salesperson B generated $1.5 million. Should salesperson B automatically receive a significantly higher evaluation? Now consider that salesperson B's territory has twice as much potential as salesperson A's. Knowing this, we might suppose that salesperson A has actually done a better job. For this reason, firms use ratios like profit per customer, orders per call, sales per hour, or expenses compared to sales as their objective measures.

Whereas objective measures are quantitative, subjective measures seek to assess sales people's behavior: what they do and how well they do it. By their very nature, subjective measures reflect one person's opinion about another's performance. Thus, subjective evaluations can be biased and should be used cautiously and only in conjunction with multiple objective measures.

Personal selling is an integral component of some firms' integrated marketing communications strategy. Although it doesn't make sense for all firms, it is widely used in B2B markets, as well as in B2C markets in which the price of the merchandise is high and customers need some one-to-one assistance before they feel ready to buy. Because of the relatively high expense of maintaining a personal selling force, it is important that sales people be adequately trained, motivated, and compensated.

CHECK YOURSELF

1. What do sales managers need to do to successfully manage their sales force?
2. What is the difference between monetary and nonmonetary incentives?

Summing Up

1. How does personal selling add value?

Although the cost of an average B2B sales call is expensive (about $330), many firms believe they couldn't do business without their sales force. Customers can buy many products and services without the help of a salesperson, but in many other cases, it is worth the extra cost built into the price of a product to be educated about the product or get valuable advice. Sales people can also simplify the buying process and therefore save the customer time and hassle.

2. What is the personal selling process?

Although we discuss selling in terms of steps, it truly represents a process, and the time spent in each step varies according to the situation. In the first step, the salesperson generates a list of viable customers. During the second step, the preapproach, the salesperson gathers information about the customer and prepares for the presentation. The third step, the sales presentation, consists of a personal meeting between the salesperson and the customer. Through discussion and by asking questions, the salesperson learns where the customer is in the buying process and tailors the discussion around what the firm's product or service can do to meet that customer's needs. During the fourth step, the close, the salesperson asks for the order. Finally, during the follow-up, the salesperson and support staff solidify the long-term relationship by making sure the customer is satisfied with the purchase and addressing any complaints. The follow-up therefore sets the stage for the next purchase.

3. How do technology and the Internet affect personal selling?

Technology in general and the Internet in particular have caused fundamental changes in the lives of professional sales people. The ability to be in constant contact with customers and the home office enables sales people to instantly make appointments; answer questions; and get customer, product, and shipping information. Technology has also streamlined the sales training process.

4. **What are the key functions of a sales manager?**

The first task of a sales manager, assuming a firm is starting a sales force from scratch, is to determine whether to use a company sales force or manufacturer's representatives. Then sales managers must determine what the primary selling responsibilities will be—order getter, order taker, or sales support. The sales manager recruits and selects sales people, but because there are all sorts of sales jobs, he or she must determine what it takes to be successful and then go after people with those attributes. In the next step, training, firms can choose between on-the-job and online training. Sales managers are also responsible for motivating and compensating sales people. Most sales people appreciate a balance of financial and nonfinancial rewards for doing a good job. Finally, sales managers are responsible for evaluating their sales people. Normally, sales people should be evaluated on a combination of objective measures, such as sales per hour, and subjective measures, such as how friendly they appear to customers.

Key Terms

- bonus, 602
- closing the sale, 594
- cold calls, 591
- commission, 598
- company sales force, 600
- independent agents, 600
- leads, 590
- manufacturer's representative, 600
- order getter, 600
- order taker, 600
- personal selling, 586
- preapproach, 591
- qualify, 590
- relationship selling, 587
- reps, 600
- role playing, 592
- salary, 602
- sales contest, 602
- sales management, 599
- sales support personnel, 601
- selling teams, 601
- telemarketing, 591
- trade shows, 591

Marketing Applications

1. How has your perception of what it would be like to have a career in sales changed since you read this chapter?

2. "Sales people just make products cost more." Agree or disagree with this statement and discuss why you've taken that position.

3. Choose an industry or a specific company that you would like to work for as a salesperson. How would you generate and qualify leads?

4. Why is it important for sales people to be good listeners? To be good at asking questions?

5. Suppose you are a salesperson at a high-end jewelry store. What can you do to ensure that your customers are satisfied? Now imagine you are the store manager of the same store; what can you do in your position to guarantee customers remain happy with the service they receive?

6. Imagine that a time machine has transported you back to 1957. How was a day in the life of an appliance salesperson different in 1957 than it is in 2007?

7. What are some of the potentially ethically troubling and illegal situations facing professional sales people, and how should they deal with them?

8. Why would Gillette use a company sales force, while a small independent manufacturer of organic shaving cream uses manufacturer's representatives?

9. Similar to the way a sales manager evaluates a salesperson, your instructors evaluate your performance to assign you a grade. Choose one of your classes and analyze the advantages and disadvantages of the objective and subjective bases used to evaluate your performance.

10. A customer has the following reservations. How do you respond?
    a. "I really like all the things this copier does, but I don't think it's going to be very reliable. With all those features, something's got to go wrong."
    b. "Your price for this printer is higher than the price I saw advertised on the Internet."

11. Imagine that you have just been hired by an online start-up company to sell ads on its Web site. You are asked what you think would be a "fair" compensation package for you. Using the information from the chapter, make a list of all the elements that should be included in your compensation package. What changes, if any, should be made over time?

12. You have taken a summer job in the windows and doors department of a large home improvement store. During sales training, you learn about the products, how to best address customers' needs, why the lifetime value of the customer concept is so important to a store like this, and how to sell the customer the best product to fit their needs regardless of price point. One day your manager informs you that you are to recommend Smith Windows to every window customer. Smith Windows are more expensive and don't really provide superior benefit except in limited circumstances. The manager is insistent that you recommend Smith. Not knowing what else to do, you recommend Smith Windows to customers who would have been better served by lower cost windows. The manager rewards you with a sales award. Later the manager tells you that he received an all-expenses-paid cruise for his family from Smith Windows. What, if anything, should you do with this information?

Quiz Yourself

1. Consumers often ask workers in supermarkets where something is located only to learn the worker is a vendor stacking and straightening their company's products on the store shelves. These manufacturer's sales representatives benefit retailers by _____.
   a. education
   b. advice
   c. saving them time and money
   d. adding product lines
   e. increasing marketing costs to the seller

2. Bridgette went to The Gap ready to buy a new blouse, but not sure which color or style she wanted. The sales representative, sensing Bridgette's buying mode, began with the _____ stage of the selling process.
   a. generate leads
   b. preapproach
   c. closing the sale
   d. follow-up
   e. sales presentation

(Answers to these two questions are provided on page 624.)

Go to www.mhhe.com/grewal2e to practice an additional 11 questions.

Net Savvy

1. There are many codes of conduct in the selling profession. The Direct Selling Association publishes one example. Go to www.dsa.org and click on the tab for the Code of Ethics. What type of conduct does the DSA address in the code? How is the code enforced? Do you feel this code is adequate to control the behavior of people engaged in direct selling? Why or why not?

2. To learn more about careers in sales, go to www.bls.gov, the Web site for the Bureau of Labor Statistics. This site contains a wealth of information about careers in all fields. Find the link to the Occupational Outlook Handbook. Bring up the handbook and then click on "Sales." Choose any of the sales fields listed, and explore that career field. What experience is necessary to be hired for that job? What is the median salary? What do earners in the highest 10 percent of performance earn? Is job growth anticipated in that field?

Chapter Case Study

TEL-SOFT SOLUTIONS: MAKING THE SALE[31]

When Vicki Cambridge reached her office, she had a message from Mike Smith, the regional sales manager, to meet him in his office regarding the ABC Telecom order. Vicki Cambridge is a senior sales associate for Tel-Soft Solutions Inc., a firm that markets software designed for telecommunications companies. The ABC Telecom order represents a multimillion-dollar contract for Tel-Soft and would help ABC Telecom boost its productivity levels and revenue for the region. To prepare for the meeting, Vicki reviews her sales call report notes on the ABC Telecom account.

Tel-Soft Solutions

Tel-Soft provides software solutions to large telecommunications firms and has an established track record for delivering an exceptional standard of quality and high levels of customer service. This excellent reputation allows Tel-Soft to charge a substantial premium, ranging from 10 to 20 percent above the market leader.

The telecommunications software services market has been dominated for two decades by this market leader. Tel-Soft holds the second position in the marketplace, with a considerably lower but growing market share. Only one other competitor, an aggressive, small, low-price player, holds a significant market share; this provider has made inroads into the market in the past several years through its aggressive sales tactics.

Tel-Soft has just built a new facility and hired 50 new software programmers. Therefore, the company must generate new business to meet its higher financial goals; even more important in the short run, it must keep the new programmers working on interesting projects to retain them.

ABC Telecom

ABC Telecom is a division of a major U.S.-based telecommunications firm that provides voice, data, fax, Internet, and videoconferencing services. Its purchasing department negotiates contracts for software services and coordinates the interface among a variety of members from different departments. The business environment for telephone services has become highly competitive in recent years, leading to tight budgets and higher levels of scrutiny of the value added by vendors. Competition is fierce, as large numbers of end-user customers are considering new phone providers, which results in considerably lower revenues.

ABC Telecom has been consistently buying software development services from the market leader since 1991 and is generally satisfied with its service. A recent change in corporate leadership, however, has increased concerns about its overreliance on one vendor for a particular service. Also, because of the difficult economic climate, the company is concerned about the cost of software services and whether it is necessary to provide such a high service level.

Vicki's Call Report

A call report is like a diary of sales calls made to a particular client. The notes in Vicki's ABC Telecom file pertaining to the current negotiations began on June 4:

June 4　I contacted Bethany O'Meara, Chief Purchasing Officer at ABC Telecom, to introduce myself to her and get a sense of what their future software needs might be. She told me that the slowed business climate had caused ABC Telecom to institute a program for increased efficiency in operations and that they would be looking to negotiate a new contract for software solutions. She gave me some insights into the technological aspects of their needs.

June 18　Met with Jon Aaronson, Head of R&D, to explain our productivity-enhancing solutions. Went into considerable depth explaining how Tel-Soft could service their needs and learned what they were looking for in a provider. I went over some specific product specification issues, but Jon did not seem impressed. But he did ask for a price and told me that the final decision rested with Brad Alexander, the Chief Financial Officer.

July 2　Presented to Bethany O'Meara and Jon Aaronson. They first asked about the price. I gave them a quote of $3.3 million. They suggested that

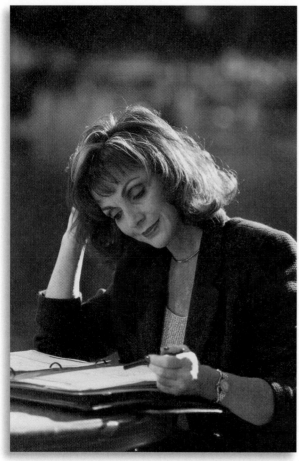

other services were much cheaper. I explained that our price reflected the latest technology and that the price differential was an investment that could pay for itself several times over through faster communication speeds. I also emphasized our reputation for high-quality customer service. While the presentation appeared to meet their software needs, they did not seem impressed with the overall value. I also sent a copy of the presentation in report form to Brad Alexander and attempted to get an appointment to see him.

July 9   Contacted Jon Aaronson by phone. He told me that we were in contention with three other firms and the debate was heated. He stated that the other firms were also touting their state-of-the-art technology. Discussed a lower price of $3.1 million. Also encouraged him to visit Tel-Soft headquarters to meet with the product manager who oversaw the product development efforts and would manage the implementation of the product. He wasn't interested in making the two-day trip even though it would spotlight our core competencies.

July 15   Received a conference call from Brad Alexander and Jon Aaronson to discuss the price. Brad said the price was still too high and that he could not depreciate that amount over the life of the software and meet target levels of efficiency. He wanted a final quote by August 6.

What are the key points Vicki should make in her presentation?

The Final Pitch

Vicki prepared for her meeting with Mike by going over her notes and market data about the competitors. Mike's voicemail indicated that they would be meeting to put together their best possible proposal.

Questions

Help Vicki prepare her sales presentation.

1.   Who should be at the presentation?
2.   How should Vicki start the meeting?
3.   What are the key points she should make in her presentation?
4.   What reservations should she expect? How should she handle them?

glossary

administered vertical marketing system A *supply chain* system in which there is no common ownership and no contractual relationships, but the dominant channel member controls the channel relationship.

advanced shipping notice An electronic document that the supplier sends the retailer in advance of a shipment to tell the retailer exactly what to expect in the shipment.

advertising A paid form of communication from an identifiable source, delivered through a communication channel, and designed to persuade the receiver to take some action, now or in the future.

advertising allowance Tactic of offering a price reduction to channel members if they agree to feature the manufacturer's product in their advertising and promotional efforts.

advertising plan A section of the firm's overall marketing plan that explicitly outlines the objectives of the advertising campaign, how the campaign might accomplish those objectives, and how the firm can determine whether the campaign was successful.

advertising schedule The specification of the timing and duration of advertising.

affective component A component of *attitude* that reflects what a person feels about the issue at hand—his or her like or dislike of something.

AIDA model A common model of the series of mental stages through which consumers move as a result of marketing communications: Awareness leads to Interests, which lead to Desire, which leads to Action.

aided recall Occurs when consumers recognize a name (e.g., of a brand) that has been presented to them.

alpha testing An attempt by the firm to determine whether a product will perform according to its design and whether it satisfies the need for which it was intended; occurs in the firm's research and development (R&D) department.

attitude A person's enduring evaluation of his or her feelings about and behavioral tendencies toward an object or idea; consists of three components: *cognitive, affective,* and *behavioral.*

autocratic buying center A buying center in which one person makes the decision alone, though there may be multiple participants.

B2B (business-to-business) The process of selling merchandise or services from one business to another.

B2C (business-to-consumers) The process in which businesses sell to consumers.

Baby Boomers Generational cohort of people born after World War II, between 1946 and 1964.

background In an advertisement, the backdrop, which is usually a single color.

bait and switch A deceptive practice of luring customers into the store with a very low advertised price on an item (the bait), only to aggressively pressure them into purchasing a higher-priced model (the switch) by disparaging the low-priced item, comparing it unfavorably with the higher-priced model, or professing an inadequate supply of the lower-priced item.

behavioral component A component of *attitude* that comprises the actions a person takes with regard to the issue at hand.

benefit segmentation The grouping of consumers on the basis of the benefits they derive from products or services.

beta testing Having potential consumers examine a product prototype in a real-use setting to determine its functionality, performance, potential problems, and other issues specific to its use.

big box retailer Discount stores that offer a narrow but deep assortment of merchandise; see *category killer.*

blog (weblog or Web log) A Web page that contains periodic posts; corporate blogs are a new form of marketing communications.

body copy The main text portion of an ad.

bonus A payment made at management's discretion when the salesperson attains certain goals; usually given only periodically, such as at the end of the year.

boycott A group's refusal to deal commercially with some organization to protest against its policies.

brand The name, term, design, symbol, or any other features that identify one seller's good or service as distinct from those of other sellers.

brand association The mental links that consumers make between a brand and its key product attributes; can involve a logo, slogan, or famous personality.

brand awareness Measures how many consumers in a market are familiar with the brand and what it stands for; created through repeated exposures of the various brand elements (brand name, logo, symbol, character, packaging, or slogan) in the firm's communications to consumers.

brand dilution Occurs when a brand extension adversely affects consumer perceptions about the attributes the core brand is believed to hold.

brand equity The set of assets and liabilities linked to a brand that add to or subtract from the value provided by the product or service.

brand extension The use of the same brand name for new products being introduced to the same or new markets.

branding In an advertisement, the portion that identifies the sponsor of the ad.

brand licensing A contractual arrangement between firms, whereby one firm allows another to use its brand name, logo, symbols, or characters in exchange for a negotiated fee.

brand loyalty Occurs when a consumer buys the same brand's product or service repeatedly over time rather than buying from multiple suppliers within the same category.

brand personality Refers to a set of human characteristics associated with a brand, which has symbolic or self-expressive meanings for consumers.

brand repositioning (rebranding) A strategy in which marketers change a brand's focus to target new markets or realign the brand's core emphasis with changing market preferences.

breadth Number of product lines offered by a firm; also known as variety.

break-even analysis Technique used to examine the relationships among cost, price, revenue, and profit over different levels of production and sales to determine the *break-even point*.

break-even point The point at which the number of units sold generates just enough revenue to equal the total costs; at this point, profits are zero.

breakthroughs See *pioneers*.

bricks-and-mortar retailer A traditional, physical store.

business ethics Refers to a branch of ethical study that examines ethical rules and principles within a commercial context, the various moral or ethical problems that might arise in a business setting, and any special duties or obligations that apply to persons engaged in commerce.

business-to-business (B2B) marketing The process of buying and selling goods or services to be used in the production of other goods and services, for consumption by the buying organization, or for resale by wholesalers and retailers.

buyer The buying center participant who handles the paperwork of the actual purchase.

buying center The group of people typically responsible for the buying decisions in large organizations.

C2C (consumer-to-consumer) The process in which consumers sell to other consumers.

cash discount Tactic of offering a reduction in the invoice cost if the buyer pays the invoice prior to the end of the discount period.

category depth The number of stock keeping units (SKUs) within a category.

category killer A specialist that offers an extensive assortment in a particular category, so overwhelming the category that other retailers have difficulty competing.

category specialist A retailer that offers a narrow variety but a deep assortment of merchandise.

cause-related marketing Commercial activity in which businesses and charities form a partnership to market an image, a product, or a service for their mutual benefit; a type of promotional campaign.

checking The process of going through the goods upon receipt to ensure they arrived undamaged and that the merchandise ordered was the merchandise received.

churn The number of consumers who stop using a product or service, divided by the average number of consumers of that product or service.

click-through tracking A way to measure how many times users click on banner advertising on Web sites.

clinical trial Medical test of the safety and efficacy of a new drug or treatment with human subjects.

close-out retailers Stores that offer an inconsistent assortment of low priced, brand name merchandise.

closing the sale Obtaining a commitment from the customer to make a purchase.

cobranding The practice of marketing two or more brands together, on the same package or promotion.

cognitive component A component of *attitude* that reflects what a person believes to be true.

cold calls A method of prospecting in which salespeople telephone or go to see potential customers without appointments.

collaboration, planning, forecasting, and replenishment (CPFR) An inventory management system that uses an electronic data interchange (EDI) through which a retailer sends sales information to a manufacturer.

commercial speech A message with an economic motivation, that is, to promote a product or service, to persuade someone to purchase, and so on.

commission Compensation or financial incentive for salespeople based on a fixed percentage of their sales.

communication channel The medium—print, broadcast, the Internet—that carries the message.

communication gap A type of *service gap*; refers to the difference between the actual service provided to customers and the service that the firm's promotion program promises.

company sales force Comprised of people who are employees of the selling company and are engaged in the selling process.

compensatory decision rule At work when the consumer is evaluating alternatives and trades off one characteristic against another, such that good characteristics compensate for bad ones.

competitive intelligence (CI) Used by firms to collect and synthesize information about their position with respect to their rivals; enables companies to anticipate market developments rather than merely react to them.

competitive parity A firm's strategy of setting prices that are similar to those of major competitors.

competitor orientation A company objective based on the premise that the firm should measure itself primarily against its competition.

competitor-based pricing A strategy that involves pricing below, at, or above competitors' offerings.

competitor-based pricing method An approach that attempts to reflect how the firm wants consumers to interpret its products relative to the competitors' offerings; for example, setting a price close to a competitor's price signals to consumers that the product is similar, whereas setting the price much higher signals greater features, better quality, or some other valued benefit.

complementary products Products whose demand curves are positively related, such that they rise or fall together; a percentage increase in demand for one results in a percentage increase in demand for the other.

concentrated segmentation strategy A marketing strategy of selecting a single, primary target market and focusing all energies on providing a product to fit that market's needs.

concept testing The process in which a concept statement that describes a product or a service is presented to potential buyers or users to obtain their reactions.

concepts Brief written descriptions of a product or service; its technology, working principles, and forms; and what customer needs it would satisfy.

conclusive research Provides the information needed to confirm preliminary insights, which managers can use to pursue appropriate courses of action.

consensus buying center A buying center in which all members of the team must reach a collective agreement that they can support a particular purchase.

consultative buying center A buying center in which one person makes the decision but he or she solicits input from others before doing so.

consumer decision rules The set of criteria that consumers use consciously or subconsciously to quickly and efficiently select from among several alternatives.

contest A brand-sponsored competition that requires some form of skill or effort.

continuous advertising schedule Runs steadily throughout the year and therefore is suited to products and services that are consumed continually at relatively steady rates and that require a steady level of persuasive or reminder advertising.

contractual vertical marketing system A system in which independent firms at different levels of the supply chain join together through contracts to obtain economies of scale and coordination and to reduce conflict.

contribution per unit Equals the price less the variable cost per unit. Variable used to determine the break-even point in units.

control phase The part of the strategic marketing planning process when managers evaluate the performance of the marketing strategy and take any necessary corrective actions.

convenience goods/services Those for which the consumer is not willing to spend any effort to evaluate prior to purchase.

convenience store Type of retailer that provides a limited number of items at a convenient location in a small store with speedy checkout.

conventional supermarket Type of retailer that offers groceries, meat, and produce with limited sales of nonfood items, such as health and beauty aids and general merchandise, in a self-service format.

conversion rates Percentage of consumers who buy a product after viewing it.

cookie Computer program, installed on hard drives, that provides identifying information.

cooperative (co-op) advertising An agreement between a manufacturer and retailer in which the manufacturer agrees to defray some advertising costs.

copycat brands Mimic a manufacturer's brand in appearance but generally with lower quality and prices.

corporate brand (family brand) The use of a firm's own corporate name to brand all of its product lines and products.

corporate social responsibility Refers to the voluntary actions taken by a company to address the ethical, social, and environmental impacts of its business operations and the concerns of its stakeholders.

corporate vertical marketing system A system in which the parent company has complete control and can dictate the priorities and objectives of the supply chain; it may own facilities such as manufacturing plants, warehouse facilities, retail outlets, and design studios.

cost of ownership method A value-based method for setting prices that determines the total cost of owning the product over its useful life.

cost-based pricing A pricing strategy that involves first determining the costs of producing or providing a product and then adding a fixed amount above that total to arrive at the selling price.

cost-based pricing method An approach that determines the final price to charge by starting with the cost, without recognizing the role that consumers or competitors' prices play in the marketplace.

countertrade Trade between two countries where goods are traded for other goods and not for hard currency.

country culture Entails easy-to-spot visible nuances that are particular to a country, such as dress, symbols, ceremonies, language, colors, and food preferences, and more subtle aspects, which are trickier to identify.

coupon Provides a stated discount to consumers on the final selling price of a specific item; the retailer handles the discount.

cross-docking distribution center A distribution center to which vendors ship merchandise prepackaged and ready for sale. So the merchandise goes to a staging area rather than into storage. When all the merchandise going to a particular store has arrived in the staging area, it is loaded onto a truck, and away it goes. Thus, merchandise goes from the receiving dock to the shipping dock—cross dock.

cross-price elasticity The percentage change in demand for product A that occurs in response to a percentage change in price of product B; see *complementary products*.

cross-promoting Efforts of two or more firms joining together to reach a specific target market.

cross-shopping The pattern of buying both premium and low-priced merchandise or patronizing both expensive, status-oriented retailers and price-oriented retailers.

cultural imperialism The belief that one's own culture is superior to that of other nations; can take the form of an active, formal policy or a more subtle general attitude.

culture The set of values, guiding beliefs, understandings, and ways of doing things shared by members of a society; exists on two levels: visible artifacts (e.g., behavior, dress, symbols, physical settings, ceremonies) and underlying values (thought processes, beliefs, and assumptions).

cumulative quantity discount Pricing tactic that offers a discount based on the amount purchased over a specified period and usually involves several transactions; encourages resellers to maintain their current supplier because the cost to switch must include the loss of the discount.

customer excellence Involves a focus on retaining loyal customers and excellent customer service.

customer orientation A company objective based on the premise that the firm should measure itself primarily according to whether it meets its customers' needs.

customer relationship management (CRM) A business philosophy and set of strategies, programs, and systems that focus on identifying and building loyalty among the firm's most valued customers.

customer service Specifically refers to human or mechanical activities firms undertake to help satisfy their customers' needs and wants.

cycle time The time between the decision to place an order and the receipt of merchandise.

data Raw numbers or facts.

data mining The use of a variety of statistical analysis tools to uncover previously unknown patterns in the data stored in databases or relationships among variables.

data warehouses Large computer files that store millions and even billions of pieces of individual data.

deal A type of short-term price reduction that can take several forms, such as a "featured price," a price lower than the regular price; a "buy one, get one free" offer; or a certain percentage "more free" offer contained in larger packaging; can involve a special financing arrangement, such as reduced percentage interest rates or extended repayment terms.

deceptive advertising A representation, omission, act, or practice in an advertisement that is likely to mislead consumers acting reasonably under the circumstances.

decider The buying center participant who ultimately determines any part of or the entire buying decision—whether to buy, what to buy, how to buy, or where to buy.

decision heuristics Mental shortcuts that help consumers narrow down choices; examples include price, brand, and product presentation.

decline stage Stage of the product life cycle when sales decline and the product eventually exits the market.

decoding The process by which the receiver interprets the sender's message.

delivery gap A type of *service gap;* the difference between the firm's service standards and the actual service it provides to customers.

demand curve Shows how many units of a product or service consumers will demand during a specific period at different prices.

democratic buying center A buying center in which the majority rules in making decisions.

demographic segmentation The grouping of consumers according to easily measured, objective characteristics such as age, gender, income, and education.

demographics Information about the characteristics of human populations and segments, especially those used to identify consumer markets such as by age, gender, income, and education.

department store A retailer that carries many different types of merchandise (broad variety) and lots of items within each type (deep assortment); offers some customer services; and is organized into separate departments to display its merchandise.

depth The number of categories within a product line.

derived demand The linkage between consumers' demand for a company's output and its purchase of necessary inputs to manufacture or assemble that particular output.

determinant attributes Product or service features that are important to the buyer and on which competing brands or stores are perceived to differ.

differentiated segmentation strategy A strategy through which a firm targets several market segments with a different offering for each.

diffusion of innovation The process by which the use of an innovation, whether a product or a service, spreads throughout a market group over time and over various categories of adopters.

direct investment When a firm maintains 100 percent ownership of its plants, operation facilities, and offices in a foreign country, often through the formation of wholly owned subsidiaries.

direct marketing Sales and promotional techniques that deliver promotional materials individually to potential customers.

disintermediation A manufacturer sells directly to consumers and bypasses retailers.

discount store A type of retailer that offers a broad variety of merchandise, limited service, and low prices.

dispatcher The person who coordinates deliveries to distribution centers.

distribution center A facility for the receipt, storage, and redistribution of goods to company stores or customers; may be operated by retailers, manufacturers, or distribution specialists.

distribution intensity The number of supply chain members to use at each level of the supply chain.

distributive fairness Pertains to a customer's perception of the benefits he or she received compared with the costs (inconvenience or loss) that resulted from a service failure.

diversification strategy A growth strategy whereby a firm introduces a new product or service to a market segment that it does not currently serve.

drugstore A specialty store that concentrates on health and personal grooming merchandise, though pharmaceuticals may represent more than 60 percent of its sales.

dumping The practice of selling a good in a foreign market at a price that is lower than its domestic price or below its cost.

duty See *tariff.*

early adopters The second group of consumers in the diffusion of innovation model, after *innovators,* to use a product or service innovation; generally don't like to take as much risk as innovators but instead wait and purchase the product after careful review.

early majority A group of consumers in the diffusion of innovation model that represents approximately 34 percent of the population; members don't like to take much risk and therefore tend to wait until bugs are worked out of a particular product or service; few new products and services can be profitable until this large group buys them.

economic situation Macroeconomic factor that affects the way consumers buy merchandise and spend money, both in a marketer's home country and abroad; see *inflation, foreign currency fluctuations,* and *interest rates.*

elastic Refers to a market for a product or service that is price sensitive; that is, relatively small changes in price will generate fairly large changes in the quantity demanded.

electronic data interchange (EDI) The computer-to-computer exchange of business documents from a retailer to a vendor and back.

emotional appeal Aims to satisfy consumers' emotional desires rather than their utilitarian needs.

emotional support Concern for others' well-being and support of their decisions in a job setting.

employment marketing Marketing programs to attract applicants to the hiring firm.

empowerment In context of service delivery, means allowing employees to make decisions about how service is provided to customers.

encoding The process of converting the sender's ideas into a message, which could be verbal, visual, or both.

English auction Goods and services are simply sold to the highest bidder.

environmental concerns Include, but are not limited to, the excessive use of natural resources and energy, refuse from manufacturing processes, excess trash created by consumer goods packages, and hard-to-dispose-of products like tires, cell phones, and computer monitors.

esteem needs Needs that enable people to fulfill inner desires.

ethical climate The set of values within a marketing firm, or in the marketing division of any firm, that guide decision making and behavior.

evaluative criteria Consist of a set of salient, or important, attributes about a particular product.

event sponsorship Popular PR tool; occurs when corporations support various activities (financially or otherwise), usually in the cultural or sports and entertainment sectors.

everyday low pricing (EDLP) A strategy companies use to emphasize the continuity of their retail prices at a level somewhere between the regular, nonsale price and the deep-discount sale prices their competitors may offer.

evoked set Comprises the alternative brands or stores that the consumer states he or she would consider when making a purchase decision.

exchange The trade of things of value between the buyer and the seller so that each is better off as a result.

exchange control Refers to the regulation of a country's currency *exchange rate*.

exchange rate The measure of how much one currency is worth in relation to another.

exclusive cobrand Developed by national brand vendor and retailer and sold only by that retailer.

exclusive distribution Strategy in which only selected retailers can sell a manufacturer's brand.

exclusive geographic territories Territories granted to one or very few retail customers by a manufacturer using an exclusive distribution strategy; no other customers can sell a particular brand in these territories.

experience curve effect Refers to the drop in unit cost as the accumulated volume sold increases; as sales continue to grow, the costs continue to drop, allowing even further reductions in the price.

experimental research A type of quantitative research that systematically manipulates one or more variables to determine which variable has a causal effect on another variable.

exploratory research Attempts to begin to understand the phenomenon of interest; also provides initial information when the problem lacks any clear definition.

exporting Producing goods in one country and selling them in another.

extended problem solving A purchase decision process during which the consumer devotes considerable time and effort to analyzing alternatives; often occurs when the consumer perceives that the purchase decision entails a lot of risk.

external locus of control Refers to when consumers believe that fate or other external factors control all outcomes.

external reference price A higher price to which the consumer can compare the selling price to evaluate the purchase.

external search for information Occurs when the buyer seeks information outside his or her personal knowledge base to help make the buying decision.

extranet A collaborative network that uses Internet technology to link businesses with their suppliers, customers, or other businesses.

extreme value food retailer See *limited assortment supermarkets*.

extreme value retailer A general merchandise discount store found in lower-income urban or rural areas.

factory outlets Outlet stores owned by manufacturers

feedback loop Allows the receiver to communicate with the sender and thereby informs the sender whether the message was received and decoded properly.

financial risk Risk associated with a monetary outlay; includes the initial cost of the purchase, as well as the costs of using the item or service.

first movers Product pioneers that are the first to create a market or product category, making them readily recognizable to consumers and thus establishing a commanding and early market share lead.

fixed costs Those costs that remain essentially at the same level, regardless of any changes in the volume of production.

flighting advertising schedule An advertising schedule implemented in spurts, with periods of heavy advertising followed by periods of no advertising.

floor-ready merchandise Merchandise that is ready to be placed on the selling floor immediately.

focus group interview A research technique in which a small group of persons (usually 8 to 12) comes together for an intensive discussion about a particular topic, with the conversation guided by a trained moderator using an unstructured method of inquiry.

foreground In an advertisement, everything that appears on top of the *background*.

foreign currency fluctuations Changes in the value of a country's currency relative to the currency of another country; can influence consumer spending.

franchisee See *franchising*.

franchising A contractual agreement between a *franchisor* and a *franchisee* that allows the franchisee to operate a business using a name and format developed and supported by the franchisor.

franchisor See *franchising*.

frequency Measure of how often the audience is exposed to a communication within a specified period of time.

functional needs Pertain to the performance of a product or service.

full-line discount stores Retailers that offer low prices, limited service, and a broad variety of merchandise.

gatekeeper The buying center participant who controls information or access to decision makers and influencers.

General Agreement on Tariffs and Trade (GATT) Organization established to lower trade barriers, such as high tariffs on imported goods and restrictions on the number and types of imported products that inhibited the free flow of goods across borders.

Generation X Generational cohort of people born between 1965 and 1976.

Generation Y Generational cohort of people born between 1977 and 1995; biggest cohort since the original postwar baby boom.

generational cohort A group of people of the same generation—typically have similar purchase behaviors because they have shared experiences and are in the same stage of life.

generic (house) brand No-frills products offered at a low price without any branding information.

geodemographic segmentation The grouping of consumers on the basis of a combination of geographic, demographic, and lifestyle characteristics.

geographic segmentation The grouping of consumers on the basis of where they live.

global labor issues Includes concerns about working conditions and wages paid to factory workers in developing countries.

globalization Refers to the processes by which goods, services, capital, people, information, and ideas flow across national borders.

globalization of production Also known as *offshoring;* refers to manufacturers' procurement of goods and services from around the globe to take advantage of national differences in the cost and quality of various factors of production (e.g., labor, energy, land, capital).

goods Items that can be physically touched.

gray market Employs irregular but not necessarily illegal methods; generally, it legally circumvents authorized channels of distribution to sell goods at prices lower than those intended by the manufacturer.

green marketing Involves a strategic effort by firms to supply customers with environmentally friendly merchandise.

gross domestic product (GDP) Defined as the market value of the goods and services produced by a country in a year; the most widely used standardized measure of output.

gross national income (GNI) Consists of GDP plus the net income earned from investments abroad (minus any payments made to nonresidents who contribute to the domestic economy).

gross rating points (GRP) Measure used for various media advertising—print, radio, or television; GRP = reach × frequency.

growth stage Stage of the product life cycle when the product gains acceptance, demand and sales increase, and competitors emerge in the product category.

habitual decision making A purchase decision process in which consumers engage with little conscious effort.

headline In an advertisement, large type designed to draw attention.

high/low pricing A *pricing* strategy that relies on the promotion of sales, during which prices are temporarily reduced to encourage purchases.

home improvement center Category specialist that offers home improvement tools for contractors and do-it-yourselfers.

horizontal price fixing Occurs when competitors that produce and sell competing products collude, or work together, to control prices, effectively taking price out of the decision process for consumers.

human development index (HDI) A composite measure of three indicators of the quality of life in different countries:

life expectancy at birth, educational attainment, and whether the average incomes are sufficient to meet the basic needs of life in that country.

ideal point The position at which a particular market segment's ideal product would lie on a *perceptual map.*

ideas Intellectual concepts—thoughts, opinions, and philosophies.

implementation phase The part of the strategic marketing planning process when marketing managers (1) identify and evaluate different opportunities by engaging in segmentation, targeting, and positioning (see *STP*) and (2) implement the marketing mix using the four Ps.

improvement value Represents an estimate of how much more (or less) consumers are willing to pay for a product relative to other comparable products.

impulse buying A buying decision made by customers on the spot when they see the merchandise.

income effect Refers to the change in the quantity of a product demanded by consumers due to a change in their income.

independent (conventional) supply chain A loose coalition of several independently owned and operated supply chain members—a manufacturer, a wholesaler, and a retailer—all attempting to satisfy their own objectives and maximize their own profits, often at the expense of the other members.

independent agents Salespeople who sell a manufacturer's products on an extended contract basis but are not employees of the manufacturer; also known as *manufacturer's representatives* or *reps.*

in-depth interview An exploratory research technique in which trained researchers ask questions, listen to and record the answers, and then pose additional questions to clarify or expand on a particular issue.

individual brands The use of individual brand names for each of a firm's products.

inelastic Refers to a market for a product or service that is price insensitive; that is, relatively small changes in price will not generate large changes in the quantity demanded.

inflation Refers to the persistent increase in the prices of goods and services.

influencer The buying center participant whose views influence other members of the buying center in making the final decision.

information Organized, analyzed, interpreted data that offers value to marketers.

informational appeal Used in a promotion to help consumers make purchase decisions by offering factual information and strong arguments built around relevant issues that encourage them to evaluate the brand favorably on the basis of the key benefits it provides.

informative advertising Communication used to create and build brand awareness, with the ultimate goal of moving the consumer through the buying cycle to a purchase.

infrastructure The basic facilities, services, and installations needed for a community or society to function, such as transportation and communications systems, water and power lines, and public institutions like schools, post offices, and prisons.

initiator The buying center participant who first suggests buying the particular product or service.

innovation The process by which ideas are transformed into new products and services that will help firms grow.

innovators Those buyers who want to be the first to have the new product or service.

inseparable A characteristic of a service: it is produced and consumed at the same time; that is, service and consumption are inseparable.

instrumental support Providing the equipment or systems needed to perform a task in a job setting.

intangible A characteristic of a service; it cannot be touched, tasted, or seen like a pure product can.

integrated marketing communications (IMC) Represents the promotion dimension of the four Ps; encompasses a variety of communication disciplines—general advertising, personal selling, sales promotion, public relations, direct marketing, and electronic media—in combination to provide clarity, consistency, and maximum communicative impact.

intensive distribution A strategy designed to get products into as many outlets as possible.

interest rates These represent the cost of borrowing money.

internal locus of control Refers to when consumers believe they have some control over the outcomes of their actions, in which case they generally engage in more search activities.

internal reference price Price information stored in the consumer's memory that the person uses to assess a current price offering—perhaps the last price he or she paid or what he or she expects to pay.

internal search for information Occurs when the buyer examines his or her own memory and knowledge about the product or service, gathered through past experiences.

International Monetary Fund (IMF) Established with the original General Agreement on Tariffs and Trade (GATT); primary purpose is to promote international monetary cooperation and facilitate the expansion and growth of international trade.

intranet A secure communication system contained within one company, such as between the firm's buyers and distribution centers.

introduction stage Stage of the product life cycle when innovators start buying the product.

introductory price promotion Short-term price discounts designed to encourage trial.

involvement Consumer's interest in a product or service.

irregulars Merchandise with minor construction errors.

joint venture Formed when a firm entering a new market pools its resources with those of a local firm to form a new company in which ownership, control, and profits are shared.

just-in-time (JIT) inventory systems Inventory management systems designed to deliver less merchandise on a more frequent basis than traditional inventory systems; the firm gets the merchandise "just in time" for it to be used in the manufacture of another product, in the case of parts or components, or for sale when the customer wants it, in the case of consumer goods; also known as *quick response (QR) systems* in retailing.

knowledge gap A type of *service gap;* reflects the difference between customers' *expectations* and the firm's perception of those expectations.

laggards Consumers who like to avoid change and rely on traditional products until they are no longer available.

lagged effect A delayed response to a marketing communication campaign.

late majority The last group of buyers to enter a new product market; when they do, the product has achieved its full market potential.

lead time The amount of time between the recognition that an order needs to be placed and the arrival of the needed merchandise at the seller's store, ready for sale.

lead users Innovative product users who modify existing products according to their own ideas to suit their specific needs.

leader pricing Consumer pricing tactic that attempts to build store traffic by aggressively pricing and advertising a regularly purchased item, often priced at or just above the store's cost.

leads A list of potential customers.

learning Refers to a change in a person's thought process or behavior that arises from experience and takes place throughout the consumer decision process.

lease A written agreement under which the owner of an item or property allows its use for a specified period of time in exchange for a fee.

licensed brand An agreement allows one brand to use another's name, image, and/or logo for a fee.

lifestyles A component of *psychographics;* refers to the way a person lives his or her life to achieve goals.

lift Additional sales caused by advertising.

limited assortment supermarkets Retailers that offer only one or two brands or sizes of most products (usually including a store brand) and attempt to achieve great efficiency to lower costs and prices.

limited problem solving Occurs during a purchase decision that calls for, at most, a moderate amount of effort and time.

locational excellence A method of achieving excellence by having a strong physical location and/or Internet presence.

logistics management The integration of two or more activities for the purpose of planning, implementing, and controlling the efficient flow of raw materials, in-process inventory, and finished goods from the point of origin to the point of consumption.

loss leader pricing Loss leader pricing takes the tactic of *leader pricing* one step further by lowering the price below the store's cost.

love needs Needs expressed through interactions with others.

loyalty program Specifically designed to retain customers by offering premiums or other incentives to customers who make multiple purchases over time.

loyalty segmentation Strategy of investing in loyalty initiatives to retain the firm's most profitable customers.

macroenvironmental factors Aspects of the external environment that affect a company's business, such as the culture, demographics, social issues, technological advances, economic situation, and political/regulatory environment.

manufacturer brands (national brands) Brands owned and managed by the manufacturer.

manufacturer's representative See *independent agents.*

markdowns Reductions retailers take on the initial selling price of the product or service.

market development strategy A growth strategy that employs the existing marketing offering to reach new market segments, whether domestic or international.

market growth rate The annual rate of growth of the specific market in which the product competes.

market penetration strategy A growth strategy that employs the existing marketing mix and focuses the firm's efforts on existing customers.

market positioning Involves the process of defining the marketing mix variables so that target customers have a clear, distinctive, desirable understanding of what the product does or represents in comparison with competing products.

market segment A group of consumers who respond similarly to a firm's marketing efforts.

market segmentation The process of dividing the market into groups of customers with different needs, wants, or characteristics—who therefore might appreciate products or services geared especially for them.

market share Percentage of a market accounted for by a specific entity.

marketing An organizational function and a set of processes for creating, *capturing,* communicating, and delivering value to customers and for managing customer relationships in ways that benefit the organization and its stakeholders.

marketing channel The set of institutions that transfer the ownership of and move goods from the point of production to the point of consumption; consists of all the institutions and marketing activities in the marketing process.

marketing ethics Refers to those ethical problems that are specific to the domain of marketing.

marketing information system (MkIS) A set of procedures and methods that apply to the regular, planned collection, analysis, and presentation of information that then may be used in marketing decisions.

marketing mix (four Ps) Product, price, place, and promotion—the controllable set of activities that a firm uses to respond to the wants of its target markets.

marketing plan A written document composed of an analysis of the current marketing situation, opportunities and threats for the firm, marketing objectives and strategy specified in terms of the four Ps, action programs, and projected or pro forma income (and other financial) statements.

marketing research A set of techniques and principles for systematically collecting, recording, analyzing, and interpreting data that can aid decision makers involved in marketing goods, services, or ideas.

marketing strategy A firm's target market, marketing mix, and method of obtaining a sustainable competitive advantage.

Maslow's hierarchy of needs A paradigm for classifying people's motives. It argues that when lower-level, more basic needs (physiological and safety) are fulfilled, people turn to satisfying their higher-level human needs (social and personal); see *physiological, safety, social,* and *personal needs.*

mass customization The practice of interacting on a one-to-one basis with many people to create custom-made products or services; providing one-to-one marketing to the masses.

mass media Channels that are ideal for reaching large numbers of anonymous audience members; include national newspapers, magazines, radio, and television.

maturity stage Stage of the product life cycle when industry sales reach their peak, so firms try to rejuvenate their products by adding new features or repositioning them.

maximizing profits A profit strategy that relies primarily on economic theory. If a firm can accurately specify a mathematical model that captures all the factors required to explain and predict sales and profits, it should be able to identify the price at which its profits are maximized.

m-commerce (mobile commerce) Communicating with or selling to consumers through wireless handheld devices such as cellular phones.

media buy The actual purchase of airtime or print pages.

media mix The combination of the media used and the frequency of advertising in each medium.

media planning The process of evaluating and selecting the *media mix* that will deliver a clear, consistent, compelling message to the intended audience.

micromarketing An extreme form of segmentation that tailors a product or service to suit an individual customer's wants or needs; also called *one-to-one marketing.*

mission statement A broad description of a firm's objectives and the scope of activities it plans to undertake; attempts to answer two main questions: What type of business is it? What does it need to do to accomplish its goals and objectives?

modified rebuy Refers to when the buyer has purchased a similar product in the past but has decided to change some specifications, such as the desired price, quality level, customer service level, options, or so forth.

monopolistic competition Occurs when there are many firms that sell closely related but not homogeneous products; these products may be viewed as substitutes but are not perfect substitutes.

motive A need or want that is strong enough to cause the person to seek satisfaction.

multichannel retailers Retailers that sell merchandise in more than one retail channel (e.g., store, catalog, and Internet).

multichannel strategy Selling in more than one channel (e.g., stores, Internet, catalog).

need recognition The beginning of the consumer decision process; occurs when consumers recognize they have an unsatisfied need and want to go from their actual, needy state to a different, desired state.

negative word of mouth Occurs when consumers spread negative information about a product, service, or store to others.

new buy In a B2B setting, a purchase of a good or service for the first time; the buying decision is likely to be quite involved because the buyer or the buying organization does not have any experience with the item.

niche media Channels that are focused and generally used to reach narrow segments, often with unique demographic characteristics or interests.

noise Any interference that stems from competing messages, a lack of clarity in the message, or a flaw in the medium; a problem for all communication channels.

noncommercial speech A message that does not have an economic motivation and therefore is fully protected under the First Amendment.

noncompensatory decision rule At work when consumers choose a product or service on the basis of a subset of its characteristics, regardless of the values of its other attributes.

noncumulative quantity discount Pricing tactic that offers a discount based on only the amount purchased in a single order; provides the buyer with an incentive to purchase more merchandise immediately.

North American Industry Classification System (NAICS) codes U.S. Bureau of Census classification scheme that categorizes all firms into a hierarchical set of six-digit codes.

objective-and-task method An IMC budgeting method that determines the cost required to undertake specific tasks to accomplish communication objectives; process entails setting objectives, choosing media, and determining costs.

observation An exploratory research method that entails examining purchase and consumption behaviors through personal or video camera scrutiny.

odd prices Prices that end in odd numbers, usually 9, such as $3.99.

off-price retailer A type of retailer that offers an inconsistent assortment of merchandise at relatively low prices.

offshoring See *globalization of production*.

oligopolistic competition Occurs when only a few firms dominate a market.

one-to-one marketing See *micromarketing*.

online chat Instant messaging or voice conversation with an online sales representative.

online couponing A promotional Web technique in which consumers print a coupon directly from a site and then redeem the coupon in a store.

online referring A promotional Web technique in which consumers fill out an interest or order form and are referred to an offline dealer or firm that offers the product or service of interest.

operational excellence Involves a firm's focus on efficient operations and excellent supply chain management.

opt in The option giving consumer complete control over the collection and dissemination of his/her personal information, usually referred to in an Internet setting.

opt out The option whereby consumer must actively choose to prevent personal information from being used or shared with third parties, usually referred to in an Internet setting. .

order getter A salesperson whose primary responsibilities are identifying potential customers and engaging those customers in discussions to attempt to make a sale.

order taker A salesperson whose primary responsibility is to process routine orders or reorders or rebuys for products.

organizational culture Reflects the set of values, traditions, and customs that guide a firm's employees' behavior.

outlet stores Off-price retailers that often stock irregulars, out-of-season merchandise, or overstocks from the parent company.

own brands See *private-label brands*.

panel research A type of quantitative research that involves collecting information from a group of consumers (the panel) over time; data collected may be from a survey or a record of purchases.

perceived value The relationship between a product or service's benefits and its cost.

perception The process by which people select, organize, and interpret information to form a meaningful picture of the world.

perceptual map Displays, in two or more dimensions, the position of products or brands in the consumer's mind.

performance risk Involves the perceived danger inherent in a poorly performing product or service.

perishability A characteristic of a service: it cannot be stored for use in the future.

personal needs Relate to ways people satisfy their inner desires.

personal selling The two-way flow of communication between a buyer and a seller that is designed to influence the buyer's purchase decision.

persuasive advertising Communication used to motivate consumers to take action.

physiological needs Those relating to the basic biological necessities of life: food, drink, rest, and shelter.

pioneers New product introductions that establish a completely new market or radically change both the rules of competition and consumer preferences in a market; also called *breakthroughs*.

planning phase The part of the strategic marketing planning process when marketing executives, in conjunction with other top managers, (1) define the mission or vision of the business and (2) evaluate the situation by assessing how various players, both in and outside the organization, affect the firm's potential for success.

point-of-purchase (POP) display A merchandise display located at the point of purchase, such as at the checkout counter in a grocery store.

political/regulatory environment Comprises political parties, government organizations, and legislation and laws.

pop-up stores Temporary storefronts that exist for only a limited time and generally focus on a new product or a limited group of products offered by a retailer, manufacturer, or service provider; give consumers a chance to interact with the brand and build brand awareness, but are not designed primarily to sell the product.

postpurchase dissonance The psychologically uncomfortable state produced by an inconsistency between beliefs and behaviors that in turn evokes a motivation to reduce the dissonance; buyers' remorse.

posttesting The evaluation of an IMC campaign's impact after it is has been implemented.

preapproach In the personal selling process, occurs prior to meeting the customer for the first time and extends the qualification of leads procedure; in this step, the salesperson conducts additional research and develops plans for meeting with the customer.

predatory pricing A firm's practice of setting a very low price for one or more of its products with the intent to drive its competition out of business; illegal under both the Sherman Act and the Federal Trade Commission Act.

premarket test Conducted before a product or service is brought to market to determine how many customers will try and then continue to use it.

premium An item offered for free or at a bargain price to reward some type of behavior, such as buying, sampling, or testing.

premium brand A branding strategy that offers consumers a private label of comparable or superior quality to a manufacturer brand.

premium pricing A competitor-based pricing method by which the firm deliberately prices a product above the prices set for competing products to capture those consumers who always shop for the best or for whom price does not matter.

prestige products or services Those that consumers purchase for status rather than functionality.

pretesting Assessments performed before an ad campaign; is implemented to ensure that the various elements are working in an integrated fashion and doing what they are intended to do.

price The overall sacrifice a consumer is willing to make—money, time, energy—to acquire a specific product or service.

price bundling Consumer pricing tactic of selling more than one product for a single, lower price than what the items would cost sold separately; can be used to sell slow-moving items, to encourage customers to stock up so they won't purchase competing brands, to encourage trial of a new product, or to provide an incentive to purchase a less desirable product or service to obtain a more desirable one in the same bundle.

price discrimination The practice of selling the same product to different resellers (wholesalers, distributors, or retailers) or to the ultimate consumer at different prices; some, but not all, forms of price discrimination are illegal.

price elasticity of demand Measures how changes in a price affect the quantity of the product demanded; specifically, the ratio of the percentage change in quantity demanded to the percentage change in price.

price fixing The practice of colluding with other firms to control prices.

price lining Consumer market pricing tactic of establishing a price floor and a price ceiling for an entire line of similar products and then setting a few other price points in between to represent distinct differences in quality.

price skimming A strategy of selling a new product or service at a high price that *innovators* and *early adopters* are willing to pay in order to obtain it; after the high-price market segment becomes saturated and sales begin to slow down, the firm generally lowers the price to capture (or skim) the next most price sensitive segment.

price war Occurs when two or more firms compete primarily by lowering their prices.

pricing tactics Short-term methods, in contrast to long-term pricing strategies, used to focus on company objectives, costs, customers, competition, or channel members; can be responses to competitive threats (e.g., lowering price temporarily to meet a competitor's price reduction) or broadly accepted methods of calculating a final price for the customer that is short term in nature.

primary data Data collected to address specific research needs.

primary demand advertising Ads designed to generate demand for the product category or an entire industry.

primary package The packaging the consumer uses, such as the toothpaste tube, from which he or she typically seeks convenience in terms of storage, use, and consumption.

private exchange Occurs when a specific firm, either buyer or seller, invites others to join to participate in online information exchanges and transactions; can help streamline procurement or distribution processes.

private-label brands Brands developed and marketed by a retailer and available only from that retailer; also called *store brands*.

procedural fairness Refers to the customer's perception of the fairness of the process used to resolve complaints about service.

product Anything that is of value to a consumer and can be offered through a voluntary marketing exchange.

product assortment The complete set of all products offered by a firm; also called the *product mix*.

product category An assortment of items that the customer sees as reasonable substitutes for one another.

product design See *product development*.

product development Also called *product design;* entails a process of balancing various engineering, manufacturing, marketing, and economic considerations to develop a product's form and features or a service's features.

product development strategy A growth strategy that offers a new product or service to a firm's current target market.

product excellence Involves a focus on achieving high-quality products; effective branding and positioning is key.

product life cycle Defines the stages that new products move through as they enter, get established in, and ultimately leave the marketplace and thereby offers marketers a starting point for their strategy planning.

product lines Groups of associated items, such as those that consumers use together or think of as part of a group of similar products.

product mix See *product assortment*.

product placement Inclusion of a product in nontraditional situations, such as in a scene in a movie or television program.

product-focused advertisements Used to inform, persuade, or remind consumers about a specific product or service.

profit orientation A company objective that can be implemented by focusing on *target profit pricing, maximizing profits,* or *target return pricing*.

projective technique A type of qualitative research in which subjects are provided a scenario and asked to express their thoughts and feelings about it.

prototype The first physical form or service description of a new product, still in rough or tentative form, that has the same properties as a new product but is produced through different manufacturing processes, sometimes even crafted individually.

psychographics Used in segmentation; delves into how consumers describe themselves; allows people to describe themselves using those characteristics that help them choose how they occupy their time (behavior) and what underlying psychological reasons determine those choices.

psychological needs Pertain to the personal gratification consumers associate with a product or service.

psychological risk Associated with the way people will feel if the product or service does not convey the right image.

public relations The organizational function that manages the firm's communications to achieve a variety of objectives, including building and maintaining a positive image, handling or heading off unfavorable stories or events, and maintaining positive relationships with the media.

public service advertising (PSA) Advertising that focuses on public welfare and generally is sponsored by nonprofit institutions, civic groups, religious organizations, trade associations, or political groups; a form of *social marketing*.

puffery The legal exaggeration of praise, stopping just short of deception, lavished on a product.

pull strategy Designed to get consumers to pull the product into the supply chain by demanding it.

pull supply chain Strategy in which orders for merchandise are generated at the store level on the basis of demand data captured by point-of-sales terminals.

pulsing advertising schedule Combines the continuous and flighting schedules by maintaining a base level of advertising but increasing advertising intensity during certain periods.

purchasing power parity (PPP) A theory that states that if the exchange rates of two countries are in equilibrium, a product purchased in one will cost the same in the other, expressed in the same currency.

pure competition Occurs when different companies sell commodity products that consumers perceive as substitutable; price usually is set according to the laws of supply and demand.

push strategy Designed to increase demand by motivating sellers—wholesalers, distributors, or salespeople—to highlight the product, rather than the products of competitors, and thereby push the product onto consumers.

push supply chain Strategy in which merchandise is allocated to stores on the basis of historical demand, the inventory position at the distribution center, and the stores' needs.

qualify The process of assessing the potential of sales leads.

quantity discount Pricing tactic of offering a reduced price according to the amount purchased; the more the buyer purchases, the higher the discount and, of course, the greater the value.

questionnaire A form that features a set of questions designed to gather information from respondents and thereby accomplish the researchers' objectives; questions can be either unstructured or structured.

quick response An inventory management system used in retailing; merchandise is received just in time for sale when the customer wants it; see *just-in-time (JIT) systems*.

quota Designates the maximum quantity of a product that may be brought into a country during a specified time period.

radio frequency identification (RFID) tags Tiny computer chips that automatically transmit to a special scanner all the information about a container's contents or individual products.

reach Measure of consumers' exposure to marketing communications; the percentage of the target population exposed to a specific marketing communication, such as an advertisement, at least once.

rebate A consumer discount in which a portion of the purchase price is returned to the buyer in cash; the manufacturer, not the retailer, issues the refund.

receiver The person who reads, hears, or sees and processes the information contained in the message or advertisement.

receiving The process of recording the receipt of merchandise as it arrives at a distribution center or store.

reference group One or more persons whom an individual uses as a basis for comparison regarding beliefs, feelings, and behaviors.

reference price The price against which buyers compare the actual selling price of the product and that facilitates their evaluation process.

regional culture The influence of the area within a country in which people live.

relational orientation A method of building a relationship with customers based on the philosophy that buyers and sellers should develop a long-term relationship.

relationship selling A sales philosophy and process that emphasizes a commitment to maintaining the relationship over the long term and investing in opportunities that are mutually beneficial to all parties.

relative market share A measure of the product's strength in a particular market, defined as the sales of the focal product divided by the sales achieved by the largest firm in the industry.

reminder advertising Communication used to remind consumers of a product or to prompt repurchases, especially for products that have gained market acceptance and are in the maturity stage of their life cycle.

reps See *independent agents*.

request for proposals (RFP) A process through which buying organizations invite alternative suppliers to bid on supplying their required components.

resellers Marketing intermediaries that resell manufactured products without significantly altering their form.

retailing The set of business activities that add value to products and services sold to consumers for their personal or family use; includes products bought at stores, through catalogs, and over the Internet, as well as services like fast-food restaurants, airlines, and hotels.

retrieval set Includes those brands or stores that the consumer can readily bring forth from memory.

reverse auction The buyer provides specifications to a group of sellers, who then bid down the price until the buyer accepts a specific bid.

reverse engineering Involves taking apart a competitor's product, analyzing it, and creating an improved product that does not infringe on the competitor's patents, if any exist.

ritual consumption Refers to a pattern of behaviors tied to life events that affect what and how people consume.

role playing A good technique for practicing the sales presentation prior to meeting with a customer; the salesperson acts out a simulated buying situation while a colleague or manager acts as the buyer.

rule-of-thumb methods Budgeting methods that base the IMC budget on either the firm's share of the market in relation to competition, a fixed percentage of forecasted sales, or what is left after other operating costs and forecasted sales have been budgeted.

safety needs One of the needs in the PSSP hierarchy of needs; pertain to protection and physical well-being.

salary Compensation in the form of a fixed sum of money paid at regular intervals.

sales contest A short-term incentive designed to elicit a specific response from the sales force.

sales management Involves the planning, direction, and control of personal selling activities, including recruiting, selecting, training, motivating, compensating, and evaluating, as they apply to the sales force.

sales orientation A company objective based on the belief that increasing sales will help the firm more than will increasing profits.

sales promotions Special incentives or excitement-building programs that encourage the purchase of a product or service, such as coupons, rebates, contests, free samples, and point-of-purchase displays.

sales support personnel Employees who enhance and help with a firm's overall selling effort, such as by responding to the customer's technical questions or facilitating repairs.

sampling Offers potential customers the opportunity to try a product or service before they make a buying decision.

scanner research A type of quantitative research that uses data obtained from scanner readings of UPC codes at checkout counters.

scenario planning A process that integrates macroenvironmental information in an attempt to understand the potential outcomes of different applications of a firm's marketing mix; enables a firm to predict, monitor, and adapt to the ever-changing future.

seasonal discount Pricing tactic of offering an additional reduction as an incentive to retailers to order merchandise in advance of the normal buying season.

secondary data Pieces of information that have already been collected from other sources and usually are readily available.

secondary package The wrapper or exterior carton that contains the primary package and provides the UPC label used by retail scanners; can contain additional product information that may not be available on the primary package.

selective demand Demand for a specific brand.

selective demand advertising Ads designed to generate demand for a specific brand, firm, or item.

selective distribution Lies between the intensive and exclusive distribution strategies; uses a few selected customers in a territory.

self-actualization When a person is completely satisfied with his or her life.

self-concept The image a person has of him- or herself; a component of *psychographics*.

self-values Goals for life, not just the goals one wants to accomplish in a day; a component of *psychographics* that refers to overriding desires that drive how a person lives his or her life.

selling teams Combinations of sales specialists whose primary duties are order getting, order taking, or sales support but who work together to service important accounts.

sender The firm from which an IMC message originates; the sender must be clearly identified to the intended audience.

Seniors America's fastest-growing generational cohort; people aged 55 to 64 years.

service Any intangible offering that involves a deed, performance, or effort that cannot be physically possessed; intangible customer benefits that are produced by people or machines and cannot be separated from the producer.

service gap Results when a service fails to meet the expectations that customers have about how it should be delivered.

service quality Customers' perceptions of how well a service meets or exceeds their expectations.

share of wallet The percentage of the customer's purchases made from a particular retailer.

shopping goods/services Those for which consumers will spend time comparing alternatives, such as apparel, fragrances, and appliances.

situation analysis Second step in a marketing plan; uses a SWOT analysis that assesses both the internal environment with regard to its **S**trengths and **W**eaknesses and the external environment in terms of its **O**pportunities and **T**hreats.

situational factors Factor affecting the consumer decision process; those that are specific to the situation that may override, or at least influence, psychological and social issues.

size discount The most common implementation of a quantity discount at the consumer level; the larger the quantity bought, the less the cost per unit (e.g., per ounce).

slotting allowances Fees firms pay to retailers simply to get new products into stores or to gain more or better shelf space for their products.

social marketing The application of marketing principles to a social issue to bring about attitudinal and behavioral change among the general public or a specific population segment.

social shoppers Consumers who seek emotional connections through shopping.

social shopping The use of the Internet to communicate about product preferences with other shoppers.

specialty goods/services Products or services toward which the customer shows a strong preference and for which he or she will expend considerable effort to search for the best suppliers.

specialty store A type of retailer that concentrates on a limited number of complementary merchandise categories in a relatively small store.

standards gap A type of *service gap*; pertains to the difference between the firm's perceptions of customers' expectations and the service standards it sets.

status quo pricing A competitor-oriented strategy in which a firm changes prices only to meet those of competition.

stock keeping units (SKUs) Individual items within each product category; the smallest unit available for inventory control.

store brands See *private-label brands*.

STP The processes of segmentation, targeting, and positioning that firms use to identify and evaluate opportunities for increasing sales and profits.

straight rebuy Refers to when the buyer or buying organization simply buys additional units of products that have previously been purchased.

strategic alliance A collaborative relationship between independent firms, though the partnering firms do not create an equity partnership; that is, they do not invest in one another.

strategic business unit (SBU) A division of the firm itself that can be managed and operated somewhat independently from other divisions and may have a different mission or objectives.

strategic relationship (partnering relationship) A supply chain relationship that the members are committed to maintaining long term, investing in opportunities that are mutually beneficial; requires mutual trust, open communication, common goals, and credible commitments.

structured questions Closed-ended questions for which a discrete set of response alternatives, or specific answers, is provided for respondents to evaluate.

substitute products Products for which changes in demand are negatively related; that is, a percentage increase in the quantity demanded for product A results in a percentage decrease in the quantity demanded for product B.

substitution effect Refers to consumers' ability to substitute other products for the focal brand, thus increasing the price elasticity of demand for the focal brand.

supercenter Large stores combining full-line discount stores with supermarkets in one place.

supply chain The group of firms that make and deliver a given set of goods and services.

supply chain conflict (channel conflict) Results when supply chain members are not in agreement about their goals, roles, or rewards.

supply chain management Refers to a set of approaches and techniques firms employ to efficiently and effectively integrate their suppliers, manufacturers, warehouses, stores, and transportation intermediaries into a seamless value chain in which merchandise is produced and distributed in the right quantities, to the right locations, and at the right time, as well as to minimize systemwide costs while satisfying the service levels their customers require.

survey A systematic means of collecting information from people that generally uses a *questionnaire*.

sustainable competitive advantage Something the firm can persistently do better than its competitors.

sweepstakes A form of sales promotion that offers prizes based on a chance drawing of entrants' names.

syndicated data Data available for a fee from commercial research firms such as Information Resources Inc. (IRI), National Purchase Diary Panel, and ACNielsen.

target marketing/targeting The process of evaluating the attractiveness of various segments and then deciding which to pursue as a market.

target profit pricing A pricing strategy implemented by firms when they have a particular profit goal as their overriding concern; uses price to stimulate a certain level of sales at a certain profit per unit.

target return pricing A pricing strategy implemented by firms less concerned with the absolute level of profits and more interested in the rate at which their profits are generated relative to their investments; designed to produce a specific return on investment, usually expressed as a percentage of sales.

tariff A tax levied on a good imported into a country; also called a *duty*.

technological advances Macroenvironmental factor that has greatly contributed to the improvement of the value of both products and services in the past few decades.

telemarketing A method of prospecting in which salespeople telephone potential customers.

test marketing Introduces a new product or service to a limited geographical area (usually a few cities) prior to a national launch.

ticketing and marking Creating price and identification labels and placing them on the merchandise.

top-of-the-mind awareness A prominent place in people's memories that triggers a response without them having to put any thought into it.

total cost The sum of the *variable* and *fixed costs*.

tracking Includes monitoring key indicators, such as daily or weekly sales volume, while the advertisement is running to shed light on any problems with the message or the medium.

trade agreements Intergovernmental agreements designed to manage and promote trade activities for specific regions.

trade area The geographical area that contains the potential customers of a particular retailer or shopping center.

trade deficit Results when a country imports more goods than it exports.

trade shows Major events attended by buyers who choose to be exposed to products and services offered by potential suppliers in an industry.

trading bloc Consists of those countries that have signed a particular trade agreement.

traditional distribution center A warehouse in which merchandise is unloaded from trucks and placed on racks or shelves for storage.

transactional orientation Regards the buyer-seller relationship as a series of individual transactions, so anything that happened before or after the transaction is of little importance.

transmitter An agent or intermediary with which the sender works to develop the marketing communications; for example, a firm's creative department or an advertising agency.

Tweens Generational cohort of people born between 1996 and 2000; not quite teenagers, but not young children either: in between.

undifferentiated segmentation strategy (mass marketing) A marketing strategy a firm can use if the product or service is perceived to provide the same benefits to everyone, with no need to develop separate strategies for different groups.

uniform delivered pricing The shipper charges one rate, no matter where the buyer is located.

unique selling proposition (USP) A strategy of differentiating a product by communicating its unique attributes; often becomes the common theme or slogan in the entire advertising campaign.

universal product code (UPC) The black-and-white bar code found on most merchandise.

universal set Includes all possible choices for a product category.

unstructured questions Open-ended questions that allow respondents to answer in their own words.

user The person who consumes or uses the product or service purchased by the buying center.

value Reflects the relationship of benefits to costs, or what the consumer *gets* for what he or she *gives*.

Value and Lifestyle Survey (VALS2) A psychographic tool developed by SRI Consulting Business Intelligence; classifies consumers into eight segments: innovators, thinkers, believers, achievers, strivers, experiencers, makers, or survivors.

value-based pricing A pricing strategy that involves first determining the perceived value of the product from the customer's point of view and then pricing accordingly.

value-based pricing method An approach that focuses on the overall value of the product offering as perceived by consumers, who determine value by comparing the benefits they expect the product to deliver with the sacrifice they will need to make to acquire the product.

variability A characteristic of a service: its quality may vary because it is provided by humans.

variable costs Those costs, primarily labor and materials, that vary with production volume.

vertical marketing system A supply chain in which the members act as a unified system; there are three types: *administrated, contractual,* and *corporate*.

vertical price fixing Occurs when parties at different levels of the same marketing channel (e.g., manufacturers and retailers) collude to control the prices passed on to consumers.

viral marketing A marketing phenomenon that encourages people to pass along a marketing message to other potential consumers.

viral marketing campaign See *viral marketing*.

virtual community Online networks of people who communicate about specific topics.

voice-of-customer (VOC) program An ongoing marketing research system that collects customer inputs and integrates them into managerial decisions.

warehouse clubs Large retailers with an irregular assortment, low service levels, and low prices that often require membership for shoppers.

Web tracking software Used to assess how much time viewers spend on particular Web pages and the number of pages they view.

wholesalers Those firms engaged in buying, taking title to, often storing, and physically handling goods in large quantities, then reselling the goods (usually in smaller quantities) to retailers or industrial or business users.

World Bank Group A development bank that provides loans, policy advice, technical assistance, and knowledge-sharing services to low- and middle-income countries in an attempt to reduce poverty in the developing world.

World Trade Organization (WTO) Replaced the GATT in 1994; differs from the GATT in that the WTO is an established institution based in Geneva, Switzerland, instead of simply an agreement; represents the only international organization that deals with the global rules of trade among nations.

zone of tolerance The area between customers' expectations regarding their desired service and the minimum level of acceptable service—that is, the difference between what the customer really wants and what he or she will accept before going elsewhere.

zone pricing The shipper sets different prices depending on a geographical division of the delivery areas.

Quiz Yourself answer key

Chapter 1

1. The "Got Milk" advertising campaign was designed to help market an:
   Answer: (c) industry

2. The evolution of marketing progressed along the continuum:
   Answer: (d) production, sales, marketing, value-based marketing

Chapter 2

1. In 2006, Ford Motor Company announced it would severely cut back automobile production. For parts companies supplying Ford Motor this represented a:
   Answer: (d) threat

2. Carla a manager of a local coffee shop, in response to increased competition from Starbucks, has been directed by her regional marketing manager to cut prices on seasonal items, run an ad in the local paper, and tell distributors to reduce deliveries for the next month. In which stage of the strategic marketing planning process is Carla engaged?
   Answer: (d) implement marketing mix and resources

Chapter 3

1. Johnson & Johnson's 1943 "Credo" was considered radical at the time because it:
   Answer: (c) put customers first

2. Recognizing that parents, children, teachers, staff, and taxpayers all have a vested interest in the problem of deteriorating school facilities, and then listening to each group's concerns, a school board would most likely next:
   Answer: (c) engage in brainstorming and evaluate alternatives

Chapter 4

1. When marketers look at advertising media they often begin with viewer or listener profiles such as, age, income, gender, and race. They then compare the media profile with their target audience. These marketers are using _____ to see if the media "fits" with their advertising agenda.
   Answer: (c) demographics

2. Many American consumers are purchasing hybrid automobiles even though they are more expensive and sometimes less fuel efficient when compared to compact conventional autos. Automobile marketers recognize these consumers:
   Answer: (a) value contributing to a greener environment

Chapter 5

1. Dawn flies regularly between Atlanta and Los Angeles. She almost always uses Delta and has a large amount of Delta Sky miles but she uses an online fare comparison site each time to see if competitors have a better price or more convenient schedule. Dawn uses a _____ decision rule.
   Answer: (a) compensatory

2. Natalie and her fiancé Dow are planning their wedding. She knows her mother wants her to have a traditional church ceremony. She would like to have a ceremony on the beach like many of her friends had. Then there is the problem of who should officiate. Dow is from Thailand and would like to have a monk officiate. Natalie and Dow's wedding decisions are influenced by:
   Answer: (e) family, reference groups, and culture

Chapter 6

1. After posting an RFP for telecommunication equipment, USF received six proposals from qualified vendors. Next, USF will:
   Answer: (e) evaluate the proposals and likely narrow the choice to a few suppliers

2. Raycom Construction needs heavy duty equipment to install a new pipeline in northern Alaska. Raycom engineers will specify the type and capability requirements for the equipment to be purchased. The Raycom engineers will primarily play the _____ role in the company's buying center.
   Answer: (c) influencer

Chapter 7

1. The Big Mac Index is a novel measure of:
   Answer: (b) purchasing power parity

2. Many of the best-known American retailers, like KFC and McDonald's, have expanded globally using:
   Answer: (a) franchising

Chapter 8

1. Adidas Group owns Reebok, Adidas, and Taylor-Made brands. Adidas uses the different brands to pursue a(n) _____ strategy.
   Answer: (d) differentiated segmentation

2. Talbots target customers are college-educated women between 35 and 55 years old with average household income of $75,000 or more. This is Talbots' _____ segment.
   Answer: (d) demographic

Chapter 9

1. Company sales invoices, Census data, and trade association statistics are examples of:
   Answer: (c) secondary data

2. Bianca's discount home furnishings store is in a strip mall. She wants to know what other businesses in the strip mall her customers visit when they come to her store. To collect information for this objective, Bianca will most likely use:
   Answer: (c) observation

Chapter 10

1. Toothpaste, toothbrush, whitening products, kids' oral products, and floss are all _____ within Colgate-Palmolive's Oral Care product line.
   Answer: (a) product categories

2. It is almost impossible to watch a sporting event on television without seeing Nike's "swoosh" check mark, which is Nike's:
   Answer: (b) symbol

Chapter 11

1. Whenever Donald considers upgrading his personal computer system, he consults with Jeremy, a knowledgeable friend who always has the latest technology. For Donald, Jeremy is an _____ in the diffusion of innovation curve.
   Answer: (a) innovator

2. Zappos.com, an online shoe store, worked to overcome the problem of new product _____ with its easy, no hassle return procedure.
Answer: (e) trialability

Chapter 12

1. A _____ gap reflects the difference between customers' expectations and the firm's perception of those customer expectations.
Answer: (b) knowledge

2. When approached by a customer, Nordstrom's employees have been trained to drop whatever they are doing, listen carefully, and provide caring, individualized attention to that customer. Nordstrom employees have been trained to emphasize _____ in the five service quality dimensions.
Answer: (e) empathy

Chapter 13

1. If a shoe company has $1 million in fixed costs and its average shoe sells for $50.00 per pair and it has variable costs of $30 per unit, how many units does the company need to sell to break even?
Answer: (c) 50,000

2. Ferrari and Lamborghini are manufacturers of very expensive automobiles. Their limited edition cars often sell for $300,000 or more. The cars are considered by most consumers a prestige product, for which demand is likely to be:
Answer: (b) price inelastic

Chapter 14

1. In determining the price for his company's new pocket digital camera, Matt is assessing what consumers consider the regular or original price for similar cameras available in the market. Matt is assessing the _____ influence on pricing strategy.
Answer: (a) improvement value

2. When Apple Computer Company introduced their iPhone in 2007, they priced the new combination iPod, Internet, and cellular telephone at $499, considerably higher than either their iPod or competing cellular phones. Apple Computer was probably pursuing a _____ pricing strategy.
Answer: (e) skimming

Chapter 15

1. Franchising involves a _____ supply chain.
Answer: (c) contractual

2. Flora is frustrated with her company's supply chain management information system. She wants to be able to receive sales data, initiate purchase orders, send and receive invoices, and receive returned merchandise documentation. Flora needs an:
Answer: (b) electronic data interchange

Chapter 16

1. The Gap, Lens Crafters, and Foot Locker are all examples of:
Answer: (d) specialty stores

2. Wal-Mart and Target dominate the _____ industry in the United States.
Answer: (c) discount store

Chapter 17

1. Often an _____ accomplishes the task of encoding IMC messages.
Answer: (a) advertising agency

2. Ingrid wants her company to expand its use of public relations. She argues that as other IMC alternatives become more expensive and _____, public relations should be a larger part of her company's IMC efforts.
Answer: (b) consumers have become more skeptical of marketing claims

Chapter 18

1. Smokey the Bear, Mothers Against Drunk Driving (MADD), and crash test dummies Vince and Larry are examples of successful:
Answer: (e) public service announcements

2. Campbell Soup Company ran a series of radio ads tied to local weather forecasts. Before an impending storm, the ads said "Time to stock up on Campbell Soup." During the storm, the ads said, "Stay home and stay warm with Campbell Soup."

The first ad was _____ advertising, while the second ad was _____ advertising.
Answer: (b) persuasive; reminder

Chapter 19

1. Consumers often ask workers in supermarkets where something is located only to learn the worker is a vendor stacking and straightening their company's products on the store shelves. These manufacturers' sales representatives benefit retailers by _____.
Answer: (c) saving them time and money

2. Bridgette went to the Gap ready to buy a new blouse, but not sure which color or style she wanted. The sales representative, sensing Bridgette's buying mode, began with the _____ stage of the selling process.
Answer: (e) sales presentation

endnotes

Chapter 1

1. http://blog.facebook.com/blog.php?post=2535632130 (accessed November 27, 2007); http://www.facebook.com/press/info.php?factsheet (accessed November 27, 2007); Ellen McGirt, "Facebook Is," *Fast Company*, November 2007; and Laura Locke, "The Future of Facebook," *Time*, July 17, 2007, http://www.time.com/time/business/article/0,8599,1644040,00.html (accessed January 2, 2008).

2. The American Marketing Association, http://www.marketingpower.com/content4620.php (accessed December 26, 2008). Word in italics was added by the authors. The latest revision of the marketing definition by AMA is discussed in a number of articles; see: Gregory Gundlach, "The Journal of Public Policy & Marketing's 2004 Definition of Marketing: Perspectives on Its Implications for Scholarship and the Role and Responsibility of Marketing in Society," *Journal of Public Policy & Marketing*, 26, no. 2 (2007), pp. 243–250; David Glen Mick, "The End(s) of Marketing and the Neglect of Moral Responsibility by the Journal of Public Policy & Marketing," *Journal of Public Policy & Marketing*, 26, no. 2 (2007), pp. 289–292; Clifford J. Shultz II, "Marketing as Constructive Engagement," *Journal of Public Policy & Marketing*, 26, no. 2 (2007), pp. 293–301; Jagdish N. Sheth, "Implications of the Revised Definition of Marketing: From Exchange to Value Creation," *Journal of Public Policy & Marketing*, 26, no. 2 (2007), pp. 302–307; George M. Zinkhan and Brian C. Williams, "The New Journal of Public Policy & Marketing Definition of Marketing: An Alternative Assessment," *Journal of Public Policy & Marketing*, 26, no. 2 (2007), pp. 284–288; William L. Wilkie and Elizabeth S. Moore, "What Does the Definition of Marketing Tell Us About Ourselves?" *Journal of Public Policy & Marketing*, 26, no. 2 (2007), pp. 269–276; Robert F. Lusch, "Marketing's Evolution Identity: Defining Our Future," *Journal of Public Policy & Marketing*, 26, no. 2 (2007), pp. 261–268; and Debra Jones Ringold and Barton Weitz, "The Journal of Public Policy & Marketing Definition of Marketing: Moving from Lagging to Leading Indicator," *Journal of Public Policy & Marketing*, 26, no. 2 (2007), pp. 251–260. More discussion on marketing is provided by Stephen L. Vargo and Robert F. Lusch, "Evolving to a New Dominant Logic for Marketing," *Journal of Marketing*, 68 (January 2004), pp. 1–17; George S. Day, John Deighton, Das Narayandas, Evert Gummesson, Shelby D. Hunt, C.K. Prahalad, Roland T. Rust, and Steven M. Shugan, "Invited Commentaries on 'Evolving to a New Dominant Logic for Marketing,'" *Journal of Marketing*, 68 (January 2004), pp. 18–27; Also see W. Stephen Brown, Frederick E. Webster Jr., Jan-Benedict E.M. Steenkamp, William L. Wilkie, Jagdish N. Sheth, Rajendra S. Sisodia, Roger A. Kerin, Deborah J. MacInnis, Leigh McAlister, Jagmohan S. Raju, Ronald J. Bauerly, Don T. Johnson, Mandeep Singh, and Richard Staelin, "Marketing Renaissance: Opportunities and Imperatives for Improving Marketing Thought, Practice, and Infrastructure," *Journal of Marketing*, 69, no. 4 (2005), pp. 1–25.

3. Jeff Sabatini, "Pale Green Lexus's $100,000 Hybrid," *The Wall Street Journal*, November 2, 2007.

4. The idea of the four Ps was conceptualized by E. Jerome McCarthy, *Basic Marketing: A Managerial Approach* (Homewood, IL: Richard D. Irwin, 1960). Also see Walter van Watershoot and Christophe Van den Bulte, "The 4P Classification of the Marketing Mix Revisited," *Journal of Marketing*, 56 (October 1992), pp. 83–93.

5. Beverage Marketing Corporation, a New York–based research and consulting firm, http://www.bottledwaterweb.com (accessed November 27, 2007).

6. "Scarlett's Inspiration," http://www.rbk.com/us/scarlett (accessed December 5, 2007).

7. Based on David Simchi-Levi, Philip Kaminsky, and Edith Simchi-Levi, *Designing and Managing the Supply Chain: Concepts, Strategies and Case Studies*, 3rd ed. (New York: McGraw-Hill Irwin, 2008); and Michael Levy and Barton A. Weitz, *Retailing Management*, 7th ed. (New York: McGraw-Hill Irwin, 2009).

8. Carmine Gallo, "How Ritz-Carlton Maintains Its Mystique," *BusinessWeek*, February 13, 2007, accessed electronically; Peter Sanders, "Takin' Off the Ritz—a Tad," *The Wall Street Journal*, June 23, 2006, p. B1; Carmine Gallo, "How Ritz-Carlton Maintains Its Mystique; The Luxury Hotel Chain Reinforces Customer-Service Values among Employees by Investing in Daily Training That Revolves around Storytelling," *BusinessWeek Online*, February 14, 2007.

9. http://www.joesstonecrab.com/today/intro.html (accessed November 28, 2007).

10. Connie Robbins Gentry, "Zappos' Lifestyle-driven CEO Measures Value in Service, Not Sales," *Chain Store Age*, December 2007; "How Zappos.com Grew So Big So Fast—10 Strategies Behind Their Success," www.marketingsherpa.com, August 7, 2007.

11. Stuart Elliot, "No Polo Pony, but Penney's New Label Is Pure Ralph Lauren Americana," *The New York Times*, February 19, 2008 (accessed electronically March 31, 2008).

12. Stewart Black, "The Employee Value Proposition: How to Be the Employer of Choice," Knowledge @ INSEAD, accessed electronically October 9, 2007; Dina Berta, "Chains Build Employment Brands to Compete for Workers," *Nation's Restaurant News*, December 18, 2006, pp. 10–8; and "'Brand' Your Company to Get—and Keep—Top Employees," *HR Focus*, October 2006, pp. 7–10.

13. Web sites such as http://www.whymilk.com/ and http://www.milkdelivers.org/campaign/index.cfm provide examples of this popular campaign (accessed November 27, 2007).

14. George S. Day, "Aligning the Organization with the Market," *Marketing Science Institute*, 5, no. 3 (2005), pp. 3–20.

15. Dhruv Grewal, Kent B. Monroe, and R. Krishnan, "The Effects of Price Comparison Advertising on Buyers' Perceptions of Acquisition Value and Transaction Value," *Journal of Marketing* 62 (April 1998), pp. 46–60; Kent B. Monroe, *Pricing: Making Profitable Decisions*, 3rd ed. (New York: McGraw-Hill, 2004); Dhruv Grewal and Larry Compeau, "Consumer Responses to Price and Its Contextual Information Cues: A Synthesis of Past Research, a Conceptual Framework, and Avenues for Further Research," *Review of Marketing Research*, 3 (2005), Naresh Malhotra (ed.); M. E. Sharpe. Dhruv Grewal, Michael Levy, R. Krishnan, and Jeanne Munger, "Retail Success and Key Drivers," *Retailing in the 21st Century: Current and Future Trends*, Manfred Krafft and Murali Mantrala (eds.) (New York: Springer, 2006) pp. 13–26.

16. Neeli Bendapudi and Robert P. Leone, "Psychological Implications of Customer Participation in Co-Production," *Journal of Marketing*, 67 (January 2003), pp. 14–28; Beibei Dong, Kenneth R. Evans, and Shaoming Zou, "The Effects of Customer Participation in Co-created Service Recovery," working paper (2007); C. K. Prahalad and Venkatram Ramaswamy, "Co-opting Customer Competence," *Harvard Business Review*, 78 (January–February 2000), pp. 79–87; C. K. Prahalad and Venkatram Ramaswamy, *The Future of Competition: Co-Creating Unique Value with Customers* (Cambridge, MA: Harvard Business School

Press, 2004); Stephen L. Vargo and Robert F. Lusch, "Evolving to a New Dominant Logic for Marketing," *Journal of Marketing*, 68 (January 2004), pp. 1–17; Stephen L. Vargo, Robert F. Lusch, and Matthew O'Brien, "Competing through Service: Insights from Service-Dominant Logic," *Journal of Retailing*, 83 (1) (2007), pp. 5–18; Jerry Wind and Arvind Rangaswamy, "Customerization: The Next Revolution in Mass Customization," *Marketing Science Institute Working Paper No. 00-108* (Cambridge, MA: Marketing Science Institute, 2000).

17. Michelle Nichols, "Softening Them Up," *BusinessWeek*, August 24, 2006; http://www.businessweek.com/smallbiz/content/aug2006/sb20060824_240150.htm?chan=smallbiz_smallbiz+index+page_michelle+nichols (accessed January 2, 2008); http://www.marsnewsroom.com/products_detail.asp?zx=332&mode=arc (accessed October 20, 2007); http://www.marsnewsroom.com/products_detail.asp?zx=299&mode=arc (accessed October 20, 2007).

18. www.mymms.com (accessed December 6, 2007).

19. Lauren Coleman-Lochner, "Wal-Mart Is Bringing Santas Back to Its Stores in Bid to Lure Christmas Shoppers," *International Herald Tribune*, December 10, 2006.

20. Shelley Emling, "Low-Cost Flying No Longer Just a U.S. Sensation," *Atlanta Journal*, December 26, 2003, p. F1.

21. Robert W. Palmatier, Rajiv Dant and Dhruv Grewal, "A Longitudinal Analysis of Theoretical Perspectives of Interorganizational Relationship Performance," *Journal of Marketing*, 71 (October 2007). In 2005, the *Journal of Marketing* ran a special section entirely devoted to relationship marketing. The section included these articles: William Boulding, Richard Staelin, Michael Ehret, and Wesley J. Johnston, "A Customer Relationship Management Roadmap: What Is Known, Potential Pitfalls, and Where to Go," *Journal of Marketing*, 69, no. 4 (2005), pp. 155–166; Jacquelyn S. Thomas and Ursula Y. Sullivan, "Managing Marketing Communications with Multichannel Customers," *Journal of Marketing*, 69, no 4 (2005), pp. 239–251; Lynette Ryals, "Making Customer Relationship Management Work: The Measurement and Profitable Management of Customer Relationships," *Journal of Marketing*, 69, no. 4 (2005), pp. 252–261; and Martha Rogers "Customer Strategy: Observations from the Trenches," *Journal of Marketing*, 69, no. 4 (2005), pp. 262–263.

22. V. Kumar, Denish Shah, and Rajkumar Venkatesan, "Managing Retailer Profitability—One Customer at a Time!" *Journal of Retailing*, 82, no.4 (2006), pp. 277–294; R. Venkatesan and V. Kumar, "A Customer Lifetime Value Framework for Customer Selections and Resource Allocation Strategy," *Journal of Marketing*, 68, no. 4 (2004) pp. 106–125; V. Kumar, G. Ramani and T. Bohling, "Customer Lifetime Value Approaches and Best Practice Applications," *Journal of Interactive Marketing*, 18, no. 3 (2004), pp. 60–72; and J. Thomas, W. Reinartz, and V. Kumar, "Getting the Most Out of All Your Customers," *Harvard Business Review*, July–August 2004, pp. 116–123.

23. http://www.hm.com/us/abouthm/theworldofhm__worldofhm.nhtml (accessed November 28, 2007).

24. http://www.zara.com (accessed November 28, 2007).

25. http://www.ahold.com (accessed November 28, 2007).

26. Julia Werdigier, "To Woo Europeans, McDonald's Goes Upscale, *The New York Times*, August 25, 2007, accessed electronically.

27. Royal Ford, "Automobilia: Toyota Makes Emotional Appeal with Zippy New Line," *Boston Globe*, March 13, 2003, p. E1; Zachary Rodgers, "Toyota Bows Web/Mobile Gaming Campaign for Scion," *Clickz*, July 8, 2004; "Forehead Advertising Goes Mainstream with Toyota," *Adrants*, April 8, 2004, http://www.adrants.com (accessed January 16, 2008); Jason Stein, "Scion National Launch Gets Offbeat Support," *Automotive News*, 78, no. 6104 (2004), p. 18.

28. http://www.pressroom.ups.com/pressreleases/current/0,1088,4384,00.html (accessed January 7, 2006).

29. http://www.kelloggcompany.com/commitments.aspx (accessed November 27, 2007).

30. http://www.colgate.com/app/Colgate/US/Corp/LivingOurValues/CoreValues.cvsp (accessed November 27, 2007).

31. http://www.benjerry.com/our_company/our_mission/ (accessed November 27, 2007).

32. Calvert, "Corporate Responsibility and Investor Confidence Survey," November 18, 2003, http://www.harrisinteractive.com (accessed January 3, 2008); also see The Trustees of Boston College, "The State of Corporate Citizenship in the United States: 2003," July 2003.

33. http://www.bbb.org/alerts/article.asp?ID=728 (accessed November 24, 2007); "Are Children Turning into Brand Junkies?" *Western Morning News*, December 15, 2006.

34. Lindsey Tanner, "Marketing Tricks Tots' Taste Buds," *USA Today*, August 6, 2007, http://www.usatoday.com/news/health/2007-08-06-tots-mcdonalds_N.htm (accessed November 23, 2007).

35. Elizabeth Olson, "Study Says Junk Food Still Dominates Youth TV," *The New York Times*, March 29, 2007; http://www.usatoday.com/news/health/2007-08-06-tots-mcdonalds_N.htm (accessed November 23, 2007).

36. http://csr.blogs.mcdonalds.com/default.asp?item=270544 (accessed November 22, 2007).

37. http://dictionary.reference.com/search?q=Entrepreneurship (accessed May 16, 2005).

38. http://www.macworld.com/news/2006/01/24/disneypixar/index.php (accessed January 27, 2006).

39. http://www.oprah.com/harpofilms/harpofilms_landing.jhtml (accessed November 1, 2007); http://www.oprah.com/about/press/about_press_bio.jhtml (accessed November 1, 2007).

40. This case was written by Colin Fox in conjunction with the textbook authors (Dhruv Grewal and Michael Levy) as the basis of class discussion rather than to illustrate either effective or ineffective marketing practice.

41. Catherine Holahan, "Viacom's Suit Won't Snuff Out YouTube," *BusinessWeek*, March 14, 2007; http://www.google.com/press/pressrel/google_youtube.html (accessed October 20, 2007); http://www.businessweek.com/technology/content/mar2007/tc20070314_729711.htm (accessed October 20, 2007).

42. http://www.youtube.com/advertise (accessed October 30, 2007).

43. http://www.youtube.com/t/fact_sheet (accessed October 30, 2007).

44. Rob Hof, "YouTube Intros Video I.D. System; Will Studios Go Along?" *BusinessWeek*, October 15, 2007, http://www.businessweek.com/the_thread/techbeat/archives/2007/10/youtube_intros.html (accessed October 15, 2007).

Chapter 2

1. http://www.starbucks.com/aboutus/Company_Factsheet.pdf (accessed November 23, 2007); Joe Nocera, "Give Me a Double Shot of Starbucks Nostalgia," *The New York Times*, March 3, 2007, http://select.nytimes.com/2007/03/03/business/03nocera.html (accessed October 6, 2008).

2. Tom Anderson, "Howard Shultz: The Star of Starbucks," *CBS News*, April 23, 2006, http://www.cbsnews.com/stories/2006/04/21/60minutes/main1532246.shtml (accessed October 6, 2008).

3. https://www.dunkindonuts.com/aboutus/company/History.aspx (accessed November 25, 2007).

4. Ibid.

5. Julie Bosman, "This Joe's For You?" *The New York Times*, June 8, 2006, http://www.nytimes.com/2006/06/08/business/media/08adco.html?n=Top/News/Business/Small%20Business/Marketing%20and%20Advertising&_r=2&adxnnl=1&oref=slogin&adxnnlx=1196532133-L3wDL9xcdseFDUFhUyxMlQ (accessed November 8, 2006).

6. Ibid.; Janet Adamy, "Dunkin' Donuts Whips Up a Recipe for Expansion," *The Wall Street Journal*, May 3, 2007; Richard Kirstein, "Music Marketplace: Brands as Music Moguls," *Brand Strategy*, June 12, 2007.

7. Michael Treacy and Fred Wiersema, *The Disciplines of Market Leaders* (Reading, MA: Addison Wesley, 1995). Treacy and Weirsema suggest the first three strategies. We suggest the fourth—locational excellence.

8. Lars Meyer-Waarden, "The Effects of Loyalty Programs on Customer Lifetime Duration and Share of Wallet," *Journal of Retailing*, 83, no.2 (2007), pp. 223–236; Seigyoung Auh, Simon J. Bell, Colin S. McLeod, and Eric Shih, "Co-production and Customer Loyalty in Financial Services," *Journal of Retailing*, 83, no.3 (2007), pp. 359–370; Ruth N. Bolton, Dhruv Grewal, and Michael Levy, "Six Strategies for Competing through Service: An Agenda for Future Research," *Journal of Retailing*, 83, no. 1 (2007), pp. 1–4; Lloyd C. Harris and Mark M. H. Goode, "The Four Levels of Loyalty and the Pivotal Role of Trust: A Study of Online Service Dynamics" *Journal of Retailing*, 80, no. 2 (2004), pp. 139–158; Hean Tat Keh, Yih Hwai Lee, V. Kumar, Denish Shah, and Rajkumar Venkatesan, "Managing Retailer Profitability—One Customer at a Time!" *Journal of Retailing*, 82, no. 4 (2006), pp. 277–294; Stephanie M. Noble, David A. Griffith, and Mavis T. Adjei, "Drivers of Local Merchant Loyalty: Understanding the Influence of Gender and Shopping Motives," *Journal of Retailing*, 82, no.3 (2006), pp. 177–188.

9. Meyer-Waarden, "The Effects of Loyalty Programs"; Mert Tokman, Lenita M. Davis, and Katherine N. Lemon, "The WOW Factor: Creating Value through Win-Back Offers to Reacquire Lost Customers," *Journal of Retailing*, 83, no. 1 (2007), pp. 47–64; Kumar et al., "Managing Retailer Profitability—One Customer at a Time!"

10. "Do Reward Programs Build Loyalty for Services? The Moderating Effect of Satisfaction on Type and Timing of Rewards," *Journal of Retailing*, 82, no. 2 (2006), pp. 127–136.

11. Mary Jo Bitner, "Self Service Technologies: What Do Customers Expect?" *Marketing Management*, Spring 2001, pp. 10–34; Mary Jo Bitner, Stephen W. Brown, and Matthew L. Meuter, "Technology Infusion in Service Encounters," *Journal of Academy of Marketing Science*, 28, no. 1 (2000), pp. 138–149; Matthew L. Meuter, Amy L. Ostrom, Robert I. Roundtree, and Mary Jo Bitner, "Self-Service Technologies: Understanding Customer Satisfaction with Technology-Based Service Encounters," *Journal of Marketing*, 64, no. 3 (2000), pp. 50–64; A. Parasuraman and Dhruv Grewal, "The Impact of Technology on the Quality-Value-Loyalty Chain: A Research Agenda," *Journal of the Academy of Marketing Science*, 28, no. 1 (2000), pp. 168–174.

12. http://www.virgin-atlantic.com/en/us/whereintheworld/index.jsp, accessed December 1, 2007; http://www.virgin-atlantic.com/our_story_history.view.do (accessed December 1, 2007).

13. S. A. Shaw and J. Gibbs, "Procurement Strategies of Small Marketers Faced with Uncertainty: An Analysis of Channel Choice and Behavior," *International Review of Market, Distribution and Consumer Research*, 9, no. 1 (1999), pp. 61–75.

14. David Lei and John Slocum Jr., "Strategic and Organizational Requirements for Competitive Advantage," *Academy of Management Executive*, February 2005, pp. 31–46.

15. Maria Halkias, "Penney Remakes Culture to Remake Image," *The Dallas Morning News*, February 12, 2007.

16. *BusinessWeek*, "The Top 100 Brands," http://bwnt.businessweek.com/brand/2006/ (accessed December 17, 2007).

17. http://www.lexus.com/about/corporate/lexus_history.html (accessed December 17, 2007).

18. http://www.marketingpower.com/live/mg-dictionary.php?SearchFor=marketing+plan&Searched=1 (accessed August 31, 2006).

19. Donald Lehman and Russell Winer, *Analysis for Marketing Planning*, 5th ed. (Burr Ridge, IL: McGraw-Hill/Irwin, 2001); David Aaker, *Strategic Market Management*, 6th ed. (New York: John Wiley, 2001).

20. Andrew Campbell, "Mission Statements," *Long Range Planning*, 30 (1997), pp. 931–933.

21. Alfred Rappaport, *Creating Shareholder Value: The New Standard for Business Performance* (New York: Wiley, 1988); Robert C. Higgins and Roger A. Kerin, "Managing the Growth-Financial Policy Nexus in Marketing," *Journal of Marketing*, 59, no. 3 (1983), pp. 19–47; and Roger Kerin, Vijay Mahajan, and P. Rajan Varadarajan, *Contemporary Perspectives on Strategic Market Planning* (Boston: Allyn & Bacon, 1991), chapter 6.

22. http://www.starbucks.com/aboutus/environment.asp (accessed December 1, 2007).

23. Web sites such as http://www.whymilk.com/ and http://www.milkdelivers.org/campaign/index.cfm provide examples of this popular campaign.

24. http://www.tateandlyle.com/NR/rdonlyres/emdassaqn-curzjsqjysjcgnleqm76mdxmobnapwew52hhpgy6vy7gm-2gmfabk4z2z2hjz35ror3xlllnjfrsjcis7ec/TateLyleDeutscheBankJune2007presentation.pdf (accessed December 17, 2007); http://www.tateandlyle.com/TateAndLyle/products_applications/_products/sucralose/default.htm (accessed December 17, 2007).

25. http://www.starbucks.com/aboutus/Company_Factsheet.pdf (accessed November 23, 2007); http://www.starbucks.com/aboutus/Company_Factsheet.pdf (accessed November 23, 2007); http://www.shareholder.com/visitors/dynamicdoc/document.cfm?CompanyID=SBUX&DocumentID=1382&PIN=&Page=6&Zoom=1x&Section=33412#33412 (accessed October 26, 2008).

26. http://www.shareholder.com/visitors/dynamicdoc/document.cfm?CompanyID=SBUX&DocumentID=1382&PIN=&Page=6&Zoom=1x&Section=33412#33412 (accessed October 6, 2008).

27. "Striking Gold-Winning Spot Sends a Powerful Message to Women Everywhere," *One*, November 2007, accessed electronically; Rosaura Lezama, Sarah Henry, and Heidi Dangelmaier, "Dove (D)evolution," *BusinessWeek*, November 12, 2007.

28. Raju Mudhar, "Dove's 'Evolution' Ad Wins at Cannes," *The Star*, June 22, 2007, accessed electronically.

29. http://dovecreamoil.msn.com (accessed December 19, 2007).

30. Andrew Martin, "Decaf Being Joined by De-Heartburn" *The New York Times*, March 14, 2007; http://www.folgers.com/pressroom/press_release_05122006.shtml (accessed December 17, 2007).

31. Merissa Marr, "Fairy-Tale Wedding? Disney Can Supply the Gown," *The Wall Street Journal*, February 22, 2007; http://www.disneybridal.com/about.html (accessed December 1, 2007).

32. http://www.goodyear.com/corporate/about/about_sbup.html (accessed December 17, 2007).

33. Paul W. Farris, Neil T. Bendle, Phillip E. Pfeifer, and David J. Reibstein, *Marketing Metrics: 50+ Metrics Every Executive Should Master* (Philadelphia: Wharton School Publishing, 2006), p. 1.

34. http://media.corporate-ir.net/media_files/irol/99/99518/reports/StarbucksAnnualReport.pdf (accessed December 20, 2007).

35. http://www.shareholder.com/visitors/dynamicdoc/document.cfm?CompanyID=MCD&DocumentID=1545&PIN=&Page=4&Zoom=1x (accessed December 20, 2007). The reported net profit of $3.5 billion included $671 million from the sale of Chipotle. This was subtracted to estimate the net profits.

36. This discussion is adapted from Roger A. Kerin, Eric N. Berkowitz, Steven W. Hartley, and William Rudelius, *Marketing*, 9th ed. (Burr Ridge, IL: McGraw-Hill/Irwin, 2009).

37. Farris et al., *Marketing Metrics: 50+ Metrics Every Executive Should Master*, p. 17.

38. Relative market share = brand's market share ÷ largest competitor's market share. If, for instance, there are only two products in a market, A and B, and product B has 90 percent market share, then A's relative market share is 10 ÷ 90 = 11.1 percent. If, on the other hand, B only has 50 percent market share, then A's relative market share is 10 ÷ 50 = 20 percent. Farris et al., *Marketing Metrics: 50+ Metrics Every Executive Should Master*, p. 19.

39. Roger Kerin, Vijay Mahajan, and P. Rajan Varadarajan, *Contemporary Perspectives on Strategic Market Planning* (Boston: Allyn & Bacon, 1991), chapter 6; Susan Mudambi, "A Topology of Strategic Choice in Marketing," *International Journal of Market & Distribution Management* (1994), pp. 22–25.

40. David Carr, "Do They Still Want Their MTV?" *The New York Times*, February 19, 2007.

41. https://jobhuntweb.viacom.com/jobhunt/main/us.asp (accessed December 1, 2007).

42. Loran Braverman, "Procter and Gamble," *Standard & Poor's Stock Report*, December 15, 2007, http://www.netadvantage.standardandpoors.com (accessed December 19, 2007).

43. Dexter Roberts, "Scrambling to Bring Crest to the Masses in China," *BusinessWeek*, June 25, 2007, http://www.businessweek.com/magazine/content/07_26/b4040058.htm (accessed December 19, 2007).

44. Jeremy Caplan, "The Smell Factory," *Time*, May 8, 2007.

45. Jeremy Caplan, "The Smell of Competition," *Time*, May 3, 2007.

46. http://www.basenotes.net/cgi-bin/basenotes.cgi?Perfumer=IFF (accessed December 19, 2007).

47. http://www.fedex.com/us/customersupport/officeprint/faq/general.html#o (accessed December 17, 2007).

48. http://www.speaking.com/speakers/paulorfalea.html (accessed December 27, 2007).

49. The scenario planning process presented here was adapted from that used first by Royal Dutch/Shell in the early 1970s and follows the steps set forth by consultants at Bain & Co., http://www.bain.com/management_tools/tools_scenario_contingency.asp?groupCode=2 (accessed December 17, 2007); Gill Ringland, *Scenario Planning: Managing for the Future*, 2nd ed. (New York: John Wiley & Sons, 2006).

50. http://www.walmartfacts.com/FactSheets/Corporate_Facts.pdf (accessed December 27, 2007); David B. Yofee, "Wal-Mart, 2005," *Harvard Business School*, April 14, 2005; "Is Wal-Mart Food for America?" *The Asian Wall Street Journal*, December 6, 2005, p. 1; www.census.gov; "Wal-Mart Saves Working Families," *PR Newswire*, November 4, 2005; Lauren Weber, "The Debate Intensifies: Is the Corporate Giant Good for Our Communities?" *Newsday*, November 21, 2005.

51. http://www.walmartfacts.com/FactSheets/Corporate_Facts.pdf (accessed December 27, 2007).

52. Jason Furman, "Wal-Mart: A Progressive Success Story," *The New York Times*, November 28, 2005; Arindrajit Dube, T. William Lester, and Barry Eidlin, "Firm Entry and Wages: Impact of Wal-Mart Growth on Earnings Throughout the Retail Sector," August 6, 2007, Institute for Research on Labor and Employment Working Paper Series, paper IIRWPS-126-05, http://repositories.cdlib.org/iir/iirwps/iirwps-126-05; Wayne F. Cascio, "The High Cost of Low Wages," *Harvard Business Review*, 84, no. 12 (2006), p. 23; Joshua Green, "The New War over Wal-Mart," *Atlantic Monthly*, June 2006.

53. Pallavi Gogoi, "Wal-Mart's Next Growth Opportunities," *BusinessWeek*, October 9, 2007, http://www.businessweek.com/bwdaily/dnflash/content/oct2007/db2007108_116420.htm (accessed December 27, 2007).

54. Anand Giridharadas and Saritha Rai, "Wal-Mart's Superstores Gain Entry into India," *New York Times*, November 28, 2006; Parija Bhatnagar, "Wal-Mart's Hot on India, No. 1 Retailer Sings Nation's Praises to Analysts; Calls Market a 'Huge Organic Growth Opportunity,'" http://money.cnn.com/2005/06/06/news/fortune500/walmart_india/ (accessed December 27, 2007).

55. Eric Bellman, "In India, a Retailer Finds Key to Success Is Clutter," *The Wall Street Journal*, August 8, 2007, p. A1.

56. This case was written by Colin Fox in conjunction with the textbook authors (Dhruv Grewal and Michael Levy) as a basis of class discussion rather than to illustrate either effective or ineffective marketing practice.

57. John Markoff, "Apple Cuts iPhone Price Ahead of Holidays," *The New York Times*, September 5, 2007, http://www.nytimes.com/2007/09/06/technology/06apple.html?_r=1&oref=login (accessed October 6, 2008); Nick Wingfield, "A New Wireless Player Hopes to Challenge iPod," *The Wall Street Journal*, April 9, 2007.

58. www.apple.com/investor/ (accessed November 27, 2007).

59. Tom Hormby, "Birth of the PowerBook: How Apple Took Over the Portable Market in 1991," *Low End Mac*, November 23, 2005, http://lowendmac.com/orchard/05/1123.html (accessed October 6, 2008).

60. Wingfield, "A New Wireless Player Hopes to Challenge iPod."

61. http://www.newswireless.net/index.cfm/article/2463 (accessed November 24, 2007).

62. Ibid.

63. Frank Rose, "Battle for the Soul of the MP3 Phone," *Wired*, November 24, 2005.

64. Ibid.

65. Lev Grossman, "Invention of the Year: iPhone," *Time*, October 31, 2007, http://www.time.com/time/business/article/0,8599,1678581,00.html (accessed November 24, 2005).

Appendix 2A

1. This Appendix was written by Tom Chevalier, Britt Hackmann, and Elisabeth Nevins Caswell, in conjunction with the textbook authors (Dhruv Grewal and Michael Levy) as the basis of class discussion rather than to illustrate either effective or ineffective marketing practice.

2. http://www.knowthis.com/tutorials/principles-of-marketing/how-to-write-a-marketing-plan.htm (accessed May 16, 2008); see also "Marketing Plan Online," http://www.quickmba.com/marketing/plan/ (accessed May 16, 2008); "Marketing Plan," http://www.businessplans.org/Market.html (accessed May 18, 2008).

3. Roger Kerin, Steven Hartley, and William Rudelius, *Marketing* (New York: McGraw-Hill/Irwin, 2008), p. 53.

4. Ibid., p. 54; http://www.knowthis.com/tutorials/principles-of-marketing/how-to-write-a-marketing-plan.htm (accessed May 16, 2008).

5. This listing of sources largely comes from the Babson College Library Guide, http://www3.babson.edu/Library/research/marketingplan.cfm, May 12, 2008 (accessed May 15, 2008). Special thanks to Nancy Dlott.

6. This marketing plan presents an abbreviated version of the actual plan for PeopleAhead. Some information has been changed to maintain confidentiality.

7. Publishers' and Advertising Directors' Conference, September 21, 2005.

8. Mintel International Group, "Online Recruitment–US," January 1, 2005, http://www.marketresearch.com (accessed September 1, 2005).

9. Corzen Inc., May 1, 2004, http://www.wantedtech.com/ (accessed May 17, 2004).

10. Mintel International Group, "Online Recruitment–US."

Chapter 3

1. "Plenty of Blame to Go Around," *Economist,* September 29, 2007.

2. Jane Simms, "Toy Story Without a Happy Ending," *Marketing,* October 10, 2007, accessed electronically.

3. Kim Nash, "Recalls Test Mattel IT," *CIO,* October 2007, p. 21.

4. Joseph Ogando, "A Virtual Hall of Shame," *Design News,* October 8, 2007, p. 62.

5. Theodore Levitt, *Marketing Imagination* (Detroit, MI: The Free Press, 1983).

6. For a detailed compilation of articles that are involved with ethical and societal issues, see: Gregory T. Gundlach, Lauren G. Block, and William W. Wilkie, *Explorations of Marketing in Society* (Mason, OH: Thompson Higher Education, 2007); G. Svensson and G. Wood, "A Model of Business Ethics," *Journal of Business Ethics,* 77, no. 3 (2007), pp. 303–322.

7. William L. Wilkie and Elizabeth S. Moore, "Marketing's Contributions to Society," *Journal of Marketing,* 63 (Special Issue, 1999), pp. 198–219.

8. http://www.gallup.com (accessed September 1, 2008).

9. http://www.ethics.org/nbes2003/2003nbes_summary.html (accessed August 3, 2005).

10. http://www.jnj.com/our_company/our_credo/index.htm (accessed December 29, 2007).

11. Erin Cavusgil, "Merck and Vioxx: An Examination of an Ethical Decision-Making Model," *Journal of Business Ethics,* 76 (2007), pp. 451–461.

12. http://www.cmomagazine.com/info/release/090104_ethics.html (accessed September 1, 2006).

13. http://www.webopedia.com/TERM/P/phishing.html (accessed January 11, 2008).

14. Catherine Holahan, "'Tis the Season for Scams," *BusinessWeek Online,* December 26, 2007, p. 1.

15. http://www.bsr.org (accessed December 15, 2007).

16. "Corporate Philanthropy's Biggest Givers," *BusinessWeek,* Special Report, December 2, 2007, accessed electronically.

17. Coca Cola Corporate Social Responsibility Report, 2006, http://www.thecoca-colacompany.com/citizenship/pdf/corporate_responsibility_review2006.pdf (accessed December 29, 2007); "Business Ethics: Corporate Social Responsibility Report," *Business Ethics,* Spring 2004 (accessed September 1, 2006).

18. Coca Cola Corporate Social Responsibility Report, 2006; Africa Employee HIV/AIDS Programmes—Africa, http://www.comminit.com/en/node/120915 (accessed December 29, 2007).

19. A. Parasuraman, Dhruv Grewal, and R. Krishnan, *Marketing Research,* 2nd ed. (Boston, MA: Houghton Mifflin Company, 2007), pp. 44–49; Allan J. Kimmel and N. Craig Smith, "Deception in Marketing Research: Ethical, Methodological and Disciplinary Implications," *Psychology & Marketing,* 18, no. 7 (2001) p. 663; Ralph W. Giacobbe and Madhav N. Segal, "A Comparative Analysis of Ethical Perceptions in Marketing Research: U.S.A. vs. Canada," *Journal of Business Ethics,* 27 (October 2000), pp. 229–246; Naresh K. Malhotra and Gina L. Miller, "An Integrated Model for Ethical Decisions in Marketing Research," *Journal of Business Ethics,* 17 (February 1988), pp. 263–280; J. R. Sparks and S. D. Hunt, "Marketing Researcher Ethical Sensitivity: Conceptualization, Measurement, and Exploratory Investigation," *Journal of Marketing,* April 1988, pp. 92–109.

20. This question is based on deontological theory, an ethical theory concerned with duties and rights. Deontological ethical theories are based on the existence of a universal principle—such as respect for others, honesty, fairness, or justice—that forms the basis for determining what is right. See: E. Cavusgil, "Merck and Vioxx: An Examination of an Ethical Decision-Making Model," *Journal of Business Ethics,* 76, no. 4 (2007), pp. 451–461; Kate McKone-Sweet, Danna Greenberg, and Lydia Moland, "Approaches to Ethical Decision Making," Babson College Case Development Center, 2003.

21. This question is based on the theory of act utilitarianism, which requires that a person act so that his or her actions result in more good than harm to his or her society. In essence, act utilitarianism involves a cost/benefit analysis in which the decision maker accounts for all the possible costs and benefits and arrives at the solution that is optimal for the greatest number of interested parties. In other words, the best decision is the one by which everyone benefits without incurring loss. See McKone-Sweet, Greenberg, and Moland, "Approaches to Ethical Decision Making."

22. This question is based on the theory of rule utilitarianism, which requires that a person act in such a way that the rule on which his or her action is based produces more benefit than harm. For example, the rule "I will do whatever it takes to get ahead" may not always produce the most benefit if getting ahead requires that the person ignore the consequences of his or her actions to others; in this case, the rule is immoral. See McKone-Sweet, Greenberg, and Moland, "Approaches to Ethical Decision Making."

23. This question is based on the theory of personal virtue, which requires a person to act only in such a way that cultivates character traits that enable that person to live peacefully with himself or herself and with others. According to theories promoted by Aristotle, individuals should develop the virtues of honesty, bravery, generosity, and justice for others. See McKone-Sweet, Greenberg, and Moland, "Approaches to Ethical Decision Making."

24. http://www.generalmills.com/corporate/commitment/corp.aspx. (accessed December 4, 2007).

25. http://www.newmansown.com/faqs.cfm (accessed December 29, 2007); Newman's Own Inc.: Our Story, http://www.newmansown.com/ (accessed December 29, 2007); "Mission Possible: Companies Embrace Social Responsibility as a Core Value," *Nutrition Business Journal,* 12 (April 2007), pp. 21–23; J. T. Ziegenfuss, "'Each One, Reach One': Newman's Own, Ethics & Entrepreneurship," *Business Renaissance Quarterly,* 2 (Fall 2007), pp. 17–12, accessed electronically; Jennifer Barrett, Paul Newman, and A. E. Hotchner, "A Secret Recipe for Success," *Newsweek,* November 3, 2003.

26. http://www.newstarget.com/007572.html (accessed August 29, 2006).

27. Douglas MacMillan and Helen Walters, "Guerilla Marketing Gone Wild," *BusinessWeek*, February 9, 2007, accessed electronically; "Aqua Teen Hunger Force," *Wikipedia*, accessed December 3, 2007.

28. http://www.caru.org/news/2005/sparkle.pdf (accessed August 30, 2006).

29. E. T. Cheah and W. L. Chan, "The Corporate Social Responsibility of Pharmaceutical Product Recalls: An Empirical Examination of U.S. and U.K. Markets," *Journal of Business Ethics*, 76, no. 4 (2007), pp. 427–449.

30. M. Whellams, "The Approval of Over-the-Counter HIV Tests: Playing Fair When Making the Rules," *Journal of Business Ethics*, 77, no. 1 (2007), pp. 5–15.

31. http://www.tobaccofreekids.org/pressoffice/RJRBadActs.pdf; http://www.tabaccofreekids.org/reports/camel/sample4php; http://www.tobaccofreekids.org/reports/targeting (accessed October 10, 2008).

32. Presentation made by Leonard Schlesinger, former COO Limited Brands, at Babson college in February 2008.

33. "Jamie Lynn Spears' TV show Cancelled by Nickelodeon," *Herald sun*, January 4, 2008 (accessed electronically April 2, 2008).

34. Carolyn Hotchkiss, "Business Ethics: One Slide Cases," Babson College, Wellesley, MA, 2004; Star 38 is no longer in business.

35. "West Virginia Governor Seeks Halt of Abercrombie T-shirts," *USA Today*, March 23, 2003, accessed electronically.

36. Emily Steel, "How Marketers Hone Their Aim Online," *The Wall Street Journal*, June 19, 2007, p. B6.

37. "Mr. Mackey's Offense," *The Wall Street Journal*, July 16, 2007, p. A12.

38. http://www.marketingpower.com/live/mg-dictionary.php?SearchFor=direct+marketing&Searched=1 (accessed December 4, 2007).

39. This case was written by Catharine Curran-Kelly (University of Massachusetts at Dartmouth) in conjunction with the textbook authors (Dhruv Grewal and Michael Levy) as the basis of class discussion rather than to illustrate either effective or ineffective marketing practice.

Chapter 4

1. Marc Gunther, "Sustainability: GE Unveils New 'Green' Card," *Fortune*, August 24, 2007.

2. Francesco Guerrera and Ben White, "GE to Launch 'Green Credit Card' in US," *Financial Times*, July 24, 2007.

3. http://ge.ecomagination.com/site/index.html#vision/intro (accessed December 19, 2007).

4. http://www.myearthrewards.com/emission.html?ProspectID (accessed December 19, 2007).

5. Gunther, "Sustainability: GE Unveils New 'Green' Card."

6. Claudia Deutsch, "G.E. Unveils Credit Card Aimed at Relieving Carbon Footprints," *New York Times*, July 25, 2007.

7. Peter F. Drucker, *The Essential Drucker* (New York: Harper Collins, 2001).

8. Matt Fish, "Silicon Belly: The Value of Competitive Intelligence," November 10, 2003, http://lexis-nexis.com (accessed September 6, 2006).

9. Jon Van, "Corporate Covertness: More Firms Use 'CI' Analysts to Gather Data on Rivals, but It's Mostly Hush-Hush," *Tribune Business News*, December 10, 2007.

10. Steven Gray, "Gillette in a Lather over Schick's Challenge for $1.7 Billion Razor Market," *The Washington Post*, January 14, 2004.

11. Jack Neff, "Gillette, Schick Fight with Free Razors," *Advertising Age* 74, no. 48, p. 8.

12. Justin Pope, "Schick Says Judge Ruled in Its Favor in Gillette Patent Case," AP *Worldstream*, January 16, 2004; Justin Pope, "When Rivals Get Each Other's Secret Products," AP *Worldstream*, September 16, 2003; Gillette Company, "The Gillette Company Files Suit against Energizer Holdings, Inc., Charges Violation of Gillette Mach3 Patent by Schick Quattro," August 12, 2003, http://www.Gillette.com (accessed September 5, 2007).

13. Andrew Caffey, "Gillette Wins Legal Fight with Schick," *Knight Ridder Tribune Business News*, April 30, 2005.

14. http://www.shavingstuff.com/archives/004938.php (accessed December 28, 2007); Abelson, Jean, "For Fusion, Gillette Plans a Super Bowl Blitz," *Knight Ridder Tribune Business News*, January 27, 2006, p.1.

15. Polly Labarre, "Leap of Faith," *Fast Company*, June 2007, http://www.fastcompany.com/magazine/116/features-leap-of-faith.html (accessed December 8, 2007).

16. Michael Solomon, *Consumer Behavior: Buying, Having and Being* (Upper Saddle River, NJ: Prentice Hall, 2006).

17. www.drpepper.com (accessed December 26, 2007).

18. John Feto, "Name Games," *American Demographics*, February 15, 2003.

19. "Orthodox," *American Demographics*, May 2004, p. 35.

20. http://www.idahostatesman.com/103/story/103077.html (accessed December 1, 2006).

21. http://www.pewinternet.org/trends.asp (accessed December 16, 2007).

22. http://pewinternet.org/pdfs/PIP_Generations_Memo.pdf (accessed December 16, 2007).

23. Kristin Davis, "Oldies but Goodies; Marketers, Take Note: Baby Boomers Have Lots of Money to Spend," *U.S. News & World Report*, Washington edition, March 14, 2005, p. 45.

24. Steve Thompson, "Which Is Getting Played: The Organ or the Owner?" *St. Petersburg Times*, July 31, 2005.

25. http://www.calreinvest.org/PredatoryLending/Top10PredatoryPractices7.2.html (accessed August 7, 2005).

26. Michael Weiss, "Chasing Youth," *American Demographics*, October 2002, pp. 35–41.

27. Heidi Benson, "'Brain Gym' May Exercise Boomers' Fears about Aging," *San Francisco Chronicle*, December 13, 2007.

28. Mavis Scanlon, "Aging Boomers Spur Reverse Mortgage Biz," *East Bay Business Times*, December 14, 2007.

29. James Tenser, "Ageless Aging of Boom-X," *Advertising Age*, January 2, 2006, pp. 18–19; Tabitha Armstrong, "GenX Family Values," *The Lane Report*, January 1, 2005, p. 41.

30. Pamela Paul, "Getting Inside Gen Y," *American Demographics* 23, no. 9.

31. Tammy Erickson, "Why Gen Y'ers Are Slow to Leave the Nest," in *Across the Ages* (Boston: Harvard Business School, 2007); http://discussionleader.hbsp.com/erickson/2007/09/when_does_our_home_become_my_h.html (accessed September 4, 2007).

32. David Cay Johnston, "Report Says That the Rich Are Getting Richer Faster, Much Faster," *New York Times*, December 15, 2007, accessed electronically.

33. http://www.Hammacher.com (accessed December 6, 2006).

34. http://www.census.gov/population/www/socdemo/educ-attn.html (accessed December 6, 2007).

35. http://www.billsaver.com/household.html (accessed September 3, 2006).

36. Marti Barletta, "How Nike Women's Marathon Wins the Gold in Marketing to Women," MarketingProfs.com, October 23, 2007.

37. Natalie Y. Moore, "Boutiques Aim to Let Men Enjoy Shopping," *Chicago Tribune*, October 16, 2006; Blanca Torres, "More and More, Men Like Shopping," *Contra Costa Times*, October 12, 2006; Nanette Byrnes, "Secrets of the Male Shopper," *BusinessWeek*, September 4, 2006.

38. Rebecca Gardyn and John Fetto, "Race, Ethnicity and the Way We Shop," *American Demographics*, February 2003, pp. 30–33; Alison Stein Wellner, "Diversity in America," *American Demographics*, November 2002; Alison Stein Wellner, "Hispanics: The Growing Force," *American Demographics*, November 2002, pp. S8–S10.

39. Chris Hammer and John Skolnicki, "Ethnic Marketing by the Numbers: Integrating Diverse Data Can Reveal New Opportunities," The ACNielsen Company, Spring 2005.

40. William H. Frey, "Zooming in on Diversity," *American Demographics*, July/August 2004, pp. 24–32.

41. Kate King, "Hispanic Entrepreneurship, Buying Power on the Rise," CNN.com/US, October 1, 2007, http://www.cnn.com/2007/US/10/01/hispanics.economy/index.html (accessed December 16, 2007).

42. "Surging Hispanic Market Draws Interest at Retail," *Discount Store News*, October 26, 1998, p. 112.

43. King, "Hispanic Entrepreneurship, Buying Power on the Rise."

44. This definition of green marketing draws on work by Jacquelyn A. Ottman, *Green Marketing: Opportunity for Innovation* (Chicago: NTC Publishing, 1997).

45. Nikki Hopewell, "In the News," *Marketing News*, July 15, 2007; Pierce Hollingsworth, "Healthy—The New Green for Wall Street," *Stagnito's New Products Magazine*, July 2007; Bruce Horovitz, "General Mills Cereals Go Totally Whole Grain," *USA Today*, September 9, 2004, http://www.usatoday.com/money/industries/food/2004-09-30-whole-grain_x.htm (accessed December 10, 2007); Mark Dolliver, "Examining Kids' Heavy Consumption of Television Advertising for Foods," *Adweek*, April 2, 2007; Lorraine Heller, "General Mills' Whole Grain Cereal Conversion in Retrospect," *Food Navigator USA*, September 19, 2006, http://www.foodnavigator-usa.com/news/ng.asp?id=70651-general-mills-whole-grain-cereal Conversion-in-retrospect (accessed December 10, 2007).

46. "Guidelines for Marketing Food to Kids Proposed," CSPI Press Release, January 5, 2005.

47. Mark Jewell, "T.J. Maxx Theft Believed Largest Hack Ever," MSNBC, March 30, 2007; Joris Evers, "T.J. Maxx Hack Exposes Consumer Data," CNET.com, January 18, 2007.

48. http://blogs.pcworld.com/staffblog/archives/006092.html (accessed December 28, 2007).

49. Martin Peers, "Buddy, Can You Spare Some Time?" *The Wall Street Journal*, January 26, 2004, pp. B1, B3; statistics from Harris Interactive.

50. Ibid.

51. Kevin Coupe, "Fresh Takes on Food," *Chain Store Age*, January 2007.

52. www.freshandeasy.com (accessed January 21, 2008).

53. www.hannaford.com (accessed January 21, 2008).

54. Deena M. Amato-McCoy, "The 'Alpha Mom' Argument," *Chain Store Age*, December 2007.

55. Jessica Tsai, "Power to the People," CRM.com, December 1, 2007.

56. Ibid.

57. http://www.yourdictionary.com (accessed September 5, 2006).

58. Gregory T. Gundlach, Lauren G. Bloch, and William W. Wilkie, *Explorations of Marketing in Society* (Mason, OH: Thompson, 2007).

59. http://www.bsr.org (accessed September 1, 2006); C. B. Bhattacharya and Sankar Sen, "Doing Better at Doing Good: When, Why and How Consumers Respond to Corporate Social Initiatives," *California Management Review*, 47, no. 1 (2004), pp. 9–24; Tom J. Brown and Peter A. Dacin, "The Company and the Product: Corporate Associations and Consumer Product Responses," *Journal of Marketing*, 61, no. 1 (1997), pp. 68–84.

60. Richard Reeves, "Ethical Evangelists," *Management Today*, September 28, 2007, http://www.managementtoday.co.uk/channel/GovernanceCSR/news/741086/ethical-evangelists/ (accessed December 13, 2007).

61. Donald R. Lichtenstein, Minette E. Drumwright, and Bridgette M. Braig, "The Effect of Corporate Social Responsibility on Customer Donations to Corporate-Supported Nonprofits," *Journal of Marketing*, 68, no.4 (2004), pp. 16–32; Sankar Sen and C. B. Bhattacharya, "Does Doing Good Always Lead to Doing Better? Consumer Reactions to Corporate Social Responsibility," *Journal of Marketing Research*, 38 (May 2001), pp. 225–243.

62. www.ge.com (accessed December 20, 2007); http://ge.ecomagination.com/site/#vision/commitments (accessed December 20, 2007).

63. http://ge.ecomagination.com/site/ (accessed December 20, 2007).

64. GE 2007 Citizenship Report, www.ge.com/citizenship/ (accessed December 20, 2007).

65. www.greenisuniversal.com (accessed December 20, 2007); http://www.nbcuni.com/ (accessed December 20, 2007).

66. http://nccsdataweb.urban.org/PubApps/profile1.php?state=US (accessed December 28, 2007).

67. Johyn Vomhof, Jr., "Target Starts Solar-power Rollout," mlive.com, April 30, 2007; Steve Hochman, "Logistics: Green Supply Chains," Forbes.com, April 20, 2007; "Best Practices: It's Good to Be Green," www.smartreply.com (accessed December 20, 2007); Michael Levy and Barton Weitz, *Retail Management* (Burr Ridge, IL; McGraw-Hill, 2009).

68. This case was written by Jeanne L. Munger and Jacquelyn Ottman in conjunction with the textbook authors (Dhruv Grewal and Michael Levy) for use in a class discussion rather than to illustrate either effective or ineffective marketing practices. It builds on a case written and published by Jacquelyn Ottman in her book *Green Marketing: Opportunity for Innovation*. Jeanne Munger is an associate professor at the University of Southern Maine. Jacquelyn Ottman is the president of J. Ottman Consulting Inc., a New York–based marketing consulting firm that specializes in helping businesses derive competitive advantage from eco-innovation and green marketing.

69. Stonyfield Farms, http://www.stonyfield.com (accessed December 21, 2007).

70. Tara Weiss, "Milking It," *Forbes*, March 7, 2007, http://www.forbes.com/2007/07/02/organic-dairy-farms-biz-cx_tw_0703stonyfield.html (accessed December 9, 2007).

Chapter 5

1. National Geographic Society, "Environment: Going Green Across Society," 2007, http://green.nationalgeographic.com/environment/going-green/going-green-society.html (accessed December 7, 2007); Andrew Gillies, "S.E.E. Change? S.E.E. Change Go Slow," *Forbes*, March 7, 2007 (accessed electronically December 8, 2007); Dan Bigman, "Going Green," *Forbes*, March 7, 2007 (accessed December 7, 2007).

2. Reena Jana, "The Business Benefits of Going Green," *BusinessWeek*, June 22, 2007 (accessed electronically December 8, 2007).

3. Norihiko Shirouzu, "Toyota Faces New Hybrid Drought," *Wall Street Journal Online,* August 9, 2007 (accessed December 7, 2007).

4. Rajesh Chandrashekaran and Dhruv Grewal, "Anchoring Effects of Advertised Reference Price and Sale Price: The Moderating Role of Saving Presentation Format," *Journal of Business Research,* 59 (October 2006), pp. 1063–1071; Dhruv Grewal, Gopalkrishnan R. Iyer, R. Krishnan, and Arun Sharma, "The Internet and the Price-Value-Loyalty Chain," *Journal of Business Research,* 56 (May 2003), p. 391.

5. For a detailed discussion of customer behavior, see J. Paul Peter and Jerry C. Olson, *Consumer Behavior and Marketing Strategy,* 8th ed. (New York: McGraw-Hill, 2008); Michael R. Solomon, *Consumer Behavior: Buying, Having, and Being,* 7th ed. (Upper Saddle River, NJ: Prentice Hall, 2006).

6. Liz C. Wang, Julie Baker, Judy A. Wagner, and Kirk Wakefield, "Can a Retail Website Be Social?" *Journal of Marketing,* 71, no. 3 (2007), pp. 143–157; Guido Gianluigi, Mauro Capestro, and Alessandro M. Peluso, "Experimental Analysis of Consumer Stimulation and Motivational States in Shopping Experiences," *International Journal of Market Research,* 49, no. 3 (2007), pp. 365–386; Woonbong Na, Youngseok Son, and Roger Marshall, "Why Buy Second-Best? The Behavioral Dynamics of Market Leadership," *Journal of Product & Brand Management,* 15, no. 1 (2007), pp. 16–22; Min-Young Lee, Kelly Green Atkins, Youn-Kyung Kim, and Soo-Hee Park, "Competitive Analyses Between Regional Malls and Big-box Retailers: A Correspondence Analysis for Segmentation and Positioning," *Journal of Shopping Center Research,* April 2006, pp. 81–98; Pamela Sebastian, "'Aspirational Wants' Form the Basis of a Modern Retailing Strategy," *The Wall Street Journal,* October 15, 1998, p. A1; Barry Babin, William Darden, and Mitch Griffin, "Work and/or Fun: Measuring Hedonic and Utilitarian Shopping Value," *Journal of Consumer Research,* 20 (March 1994), pp. 644–656.

7. Cindy Clark, "Christian Louboutin's Red-soled Shoes Are Red-hot," *USA Today,* http://www.usatoday.com/life/lifestyle/fashion/2007-12-25-louboutin-shoes_N.htm (accessed January 2, 2008).

8. http://www.harley-davidson.com/wcm/Content/Pages/HOG/HOG.jsp?locale=en_usu (accessed December 24, 2007).

9. "Harley Owners Group Members Ready to Rendezvous In Adirondacks," *Motorcyclist,* August 30, 2007 (accessed December 26, 2007).

10. Brian T. Ratchford, Debabrata Talukdar, and Myung-Soo Lee, "The Impact of the Internet on Consumers' Use of Information Sources for Automobiles: A Re-Inquiry," *Journal of Consumer Research,* 34, no. 1 (2007), pp. 111–119; Glenn J. Browne, Mitzi G. Pitts, and James C. Wetherbe, "Cognitive Shopping Rules for Terminating Information Search in Online Tasks," *MIS Quarterly,* 31, no.1 (2007), pp. 89–104

11. http://www.truejeans.com (accessed December 26, 2007).

12. http://www.google.com/corporate/history.html (accessed September 3, 2006).

13. "Why Index Size Is Important," *Search Engine Watch,* October 1, 2007 (accessed December 26, 2007).

14. Abbey Klaassen, "Guess Who Gained Search Share; Despite Their Best Efforts, Yahoo, Microsoft and Ask Are No Match for Google," *Advertising Age,* 78, no. 50 (December 17, 2007) (accessed December 26, 2007).

15. The term *determinance* was first coined by James Myers and Mark Alpert nearly three decades ago; http://www.sawtoothsoftware.com/productforms/ssolutions/ss12.shtml (accessed September 4, 2006).

16. http://www.sawtoothsoftware.com/productforms/ssolutions/ss12.shtml (accessed September 4, 2006).

17. Chris T. Allen, Karen A. Machleit, Susan Schultz Kleine, and Arti Sahni Notani, "A Place for Emotion in Attitude Models," *Journal of Business Research,* 58, no. 4 (2005), pp. 494–499; Armin Scholl, Laura Manthey, Roland Helm, and Michael Steiner, "Solving Multiattribute Design Problems with Analytic Hierarchy Process and Conjoint Analysis: An Empirical Comparison," *European Journal of Operational Research,* 164, no. 3 (2005), pp. 760–777; Richard Lutz, "Changing Brand Attitudes through Modification of Cognitive Structure," *Journal of Consumer Research,* 1, no. 1 (1975), pp. 125–136.

18. Jim Oliver, "Finding Decision Rules with Genetic Algorithms," http://www.umsanet.edu.bo/docentes/gchoque/MAT420L07.htm (accessed June 2004).

19. Anne Roggeveen, Dhruv Grewal, and Jerry Gotlieb, "Does the Frame of a Comparative Ad Moderate the Effectiveness of Extrinsic Information Cues?" *Journal of Consumer Research,* 33 (June 2006), pp. 115–122; Anthony Miyazaki, Dhruv Grewal, and Ronald C. Goodstein, "The Effect of Multiple Extrinsic Cues on Quality Perceptions: A Matter of Consistency," *Journal of Consumer Research,* 32 (June 2005), pp. 146–153; Paul S. Richardson, Alan S. Dick, and Arun K. Jain, "Extrinsic and Intrinsic Cue Effects on Perceptions of Store Brand Quality," *Journal of Marketing* 58 (October 1994), pp. 28–36; Rajneesh Suri and Kent B. Monroe, "The Effects of Time Constraints on Consumers' Judgments of Prices and Products," *Journal of Consumer Research* 30 (June 2003), pp. 92–104.

20. Merrie Brucks, Valerie A. Zeithaml, and Gillian Naylor, "Price and Brand Name as Indicators of Quality Dimensions for Consumer Durables," *Journal of the Academy of Marketing Science* 28, no. 3 (2000), pp. 359–374; Niraj Dawar and Philip Parker, "Marketing Universals: Consumers' Use of Brand Name, Price, Physical Appearance, and Retailer Reputation as Signals of Product Quality," *Journal of Marketing,* 58 (April 1994), pp. 81–95; William B. Dodds, Kent B. Monroe, and Dhruv Grewal, "Effects of Price, Brand, and Store Information on Buyers' Product Evaluations," *Journal of Marketing Research* 28 (August 1991), pp. 307–19.

21. Mary Jo Bitner, "Servicescapes: The Impact of Physical Surroundings on Customers and Employees," *Journal of Marketing* 56 (April 1992), pp. 57–71; Dhruv Grewal and Julie Baker, "Do Retail Store Environmental Factors Affect Consumers' Price Acceptability? An Empirical Examination," *International Journal of Research in Marketing* 11 (1994), pp. 107–15; Eric R. Spangenberg, Ayn E. Crowley, and Pamela W. Henderson, "Improving the Store Environment: Do Olfactory Cues Affect Evaluations and Behaviors?" *Journal of Marketing* 60 (April 1996), pp. 67–80; Kirk L. Wakefield and Jeffrey G. Blodgett, "Customer Response to Intangible and Tangible Service Factors," *Psychology and Marketing* 16 (January 1999), pp. 51–68.

22. "Beware of Dissatisfied Consumers: They Like to Blab," *Knowledge@Wharton,* March, 8, 2006, based on the "Retail Customer Dissatisfaction Study 2006" conducted by the Jay H. Baker Retailing Initiative at Wharton and The Verde Group, accessed electronically; "The Lowdown on Customer Loyalty Programs: Which Are the Most Effective and Why," *Knowledge@Wharton,* September 6, 2006; Sandra Kennedy, "Keeping Customers Happy," *Chain Store Age,* February 2005, p. 24; Heiner Evanschitzky, Gopalkrishnan Iyer, Josef Hesse, and Dieter Ahlert, "E-satisfaction: A Re-examination," *Journal of Retailing,* 80, no. 3 (2004), pp. 239–252; Emin Babakus, Carol Bienstock, and James Van Scotter, "Linking Perceived Quality and Customer Satisfaction to Store Traffic and Revenue Growth," *Decision Sciences,* 35 (Fall 2004), pp. 713–738; Jarrad Dunning, Anthony Pecotich, and Aron O'Cass, "What Happens When Things Go Wrong? Retail Sales Explanations and Their Effects," *Psychology & Marketing* (July 2004), pp. 553–568; Richard Oliver, Roland Rust, and Sajeev Varki, "Customer Delight: Foundations, Findings, and Managerial Insights," *Journal of Retailing,* 73 (Fall 1997), pp. 311–336; Chezy Ofir and

Itamar Simonson, "The Effect of Stating Expectations on Customer Satisfaction and Shopping Experience," *Journal of Marketing Research*, 44, no.1 (2007), pp. 164–174.

23. http://www.expedia.com/daily/service/about.asp?rfrr=-1087 (accessed December 24, 2007).

24. Spencer E. Ante with Cliff Edwards, "The Science of Desire," *BusinessWeek Online,* June 6, 2006 (accessed December 27, 2007).

25. For a more extensive discussion on these factors, see: Banwari Mittal, *Consumer Behavior* (Cincinnati, OH: Open Mentis, 2008); Peter and Olson, *Consumer Behavior and Marketing Strategy;* Solomon, *Consumer Behavior: Buying, Having, and Being.*

26. A. H. Maslow, *Motivation and Personality* (New York: Harper & Row, 1970).

27. For more discussion on these factors, see: Mittal, *Consumer Behavior;* Peter and Olson, *Consumer Behavior and Marketing Strategy;* Solomon, *Consumer Behavior: Buying, Having, and Being;* Michael Levy and Barton A. Weitz, *Retailing Management,* 7th ed. (Burr Ridge IL: Irwin/Mc-Graw-Hill, 2009), chapter 4.

28. Margaret Magnarelli, "Big Spenders," *Parents,* March 2004.

29. "Grandparents in U.S. Spend $27.5 Billion Annually on Their Grandchildren," *Senior News,* September 4, 2007 (accessed December 26, 2007).

30. Sandra Yin, "Kids' Hot Spots," *American Demographics,* December 1, 2003; Peter Francese, "Trend Ticker: Trouble in Store," *American Demographics,* December 1, 2003.

31. http://www.oxo.com/oxo/about.htm (accessed December 24, 2007).

32. Helen Walters, "OXO, Remade in Japan," *BusinessWeek Online,* December 8, 2006 (accessed December 24, 2007).

33. For a greater discussion on these factors, see: Mittal, *Consumer Behavior;* Peter and Olson, *Consumer Behavior and Marketing Strategy;* Solomon, *Consumer Behavior: Buying, Having, and Being.*

34. The concept of atmospherics was introduced by Philip Kotler, "Atmosphere as a Marketing Tool," *Journal of Retailing,* 49 (Winter 1973), pp. 48–64.

35. Sylvie Morin, Laurette Dubé and Jean-Charles Chebat, "The Role of Pleasant Music in Servicescapes: A Test of the Dual Model of Environmental Perception," *Journal of Retailing,* 83, no. 1 (2007), pp. 115–130; Nicole Bailey and Charles S. Areni, "When a Few minutes Sound Like a Lifetime: Does Atmospheric Music Expand or Contract Perceived Time?" *Journal of Retailing,* 82, no. 3 (2006), pp. 189–202; Dhruv Grewal, Julie Baker, Michael Levy, and Glenn B. Voss, "The Effects of Wait Expectations and Store Atmosphere Evaluations on Patronage Intentions in Service-intensive Retail Stores," *Journal of Retailing,* 79, no. 4 (2003), pp. 259–268; Anna S. Mattila and Jochen Wirtz, "Congruency of Scent and Music as a Driver of In-Store Evaluations and Behavior," *Journal of Retailing,* 77, no. 2 (Summer 2001), pp. 273–89; Teresa A. Summers and Paulette R. Hebert, "Shedding Some Light on Store Atmospherics; Influence of Illumination on Consumer Behavior," *Journal of Business Research,* 54, no. 2 (November 2001), pp. 145–150; for a review of this research, see Joseph A. Bellizzi and Robert E. Hite, "Environmental Color, Consumer Feelings, and Purchase Likelihood," *Psychology and Marketing,* 9, no. 5 (September–October 1992), pp. 347–63; J. Duncan Herrington and Louis Capella, "Effects of Music in Service Environments: A Field Study," *Journal of Services Marketing,* 10, no. 2 (1996), pp. 26–41; Richard F. Yalch and Eric R. Spangenberg, "The Effects of Music in a Retail Setting on Real and Perceived Shopping Times," *Journal of Business Research,* 49, no. 2 (August 2000), pp. 139–148; Michael Hui, Laurette Dube, and Jean-Charles Chebat, "The Impact of Music on Consumer's Reactions to Waiting for Services," *Journal of Retailing,* 73, no. 1 (1997), pp. 87–104; Julie Baker, Dhruv Grewal, and Michael Levy, "An Experimental Approach to Making Retail Store Environmental Decisions," *Journal of Retailing,* 68 (Winter 1992), pp. 445–460; Maxine Wilkie, "Scent of a Market," *American Demographics,* August 1995, pp. 40–49; Spangenberg, Crowley, Henderson, "Improving the Store Environment: Do Olfactory Cues Affect Evaluations and Behaviors?"; Paula Fitzgerald Bone and Pam Scholder Ellen, "Scents in the Marketplace: Explaining a Fraction of Olfaction," *Journal of Retailing,* 75, no. 2 (Summer 1999), pp. 243–263.

36. Hitha Prabhakar, "Top Shops 2006," *Forbes,* December 15, 2006 (accessed electronically January 12, 2008).

37. Chris Serres, "Best Buy Displays a Feminine Side," *Minneapolis Star Tribune,* November 15, 2006 (accessed electronically January 23, 2008.)

38. www.mitchellsonline.com, (accessed January 23, 2008); Keiko Morris," Venerable Men's Store 'Hugs' Women," *Knight Ridder Tribune Business News,* September 11, 2006. p. 1.

39. Katherine Field, "Containing Culture," *Chain Store Age,* April 2007, pp. 22–24; Sara Schaefer Munoz, "Why The Container Store Guy Wants to Be Your Therapist," *The Wall Street Journal,* March 29, 2007, p. D.1, www.containerstore.com (accessed July 16, 2007).

40. Bob Tedeshi, "Salesmanship Comes to the Online Stores, But Please Call It a Chat," *New York Times,* August 7, 2006, accessed electronically; Subramanian Sivaramakrishnan, Fang Wan, Zaiyong Tang, "Giving an 'E-human Touch' to E-tailing: The Moderating Roles of Static Information Quantity and Consumption Motive in the Effectiveness of an Anthropomorphic Information Agent," *Journal of Interactive Marketing,* 21, no. 1 (2007), pp. 60–75.

41. Julie Baker, Dhruv Grewal, Michael Levy, and Glenn Voss, "Wait Expectations, Store Atmosphere and Store Patronage Intentions," *Journal of Retailing* 79, no. 4 (2003), pp. 259–268.

42. Charles Delafuente, "Pushing Colleges to Limit Credit Offers to Students," *The New York Times,* October 17, 2007 (accessed December 26, 2007).

43. Jessica Silver-Greenberg, "Selling Students into Credit-Card Debt," *BusinessWeek Online,* October 3, 2007 (accessed December 26, 2007).

44. Mittal, *Consumer Behavior;* Peter and Olson, *Consumer Behavior and Marketing Strategy;* Solomon, *Consumer Behavior: Buying, Having, and Being.*

45. R. Puri, "Measuring and Modifying Consumer Impulsiveness: A Cost-Benefit Accessibility Framework," *Journal of Consumer Psychology* 5 (1996), pp. 87–113.

46. This case was written by Jeanne L. Munger in conjunction with Dhruv Grewal and Michael Levy as the basis of class discussion rather than to illustrate either effective or ineffective marketing practices. Jeanne Munger is an associate professor at the University of Southern Maine.

47. http://www.smartusa.com/smart-media-press-pricing-announcement.aspx (accessed December 24, 2007).

48. A. Pawlowski, "Mini to the Max: Will the Smart Car Grow on U.S. Drivers?" CNN.com, November 8, 2007 (accessed December 24, 2007).

49. Kara Rowland, "Think Small, Get Smart; Little German Car Rated at 45 Highway Miles per Gallon," *The Washington Times,* December 5, 2007 (accessed December 26, 2007).

50. "Buyers Thinking Smart Can Reserve fortwo Now, before 2008 Launch," *The Record,* December 16, 2007 (accessed December 26, 2007).

51. David Shepardson, "Brains over Brawn; Daimler's Smart Car Set to Go on Sale Next Month, Giving Consumers an Alternative to Gas-Chugging SUVs," *The Detroit News*, December 5, 2007 (accessed December 26, 2007).

52. "SmartUSA Offering $99 Reservations to Gauge Interest in the ForTwo," Autoblog.com, February 5, 2007 (accessed December 24, 2007).

53. Ken Thomas, "Smart Car Is in High Demand," *Deseret Morning News*, December 16, 2007 (accessed December 26, 2007).

Chapter 6

1. www.eastman.com (accessed January 3, 2008).

2. "CamelBak Improves Water Bottle Convenience and Performance Using New Eastman Tritan Copolyester," http://www.eastman.com/Company/News_Center/News_Archive/2007/English/Product_News/071024f.htm (accessed January 7, 2008).

3. Kate Maddox, "Eastman Chemical Rolls Out Campaign," *B to B Online*, December 10, 2007.

4. Arun Sharma, R. Krishnan, and Dhruv Grewal, "Value Creation in Markets: A Critical Area of Focus for Business-to-Business Markets," *Industrial Marketing Management*, 30, no. 4 (2001), pp. 391–402; Ajay K. Kohli and Bernard J. Jaworski, "Market Orientation: The Construct, Research Propositions, and Managerial Implications," *Journal of Marketing*, 54, no. 2 (1990), pp. 1–13; John C. Narver and Stanly F. Slater, "The Effect of Market Orientation on Business Profitability," *Journal of Marketing*, 54, no. 4 (1990), pp. 20–33.

5. Danny Peltz, "When Clients Speak, Wells Fargo Listens," *Bank Systems & Technology*, May 25, 2006.

6. Kate Maddox, "Marketers Face Challenges from Economy to Ecology," *B to B Online*, December 10, 2007.

7. "Our Mission and Vision," http://www.burtsbees.com (accessed January 4, 2008).

8. "Burt's Bees Focuses on Production Efficiency," *Cosmetics Design*, November 2, 2006.

9. "Illinois State Board of Education FY08 Budget," www.isbe.net (accessed January 3, 2007); Brian Chapman and Chip W. Hardt, "Purchasing Lessons for Schools," *The McKinsey Quarterly*, no. 4 (2003), electronically accessed.

10. Christina Binkley, "Fashion Journal: After the Show: The Real Business of Fashion," *The Wall Street Journal*, March 2, 2007.

11. Amanda Fortini, "How the Runway Took Off: A Brief History of the Fashion Show," *Slate Magazine*, February 8, 2006.

12. "Budget of the United States Government: Fiscal Year 2007," *Executive Office of the United States: Office of Management and Budget* (accessed electronically January 4, 2008).

13. "Budget of the United States Government: Fiscal Year 2007," www.gpoaccess.gov (accessed January 4, 2008).

14. Navi Radjou with Laurie M. Orlov and Nicole Belanger, "The Defense Contractors' Supply Chain Imperative," *Forrester Research*, August 15, 2003. This text provides citings from the December 2002 Forrester Report, "SCM Processes Replace Apps: 2003–2008."

15. http://www.census.gov/epcd/naics07/ (accessed January 22, 2008).

16. http://www.census.gov/epcd/naics02/N2SIC51.HTM (accessed January 22, 2008); http://www.census.gov/epcd/naics07/ (accessed January 22, 2008).

17. http://www.census.gov/epcd/naics02/SICN02E.HTM#S48 (accessed January 22, 2008).

18. This illustration, which exemplifies how Toyota works with its suppliers, is based on Jeffrey K. Liker and Thomas Y. Choi, "Building Deep Supplier Relationships," *Harvard Business Review*, December 2004, pp. 104–114.

19. http://Toyotasupplier.com (accessed January 4, 2008).

20. Ibid.

21. http://www.marketingpower.com/live/mg-dictionary-view435.php. These definitions are provided by www.marketingpower.com (the American Marketing Association's Web site). We have bolded our key terms.

22. "Study: U.S. Drug Industry Spends Almost Double on Marketing Over R&D," *BrandWeek*, January 3, 2007.

23. http://www.pulsus.com/clin-pha/08_02/lexc_ed.htm (accessed September 6, 2006).

24. John Simons, "A Big Pharma Whistleblower Blogs on Drugs," *Fortune*, June 6, 2007; http://peterrost.blogspot.com (accessed January 8, 2008).

25. http://www.goer.state.ny.us/train/onlinelearning/FTMS/500s1.html (accessed January 22, 2008).

26. "The Purchasing Department of Volkswagen," presentation, http://www.volkswagen-ir.de/download/InvPres_01/20010518VWSanzENG.pdf (accessed May 16, 2005); Martin Hofmann, Emily-Sue Sloane, and Elena Malykhina, "VW Revs Its B2B Engine," *Optimize*, March 2004, pp. 22–26; "FAQ," http://www.vwgroupsupply.com/; "Volkswagen Expands B2B Platform: Volkswagen Has Expanded its Business-to-Business Platform to Allow Suppliers to Easily Manage Their Financial Dealings with the Company via the Internet," *Computer World*, 9, no. 7 (2002); Erika Morphy, "Volkswagen Takes on Covisint in the B2B Auction Arena," *CRM Daily*, July 13, 2001.

27. http://www.volkswagenag.com/vwag/vwcorp/content/en/brands_and_companies/automotive_and_financial.html (accessed January 18, 2008); Volkswagen AG, "2006 Annual Report," Wolfsburg, Germany, Volkswagen AG, 2007.

28. "Volkswagen's World-Class Procurement Strategy Produces Breakthrough Productivity Gains," http://www.ibm.com (accessed January 3, 2008).

29. Doug Lesmerises, "Ohio State Football Reaches New Deal with Nike," *The Plain Dealer*, September 13, 2007 (accessed electronically January 4, 2007).

30. Barton A. Weitz, Stephen B. Castleberry, and John F. Tanner, *Selling Building Partnerships*, 5th ed. (Burr Ridge, IL: McGraw-Hill/Irwin, 2003), p. 93.

31. "OVU Basketball Nets 3-Year Contract with New Balance," www.ovu.edu/base.cfm?page_id=3229 (accessed January 4, 2007).

32. Lesmerises, "Ohio State Football Reaches New Deal."

33. Maddox, "Marketers Face Challenges from Economy to Ecology."

34. Amanda C. Kooser, "Virtual Trade Shows Take Care of Some Very Real Business," *Entrepreneur*, August 2007.

35. Ibid.

36. www.onforce.com (accessed January 4, 2008).

37. Raymund Flandez, "Managing Technology—In Search of Help: For Small Firms Seeking IT Services, the Choices Have Never Been More Varied—or More Confusing," *The Wall Street Journal*, March 19, 2007.

38. K. C. Laudon and C. G. Traver, *E-Commerce: Business, Technology, Society*, 2nd ed. (Boston: Pearson, 2004).

39. http://www.Guru.com (accessed January 3, 2008).

40. David Whitford, "Hired Guns on the Cheap," *Fortune Small Business*, January 3, 2008.

41. R. Tassabehji, W. A. Taylor, R. Beach, A. Wood, "Reverse E-auctions and Supplier-Buyer Relationships: An Exploratory Study," *International Journal of Operations and Production Management*, 26, no. 2 (2006), pp. 1–19; Sandy Jap, "An Exploratory Study of the Introduction of Online Reverse Auctions," *Journal of Marketing*, 67, no. 3 (2003), electronically accessed; Sandy Jap, "Going Going, Gone," *Harvard Business Review*, 78, no. 6, electronically accessed; "Reverse Auctions Gain Momentum as Cost Tool-Chipmakers Grudgingly Join in Online Bids," *Spencer Chin*, March 3, 2003, p. 1.

42. This case was written by Jeanne L. Munger in conjunction with the textbook authors (Dhruv Grewal and Michael Levy) as the basis of class discussion rather than to illustrate either effective or ineffective marketing practices. Jeanne Munger is an associate professor at the University of Southern Maine.

43. http://www.weyerhaeuser.com/aboutus/ (accessed January 18, 2008).

44. Weyerhaeuser, www.weyerhaeuser.com (accessed January 18, 2008).

45. http://www.realtor.org/referral.nsf/pages/WhatpercentageofthemeGrossDomest (accessed January 18, 2008); *2004 Housing Facts, Figures and Trends*, National Association of Home Builders.

46. Ken Leon, "Homebuilding," *Standard & Poor's Industry Surveys*, January 3, 2008, p. 28.

47. Barry A. Rappaport and Tamara A. Cole, *1997 Economic Census—Construction Sector Special Study, Housing Starts Statistics: A Profile of the Homebuilding Industry* (July 2000).

Chapter 7

1. Marriott International Inc., *2006 Annual Report* (accessed electronically January 10, 2008).

2. "December 5, 2007 Wachovia Investor Conference," http://ir.shareholder.com/mar/downloads/LP-NYC-Wachovia-Conf-12-6-07.pdf (accessed January 9, 2008).

3. "What's Your World Wonder?" http://www.marriott.com/news/detail.mi?marrArticle=290999 (accessed January 9, 2008).

4. Loretta Chao, "Ritz Makes China Push, Plans 7 New Sites by 2010," *The Wall Street Journal*, December 5, 2007, p. D10 (accessed electronically January 10, 2008).

5. "Marriott Launches Dynamic, Integrated Global Advertising Campaign," November 29, 2007, http://www.marriott.com/news/detail.mi?marrArticle=295788.

6. "Marriott Launches Global Advertising Campaign," *Asia Travel Tips*, December 10, 2007 (accessed electronically January 8, 2008).

7. Pierre-Richard Agenor, *Does Globalization Hurt the Poor?* (Washington, DC: World Bank, 2002); "Globalization: Threat or Opportunity," International Monetary Fund, http://www.imf.org/external/np/exr/ib/2000/041200.htm#II (accessed September 18, 2006).

8. Charles W. L. Hill, *Global Business Today*, 5th ed. (New York: McGraw-Hill/Irwin 2008).

9. Joel D. Pinaroc, "China, India Hold Offshoring Ground," *ZDnet Asia*, October 31, 2007 (accessed electronically January 7, 2008).

10. Andy McCue, "More Firms Setting Up Own Offshoring," *Silicon*, July 13, 2007 (accessed electronically January 7, 2008).

11. Pinaroc, "China, India Hold Offshoring Ground."

12. McCue, "More Firms Setting Up Own Offshoring."

13. Rachael King, "The Outsourcing Upstarts," *BusinessWeek*, July 31, 2007 (accessed electronically January 7, 2007).

14. Jack Ewing, "Why Krakow Still Works for IBM," *BusinessWeek*, September 25, 2007 (accessed electronically January 7, 2008).

15. http://www.econ.iastate.edu/classes/econ355/choi/wtoroots.htm (accessed October 7, 2007).

16. http://www.wto.org/english/thewto_e/whatis_e/tif_e/org6_e.htm (accessed October 8, 2007).

17. Social Science Research Council, http://www.ssrc.org/sept11/essays/teaching_resource/tr_globalization.htm (accessed February 5, 2008).

18. http://web.worldbank.org/WBSITE/EXTERNAL/EXTABOUTUS/0,,pagePK:50004410~piPK:36602~theSitePK:29708,00.html (accessed January 3, 2008).

19. For a full description of criticisms of the IMF, see http://www.imf.org/external/np/exr/ccrit/eng/cri.htm; for a list of criticisms of the World Bank, see http://www.artsci.wustl.edu/~nairobi/wbissues.html (accessed August 28, 2005).

20. http://www.acdi-cida.gc.ca/CIDAWEB/webcountry.nsf/VLUDocEn/Cameroon-Factsataglance#def (accessed January 3, 2008).

21. http://en.wikipedia.org/wiki/Purchasing_power_parity (accessed February 5, 2008); Arthur O'Sullivan, Steven Sheffrin, and Steve Perez, *Macroeconomics: Principles and Tools Activebook*, 5th ed. (Upper Saddle River, NJ: Prentice Hall, 2007).

22. http://hdr.undp.org/reports/global/2001/en/; Nobel Prize–winning economist Amartya Sen has proposed that developing countries should also be measured according to the capabilities and opportunities that people within that particular country possess.

23. T. N. Ninan, "Six Mega-Trends That Define India's Future," Rediff.com, January 6, 2007 (accessed January 7, 2007).

24. "India," *The CIA World Factbook*, December 13, 2007 (accessed electronically January 8, 2008).

25. "United States," *The CIA World Factbook*, December 13, 2007 (accessed electronically January 8, 2008).

26. "India," *The CIA World Factbook*.

27. Mayur Shekhar Jha and Chaitali Chakravarty, "Specialty Retailers Say No to India Call," *The Economic Times*, May 9, 2007 (accessed electronically on January 30, 2008).

28. "Coming to Market," *The Economist*, April 12, 2006 (accessed electronically January 30, 2008).

29. Ibid.

30. Eric Bellman, "In India, a Retailer Finds Key to Success Is Clutter," *The Wall Street Journal*, August 8, 2007, p. A1

31. "What's Ahead for the Global Economy in 2008?" Reports from the Knowledge@Wharton Network, *Knowledge@Wharton*, January 9, 2008 (accessed January 10, 2008).

32. Ellen Byron, "Emerging Ambitions—P&G's Global Target: Shelves of Tiny Stores," *The Wall Street Journal*, July 16, 2007, p. A1 (accessed electronically January 8, 2008).

33. Kelly Crow, "Buoyant Art Market Draws International Buyers," *The Wall Street Journal*, January 2, 2008, p. R19 (accessed electronically January 10, 2008).

34. David L. Scott, *Wall Street Words: An A to Z Guide to Investment Terms for Today's Investor* (Boston: Houghton Mifflin, 2003).

35. John McKinnon, "Biofuels Pact Likely to Hit Hurdles," *The Wall Street Journal*, March 10, 2007, p. A2 (accessed electronically January 7, 2007).

36. Ben Lieberman, "Lift Tariffs on Foreign Ethanol," *The Heritage Foundation*, May 12, 2006 (accessed electronically January 7, 2007).

37. http://economics.about.com/library/glossary/bldef-dumping.htm (accessed February 5, 2008); Scott, *Wall Street Words*.

38. Greg Hitt and James Hookway, "Seafood Fight: U.S. Shrimpers Haul Cash From Lower-Cost Rivals," *The Wall Street Journal,* April 2, 2007, p. A1 (accessed electronically January 7, 2007).

39. http://www.bloomberg.com/apps/news?pid=10000103&sid=ajtpC2UYVKwk&refer=us (accessed January 3, 2008).

40. "Half of Europeans Distrust American Companies," 2004, http://www.gmimr.com/gmipoll/press_room_wppk_pr_12272004.phtml (accessed September 11, 2006).

41. "Exchange Rate," http://en.wikipedia.org/wiki/Exchange_rate (accessed January 3, 2008).

42. "Philippines Implement Countertrade Program for Vietnamese Rice," *Asia Pulse Pte Limited,* April 27, 2005.

43. http://ucatlas.ucsc.edu/trade/subtheme_trade_blocs.php (accessed February 5, 2008).

44. http://www.unescap.org/tid/mtg/postcancun_rterta.pps#1 (accessed January 3, 2008).

45. http://europa.eu/abc/european_countries/index_en.htm (accessed January 8, 2008).

46. http://ec.europa.eu/enlargement/countries/index_en.htm (accessed January 8, 2008).

47. http://www.fas.usda.gov/itp/CAFTA/cafta.html (accessed September 10, 2006).

48. Danielle Medina Walker and Thomas Walker, *Doing Business Internationally: The Guide to Cross-Cultural Success,* 2nd ed. (Princeton, NJ: Trade Management Corporation, 2002).

49. Geert Hofstede and Gert Jan Hofstede, *Cultures and Organizations: Software of the Mind* (New York: McGraw-Hill/Irwin, 2004); Geert Hofstede, "Management Scientists Are Human," *Management Science,* 40 (January 1994), pp. 4–13; Geert Hofstede and Michael H. Bond, "The Confucius Connection from Cultural Roots to Economic Growth," *Organizational Dynamics,* 16 (Spring 1988), pp. 4–21; Masaaki Kotabe and Kristiaan Helsen, *Global Marketing Management,* 3rd ed. (Hoboken, NJ: John Wiley & Sons, 2004).

50. http://www.geert-hofstede.com/ (accessed February 6, 2008).

51. Tian Feng and Julian Lowe, "The Influence of National and Organizational Culture on Absorptive Capacity of Chinese Companies," *The International Journal of Knowledge, Culture and Change Management,* 7, no. 10, (2007), pp. 9–16; Donghoon Kim, Yigang Pan, and Heung Soo Park, "High versus Low Context Culture: A Comparison of Chinese, Korean and American Cultures," *Psychology and Marketing,* 15, no. 6 (1998), pp. 507–521.

52. Dexter Roberts, "China Autos: Chery Keeps Accelerating," *BusinessWeek,* January 4, 2008 (accessed electronically January 8, 2008).

53. Ibid.

54. http://audi.ogilvy.com.cn/en/about/history/audi_inchina/audi_inchina.html (accessed January 8, 2008).

55. "ING Overview," http://home.ingdirect.com/about/about.asp (accessed January 8, 2008).

56. Arkadi Kuhlmann, "First State Boasts First-Class Thinkers," *News Journal,* January 1, 2008 (accessed electronically January 8, 2008).

57. http://www.cyber-ark.com/networkvaultnews/pr_20031110.asp (accessed September 10, 2007).

58. Bruce D. Keillor, Michael D'Amico, and Veronica Horton, "Global Consumer Tendencies," *Psychology and Marketing* 18, no. 1 (2001), pp. 1–20.

59. Jessica E. Vascellaro, "MySpace Aims for Trickier Markets," *The Wall Street Journal,* December 13, 2007, p. B3 (accessed electronically January 8, 2008).

60. http://ro.unctad.org/infocomm/anglais/orange/market.htm; http://www.tropicana.com/index.asp?ID=27 (accessed January 3, 2008).

61. Daniel Lovering, "Heinz Researchers Cook Up New Food Items," The Associated Press, January 14, 2008.

62. Charles W. L. Hill, *Global Business Today,* 5th ed. (New York: McGraw-Hill/Irwin, 2008).

63. Julie Jargon, "Can M'm, M'm Good Translate?" *The Wall Street Journal,* July 9, 2007, p. A16 (accessed electronically January 9, 2008); "Campbell Outlines Entry Strategy and Product Plans for Russia and China," July 9, 2007, http://investor.shareholder.com/campbell/releasedetail.cfm?releaseid=252914 (accessed January 16, 2008).

64. http://www.pringles.it/ (accessed February 5, 2008).

65. "Nestle to Buy U.S. Baby-Food Giant Gerber," The Associated Press, April 12, 2007 (accessed electronically January 9, 2008).

66. "At a Glance," http://www.nestle.com/AllAbout/AtGlance/KeyDates/KeyDates.htm (accessed January 9, 2008).

67. Mary Anne Raymond, John F. Tanner Jr., and Jonghoon Kim, "Cost Complexity of Pricing Decisions for Exporters in Developing and Emerging Markets," *Journal of International Marketing* 9, no. 3 (2001), pp. 19–40.

68. Amanda J. Broderick, Gordon E. Greenley, and Rene Dentiste Mueller, "The Behavioural Homogeneity Evaluation Framework: Multi-level Evaluations of Consumer Involvement in International Segmentation," *Journal of International Business Studies,* 38 (2007), pp. 746–763; Terry Clark, Masaaki Kotabe, and Dan Rajaratnam, "Exchange Rate Pass-Through and International Pricing Strategy: A Conceptual Framework and Research Propositions," *Journal of International Business Studies* 30, no. 2 (1999), pp. 249–268.

69. "Fashion Conquistador," *BusinessWeek,* September 4, 2006 (accessed electronically January 31, 2008).

70. Jane Wardell, "Whole Foods Aims for British Food Market," *International Business Times,* June 1, 2007 (accessed electronically January 9, 2008).

71. Jos Poels, "Retail Profile: Whole Foods Market Kensington, London," *Elsevier Food International,* September 2007 (accessed electronically January 10, 2008).

72. Kim Murphy, "Whole Foods Enters British Market," *Miami Herald,* June 20, 2007 (accessed electronically January 9, 2008).

73. Loretta Chao, "Chinese Ticket Brokers Go High Tech," *The Wall Street Journal,* November 20, 2007 (accessed electronically January 10, 2008).

74. Satish Shankar, Charles Ormiston, Nicolas Bloch, Robert Schaus, and Vijay Vishwanath, "How to Win in Emerging Markets," *Bain Briefs,* November 29, 2007 (accessed electronically January 9, 2008).

75. http://www.literacyonline.org/explorer/compare.iphtml?ID1=78&ID2=79&ID3=27&ID4=12&ID5=127 (accessed January 8, 2008).

76. http://www.aeforum.org/latest.nsf (accessed September 6, 2007).

77. http://www.brandchannel.com/features_effect.asp?pf_id=274 (accessed September 6, 2007).

78. "China: Online Marketing Comes of Age," *BusinessWeek,* June 12, 2007 (accessed electronically January 10, 2008).

79. Normandy Madden, "Chinese Net Stars Tapped by Brands," *Ad Age China,* September 20, 2006 (accessed electronically January 10, 2008).

80. Loretta Chao and Betsy Mckay, "Pepsi Steps into Coke Realm: Red, China," *The Wall Street Journal,* September 12, 2007, p. B4 (accessed electronically January 9, 2008).

81. Joan Voight, "How to Customize Your U.S. Branding Effort to Work Around the World," *Adweek*, September 3, 2008 (accessed electronically January 9, 2008).

82. http://www.fas.usda.gov/htp/Hort_Circular/2002/02-08/OJ%20FEA.htm (accessed February 5, 2008); George Hager, "Bush Plays Free-Trade Game," *USA Today*, May 2, 2002.

83. Paul Meller, "The W.T.O. Said to Weigh In on Product Names," *The New York Times*, November 18, 2004, p. 1; Mark Jarvis, "Which Bud's for You?" *BrandChannel*, January 5, 2004, http://www.brandchannel.com/start1.asp?fa_id=191 (accessed September 5, 2005); Paul Byrne, "Austrian Court Rules in Favor of Anheuser Busch," *PR Newswire*, December 31, 2004.

84. BBC News, "Disposable Planet," http://news.bbc.co.uk/hi/english/static/in_depth/world/2002/disposable_planet/waste/ (accessed January 31, 2008).

85. Alladi Venkatesh, "Postmodernism Perspective for Macromarketing: An Inquiry into the Global Information and Sign Economy," *Journal of Macromarketing*, 19, no. 12 (1999), pp. 153–169.

86. Michael R. Czinkota and Ilkka A. Ronkainen, "An International Marketing Manifesto," *Journal of International Marketing*, 11, no. 1 (2003), pp. 13–27.

87. Bruce Einhorn, "Apple's Chinese Supply Lines," *BusinessWeek*, January 8, 2008 (accessed electronically January 9, 2008).

88. David Vogel, "Apple's iPod and the Market for Virtue," *San Francisco Chronicle*, August 14, 2006 (accessed electronically January 10, 2008).

89. Arik Hesseldahl, "Apple Answers 'Sweatshop' Claims," *BusinessWeek*, August 21, 2006 (accessed electronically January 9, 2008).

90. "Electronic Industry Code of Conduct," http://www.eicc.info/code.html (accessed January 9, 2008).

91. "Responsible Supplier Management," http://www.apple.com/supplierresponsibility/ (accessed January 9, 2008).

92. http://users.aber.ac.uk/pjm04/linguisticimperialism.html#culturalimperialism (accessed September 6, 2007).

93. Shaghayegh Azimi, "Valentine's Day in Iran," *Frontline World*, February 14, 2006 (accessed electronically January 10, 2008).

94. "Scrambling to Bring Crest to the Masses in China," *BusinessWeek*, June 25, 2007 (accessed electronically January 10, 2008).

95. "The World Factbook: China," https://www.cia.gov/library/publications/the-world-factbook/geos/ch.html (accessed January 9, 2008).

96. "Country Report: China," *The Economist Intelligence Unit*, January 2008 (accessed electronically January 10, 2008).

97. "The World Factbook: China."

Chapter 8

1. "Heritage," http://www.thecoca-colacompany.com/heritage/ourheritage.html (accessed January 14, 2008).

2. "Coca-Cola Announces Plans to Launch Coca-Cola Zero," Coca-Cola Company News Release, March 21, 2005 (accessed electronically January 14, 2008).

3. Betsy McKay, "Zero Is Coke's New Hero," *The Wall Street Journal*, April 17, 2007 (accessed electronically January 14, 2008).

4. "The Chronicle of Coca-Cola," http://www.thecoca-cola-company.com/heritage/chronicle_global_business.html (accessed January 15, 2008).

5. Kate Fitzgerald, "Coke Zero," *Advertising Age*, November 12, 2007 (accessed electronically January 14, 2008).

6. "Brands," http://www.thecoca-colacompany.com/brands/index.html (accessed January 14, 2008).

7. "Coca-Cola Announces Plans to Launch Coca-Cola Zero."

8. "'Coca-Cola' Zero Has Landed Marketing Campaign Set to Boost Nationwide Roll Out," http://www.cokecce.co.uk/cce/news_art.jsp?aid=267 (accessed July 4, 2006).

9. Kate MacArthur, "Coke Bets on Zero to Save Cola Category," *Advertising Age*, January 1, 2007 (accessed electronically January 14, 2008).

10. Marie Driscoll, "Abercrombie & Fitch: Power Shopper," *Standard & Poor's Equity Research*, October 30, 2007 (accessed electronically January 16, 2008).

11. Nicholas Köhler, "Abercrombie and Fitch: Come Shop in Our Dungeon," *Maclean's*, November 13, 2006 (accessed electronically January 16, 2008).

12. Thorsten Blecker, *Mass Customization: Challenges and Solutions* (New York: Springer, 2006); B. Joseph Pine, *Mass Customization: The New Frontier in Business Competition* (Cambridge, MA: Harvard Business School Publishing, 1999); James H. Gilmore and B. Joseph Pine, eds., *Markets of One: Creating Customer-Unique Value through Mass Customization* (Cambridge, MA: Harvard Business School Publishing, 2000).

13. Vanessa O'Connell, "Park Avenue Classic or Soho Trendy?" *The Wall Street Journal*, April 20, 2007.

14. Natalie Y. Moore, "Boutiques Aim to Let Men Enjoy Shopping," *Chicago Tribune*, October 16, 2006 (accessed electronically January 1, 2008); Blanca Torres, "More and More, Men Like Shopping," *Contra Costa Times*, October 12, 2006 (accessed electronically January 1, 2008); Nanette Byrnes, "Secrets of the Male Shopper," *BusinessWeek*, September 4, 2006 (accessed electronically January 1, 2008); Melanie Shortman, "Gender Wars," *American Demographics*, April 2002, p. 22.

15. Banwari Mittal, *Consumer Behavior* (Cincinnati, OH: Open Mentis, 2008); J. Paul Peter and Jerry C. Olson, *Consumer Behavior and Marketing Strategy*, 8th ed. (New York: McGraw-Hill, 2008); Michael R. Solomon, *Consumer Behavior: Buying, Having, and Being*, 7th ed. (Upper Saddle River, NJ: Prentice Hall, 2006); Jagdish Sheth, Banwari Mittal, and Bruce I. Newman, *Customer Behavior: Consumer Behavior and Beyond* (Fort Worth, TX: The Dryden Press, 1999).

16. Chi Kin (Bennett) Yim, Kimmy Wa Chan, and Kineta Hung, "Multiple Reference Effects in Service Evaluations: Role of Alternative Attractiveness and Self-Image Congruity," *Journal of Retailing*, 83, no. 1 (2007), pp. 147–157; Tamara Mangleburg, M. Joseph Sirgy, Dhruv Grewal, Danny Axsom, Maria Hatzios, C. B. Claiborne, and Trina Bogle, "The Moderating Effect of Prior Experience in Consumers' Use of User-Image Based versus Utilitarian Cues in Brand Attitude," *Journal of Business & Psychology*, 13 (Fall 1998), pp. 101–113; M. Joseph Sirgy et al., "Direct versus Indirect Measures of Self-Image Congruence," *Journal of the Academy of Marketing Science*, 25, no. 3 (1997), pp. 229–241.

17. Mittal, *Consumer Behavior*; Peter and Olson, *Consumer Behavior and Marketing Strategy*; Solomon, *Consumer Behavior: Buying, Having, and Being*; Sheth, Mittal, and Newman, *Customer Behavior: Consumer Behavior and Beyond*.

18. Elena Malykhina, "MTV's ThinkMTV, A Socially Conscious Social Network," *Information Week*, September 20, 2007 (accessed electronically January 16, 2008).

19. "Think," http://www.labsblog.mtv.com/2007/09/21/think/comment-page-1/ (accessed January 16, 2008).

20. "MTV Launches First Online Community to Make Youth Famous for Doing Good," http://www.prdomain.com/companies/V/Viacom/newsreleases/200792146424.htm (accessed January 14, 2008).

21. "Who We Are," http://www.mediacsrforum.org/who.jsp (accessed January 16, 2008).

22. Arundhati Parmar, "The Positive Alternative," *Marketing News*, September 1, 2007 (accessed electronically January 14, 2008).

23. "MTV Gives 'The Real World' Green Slant," *Environmental Leader*, August 16, 2007 (accessed electronically January 16, 2008).

24. VALS1, the original lifestyle survey, assessed general values and lifestyles. The VALS survey focuses more on values and lifestyles related to consumer behavior and thus has more commercial applications. Another lifestyle segmentation system is Yankelovich's Monitor Mindbase; see yankelovich.com.

25. www.sric-bi.com/VALS/projects.shtml (accessed April 8, 2008.)

26. "Segmentation and Targeting," http://www.kellogg. northwestern.edu/faculty/sterntha/htm/module2/1.html (accessed January 24, 2008); Michael D. Lam, "Psychographic Demonstration: Segmentation Studies Prepare to Prove Their Worth," *Pharmaceutical Executive*, January 2004.

27. Kathleen Khiralla, "CRM Case Study: The Analytics That Power CRM at Royal Bank [of Canada]," http://www.teradata.com/ library/pdf/towergroup_020701.pdf (accessed January 24, 2008).

28. "flyPhone," http://www.fireflymobile.com/flyphone/ ?osCsid=I64huuvkuv66c55l78d3eg4g75 (accessed January 16, 2008).

29. A.M.Tomczyk,"Firefly Mobile: Calling All Tweens," *BusinessWeek Online*, November 8, 2008.

30. Stowe Shoemaker and Robert Lewis, "Customer Loyalty: The Future of Hospitality Marketing," *Hospitality Management*, 18 (1999), p. 349.

31. Yuping Liu, "The Long-Term Impact of Loyalty Programs on Consumer Purchase Behavior and Loyalty," *Journal of Marketing* 71, no. 4 (October 2007), pp. 19–35; V. Kumar and Denish Shah, "Building and Sustaining Profitable Customer Loyalty for the 21st Century," *Journal of Retailing*, 80, no. 4 (2004), pp. 317–330.

32. http://www.united.com/page/article/0,6722,1171,00.html (accessed September 12, 2006).

33. Chris Reidy, "CVS Ad Campaign's Focus Is Women," *The Boston Globe*, October 9, 2007 (accessed electronically January 15, 2008).

34. Kimberly Palmer, "An Rx for Women," *US News and World Report*, November 1, 2007 (accessed electronically January 15, 2008).

35. Mya Fazier, "Need a Doctor? Try Target or Wal-Mart," *Advertising Age*, November 28, 2005 (accessed electronically January 15, 2008).

36. Bob Garfield, "The Women Who Care for Us All Won't Care for CVS's Sappy Spot," *Advertising Age*, October 29, 2007 (accessed electronically January 15, 2008).

37. "CVS Targets Women in New Ad Campaign," *The Providence Journal*, October 9, 2007 (accessed electronically January 15, 2008).

38. Cannon Consulting, "Growth Specialty Retail Opportunity Retailer Profile: Talbots," February 2005, available at http:// www.naa.org/horizon/specialty_retail/256,1,Growth Specialty Retail Opportunity.

39. "Talbots Will Exit Kids' and Men's Businesses," *The Boston Globe*, January 4, 2008, http://www.boston.com/business/ticker/2008/01/talbots_will_ex.html (accessed January 24, 2008).

40. "Disaboom CEO Donates Stock to Non-Profit Organizations," *Fox Business News*, December 27, 2007 (accessed electronically January 15, 2008).

41. "Disaboom Company Overview: October 2007," http://files. shareholder.com/downloads/DISA/219815542x0x123379/ d90d881f-135e-4d22-923f-f0db20d10328/DSBO%20Company %20Overview.Final.UPDATED.PPT.pdf (accessed January 14, 2008).

42. "About Us," http://aboutus.disaboom.com/About-Us.aspx (accessed January 14, 2008).

43. Bill Radford, "Linking People with Disabilities," *Colorado Springs Gazette*, April 29, 2007 (accessed electronically January 15, 2008).

44. "Disaboom News Releases," http://aboutus.disaboom.com/ Press-Room.aspx (accessed January 15, 2008).

45. Andrew Adam Newman, "Web Marketing to a Segment Too Big to Be a Niche," *The New York Times*, October 30, 2007 (accessed January 15, 2008).

46. Dhruv Grewal, "Marketing Is All About Creating Value: 8 Key Rules," in *Inside the Mind of Textbook Marketing* (Boston, MA: Aspatore Inc., 2003), pp. 79–96.

47. "Frequently Asked Questions," http://corporate.hallmark. com/FAQ/FAQ-About-Hallmark (accessed January 15, 2008).

48. G. R. Iyer, A. D. Miyazaki, D. Grewal, and M. Giordano, "Linking Web-Based Segmentation to Pricing Tactics," *Journal of Product & Brand Management*, 11, no. 5 (2002), pp. 288–302; B. Jaworski and K. Jocz, "Rediscovering the Consumer," *Marketing Management*, September/October 2002, pp. 22–27; L. Rosencrance, "Customers Balk at Variable DVD Pricing," *Computer World*, September 11, 2000, p. 4; M. Stephanek, "None of Your Business: Customer Data Were Once Gold to E-Commerce. Now, Companies Are Paying a Price for Privacy Jitters," *BusinessWeek*, June 26, 2000, p. 78; D. Wessel, "How Technology Tailors Price Tags," *The Wall Street Journal*, June 23, 2001, p. A1.

49. http://www.aa.com/content/AAdvantage/programDetails/ eliteStatus/main.jhtml (accessed March 16, 2008).

50. Jessica Tsai, "Cast a Narrow Net," *Destination CRM*, November 2007 (accessed January 16, 2008).

51. "What's on the Horizon for Marketing to Hispanics," *Marketing News*, September 1, 2007.

52. Vanessa O'Connell, "Fashion Journal: Bubble Gum at Bergdorf's," *The Wall Street Journal*, February 15, 2008 (accessed electronically January 15, 2008).

53. Vanessa O'Connell, "Fashion Bullies Attack—In Middle School," *The Wall Street Journal*, October 25, 2007 (accessed electronically January 15, 2008).

54. Jeanine Poggie, "Designer Brands a High-End Teen Attraction," *Women's Wear Daily*, June 11, 2008 (accessed electronically January 15, 2008).

55. Jack Neff, "Value Positioning Becomes a Priority," *Advertising Age*, 75, no. 8 (2004), p. 24.

56. Stuart Schwartzapfel, "Volvo S80: Playing It Too Safe?" *BusinessWeek*, July 23, 2007; Jean Halliday, "Maloney Wants Volvo Viewed as Both Safe and Luxurious," *Advertising Age*, 75, no. 12 (2004), p. 22.

57. Ellen Byron, "To Refurbish Its Image, Tiffany Risks Profits," *The Wall Street Journal*, January 10, 2007 (accessed electronically February 12, 2008).

58. This case was written by Colin Fox in conjunction with the textbook authors (Dhruv Grewal and Michael Levy) for class discussion rather than to illustrate either effective or ineffective marketing practice.

59. Dexter Roberts, "China Mobile's Hot Signal," *BusinessWeek*, February 5, 2007 (accessed electronically January 18, 2008).

60. Janet Ong, "China Mobile Profit Surges 29%," *China Daily*, August 17, 2007 (accessed electronically January 17, 2008).

61. "Business Review," http://www.chinamobileltd.com/ op.php?menu=3 (accessed January 18, 2008).

62. Dexter Roberts, "China Mobile: Everything to Everyone," *BusinessWeek,* July 6, 2007 (accessed electronically January 17, 2008).

63. Frederik Balfour, "China Mobile Is Growing Rural," *BusinessWeek,* December 20, 2006 (accessed electronically January 18, 2008).

64. Clay Chandler, "China's Mobile Maestro," *Fortune,* July 31, 2007 (accessed electronically January 18, 2008).

65. "IT 100 Special Report 2006: 8 China Mobile," *BusinessWeek,* July 3, 2006 (accessed electronically January 17, 2008).

66. Roberts, "China Mobile's Hot Signal."

67. "Business Review."

68. "China Mobile's CEO Talks Expansion," *BusinessWeek Online,* February 5, 2007 (accessed electronically January 18, 2008).

69. "Business Review."

Chapter 9

1. "About McDonald's . . . ," http://mcdonalds.com/corp/about.html (accessed January 18, 2008).

2. Zachary Lewis, "New Look Coming to a Local McDonald's," *The Plain Dealer,* October 19, 2007 (accessed electronically January 23, 2008).

3. "Innovators Summit: Abstracts," http://www.jmp.com/about/events/summit2007/abstracts.shtml (accessed January 23, 2008).

4. Amy Choate-Nielsen, "New McDonald's Goes Upscale," *Deseret Morning News,* March 25, 2007 (accessed electronically January 23, 2008).

5. Pallavi Gogoi, Michael Arndt, and Abed Moiduddin, "Mickey D's McMakeover," *BusinessWeek,* May 15, 2006 (accessed electronically January 21, 2008).

6. A. Parasuraman, Dhruv Grewal, and R. Krishnan, *Marketing Research,* 2nd ed. (Boston: Houghton Mifflin, 2007), p. 9.

7. http://www.marketingpower.com/content19685.php (accessed electronically January 22, 2008).

8. "About Us," http://www.overstock.com (accessed January 31, 2008).

9. Richard H. Levey, "Letter Perfect," *Direct,* March 1, 2007 (accessed electronically January 31, 2008).

10. Jessica Vascellaro, "Online Retailers Are Watching You," *The Wall Street Journal,* November 28, 2006.

11. Thomas Claburn, "GE Money Backup Tape with 650,000 Records Missing at Iron Mountain," *InformationWeek,* January 18, 2008 (accessed electronically January 31, 2008).

12. Bill Brenner, "Data Breach Costs Soar," SecuritySearch.com, November 29, 2007 (accessed January 31, 2008), attributed to the Ponemon Institute.

13. http://www.copia.com/tcpa/ (accessed January 16, 2008).

14. Lona M. Farr, "Whose Files Are They Anyway? Privacy Issues for the Fundraising Profession," *International Journal of Nonprofit and Voluntary Sector Marketing,* 7, no. 4 (November 2002), p. 361.

15. http://www.whirlpool.com/home.jsp (accessed January 16, 2008); Parasuraman, Grewal, and Krishnan, *Marketing Research;* Greg Steinmetz and Carl Quintanilla, "Whirlpool Expected Easy Going in Europe, and It Got a Big Shock," *The Wall Street Journal,* April 10, 1998, pp. A1, A6.

16. "AquaSteam," http://www.whirlpool.co.uk/app.cnt/whr/en_GB/pageid/pgdswprmhome001/rqpg/detail/id/293 (accessed February 5, 2008).

17. Relative market share = brand's market share ÷ largest competitor's market share. If, for instance, there are only two products in a market, A and B, and product B has 90 percent market share, then A's relative market share is 10 ÷ 90 = 11.1 percent. If, on the other hand, B only has 50 percent market share, then A's relative market share is 10 ÷ 50 = 20 percent. Paul W. Farris, Neil T. Bendle, Phillip E. Pfeifer, and David J. Reibstein, *Marketing Metrics: 50+ Metrics Every Executive Should Master* (Philadelphia: Wharton School Publishing, 2006), p. 19.

18. "CVS Press Kit—ExtraCare," http://www.phx.corporate-ir.net/phoenix.zhtml?c=183405&p=irol-cvsextracare (accessed February 1, 2008).

19. Bill Brohaugh, "Three Women," *Colloquy,* Summer 2007 (accessed electronically January 30, 2008).

20. http://www.marketingpower.com/live/content19312.php (accessed July 16, 2005); http://www.infores.com/public/us/default.htm (accessed July 16, 2005); "Sophisticated Data Gives Insights into What's Shaping the H&BA Market," *Chain Drug Review,* 26, no. 11 (June 21, 2004), p. 211; "Are You Season-Savvy? Celebrate the Opportunity to Manage Seasonal Candy Sales More Strategically," *Confectioner,* 89, no. 3 (April 2004), p. 38.

21. "Company Overview," http://us.infores.com/page/about/company_overview (accessed January 29, 2008).

22. Sheila McCusker, "Private Label 2007: U.S. & Europe," *Times and Trends,* October 2007 (accessed electronically February 4, 2008).

23. Linda Tischler, "Every Move You Make," *Fast Company,* 81 (April 2004), p. 73; "Miller Launches Beer in Fridge Pack Cans," August 2004, http://www.foodproductiondaily.com; Richard Elliot and Nick Janket-Elliot, "Using Ethnography in Strategic Consumer Research," *Qualitative Market Research,* 6, no. 4 (2003), p. 215; http://www.envirosell.com/case_studies.html# (accessed September 20, 2006).

24. Becky Ebencamp, "People: Gilding Offers In: site to Agencies," *Brandweek,* November 6, 2006 (accessed electronically February 2, 2008).

25. Kate Maddox, "Marketers Focus on Behavior with Help from Anthropologists and Documentary Filmmakers," *B to B,* April 3, 2006 (accessed electronically February 2, 2008).

26. "Our Brands," http://www.jny.com/brand.jsp?event=brands (accessed February 2, 2008).

27. Ross Tucker, "L.E.I. Gets New Look for Back-to-School," *Women's Wear Daily,* July 5, 2007 (accessed electronically February 2, 2008).

28. Allison Fass, "Collective Opinion," Forbes.com, November 11, 2005.

29. Richard Siklos, "Not in the Real World Anymore," *The New York Times,* September 18, 2006 (accessed electronically February 5, 2008).

30. http://vmtv.com.

31. "User Experience Testing," http://www.mauronewmedia.com/testing/virtual-reality.php (accessed February 5, 2008).

32. Louise Story, "Coke Promotes Itself in a New Virtual World," *The New York Times,* December 7, 2008 (accessed electronically February 5, 2008).

33. Daniel Terdimanu, "A Winning Business Plan for 'Second Life,'" CNet News.com, February, 19, 2007 (accessed February 5, 2008).

34. Stanley E. Griffis, Thomas J. Goldsby, and Martha Cooper, "Web-Based and Mail Surveys: A Comparison of Response, Data and Cost," *Journal of Business Logistics,* 24, no. 2 (2003), pp. 237–259; Chris Gautreau, "Getting the Answers," *The Greater Baton Rouge Business Report,* 22, no. 29 (September 28, 2004), p. 17; Alf Nucifora, "Weaving Web Surveys That Work," *njbiz,* 15, no. 46 (November 11, 2002), p. 28.

35. Detailed illustrations of scales are provided in these two books: Gordon C. Bruner, Karen E. James, and Paul J. Hensel, *Marketing Scales Handbook,* Volume IV: *A Compilation of Multi-Item Measures* (Mason, OH: South-Western, 2005); Willian O. Bearden and Richard G. Netemeyer, *Handbook of Marketing Scales: Multi-Item Measures for Marketing and Consumer Behavior Research* (Thousand Oaks, CA: Sage Publications, 1999). Sources for the scales used in the exhibit are: Dhruv Grewal, Gopalkrishnan Iyer, Jerry Gotlieb, and Michael Levy, "Developing a Deeper Understanding of Post-Purchase Perceived Risk and Repeat Purchase Behavioral Intentions in a Service Setting," *Journal of the Academy of Marketing Science,* 35, no. 2 (2007), pp. 250–258; Anthony Miyazaki, Dhruv Grewal, and Ronald C. Goodstein, "The Effect of Multiple Extrinsic Cues on Quality Perceptions: A Matter of Consistency," *Journal of Consumer Research,* 32 (June 2005), pp. 146–153; Dhruv Grewal, Joan Lindsey-Mullikin, and Jeanne Munger, "Loyalty in e-Tailing: A Conceptual Framework," *Journal of Relationship Marketing,* 2, no. 3–4 (2003), pp. 31–49; Julie Baker, A. Parasuraman, Dhruv Grewal, and Glenn Voss, "The Influence of Multiple Store Environment Cues on Perceived Merchandise Value and Patronage Intentions," *Journal of Marketing,* 66 (April 2002), pp. 120–141; Dhruv Grewal, Kent B. Monroe, and R. Krishnan, "The Effects of Price Comparison Advertising on Buyers' Perceptions of Acquisition Value and Transaction Value," *Journal of Marketing,* 62 (April 1998), pp. 46–60; Jerry B. Gotlieb, Dhruv Grewal, and Stephen W. Brown, "Consumer Satisfaction and Perceived Quality: Complementary or Divergent Constructs?" *Journal of Applied Psychology,* 79, no. 6 (1994), pp. 875–885; Parasuraman, Grewal, and Krishnan, *Marketing Research.*

36. Gary Loveman, "Diamonds in the Data Mine," *Harvard Business Review* 81, no. 5 (May 2003), pp. 109–13; http://www.harrahs.com (accessed September 20, 2006); Thomas Hoffman, "Harrah's Bets on Loyalty Program in Caesars Deal," computerworld.com, June 27, 2005 (accessed February 22, 2006).

37. http://www.harrahs.com (accessed February 5, 2008).

38. Sudhir H. Kale and Peter Klugsberger, "Reaping Rewards," *Marketing Management,* July/August 2007.

39. Gary Loveman, "Diamonds in the Data Mine," Harvard Business Review 81, no. 5 (May 2003), pp. 109–13; http://www.harrahs.com (accessed September 20, 2006); Hoffman, Thomas, "Harrah's Bets on Loyalty Program in Caesars Deal," computerworld.com, June 27, 2005 (accessed February 22, 2006).

40. "About Cablecom," http://www.cablecom.ch/en/wirueberuns.htm (accessed February 5, 2008).

41. "Cablecom," http://www.spss.com/success/template_view.cfm?Story_ID=208 (accessed February 5, 2008).

42. For a more thorough discussion of effective written reports, see Parasuraman, Grewal, and Krishnan, *Marketing Research,* chapter 16.

43. This case was written by Colin Fox in conjunction with the textbook authors Dhruv Grewal and Michael Levy as the basis of class discussion rather than to illustrate either effective or ineffective marketing practices.

44. Maureen Nevin Duffy, "Cantor Fitzgerald's Virtual Trading Platform Helps Film Producers Project Their Grosses," *Securities Industry News,* September 3, 2007 (accessed electronically February 5, 2008).

45. "Nielsen NRG," http://www.nielsen.com/solutions/nrg.html (accessed February 5, 2008).

46. Parasuraman, Grewal, and Krishnan, *Marketing Research.*

47. "Corporate Overview," http://www.hsxresearch.com/corporate_overview.htm (accessed February 5, 2008).

48. Anita Elberse and Bharat Anand, "The Effectiveness of Pre-Release Advertising for Motion Pictures: An Empirical Investigation Using a Simulated Market," *Information Economics and Policy,* July 10, 2007 (accessed electronically February 5, 2008).

Appendix 9A

1. V. Kumar, A. Petersen and R. P. Leone, "How Valuable Is the Word of Mouth?" *Harvard Business Review,* October 2007, pp. 139–146; V. Kumar and Morris George, "Measuring and Maximizing Customer Equity: A Critical Analysis," *Journal of the Academy of Marketing Science,* 35, no. 2 (June 2007), pp. 157–171; V. Kumar, Denish Shah, and Rajkumar Venkatesan, "Managing Retailer Profitability: One Customer at a Time!" *Journal of Retailing,* 82, no. 4 (October 2006), pp. 277–294; V. Kumar, "Profitable Relationships," *Marketing Research: A Magazine of Management and Applications,* 18, no. 3 (Fall 2006), pp. 41–46; V. Kumar, "Customer Lifetime Value: A Databased Approach," *Journal of Relationship Marketing,* 5, no. 2/3 (2006), pp. 7–35; Sunil Gupta, Dominique Hanssens, Bruce Hardie, William Kahn, V. Kumar, Nathaniel Lin, Nalini Ravishanker, and S. Sriram, "Modeling Customer Lifetime Value," *Journal of Service Research,* 9 (November 2006), pp. 139–155; V. Kumar, R. Venkatesan, and Werner Reinartz, "Knowing What to Sell, When and to Whom," *Harvard Business Review,* March, 2006, pp. 131–137; Werner Reinartz, J. Thomas, and V. Kumar, "Balancing Acquisition and Retention Resources to Maximize Profitability," *Journal of Marketing,* 69 (January 2005), pp. 63–79; R. Venkatesan and V. Kumar, "A Customer Lifetime Value Framework for Customer Selection and Resource Allocation Strategy," *Journal of Marketing,* 68 (October 2004), pp. 106–125; V. Kumar and J. Andrew Petersen, "Maximizing ROI or Profitability: Is One Better than the Other," *Marketing Research: A Magazine of Management and Applications,* 16, no. 3 (Fall 2004), pp. 28–34; V. Kumar, G. Ramani, and T. Bohling, "Customer Lifetime Value Approaches and Best Practice Applications," *Journal of Interactive Marketing* 18, no. 3 (Summer 2004), pp. 60–72; J. Thomas, Werner Reinartz, and V. Kumar, "Getting the Most out of All Your Customers," *Harvard Business Review* (July–August 2004), pp. 116–123; Werner Reinartz and V. Kumar, "The Impact of Customer Relationship Characteristics on Profitable Lifetime Duration," *Journal of Marketing,* 67 (January 2003), pp. 77–99; Werner Reinartz and V. Kumar, "The Mismanagement of Customer Loyalty," *Harvard Business Review* (July 2002), pp. 86–97; W. Reinartz and V. Kumar, "On the Profitability of Long Lifetime Customers: An Empirical Investigation and Implications for Marketing," *Journal of Marketing,* 64 (October 2000), pp. 17–32.

2. We have made some minor adjustments to the formula suggested by Gupta et al., "Modeling Customer Lifetime Value."

3. Sunil Gupta and Donald R. Lehmann, *Managing Customers as Investments* (Philadelphia, PA: Wharton School Publishing, 2005); Gupta et al., "Modeling Customer Lifetime Value."

Chapter 10

1. "Jordan Brand History," www.sneakerhead.com (accessed January 28, 2007).

2. Rigel Gregg, "Michael Jordan's Pricey and Sustainable Sneakers," January 10, 2008, http://www.luxist.com/2008/01/10/michael-jordans-pricey-and-sustainable-sneakers/ (accessed January 28, 2008).

3. Lisa DeCarlo, "With Tiger Woods, It's Nike, Nike Everywhere," http://www.msnbc.msn.com/id/4554944/ (accessed January 28, 2007).

4. American Marketing Association, *Dictionary of Marketing Terms* (Chicago: American Marketing Association), available at http://www.marketingpower.com/live/mg-dictionary-view329.php? (accessed December 21, 2007).

5. "All Colgate Toothpastes," http://www.colgate.com (accessed December February 1, 2008).

6. Kostas Axarloglou, "Product Line Extensions: Causes and Effects," *Managerial & Decision Economics,* 29, no. 1 (2008), pp. 9–21; Michaela Draganska and Dipak C. Jain, "Product-Line Length as a Competitive Tool," *Journal of Economics & Management Strategy,* 14, no. 1 (2005), pp. 1–28; William P. Putsis Jr. and Barry L. Bayus, "An Empirical Analysis of Firms' Product Line Decisions," *Journal of Marketing Research,* 38, no. 1 (February 2001), pp. 110–118.

7. Bruce G. S. Hardie and Leonard M. Lodish, "Perspectives: The Logic of Product-Line Extensions," *Harvard Business Review,* November–December 1994, p. 54; Kate MacArthur, "Pepsi Goes on $55 mil Binge for Diet Max," *Advertising Age,* June 25, 2007.

8. Paraskevas C. Argouslidis and George Baltas, "Structure in Product Line Management: The Role of Formalization in Service Elimination Decisions," *Journal of the Academy of Marketing Science,* 35, no. 4 (2007), pp. 475–491; John A. Quelch and David Kenny, "Extend Profits, Not Product Lines," *Harvard Business Review,* September–October 1994, pp. 153–160.

9. Simon Pittman, "Revlon Switches CEO as Pressure Mounts over Performance," http://www.cosmeticsdesign.com/news/ng.asp?n=70686-revlon-ceo-stahl-vital-radiance (accessed January 28, 2008).

10. "True Religion Unveils Handbags at Vegas Trade Show," www.reuters.com (accessed August 28, 2007).

11. Elizabeth Gillespie, "Starbucks Axes Sandwiches as Part of Fix," Associated Press, January 31, 2008, http://ap.google.com/article/ALeqM5j8VQuhjO_4goc_oXvyrtQRdAgF3wD8UGLEMOo (accessed January 31, 2008).

12. Molly Knight, "Cold Competition," *Shopping Centers Today,* February 2008.

13. www.band-aid.com (accessed March 15, 2008).

14. "Discontinued Products List," http://www.mccormick.com/content.cfm?id=12157 (accessed February 2, 2008); http://media.corporate-ir.net/media_files/irol/65/65454/reports/AR2007/27.html (accessed March 15, 2008).

15. http://newsroom.bankofamerica.com/index.php?s=press_releases&item=7964 (accessed January 29, 2008).

16. http://www.bankofamerica.com/deposits/checksave/index.cfm (accessed January 29, 2008).

17. Kevin Lane Keller, *Strategic Brand Management: Building, Measuring, and Managing Brand Equity,* 2nd ed. (Upper Saddle River, NJ: Prentice Hall, 2003).

18. This discussion of the advantages of strong brands is adapted from Keller, *Strategic Brand Management,* pp. 104–112; Elizabeth S. Moore, William L. Wilkie, and Richard J. Lutz, "Passing the Torch: Intergenerational Influences as a Source of Brand Equity," *Journal of Marketing,* 66, no. 2 (2002), p. 17.

19. Angela Y. Lee and Aparna A. Labroo, "The Effect of Conceptual and Perceptual Fluency on Brand Evaluation," *Journal of Marketing Research,* 41, no. 2 (2002), pp. 151–165.

20. Elva Ramirez, "Fashion's Elite Expand Online," *The Wall Street Journal,* August 11, 2007 (accessed electronically April 8, 2008).

21. Linda Rosencrance, "American Airlines Sues Google over Keyword Ads," http://www.computerworld.com/action/article.do?command=viewArticleBasic&articleId=9031218, August 17, 2007 (accessed January 31, 2008).

22. http://www.ourfishbowl.com/images/surveys/Interbrand_BGB_2007.pdf (accessed March 15, 2008). The net present value of the earnings over the next 12 months is used to calculate the value.

23. David Aaker, *Brand Portfolio Strategy: Creating Relevance, Differentiation, Energy, Leverage, and Clarity* (New York: Free Press, 2004); David A. Aaker, *Managing Brand Equity* (New York: Free Press, 1991).

24. Polo Ralph Lauren Corporate Annual Report 2007, available at http://library.corporate-ir.net/library/65/659/65933/items/251536/rl_07ar.pdf (accessed March 15, 2008).

25. Keller, *Strategic Brand Management: Building, Measuring, and Managing Brand Equity.*

26. David Aaker, *Building Strong Brands* (New York: Simon & Schuster, 2002); David A. Aaker, "Measuring Brand Equity Across Products and Markets," *California Management Review,* 38 (1996), pp. 102–120.

27. Keller, *Strategic Brand Management: Building, Measuring, and Managing Brand Equity.*

28. Paul R. La Monica, "Super Prices for Super Bowl Ads," CNNMoney.com, January 3, 2007.

29. Elizabeth A. Smith and Ruth E. Malone, "Altria Means Tobacco: Philip Morris's Identity Crisis," *American Journal of Public Health,* 93, no. 4 (2003), pp. 553–556; www.altriameanstobacco.com (accessed March 16, 2008).

30. Kara G. Morrison, "Chic on the Cheap," *The Detroit News,* February 15, 2008; http://www.fxmagazine.co.uk/story.asp?storyCode=1632 (accessed March 15, 2008).

31. http://www.nyama.org/initiatives/mhof_hallmark.cfm (accessed March 16, 2008).

32. Rohir Bhargava, *Personality Not Included: Why Companies Lose Their Authenticity and How Great Brands Get It Back* (New York: McGraw Hill, 2008); Jennifer L. Aaker, "Dimensions of Brand Personality," *Journal of Marketing Research,* 34, no. 3 (1997), pp. 347–356.

33. Kevin Lane Keller, "Conceptualizing, Measuring, and Managing Customer-Based Brand Equity," *Journal of Marketing,* 57, no. 1 (1993), pp. 1–22.

34. Dave Larson, "Building a Brand's Personality from the Customer Up," *Direct Marketing,* October 2002, pp. 17–21.

35. Julia Werdigier, "To Woo Europeans, McDonald's Goes Upscale," *The New York Times,* August 25, 2007.

36. http://www.marketingpower.com/live/mg-dictionary.php?SearchFor=brand+loyalty&Searched=1 (accessed September 17, 2006).

37. Michael Ozanian and Peter Schwartz, "We're No. 1: The World's Most Valuable Sports Brands," *Forbes,* September 27, 2007, http://www.forbes.com/2007/09/26/sports-brands-teams-biz-sports_cz_mo_0927sportsbrands.html (accessed January 28, 2008).

38. Manchester United, www.manutd.com (accessed January 29, 2008).

39. Jonathan Birchall, "Just Do It, Marketers Say," *Financial Times,* April 30, 2007 (accessed electronically January 11, 2008).

40. http://www.tide.com/en_US/index.jsp (accessed January 30, 2008); Constantine von Hoffman, "P&G's Latest Entry Joins Recent Tide of Extensions," dlmediaroundup.blogspot.com/2007/03/extensions-p-latest-entry-joins-recent.html (accessed January 30, 2008); Christine Bittar, "Big Brands: Stronger Than Dirt," *BrandWeek,* June 23, 2003, pp. S52–S53.

41. This section draws from Michael Levy and Barton A. Weitz, *Retailing Management,* 7th ed. (Burr Ridge, IL: McGraw-Hill/Irwin), chapter 14.

42. http://www2.acnielsen.com/news/20030916.shtml (accessed March 19, 2008).

43. Nirmalya Kumar and Jan-Benedict E.M. Steenkamp, "Premium Store Brands: The Hottest Trend in Retailing," in *Private Label Strategy: How to Meet the Store Brand Challenge* (Cambridge, MA: Harvard Business School Press, February 2007).

44. Ibid.

45. Mark Bergen, Shantanu Dutta, and Steven Shugan, "Branded Variants: A Retail Perspective," *Journal of Marketing Research,* February 1996, pp. 9–20.

46. http://www.forbes.com/businesswire/feeds/business-wire/2008/03/15/businesswire20080314005915r1.html (accessed March 15, 2008).

47. Teresa F. Lindeman, "Brands Expand: Retailers Work to Create Exclusive Products to Set Themselves Apart," *Pittsburgh Post-Gazette,* March 19, 2008, accessed electronically.

48. Ibid.

49. Clint Engel, "Serta to Make Furniture First Private Label Line," *Furniture Today,* January 11, 2008.

50. http://www.pg.com (accessed March 18, 2008).

51. Renee Alexander, "A Brand by Any Other Name," http://www.brandchannel.com, September 11, 2006 (accessed January 31, 2008).

52. For recent research on brand extensions, see Byung Chul Shine, Jongwon Park, and Robert S. Wyer, "Brand Synergy Effects in Multiple Brand Extensions," *Journal of Marketing Research,* 44, no. 4 (2007), pp. 663–670; Gochen Wu and Yung-Ghien Yen, "How the Strength of Parent Brand Associations Influences the Interaction Effects of Brand Breadth and Product Similarity with Brand Extension Evaluations," *Journal of Product & Brand Management,* 16, no. 4–5 (2007), pp. 334–341; Franziska Volckner and Henrik Sattler, "Drivers of Brand Extension Success," *Journal of Marketing,* 70, no. 2 (2006), pp. 18–34; Subramanian Balachander and Sanjoy Ghose, "Reciprocal Spillover Effects: A Strategic Benefit of Brand Extensions," *Journal of Marketing,* 67, no. 1 (2003), pp. 4–13; Kalpesh Kaushik Desai and Kevin Lane Keller, "The Effects of Ingredient Branding Strategies on Host Brand Extendibility," *Journal of Marketing,* 66, no. 1 (2002), pp. 73–93; Tom Meyvis and Chris Janiszewski, "When Are Broader Brands Stronger Brands? An Accessibility Perspective on the Success of Brand Extensions," *Journal of Consumer Research,* 31, no. 2 (2004), pp. 346–357.

53. David Aaker, "Brand Extensions: The Good, the Bad, and the Ugly," *Sloan Management Review,* 31 (Summer 1990), pp. 47–56.

54. http://www.braun.com (accessed December 19, 2007).

55. http://www.dell.com (accessed December 19, 2007).

56. Vanitha Swaminathan, Richard J. Fox, and Srinivas K. Reddy, "The Impact of Brand Extension Introduction on Choice," *Journal of Marketing,* 65, no. 3 (2001), pp. 1–15.

57. http://www.fritolay.com/consumer.html (accessed December 19, 2007).

58. http://corporate.disney.go.com/investors/fact_books/2007/book.html (accessed March 29, 2008).

59. Merissa Marr, "Fairy-Tale Wedding? Disney Can Supply the Gown," *The Wall Street Journal,* February 22, 2007.

60. Susan Gunelius, "Disney Extends Its Brand Presence Everywhere," www.brandcurve.com (accessed July 1, 2007).

61. Jennifer Aaker, Susan Fournier, and S. Adam Brasel, "When Good Brands Do Bad," *Journal of Consumer Research,* 31, no. 1 (2004), pp. 1–16.

62. Barbara Loken and Deborah Roedder John, "Diluting Brand Beliefs: When Do Brand Extensions Have a Negative Impact?" *Journal of Marketing,* 57, no. 3 (1993), pp. 71–84.

63. http://www.virgin.com (accessed January 30, 2008).

64. Costas Hadjicharalambous, "A Typology of Brand Extensions: Positioning Cobranding as a Sub-Case of Brand Extensions," *Journal of American Academy of Business,* 10, no. 1 (2006), pp. 372–377; David A. Aaker and Kevin Lane Keller, "Consumer Evaluations of Brand Extensions," *Journal of Marketing,* 54, no. 1 (1990), pp. 27–41.

65. Kenneth Hein, "A Look Back: Line Extensions That Crossed the Line in 07," *Brandweek,* December 10, 2007; http://www.brandweek.com/bw/news/recent_display.jsp?vnu_content_id=1003683002 (accessed January 30, 2008).

66. Raisa Yakimova and Michael Beverland, "The Brand-Supportive Firm: An Exploration of Organisational Drivers of Brand Updating," *Journal of Brand Management,* 12, no. 6 (2005), pp. 445–460; Susan M. Broniarczyk and Joseph W. Alba, "The Importance of the Brand in Brand Extension," *Journal of Marketing Research,* 31, no. 2 (1994), pp. 214–228.

67. Hein, "A Look Back."

68. http://www.ritzcarlton.com/corporate/about_us/history.asp (accessed September 16, 2006).

69. Michael H Jalili, "Potential Seen in Small-Business Cobranding Pacts," *American Banker,* 172, no. 173 (2007), p. 8; Kate Fitzgerald, "A New Addition to Cobranding's Menu," *Credit Card Management,* 16 (November 2003), pp. 40–44.

70. This section is based on Akshay R. Rao and Robert W. Ruekert, "Brand Alliances as Signals of Product Quality," *Sloan Management Review,* 36 (Fall 1994), pp. 87–97.

71. http://www.syncmyride.com/default.aspx?UserCulture=en-US#/home/ (accessed February 1, 2008).

72. "FedEx Expands Alliance with Kinko's," *Journal of Commerce,* August 11, 2000, p. WP.

73. "FedEx and Kinko's to Deliver Increased Threat," *DSN Retailing Today,* May 17, 2004, p. 17.

74. "FedEx Kinko's and Adobe Collaborate to Deliver Print on Demand," press release, June 6, 2007, http://www.adobe.com/aboutadobe/pressroom/pressreleases/200706/060607FedExKinkos.html (accessed February 1, 2008).

75. John Loiacono, "Adobe and FedEx Kinko's Update," August 1, 2007, http://blogs.adobe.com/johnnyl/2007/08/adobe_and_fedex_kinkos_update.html (February 1, 2008); Rebecca Buckman and Corey Dade, "Adobe-FedEx Link Pushes a Hot Button," *The Wall Street Journal,* July 30, 2007.

76. T. Kippenberger, "Co-Branding as a Competitive Weapon," *Strategic Direction,* 18, no. 10 (2002), pp. 31–33.

77. Tom Blacket and Bob Boad, eds., *Co-Branding: The Science of Alliance* (London: Macmillan Press, 1999).

78. Piyush Kumar, "The Impact of Cobranding on Customer Evaluation of Brand Counterextensions," *Journal of Marketing,* 69, no. 3 (2005), pp. 1–18; David A. Aaker, *Brand Portfolio Strategy* (New York: The Free Press, 2004).

79. Keller, *Strategic Brand Management: Building, Measuring, and Managing Brand Equity.*

80. Doug Desjardins, "LIMA Foresees Huge 2nd Half for Entertainment Properties," *DSN Retailing Today,* June 21, 2004, pp. 6, 37.

81. Stacy Meichtry, "Armani Links with Samsung for Electronics Line," *The Wall Street Journal,* September 24, 2007.

82. Keller, *Strategic Brand Management: Building, Measuring, and Managing Brand Equity.*

83. http://www.lacoste.com/usa/.

84. Dwight Oestricher, "Marvel: Powerhouse Potential? Other Heroes Spawned by Spider-Man Creator Could Pay Off," *The Wall Street Journal,* May 8, 2002, p. B9 ff.

85. Yakimova and Beverland, "The Brand-Supportive Firm"; Stephen Brown, Robert V. Kozinets, and John F. Sherry Jr., "Teaching Old Brands New Tricks: Retro Branding and the Revival of Brand Meaning," *Journal of Marketing*, 67, no. 2 (2003), p. 19.

86. www.fragrancex.com/products/_bid_Abercrombie---am---Fitch-am-cid_perfume-am-lid_A__brand_history.html (accessed March 17, 2008).

87. Rick Spence, "Don't Let Your Brand Stray from the Herd," *Financial Post*, March 10, 2008; Sangeeta Mulchand, "Category Report: Shampoo," *Media*, September 22, 2006; "P&G Aims to Clean Up," *Marketing Week*, January 19, 2006.

88. Kate Bertrand, "Marketing Misfires," www.brandpackaging.com, August 2005.

89. Simon Pitman, "Cenveo Makes Move into Cosmetics Industry," www.cosmeticsdesign.com, January 2, 2008; http://www.cpcp-kg.com/magazine/07_11_sample_packaging.php (accessed March 19, 2008); William Makely, "Being the Beauty, Being the Brand," *Global Cosmetic Industry*, January 2004, pp. 28–30.

90. http://www2.dupont.com/Packaging/en_US/news_events/19th_dupont_packaging_award_winners.html (accessed March 19, 2008).

91. "MarketLooks: Ready Meals & Side Dishes," *PackagedFacts*, May 2004, http://www.packagedfacts.com; Deborah Ball, Sarah Ellison, Janet Adamy, and Geoffrey A. Fowler, "Recipes without Borders?" *The Wall Street Journal*, August 18, 2004.

92. "Expert: Many Underestimate Calories," November 18, 2007, http://www.cbsnews.com/stories/2007/11/16/60minutes/main3513549.shtml (accessed February 1, 2008).

93. This case was written by Jeanne L. Munger and Julie Rusch in conjunction with the textbook authors Dhruv Grewal and Michael Levy as the basis of class discussion rather than to illustrate either effective or ineffective marketing practices. Jeanne Munger is an associate professor at the University of Southern Maine.

94. "O-T-C Health Care: United States Over-the-Counter Heath Care Product Sales in Dollars and Percent Change for 2003," *Chain Drug Review*, May 24, 2004, p. 32; http://www.bandaid.com/brand_story.shtml; http://www.bandaid.com/new_products.shtml; Christine Bittar, "J&J Stuck on Expanding BAND-AID® Franchise," *Brandweek*, March 3, 2003, p. 4; "United States Top 10 First Aid Tape/Bandages/Gauze Brands Ranked by Dollar Sales and Unit Volume for 2003," *Chain Drug Review*, June 21, 2004, p. 238; Richard Gutwillig, "Billion-Dollar Bandages," *Supermarket Business*, August 15, 2000, p. 58; Andrea M. Grossman, "Personal and Beauty Care: News Bites," *Drug Store News*, January 11, 1999, p. 61.

95. http://www.bandaid.com/ourProducts.jsp (accessed March 29, 2008).

96. Christine Bittar, "J&J Stuck on Expanding Band-Aid Franchise," *Brandweek* 44, no. 9 (March 3, 2003), p. 4.

Chapter 11

1. http://www.inventables.com (accessed January 28, 2008).

2. http://www.dove.com (accessed January 28, 2008).

3. Koen Pauwels, Jorge Silva-Risso, Shuba Srinivasan, and Dominique M. Hanssens, "New Products, Sales Promotions, and Firm Value: The Case of the Automobile Industry," *Journal of Marketing*, 68, no. 4 (2008), p. 142.

4. Andrea Morales, Barbara E. Kahn, Cynthia Huffman, Leigh McAlister, and Susan M. Bronizrszyk, "Perceptions of Assortment Variety: The Effects of Congruency between Consumer's Internal and Retailer's External Organization," *Journal of Retailing*, 81, no. 2 (2005), pp. 159–169.

5. Kalpesh Kaushik Desai and Kevin Lane Keller, "The Effects of Ingredient Branding Strategies on Host Brand Extendibility," *Journal of Marketing*, 66, no. 1 (2002), pp. 73–93.

6. Rajesh K. Chandy, Jaideep C. Prabhu, and Kersi D. Antia, "What Will the Future Bring? Dominance, Technology Expectations, and Radical Innovation," *Journal of Marketing*, 67, no. 3 (2003), pp. 1–18; Harald J. van Heerde, Carl F. Mela, and Puneet Manchanda, "The Dynamic Effect of Innovation on Market Structure," *Journal of Marketing Research*, 41, no. 2 (2004), pp. 166–183.

7. Angus Loten, "The iPhone Economy Emerges," Inc.com, June 1, 2007 (accessed January 30, 3008); Clayton M. Christensen and Michael E. Raynor, *The Innovator's Solution* (Boston: Harvard Business School Press, 2003).

8. James L. Oakley, Adam Duhachek, Subramanian Balachander, and S. Sriram, "Order of Entry and the Moderating Role of Comparison Brands in Brand Extension Evaluation," *Journal of Consumer Research*, 34, no. 5 (2008), pp. 706–712; Fernando F. Suarez and Gianvito Lanzolla, "Considerations for a Stronger First Mover Advantage Theory," *Academy of Management Review*, 33, no. 1 (2008), pp. 269–270; Ralitza Nikolaeva, "The Dynamic Nature of Survival Determinants in E-commerce," *Journal of the Academy of Marketing Science*, 35, no. 4 (2007), pp. 560–571; Philip Kotler, *Marketing Management*, 11th ed. (Upper Saddle River, NJ: Prentice-Hall, 2003), pp. 330–331; G. S. Carpenter and Kent Nakamoto, "Consumer Preference Formation and Pioneering Advantage," *Journal of Marketing Research*, 26, no. 3 (1989), pp. 285–298; Glen L. Urban, T. Carter, S. Gaskin, and Z. Mucha, "Market Share Rewards to Pioneering Brands: An Empirical Analysis and Strategic Implications," *Management Science*, 32 (1986), pp. 645–659. Kotler's work was based on the following research: William T. Robinson and Claes Fornell, "Sources of Market Pioneer Advantages in Consumer Goods Industries," *Journal of Marketing Research*, 22, no. 3 (1985), pp. 305–317.

9. Raji Srinivasan, Gary L. Lilien, and Arvind Rangaswamy, "First in, First out? The Effects of Network Externalities on Pioneer Survival," *Journal of Marketing*, 68, no. 1 (2004), p. 41.

10. Rajeev K. Tyagi, "New Product Introductions and Failures under Uncertainty," *International Journal of Research in Marketing*, 23, no. 2 (2006), pp. 199–213; Lori Dahm, "Secrets of Success: The Strategies Driving New Product Development at Kraft," *Stagnito's New Products Magazine*, 2 (January 2002), p. 18ff; Cyndee Miller, "Little Relief Seen for New Product Failure Rate," *Marketing News*, June 21, 1993, pp. 1, 10; *BusinessWeek*, "Flops," August 16, 1993, p. 76ff.

11. http://www.marketingpower.com (accessed September 18, 2006).

12. http://www.quickmba.com (accessed September 16, 2006).

13. Subin Im and John P. Workman Jr., "Market Orientation, Creativity, and New Product Performance in High-Technology Firms," *Journal of Marketing*, 68, no. 2 (2004), p. 114.

14. http;//www.arimidex.com/glossary/index.asp (accessed April 9, 2008).

15. Ted Agres, "Support for Orphan Diseases," *Drug Discovery & Development*, 9, no. 7 (2006), pp. 6–8.

16. Standard & Poor's, *Industry Surveys: Healthcare: Pharmaceuticals*, June 24, 2004.

17. Glen L. Urban and John R. Hauser, "'Listening In' to Find and Explore New Combinations of Customer Needs," *Journal of Marketing*, 68, no. 2 (2004), p. 72; Steve Hoeffler, "Measuring Preferences for Really New Products," *Journal of Marketing Research*, 40, no. 4 (2003), pp. 406–420.

18. Glen L. Urban and John R. Hauser, *Design and Marketing of New Products*, 2nd ed. (Upper Saddle River, NJ: Prentice Hall, 1993), pp. 120–121.

19. Kate Bertrand Connelly, "Facing Off Against 'Wrap Rage'," October 2006, http://www.brandpackaging.com/content.php?s=BP/2006/10&p=2 (accessed February 1, 2008).

20. http://www.betterproductdesign.net/tools/user/lead-user.htm (accessed November 12, 2004); Eric von Hippel, *The Sources of Innovation* (New York: Oxford University Press, 1988); Glen L. Urban and Eric von Hippel, "Lead User Analysis for the Development of Industrial Products," *Management Science*, 34 (May 1988), pp. 569–582; Eric von Hippel, "Lead Users: A Source of Novel Product Concepts," *Management Science*, 32 (1986), pp. 791–805; Eric von Hippel, "Successful Industrial Products from Consumers' Ideas," *Journal of Marketing*, 42, no. 1 (1978), pp. 39–49.

21. William Bulkeley, "Got a Better Letter Opener?" *The Wall Street Journal*, July 13, 2006.

22. Karl T. Ulrich and Steven D. Eppinger, *Product Design and Development*, 4th ed. (Boston: Irwin-McGraw-Hill, 2008).

23. http://www.marketingpower.com (accessed September 18, 2006).

24. Ulrich and Eppinger, *Product Design and Development*.

25. http://www.marketingpower.com (accessed September 18, 2006).

26. "A New Way to Prevent Lost Luggage," *The Wall Street Journal*, February 27, 2007.

27. Ulrich and Eppinger, *Product Design and Development*.

28. Ellen Byron, "A Virtual View of the Store Aisle," *The Wall Street Journal*, October 3, 2007.

29. "Animal Testing," http://www.hsus.org/animals-in-research/animal_testing (accessed February 1, 2008); "EU to Ban Animal Tested Cosmetics," www.cnn.com (accessed March 31, 2006); Tonya Vinas, "P&G Seeks Alternatives to Animal Tests," *Industry Week*, 253, no. 7 (2004), p. 60; Guy Montague-Jones, "Search for Alternatives to Animal testing Remains Slow," January 11, 2008, http://www.cosmeticsdesign-europe.com/news/ng.asp?n=82494-animal-testing-cosmetics-allergens (accessed February 1, 2008); Gary Anthes, "P&G Uses Data Mining to Cut Animal Testing," http://www.computerworld.com (accessed December 6, 1999).

30. http://www.peta.org; "Mars Candy Kills," http://www.marscandykills.com (accessed February 1, 2008).

31. http://www2.acnielsen.com/products/crs_bases2.shtml (accessed September 20, 2006).

32. Patricia Sellers, "P&G: Teaching an Old Dog New Tricks," *Fortune*, May 31, 2004, pp. 166–180.

33. Andrew Martin, "Decaf Being Joined by De-Heartburn" *The New York Times*, March 14, 2007.

34. http://www.infores.com/public/us/analytics/productportfolio/bscannewprodtest.htm (accessed April 2, 2006).

35. Product Development Management Association, *The PDMA Handbook of New Product Development*, 2nd ed., Kenneth K. Kahn, ed. (New York: John Wiley & Sons, 2004).

36. Ashwin W. Joshi and Sanjay Sharma, "Customer Knowledge Development: Antecedents and Impact on New Product Success," *Journal of Marketing*, 68, no. 4 (2004), p. 47.

37. http://www.beiersdorf.com/Area-Brands/News-Innovations/ (accessed February 2, 2008); http://www.nivea.com/highlights/int_product/show/nhc_diamond_gloss/ (accessed February 2, 2008).

38. Yuhong Wu, Sridhar Balasubramanian, and Vijay Mahajan, "When Is a Preannounced New Product Likely to Be Delayed?" *Journal of Marketing*, 68, no. 2 (2004), p. 101.

39. http://www.pdma.org/ (accessed September 15, 2006).

40. Theodore Levitt, *Marketing Imagination* (New York: The Free Press, 1986).

41. Donald R. Lehmann and Russell S. Winer, *Analysis for Marketing Planning*, 6th ed. (Boston: McGraw-Hill/Irwin, 2004).

42. Glen L. Urban and John R. Hauser, *Design and Marketing of New Products*, 2nd ed. (Upper Saddle River, NJ: Prentice Hall, 1993), pp. 120–121.

43. http://www.organicearthday.org/DelMonteFoods.htm (accessed January 31, 2008); http://www.delmonte.com/Products/ (accessed January 31, 2008).

44. Ned Randolph, "DVR Penetration to Double in Five Years," January 3, 2008, http://www.contentagenda.com/article/CA6516778.html (accessed February 1, 2008); Todd Spangler, "TiVo Debuts $299 HD DVR for Cable," July 24, 2007, http://www.multichannel.com/article/CA6462451.html (accessed February 1, 2008); *The Economist*, "Business: A Farewell to Ads? Advertising and Television," April 17, 2004, p. 70; *Technology Review*, "Technology: How TiVo Works," May 2004, pp. 80–81; Mark Basch, "Digital Video Recorder to Change How People View TV," *Knight Ridder Tribune Business News*, June 30, 2004; Scott Kirsner, "Can TiVo Go Prime Time?" *Fast Company*, August 2000, p. 82.

45. Miriam Jordan and Jonathan Karp, "Machines for the Masses; Whirlpool Aims Cheap Washer at Brazil, India and China; Making Do with Slower Spin," *The Wall Street Journal*, December 9, 2003, p. A19.

46. Om Malik, "The New Land of Opportunity," *Business 2.0*, July 2004, pp. 72–79.

47. Claire Briney, "Wiping Up the Market," *Global Cosmetic Industry*, 172, no. 4 (April 2004), pp. 40–43.

48. Kara Swisher, "Home Economics: The Hypoallergenic Car; Wave of Cleaning Products Caters to Finicky Drivers; Premoistened Auto Wipes," *The Wall Street Journal* (eastern edition), May 6, 2004, p. D.1.

49. http://www.toiletwand.com (accessed September 20, 2006).

50. http://www.dfj.com/nanocar/ (accessed March 19, 2008); "Light Engine Drives Nanocar," *Laser Focus World*, 42, no. 6 (2006), p. 15.

51. Steven Levenstein, "Sony's New USB Turntable Sparks Vinyl Revival," www.inventospot.com, March 14, 2008; http://www.electronichouse.com/article/vinyl_the_classic_format/C155 (accessed March 16, 2008); Roy Bragg, "LP Vinyl Records Are Making a Comeback in Audiophile Circles," *Knight Ridder Tribune Business News*, January 3, 2004 (ProQuest Document ID: 521358371); Susan Adams, "You, the Record Mogul," *Forbes*, October 27, 2003, p. 256ff.

52. Kevin J. Clancy and Peter C. Krieg, "Product Life Cycle: A Dangerous Idea," *Brandweek*, March 1, 2004, p. 26; Nariman K. Dhalla and Sonia Yuseph, "Forget the Product Life-Cycle Concept," *Harvard Business Review* (January–February 1976), p. 102ff.

53. Peter Golder and Gerard Tellis, "Cascades, Diffusion, and Turning Points in the Product Life Cycle," MSI Report No. 03-120, 2003.

54. Jay Bolling, "DTC: A Strategy for Every Stage," *Pharmaceutical Executive*, November 2003, pp. 110–117.

55. This case was written by Elisabeth Nevins Caswell in conjunction with the textbook authors Dhruv Grewal and Michael Levy as a basis of class discussion rather than to illustrate either effective or ineffective marketing practice.

56. http://www.metronaps.com/ (accessed February 2, 2008); Michael Myser, "$20 Billion for a Good Night's Rest," *Business 2.0*, March 15, 2007; http://money.cnn.com/magazines/business2/business2_archive/2006/10/01/8387112/index.htm?postversion=2006092517 (accessed February 2, 2008).

Chapter 12

1. "Enterprise Rent-A-Car Ranked Highest by J.D. Power and Associates for Fourth Straight Year," *Business Wire,* November 13, 2007; "A Simple, Sustainable Choice: Enterprise Rent-A-Car, National Car Rental and Alamo Rent A Car Launch Customer Carbon Offset Program," www.enterprise.com, January 15, 2008; Rhymer Rigby, "Turn Your Staff into Recruitment Consultants: Rhymer Rigby Finds Recruits Who Are Recommended Can Be More Loyal and Motivated," *Financial Times,* January 15, 2008.

2. "Corporate Fact Sheet," http://aboutus.enterprise.com/files/rent_a_car_fact_sheet.pdf (accessed April 2, 2008).

3. "Book Excerpt," http://www.exceedingcustomerexpectations.com (accessed April 2, 2008).

4. "Culture of Customer Service," http://aboutus.enterprise.com/who_we_are/customer_service.html (accessed April 2, 2008).

5. Leonard L. Berry and A. Parasuraman, *Marketing Services: Competing through Quality* (New York: The Free Press, 1991), p. 5.

6. "Table 1.1.5. Gross Domestic Product," http://www.bea.gov/national/nipaweb/TableView.asp?SelectedTable=5&FirstYear=2006&LastYear=2007&Freq=Qtr (accessed February 19, 2008).

7. Ron Scherer, "Service Work Props Up U.S. Job Market," *The Christian Science Monitor,* July 9, 2007, http://www.csmonitor.com/2007/0709/p01s05-usec.html (accessed April 14, 2008).

8. Valarie A. Zeithaml, A. Parasuraman, and Leonard L. Berry, *Delivering Quality Service: Balancing Customer Perceptions and Expectations* (New York: The Free Press, 1990).

9. Parija B. Kavilanz, "Musical Chairs at the Mall," CNNMoney.com, March 21, 2008 (accessed April 4, 2008).

10. "Frequently Asked Questions," April 4, 2008, http://www.ipic.com/.

11. "Center for Professional Responsibility," http://www.abanet.org/cpr/professionalism/lawyerAd.html (accessed February 20, 2008).

12. Choice Hotels, "Special Guest Policies," http://www.choice-hotels.com/ires/en-US/html/GuestPolicies (accessed April 14, 2008).

13. Peter H. Geraghty, "New New York Rules on Lawyer Advertising," ABA EthicSearch (accessed electronically February 20, 2008).

14. Dhruv Grewal, Michael Levy, Gopal Iyer, and Jerry Gotlieb, "Developing a Deeper Understanding of Post-Purchase Perceived Risk and Repeat Purchase Behavioral Intentions in a Service Setting," *Journal of the Academy of Marketing Science,* 35, no. 2 (2007), pp. 250–258; Mary Jo Bitner, Stephen W. Brown, and Matthew L. Mueter, "Technology Infusion in Service Encounters," *Journal of the Academy of Marketing Science,* 28, no. 1 (2000), pp. 138–149; Jerry Gotlieb, Dhruv Grewal, Michael Levy, and Joan Lindsey-Mullikin, "An Examination of Moderators of the Effects of Customers' Evaluation of Employee Courtesy on Attitude toward the Service Firm," *Journal of Applied Social Psychology,* 34 (April 2004), pp. 825–847.

15. "The Charles Schwab Corporation," http://www.aboutschwab.com/about/facts/index.html (accessed April 4, 2008).

16. "The Charles Schwab Corporation Company Profile," http://biz.yahoo.com/ic/10/10320.html (accessed April 4, 2008).

17. Jeff Bennett, "Technology Trends: More Shoppers Find Self-Checkout Easy; Major Retailers Turn to Automation for Customers," *Detroit Free Press Business,* March 1, 2003, http://www.freep.com/money/business/scan1_20030301.htm (accessed November 10, 2004); http://www.ncr.com/products/pdf/hardware/fastlane_capabilities.pdf (accessed

November 11, 2004); Matt Pillar, "Self-Checkout: Self-Serving or Customer Centric?" *Integrated Solutions for Retailers,* July 2004, http://ismretail.com/articles/2004_07/040710.htm (accessed November 10, 2004).

18. "Self-Service Kiosks Aiding Best-in-Class Success," CNN Money.com, August 7, 2007; "Kiosks Touch More Self-Service Areas," *Los Angeles Times,* August 3, 2007.

19. The discussion of the Gaps Model and its implications draws heavily from Michael Levy and Barton A. Weitz, *Retailing Management,* 6th ed. (Burr Ridge, IL: Irwin/McGraw-Hill, 2007) and also is based on Deon Nel and Leyland Pitt, "Service Quality in a Retail Environment: Closing the Gaps," *Journal of General Management,* 18 (Spring 1993), pp. 37–57; Zeithaml, Parasuraman, and Berry, *Delivering Quality Service;* Valerie Zeithaml, Leonard Berry, and A. Parasuraman, "Communication and Control Processes in the Delivery of Service Quality," *Journal of Marketing,* 52, no. 2 (April 1988), pp. 35–48.

20. Mary Jo Bitner, "Self-Service Technologies: What Do Customers Expect? In This High-Tech World, Customers Haven't Changed—They Still Want Good Service," *Marketing Management,* Spring 2001, pp. 10–15; Chezy Ofir and Itamar Simonson, "The Effect of Stating Expectations on Customer Satisfaction and Shopping Experience." *Journal of Marketing Research,* 44 (February 2007), p. 37; Jackie L M Tam, "Managing Customer Expectations in Financial Services: Opportunities and Challenges," *Journal of Financial Services Marketing,* 11 (May 2007), pp. 281–289.

21. Kenneth Clow, David Kurtz, John Ozment, and Beng Soo Ong, "The Antecedents of Consumer Expectations of Services: An Empirical Study across Four Industries," *The Journal of Services Marketing,* 11 (May–June 1997), pp. 230–248; Ann Marie Thompson and Peter Kaminski, "Psychographic and Lifestyle Antecedents of Service Quality Expectations," *Journal of Services Marketing,* 7 (1993), pp. 53–61.

22. Kemba J. Dunham, "Beyond Satisfaction," The *Wall Street Journal,* October 30, 2006, p. R4.

23. http://www.consumerreports.org/cro/home-garden/resource-center/home-improvement/return-policies-of-the-leading-home-improvement-retailers-9-07/retailers-return-policies/home-improvement-return-policies-retailers-return-policies.htm (accessed November 7, 2007); Zhen Zhu, K. Sivakumar, and A. Parasuraman, "A Mathematical Model of Service Failure and Recovery Strategies," *Decision Science,* 35 (Summer 2004), pp. 493–525; Roland T. Rust and Tuck Siong Chung, "Marketing Models of Service and Relationships," *Marketing Science,* 25 (November 2006), pp. 560–580; A. Parasuraman, "Modeling Opportunities in Service Recovery and Customer-Managed Interactions," *Marketing Science,* 25 (November 2006), pp. 590–593; Zeithaml, Parasuraman, and Berry, *Delivering Quality Service.*

24. Stephen L. Vargo, Kaori Nagao, Yi He, and Fred W. Morgan, "Satisfiers, Dissatisfiers, Criticals, and Neutrals: A Review of Their Relative Effects on Customer (Dis)Satisfaction," *Academy of Marketing Science Review* (January 2007), p. 1; Chezy Ofir and Itamar Simonson, "The Effect of Stating Expectations on Customer Satisfaction and Shopping Experience," *Journal of Marketing Research,* 44 (February 2007), p. 37; Torsten Ringberg, Gaby Odekerken-Schröder, and Glenn L Christensen, "A Cultural Models Approach to Service Recovery," *Journal of Marketing,* 71 (July 2007), p. 194; Leonard Berry and A. Parasuraman, "Listening to the Customer—The Concept of a Service-Quality Information System," *Sloan Management Review,* 38, no. 3 (1997), pp. 65–77; A. Parasuraman and Dhruv Grewal, "Serving Customers and Consumers Effectively in the 21st Century," working paper (1998), University of Miami, Coral Gables, FL.

25. Teena Lyons, "Complain to Me—If You Can," *Knight Ridder Tribune News*, December 4, 2005, p. 1.

26. Hazel-Anne Johnson and Paul Spector, "Service With a Smile: Do Emotional Intelligence, Gender, and Autonomy Moderate the Emotional Labor Process?" *Journal of Occupational Health Psychology*, October 2007, pp. 319–333; Merran Toerien and Celia Kitzinger, "Emotional Labour in Action: Navigating Multiple Involvements in the Beauty Salon," *Sociology*, August 2007, pp. 645–662.

27. "Homewood Suites by Hilton Rolls out iPod Mobile Training," *Business Wire*, August 8, 2007.

28. "Whole Foods Market Benefits: US Team Members," http://www.wholefoodsmarket.com/careers/benefits_us.html (accessed April 2, 2008).

29. George Gombossy, "Whole Foods Shows You Can Get Something for Nothing," *Hartford Courant*, December 21, 2007 (accessed April 2, 2008).

30. Kemba J. Dunham, "Beyond Satisfaction," *The Wall Street Journal*, October 30, 2006, p. R4.

31. James R. Detert and Ethan R. Burris, "Leadership Behavior and Employee Voice: Is the Door Really Open?" *Academy of Management Journal,* 50 (August 2007), pp. 869–884; Gilad Chen, Bradley L. Kirkman, Ruth Kanfer, Don Allen, and Benson Rosen, "A Multilevel Study of Leadership, Empowerment, and Performance in Teams," *Journal of Applied Psychology,* 92 (March 2007), p. 331; Adam Rapp, Michael Ahearne, John Mathieu, and Niels Schillewaert, "The Impact of Knowledge and Empowerment on Working Smart and Working Hard: The Moderating Role of Experience," *International Journal of Research in Marketing,* 23 (September 2006), pp. 279–293; Jim Poisant, *Creating and Sustaining a Superior Customer Service Organization: A Book about Taking Care of the People Who Take Care of the Customers* (Westport, CT: Quorum Books, 2002); "People-Focused HR Policies Seen as Vital to Customer Service Improvement," *Store,* January 2001, p. 60; Michael Brady and J. Joseph Cronin, "Customer Orientation: Effects on Customer Service Perceptions and Outcome Behaviors," *Journal of Service Research,* February 2001, pp. 241–251; Michael Hartline, James Maxham III, and Daryl McKee, "Corridors of Influence in the Dissemination of Customer-Oriented Strategy to Customer Contact Service Employees," *Journal of Marketing,* 64, no. 2 (April 2000), pp. 25–41.

32. "Quicken Loans Ranked #2 on Fortune's 100 Best Companies to Work For' in America List,'" http://www.quickenloans.com (accessed April 1, 2008).

33. "Oregon Home Loans," http://www.quickenloans.com (accessed April 1, 2008).

34. "100 Best Companies to Work For 2008," *Fortune,* February 4, 2008 (accessed electronically April 1, 2008).

35. Julie Holliday Wayne, Amy E. Randel, and Jaclyn Stevens, "The Role of Identity and Work-family Support in Work-family Enrichment and Its Work-related Consequences," *Journal of Vocational Behavior,* 69 (December 2006), p. 445; Alicia Grandey and Analea Brauburger, "The Emotion Regulation behind the Customer Service Smile," in *Emotions in the Workplace: Understanding the Structure and Role of Emotions in Organizational Behavior,* eds. R. Lord, R. Klimoski, and R. Kanfer (San Francisco: Jossey-Bass, 2002); Mara Adelman and Aaron Ahuvia, "Social Support in the Service Sector: The Antecedents, Processes, and Consequences of Social Support in an Introductory Service," *Journal of Business Research,* 32 (March 1995), pp. 273–282.

36. Johnson and Spector, "Service with a Smile"; Toerien and Kitzinger, "Emotional Labour in Action"; Jarrrad Dunning, Aron O'Cass, Anthony Pecotich, "Retail Sales Explanations: Resolving Unsatisfactory Sales Encounters," *European Journal of Marketing,* 38 (2004), pp. 1541–1561; Margaret Pressler, "The Customer Isn't Always Right; Retail Staff Say Shoppers' Behavior Is Going from Bad to Worse," *The Washington Post,* March 24, 2002, p. H.05; Chris Penttila, "Touch Customer: Managing Abusive Customers," *Entrepreneur,* May 2001, pp. 5, 95.

37. http://www.threadless.com (accessed April 14, 2008).

38. Justin Martin, "6 Companies Where Customers Come First," http://money.cnn.com/galleries/2007/fsb/0709/gallery.where_customers_come_first.fsb/6.html (accessed April 14, 2008).

39. Fons Naus, Ad van Iterson, and Robert Roe, "Organizational Cynicism: Extending the Exit, Voice, Loyalty, and Neglect Model of Employees' Responses to Adverse Conditions in the Workplace," *Human Relations,* 60 (May 2007), pp. 683–718; Richard Netemeyer and James G. Maxham III, "Employee versus Supervisor Ratings of Performance in the Retail Customer Service Sector: Differences in Predictive Validity for Customer Outcomes," *Journal of Retailing,* 83 (January 2007), pp. 131–146.

40. Carmine Gallo, "Bringing Passion to Starbucks, Travelocity," *BusinessWeek,* January 9, 2008 (accessed electronically April 1, 2008).

41. "Travelocity," http://www.sabre-holdings.com/ourBrands/travelocity.html (accessed April 1, 2008).

42. Smith Joyce, "Positive Customer Service Pays Off, Consumer Loyalty May Take Financial Investment," *Myrtle Beach Sun News,* November 5, 2006, accessed electronically.

43. "Marriott Deploys NCR Self-Service Kiosks; Global Hotel Chain Pilots Check-In, Check-Out Solution from World's Leading Self-Service Technology Provider," *TMC Net,* June 3, 2004, http://www.tmcnet.com/usubmit/2004/jun/1045424.htm (accessed September 20, 2006).

44. Jason Friedman, "Tracking Success In-Store," MarketingAtRetail.com, December 21, 2006; Dennis Viehland and Aaron Wong, "The Future of Radio Frequency Identification," *Journal of Theoretical and Applied Electronic Commerce Research,* 2 (August 2007), pp. 74–81; Claudia Loebbecke "Use of Innovative Content Integration Information Technology at the Point of Sale," *European Journal of Information Systems,* 16 (July 2007), pp. 228–236.

45. Erica Ogg, "HP Developing Shopping Kiosks of the Future," silicon.com, May 30, 2007, accessed electronically.

46. http://www.stopandshop.com/stores/shopping_buddy.htm (accessed November 7, 2007); Shia Kapos, "High-Tech Shopping Lists Guide Grocery Shoppers," *Chicago Tribune,* June 20, 2005, p. C1.

47. "Telematics," *Wikipedia, The Free Encyclopedia,* March 27, 2008, http://en.wikipedia.org/w/index.php?title=Telematics&oldid=201429114 (accessed April 3, 2008).

48. "Drivers," http://atxg.stationhq.com/en-US/drivers (accessed April 2, 2008).

49. Rhett H. Walker, Margaret Craig-Lees, Robert Hecker, and Heather Francis, "Technology-Enabled Service Delivery: An Investigation of Reasons Affecting Customer Adoption and Rejection," *International Journal of Service Industry Management,* 13, no. 1 (2002), pp. 91–107; Bitner, Brown, and Meuter, "Technology Infusion in Service Encounters"; Stephen W. Brown, "Service Recovery through IT," *Marketing Management,* 6 (Fall 1997), pp. 25–27; P. A. Dabholkar, "Technology-Based Service Delivery: A Classification Scheme for Developing Marketing Strategies," in *Advances in Services Marketing and Management,* vol. 3, eds. T. A. Swartz, Deborah E. Bowen, and Stephen W. Brown (Greenwich, CT: JAI Press, 1994), pp. 241–271.

50. Colin Armistead and Julia Kiely, "Creating Strategies"; A. Parasuraman, "Technology Readiness Index—A Multiple–Item Scale to Measure Readiness to Embrace New Technologies," *Journal of Service Research*, 2, no. 4 (2000), pp. 307–320; C. Voss, "Developing an e-Service Strategy," *Business Strategy*, 11, no. 1 (2000), pp. 21–33; J. Walsh and S. Godfrey, "The Internet: A New Era in Customer Service," *European Management Journal*, 18, no. 1 (2000), pp. 85–92.

51. Subimal Chatterjee, Susan A. Slotnick, and Matthew J. Sobel, "Delivery Guarantees and the Interdependence of Marketing and Operations," *Production and Operations Management*, 11, no. 3 (Fall 2002), pp. 393–411; Piyush Kumar, Manohar Kalawani, and Makbool Dada, "The Impact of Waiting Time Guarantees on Customers' Waiting Experiences," *Marketing Science*, 16, no. 4 (1999), pp. 676–785.

52. Hui Liao, "Do It Right This Time: The Role of Employee Service Recovery Performance in Customer-Perceived Justice and Customer Loyalty after Service Failures," *Journal of Applied Psychology*, 92 (March 2007), p. 475; K. Douglas Hoffman, Scott W. Kelley, and H. M. Rotalsky, "Tracking Service Failures and Employee Recovery Efforts," *Journal of Services Marketing*, 9, no. 2 (1995), pp. 49–61; Scott W. Kelley and Mark A. Davis, "Antecedents to Customer Expectations for Service Recovery," *Journal of the Academy of Marketing Science*, 22 (Winter 1994), pp. 52–61; Terrence J. Levesque and Gordon H. G. McDougall, "Service Problems and Recovery Strategies: An Experiment," *Canadian Journal of Administrative Sciences*, 17, no. 1 (2000), pp. 20–37; James G. Maxham III and Richard G. Netemeyer, "A Longitudinal Study of Complaining Customers' Evaluations of Multiple Service Failures and Recovery Efforts," *Journal of Marketing*, 66, no. 3 (October 2002), pp. 57–71; Amy K. Smith, Ruth N. Bolton, and Janet Wagner, "A Model of Customer Satisfaction with Service Encounters Involving Failure and Recovery," *Journal of Marketing Research*, 36, no. 3 (August 1999), pp. 356–372; Scott R. Swanson and Scott W. Kelley, "Attributions and Outcomes of the Service Recovery Process," *Journal of Marketing Theory and Practice*, 9 (Fall 2001), pp. 50–65; Stephen S. Tax and Stephen W. Brown, "Recovering and Learning from Service Failure," *Sloan Management Review*, 40, no. 1 (1998), pp. 75–88; Stephen S. Tax, Stephen W. Brown, and Murali Chandrashekaran, "Consumer Evaluations of Service Complaint Experiences: Implications for Relationship Marketing," *Journal of Marketing*, 62, no. 2 (April 1998), pp. 60–76; Scott Widmier and Donald W. Jackson Jr., "Examining the Effects of Service Failure, Customer Compensation, and Fault on Customer Satisfaction with Salespeople," *Journal of Marketing Theory and Practice*, 10 (Winter 2002), pp. 63–74; Valarie A. Zeithaml and Mary Jo Bitner, *Services Marketing: Integrating Customer Focus across the Firm* (New York: McGraw-Hill, 2003).

53. James Maxham III, "Service Recovery's Influence on Consumer Satisfaction, Positive Word-of-Mouth, and Purchase Intentions," *Journal of Business Research*, October 2001, pp. 11–24; Michael McCollough, Leonard Berry, and Manjit Yadav, "An Empirical Investigation of Customer Satisfaction after Service Failure and Recovery," *Journal of Service Research*, November 2000, pp. 121–137.

54. "Correcting Store Blunders Seen as Key Customer Service Opportunity," *Stores*, January 2001, pp. 60–64; Stephen W. Brown, "Practicing Best-in-Class Service Recovery: Forward-Thinking Firms Leverage Service Recovery to Increase Loyalty and Profits," *Marketing Management*, Summer 2000, pp. 8–10; Tax, Brown, and Chandrashekaran, "Customer Evaluations"; Amy Smith and Ruth Bolton, "An Experimental Investigation of Customer Reactions to Service Failures and Recovery Encounters: Paradox or Peril?" *Journal of Service*

Research, 1 (August 1998), pp. 23–36; Cynthia Webster and D. S. Sundaram, "Service Consumption Criticality in Failure Recovery," *Journal of Business Research* 41 (February 1998), pp. 153–159.

55. Ko de Ruyter and Martin Wetsel, "The Impact of Perceived Listening Behavior in Voice-to-Voice Service Encounters," *Journal of Service Research*, February 2000, pp. 276–284.

56. Hooman Estelami, "Competitive and Procedural Determinants of Delight and Disappointment in Consumer Complaint Outcomes," *Journal of Service Research*, February 2000, pp. 285–300.

57. Michael Tsiros, Anne Roggeveen, and Dhruv Grewal, "Compensation as a Service Recovery Strategy: When Does It Work?" unpublished working paper, 2006, Babson College; Amy K. Smith, Ruth N. Bolton, and Janet Wagner, "A Model of Customer Satisfaction with Service Encounters Involving Failure and Recovery," *Journal of Marketing Research*, 36 (August 1999), pp. 356–372; Scott R. Swanson and Scott W. Kelley, "Attributions and Outcomes of the Service Recovery Process," *Journal of Marketing: Theory and Practice*, 9 (Fall 2001), pp. 50–65.

58. David Carter and Darren Rovell, "It's a Homerun: Customer Service Greatness in the Minor Leagues," *Financial Times*, June 27, 2003.

59. https://www.usaa.com/inet/ent_utils/McStaticPages?key-=about_usaa_overviews (accessed April 22, 2008).

60. Chihyung Ok, Ki-Joon Back and Carol W. Shanklin, "Mixed Findings on the Service Recovery Paradox," *The Service Industries Journal*, 27 (September 2007), p. 671; Celso Augusto de Matos, Jorge Luiz Henrique and Carlos Alberto Vargas Rossi, "Service Recovery Paradox: A Meta-Analysis," *Journal of Service Research*, 10 (August 2007), pp. 60–77; Torsten Ringberg, Gaby Odekerken-Schröder and Glenn L Christensen, "A Cultural Models Approach to Service Recovery," *Journal of Marketing*, 71 (July 2007), p. 194; Mahesh S. Bhandari, Yelena Tsarenko and Michael Jay Polonsky, "A Proposed Multi-dimensional Approach to Evaluating Service Recovery," *The Journal of Services Marketing*, 21 (April 2007), pp. 174–185; James G. Maxham III and Richard G. Netemeyer, "A Longitudinal Study of Complaining Customers' Evaluations of Multiple Service Failures and Recovery Efforts," *Journal of Marketing*, 66 (October 2002), pp. 57–71; L. Biff Motley, "Dealing with Unsatisfied Customers," *ABA Bank Marketing*, 35, no. 10 (December 2003), p. 45.

61. This case was written by Colin Fox and Britt Hackmann in conjunction with the textbook authors (Dhruv Grewal and Michael Levy) as the basis of class discussion rather than to illustrate either effective or ineffective marketing practice. Suzanne Marta, "As Ritz Opening Nears, Every Detail Counts," *Knight Ridder Tribune Business News*, August 6, 2007; Jack Gordon, "Redefining Elegance," *Training*, 44, no. 2 (2007), pp. 14–20; Jennifer Saranow, "Turning to Luxury Hotels for Service Ideas; Companies Lacking in Customer Savvy Try the Special Touch," *The Wall Street Journal*, July 19, 2006.

62. "Luxury Hotels—Business Is Up and Hotels Are Upgrading," *BusinessWeek*, January 20, 2008 (accessed electronically February 26, 2008).

63. "Fact Sheet," http://corporate.ritzcarlton.com/en/Press/FactSheet.htm (accessed February 26, 2008).

64. "Our History," http://corporate.ritzcarlton.com/en/About/OurHistory.htm (accessed February 26, 2008).

65. "Working at the Ritz Carlton," http://corporate.ritzcarlton.com/en/Careers/WorkingAt.htm (accessed February 26, 2008).

Chapter 13

1. Hooman Estelami, Dhruv Grewal, and Anne L. Roggeveen, "The Effect of Policy Restrictions on Consumer Reactions to Price-Matching Guarantees," *Journal of the Academy of Marketing Science,* 35, no. 2 (2007), pp. 208–219; Monika Kukar-Kinneyika and Dhruv Grewal, "Comparison of Consumer Reactions to Price-Matching Guarantees in Internet and Bricks-and-Mortar Retail Environments," *Journal of the Academy of Marketing Science,* 35, no. 2 (2007), pp. 197–207; Sujay Dutta, Abhijit Biswas, and Dhruv Grewal, "Low Price Signal Default: An Empirical Investigation with Low-Price Guarantees," *Journal of the Academy of Marketing Science,* 35, no. 1 (2007), pp. 76–88; Kent B. Monroe, *Pricing: Making Profitable Decisions,* 3rd ed. (New York: McGraw-Hill, 2003); Dhruv Grewal, Kent B. Monroe, and R. Krishnan, "The Effects of Price Comparison Advertising on Buyers' Perceptions of Acquisition Value and Transaction Value," *Journal of Marketing,* 62 (April 1998), pp. 46–60.

2. "American Shoppers Economize, Show Greater Interest in Nutrition and Awareness of Food Safety Issues, According to Trends in the United States: Consumer Attitudes and the Supermarket 2003," http://www.fmi.org/media/mediatext.cfm?id=534 (accessed December 10, 2005). A key finding in this study reveals that low price is the third most important feature in selecting a supermarket and is viewed as important by 83 percent of respondents; see also "The New Value Equation," *Supermarket News,* 50 (June 10, 2002), p. 12.

3. Anthony Miyazaki, Dhruv Grewal, and Ronnie Goodstein, "The Effects of Multiple Extrinsic Cues on Quality Perceptions: A Matter of Consistency," *Journal of Consumer Research,* 32 (June 2005), pp. 146–153; William B. Dodds, Kent B. Monroe, and Dhruv Grewal, "The Effects of Price, Brand, and Store Information on Buyers' Product Evaluations," *Journal of Marketing Research,* 28 (August 1991), pp. 307–319.

4. Robert J. Dolan, "Note on Marketing Strategy," *Harvard Business School* (November 2000), pp. 1–17; Dhruv Grewal and Larry D. Compeau, "Pricing and Public Policy: An Overview and a Research Agenda," *Journal of Public Policy & Marketing,* 18 (Spring 1999), pp. 3–11.

5. "British Retailer Sells Final Potter Book for $10," July 19, 2007, http://www.msnbc.msn.com/id/19858847 (accessed January 3, 2008).

6. "Delta Rescinds Fare Increase on Some of Its U.S. Routes," *Salt Lake City News,* September 11, 2007 (accessed electronically January 3, 2008).

7. Monroe, *Pricing: Making Profitable Decisions.*

8. Raymond Flandez, "Voluntary Pricing Lets Small Eateries Give—and Get Back," *The Wall Street Journal,* August 28, 2007.

9. "For Radiohead Fans, Does 'Free' + 'Download' = 'Freeload'?" press release, November 5, 2007, http://www.comscore.com/press/release.asp?press=1883 (accessed January 3, 2008).

10. Stacy Meichtry, "Golden Fleece, Seeking Edge, Fashion Firm Bets on Rare, Furry Animals," *The Wall Street Journal,* February 21, 2007.

11. Fender U.S. Price Lists, http://www.fender.com/resources/price_lists.php (accessed January 3, 2008).

12. Monroe, *Pricing: Making Profitable Decisions.*

13. http://finance.yahoo.com/currency/convert?amt=1&from=EUR&to=USD&submit=Convert (accessed December 27, 2007).

14. http://www.marketingpower.com/mg-dictionary-view669.php? (accessed December 27, 2007).

15. http://www.marketingpower.com/mg-dictionary.php?SearchFor=substitute+products&Searched=1 (accessed December 27, 2007).

16. Joan Lindsey-Mullikin and Dhruv Grewal, "Market Price Variation: The Availability of Internet Market Information," *Journal of the Academy of Marketing Science,* 34, no. 2 (2006), pp. 236–243.

17. Suzanne Marta, "As Ritz Opening Nears, Every Detail Counts," *Knight Ridder Tribune Business News,* August 6, 2007.

18. Jack Gordon, "Redefining Elegance, *Training* 44, no. 2 (2007), pp. 14–20.

19. Ibid.

20. Lori Calabro, "At Your Beck and Call," *CFO Magazine,* September 1, 2007 (accessed electronically February 4, 2008).

21. Vanessa O'Connell, "Posh Retailers Pile on Perks for Top Customers," *The Wall Street Journal,* April 26, 2007 (accessed electronically February 4, 2008).

22. Julie Jargon and Lauren Etter, "Food Makers Struggle to Pass on High Costs," *The Wall Street Journal,* October 3, 2007, p. A2.

23. "Popcorn Prices Pop Up on Ethanol Demand," *Morning Edition,* July 24, 2007 (accessed electronically January 3, 2008).

24. Cenk Koça and Jonathan D. Bohlmann, "Segmented Switchers and Retailer Pricing Strategies," *Journal of Marketing,* 72, no. 3 (2008), pp. 124–142; Ruth N. Bolton and Venkatesh Shankar, "An Empirically Derived Taxonomy of Retailer Pricing and Promotion Strategies," *Journal of Retailing,* 79, no. 4 (2003), pp. 213–224; Rajiv Lal and Ram Rao, "Supermarket Competition: The Case of Every Day Low Pricing," *Marketing Science,* 16, no. 1 (1997), pp. 60–80.

25. A. R. Rao, M. E. Bergen, and S. Davis, "How to Fight a Price War," *Harvard Business Review,* 78 (March–April 2000), pp. 107–116.

26. Ibid.

27. "Retail Price Maintenance Policies: A Bane for Retailers, but a Boon for Consumers?" *Knowledge@Wharton,* August 8, 2007.

28. *Merriam-Webster's Dictionary of Law,* 1996.

29. http://www.plasmavision.com/warranty.htm (accessed April 17, 2008).

30. Dhruv Grewal, Gopalkrishnan R. Iyer, R. Krishnan, and Arun Sharma, "The Internet and the Price-Value-Loyalty Chain," *Journal of Business Research,* 56 (May 2003), pp. 391–398; Gopalkrishnan R. Iyer, Anthony D. Miyazaki, Dhruv Grewal, and Maria Giordano, "Linking Web-Based Segmentation to Pricing Tactics," *Journal of Product & Brand Management,* 11, no. 4–5 (2002), pp. 288–302; Xing Pan, Brian T. Ratchford, and Venkatesh Shankar, "Can Price Dispersion in Online Markets Be Explained by Differences in E–Tailer Service Quality?" *Journal of the Academy of Marketing Science,* 30, no. 4 (2002), pp. 433–445; Michael D. Smith, "The Impact of Shopbots on Electronic Markets," *Journal of the Academy of Marketing Sciences,* 30, no. 4 (2002), pp. 446–454; Michael D. Smith and Erik Brynjolfsson, "Consumer Decision-Making at an Internet Shopbot: Brand Still Matters," *The Journal of Industrial Economics,* 49 (December 2001), pp. 541–558; Fang-Fang Tang and Xiaolin Xing, "Will the Growth of Multi-Channel Retailing Diminish the Pricing Efficiency of the Web?" *Journal of Retailing,* 77, no. 3 (2001), pp. 319–333; Erik Brynjolfsson and Michael D. Smith, "Frictionless Commerce? A Comparison of Internet and Conventional Retailers," *Management Science,* 46, no. 4 (2000), pp. 563–585; Florian Zettlemeyer, "Expanding to the Internet: Pricing and Communications Strategies When Firms Compete on Multiple Channels," *Journal of Marketing Research,* 37 (August 2000), pp. 292–308; Rajiv Lal and Miklos Sarvary, "When and How Is the Internet Likely to Decrease Price Competition?" *Marketing Science,* 18, no. 4 (1999), pp. 485–503; Joseph P. Bailey, "Electronic Commerce: Prices and Consumer Issues for Three Products: Books, Compact Discs, and Software," *Organization for Economic Cooperation and*

Development, OECD, GD 98 (1998), p. 4; J. Yannis Bakos, "Reducing Buyer Search Costs: Implications for Electronic Marketplaces," *Management Science,* 43, no. 12 (1997), pp. 1676–1692.

31. Kerry Miller, "eBay Sellers Go Back to School: 10 Tips," September 7, 2006.

32. Gillian Ku, Adam D. Galinsky, and J. Keith Murnighan, "Starting Low but Ending High: A Reversal of the Anchoring Effect in Auctions," *Journal of Personality and Social Psychology,* 90, no. 6 (2006), pp. 975–986.

33. Patrick Bajari and Ali Hortacsu, "The Winner's Curse, Reserve Prices and Endogenous Entry: Empirical Insights from eBay Auctions," *Journal of Economics,* 34, no. 2 (2002), p. 329.

34. Barbara Stern and Maria Royne Stafford, "Individual and Social Determinants of Winning Bids in Online Auctions," *Journal of Consumer Behavior,* 5 (July 2006), pp. 43–55.

35. Ku, Galinsky, and Murnighan, "Starting Low but Ending High."

36. Stern and Stafford, "Individual and Social Determinants of Winning Bids in Online Auctions;" Ku, Galinsky, and Murnighan, "Starting Low but Ending High."

37. David Lucking-Reiley, Doug Bryan, Naghi Prasad, and Daniel Reeves, "Pennies from eBay: The Determinants of Price in Online Auctions," *Journal of Industrial Economics,* forthcoming.

38. Uri Simonsohn and Dan Ariely, "eBay's Happy Hour: Non-Rational Herding in Online Auctions," unpublished manuscript.

39. Tanjim Hossain and John Morgan, " . . . Plus Shipping and Handling: Revenue (Non) Equivalence in Field Experiments on eBay," *Advances in Economic Analysis and Policy,* 6, no. 2 (2006), Article 3.

40. Jeffrey A. Livingston, "How Valuable Is a Good Reputation? A Sample Selection Model of Internet Auctions," *Review of Economics and Statistics,* 87, no. 3 (2005), pp. 453–465; Steven T. Anderson, Daniel Friedman, Garrett H. Daniel, and Nirvikar Singh, "Seller Strategies on eBay," April 2004, UC Santa Cruz Economics Working Paper No. 564.

41. This case was written by Larry D. Compeau in conjunction with the textbook authors (Dhruv Grewal and Michael Levy) as the basis of class discussion rather than to illustrate either effective or ineffective marketing practice.

Chapter 14

1. Brian Russak, "The Giant Awakens—With a Host of High-Profile Marketing Initiatives," *Footwear News,* December 4, 2006; Stephanie Kang, "After a Slump, Payless Tries on Fashion for Size," *The Wall Street Journal,* February 10, 2007.

2. Karyn McCormick, "Price War Leaves AMD Reeling," *BusinessWeek,* January 4, 2007, http://www.business-week.com/investor/content/jan2007/pi20070124_029733. htm?chan=technology_technology+index+page_computers (accessed January 19, 2008).

3. David Henderson, "What Are Price Wars Good For? Absolutely Nothing," *Fortune,* May 12, 1997, http://money.cnn.com/magazines/fortune/fortune_archive/1997/05/12/226238/index.htm (accessed January 19, 2008).

4. "How and Why Chinese Firms Excel in 'The Art of Price War'," *Knowledge@Wharton,* December 13, 2006, http://knowledge.wharton.upenn.edu/article.cfm?articleid=1625&CFID=1726362&CFTOKEN=46286770 (accessed January 19, 2008).

5. "Organic Clothing—Not Just for Hippies Anymore," *Dow Jones News,* February 9, 2007.

6. Thomas T. Nagle and Reed K. Holden, *The Strategy and Tactics of Pricing,* 3rd ed. (Upper Saddle River, NJ: Pearson, 2002).

7. Ethan Smith, "Hannah Montana Battles the Bots," *The Wall Street Journal,* October 5, 2007.

8. Sarah Hall, "Hannah Montana's Total Sellout," October 5, 2007, http://www.eonline.com/news/article/index.jsp?uuid=-5da8154b-e76a-478e-ada7-09594d5e5313 (accessed January 20, 2008).

9. "Mother Lied to Win Hannah Montana Contest," December 29, 2007, http://www.msnbc.msn.com/id/22429882/ (accessed January 20, 2008).

10. Lisa E. Bolton, Luk Warlop, and Joseph W. Alba, "Consumer Perceptions of Price (Un)Fairness," *Journal of Consumer Research,* 29 (March 2003), pp. 474–491; Peter R. Darke and Darren W. Dahl, "Fairness and Discounts: The Subjective Value of a Bargain," *Journal of Consumer Psychology,* 13, no. 3 (2003), pp. 328–338; Margaret C. Campbell, "Perceptions of Price Unfairness: Antecedents and Consequences," *Journal of Marketing Research,* 36 (May 1999), pp. 187–199; Sarah Maxwell, "What Makes a Price Increase Seem 'Fair'?" *Pricing Strategy & Practice,* 3, no. 4 (1995), pp. 21–27.

11. Rajesh Chandrashekaran and Dhruv Grewal, "Assimilation of Advertised Reference Prices: The Moderating Role of Involvement," *Journal of Retailing,* 79, no. 1 (2003), pp. 53–62; David M. Hardesty and William O. Bearden, "Consumer Evaluations of Different Promotion Types and Price Presentations: The Moderating Role of Promotional Benefit Level," *Journal of Retailing,* 79, no. 1 (2003), pp. 17–25; Larry D. Compeau and Dhruv Grewal, "Comparative Price Advertising: An Integrative Review," *Journal of Public Policy & Marketing,* 17 (Fall 1998), pp. 257–273; A. Biswas, E. J. Wilson, and J. W. Licata, "Reference Pricing Studies in Marketing: A Synthesis of Research Results," *Journal of Business Research,* 27, no. 3 (1993), pp. 239–256; A. Biswas, "The Moderating Role of Brand Familiarity in Reference Price Perceptions," *Journal of Business Research,* 25 (1992), pp. 251–262; A. Biswas and E. Blair, "Contextual Effects of Reference Prices in Retail Advertisements," *Journal of Marketing,* 55 (1991), pp. 1–12.

12. Dhruv Grewal, Kent B. Monroe, and R. Krishnan, "The Effects of Price Comparison Advertising on Buyers' Perceptions of Acquisition Value and Transaction Value," *Journal of Marketing,* 62, April 1998, pp. 46–60.

13. Noreen M. Klein and Janet E. Oglethorpe, "Reference Points in Consumer Decision Making," in *Advances in Consumer Research,* vol. 14, eds. Melanie Wallendorf and Paul Anderson (Provo, UT: Association for Consumer Research, 1987), pp. 183–187.

14. J. E. Urbany, W. O. Bearden, and D. C. Weilbaker, "The Effect of Plausible and Exaggerated Reference Prices on Consumer Perceptions and Price Search," *Journal of Consumer Research,* 15 (1988), pp. 95–110.

15. Michael Levy and Barton A. Weitz, *Retailing Management,* 7th ed. (Burr Ridge, IL: Irwin/McGraw-Hill, 2008).

16. Robert Schindler, "The 99 Price Ending as a Signal of a Low-Price Appeal," *Journal of Retailing,* 82, no. 1 (2006).

17. Ibid.

18. Merrie Brucks, Valerie A. Zeithaml, and Gillian Naylor, "Price and Brand Name as Indicators of Quality Dimensions for Consumer Durables," *Journal of the Academy of Marketing Science,* 28, no. 3 (2008), pp. 359–374; William B. Dodds, Kent B. Monroe, and Dhruv Grewal, "Effects of Price, Brand, and Store Information on Buyers' Product Evaluations," *Journal of Marketing Research,* 28 (August 1991), pp. 307–319.

19. Anthony Miyazaki, Dhruv Grewal, and Ronnie Goodstein, "The Effect of Multiple Extrinsic Cues on Quality Perceptions: A Matter of Consistency," *Journal of Consumer Research*, 32 (June 2005), pp. 146–153; Merrie Brucks, Valerie A. Zeithaml, and Gillian Naylor, "Price and Brand Name as Indicators of Quality Dimensions for Consumer Durables," *Journal of the Academy of Marketing Science*, 28, no. 3 (2008); Niraj Dawar and Philip Parker, "Marketing Universals: Consumers' Use of Brand Name, Price, Physical Appearance, and Retailer Reputation as Signals of Product Quality," *Journal of Marketing*, 58 (April 1994) pp. 81–95; Dodds, Monroe, and Grewal, "Effects of Price, Brand, and Store Information on Buyers' Product Evaluations"; Paul S. Richardson, Alan S. Dick, and Arun K. Jain, "Extrinsic and Intrinsic Cue Effects on Perceptions of Store Brand Quality," *Journal of Marketing*, 58, October 1994, pp. 28–36.

20. "Cervical Cancer Vaccine: Who Needs It, How It Works," http://www.mayoclinic.com/health/cervical-cancer-vaccine/WO00120 (accessed January 19, 2008); Gardiner Harris, "U.S. Approves Cervical Cancer Vaccine," *The New York Times*, June 8, 2006 (accessed January 19, 2008).

21. Steve Jobs, "To All iPhone Customers," http://www.apple.com/hotnews/openiphoneletter/ (accessed January 19, 2008).

22. J. J. Martin, "Keeping Ahead in Fashion's Slow Lane," *International Herald Tribune*, June 28, 2005, http://www.iht.com/articles/2005/06/27/opinion/rslow.php?page=1 (accessed January 19, 2008); http://www.zara.com (accessed January 19, 2008).

23. Adena Halpern, *Target Underwear and a Vera Wang Gown: Notes from a Single Girl's Closet* (New York: Gotham, 2006).

24. http://www.brooksbrothers.com (accessed January 19, 2008).

25. This section draws from Levy and Weitz, *Retailing Management*.

26. Mike Snider, "PlayStation 3 Price Cut by $100," *USA Today*, July 9, 2007, http://www.usatoday.com/tech/gaming/2007-07-09-playstation-price_N.htm?csp=34 (accessed January 20, 2008).

27. Sha Yang and Priya Raghubir, "Can Bottles Speak Volumes? The Effect of Package Shape on How Much to Buy," *Journal of Retailing*, 81, no. 4 (2005), pp. 269–281.

28. This section is adapted from Levy and Weitz, *Retailing Management*.

29. Cotten Timberlake, "Macy's Loses Sales as It Weans Shoppers from Coupons," Bloomberg.com, May 16, 2007.

30. Michael Johnsen, "Ukrop's Launches Personalized Loyalty Shopper Program," *C Drug Store News*, May 15, 2007 (accessed electronically).

31. Alice Park, "The Leasing Life," *Time*, April 1, 2007.

32. Larry Compeau, Joan Lindsey–Mullikin, Dhruv Grewal, and Ross Petty, "An Analysis of Consumers' Interpretations of the Semantic Phrases Found in Comparative Price Advertisements," *Journal of Consumer Affairs*, 38 (Summer 2004), pp. 178–187; Larry D. Compeau, Dhruv Grewal, and Diana S. Grewal, "Adjudicating Claims of Deceptive Advertised Reference Prices: The Use of Empirical Evidence," *Journal of Public Policy & Marketing*, 14 (Fall 1994), pp. 52–62; Dhruv Grewal and Larry D. Compeau, "Comparative Price Advertising: Informative or Deceptive?" *Journal of Public Policy & Marketing*, 11 (Spring 1992), pp. 52–62.

33. Amy Feldman, "The Tiger in Costco's Tank," *Fast Company*, 117 (July/August 2007), p. 35; "The Pantry Files Lawsuit Against Costco," AllBusiness.com, January 3, 2007, http://www.allbusiness.com/retail-trade/food-stores/4490673-1.html (accessed January 20, 2008).

34. "Wal-Mart Cuts Prices of Generic Drugs as Competitors Follow Suit," September 22, 2006, http://www.pbs.org/newshour/bb/health/july-dec06/walmart_09-22.html (accessed January 18, 2008).

35. Joanna Grossman, "The End of Ladies Night in New Jersey," *Find Law's Legal Commentary*, 2004, http://writ.news.findlaw.com/grossman/20040615.html (accessed November 29, 2005); http://washingtontimes.com/national/20040602-111843-2685r.htm (accessed November 29, 2005); Joyce Howard Price, "Ladies Night Ruled Discriminatory," *The Washington Times*, 2004.

36. Ibid.

37. Steven Friess, "Gym Faces 'Ladies' Night' Bias Case," *The New York Times*, December 12, 2007.

38. http://www.usatoday.com/life/music/news/2002-09-30-cd-settlement_x.htm (accessed November 11, 2008).

39. http://www.cnn.com/US/9711/04/scotus.antitrust/ (accessed September 20, 2006).

40. This case was written by Elisabeth Nevins Caswell in conjunction with the textbook authors (Dhruv Grewal and Michael Levy) for the basis of class discussion rather than to illustrate either effective or ineffective marketing practice. David Kravets, "Like Amazon's DRM-Free Music Downloads? Thanks Apple," *Wired.com*, September 25, 2007 (accessed January 20, 2008); Kevin Kelleher, "Let the MP3 Price Wars Begin," TheStreet.com, September 28, 2007, http://www.thestreet.com/newsanalysis/technet/10381387.html (accessed January 20, 2008).

41. This case was written by Larry D. Compeau in conjunction with the textbook authors (Dhruv Grewal and Michael Levy) as the basis of class discussion rather than to illustrate either effective or ineffective marketing practice.

Chapter 15

1. Stacey Kusterbeck, "Nicole Miller: Moving from 'Mom and Pop' to Major Player," *Apparel Magazine*, 49, no. 2 (2007), pp. 22–24.

2. This chapter draws from Michael Levy and Barton A. Weitz, *Retailing Management*, 7th ed. (Burr Ridge, IL: McGraw-Hill/Irwin, 2009).

3. Based on David Simchi-Levi, Philip Kaminsky, and Edith Simchi-Levi, *Designing and Managing the Supply Chain: Concepts, Strategies and Case Studies*, 2nd ed. (New York: McGraw-Hill Irwin, 2003); and Levy and Weitz, *Retailing Management*.

4. http://www.marketingpower.com/_layouts/Dictionary.aspx.

5. Ibid.

6. Ibid.

7. http://www.zara.com/v04/eng/home.php (accessed September 20, 2006); Pankaj Ghemawat and Jose Luis Nueno, "Zara: Fast Fashion," Harvard Business School Case Number 9-703-497 (April 1, 2003); http://www.inditex.com/english/home.htm (accessed July 20, 2006); Guillermo D'Andrea and David Arnold, "Zara," Harvard Business School Case Number 9-503-050 (March 12, 2003); http://www.gapinc.com/financmedia/financmedia.htm (accessed March 13, 2005); http://www.hm.com/us/start/start/index.jsp# (accessed June 4, 2005); http://www.benetton.com/press/ (accessed September 3, 2006); Stephen Tierney, "New Look's Supply Chain Obsession," *Frontline Solutions*, 12, no. 6 (October 2003), pp. 24–25; David Bovet and Joseph Martha, "E-Business and Logistics Unlocking the Rusty Supply Chain," *Logistics Quarterly*, 6, no. 4 (Winter 2000), pp. 1–3; Jane M. Folpe, "Zara Has a Made-to-Order Plan for Success," *Fortune*, 142, no. 5 (September 2000), pp. 80–82; Carlta Vitzthum, "Just-in-Time Fashion: Spanish Retailer Zara Makes Low-Cost Lines in Weeks by Running Its Own Show," *The Wall Street Journal* (Eastern Edition), May 18, 2001, p. B1.

8. Cecilie Rohwedder and Keith Johnson, "Pace-Setting Zara Seeks More Speed to Fight Its Rising Cheap-Chic Rivals," *The Wall Street Journal,* February 20, 2008.

9. http://www.marketingpower.com/_layouts/Dictionary.aspx.

10. Jean Thilmany, "Neiman Marcus Sails through Customs," *Apparel Magazine,* 49, no. 2 (2007).

11. Anthony Coia, "How Cabela's Is Maximizing Fulfillment Efficiency," *Apparel Magazine,* 46, no. 10 (June 2005).

12. http://www.vendormanagedinventory.net (accessed May 28, 2008).

13. S. P Nachiappan, A. Gunasekaran, and N. Jawahar, "Knowledge Management System for Operating Parameters in Two-Echelon VMI Supply Chains," *International Journal of Production Research,* 45, no. 11 (2007), pp. 2479–2505; Andres Angulo, Heather Nachtmann, and Matthew A. Waller, "Supply Chain Information Sharing in a Vendor Managed Inventory Partnership," *Journal of Business Logistics,* 25 (2004), pp. 101–120.

14. Mohsen Attaran and Sharmin Attaran, "Collaborative Supply Chain Management: The Most Promising Practice for Building Efficient and Sustainable Supply Chains," *Business Process Management Journal,* 13, no. 3 (2007), pp. 390–404; http://www.ediuniversity.com/glossary (accessed January 8, 2008); Mark Barratt, "Positioning the Role of Collaborative Planning in Grocery Supply Chains," *International Journal of Logistics Management,* 14 (2003), pp. 53–67.

15. Jerold P. Cederlund, Rajiv Kohil, Susan A Sherer, and Yuliang Yao, "How Motorola Put CPFR into Action, *Supply Chain Management Review,* October 1, 2007.

16. BJ's Wholesale Club Case Study, "BJ's Wholesale Club and Pharmavite Reap the Benefits of a Collaborative Program for Increased Sales, Forecast Accuracy and Reduced Inventory," JDA Software Group, 2007.

17. Lingxziu Dong and Kaijie Zhu, "Two-Wholesale-Price Contracts: Push, Pull and Advance-Purchase Discount Contracts," *Manufacturing & Service Operations Management,* 9, no. 3 (2007), pp. 291–311; Hyun-Soo Ahn and Philip Kaminsky, "Production and Distribution Policy in a Two-Stage Stochastic Push-Pull Supply Chain," *IIE Transactions,* 37, no. 7 (2005), pp. 609–621; W. Masuchun, S. Davis, and J. Patterson, "Comparison of Push and Pull Control Strategies for Supply Network Management in a Make-to-Stock Environment," *International Journal of Production Research,* 42, no. 20 (2004), pp. 4401–4420.

18. Sharon Gaudin, "American Apparel Uses RFID to Take Better Stock of Its Stores," Computerworld.com, April 16, 2008.

19. Mary Catherine O'Connor, "American Apparel Makes a Bold Fashion Statement with RFID," *RFID Journal,* April 14, 2008; Terry Sweeney, "American Apparel Taking Wireless Inventory with RFID," *Information Week,* April 14, 2008.

20. Gary McWilliams, "Wal-Mart's Radio-Tracked Inventory Hits Static," *The Wall Street Journal,* February 15, 2007, p. B1; Zeynep Ton, Vincent Dessain, and Monika Stachowiak-Joulain, "RFID at the Metro Group," Harvard Business School Publications, 9-606-053, November 9, 2005.

21. Michael Garry, "Supply Chain Systems Seen Boosting Tesco's U.S. Stores," *Supermarket News,* 55, no. 43 (2007).

22. Ayse Akbalik, Sekoun Kebe, Bernard Penz, and Najiba Sbihi, "Exact Methods and a Heuristic for the Optimization of an Integrated Replenishment-Storage Planning Problem," *International Transactions in Operational Research,* 15, no. 2 (March 2008), pp. 195–214.

23. http://www.tubularsteel.com/solutions_so1006.asp (accessed May 9, 2008).

24. "How Zappos.com Grew So Big So Fast—10 Strategies Behind Their Success," www.marketingsherpa.com, August 7, 2007.

25. UPS Supply Chain Solutions Case Study, "Adidas Goes for the Gold in Customer Service," 2005.

26. http://www.marketingpower.com/live/mg-dictionary.

27. http://www.franchise.org/defaultindustry.aspx (accessed May 19, 2008); http://www.census.gov/marts/www/marts_current.pdf (accessed May 9, 2008).

28. *Entrepreneur's* Top 10 Franchise 500, http://www.entrepreneur.com/franchises/rankings/franchise500-115608/2008.html (accessed May 28, 2008).

29. Pankaj Ghemawat and Jose Luis Nueno, "Zara: Fast Fashion," Harvard Business School Case Number 9-703-497 (April 1, 2003).

30. Laurie Sullivan, "Best Buy Puts a Spin on RFID," *CommDesign,* October 17, 2005, http://www.commsdesign.com/show-Article.jhtml?articleID=172301609 (accessed May 20, 2008); "Security System to Balance Privacy and Supply Chain," *RFID Update,* August 12, 2005, www.rfidupdate.com/articles/index.php?id=932 (accessed May 20, 2008); Miyako Ochkubo, Koutarou Suzuki, and Shingo Kinoshita, "RFID Privacy Issues and Technical Challenges," *Communications of the ACM,* 48, no. 9 (September 2005), pp. 66–71.

31. Erin Anderson and Barton Weitz, "The Use of Pledges to Build and Sustain Commitment in Distribution Channels," *Journal of Marketing Research* 29 (February 1992), pp. 18–34.

32. This case was written by Jeanne L. Munger in conjunction with the textbook authors (Dhruv Grewal and Michael Levy) as the basis of class discussion rather than to illustrate either effective or ineffective marketing practice. Jeanne Munger is an associate professor at the University of Southern Maine.

33. Melissa S. Monroe, "Wal-Mart Is Rewriting Rules, Dominating World's Supply Chain," *Knight Ridder Tribune Business News,* November 10, 2003, p. 1.

34. David Biederman, "Keep It Moving," *Journal of Commerce,* 7, no. 6 (2006), pp. 20–23; Richard J. Schonberger, "The Right Stuff, Revisited," *MSI* 21, no. 9 (September 2003), p. 26.

35. Sharon Gaudin, "Some Suppliers Gain from Failed Wal-Mart RFID Edict," Computerworld.com, April 28, 2008; Marc L. Songini, "Wal-Mart Shifts RFID Plans," Computerworld.com, February 26, 2007.

Chapter 16

1. Stephen Fenech, "Apple's Theme Park," *Herald Sun,* May 28, 2008; http://www.apple.com (accessed May 28, 2008); Jerry Useem, "Apple: America's Best Retailer," *Fortune,* March 8, 2007.

2. David Chartier, "Apple Retail Stores Stomping Competition Foot by Foot," *InfiniteLoop,* January 8, 2008.

3. http://www.nxtbook.com/nxtbooks/nrfe/stores-globalretail08/, p. 8 (accessed May 28, 2008).

4. This chapter draws heavily from Michael Levy and Barton A. Weitz, *Retailing Management,* 7th ed. (Burr Ridge, IL: McGraw-Hill/Irwin, 2009), Chapters 2 and 3.

5. *Industry Outlook: Food Channel* (Columbus, OH: Retail Forward, April 2007).

6. Ibid., p. 12.

7. Ibid., p. 13.

8. http://www.fmi.org/facts_figs/keyfacts/superfact.htm (accessed May 28, 2008).

9. Ibid.

10. Ibid.

11. "Limited Assortment Supermarkets," http://www.wikipedia.com (accessed May 28, 2008).

12. Mary Ellen Burris, "New PA Service Center," http://www. wegmans.com (accessed September 19, 2005); Mary Ellen Burns, "ACHOOOO . . . ," http://www.wegmans.com (accessed September 19, 2005); "The Wegmans Way," *Fortune* 151, no. 2 (January 24, 2005), pp. 62–64, 66, 68; Mary Glynn, "Wegmans Plans to Rebuild a Depew Store," *Knight Ridder Tribune Business News,* June 8, 2005, p. 1.

13. Kelly Trackett, *Industry Outlook: Department Stores* (Columbus, OH: Retail Forward, July 2006), p. 7.

14. Christopher Palmeri, "Trader Joe's Recipe for Success," *BusinessWeek,* February 21, 2008 (accessed electronically May 27, 2008); "Trader Joe's . . . The Forgotten Supermarket Giant," *Autopsy,* June 10, 2007.

15. *Industry Channel: Mass Channel* (Columbus, OH: Retail Forward, June 2006), p. 29.

16. Sandra J. Skrovan, *Drug Stores on Acquisition Trail* (Columbus, OH: Retail Forward, August 2006).

17. Rusty Williamson, "Walgreens Raising Its Fashion Quotient," *WWD,* December 13, 2006 (accessed electronically November 11, 2008).

18. "Variety Store," http://en.wikipedia.org/wiki/Variety_store (accessed May 28, 2008).

19. "T.J. Maxx," http://en.wikipedia.org/wiki/T.J._Maxx (accessed May 28, 2008).

20. Sylvie Morin, Laurette Dube, and Jean-Charles Chebat, "The Role of Pleasant Music in Servicescapes: A Test of the Dual Model of Environmental Perception," *Journal of Retailing,* 83, no.1 (2007), pp. 115–130; Nancy M. Pucinelli, Dhruv Grewal, Susan Andrzejewski, Ereni Markos, and Tracy Noga, "The Value of Knowing What Customers Really Want: Interpersonal Accuracy as an Environmental Cue," working paper (2008); Liz C. Wang, Julie Baker, Judy A. Wagner, and Kirk Wakefield, "Can a Retail Web Site Be Social?" *Journal of Marketing,* 71, (July 2007), pp. 143–157; Julie Baker, A. Parasuraman, Dhruv Grewal, and Glenn Voss, "The Influence of Multiple Store Environment Cues on Perceived Merchandise Value and Patronage Intentions," *Journal of Marketing,* 66 (April 2001), pp. 120–141; Eric R. Spangenberg, Ayn E. Crowley, and Pamela W. Henderson, "Improving the Store Environment: Do Olfactory Cues Affect Evaluations and Behaviors?" *Journal of Marketing,* 60 (April 1996), pp. 67–80; Michael K. Hui and John E. G. Bateson, "Perceived Control and the Effects of Crowding and Consumer Choice on the Service Experience," *Journal of Consumer Research,* 18 (September 1991), pp. 174–184.

21. Leonard Berry, Kathleen Seiders, and Dhruv Grewal, "Understanding Service Convenience," *Journal of Marketing,* 66 (July 2002), pp. 1–17.

22. "Can't Find That Dress on the Rack? Retailers Are Pushing More Shoppers to the Net," *Knowledge@Wharton,* November 1, 2006.

23. John P. Mello Jr., "Solo Hunters, Social Gatherers and the Online Marketplace," *E-Commerce Times,* May 25, 2007 (accessed electronically May 28, 2008).

24. James Covert, "Online Clothes Reviews Give 'Love That Dress' New Clout," *The Wall Street Journal,* December 7, 2006, p. B1.

25. Bob Tedeschi, "Like Shopping? Social Networking? Try Social Shopping," *The New York Times,* September 11, 2006 (accessed electronically May 28, 2008).

26. Satish Nambisan and Robert A. Baron, "Interactions in Virtual Customer Environments: Implications for Product Support and Customer Relationship Management," *Journal of Interactive Marketing,* 21, no. 2 (2007), pp. 42–62.

27. Kenneth Hein, "Study: Web Research Nets In-Store Sales," *Brandweek,* May 7, 2007 (accessed electronically December 24, 2007).

28. Jessica E. Vascellaro, "Online Retailers Are Watching You," *The Wall Street Journal,* November 28, 2006, p. D1.

29. "Internet Retailer Best of the Web 2007," *Internet Retailer,* June 18, 2007 (accessed electronically May 28, 2008).

30. Alexandria Sage, "Consumers Find a Personal Shopper in the Web," *Boston Globe,* August 19, 2006 (accessed electronically May 28, 2008).

31. Brad Stone, "Amazon Accelerates Its Move to Digital," *The New York Times,* April 7, 2008; Joe Nocera, "Put Buyers First? What a Concept," *The New York Times,* January 5, 2008.

32. Gianluigi Guido, Mauro Capestro, and Alessandro M. Peluso, "Experimental Analysis of Consumer Stimulation and Motivational States in Shopping Experiences," *International Journal of Market Research,* 49, no. 3 (2007), pp. 365–386.

33. Sandra Forsythe, Liu Chuanlan Liu, David Shannon, and Liu Chun Gardner, "Development of a Scale to Measure the Perceived Benefits and Risks of Online Shopping," *Journal of Interactive Marketing,* 20, no. 2 (2006), pp. 55–75.

34. Jon Brodkin, "TJX Breach: Rethinking Corp. Security," *Network World,* 24, no. 13 (2007) (accessed electronically December 14, 2007).

35. Forsythe et al., "Development of a Scale to Measure the Perceived Benefits and Risks of Online Shopping."

36. Brodkin, "TJX Breach: Rethinking Corp. Security."

37. Ibid.

38. For more information on approaches for increasing share of wallet, see Tom Osten, *Customer Share Marketing* (Upper Saddle River, NJ: Prentice Hall, 2002).

39. This case was written by Jeanne L. Munger (University of Southern Maine) in conjunction with the textbook authors Dhruv Grewal and Michael Levy as the basis of class discussion rather than to illustrate either effective or ineffective marketing practice. The authors thank Max Ward, vice president of technology at Staples, who provided valuable input for the development of this case. They also acknowledge that parts of the case are based on information provided by W. Caleb McCann (in collaboration with J. P. Jeannet, Dhruv Grewal, and Martha Lanning), "Staples," in *Fulfillment in E-Business,* eds. Petra Schuber, Ralf Wolfle, and Walter Dettling (Germany: Hanser, 2001) pp. 239–252 (in German).

40. http://www.bizjournals.com/boston/stories/2004/03/01/daily53.html (accessed September 20, 2006).

41. http://multichannelmerchant.com/news/marketing_electronic_catalog_key (accessed May 28, 2008).

Chapter 17

1. http://www.wakeuppeople.com (accessed February 14, 2008).

2. "Coke Zero Pulls Fast One on Top NASCAR Drivers," *Business Wire,* February 12, 2008, http://www.foxbusiness.com/markets/industries/retail/article/coke-zero-pulls-fast-nascar-drivers_476241_7.html (accessed February 14, 2008).

3. Kate MacArthur, "Pepsi Goes on $55 mil Binge for Diet Max," *Advertising Age,* June 25, 2007.

4. http://www.cocacolazero.com/sueafriend.html (accessed February 14, 2008).

5. T. Duncan and C. Caywood, "The Concept, Process, and Evolution of Integrated Marketing Communication," in *Integrated Communication: Synergy of Persuasive Voices,* eds. E. Thorson and J. Moore (Mahwah, NJ: Lawrence Erlbaum Associates, 1996); http://jimc.medill.northwestern.edu/2000/pettegrew.htm.

6. Deborah J. MacInnis and Bernard J. Jaworski, "Information Processing from Advertisements: Toward an Integrative

Framework," *Journal of Marketing,* 53, no. 4 (October 1989), pp. 1–23.

7. Deborah J. MacInnis, Christine Moorman, and Bernard J. Jaworski, "Enhancing and Measuring Consumers' Motivation, Opportunity," *Journal of Marketing,* 55, no. 4 (October 1991), pp. 32–53; Joan Meyers-Levy, "Elaborating on Elaboration: The Distinction between Relational and Item-Specific Elaboration," *Journal of Consumer Research,* 18 (December 1991), pp. 358–367.

8. Carleen Hawn, "Marketing's New Vanguard: The Cubicle," Inc.com, August 2006, http://www.inc.com/magazine/20060801/handson-advertising.html (accessed February 14, 2008).

9. E. K. Strong, *The Psychology of Selling* (New York: McGraw Hill, 1925).

10. Karl Greenber, "Toyota Promotes Yaris in 'TV Guide,' Fox Deal," *Marketing Daily,* October 3, 2007, http://publications.mediapost.com/index.cfm?fuseaction=Articles.showArticle&art_aid=68554 (accessed February 14, 2008).

11. Seth Stevenson, "Toyota's Violent Yaris Car Ads," July 6, 2007, http://www.npr.org/templates/story/story.php?storyId=5538263 (accessed February 14, 2008).

12. Ibid.

13. William F. Arens, Michael F. Weigold, and Christian Arens, *Contemporary Advertising,* 11th ed. (New York: McGraw-Hill, 2008), p. 255.

14. John Philip Jones, "What Makes Advertising Work?" *The Economic Times,* July 24, 2002.

15. http://www.legamedia.net/lx/result/match/0591dfc9787c111b1b24dde6d61e43c5/index.php.

16. http://www.mediafinder.com (accessed February 18, 2008).

17. Samir Husni, *Samir Husni's Guide to New Magazines* (Oxford, MS: Nautilus Publishing, 2005).

18. American Marketing Association, *Dictionary of Marketing Terms* (Chicago: American Marketing Association, 2008).

19. George E. Belch and Michael A. Belch, *Advertising and Promotion: An Integrated Marketing Communications Perspective* (New York: McGraw-Hill, 2007).

20. http://about.telus.com/investors/en/glossaryBot.html (accessed October 26, 2007).

21. Joseph Tarnowski, "Technology: The 'Extended Peripheral'." *Progressive Grocer,* September 14, 2006 (accessed electronically January 25, 2008).

22. Jayne O'Donnell, "Teens Targeted with Cellphone Marketing," *USA Today,* March 20, 2007.

23. Ibid.

24. Louise Story, "New Form of Impulse: Shopping via Text Message," *The New York Times,* April 16, 2007 (accessed electronically January 25, 2008).

25. "What's on the Horizon for Marketing to Hispanics," *Marketing News,* September 1, 2007.

26. Emily Steel, "How Marketers Hone Their Aim Online," *The Wall Street Journal,* June 19, 2007.

27. "iUpload Takes Datamation's First Blogging Win," February 28, 2006, www.itmanagement.earthweb.com (accessed April 19, 2006); Nicole Ziegler Dizon, "Corporations Enter into World of Blogs," *San Francisco Gate,* June 6, 2006, www.sfgate.com (accessed September 26, 2006); Mark Berger, "Annie's Homegrown: 'Bernie's Blog' Case Study," www.backbonemedia.com (accessed September 26, 2006); "Corporate Blogging Survey" www.backbonemedia.com (accessed September 26, 2006).

28. "Mr. Mackey's Offense," *The Wall Street Journal,* July 16, 2007 (accessed May 9, 2008).

29. www.blogsouthwest.com (accessed May 13, 2008).

30. http://wholefoodsmarket.com/socialmedia/blogs/ (accessed May 13, 2008).

31. http://community.overstock.com/ (accessed May 13, 2008).

32. Greet Van Hoye and Filip Lievens, "Social Influences on Organizational Attractiveness: Investigating If and When Word of Mouth Matters," *Journal of Applied Social Psychology,* 37, no. 9 (2007), pp. 2024–2047; Robert East, Kathy Hammond, and Malcom Wright, "The Relative Incidence of Positive and Negative Word of Mouth: A Multi-Category Study," *International Journal of Research in Marketing,* 24, no. 2 (2007), pp. 175–184; Tom Brown, Thomas Barry, Peter Dacin, and Richard Gunst, "Spreading the Word: Investigating Antecedents of Consumers' Positive Word-of-Mouth Intentions and Behaviors in a Retailing Context," *Journal of the Academy of Marketing Science,* 33 (Spring 2005), pp. 123–139.

33. Bob Tedeschi, "Like Shopping? Social Networking? Try Social Shopping," *The New York Times,* September 16, 2006 (accessed electronically January 25, 2008).

34. Joan Voight, "Getting a Handle on Customer Reviews," *Adweek,* July 5, 2007, based on research by Top 40 Online Retail from Foresee Results and the University of Michigan (accessed electronically January 25, 2008).

35. Cheryl Lu-Lien Tan, "That's So You! Just Click Here to Buy It," *The Wall Street Journal,* June 7, 2007, p. D8.

36. Ibid.

37. Voight, "Getting a Handle on Customer Reviews."

38. This section draws from Michael Levy and Barton A. Weitz, *Retailing Management,* 7th ed. (Burr Ridge, IL: McGraw-Hill/Irwin, 2009).

39. Murali Mantrala, "Allocating Marketing Resources," in *Handbook of Marketing,* eds. Barton Weitz and Robin Wensley (London: Sage, 2002), pp. 409–435.

40. http://www.riger.com/know_base/media/understanding.html (accessed November 15, 2004).

41. "Marketing and Advertising Using Google," Google, 2007.

42. http://publishing2.com/2008/05/27/google-adwords-a-brief-history-of-online-advertising-innovation/ (accessed June 1, 2008).

43. http://www.cdc.gov/tobacco/overview/chron96.htm (accessed September 26, 2006).

44. In general, commercial speech is defined as a communication that proposes a commercial transaction, such as a specific offer to buy or sell a product (e.g., Virginia Pharmacy sells prescription drugs). Speech that does not specifically propose a commercial transaction may still be considered commercial speech. Factors to consider (*Bolger v. Youngs Drug Products*) include (1) appearance in an advertisement, (2) reference to a specific product, (3) reference to a product generically when the speaker has strong market position, and (4) the economic motivation of the speaker. However, the mere fact that a speech is made for an economic motive does not make it commercial speech (*New York Times v. Sullivan*). Speech may be "commercial" even if it includes references that "link the product to a current public debate." http://www.kylewood.com/firstamendment/commercial.htm.

45. Beverly Rice, "Pepsi Accuses Coke of Deceptive Advertising," *Legal Zoom,* https://www.legalzoom.com/legal-articles/pepsi-accuses-coke-deceptive-advertising.html (accessed February 28, 2008).

46. Richard Kielbowicz and Linda Lawson, "Unmasking Hidden Commercials in Broadcasting: Origins of the Sponsorship Identification Regulations 1927–1963," 2004, http://www.law.indiana.edu/fclj/pubs/v56/no2/Kielbowicz%20around%20IV.pdf (accessed September 4, 2005). More case/settlement details in IM.

47. This case was written by Elisabeth Nevins Caswell in conjunction with the textbook authors, Dhruv Grewal and Michael Levy, as the basis of class discussion rather than to illustrate either effective or ineffective marketing practice.

48. "Adweek Magazine's Special Report: Best Laid Plans," June 18, 2007, http://www.mediaweek.com/mediaweek/images/pdf/MediaPlan6_18.pdf (accessed March 3, 2008).

49. "Lionsgate and Warcon Records Promote 'Saw III' with Live Musical Event," October 13, 2007, http://www.indiescene.net/archives/lionsgate_films/lionsgate_and_warcon_records_p.htm (accessed March 3, 2008).

50. http://vids.myspace.com/index.cfm?fuseaction=vids.channel&ChannelID=77571500 (accessed March 3, 2008).

Chapter 18

1. The Gap Inc., http://www.gapinc.com/public/About/abt_milestones.shtml (accessed March 7, 2008).

2. Phil Wahba, "The Politics of Gap's Advertising," *The New York Sun*, January 23, 2007, http://www.nysun.com/article/47171?page_no=1 (accessed March 7, 2008).

3. Claire Atkinson, "Gap Tries a Somewhat Old-Fashioned Campaign," *The New York Times*, August 3, 2007.

4. George E. Belch and Michael A. Belch, *Advertising and Promotion: An Integrated Marketing Communications Perspective* (New York: McGraw-Hill, 2007); Jef I. Richards and Catherine M. Curran, "Oracles on 'Advertising': Searching for a Definition," *Journal of Advertising* 31, no. 2 (Summer 2002), pp. 63–77.

5. "U.S. Ad Spend to Grow 3.7% in '08, Up from 2.8% in '07; Global to Grow 7%," http://www.mediabuyerplanner.com/2007/12/05/us-ad-spend-to-grow-37-in-08-up-from-28-in-07-global-to-grow-7/ (accessed March 7, 2008); "Global Ad Spending Expected to Grow 6%," *Brandweek*, December 6, 2005.

6. Raymond R. Burke and Thomas K. Srull, "Competitive Interference and Consumer Memory for Advertising," *Journal of Consumer Research*, 15 (June 1988), pp. 55–68; Kevin Lane Keller, "Memory Factors in Advertising: The Effect of Advertising Retrieval Cues on Brand Evaluation," *Journal of Consumer Research*, 14 (December 1987), pp. 316–333; Kevin Lane Keller, "Memory and Evaluation Effects in Competitive Advertising Environments," *Journal of Consumer Research*, 17 (March 1991), pp. 463–477; Robert J. Kent and Chris T. Allen, "Competitive Interference Effects in Consumer Memory for Advertising: The Role of Brand Familiarity," *Journal of Marketing*, 58, no. 3 (July 1994), pp. 97–106.

7. Terry Daugherty, Matthew Eastin, and Laura Bright, "Exploring Consumer Motivations for Creating User-Generated Content," *Journal of Interactive Advertising*, 8, no. 2 (2008); Anthony Bianco, "The Vanishing Mass Market," *BusinessWeek*, July 12, 2004, pp. 61–68.

8. "Jewelry: A Cross-Generation Purchase," *Idex Magazine*, October 10, 2006, http://www.idexonline.com/portal_FullMazalUbracha.asp?id=26293 (accessed March 7, 2008); http://retailindustry.about.com/library/bl/q2/bl_um041701.htm (accessed September 26, 2006).

9. http://www.inastrol.com/Articles/990601.htm (accessed September 26, 2006).

10. Karl Greenburg, "Chrysler Turns to Nickelodeon to Plug Backseat TV, Swivel Seats," *Marketing Daily*, June 26, 2007, http://publications.mediapost.com/index.cfm?fuseaction=Articles.showArticle&art_aid=62953 (accessed March 7, 2008).

11. William F. Arens, Michael F. Weigold, and Christian Arens, *Contemporary Advertising*, 11th ed. (New York: McGraw-Hill, 2007).

12. Gina Chon, "Chrysler Challenge: Burnish Image," *The Wall Street Journal*, August 24, 2007.

13. Matthew Shum, "Does Advertising Overcome Brand Loyalty? Evidence from the Breakfast Cereal Market," *Journal of Economics and Management Strategy* 13, no. 2 (2004), pp. 77–85.

14. "Got Milk?" http://www.gotmilk.com/fun/ads.html (accessed March 7, 2008).

15. http://advertising.utexas.edu/research/terms/index.asp#P (accessed November 15, 2004).

16. http://www.grantstream.com/glossary.htm (accessed September 26, 2006).

17. The Ad Council, "Campaigns," http://www.adcouncil.org/default.aspx?id=15 (accessed March 7, 2008).

18. The Ad Council, "Historic Campaigns," http://www.adcouncil.org/default.aspx?id=61 (accessed March 7, 2008).

19. Protect the truth, "truth Campaign," http://www.protectthetruth.org/truthcampaign.htm (accessed March 7, 2008).

20. http://www.apha.org/journal/nation/truthcover0504.htm (accessed September 26, 2006).

21. Alina Tugend, "Cigarette Makers Take Anti-Smoking Ads Personally," *The New York Times*, October 27, 2002, Business section.

22. "The Sunny Side of truth: The Useful Cigarette," http://www.thetruth.com/facts/useFulCig/ (accessed March 7, 2008).

23. "The Sunny Side of truth: About Us," http://www.thetruth.com/aboutUs.cfm (accessed March 7, 2008).

24. Protect the truth, http://www.protectthetruth.org/truth-campaign.htm (accessed March 7, 2008).

25. Theodore Leavitt, *The Marketing Imagination* (New York: The Free Press, 1986).

26. Belch and Belch, *Advertising and Promotion: An Integrated Marketing Communications Perspective*.

27. http://www2.kleenex.com/au/range/anti-viral/ (accessed May 8, 2008).

28. Bret A. S. Martin, Bodo Lang, and Stephanie Wong, "Conclusion, Explicitness in Advertising: The Moderating Role of Need for Cognition and Argument Quality on Persuasion," *Journal of Advertising*, 32, no. 4 (2004), pp. 57–65.

29. Michael Petracca and Madeleine Sorapure, eds., *Common Culture: Reading and Writing about American Popular Culture* (Upper Saddle River, NJ: Prentice Hall, 1998).

30. http://wps.prenhall.com/ca_ph_ebert_busess_3/0,6518,224378-,00.html.

31. TNS Media Intelligence, January 7, 2008, http://www.tns-mi.com/news/01072008.htm (accessed March 8, 2008); http://www.admedia.org/ (accessed September 26, 2006).

32. http://www.marketingpower.com/_layouts/Dictionary.aspx, (accessed November 13, 2008).

33. Jeff Borden, "Good Cheer," *Marketing News*, March 15, 2008.

34. Arens, Weigold, and Arens, *Contemporary Advertising*.

35. Media guru Marshall McLuhan first discussed the notion of "The Medium is the Message" in the 1960s.

36. http://adsoftheworld.com/media/print/buenos_aires_zoo_ape.

37. Dean M. Krugman, Leonard N. Reid, S. Watson Dunn, and Arnold M. Barban, *Advertising: Its Role in Modern Marketing* (New York: The Dryden Press, 1994), pp. 221–226.

38. Stanford L. Grossbart and Lawrence A. Crosby, "Understanding Bases of Parental Concern and Reaction to Children's Food Advertising," *Journal of Marketing*, 48, no. 3 (1984), pp. 79–93; Brian M. Young, "Does Food Advertising Influence Children's Food Choices? A Critical Review of Some of the Recent Literature," *International Journal of Advertising*, 22, no. 4 (2003), p. 441.

39. http://ods.od.nih.gov/factsheets/DietarySupplements.asp (accessed September 26, 2006).

40. Alexandra Zendrian, "Airborne Settles Lawsuit," *The New York Times*, March 7, 2008.

41. Neil Merrett, "Dannon Heads to Courts over 'Fraud' Probiotic Claims," NUTRAUSAingredients.com, January 24, 2008. This case had not been settled at press time.

42. Debra Harker, Michael Harker, and Robert Burns, "Tackling Obesity: Developing a Research Agenda for Advertising Researchers," *Journal of Current Issues & Research in Advertising*, 29, no. 2 (2007), pp. 39–51; N. Kapoor and D. P. S. Verma, "Children's Understanding of TV Advertisements: Influence of Age, Sex and Parents," *Vision*, 9, no. 1 (2005), pp. 21–36; Catharine M. Curran and Jef I. Richards, "The Regulation of Children's Advertising in the U.S.," *The International Journal of Advertising and Marketing to Children*, 2, no. 2 (2002).

43. http://advertising.utexas.edu/research/terms/index.asp#O (accessed May 12, 2008).

44. Bob Hunt, "Truth in Your Advertising: Avoid Puffery?" *Realty Times*, June 20, 2007.

45. *American Italian Pasta Company v. New World Pasta Company*, 371 F.3d 387 (8th Cir. 2004); Craig Barkacs, "Must a Claim to Be 'America's Favorite' Be Verifiable?," *Journal of the Academy of Marketing Science*, 33, no. 4, (Fall 2005), pp. 634–636.

46. Hunt, "Truth in Your Advertising: Avoid Puffery?"

47. Katherine Rosman, "And the Loser Is . . . Fashion," *The Wall Street Journal*, January 9, 2008.

48. Erin Carlson, "Diablo Cody's Oscar Success with Juno Was Bound to Have a Backlash," *Chicago Sun-Times*, February 27, 2008, http://www.suntimes.com/entertainment/movies/815295,cody022708.article (accessed February 28, 2008).

49. Carl Obermiller and Eric R. Spangenberg, "On the Origin and Distinctness of Skepticism toward Advertising," *Marketing Letters*, 11, no. 4 (2000), p. 311.

50. http://www.tomsshoes.com/ourcause.aspx (accessed February 23, 2008).

51. Jackie Huba, "A Just Cause Creating Emotional Connections with Customers," 2003, http://www.inc.com/articles/2003/05/25537.html.

52. http://www.insightargentina.org (accessed February 23, 2008).

53. Carol Angrisani, "CVS Moves to Personalization," *SN: Supermarket News*, 56, no. 2 (March 24, 2008), p. 29.

54. Carol Angrisani, "Thousands of Kroger Shoppers Embrace E-Coupons," *SN: Supermarket News*, 56, no. 14 (April 7, 2008), p. 27.

55. "Mobile Coupons Find More Favor with Consumers than Advertisers," *Internet Retailer*, May 11, 2008.

56. Peter Meyers and Steve Litt, "Finding the Redemption Sweet Spot: Debunking the Top Ten Myths about Couponing," *Journal of Consumer Marketing*, 25, no. 1 (2008), pp. 57–59; Michelle Roehm, " The Relationship between FSI Advertising Style and Coupon Redemption," *Marketing Letters*, 18, no. 4 (October 2007), pp. 237–247.

57. "Post-it Notes Holds Video Contest on YouTube," http://promote.3m.com/notepad_youtube.jsp;jsessionid=avmFtZ6_-VRa (accessed May 11, 2008).

58. Daniel B. Honigman, "Hotels at Home," *Marketing News*, March 15, 2008.

59. Brent Bowers, "Waiting (and Waiting) for the Rebate Check," *The New York Times*, March 19, 2008 (accessed electronically March 19, 2008).

60. https://www.stapleseasyrebates.com/img/staples/paper-less/pages/Landing.html (accessed March 19, 2008).

61. Elizabeth Cowley and Chris Barron, "When Product Placement Goes Wrong," *Journal of Advertising*, 37, no. 1 (Spring 2008), pp. 89–98.

62. http://www.hersheys.com/products/details/reesespieces.asp (accessed May 8, 2008).

63. Bill Shepard, "Jumping on the Brand Wagon: The Allure of Product Placement," *Wisconsin Business Alumni Update*, 25, no. 1 (June 2007).

64. Motoko Rich, "Product Placement Deals Make Leap from Film to Books," *The New York Times*, June 12, 2006 (accessed electronically March 10, 2008); Motoko Rich, "In Books for Young, Two Views on Product Placement," *The New York Times*, February 19, 2008 (accessed electronically March 10, 2008).

65. David Kiley, "Hip Hop Two-Step over Product Placement," *BusinessWeek*, April 6, 2006 (accessed electronically March 20, 2008).

66. Cristel A. Russell and Michael Belch, "A Managerial Investigation into the Product Placement Industry," *Journal of Advertising Research*, 45, no. 1 (2005), pp. 73–92.

67. Ronald Curhan and Robert Kopp, "Obtaining Retailer Support for Trade Deals: Key Success Factors," *Journal of Advertising Research*, 27 (December 1987–January 1988), pp. 51–60.

68. This case was written by Elisabeth Nevins Caswell in conjunction with the textbook authors, Dhruv Grewal and Michael Levy, as the basis of class discussion rather than to illustrate either effective or ineffective marketing practice.

69. Guy Trebay, "She's Famous (and So Can You)," *The New York Times*, October 28, 2007; Lev Grossman, "Tila Tequila," *Time*, December 16, 2006.

70. http://www.facebook.com/ads/?src=awo5 (accessed March 19, 2008).

71. http://www.myspace.com/ (accessed March 19, 2008).

72. Elisabeth A. Sullivan, "Be Sociable," *Marketing News*, January 15, 2008.

Chapter 19

1. http://www.cnbc.com/id/23155570 (accessed April 15, 2008); http://www.charismafactor.com/speakers/gloria-mayfield-banks.asp (accessed April 15, 2008); Ronda Racha Penrice, "Positively Fabulous," *Turning Point Magazine*, http://www.turningpointmagazine.com/index.php (accessed April 15, 2008); http://abcnews.go.com/Video/playerIndex?id=3715173 (accessed April 15, 2008).

2. U.S. Department of Labor, "Occupational Employment and Wages: Sales and Related Occupations," May 2006.

3. This section draws from Mark W. Johnston and Greg W. Marshall, *Relationship Selling and Sales Management*, 2nd ed. (Burr Ridge, IL: Irwin/McGraw-Hill, 2007).

4. http://www.workz.com/content/view_content. html?section_id=557&content_id=7086 (accessed April 15, 2008).

5. Steve McKee, "How to Generate Real Customer Loyalty," *BusinessWeek*, June 6, 2007; Michael Beverland, "Contextual Influences and the Adoption and Practice of Relationship Selling in a Business-to-Business Setting: An Exploratory Study," *Journal of Personal Selling and Sales Management*, Summer 2001, p. 207.

6. McKee, "How to Generate Real Customer Loyalty."

7. Bill Stinnett, *Think Like Your Customer* (Burr Ridge, IL: McGraw-Hill, 2004).

8. Prashant Gopal, "How the Super-Rich Buy Homes," *BusinessWeek*, April 11, 2008.

9. Mark W. Johnston and Greg W. Marshall, *Relationship Selling and Sales Management*, 2nd ed. (Burr Ridge, IL: Irwin/McGraw-Hill, 2007).

10. Michael Levy and Barton A. Bart Weitz, *Retailing Management*, 7th ed. (New York: McGraw-Hill/Irwin, 2008); http://www.cesweb.org/about_ces/fact_sheet.asp (accessed October 11, 2007).

11. Christine Comaford, "Sales Stuck? Try Sticking to a Script," *BusinessWeek*, April 4, 2008.

12. Christine Comaford-Lynch, "A Bad Lead Is Worse Than No Lead at All," *BusinessWeek*, March 26, 2008.

13. Barton A. Weitz, Harish Sujan, and Mita Sujan, "Knowledge, Motivation, and Adaptive Behavior: A Framework for Improving Selling Effectiveness," *Journal of Marketing*, October 1986, pp. 174–191.

14. http://www.quotedb.com/quotes/1303 (accessed April 15, 2008).

15. Mark W. Johnston and Greg W. Marshall, *Churchill/Ford/Walker's Sales Force Management*, 8th ed. (Burr Ridge, IL: McGraw-Hill/Irwin, 2005).

16. "He Works Hard for the Money," Businessweek.com, January 24, 2008.

17. Marshall Lager, "Selling CRM to Your Sales Force," CRM.com, March 1, 2008.

18. Vauhini Vara, "'That Looks Great on You': Online Salespeople Get Pushy," *The Wall Street Journal*, January 3, 2007.

19. David H. Holtzman, "Big Business Knows Us Too Well," *BusinessWeek*, June 22, 2007.

20. Johnston and Marshall, *Churchill/Ford/Walker's Sales Force Management*.

21. "Ethical Breach," *Sales & Marketing Management*, July 2004.

22. Erin Stout, "Doctoring Sales," Salesandmarketing.com, May 2001; "Pushing Pills; Pharmaceuticals," *The Economist*, 366, no. 8311 (February 15, 2003), p. 65; R. Stephen Parker and Charles E. Pettijohn, "Ethical Considerations in the Use of Direct-to-Consumer Advertising and Pharmaceutical Promotions: The Impact on Pharmaceutical Sales and Physicians," *Journal of Business Ethics*, 48, no. 3 (December 2, 2003), p. 279; "Pharmaceutical Sales Ethics: New Reforms or Business As Usual?" press release, July 23, 2004, http://www.medzilla.com/press72304.html (accessed September 26, 2006); Kate Moore and Jahi Harvey, "Drug Companies Push Pills to Doctors," MorningJournal.com, August 7, 2002.

23. http://www.marketingpower.com/live/mg-dictionary (accessed April 15, 2008).

24. Johnston and Marshall, *Relationship Selling and Sales Management*, pp. 375–376; Johnston and Marshall, *Churchill/Ford/Walker's Sales Force Management*.

25. Rene Y. Darmon, "Where Do the Best Sales Force Profit Producers Come From?" *Journal of Personal Selling and Sales Management*, 13, no. 3 (1993), pp. 17–29.

26. Julie Chang, "Born to Sell?" *Sales and Marketing Management*, July 2003, p. 36.

27. Laura Heller, "Cutting Commissions Is the Key That Turns Merchandise—and Turns on the Fun," *DSN Retailing Today* 42 (September 8, 2003), p. 17.

28. "Mary Kay: Where's the Money?" http://www.marykay.com (accessed September 5, 2006); http://www.Marykay.com/lsoulier; "Mary Kay Museum," www.addisontexas.net (accessed September 5, 2006).

29. Johnston and Marshall, *Relationship Selling and Sales Management*, p. 368; Bill Kelley, "Recognition Reaps Rewards," *Sales and Marketing Management*, June 1986, p. 104 (reprinted from Thomas R. Wotruba, John S. Macfie, and Jerome A. Collem, "Effective Sales Force Recognition Programs," in *Industrial Marketing Management*, 20, pp. 9–15).

30. For a discussion of common measures used to evaluate sales people, see Johnston and Marshall, *Churchill/Ford/Walker's Sales Force Management*.

31. This case was written by Jeanne Munger in conjunction with the textbook authors Dhruv Grewal and Michael Levy as the basis of class discussion rather than to illustrate either effective or ineffective marketing practice. For a discussion of common measures used to evaluate sales people, see Johnston and Marshall, *Churchill/Ford/Walker's Sales Force Management*.

credits

Chapter 1

Photos/ads: P. 2, AP Photo. P. 4, AP Photo/Keystone, Walter Bieri. P. 5, ©The Procter & Gamble Company. Used by permission. P. 6, Photo by Carlos Alvarez/Getty Images. P. 7, ©M. Hruby. P. 8, Photo by Chris Gordon/Getty Images. P. 9, Courtesy The Ritz Carlton Hotel Company, LLC; Agency: Team One/El Segundo, CA. P. 10, Courtesy Zappos.com. P. 11, Photo by Paul Hawthorne/Getty Images. P. 12, Courtesy National Fluid Milk Processor Promotion Board; Agency: Lowe Worldwide, Inc. P. 12, Courtesy National Fluid Milk Processor Promotion Board; Agency: Lowe Worldwide, Inc. P. 13, H. Armstrong Roberts/Retrofile/Getty Images. P. 13, Jamie Grill/Iconica/Getty Images. P. 13, ©Ted Dayton Photography/Beateworks/Corbis. P. 13, Ciaran Griffin/Stockbyte/Getty Images. P.13, ©Colin Anderson/Blend Images/Corbis. P. 15, Courtesy Mars Incorporated. P. 16, Courtesy Starwood Hotels & Resorts; Agency: Deutsch Inc./New York. P. 17, Courtesy Zara International, Inc. P. 18, Courtesy easyJet. P. 19, Jason Reed/Getty Images. P. 19, ©Digital Vision/PunchStock. P. 19, ©Edward Rozzo/Corbis. P. 19, Andrew Ward/Life File/Getty Images. P. 19, Â©Roy McMahon/Corbis. P. 19, ©Brand X Pictures/PunchStock. P. 19, BananaStock/JupiterImages. P. 19, Digital Vision/Getty Images. P. 20, Courtesy Scion, Toyota Motor Sales, U.S.A., Inc. P. 22, Jeff Zelevansky/Bloomberg News/Landov. P. 23, ©M. Hruby. P. 25, Courtesy Shooting Star. P. 25, Photo by Thomas Cooper/Getty Images.

Chapter 2

Photos/ads: P. 30, ©Henry Yung. P. 33, Photo by Amy Sussman/Getty Images. P. 35, Photo by Mario Tama/Getty Images. P. 36, Roger Tully/Stone/Getty Images. P. 37, Courtesy Team One Advertising; Photographer: Brian Garland. P. 38, Courtesy of Southwest Airlines. P. 40, Used with permission. ©Mother Against Drunk Drivers 2005. P. 41, ©M. Hruby. P. 42, Gabriel Bouys/AFP/Getty Images. P. 43, *Both ads:* Courtesy of The Coca-Cola Company. P. 44, Courtesy Unilever U.S., Inc. P. 45, ©The Procter & Gamble Company. Used by permission. P. 46, Photo courtesy Staples, Inc. P. 47, AP Photo/Stuart Ramson. P. 47, Courtesy ©2008 The Goodyear Tire & Rubber Company. All rights reserved. Agency: McCann Erickson/New York, NY. Creative Director: Craig Markus; Art Director: Tim Dillingham; Copywriter: Mark Ronquillo; Photographer: ©2007 Graham Westmoreland/Friend and Johnson. P. 50, Photo by Chip Somodevilla/Getty Images. P. 53, Photo by Theo Wargo/WireImage/Getty Images. P. 54, Frederic J. Brown/AFP/Getty Images. P. 55, Courtesy FedEx Corporation. P. 57, Courtesy Wal-Mart Stores, Inc. P. 58, Sebastian D'Souza/AFP/Getty Images. P. 63, Courtesy of Apple.

Chapter 3

Photos/ads: P. 84, AP Photo/CSPS. P. 85, Chip Somodervilla/Getty Images. P. 87, GRANTLANDD®. Copyright Grantland Enterprises; www.grantland.net. P. 88, Dyamic Graphics/JupiterImages. P. 89, AP Photo/Pat Sullivan. P. 92, ©Dennis MacDonald/PhotoEdit. P. 93, Ryan McVay/Getty Images. P. 94, Courtesy The Coco-Cola Company. P. 97, GRANTLAND®. Copyright Grantland Enterprises; www.grantland.net. P. 99, ©M. Hruby. P. 100, ©Newman's Own, Inc. P. 101, Royalty-Free/CORBIS. P. 101, AP Photo/Steven Senne. P. 104, GRANTLAND®. Copyright Grantland Enterprises; www.grantland.net. P. 106, GRANTLAND®. Copyright Grantland Enterprises; www.grantland.net. P. 107, GRANTLAND®. Copyright Grantland Enterprises; www.grantland.net. P. 110, DynamicGraphics/Jupiter Images.

Exhibits: Exhibit 3.3, "American Marketing Association's Code of Ethics, Ethical Norms and Values for Marketers" (www.marketingpower.com). Used by permission of The American Marketing Association; Exhibit 3.7, Adapted from Kate McKone-Sweet, Danna Greenberg, and Lydia Moland, "Approaches to Ethical Decision Making," Babson College Case Development Center, 2003. Used by permission; Exhibit 3.9, Tom Morris, The Art of Achievement: Mastering the 7Cs of Success in Business and in Life, Fine Communications, 2003.

Chapter 4

Photos/ads: P. 112, Courtesy GE Money. P. 117, © M. Hruby. P. 118, Courtesy Nau, Inc.; Photographer: Jimmy Chin. P. 120, *Both ads:* Courtesy MINI USA. P. 120, Jack Hollingsworth/Getty Images. P. 122, ©Royalty-Free/Corbis. P. 123, Photo by Brian Bahr/Getty Images. P. 124, ©Chuck Savage/CORBIS. P.125, BananaStock/JupiterImages. P. 125, Courtesy of Hammacher Schleemmer, www.hammacher.com. P. 126, *No credit.* P. 127, Jochen Sand/Digital Vision/Getty Images. P. 127, ©2006 Oldemarak, LLC. Reprinted with permission. The Wendy's name, design and logo are registered trademarks of Oldemark, Llc and are licensed to Wendy's International, Inc. P. 128, Comstock/PictureQuest. P. 128, Courtesy Ford Motor Company. P. 130, Photo by CBS Photo Archive/Getty Images. P. 130, AP Photo/Ric Feld. P. 132, Kaz Chiba/Digital Vision/Getty Images. P. 137, Courtesy General Electric Company. P. 139, Courtesy America on the Move Foundation. P. 144, Courtesy Stonyfield Farm. P. 145, Courtesy Stonyfield Farm.

Exhibits: Exhibit 4.5, Reprinted with permission from the Dec 2002 issue of American Demographics. Copyright, Crain Communications Inc. 2002; Exhibit 4.10, "America's Most Admired Companies," March 17, 2008 issue, FORTUNE, top 20 most admired companies over all industries. Copyright © 2008 Time Inc. All rights reserved. Used by permission; Exhibit 4.12, Adapted from C.B. Bhattacharya and Sankar Sen (2004), "Doing Better at Doing Good" When, Why and How Consumers Respond to Corporate Social Responsibilities," California Management Revew, 47 (Fall), 9–24.

Chapter 5

Photos/ads: P. 148, Courtesy Toyota Motor Sales, U.S.A., Inc. P. 151, Photo by Timothy A. Clary/AFP/Getty Images. P. 152, AP Photo/Ann Johansson. P. 153, Courtesy SeenOn! P. 154, ©M. Hruby. P. 155, Andrew Wakeford/Getty Images. P. 156, Photo by Mark Renders/Getty Images. P. 157, Used by permission of Sony Electronics, Inc. P. 159, Courtesy Expedia, Inc. P. 161, Photo by Warner Bros./Getty Images. P. 163, Courtesy Taco Bell. P. 164, McGruff® and Scruff® are a part of the National Crime Prevention Council's ongoing crime prevention education campaign. P. 164, 2007 Subway FreshFit for Kids™ Meal. P. 165, Courtesy Hallmark Cards, Inc. P. 166, The McGraw-Hill Companies, Inc./Andrew Resek, photographer. P. 166, ©Shooting Star. P. 167, General Motors Corp. Used with permission, GM Media Archives. P. 168, Thinkstock/JupiterImages. P. 170, Courtesy Outback Steakhouse; Photographer: Tim Healy/People; Photographer: Terry Zelen/Interior. P. 171, Courtesy Albertson's, Inc. P. 173, The McGraw-Hill Companies, Inc./Emily & David Tietz, photographers. P. 173, ©Digital Vision. P. 173, The McGraw-Hill Companies, Inc./Andrew Resek, photographer. P. 178, Courtesy smart GmbH.

Chapter 6

Photos/ads: P. 180, Courtesy Eastman Chemical Company. P. 182, Courtesy Wells Fargo Auto Finance. P. 183, Courtesy Siemen's Corporation. P. 184, Courtesy of Burt's Bees, Inc. P. 185, Photo by Eric Ryan/Getty Images. P. 186, Royalty-Free/CORBIS. P. 186, ©Comstock Images/Alamy. P. 186, ©Myrleen Ferguson Cate/PhotoEdit. P. 188, Copyright ©Ron Kimball/Ron Kimball Stock—All rights reserved. P. 188, GRANTLAND®. Copyright Grantland Enterprises; www.grantland.net. P. 189, ©Toyota Motor Engineering & Manufacturing North America, Inc. P. 189, ©Worth Canoy/Icon SMI/Corbis. P. 191, *GRANTLAND®.* Copyright Grantland Enterprises; www.grantland.net. P. 193, ©Custom Medical Stock Photo. P. 195, AP Photo/Fabian Bimmer. P. 196, Courtesy LSU Athletic Department. P. 198, dynamicgrapics/Jupiterimages. P. 203, Courtesy Weyerhaeuser Company.

Chapter 7

Photos/ads: P. 206, Courtesy Marriott International, Inc.; Agency: McGarry Bowen/New York. P. 209, Courtesy LEGO Company. P. 210, STR/AFP/Getty Images. P. 210, AP Photo/J. Scott Applewhite. P. 216, ©Dhruv Grewal, Ph.D. P. 217, Dan Kitwood/Getty Images. P. 218, AP Photo/Greg Baker. P. 219, Photo by Tim Boyle/Getty Images. P. 219, ©Gail Mooney/CORBIS. P. 220, Stephen Alvarez/National Geographic/Getty Images. P. 222, ©Digital Vision/Getty Images. P. 226, *No credit.* P. 228, AP Photo/Jay LaPrete. P. 228, AP Photo/Gurinder Osan. P. 230, Courtesy Whole Foods Market, Inc. P. 232, Courtesy Pepsi-Cola Company. P. 233, AP Photo/Michele Limina. P. 238, Mark Leong/Redux.

Exhibits: Exhibit 7.2, "Big Mac Index," The Economist, January 12, 2006. Exhibit 7.3, From www.nationmaster.com. Used by permission; Exhibit 7.4, ©Copyright 2006 SASI Group (University of Sheffield) and Mark Newman (University of Michigan); Exhibit 7.7, Permission

Chapter 8

Photos/ads: P. 242, ©M. Hruby. P. 247, CourtesyAu Bon Pain. P. 248, Photo by Michael Loccisano/ FilmMagic for Paul Wilmot Comunications/Getty Images. P. 248, Courtesy Build-a-Bear Workshop, Inc. P. 250, Photo by Jemal Countess/WireImage/ Getty Images. P. 251, *Both* Courtesy The Gillette Company. P. 252, ©Benetton Group SPA; Photo by: Oliviero Toscani. P. 254, Ryan McVay/Getty Images. P. 254, Ryan McVay/Getty Images. P. 255, Stockbyte/ Punchstock Images. P. 255, Jack Hollingsworth/ Getty Images. P. 255, Ryan McVay/Getty Images. P. 258, ©Jerry Arcieri/Corbis. P. 258, The McGraw-Hill Companies, Inc./Andrew Resek, photographer. P 259, ©Ron Kimball. P. 261, Courtesy Shooting Star. P. 261, Courtesy Carhartt, Inc. P. 261, Courtesy Hallmark Cards, Inc. P. 264, Courtesy Volvo Cars of North America, LLC. P. 265, Green Giant for Business Wire via Getty Images. P. 266, Photo by Doug Benc/Getty Images. P. 266, Photo by Ezra Shaw/Getty Images. P. 272, ©Index Stock. P. 272, James Hardy/Reflex Stock.

Chapter 9

Photos/ads: P. 274, AP Photo/M. Spencer Green. P. 276, ©Bill Aron/PhotoEdit, Inc. P. 277, The McGraw-Hill Companies, Inc./John Flournoy, Photographer. P. 279, Courtesy Whirlpool Corporation. P. 280, Photo by Charley Gallay/Getty Images. P. 283, ©M. Hruby. P. 283, Courtesy Information Resources, Inc. P. 284, ©Spencer Grant/PhotoEdit, Inc. P. 286, The McGraw-Hill Companies, Inc./ John Flournoy, Photographer. P. 287, Mark Douet/Riser/Getty Images. P. 288, Courtesy Jones Apparel Group, Inc. P. 288, ©2006 The LEGO Group. P. 289, Courtesy Makena Technologies. P. 291, The McGraw-Hill Companies, Inc./John Flournoy, Photographer. P. 294, AP Photo/Mary Altaffer. P. 296, Royalty-Free/CORBIS.

Exhibits: Exhibit 9.7, Chart adapted from Parasuramn, Grewal and Krishnan, Marketing Research, 2nd ed, Houghton Mifflin, 2007, Ch 10.

Appendix 9A

Photos/ads: P. 304, ©Don Mason/CORBIS.

Chapter 10

Photos/ads: P. 308, Photo by George Napolitano/ Film Magic/Getty Images. P. 312, Courtesy Pepsi Cola Company. P. 313, Lime Public Relations & Promotions. P. 313, ©M. Hruby. P. 314, Courtesy Mercedes-Benz USA, LLC; Merkley & Partners/ New York. P. 315, ©M. Hruby. P. 316, Courtesy of Rolex USA. P. 318, ©M. Hruby. P. 319, Photo by Peter Kramer/Getty Images. P. 321, Courtesy REI. P. 323, McGraw-Hill Companies. P. 325, Courtesy FritoLay, Inc. P. 325, ©M. Hruby. P. 326, Photo by Stephane L'hostis/Getty Images. P. 328, *Both ads:* LaCoste S.A. P. 330, ©M. Hruby. P. 331, ©M. Hruby. P. 334, Courtesy Bank of America. P. 335, ©M. Hruby.

Exhibits: Exhibit 10.2, Kevin Lane Keller, Strategic Brand Management, 2nd ed, Prentice Hall, 2003. Exhibit 10.3, The World's Ten Most Valuable Brands, Best Global Brands 2007

Chapter 11

Photos/ads: P. 338, ©M. Hruby. P. 341, ©Michael Newman/Photo Edit. P. 341, Courtesy Tivo, Inc. P. 341, Courtesy Polaroid Corporation. P. 341, ©The Procter & Gamble Company. Used by permission. P. 341, ©M. Hruby. P. 342, *All* Courtesy of NewProductWorks, www.newproductworks.com. P. 343, ©Derrick Donnelly, Blackbag Technologies. P. 345, ©Shooting Star. P. 346, ©Michael Newman/ PhotoEdit. P. 348, Courtesy Black & Decker Corporation. P. 349, Photo by Dave Hogan/Getty Images. P. 352, Courtesy Coalition for Consumer Information on Cosmetics. P. 354, *First four photos:* Courtesy of NewProductWorks, www.new-productworks.com. P. 354, Courtesy Hammacher Schlemmer catalog. P. 355, ©The Procter & Gamble Company. Used by permission. P. 356, ©M. Hruby. P. 359, *No credit.* P. 359, ©Comstock Images/Alamy. P. 359, Courtesy TiVo, Inc. P. 360, ©M. Hruby. P. 361, *No credit.* P. 365, Courtesy MetroNaps.

Exhibits: Exhibit 11.1, Adapted from Everett M. Rodgers, Diffusion of Innovation, The Free Press, 1983.

Chapter 12

Photos/ads: P. 366, Courtesy Enterprise Rent-A-Car. P. 369, Dynamic Graphics/Jupiter Images. P. 369, ©Jose Fuste Raga/CORBIS. P. 369, The McGraw-Hill Companies, Inc./Andrew Resek, Photographer. P. 369, John A. Rizzo/Getty Images. P. 369, ©Charles Bowman/Alamy. P. 369, ©Photodisc. P. 369, Brand X Pictures/Getty Images. P. 370, Courtesy iPic Entertainment, LLC. P. 372, Courtesy Choice Hotels. P. 373, Courtesy The Charles Schwab Corporation. P. 373, Courtesy Geek Housecalls, Inc. P. 374, Courtesy NCR Corporation. P. 375, ©Buddy Mays/CORBIS. P. 377, ©Dan Holmberg/CORBIS. P. 380, ©Dynamic Graphics Group/Creatuas/Alamy. P. 381, ©Royalty-Free/CORBIS. P. 384, Courtesy Threadless T-Shirts. P. 385, Courtesy The Home Depot, Inc. P. 386, Courtesy IBM Corporation. P. 388, ©Royalty-Free/Corbis. P. 389, ©Michael Newman/PhotoEdit, Inc. P. 393, Royalty-Free/ CORBIS.

Chapter 13

Photos/ads: P. 396, Photo by George Pimentel/ WireImage/Getty Images. P. 398, Daniel Acker/ Bloomberg News/Landov. P. 399, Courtesy IKEA. P. 402, Photo by Justin Sullivan/Getty Images. P. 403, Courtesy Saturn Corporation. P. 403, *Both:* Courtesy Paradigm Electronics, Inc. P. 404, ©The Seattle Times. P. 405, Photo by Simon Frederick/ Getty Images. P. 406, ©Bill Aron/PhotoEdit, Inc. P. 406, ©Dennis MacDonald/PhotoEdit, Inc. P. 407, Courtesy Mercedes-Benz USA, LLC; Merkley & Partners/New York. P. 408, ©David Young-Wolff/ PhotoEdit, Inc. P. 410, AP Photo/Brian Kersey. P. 410, Michael Rosenfeld/Stone/Getty Images. P. 413, Allan Danahar/Digital Vision/Getty Images.

P. 413, Inti St Clair/Photodisc Red/Getty Images. P. 414, ©M. Hruby. P. 416, Courtesy Fujitsu General America, Inc. P. 417, Photo by Chris Jackson/Getty Images. P. 419, AP Photo/Richard Vogel.

Exhibits: Exhibit 13.3, Fujitsu General America, Inc. Used by permission.

Chapter 14

Photos/ads: P. 424, Photo by Donald Bowers/ Getty Images for Payless ShoeSource. P. 427, AP Photo/Paul Sakuma. P. 427, AP Photo/Matthias Rietschel. P. 428, Courtesy Ferrari S.p.A. P. 429, Courtesy Motorola, Inc. P. 430, Photo by Gregg DeGuire/WireImage/Getty Images. P. 431, AP Photo/William Thomas Cain. P. 432, Courtesy Sears, Roebuck and Co. P. 432, Courtesy Wal-Mart Stores, Inc. P. 433, ©Jeff Greenberg/PhotoEdit. P. 435, Photo by Michael Nagle/Getty Images. P. 439, ©M. Hruby. P. 439, ©M. Hruby. P. 441, ©M. Hruby. P. 442, ©M. Hruby. P. 442, Courtesy PR Newswire. P. 444, Courtesy Classic Car Club Manhattan. P. 445, ©Jeff Greenberg/PhotoEdit, Inc. P. 446, ©Tom Prettyman/PhotoEdit. P. 447, ©Royalty-Free/Corbis.

Chapter 15

Photos/ads: P. 454, AP Photo/Luis Romero. P. 459, ©Thinkstock/Alamy/Getty Images. P. 461, *Both:* Courtesy Zara International, Inc. P. 465, Photo by Cabela's. P. 467, AP Photo/Danny Johnston. P. 469, Mario Tama/Getty Images. P. 470, David Buffinton/Photodisc/Getty Images. P. 471, Photo by Scott Olson/Getty Images. P. 471, Walter Hodges/Digital Vision/Getty Images. P. 473, Courtesy Tubular Steel, Inc. P. 474, Courtesy Zappos.com. P. 475, Courtesy The Stanley Works. P. 477, ©Tessuto E Colore srl. P. 480, Ryan T. Conaty/Bloomberg News/Landov. P. 480, Keith Bedford/Reuters/Landov. P. 480, Keith Bedford/ Reuters/Landov. P. 484, ©Wal-Mart Stores, Inc. P. 484, ©Wal-Mart Stores, Inc.

Exhibits: Exhibit 15.4, Copyright © 2008. SAS Institute Inc. All rights reserved. Reproduced with permission of SAS Institute Inc., Cary, NC, USA; Exhibit 15.7, Source: http://www.entrepreneur.com/franchise500/with permission of Entrepreneur.com, Inc. All rights reserved.

Chapter 16

Photos/ads: P. 486, Photo by Jerry T. Lai/Getty Images. P. 489, Photo by John Parra/WireImage/ Getty Images. P. 489, Photo by Todd Williamson/ WireImage\Getty Images. P. 490, ©M. Hruby. P. 492, ©Jeff Greenberg/PhotoEdit. P. 492, ©Susan Van Etten/PhotoEdit. P. 494, ©M. Hruby. P. 494, ©M. Hruby. P. 495, Courtesy Wegmans Food Markets, Inc. P. 496, AP Photo/Paul Sakuma. P. 497, Photo by Michael Nagel/Getty Images. P. 498, Photo by Justin Sullivan/Getty Images. P. 500, Tony Avelar/Bloomberg News/Landov. P. 501, AP Photo/ MarkHumphrey. P. 501, Courtesy Prime Retail. P. 502, AP Photo/Al Behrman. P. 503, Courtesy Bass Pro Shops. P. 504, Photo by Mike Moore/ WireImage/Getty Images. P. 505, ©M. Hruby. P. 506, Courtesy Mall of America. P. 507, Photo by Charley Gallay/WireImage/Getty Images. P. 508, Courtesy Harrah's Entertainment, Inc. P. 509, Courtesy Bluefly, Inc. P. 511, Courtesy H&M, Hennes & Mauritz L.P. P. 515, Andy Kropa/Redux.

Chapter 17

Photos/ads: P. 527, Courtesy The Coca-Cola Company. Used with permission. P. 527, Courtesy The Home Depot, Inc. P. 528, ©M. Hruby. P. 528, Courtesy Peapod. P. 529, Courtesy LG Electronics. P. 530, Courtesy Saatchi LA. P. 531, ©M. Hruby. P. 534, ©M. Hruby. P. 535, *Both:* ©Nokia 2008. P. 537, Courtesy Southwest Airlines. P. 538, Courtesy Sugar, Inc. P. 538, ©Tag Fragrance Co. P. 539, Courtesy REI. P. 542, Courtesy Hugo Boss. P. 543, Rob Kim/Landov. P. 543, Courtesy Google, Inc. P. 549, Courtesy Initiative Public Relations.

Exhibits: Exhibit 17.4, Used by permission of TNS Media Intelligence.

Chapter 18

Photos/ads: P. 550, Photo by David Paul Morris/Getty Images. P. 552, J. Leynse/REA/Redux Pictures. P. 554, Courtesy The Diamond Trading Company; Agency: J. Walter Thompson U.S.A., Inc. P. 555, Courtesy Chrysler, Inc. P. 556, ©TJX Companies, Inc. P. 556, ©The Procter & Gamble Company. Used by permission. P. 557, Courtesy The Coca-Cola Company. P. 557, Courtesy National Fluid Milk Processor Promotion Board; Agency: Lowe Worldwide, Inc. P. 557, Courtesy The Coca-Cola Company. P. 557, Courtesy McDonald's USA, LLC. P. 557, ©Michael Newman/PhotoEdit. P. 558, Courtesy National Fluid Milk Processor Promotion Board; Agency: Lowe Worldwide, Inc. P. 558, California Milk Processor Board; Agency: Goodby, Silverstein & Partners. P. 558, Courtesy of the National Crime Prevention Council, ww.ncpc.org. P. 559, Courtesy American Legacy Foundation. P. 561, Courtesy The Black & Decker Corporation.P. 561, *Both ads* Courtesy IBM Corporation. P. 561, Courtesy Lufthansa German Airlines. P. 563, Courtesy Alliance for Climate Protection. P. 563, Courtesy BBH Tokyo. P. 565, Courtesy Office Max. P. 566, Courtesy IKEA. P. 566, Courtesy MINI USA. P. 567, Courtesy Del Campo/Nazca Saatchi & Saatchi/Buenos Aires. P. 570, ©Bill Aron/PhotoEdit. P. 573, Courtesy Payless Shoe Source, Inc. P. 574, Courtesy David Brice. P. 575, Kate Fisher/CBS/Landov. P.575, Courtesy Hotels at Home. P. 576, *No credit* P.577, Ron P. Jaffe/CBS/Landov. P. 577, Photo by Chris Polk/FilmMagic/Getty Images.

Chapter 19

Photos/ads: P. 584, Courtesy Mary Kay, Inc. P. 586, ©Royalty-Free/Corbis. P. 587, Thinkstock/JupiterImages. P. 587, Â©Royalty-Free/Corbis. P. 588, Daniel Acker/Bloomberg News/Landov. P. 591, ©Royalty-Free/Corbis. P. 591, Photo by Evan Agostini/Getty Images. P. 592, ©Susan Van Etten/PhotoEdit, Inc. P. 594, ©Susan Van Etten/PhotoEdit, Inc. P. 595, AP Photo/Andy Wong. P. 596, Ryan McVay/Getty Images. P. 597, Courtesy Sam Hussey; ©McGraw-Hill Irwin. P. 598, AP Photo/Charlie Riedel. P. 599, ©Custom Medical Stock Photo. P. 600, AP Photo/Nati Harnik. P. 600, ©Mark Tuschman/CORBIS. P. 601, ©Royalty-Free/Corbis. P. 608, Dynamic Graphics/JupiterImages.

name index

company index

subject index

An f next to a page number indicates a figure on that page; an n, a note.

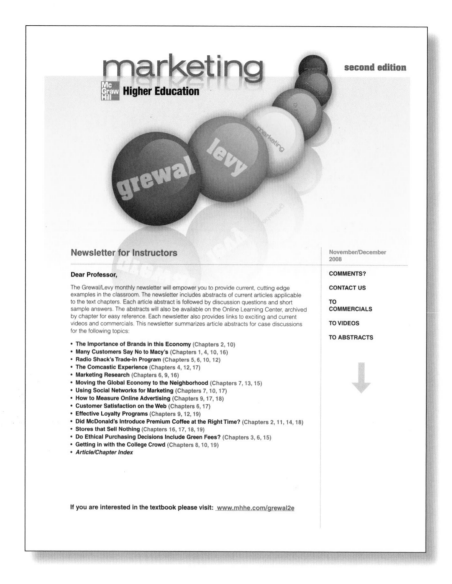

monthly newsletter

Each month instructors using *Marketing 2e* will receive a newsletter which includes many of the hottest topics in marketing today. Each newsletter contains 8-10 articles, videos and podcasts on the latest happenings in the Marketing discipline, with abstracts and a guide that explains where the information can be implemented in a Principles of Marketing course.